JURISDICTION AND ENFORCEMENT OF JUDGMENTS IN CIVIL AND COMMERCIAL MATTERS

ECJ JUDGMENTS

VOLUME II

JURISDICTION AND ENFORCEMENT OF JUDGMENTS IN CIVIL AND COMMERCIAL MATTERS ECJ JUDGMENTS

VOLUME II

Edited by
Paolo Galizzi

BIICL
British Institute of
International and
Comparative Law

Published and Distributed by
The British Institute of International and Comparative Law
Charles Clore House, 17 Russell Square, London WC1B 5JP

British Library Cataloguing in Publication Data
A Catalogue record of this book is available from the British Library

ISBN 0–903067–85–4

Printed in Great Britain by Biddles Ltd.,
Guildford and King's Lynn

TITLE II *[Chapter II]*

JURISDICTION *[Jurisdiction]*

Prorogation of jurisdiction by consent – Article 17 *[Article 23]*

See also

Case 24/76 - 14 December 1976

Estasis Salotti di Colzani Aimo e Gianmario Colzani
v
RÜWA Polstereimaschinen GmbH

Article 17 - Jurisdiction by consent - Effect - Validity - Manner in which applied - Strict interpretation - Consensus between the parties - Courts having jurisdiction - Consent in writing - Contract signed by the parties - General conditions of sale printed on the back - Clause conferring jurisdiction - Necessity for an express reference to those conditions in the contract - Contract - Entered into by reference to prior offers - Reference to general conditions of sale - Clause conferring jurisdiction - Necessity for an express reference.

Summary

1. The way in which Article 17 of the Convention of 27 September 1968 is to be applied must be interpreted in the light of the effect of the conferment of jurisdiction by consent, which is to exclude both the jurisdiction determined by the general principle laid down in Article 2 and the special jurisdictions provided for in Articles 5 and 6 of that Convention. In view of the consequences that such an option may have on the position of the parties to the action, the requirements set out in Article 17 governing the validity of clauses conferring jurisdiction must be strictly construed. By making the validity of clauses conferring jurisdiction subject to the existence of an 'agreement' between the parties, Article 17 imposes on the court before which the matter is brought the duty of examining, first, whether the clause conferring jurisdiction upon it was in fact the subject of a consensus between the parties, which must be clearly and precisely demonstrated, for the purpose of the formal requirements imposed by Article 17 is to ensure that the consensus between the parties is in fact established.

2. In the case of a clause conferring jurisdiction, which is included among the general conditions of sale of one of the parties, printed on the back of the contract, the requirement of a writing under the first paragraph of Article 17 of the Convention of 27 September 1968 is only fulfilled if the contract signed by the two parties includes an express reference to those general conditions.

3. In the case of a contract concluded by reference to earlier offers, which were themselves made with reference to the general conditions of one of the parties including a clause conferring jurisdiction, the requirement of a writing under the first paragraph of Article 17 of the Convention of 27 September 1968 is satisfied only if the reference is express and can therefore be checked by a party exercising reasonable care.

JUDGMENT OF THE COURT

Kutscher, President, Donner and Pescatore, Presidents of Chambers, Mertens de Wilmars, Sorensen, Lord Mackenzie Stuart and O'Keeffe, Judges

1. By an order of 18 February 1976, received at the Court Registry on 11 March 1976, the Bundesgerichtshof referred to the Court of Justice pursuant to the Protocol of 3 June 1971 on the Interpretation of the Convention of 27 September 1968 on Jurisdiction and the Enforcement of Judgments in Civil and Commercial Matters (hereinafter referred to as 'the Convention', certain questions concerning the interpretation of Article 17 of the said Convention.

2. It appears from the order making the reference that at the present stage the action, which was brought before the Bundesgerichtshof by way of appeal on a point of law, concerns the jurisdiction of the Landgericht Köln to hear an action brought by an undertaking established within the area of jurisdiction of that Court against an Italian undertaking whose registered office is at Meda (Milan), for failure to perform a contract relating to the supply by the German undertaking to the Italian undertaking of machines for the manufacture of upholstered furniture.

3. It appears from the facts stated in the order making the reference that the delivery in question had been agreed in a written contract, signed at Milan on commercial paper bearing the letter-head of the German

undertaking, on the reverse of which the general conditions of sale of that undertaking were printed.

Those general conditions include a clause conferring jurisdiction on the courts of Cologne to settle any dispute which might arise between the parties concerning the contract.

Although it is true that the text of the contract does not expressly mention the said general conditions, it refers to previous offers made by the German undertaking which contained an express reference to the same general conditions, which were also printed on the reverse of the papers in question.

4. In a judgment delivered on 9 April 1974, the Landgericht Köln, before which the matter was brought by the German undertaking, declared that it had no jurisdiction to hear the dispute.

It held that the clause conferring jurisdiction had not validly been agreed between the parties, having regard to the provisions of Italian law, to which, in the view of that court, the contract between the parties is subject.

That judgment was reversed by a judgment of 18 November 1974 of the Oberlandesgericht Köln which, taking the view that the contract in question is subject to the provisions of German law, overruled the judgment of the lower court, declared that the Landgericht had jurisdiction and remitted the case to it.

5. The Italian undertaking appealed on a point of law to the Bundesgerichtshof, and that court is of the opinion that the question at issue must be resolved on the basis of Article 17 of the Convention.

In this connexion, the Bundesgerichtshof has referred two questions on the interpretation of the first paragraph of that article.

On the interpretation of Article 17 of the Convention in general

6. The first paragraph of Article 17 of the Convention provides: 'If the parties, one or more of whom is domiciled in a Contracting State, have, by agreement in writing or by an oral agreement confirmed in writing, agreed that a court or the courts of a Contracting State are to have jurisdiction to settle any disputes which have arisen or which may arise in connexion with a particular legal relationship, that court or those courts shall have exclusive jurisdiction'.

7. The way in which that provision is to be applied must be interpreted in the light of the effect of the conferment of jurisdiction by consent,

which is to exclude both the jurisdiction determined by the general principle laid down in Article 2 and the special jurisdictions provided for in Articles 5 and 6 of the Convention.

In view of the consequences that such an option may have on the position of the parties to the action, the requirements set out in Article 17 governing the validity of clauses conferring jurisdiction must be strictly construed.

By making such validity subject to the existence of an 'agreement' between the parties, Article 17 imposes on the court before which the matter is brought the duty of examining, first, whether the clause conferring jurisdiction upon it was in fact the subject of a consensus between the parties, which must be clearly and precisely demonstrated.

The purpose of the formal requirements imposed by Article 17 is to ensure that the consensus between the parties is, in fact, established.

The questions referred to the Court by the Bundesgerichtshof must be examined in the light of these considerations.

On the questions referred by the Bundesgerichtshof

8. The *first question* asks whether a clause conferring jurisdiction, which is included among general conditions of sale printed on the back of a contract signed by both parties, fulfils the requirement of a writing under the first paragraph of Article 17 of the Convention.

9. Taking into account what has been said above, it should be stated that the mere fact that a clause conferring jurisdiction is printed among the general conditions of one of the parties on the reverse of a contract drawn up on the commercial paper of that party does not of itself satisfy the requirements of Article 17, since no guarantee is thereby given that the other party has really consented to the clause waiving the normal rules of jurisdiction.

It is otherwise in the case where the text of the contract signed by both parties itself contains an express reference to general conditions including a clause conferring jurisdiction.

10. Thus, it should be answered that where a clause conferring jurisdiction is included among the general conditions of sale of one of the parties, printed on the back of a contract, the requirement of a writing under the first paragraph of Article 17 of the Convention is fulfilled only if the contract signed by both parties contains an express reference to those general conditions.

11. The *second question* asks whether the requirement of a writing under the first paragraph of Article 17 of the Convention is fulfilled if the parties expressly refer in the contract to a prior offer in writing in which reference was made to general conditions of sale including a clause conferring jurisdiction.

12. In principle, the requirement of a writing under the first paragraph of Article 17 is fulfilled if the parties have referred in the text of their contract to an offer in which reference was expressly made to general conditions including a clause conferring jurisdiction.

This view of the matter, however, is valid only in the case of an express reference, which can be checked by a party exercising reasonable care, and only if it is established that the general conditions including the clause conferring jurisdiction have in fact been communicated to the other contracting party with the offer to which reference is made.

But the requirement of a writing in Article 17 would not be fulfilled in the case of indirect or implied references to earlier correspondence, for that would not yield any certainty that the clause conferring jurisdiction was, in fact, part of the subject-matter of the contract properly so-called.

13. Thus it should be answered that in the case of a contract concluded by reference to earlier offers, which were themselves made with reference to the general conditions of one of the parties including a clause conferring jurisdiction, the requirement of a writing under the first paragraph of Article 17 of the Convention is satisfied only if the reference is express and can therefore be checked by a party exercising reasonable care.

On those grounds, the court in answer to the questions referred to it by the Bundesgerichtshof by order of 18 February 1976, hereby rules:

> **Where a clause conferring jurisdiction is included among the general conditions of sale of one of the parties, printed on the back of a contract, the requirement of a writing under the first paragraph of Article 17 of the Convention of 27 September 1968 on Jurisdiction and the Enforcement of Judgments in Civil and Commercial Matters is fulfilled only if the contract signed by both parties contains an express reference to those general conditions.**
>
> **In the case of a contract concluded by reference to earlier offers, which were themselves made with reference to the general**

conditions of one of the parties including a clause conferring jurisdiction, the requirement of a writing under the first paragraph of Article 17 of the Convention is satisfied only if the reference is express and can therefore be checked by a party exercising reasonable care.

OPINION OF MR ADVOCATE GENERAL CAPOTORTI

1. In the present case the Court is called upon to resolve a question of interpretation of Article 17 of the Brussels Convention of 27 September 1968 on jurisdiction and the enforcement of judgments in civil and commercial matters. I take the liberty of reminding the Court that the question is concerned with the article governing jurisdiction by consent: it covers the situation when 'the parties, one or more of whom is domiciled in a Contracting State, have ... agreed that a court or the courts of a Contracting State are to have jurisdiction to settle any disputes which have arisen or which may arise in connexion with a particular legal relationship, and confers exclusive jurisdiction on the court or courts designated provided that the agreement between the parties takes the form of an agreement in writing or ... an oral agreement confirmed in writing'. The meaning of this formal requirement is, in fact, the subject of the questions referred to the Court by the Bundesgerichtshof of the Federal Republic of Germany.

The parties in the main action, the German company RÜWA, as vendor, and the Italian company Estasis Salotti, as purchaser, had on 31 October 1969 concluded a sales contract in Milan on the vendor's letter-head, on the back of which were printed the general conditions of sale laid down by the company. There was no mention in the contract of those conditions and no reference to them; it stated that the purchaser was placing an order with the vendor for the 'machines offered, in accordance with your letter of 18 September 1969'. In fact, the letter of 18 September was sent with seven offers of sale, dated 11 September, each of which referred to the general conditions of sale printed at the back of the letter, but there was no corresponding reference in the letter.

Subsequently the purchaser refused to take delivery of the machines and the vendor brought proceedings against it before the German court designated in the jurisdiction clause contained in its general conditions of sale. The court, applying Articles 1341 and 1342 of the Italian civil code, which require specific acceptance in writing of printed clauses excluding jurisdiction, upheld the objection of lack of jurisdiction raised by the purchaser. The appeal court held that it was bound by paragraph 38 of the German code of civil procedure in determining the validity or otherwise of the assignment of jurisdiction relied upon by the vendor, and recognized the German court as having jurisdiction in the matter.

In further appeal proceedings, the Bundesgerichtshof referred the following questions for a ruling by the Court of Justice pursuant to Article 3 of the Protocol of 3 June 1971 on the interpretation of the Convention of 27 September 1968:

(1) Does an agreement assigning jurisdiction, which is included among general conditions of sale printed on the back of a contract signed by both parties, fulfil the requirement of a writing under the first paragraph of Article 17 of the Convention?

(2) In particular, is the requirement of a writing under the first paragraph of Article 17 of the Convention fulfilled if the parties expressly refer in the contract to a prior offer in writing in which reference was made to general conditions of sale including an agreement assigning jurisdiction and to which these conditions of sale were annexed?

2. The general question of the choice between an independent interpretation of the provisions of the Convention and reference to the substantive law applicable in accordance with the private international law of the court before which the matter is brought - to which attention was drawn by the Court of Justice in its judgment in *Industrie Tessili* v. *Dunlop* - also arises in the present case. Form is, of course, only one aspect of a private agreement providing for the assignment of jurisdiction, and the connexion between the various aspects of the agreement becomes even more evident when the assignment of jurisdiction is the subject of only one of a group of clauses of the contract relating to questions of substance. This explains why, in the context of national law, it has been held by some authorities that the form of the agreement or of the clause assigning jurisdiction must be determined in accordance with the rule of private international law governing the form of contracts (which, in the majority of the States, is based on the principle *locus regit actum*). Does this view have any bearing on the question of interpretation which the Court now has to decide?

In my view it does not, for two reasons. In the first place, Article 17 of the Convention, which is concerned with the requirements which, in order to produce the effect desired by the parties, must be satisfied by the clause or the agreement assigning jurisdiction, is, in my view, strictly concerned with the procedural function proper to the Convention and does not prejudice in any way either such questions of substance as may be inherent in that expression of intent (capacity to act and any deficiencies vitiating the agreement), or the question of the form to be observed for the agreement of which the clause forms part. In other words, Article 17 does no more than lay down conditions required to produce the procedural effect of assigning jurisdiction. In the second place it is clearly important that there should be uniform treatment, in all the Member States, of private parties between whom there exist agreements assigning jurisdiction; this purpose would not be served if reference were made to this or that substantive law applicable to the form of instruments according to the private international law of each Member State. For this reason Article 17 of the Brussels Convention must be interpreted independently of national law.

3. The wording of Article 17 of the Brussels Convention closely resembles that of Article 3(2) of the Germano-Belgian Convention of 30 June 1958, which came into force on 27 January 1961, an article which was in turn based on the rule in Article 2 of the Hague Convention of 15 April 1958 on the jurisdiction of the selected forum in international sales of goods.

As emphasized in the Jenard report on the Brussels Convention, insistence on writing was intended to ensure legal certainty. This means that what was required was clear proof that the parties were *ad idem* on the clause specifying the court having jurisdiction so as to avoid those uncertainties and conflicting views on the existence and terms of the contract in question which might arise if the principle were accepted that there should be no requirement whatever as to form. Again according to the Jenard report, the provision in Article 17 ought to - make it possible to enforce those requirements without creating such unnecessary formalities as to impede business practices. In fact the authors of the Convention tried to ensure that, in the interests of trade, legal formalities should be rapid and flexible in operation, especially by enabling the contracting parties to make a valid, even though oral, agreement on the assignment of jurisdiction, provided that it is 'confirmed in writing'. The procedure for confirmation is not specified in clear terms and may make interpretation somewhat difficult, especially when there is confirmation by only one of the parties but this goes beyond the ambit of the present case. I shall have occasion to return to this point in my opinion in Case 25/76.

The central issue raised by the present case is a different one; it is that of clauses for jurisdiction by consent drawn up in advance, in writing, for its own benefit by one of the contracting parties, and in most cases pre-printed on blanks or forms used for contracts or offers of contracts. We know that, in some cases, to avoid the possibility of those clauses being accepted by the other party without his being fully aware of the extent of his commitment, national regulations prescribe what might be called more substantial requirements as to form: not only must there be writing, a requirement which is obviously fulfilled when the clause has been drawn up in advance, especially when it is printed, but also a specific acceptance in writing. The Convention does not contain a provision of this kind. Moreover, the reservation by Luxembourg laying down that an agreement conferring jurisdiction shall be valid with respect to a person domiciled in that State only if that person has expressly and specifically so agreed (second paragraph of Article I of the Protocol annexed to the Convention) shows that specific acceptance in writing is not necessarily required by Article 17. This, again, is probably the result of anxiety not to obstruct business practice with requirements of form which might appear unnecessarily restrictive. But the Jenard report, quoting the report accompanying the Germano-Belgian Convention of 1958, contains a very significant reference to this subject, in a sentence stating that the object is to 'render ineffective clauses in contracts which are liable to escape notice'. And it adds: 'Account will, therefore, be taken of such clauses only when they are the subject of an agreement, which assumes the parties to be *ad idem*. Accordingly, clauses which appear on printed matter used for correspondence or invoices and which have not been accepted by the party against whom they are to be applied will be of no effect.

There can be no doubt that, since they refer to 'clauses which are liable to escape notice' the passages quoted refer, by implication, to clauses pre-determined by one of the parties.

In my opinion, the principle embodied in the Jenard report can be described as follows: although the contracting party who did not participate in laying down the clauses in advance has the opportunity to acquaint himself with them (by reading, for example, what is printed at the back of a form), this does not suffice; there must be proof of a consensus, that the parties are *ad idem*, which is obviously something more than merely knowing or being in a position to know the clauses which the other party has drafted for his own benefit. I have no doubt that this principle is a fair one: it not only accords with the general principle, on which Article 17 is based, that the weaker party should be protected but it also covers the extreme case where failure to comply with a requirement of form may indicate total absence of agreement.

In practice, this possibility is especially likely to exist where the pre-determined clauses are not contained in the text of the contract; I have already quoted the example which, incidentally, applies in the present case, of clauses printed on the back of the sheet on which the contract is written. In a case of that kind, the contract might contain a reference to the clauses but use of this technique of reference creates further difficulty. I make no attempt to give here an exhaustive list of the ways in which the reference may be formulated, but shall confine myself to saying that it must be sufficiently clear to make it reasonable to assume that the party against whom the assignment of jurisdiction is being invoked has agreed to it.

Finally, in cases where the clause assigning jurisdiction has been formulated in advance and, in particular, when it is included in the general conditions of sale, the requirement of written form laid down by Article 17, which acts as a guarantee that there is a consensus, involves strict proof of the purchaser's agreement to the assignment of jurisdiction. This strictness is justified by the seriousness at the international level of removing one of the parties to the contract from the jurisdiction natural to him as indicated in Articles 2 and 5 of the Brussels Convention.

4. In the light of the general considerations set out above, I can now consider the two questions submitted by the Bundesgerichtshof.

To deal with the first question, I would say that when the clause assigning jurisdiction is included in the general conditions of sale printed on the back of the sheet containing the text of the contract, then in order to prevent the purchaser from having that clause set up against him without his being aware of it at the time when the contract is signed and, accordingly, to ensure that the parties have agreed upon such assignment, there must, in the body of the instrument signed at the foot by the purchaser, be a clear reference to such clause or at least to the general conditions of sale. The mere fact that a contract has been drawn up on a form on the back of which the vendor's pre-determined conditions, including the clause assigning jurisdiction, are printed does not amount to proof that the purchaser was in fact aware of the assignment clause or, even if he has become aware of it in some other way. that he intended to accept it.

Bearing in mind, therefore, that the written form required by Article 17 serves mainly to ensure that the agreement on jurisdiction by consent is a real one, it is impossible to regard the provision contained in that article as having been observed in the case under consideration. To take a different view would be to place at risk the principle of legal certainty which was the purpose of the rule in question. Nor, in my view, is it unnecessarily formal to require a clear and express reference if not specifically to the clause itself at least to the general conditions in which the assignment clause appears.

5. The second question is concerned with a more complicated situation, in which the parties expressly refer to a prior offer in which reference was made to the general conditions annexed thereto and containing the clause relating to the court having jurisdiction.

It is not possible to state with certainty whether an indirect reference to an assignment clause fulfils or does not fulfil the requirements of Article 17. It is a question for determination in each individual case whether the reference is made in sufficiently clear terms and in such a way as to meet objectively the requirement of certainty which the rule in question is intended to enforce.

In order, therefore, that the question put by the Bundesgerichtshof may be answered correctly, it is necessary to go more closely into the circumstances on which its question is based.

The letter of 18 September 1969, which accompanied the seven offers of sale and which was referred to in the contract of the following 31 October, did not in fact include any reference to the general conditions of sale which appeared at the back of the individual offers but merely referred to the offers. These in turn referred to the conditions of sale printed at the back of each offer. Beginning, therefore, with the contract, there is a series of three references: by the contract to the letter, by the letter to the offers of sale, and by each offer to the general conditions of sale. And it must be borne in mind that the assignment clause was only one of the general conditions, that is to say, it was not particularly prominent.

Can such an indirect reference be regarded as sufficient to satisfy the requirements of form laid down in the first paragraph of Article 17?

If the point were to be decided by applying the municipal law of the States which subscribed to the Convention the answer might differ according to the national legal system involved. There can be no doubt that the assignment would not have been validly effected under Italian law because Article 1341, quoted above, of the Civil Code lays down that the general conditions of contract determined in advance by one of the parties cannot be set up against the other party unless it is the subject of a specific agreement in writing. It seems likely that the situation would be the same under French law as under Italian law. In fact, Article 48 of the new Code of Civil Procedure, which came into force on 1 January 1976, provides that any clause derogating from the rules of territorial jurisdiction shall be deemed not to be in writing unless it has been the subject of agreement between persons who have all contracted in their capacity as traders and unless it has been set out in very clear terms in the obligations undertaken by the party against whom it is being invoked.

On the other hand, the position in German law may enable the assignment clause to be invoked in pursuance of paragraph 38 of the Code of Civil Procedure, as interpreted in the present case by the Oberlandesgericht Köln whose decision is being contested in proceedings before the Court which submitted the present questions.

I do not propose to comment on the question in respect of cases in which a contract of sale is entered into in the context of continuous business transactions between two undertakings, in the scope of which the application of a clause assigning jurisdiction is customary; this does not appear to apply in the present case. In my view, a method of reference so complex and, by its nature, generally so indirect as that revealed by the circumstances underlying the question referred by the Bundesgerichtshof cannot be regarded as sufficient to meet the requirements of form laid down in the first paragraph of Article 17 of the Brussels Convention. It is in fact incapable of satisfying the requirement of certainty in the purported agreement between the party which has laid down the general provisions of sale in advance and the party against whom the clause assigning jurisdiction is invoked.

My recommendation is therefore that the Court should reply in the following terms to the two questions which has been submitted by the Bundesgerichtshof:

(a) The requirement of confirmation in writing laid down in the first paragraph of Article 17 of the Convention of 27 September 1968 on jurisdiction and the enforcement of judgments in civil and commercial matters is not fulfilled if the clause relating to jurisdiction by consent is included in the conditions printed on the back of a contract signed by both parties unless there is a clear reference to those conditions in the body of the contract;

(b) Nor are the requirements of Article 71 sufficiently met by a reference in the contract to a prior document which, without itself containing the text of the general conditions of sale, which include the assignment clause, and without including a reference to that clause, does no more than refer to another document which contains a reference to the conditions of sale appearing on the back thereof.

Case 25/76 - 14 December 1976

Galeries Segoura SPRL
v
Rahim Bonakdarian

Article 17 - Conferment of jurisdiction by consent - Effect - Validity - Requirement - Strict construction - Consensus between parties - Form - Contract orally concluded - Vendor's confirmation in writing - Notification of general conditions of sale - Clause conferring jurisdiction - Need for acceptance in writing by the purchaser - Oral agreement within the framework of a continuing trading relationship - Implied acceptance of the clause conferring jurisdiction.

Summary

1. The way in which Article 17 of the Convention of 27 September 1968 is to be applied must be interpreted in the light of the effect of the conferment of jurisdiction by consent, which is to exclude both the jurisdiction determined by the general principle laid down in Article 2 and the special jurisdictions provided for in Articles 5 and 6 of the Convention. In view of the consequences that such an option may have on the position of the parties to the action, the requirements set out in Article 17 governing jurisdiction must be strictly construed. By making such validity subject to the existence of an 'agreement' between the parties, Article 17 imposes upon the court before which the matter is brought the duty of examining, first, whether the clause conferring jurisdiction upon it was, in fact, the subject of a consensus between the parties, which must be clearly and precisely demonstrated, the purpose of the formal requirements imposed by Article 17 being to ensure that the consensus between the parties is, in fact, established.

2. In the case of an orally concluded contract, the requirements of the first paragraph of Article 17 of the Convention of 27 September 1968 as to form are satisfied only if the vendor's confirmation in writing accompanied by notification of the general conditions of sale has been accepted in writing by the purchaser. The fact that the purchaser does not raise any objections against a confirmation issued unilaterally by the other party does not amount to acceptance on his part of the clause conferring jurisdiction, unless the oral agreement comes within the framework of a continuing trading relationship between the parties which is based on the general conditions of one of them, and those conditions contain a clause conferring jurisdiction.

JUDGMENT OF THE COURT

Kutscher, President, Donner, Pescatore, Presidents of Chambers, Mertens de Wilmars, Sorensen, Lord Mackenzie Stuart and O'Keeffe, Judges

1. By an order of 18 February 1976, received at the Court Registry on 11 March 1976, the Bundesgerichtshof referred to the Court of Justice, pursuant to the Protocol of 3 June 1971 on the interpretation of the Convention of 27 September 1968 on Jurisdiction and the Enforcement of Judgments in Civil and Commercial Matters (hereinafter referred to as 'the Convention') two questions concerning the interpretation of Article 17 of the said Convention.

2. It appears from the order making the reference that at the present stage the action, which was brought before the Bundesgerichtshof by way of appeal on a point of law, concerns the jurisdiction of the Landgericht Hamburg to hear an action brought by a trading undertaking established within the area of its jurisdiction against a trading company having its registered office in Brussels, for payment of the balance of the price of a batch of carpets bought in Hamburg by the Brussels firm.

The contract was concluded orally between the parties, and the vendor performed his side of it on the same day in consideration of a part-payment made by the purchaser.

On handing over the goods, the vendor delivered to the purchaser a document described as 'Confirmation of order and invoice', which stated that the sale and the delivery had taken place 'subject to the conditions stated on the reverse'.

The 'Conditions of Sale, Delivery and Payment' printed on the reverse of this document contained *inter alia* a clause stipulating that all disputes were to be decided exclusively by the Hamburg courts.

This document was not confirmed by the purchaser.

3. After the purchaser had received formal notice to pay the balance of the purchase price, the vendor brought an action before the Landgericht Hamburg which, by a judgment in default delivered on 16 May 1973, ordered the purchaser to pay the balance with interest thereon for delay. On the purchaser's entering an objection, the Landgericht, by a judgment of 17 December 1973, withdrew its first judgment and declared that it had no jurisdiction, on the ground that the parties had not concluded any agreement conferring jurisdiction within the meaning of Article 17 of the Convention.

The vendor brought an appeal before the Hanseatisches Oberlandesgericht which quashed the decision of the Landgericht and remitted the case to that court, holding that an agreement conferring jurisdiction had been validly concluded between the parties under Article 17 of the Convention.

4. An appeal on a point of law by the purchaser against this judgment is at present before the Bundesgerichtshof.

In this connexion, the Bundesgerichtshof has referred to the Court two questions concerning the interpretation of the first paragraph of Article 17.

The interpretation of Article 17 of the Convention in general

5. The first paragraph of Article 17 of the Convention provides: 'If the parties, one or more of whom is domiciled in a Contracting State, have, by agreement in writing or by an oral agreement confirmed in writing, agreed that a court or the courts of a Contracting State are to have jurisdiction to settle any disputes which have arisen or which may arise in connexion with a particular legal relationship, that court or those courts shall have exclusive jurisdiction'.

6. The way in which that provision is to be applied must be interpreted in the light of the effect of the conferment of jurisdiction by consent, which is to exclude both the jurisdiction determined by the general principle laid down in Article 2 and the special jurisdictions provided for in Articles 5 and 6 of the Convention.

In view of the consequences that such an option may have on the position of the parties to the action, the requirements set out in Article 17 governing the validity of clauses conferring jurisdiction must be strictly construed.

By making such validity subject to the existence of an 'agreement' between the parties, Article 17 imposes upon the court before which the matter is brought the duty of examining, first, whether the clause conferring jurisdiction upon it was in fact the subject of a consensus between the parties, which must be clearly and precisely demonstrated.

The purpose of the formal requirements imposed by Article 17 is to ensure that the consensus between the parties is in fact established.

The questions referred to the Court by the Bundesgerichtshof must be examined in the light of these considerations.

The questions referred by the Bundesgerichtshof

7. The *first question* is whether the requirements of Article 17 of the Convention are satisfied if, at the oral conclusion of a contract of sale, a vendor has stated that he wishes to rely on his general conditions of sale and if he subsequently confirms the contract in writing to the purchaser and annexes to this confirmation his general conditions of sale which contain a clause conferring jurisdiction.

8. In accordance with the foregoing general considerations, it cannot be presumed that one of the parties waives the advantage of the provisions of the Convention conferring jurisdiction.

Even if, in an orally concluded contract, the purchaser agrees to abide by the vendor's general conditions, he is not for that reason to be deemed to have agreed to any clause conferring jurisdiction which might appear in those general conditions.

It follows that a confirmation in writing of the contract by the vendor, accompanied by the text of his general conditions, is without effect, as regards any clause conferring jurisdiction which it might contain, unless the purchaser agrees to it in writing.

9. The *second question* then asks whether Article 17 of the Convention applies if, in dealings between merchants, a vendor, after the oral conclusion of a contract of sale, confirms in writing to the purchaser the conclusion of the contract subject to his general conditions of sale and annexes to this document his conditions of sale which include a clause conferring jurisdiction and if the purchaser does not challenge this written confirmation.

10. It emerges from a comparison of the wording of the two questions

and from the explanations given during the proceedings before the Court that the second of the two questions concerns the hypothetical situation of a sale being concluded without any reference being made at all to the existence of general conditions of sale.

In such a case, it is patent that a clause conferring jurisdiction which might be included in those general conditions did not form part of the subject-matter of the contract concluded orally between the parties.

Therefore, subsequent notification of general conditions containing such a clause is not capable of altering the terms agreed between the parties, except if those conditions are expressly accepted in writing by the purchaser.

11. It follows from the foregoing, in both of the alternative cases suggested by the Bundesgerichtshof, that a unilateral declaration in writing such as the one in the present case is not sufficient to constitute an agreement on jurisdiction by consent.

However, it would be otherwise where an oral agreement forms part of a continuing trading relationship between the parties, provided also that it is established that the dealings taken as a whole are governed by the general conditions of the party giving the confirmation, and these conditions contain a clause conferring jurisdiction.

Indeed, in such a context, it would be contrary to good faith for the recipient of the confirmation to deny the existence of a jurisdiction conferred by consent, even if he had given no acceptance in writing.

12. It is, therefore, possible to give a single answer to the two questions referred to the Court as follows: in the case of an orally concluded contract, the requirements of the first paragraph of Article 17 as to form are satisfied only if the vendor's confirmation in writing accompanied by notification of the general conditions of sale has been accepted in writing by the purchaser.

The fact that the purchaser does not raise any objections against a confirmation issued unilaterally by the other party does not amount to acceptance on his part of the clause conferring jurisdiction unless the oral agreement comes within the framework of a continuing trading relationship between the parties which is based on the general conditions of one of them, and those conditions contain a clause conferring jurisdiction.

On those grounds, the court in answer to the questions referred to it by the Bundesgerichtshof by order of 18 February 1976, hereby rules:

In the case of an orally concluded contract, the requirements of the first paragraph of Article 17 of the Convention of 27 September 1968 on Jurisdiction and the Enforcement of Judgments in Civil and Commercial Matters as to form are satisfied only if the vendor's confirmation in writing accompanied by notification of the general conditions of sale has been accepted in writing by the purchaser.

The fact that the purchaser does not raise any objections against a confirmation issued unilaterally by the other party does not amount to acceptance on his part of the clause conferring jurisdiction, unless the oral agreement comes within the framework of a continuing trading relationship between the parties which is based on the general conditions of one of them, and those conditions contain a clause conferring jurisdiction.

OPINION OF MR ADVOCATE GENERAL CAPOTORTI

1. This case, like Case 24/76, is concerned with the interpretation of Article 17 of the Brussels Convention of 27 September 1968 on jurisdiction and the enforcement of judgments in civil and commercial matters; here too, therefore, we have to consider the requirements which need to be satisfied by an agreement assigning jurisdiction (which, in the present case, is invoked by the vendor against the purchaser). But, in contrast to Case 24/76, the questions referred by the German Bundesgerichtshof for a preliminary ruling on this occasion are concerned with the case of an oral contract. The issues raised thereby are concerned both with the conditions necessary for an oral agreement assigning jurisdiction to be deemed to exist and with the way in which the assignment agreement is, as required by Article 17, to be confirmed in writing for it to be recognized as valid.

A contract of sale was orally entered into on 14 September 1971 between Bonakdarian, whose registered office is in Hamburg, the vendor, and Segoura, whose registered office is in Brussels, the purchaser. At the same time the purchaser made a payment on account. On the same day, it received the goods which were the subject of the contract together with a document serving as a 'confirmation letter and invoice' which made an express reference to the general conditions of sale, delivery and payment printed on the back. Those conditions included a clause conferring on the Hamburg court exclusive jurisdiction to decide any dispute which might arise. This evoked no comment from the purchaser.

A dispute subsequently arose concerning payment of the outstanding amount and the German court of first instance at first ordered Segoura in its absence to pay a sum equivalent to the outstanding amount, together with interest but later, following an objection, cancelled its judgment and ruled that it had no jurisdiction because there had been no agreement for jurisdiction by consent within the meaning of the first paragraph of Article 17 of the Brussels Convention of 27 September 1968. The court declared that, in the absence of any evidence proving that the assignment clause had been the subject of an oral agreement, there was no such agreement. With regard to the contention of the vendor that the consent of the purchaser to the assignment of jurisdiction was evidenced by the absence of any comment after it had received the invoice letter referring to the general conditions of sale, the court observed that, in those circumstances, the invoice letter, which referred for the first time to the clause assigning jurisdiction, amounted at most to a contractual offer amending the original contract, and that, in any case, there was a total absence of the written acceptance required by Article 17.

A different view was, however, taken by the appeal court, which held that the reference to the general conditions of sale contained in the invoices sent to the purchaser constituted confirmation of an oral agreement which also covered the general conditions of sale, including the clause assigning jurisdiction. According to the appeal court such confirmation, which was not disputed, was sufficient to satisfy the relevant requirements as to form laid down in Article 17.

The difference between the two courts dealing with the substance in their appraisal of the facts and concerning the existence in the present case of an oral agreement assigning jurisdiction may perhaps explain why the Bundesgerichtshof, to which the purchaser appealed against the judgment of the appeal court, has submitted two separate questions on the interpretation of Article 17 relating to two separate sets of circumstances, the first concerning the interpretation placed on the facts by the appeal court, the second appearing to be framed in accordance with the different view of the facts taken by the court of first instance.

The questions are as follows:

(1) Are the requirements of Article 17 of the Convention of 27 September 1968 on jurisdiction and the enforcement of judgments in civil and commercial matters satisfied if, at the oral conclusion of a contract of sale, a vendor has stated that he wishes to rely on his general conditions of sale and if he subsequently confirms the contract in writing to the purchaser and annexes to this confirmation his general conditions of sale which contain a clause assigning jurisdiction?

(2) Are the requirements of the said article satisfied if, in dealings between merchants, a vendor, after the oral conclusion of a contract of sale, confirms in writing to the purchaser the conclusion of the contract subject to his general conditions of sale and annexes to this document his conditions of sale which include a clause assigning jurisdiction and if the purchaser does not challenge this confirmatory letter?

2. Under Article 17 an oral agreement for jurisdiction by consent is, with a view to expediting trade, a valid means of conferring exclusive jurisdiction on the selected court but, out of consideration for the certainty of legal relationships and the protection of the weaker party, such an agreement has effect only if it is

followed by confirmation in writing (the article cited requires in terms an 'oral agreement confirmed in writing'). Such confirmation must obviously be such as to fulfil the purpose for which it was required. Furthermore, especially when the clause assigning jurisdiction is one of a set of general conditions pre-determined by one of the parties, particular care must be taken to ensure that confirmation is effected in such a way as to leave no doubt concerning the agreement of the other party to the assignment of jurisdiction.

At this juncture there arises the issue of confirmation forthcoming from one only of the parties. The Jenard report, which was presented with the Brussels Convention, stated that the wording of Article 17 is 'very similar' to that of the Germano-Belgian Convention, which is in turn based on the Hague Convention of 15 April 1958 on selected jurisdiction in connexion with international sales of goods. As regards the effectiveness of oral agreements assigning jurisdiction the Germano-Belgian Convention requires 'confirmation in writing which has not been disputed' (Article 3(2)) and the Hague Convention confirmation 'by declaration in writing by one of the parties or by a broker without having been contested' (Article 2), both of them, of course, with specific reference to the designation of the Court which is to have jurisdiction. The Jenard report adds that 'since the clause conferring jurisdiction presupposes a genuine agreement between the parties, the court may not necessarily regard a writing made by the party invoking it as proof of an oral agreement'.

In the light of these considerations, it is, in my opinion, clearly impossible to justify so strict a view with regard to the requirements for confirmation as that suggested by Segoura, the effect of which would be wholly and absolutely to rule out any possibility of valid confirmation being supplied by the party which has pre-determined the clause assigning jurisdiction. The wording of Article 17 does not appear to require this, nor would it be necessary for the protection of the party against whom the assignment of jurisdiction is being invoked because the latter still retains the right, after receiving the letter of confirmation, to challenge anything stated therein which relates to the oral agreement on assignment. The essential purpose of confirmation in writing of an oral agreement assigning jurisdiction is to express the oral clause in words which are objectively certain, and to define its precise terms as they affect the parties and the selected court which, under the clause, is assigned jurisdiction in disputes arising in connexion with a specific legal relationship. The same purpose can be achieved even when the written document containing the confirmation is supplied by the party which pre-determined the assignment clause provided that, having regard to the previous and subsequent conduct of the two parties to the agreement, this is done in such a way as to amount to objective verification of the agreement reached on the clause reduced to writing in the 'confirmation'.

Apart, therefore, from the case of a bilateral confirmation which obviously presents no difficulty, it is possible to distinguish two separate examples of written confirmation given by one party only in the context of general conditions, including assignment of jurisdiction, pre-determined in its own interests by one of the contracting parties. In the first example, confirmation is given by the party which did not pre-determine the general conditions and to whom the clause is disadvantageous. Even if such confirmation refers to the general conditions as a whole it can be regarded as sufficient to give effect to the assignment clause. The second example occurs when confirmation is forthcoming from the party which has pre-determined the general conditions. It is clear that, in this case, there must be stricter approach: that is to say, confirmation in writing must record not only the oral agreement concerning the general conditions but, in particular, the agreement regarding the clause assigning jurisdiction. What must be avoided is the possibility that the clause has gone unnoticed or has simply not been mentioned in a comprehensive reference to the general conditions of contract. It must, of course, be borne in mind that the above-mentioned rules of the Conventions all provide for written confirmation of an oral agreement assigning jurisdiction; it is therefore the conclusion of that agreement which must be proved. And, as is usual, the weaker party must have played its part in the conclusion of such agreement not only by being aware of the assignment clause but also by being willing to accept it.

3. In the light of the foregoing considerations, I come now to consider the case, set out in the first question, where, at the time of the oral conclusion of a contract of sale, the vendor did no more than make a unilateral and very general declaration of his intention to contract on the basis of the general conditions which he himself had laid down. In a case of this kind can the jurisdiction clause be regarded as having been incorporated in the agreement although there has never been any direct mention of it?

It will be noted that the case in question is very different from that in which a comprehensive reference to conditions of sale laid down in advance by the vendor is included in the text of a written contract on the back of which those conditions, including the clause on jurisdiction, are printed. In that case the purchaser has ample opportunity to acquaint himself with the clause before concluding the contract.

On the other hand, when an oral contract is entered into it is, as the vendor itself agrees in its observations in the present case, reasonable to assume that the parties concentrate their attention on the essential points of the agreement without specifically considering the general conditions, of which, therefore, the purchaser really becomes aware only when it receives the letter from the vendor confirming the oral agreement relating to the essential points and to which the text of the general conditions is annexed. If the purchaser has not been aware of the assignment clause he cannot conceivably have agreed to it; the purchasers presumed agreement to an indefinite number of general conditions would be tantamount to leaving the vendor free to determine the court which is to have jurisdiction, and this is not the same as an agreement specifically designating the court which is to have jurisdiction, as provided for by Article 17.

The situation might well be different in the case, on which we need not however express a view here, where there is a continuous business relationship between two undertakings by virtue of which it is customary to apply the assignment clause in accordance with the general conditions laid down in advance by one of the parties. In such circumstances it is not inconceivable that a straightforward general reference by word of mouth to such conditions by the vendor and agreed to by the purchaser may amount to consent by the latter to the assignment clause. When, therefore, in the conclusion of a sales agreement the facts are as described in the first question, the attachment of the written text of the conditions of sale to the subsequent letter of confirmation referring to them cannot constitute confirmation within the meaning of Article 17 because its essential premise is lacking, namely prior agreement on the assignment of jurisdiction. Such a letter may constitute a draft amendment of the oral contract but, as such, it is capable of having effect only if the other party has agreed to it in writing.

4. Nor is the view which I have developed up to this point invalidated by the objection that it goes beyond consideration of the formal requirements provided for by Article 17 of the Convention since it broaches the question of the conditions required for the existence of an agreement selecting jurisdiction to be valid. In fact, the questions submitted by the national court are concerned with the extent to which particular circumstances meet the requirements (all the requirements) laid down by Article 17, and the 'sufficiency' of particular conduct for the purposes of that article. Article 17 must accordingly be viewed as a whole and it is clear that, even before laying down specific requirements as to form, its purpose is to ensure that the parties have concluded an agreement (or agreed on a clause) the purpose of which is to select a forum which is to be seised of disputes which have arisen or are liable to arise out of a given legal relationship. That is to say, the rule in question also includes conditions of substance, the first of which is the existence of an agreement of a certain type and which has a particular purpose. In this connexion, the question legitimately arises whether the substantive aspects of the agreement assigning jurisdiction are to be deduced from Article 17, interpreted by itself, or whether these aspects ought not rather to be left for determination under the law of the different States. The issue is similar to that described in my opinion in Case 24/76 regarding the form of the agreement in question and, in particular, the possibility that the meaning at the words 'in writing' should be interpreted in accordance with the law applicable in the various States. And the answer in this case must follow the same lines: in so far as such requirements, whether relating to substance or to form, have been laid down by the Convention as conditions precedent for the formalities required by the Convention to be fulfilled, an independent interpretation must be found on the basis of the logic and wording of the Convention. All this is, of course, without prejudice to national requirements in other respects, whether of form or of substance, which do not come within the ambit of the Convention rules subject to Community interpretation.

The close connexion between the question of confirmation in writing of an oral agreement assigning jurisdiction and that of the existence of such an agreement is abundantly clear. To distinguish between the existence of an oral agreement and its confirmation by regarding the first as exclusively subject to national law and, accordingly, to different legal rules and case-law, while the other was governed by a single legal system would be liable to create serious discrepancies in the application of Article 17 within the Contracting States. I may add that, if the definition of the requirements for the creation of an agreement were beyond the scope of the Convention, the appraisal by this Court of the formal requirement of confirmation in writing might prove too restrictive or too liberal, according to the standpoint of the particular national legal system which is regarded as having jurisdiction to verify the existence of the assignment clause. This would produce a situation contrary to the principle of uniformity which the Convention seeks to establish.

5. Consideration of the second question submitted by the national Court does not, at this juncture, call for much comment. As this Court is aware, the difference between the case stated in the first question and that in the second question is the following: in the first, the vendor's statement that he intends to apply his own general conditions to the contract is assumed to have been made at the time when the contract was orally concluded; in the second, the declaration is assumed to have been made in writing only after the oral conclusion of the contract and without protest on the part of the purchaser. In these circumstances, it seems clear that when, during the negotiations which lead to the oral contract of sale, there is not even any reference to the general conditions including the assignment clause, that consensus of wills on the assignment of jurisdiction without which there cannot be any 'confirmation' within the meaning of Article 17 is absolutely lacking.

6. It is accordingly my opinion that the Court should reply to the questions of the Bundesgerichtshof by ruling that the requirements of Article 17 of the Brussels Convention of 27 September 1961 are not satisfied if, during the oral conclusion of a contract of sale, the vendor indicates that he wishes to rely on the general conditions of sale laid down by himself and does no more than make a general reference to those conditions without specifically mentioning the assignment of jurisdiction and subsequently sends to the purchaser a written confirmation of the contract to which are annexed his general conditions, including a clause assigning jurisdiction.

The reply must be the same even if, after the conclusion between merchants of an oral contract of sale, the vendor confirms the contract in writing and, simultaneously, for the first time states that the contract is to be regarded as subject to the general conditions of sale - which include a clause assigning jurisdiction - laid down by the vendor himself and attached to the writing, and the purchaser does not indicate his dissent.

Case 23/78 - 9 November 1978

Nikolaus Meeth
v
Glacetal

Article 17, first paragraph - Agreement conferring jurisdiction - Mutual assent to the jurisdiction of the courts of the State of domicile of the defendant - Lawfulness - Power of such courts to take into account a set-off connected with the legal relationship in dispute - Conditions.

Summary

1. Although, with regard to an agreement of conferring jurisdiction, Article 17 of the Brussels Convention, as it is worded, refers to the choice by the parties to a contract of a single court or the courts of a single State, that wording cannot be interpreted as prohibiting an agreement under which the two parties to a contract, who are domiciled in different States, can be sued only in the courts of their respective States.

2. Having regard to the need to respect individuals' right of independence, upon which Article 17 is based, and the need to avoid superfluous procedure, which forms the basis of the Convention as a whole, the first paragraph of Article 17 cannot be interpreted as preventing a Court before which proceedings have been instituted pursuant to a clause of the type described above from taking into account a claim for a set-off connected with the legal relationship in dispute if such court considers that course to be compatible with the letter and spirit of the clause conferring jurisdiction.

JUDGMENT OF THE COURT

Kutscher, President, Mertens de Wilmars and Lord Mackenzie Stuart, Presidents of Chambers, Pescatore, Sorensen, O'Keeffe and Bosco, Judges

1. By an order of 1 February 1978, which was received at the Court Registry on 27 February 1978, the Bundesgerichtshof submitted pursuant to the Protocol of 3 June 1971 on the Interpretation by the Court of Justice of the Convention of 27 September 1968 on Jurisdiction and the Enforcement of Judgments in Civil and Commercial Matters (hereinafter referred to as 'the Convention') certain questions concerning the interpretation of Article 17 of the Convention.

2. The file shows that the undertaking Nikolaus Meeth, window manufacturers and wood processors, established in Piesport/Mosel, Federal Republic of Germany, the defendant in the main action and appellant on a point of law, entered into a contract with Glacetal S. à R. L., the plaintiff in the main action and respondent to the appeal, for the supply of glass by the French company to the German undertaking.

3. The parties agreed that the contract should be governed by German law, that the place of performance of the contract was Piesport and that 'if Meeth sues Glacetal the French courts alone shall have jurisdiction. If Glacetal sues Meeth the German courts alone shall have jurisdiction'.
When Meeth failed to pay for certain deliveries effected by Glacetal the latter commenced proceedings to obtain payment of the sums due before the Landgericht Trier - the court having jurisdiction on the basis of the defendant's domicile - which ordered the German undertaking to make payment.

In the course of that procedure Meeth raised against Glacetal's claim a defence of set-off relating to the damage which it claimed to have suffered owing to delay or default on the part of the French company in performing its obligations under the contract.

The court of first instance, however, refused to allow that sum to be set off against the sale-price claimed by the French company since it considered that Meeth had failed to adduce sufficient proof in support of its claim for damages.

Meeth appealed against that judgment to the Oberlandesgericht Koblenz, which in turn found that the French undertaking was entitled to the payments it claimed, subject, however, to the effects of a composition in bankruptcy which had in the meantime been arranged.

With regard to the set-off between the selling price and the claim submitted by Meeth, the Oberlandesgericht did not allow this defence on the ground that the clause conferring jurisdiction contained in the agreement between the parties did not permit a set-off to be claimed before the German courts.

An appeal was made against this judgment on a point of law to the Bundesgerichtshof which considers that the answer to this question depends on the interpretation of Article 17 of the Convention and has referred two preliminary questions on this point to the Court of Justice.

The first question

4. The first question asks: 'Does the first paragraph of Article 17 of the Convention permit an agreement under which the two parties to a contract for sale, who are domiciled in different States, can be sued only in the courts of their respective States?'

5. According to the first paragraph of Article 17 'if the parties … have agreed that a court or the courts of a Contracting State are to have jurisdiction to settle any disputes which have arisen or which may arise in connection with a particular legal relationship, that court or those courts shall have exclusive jurisdiction'.

With regard to an agreement conferring reciprocal jurisdiction in the form in which it appears in the contract whose implementation forms the subject-matter of the dispute, the interpretation of that provision gives rise to difficulty because of the fact that Article 17, as it is worded, refers to the choice by the parties to the contract of a single court or the courts of a single State.

That wording, which is based on the most widespread business practice, cannot, however, be interpreted as intending to exclude the right of the parties to agree on two or more courts for the purpose of settling any disputes which may arise.

This interpretation is justified on the ground that Article 17 is based on a recognition of the independent will of the parties to a contract in deciding which courts are to have jurisdiction to settle disputes falling within the scope of the Convention, other than those which are expressly excluded pursuant to the second paragraph of Article 17.

This applies particularly where the parties have by such an agreement reciprocally conferred jurisdiction on the courts specified in the general rule laid down by Article 2 of the Convention.

Although such an agreement coincides with the scope of Article 2 it is, nevertheless, effective in that it excludes, in relations between the parties, other optional attributions of jurisdiction, such as those detailed in Articles 5 and 6 of the Convention.

6. The reply to the first question must accordingly be that the first paragraph of Article 17 of the Convention cannot be interpreted as prohibiting an agreement under which the two parties to a contract for sale, who are domiciled in different States, can be sued only in the courts of their respective States.

The Second Question

7. The Second question asks: 'Where an agreement permitted by the first paragraph of Article 17 of the Convention contains the clause mentioned in Question 1, does it automatically rule out any off-set which one of the parties to the contract wishes to propose in pursuance of a claim arising under the said agreement in answer to the claim made by the other party in the court having jurisdiction to hear the latter claim?'

8. According to the first paragraph of Article 17, jurisdiction is conferred on a given court or courts in order to settle any disputes which have arisen or which may arise 'in connection with a particular legal relationship'.

The question of the extent to which a court before which a case is brought pursuant to a reciprocal jurisdiction clause, such as that appearing in the contract between the parties, has jurisdiction to decide on a set-off claimed by one of the parties on the basis of the disputed contractual obligation must be determined with regard both to the need to respect individuals' right of independence, upon which Article 17, as has been noted above, is based, and the need to avoid superfluous procedure, which forms the basis of the Convention as a whole of which Article 17 is part.

In the light of both of these objectives Article 17 cannot be interpreted as preventing a court before which proceedings have been instituted pursuant to a clause conferring jurisdiction of the type described above from taking into account a claim for a set-off connected with the legal relationship in dispute if such court considers that course to be compatible with the letter and spirit of the clause conferring jurisdiction.

9. Accordingly, the reply to the second question must be that where there is a clause conferring jurisdiction such as that described in the reply to the first question the first paragraph of Article 17 of the Convention

cannot be interpreted as prohibiting the court before which a dispute has been brought in pursuance of such a clause from taking into account a set-off connected with the legal relationship in dispute.

On those grounds, the court, in answer to the questions referred to it by the Bundesgerichtshof by an order of 1 February 1978, hereby rules:

1. The first paragraph of Article 17 of the Convention of 27 September 1968 on Jurisdiction and the Enforcement of Judgments in Civil and Commercial Matters cannot be interpreted as prohibiting an agreement under which the two parties to a contract for sale, who are domiciled in different States, can be sued only in the courts of their respective States.

2. Where there is a clause conferring jurisdiction such as that described in the reply to the first question the first paragraph of Article 17 of the Convention of 27 September 1968 cannot be interpreted as prohibiting the court before which a dispute has been brought in pursuance of such a clause from taking into account a set-off connected with the legal relationship in dispute.

OPINION OF MR ADVOCATE GENERAL CAPOTORTI

1. In exercising its jurisdiction to interpret the Brussels Convention of 27 September 1968 on Jurisdiction and the Enforcement of Judgments in Civil and Commercial Matters the Court of Justice has already had occasion to consider Article 17 which, as the Court is aware, governs ‘prorogation of jurisdiction’. In two judgments of 14 December 1976 delivered in Cases 24/76 *Estasis Salotti* v *Ruwa* and 25/76 *Galeries Segoura* v *Bonakdarian* [1976] ECR 1831 and 1851) the Court gave particular attention to the form of clauses conferring jurisdiction. Two different questions have now been submitted, one of which concerns the conditions for the permissibility of a clause of that nature with regard to its content, whilst by the other it is intended to establish whether that prorogation of jurisdiction must also cover a claim of set-off submitted by the defendant.

It is sufficient with regard to the fact to recall that: (a) in August 1972 a contract for the supply of glass was concluded between the company Glacetal, having its registered office in France, and the undertaking Meeth, having its registered office in the Federal Republic of Germany. The contract contained in addition to a clause assenting to the jurisdiction of the German courts, a clause prorogating jurisdiction whereby proceedings instituted by Meeth were to come under the jurisdiction of the French courts whilst proceedings initiated by Glacetal had to be brought before the German courts; (b) subsequently, Glacetal, in order to obtain payment of the balance of the price remaining unpaid, instituted proceedings against the defendant in the Landgericht (Regional Court) Trier which, by judgment of 13 January 1975, found in favour of the plaintiff. In the course of an appeal to the Oberlandesgericht (Higher Regional Court) Koblenz the undertaking Meeth claimed a set-off in respect of an alleged credit arising out of its right to compensation for damages caused through delay in delivery of the goods; however, the Oberlandesgericht, in its judgment of 17 September 1976, declared that defence was inadmissible since, under the clause conferring jurisdiction, the French courts alone were entitled to pronounce judgment on Meeth's claim; (c) following a further appeal the proceedings are now before the Bundesgerichtshof (Federal Court of Justice) which, by an order of 1 February 1978, has submitted the following two questions to the Court of Justice:

1. Does the first paragraph of Article 17 of the Convention permit an agreement under which the two parties to a contract for sale, who are domiciled in different States, can be sued only in the courts of their respective States?

2. Where an agreement permitted by the first paragraph of Article 17 of the Convention contains the clause mentioned in Question 1, does it automatically rule out any set-off which one of the parties to the contract wishes to propose in pursuance of a claim arising under the said agreement in answer to the claim made by the other party in the court having jurisdiction to hear the latter claim?

2. The doubt which is expressed by the first question concerns the following point: the first paragraph of Article 17 of the Convention relates to a clause whereby 'the parties have .... agreed that a court or the courts *of a Contracting State* are to have jurisdiction to settle any disputes which have arisen in connection with a particular legal relationship', whereas a clause such as that in the present case confers jurisdiction on the courts *of two Contracting States* to settle disputes arising from the contract and the disputes are assigned to the courts of one or other State depending on which of the parties to the contract initiates proceedings.

In my view the validity of a clause of this nature can be recognized without misgivings. Indeed, it is probable that no doubt would have arisen if the clause had been worded differently; that is, if it had prescribed that each party could be sued only before the courts of his domicile (or perhaps of the State of which he is a national: in the present case the two links coincide). In those circumstances an identical intention would have been expressed in such a way as to emphasize the concern of the parties to establish a single criterion as being decisive: the domicile (or the nationality) of the defendant. Nevertheless, quite apart from the foregoing, it can be recognized that the parties to a contract may stipulate that the courts of two States shall have jurisdiction to settle disputes arising from that contract, provided that each jurisdiction is restricted to a specified class of dispute. In short, there is nothing to preclude the parties, instead of treating all disputes which could arise from their contract as a whole, from dividing them into two of more groups in accordance with criteria which they are free to establish and prescribing the courts of a different State for each group. This is not a common step but there are no grounds for considering it unlawful.

The Commission is accordingly correct in observing that the parties to the contract could have concluded two separate agreements (one for proceedings which Meeth might institute and the other for proceedings initiated by Glacetal), thus specifying in each of such agreements a single jurisdiction (the French courts in the former case, the German in the latter). The simpler form, whereby two separate, national agreements are combined in a single clause, clearly cannot affect the problem of the substantive validity of such expression of the joint intention of the parties.

It is scarcely necessary to state that the specific choice made by the parties in the present case is undoubtedly compatible with Article 17 of the Convention. We have seen that the Bundesgerichtshof has referred exclusively to the first paragraph of Article 17, which does not prescribe limits to the right to such choice in that it does not require that there be any material link between the contract and the State to which the court or tribunal specified by the clause pertains. But even if regard be had to the second paragraph of Article 17, the conditions concerning validity which it prescribes - a requirement that Articles 12, 15 and 16 must in all circumstances be observed - it will simply be found that the clause in question does not infringe any of those conditions. Accordingly it is merely superfluous to point out that the choice expressed in the clause is fully in accordance with the general system of the Convention: the courts specified are those of the defendant's country of domicile, as is provided in the first paragraph of Article 2. The only effect of the clause is thus that the jurisdiction based on domicile is rendered exclusive.

It remains, finally, to point out that the Commission has further doubted whether the generic description in the clause conferring jurisdiction of the courts of a State is sufficient in the absence of further specification of the level or type of court. The Commission has itself affirmed that it is sufficient, and indeed it appears to me that nothing could conform more completely with Article 17 than the literal repetition of the wording adopted by that article ('the courts of a Contracting State are to have jurisdiction...'). It seems to me clear that a clause so worded refers by implication to the system of rules of territorial jurisdiction relating to value and subject-matter in force in the State in question in order to determine precisely the court before which proceedings must be instituted.

3. I shall now turn to consider the second question, which is undoubtedly more complex. It appears to me proper, first of all, to clarify the wording of the question in order to avoid any confusion which might arise from the question as it has been formulated by the Bundesgerichtshof. That court has, in fact, asked whether an agreement prorogating jurisdiction such as that at issue in the present case precludes any possibility on the part of the defendant to put forward a defence of set-off in the court before which the plaintiff has brought his action and which has jurisdiction under the agreement to settle the main action. The problem which the Court of Justice is required to decide is not that of the interpretation of the intention of the parties to the contract and the scope which they attributed, whether expressly or by implication, to that jurisdiction clause. That is for the national court to settle. The interpretation of the clause must, however, be preceded by an interpretation of the rules of the Brussels

Convention with a view to attaining two ends: to ascertain, on the one hand, whether or not the parties to a contract who draw up a clause prorogating jurisdiction have the power, if they wish, to exclude the hypothesis of a defence of set-off before the court having jurisdiction under the clause; and to establish, on the other, how to resolve the problem of jurisdiction concerning a set-off where jurisdiction over the main action has been determined by an agreement prorogating jurisdiction of the type described above and where the parties have made no provision whatever for dealing with claims of this nature.

Another essential point appears to me that concerning the nature of the claim in question. In its observations the German Government was rightly concerned to point out that for the purposes of this procedure 'set-off' ('Aufrechnung') must be taken to mean only 'reliance by one party as a defence, on the substantive effects of a set-off in court proceedings', and that we are not concerned either with a case in which a set-off agreement is invoked or with a case in which the defendant submits a counterclaim based on sums due to him to be offset against his debt. In this matter I have to point out that, whilst the first of those cases is certainly irrelevant to the question submitted by the Bundesgerichtshof, the file does not make it sufficiently clear whether in the present proceedings the German undertaking has put forward a defence of set-off strictly so-called or a counter-claim. Investigation of this matter falls within the jurisdiction of the court dealing with the substance of the case. However, since the distinction between a counterclaim and a defence is very important for the reply to the question in point, I think it appropriate to take account of both possibilities.

In substantive law the mechanism of a set-off is clear: a debt owed by one person to another is extinguished because the debtor is also the creditor of the opposite party; naturally, the debt and the credit are cancelled out up to an equal amount. With regard to procedure, however, two situations may arise: the case where the defendant relies on the plaintiff's debt exclusively as a defence and the case where the defendant submits a counterclaim. The difference is that the defence is concerned exclusively to obtain the dismissal of the plaintiff's claim, whilst the counterclaim is intended to establish a claim by the defendant and accordingly to obtain a ruling against the plaintiff. In the case of the set-off the defendant may rely on this defence to justify his non-payment of the debt claimed by the plaintiff; but he must introduce a counterclaim if he wishes his own debt to be recognized in its entirety and to obtain a ruling compelling the plaintiff to make payment (full payment if the court rules that the plaintiff's claim is unfounded; partial payment if it upholds the plaintiff's claim but the amount to which the defendant is entitled exceeds that owing to the plaintiff).

4. The above considerations are, I think, sufficient guidance for an inquiry. Let us suppose that the set-off is claimed purely as a defence. In that case it appears to me that the parties to a contract who draw up a clause prorogating jurisdiction do not have power to preclude the court on which jurisdiction is conferred from taking cognizance in addition of any defence, provided that the set-off is claimed in respect of a right arising from the same contract. In fact, in accordance with Article 17 of the Convention, all jurisdiction clauses confer

upon the court or courts chosen by the parties jurisdiction 'to settle *any disputes* which have arisen or which may arise in connection with a particular legal relationship'. The set-off, the defence relied upon by the defendant, remains within the context of the dispute which the plaintiff has brought before the court; that dispute continues to be classified as arising from the contractual relationship binding the parties where the set-off too expresses a claim originating in that relationship. To consider that the defence should be brought before a different court from that seized of the main action would entail dissolving the unity of the procedure and would disregard the rights of the defence, since it would, in fact, oblige the defendant to change his defence into an independent claim. Accordingly, I consider that, despite anything which may have been included in the prorogating agreement, jurisdiction to hear a set-off must always be attributed to the court having jurisdiction to hear the main action. Likewise, I think it unnecessary in this context to refer to the principles of the proper administration of justice and economy of procedure, which were no doubt amongst the principles which prompted the Convention of 1968, and to which both the Commission and the German Government have referred in their observations.

If the defence takes the form of a counterclaim, quite different considerations apply. Article 6(3) of the Convention lays down a special rule on counterclaims arising from the same contract or facts on which the original claim was based, providing that the court in which the original claim is pending has jurisdiction. Likewise in the context of the provisions on jurisdiction in matters relating to insurance and instalment sales and loans, it is expressly stated that they do not affect the right to bring a counterclaim in the court in which, in accordance with Sections 3 and 4 of Title II, the original claim is pending (second paragraph of Article 11 and third paragraph of Article 14). The said Article 6, however, is one of those special jurisdiction provisions which are to be considered as being excluded by the prorogation of jurisdiction: the Court of Justice made this clear in the said judgments in the *Salotti* v *Rüwa* case (paragraph 7 of the decision) and in the *Segoura* v *Bonakdarian* case (paragraph 6 of the decision). The decisive factor here, in other words, is the exclusive nature of the jurisdiction conferred; the independent nature of a counterclaim, precisely because it is a positive action and not merely a defence, allows it to be separated from the main procedure, as of necessity, happens if a clause of the type in question requires one party to the agreement to bring proceedings before a court other than that before which proceedings must be instituted by the other party. This point is also supported by legal writers: I shall only indicate Weser ('Convention Communautaire sur la Compétence Judiciaire et l'Exécution des Décisions', p. 266). The celebrated Jenard Report also makes clear that any clause based on Article 17 which is inserted in an agreement concerning a guarantee takes precedence over the special provision on jurisdiction contained in Article 6(2), although it does not deal with the relation between a clause conferring jurisdiction and the rule in Article 6(3); however, I think it can be taken that the reasoning applied with regard to Article 6(2) also applies to the next paragraph.

If the foregoing is correct, it must follow that the parties to a contract may, if such is their intention, expressly provide that counterclaims cannot be brought before the court on which jurisdiction has been conferred by a clause of the type in question. If the parties make no provision on this point such exclusion of jurisdiction follows from the relationship between Article 17 and Article 6 of the Convention. Finally, in view of the breadth of the discretion attributed to parties to contracts by the said Article 17, it would naturally be possible for them, whilst making provision in general terms for the exclusive jurisdiction of the courts of the domicile of the defendant, at the same time to provide (always subject to observance of the formal requirements prescribed in that article) that counterclaims should be 'drawn into' the jurisdiction specified for main actions.

5. In conclusion I suggest that the Court, in reply to the questions referred to it by the Bundesgerichtshof by its order of 1 February 1978, should rule that:

(a) An agreement to the effect that each of the parties to a contract for sale, who are domiciled in different States and have different nationalities, may be sued only before the courts of his domicile or of the State of which he is a national, is valid in accordance with Article 17 of the Brussels Convention of 27 September 1968 on Jurisdiction and the Enforcement of Judgments in Civil and Commercial Matters.

(b) The fact that it has been agreed in the context of a contract for sale between persons domiciled in different States and having different nationalities that the courts of the domicile of the defendant (or of the State of which he is a national) shall have exclusive jurisdiction does not prevent those courts from having sole jurisdiction to settle a claim of set-off submitted purely as a defence by the defendant in proceedings instituted by the other party to the contract.

(c) An agreement in a contract for sale to the effect that each of the parties, who are domiciled in different States and have different nationalities, may be sued only before the courts of his domicile (or of the State of which he is a national) precludes the submission of a counterclaim before the court having jurisdiction to take cognizance of the main action unless this has been expressly provided for by the parties.

Case 25/79 - 13 November 1979

Sanicentral GmbH
v
René Collin

Field of application of the Convention - Employment law - Inclusion - Object of the Convention - Precedence over national laws - Articles 17 and 54 - Transitional provisions - Judicial proceedings instituted after the coming into force of the Convention - Prior clauses conferring jurisdiction which according to national rules in force at the time of agreement were void - Validity.

Summary

1. Employment law comes within the substantive field of application of the Convention on Jurisdiction and the Enforcement of Judgments in Civil and Commercial Matters signed at Brussels on 27 September 1968.

2. As the Brussels Convention seeks to determine the jurisdiction of the courts of the contracting States in the intra-Community legal order in regard to matters of civil jurisdiction, the national procedural laws applicable to the cases concerned are set aside in the matters governed by the Convention in favour of the provisions thereof.

3. Articles 17 and 54 of the Brussels Convention must be interpreted to mean that, in judicial proceedings instituted after the coming into force of the Convention, clauses conferring jurisdiction included in contracts of employment concluded prior to that date must be considered valid even in cases in which they would have been regarded as void under the national law in force at the time when the contract was entered into.

JUDGMENT OF THE COURT

Kutscher, President, O'Keeffe and Touffait, Presidents of Chambers, Mertens de Wilmars, Pescatore, Lord Mackenzie Stuart and Bosco, Judges

1. By a judgment dated 10 January 1979, received at the Court Registry on 12 February 1979, the French Cour de Cassation (Social Chamber) referred to the Court of Justice under the Protocol of 3 June 1971 on the Interpretation by the Court of Justice of the Convention of 27 September 1968 on Jurisdiction and the Enforcement of Judgments in Civil and Commercial Matters (hereinafter referred to as 'the Convention') a question relating to the interpretation of Articles 17 and 54 of the said Convention which, in accordance with Article 62 thereof, entered into force on 1 February 1973. This question is raised in the course of an action, concerned with the breach - on 8 December 1971 - of a contract of employment containing a clause conferring jurisdiction upon a German court, between a French worker, resident in France, and a German company which had engaged him to work in the Federal Republic of Germany, independently of any establishment.

This contract of employment was concluded on 27 October 1971 and the court proceedings were commenced on 27 November 1973.

2. In view of these facts the Cour de Cassation asks whether the clause conferring jurisdiction is effective in the case of contracts of employment concluded prior to the Convention or whether 'insofar as they concern the protection of employed workers those provisions relate to the very substance of agreements and must be given effect only in relation to subsequent contracts'. The Cour de Cassation accordingly framed the following question:

'Whether, in application of Article 54 of the Brussels Convention, Article 17 of that Convention must be interpreted to mean that, when proceedings have been commenced after 1 February 1973, clauses conferring jurisdiction inserted into a contract of employment concluded before 1 February 1973 which would have been regarded as void by the internal legislation in force at that time must henceforward be deemed to be valid, regardless of the date of the agreements between the parties and the date of the performance of the work in question'.

3. It follows from this question that the Cour de Cassation rightly accepts that employment law comes within the substantive field of application of the Convention and that litigation arising out of a contract

of employment concluded after 1 February 1973 is subject to the Convention and particularly to Article 17 thereof relating to prorogation of jurisdiction.

4. In view of the fact that the contract of employment was broken off on 8 December 1971 and that the judicial proceedings were not commenced until 27 November 1973, that is after the Convention had come into force, the Cour de Cassation is concerned as to the meaning of Article 54 of the Convention which provides that 'the provisions of this Convention shall apply only to legal proceedings instituted and to documents formally drawn up or registered as authentic instruments after its entry into force'and asks whether the clause in the contract of employment conferring jurisdiction, which could have been regarded under French legislation prior to 1 February 1973 as being void, recovers its validity at the date of the entry into force of the Convention.

5. It is appropriate to answer this point by stating, on the one hand, that the Convention does not affect rules of substantive law and, on the other hand, that, as the Convention seeks to determine the jurisdiction of the courts of the Contracting States in the intra-Community legal order in regard to matters of civil jurisdiction, the national procedural laws applicable to the cases concerned are set aside in the matters governed by the Convention in favour of the provisions thereof.

6. By its nature a clause in writing conferring jurisdiction and occurring in a contract of employment is a choice of jurisdiction; such a choice has no legal effect for so long as no judicial proceedings have been commenced and only becomes of consequence at the date when judicial proceedings are set in motion.

That is, therefore, the relevant date for the purposes of an appreciation of the scope of such a clause in relation to the legal rules applying at that time.

The judicial proceedings were instituted on 27 November 1973 and the Convention thus applies in pursuance of Article 54 thereof.

The effect of that article indeed is that the only essential for the rules of the Convention to be applicable to litigation relating to legal relationships created before the date of the coming into force of the Convention is that the judicial proceedings should have been instituted subsequently to that date, which is the position in the present instance.

7. Consequently, the answer to the question raised by the French Cour de Cassation (Social Chamber) must be that Articles 17 and 54 of the

Convention must be interpreted to mean that, in judicial proceedings instituted after the coming into force of the Convention, clauses conferring jurisdiction included in contracts of employment concluded prior to that date must be considered valid even in cases in which they would have been regarded as void under the national law in force at the time when the contract was entered into.

On those grounds, the court, in answer to the question referred to it by the Cour de Cassation (Social Chamber) by a judgment of 10 January 1979, hereby rules:

> **Articles 17 and 54 of the Convention of Brussels of 27 September 1968 on Jurisdiction and the Enforcement of Judgments in Civil and Commercial Matters must be interpreted to mean that, in judicial proceedings instituted after the coming into force of the Convention, clauses conferring jurisdiction included in contracts of employment concluded prior to that date must be considered valid even in cases in which they would have been regarded as void under the national law in force at the time when the contract was entered into.**

OPINION OF MR ADVOCATE GENERAL CAPOTORTI

1. The preliminary proceedings of which my opinion of today forms part, raise two interesting problems of the interpretation of the Convention of Brussels of 27 September 1968 on Jurisdiction and the Enforcement of Judgments in Civil and Commercial Matters. First, one has the opportunity of clarifying whether clauses conferring jurisdiction which the parties to a contract of employment have agreed upon are in every case effective in accordance with Article 17 of the Convention, notwithstanding the contrary provisions of some statutory legislation in regard to the exclusion of the jurisdiction of the national courts dealing with labour relations. If that issue fails to be resolved in the affirmative, the question remains whether in the case of contracts of employment entered into and executed prior to the date of the coming into force of the Convention (that is to say, prior to 1 February 1973) the clauses in question must be considered as effective under Article 54 of the same Convention whenever a court is called upon to deal with a dispute after the aforementioned date.

To summarise briefly the facts of the case before us I would recall that on 27 October 1971 René Collin, a French national, contracted in the capacity of an employee with Sanicentral, of Saarbrücken, a company with limited liability incorporated under German law, to work in the Federal Republic independently of any establishment. A specific clause of the contract of employment, which was reduced to writing, conferred upon the German courts jurisdiction to decide any disputes arising between the parties in relation to their respective obligations. The employment relationship was terminated on 8 December 1971 and Mr Collin, by a summons dated 26 November 1973, applied to the Tribunal d'Instance, Molsheim (Bas-Rhin), sitting as an industrial relations tribunal for a decree obliging the German company to pay to him certain salary supplements and various allowances. The French court assumed jurisdiction on the view that, under French law, clauses inserted in contracts of employment and purporting to exclude territorial jurisdiction are void.

The Cour d'Appel [Court of Appeal], Colmar, to which the employer applied at second instance, by its judgment of 23 September 1976, confirmed the decision of the court of first instance insofar as it was concerned with the impossibility of excluding jurisdiction, adding that, in any event, Article 17 of the Convention of Brussels could not have been applied insofar as the Convention came into force in France subsequently to the date of the contract of employment concerned. The case was finally brought before the Cour de Cassation [Court of Cassation] (Social Chamber) and that court, by a judgment dated 10 October 1979, submitted to the Court of Justice, by means of a preliminary reference, the following question: 'Whether, in application of Article 54 of the Brussels Convention, Article 17 of that Convention must be interpreted to mean that, when proceedings have been commenced after 1 February 1973, clauses conferring jurisdiction inserted into a contract of employment concluded before 1 February 1973 which would have been regarded as void by the internal legislation in force at that time must henceforward be deemed to be valid, regardless of the date of the agreements between the parties and of the date of the performance of the work in question'.

2. That the Convention must apply in its entirety to contracts of employment appears to me not to be open to question. It is true that the field of employment presents particular aspects which differentiate it considerably from other fields of private law and endow it with numerous elements of public law; it is also true that in more than one State the system of employment relations courts takes account, both in the composition of the tribunal and in certain specialities of procedure, of the need to ensure certain protection for the employee in the course of the litigation, he being the weaker party in the substantive legal relationship . However, it has to be borne in mind that traditionally the individual contract of employment is regarded as falling within the field of private law obligations and that, at all events, the Brussels Convention not only does not exclude the subject of employment from its proper area of application (in distinction to what is provided in regard to social security - see subparagraph (3) of the second paragraph of Article 1) but also does not apply to it rules differing from those by which contractual obligations in general are governed. It is to be observed also that specific provision has been made in regard to certain matters according to the special nature of the interests involved (insurance, instalment sales and loans; the matters assigned by Article 16 to the exclusive jurisdiction of a court of one of the Contracting States) and accordingly, had the States wished disputes arising out of employment to be

subject to special rules they would without doubt have made express provision for that. The lack of any special provision justifies the view that it was intended to include employment within the Convention's sphere of application.

Strong confirmation for this view is to be found in the report of the committee of experts which was put before all the governments together with the draft Convention (the so-called 'Jenard Report'). It is to be noted (at p. 24) that indeed the preliminary proposals envisaged conferring exclusive jurisdiction in regard to disputes arising out of contracts of employment on the courts of the State in which the work is performed, which would have removed any possibility of any contractual prorogation of jurisdiction. But after lengthy debate this approach was rejected for various reasons which the report lists: the expectation that the Community would prepare rules concerning the law applicable to contracts of employment; the existence of numerous categories of employees in different situations and finally, indeed, the concern not to impede parties from expressing their own wishes in regard to the selection of the proper *forum*. The report concludes, therefore, that the general rules of the Convention - including Articles 17 and 18 - apply in regard to contracts of employment at least for such time as the Convention is not amended by agreed provisions regulating the matter.

3. What I have said may be sufficient for it to be recognised that a clause conferring jurisdiction contained in a contract of employment is lawful and effective if it meets the conditions laid down by Article 17 of the Convention. Moreover, further support for this is to be found in the fact that that article makes mention of the exceptions to the freedom to exclude jurisdiction (referring to the provisions of Articles 12, 15 and 16) and does not include contracts of employment in those cases.

The approach adopted by the Convention therefore appears to be different from and in contrast to that of some of the national legal systems: in particular it contrasts with French law which regards clauses excluding jurisdiction in contracts of employment as void (Article R 517-1 of the Labour Code in the form approved by decree dated 12 September 1974) and also with Italian law (Article 413, last paragraph, of the Code of Civil Procedure as amended by the Law of 11 August 1973 No 533). Such a situation prompts one to ask whether explanations may exist for the difference in approach, and in any event, what consequences that difference may have on the field of application of the Convention. In regard to the first point, a formalistic argument may be found in the fact that the nullity of clauses excluding jurisdiction in accordance with the above-mentioned national laws has the purpose of safeguarding the rule of territorial jurisdiction; however, what is at stake here is the international jurisdiction of courts, that is to say a different kind of jurisdiction. It could at all events be argued that at the basis of the prohibition against clauses excluding jurisdiction in labour matters is the need to afford the employee more appropriate protection in the area of litigation and that this need exists in not dissimilar manner in both relationships which operate entirely within the national context and relationships which present an international element and fall within the framework of the Convention. It may be added that the relationship between the two positions becomes more prominent when one considers that the Brussels

Convention, by means of its rules, seeks to unify Community judicial activity in civil matters and that in accordance with that approach it seeks to place relationships between courts of the Contracting Member States on a similar level to those between courts of a single country.

Accordingly, in the final analysis, the approach chosen by the authors of the Convention appears to have its roots in a different conception of the employment relationship from that which inspired the provisions of the French and Italian legal systems; I should like to mention also that the approach is probably linked with the expectation of a greater harmonisation in the field of employment law as the Jenard Report clearly indicated. Such a harmonisation is in my opinion made all the more necessary by the fact that under the present state of affairs the selection of the court, in accordance with Article 17, does not require the existence of any objective connection between the dispute and the judicial authority upon which jurisdiction is conferred; consequently even a judge who has no links with the socio-economic reality in which the employment relationship itself has developed may, on the basis of a clause conferring jurisdiction, be called upon to take cognisance of a dispute arising out of a contract of employment.

Lastly, it appears to me to be of interest to mention that according to Article 6 of the Draft Convention on the Law applicable to Contractual Obligations a choice of law made by the parties to an employment contract 'shall not have the result of depriving the employee of the protection afforded to him by the mandatory rules of law which would be applicable ... in the absence of choice'. There is no doubt a certain degree of similarity between the two problems of the choice of law and the designation of the court which is to have jurisdiction even if, as already noted, they are in fact different matters; and accordingly find significant the concern shown by that draft Convention not to sacrifice the protection of the worker to complete observance of the principle of freedom of choice.

I pass now to the other question which I set out: Where certain internal legislation of a Member State enacted after the entry into force of the Convention is in conflict with the Convention, *quid juris*? Independently of the question of whether or not international treaties prevail over the laws of a State - which is answered in the affirmative in certain national constitutions but ignored in others - I consider that the link between Community law and the Convention created in Article 220 of the Treaty of Rome and the function entrusted to the Court of uniformly interpreting the law are sufficient for one to reply that the rules of the Convention must prevail over national law, even the subsequent national law, of a Member State. (As we are aware, after the Convention of Accession the positions of the Contracting Parties and the Member States now coincide.) In other words the position regarding the relationship between Community law and the laws of the Member States which has been laid down on several occasions by this Court must also apply to the Convention envisaged by Article 220 of the EEC Treaty, the uniform interpretation of which this Court is called upon to ensure.

4. I stated at the outset the terms of the questions of transitional law which has been presented by the national court. Its solution involves the interpretation of the first paragraph of Article 54 of the Convention.

That provision lays down that the Convention applies to legal proceedings brought subsequently to its coming into force. Consequently the only condition necessary for the operation of the new system of rules, even in regard to disputes relating to relationships entered into prior to the date of the Convention's coming into force, is that the action be brought after that date. The transitional provisions, following techniques already tested in systems of municipal law, attribute significance to the time of commencement of proceedings, thus limiting the application of the new system of rules to proceedings commenced after such time. If a rule of that nature had not been made, it might have been maintained that, on the principle *tempus regit actum*, the Convention ought to apply also to current proceedings. In order to avoid the inconvenience, especially the practical inconvenience, which a solution of that nature would have brought, the Convention has expediently provided for the transition from the old to the new system and restricted within rational limits the temporal aspect of the application of the new rules.

The criterion adopted in Article 54 does not give rise to any difficulty if the question is one of the regulation of conflicts in time of provisions relating to events or documents which are strictly forensic, that is to say events or documents which are connected with the litigation proceedings themselves. If, however, the rule of the Convention which has to be applied pre-supposes the existence of a document or a relationship which may have come into being before the court proceedings it may be questioned whether the same criterion continues to be valid. A theory might indeed be propounded where Article 54 refers to provisions of the Convention of the first type whereas for those linked to the working of the substantive relationship between individuals their applicability would be limited to cases in which the relationship had been formed after the entry into force of the Convention.

I have already had occasion to note, in the opinion delivered on 17 November 1976 in Case 25/76 *Segura* v *Bonakdarian* [1976] ECR 1851 at p.1867, that the Convention lays down certain features of substantive law 'as conditions precedent for the formalities required by the Convention to be fulfilled', which it is the function of the Convention to regulate. In other instances (as in the cases envisaged in Article 17), the expression of the parties'desire to achieve a certain forensic result is set in a contractual context, that is, in a context of substantive law. But what is important, for the purposes of the Convention, is the effect to be given to a specific instrument (in this case the clause of exclusion inserted in the contract of employment): to be more precise the forensic effect - which cannot take place except in the context of litigation and therefore after the litigation has been commenced - independently of the contractual context.

In these circumstances I consider that Article 54 falls to be interpreted in a manner which makes provisions of the Convention of the nature of Article 17 applicable even if the legal relationship in question pre-dated the entry into force of the Convention. Accordingly, the rule which recognises the lawfulness of clauses excluding jurisdiction applies also to those contracts which were entered into prior to that date.

In this case the view adopted by the French appellate court was influenced by the fact that at the time when the clause excluding jurisdiction was entered into it was subject only to national law (the Convention not then being in force) and under that law, as has been seen, the clause was regarded as void. This kind of situation might raise a doubt as to whether Article 54 had, so to speak, the power of reviving an agreement which *ab initio* had been denied legal validity. But this doubt may be removed by three classes of consideration. First, a finding of nullity made by the law of one State does not prevent a different finding being arrived at by another judicial yardstick (that being, in this case, the Convention). The actual existence of the agreement being beyond dispute, its legal effect may be determined in a different manner if looked at from the standpoint of a different set of rules. Secondly, insofar as it has to be accepted that what is involved is the subsequent revival of a clause which was radically defective at the date of the agreement, the point may be made that there is no reason why a legislative provision may not regulate a particular matter with retroactive effect; and particularly so in the field of the validation of instruments which were initially radically defective, given that the possibility of such validation is conferred by many systems of law even on private individuals, subject to certain conditions. It is to be noted that in the field of private law retroactive acts encounter a limit only in certain particular situations: and that is, as a rule, in the case of accrued rights and decrees judicially pronounced: apart from cases such as that the legislature is free to lay down rules even for the past. But the consideration which appears to me to be compelling is a further one. It is not necessary to attribute a retroactive effect to Article 17 as read with Article 54 for the simple reason that the question of the validity or nullity of the clause excluding jurisdiction was relevant only for the purposes of the litigation and, as I have already noted, its effect in terms of litigation only came in for debate after the Convention had come into force. In short, in my opinion, the annulling effect of French law in the present case has always remained inoperative in as much as only the substantive and not the procedural aspects of the contract of employment had been acted upon prior to 1 February 1973 When the prerequisite for the creation of any procedural effects - namely, the commencement of judicial proceedings - was met the Convention had then entered into force.

5. In conclusion I consider that the Court should reply to the question raised by the French Cour de Cassation (Social Chamber) by judgment of 10 January 1979 as follows: 'Articles 17 and 54 of the Brussels Convention of 27 September 1968 on Jurisdiction and the Enforcement of Judgments in Civil an Commercial Matters must be interpreted to mean that in judicial proceedings commenced after the entry into force of the Convention clauses conferring jurisdiction agreed upon in the context of contracts of employment prior in date to 1 February 1975 are to be regarded as valid even if they would have been considered void according to the national law in force at the time when the contract was entered into'.

Case 201/82 - 14 July 1983

Gerling Konzern Speziale Kreditversicherungs-AG and Others
v
Amministrazione del Tesoro dello Stato

Article 17 - Jurisdiction by consent - Agreement conferring jurisdiction - Contract of insurance - Jurisdiction clause for the benefit of third parties who have not signed the clause - Right of third parties to avail themselves of the said clause - Conditions - Article 18 - Jurisdiction by consent - Appearance of the defendant before the court seised of the matter - Appearance not only to contest jurisdiction but also to plead as to the substance - Appearance not conferring jurisdiction.

Summary

1. The first paragraph of Article 17 of the Convention of 27 September 1968 on Jurisdiction and the Enforcement of Judgments in Civil and Commercial Matters must be interpreted as meaning that where a contract of insurance, entered into between an insurer and a policy-holder and stipulated by the latter to be for his benefit and to enure for the benefit of third parties to such a contract, contains a clause conferring jurisdiction relating to proceedings which might be brought by such third parties, the latter, even if they have not expressly signed the said clause, may rely upon it provided that, as between the insurer and the policy-holder, the condition as to writing laid down by Article 17 of the Convention has been satisfied and provided that the consent of the insurer in that respect has been clearly manifested.

2. Article 18 of the Convention of 27 September 1968 on Jurisdiction and the Enforcement of Judgments in Civil and Commercial Matters must be interpreted as meaning that it allows a defendant not merely to contest jurisdiction but at the same time to submit, in the alternative, a

defence on the substance of the case without thereby losing the right to raise an objection of want of jurisdiction.

JUDGMENT OF THE COURT

Everling, President, Galmot and Kakouris, Judges

1. By order of 25 July 1982, received at the Court Registry on 6 August 1982, the Corte Suprema di Cassazione, Sezioni Unite Civili [Supreme Court of Cassation, Combined Civil Sections] pursuant to the Protocol of 3 June 1971 on the Interpretation by the Court of Justice of the Convention of 27 September 1968 on Jurisdiction and the Enforcement of Judgments in Civil and Commercial Matters (hereinafter referred to as 'the Convention'), referred to the Court for a preliminary ruling two questions on the interpretation of Articles 17 and 18 of the Convention.

2. Those questions arose in proceedings between the Amministrazione del Tesoro dello Stato [Treasury Administration] and Gerling Konzern Speziale Kreditversicherungs-AG and Others (hereinafter referred to as 'Gerling'), whose registered office is in Cologne, in which the plaintiff sought to recover a sum representing pecuniary penalties, taxes, duties and supplementary charges in connection with a series of transport operations under the TIR system, which it subsequently appeared were illegal under Italian law and as such became liable for the above-mentioned charges and taxes.

3. To enjoy the facilities provided for by the Customs Convention on the International Transport of Goods under cover of TIR carnets adopted in Geneva on 15 January 1959, transport must in particular be effected under a TIR carnet issued by the authorised association in each country signatory to the Customs Convention and the carriage takes place under its guarantee. The national association which gives the guarantee is liable for payment of the duties and taxes held to be payable and for penalties incurred by the holder of the TIR carnet.

4. The authorised national association in Italy at the material time was the Ente Autotrasporti Merci. Since it has been wound up its rights have been vested in the Italian Ministry of the Treasury pursuant to the combined provisions of Law No 1404 of 4 December 1956, Law No 413 of 18 March 1968 and Law No 1139 of 23 December 1970.

5. The national associations are affiliated to the International Road Transport Union. Each of those national associations enjoys in turn insurance cover from an international group of insurers represented by Gerling pursuant to a contract made in 1961 by the International Road Transport Union on its own behalf and on behalf of each of the national associations on the one hand and by the aforesaid international group of insurers on the other.

6. Article 8 of the contract of insurance provides: 'In case of a dispute between the pool and one of the national associations the latter shall be entitled to insist on proceedings before the court having jurisdiction in the country in which it has its registered office, for the application of the law of that country'.

7. Since the Italian Customs Administration claimed payment of a series of penalties, charges and duties connected with road transport under the TIR system in Italy the Ministry of the Treasury brought an action before the Tribunale di Roma [District Court, Rome] against the aforesaid group of insurers claiming payment of a total sum of LIT 812 134 310.

8. During the proceedings the group of insurers brought an interlocutory action before a section of the Corte di Cassazione pursuant to Article 41 of the Italian Code of Civil Procedure for a preliminary ruling on jurisdiction. The insurers deny that the aforesaid clause conferring jurisdiction may be relied upon in as much as it was not signed by the Ente Autotrasporti Merci (or by the Treasury Administration) whereas Article 17 of the Convention required such a clause conferring jurisdiction to be in writing and signed by the parties.

9. It is against that background that the Corte di Cassazione has referred the following two questions to the Court for a preliminary ruling: '1. Where a contract has been duly signed by the contracting parties and there has been included by one of those parties, on its own behalf and in the interests of other beneficiaries under the contract, the jurisdiction clause agreed upon therein with reference to proceedings which may be brought by the said beneficiaries, does the requirement as to written form laid down by Article 17 of the Brussels Convention of 27 September 1968 on Jurisdiction and the Enforcement of Judgments in Civil and Commercial Matters also apply in favour of those beneficiaries? 2. Is the effect of confirming the jurisdiction of the court before which an action is brought - which comes about, under Article 18 of the said Convention,

as a result of the entry of an appearance by the defendant - also produced when the defendant, in entering an appearance, besides lodging a preliminary objection to the court's jurisdiction, sets out, purely in the alternative, a defence on the substance of the case?'

1. First Question

10. The Corte di Cassazione is asking the Court basically to clarify whether the Convention, and in particular Article 17 thereof, may be interpreted as meaning that under a contract of insurance a person in whose favour the contract is made but who is not a party to the contract and is separate from the insured, is entitled to rely on a clause extending jurisdiction inserted for his benefit although he has not himself signed it, albeit the insurer and insured have duly done so.

11. In applying the Convention it is necessary to interpret it by reference mainly to its structure and objectives in order to make it fully effective.

12. The first paragraph of Article 17 of the Convention provides: 'If the parties, one or more of whom is domiciled in a Contracting State, have, by agreement in writing or by an oral agreement evidenced in writing, agreed that a court or the courts of a Contracting State are to have jurisdiction to settle any disputes which have arisen or which may arise in connection with a particular legal relationship, that court or those courts shall have exclusive jurisdiction.'

13. As the Court has repeatedly held, in particular in its judgments of 14 December 1976 in Case 24/76 *Estasis Salotti* [1976] ECR 1831 and Case 25/76 *Segoura* [1976] ECR 1851 and of 6 May 1980 in Case 784/79 *Porta Leasing* [1980] ECR 1517, the purpose of the requirement of writing under Article 17 of the Convention is to ensure that the consent of the parties, who, by an agreement conferring jurisdiction depart from the general rules for determining jurisdiction laid down in Articles 2, 5 and 6 of the Convention, is clearly and precisely demonstrated and is actually established.

14. Moreover, Article 17 of the Convention in requiring writing between the parties does not have either the object or the effect of subjecting a third party benefiting from the requirement imposed on others to the same requirement of writing where the clause conferring jurisdiction is made for his benefit and he seeks to rely on it in proceedings between him and the insurer.

15. In such circumstances it appears to the Court that the insurer, if his original consent has been made clear in the provisions of the contract, cannot object to such an exclusion of jurisdiction on the sole ground that the party benefiting from the requirement imposed on others, not being a party to the contract, has not himself satisfied the requirement of writing prescribed by Article 17 of the Convention.

16. Consideration of the provisions of Section 3 of the Convention relating to jurisdiction in matters relating to insurance confirms that view.

17. It is apparent from a consideration of the provisions of that section in the light of the documents leading to their enactment that in affording the insured a wider range of jurisdiction than that available to the insurer and in excluding any possibility of a clause conferring jurisdiction for the benefit of the insurer their purpose was to protect the insured who is most frequently faced with a predetermined contract the clauses of which are no longer negotiable and who is in a weaker economic position.

18. Moreover, Article 12 of the Convention allows the parties to depart from the provisions of Section 3 'by an agreement....(2) which allows the policy-holder, the insured or a beneficiary to bring proceedings in courts other than those indicated in this section'. It is thus clear that the Convention has expressly provided for the possibility of stipulating clauses conferring jurisdiction not only in favour of the policy-holder, being a party to the contract, but also in favour of the insured and the beneficiary who may not be parties to the contract when, as in the present case, they are different persons whose identity may even be unknown when the contract is signed.

19. Consequently if the requirement as to form referred to in Article 17 were to be regarded as requiring the insured or beneficiary, not being a party to the contract but a person for whose benefit the clause conferring jurisdiction is made, expressly to sign the said clause so as to validate it and to entitle him to rely on it, the effect of such an interpretation would be to place on the latter, in view of the fact that originally the insurer has unequivocally given his consent to an open and general system of extension of jurisdiction, a pointless restriction amounting even, it may be, to a formality with which it would be difficult to comply if, before any proceedings, the insured has not been informed by the policy-holder of the existence of a clause conferring jurisdiction which has been made for his benefit.

20. It follows from all the foregoing that the answer should be that where in a contract of insurance a clause conferring jurisdiction is inserted for the benefit of the insured who is not a party to the contract but a person distinct from the policy-holder, it must be regarded as valid within the meaning of Article 17 of the Convention provided that, as between the insurer and the policy-holder, the condition as to writing laid down therein has been satisfied and provided that the consent of the insurer in that respect has been clearly and precisely manifested.

2. Second question

21. As regards this question it is sufficient to recall that the Court in its judgments of 24 June 1981 in Case 150/80 *Elefanten Schuh GmbH* [1981] ECR 1671, of 22 October 1981 in Case 27/81 *Rohr* [1981] ECR 2431 and of 31 March 1982 in Case 25/81 *CHW* [1982] ECR 1189 has recognized that Article 18 of the Convention must be interpreted as meaning that it allows a defendant not merely to contest jurisdiction but at the same time to submit, in the alternative, a defence on the substance of the case without thereby losing the right to raise an objection of want of jurisdiction.

On those grounds, the Court (Third Chamber), in answer to the questions referred to it by the Corte Suprema di Cassazione (Sezioni Unite Civili), by order of 28 July 1982, hereby rules:

> **1. The first paragraph of Article 17 of the Convention of 27 September 1968 on Jurisdiction and the Enforcement of Judgments in Civil and Commercial Matters must be interpreted as meaning that where a contract of insurance, entered into between an insurer and a policy-holder and stipulated by the latter to be for his benefit and to enure for the benefit of third parties to such a contract, contains a clause conferring jurisdiction relating to proceedings which might be brought by such third parties, the latter, even if they have not expressly signed the said clause, may rely upon it provided that, as between the insurer and the policy-holder, the condition as to writing laid down by Article 17 of the Convention has been satisfied and provided that the consent of the insurer in that respect has been clearly manifested.**
>
> **2. Article 18 of the Convention of 27 September 1968 on Jurisdiction and the Enforcement of Judgments in Civil and**

Commercial Matters must be interpreted as meaning that it allows a defendant not merely to contest jurisdiction but at the same time to submit, in the alternative, a defence on the substance of the case without thereby losing the right to raise an objection of want of jurisdiction.

OPINION OF MR ADVOCATE GENERAL MANCINI

1. In this reference for a preliminary ruling the Court is called upon to interpret certain aspects of the Brussels Convention of 27 September 1968 on Jurisdiction and the Enforcement of Judgments in Civil and Commercial Matters. The Court has first of all to decide the scope of the requirement of writing in Article 17 as regards a clause in a contract of insurance in which there is a jurisdiction clause for the benefit of the insured who is not a party to the contract. Then it is necessary to decide whether pursuant to Article 18 a party who pleads that the national court has no jurisdiction may at the same time and in the alternative deliver a defence on the substance of the case. Whilst the Court has already given a ruling on the second issue (judgment of 22 October 1981 in Case 27/81 *Rohr* v *Ossberger* [1981] ECR 2341), there is no precedent on the first.

2. In order better to understand the problems of interpretation raised by this case it is worthwhile at this stage calling to mind all the circumstances and the background to the case. That requires a reference to the provisions which govern international road transport and the special forms of insurance which apply to the sector in question.

Certain important aspects of the case are governed by the Customs Convention on the International Transport of Goods adopted in Geneva on 15 January 1959 and brought into force in Italy by Law No 1517 of 12 August 1962. The Convention lays down that vehicles which (a) are provided with a special document (a TIR carnet) issued in the State of departure by authorised associations affiliated to the International Road Transport Union (hereinafter referred to as 'the Union') and which (b) have been sealed by the customs office of departure, may cross frontiers en route without examination and without paying import or export duties or taxes. The payment is made in the country where it is due by the national organisations which issue the TIR carnet even if they are from another State. For that purpose they give a guarantee.

The said organisations are covered in turn by a guarantee given by an international pool of insurers comprising seven banks, represented in the main proceedings by Gerling Konzern Speziale Kreditversicherungs-AG whose registered office is in Cologne in the Federal Republic of Germany. Article 8 of the contract in question made in 1961 in Geneva by the Union on its own behalf and on behalf of those affiliated to it provides that 'in case of a dispute between the pool and one of the national associations the latter shall be entitled to insist on proceedings before the Court having jurisdiction in the country in which it has its registered office for the application of the law of that country'. In Italy the organisation authorised to issue TIR carnets was at the material time the Ente Autotrasporti Merci [Bureau for Motor Transport of Goods], (hereinafter referred to as 'the Bureau'); it was subsequently put into liquidation and its activities continued in accordance with the law by the Ministry of the Treasury.

3. Against that background I can now summarise the facts. The case goes back to a claim by the Italian customs administration against the Ministry of the Treasury in its capacity as liquidator of the Bureau for the payment of pecuniary penalties, taxes, duties and incidental fees in connection with a series of infractions committed in Italy in the course of transport operations under the TIR system. Subsequently, the Ministry brought an action before the Tribunale di Roma [District Court, Rome] on 17 July 1974 against the banks guaranteeing the national organisations, of which the Bureau was one, claiming that they should be ordered to pay jointly, or at least severally as regards their respective shares, a sum equal to the amount of the claim against them by the customs administration (some LIT 812 000 000).

In the proceedings the defendants objected that the Italian court lacked jurisdiction but in the alternative put forward a defence on the substance of the case. In the course of the proceedings they applied to the Sezioni Unite [Combined Sections] of the Corte di Cassazione [Court of Cassation] pursuant to Article 41 of the Italian Code of Civil Procedure for a preliminary ruling on jurisdiction. By order of 28 July 1982 the Sezioni Unite stayed the proceedings and referred the following questions to the Court pursuant to the Protocol on the Interpretation of the Brussels Convention: '1. Where a contract has been duly signed by the contracting parties and there has been included by one of those parties, on its own behalf and in the interests of other beneficiaries under the contract, the jurisdiction clause agreed upon therein with reference to proceedings which may be brought by the said beneficiaries, does the requirement as to written form laid down by Article 17 of the Brussels Convention of 27 September 1968 on Jurisdiction and the Enforcement of Judgments in Civil and Commercial Matters also apply in favour of those beneficiaries? 2. Is the effect of confirming the jurisdiction of the court before which an action is brought - which comes about, under Article 18 of the said Convention, as a result of the entry of an appearance by the defendant - also produced when the defendant, in entering an appearance, besides lodging a preliminary objection to the court's jurisdiction, sets out, purely in the alternative, a defence on the substance of the case?'

4. The case submitted to the Corte di Cassazione concerns a contract of insurance made between an international insurance group and the International Road Transport Union. Its special feature lies in the fact, as the Court of reference clearly points out, that the Union entered into the contract in its own name but in favour of the national organisations affiliated to it: the latter are thus not parties to the contract. Let us suppose that the parties to such a contract insert a jurisdiction clause, as the Pool and the Union have done in Article 8, can the insured claim the benefit of it even though, since it is a *res inter alios acta*, he has not approved it in writing? To answer that question requires the precise scope of Article 17 of the Brussels Convention to be determined.

As the Court is aware, according to that provision, if the parties have 'agreed that a court or the courts of a Contracting State are to have jurisdiction to settle any disputes which have arisen or which may arise in connection with a particular legal relationship, that court or those courts shall have exclusive jurisdiction'; it stipulates, however, and that is the issue, that the agreement in question must be in writing or, if oral, evidenced in writing. I think that in the case of a contract for the benefit of a third person that requirement is satisfied when the parties have agreed or confirmed the jurisdiction clauses in writing. The written agreement of the third person is not necessary.

I come to that conclusion on the basis of various arguments. First of all, there is the purpose of the requirement in question. As the Jenard report states (Official Journal, C 59, 5. 3. 1979, p.1), that requirement is intended to ensure legal certainty that is to say, as Mr Advocate General Capotorti observed, what is required is 'clear proof that the parties were ad idem on the clause specifying the Court having jurisdiction' (Opinion in Case 24/76 *Estasis Salotti* v *RUWA* [1976] ECR 1845). *A fortiori* that requirement applies where one of the parties is weaker as in the case of contracts the terms of which are not negotiable but drawn up unilaterally by one party and merely accepted by the other.

The Court has repeatedly recognized that reality. Thus the first of two judgments of 14 December 1976 states that where 'a clause conferring jurisdiction is included among the general conditions of sale of one of the parties, printed on the back of a contract, the requirement of a writing.....is fulfilled only if the contract....contains an express reference to those general conditions' (Case 24/76 above) and the second states that 'in the case of an orally concluded contract' the same requirement is satisfied 'only if the vendor's confirmation in writing accompanied by notification of the general conditions of sale has been accepted in writing by the purchaser' (Case 25/76 *Segoura* v *Bonakdarian* [1976] ECR 1851). In brief, the requirement of writing serves to draw the attention of the parties to the risks involved in the jurisdiction clause. It will not be forgotten that the latter excludes both the general jurisdiction provided for in Article 2 of the Convention (which refers to the domicile of the defendant) and the special jurisdiction provided for in Articles 5 and 6, unless the clause conferring jurisdiction is concluded for the benefit of only one of the parties, in which case - though this merely increases the risks - that party retains the right to bring proceedings in any other court having jurisdiction by virtue of the Convention (third paragraph of Article 17).

It is necessary, however, to be careful. All I have said so far applies to the parties. Third parties who benefit from the contract without incurring the obligations and running any risks need no protection; to subject the validity of the clause to their signature would, therefore, make no sense. Moreover, there is no legal system which requires such a measure especially in written form unless to avoid revocation of the stipulation (cf. the second paragraph of Article 1411 of the Italian Civil Code); in any event the very wording of Article 17 excludes the need in the present case. When its opening words are read '*If the parties*, have, by agreement in writing or by an oral agreement confirmed in writing' it is difficult not to find it decisive. It is not possible for an article of that kind to use an expression - 'the parties' - otherwise than in a technical sense. Any first year law student would be ready to swear that it is not possible to include the concept of third party in that expression. By 'parties' the Convention thus means 'the promisee' and the 'promisor', that is to say, the parties who have agreed to bring the contract into being, the one by requiring and the other by assuming the obligation as against the third party.

5. The purpose and wording of Article 17, however, are not alone in demonstrating that the requirement of writing binds only such persons and that, therefore, a third party may rely on the clause conferring jurisdiction without having fulfilled the said condition. The provisions of the Brussels Convention on contracts of insurance provide additional arguments to the same effect.

On that subject Articles 7 to 12 lay down *ad hoc* rules of jurisdiction. Their object is to give the policy-holder, the insured and the beneficiary, namely the persons regarded as weaker, greater protection than that given by the general rules. Thus, it is provided that the insurer may be sued in the courts 'for the place where the policy-holder is domiciled' (Article 8(1)) or 'in respect of liability insurance or insurance of immovable property in the courts for the place where the harmful event occurred' (Article 9); to the same end it is provided that 'an insurer may bring proceedings only in the courts of the Contracting State in which the defendant is domiciled' (Article 11). In my view, however, the most significant provision is that of Article 12. It deals with derogations from the principles governing jurisdiction in relation to insurance and provides *inter alia*: 'The provisions of this section' (namely that appertaining to insurance) 'may be departed from only by an agreement: ... which allows the policy-holder, the insured or a beneficiary to bring proceedings in courts other than those indicated in this section'.

The fact that the article expressly contemplates clauses giving rights to third parties such as the insured, even though not a party, and a beneficiary implies that such clauses are valid and effective even if such persons have not approved them in writing. Moreover, Article 17 (second paragraph) itself supports that interpretation insofar as it provides that agreements conferring jurisdiction shall have no legal force if they are contrary to the provisions of Article 12 (2). Obviously the needs to which Article 12 related have been regarded by the draughtsmen of the Convention as special and as prevailing over those protected by Article 17.

Counsel for Gerling ultimately recognises the force of that observation and, to find an escape, it is forced to deny that the agreement made in 1961 between the Union and the Pool is one of insurance, thus preventing the possibility of applying Article 12 to it. That point of view, however, (which in any event does not answer the arguments I have put forward at point 4) is far from convincing. The fact, put forward, moreover, vaguely, that the organisations associated with the Union have sometimes issued TIR carnets after events have taken place to give rise to liability on the part of the insurer, is part, or so it seems to me, of the pathology of the relationship. In view of its probably marginal nature it cannot affect the character of the transaction, which is one of insurance insofar as the issue of carnets implies the acceptance of a risk - namely the one which the national organisations will pass on to the Pool under the aforesaid contract.

6. In support of my contentions the Commission derives a final argument from the principle of good faith governing the making and performance of contracts. It observes that if the Brussels Convention allowed an insurer, the promisor, not to respect the undertaking which he has assumed with regard to third parties in agreeing the jurisdiction clause with the promisee, that would amount to rewarding deliberately unfair conduct and bad faith, which would be absurd. The observation seems to me pertinent (even though I should have based it on the principle pacta sunt servanda) and supports the interpretation of Article 17 which I have proposed.

7. In its second question the Corte di Cassazione puts the case of a defendant who in entering appearance does not confine himself to challenging the jurisdiction of the Court but in the alternative puts forward a defence on the substance of the case and asks whether in the light of Article 18 of the Brussels Convention such conduct may imply tacit acknowledgement of the jurisdiction of the court before which the matter has been brought.

As I said at the beginning, that problem is not new. Two years ago the Court settled it by stating that Article 18 'allows the defendant not only to contest the jurisdiction but to submit at the same time in the alternative a defence on the substance of the action without losing his right to raise an objection of lack of jurisdiction' (judgment of 22 October 1981 in Case 27/81 *Rohr* v *Ossberger* [1981] ECR 2431). There is no reason, and it seems to me that the parties have not put forward any, to depart from that view.

8. For all the reasons set out I propose that the Court should give the following answer to the questions referred to it for a preliminary ruling by the Italian Corte di Cassazione by order of 28 July 1982 in the case brought by the Ministero del Tesoro in its capacity as liquidator of Ente Autotrasporti Merci against Gerling Konzern Speziale Kreditversicherungs-AG, Cologne, and others:

1. *First question*: the first paragraph of Article 17 of the Brussels Convention of 27 September 1968 on Jurisdiction and the Enforcement of Judgments in Civil and Commercial Matters must be interpreted as meaning that in the case of a contract made by a party for himself and for the benefit of third parties and containing a jurisdiction clause relating to actions likely to be brought by the said third parties the latter may rely on application of the clause provided that the parties to the contract have made it or approved it in writing.

2. *Second question*: Article 18 of the above-mentioned Convention must be interpreted as meaning that it allows the defendant not only to claim a lack of jurisdiction but also to submit at the same time in the alternative a defence on the substance of the action without losing his right to raise the objection of lack of jurisdiction.

Case 71/83 - 19 June 1984

Partenreederei ms Tilly Russ and Ernest Russ
v
NV Haven- & Vervoerbedrijf Nova and NV Goeminne Hout

Article 17 - Jurisdiction agreement - Jurisdiction clause in a bill of lading - Validity - Conditions.

Summary

A jurisdiction clause contained in the printed conditions on a bill of lading satisfies the conditions laid down by Article 17 of the Convention: if the agreement of both parties to the conditions containing that clause has been expressed in writing; or if the jurisdiction clause has been the subject-matter of a prior oral agreement between the parties expressly relating to that clause, in which case the bill of lading, signed by the carrier, must be regarded as confirmation in writing of the oral agreement; or if the bill of lading comes within the framework of a continuing business relationship between the parties, insofar as it is thereby established that the relationship is governed by general conditions containing the jurisdiction clause.

As regards the relationship between the carrier and a third party holding the bill of lading, the conditions laid down by Article 17 of the Convention are satisfied if the jurisdiction clause has been adjudged valid as between the carrier and the shipper and if, by virtue of the relevant national law, the third party, upon acquiring the bill of lading, succeeded to the shipper's rights and obligations.

JUDGMENT OF THE COURT

Lord Mackenzie Stuart, President, Koopmans, Bahlmann, Galmot, Presidents of Chambers, Pescatore, O'Keeffe, Bosco, Due and Everling, Judges

1. By an order dated 8 April 1983, which was received at the Court on 28 April 1983, the Hof van Cassatie [Court of Cassation], Belgium, submitted, in accordance with the Protocol of 3 June 1971 on the Interpretation by the Court of Justice of the Convention of 27 September 1968 on Jurisdiction and the Enforcement of Judgments in Civil and Commercial Matters [hereinafter referred to as 'the Convention'], a question for a preliminary ruling on the interpretation of Article 17 of that Convention.

2. The question was raised in proceedings brought by the Belgian limited company 'NV Goeminne Hout' against the German shipowner 'Partenreederei ms Tilly Russ' and Mr Ernest Russ, both of Hamburg, concerning the validity of a jurisdiction clause contained in bills of lading Nos CT 108 and CT 118 dated 16 August 1976. It appears from the documents before the Court that those bills of lading were drawn up for the carrier by Tolmar International Inc., Cleveland, as agent for Europe Canada Lakes Line, Ernest Russ - North America, Inc., Chicago, to the order of the shipper, American Lumber International Inc., Union City, Pennsylvania, Goeminne Hout being indicated as 'notify party' and Tilly Russ as 'exporting carrier'.

3. When the cargo was delivered in Antwerp on 7 September 1976 the packaging of two lots was found to be damaged and about 10 planks were missing. Goeminne Hout therefore claimed USD 304 in damages before the Rechtbank van Koophandel [Commercial Court], Antwerp.

4. Tilly Russ objected to the jurisdiction of the Antwerp court, relying on a jurisdiction clause appearing on the reverse of each of the bills of lading which stated as follows: 'Any dispute arising under this bill of lading shall be decided by the Hamburg courts'.

5. Nevertheless, by judgment of 31 October 1978, the Antwerp court held that it had jurisdiction and gave judgment in favour of Goeminne Hout; that judgment was confirmed by the Hof van Beroep [Court of Appeal], Antwerp, by judgment of 7 October 1981 and, on 1 March 1982, Tilly Russ appealed to the Hof van Cassatie.

6. The Hof van Cassatie submitted the following question for a preliminary ruling: 'Can the bill of lading issued by the carrier to the shipper be considered, having regard to the relevant generally accepted practices, to be 'an agreement in writing' or an 'agreement evidenced by writing' between the parties within the meaning of Article 17 of the Convention of 27 September 1968 on Jurisdiction and the Enforcement of Judgment in Civil and Commercial Matters and, if so, does that also apply in relation to a third party holding the bill of lading?'

7. That question must be construed as asking whether the jurisdiction clause contained in the bills of lading satisfies the conditions laid down in Article 17 of the Convention as regards, first, the relationship between the shipper and the carrier and, secondly, the relationship between the carrier and a third party holding the bill.

The first part of the question

8. According to Goeminne Hout and the Commission of the European Communities, Article 17 of the Convention should be interpreted as meaning that where a jurisdiction clause is not expressly accepted by the shipper and the carrier it is not valid within the meaning of that provision.

9. The Commission adds, however, that even if it was not signed by the shipper such a clause may nevertheless be valid under Article 17 of the Convention, provided that there is a continuing trading relationship between the parties.

10. The Italian Government considers that a bill of lading is a document proving the existence of the contract of carriage and that the jurisdiction clause therefore constitutes an oral agreement evidenced in writing if it is signed by the party against whom it is invoked forms part of the general conditions of the contract, then it may be in conformity with Article 17 of the Convention. However, according to the Italian Government, it is for the national court to ascertain whether there is a signature in the sense indicated above and in what circumstances the jurisdiction clause was incorporated in the bill of lading.

11. At the hearing, the United Kingdom emphasised the importance of the issue raised and suggested that the question submitted by the national court should be reformulated as follows: 'Was the jurisdiction clause incorporated in the bill of lading in a manner enabling it to be, shown that there was a genuine agreement between the parties, account being taken

of the principle of good faith?' A reply to that question is possible, according to the United Kingdom, only if the precise facts of the case are known; however, since in this instance they have not been established no general reply should be given to the first question, on the ground that there are several possibilities and the national court should be left to determine the precise nature of the bill of lading.

12. The first paragraph of Article 17 of the Convention, as now in force, states: 'If the parties, one or more of whom is domiciled in a Contracting State have, by agreement in writing or by an oral agreement evidenced in writing agreed that a court or the courts of a Contracting State are to have jurisdiction to settle any disputes which have arisen or which may arise in connection with a particular legal relationship, that court or those courts shall have exclusive jurisdiction'.

13. It may be observed that for Article 17 of the Convention to apply at least one of the parties must be domiciled in a Contracting State, that being a matter for the national court to determine.

14. As the Court held in its judgments of 14 December 1976 (Case 24/76, *Salotti* v *Rüwa*, [1976] ECR 1831, and Case 25/76, *Segoura* v *Bonakdarian* [1976] ECR 1851) and of 6 May 1980 (Case 784/79, *Porta-Leasing* v *Prestige International* [1980] ECR 1517), the requirements set out in Article 17 governing the validity of jurisdiction clauses must be strictly construed since the purpose of Article 17 is to ensure that the parties have actually consented to such a clause, which derogates from the ordinary jurisdiction rules laid down in Articles 2, 5 and 6 of the Convention, and that their consent is clearly and precisely demonstrated.

15. In order to decide whether the conditions laid down in Article 17 are satisfied, it is necessary to consider separately whether the agreement of the parties to the choice of jurisdiction was expressed in the form of a written agreement or in the form of an oral agreement evidenced in writing.

16. In the first place, it must be observed that, where a jurisdiction clause appears in the conditions printed on a bill of lading signed by the carrier, the requirement of an 'agreement in writing' within the meaning of Article 17 of the Convention is satisfied only if the shipper has expressed in writing his consent to the conditions containing that clause, either in the document in question itself or in a separate document. It must be added that the mere printing of a jurisdiction clause on the reverse of the

bill of lading does not satisfy the requirements of Article 17 of the Convention, since such a procedure gives no guarantee that the other party has actually consented to the clause derogating from the ordinary jurisdiction rules of the Convention.

17. Secondly, if it was established that the jurisdiction clause contained in the conditions printed on a bill of lading was the subject of a prior oral agreement between the parties expressly relating to the jurisdiction clause and that the bill of lading, signed by the carrier, was to be regarded as the written conformation of that oral agreement, such a clause would satisfy the conditions laid down in Article 17 of the Convention, even if it was not signed by the shipper and therefore bore only the signature of the carrier. In fact, not only is the letter of Article 17, which expressly provides for the possibility of an oral agreement evidenced in writing, thereby observed but in addition its function, which is to ensure that the agreement of the parties is clearly established, is also fulfilled.

18. Finally, such a jurisdiction clause not signed by the shipper may still satisfy the requirements laid down in Article 17 of the Convention, even in the absence of a prior oral agreement relating to that clause, provided that the bill of lading comes within the framework of a continuing business relationship between the shipper and the carrier, insofar as it is thereby established that that relationship is governed as a whole by general conditions containing the jurisdiction clause drawn up by the author of the written confirmation, in this case the carrier (see the Segoura judgment, cited above), and provided that the bills of lading are all issued on pre-printed forms systematically containing such a jurisdiction clause. In those circumstances, it would be contrary to good faith to deny the existence of a jurisdiction agreement.

19. Consequently, the reply to the first part of the question submitted must be that a jurisdiction clause contained in the printed conditions on a bill of lading satisfies the conditions laid down by Article 17 of the Convention: 'If the agreement of both parties to the conditions of the bill of lading containing that clause has been expressed in writing; or if the jurisdiction clause has been the subject of a prior oral agreement between the parties expressly relating to that clause, in which case the bill of lading, signed by the carrier, must be regarded as confirmation in writing of the oral agreement; or if the bill of lading comes within the framework of a continuing business relationship between the parties, insofar as it is thereby established that that relationship is governed by general conditions containing the jurisdiction clause'.

The second part of the question

20. As regards the validity of the jurisdiction clause as between the carrier and a third party holding the bill of lading, Goeminne Hout and the Commission are of the Opinion that if the third party has not signed the bill of lading the jurisdiction clause appearing on it is not enforceable against him since the agreement between the parties is not established.

21. According to the Commission, an exception may be made to that rule only if the national legal order in question embodies a theory of assignment whereby the shipper assigns his rights and obligations to the third party.

22. The Governments of the Italian Republic and the United Kingdom consider that, insofar as the jurisdiction clause is valid as between the shipper and the carrier, it should also be valid as against a third party holding the bill of lading, on the ground that if, by acquiring the bill of lading, such a third party becomes entitled to exercise the rights mentioned therein he must at the same time also become subject to the obligations and limitations deriving thereform; both governments base their view on the judgment of the Court of 14 July 1983 in Case 201/82 (*Gerling* v *Amministrazione del Tesoro dello Stato* [1983] ECR 2503).

23. In this regard, it must be noted that the *Gerling* decision concerned a case in which a third party to an insurance contract, containing a stipulation made for his benefit by the insured, relied upon a jurisdiction clause as against the insurer, the clause being inspired, as the Court pointed out by a concern to protect the insured, who 'is in a weaker economic position'. The same considerations are not necessarily relevant to the carriage of goods by sea.

24. Insofar as a jurisdiction clause incorporated in a bill of lading is valid under Article 17 of the Convention as between the shipper and the carrier, and insofar as a third party, by acquiring the bill of lading, has succeeded to the shipper's rights and obligations under the relevant national law, the fact of allowing the third party to remove himself from the compulsory jurisdiction provided for in the bill of lading on the ground that he did not signify his consent thereto would be alien to the purpose of Article 17, which is to neutralise the effect of jurisdiction clauses that might pass unnoticed in contracts.

25. In fact, in the circumstances outlined above acquisition of the bill of lading could not confer upon the third party more rights than those attaching to the shipper under it. The third party holding the bill of lading thus becomes vested with all the rights, and at the same time becomes subject to all the obligations, mentioned in the bill of lading, including those relating to the agreement on jurisdiction.

26. It is apparent from all the foregoing considerations that the reply to the second part of the question submitted must be that the conditions laid down in Article 17 of the Convention are satisfied in the case of a jurisdiction clause contained in a bill of lading, provided that the clause has been adjudged valid as between the carrier and the shipper and provided that by virtue of the relevant national law, the third party, upon acquiring the bill of lading, succeeded to the shipper's rights and obligations.

On those grounds, the Court, in reply to the question submitted to it by the Belgian Hof van Cassatie by order of 8 April 1983, hereby rules:

1. A jurisdiction clause contained in the printed conditions on a bill of lading satisfies the conditions laid down by Article 17 of the Convention: if the agreement of both parties to the conditions containing that clause has been expressed in writing, or if the jurisdiction clause has been the subject-matter of a prior oral agreement between the parties expressly relating to that clause, in which case the bill of lading, signed by the carrier, must be regarded as confirmation in writing of the oral agreement, or if the bill of lading comes within the framework of a continuing business relationship between the parties, insofar as it is thereby established that that relationship is governed by general conditions containing the jurisdiction clause;

2. As regards the relationship between the carrier and a third party holding the bill of lading, the conditions laid down by Article 17 of the Convention are satisfied if the jurisdiction clause has been adjudged valid as between the carrier and the shipper and if, by virtue of the relevant national law, the third party, upon acquiring the bill of lading, succeeded to the shipper's rights and obligations.

OPINION OF ADVOCATE GENERAL SIR GORDON SLYNN

NV Goeminne Hout, a Belgian company, is apparently the holder of two bills of lading relating to consignments of timber which it had purchased and which were shipped from Canada. When the timber arrived in Antwerp, on 7 September 1976, it was found that some was missing. The company and its agents sued, apparently, the shipowner in the commercial court in Antwerp. They were met by the objection that the bills of lading contained the provision '4(e): Any dispute arising under this bill of lading, shall be decided by the Hamburg courts', and that, accordingly, by virtue of Article 17 of the Brussels Convention on Jurisdiction and the Enforcement of Judgments in Civil and Commercial Matters of 27 September 1968, the courts of Antwerp had no jurisdiction. The commercial court, and the court of appeal, on 7 October 1981, rejected that objection. When the matter came before the Court of Cassation (Hof van Cassatie) that court stayed proceedings pending a reference to the Court of Justice of the following question: 'Can the bill of lading issued by the carrier to the shipper be considered having regard to the relevant generally accepted practices, to be an 'agreement in writing' or an 'agreement evidenced in writing' between the parties within the meaning of Article 17 of the [Convention], and if so, does that also apply in relation to a third party holding the bill of lading?'

Article 17, a derogation from the general rule that a person domiciled in a Contracting State shall be sued there and from the special jurisdictions available under Articles 5 and 6 for particular obligations, grants, subject to exceptions, exclusive jurisdiction to the courts of a Contracting State, if the parties, one or more of whom is domiciled in a Contracting State, have by agreement in writing or by an oral agreement evidenced in writing agreed that those Courts are to have jurisdiction to settle any disputes which have arisen or which may arise in connection with a particular legal relationship.

In the French text, which I understand to be similar to other language versions the phrase is 'par une convention écrite ou par une convention verbale confirmée par écrit'. It does not seem to me that for present purposes a distinction is to be made between 'evidenced in writing' and 'confirmée par écrit'.

Article 17 has been amended by the Convention of Accession to the Brussels Convention by Denmark, Ireland and the United Kingdom dated 9 October 1978. So far as relevant, the agreement conferring jurisdiction must under the amendment 'be either in writing or evidenced in writing or, in international trade or commerce, in a form which accords with practices in that trade or commerce of which the parties are or ought to have been aware'. Since, however, that amendment is not yet in force, it seems to me that, in considering the forms in which the consent to jurisdiction can be proved, it is right not to take any account of it.

The article as it stands thus requires that consent to a choice of jurisdiction clause shall be established, and prescribes the ways in which such consent can be proved. Whether there has been in fact an agreement as to choice of jurisdiction, the ambit and effect of the clause agreed and the resolution of the dispute between the parties is for the national court to decide in accordance with the system of national law applicable. What is capable of constituting 'an agreement in writing' or 'an oral agreement evidenced in writing', in other words how the agreement can be proved, is a matter of Community law for this Court in the last resort. If it were otherwise the requirements as to form set out in Article 17 might be interpreted differently in the courts of the various Member States and that degree of uniformity which the Convention seeks to achieve would not be achieved.

It is accordingly, as I see it, not for this Court under the Convention to decide the broad question whether a bill of lading can, let alone in this case does, constitute a contract of carriage or evidence in writing of an oral contract of carriage, or whether, as is contended, it is a mere receipt for goods shipped or a document of title separate from the contract of carriage. That remains a question of national law. The sole question is whether the bill of lading is capable of constituting or providing proof of an agreement as to jurisdiction. In dealing with this kind of question which arises under the Convention, the Court has already established that the overriding rule is that jurisdiction can only validly be conferred on the courts of a Contracting State where a consensus to that effect between the parties is 'clearly and precisely demonstrated'. 'The purpose of the formal requirements imposed by Article 17 is to ensure that the consensus between the parties is in fact established' (Case 24/76 *Estasis Salotti* v *RUWA* [1976] ECR 1831 and Case 25/76 *Galeries Segoura* v *Bonakdarian* ib. p 1851). True consent, the condition precedent, may thus be satisfied where the clause conferring jurisdiction appears in the body of the contract or of the writing said to be evidence of the contract, or is clearly referred to in it or is to be found in conditions clearly and expressly incorporated in the agreement. There must be a sufficient and express notice that conditions exist which include a choice of jurisdiction clause which the other party can reasonably ascertain and identify. Where an oral agreement has been made, expressly incorporating conditions which include a choice of jurisdiction clause, the written evidence must either expressly, or in my view impliedly, refer to those conditions. These basic rules may, however, not have to be satisfied where there is a continuous trading relationship between the parties in which the choice of jurisdiction clause has been included and where it would be mala fide for one side to seek to rely on the non-compliance with the formal rules laid down by Article 17. See, in addition to the two cases referred to, Case 23/78 *Meeth* v *Glacetal* [1978] ECR 2133 at para. 5; Case 784/79 *Porta-Leasing* v *Prestige International* [1980] ECR 1517 at paras 5-7; Case 150/80 *Elefanten Schuh* v *Jacqmain* [1981] ECR 1671 at paras 25 and 26; and Case 201/82 *Gerling Konzern Speziale Kreditversicherung* v *Amministrazione del Tesoro*, 14 July 1983, at paras 14,15, 17-18 and 20.

Thus, in summary, the formal requirements may be satisfied if a party actually knew that a jurisdiction clause was incorporated or if he was given notice that such a clause was incorporated and had reasonable opportunity of ascertaining its terms.

Such an agreement as to jurisdiction can be found either in the primary contract between the parties (sale of goods, carriage by sea, leasing) or be introduced by way of amendment to the primary contract or be contained in a separate contract relating to the choice of jurisdiction for the settlement of defined disputes. A clause will only be effective in respect of disputes in connection with the particular relationship envisaged in the agreement conferring jurisdiction, though it may be capable of including disputes as to the rights of third parties derived from the original agreement (Case 201/82 *Gerling* supra).

The dispute in the present case, it is said, concerns the holder of a bill of lading and the carrier. Since the position between them may turn on whether the clause in issue in the bill of lading is valid for the purposes of Article 17 as between the shipper and the carrier, the latter question in argument has been, and I think has to be, considered first.

It seems to me quite impossible to say that a bill of lading can never be a contract in writing or evidence of a contract in writing between shipper and carrier for the purpose of proving a choice of jurisdiction clause within the meaning of Article 17. It must depend on the facts and the legal relationship created by the issue and acceptance of the bill.

In this case it is not possible to give a precise answer to the question related to the facts, since the reference does not make any finding as to essential facts or recite the findings made (if any) by the lower courts. The factual position is far less clear than it was in the other cases to which I have referred. I agree that this should be so for the reasons given in my Opinion in Case 227/81 *Aubin* v *Unedic* [1982] ECR 1991 at p 2008.

For example, the original bills of lading refer to a shipper and a carrier with addresses in the United States; there is no finding that either is domiciled in a Contracting State, and the carrier cited in the proceedings has a different name from the carrier mentioned in the bill of lading. Before Article 17 can apply at all, it, thus, has to be ascertained by the national court whether the original shipper or carrier was domiciled in a Contracting State. If neither was so domiciled it must be ascertained by the national court whether there is a separate contract between the holder and the carrier incorporating the jurisdiction clause in the bill of lading. If there is no such contract, the question will arise as to whether in such a position the holder (which is domiciled in a Contracting State) is substituted under national law for the shipper by transfer or assignment of the bill and whether he has actual knowledge of the choice of jurisdiction clause (or is given sufficient notice of it to enable him reasonably to ascertain its terms). If the holder is so substituted, with notice or knowledge of the clause, the question would then also arise as to whether the resulting contractual position fell within Article 17. This matter has not been argued, and since it may not be the relevant position to be considered, it seems to me that it is not necessary to decide it. My tentative view is that where a holder domiciled in a Member State is substituted for one of two contracting parties not so domiciled, the agreement as to jurisdiction with the holder does not fall within Article 17.

It seems from the copies of the bills which have been produced to the Court that a company called American Lumber International Inc., with an address in Pennsylvania, USA, shipped the timber on board the vessel 'Tilly Russ' at

Toronto, Canada. The bills were issued by Tolmar International Inc., with an address in Cleveland, Ohio, acting as agents for the carrier, Europe Canada Lakes Line, Ernest Russ America Inc. in Chicago.

Page 1 of the bills is headed 'Europe Canada Lakes Line Ernest Russ, Hamburg'. Described as the 'Short form bill of lading (not negotiable unless consigned 'to order')', the bill incorporates, by reference the terms of the carrier's 'Long form bill of lading'. The print is small but clause 4 is headed in large type 'Responsibility and jurisdiction'. Clause 4(a) incorporates, in respect of the carriage of goods from a Canadian port, the Water Carriage of Goods Act of Canada 1936. Clause 4(e) provides that any dispute under the bill shall be decided by the courts of Hamburg and 'as far as not otherwise provided for in this bill of lading, according to German law'. The concluding words of page 1 are 'Conditions continued on reverse side hereof'. The reverse side (marked page 2) contains the details of the shipment which have been typed in. The consignee is 'Order of shipper' but Goeminne Hout in Belgium appears in the box 'Notify party'. The bills are said to be dated at Cleveland, 16 August 1976.

The reference asked the Court to proceed 'having regard to the relevant generally accepted practices'. These practices can at most be relevant in assisting the Court to decide whether under the version of Article 17 in force, the material tendered can constitute an agreement in writing or evidence in writing of an oral agreement as to jurisdiction. They cannot extend the effect of those words.

These generally accepted practices are in any event not set out and there is no agreement as to them between the parties appearing before the Court or as to the practice on the Great Lakes.

Thus, counsel for Goeminne Hout contends, in a case like the present where there is no charterparty, that in practice the contract of carriage is made by an exchange of telexes between shipper and shipping agent merely reserving space for the cargo on the vessel. The bill of lading is issued after the contract is made, and, as in this case the bill states goods 'on board', would be issued after loading. He contends that the shipper and its agents did not sign the bill. The fact that the 'copy not negotiable' which has been produced to the Court is not signed, however, is in my opinion not conclusive that the original was not signed or stamped. Moreover, although there is no section for the shipper to sign, it looks as if the name and address of the shipper's agent 'Seaway Forwarding Corporation' was placed on the bill by a stamp.

The written arguments on behalf of the Italian Government appear to proceed on the basis that one copy of the bill is signed by the shipper and kept by the carrier, another is signed by the carrier and kept by the shipper. The Commission on the other hand supports the holder in arguing that the shipper does not know the terms of the bill of lading, which in practice he rarely signs, at the time the contract of carriage is concluded, so that a choice of jurisdiction clause is only valid if the shipper expressly agrees to it in writing. Counsel for the United Kingdom contends that the normal practice in London is for preprinted forms of a bill of lading, issued by different shipping lines, to be bought from a stationers and a shippers agent is likely to have a stock of them. The shipper or his agent fills in the blank spaces on the bill and takes it to the carrier's agent who signs it on behalf of the carrier and hands it back to the shipper or his agent (see also *Heskell* v *Continental Express Ltd* [1950] 1 AER 1033 at p. 1037 where such practice is found to exist by Mr Justice Devlin). Since these bills are drawn up in Cleveland, Ohio, it is also appropriate to note that according to 'American Jurisprudence' Second Edition, Vol. 13, 'Carriers' para. 276, 'It is customary for a shipper making frequent shipments to have blank bills of lading in his possession and to fill them out himself and to present them for signature to the carrier at the time the goods are delivered'.

On these divergent views as to what might have happened, which must be resolved by the national court, it seems to me that the most that can be said in answer to the first part of the question raised is on the following lines. If, as a matter of national law, the bill of lading is the contract of carriage and the jurisdiction clause is clearly incorporated in it in a way already indicated by this Court, that clause is valid.

If the contract of carriage is made, whether orally or in writing, prior to the issue of the bill of lading

(a) The jurisdiction clause in the bill is valid if the bill is under national law to be treated as, or as evidence of, a legal transaction incorporating an agreement as to jurisdiction separate from the contract of carriage.

(b) The jurisdiction clause in the bill is valid if the oral or written contract of carriage expressly incorporates the jurisdiction clause to be contained in the bill or the general conditions contained in the bill, including the jurisdiction clause, and such clause or conditions are either known to the shipper or could by reasonable diligence have been ascertained by him before entering into the contract of carriage.

(c) The clause in the bill is valid if there has been a course of dealing (or continuing trading relationship) between shipper and carrier, directly or through agents, during which contracts of carriage between them were subject to the terms of the bill of lading. From such course of dealing the shipper must have known, or been in a position where reasonably he could have known, that the carriage was on the terms of the bill, including the jurisdiction clause, so that he must be taken to have accepted this expressly or by conduct in such a way that it would be a breach of good faith to deny their applicability. I would reject the Commission's argument that over 70% of the shipper's trade must be with the carrier before he can establish such a course of dealing. It is a question of fact in each case as to whether from a series of transactions the shipper has, or must be taken to have, known of the clause and to have accepted it.

If a dispute arises as to, or under, the bill of lading itself, regardless of the question as to whether a separate contract of carriage exists.

(a) If the bill is completed by the shipper or his agent who writes or stamps the shipper's name on it, and is handed to the carrier or his agent who accepts it by signing or stamping the carrier's name on it, that is a sufficient agreement in writing or an agreement evidenced in writing as to the jurisdiction clause for the purposes of Article 17.

(b) If the bill is completed by the carrier and delivered to the shipper who signs it or otherwise recognises it in writing, or who with actual knowledge or reasonable notice of its terms, accepts or acts upon the bill, that is sufficient to constitute an agreement evidenced in writing as to the jurisdiction clause for the purposes of Article 17. In the present case the fact that the typed insertions are on page 2 of the bill is to my mind sufficient to give notice that there is a page 1, although plainly the carrier would be wiser to include on page 2 a reference to the terms of page 1.

In all these cases, however, the agreement is limited to disputes arising 'in connection with a particular legal relationship' as defined expressly or impliedly in the clause. Disputes outside the ambit of such clause would not be subject to the choice of jurisdiction clause.

The case of *Gerling* (supra), which has been relied on in arguments dealing with the position of the holder of the bill of lading as against the carrier, clearly recognises that a beneficiary under an insurance policy, who is not a party to the contract of insurance, may plead a choice of jurisdiction clause against the insurer, if the policy was taken out in his favour and if the clause is wide enough to cover disputes between the beneficiary and the insurer, even though the beneficiary has not signed the clause but so long as the insurer has clearly evinced his acceptance of the clause relied on. That was a case where Article 12 of the Convention gave some guidance (which is not so here) and, of course, was a case where the clause was invoked against a party to the original agreement. Thus, the choice of jurisdiction clause can be wide enough to cover third parties, who can be 'parties' for the purpose of Article 17. It does not, however, automatically follow that such a clause can be relied on by a party to the contract against a third party as assignee or transferee of the benefit of the contract. On the other hand, the *Gerling* judgment does not indicate that it may not be relied on and the question seems to me to be open.

Again, the answer to the question must, in my view, turn on the facts and the nature of the third party's relationship with the adversary, a party to the agreement on the choice of jurisdiction clause. In my opinion, if the holder's rights against the carrier derive under the applicable national law from the transfer of the bill from the shipper by endorsement or assignment or otherwise, then a jurisdiction clause valid as between shipper and carrier will, in the ordinary way, be equally valid as between the holder and the carrier. If the holder takes subject to all the clauses in the bill, they include the jurisdiction clause (if it was validly proved as between the original parties), even if the assignee or endorsee has not specifically signed the clause. In the present case it is plain to my mind that the third parties were contemplated by the terms of the bill of lading including the choice of jurisdiction clause. The bill was expressed to be not negotiable unless consigned to order, it was specifically declared to be consigned to order of shipper. Moreover, it is clear that a substantial number of disputes over bills of lading involve endorsees and the carrier rather than the original parties to the bill, and the holders can be seen to be within the ambit of the clauses included in the bill including the jurisdiction clause.

If the holder does not stand in the shoes of the original shipper under the applicable national law, then a new agreement has to be found between the holder and the carrier, either in writing or evidenced by writing, on a choice of jurisdiction clause. It does not seem to me that the mere presentation by the holder of the bill, who has already purchased the goods to the carrier would in itself constitute such an agreement or evidence of an agreement for the purposes of Article 17. If there is, on the other hand, a specific contract between carrier and third party holder as to choice of jurisdiction (which may be unlikely) then the validity of the clause will depend on the rules already indicated by the Court.

I conclude accordingly that the question referred should be answered on the lines:

1. If under the applicable national law a bill of lading constitutes an agreement between the carrier and the shipper, which expressly states or clearly incorporates by reference a choice of jurisdiction clause, the bill of lading can be an agreement in writing for the purpose of Article 17 of the Brussels Convention 1968. A bill of lading may constitute evidence in writing of an oral agreement as to a choice of jurisdiction for the purpose of Article 17, if the oral agreement expressly incorporates the conditions in the bill including the choice of jurisdiction clause, and the clause is known to the shipper (or could with reasonable diligence have been ascertained by him prior to the making of the contract), or if such a clause has been adopted in a course of dealing between the parties.

2. A holder of such a bill may be bound by a choice of jurisdiction clause if he has expressly agreed to be bound by it in writing, or in a written statement evidencing an oral agreement to be bound by it, or if, under the law applicable to the transfer of the bill, the holder succeeds to all the rights and obligations of the shipper under the bill which, as between shipper and carrier, constituted an agreement in writing, or written evidence of an oral contract for the purposes of Article 17, and in either case so long as the dispute between the carrier and the holder of the bill is one falling within the scope of the choice of jurisdiction clause.

Case 221/84 - 11 July 1985

F. Berghoefer GmbH
v
Co. KG v. ASA SA

Article 17, first paragraph - Jurisdiction agreement - Oral agreement confirmed in writing - Formal requirements.

Summary

The first paragraph of Article 17 of the Convention of 27 September 1968 on Jurisdiction and the Enforcement of Judgments in Civil and Commercial Matters must be interpreted as meaning that the formal requirements therein laid down are satisfied if it is established that jurisdiction was conferred by express oral agreement, that written confirmation of that agreement by one of the parties was received by the other and that the latter raised no objection.

JUDGMENT OF THE COURT

Due, President of Chamber, Kakouris, Everling, Galmot and Joliet, Judges

1. By an order of 28 June 1984, which was received at the Court on 18 August 1984, the Bundesgerichtshof referred to the Court for a preliminary ruling under Article 3 of the Protocol of 3 June 1971 on the interpretation by the Court of Justice of the Convention of 27 September 1968 on Jurisdiction and the Enforcement of Judgments in Civil and Commercial Matters two questions on the interpretation of the first paragraph of Article 17 of that Convention.

2. Those questions were raised in the context of litigation between Berghoefer GmbH (the plaintiff), whose registered office is at Mönchengladbach (Federal Republic of Germany), and ASA SA (the defendant), whose registered office is at Villeurbanne (France), on the validity of a jurisdiction clause initially agreed in writing and subsequently amended orally.

3. For about 20 years, the plaintiff acted as agent ('Handelsvertreter') for the defendant. Following the termination of the agency contract, the plaintiff sought compensation from the defendant pursuant to Paragraph 89(b) of the German Commercial Code and an indemnity in respect of the restriction imposed on its right to compete.

4. The parties to the main proceedings disagreed as to whether the Landgericht [Regional Court] Mönchengladbach, before which the plaintiff had brought proceedings, had jurisdiction. Although the parties had agreed in the agency contract, concluded in 1964, that the Tribunal de Commerce [Commercial Court], Roanne (France), would have jurisdiction over any dispute, the plaintiff claimed that it had agreed orally with the defendant on 8 October 1975 to modify the initial jurisdiction agreement and to confer jurisdiction on the courts sitting at Mönchengladbach, in return for which the plaintiff, rather than the defendant, would thereafter bear the costs of translation arising from their correspondence.

5. The plaintiff claimed to have confirmed that oral agreement by a letter of 27 October 1975 addressed to the defendant. According to the plaintiff, the defendant received that letter and expressed no disagreement with its contents. The defendant, on the other hand, denied that there had been any oral agreement and claimed that he had never received the letter which was supposed to have confirmed it.

6. By judgment of 19 February 1981, the Landgericht Mönchengladbach declared that it had jurisdiction to settle the dispute since it considered that it was proven that the parties had in fact agreed orally to confer jurisdiction on the courts at Mönchengladbach and that the confirmation of that agreement had been received by the defendant.

7. On appeal, the Oberlandesgericht [Higher Regional Court] Düsseldorf decided, in a judgment of 12 March 1982, that even if the facts set out by the plaintiff were correct they would not constitute sufficient grounds for concluding that the courts sitting at

Mönchengladbach had jurisdiction since the written confirmation which the plaintiff claimed to have sent did not meet the requirements of the first paragraph of Article 17 of the Convention. In the view of the Oberlandesgericht, an oral agreement conferring jurisdiction was only valid if it had been confirmed in writing by the party against whom it was to be raised in the event of a dispute. In this case, however, the written confirmation emanated from the plaintiff, the party for whose benefit the agreement was made, and not from the defendant, against whom it was being raised.

8. The plaintiff then brought an appeal on a point of law before the Bundesgerichtshof in which it disputed the Oberlandesgericht's conclusion. It contended firstly that, according to the letter and the spirit of the first paragraph of Article 17 of the Convention, a jurisdiction agreement could also be validly confirmed by the party for whose benefit it had been concluded. Secondly, it pleaded the bad faith of the defendant, which was now relying on the alleged formal defect in the jurisdiction agreement even though it had previously availed itself, without contesting the agreement, of the provision favourable to it which had been agreed on in consideration of the oral modification of the jurisdiction clause.

9. It was in those circumstances that the Bundesgerichtshof stayed the proceedings and referred the following two questions to the Court of Justice for a preliminary ruling: '(1) Are the requirements of the first paragraph of Article 17 of the Convention of 27 September 1968 on Jurisdiction and the Enforcement of Judgments in Civil and Commercial Matters relating to the formal validity of an oral jurisdiction agreement satisfied where the agreement has been confirmed in writing by the party for whose benefit it was concluded?

If Question 1 is answered in the negative: (2) Is the party against whom the jurisdiction agreement is raised estopped from pleading its formal invalidity where that party did not contradict the written confirmation of the agreement and has enjoyed the consideration given for it, and where, moreover, the parties, both commercial firms, have been doing business with each other continuously for a prolonged period?'

10. In their observations to the Court the plaintiff in the main proceedings, the United Kingdom and the Commission all agree that the first question should be answered in the affirmative. In support of that proposition the following arguments were advanced: first, textual

arguments based on the actual terms of the first paragraph of Article 17 of the Convention, on an analysis *a contrario* of the second paragraph of Article 1 of the Protocol annexed to the said Convention and on an examination of the Convention of 9 October 1978, on the accession of the Kingdom of Denmark, Ireland and the United Kingdom of Great Britain and Northern Ireland to the Convention (Official Journal, L 304 of 30 October 1978); secondly, arguments based on an analysis of the working documents which preceded the adoption of the Convention, from which it appears that it is necessary to avoid excessive formality incompatible with commercial practice and that it is often difficult to determine for whose benefit a jurisdiction agreement has actually been concluded; thirdly, arguments based on an analysis of the Court's case-law on the purposes of the formal requirement laid down in the first paragraph of Article 17 of the Convention.

11. According to the first paragraph of Article 17 of the Convention: 'If the Parties, one or more of whom is domiciled in a Contracting State, have, by agreement in writing or by an oral agreement evidenced in writing, agreed that a court or the courts of a Contracting State are to have jurisdiction to settle any disputes which have arisen or which may arise in connection with a particular legal relationship, that court or those courts shall have exclusive jurisdiction.

12. The Court observes that in order to give full effect to those provisions, reference should, in applying them, be made principally to the general scheme and the purposes of the Convention.

13. According to settled case-law (judgment of 14 December 1976 in Case 24/76, *Salotti* v *RÜWA*, [1976] ECR 1831; judgment of 14 December 1976 in Case 25/76, *Segoura* v *Bonakdarian*, [1976] ECR 1851; judgment of 6 May 1980 in Case 784/79, *Porta-Leasing* v *Prestige International*, [1980] ECR 1517; judgment of 19 June 1984 in Case 71/83, *Tilly Russ* v *Haven en Vervoerbedrijf Nova* [1984] ECR 2417), the requirements set out in Article 17 governing the validity of jurisdiction clauses must be strictly construed since the purpose of Article 17 is to ensure that the parties have actually consented to such a clause and that their consent is clearly and precisely demonstrated.

14. It must be pointed out that, unlike the provisions concerning persons domiciled in Luxembourg contained in the second paragraph of Article 1 of the Protocol annexed to the Convention, Article 17 of the Convention does not expressly require that the written confirmation of an oral

argument should be given by the party who is to be affected by the agreement. Moreover, as the various observations submitted to the Court have rightly emphasised, it is sometimes difficult to determine the party for whose benefit a jurisdiction agreement has been concluded before proceedings have actually been instituted.

15. If it is actually established that jurisdiction has been conferred by express oral agreement and if confirmation of that oral agreement by one of the parties has been received by the other and the latter has raised no objection to it within a reasonable time thereafter, the aforesaid literal interpretation of Article 17 will also, as the Court has already decided in another context (see judgment of 19 June 1984, cited above), be in accordance with the purpose of that article, which is to ensure that the parties have actually consented to the clause. It would therefore be a breach of good faith for a party who did not raise any objection subsequently to contest the application of the oral agreement. It is not necessary in this case to decide the question of whether and to what extent objections raised by the other party to the written confirmation of an oral agreement could, in an appropriate case, be taken into consideration.

16. The reply to the question referred to the Court must therefore be that the first paragraph of Article 17 of the Convention of 27 September 1968 on Jurisdiction and the Enforcement of Judgments in Civil and Commercial Matters must be interpreted as meaning that the formal requirements therein laid down are satisfied if it is established that jurisdiction was conferred by express oral agreement, that written confirmation of that agreement by one of the parties was received by the other and that the latter raised no objection.

17. Having regard to the reply to the first question submitted by the national court, the second question no longer has any purpose.

On those grounds, the Court (Fifth Chamber), in answer to the questions referred to it by the Bundesgerichtshof (First Civil Chamber) by order of 28 June 1984, hereby rules:

The first paragraph of Article 17 of the Convention of 27 September 1968 on Jurisdiction and the Enforcement of Judgments in Civil and Commercial Matters must be interpreted as meaning that the formal requirements therein laid down are satisfied if it is established that jurisdiction was

conferred by express oral agreement, that written confirmation of that agreement by one of the parties was received by the other and that the latter raised no objection.

OPINION OF ADVOCATE GENERAL SIR GORDON SLYNN

In the present proceedings, the Bundesgerichtshof has referred two questions on the interpretation of Article 17 of the Convention on Jurisdiction and the Enforcement of Judgments in Civil and Commercial Matters.

The plaintiffs are a company whose head office is in Mönchengladbach in the Federal Republic of Germany. From 1964 they acted as commercial agents for the defendants, who are based in Villeurbanne in France. Initially the parties agreed to confer jurisdiction on the commercial court at Roanne in France. However, the plaintiffs allege that on 8 October 1975 at the Milan trade fair they agreed orally with the defendants that the courts of Mönchengladbach should have jurisdiction instead. In return for this, according to the plaintiff's version of events, the plaintiffs agreed to bear the costs of translation in lieu of the defendants. The plaintiffs claim to have sent the defendants written confirmation of this oral agreement on 27 October 1975. The defendants are said to have received that letter and never to have disputed its contents.

When the agency agreement was terminated, the plaintiffs brought an action for compensation before the court at Mönchengladbach. The defendants contested the jurisdiction of that court. They denied having entered into the agreement of 8 October 1975 or having received the plaintiffs' letter of 27 October 1975. When the case came by way of appeal to the Oberlandesgericht at Düsseldorf, that court held that the courts at Mönchengladbach had no jurisdiction because the conditions of Article 17 of the Convention were not satisfied. In its view, Article 17 required an oral agreement of the type in question to be confirmed in writing by the party who stood to lose from it.

The case subsequently reached the Bundesgerichtshof which made the present reference on the basis that the plaintiffs' allegations of fact were well-founded. The first question asks 'Are the requirements of the first paragraph of Article 17 of the Convention of 27 September 1968 on Jurisdiction and the Enforcement of Judgments in Civil and Commercial Matters relating to the formal validity of an oral jurisdiction agreement satisfied where the agreement has been confirmed in writing by the party for whose benefit it was concluded?'

Written observations have been put in by the United Kingdom, the Commission and the plaintiffs in the main case. The content of the three sets of written pleadings is to similar effect. The first paragraph of Article 17 reads as follows: 'If the Parties, one or more of whom is domiciled in a Contracting State have, by agreement in writing or by an oral agreement evidenced in writing, agreed that a court, or the courts of a Contracting State are to have jurisdiction to settle any disputes which have arisen or which may arise in connection with a particular legal relationship, that court or those courts shall have exclusive jurisdiction.'

The first question referred presupposes that an agreement as to jurisdiction has been concluded. Accordingly, the judgments in Cases 24/76 *Estasis Salotti* v *RÜWA* (1976) ECR 1831 and 25/76 *Galeries Segoura* v *Bonakdarian* (1976) ECR 1851, in which the existence of mutual consent as required by Article 17 was in issue, are not in point in relation to this question.

All those who have put in observations have referred to the Report on the Convention by Mr Jenard (Official Journal 1979, C 59). The passage devoted to Article 17 makes it clear that that provision aimed to strike a balance between excessive formality, on the one hand, and the legal uncertainty resulting from the absence of sufficient formal requirements, on the other. The Report then states: 'In this respect, the version adopted is similar to that of the Convention between Germany and Belgium, which was itself based on the rules of the Hague Convention of 15 April 1958, in that a clause conferring jurisdiction is valid only if it is in writing, or if at least one of the parties has confirmed in writing an oral agreement.'

Consequently, according to the Jenard Report, the requirement in Article 17 that an oral agreement be evidenced in writing is fulfilled when either of the parties has confirmed that agreement in writing.

Confirmation for this view is said to be found in Article 1(2) of the 1968 Protocol to the Convention which provides that: 'An agreement conferring jurisdiction within the meaning of Article 17, shall be valid with respect to a person domiciled in Luxembourg only if that person has expressly and specifically so agreed.'

It is argued that this necessarily implies that, with respect to persons domiciled in other Member States, the evidence in writing required by Article 17 may fall short of 'express and specific' agreement. There may be some force in this but in view of the judgment of the Court in Case 784/79 *Porta-Leasing* v *Prestige International* (1980) ECR 1517 which emphasises the stringent requirements of this Article I doubt whether much weight should be attached to the distinction.

The interpretation advanced in the Jenard Report has, however, been endorsed by the Court in Case 71/83 *Partenreederei Tilly Russ* v *Goeminne Hout* (judgment of 19 June 1984). Paragraph 17 of that judgment reads as follows: 'Secondly, if it was established that the jurisdiction clause contained in the conditions printed on the bill of lading was the subject of a prior oral agreement between the parties expressly relating to the jurisdiction clause and that the bill of lading, signed by the carrier, was to be regarded as the written confirmation of that oral agreement, such a clause would satisfy the conditions laid down in Article 17 of the Convention, even if it was not signed by the shipper and therefore bore only the signature of the carrier. In fact, not only is the letter of Article 17, which expressly provides for the possibility of an oral agreement evidenced in writing, thereby observed, but in addition its function, which is to ensure that the agreement of the parties is clearly established, is also fulfilled.'

There is, however, one matter which is raised by the first question in this case but which did not arise expressly in *Tilly Russ*. That is the question as to whether it suffices for an agreement to be evidenced in writing only by the party for whose benefit it was concluded. To my mind it is so sufficient. If it were otherwise, considerable legal uncertainty would ensue: in any given case it is not always clear which party benefits from such an agreement, especially at the time when it is concluded. As a general rule, it is in a party's interest to litigate in his own State. Yet that is not necessarily so, since it may be that the law of another State is more favourable to him. There may also be other circumstances making it unclear which of the two parties derives the greater benefit from the agreement. This is true of the present case since the plaintiffs have undertaken to bear the costs of translation in return for the defendants agreeing to confer jurisdiction on the courts of Mönchengladbach.

On the other hand, although the point has not been contested in this case, it seems to me that the fact of recording in writing is not in itself enough. The document must be communicated to the other party by or on behalf of the party who signs. It is not enough for the party who records the agreement in writing to file it away in a drawer. While this does not emerge clearly from the words 'evidenced in writing' in the English version of Article 17, it seems to me to be an essential element. The French and German texts ('confirmée par écrit' and 'schriftlich bestätigt' respectively) seem to support that view.

I therefore conclude that a contract is evidenced in writing within the meaning of Article 17 where either of the parties has recorded it in writing and communicated the ensuing document to the other party. It is of no consequence whether or not the agreement was concluded for the benefit of the party who has recorded the agreement in writing.

By its second question the Bundesgerichtshof asks: 'If Question 1 is answered in the negative: Is the party against whom the jurisdiction is raised estopped from pleading its formal invalidity where that party did not contradict written confirmation of the agreement and has enjoyed the consideration given for it, and where, moreover, the parties, both commercial firms, had been doing business with each other continuously for a prolonged period?'

This question is asked only in the event that the first question is answered in the negative. Since I take the view that the answer to the initial question is in the affirmative, there is strictly speaking no need to answer the second question. Nevertheless, it seems appropriate to consider that question.

It seems to me from the existing case law that the recipient of a document purporting to confirm an oral agreement is estopped from contesting its contents unless he does so within a reasonable time. The Court has held that, where there is a continuous course of dealing between the parties and a jurisdiction agreement forms part of the general conditions of trading of one of them, then it would be contrary to good faith for the other party to deny the existence of the jurisdiction agreement: paragraph 11 of the judgment in *Segoura*, paragraph 18 of the judgment in *Tilly Russ*. A fortiori the same principle must apply to an oral agreement relating solely to a choice of jurisdiction.

This is all the more so where a party has enjoyed the consideration given for an agreement, e.g. as here the translation of the relevant papers at the expense of the other party.

In the light of these considerations, the questions referred by the Bundesgerichtshof should in my opinion be answered as follows:

(1) An oral agreement is evidenced in writing for the purposes of the first paragraph of Article 17 of the Convention of 27 September 1968 on Jurisdiction and the Enforcement of Judgments in Civil and Commercial Matters where either of the parties has recorded it in writing and communicated the ensuing document to the other party. It is of no consequence whether or not the agreement was concluded for the benefit of the party who has recorded the agreement in writing.

(2) The party against whom the jurisdiction agreement is raised is estopped from contesting its existence or its formal validity where he did not contradict the document constituting written confirmation of the agreement within a reasonable time and has enjoyed the consideration given for it, and where there is a continuous course of dealing between the parties, both of which are commercial firms.

Case 22/85 - 24 June 1986

Rudolf Anterist
v
Crédit Lyonnais

Article 17, third paragraph - Prorogation of jurisdiction - Agreement conferring jurisdiction 'concluded for the benefit of only one of the parties' - Definition - Criteria

Summary

Since Article 17 of the Convention of 27 September 1968 embodies the principle of the parties' autonomy to determine the court or courts with jurisdiction, the third paragraph of that provision must be interpreted in such a way as to respect the parties' common intention when the contract was concluded. Therefore, if an agreement conferring jurisdiction is to be regarded as having been 'concluded for the benefit of only one of the parties', the common intention to confer an advantage on one of the parties must be clear from the terms of the jurisdiction clause or from all the evidence to be found therein or from the circumstances in which the contract was concluded.

It follows that an agreement conferring jurisdiction is not to be regarded as falling within the third paragraph of Article 17 of the Convention where all that is established is that the parties have agreed that a court or the courts of the Contracting State in which that party is domiciled are to have jurisdiction.

JUDGMENT OF THE COURT

Everling, President of the Chamber, Joliet, Due, Galmot and Kakouris, Judges

1. By order of 20 December 1984, which was received at the Court on 24 January 1985, the Bundesgerichtshof referred to the Court for a preliminary ruling under the Protocol of 3 June 1971 on the Interpretation by the Court of Justice of the Convention of 27 September 1968 on Jurisdiction and the Enforcement of Judgments in Civil and Commercial Matters (hereinafter referred to as 'the Convention') a question concerning the interpretation of the third paragraph of Article 17 of the Convention.

2. The question arose in a dispute between Crédit Lyonnais, a bank, and Mr Anterist concerning the performance of a contract of guarantee.

3. By an agreement of 16 May 1967, Mr Anterist, who resides in Saarbrücken (Federal Republic of Germany) stood surety for the liabilities of Anterist & Schneider Sàrl, a company with limited liability whose registered office is in France, to Crédit Lyonnais, which was represented by its branch in Forbach, which is within the jurisdiction of the court of Sarreguemines (France). The terms of that agreement, which were set out on a printed form provided by the bank, included a clause providing that: 'the court within whose jurisdiction that branch is situated shall have exclusive jurisdiction to adjudicate upon all matters concerning the performance of this agreement, irrespective of who is the defendant'.

4. Since Anterist & Schneider was unable to pay its debt to the bank when it fell due, Crédit Lyonnais brought an action against Mr Anterist in the Landgericht [Regional Court] Saarbrücken for performance of the contract of guarantee. Mr Anterist challenged the jurisdiction of the Landgericht on the ground that the guarantee conferred exclusive jurisdiction on the court of Sarreguemines. The Landgericht upheld Mr Anterist's arguments. On appeal by Crédit Lyonnais, the Oberlandesgericht [Higher Regional Court] took the view that the clause in question was advantageous only to Crédit Lyonnais and was therefore to be regarded as having been agreed for the benefit of that party alone within the meaning of the third paragraph of Article 17 of the Convention. Consequently, the Oberlandesgericht quashed the Landgericht's judgment and remitted the case to that court. Mr Anterist

then lodged an appeal on a point of law with the Bundesgerichtshof in which he sought to have the Landgericht's judgment restored.

5. The Bundesgerichtshof considers that the Oberlandesgericht's decision is by implication based on the view that any agreement conferring jurisdiction on the courts of the State in which one of the parties is domiciled must be regarded as having been concluded for the benefit of that party alone within the meaning of the third paragraph of Article 17 of the Convention.

6. Since an interpretation of the Convention is necessary in order to determine whether that conclusion is well founded, the Bundesgerichtshof has referred the following question to the Court for a preliminary ruling: 'Is an agreement conferring jurisdiction to be regarded as "concluded for the benefit of only one of the parties" within the meaning of the third paragraph of Article 17 of the Convention where all that is established is that the parties have effectively agreed, in accordance with the first paragraph of Article 17, that a court or the courts of the Contracting State in which that party is domiciled are to have international jurisdiction?'

7. Mr Anterist takes the view that the question submitted for a preliminary ruling should be answered in the negative. In order to determine whether an agreement conferring jurisdiction was concluded for the benefit of only one of the parties, it is necessary to ascertain the intention of the parties. That intention must be reflected in the wording of the clause. As an example of the kind of clause covered by the third paragraph of Article 17 of the Convention, Mr Anterist refers to a clause entitling one of the parties to sue the other party either in the court of the latter's domicile or in the court of his own domicile whereas he himself may be sued only in the court of his own domicile. Mr Anterist then argues that an affirmative answer to the question submitted would be contrary to the scheme of Article 17 of the Convention. The exception provided for in the third paragraph of Article 17 would then become the rule since in practice most jurisdiction clauses confer jurisdiction on the court of the domicile of one of the parties. Moreover, such a solution would lead to disputes arising from the same contractual relationship being scattered between the courts of different States, which is precisely what the first paragraph of Article 17 of the Convention is meant to avoid. Finally, even if the question submitted were given an affirmative answer in principle, exceptions would have to be permitted since the advantage referred to in the third paragraph of Article 17 must be exclusive. The

advantages which the jurisdiction clause might have for the other party would have to be assessed with reference to the applicable national law, which would create considerable uncertainty with regard to the applicability of the third paragraph of Article 17 in each individual case.

8. Crédit Lyonnais, which confined itself to submitting oral argument, takes the view that the question referred to the Court should be answered in the affirmative. From the choice of the court of the domicile of one of the parties it would always be possible to draw the conclusion that the jurisdiction agreement was concluded for the benefit of that party alone owing to the practical advantages which it gained from that choice (time saved, knowledge of national law, language, choice of lawyer).

9. The United Kingdom considers that the question submitted for a preliminary ruling should be answered in the negative. The opposite solution would render the first paragraph of Article 17 of the Convention wholly ineffective. The most usual jurisdiction clauses confer exclusive jurisdiction of the courts of the State in which one party, but not the other, is domiciled. If proceedings our instituted by the party domiciled in the State on whose courts the jurisdiction clause confers jurisdiction, that party would be able to evade the rule concerning exclusive jurisdiction laid down in the first paragraph of Article 17 by relying on the third paragraph thereof. If it is the other party who institutes proceedings, the first paragraph of Article 17 would admittedly require it to commence them in the court of the defendant's domicile but the application of the general rule in Article 2 of the Convention would lead to the same result. In such cases the jurisdiction clause would be otiose, as would the first paragraph of Article 17, which confers exclusive jurisdiction on the court designated in the clause.

10. The United Kingdom therefore suggests that the third paragraph of Article 17 of the Convention should be interpreted as applying only to clauses indicating the court or courts in which one of the parties must institute proceedings without specifying the court or courts with jurisdiction to hear and determine proceedings instituted by the other party. The third paragraph of Article 17 is precisely intended to prevent proceedings instituted by the latter party from being regarded. As a result of the application of the first paragraph of Article 17, as falling within the exclusive jurisdiction of the court or courts designated to hear and determine proceedings instituted by the other party.

11. The Government of the Italian Republic suggests that the answer to

the question submitted for a preliminary ruling should be that the designation of the court of the domicile of one of the parties may be evidence of that party's exclusive interest in the clause conferring jurisdiction but not necessarily conclusive evidence. The national court before which the case is brought must determine, on the basis of all the information available, whether the clause was also agreed in the interests of this other party, even if they are only secondary.

12. In the Commission's view, the question referred to the Court should be answered in the affirmative. The third paragraph of Article 17 of the Convention should be interpreted so as to restrict the scope of the first paragraph of that article, which constitutes an exception to the general rules on jurisdiction laid down in Articles 2, 5 and 6 of the Convention. The fact that jurisdiction is conferred on the courts of the place where one of the parties is domiciled allows the presumption to be made that the jurisdiction clause was agreed for the benefit of that party only, within the meaning of the third paragraph of Article 17. Any jurisdiction clause which departs from the general principle laid down in Article 2 of the Convention, which favours the defendant, should be presumed to be for the benefit of the plaintiff within the meaning of the third paragraph of Article 17.

13. It should be pointed out in the first place that Article 17 of the Convention, which appears in Section 6 of Title II headed 'Prorogation of jurisdiction', allows the parties, within the limits laid down by the second paragraph of that provision, to choose by mutual agreement a court or the courts of a Contracting State. The parties may thus confer jurisdiction on courts which would not have jurisdiction under the general or special provisions of the Convention or exclude the jurisdiction of courts which would normally have jurisdiction under those rules. According to the first paragraph of Article 17, the jurisdiction of a court or courts designated by a jurisdiction clause is exclusive, whilst the third paragraph of that article maintains the right of the party for whose benefit the clause was agreed to institute proceedings in any other court having jurisdiction under the Convention.

14. Since Article 17 of the Convention embodies the principle of the parties' autonomy to determine the court or courts with jurisdiction, the third paragraph of that provision must be interpreted in such a way as to respect the parties' common intention when the contract was concluded. The common intention to confer an advantage on one of the parties must therefore be clear from the terms of the jurisdiction clause or from all the

evidence to be found therein or from the circumstances in which the contract was concluded.

15. Clauses which expressly state the name of the party for whose benefit they were agreed and those which, whilst specifying the courts in which either party may sue the other, give one of them a wider choice of courts must be regarded as clauses whose wording shows that they were agreed for the exclusive benefit of the parties.

16. The designation of a Court or the courts of the Contracting State in which one of the parties is domiciled is not sufficient in itself, having regard to the wide variety of reasons which may have led to the choice of such a clause, to support the conclusion that the common intention of the parties was to confer an advantage on that party.

17. It follows from those considerations that the answer to the question submitted by the Bundesgerichtshof must be that an agreement offering jurisdiction is not to be regarded as having been concluded for the benefit of only one of the parties, within the meaning of the third paragraph of Article 17 of the Convention, where all that is established is that the parties, have agreed that a court or the courts of the Contracting State in which that party is domiciled are to have jurisdiction.

On those grounds, the Court (Fifth Chamber), in answer to the question referred to it by the Bundesgerichtshof by order of 20 December 1954 hereby rules:

> **An agreement conferring jurisdiction is not to be regarded as having been concluded for the benefit of only one of the parties, within the meaning of the third paragraph of Article 17 of the Convention of 27 September 1968 on Jurisdiction and the Enforcement of Judgments in Civil and Commercial Matters, where all that is established is that the parties have agreed that a court or the courts of the Contracting State in which that party is domiciled are to have jurisdiction.**

OPINION OF MR ADVOCATE GENERAL DARMON

1. The parties to the main proceedings are French bank, Crédit Lyonnais, Forbach branch, and Mr Rudolf Anterist, residing in Saarbrücken (Federal Republic of Germany), who had jointly and severally guaranteed to the bank the

debts of Anterist & Schneider, a company whose registered office is situated at Stiring-Tendel (France). The printed contract of guarantee signed on 16 May contained the following clause: 'All claims and notices shall be served upon Crédit Lyonnais at its ... branch at present situated at No ... rue ... and the court within whose jurisdiction that branch is situated shall have exclusive jurisdiction to adjudicate upon all matters concerning the performance of this agreement, irrespective of who is the defendant.'

The parties had thus agreed that the tribunal de grande instance [Regional Court], Sarreguemines, within whose jurisdiction the Forbach branch of the Crédit Lyonnais is situated, was to have jurisdiction.

Several years later, Anterist & Schneider was unable to pay its debts when they fell due. Crédit Lyonnais therefore brought an action against the guarantors before the Landgericht [Regional Court] Saarbrücken within whose jurisdiction Mr Anterist was residing. Mr Anterist challenged the jurisdiction of that court. An appeal on a point of law was lodged and the case came before the Bundesgerichtshof [Federal Court of Justice], which, by order of 20 December 1984, referred to the Court of Justice for a preliminary ruling a question concerning the interpretation of the third paragraph of Article 17 of the Convention of 27 September 1968 on Jurisdiction and the Enforcement of Judgments in Civil and Commercial Matters (hereinafter referred to as 'the Convention'). The question is as follows: 'Is an agreement conferring jurisdiction to be regarded as "concluded for the benefit of only one of the parties" within the meaning of the third paragraph of Article 17 of the Convention even where all that is established is that the parties have effectively agreed, in accordance with the first paragraph of Article 17, that a court or the courts of the Contracting State in which that party is domiciled are to have international jurisdiction?'

The two paragraphs of Article 17 referred to by the national court are worded as follows: *First paragraph*: 'If the parties, one or more of whom is domiciled in a Contracting State, have, by agreement in writing or by an oral agreement evidenced in writing, agreed that a court or the courts of a Contracting State are to have jurisdiction to settle any disputes which have arisen or which may arise in connection with a particular legal relationship, that court or those courts shall have exclusive jurisdiction.' *Third paragraph*: 'If the agreement conferring jurisdiction was concluded for the benefit of only one of the parties, that party shall retain the right to bring proceedings in any other court which has jurisdiction by virtue of this Convention.'

2. The parties to the main proceedings, the Commission and two Member States, Italy and the United Kingdom, have submitted observations which are summarised below.

According to Mr Anterist, who considers that the question submitted should be answered in the negative, the choice of the court of a party's domicile should not be regarded as a criterion for assessing the benefit referred to in the exception set out in the third paragraph of Article 17, since that would in effect render the rule in the first paragraph of Article 17 meaningless.

In his view, that paragraph enables the parties to know in advance which court has exclusive jurisdiction. The inquiries which the court would necessarily have to carry out in order to ascertain whether the choice of the court of a party's domicile constitutes an advantage solely for the party claiming the application of the third paragraph would scarcely be compatible with the aim of the Convention, which is to clarify and simplify proceedings.

3. The *United Kingdom* also submitted that the third paragraph of Article 17 constituted an exception to the first paragraph of that article. Since most clauses conferring jurisdiction are identical to that at issue in this case, an affirmative answer to the question submitted would render wholly ineffective the rule in the first paragraph of Article 17 conferring exclusive jurisdiction.

Furthermore, in its view, the third paragraph of Article 17 applies only to clauses specifying the court in which a party may institute proceedings whilst leaving the other party free to rely on the general provisions of the Convention.

4. The *Italian Government* considers that the provision in question is applicable if one party for whatever reason, has compelled the other party to accept the jurisdiction of a particular court. However, it is not always clear from jurisdiction clauses whether they were agreed in the common interest of the parties - in which case the first paragraph of Article 17 applies - or in the interest of only one of the parties. Consequently, the national court must carefully ascertain the intention of the parties and determine whether the agreement was concluded in the interests of only one of the parties. The choice of the court of a party's domicile may suggest that the jurisdiction clause is in the interests of only one of the parties but it is important to determine whether it also gives an advantage to the other party, albeit a secondary one. If the clause is in the interests of only one of the parties, that party is at liberty to institute proceedings in any court which has jurisdiction under the Convention, if only to avoid objections concerning the validity of the clause.

5. The *Commission's view*, with which the representative of Crédit Lyonnais, which had not submitted any written observations, agreed at the hearing, is as follows: the first paragraph of Article 17 does not lay down a rule by exception to Articles 2, 5, and 6 of the Convention. The second and third paragraphs merely define its scope. The first paragraph of Article 17 should therefore be interpreted restrictively.

Any jurisdiction agreement that departs from the general principle laid down in Article 2 of the Convention which favours the defendant, is presumed to be in the interests of the plaintiff if he has obtained an agreement overturning the general rule laid down in Article 2. Paragraph 3 of Article 17 authorises the plaintiff not to take advantage of is objectively advantageous legal position.

The Commission considers that, in order to ensure that the aims of the Convention are respected, the 'advantage' should be assessed in accordance with objective criteria. The jurisdiction conferred on the court of the domicile of one of the parties constitutes one of those criteria. Account may also be taken of the fact that a party in a financially stronger position has imposed its standard terms and conditions of trade on the other party, even if the court on which jurisdiction is conferred is not the court of the stronger party's domicile. If the weaker party wishes to avoid the application of the third paragraph of Article 17, it must ensure that its own interest in the jurisdiction clause is clear from its wording. In those circumstances, the stronger party's advantage is no longer exclusive.

6. There is a paradox in these proceedings. Mr Anterist seeks the application of a jurisdiction clause which Crédit Lyonnais is endeavouring to prevent on the ground that the clause was agreed for its benefit only. Plainly, the paradox is only apparent. I need not inquire into the real interests at stake in that academic discussion. That is a matter for the Bundesgerichtshof and I shall merely attempt to provide some considerations to enable the Court to answer the question referred to it.

7. The third paragraph of Article 17 cannot be interpreted in isolation. The parties to the main proceedings and the interveners have attempted to set that provision in the broader context of the Convention. I shall adopt the same approach.

The purpose of the Convention, according to its preamble, is to simplify the formalities governing the reciprocal recognition and enforcement of judgments of courts or tribunals and to strengthen in the Community the legal protection of persons therein established. The preamble also sets out the means for attaining those objectives, which include first and foremost the determination of the international jurisdiction of the courts of the Member States. Briefly, the aim of the Convention is to introduce legal certainty into procedural matters by giving each individual the means of determining with certainty the court of his choice so that he can assert his rights effectively.

Article 17 forms part of Title II of the Convention, which deals with jurisdiction. It is arranged as follows: Section 1 ('General provisions') provides in Article 2 that '... persons domiciled in a Contracting State shall, whatever their nationality, be sued in the courts of that State'. The jurisdiction of the court is therefore determined by the country of the defendant's domicile. Sections 2, 3 and 4 deal with jurisdiction in special matters whilst Section 5 deals with exclusive jurisdiction, which constitutes an exception to the rule *actor sequitur forum rei*. Sections 7, 8 and 9 are concerned with the functions of the court.

Article 17 is in Section 6 ('Prorogation of jurisdiction'). The wording of that provision is significant: the first paragraph makes provision for the prorogation of jurisdiction by agreement, which is binding on the parties subject to the provisos in the second and third paragraphs.

The structure of the scheme established by the Convention in regard to jurisdiction is therefore as follows: alongside the general rules laid down in Articles 2 to 16, there is a body of rules, contained in Article 17, under which, in cases in which courts have exclusive jurisdiction under Article 16, the parties to a contract may avoid the general rules by means of a clause conferring jurisdiction.

That scheme provides the key to the interpretation of the first paragraph of Article 17.

In that regard a distinction must be drawn between the existence of a clause conferring jurisdiction and its binding force. Such a clause cannot be presumed to exist and if there is any doubt the general rules will apply. From that point of view, the first paragraph of Article 17 must be strictly construed. That approach has been confirmed by the Court, which has held that: '... the requirements set out in Article 17 governing the validity of jurisdiction clauses must be strictly construed since the purpose of Article 17 is to ensure that the parties have actually consented to such a clause, which derogates from the ordinary jurisdiction rules laid down in Articles 2, 5 and 6 of the Convention, and that their consent is clearly and precisely demonstrated' (judgment of 19 June 1984 in Case 71/83 *Tilly Russ* v *Nova* [1984] ECR 2417 at p. 2432, paragraph 14 of the decision).

8. The position with regard to the binding force of the jurisdiction clause is different. Here we return to the fundamental rule that the parties are bound by the agreement concluded between them. The clause conferring jurisdiction is binding on the contracting parties, provided that it is not contrary to the rules governing exclusive jurisdiction laid down in Article 16. Since such a clause has been permitted by the authors of the Convention, it may not, if validly agreed, enable one of the parties to repudiate it so as to bring the general rules back into operation. The fact that in examining whether there has been valid consent, recourse must be had to a strict interpretation may not, if there is such consent, be put forward as a ground for challenging the binding force of the agreement on jurisdiction.

9. The third paragraph of Article 17 remains to be interpreted.

It is arguable, and has been argued, that this provision contemplates the case in which a unilateral jurisdiction clause provides that only one of the parties is to be subject to it whilst the other party may waive it and thus bring into operation the general rules on jurisdiction laid down in the Convention. If that interpretation were correct, the third paragraph of Article 17 would have nothing to do with this case and would not be applicable to it. However, it is difficult to see what purpose is served by a provision which restores to the party which has 'the advantage' the benefit of rules of general application which, by definition, it has not waived by contract.

Therefore, in my view, the third paragraph of Article 17 applies to a clause which, although inserted exclusively in the interests of only one of the contracting parties, is nonetheless, as in this case, bilateral in nature or to a unilateral clause stipulating that proceedings brought by that contracting party must be brought in a court which is expressly designated. The third paragraph of Article 17 confers on the party which is 'at an advantage' the right to waive its advantage in order to bring into operation the general rules on jurisdiction.

So construed, the third paragraph of Article 17 constitutes a derogation from the contracting parties. Moreover, besides the jurisdiction conferred by agreement, it introduces one or more alternative jurisdictions, which detracts from legal certainty, an aim of both the Brussels Conventions and the clause conferring jurisdiction. For those two reasons, it must be regarded as an exception to the contractual rule for which the first paragraph of Article 17 makes provision and as such, must be interpreted strictly.

The parties may expressly state in the contract that the clause conferring jurisdiction was agreed upon in the interests of only one of them. This would greatly facilitate the court's task with regard to the application of the third paragraph of Article 17.

However, that was not done in this case. The court must therefore look at the contract to see whether there is an exclusive interest of that kind. Since the third paragraph of Article 17 must be strictly construed, the existence of an exclusive interest cannot be presumed. Nor can it be automatically inferred from objective evidence, since it is a question of interpreting the intention of the parties. Consequently, the fact that the clause confers jurisdiction on the court of the domicile of one of the contracting parties is a factor which may - and must - be taken into account by the national court when determining the intention of the parties. However, it is not the decisive factor. Other factors, such as the manner in which the law applicable to the contract is currently applied by the court which is designated, may show that the clause is in the interests of both parties.

I therefore suggest that the Court should answer the question referred to it for a preliminary ruling as follows:

(1) Agreements conferring jurisdiction which are validly concluded in accordance with the first paragraph of Article 17 of the Brussels Convention of 27 September 1968 on Jurisdiction and the Enforcement of Judgments in Civil and Commercial Matters are just as binding on the contracting parties as the general rules for conferring jurisdiction laid down in Articles 2 to 15 of the Convention in the absence of such agreements.

(2) The third paragraph of Article 17 of the Convention must be interpreted as meaning that, where such an agreement has been concluded for the exclusive benefit of one of the contracting parties, that party retains the right to waive that advantage and to institute proceedings in any other court which has jurisdiction by virtue of the aforesaid general rules.

(3) It is for the national court to determine, having regard to the circumstances of the case before it and to the terms of the contract, whether or not a clause conferring jurisdiction has been agreed upon for the exclusive benefit of one of the parties. The fact that the clause confers jurisdiction on the court of the domicile of one of the parties is a factor whose significance must be assessed by that court.

Case 313/85 - 11 November 1986

Iveco Fiat SpA
v
Van Hool NV

Article 17 - Prorogation of jurisdiction - Written agreement containing a jurisdiction clause and stipulating that the agreement can be renewed only in writing - Expiry of the agreement - Maintenance of business relations between the parties - Validity of the jurisdiction clause - Conditions.

Summary

Article 17 of the Convention of 27 September 1968 on Jurisdiction and the Enforcement of Judgments in Civil and Commercial Matters must be interpreted as meaning that where a written agreement containing a jurisdiction clause and stipulating that the agreement can be renewed only in writing has expired but has continued to serve as the legal basis for the contractual relations between the parties, the jurisdiction clause satisfies the formal requirements in Article 17 if, under the law applicable, the parties could validly renew the original agreement otherwise than in writing, or if, conversely, one of the parties has confirmed in writing either the jurisdiction clause or the set of terms which has been tacitly renewed and of which the jurisdiction clause forms part, without any objection from the other party to whom such confirmation has been notified.

JUDGMENT OF THE COURT

Galmot, President of the Chamber, Schockweiler, Everling, Joliet and Moitinho de Almeida, Judges

1. By order of 4 October 1985 which was received at the Court on 18 October 1985, the Belgian Court of Cassation referred to the Court of Justice for a preliminary ruling under the Protocol of 3 June 1971 on the interpretation by the Court of Justice of the Convention of 27 September 1968 on Jurisdiction and the Enforcement of Judgments in Civil and Commercial Matters (hereinafter referred to as 'the Convention') a question concerning the interpretation of Article 17 of the Convention.

2. The question arose in a dispute between Iveco Fiat SpA ('Fiat'), a company incorporated under Italian law, and Van Hool NV ('Van Hool'), a company incorporated under Belgian law, concerning the validity of a jurisdiction clause inserted in a written agreement granting an exclusive sales concession which stipulated that the agreement could be renewed only in writing but which continued, after its expiry, to serve as the legal basis for the contractual relations between the parties notwithstanding the fact that it was not renewed in writing.

3. The Belgian Court of Cassation, hearing the case, decided to stay the proceedings and refer the following question to the Court for a preliminary ruling: 'Are the requirements of Article 17 of the Convention of 27 September 1968 satisfied by a written agreement which contain a jurisdiction clause but whose expiry date has passed where that agreement has continued to serve as the legal basis for the contractual relations between the parties although the condition stipulating that the agreement could be renewed only in writing was not fulfilled?'

4. For a more detailed exposition of the facts of the case, the course of the procedure and the observations submitted under Article 20 of the Protocol on the Statute of the Court of Justice, reference is made to the Report for the Hearing. Those details are referred to hereinafter only insofar as is necessary for the reasoning of the Court.

5. In order to place the question in its proper context, it should be noted in the first place that the sole purpose of the formal requirement laid down by Article 17 of the Convention to the effect that a jurisdiction clause must be in writing if it is to be valid is to ensure that the consensus between the parties is in fact established and it imposes upon the national court the duty of examining whether the clause conferring jurisdiction upon it was in fact the subject of such a consensus, which must be clearly and precisely demonstrated (judgments of 14 December 1976 in Case 24/76 *Estasis Salotti* v *RÜWA* [1976] ECR 1831, and in Case 25/76 *Segoura* v *Bonakdarian* [1976] ECR 1851).

6. In order to answer the question raised by the national court, it is necessary to distinguish between two situations.

7. If the applicable law allows the original agreement to be renewed without complying with the clause expressly stipulated therein to the effect that renewal must be in writing, all the terms of the agreement continue to be binding on the parties, including the jurisdiction clause, in relation to which their consent must be established beyond doubt in the manner provided for by Article 17.

8. If, however, according to the applicable law, the original agreement could not be renewed otherwise than in writing, it is necessary to consider whether the jurisdiction clause, insofar as it forms part of a set of terms which were tacitly taken over from a previous written agreement that has expired and which continued to serve as the legal basis for the contractual relations between the parties, satisfies the conditions laid down by Article 17.

9. It is clear from the case-law of the Court that in the case of an unwritten agreement conferring jurisdiction, the conditions of Article 17 are satisfied if written confirmation of that agreement by one of the parties has been received by the other and the latter has raised no objection to it within a reasonable time thereafter (judgment of 11 July 1985 in Case 221/84 *Berghöfer* v *ASA* [1985] ECR 2699). Accordingly, on the assumption that the jurisdiction clause forms part of a set of terms which were tacitly taken over from a previous written agreement that expired and which continued to serve as the legal basis for the contractual relations between the parties, the formal requirements of Article 17 are satisfied only if one of the parties has confirmed in writing either the jurisdiction clause or the set of terms of which that clause forms part, without any objection from the other party to whom such confirmation has been notified.

10. The answer to the question submitted by the Belgian Court of Cassation must therefore be that Article 17 of the Convention on Jurisdiction and the Enforcement of Judgments in Civil and Commercial Matters must be interpreted as meaning that where a written agreement containing a jurisdiction clause and stipulating that the agreement can be renewed only in writing has expired but has continued to serve as the legal basis for the contractual relations between the parties, the jurisdiction clause satisfies the formal requirements in Article 17 if, under the law applicable, the parties could validly renew the original agreement

otherwise than in writing, or if, conversely, one of the parties has confirmed in writing either the jurisdiction clause or the set of terms which has been tacitly renewed and of which the jurisdiction clause forms part, without any objection from the other party to whom such confirmation has been notified.

On those grounds, the Court (Fifth Chamber), in answer to the question referred to it by the Belgian Court of Cassation, by order of 4 October 1985, hereby rules:

Article 17 of the Convention of 27 September 1968 on Jurisdiction and the Enforcement of Judgments in Civil and Commercial Matters must be interpreted as meaning that where a written agreement containing a jurisdiction clause and stipulating that an agreement can be renewed only in writing has expired but has continued to serve as the legal basis for the contractual relations between the parties, the jurisdiction clause satisfies the formal requirements in Article 17 if, under the law applicable, the parties could validly renew the original agreement otherwise than in writing, or if, conversely, one of the parties has confirmed in writing either the jurisdiction clause or the set of terms which has been tacitly renewed and of which the jurisdiction clause forms part, without any objection from the other party to whom such confirmation has been notified.

OPINION OF MR ADVOCATE GENERAL DA CRUZ VILAÇA

1. Pursuant to Article 3(1) of the Protocol of 3 June 1971 on the interpretation by the Court of Justice of the Convention of 27 September 1968 on Jurisdiction and the Enforcement of Judgments in Civil and Commercial Matters (Official Journal 1978, L 304, p. 36) (hereinafter referred to as 'the Convention'), the Belgian Court of Cassation has asked the Court of Justice for an interpretation of Article 17 of the Convention in connection with a dispute concerning the enforcement of an agreement containing a clause conferring jurisdiction on a court of a State of which one of the parties is a national.

In the light of the documents before the Court, the facts of the case are as follows.

2. Two undertakings, Iveco Fiat SpA ('Fiat'), having its registered office in Turin (Italy) and Van Hool) NV ('Van Hool'), having its registered office in Koningshooikt-Lier (Belgium), entered into a one-year agreement on 28 December 1956 with effect from 1 January 1957 whereby Fiat granted Van Hool exclusive rights within the territory of the Benelux States to assemble or sell certain Fiat motor vehicles or spare parts.

A further agreement was concluded on 1 January 1958 extending co-operation between the two undertakings to another category of Fiat motor vehicles. Van Hool's place in that relationship was subsequently taken, according to the terms of an agreement concluded on 30 December 1961, by another undertaking, Catrabel PVBA ('Catrabel'), whilst Van Hool continued to exercise the other exclusive rights resulting from the agreement concluded in December 1956.

Both the 1956 agreement (Article 10) and the 1958 agreement (Article 18) contained a clause conferring exclusive jurisdiction in disputes arising from the performance of the agreements concerned on the Tribunale di Torino [the district court of Turin].

However - and this is where the problem arises - the agreement concluded in 1956 stipulated in Article 9 that in order to be renewed beyond 31 December 1957 'written confirmation by Fiat' was necessary, and a similar clause was to be found in Article 16 of the agreement concluded on 1 January 1958 granting the concession subsequently taken over by Catrabel.

Fiat wrote to Van Hool renewing the 1956 agreement for a period of one year until 31 December 1958, and continued to renew it from year to year until 31 December 1961.

From 1962 onwards, Fiat ceased to express in writing its intention to renew the agreement from year to year, although both undertakings continued to maintain business relations until the end of 1981 on the terms, it would appear, of the original agreement.

However, as a result of certain disagreements which had arisen in the meantime, Fiat broke off business relations with Van Hool as from 1 January 1982.

Since business relations were broken off unilaterally, Van Hool brought an action against Fiat in the Tribunal de commerce [Commercial Court] of Malines, in Belgium. In those proceedings Fiat objected that the Tribunal de commerce lacked jurisdiction on the ground that, in Fiat's view, the clause conferring jurisdiction on the Turin court was applicable to the contractual relations which had continued to exist between the parties after 31 December 1961, the last year for which the agreement had been renewed in writing by Fiat. The Tribunal de commerce of Malines considered, however, that it had jurisdiction on the ground that the conditions laid down by the first paragraph of Article 17 of the Convention governing the validity of jurisdiction clauses had not been satisfied. That decision was later upheld by the cour d'appel [Appeal Court] of Antwerp, against whose judgment Fiat lodged an appeal with the Belgian Court of Cassation.

The Court of Cassation decided to stay the proceedings until the Court of Justice of the European Communities had given a preliminary ruling on the following question: 'Are the requirements of Article 17 of the Convention of 27 September 1968 satisfied by a written agreement which contains a jurisdiction clause but whose expiry date has passed where that agreement continued to serve as the legal basis for the contractual relations between the parties although the condition stipulating that the agreement could be renewed only in writing was not fulfilled?'

3. The first paragraph of Article 17 of the Convention provides that 'if the parties ... have ... agreed that a court or the courts of a Contracting State are to have jurisdiction to settle any disputes which have arisen or which may arise in connection with a particular legal relationship, that court or those courts shall have exclusive jurisdiction'.

According to that article, however, the agreement conferring jurisdiction must be *in writing* or *evidenced in writing.*

The origin of those formal requirements is, of course, as was pointed out in the Jenard report on the Convention (Official Journal 1979, C 159, p. 1) the fundamental concern 'to ensure legal certainty'.

The Court has already on several occasions clearly stated in its decisions the reasons for, and the meaning of, those requirements. The purpose of the conditions laid down in Article 17 for the validity of jurisdiction clauses is to ensure that the parties 'have actually consented' to such a clause, which in addition derogates from the general rules for determining jurisdiction, and that their consent 'is clearly and precisely demonstrated'.

In the words of Advocate General Capotorti (Opinion in *Estasis Salotti*) what is required is 'clear proof that the parties were *ad idem* on the clause specifying the court having jurisdiction'. For that reason, the Court has consistently held that the requirements set out in Article 17 governing the validity of jurisdiction clauses 'most be strictly construed'.

There is no doubt, as was also made clear in the Jenard Report, that the authors of the Convention were concerned to avoid excessive formality which is incompatible with commercial practice'.

Article 17 may thus be said to be the result of a compromise between the requirements of *legal certainty* and *commercial flexibility*, which, moreover, led to recognition of a mere oral agreement as valid if *evidenced in writing*.

In my view, however, those requirements are not of equal importance under the Convention. As is clear from the case-law of this Court, in any attempt to compromise between certainty and flexibility priority must be given to the former, inasmuch as the requirements of speed and facility in commercial practice cannot justify the acceptance of any doubts or ambiguities concerning the consent of the parties to the insertion in an agreement of a jurisdiction clause which derogates from the general criteria for determining jurisdiction set out in Articles 2, 5 and 6 of the Convention. The requirement of writing serves to draw the attention of the parties to the risks involved in the jurisdiction clause' (Opinion of Advocate General Mancini in Case 201/82 *Gerling* v *Amministrazione del Tesoro* [1983] ECR 2503 at p. 2521).

In some respects the difficulty here may be likened to a problem of linear programming, in which a variable factor - certainty - must be given *maximum effect* within the parameters of concern to ensure the normal development of business relations, in accordance with the criteria of current practice and the requirements of good faith.

In my view, that is the meaning of Article 17, having regard to its wording, although it might be construed differently if the new version of Article 17 had come into force, namely that contained in the Convention of Accession of 9

October 1978 of the Kingdom of Denmark, of Ireland and of the United Kingdom of Great Britain and Northern Ireland to the 1968 Convention on Jurisdiction and the Enforcement of Judgments in Civil and Commercial Matters. That version of Article 17 provides that an agreement conferring jurisdiction may be either 'in writing' or an oral agreement 'evidenced in writing' or, in international trade or commerce, 'in a form which accords with practices in that trade or commerce of which the parties are or ought to have been aware'.

In the light of that, it would also be possible to take the opposite approach to the one which I have adopted, recognising the standards and requirements of commercial practice as the principal variable factor which is *restricted* in its development by the need to ensure an appropriate degree of legal certainty for the parties.

As matters stand, however, and as the new version of that article has not yet come into force, it is premature in my view to take that alternative approach.

Moreover, the approach which I have adopted strikes me as being the one which comes closest to an interpretation of the Convention which takes account, as the Court has advocated, of its *structure* and *objectives*.

I also believe that recognition of an oral agreement evidenced in writing is the essential feature of the concessions made in Article 17 of the Convention to flexibility in commercial practices with regard to jurisdiction clauses, and great stringency and caution must be exercised with the regard to the requirements relating to evidence of actual consent by the parties.

4. In the decisions to which I have referred, the Court laid down on several occasions the conditions in which jurisdiction clauses exhibiting certain characteristics must be regarded as valid for the purposes of Article 17 of the Convention.

However, there is an important factor which distinguishes this case from those in which the judgments referred to earlier were given, and which raises a fresh question that is still unresolved.

The question referred to the Court of Justice by the Belgian Court of Cassation is concerned - notwithstanding the terms in which it is couched - with the question whether a jurisdiction clause in a written agreement which has expired and, contrary to its terms, has not been renewed in writing, although the parties have continued to maintain normal business relations, satisfies the requirements of Article 17.

That raises the problem of the scope *ratione temporae* of the agreement containing the jurisdiction clause, which has not arisen in any of the previous cases.

Those cases were concerned with agreements which did not give rise to any questions relating to the existence of any clauses restricting their duration.

How then are the general principles referred to earlier to be applied to the question at issue?

5. It is indisputable that, in the case under consideration, the parties inserted in the original written agreement between them - without there being any risk of its passing unnoticed - a jurisdiction clause which clearly satisfied the formal requirements laid down in Article 17 of the Convention.

If that agreement had been concluded for an indeterminate period or had been properly renewed in writing in the stipulated manner, no problem would arise.

Moreover, the problem would be entirely different if the agreement did not contain a clause providing for renewal in writing and either made provision for tacit renewal or was silent as regards the form of renewal.

Nor would there be any problem as regards any dispute which might have arisen during the initial period of validity of the agreement or during any of the periods for which it was renewed in writing.

As the Court is aware, however, that is not the case. The validity of the jurisdiction clause was not called in question until the final breach occurred between the parties, that is to say the termination of business relations between them 20 years after the agreement was last renewed in writing.

There is no doubt as to the *existence* of a valid jurisdiction clause, but there is doubt as to its *validity* at the time when a party sought to rely on it in legal proceedings.

Even if the problem had arisen after contractual relations between the parties had come to an end (as a result of a breach during the period of validity of the agreement, expiry of the stipulated period or any other cause), but still in connection with a dispute concerning the performance of the original agreement, there would not, in principle, be any particular difficulties to resolve. In that respect the question of which court has jurisdiction would naturally be covered by a jurisdiction clause (on the assumption that it was validly stipulated in accordance with Article 17) expressly adopted by the parties and intended to apply in any dispute concerning the performance of the agreement in which the clause was inserted. The validity of the clause naturally extends beyond that of the agreement or, to put it another way, continues to be valid after the expiry of the agreement. That possibility could arise even in the circumstances of this case. I believe, however, that it is not necessary to take that possibility into consideration in the answers to be given to the Court of Cassation since there is general agreement on the matter and the question submitted by the Belgian court may be taken as referring by implication only to disputes arising after the expiry of the written agreement.

The distinguishing feature of the case before the Court is undoubtedly the considerable period which elapsed after the original agreement was last renewed in writing and during which the parties continued to maintain business relations 'within the framework' of that agreement.

A further complication arises where, as in this case, there is no unanimity between the parties to the proceedings concerning the scope or the nature of those relations.

Admittedly, the Court of Cassation found in its judgment requesting a preliminary ruling that the original agreement 'has continued to serve as the *legal basis* for the contractual relations between the parties'. But the wording - particularly in the context in which it is set, since the national court recognises in the same question that the agreement has expired - is not unequivocal and is capable of supporting various interpretations.

On the other hand, although Fiat states, in its written observations, that 'business relations between the parties *continued to be governed* by the said co-operation agreement, Van Hool maintains that, as from 31 December 1961, the parties continued to deal with one another merely on the basis of '*de facto* contractual co-operation', that is to say by applying rules differing from those laid down in writing in previous agreements, since some of the terms of those agreements (concerning the territorial limits of the concession and fixing the minimum purchase quotas, prices and means of payment) were amended subsequently.

Naturally, the parties endeavour to reinforce their respective standpoints by relying on facts and documents relating to the 'grey' period between the end of 1958 and the end of 1981. Fiat has produced the letter of 5 November 1968, the document dated 20 November 1968 and the note of 7 September 1983 addressed to the experts appointed by the Tribunal de commerce de Malines, all emanating from Van Hool, and also the agreements entered into with Catrabel which remained in force until 1981. Van Hool has produced Fiat's letter of 27 March 1964.

6. It is not for the Court of Justice to take the place of the national court by fixing on the basis of facts concerning the conduct of the parties which it is for the national court to establish, the nature of the legal uncertainty between the last time the original agreement was renewed in writing and the termination of the business relations which the parties continued to maintain for a number of years thereafter.

Similarly, it is not for the Court to resolve the general question of whether the original agreement was valid following its last renewal in writing, or to state its views concerning the terms on which the agreement was validly concluded or otherwise.

As the United Kingdom and the Commission rightly point out in their written observations, those are matters which fall outside the ambit of Article 17 and, consequently, are not governed by its interpretation. They must be resolved by the national court in accordance with the law which is applicable to the agreement in the light of national rules on the conflict of laws.

It is the task of the Court of Justice, according to the circumstances of each case, to interpret Article 17 within its sphere of application, particularly in relation to the formal requirements which that provision lays down with regard to jurisdiction clauses, thereby making it possible to determine whether such clauses - and such clauses alone - are valid in the light of those requirements.

Having said that, however, it is necessary to see matters in their proper perspective: in view of the specific nature of the formal requirements laid down in Article 17 regarding jurisdiction clauses, it is necessary, in order to determine the validity of those clauses, to consider separately the other terms of the agreements in which those clauses are inserted.

The fate of jurisdiction clauses is not necessarily linked to that of the agreements in which they are inserted. That is the principle which may be elicited from the consistent case-law of the Court in this field.

For that reason, I would not go as far as the United Kingdom appears to in its written observations in these proceedings. The scope *ratione temporae* of a jurisdiction clause cannot be linked automatically to the continued existence of the agreement of which it forms part, on the assumption that that question 'can only be determined under the relevant national law'.

For instance, the competent court may decide that the original agreement was indisputably valid after it was last renewed and therefore constituted the 'legal basis' for business relations between the parties. That will not *necessarily* mean that the jurisdiction clause was still valid, in the light of the requirements in Article 17, as interpreted by the Court of Justice.

As a rule, this Court is bound by the nature of the Convention, which is based on the principle of direct jurisdiction, to provide an independent interpretation of its provisions in the light of its scheme and context. That is, moreover, as has already been observed (see the Opinion of Advocate General Capotorti in *Estasis Salotti* [1976] ECR 1831 at p. 1845 and *Segoura* [1976] ECR 1851 at p. 1867), a necessary condition in order to ensure that the Convention is applied uniformly in the various Contracting States and, consequently, in order to ensure equal treatment of natural and legal persons in the Community by the various national courts.

The question whether a jurisdiction clause complies with the formal requirements of Article 17 of the Convention is 'a matter of Community law for this Court in the last resort (see the Opinion of Advocate General Sir Gordon Slynn in *Tilly Russ* [1984] ECR 2417 at p. 2438) and is to be resolved in accordance with the requirements of an 'interpretation subject to Community law'.

7. Before I reach my conclusion, I must rapidly recapitulate the essential facts of the case *sub judice*, as reflected in the question submitted by the Belgian Court of Cassation.

Two undertakings, each having its registered office in a different Member State of the Community, concluded at the end of 1956 a one-year written agreement in which one party assigned an exclusive concession to the other and which contained a clause providing for renewal of the agreement in writing and a clause conferring jurisdiction.

The agreement was last renewed in writing in 1961, however, the parties continued to maintain normal business relations *on the basis or within the framework* (which had, it would appear, been amended) of the agreement previously concluded, until in 1981 one of the parties decided to bring those relations to an end, with the result that the other party was obliged to institute legal proceedings against the first party.

8. That statement of the essential facts which are set out in the documents before the Court (and in particular in the judgment of the Court of Cassation) does not, as I said earlier, dispel certain doubts or ambiguities concerning the facts of the case. Allow me, however, in the light of the considerations which I have set forth, to consider two possibilities and to draw symmetrical conclusions from them.

The first possibility is that the original agreement is regarded by the court having jurisdiction as legally valid and applicable even though it has not been renewed in writing; that is the sense in which the reference to the fact that it continued to serve as the 'legal basis' for the contractual relations between the parties is to be understood.

That possibility arises - as the Commission points out in its observations - where, for instance, the national law applicable to the agreement recognises the validity of a mere oral revocation of the original clause providing for renewal of the original agreement in writing and the parties subsequently renew it either orally or tacitly. In that case, as the Commission concedes, the jurisdiction clause in the original agreement could be regarded simply as valid in every respect. That would be consistent with the requirements of flexibility in commercial practice also because oral renewal, which relates to the written agreement as a whole, would encompass all of its terms, which were undoubtedly inserted with the consent of the parties. Renewal of the agreement in writing would also have the same effect, without there being any need for express or specific confirmation of the jurisdiction clause.

However, I consider that, whilst that is the first element to be taken into account in the answer to be given to the question submitted to the Court, it is not the sole element and, perhaps for that reason, is not decisive.

Attention must be drawn to the following circumstances, which have been established or may have arisen in this case, and which should be taken into account over and above purely legal considerations in assessing the facts: the original agreement was no longer renewed in writing beyond a certain date; a considerable period (20 years) elapsed between the last date on which the agreement was renewed in writing and the termination of business relations between the parties; it is unclear to what extent the parties relied during that period on the original agreement, whether its terms were expressly relied upon as between the parties or in the proceedings or whether the agreement only continued to serve as a vague and general frame of reference; it may be true, as one of the parties alleged, that there was an agreement between them (oral or written? How important was it?) to replace the requirement of written renewal with a system of tacit renewal; throughout the period in question the written terms of the agreement may have been amended in various ways without its being possible to ascertain the precise manner in which they were amended (orally or in writing, expressly or tacitly)

Hence, even on the assumption that the original agreement continued to be legally valid, there are doubts as to the manner in which it continued to serve as the 'legal basis' for relations between the parties.

In view of the circumstances, and notwithstanding the terms in which it was originally couched, the form of the jurisdiction clause does not constitute sufficient evidence of valid consent by the parties for the purposes of Article 17 of the Convention. It should be noted that, in the circumstances of this case, legal certainty requires two things: in the first place Article 17 of the Convention requires an 'agreement in writing or ... oral agreement evidenced in writing', which must be strictly interpreted by the Court, and secondly between the appellant and the respondent in the main proceedings requires renewal to be confirmed in writing. In those circumstances, a rigorous assessment is essential in whether the formal determining for the validity of the jurisdiction clause are satisfied.

The second possibility is that the original agreement is not regarded as valid and applicable (and may not therefore be relied upon as it stands against either of the law parties) under the applicable national law, but continues to serve as a legal framework for business relations between the parties, with the result that it may be said, for instance, to the extent to which the applicable national law permits them to do so, that the parties accept the agreement as a set of general conditions governing current business relations between them an any oral agreements which they may make.

The result is that if the parties actually rely upon that agreement, whether in legal proceedings or otherwise, and comply with its terms, which they originally stipulated in writing freely and in full knowledge of the facts, they can no longer seriously maintain that they were unaware of those terms, and it would thus be contrary to the principle of *good faith* if one of the parties were able to invoke the requirements of Article 17 in order to escape the application of a jurisdiction clause (with regard to the principle of good faith in this area, I would refer to the case-law cited earlier).

That second possibility assumes quite a different form if the national court finds, in the light of national legislation interpreted and applied by it in the specific circumstances of the case, that the agreement ceased to have any force after the expiry of the period for which it was last renewed in writing.

The agreement before the Court would then be entirely distinct from the agreement that preceded it; it would be based on an oral or tacit agreement and might or might not be in conformity with national law but, in any event, would be incapable of satisfying the requirements of Article 17 of the Convention (even on the assumption that the terms of the two agreements are identical) not being evidenced in writing.

If it were otherwise, there would be a risk (as in the case of the first possibility) of recognising as valid for the purposes of Article 17 what is no more than an implied reference to a written agreement which was concluded earlier (and has in this case expired); this the Court has refused to do, albeit in another context (see the judgment in *Salotti* [1976] ECR 1831 at p. 1842).

9. In conclusion, therefore, I suggest that the Court of Justice answer the question submitted to it for a preliminary ruling by the Belgian Court of Cassation as follows: 'A jurisdiction clause validly inserted in a written agreement which continued to serve as the legal basis for relations between the parties after the period of validity of the agreement had expired because the condition stipulating that the agreement could be renewed only in writing was not fulfilled must be deemed to be in conformity with the requirements of the first paragraph of Article 17 of the Convention on Jurisdiction and the Enforcement of Judgments in Civil and Commercial Matters provided that:

- the original agreement is still valid under the national law applicable, notwithstanding the fact that it has not been renewed in writing, and the conduct of the parties does not support the conclusion that they ceased to regard it as a frame of reference for business relations between them so as to remove or seriously reduce the scope of the original guarantees concerning their consent to the insertion of the jurisdiction clause;

- the original agreement, although it is deemed to have expired under the national law applicable, continued to serve in practice as a set of general conditions and as a legal frame of reference for the parties in current business relations between them, with the result that it would be contrary to the principle of good faith for either of them to challenge the application of the jurisdiction clause'.

Case C-214/89 - 10 March 1992

Powell Duffryn plc
v
Wolfgang Petereit

Prorogation of jurisdiction - Article 17, as amended by the 1978 Accession Convention - Agreement conferring jurisdiction - Concept - Independent interpretation - Clause conferring jurisdiction contained in the statutes of a company limited by shares - Included - Validity as against shareholders - Conditions - Prorogation of jurisdiction - Agreement conferring jurisdiction - Scope - Disputes arising from a given legal relationship - Dispute between a company and its shareholders as such.

Summary

1. The concept of 'agreement conferring jurisdiction' in Article 17 of the Convention of 27 September 1968 on Jurisdiction and the Enforcement of Judgments in Civil and Commercial Matters must be regarded as an indcpcndcnt Concept.

A clause contained in the statutes of a company limited by shares and adopted in accordance with the provisions of the applicable national law and those statutes themselves conferring jurisdiction on a court of a Contracting State to settle disputes between that company and its shareholders constitutes an agreement conferring jurisdiction.

The formal requirements laid down in Article 17 of the Convention must be considered to be complied with in regard to any shareholder, irrespective of how the shares were acquired, if the clause conferring jurisdiction is contained in the statutes of the company and those statutes are lodged in a place to which the shareholder may have access or are contained in a public register.

2. The requirement that a dispute arise in connection with a particular legal relationship, for the solution of which Article 17 of the Convention permits the assignment of jurisdiction by agreement, is satisfied if the clause conferring jurisdiction contained in the statutes of a company may be interpreted by the national court, which has exclusive competence in that regard, as referring to the disputes between the company and its shareholders as such.

JUDGMENT OF THE COURT

Due, President, Sir Gordon Slynn, Joliet, Schockweiler, Grévisse, Kapteyn, Presidents of Chambers, Mancini, Kakouris, Moitinho de Almeida, Rodríguez Iglesias, Diez de Velasco, Zuleeg and Murray, Judges

1. By order of 1 June 1989, which was received at the Court on 10 July 1989, the Oberlandesgericht (Higher Regional Court) Koblenz referred to the Court, for a preliminary ruling pursuant to the Protocol of 3 June 1971 on the interpretation by the Court of Justice of the Convention of 27 September 1968 on Jurisdiction and the Enforcement of Judgments in Civil and Commercial Matters a number of questions on the interpretation of Article 17 of that convention, as amended by the 1978 Accession Convention (Official Journal 1978 L 304, p. 1, hereinafter referred to as the 'Brussels Convention').

2. The questions arose in proceedings between W. Petereit, acting as liquidator of the company IBH-Holding AG, in liquidation, and Powell Duffryn plc (hereinafter referred to as 'Powell Duffryn'). It appears from the papers in the case that Powell Duffryn, a company under English law, had subscribed for registered shares in IBH-Holding AG (hereinafter referred to as 'IBH-Holding'), a company limited by shares under German law, when the latter's capital was increased in September 1979. On 28 July 1980 Powell Duffryn participated in the proceedings of a general meeting of IBH-Holding during which by a show of hands, the shareholders adopted resolutions amending the statutes of IBH, in particular by inserting into them the following clause: 'By subscribing for or acquiring shares or interim certificates the shareholder submits, with regard to all disputes between himself and the company or its organs, to the jurisdiction of the courts ordinarily competent to entertain suits concerning the company'.

3. In 1981 and 1982 Powell Duffryn subscribed for further shares on successive increases in the capital of IBH-Holding and also received dividends. In 1983 IBH-Holding was put into liquidation and Mr Petereit, acting as liquidator, brought an action before the Landgericht Mainz claiming that Powell Duffryn had not fulfilled its obligations to IBH-Holding to make the cash payments due in respect of the increases in capital. He also sought to recover dividends which he maintained had been wrongly paid to Powell Duffryn.

4. The Landgericht dismissed the plea of lack of jurisdiction raised by Powell Duffryn whereupon the latter appealed to the Oberlandesgericht Koblenz. That court considered that the dispute raised a question of interpretation of Article 17 of the Brussels Convention, stayed the proceedings and referred the following questions to the Court of Justice for a preliminary ruling:

'1. Does the rule contained in the statutes of a company limited by shares on the basis of which the shareholder by subscribing for or acquiring shares submits, with regard to all disputes with the company or its organs, to the jurisdiction of the courts ordinarily competent to entertain suits concerning the company constitute an agreement conferring jurisdiction within the meaning of Article 17 of the Brussels Convention which is concluded between the shareholder an the company? (Must this question be answered differently depending on whether the shareholder himself subscribes for shares on the occasion of an increase in the company's capital or acquires existing shares?)

2. If Question (1) is answered in the affirmative: (a) Does subscription for and acceptance of shares, by means of a written declaration of subscription, on the occasion of an increase in the capital of a company limited by shares comply with the requirement for writing laid down in the first paragraph of Article 17 of the Brussels Convention as regards a jurisdiction clause contained in the statutes of the company? (b) Does the jurisdiction clause satisfy the requirement that the dispute must arise in connection with a particular legal relationship within the meaning of Article 17 of the Brussels Convention? (c) Does the jurisdiction clause in the statutes also cover claims for payment arising out of a contract relating to the subscription of shares and claims for repayment of wrongly paid dividends?'

5. Reference is made to the Report for the Hearing for a fuller account of the facts of the case, the procedure and the written observations submitted to the Court, which are mentioned or discussed hereinafter only insofar as is necessary for the reasoning of the Court.

The first question

6. Article 17 of the Brussels Convention provides that if the parties, one or more of whom is domiciled in a Contracting State, have agreed that a court of a Contracting State is to have jurisdiction to settle any disputes which have arisen or which may arise in connection with a particular legal relationship, that court is to have exclusive jurisdiction.

7. It is necessary to examine whether a clause conferring jurisdiction inserted in the statutes of a company limited by shares constitutes an agreement within the meaning of Article 17 between the company and its shareholders.

8. Powell Duffryn maintains that a clause conferring jurisdiction contained in the statutes of a company limited by shares cannot constitute an agreement because the statutes are normative by nature and thus the contents are not open to discussion by shareholders; shareholders even face the risk of clauses being introduced against their express wishes if such a possibility is provided for in the statutes or the applicable national law.

9. In contrast, Mr Petereit and the Commission argue, on the basis of German law and in particular the provisions of the German Aktiengesetz (Law on share companies), that the statutes are contractual by nature and therefore a clause conferring jurisdiction contained therein constitutes an agreement within the meaning of Article 17 of the Brussels Convention.

10. In that regard, it appears from a comparative examination of the different legal systems of the Contracting States that the characterization of the nature of the relationship between a company limited by shares and its shareholders is not always the same. In some legal systems the relationship is characterized as contractual and in others it is regarded as institutional, normative or *sui generis.*

11. The question therefore arises whether the concept of 'agreement conferring jurisdiction' in Article 17 of the Brussels Convention must be given an independent interpretation or be construed as referring to the national law of one or other of the States concerned.

12. It must be emphasized that, as the Court held in its judgment in Case 12/76 *Tessili* v *Dunlop* [1976] ECR 1473, neither of those two options rules out the other since the appropriate choice can only be made in

respect of each of the provisions of the Convention to ensure that it is fully effective having regard to the objectives of Article 220 of the EEC Treaty.

13. The concept of 'agreement conferring jurisdiction' is decisive for the assignment, in derogation from the general rules on jurisdiction, of exclusive jurisdiction to the court of the Contracting State designated by the parties. Having regard to the objectives and general scheme of the Brussels Convention, and in order to ensure as far as possible the equality and uniformity of the rights and obligations arising out of the Convention for the Contracting States and persons concerned, therefore, it is important that the concept of 'agreement conferring jurisdiction' should not be interpreted simply as referring to the national law of one or other of the States concerned.

14. Accordingly, as the Court has held for similar reasons as regards, in particular, the concept of 'matters relating to a contract' and other concepts, referred to in Article 5 of the Convention, which serve as criteria for determining special jurisdiction (see the judgment in Case 34/82 *Peters* v *ZNAV* [1983] ECR 987, paragraphs 9 and 10), the concept of 'agreement conferring jurisdiction' in Article 17 must be regarded as an independent concept.

15. In that connection, it must be recalled that, when it was requested to interpret the concept of 'matters relating to a contract', referred to in Article 5 of the Convention, the Court held that the obligations imposed on a person in his capacity as member of an association were to be considered to be contractual obligations, on the ground that membership of an association created between the members close links of the same kind as those which are created between the parties to a contract (see the judgment in Case 34/82 *Peters* v *ZNAV*, referred to above, paragraph 13).

16. Similarly, the links between the shareholders of a company are comparable to those between the parties to a contract. The setting up of a company is the expression of the existence of a community of interests between the shareholders in the pursuit of a common objective. In order to achieve that objective each shareholder is assigned, as regards other shareholders and the organs of the company, rights and obligations set out in the company's statutes. It follows that, for the purposes of the application of the Brussels Convention, the company's statutes must be regarded as a contract covering both the relations between the

shareholders and also the relations between them and the company they set up.

17. It follows that a clause conferring jurisdiction in the statutes of a company limited by shares is an agreement, within the meaning of Article 17 of the Brussels Convention, which is binding on all the shareholders.

18. It is immaterial that the shareholder against whom the clause conferring jurisdiction is invoked opposed the adoption of the clause or that he became a shareholder after the clause was adopted.

19. By becoming and by remaining a shareholder in a company, the shareholder agrees to be subject to all the provisions appearing in the statutes of the company and to the decisions adopted by the organs of the company, in accordance with the provisions of the applicable national law and the statutes, even if he does not agree with some of those provisions or decisions.

20. Any other interpretation of Article 17 of the Brussels Convention would lead to a multiplication of the heads of jurisdiction for disputes arising from the same legal and factual relationship between the company and its shareholders and would run counter to the principle of legal certainty.

21. Consequently, the reply to the national court's first question must be that a clause contained in the statutes of a company limited by shares and adopted in accordance with the provisions of the applicable national law and those statutes themselves conferring jurisdiction on a court of a Contracting State to settle disputes between that company and its shareholders constitutes an agreement conferring jurisdiction within the meaning of Article 17 of the Brussels Convention.

The first part of the second question

22. In the first part of the second question the national court seeks essentially to ascertain the circumstances in which a clause conferring jurisdiction contained in a company's statutes satisfies the formal requirements laid down in Article 17 of the Brussels Convention.

23. Pursuant to Article 17 of the Brussels Convention an agreement conferring jurisdiction must be either in writing or evidenced in writing or, in international trade or commerce, in a form which accords with usage in that area and of which the parties are or ought to be aware.

24. As the Court held in Case 24/76 *Estasis Salotti* v *Rüwa* [1976] ECR 1831, paragraph 7, the purpose of the formal requirements imposed by Article 17 is to ensure that the consensus between the parties is in fact established.

25. It must nevertheless be emphasized that the situation of shareholders as regards the statutes of a company - which are the expression of the existence of a community of interests between the shareholders in the pursuit of a common objective - is different from that, referred to in the above-mentioned judgment, of a party to a contract of sale as regards general conditions of sale.

26. First of all, in the legal systems of all the Contracting States the statutes of a company are in writing. Moreover, in the company law of all the Contracting States it is acknowledged that the statutes of companies play a particular role insofar as they constitute the basic instrument governing the relations between a shareholder and the company.

27. Furthermore, irrespective of how shares are acquired, every person who becomes a shareholder of a company knows, or ought to know, that he is bound by the company's statutes and by the amendments made to them by the company's organs in accordance with the provisions of the applicable national law and the statutes.

28. Consequently, when the company's statutes contain a clause conferring jurisdiction, every shareholder is deemed to be aware of that clause and actually to consent to the assignment of jurisdiction for which it provides if the statutes are lodged in a place to which the shareholder may have access, such as the seat of the company, or are contained in a public register.

29. Having regard to the foregoing, the reply to the first part of the national court's second question must be that, irrespective of how shares are acquired, the formal requirements laid down in Article 17 must be considered to be complied with in regard to any shareholder if the clause conferring jurisdiction is contained in the statutes of the company and those statutes are lodged in a place to which the shareholder may have access or are contained in a public register.

The second part of the second question

30. Pursuant to Article 17 of the Brussels Convention, jurisdiction is

conferred for the purpose of settling disputes which have arisen or which may arise 'in connection with a particular legal relationship'.

31. That requirement is intended to limit the scope of an agreement conferring jurisdiction solely to disputes which arise from the legal relationship in connection with which the agreement was entered into. Its purpose is to avoid a party being taken by surprise by the assignment of jurisdiction to a given *forum* as regards all disputes which may arise out of its relationship with the other party to the contract and stem from a relationship other than that in connection with which the agreement conferring jurisdiction was made.

32. In that regard, a clause conferring jurisdiction contained in a company's statutes satisfies that requirement if it relates to disputes which have arisen or which may arise in connection with the relationship between the company and its shareholders as such.

33. The question whether in the present case the clause conferring jurisdiction is to be regarded as having such an effect is a question of interpretation which is a matter for the national court to resolve.

34. Consequently, the reply to the second part of the national court's second question must be that the requirement that a dispute arise in connection with a particular legal relationship within the meaning of Article 17 is satisfied if the clause conferring jurisdiction contained in the statutes of a company may be interpreted as referring to the disputes between the company and its shareholders as such.

The third part of the second question

35. In the third part of the second question the national court is essentially seeking to ascertain whether the clause conferring jurisdiction raised before it applies to the disputes brought before it.

36. In that regard, it should be observed that it is for the national court to interpret the clause conferring jurisdiction invoked before it.

37. Consequently, the reply to the third part of the national court's second question must be that it is for the national court to interpret the clause conferring jurisdiction invoked before it in order to determine which disputes fall within its scope.

On those grounds, the Court, in answer to the questions referred to it by the Oberlandesgericht Koblenz, order of 1 June 1989, hereby rules:

1. A clause contained in the statutes of a company limited by shares and adopted in accordance with the provisions of the applicable national law and those statutes themselves conferring jurisdiction on a court of a Contracting State to settle disputes between that company and its shareholders constitutes an agreement conferring jurisdiction within the meaning of Article 17 of the Brussels Convention;

2. Irrespective of how shares are acquired, the formal requirements laid down in Article 17 must be considered to be complied with in regard to any shareholder if the clause conferring jurisdiction is contained in the statutes of the company and those statutes are lodged in a place to which the shareholder may have access or are contained in a public register;

3. The requirement that a dispute arise in connection with a particular legal relationship within the meaning of Article 17 is satisfied if the clause conferring jurisdiction contained in the statutes of a company may be interpreted as referring to the disputes between the company and its shareholders as such;

4. It is for the national court to interpret the clause conferring jurisdiction invoked before it in order to determine which disputes fall within its scope.

OPINION OF MR ADVOCATE GENERAL TESAURO

1. These proceedings concern certain questions referred to the Court by the Oberlandesgericht (Higher Regional Court), Koblenz, for a preliminary ruling on the interpretation of Article 17 of the Convention of 27 September 1968 on Jurisdiction and the Enforcement of Judgments in Civil and Commercial Matters, as amended by the 1978 Accession Convention.

2. I shall briefly recall the facts underlying these proceedings, referring for a more detailed account to the Report for the Hearing.

In 1979, and then in 1980 and 1981, Powell Duffryn plc, an undertaking governed by English law, participated in the increase of capital in IBH-holding AG (referred to as 'IBH'), an undertaking governed by German law, and subscribed for shares in it.

In 28 July 1980 the statutes of IBH were altered in general meeting and a new clause was inserted into Article 4 of the statutes with the following wording: '*By subscribing for or purchasing shares or interim certificates the shareholder submits with regard to all disputes with the company or its organs, to the jurisdiction of the courts ordinarily competent to entertain suits concerning the company.*' It should be emphasized that Powell Duffryn took part in the meeting and was therefore present when the amendment was introduced and approved by a show of hands.

Subsequently to the declaration of insolvency of IBH, Mr Petereit, a lawyer acting as the trustee in bankruptcy, commenced proceedings before the Landgericht (Regional Court), Mainz, maintaining that Powell Duffryn had not fulfilled its obligations under the agreement to subscribe for shares, and seeking reimbursement of dividends wrongly paid. Powell Duffryn contended that the Landgericht Mainz lacked jurisdiction but the latter, by interlocutory decision, declared itself to have jurisdiction, and considered that the jurisdiction clause contained in Article 4 of the statutes was valid under Article 17 of the Convention.

Powell Duffryn appealed against that decision to the Oberlandesgericht, Koblenz, which stayed the proceedings and, in essence, referred the following questions to the Court for a preliminary ruling:

1. Does a jurisdiction clause in the statutes of a company limited by shares constitute an agreement conferring jurisdiction within the meaning of Article 17 of the Convention, and must this question be answered differently depending upon whether the shareholder subscribes for shares or purchases existing shares?

2. If the first question is answered in the affirmative: (a) does a written declaration of subscription for and acceptance of shares, on the occasion of an increase in capital, comply with the requirements for writing laid down in the first paragraph of Article 17; (b) does the jurisdiction clause satisfy the requirement that the dispute must arise in connection with a particular legal relationship within the meaning of Article 17; (c) finally, does the jurisdiction clause also cover claims to payment arising out of a contract for the subscription of shares and claims to the repayment of wrongly paid dividends?

3. The main point to be decided is therefore whether a jurisdiction clause contained in the statutes of a company limited by shares constitutes an agreement conferring jurisdiction within the meaning of Article 17, thus complying with the formal requirements laid down in that article.

Article 17, in the wording formulated in the Accession Agreement in respect of Denmark, Ireland and the United Kingdom of 1978, provides for the situation in which 'the parties, one or more of whom is domiciled in a Contracting State, have agreed that a court or the courts of a Contracting State are to have jurisdiction to settle any disputes which have arisen or may arise in connection with a particular legal relationship', as well as requiring that 'such an agreement conferring jurisdiction shall be either in writing or evidenced in writing, or, in international trade or commerce, in a form which accords with a usage of which the parties are or ought to have been aware. In view of the terms of the aforementioned provision, the question to be determined in the first place is whether the provision in question contained in the statutes (the clause conferring jurisdiction) is of a contractual nature within the meaning of Article 17. In order to reply to that question it is essential to clarify as a preliminary point the scope of the concept of an agreement between the parties (literally 'if the parties ... have agreed...') referred to in Article 17.

On that point it is clear that an autonomous meaning, and thus one common to all the Contracting States, may be attributed to concepts used in the Convention, where they are not defined by it, or regard may be had to national law. And it is well known that the Court has not in principle opted for the 'national' interpretation or for an autonomous interpretation, but has allowed that choice to be determined by an examination of the individual concepts in order to establish on a case-by-case basis which of the two options is likely to contribute most fully to the efficacy of the Convention.

Nevertheless, in its most recent judgment the Court has shown a clear preference for the autonomous interpretation of the Convention, to the extent to which it may be affirmed that practice in the matter has developed towards a situation in which there exists a general rule (autonomous interpretation) subject to exceptions (renvoi to national law).

I therefore consider that the concept of an agreement between the parties within the meaning of Article 17 must be interpreted in an autonomous manner. In so doing, I am taking account both of the objectives and of the scheme of the Convention, and in particular, therefore, of the objective of avoiding divergences in the application of the Convention itself, and of thus ensuring greater legal certainty by means of a clear and uniform interpretation for all the Contracting States, and also of the general principles common to all the national legal systems.

4. Indeed a comparison of the various legal orders of the Member States demonstrates, on the one hand, that the nature of corporate relationships and in particular - of relevance here - the relationships between a company and its shareholders, are not treated uniformly, although at the same time the differences do not entail substantially different consequences.

In fact, in the legal systems in which the contractual conception prevails, and they are the largest majority, it is clearly established that the obligation stemming from status as a shareholder may subsist irrespective of the will of the individual. Thus, for example, it is not disputed that a resolution adopted by a majority at a meeting of the company, which in principle resists inclusion in any contractual classification, is binding on all the shareholders including those in disagreement, and on persons who subsequently become shareholders. Conversely, in the legal systems where the institutional concept prevails, whereby the statutes (and indeed the deed of incorporation) are *sui generis* acts having the value of objective law for the shareholders, it may be that certain clauses of the statutes are enforceable only against those who expressly consented to them, in the strict contractual sense of the term.

The contractual-institutional dichotomy in the categorization of corporate relationships seems to me in the end rather theoretical and thus of little relevance in the solution of the problem in question. What is important, in my opinion, is rather the fact that, regardless of the view adhered to and of the academic discussion on this subject, there is underlying the corporate phenomenon an expression of an intention to enter into legal relations which manifests itself in the deed of incorporation of the company, of which the statutes form an integral part, which leads to close links being established between the shareholders and between the shareholders and the company, reciprocal obligations which are provided for most fully and completely in the statutes and, for present purposes, are in essence at least analogous to contractual obligations in their effects.

5. That is specifically confirmed in the *Peters* judgment in which the Court held that an action for the recovery of monies brought by an association having legal personality against one of its members was a matter relating to a contract. That judgment has a twofold significance: on the one hand, the Court therein stated that, in order to ensure as far as possible the equality and uniformity of the rights and obligations arising out of the Convention for the Contracting States and the persons concerned, the concept of matters relating to a contract (referred to in Article 5 of the Convention), cannot be interpreted 'simply as referring to the national law of one or other of the States concerned'; it then went on to state that 'membership of an association creates between the members close links of the same kind as those which are created between the parties to a contract'.

It is hardly necessary to point out that the general and definitive terms of that description by the Court of corporate relationships preclude its scope from being confined to the, concept of 'matters relating to a contract' in Article 5(1) of the Convention, which was specifically at issue in the *Peters* judgment. Nor do I see any reason to depart in this case from the above-mentioned case-law.

In the final analysis I consider that, in the context of an independent and uniform interpretation of the concepts contained in the Convention and having regard to the essence of the corporate phenomenon (transcending the various formal definitions adopted in the various legal orders), it is legitimate and reasonable for present purposes to recognize the provisions of statutes governing relations between the company and its shareholders as being of a contractual nature, or at least of a nature analogous to contract; and that, obviously, also applies to a clause conferring jurisdiction such as the clause at issue in the present proceedings. A clause of that kind may therefore be regarded as falling within the concept of an agreement between the parties, within the meaning of Article 17.

6. Once it is established on the basis of the foregoing that a clause conferring jurisdiction contained in the statutes of a company falls within the concept of an agreement between the company and its shareholders, it is necessary to ascertain whether that clause complies with the conditions laid down in Article 17 of the Convention.

I nevertheless consider that it is useful, before ascertaining that question, briefly to review the Court's case-law in the matter.

The Court has always held that the provisions of the article in question must be interpreted in accordance with a restrictive and strict criterion, given that they constitute an exception to the general principle of the defendant's forum (Article 2) and the special jurisdiction referred to in Articles 5 and 6.

In particular, the Court has held that, by making the validity of the prorogation of jurisdiction subject to 'the existence of an agreement between the parties, Article 17 imposes on the court before which the matter is brought the duty of examining first, whether the clause conferring jurisdiction upon it was in fact the subject of a consensus between the parties, which must be clearly and precisely demonstrated.' The manner in which that consensus is to be demonstrated is therefore, according to the interpretation given by the Court, closely linked to proof of the existence of the agreement between the parties. In fact 'the purpose of the formal requirements imposed by Article 17 is to ensure that the consensus between the parties is in fact established.'

Moreover, the practical solutions adopted demonstrate that the Court has to some extent mitigated the strictness of the formal requirements laid down in the provisions in question.

In fact it is clear from the relevant case-law that the consensus between the parties may be ascertained on the basis of presumptions of logic (for example, where a party receives an advantage under a clause, he must be presumed to have accepted that clause), or on the basis of conclusive conduct (for example where a written confirmation was not contested by the other party, or the acceptance of a benefit provided for in return for a clause conferring jurisdiction favouring the other party), or again on the basis of the application of reasonable care, as in the case of clauses which the party concerned could or should have been aware of by exercising reasonable care, or of usages which he should or could have been aware of, etc.

The mitigation by the Court of the strict application of the formal requirements was confirmed and amplified by the new wording of Article 17, as amended by the Accession Convention of 1978 which, I recall, refers to the usages of international trade or commerce and provides that a clause conferring jurisdiction may also be accepted in a form permitted by usages which the parties were or ought to have been aware of.

All that shows a very considerable (and necessary) attention and sensitivity to the demands of international trade and, more generally, to the actual functioning of the business world. For it is clear that an excessively strict application of the principles laid down in Article 17 would render it practically impossible to apply clauses conferring jurisdiction contained in contractual documents or documents arising out of contractual relationships (for example credit documents) which owing to their specific characteristics are not, and only with difficulty could be, signed by one of the Contracting Parties.

7. Having said that, it is also true that the Court has always stressed that the reality of the consensus between the parties with regard to the clause in question must be proved, as must the fact that they agreed to it knowingly. The purpose is always to avoid a jurisdiction clause being inserted surreptitiously, that is to say in a situation in which one of the parties is not in fact aware of it, whether under the reasonable care doctrine or under the presumption of awareness of usages, as referred to in the *Salotti* and *Tilly Russ* judgments cited above.

With regard to the case before the Court, it is necessary to establish whether there was conscious acceptance, or at least awareness, of a clause contained in the statutes of the company which, by way of derogation from the general principle of the defendant's forum and the special jurisdictions laid down in Articles 2, 5 and 6 of the Convention respectively, provides that the competent courts for disputes involving the company are to be those of the company's principal office, irrespective of the nature of the dispute.

Situations raising the problem of the validity and therefore the applicability of the derogating provision may occur at various times in the life of the company.

The first situation relates, shall I say, to the 'original' validity of the clause, that is to say its insertion in the statutes at the time when the company was incorporated. I do not consider that this situation poses particular problems where the corporate obligations are essentially given a contractual designation, as I have already suggested. As to the formal requirements laid down in Article 17 it is inconceivable that those requirements, as elucidated by the Court, are not complied with in the case of a deed of incorporation of a company.

Nor are any greater or different problems posed by the situation in which the clause assigning jurisdiction is introduced subsequently by an alteration of the statutes by a resolution of the general meeting, in particular as regards those members expressing by a vote in favour their agreement to the introduction of the clause. In that case as well, it is undeniable that both the substantive conditions (consensus), and the formal conditions (reduction to writing) required by Article 17 of the Convention are met.

It is hardly necessary to point out that, as is evident from the file, the clause in the present case is valid and fully enforceable against Powell Duffryn which voted in favour of it when it was resolved to insert the clause into the statutes of IBH.

8. Perplexity and disagreement have arisen on the question whether the clause assigning jurisdiction is to be deemed valid and enforceable also as against members who (a) voted against the insertion of the clause into the statutes; (b) have subsequently become members of the company, perhaps by acquiring shares by telephonic means or,according to the very infelicitous example given at the hearing, by finding the security by chance or even by stealing it, or by subscribing for new shares on the occasion of an increase of capital. Essentially, in both situations mentioned the conditions laid down in Article 17 are not satisfied: in the former situation there is no consensus since there was in fact disagreement; in the latter there is no proof of actual consent to the clause.

I do not share this perplexity and consider instead that a clause assigning jurisdiction contained in the statutes of a company is binding on all its members, including future members and members who were against the introduction of the clause and who have remained as shareholders. I consider therefore that the argument to the contrary must be rejected since it does not foresee or resolve either immediate problems or remote and general ones.

As regards the situation of the shareholder who has expressed his disagreement to the insertion of a clause conferring jurisdiction, it may be stated straight away that, whilst the purpose of Article 17 is to prevent such a clause from being introduced into a contract surreptitiously, its purpose is not to render it inapplicable as against those persons who, though being perfectly aware of its existence but disagreeing with it, continue to be shareholders. Indeed, whereas normally the non-acceptance of a clause assigning jurisdiction precludes the relevant contract from coming into existence, or causes that clause to be excluded from the contract, it would be very curious if, in the case of a company, such disagreement were to bring about an extremely advantageous situation, namely continued membership of the company and at the same time inapplicability of the clause in question as against the dissenting shareholder.

As regards, then, the situation in which a person becomes a shareholder on the acquisition of or the subscription for a share, it has been authoritatively argued, and rightly so, that such an event is usually marked by some written formality, which is either contemporaneous or subsequent and confirmatory and specifically refers to the statutes of the company and to all the rights and obligations flowing therefrom, in such a way as to observe the strict conditions laid down in Article 17 of the Convention, as interpreted by the Court.

However, it is apparent from a research note drawn up by the Court's departments that, although it is true that the subscription for and the acquisition of shares are carried out in such a way as to require written form, the form of subscription for and/or the acquisition of a share do not normally contain any reference to the statutes. On the other hand, contrary to arguments put forward during the hearing, I do not think that an express reference to the statutes is necessary in order for the clause assigning jurisdiction contained in them to be valid, since the Court's case-law on such clauses inserted in general conditions or standard contracts is not relevant here.

It is perhaps superfluous to emphasize that, whilst a reference to general conditions of sale is doubtless necessary since those conditions might even be missing, reference to statutes contained in a document attesting the acquisition of or subscription for shares would constitute excessive and unnecessary formalism. Even the most heedless and casual acquirer of shares is in fact well aware of the fact that he is always subject to the rules contained in the statutes, regardless of any reference to their applicability.

9. I am, moreover, persuaded that the solution of the problem calls for a wider perspective which does justice both to the specific nature of the jurisdiction clause contained in the statutes of a company and to the relevance in the 'legal' as opposed to the economic life of the company of the collective will as against the consent of an individual. Were one to fail to appreciate that the problem raised by the national court does not call for a solution dependent on the sole consent of the individual and on traditional contractual aspects, one would not go very far; perhaps one would manage to resolve the present case, somehow: it would, however, be on a narrow ground and unsatisfactory.

In particular, to seek the consent of the individual shareholder in the traditional manner, applying to the jurisdiction clause the criteria used for the contract of a sale of a consignment of beetroot, would lead inexorably and primarily to an intolerable duality of regimes as between shareholders. That would be in this way: although falling within the sphere of Article 17, such a clause would be enforceable only against those persons taking part in the adoption of the statutes contemporaneously with the deed of incorporation, or in the case of a clause introduced subsequently, only against those expressing a vote in favour of such a clause. But not only in that way: in the case of subsequent shareholders acquiring existing shares it may be possible to come to the conclusion that such a clause is enforceable against them or not depending on whether they acquired the shares of members in respect of whom that clause was applicable; clearly that unacceptable result would be achieved, for example, if the solution adopted by the Court in the *Tilly Russ* judgment were to be followed literally.

It is certainly not a coincidence that all the parties to the proceedings are opposed to a solution involving a duality of regimes as between shareholders. In fact, a duality of regimes would lead to a very paradoxical situation, especially in a company with many shareholders in many different countries. The company would be compelled, in the absence of a clause such as the one now before the Court, to proceed against its members before courts throughout the whole of Europe, America, Asia in order to recover contributions.

On the other hand, it is precisely the principle of equality between shareholders together with the requirements of transparency emphasized at the outset, which have inspired the most enlightened legislatures to affirm the criterion of *forum societatis*. Indeed it is well known that the exclusive or concurrent jurisdiction of the court of the place in which the company has its principal office is consistently applied in disputes between members and as between the company and its members, irrespective, evidently, of the nature of the dispute and of whether the company is the plaintiff or the defendant.

It is symbolic that in the jurisdiction clause now before the Court the term used, which is a habitual one, is the courts ordinarily competent to entertain suits concerning the company.

Nor obviously would it be reasonable to suggest that each shareholder, in the process of acquiring that status, should have to subscribe to an express and specific acceptance of the derogation of jurisdiction in favour of the *forum societatis*. Such a solution, which has already been by-passed by the Court's case law, would in any event be unfeasible having regard to the methods and techniques applicable to the movement of securities, and would not eliminate the two-fold regime as between shareholders: in essence it would amount to affirming the radical impossibility for a company limited by shares to enjoy the benefit of a clause of the type now before the Court.

As may be seen, it is necessary to adopt a different and broader perspective which, whilst fully doing justice to the ratio of Article 17 of the Convention and eschewing excessive and damaging formalism, takes account of the reality of the corporate phenomenon and its specific features in relation to contracts for valuable consideration, and of the requirements relating to the circulation of shares.

10. In the case of companies, there is undeniably underpinning the constitution of the company (whatever may be the legal description given to the

corporate 'contract') a convergence of economic interests directed at the pursuit of common purposes. There is in the deed incorporating the company a community of interests whereby all the Contracting Parties seek through the pursuit of a common (economic) activity, profits and advantages. That is so, regardless of the individual reasons prompting each member to pursue the common interests, reasons which obviously may vary, but not in any significant way.

Thus, the original convergence of interests and the identical legal position of the members equality of status subsists not merely as between the founder members at the time of incorporation but also as between them and persons joining the company subsequently since the same community of interests in pursuit of common ends extends to them as well) include an inherent possibility of sacrificing the interest of the individual seen in the light of the objectives pursued by the company which are in any event common to all the participants.

In fact, acceptance of all the provisions of the statutes, even if by definition there is not unanimity on one of them, flows from observance of the rules as to the formation of the corporate will, part of the rules governing the company's functioning. Those rules, which may be defined as the 'rules of the game', imply by definition that the shareholder agrees to be bound by the decisions of the general meeting, even if he is in disagreement with regard to a specific clause, in the same way as the shareholder who subsequently joins the company agrees to be bound by the matters hitherto occurring in the company's life.

In the final analysis, the acceptance of the rights and obligations flowing from statutes is inherent in the acquisition of status of member and, moreover, entails acquiescence in all past and future decisions of the organs of the company adopted in accordance with the provisions of the statutes and of the law concerning the formation of the corporate will.

11. Corporate logic and its underlying principles, as I have described them, clearly demonstrate that the consent of the parties to the statutes, thus to the rules governing the functioning of the company, constitute the expression of the collective will of the shareholders namely the corporate will. Similarly, it is the corporate will, and the acts giving expression to it, which regulate the obligations as between members and company, and, again, it is the corporate will in which the contractual origins of the company are subsumed. So much is that so that it is inconceivable to seek an agreement between the parties in the strict sense of the term, as an exclusive source of the obligations in question.

It is therefore in the light of the corporate will, and not in relation to the consent of the individual shareholder, that the conformity of the clause in question with the conditions laid down in Article 17 falls to be assessed.

Any other conclusion would entirely misapprehend the reality of the corporate phenomenon and lead to consequences which are certainly undesirable and which, in any event, do not correspond to the logic of the article in question: in particular, the risk of a *duality of regimes averted to as between the shareholders with regard to the competent court, a situation which would surely be at variance with the objective of Article 17.*

In the light of the foregoing considerations I therefore consider that the formal requirements laid down in Article 17 of the Convention are fulfilled if the corporate will, that is to say the expression of the overall will of the shareholders, has been arrived at in conformity with the rules of national law applicable in that respect.

That reference to the applicable national law, in the terms stated, seems to me essential in order to establish the valid formation of the corporate will (the provisions governing its formation and, specifically the majorities required, being different in the various Member States) and, at the same time, specifically to mark the limits thereof. It is in fact hardly necessary to stress that any such reference may in no way enable the Contracting States to impose different formal requirements going beyond those provided for in Article 17 as interpreted in these proceedings.

In the present case, those conditions are fully satisfied since written form, often satisfied by a notarial deed, is required in all the legal systems of the Contracting States for the adoption of the deed incorporating the company, and containing the statutes or, in any event, making express reference to them. Similarly, alteration of the statutes is required to be in written form or, at the very least, confirmed in writing, in order generally to comply with the same formal conditions as those prescribed for the deed of incorporation.

From the foregoing observations it may evidently be inferred that the same conclusion is arrived at whether the clause in question was originally contained in the statutes or whether it was inserted subsequently as a result of an alteration thereto.

As regards, then, those shareholders who did not take part in the adoption of the clause in question, the same conclusion must be arrived at, regard being had to the specific characteristics of companies and the requirements inherent in the circulation of shares. Thus, the acquisition of the status of shareholder (regardless of whether already existing shares are acquired or whether new shares are subscribed for on an increase in capital) entails acceptance of all the obligations flowing from the statutes including any clause conferring jurisdiction.

12. I do not think it appropriate to go into the preoccupations concerning any perverse effects which may arise from the solution which I have suggested, such as the risk of frivolous choices of courts or the choice of a *forum non conveniens* (the courts of Heidelberg for a company with its principal office and main establishment in Naples).

Above all else, the Court is called upon to interpret the Convention with regard to a concrete case in which the jurisdiction clause provides for 'the jurisdiction of the courts ordinarily competent to entertain suits concerning the company', that is to say the courts of the place in which the company has its principal office. Having said that, I consider that the problem deserves to be examined in a manner which goes beyond the present case, both in view of the importance of the question raised, and the fact that the question raised by the national court is formulated in general terms.

On a first reading, indeed, the choice made by the parties as to the competent court might appear irrelevant from the point of view of the

Convention and the Court's case-law. But on a closer and more thorough examination it is certainly not to be excluded that the Court's case-law (the *Tilly Russ* and the *Salotti* judgments) and specifically Article 17 itself, as amended by the 1978 Convention, (the reference to international trade, and in particular the usages which the parties were or ought to have been aware of) very opportunely provide hints for that choice, in fact, hints as to the coherence and rationality of the choice of the competent courts in relation to practice.

In any event, I consider that the sole manner in which one may be certain of not depriving the new wording of Article 17 of all significance, and of paying heed to the specific requirements of the actual functioning of the business world (without, moreover, distorting the original purpose of that provision which continues to be that of ensuring certainty and awareness of such clauses), consists precisely in laying down specific conditions relating to consent, which do justice to the particular sector in question.

In that context, in examining the validity of clauses assigning jurisdiction in the light of usages in force in international commerce, as well as ensuring observance of the formal requirements which guarantee that attention is drawn to the clauses themselves, it is appropriate also to review their contents, thus ensuring the consistency and the reasonableness of the rules in the light of current usages in the specific commercial sector under consideration.

Returning to the case under examination and in order to seek further clarity, I would observe that, having regard to the choice of the *forum societatis* made by the large majority of legal systems, the same choice made by the shareholders and enshrined in the statutes of the company not only complies with the formal requirements laid down, but is also the only coherent and reasonable choice out of the actual or legally permissible choices available in the sector before the court.

I therefore suggest that the Court should limit the validity of a clause conferring jurisdiction to the situation in which, as in the present case, it is provided that the courts ordinarily competent to entertain suits concerning the company are to have jurisdiction, and should affirm that a provision contained in the statutes conferring such jurisdiction constitutes a valid agreement within the meaning of Article 17, where it comes into existence in accordance with the applicable national rules governing the formation of the corporate will. That conclusion also replies to question 2(a).

13. As regards, then, the question whether the clause conferring jurisdiction satisfies the requirement that the dispute must arise in connexion with a particular legal relationship within the meaning of Article 17 (question 2(b)), I would first of all recall that the purpose of that provision is to prevent the party in a stronger bargaining position from imposing on the other party the jurisdiction of any other court. In view of that fact, the provision in question is observed in Article 4 of the statutes, whose interpretation is in the end a matter for the national court, is interpreted as referring to all disputes between the shareholder and the company arising out of the reciprocal corporate obligations.

Finally, as regards question 2(c), in which the national court asks whether the clause referred to in Article 4 of the statutes also covers claims to payment arising out of a contract relating to the subscription for shares and claims to the repayment of wrongly paid dividends, the interpretation of the article in question is a matter for the court hearing the main dispute. It is that court which is required to give a decision on the jurisdiction clause in order to determine to what extent and subject to what limits it is applicable to money owing to the company and to claims for the recovery of wrongly paid dividends.

14. In the light of the foregoing observations, I conclude that the Court should reply as follows to the questions raised by the Oberlandesgericht, Koblenz:

1. A clause conferring jurisdiction contained in the statutes of a company limited by shares, pursuant to which the shareholder is bound to accept the jurisdiction of the courts, ordinarily competent to entertain suits concerning the company in respect of disputes with it or its organs, constitutes for all shareholders a valid agreement conferring jurisdiction within the meaning of Article 17 of the Convention, if it is concluded in compliance with the applicable rules of national law concerning the formation of the corporate will.

2. The requirement that a dispute must arise in connection with a particular legal relationship within the meaning of Article 17 is satisfied if Article 4 of the statutes is interpreted as referring to all disputes between the shareholders and the company arising out of the reciprocal corporate obligations.

3. It is for the national court to interpret the clause conferring jurisdiction in order to determine which disputes fall within its scope.

Case C-106/95 - 20 February 1997

Mainschiffahrts-Genossenschaft e.G. (MSG)
v
Les Gravières Rhénanes SARL

Article 17 - Prorogation of jurisdiction - Agreement conferring jurisdiction - Conditions as to form - Agreement concluded in a form according with practices in international trade or commerce - Concept - Contract concluded orally - Clause included in a commercial letter of confirmation and in invoices paid - Unchallenged - Validity of the clause - Conditions - Special jurisdiction - Court for the place of performance of the contractual obligation - Oral agreement between the parties on a place other than that of actual performance with the sole purpose of establishing that the courts of a particular place have jurisdiction - Applicability of Article 5(1) - Applicability of the conditions as to form for agreements conferring jurisdiction.

Summary

1. The third hypothesis in the second sentence of the first paragraph of Article 17 of the Convention of 27 September 1968 on jurisdiction and the enforcement of judgments in civil and commercial matters must be interpreted as meaning that, under a contract concluded orally in international trade or commercial matters must be interpreted as meaning that, under a contract concluded orally in international trade or commerce, an agreement conferring jurisdiction will be deemed to have been validly concluded under that provision by virtue of the fact that one party to the contract did not react to a commercial letter of confirmation sent to it by the other party to the contract or repeatedly paid invoices

without objection where those documents contained a pre-printed reference to the courts having jurisdiction, provided that such conduct is consistent with a practice in force in the field of international trade or commerce in which the parties in question operate and the latter are aware or ought to have been aware of the practice in question.

In this regard, a practice exists in a branch of international trade or commerce in particular where a particular course of conduct is generally followed by contracting parties operating in that branch when they conclude contracts of a particular type. The fact that the contracting parties were aware of that practice is made out in particular where they had previously had trade or commercial relations between themselves or with other parties operating in the branch of trade or commerce in question or where, in that branch, a particular course of conduct is generally and regularly followed when concluding a certain type of contract, with the result that it may be regarded as being a consolidated practice.

2. The Convention must be interpreted as meaning that an oral agreement on the place of performance which is designed not to determine the place where the person liable is actually to perform the obligations incumbent upon him, but solely to establish that the courts for a particular place have jurisdiction, is not governed by Article 5(1) of the Convention, but by Article 17, and is valid only if the requirements set out therein are complied with. Whilst the parties are free to agree on a place of performance for contractual obligations which differs from that which would be determined under the law applicable to the contract, without having to comply with specific conditions as to form, they are nevertheless not entitled, having regard to the system established by the Convention, to designate, with the sole aim of specifying the courts having jurisdiction, a place of performance having no real connection with the reality of the contract at which the obligations arising under the contract could not be performed in accordance with the terms of the contract.

JUDGMENT OF THE COURT

Murray (President), Kakouris, Kapteyn, Hirsch and Ragnemalm, Judges

1. By order of 6 March 1995, received at the Court on 31 March 1995, the Bundesgerichtshof (Federal Court of Justice) referred to the Court for a preliminary ruling under the Protocol of 3 June 1971 on the

interpretation by the Court of Justice of the Convention of 27 September 1968 on Jurisdiction and the Enforcement of Judgments in Civil and Commercial Matters (OJ 1978 L 304, p.36) as amended by the Convention of 9 October 1978 on the accession of the Kingdom of Denmark, Ireland and the United Kingdom of Great Britain and Northern Ireland (OJ 1978 L 304, p.1; amended version of the Convention at p.77; hereinafter 'the Convention'), two questions on the interpretation of Article 5(1) and the third hypothesis mentioned in the second sentence of the first paragraph of Article 17 of the Convention.

2. The questions arose in proceedings between Mainschiffahrts-Genossenschaft eG (MSG) ('MSG'), an inland-waterway transport co-operative based at Würzburg (Germany), and Les Gravières Rhénanes SARL ('Gravières Rhénanes'), whose registered office is in France, concerning compensation for damage caused to an inland-waterway vessel which MSG owned and had chartered to Gravières Rhénanes by a time charter concluded orally between the parties.

3. According to the case-file, that vessel operated a shuttle service on the Rhine between 1 June 1989 and 10 February 1991, chiefly carrying shipments of gravel. With some exceptions, the places of loading were all located in France, whilst the cargo was invariably unloaded in France. According to MSG, the handling equipment used by Gravières Rhénanes to unload the cargo damaged its vessel. The main proceedings are for the sum of DM 197 284, namely the difference between the amount paid by Gravières Rhénanes' insurers and the amount claimed by MSG.

4. MSG brought an action before the Schiffahrtsgericht (Maritime Court) Würzburg, taking the view that the third hypothesis mentioned in the second sentence of the first paragraph of Article 17 of the Convention entitled it to do so on the ground that the parties had validly designated Würzburg, MSG's principal place of business, as the place of performance and the Würzburg courts as having jurisdiction.

5. The first and second sentences of the first paragraph of Article 17 of the Convention provide as follows: 'If the parties, one or more of whom is domiciled in a Contracting State, have agreed that a court or the courts of a Contracting State are to have jurisdiction to settle any disputes which have arisen or which may arise in connection with a particular legal relationship, that court or those courts shall have exclusive jurisdiction. Such an agreement conferring jurisdiction shall be either in writing or evidenced in writing or, in international trade or commerce, in a form

which accords with practices in that trade or commerce of which the parties are or ought to have been aware'.

6. It appears from the order for reference that, when the contractual negotiations had been completed, MSG sent Gravières Rhénanes a commercial letter of confirmation containing the following pre-printed statement: 'The place of performance is Würzburg and the courts for that place have exclusive jurisdiction'.

Moreover, MSG's invoices also mentioned that forum directly and by reference to the conditions of the bill of lading. Gravières Rhénanes did not challenge the commercial letter of confirmation and paid all invoices without objection. The Schiffahrtsgericht Würzburg declared the action admissible.

7. On an appeal brought by Gravières Rhénanes, the Oberlandesgericht (Higher Regional Court) Nürnberg rejected the application as inadmissible on the ground that there was no international jurisdiction. MSG appealed on a point of law to the Bundesgerichtshof.

8. The Bundesgerichtshof found, in the first place, that the jurisdiction of the French courts was borne out by the general rule set forth in the first paragraph of Article 2 of the Convention (place of the defendant's domicile), by Article 5(3) (place where the harmful event occurred) and likewise by Article 5(1) (place of performance of the obligation in question). The contractual obligations arising under the contract of carriage had to be performed in France and MSG was under an obligation to present the vessel at Gravières Rhénanes' principal place of business, which was in France. In the Bundesgerichtshof's view, this case affords two possible approaches by which the jurisdiction of the French courts might be ousted in favour of the international jurisdiction of the German courts.

9. In the first place, Würzburg might be regarded as the place of performance within the meaning of Article 5(1) of the Convention, on the ground that it was identified as such by the parties'oral agreement. The Bundesgerichtshof observes that in this case the agreement was 'abstract'. It characterises an agreement on the place of performance as abstract where it does not set out to designate the place where the person liable has to perform his obligations, but only to determine the courts having jurisdiction, without complying with the requirements as to form set out in Article 17 of the Convention. The only aim of such an agreement, therefore, is to disguise an agreement conferring jurisdiction.

In this case, the contractual obligations had to be performed in any event in France, where in all cases the place of unloading was located.

10. Whilst stressing that, under the applicable German law, the agreement at issue on the place of performance was validly concluded, the Bundesgerichtshof has doubts about whether such 'abstract' agreements are valid under the Convention insofar as they involve a risk of abuse, that is to say, circumvention of the rules as to form set out in Article 17 of the Convention.

11. Secondly, in the event that an 'abstract' agreement on the place of performance is regarded as invalid, the Bundesgerichtshof considers that the German courts might have jurisdiction in this case by virtue of the third hypothesis mentioned in the second sentence of the first paragraph of Article 17 of the Convention.

12. In those circumstances, the Bundesgerichtshof stayed proceedings and referred the following questions to the Court for a preliminary ruling:

'1. Is an oral agreement on the place of performance (Brussels Convention, Article 5) to be recognised even if it is not intended to fix the place at which the person liable has to perform the obligations incumbent on him, but is intended solely to establish - informally - that the courts for a particular place are to have jurisdiction (a so-called "abstract" agreement on the place of performance)?

2. In the event that the Court of Justice should answer Question 1 in the negative:

(a) Can an agreement conferring jurisdiction in international trade or commerce in accordance with the third hypothesis mentioned in the second sentence of the first paragraph of Article 17 of the 9178 version of the Brussels Convention also be concluded by one party's not contradicting a commercial letter of confirmation containing a pre-printed reference to the courts of the consignors' place of business having sole jurisdiction or must there have been in every case prior consensus with regard to the content of the letter of confirmation?

(b) Is it sufficient in order for there to be an agreement conferring jurisdiction within the meaning of the aforesaid provision if the invoices sent by one party all contain a reference to the courts of the carrier's place of business having sole jurisdiction and to the conditions of the bill of lading used by the carrier which also stipulate the courts of the same place as having jurisdiction, and the other party invariably paid the invoices without objecting, or is prior consensus also required in this respect?

The second question

13. By its second question, which, being concerned with exclusive jurisdiction, may conveniently be considered first, the national court essentially asks whether, under a contract concluded orally, an agreement conferring jurisdiction may be deemed to have been concluded in international trade or commerce in the form required by the third hypothesis mentioned in the second sentence of the first paragraph of article 17 of the Convention simply by virtue of the fact that one party to the contract did not react to a commercial letter of confirmation sent to him by the other party to the contract or repeatedly paid invoices without objection where those documents contained a pre-printed reference to the courts having jurisdiction, or whether there should in any event be prior consensus on the part of the persons concerned, only written confirmation of the agreement being unnecessary.

14. It should be observed in this regard that, according to the Court's case-law, the requirements laid down by Article 17 of the Convention must be strictly interpreted insofar as that article excludes both jurisdiction as determined by the general principle of the defendant's court laid down in Article 2 and the special jurisdictions provided for in Articles 5 and 6 (see, to this effect, Case 24/76 *Estasis Salotti* [1976] ECR 1831, paragraph 7, and Case 25/76 *Segoura* [1976] ECR 1851, paragraph 6).

15. The Court has further held with regard to the initial version of Article 17 that, by making the validity of a jurisdiction clause subject to the existence of an 'agreement' between the parties, Article 17 imposes on the court before which the matter is brought the duty of examining, first, whether the clause conferring jurisdiction upon it was in fact the subject of consensus between the parties, which must be clearly and precisely demonstrated, and that the purpose of the requirements as to form imposed by Article 17 is to ensure that consensus between the parties is in fact established (*Estasis Salotti*, paragraph 7, and *Segoura*, paragraph 6).

16. However, in order to take account of the specific practices and requirements of international trade, the aforementioned Accession Convention of 9 October 1978 added to the second sentence of the first paragraph of Article 17 of the Convention a third hypothesis providing that, in international trade or commerce, a jurisdiction clause may be validly concluded in a form which accords with practices in that trade or commerce of which the parties are or ought to have been aware.

17. Yet that relaxation incorporated in Article 17 by the 1978 Accession Convention does not mean that there is not necessarily any need for consensus between the parties on a jurisdiction clause, since it is still one of the aims of that provision to ensure that there is real consent on the part of the persons concerned. The weaker party to the contract should be protected by avoiding jurisdiction clauses incorporated in a contract by one party alone going unnoticed.

18. To take the view, however, that the relaxation thus introduced relates solely to the requirements as to form laid down by Article 17 by merely eliminating the need for a written form of consent would be tantamount to disregarding the requirements of non-formalism, simplicity and speed in international trade or commerce and to depriving that provision of a major part of its effectiveness.

19. Thus, in the light of the amendment made to Article 17 by the 1978 Accession Convention, consensus on the part of the contracting parties as to a jurisdiction clause is presumed to exist where commercial practices in the relevant branch of international trade or commerce exist in this regard of which the parties are or ought to have been aware.

20. It must therefore be considered that the fact that one of the parties to the contract did not react or remained silent in the face of a commercial letter of confirmation from the other party containing a pre-printed reference to the courts having jurisdiction and that one of the parties repeatedly paid without objection invoices issued by the other party containing a similar reference may be deemed to constitute consent to the jurisdiction clause in issue, provided that such conduct is consistent with a practice in force in the area of international trade or commerce in which the parties in question are operating and the parties are or ought to have been aware of that practice.

21. Whilst it is for the national court to determine whether the contract in question comes under the head of international trade or commerce and to find whether there was a practice in the branch of international trade or commerce in which the parties are operating and whether they were aware or are presumed to have been aware of that practice, the Court should nevertheless indicate the objective evidence which is needed in order to make such a determination.

22. It should first be considered that a contract concluded between two companies established in different Contracting States in a field such as

navigation on the Rhine comes under the head of international trade or commerce.

23. Next, whether a practice exists must not be determined by reference to the law of one of the Contracting Parties. Furthermore, whether such a practice exists should not be determined in relation to international trade or commerce in general, but to the branch of trade or commerce in which the parties to the contract are operating. There is a practice in the branch of trade or commerce in question in particular where a particular course of conduct is generally and regularly followed by operators in that branch when concluding contracts of a particular type.

24. Lastly, actual or presumptive awareness of such practice on the part of the parties to a contract is made out where, in particular, they had previously had commercial or trade relations between themselves or with other parties operating in the sector in question or where, in that sector, a particular course of conduct is sufficiently well known because it is generally and regularly followed when a particular type of contract is concluded, with the result that it may be regarded as being a consolidated practice.

25. The answer to the second question must therefore be that the third hypothesis in the second sentence of the first paragraph of Article 17 of the Convention, as amended by the Accession Convention of 9 October 1978, must be interpreted as meaning that, under a contract concluded orally in international trade or commerce, an agreement conferring jurisdiction will be deemed to have been validly concluded under that provision by virtue of the fact that one party to the contract did not react to a commercial letter of confirmation sent to it by the other party to the contract or repeatedly paid invoices without objection where those documents contained a pre-printed reference to the courts having jurisdiction, provided that such conduct is consistent with a practice in force in the field of international trade or commerce in which the parties in question operate and the latter are aware or ought to have been aware of the practice in question. It is for the national court to determine whether such a practice exists and whether the parties to the contract were made aware of it. A practice exists in a branch of international trade or commerce in particular where a particular course of conduct is generally followed by contracting parties operating in that branch when they conclude contracts of a particular type. The fact that the contracting parties were aware of that practice is made out in particular where they had previously had trade or commercial relations between themselves or

with other parties operating in the branch of trade or commerce in question or where, in that branch, a particular course of conduct is generally and regularly followed when concluding a certain type of contract, with the result that it may be regarded as being a consolidated practice.

The first question

26. The first question has to be answered in case the national court concludes that there is in this case no practice in the branch of trade or commerce in question of which the parties were or ought to have been aware and that, as a result, a jurisdiction clause was not validly concluded.

27. By this question, the national court essentially asks whether an oral agreement on the place of performance, which is designed not to determine the place where the person liable is actually to perform the obligations incumbent upon him, but solely to establish that the courts for a particular place have jurisdiction, is valid under Article 5(1) of the Convention.

28. Article 5(1) of the Convention provides as follows: 'A person domiciled in a Contracting State may, in another Contracting State, be sued: 1. in matters relating to a contract, in the courts for the place of the performance of the obligation in question'.

29. According to the case-law of the Court, jurisdiction derogating from the general rule that the defendant's courts should have jurisdiction was introduced by Article 5(1) in view of the existence in certain well-defined cases of a particularly close relationship between a dispute and the court which may be called upon to take congizance of the matter, with a view to the effective organisation of the proceedings (Case 12/76 *Tessili* v. *Dunlop* [1976] ECR 1473, paragraph 13).

30. Moreover, the Court has also held that the place of performance of a contractual obligation may also be fixed by agreement between the parties and that, if the parties to the contract are permitted by the applicable law, subject to the conditions imposed thereby, to specify the place of performance without satisfying any special condition of form, an agreement on the place of performance of the obligation is sufficient to found jurisdiction in that place within the meaning of Article 5(1) of the Convention (Case 56/79 *Zelger* v. *Salinitri* [1980] ECR 89, paragraph 5).

31. It should be noted, however, that whilst the parties are free to agree on a place of performance for contractual obligations which differs from that which would be determined under the law applicable to the contract, without having to comply with specific conditions as to form, they are nevertheless not entitled, having regard to the system established by the Convention, to designate, with the sole aim of specifying the courts having jurisdiction, a place of performance having no real connection with the reality of the contract at which the obligations arising under the contract could not be performed in accordance with the terms of the contract.

32. This approach is based, in the first place, on the terms of Article 5(1) of the Convention, which confers jurisdiction on the courts for the place 'of performance' of the contractual obligation on which the claim is based. Consequently, that provision has in mind the place of actual performance of the obligation as the jurisdictional criterion by reason of its direct connection with the courts on which it confers jurisdiction.

33. Secondly, it should be considered that to specify a place of performance which has no actual connection with the real subject-matter of the contract becomes fictitious and has as its sole purpose the determination of the place of the courts having jurisdiction. Such agreements conferring jurisdiction are governed by Article 17 of the Convention and are therefore subject to specific requirements as to form.

34. Thus, where there is such an agreement, there is not only no direct connection between the dispute and the courts called upon to determine it, but there is also circumvention of Article 17, which, whilst providing for exclusive jurisdiction by dispensing with any objective connection between the relationship in dispute and the court designated (Zelger v. Salinitri, paragraph 4), requires, for that very reason, compliance with the strict requirements as to form which it sets out.

35. The answer to the national court's first question must therefore be that the Convention must be interpreted as meaning than an oral agreement on the place of performance which is designed not to determine the place where the person liable is actually to perform the obligations incumbent upon him, but solely to establish that the courts for a particular place have jurisdiction, is not governed by Article 5(1) of the Convention, but by Article 17, and is valid only if the requirements set out therein are complied with.

On those grounds, the Court in answer to the questions referred to it by the Bundesgerichtshof, by order of 6 March 1995, hereby rules:

1. The third hypothesis in the second sentence of the first paragraph of Article 17 of the Convention of 27 September 1968 on jurisdiction and the enforcement of judgments in civil and commercial matters, as amended by the Convention of 9 October 1978 on the accession of the Kingdom of Denmark, Ireland and the United Kingdom of Great Britain and Northern Ireland, must be interpreted as meaning that, under a contract concluded orally in international trade or commerce, an agreement conferring jurisdiction will be deemed to have been validly concluded under that provision by virtue of the fact that one party to the contract did not react to a commercial letter of confirmation sent to it by the other party to the contract or repeatedly paid invoices without objection where those documents contained a pre-printed reference to the courts having jurisdiction, provided that such conduct is consistent with a practice in force in the field of international trade or commerce in which the parties in question operate and the latter are aware or ought to have been aware of the practice in question. It is for the national court to determine whether such a practice exists and whether the parties to the contract were aware of it. A practice exists in a branch of international trade or commerce in particular where a particular course of conduct is generally followed by contracting parties operating in that branch when they conclude contracts of a particular type. The fact that the contracting parties were aware of that practice is made out in particular where they had previously had trade or commercial relations between themselves or with other parties operating in the branch of trade or commerce in question or where, in that branch, a particular course of conduct is generally and regularly followed when concluding a certain type of contract, with the result that it may be regarded as being a consolidated practice.

2. The Convention of 27 September 1968 must be interpreted as meaning that an oral agreement on the place of performance which is designed not to determine the place where the person liable is actually to perform the obligations incumbent upon him, but solely to establish that the courts for a particular place have jurisdiction, is not governed by Article

5(1) of the Convention, but by Article 17, and is valid only if the requirements set out therein are complied with.

OPINION OF MR ADVOCATE GENERAL TESAURO

1. The questions referred to the Court for a preliminary ruling by the Bundesgerichtshof (Federal Court of Justice) are concerned with the interpretation of Articles 5(1) and 17 of the Convention of 27 September 1968 on jurisdiction and the enforcement of judgments in civil and commercial matters ('the Convention'), as amended by the 1978 Accession Convention.

More specifically, the national court wishes to establish whether an 'abstract' agreement on the place of performance - that is to say, an agreement concluded, not to establish the place at which the person liable actually has to perform his obligations, but simply and exclusively to designate the courts having jurisdiction - is valid under Article 5(1) of the Convention and hence whether the courts for the place of performance thus identified have jurisdiction to rule on disputes relating to the obligation in question. If that question is answered in the negative, the Court is asked whether in this case the 'abstract' agreement fulfils the requirements of Article 17 of the Convention, that is to say, whether a jurisdiction clause has been validly concluded.

2. I would first hark back to the origins of these proceedings. By a time charterparty concluded orally, the inland waterway company Mainschiffahrts-Genossenschaft e.G. ('MSG'), having its seat in Germany (Würzburg), made an inland waterway vessel available to the undertaking Les Gravières Rhénanes SARL ('the defendant'), having its registered office in France. The vessel was used on the Rhine between 1 June 1989 and 10 February 1991 to transport gravel from the place of loading to the place of unloading, both of which were located in France.

During unloading operations, the vessel was damaged by the unloading equipment used by the defendant on its responsibility. The damage, which was made good after the contract had expired, was assessed at different levels by the respective assessors appointed by the parties.

What is at issue in these proceedings is the sum of DM 197,284, namely the difference between the amount paid by the defendant's insurers and the amount claimed by MSG. With a view to obtaining that sum, MSG brought an action for damages for breach of the charterparty before the Schiffahrtsgericht (Maritime Court) Würzburg, the competent inland waterways court.

3. MSG claims that the German courts have jurisdiction on the ground that the defendant did not express any objections to a commercial letter of confirmation containing a pre-printed reference to Würzburg - the place at which MSG itself had its principal place of business - as the place of performance and the forum having jurisdiction or to the invoices, including a similar reference, issued by it, which the defendant paid without challenging them in any way.

By interlocutory judgment, the Schiffahrtsgericht declared the application admissible. On appeal, the Oberlandesgericht (Higher Regional Court)

Nürnberg upheld the defendant's claim that it could be sued only in the French courts, and dismissed the application as inadmissible for want of jurisdiction.

4. The plaintiff appealed on a point of law against that judgment to the Bundesgerichtshof, in which it claims that the judgment of the court of first instance should be upheld. In the order for reference, the Bundesgerichtshof found, *inter alia*, that 'the contractual obligations under the time charterparty which was concluded were to be performed in France; this is where the main element of the performance of the contract took place: it was not only there that the defendant, as the party determining the use of the vessel, had its seat, but it was there that the vessel was almost invariably loaded and always unloaded, with the result that it was not necessary to have an agreement deviating from Article 5 of the Brussels Convention in order to safeguard the - by all means - legitimate interest of the plaintiff in having a single place of performance'.

After finding that all the - principal and ancillary - contractual obligations could be performed only in France, the Bundesgerichtshof therefore concluded that the determination of the place of performance was fictitious and that 'the reference in [the plaintiff's] general conditions of business to Würzburg as the place of performance was intended solely to enable legal disputes to be brought before the courts of the place at which its principal place of business was located'. The decision had therefore been taken solely in order to give jurisdiction to the plaintiff's courts and hence to avoid complying with the formal requirements imposed by Article 17 of the Brussels Convention. Nevertheless, as the Bundesgerichtshof points out, under German law 'an effective agreement on the place of performance was made'.

5. In view of those circumstances, the Bundesgerichtshof deemed it necessary to refer the following questions to the Court in order to resolve the dispute pending before it:

'1. Is an oral agreement on the place of performance (Brussels Convention, Article 5) to be recognized even if it is not intended to fix the place at which the person liable has to perform the obligations incumbent on him, but is intended solely to establish - informally - that the courts for a particular place are to have jurisdiction (a so-called 'abstract' agreement on the place of performance)?

2. In the event that the Court of Justice should answer question 1 in the negative:

(a) Can an agreement conferring jurisdiction in international trade or commerce in accordance with the third hypothesis mentioned in the second sentence of the first paragraph of Article 17 of the 1978 version of the Brussels Convention also be concluded by one party's not contradicting a commercial letter of confirmation containing a pre-printed reference to the courts of the consignors' place of business having sole jurisdiction or must there have been in every case prior consensus with regard to the content of the letter of confirmation?

(b) Is it sufficient in order for there to be an agreement conferring jurisdiction within the meaning of the aforesaid provision if the invoices sent by one party all contain a reference to the courts of the carrier's place of business having sole jurisdiction and to the conditions of the bill of lading used by the carrier which also stipulate the courts of the same place as having jurisdiction, and the other party invariably paid the invoices without objecting, or is prior consensus also required in this respect?'

6. What therefore has to be established in the first place is whether an abstract agreement on the place of performance - which simply conceals a jurisdiction clause, which, as such, would be subject to formal requirements - is to be considered valid under Article 5(1). If that question is answered in the negative, it has to be determined whether in the case in point the agreement on the place of performance may be regarded as a validly concluded jurisdiction clause under Article 17.

The Commission has suggested reversing the order of the preliminary questions on the ground that, if only on logical grounds, it should be determined whether there is a valid jurisdiction clause within the meaning of Article 17 before any finding is made as to whether there is a valid agreement on the place of performance within the meaning of Article 5(1). This is precisely because Article 17 provides for exclusive jurisdiction, which therefore prevails over every other jurisdiction, even special jurisdiction under Article 5(1). In addition - the Commission further maintains - if there were to be a validly concluded jurisdiction clause this would mean that the Court would have no need to answer a question on the validity of an abstract agreement on the place of performance which is undoubtedly more complex and thornier (sic!).

7. For my part, I consider that the order of the questions as they have been put by the national court should be respected. Over and above the different (or allegedly different) degree of difficulty of the two questions - a criterion which, to my mind, cannot or should not influence the Court's decision - I consider that the Bundesgerichtshof's decision to place the question on the interpretation of Article 5(1) first is anything but a matter of chance. Whilst an affirmative answer to that question would mean that the German courts certainly have jurisdiction, it is possible that the Court's answer with regard to Article 17 may require further findings of fact on the part of the national court in order to establish which courts have jurisdiction, which it is not competent to the Bundesgerichtshof to make. Consequently, should the Court decide to answer the second question only, this might make a second reference to the Court necessary with regard to the same dispute.

In addition, there is the fact that the question of abstract clauses on the place of performance certainly should not be underestimated and, as will be seen, has been tackled and resolved by the various national courts in different ways. In those circumstances, clarification from the Court seems necessary. I shall therefore consider the questions in the order in which they have been put.

The first question

8. Article 5(1) of the Convention, which is the subject of the national court's first question, provides that 'a person domiciled in a Contracting State may, in another Contracting State, be sued: in matters relating to a contract, in the courts for the place of performance of the obligation in question; ...'.

Next, it should be observed that Article 5(1), which appears in Section 2, 'Special jurisdiction', provides for an exception to the general rule contained in Article 2 that the courts having jurisdiction should be those of the State in which the defendant is domiciled. This derogation in favour of the place of performance of the obligation in question is justified, as the Jenard Report points out, by the fact that there is 'a close connecting factor between the dispute and the court with jurisdiction to resolve it'.

9. The same reasoning is to be found in the relevant case-law of the Court, which has repeatedly held that that freedom of choice on the part of the plaintiff under Article 5 'was introduced in view of the existence in certain well-defined cases of a particularly close relationship between a dispute and the court which may be most conveniently called upon to take cognizance of the matter'. In other words, the reason why the courts of the place of performance should have jurisdiction is that there is a direct and, above all, objective connection between the dispute and the courts having jurisdiction to entertain it. It is consequently the physical proximity of those courts to the relationship at issue which, at least in the intention of the authors of the Convention, justifies their having jurisdiction.

The jurisdictional criterion set out in Article 5(1), however, is not, or at least not directly, the 'proximity'of the courts to the dispute, but the place of 'performance of the obligation in question'.

10. It should next be recalled that the Court has consistently held, except in relation to employment contracts, that for the purposes of determining the place of performance within the meaning of Article 5(1) 'the obligation to be taken into account is that which corresponds to the contractual right on which the plaintiff's action is based'. The place of performance of that obligation is determined by referring to the national law. The Court has in fact stated that for this purpose the court seised must 'determine in accordance with its own rules of conflict of laws what is the law applicable to the legal relationship in question and define in accordance with that law the place of performance of the contractual obligation in question'.

In brief, Article 5(1) must be interpreted as meaning that the courts of the place of performance of the contractual obligation actually relied on in the proceedings have jurisdiction; the place of performance of that obligation is to be determined on the basis of the substantive law applicable thereto under the provisions of the private international law of the court seised.

11. Having said this, the place of performance may also be determined contractually as between the parties. This may be inferred from *Zelger* v *Salinitri*, in which the Court specifically considered the relationship between Article 5(1) and Article 17. In that case, the Court was called upon to decide

whether the validity of an agreement between the parties on the place of performance of the obligation in question was or was not dependent upon compliance with the formal requirements laid down by Article 17.

Starting from the premiss that 'the jurisdiction of the court for the place of performance (provided for in Article 5(1)) and that of the selected court (provided for in Article 17) are two distinct concepts and only agreements selecting a court are subject to the requirements of form prescribed by Article 17 of the Convention'(paragraph 4 of the judgment), the Court reached the conclusion that 'if the parties to the contract are permitted by the law applicable to the contract, subject to any conditions imposed by that law, to specify the place of performance of an obligation without satisfying any special condition of form, an agreement on the place of performance of the obligation is sufficient to found jurisdiction in that place within the meaning of Article 5(1) of the Convention'(paragraph 5).

12. In accordance with *Zelger* v *Salinitri* it is therefore enough, in order for a clause specifying the place of performance to be valid under Article 5(1), that 'the place of performance of a contractual obligation has been specified by the parties in a clause which is valid according to the national law applicable to the contract'(paragraph 6).

If that solution were to be applied to the case now before the Court, it would have to be held that the agreement on the place of performance - in so far as it was valid under the German law applicable to the contract - was also valid for the purposes and effects of Article 5(1). However, as the Bundesgerichtshof itself observes in the order for reference, it cannot, however, be inferred without question from the judgment in *Zelger* v *Salinitri* whether oral agreements on the place of performance which are not concerned with fixing the place at which the person liable has to carry out the performance due from him, but are intended instead solely to determine the courts of a particular place as having jurisdiction, without the requirements of Article 17 of the Brussels Convention having to be fulfilled (so-called abstract agreements on the place of performance), must also be recognized'.

13. I would start by observing that the solution adopted by the Court in *Zelger* v *Salinitri*, which I concur with in principle, did indeed leave the issue now before the Court open. This is evidenced by the fact that that judgment does not make any mention of the problem of possible circumvention of Article 17 by means of fictitious determinations of the place of performance, even though that problem was discussed during the proceedings and tackled by the Advocate General in his Opinion. In any case, suffice it to say that, unlike in the present case, what was in issue in *Zelger* v *Salinitri* was not an 'abstract' agreement: the place of performance specified by the parties was in fact the same as that determined by the law.

In addition, in that case, while stating that provided that an agreement between the parties on the place of performance within the meaning of Article 5(1) is in accordance with the applicable national law, it does not have to comply with the formal requirements imposed by Article 17, the Court did not confine itself to pointing out that the provisions in question have different functions and therefore operate on different levels. It stressed in particular that whilst jurisdiction determined by virtue of Article 5 is justified by 'the existence of a direct link between the dispute and the court called upon to take cognizance of it'(paragraph 3), exclusive jurisdiction under Article 17 'dispenses with any objective connection between the legal relationship in dispute and the court designated'(paragraph 4).

14. It is undisputed that the place of performance indicated in the 'abstract' agreement which is at issue in these proceedings dispenses with an objective connection between the legal relationship at issue and the court designated. Moreover, according to the national court, in this case the only purpose of the agreement on the place of performance is precisely that of designating the courts having jurisdiction. Since this is the way matters stand, it is unquestionable that the agreement at issue tends to come within the *ratio legis* of Article 17 and should therefore come within its scope, if only logically. Consequently, it should be declined validity under Article 5.

This solution, however, would seem to come up against a not inconsiderable number of obstacles, in view, among other things, of the fact that the Court's case-law has established unequivocally: (a) that the place of performance should be determined by reference to national law (*Tessili* v *Dunlop*); (b) that national law may provide that the parties can determine the place of performance, in which case it is unnecessary to comply with the formal requirements of Article 17 (*Zelger* v *Salinitri*); and lastly (c) that the place of performance thus identified may dispense with any objective connection with the dispute (*Custom Made Commercial*). The obvious conclusion to which reading those three judgments together brings one is precisely that possible fictitious determinations of the place of performance are invariably and in any event valid under Article 5(1). This, moreover, was the proposition put forward by the Commission during these proceedings, a proposition which - if the judgments in question are read in isolation from their context - leads one to a conclusion which, albeit on the face of it unobjectionable and certainly simpler, completely fails to take account [of] the function played by Article 17 within the system of the Brussels Convention.

15. In the final analysis, on the basis of this proposition, once it is conceded that the parties may locate the constituent elements of the contract as and where they wish - which allegedly may be inferred from the above mentioned judgments - the inevitable consequence would be that the parties themselves are entitled to 'utilize' the determination of the place of performance also in order to choose a forum other than the one which would normally have jurisdiction (under Article 2 or under Article 5 if the place of performance were to be determined by virtue of the law). In other words, there would be no limit to the parties' will, apart from any laid down by national law itself, either as a result of the imposition of formal requirements or as a result of case-law referring to institutions such as fraud on a statute. Otherwise, agreements on the place of performance would have to be recognized as being valid invariably and in any event.

That interpretation of the aforementioned three judgments, which is admittedly based only on syllogisms, is to my mind somewhat over-simplistic.

In the first place, whilst it is true that the place of performance is determined by reference to the substantive law, this does not automatically mean that the Community Court is precluded from laying down limits designed to prevent some other provision of the Convention, in this case Article 17, from being circumvented. Secondly, it seems to me that, in view of the reference which it makes to the direct connection between the dispute and the court called upon to decide it, *Zelger* v *Salinitri* should instead be interpreted as meaning that the parties may indeed decide to locate the performance of the contract at a place other than the one which would be fixed by the law, but that place must at all events be the actual place of performance: only then are the parties not obliged to comply with the formal requirements set out in Article 17. Lastly, for present purposes I consider that the Court's *dictum* in *Custom Made Commercial* that 'under Article 5(1), in matters relating to a contract, a defendant may be sued in the courts for the place of performance of the obligation in question, even where the court thus designated is not that which has the closest connection with the dispute has no bearing on the matter'. What was at issue in *Custom Made Commercial* was the possibility of excluding reference to the lex causae as the criterion for determining the place of performance: this was simply because, if that criterion were to be applied, the court which would have jurisdiction would be the one less connected with the relationship at issue.

16. In the case now before the Court, in contrast, it is undisputed that the agreement in question is not confined to conferring jurisdiction on the courts for a place which has no connection with the case, except for the fact that it is the plaintiff's domicile, but is designed simply to evade the formal requirements laid down by Article 17. The issue raised by these proceedings therefore goes considerably further than whether jurisdiction under Article 5 must invariably and in any event be vested in the courts for the place which has the greater physical connection with the case in question.

In the final analysis, here the question is that of establishing whether, where the contractual obligation cannot in fact be performed in the place agreed as the place of performance either because that place is at odds with the very nature of the contract or because it is not consistent with geographical fact, Article 5(1) nevertheless remains a valid jurisdictional criterion.

17. To allow such a solution would manifestly mean that the parties are in fact entitled, by means of a fictitious determination of the place of performance, to circumvent the formal obstacles placed in the way of jurisdiction clauses. Should the Court accept this solution, it would therefore be giving its blessing to an alternative use of Article 5(1), in that the parties would be authorized to designate a court other than the one which generally has jurisdiction by certainly simpler means than those provided for by Article 17, and this would result in both the wording and the purpose of that provision being breached or at least devalued. It is hardly necessary to point out in this connection that the formal requirements imposed by Article 17 are not aims in themselves, but seek to protect the weaker party to the contract; the aim pursued by them, or rather by means of them, is therefore to avoid jurisdiction clauses incorporated in the contract by only one party passing unobserved.

It is only too obvious from this point of view that Article 5(1) may not be interpreted in such a way as to enable the outcome to be brought about which, through the imposition of rigid formal requirements, Article 17 set out to avoid. The question would arise as to how making use of that state of affairs could be regarded as correct having regard to Article 5(1) and consistent with the system and aims of the Convention as a whole and in particular with regard to Article 17.

18. Although it recognizes that a fictitious determination of the place of performance may be a means of circumventing the formal requirements laid down by Article 17, the Commission nevertheless considers that this is permitted by the Convention itself. It simply points out in this connection that Article 5(1) does not require the parties to indicate the actual place of performance of the contractual obligations.

That argument goes too far. In fact, the only criterion which can be inferred from the provision in question, which however contains no indication as to how the place of performance may be determined contractually, is that the place must be the place of performance of the obligation in question. Now, it seems reasonable to me to consider that that criterion, far from enabling any place in the world to be chosen, requires there to be a connection with the place at which the obligation in question actually has been or should be performed. In brief, even if the place is different from that fixed under the law, it must still be a place which is connected with, or at least appropriate to, the subject-matter of the contract.

Neither does the argument that such an approach would lead parties no longer to stipulate clauses on the place of performance, which would end up by devoiding Article 5(1) of its substance, seem to me to have any particular importance. I would merely observe in this connection that the place of performance certainly is not destined to *disappear* simply because agreements on the place of performance in certain circumstances do not have the effect of conferring jurisdiction: the plaintiff may still sue in the courts for the place of performance of the obligation in question under the law.

19. In the final analysis, I consider it absurd even only to conjecture that the Convention might be interpreted in such a way as to enable Article 17 to be circumvented, bearing in mind moreover the importance of Article 17 within the system of the Convention. In view of this, I am unable to agree with the Commission's proposition that this is the price to be paid in order for there to be legal certainty and foreseeability of the courts having jurisdiction. In point of fact, those objectives are certainly not aims in themselves; for example, making the application of the rules on jurisdiction foreseeable means first and foremost reinforcing the legal protection available to persons established in the Community by allowing the plaintiff easily to identify the court before which he may bring an action and the defendant reasonably to foresee the court before which he may be sued. I am unable to see, moreover, in what way legal certainty might be strengthened by a breach of Article 17.

It is true that to superimpose the two provisions without any interpretative review is unacceptable, especially bearing in mind the need to safeguard balance between the parties as sought by Article 17.

20. Unless *Zelger* v *Salinitri* is called in question and the place of performance is accordingly determined independently where it is decided upon contractually as between the parties - a solution which is in principle desirable and would have the merit of being linear and unequivocal, but would oblige the parties to comply with particularly strict formal conditions, even where the actual place of performance was designated - the simplest solution is for the Community Court to lay down limits designed simply and solely to obviate circumvention of Article 17.

Fixing such limits does not moreover require particular imagination or effort. In my view, it is sufficient to establish that where the national court finds - as the German court found in this case - that the place of performance determined by the parties has no substantial connection with the subject-matter of the contract and that that place was determined solely in order to introduce a jurisdiction clause without having to comply with the formal requirements laid down by Article 17, the place of performance thus identified cannot be regarded as complying with Article 5(1) of the Convention.

The second question

21. By this question, which is asked in the event that the Court should consider, as I have suggested it should, that agreements on the place of performance having the sole aim of formally designating the court having jurisdiction as a court other than that for the actual place of performance are unlawful, the Bundesgerichtshof seeks to establish whether in such case it may considered that there is a jurisdiction clause under Article 17 of the Convention. More specifically, the question is whether, in international trade or commerce, a jurisdiction clause can be regarded as having been validly concluded even through one party's lack of response to a commercial letter of confirmation [question 2(a)] or through that party's having paid without objection invoices referring to the courts having jurisdiction [question 2(b)], or whether there should in every case have been prior consensus between the parties and that consensus must necessarily have been evidenced in writing.

The question therefore relates to the interpretation of the second sentence of the first paragraph of Article 17, as amended by the 1978 Accession Convention. That convention added to the possible ways of concluding an agreement conferring jurisdiction - 'in writing'(first hypothesis) or 'evidenced in writing'(second hypothesis) - a third hypothesis to the effect that a jurisdiction clause may be concluded 'in international trade or commerce, in a form which accords with practices in that trade or commerce of which the parties are or ought to have been aware'.

22. The Court has not yet had occasion to rule on the interpretation of that provision. Before I even proceed to consider the aims and innovations introduced by that provision and draw conclusions with regard to the case before the Court, I consider it nevertheless appropriate to call to mind the interpretation which the Court gave to the version of Article 17 which was in force before the amendment under discussion, naturally in so far as that interpretation is relevant to the present case.

The Court has consistently held that the provisions of Article 17 must be interpreted restrictively and strictly, given that they constitute an exception to the general principle that the defendant's courts have jurisdiction (Article 2) and to the special jurisdictions provided for in Articles 5 and 6. In particular, the Court has made it clear that by making the validity of the conferment of jurisdiction subject to the 'existence of an "agreement" between the parties, Article 17 imposes on the court before which the matter is brought the duty of examining, first, whether the clause conferring jurisdiction upon it was in fact the subject of a consensus between the parties, which must be clearly and precisely demonstrated'.

Thus, for example, the Court denied any validity to a jurisdiction clause set out on the reverse of a letter of confirmation delivered by the seller to the purchaser after the conclusion of an oral agreement on the ground that it did not comply with the formal requirements laid down by Article 17, which is a very similar case to the one at issue in these proceedings. Even in those circumstances the Court held that there was a need for written confirmation on the part of offeree, the only attenuation consisting in the possibility of departing from the requirement for writing in the case of a continuing trading relationship.

23. The new version of Article 17 seems to have been drawn up precisely because of the excessive formalism of such an approach in regard to international trade. Indeed, it is stated in the Schlosser Report that the Court's interpretation of Article 17 'does not cater adequately for the customs and requirements of international trade. In particular, the requirement that the other party to a contract with anyone employing general conditions of trade has to give written confirmation of their inclusion in the contract before any jurisdiction clause in those conditions can be effective is unacceptable in international trade. International trade is heavily dependent on standard conditions which incorporate jurisdiction clauses.'

Seen in that light, the amendment introduced by the 1978 Accession Convention certainly reflects greater (perhaps necessary) attention and sensitivity to the requirements of international trade and, more generally, to the actual workings of the business world. It is obvious that too strict an application of the principles set out in Article 17 would make it virtually impossible for jurisdiction clauses to operate where they were contained in contractual documents which because of their specific characteristics are not signed by one of the parties.

24. Whilst those were the considerations which prompted the amendment of Article 17, the fact remains, as the Schlosser Report itself emphasizes, that 'This is however, as should be clearly emphasized, *only a relaxation of the formal requirements. It must be proved that a consensus existed on the inclusion in the contract of the general conditions of trade and the particular provisions'*.

In the final analysis, the intention behind that amendment would seem to have been to attenuate only the formal requirements laid down by Article 17 in order to bring them into line with the requirements of international trade, yet without losing sight of the aim of actual consensus. The conflict between those two requirements - or in any event the difficulty in reconciling them - is only too obvious. The way in which consensus is manifested, according to the Court's interpretation, is closely connected with proving actual consensus between the parties. Whilst it is therefore true - and how could it be doubted? - that the formal requirements are not an end in themselves but serve precisely to prove that there was genuine consensus between the parties and hence that the agreement on the conferment of jurisdiction is valid, it follows from this, as has been pointed out in academic writings, that any relaxation of the formal requirements is bound to have repercussions on the reality of the consensus.

25. On top of this, it is extremely difficult to establish that there are trade or commercial practices with regard only to formal requirements - these being procedural rules which are liable to be changed by the States at any time - and doing so would therefore devoid the new version of Article 17, as amended by the 1978 Accession Convention, of any meaning. It must therefore be held that the amendment entails not only a relaxation of the ways in which consensus is manifested, but also, for that very reason, less strictness with regard to the formation of the parties' consensus with regard to designating the court having jurisdiction. In other words, actual consensus, which was initially essential and guaranteed only by writing or evidence in writing of an oral agreement, now yields in international trade to a presumption of actual consensus. This is confirmed by the very wording of the provision in question in so far as it provides that the practice in question must be one of which the parties were aware or 'ought to have been aware'.

However, the foregoing must not cause it to be overlooked that the essential aim of Article 17 is to protect the weaker party to the contract and, to that end, to avoid jurisdiction clauses incorporated in the contract by one party alone from going unnoticed. It follows that the interpretation of the provision in question must necessarily and rigorously be strict. Furthermore, the interpretation cannot in any event be such as to cause the objective of 'actual' consent to be lost sight of, if only through awareness or reasonably imputable knowledge of customary practices in international trade or commerce. To my mind, this is the criterion which should guide the interpretation of the provision in question.

26. Given all these considerations, when and in what way may it be considered that there is a trade or commercial practice with regard to manners of achieving consensus of which the parties are or ought to have been aware?

I would immediately exclude determination of the existence of such a practice by referring to the lex causae or the lex fori, as some commentators have suggested, and hence to the legal system identified thereby. In the first place, it is all too obvious that such a solution would be liable to conflict with the *ratio legis* of the provision in question: it might have the perverse effect of endorsing as 'trade or commercial practices' within the meaning of Article 17 practices, not of international trade, but of only one or more legal systems, with the result that validity would be conferred on jurisdiction clauses based (possibly) on only local practices or on 'practices'[which] have not yet taken hold as such. On top of this, the Court has to date interpreted the concept of 'agreement' between the parties within the meaning of Article 17 independently. There does not seem to me to be any ground for diverging from this approach where the manners of reaching a consensus are attributable to trade or commercial practices.

27. Consequently, it is appropriate, also with regard to the third hypothesis provided for in Article 17, that the Court itself should indicate the objective evidence and/or conclusive conduct from which it can be inferred that one is in the presence of a trade or commercial practice which may appropriately be 'utilized' for the purposes of the valid conclusion of a jurisdiction clause. Seen from that perspective and bearing in mind the importance of consensus on the part of the parties concerned, the concept of trade or commercial practices for the purposes and effects of Article 17 can only be based, as Advocate General Lenz has suggested, on the existence of 'a practice ... which is followed generally, continuously and regularly by the circles concerned in transactions which correspond, both objectively and in point of their localization, to the transaction at issue'. In brief, the practice must be such as to lead to the conviction that the parties' conduct is conclusive, that is to say that it implies a meeting of the minds and hence actual consensus as regards the conferment of jurisdiction. From that perspective, the existence of a specific trade or commercial practice in a particular sector should in any event be proved: it is only in those circumstances that the practice acquires legal effectiveness under Article 17.

This interpretation is moreover confirmed by the 1988 Lugano Convention and the Brussels Convention as amended by the 1989 San Sebastian Convention. Apart from the requirements set out in the 1978 version, Article 17 of the Lugano and San Sebastian Conventions requires the trade or commercial usage in question to be 'widely known to, and regularly observed by, parties to contracts of the type involved in the particular trade or commerce concerned'. Accordingly, it is not enough for a jurisdiction clause to have been concluded in a form which accords with a usage in the particular trade or commerce concerned of which the parties were or ought to have been aware; the usage must have been 'on the one hand, widely known in international trade or commerce, and, on the other, regularly observed by parties to contracts of the type involved in the particular trade or commerce concerned'.

28. In my view, this suggested interpretation of the notion of a trade or commercial usage also enables it more easily to be established in what circumstances it should be considered, at least in principle, that the parties were or ought to have been aware of the usage in question. It is self-evident that it may reasonably be presumed that there was reasonably imputable knowledge of a practice which was continually followed in relation to contracts of the same type in the particular trade or commerce concerned.

Having said this, it is true that there cannot be an absolute presumption of reasonably imputable knowledge, it should be proved by objective evidence. To this end, particular importance attaches to factual circumstances, such as previous contractual dealings between the same parties or even with other parties but with regard to contracts of the same geographical and substantive type. Again, it may be important to ascertain whether or not the relevant usage was recognized by the legal system of the trader against whom the jurisdiction clause is sought to be enforced.

29. Let us return to the case before the Court. Since the contract in question was a charterparty concluded between traders in the relevant sector, there is no doubt that we are in the realm of international trade or commerce and hence within the field of application of the provision in question. I would go on to point out once again that the national court asks whether one party's lack of response to a commercial letter of confirmation containing a pre-printed indication of the courts having jurisdiction constitutes a practice within the meaning of Article 17 and hence should be deemed to constitute acceptance of the conferment of jurisdiction. In the alternative, the national court asks whether that conferment of jurisdiction may be deemed valid as a result of the defendant's having paid all MSG's invoices containing a similar indication of the competent courts.

In view of foregoing considerations it is only too plain that the existence of commercial practices of the type contemplated by the national court's questions with regard to the manner of achieving and manifesting consensus has to be proved in relation to the trade or commerce in question.

30. I therefore cannot accept the proposition put forward by the plaintiff and the German Government in the proceedings to the effect that, under Article 17, lack of response to a commercial letter of confirmation is to be deemed to constitute tacit acquiescence, irrespective as to whether any inquiry has been made whether there exists a practice to that effect in the relevant trade or commerce. That proposition, which relies, on the one hand, on the existence of a presumed, generalized - that is to say, Europe-wide - practice and, on the other, on the fact that the amendment made by the 1978 Accession Convention was adopted precisely in order to avoid the excessive formalism of the case-law with regard to cases of this type, is in fact without any foundation.

Admittedly, it emerges from the Schlosser Report that one of the reasons for the amendment in question was the desire to avoid the requirement for writing with regard to a commercial letter of confirmation. However, this does not mean, or at least not automatically, that the practice in question is recognized invariably and in any event as having the status of a commercial practice within the meaning of Article 17. What is more, the legal significance of silence in international trade is not recognized as broadly and generally as it is in Germany. I would just refer, for example, to Article 18(1) of the Vienna Convention of 11 April 1980 on Contracts for the International Sale of Goods, according to which 'A statement made by or other conduct of the offeree indicating assent to an offer is an acceptance. *Silence or inactivity does not in itself amount to acceptance.'*

31. In the final analysis, in order to establish whether the silence of one party in relation to a commercial letter of confirmation constitutes a manner of acceptance and hence means that a jurisdiction clause has validly been concluded, it is necessary to prove the existence of such a usage on the basis of the criteria set out above.

The national court has not provided the Court with any evidence enabling any view to be given in this regard. In these circumstances, it is therefore for the national court to establish whether in the sector of inland waterway transport on the Rhine there is a consolidated, habitually followed practice in relation to charterparties on the basis of which silence in response to a commercial letter of confirmation is deemed to constitute acceptance of the jurisdiction clause. In the event that it is found that there is such a usage, it will then have to be established whether the party against whom the jurisdiction clause is relied was or ought to have been aware of the existence of such a usage. Whether such reasonably imputable knowledge existed of the usage in question will depend, in turn, on the importance of that usage in the country in which the party against which the clause is relied is habitually resident and on whether or not this was the first contract concluded with that party and/or in that sector.

32. The solution just put forward can also be applied in order to determine whether there was a presumed trade or commercial usage consisting in the fact that the defendant paid without any objection the invoices issued by MSG, all of which contained a statement to the effect that the place at which MSG had its principal place of business was the competent forum. It will therefore be necessary to show also with regard to this hypothesis that, on the basis of the same criteria listed above, there was a commercial usage of which the parties were or ought to have been aware.

33. In the light of the foregoing considerations, I therefore propose that the Court should answer the Bundesgerichtshof's questions as follows:

(1) Article 5(1) of the Brussels Convention of 27 September 1968 must be interpreted as precluding jurisdiction being vested in the courts for the place of performance of a contractual obligation where that place, determined contractually by the parties, has no substantial connection with the subject matter of the contract and it appears that that determination was made with the sole aim of designating the courts having jurisdiction without complying with the formal requirements laid down by Article 17 of the Convention.

(2) The third hypothesis provided for in the second sentence of the first paragraph of the Brussels Convention of 27 September 1968, in the version as amended by the 1978 Accession Convention, must be interpreted as meaning that a jurisdiction clause may be regarded as having been validly concluded by reason of the silence of one party with regard to a commercial letter of confirmation containing a pre-printed reference to the courts having jurisdiction or by reason of that party's having paid without objection invoices issued by the other party containing a similar reference. To that end, however, it is for the national court to ascertain: (a) whether there exists in the trade or commerce concerned a practice to that effect which is followed continuously and generally and whether that practice is followed in contracts which are similar from both the substantive and geographical points of view to the contract at issue; (b) whether the defendant was or ought to have been aware of that usage, in particular because it was known also in his country of residence and/or having regard to previous contractual relations with the same contracting party and/or in the same sector.

Case C-159/97 - 16 March 1999

Transporti Castelletti Spedizioni Internazionali SpA
v
Hugo Trumpy SpA

Prorogation of jurisdiction - Agreement conferring jurisdiction - Conditions as to form - Written form - Clause included in the general conditions on the reverse of the contract - Need for an express reference to those conditions in the contract.

Agreement made in a form according with usages in international trade or commerce - Concept - Criteria of assessment - Consent of the parties - Proof of the usage and of the parties' awareness of it.

Scheme of the Convention - Exhaustive nature - Application of other conditions concerning the choice of court by the parties - Excluded.

Protocol on the interpretation of the Convention by the Court of Justice - Preliminary rulings - Jurisdiction of the Court of Justice - Limits

Summary

1. Whilst the mere fact that a clause conferring jurisdiction is printed on the reverse of a contract drawn up on the commercial paper of one of the parties does not of itself satisfy the requirements as to written form laid down in Article 17 of the Convention of 27 september 1968 on Jurisdiction and the Enforcement of Judgements in Civil and Commercial matters, it is otherwise where the text of the contract signed by both parties itself contains an express reference to general conditions which include a clause conferring jurisdiction.

2. Under the division of responsibilities in the preliminary ruling

procedure laid down by the Protocol of 3 June 1971 on the interpretation by the Court of Justice of the Convention of 27 September 1968 on Jurisdiction and the Enforcement of Judgments in Civil and Commercial Matters, it is solely for the national court before which the dispute has been brought, and which must assume responsibility for the subsequent judicial decision, to determine in the light of the particular circumstances of each case both the need for a preliminary ruling in order to enable it to deliver judgment and the relevance of the questions which it submits to the Court.

3. The third case mentioned in the second sentence of the first paragraph of Article 17 of the Convention of 27 September 1968 is to be interpreted as follows:

- The contracting parties' consent to the jurisdiction clause is presumed to exist where their conduct is consistent with a usage which governs the area of international trade or commerce in which they operate and of which they are, or ought to have been, aware.
- The existence of such a usage, which must be determined in relation to the branch of trade or commerce in which the parties to the contract operate, is established where a particular course of conduct is generally and regularly followed by operators in that branch when concluding contracts of a particular type. It is not necessary for such a course of conduct to be established in specific countries or, in particular, in all the Contracting States. In addition, in establishing the existence of a usage, although any publicity which might be given in associations or specialised bodies to the standard forms on which a jurisdiction clause appears may help to prove that a practice is generally and regularly followed, such publicity cannot be a requirement. Furthermore, a course of conduct satisfying the conditions indicative of a usage does not cease to be a usage because it is challenged before the courts, whatever the extent of the challenges, provided that it still continues to be generally and regularly followed in the trade with which the type of contract in question is concerned.
- The specific requirements covered by the expression 'form which accords' must be assessed solely in the light of the commercial usages of the branch of international trade or commerce concerned, without taking into account any particular requirements which national provisions might lay down.
- Awareness of the usage must be assessed with respect to the original parties to the agreement conferring jurisdiction, their nationality being irrelevant in this regard. Awareness of the usage will be established when, regardless of any specific form of publicity, in the branch of trade

or commerce in which the parties operate a particular course of conduct is generally and regularly followed in the conclusion of a particular type of contract, so that it may be regarded as an established usage.

4. The choice of court in a jurisdiction clause may be assessed only in the light of considerations connected with the requirements laid down in Article 17 of the Convention of 27 september 1968. Considerations about the links between the court designated and the relationship at issue, about the validity of the clause, or about the substantive rules of liability applicable before the chosen court are unconnected with those requirements.

JUDGMENT OF THE COURT

Iglesias, President, Kapteyn and Jann, Rapporteur, Presidents of Chambers, Mancini, Gulmann, Murray, Edward, Ragnemalm, Sevón, Wathelet and Schintgen, Judges

1. By order of 24 October 1996, received at the Court on 25 April 1997, the Corte Suprema di Cassazione (Supreme Court of Cassation) referred to the Court for a preliminary ruling under the Protocol of 3 June 1971 on the interpretation by the Court of Justice of the Convention of 27 September 1968 on Jurisdiction and the Enforcement of Judgments in Civil and Commercial Matters fourteen questions on the interpretation of Article 17 of the Convention of 27 September 1968 (OJ 1972 L 299, p. 32), as amended by the Convention of 9 October 1978 on the Accession of the Kingdom of Denmark, Ireland and the United Kingdom of Great Britain and Northern Ireland (OJ 1978 L 304, p. 1; amended version of the Convention at p. 77; hereinafter 'the Convention').

2. The questions have been raised in proceedings for compensation for damage allegedly caused during the unloading of goods carried under a number of bills of lading from Argentina to Italy, between Trasporti Castelletti Spedizioni Internazionali SpA ('Castelletti'), having its registered office in Milan, Italy, to which the goods were delivered, and Hugo Trumpy SpA ('Trumpy'), having its registered office in Genoa, Italy, in its capacity as agent for the vessel and for the carrier Lauritzen Reefers A/S ('Lauritzen'), whose registered office is in Copenhagen.

The Convention

3. The first and second sentences of the first paragraph of Article 17 of the Convention provide: 'If the parties, one or more of whom is domiciled in a Contracting State, have agreed that a court or the courts of a Contracting State are to have jurisdiction to settle any disputes which have arisen or which may arise in connection with a particular legal relationship, that court or those courts shall have exclusive jurisdiction. Such an agreement conferring jurisdiction shall be either in writing or evidenced in writing or, in international trade or commerce, in a form which accords with practices (1) in that trade or commerce of which the parties are or ought to have been aware.'

4. That version was amended, after the events which are the subject of the main proceedings, by the Convention of 26 May 1989 on the Accession of the Kingdom of Spain and the Portuguese Republic (OJ 1989 L 285, p. 1). The first paragraph of Article 17 now provides: 'If the parties, one or more of whom is domiciled in a Contracting State, have agreed that a court or the courts of a Contracting State are to have jurisdiction to settle any disputes which have arisen or which may arise in connection with a particular legal relationship, that court or those courts shall have exclusive jurisdiction. Such an agreement conferring jurisdiction shall be either:

(a) in writing or evidenced in writing, or

(b) in a form which accords with practices which the parties have established between themselves, or

(c) in international trade or commerce, in a form which accords with a usage (1) of which the parties are or ought to have been aware and which in such trade or commerce is widely known to, and regularly observed by, parties to contracts of the type involved in the particular trade or commerce concerned.'

The main proceedings

5. The goods at issue in the main proceedings were, according to 22 bills of lading issued in Buenos Aires on 14 March 1987, placed by various Argentine shippers on board a vessel operated by Lauritzen, bound for Savona, Italy, where they were to be delivered to Castelletti. As a result of problems which arose during the unloading of the goods, Castelletti brought an action against Trumpy before the Tribunale di Genova (Genoa District Court) seeking an order for payment of compensation.

6. Trumpy, relying on clause 37 of the bills of lading, which confers jurisdiction on the High Court of Justice, London, argued that the Genoa court had no jurisdiction.

7. Clause 37, which is drawn up in English as are all the bills of lading in which it is inserted in small, but legible, characters, is the last to appear on the reverse of the printed document. It is worded as follows: 'The contract evidenced by this Bill of Lading shall be governed by English Law and any disputes thereunder shall be determined in England by the High Court of Justice in London according to English Law to the exclusion of the Courts of any other country'.

8. On the face of the bills of lading there is, inter alia, a box to be filled in with particulars of the cargo, and a reference, in characters more obvious than those used for the other clauses, to the conditions set out on the reverse side. Below that reference are added the date and place of issue of the bill of lading and the signature of the carrier's local agent. The signature of the original shipper appears below the particulars of the cargo and above the reference to the reverse side.

9. By judgment of 14 December 1989, the Tribunale di Genova upheld the objection, taking the view that, having regard to the bill of lading produced before it, the clause conferring jurisdiction, although contained in a form which had not been signed by the shipper, was valid in the light of the usages of international trade. By decision of 7 December 1994, the Corte d'Appello (Court of Appeal), Genoa, upheld that judgment, but on different grounds. After examining all the bills of lading, it found that the shipper's signature on their face implied Castelletti's acceptance of all the clauses, including those on the reverse.

10. Castelletti therefore appealed on a point of law, claiming that the signature of the original shipper could not have entailed acceptance by it of all the clauses, but only, as is clear from its location, those relating to the particulars of the cargo.

11. The Corte Suprema di Cassazione found that this plea was admissible and that the signature of the original shipper could not be deemed to imply consent to all the clauses of the bill of lading. Since the court had thus ruled out the possibility that an agreement conferring jurisdiction had been made in writing or even evidenced in writing, it considered that the resolution of the dispute depended upon the interpretation of Article 17 of the Convention, in that it provides that an

agreement conferring jurisdiction can be made, 'in international trade or commerce, in a form which accords with practices (usages) in that trade or commerce of which the parties are or ought to have been aware.'

12. In those circumstances, the Corte Suprema di Cassazione decided to stay the proceedings and to refer the following questions to the Court for a preliminary ruling: '1. The first question to be put to the Court of Justice is as follows: In the case-law of the Court of Justice relating to the original wording of Article 17, reference has been made to the need to ascertain and protect the actual will of the parties with regard to the jurisdiction clause by means of the requirements laid down by that provision in respect of the validity of such clauses; that is also the case where the clause is adjudged valid, when the bill of lading containing the clause comes within the framework of a continuing business relationship between the parties, and it is thereby established that the relationship is governed by the general terms and conditions (drawn up by one of the parties, namely the carrier) containing that clause (see Case 71/83 *Tilly Russ* v *Nova* [1984] ECR 2417, which cites earlier judgments underscoring the need for the consent of the parties to be clearly and precisely demonstrated).

However, in the light of the insertion into the new wording of the provision of the reference to usage, which is prescriptive (and thus unconnected to the will of the parties, at least so far as specifically concerns a particular contract), the question arises whether the requirement of (actual) knowledge, or of lack of awareness arising out of negligent and inexcusable ignorance, is sufficient in view of the consistent incorporation (in all agreements similar to that in issue) of the jurisdiction clause. The question arises, in other words, whether it is any longer necessary to ascertain the will of the parties, despite the fact that Article 17 uses the word "concluded" [in the Italian version], which implies an expression of will and thus "commercial" usage (customary clauses).

2. The second question concerns the meaning of the expression "form which accords". The first aspect concerns the way in which the clause appears, that is whether it must necessarily be in writing signed by the party who has drawn it up and who has therefore expressed the intention of relying upon it - for example - by signing the bill of lading referring specifically to a clause which in turn refers to an agreement conferring exclusive jurisdiction, even in the absence of the signature of the other party (the shipper).

The second aspect consists in establishing whether it is necessary for the jurisdiction clause to stand out prominently on its own within the contract as a whole, or whether it is sufficient (and therefore of no consequence as regards the validity of the clause) for it to be inserted amongst numerous other clauses drawn up in order to regulate the contract of carriage in every respect.

The third aspect relates to the language in which the clause is drawn up, that is to say, whether it must be in some way related to the nationality of the parties to the contract or whether it is sufficient for it to be a language regularly used in international trade or commerce.

3. The third question is concerned with whether the designated court must, as well as being a court of a Contracting State, be in some way related to the nationality and/or the residence of the parties to the contract or to the place of performance and/or conclusion of the contract, or whether the first condition is sufficient without there being any other link with the substance of the relationship.

4. The fourth question concerns the process by which usage comes into being; that is, whether consistent incorporation of the clause in bills of lading issued by trade associations or a significant number of maritime transport undertakings is sufficient or whether it must be demonstrated that since users of such transport (whether traders or otherwise) have not made any observations or expressed reservations regarding consistent incorporation of the clause, they have tacitly acquiesced to the conduct of the other party, so that there may no longer be considered to be a dispute between them.

5. The fifth question concerns the form in which such consistent practice is publicised: must the form of bill of lading in which the jurisdiction clause appears be lodged at a particular office (trade association, chamber of commerce, port authorities, and so on) for consultation or made public in some other way?

6. The sixth question concerns the validity of the clause, even where, by virtue of the substantive rules applicable in the chosen court, it takes the form of a clause exempting the carrier from, or limiting, his liability.

7. The seventh question is concerned with whether the court (other than the chosen court) which has been called upon to assess the validity of the clause may examine the reasons for it, that is to say, the intention of the carrier in the choice of court made, as distinct from the court which would have had jurisdiction according to the usual criteria laid down in the Brussels Convention or by the *lex fori*.

8. The eighth question consists in ascertaining whether the fact that many shippers and/or endorsees of bills of lading have challenged the validity of the clause by bringing an action before a court other than that designated by the clause itself is indicative of the fact that usage

regarding the insertion of the clause in forms has not become well established.

9. The ninth question consists in ascertaining whether the usage must exist in all the countries of the European Community or whether the expression "international trade or commerce" is intended to mean that it is sufficient for the usage to be practised in those countries which, in the context of international trade or commerce, have traditionally played a prominent role.

10. The tenth question consists in ascertaining whether the usage in question may derogate from mandatory statutory provisions of individual States, such as, in Italy, Article 1341 of the Civil Code which, with regard to the general contractual terms and conditions drawn up by one of the parties, provides that, in order for the usage to be valid, the other party must be or ought to have been aware of it and provides that clauses laying down particular limitations to or derogating from the jurisdiction of the courts must be specifically approved in writing.

11. The eleventh question concerns the circumstances in which insertion of the clause in question in a standard form, not signed by the party not involved in drawing it up, may be considered to be grossly unfair or even abusive.

12. The twelfth question involves ascertaining whether the party concerned was or ought to have been aware of the usage, other than with regard to the condition set forth in paragraph 5, above, as regards the bill of lading itself, which contained numerous clauses appearing on the reverse (paragraph 2, above).

13. The thirteenth question involves identifying the person who is or ought to have been aware of the usage; whether it must be the original shipper, even if he is a national of a non-Contracting State (such as, in the present case, Argentina), or whether it is sufficient for it to be the endorsee of the bill, who is a national of a Contracting State (in the present case, Italy).

14. The fourteenth question is concerned with whether the phrase "ought to have been aware" refers to a criterion of good faith and honesty when a particular contract was drawn up or to a criterion of ordinary care on the part of individuals who must be fully informed of current practices in international trade, for the purposes of paragraph 9, above.'

The questions submitted for a preliminary ruling

13. In Case 24/76 *Estasis Salotti* v *RÜWA* [1976] ECR 1831, paragraph 9, the Court of Justice held that, whilst the mere fact that a clause conferring jurisdiction is printed on the reverse of a contract drawn up on

the commercial paper of one of the parties does not of itself satisfy the requirements of Article 17, it is otherwise where the text of the contract signed by both parties itself contains an express reference to general conditions which include a clause conferring jurisdiction.

14. Further, under the division of responsibilities in the preliminary ruling procedure laid down by the Protocol of 3 June 1971 on the interpretation by the Court of Justice of the Convention, it is for the national court alone to define the subject-matter of the questions which it proposes to refer to the Court. According to settled case-law, it is solely for the national court before which the dispute has been brought, and which must assume responsibility for the subsequent judicial decision, to determine in the light of the particular circumstances of each case both the need for a preliminary ruling in order to enable it to deliver judgment and the relevance of the questions which it submits to the Court (Cases C-220/95 *Van den Boogaard* v *Laumen* [1997] ECR I-1147, paragraph 16, and C-295/95 *Farrell* v *Long* [1997] ECR I-1683, paragraph 11).

15. It is apparent from the wording of the questions submitted that the national court seeks clarification of four factors affecting the validity of a jurisdiction clause which is drawn up in a form which accords with established practices (usages) - the third case mentioned in the second sentence of the first paragraph of Article 17 of the Convention - namely:

- the consent of the parties to the clause (first question);
- the notion of usage in international trade or commerce (ninth, fourth, fifth and eighth questions);
- the notion of form which accords with established usages (second, eleventh and tenth questions);
- the parties' awareness of the usage (thirteenth, fourteenth and twelfth questions).

16. It is also clear from its questions that the national court is unsure whether there are any restrictions as to the choice of court under Article 17 of the Convention (third, seventh and sixth questions).

The first question: parties' consent to the jurisdiction clause

17. By its first question, the national court is asking essentially whether Article 17 of the Convention, as amended by the Accession Convention of 9 October 1978, in so far as it refers to the notion of 'practices' (usages) whilst using the term 'concluded' [in the Italian version],

necessarily requires that the consent of the parties to the jurisdiction clause be established.

18. In its original version, Article 17 made the validity of a jurisdiction clause subject to the existence of an agreement in writing or an oral agreement evidenced in writing. It was in order to take account of the specific practices and requirements of international trade that the Accession Convention of 9 October 1978 added to the second sentence of the first paragraph of Article 17 a third case providing that, in international trade or commerce, a jurisdiction clause may be validly concluded in a form which accords with usages in that trade or commerce of which the parties are, or ought to have been, aware (Case C-106/95 *MSG* v *Gravières Rhénanes* [1997] ECR I-911, paragraph 16).

19. At paragraph 17 of *MSG*, the Court held that, in spite of the flexibility introduced into Article 17, the provision's aim was still to ensure that there was real consent on the part of the persons concerned so as to protect the weaker party to the contract by avoiding jurisdiction clauses, incorporated in a contract by one party, going unnoticed.

20. The Court went on to state, however, that the amendment made to Article 17 makes it possible to presume that such consent exists where commercial usages of which the parties are or ought to have been aware exist in this regard in the relevant branch of international trade or commerce (*MSG*, paragraphs 19 and 20).

21. The answer to the first question must therefore be that the third case mentioned in the second sentence of the first paragraph of Article 17 of the Convention is to be interpreted as meaning that the contracting parties' consent to the jurisdiction clause is presumed to exist where their conduct is consistent with a usage which governs the area of international trade or commerce in which they operate and of which they are, or ought to have been, aware.

The ninth, fourth, fifth and eighth questions: usage in international trade or commerce

22. By these questions, the national court seeks to ascertain the countries in which a usage must be found to exist, the process by which it comes into being, the forms in which it must be publicised, and the consequences to be drawn, as to the existence of a usage in this area, from actions challenging the validity of jurisdiction clauses inserted in bills of lading.

23. At paragraph 21 of *MSG*, the Court stated that it is for the national court to determine, first, whether the contract in question is one forming part of international trade or commerce and, second, whether there is a usage in the branch of international trade or commerce in which the parties operate.

24. As to the first point, it is common ground that, in the main proceedings, the contract is one forming part of international trade or commerce.

25. As to the second point, the Court explained in *MSG*, at paragraph 23, that whether a usage exists is not to be determined by reference to the law of one of the Contracting Parties or in relation to international trade or commerce in general, but in relation to the branch of trade or commerce in which the parties to the contract operate.

26. It went on to hold in the same paragraph that there is a usage in the branch of trade or commerce in question where in particular a certain course of conduct is generally and regularly followed by operators in that branch when concluding contracts of a particular type.

27. It follows that it is not necessary for such a course of conduct to be established in specific countries or, in particular, in all the Contracting States. The fact that a practice is generally and regularly observed by operators in the countries which play a prominent role in the branch of international trade or commerce in question can be evidence which helps to prove that a usage exists. The determining factor remains, however, whether the course of conduct in question is generally and regularly followed by operators in the branch of international trade in which the parties to the contract operate.

28. Since Article 17 of the Convention does not contain any reference to forms of publicity, it must be held, as the Advocate General considered at point 152 of his Opinion, that, although any publicity which might be given in associations or specialised bodies to the standard forms on which a jurisdiction clause appears may help to prove that a practice is generally and regularly followed, such publicity cannot be a requirement for establishing the existence of a usage.

29. A course of conduct satisfying the conditions indicative of a usage does not cease to be a usage because it is challenged before the courts, whatever the extent of the challenges, provided that it still continues to be generally and regularly followed in the trade with which the type of

contract in question is concerned. Therefore, the fact that numerous shippers and/or endorsees of bills of lading have challenged the validity of a jurisdiction clause by bringing actions before courts other than those designated would not cause the incorporation of that clause in those documents to cease to constitute a usage, as long as it is established that it amounts to a usage which is generally and regularly followed.

30. The answer to the ninth, fourth, fifth and eighth questions must therefore be that the third case mentioned in the second sentence of the first paragraph of Article 17 of the Convention is to be interpreted as follows: The existence of a usage, which must be determined in relation to the branch of trade or commerce in which the parties to the contract operate, is established where a particular course of conduct is generally and regularly followed by operators in that branch when concluding contracts of a particular type.

It is not necessary for such a course of conduct to be established in specific countries or, in particular, in all the Contracting States.

A specific form of publicity cannot be required in all cases.

The fact that a course of conduct amounting to a usage is challenged before the courts is not sufficient to cause the conduct no longer to constitute a usage.

The second, eleventh and tenth questions: 'form which accords with practices'

31. By its second question, the national court seeks to ascertain what is specifically required for there to be a 'form which accords' within the meaning of Article 17 of the Convention. It asks more precisely whether the jurisdiction clause must be contained in a written document, bearing the signature of the party stipulating it, with the signature itself being accompanied by a reference to the clause, whether that clause must stand out prominently from the other clauses and whether the language in which it is drawn up must be related to the nationality of the parties.

32. By its eleventh question, the national court seeks to ascertain the circumstances in which insertion of the clause in question in a standard form, which has not been signed by the party not involved in drawing it up, may be considered to be grossly unfair or even abusive.

33. By its tenth question, the national court asks whether it is acceptable, in the context of Article 17 of the Convention, to rely on a usage which

would derogate from mandatory statutory provisions adopted by certain Contracting States as regards the form of jurisdiction clauses.

34. As the Court held in Case 150/80 *Elefanten Schuh* v *Jacqmain* [1981] ECR 1671, paragraph 25, Article 17 is intended to lay down itself the conditions as to form which jurisdiction clauses must meet, so as to ensure legal certainty and to ensure that the parties have given their consent.

35. It follows that the validity of a jurisdiction clause may be subject to compliance with a particular condition as to form only if that condition is linked to the requirements of Article 17.

36. It is therefore for the national court to refer to the commercial usages in the branch of international trade or commerce concerned in order to determine whether, in the case before it, the physical appearance of the jurisdiction clause, including the language in which it is drawn up, and its insertion in a standard form, which has not been signed by the party not involved in drawing it up, are consistent with the forms according with those usages.

37. In *Elefanten Schuh*, at paragraph 26, the Court stated that Contracting States are not at liberty to lay down formal requirements other than those laid down in the Convention.

38. Therefore, the usages to which Article 17 refers cannot be nullified by national statutory provisions which require compliance with additional conditions as to form.

39. The answer to the second, eleventh and tenth questions must therefore be that the third case mentioned in the second sentence of the first paragraph of Article 17 of the Convention is to be interpreted as meaning that the specific requirements covered by the expression 'form which accords' must be assessed solely in the light of the commercial usages of the branch of international trade or commerce concerned, without taking into account any particular requirements which national provisions might lay down.

The thirteenth, fourteenth and twelfth questions: the parties' awareness of the usage

40. By these questions, the national court seeks to ascertain, first, which party must be aware of the usage and whether his nationality is relevant

in this regard, next, what degree of awareness that party must have of the usage and, finally, whether any publicity must be given to the standard forms containing jurisdiction clauses and, if so, in what form.

41. As to the first point, the Court of Justice held in *Tilly Russ*, at paragraph 24, that, in so far as a jurisdiction clause incorporated in a bill of lading is valid under Article 17 of the Convention as between the shipper and the carrier, it can be pleaded against the third party holding the bill of lading so long as, under the relevant national law, the holder of the bill of lading succeeds to the shipper's rights and obligations.

42. Since the validity of the clause under Article 17 must be assessed by reference to the relationship between the original parties, it follows that it is those parties whose awareness of the usage must be assessed, the parties' nationality being irrelevant for the purposes of that investigation.

43. As to the second point, it is clear from paragraph 24 of *MSG* that actual or presumed awareness of a usage on the part of the parties to a contract can be made out, in particular, by showing either that the parties had previously had commercial or trade relations between themselves or with other parties operating in the sector in question, or that, in that sector, a particular course of conduct is sufficiently well known because it is generally and regularly followed when a particular type of contract is concluded, so that it may be regarded as being an established usage.

44. As to the third point, given the Convention's silence on the means by which awareness of a usage may be proved, it must be held that, although any publicity which might be given in associations or specialised bodies to the standard forms containing jurisdiction clauses would make it easier to prove awareness, it cannot be essential for this purpose.

45. The answer to the thirteenth, fourteenth and twelfth questions must therefore be that the third case mentioned in the second sentence of the first paragraph of Article 17 of the Convention is to be interpreted as meaning that awareness of the usage must be assessed with respect to the original parties to the agreement conferring jurisdiction, their nationality being irrelevant in this regard. Awareness of the usage will be established when, regardless of any specific form of publicity, in the branch of trade or commerce in which the parties operate a particular course of conduct is generally and regularly followed in the conclusion of a particular type of contract, so that it may be regarded as an established usage.

The third, seventh and sixth questions: choice of court

46. By these questions, the national court seeks to ascertain whether there are, under Article 17 of the Convention, any limitations as to the choice of court. It asks whether it is necessary for the parties to choose a court having some link to the case, whether the court seised may review the validity of the clause as well as the intention of the party which inserted it, and whether the fact that the substantive provisions applicable before the chosen court tend to reduce that party's liability may affect the validity of the jurisdiction clause.

47. In that regard, it should be recalled that the Convention does not affect rules of substantive law (Case 25/79 *Sanicentral* v *Collin* [1979] ECR 3423, paragraph 5), but has the aim of establishing uniform rules of international jurisdiction (Case C-269/95 *Benincasa* v *Dentalkit* [1997] ECR I-3767, paragraph 25).

48. As the Court has repeatedly stated, it is in keeping with the spirit of certainty, which constitutes one of the aims of the Convention, that the national court seised should be able readily to decide whether it has jurisdiction on the basis of the rules of the Convention, without having to consider the substance of the case (Cases 34/82 *Peters* v *ZNAV* [1983] ECR 987, paragraph 17; C-288/92 *Custom Made Commercial* v *Stawa Metallbau* [1994] ECR I-2913, paragraph 20; and *Benincasa*, paragraph 27). In *Benincasa*, at paragraphs 28 and 29, the Court explained that the aim of securing legal certainty by making it possible reliably to foresee which court will have jurisdiction has been interpreted, in connection with Article 17 of the Convention, by fixing strict conditions as to form, since the purpose of that provision is to designate, clearly and precisely, a court in a Contracting State which is to have exclusive jurisdiction in accordance with the consensus between the parties.

49. It follows that the choice of court in a jurisdiction clause may be assessed only in the light of considerations connected with the requirements laid down by Article 17.

50. It is for those reasons that the Court has repeatedly held that Article 17 of the Convention dispenses with any objective connection between the relationship in dispute and the court designated (Case 56/79 *Zelger* v *Salinitri* [1980] ECR 89, paragraph 4; *MSG*, paragraph 34; and *Benincasa*, paragraph 28).

51. For the same reasons, in a situation such as that in the main proceedings, any further review of the validity of the clause and of the intention of the party which inserted it must be excluded and substantive rules of liability applicable in the chosen court must not affect the validity of the jurisdiction clause.

52. The answer to the third, seventh and sixth questions must therefore be that the third case mentioned in the second sentence of the first paragraph of Article 17 is to be interpreted as meaning that the choice of court in a jurisdiction clause may be assessed only in the light of considerations connected with the requirements laid down in Article 17 of the Convention. Considerations about the links between the court designated and the relationship at issue, about the validity of the clause, or about the substantive rules of liability applicable before the chosen court are unconnected with those requirements.

On those grounds, the Court, in answer to the questions referred to it by the Corte Suprema di Cassazione by order of 24 October 1996, hereby rules:

> **The third case mentioned in the second sentence of the first paragraph of Article 17 of the Convention of 27 September 1968 on Jurisdiction and the Enforcement of Judgments in Civil and Commercial Matters, as amended by the Convention of 9 October 1978 on the Accession of the Kingdom of Denmark, Ireland and the United Kingdom of Great Britain and Northern Ireland, is to be interpreted as follows:**
>
> **1. The contracting parties' consent to the jurisdiction clause is presumed to exist where their conduct is consistent with a usage which governs the area of international trade or commerce in which they operate and of which they are, or ought to have been, aware.**
>
> **2. The existence of a usage, which must be determined in relation to the branch of trade or commerce in which the parties to the contract operate, is established where a particular course of conduct is generally and regularly followed by operators in that branch when concluding contracts of a particular type.**
>
> **It is not necessary for such a course of conduct to be established in specific countries or, in particular, in all the Contracting States.**

A specific form of publicity cannot be required in all cases.

The fact that a course of conduct amounting to a usage is challenged before the courts is not sufficient to cause the conduct no longer to constitute a usage.

3. The specific requirements covered by the expression 'form which accords' must be assessed solely in the light of the commercial usages of the branch of international trade or commerce concerned, without taking into account any particular requirements which national provisions might lay down.

4. Awareness of the usage must be assessed with respect to the original parties to the agreement conferring jurisdiction, their nationality being irrelevant in this regard. Awareness of the usage will be established when, regardless of any specific form of publicity, in the branch of trade or commerce in which the parties operate a particular course of conduct is generally and regularly followed in the conclusion of a particular type of contract, so that it may be regarded as an established usage.

5. The choice of court in a jurisdiction clause may be assessed only in the light of considerations connected with the requirements laid down in Article 17 of the Convention of 27 September 1968. Considerations about the links between the court designated and the relationship at issue, about the validity of the clause, or about the substantive rules of liability applicable before the chosen court are unconnected with those requirements.

(1) - The terminology of the English text was changed by the Convention of 26 May 1989 from 'practices' to 'usages'. The majority of the other language texts use the same terminology (usage, uso, Handelsbrauch ...). In the translation of the present judgment, the term 'usages' has been adopted [although it did not appear in the text of the convention under consideration].

OPINION OF MR ADVOCATE GENERAL LÉGER

1. By the 14 questions submitted to the Court, the Corte Suprema di Cassazione asks the Court to explain the conditions for the application of Article

17 of the Convention of Brussels of 27 September 1968 on Jurisdiction and the Enforcement of Judgments in Civil and Commercial Matters, as amended by the Accession Convention of 1978 (or hereinafter 'the Convention'), in so far as it refers to usages in international trade or commerce, in order to examine the validity of a clause conferring jurisdiction appearing on the reverse side of a bill of lading, of which only the front side is signed.

Legal framework

2. Under the unified system of determination of jurisdiction that Title II of the Convention seeks to facilitate, Article 17 provides for an exclusive head of jurisdiction, derogating from both that established in principle by Article 2, for the courts of the Contracting State in which the defendant is domiciled, and the special jurisdiction provided for in Articles 5 and 6. The Court has consistently held in this regard that 'the requirements laid down by Article 17 of the Convention must be strictly interpreted in so far as that article excludes both jurisdiction as determined by the general principle of the defendant's courts laid down in Article 2 and the special jurisdictions provided for in Articles 5 and 6.'

3. Article 17, which forms part of Section 6 concerning 'Prorogation of jurisdiction', which also gives jurisdiction, under Article 18, to the courts before which the defendant appears, allows the parties, at least one of whom is domiciled in a Contracting State, by a demonstration of their will alone, to confer jurisdiction on the courts of a Contracting State which normally have no jurisdiction.

4. The article in question, Article 17, 'is probably the article of the Convention that was the most transformed by the successive accessions of new States'. It is thus useful to briefly recall the evolution of this provision.

5. In its original version, this provision was worded as follows:

'If the Parties, one or more of whom is domiciled in a Contracting State, have, by agreement in writing or by an oral agreement evidenced in writing, agreed that a court or the courts of a Contracting State are to have jurisdiction to settle any disputes which have arisen or which may arise in connection with a particular legal relationship, that court or those courts shall have exclusive jurisdiction.'

6. By the adoption of the Accession Convention of 1978, the Contracting Parties agreed, in particular, that agreements conferring jurisdiction could be concluded in a third form: beside the reference to a written agreement or oral agreement confirmed in writing there was added that of the usages of international trade or commerce. This version, which is the subject of the present reference, reads as follows:

'If the parties, one or more of whom is domiciled in a Contracting State, have agreed that a court or the courts of a Contracting State are to have jurisdiction to settle any disputes which have arisen or which may arise in connection with a particular legal relationship, that court or those courts shall have exclusive jurisdiction. Such an agreement conferring jurisdiction shall be either in writing or evidenced in writing or, in international trade or commerce, in a form which accords with practices in that trade or commerce of which the parties are or ought to have been aware. Where such an agreement is concluded by parties, none of whom is domiciled in a Contracting State, the courts of other Contracting States shall have no jurisdiction over their disputes unless the court or courts chosen have declined jurisdiction.'

7. I should, finally, refer to the latest version of Article 17, resulting from the Convention of San Sebastian of 26 May 1989, which clarifies the nature of the usage with which the form of the clause should accord and, in particular, lays down a fourth form that may be used by the parties, in order to take account of the 'practices' which they may have established between themselves.

'If the parties, one or more of whom is domiciled in a Contracting State, have agreed that a court or the courts of a Contracting State are to have jurisdiction to settle any disputes which have arisen or which may arise in connection with a particular legal relationship, that court or those courts shall have exclusive jurisdiction. Such an agreement conferring jurisdiction shall be either:

(a) in writing or evidenced in writing, or

(b) in a form which accords with practices which the parties have established between themselves, or

(c) in international trade or commerce, in a form which accords with a usage of which the parties are or ought to have been aware and which in such trade or commerce is widely known to, and regularly observed by, parties to contracts of the type involved in the particular trade or commerce concerned'

Facts

8. The questions referred to the Court originated in the following facts:

9. Consignments of fruit were loaded by various Argentinian shippers under 22 bills of lading issued in Buenos Aires on 14 March 1987 on board a vessel operated by the shipowner Lauritzen Reefers A/S, whose registered office is in Copenhagen, bound for Savona in Italy, where they were to be delivered to the company Trasporti Castelletti Spedizioni Internazionali SpA (hereinafter 'Castelletti' or 'the appellant in the main proceedings').

10. As a result of problems which arose during the unloading of the goods, Castelletti brought an action against the forwarding agent of the ship and the Danish carrier, Hugo Trumpy SpA (or hereinafter 'the respondent in the main proceedings'), having its registered office in Genoa, Italy, before the Tribunale di Genova (Genoa District Court) seeking an order for payment of compensation.

11 . The respondent in the main proceedings immediately invoked the lack of jurisdiction of the Italian court, relying on Article 17 of the Brussels Convention, as drafted following the Accession Convention of Luxembourg of 1978 and clause 37 of the bills of lading, conferring jurisdiction on the High Court of Justice, London.

12. This clause, which was drawn up in English like the rest of the bill of lading in which it was contained, and in small, but legible, characters, is the last reference to appear on the reverse side of the printed document. It reads as

follows: 'The contract evidenced by this Bill of Lading shall be governed by English Law and any disputes thereunder shall be determined in England by the High Court of Justice in London according to English Law to the exclusion of the Courts of any other country.'

On the face of the bill of lading there is, inter alia, a box to be filled in with particulars of the cargo, as well as a reference, worded in capitals, in thick letters larger than those used in the clauses, to the conditions set out on the reverse side: 'Continued on reverse side'. Below that reference are added the date and place of issue of the bill of lading, as well as the signature of the carrier; that of the original shipper appearing just below particulars of the cargo, is appended beside the reference 'above particulars declared by shipper'.

13. Having regard to the usages of international trade or commerce, the Tribunale di Genova upheld the objection of lack of jurisdiction and held the clause in question, although contained in a form not signed by the shipper, to be valid. By decision of 7 December 1994, the Corte d'Appello, Genoa, upheld the first decision, but on different grounds. It ruled that the signature on the face of the bill of lading by the original shipper implied acceptance of all the clauses, including those on the reverse side, by Castelletti.

14. Castelletti therefore appealed on a point of law, relying on Article 17 of the Convention, and, in particular, on the condition regarding the consent of the parties, on the ground that the signature of the original shipper could not have entailed acceptance by it of all the clauses, but only those which preceded it, relating to the particulars of the cargo.

15. The Corte Suprema di Cassazione ruled that: 'the plea of the applicant is admissible'. While finding that the amended 1978 Convention was applicable, it considered that there nevertheless existed a doubt as to the correct interpretation of the (new) wording of Article 17, which requires that an agreement conferring jurisdiction should be concluded 'in international trade or commerce in a form which accords with usages in that trade or commerce of which the parties are or ought to have been aware', since it ruled out the possibility that the agreement had been made in writing, or was even evidenced in writing.

16. It thus granted a stay and referred to the Court fourteen questions, reproduced in the annex, which may be regrouped under different headings, which I will now examine in turn.

Preliminary remarks

17. The extreme detail of the questions submitted to the Court is at first sight somewhat perplexing.

18 The Italian court seems to be inviting the Court to review all its already extensive case-law on Article 17 of the Convention, in particular before the amendment made in 1978, in order to ascertain that it is still relevant after that date. On the one hand, it does not follow from the Schlosser Report that the wish of the Contracting Parties was to completely change the meaning and scope of this provision: the aim was rather to resolve a number of difficulties encountered

in practice and to anticipate the particularities of new members. On the other hand, I doubt the relevance of some of the questions submitted for the resolution of the case, especially since the scant information contained in the order for reference does not assist in probing the concerns of the court that prompted them.

19. It is also true, as we shall see, that a certain number of the questions formulated have lost some relevance since the Court's rulings in recent cases, in particular *MSG*, ibid., and the judgment of 3 July 1997 in *Benincasa*.

20. I will nevertheless do my best to suggest to the Court a way which, while fully taking into account the questions submitted, provides effective clarification to the national court on the application of Article 17 of the Convention which in the end it has to apply.

21. I think it is useful to point out first of all that the Corte Suprema di Cassazione correctly holds Article 17 of the Brussels Convention, resulting from the amendment made in 1978, applicable in this case.

22. On the one hand, the bill of lading in question was issued on 14 March 1987, that is after the date of entry into force of the amended Convention in each of the Contracting States capable of having a connecting link with the facts in the present case (the Italian Republic, the Kingdom of Denmark and the United Kingdom of Great Britain and Northern Ireland).

On the other hand, neither the Accession Convention of 25 October 1982 nor - a fortiori - that of San Sebastian had entered into force at the time of the facts in question.

23. It is beyond doubt that the Convention as amended by the 1978 Accession Convention is fully applicable *ratione temporis*.

24. Moreover, the foreign element introduced into the present case by the Argentine nationality of the original shippers is not of such a nature to exclude the application of Article 17, as the Corte Suprema di Cassazione points out.

25. In requiring that at least one of the parties be 'domiciled in a Contracting State', the authors of the Convention really envisaged three types of situation, as M. Jenard emphasised in his report: 'Article 17 applies where the agreement conferring jurisdiction was made either between a persons domiciled in one Contracting State and a person domiciled in another Contracting State, or between a person domiciled in a Contracting State and a person domiciled outside the Community, if the agreement confers jurisdiction on the Courts of a Contracting State; it also applies where two person domiciled in one Contracting State agree that the Court of another Contracting State shall have jurisdiction.' For its part, the Schlosser Report observes that 'Article 17 ... [applies] only if the transaction in question is international in character.'

26. It is sufficient to recall that this is clearly the case on the facts of the present case.

27. Without at this stage resolving the question - which will be examined later - of the identification of the 'parties' envisaged by Article 17 of the Convention, it can be noted right away that, both in the relations between the original parties and those linking the appellant in the main proceedings to the respondent in the main proceedings, the condition that at least one of the parties has 'his domicile in a Contracting State' is satisfied.

28. First of all, in the context of the initial links, the disputed clause is one of those foreseen in the second instance in the Jenard Report because it was concluded between 'a person domiciled in a Contracting State' (the Danish carrier) and 'a person domiciled outside the Community' (the Argentine shippers) and it grants 'prorogation in favour of the court of a Contracting State' (the High Court of Justice, London).

29. The second relational context presents no difficulties, each of the two parties being domiciled in a Contracting State (Italy in the present case).

30. Finally, although the field of maritime transport, in particular in so far as it concerns bills of lading, is specifically dealt with by international conventions, widely cited elsewhere during the proceedings before the Court, it is clearly not excluded from the material scope of Article 17 of the Convention.

31. In this regard, it should be remembered that, with the exception of the restrictions contained in Article 12 (jurisdiction in insurance matters), Article 15 (jurisdiction over consumer contracts) and Article 16 (exclusive jurisdiction in certain matters, such as rights in immovable property) of the Convention, the choice of forum is allowed in all matters covered by the Convention.

Opinion

32. Despite their large number, the questions referred to the Court essentially seek to have the Court explain each of the three elements affecting the validity of a jurisdiction clause from the point of view of the third case mentioned in the second sentence of the first paragraph of Article 17 of the Convention in its 1978 version. They mean to identify at the outset the competent court to rule on the conditions for application of this provision.

33. I therefore propose to examine them in so far as they concern the consent of the parties to the clause (II); the notion of form which accords with usages in international trade or commerce (III); as well as the parties' awareness of the usage (IV). Some of the questions also relate to jurisdictional capacity to recognise such clauses (I); to the extent that they affect the jurisdiction of the national court, it is with these that I begin my analysis.

I - Jurisdictional capacity (third and seventh questions)

34. By its third question, the national court asks the Court whether, for the purposes of applying Article 17, the court designated by the jurisdiction clause must be linked in some way to the dispute. The question is worded as follows:

'[The Corte Suprema di Cassazione asks] whether the designated court must, as well as being a court of a Contracting State, be in some way related to the nationality and/or the residence of the parties to the contract or to the place of performance and/or conclusion of the contract, or whether the first condition is sufficient without there being any other link with the substance of the relationship.'

35. It seems to me that the case-law of the Court allows a clear negative answer to be given right away to the first alternative thus formulated.

36. In *Zelger* the Court held that, in contrast to Article 5(1) of the Convention, which provides for a ground of jurisdiction - the courts of the place in which the contractual obligation was or is to be performed - justified by the existence of a direct connecting factor between the dispute and the selected court, Article 17 '... dispenses with any objective connection between the legal relationship in dispute and the court designated'.

37. This analysis was confirmed by the Court in its most recent judgments, which emphasised that the disputed provision '... which accords with the intentions of the parties to the contract and provides for exclusive jurisdiction by dispensing with any objective connection between the relationship in dispute and the court designated.'

38. This is, as academic writers have stated, a rejection of the theory of forum conveniens, the practical difficulties for the application of which, arising from the determination of the link between the case and the court designated, can easily be imagined. On the contrary, it may be preferable to leave the parties to choose the most neutral court possible, which may be completely unconnected to their dispute. As one author states, 'If every possibility of absolute neutrality had been eliminated from the outset, it would have encouraged the parties to turn to arbitration, where the absence of an objective link between the dispute and the arbitrators is more usually the case in international matters'.

39 . It follows from this that, in so far as the court designated in the jurisdiction clause is concerned, the greatest possible freedom is left to the will of the parties, which cannot be restricted, according to the wording of the provision itself, except by the requirement that the court must be one belonging to a Contracting State.

40. In reply to the third question, it therefore suffices to say that, for the application of Article 17, it is not necessary that the jurisdiction chosen has a link with the parties or the contract.

41. The jurisdiction chosen does not, however, always necessarily coincide with the court seised. Dealings with a clause conferring jurisdiction can be a source of difficulty for the latter, as in the present case, which led the national court to ask the seventh question, which is:

'whether the court (other than the chosen court) which has been called upon to assess the validity of the clause may examine reasons for it, that is to say, the intention of the carrier in the choice of court made, as distinct from the court which would have had jurisdiction according to the usual criteria laid down in the Brussels Convention or by the lex fori.'

42. The Court is hereby invited to take a position on the twofold question of the power of the court seised to examine the validity of the clause granting jurisdiction to another court, and if the case arises, the extent of this review.

43. If the power of the court designated by the jurisdiction clause to rule on its validity is not in doubt, that of the court seised raises certain questions. It is true that the exclusive nature of the jurisdiction conferred on the court chosen by the parties could be invoked against it, under Article 17, according to which the 'court or the courts [designated by the parties] shall have exclusive jurisdiction'.

44. However, it does not seem to me that it should end at this consideration.

The case-law and the Schlosser Report, seem to me in fact to be without ambiguity in this regard.

45. In *Estasis* and *Segoura*, cited above, the Court stated that '... Article 17 imposes on the court before which the matter is brought the duty of examining, first, whether the clause conferring jurisdiction was in fact the subject of consensus between the parties', such consensus, as we shall see, affecting the validity of the clause.

46. It is true that, in those two cases, the court before which the matter was brought was the court designated by the clause. The reasoning followed should however prevail where this is not the case.

47. If the court before which the matter is brought is not recognised as having power to rule in the first place on the validity of the clauses electing a foreign jurisdiction, it should logically be allowed to stay proceedings as soon as it is seised, in order to refer the parties to the court designated, so as to leave it to the latter court to review the validity of the clause conferring jurisdiction on it, although it may mean that the latter court will refer the case back again to the court originally seised should review of this issue be negative. One can see immediately the incoherence of such a mechanism in the scheme of the Convention, one of whose objectives is to facilitate the immediate and speedy designation of a competent court.

48. The Court's recent judgment in *Benincasa*, cited above, without specifically tackling this aspect, nevertheless ruled on the related question of the court competent to determine whether or not the dispute falls within the scope of application of the clause conferring jurisdiction in favour of '... the national court...[before which] the clause conferring jurisdiction [is] invoked'. This broad formulation seems to me to designate in a general manner the court before which the matter is brought, whether this corresponds or not with the jurisdiction designated.

49. Moreover, the approach which I am suggesting to the Court is not at all detrimental to the legal certainty sought by the Convention in the designation of competent courts. In recognising the power of the court before which the matter is brought to rule on the validity of the clause, and thus on its own jurisdiction, whether it is the court chosen or not, the power of the court to rule on the substance of the dispute is not prejudiced. In the interests of economy of procedure it simply puts the court before which the matter is brought in a position to ascertain itself whether it has jurisdiction.

50. The Schlosser Report does not really say anything different when it states that '... the existence of an agreement conferring jurisdiction on a court other than the one seised of the proceedings is ... taken into account by the court of its own motion.' Thus, once it is accepted that the court seised of the proceedings has to satisfy itself that the parties have not agreed to another jurisdiction, it must be accepted that it is also allowed, by the same token as it were, to verify the validity of such an election of jurisdiction.

51. Finally, I should also point out that to deny the court seised of proceedings the power to rule on the validity of the clause would risk encouraging delaying tactics in which less scrupulous parties would not fail to

engage. Knowing that the court before which proceedings are brought has of its own motion to establish the existence of a jurisdiction clause, if it was considered that it could not, however, rule on the clause's validity, it would be very easy for a party wishing, for example, to slow down the proceedings to make up the existence of such a choice of jurisdiction in order to achieve its purpose. It is clear that the system established by the Convention could not favour such practices.

52. In my opinion, therefore, the court before which the matter is brought, whether or not it is the court designated in the jurisdiction clause, is competent to rule on its validity.

53. As regards the issue, also dealt with in the seventh question, of the extent of review over this clause by the court seised, this does not seem to me to require detailed consideration. It is sufficient to accept that, as the court seised is competent to rule on the validity of the clause, this review can also extend to all aspects affecting this validity, set out under Article 17. These are in fact the points raised in the subsequent questions, concerning the consent of the parties to the clause, the existence of a usage in international trade or commerce and the parties' awareness of the usage.

54. I therefore consider that, in reply to the seventh question, it should be stated that the court seised, whether or not it is the court designated in the clause conferring jurisdiction, is competent to rule on the validity of the clause in relation to the conditions set out under Article 17.

II - The consent of the parties to the jurisdiction clause (first and eleventh questions and the first part of the second question)

55. One of the central concerns of the Corte Suprema di Cassazione seems to be on the point whether, as was the case prior to the amendment made in 1978, the application of Article 17, since it now refers to usages, always presupposes the need to check that the parties agreed to the jurisdiction clause.

56. That is the purpose of the very detailed first question, to which the Court has in the meantime, as we shall see, logically given an affirmative response. Then, in relation to the first part of the second question, as well as the eleventh question, I will examine who are the 'parties' from which such consent is required, in a situation such as in the present case, where the parties which originally concluded and/or signed the bill of lading are not necessarily those who rely on it or against whom it is invoked subsequently.

57. The first question is worded in these terms:

'In the case-law of the Court of Justice relating to the original wording of Article 17, reference has been made to the need to ascertain and protect the actual will of the parties with regard to the jurisdiction clause by means of the requirements laid down by that provision in respect of the validity of such clauses; that is also the case where the clause is adjudged valid, when the bill of lading containing the clause comes within the framework of a continuing business relationship between the parties, and it is thereby established that the relationship is governed by the general terms and conditions (drawn up by one of the parties, namely the carrier) containing that clause (see Case 71/83 *Tilly Russ* v *Nova* [1984] ECR 2417, which cites earlier judgments underlining the need for the consent of the parties to be clearly and precisely demonstrated).

However, in light of the insertion into the new wording of the provision of the reference to usage, which is prescriptive (and thus unconnected to the will of the parties, at least so far as specifically concerns a particular contract), the question arises whether the requirement of (actual) knowledge, or of lack of awareness arising out of negligent and inexcusable ignorance, is sufficient in view of the consistent incorporation (in all agreements similar to that in issue) of the jurisdiction clause. The question arises, in other words, whether it is any longer necessary to ascertain the will of the parties, despite the fact that Article 17 uses the word "concluded", which implies an expression of will and thus "commercial" usage (customary clauses).'

58. First of all, the purpose of the provision in question is to provide for a head of voluntary prorogation of jurisdiction: the authors of the Convention intended only the will of the parties to be capable of forming a derogation from Articles 2, 4 and 5. The requirement for their consent to this derogation is thus inherent in spirit of Article 17.

59. Moreover, this is echoed in the Jenard Report, which states that: '[clauses conferring jurisdiction] will be taken into consideration only if they are the subject of an agreement, and this implies the consent of all the parties', which the Court has taken up in the following terms, in emphasising that 'by making [the validity of clauses conferring jurisdiction] subject to the existence of an "agreement" between the parties, Article 17 imposes on the court before which the matter is brought the duty of examining, first, whether the clause conferring jurisdiction upon it was in fact the subject of a consensus between the parties.'

60. In accordance with the purpose of this provision, the Court found, in its recent judgments given in the context of proceedings for which the Convention in its version prior to the amendment made in 1978 was applicable, that 'the requirements set out in Article 17 governing the validity of jurisdiction clauses must be strictly construed since the purpose of Article 17 is to ensure that the parties have actually consented to such a clause, which derogates from the ordinary jurisdiction rules laid down in Articles 2, 5 and 6 of the Convention, and that their consent is clearly and precisely demonstrated.' To this end, that is to say 'In order to decide whether the conditions laid down in Article 17 are satisfied', the Court endeavoured to consider 'separately whether the agreement of the parties to the choice of jurisdiction was expressed in the form of a written agreement or in the form of an oral agreement evidenced in writing.'

61. The requirement of the consent of the parties to the jurisdiction clause still seems to me to affect the validity of the latter under Article 17, since the amendment made in 1978. The reference to usages can only mean that the parties could in future find themselves confronted by a clause to which they would not have agreed.

62. It is true, however, as results from the Schlosser Report, that the authors of the 1978 Accession Convention wished to reduce the excessive formalism that

the old version of Article 17, in requiring in every case written confirmation of this consent, tended to promote.

63. In doing this, however, only a 'relaxation of the formal requirements' was involved, to adapt Article 17 to the conditions of international trade, since 'the requirement that the other party to a contract with anyone employing general conditions of trade has to be given written confirmation of their inclusion in the contract before any jurisdiction clause in those conditions can be effective is unacceptable in international trade. International trade is heavily dependent on standard conditions which incorporate jurisdiction clauses. Nor are those conditions in many cases unilaterally dictated by one set of interests in the market; they have frequently been negotiated by representatives of the various interests.'

64. That is why the reference to usages in the new version of Article 17 means, according to the terms of this provision, 'in international trade or commerce', 'in a form ... which the parties are or ought to have been aware'. Thus, if it no longer refers to a written undertaking of the parties, it is because it is presumed that, as professionals in the area of trade in question, they have a knowledge of the usages that are practised in it and tacitly adhere to them. To facilitate the speed of transactions, there is thus an implied consent between the parties to these usages that is recognised in the new wording of Article 17, or, according to the words of Advocate General Tesuaro, 'a presumption of actual consensus'.

65. The Court adopted this analysis in *MSG*, in finding that the 'relaxation incorporated in Article 17 by the 1978 Accession Convention does not mean that there is not necessarily any need for consensus between the parties on a jurisdiction clause, since it is still one of the aims of that provision to ensure that there is real consent on the part of the persons concerned' and concluding from that, 'in the light of the amendment made to Article 17 by the 1978 Accession Convention, consensus on the part of the contracting parties as to a jurisdiction clause is presumed to exist where commercial practices in the relevant branch of international trade or commerce exist in this regard of which the parties are or ought to have been aware.'

66. In reply to the first question, it should be explained to the national court that, notwithstanding the relaxation of the conditions of form in 1978, the actual consent of the parties to the jurisdiction clause is still required for the purposes of the validity of the clause under Article 17 of the Convention. This consent is presumed to exist where such a clause constitutes a usage, in the relevant branch of trade, adopted in a form that the parties are, or ought to have been, aware of.

67. Before defining the notion of 'usage' and 'the parties' awareness', which other questions of the national court invite the Court to do, the 'parties' whose consent to the clause is thus presumed to exist still need to be determined. This, it seems to me, is the purpose of the first part of the second question, as well as the eleventh question.

68. The eleventh question 'concerns the circumstances in which insertion of the clause in question in a standard form, not signed by the party not involved in drawing it up, may be considered to be grossly unfair or even abusive'.

69. 'The second question concerns the meaning of the expression "form which accords". The first aspect concerns the way in which the clause appears, that is whether it must necessarily be in writing signed by the party who has it drawn it up and who has therefore expressed the intention of relying upon it - for example - by signing the bill of lading referring specifically to a clause which in turn refers to an agreement conferring exclusive jurisdiction, even in the absence of the signature of the other party (the shipper).'

70. I will return to the aspect relating to the form of the clause, also raised by the Italian court in its questions, but I will concentrate for the moment on the examination of the enforceability of the clause against parties who, as in the present case, are not those who originally concluded the bill of lading in which it is contained.

71. In other words, does the notion of 'parties' within the meaning of Article 17 only mean the 'original' parties, i.e., those at the origin of the clause, or does it also mean the 'parties' to the dispute, even third parties to the original agreement, capable of being bound by an undertaking in which they did not take part?

72. One would be tempted to state a priori as a principle that a jurisdiction clause, like any contractual stipulation, only binds the parties that have agreed it and those parties only. This principle may be even more appropriate as regards arbitration and jurisdiction clauses in so far as they fall outside the normal rules.

73. There are, however, situations in which such a clause will have effect as against persons who have not signed it. A certain number of judgments illustrate this point.

74. First of all there is the judgment in *Gerling and Others*, which, although given in a specific context, recognised that the beneficiary of a stipulation in favour of a third party, while not being a party to the original agreement, can rely on it on the basis of Article 17 of the Convention in its original version.

75. Even more illuminating is the Court's judgment in *Powell Duffryn*, cited above, from which it follows that the jurisdiction clause contained in the statutes of a company is enforceable against all the shareholders - those who took part in the vote on the statutes, whether voting for or against the clause, and also all subsequent shareholders, irrespective of how their shares were acquired.

76. Finally, it should also be accepted that, if the contract containing the clause was assigned, the clause could be invoked for the benefit of or against any assignee who, by definition, did not give his consent at the time of conclusion of the contract.

77. Accordingly, in *Tilly Russ*, the Court ruled that a clause contained in a bill of lading and adjudged to be valid as between the shipper and the carrier was enforceable against third parties holding the bill of lading, since, under the applicable national law, the bearer of the bill of lading succeeded to the shipper's rights and obligations.

78. The Court considered that the third party could not escape the jurisdiction provision in the bill of lading on the ground that he did not give his consent to the latter, since, in this situation, 'acquisition of the bill of lading could not confer upon the third party more rights than those attaching to the

shipper under it. The third party holding the bill of lading thus becomes vested with all the rights, and at the same time becomes subject to all the obligations, including those relating to the agreement on jurisdiction.'

79. The fact that, as in the present case, we have not one (the third party holding the bill of lading) but two parties not privy to the original contract - bearing in mind that the dispute in the main proceedings is between the third party holding the bill of lading and the agent of the ship and of the carrier over a clause agreed between an Argentinian shipper and a Danish carrier - is not such as to change the basic outcome set out above.

80. The reasoning that should be adopted by the national court, under the Court's case-law, should therefore be broken down into two stages.

81. In order to ascertain that the jurisdiction clause binds the third party holding the bill of lading to the agent of the ship, the national court must first of all satisfy itself that the original parties - shipper and carrier - consented to the clause. We have seen that, in reality, under the wording of Article 17 following its amendment in 1978, the reference to 'usages in international trade or commerce' known to the parties allows it to be presumed that they consented to the clause.

82. The court before which the matter is brought must then ascertain that the third party to the original contract who invokes the clause, or against whom the clause is invoked, has, by virtue of the applicable national law, succeeded to the rights and obligations of one of the original parties. If this is clearly the case, his consent to the clause has to be neither verified nor presumed under Article 17.

83. It is for the Italian court in the present case to ascertain in particular that the latter condition is satisfied, before going on to hold the clause in question to be applicable between the appellant and the respondent in the main proceedings.

84. Thus, in my opinion, the parties whose consent to the jurisdiction clause is presumed under Article 17, in so far as it refers to usages, are the parties having initially concluded the agreement in relation to which it was adopted.

85. As regards the relationship between the agent of the ship and of the carrier and the third party holding the bill of lading, Article 17 of the Convention applies where the jurisdiction clause was adjudged to be valid between the shipper and the carrier, and, under the applicable national law, the third party bearer, in acquiring the bill of lading, and the agent, by virtue of his capacity, succeeded to the rights and obligations of the shipper and the carrier respectively.

III - 'Form which accords with usages in international trade or commerce' (second question, second and third limbs, fourth, eighth, tenth and ninth questions)

86. Under the amendment made to Article 17 by the 1978 Accession Convention, the consensus of the contracting parties, capable of binding, as we have seen, third parties to the contract, is presumed to be established where there exists in this regard commercial usages in the branch of international trade or commerce concerned, usages of which the parties are aware or ought to have

been aware. The Corte Suprema di Cassazione invites the Court to define more precisely the meaning and scope of the reference to 'usages' in international trade or commerce, by five questions that I will examine in turn.

87 I must point out first that the Court's decision in *MSG*, cited above, delivered after this reference was made, clarifies a number of aspects of the questions submitted to the Court.

88. I would also observe that it is not for me or for the Court to determine whether, in the present case, the insertion of a clause conferring jurisdiction on the High Court of Justice on the reverse side of a pre-printed bill of lading constitutes a usage within the meaning of Article 17 of the Convention. Our role can only be to provide guidance to the national court, which, in the final analysis, must, in the light of the interpretative elements provided to it, decide whether there is a usage within the meaning of this provision.

'Forms which accord'

89. The meaning of 'form which accords', first of all, is the subject of paragraphs 2 and 3 of the second question, which 'concerns the meaning of the expression "form which accords". The second aspect of this question consists in establishing whether it is necessary for the jurisdiction clause to stand out prominently on its own within the contract as a whole, or whether it is sufficient (and therefore of no consequence as regards the validity of the clause) for it to be inserted amongst numerous other clauses drawn up in order to regulate the contract of carriage in every respect.

The third aspect relates to the language in which the clause is drawn up, that is to say, whether it must be in some way related to the nationality of the parties to the contract or whether it is sufficient for it to be a language regularly used in international trade or commerce.'

90. On the latter point, the Court has already held, in *Elefanten Schuh*, that the validity of a clause conferring jurisdiction cannot be put into question simply because the language in which it is formulated is not that stipulated by the national law of a Contracting State.

91. It should be added that, in accordance with the freedom afforded by the wording of Article 17 to the expression of the will of the parties, it cannot be considered that it prescribes either the use of a particular language or even the use of a language having a connecting factor with the parties. It is, in this regard, for the national court to refer to the usages in the branch of international trade or commerce in question, in order to determine whether, in the present case, the wording of a jurisdiction clause in English, like the rest of the bill of lading in which it is contained, constitutes a form consistent with the usages in the matter.

92. In my view, no further information can be provided in response to the second aspect of this second question. The question of the placing of a jurisdiction clause in a prominent position compared with the other clauses also depends on the usages followed in the branch of trade concerned.

93. Certainly, as the Schlosser Report states, the contracting party should be

protected 'from the danger of finding himself inadvertently bound by standard forms of agreement, containing jurisdiction clauses without realising it.'

94. However, on the one hand, it should be noted that the disputed clause is, in the present case, printed in the same type as the other clauses which it follows. Although it does not therefore stand out, it is not concealed either.

95. Moreover, as we shall see, the third case mentioned in the second sentence of the first paragraph of Article 17 governs the relations of well-informed business people aware of, or who 'ought to have been aware of', the usage in question. If the Corte Suprema di Cassazione were to find that the form of the clause corresponds with that of the usage in the branch in question, the parties' awareness of this usage would suffice to make the form in question in conformity with the requirements of Article 17.

96. These various elements are precisely the subject of the questions that I will consider hereafter.

97. In reply to the second question, concerning the 'forms which accord' within the meaning of Article 17, I can only refer the national court to the usages followed in the relevant branch of international trade or commerce, without being able to prescribe a priori the observance of the forms provided for under the provisions of the applicable law.

Usage

98. By the fourth question, the Court is asked, in relation to the process by which the usage comes into being, whether 'consistent incorporation of the clause in bills of lading issued by trade associations or a significant number of maritime transport undertakings is sufficient or whether it must be demonstrated that since users of such transport (whether traders or otherwise) have not made any observations or expressed any reservations regarding the consistent incorporation of the clause, they have tacitly acquiesced to the conduct of the other party, so that there may no longer be considered to be a dispute between them.'

99. It is thus the process by which the usage comes into being within the meaning of Article 17 that the Court is asked to explain.

100. Whilst the reasons that were put forward at the time of the amendment in 1978 are known - the Schlosser Report emphasises that 'the interpretation of that Article, which many national courts have shown a tendency to follow, does not cater adequately for the customs and requirements of international trade. These are the factors behind the relaxation of the formal provisions for international trade in the amended version of Article 17' - no definition or understanding of the notion of usage to which reference is now made appears in the text of the report.

101. It was not until 1989, upon the amendment made by the adoption of the Convention of San Sebastian, that the text of Article 17 specified that this usage must be 'widely known to, and regularly observed by, parties to contracts of the type involved in the particular trade or commerce concerned.' The Report concerning the Lugano Convention, drawn up in this regard in the same terms,

explains the new wording thus: 'even in international trade or commerce, it is not sufficient that an agreement conferring jurisdiction be in a form which accords with practices (or a usage) in such trade or commerce of which the parties are or ought to have been aware. It is moreover required that the usage shall be, on the one hand, widely known in international trade or commerce and, on the other, regularly observed by parties to contracts of the type involved in the particular trade or commerce concerned.'

102. Although the reports throw no more light on the meaning of the notion of usage, they nevertheless allow it to be said, first, that the taking into account of these usages introduced in 1978 can obviously only concern agreements made between professional traders in international trade or commerce. The continuous reference to 'international commercial practice' and other 'commercial transactions', particularly in the Schlosser Report, cannot be understood any other way. Therefore, the reference in the wording of the fourth question to 'users (whether traders or not)' cannot be considered relevant: only the 'operators in international commerce' benefit from this relaxation as regards the forms of clauses conferring jurisdiction.

103. It should also be emphasised that the meaning of the notion of usage cannot be left to be determined by each body of national law. It will be recalled that 'the principle laid down by the case-law ... according to which the concepts used in the Convention, which may have a different content depending on the national law of the Contracting States, must be interpreted independently, by reference principally to the system and objectives of the Convention, in order to ensure that the Convention is uniformly applied in all the Contracting States.' The same should also apply to the notion of 'usage', within the meaning of Article 17.

104. So, in reality, the question of the determination of the meaning of 'usage' is no longer a novel matter for the Court. The *MSG* case concerned a clause conferring jurisdiction printed on a commercial letter of confirmation as well as on a series of invoices paid without contestation. When asked to rule on the validity of such a clause from the point of view of Article 17 of the Convention, the Court first of all stated that: 'Whilst it is for the national court ... to find whether there was a practice [French: "usage"] ... the Court should nevertheless indicate the objective evidence which is needed in order to make such a determination.'

105. The Court went on to state that: 'There is a practice [French: "usage"] in the branch of trade or commerce in question in particular where a particular course of conduct is generally and regularly followed by operators in that branch when concluding contracts of a particular type.'

106. In so doing, the Court, anticipating, it might be said, the terms of the Convention of San Sebastian, which was not applicable at the time to the facts at issue, and which in 1989 explained that the usage to which reference is made should be 'widely known to, and regularly observed by, parties to contracts of the type involved in the particular [international] trade or commerce concerned,' relied broadly on that formula.

107. Therein lies the answer to the fourth question, whereby it should be

considered that a usage comes into being when a particular course of conduct is generally and regularly followed by operators in the branch concerned when concluding contracts of a particular type.

108. The eighth question asks the Court to state:

'whether the fact that many shippers and/or endorsees of bills of lading have challenged the validity of the clause by bringing an action before a court other than that designated by the clause itself is indicative of the fact that usage regarding the insertion of the clause in forms has not become well established.'

109. In inquiring about the consequences to be drawn from actions brought to challenge a practice (the incorporation of jurisdiction clauses in bills of lading), the Italian court necessarily recognises that this practice is regularly followed, since it has to be brought before the courts in order to dispute its application. It therefore accepts that such a practice does constitute a usage.

110. Whether this usage then becomes the object of disputes as to its application or even its very existence, to a greater or lesser extent, on a local, national, or international level (all elements that the order for reference does not allow to be determined) does not deprive it of its nature as a usage if it continues to be regularly followed in the branch of trade or commerce in question.

111. One could in fact say that the very principle of jurisdiction clauses in bills of lading is controversial in the field of maritime trade, to such an extent that the Hamburg Rules, mentioned above, go so far as to suppress their use. However, so long as these arguments have not been resolved, that is, in effect, notwithstanding the criticisms to which they are subjected, so long as the jurisdiction clauses at issue continue to be the practice generally and regularly followed by traders within the particular trade or commerce concerned when contracts of the same type are concluded, they will still retain their status as a usage.

112. My proposed response to the eighth question is therefore that, merely because a practice constitutive of a usage within the meaning of Article 17 of the Convention is contested, this cannot cause it to cease to constitute a usage.

113. Regarding the meaning of usage for the purposes of Article 17, the object of the tenth question is to determine whether or not 'the usage in question may derogate from mandatory statutory provisions of individual States, such as, in Italy, Article 1341 of the Civil Code which, with regard to the general contractual terms and conditions drawn up by one of the parties, provides that, in order for the usage to be valid, the other party must be or ought to have been aware of it and provides that clauses laying down particular limitations to or derogating from the jurisdiction of the courts must be specifically approved in writing'.

114. It seems to me that this question has two aspects.

115. The first seeks to determine whether it is permissible, within the framework of Article 17 of the Convention, to invoke a usage which would derogate from the legislative provisions, applicable in principle, relating to the form of clauses conferring jurisdiction. The response can only be affirmative, to my mind, since this is the entire purpose of Article 17 of the Convention: to give to the parties' wishes a value over and above any other rule applicable in principle, and in particular to the ordinary statutory provisions.

116. Article 1341 of the Italian Civil Code cannot therefore be invoked in order to subject the validity of the clause in question to mandatory provisions of national law in addition to those laid down in Article 17: 'Contracting States are not free to lay down formal requirements other than those contained in the Convention'.

117. The second aspect raised by this question is linked to that, examined hereafter in connection with the twelfth, fifth, thirteenth and fourteenth questions, of the parties' awareness of the usage in question.

International trade or commerce

118. The *MSG* judgment, cited above, also contains the answer to the ninth question from the Corte Suprema di Cassazione, concerning the geographical delimitation of the usage to which reference is made in Article 17. This question asks:

'whether the usage must exist in all the countries of the European Community, or whether the expression "international trade or commerce" is intended to mean that it is sufficient for the usage to be practised in those countries which, in the context of international trade or commerce, have traditionally played a prominent role'.

119. The reference to the form which accords with 'usages in international trade or commerce' does not in reality follow from either of the two alternatives put forward by the referring court.

120. Since '... whether a practice [French: "usage"] exists must not be determined by reference to the law of one of the Contracting Parties', the reference to 'international trade or commerce' cannot be understood as referring to specific countries, such as those which have a dominant position in international trade or commerce, or those requiring a convergent practice in all the States party to the Convention.

121. The Court considers that the existence of a usage should 'not be determined in relation to international trade or commerce in general, but [in relation] to the branch of trade or commerce in which the parties to the contract are operating'.

122. It would seem that this consideration is enough to dispel any possibility of national links.

123. The problem does not appear to me to be whether the national court should take account of a usage accepted in certain countries, rather than in the chosen country of jurisdiction for instance, or in certain countries, rather than in those which have an objective link with the dispute.

124. To the extent that the application of Article 17 necessarily presupposes an international factual context, it would first of all be clearly inappropriate to refer to what is usage in one or other of the signatory States, since transnational situations are precisely those envisaged. Nevertheless, if one were to investigate a 'connecting factor law' in order to determine whether, under that law, there is a usage, one would be accepting a step rejected by the Court in respect of the court chosen, for which, as I have

recalled, the Court requires no connecting link with either the parties or the contract.

125. That is why I consider that the reference made by the Court clearly covers a field of activity, that of 'the particular branch of trade or commerce in which the contracting parties operate', and not a national practice. In circumstances such as those in the present case for example, this means referring to usages followed in the branch of transport, or more specifically, as the case may be, in the branch of transport of consignments of fruit by sea.

126. In other words, the referring court will not in principle need to investigate, as its question suggests, whether it is the practice in the United Kingdom, for instance, or in certain other signatory States to the Convention, to put jurisdiction clauses on the reverse side of pre-printed bills of lading. On the other hand, the court will have to verify that such clauses do form a usage in the international carriage of consignments of fruit by sea.

127. It is unlikely that, in conducting this investigation, the court would find different usages in the same trade. If, however, that were to be the case, the criterion of 'usage within the branch of trade or commerce in question' would have to be combined with the criterion of knowledge of the parties of the usage, so as to give preponderant weight to the criterion based on usages which would not be unfamiliar to the contracting parties. I will return to this point when examining the questions relating to the parties' awareness of the usage in question.

128. Therefore, in response to the ninth question, it should be stated that the reference to usages in Article 17 of the Convention does not have any geographical or territorial character whatsoever, but, on the contrary, covers a field, of the trade or commerce in question: the 'particular trade or commerce in which the parties operate'. In this regard, it is for the national court to satisfy itself that the form of the jurisdiction clause corresponds with a usage governing the field of international trade or commerce in which the contracting parties operate.

129. It is for the national court, on the basis of the answers given for the purpose of defining the notion of usage referred to in Article 17, to determine whether, in the circumstances of the case, the reference to a jurisdiction clause, such as the one which it has to examine, on the reverse side of a bill of lading, corresponds to a 'form which accords with usages of international trade or commerce'.

130. If the court decides that this is not the case, the other questions are hardly of interest, since Article 17 of the Convention, in so far as it relates to usages, will no longer be applicable. It will then be for the court to verify, if need be, compliance with the other conditions of form of jurisdiction clauses permitted by the provision of the Convention in question. It would seem, though, that the Corte Suprema di Cassazione has already excluded the existence of a written agreement or an oral agreement evidenced in writing.

131. Should that court feel, on the other hand, that such a usage exists, the other questions, relating to the parties' awareness of it, will have to be considered.

IV - The parties' awareness of the usage in question (thirteenth, fourteenth, twelfth, fifth and sixth questions)

132. Five of the questions submitted to the Court concern the last condition for the validity of a jurisdiction clause within the meaning of the Article 17 at issue: the expression of the parties' awareness of the usage in question.

133. I will first try to identify the party whose awareness of such a usage is required (thirteenth question), before considering in detail the degree of awareness required of that party (fourteenth, twelfth and fifth questions), in order to ascertain, finally, whether the fact that the clause at issue amounts to an exemption clause is not evidence of the lack of awareness of the usage in question (sixth question).

134. The thirteenth question 'involves identifying the person who is or ought to have been aware of the usage; whether it must be the original shipper, even if he is a national of a non-Contracting State (such as, in this case, Argentina), or whether it is sufficient for it to be the endorsee of the bill, who is a national of a Contracting State (in the present case, Italy)'.

135. The question of identifying the party whose awareness of the usage is required is actually linked to that, already examined, of identifying the party whose consent to the clause affects its validity.

136. I have suggested to the Court, pursuant to the *Tilly Russ* judgment, cited above, that the clause in question should be held to be enforceable against parties who have succeeded, according to the applicable national law, to the rights and obligations of the original parties, where their consent to the clause may be presumed.

137. Similarly, the parties whose awareness of the usage is required must, it seems to me, necessarily be those having originally concluded the clause in question. Such a requirement cannot apply to each successor, of which there may be many, since a bill of lading can pass from hand to hand.

138. As the commentators state 'it is difficult to accept that the formal rules of the first paragraph of Article 17 are of such primary importance that they should be respected not only when agreeing the choice of jurisdiction, but also each time that one of the parties assigns to a third party the benefit of the contract containing a jurisdiction clause'.

139. Once again, where a third party succeeds to the rights and obligations of one of the original parties to an agreement containing a clause electing a court by virtue of the applicable law, the effects of this clause are transferred to this beneficiary, without its being necessary systematically to check compliance with each of the elements affecting the validity of the clause under the Convention.

140. The court still needs to ascertain that the rights and obligations of the original party have actually been transferred to the party seeking to rely on them, according to the relevant national provisions.

141. Therefore, it is sufficient to note that the parties whose awareness of the usage is required are the same as those whose consent to the clause affects its validity. Moreover, this follows expressly from *MSG*, in which it is stated that: '... consensus on the part of the contracting parties as to a jurisdiction clause is

presumed to exist where commercial practices in the relevant branch of international trade or commerce exist in this regard of which the parties are or ought to have been aware'.

142. As regards the fact that one of the original parties to the agreement was not a national of a State party to the Convention, this has no bearing on the question now being considered. The Convention makes no reference at all to the nationality of the persons to which it applies. On the other hand, importance is, of course, attached to the criterion of domicile for determining its application and the jurisdictions it establishes. As I have already pointed out, the application of Article 17 is precisely dependent on that criterion of domicile within a Contracting State. Since the Danish carrier was domiciled within a signatory State, the Argentinian nationality of the other party does not prevent the ascertainment, for the purposes of the application of Article 17, of its knowledge of the usage in question, as in the case of the Danish carrier.

143. This approach could be criticised for its lack of realism. I do not underestimate, however, the difficulties for the court seised to find a co-contracting party, as the case may be, as in this instance, who is a national of a third-party State, then to determine that party's awareness or otherwise of the usage in question. Such an approach could greatly delay the procedure. However, it seems to me that the very wording of Article 17 suggests that this kind of difficulty could be easily avoided if it is not required that the usage always be known to the parties but it is enough that it 'ought' to be.

144. The fourteenth question of the Corte Suprema di Cassazione is specifically directed at the clarification of this part of the wording of Article 17. It is 'concerned with whether the phrase "ought to have been aware" refers to a criterion of good faith and honesty when a particular contract was drawn up or to a criterion of ordinary care on the part of individuals who must be fully informed of current practices in international trade, for the purposes of paragraph 9, above.'

145. The Court's recent judgment in *MSG*, cited above, provides an answer to this question. The Court held that 'the actual or presumed knowledge [of] the usage by the contracting parties' could be established by two alternative methods: either by demonstrating that the 'parties had on previous occasions entered into agreements or had already contracted with other parties within the considered sector', or 'where, in that sector, a particular course of conduct is sufficiently well known because it is generally and regularly followed when a particular type of contract is concluded, with the result that it may be regarded as being a consolidated practice'.

146. This last limb of the alternative in particular, explaining that awareness of the usage is presumed in the case of economic agents operating in the branch under consideration in which this usage is generally and regularly followed, should permit the referring court to determine whether the usage in question ought to have been known by the original parties. It can undoubtedly be likened to the concept of 'ordinary care', put forward by the referring court, which one expects of an operator familiar with this particular area of international trade or commerce. I should also point out that it is precisely this notion of 'ordinary

care' to which the Court has referred in previous judgments, in the case of clauses that the party concerned could or should have been aware of by exercising ordinary care, or of usages which he should or could have been aware of.

147. Consequently, the questions about the ascertainment of parties' awareness of the usage are somewhat irrelevant, since Article 17 creates an actual presumption of awareness, which does not, by hypothesis, need to be verified.

148. The first of these questions is the twelfth question, which 'involves ascertaining whether the party concerned was or ought to have been aware of the usage, other than with regard to the condition set forth in paragraph 5, above, as regards the bill of lading itself, which contained numerous clauses appearing on the reverse (paragraph 2, above)'.

149. Besides the second question, to which it also refers, the fifth question 'concerns the form in which such consistent practice is publicised: must the form of bill of lading in which the jurisdiction clause appears to be lodged at a particular office (trade association, chamber of commerce, port authorities, and so on) for consultation or made public in some other way?'

150. In the absence of specific indications, I presume that the Italian court is implicitly referring to the Court's judgment in *Powell Duffryn*, cited above, in which the Court held that 'when [a] company's statutes contain a clause conferring jurisdiction, every shareholder is deemed to be aware of that clause and actually to consent to the assignment of jurisdiction for which it provides if the statutes are lodged in a place to which the shareholder may have access, such as the seat of the company, or are contained in a public register.'

151. The reference to the lodging of company statutes in a place accessible to the shareholders, or their mention in a public register, is easily explained in the circumstances of the case in point, where the shareholders, independently of the mode of acquisition of the shares, could have seen the clause at issue invoked against them.

152. In referring to usages, Article 17 cannot, however, be read as meaning that, in order for a given usage to be taken into account, it systematically requires publicity, in a written form, of this practice regularly followed in the area at issue, within associations or specialised bodies.

153. It is true that, normally, the form of the bills of lading used by shipping companies follow the guidelines issued by the international organisations such as Bimco (Baltic and International Maritime Conference), the ICS (International Chamber of Shipping) or by national associations such as Simprofrance (The French Committee for the simplification of international trade procedures).

154. However any such publicity can be no more than a means by which to prove the existence of a usage. As it is, the Convention does not place any limitation on the means of proof that may be put forward in order to establish the existence of a usage. It is, moreover, self-evident that the reference of the invoked usage in such lists can facilitate proof of its existence.

155. The twelfth question is also related to a question of proof, outside the scope of Article 17, which is for the national court alone, on the basis of the applicable law, to resolve.

156. It remains for me to examine the sixth question, which 'concerns the validity of the clause, even where, by virtue of the substantive rules applicable in the chosen court, it takes the form of a clause exempting the carrier from, or limiting, his liability.'

157. In the absence of specific indications in the order for reference, I must presume that the referring court has in mind the situation in which, in order to justify the non-enforceability of the clause against him, one of the parties invokes as a defence his lack of awareness of the usage in question, arguing that he would never have consented to a clause which would have been unfavourable to him.

158. However, even so understood, this question seems to be referring to the law applicable in the present case by virtue of the disputed clause, which stipulates that: 'The contract evidenced by this Bill of Lading shall be governed by English Law ...'. If this is the case, this aspect of the dispute cannot be resolved on the basis of the Convention, which is not designed to resolve conflicts of law. It is for the national court to determine whether, by virtue of the applicable law, the fact that the application of English law designated by the clause amounts to a clause excluding or limiting the liability of the carrier would suggest that the initial carrier could not have wished to agree to it.

159. In response to this question, I conclude, therefore, that the Convention is not applicable for the purpose of resolving problems relating to the conflict of laws.

Conclusion

160. For the foregoing reasons, I propose that the Court gives the following answers to the questions referred by the Corte Suprema di Cassazione:

(1) The third case mentioned in the second sentence of the first paragraph of Article 17 of the Brussels Convention of 27 September 1968 on Jurisdiction and the Enforcement of Judgments in Civil and Commercial Matters, as amended by the Convention of 9 October 1978 concerning the Accession of the Kingdom of Denmark, Ireland and the United Kingdom of Great-Britain and Northern Ireland, is to be interpreted as meaning that the conditions which it sets out are satisfied by a jurisdiction clause printed on the reverse side of a bill of lading where only the face is signed by the contracting parties, by which a jurisdiction without a particular link or objective connection with the parties or the bill of lading in which it is incorporated is chosen. The court before which the matter is brought, whether or not it is the court designated, has jurisdiction to rule on the validity, with regard to the conditions set out in Article 17, of such a clause conferring jurisdiction.

(2) Article 17, cited above, is to be interpreted as meaning that the enforceability of a clause conferring jurisdiction against parties who, under the applicable national law, in acquiring the bill of lading, have succeeded to the rights and obligations of the original parties, is subject to the validity of the said clause in the relationship between those original parties, which presupposes their consent. This consent is presumed to exist where the reference to such a clause

is in a form accepted by usages in the branch of international trade or commerce in question, and the same parties are, or ought to be aware of, those usages.

(3) It is for the national court to ascertain the existence of such a usage as well as awareness of it by the contracting parties. The reference to a clause conferring jurisdiction, inserted, without standing out prominently, amongst other clauses of which it forms part, on the reverse side of a bill of lading pre-printed in English, where only the face is signed, is a form according with usages in the branch of international carriage by sea of consignments of fruit, if such a reference constitutes a practice generally followed by contracting parties operating in the branch of international trade or commerce in question when concluding contracts of the same type. The fact that such a practice, if it constitutes a usage within the meaning of Article 17, is contested is not such as to cause it to cease to constitute a usage. The usage to which reference is so made cannot be affected by the application of contrary provisions of national law.

(4) There will be actual or presumed awareness of this usage by the contracting parties, professional traders in the branch of international trade or commerce in question, where, in this branch, a certain course of conduct is sufficiently known, by reason of the fact that it is generally and regularly followed in the conclusion of a certain type of contract, such as to be capable of being regarded as an established practice. The means by which this awareness or presumed awareness may be proved to the national court are those admissible under the applicable national law.

Annex: The preliminary questions submitted by the Corte Suprema di Cassazione

'1. The first question to be put to the Court of Justice is as follows:

In the case-law of the Court of Justice relating to the original wording of Article 17, reference has been made to the need to ascertain and protect the actual will of the parties with regard to the jurisdiction clause by means of the requirements laid down by that provision in respect of the validity of such clauses; that is also the case where the clause is adjudged valid, when the bill of lading containing the clause comes within the framework of a continuing business relationship between the parties, and it is thereby established that the relationship is governed by the general terms and conditions (drawn up by one of the parties, namely the carrier) containing that clause (see Case 71/83 *Tilly Russ* v *Nova* [1984] ECR 2417, which cites earlier judgments underscoring the need for the consent of the parties to be clearly and precisely demonstrated).

However, in the light of the insertion into the new wording of the provision of the reference to usage, which is prescriptive (and thus unconnected to the will of the parties, at least so far as specifically concerns a particular contract), the question arises whether the requirement of (actual) knowledge, or of lack of awareness arising out of negligent and inexcusable ignorance, is sufficient in view of the consistent incorporation (in all agreements similar to that in issue) of the jurisdiction clause. The question arises, in other words, whether it is any longer necessary to ascertain the will of the parties, despite the fact that Article

17 uses the word "concluded" [in the Italian version], which implies an expression of will and thus "commercial" usage (customary clauses).

2. The second question concerns the meaning of the expression "form which accords". The first aspect concerns the way in which the clause appears, that is whether it must necessarily be in writing signed by the party who has drawn it up and who has therefore expressed the intention of relying upon it - for example - by signing the bill of lading referring specifically to a clause which in turn refers to an agreement conferring exclusive jurisdiction, even in the absence of the signature of the other party (the shipper).

The second aspect consists in establishing whether it is necessary for the jurisdiction clause to stand out prominently on its own within the contract as a whole, or whether it is sufficient (and therefore of no consequence as regards the validity of the clause) for it to be inserted amongst numerous other clauses drawn up in order to regulate the contract of carriage in every respect.

The third aspect relates to the language in which the clause is drawn up, that is to say, whether it must be in some way related to the nationality of the parties to the contract or whether it is sufficient for it to be a language regularly used in international trade or commerce.

3. The third question is concerned with whether the designated court must, as well as being a court of a Contracting State, be in some way related to the nationality and/or the residence of the parties to the contract or to the place of performance and/or conclusion of the contract, or whether the first condition is sufficient without there being any other link with the substance of the relationship.

4. The fourth question concerns the process by which usage comes into being; that is, whether consistent incorporation of the clause in bills of lading issued by trade associations or a significant number of maritime transport undertakings is sufficient or whether it must be demonstrated that since users of such transport (whether traders or otherwise) have not made any observations or expressed reservations regarding consistent incorporation of the clause, they have tacitly acquiesced to the conduct of the other party, so that there may no longer be considered to be a dispute between them.

5. The fifth question concerns the form in which such consistent practice is publicised: must the form of bill of lading in which the jurisdiction clause appears be lodged at a particular office (trade association, chamber of commerce, port authorities, and so on) for consultation or made public in some other way?

6. The sixth question concerns the validity of the clause, even where, by virtue of the substantive rules applicable in the chosen court, it takes the form of a clause exempting the carrier from, or limiting, his liability.

7. The seventh question is concerned with whether the court (other than the chosen court) which has been called upon to assess the validity of the clause may examine the reasons for it, that is to say, the intention of the carrier in the choice of court made, as distinct from the court which would have had jurisdiction according to the usual criteria laid down in the Brussels Convention or by the lex fori.

8. The eighth question consists in ascertaining whether the fact that many

shippers and/or endorsees of bills of lading have challenged the validity of the clause by bringing an action before a court other than that designated by the clause itself is indicative of the fact that usage regarding the insertion of the clause in forms has not become well established.

9. The ninth question consists in ascertaining whether the usage must exist in all the countries of the European Community or whether the expression "international trade or commerce" is intended to mean that it is sufficient for the usage to be practised in those countries which, in the context of international trade or commerce, have traditionally played a prominent role.

10. The tenth question consists in ascertaining whether the usage in question may derogate from mandatory statutory provisions of individual States, such as, in Italy, Article 1341 of the Civil Code which, with regard to the general contractual terms and conditions drawn up by one of the parties, provides that, in order for the usage to be valid, the other party must be or ought to have been aware of it and provides that clauses laying down particular limitations to or derogating from the jurisdiction of the courts must be specifically approved in writing.

11. The eleventh question concerns the circumstances in which insertion of the clause in question in a standard form, not signed by the party not involved in drawing it up, may be considered to be grossly unfair or even abusive.

12. The twelfth question involves ascertaining whether the party concerned was or ought to have been aware of the usage, other than with regard to the condition set forth in paragraph 5, above, as regards the bill of lading itself, which contained numerous clauses appearing on the reverse (paragraph 2, above).

13. The thirteenth question involves identifying the person who is or ought to have been aware of the usage; whether it must be the original shipper, even if he is a national of a non-Contracting State (such as, in the present case, Argentina), or whether it is sufficient for it to be the endorsee of the bill, who is a national of a Contracting State (in the present case, Italy).

14. The fourteenth question is concerned with whether the phrase "ought to have been aware" refers to a criterion of good faith and honesty when a particular contract was drawn up or to a criterion of ordinary care on the part of individuals who must be fully informed of current practices in international trade, for the purposes of paragraph 9, above.'

Case C-387/98 - 9 November 2000

Coreck Maritime
v
Handelsveem and Others

Article 17 - Clause conferring jurisdiction - Formal conditions - Effects - Article 1 Protocol of interpretation of the Convention

Summary

1. The words 'have agreed' in the first sentence of the first paragraph of Article 17 of the Convention cannot be interpreted as meaning that it is necessary for a jurisdiction clause to be formulated in such a way that the competent court can be determined on its wording alone. It is sufficient that the clause state the objective factors on the basis of which the parties have agreed to choose a court or the courts to which they wish to submit disputes which have arisen or which may arise between them. Those factors, which must be sufficiently precise to enable the court seised to ascertain whether it has jurisdiction, may, where appropriate, be determined by the particular circumstances of the case.

2. The first paragraph of Article 17 of the Convention only applies if, first, at least one of the parties to the original contract is domiciled in a Contracting State and, secondly, the parties agree to submit any disputes to a court or the courts of a Contracting State.

3. A jurisdiction clause agreed between a carrier and a shipper which appears in a bill of lading enforceable against a third party bearer of the bill of lading. If he did not, it must be ascertained whether he accepted that clause having regard to the requirements laid down in the first paragraph of Article 17 of the Convention.

4. Under Article 1 of the Protocol, the Court has jurisdiction to give rulings on the interpretation of the Convention. The question which national law is applicable for the purposes of determining the rights and obligations of a third party bearer of a bill of lading is not one of intepretation of the Convention; it falls within the jurisdiction of the national court, which must apply its rules of private international law. Similarly, the question how to supply a lacuna in the applicable national law, apart from being hypothetical, is not one of the interpretation of the Convention.

JUDGMENT OF THE COURT

Edward, President of the Chamber, Jann and Sevón, Judges

1. By judgment of 23 October 1998, lodged at the Court on 29 October 1998, the Hoge Raad der Nederlanden (Supreme Court of the Netherlands) referred for a preliminary ruling under the Protocol of 3 June 1971 on the interpretation by the Court of Justice of the Convention of 27 September 1968 on Jurisdiction and the Enforcement of Judgments in Civil and Commercial Matters (hereinafter 'the Protocol') four questions on the interpretation of the first paragraph of Article 17 of the abovementioned Convention of 27 September 1968 (OJ 1972 L 299, p. 32), as amended by the Convention of 9 October 1978 on the Accession of the Kingdom of Denmark, Ireland and the United Kingdom of Great Britain and Northern Ireland (OJ 1978 L 304, p. 1, and - amended text - p. 77), by the Convention of 25 October 1982 on the Accession of the Hellenic Republic (OJ 1982 L 388, p. 1) and by the Convention of 26 May 1989 on the Accession of the Kingdom of Spain and the Portuguese Republic (OJ 1989 L 285, p. 1, hereinafter 'the Convention').

2. Those questions were raised in proceedings relating to the validity of a jurisdiction clause in bills of lading between Coreck Maritime GmbH, a company incorporated according to German law established in Hamburg, Germany, the issuer of the bills of lading (hereinafter 'Coreck') on the one hand, and Handelsveem BV, the holder in due course of the bills of lading, V. Berg and Sons Ltd and Man Producten Rotterdam BV, the owners of the cargo under the bills of lading, and The People's Insurance Company of China, the insurer of that cargo (hereinafter referred to collectively as 'Handelsveem') on the other.

The Convention

3. The first and second paragraphs of Article 17 of the Convention provide: 'If the parties, one or more of whom is domiciled in a Contracting State, have agreed that a court or the courts of a Contracting State are to have jurisdiction to settle any disputes which have arisen or which may arise in connection with a particular legal relationship, that court or those courts shall have exclusive jurisdiction. Such an agreement conferring jurisdiction shall be either:

(a) in writing or evidenced in writing; or

(b) in a form which accords with practices which the parties have established between themselves; or

(c) in international trade or commerce, in a form which accords with a usage of which the parties are or ought to have been aware and which in such trade or commerce is widely known to, and regularly observed by, parties to contracts of the type involved in the particular trade or commerce concerned.

Where such an agreement is concluded by parties, none of whom is domiciled in a Contracting State, the courts of other Contracting States shall have no jurisdiction over their disputes unless the court or courts chosen have declined jurisdiction.

The main proceedings

4. Consignments of groundnut kernels were transported from Qingdao in China to Rotterdam in the Netherlands in 1991 aboard a ship belonging to Sevryba, a company incorporated under Russian law established in Murmansk, Russia, pursuant to a contract of carriage concluded with the shipper by Coreck, the time charterer of the vessel.

5. Various bills of lading were issued by Coreck in respect of the carriage containing, inter alia, the following clauses: '3. Jurisdiction

Any dispute arising under this Bill of Lading shall be decided in the country where the carrier has his principal place of business and the law of such country shall apply except as provided elsewhere herein.

Identity of Carrier

The Contract evidenced by this Bill of Lading is between the Merchant and the Owner of the vessel named herein (or substitute) and it is therefore agreed that the said Shipowner only shall be liable for any damage or loss due to any breach or non-performance of any obligation arising out of the contract of carriage, whether or not relating to the vessel's seaworthiness. If, despite the foregoing, it is adjudged that any other is the Carrier and/or bailee of the goods shipped hereunder, all limitations of, and exonerations from, liability provided for by law or by this Bill of Lading shall be available to such other.

It is further understood and agreed that as the Line, Company or Agents who has [sic] executed this Bill of Lading for and on behalf of the Master is not a principal in the transaction, said Line, Company or Agents shall not be under any liability arising out of the contract of carriage, nor as Carrier or bailee of the goods.

6. The following words appeared on the face of the bills of lading: 'Coreck Maritime G.m.b.H.' Hamburg.

7. By a document of 5 March 1993, Handelsveem summoned Sevryba and Coreck, under Article 5(1) of the Convention, to appear before the Rechtbank (District Court) in Rotterdam - being the court for the area where the port of discharge designated in the bills of lading was situated - for an order for payment of compensation for the damage allegedly sustained by the cargo during transportation.

8. Coreck, relying on the jurisdiction clause in the bills of lading, claimed that that court did not have jurisdiction. In a judgment of 24 February 1995 the Rechtbank in Rotterdam held the clause to be inapplicable and declared that it did have jurisdiction on the ground that, in order for such a clause to be valid, it must be possible to ascertain the court having jurisdiction without difficulty, which was not the case here. On appeal by Coreck, the Gerechtshof (Regional Court of Appeal) in The Hague, in a judgment of 22 April 1997, upheld the decision given at first instance.

9. Coreck appealed to the Hoge Raad der Nederlanden, which decided to stay the proceedings and refer the following four questions to the Court for a preliminary ruling:

'1. Must the first sentence of Article 17 of the Brussels Convention (in particular, the words have agreed), read in conjunction with the case-law of the Court of Justice according to which the purpose of Article 17 is to ensure that the [consent of the] parties ... to such a clause, which derogates from the ordinary jurisdiction rules laid down in Articles 2, 5 and 6 of the Convention, ... is clearly and precisely demonstrated, be interpreted as meaning:

(a) that, in order for a clause vesting jurisdiction in a given court, as provided for in that article, to be valid as between the parties, it is necessary in each case for that clause to be formulated in such a way that its wording alone makes it quite clear, or at least easy to ascertain, (even) for persons other than the parties - and in particular to the court concerned - which court is to have jurisdiction to settle disputes arising from the legal relationship in the context of which that clause is stipulated; or

(b) that - generally or now, in consequence of or in connection with the progressive relaxation of the rules in Article 17 of the Brussels Convention, together with the case-law of the Court of Justice concerning the circumstances in which such a clause is to be regarded as having been validly concluded -in order for such a clause to be valid, it is enough that the parties themselves clearly know, on the basis (inter alia) of the (other) circumstances of the case, which court is to have jurisdiction to settle such disputes?

2. Does Article 17 of the Brussels Convention also govern the validity, as against a third party holding a bill of lading, of a clause which specifies as the forum having jurisdiction to settle disputes under this Bill of Lading the courts of the place where the carrier has his principal place of business and which is laid down in a bill of lading also containing an identity of carrier clause, that bill of lading being issued for the purposes of the carriage of goods, where (a) the shipper and one of the possible carriers are not established in a Contracting State and (b) the second possible carrier is indeed established in a Contracting State but it is not certain whether his principal place of business is situated in that State or in a State which is not a party to the Convention?

3. If the answer to Question 2 is in the affirmative:

(a) Does the fact that the jurisdiction clause contained in the bill of lading must be regarded as valid as between the carrier and the shipper mean that it is also binding on any third party holding the bill of lading, or is that the position only as regards a third party who, upon acquiring the bill of lading, succeeds by virtue of the applicable national law to the shipper's rights and obligations?

(b) Assuming that the jurisdiction clause contained in the bill of lading must be regarded as valid as between the carrier and the shipper, does the answer to the question whether it is also binding on a third party holding the bill of lading also possibly depend to some extent on the contents of the bill of lading and/or the particular circumstances of the case, such as the particular state of knowledge of the third party concerned or the fact that the latter has a long-standing business relationship with the carrier and, if so, can the third party be deemed to be aware of the particular circumstances of the case if the contents of the bill of lading do not make it sufficiently clear to him that the clause in question is valid?

4. If the answer to Question 3(a) is as just suggested, which national law governs the decision as to whether the third party, upon acquiring the bill of lading, succeeded to the shipper's rights and obligations, and what is the position if the national law in question has not hitherto provided, either in its legislation or in its case-law, an answer to the question whether the third party, upon acquiring the bill of lading, succeeds to the shipper's rights and obligations?

The first question

10. As regards the first question, the national court essentially asks whether the words 'have agreed in the first sentence of the first paragraph of Article 17 of the Convention must be interpreted as meaning that the jurisdiction clause must be formulated in such a way that it is possible to identify the court having jurisdiction on its wording alone.

11. Handelsveem considers that that question must be answered in the affirmative, given the particular need for legal certainty where the choice of forum is concerned. The Italian and Netherlands Governments for their part emphasise how important it is that the court chosen by the parties be identified clearly and precisely, so that the court seised can determine whether it is has jurisdiction.

12. On the other hand, Coreck, the United Kingdom Government and the Commission argue that it is sufficient that the court having jurisdiction be identifiable from the wording of the clause considered in the light of the actual circumstances of the individual case.

13. The Court has held that, by making the validity of a jurisdiction clause subject to the existence of an 'agreement between the parties, Article 17 of the Convention imposes on the court before which the matter is brought the duty of examining first whether the clause conferring jurisdiction upon it was in fact the subject of consensus between the parties, which must be clearly and precisely demonstrated, and that the purpose of the requirements as to form imposed by Article 17 is to ensure that consensus between the parties is in fact established (Case 24/76 *Estasis Salotti* v *RÜWA* [1976] ECR 1831, paragraph 7, Case 25/76 *Segoura* v *Bonakdarian* [1976] ECR 1851, paragraph 6, and Case C-106/95 *MSG* v *Gravières Rhénanes* [1997] ECR 1-911, paragraph 15).

14. However, if the purpose of Article 17 of the Convention is to protect the wishes of the parties concerned, it must be construed in a manner

consistent with those wishes where they are established. Article 17 is based on a recognition of the independent will of the parties to a contract in deciding which courts are to have jurisdiction to settle disputes falling within the scope of the Convention, other than those which are expressly excluded pursuant to the fourth paragraph of Article 17 (Case 23/78 *Meeth* v *Glacetal* [1978] ECR 2133, paragraph 5).

15. It follows that the words 'have agreed in the first sentence of the first paragraph of Article 17 of the Convention cannot be interpreted as meaning that it is necessary for a jurisdiction clause to be formulated in such a way that the competent court can be determined on its wording alone. It is sufficient that the clause state the objective factors on the basis of which the parties have agreed to choose a court or the courts to which they wish to submit disputes which have arisen or which may arise between them. Those factors, which must be sufficiently precise to enable the court seised to ascertain whether it has jurisdiction, may, where appropriate, be determined by the particular circumstances of the case.

The second question

16. By its second question, the national court asks about the conditions of application of the first paragraph of Article 17 of the Convention. It essentially asks whether that provision applies if the jurisdiction clause designates the court for the area where one of the parties to the original contract has its principal place of business but it is not proven that that place of business is situated in a Contracting State.

17. As the wording of the first sentence of the first paragraph of Article 17 of the Convention itself makes clear, that provision only applies where the twofold condition is satisfied that, first, at least one of the parties to the contract is domiciled in a Contracting State and, secondly, the jurisdiction clause designates a court or the courts of a Contracting State. So, that rule, which owes its existence to the fact that the Convention is intended to facilitate the mutual recognition and enforcement of judicial decisions, lays down a requirement as to precision which the jurisdiction clause must satisfy.

18. In relation to the first condition, the first paragraph of Article 53 of the Convention provides that the seat of a company is to be treated as its domicile for the purposes of the Convention. Under that provision, the court seised must, in order to determine that seat, apply its rules of private international law. Consequently, the criteria for identifying the seat of a legal

person and particularly for determining the significance of the principal place of business in that process must be established by the national law which is applicable under the conflict of laws rules of the court seised.

19. As to the second condition, Article 17 of the Convention does not apply to clauses designating a court in a third country. A court situated in a Contracting State must, if it is seised notwithstanding such a jurisdiction clause, assess the validity of the clause according to the applicable law, including conflict of laws rules, where it sits (Report by Professor Schlosser on the Convention of 9 October 1978 on the Accession of the Kingdom of Denmark, Ireland and the United Kingdom of Great Britain and Northern Ireland to the Convention on Jurisdiction and the enforcement of judgments in Civil and Commercial matters and to the Protocol on its interpretation by the Court of Justice, OJ 1979 C 59, p. 71, paragraph 176).

20. Furthermore, it is settled case-law that the validity of a jurisdiction clause under Article 17 of the Convention must be assessed by reference to the relationship between the parties to the original contract (see to that end Case 71/83 *Tilly Russ* v *Nova* [1984] ECR 2417, paragraph 24, and Case C-159/97 *Castelletti* v *Trumpy* [1999] ECR I-1597, paragraphs 41 and 42). It follows that it is in relation to those parties, which it is for the national court to identify, that the conditions of application of Article 17 of the Convention must be assessed. The circumstances in which a jurisdiction clause may be enforced against a person who was not privy to the original contract are the subject-matter of the third question, which is considered below.

21. That being so, the reply to the second question must be that the first paragraph of Article 17 of the Convention only applies if, first, at least one of the parties to the original contract is domiciled in a Contracting State and, secondly, the parties agree to submit any disputes to a court or the courts of a Contracting State.

The third question

22. By its third question, the national court essentially asks whether a jurisdiction clause which has been agreed between a carrier and a shipper and appears in a bill of lading is valid as against any third party bearer of the bill of lading or whether it is only valid as against a third party bearer of the bill of lading who succeeded by virtue of the applicable national law to the shipper's rights and obligations when he acquired the bill of lading.

23. It is sufficient to note that the Court has held that, in so far as the jurisdiction clause incorporated in a bill of lading is valid under Article 17 of the Convention as between the shipper and the carrier, it can be pleaded against the third party holding the bill of lading so long as, under the relevant national law, the holder of the bill of lading succeeds to the shipper's rights and obligations (*Tilly Russ*, paragraph 24, and *Castelletti*, paragraph 41).

24. It follows that the question whether a party not privy to the original contract against whom a jurisdiction clause is relied on has succeeded to the rights and obligations of one of the original parties must be determined according to the applicable national law.

25. If he did, there is no need to ascertain whether he accepted the jurisdiction clause in the original contract. In such circumstances, acquisition of the bill of lading could not confer upon the third party more rights than those attaching to the shipper under it. The third party holding the bill of lading thus becomes vested with all the rights, and at the same time becomes subject to all the obligations, mentioned in the bill of lading, including those relating to the agreement on jurisdiction (*Tilly Russ*, paragraph 25).

26. On the other hand, if, under the applicable national law, the party not privy to the original contract did not succeed to the rights and obligations of one of the original parties, the court seised must ascertain, having regard to the requirements laid down in the first paragraph of Article 17 of the Convention, whether he actually accepted the jurisdiction clause relied on against him.

27. Accordingly, the reply to the third question must be that a jurisdiction clause agreed between a carrier and a shipper which appears in a bill of lading is enforceable against a third party bearer of the bill of lading if he succeeded to the rights and obligations of the shipper under the applicable national law when he acquired the bill of lading. If he did not, it must be ascertained whether he accepted that clause having regard to the requirements laid down in the first paragraph of Article 17 of the Convention.

The fourth question

28. By its fourth question, the national court is essentially asking what the applicable national law is for the purposes of determining the rights and obligations of a third party bearer of a bill of lading and, in the event that

the relevant national law provides no solution, what are the rules which should be applied.

29. Under Article 1 of the Protocol, the Court has jurisdiction to give rulings on the interpretation of the Convention.

30. The question which national law is applicable for the purposes of determining the rights and obligations of a third party bearer of a bill of lading is not one of interpretation of the Convention; it falls within the jurisdiction of the national court, which must apply its rules of private international law.

31. Similarly, the question how to supply a lacuna in the applicable national law, apart from being hypothetical, is not one of the interpretation of the Convention.

32. It follows that the fourth question is inadmissible.

On those grounds, the Court, in answer to the questions referred to it by the Hoge Raad der Nederlanden by judgment of 23 October 1998, hereby rules:

The first paragraph of Article 17 of the Convention of 27 September 1968 on Jurisdiction and the Enforcement of Judgments in Civil and Commercial Matters, as amended by the Convention of 9 October 1978 on the Accession of the Kingdom of Denmark, Ireland and the United Kingdom of Great Britain and Northern Ireland, by the Convention of 25 October 1982 on the Accession of the Hellenic Republic and by the Convention of 26 May 1989 on the Accession of the Kingdom of Spain and the Portuguese Republic, must be interpreted as follows:

1. It does not require that a jurisdiction clause be formulated in such a way that the competent court can be determined on its wording alone. It is sufficient that the clause state the objective factors on the basis of which the parties have agreed to choose a court or the courts to which they wish to submit disputes which have arisen or which may arise between them. Those factors, which must be sufficiently precise to enable the court seised to ascertain whether it has jurisdiction, may, where appropriate, be determined by the particular circumstances of the case.

2. It applies only if, first, at least one of the parties to the original contract is domiciled in a Contracting State and, secondly, the parties agree to submit any disputes before a court or the courts of a Contracting State.

3. A jurisdiction clause agreed between a carrier and a shipper which appears in a bill of lading is enforceable against a third party bearer of the bill of lading if he succeeded to the rights and obligations of the shipper under the applicable national law when he acquired the bill of lading. If he did not, it must be ascertained whether he accepted that clause having regard to the requirements laid down in the first paragraph of Article 17 of the Convention, as amended.*

* Opinion of AG not yet available in English.

TITLE II *[Chapter II]*

JURISDICTION *[Jurisdiction]*

Prorogation of jurisdiction by appearance – Article 18 *[Article 24]*

See also

Case 150/80 - 24 June 1981

Elefanten Schuh GmbH
v
Pierre Jacqmain

Articles 17 and 18 - Appearance of the defendant before the court seised - Agreement conferring jurisdiction designating another court - Effect - Prorogation of jurisdiction - Article 18 - Appearance of the defendant before the court seised - Challenge as to jurisdiction and defence on the substance - Appearance not conferring jurisdiction - Conditions - Article 17 - Prorogation of jurisdiction - Agreements conferring jurisdiction - Formal requirements - Rules of the Convention - Stipulation by a Contracting State of other requirements - Not permissible - Application to provisions on languages.

Summary

1. Article 18 of the Convention of 27 September 1968 on Jurisdiction and the Enforcement of Judgments in Civil and Commercial Matters applies even where the parties have by agreement designated a court which is to have jurisdiction within the meaning of Article 17 of that Convention.

2. Article 18 of the Convention of 27 September 1968 must be interpreted as meaning that the rule on jurisdiction which that provision lays down does not apply where the defendant not only contests the court's jurisdiction but also makes submissions on the substance of the action, provided that if the challenge to jurisdiction is not preliminary to any defence as to the substance it does not occur after the making of the submissions which under national procedural law are considered to be the first defence addressed to the court seised.

3. Since the aim of Article 17 of the Convention is to lay down the formal requirements which agreements conferring jurisdiction must meet, Contracting States are not free to lay down formal requirements other than those contained in the Convention. When those rules are applied to provisions concerning the language to be used in an agreement conferring jurisdiction they imply that the legislation of a Contracting State may not allow the validity of such an agreement to be called in question solely on the ground that the language used is not that prescribed by that legislation.

JUDGMENT OF THE COURT

Mertens de Wilmars, President, Pescatore, Lord Mackenzie Stuart, Koopmans, O'Keeffe, Bosco, Due, Everling and Chloros, Judges

1. By judgment dated 9 June 1980 which was received at the Court on 24 June 1980 the Cour de Cassation [Court of Cassation] of Belgium referred to the Court for a preliminary ruling under the Protocol of 3 June 1971 on the Interpretation by the Court of Justice of the Convention of 27 September 1968 on Jurisdiction and the Enforcement of Judgments in Civil and Commercial Matters several questions as to the interpretation of Articles 17, 18 and 22 of that Convention.

2. Those questions were put in the context of an appeal in cassation against a judgment of the Arbeidshof Antwerpen [Labour Court, Antwerp] ordering Elefanten Schuh GmbH, a company incorporated under German law, and Elefant NV, a company incorporated under Belgian law, to pay jointly the sum of BFR 3 120 597 together with interest to Mr Pierre Jacqmain for having *inter alia* dismissed Mr Jacqmain without notice.

3. It appears from the papers placed before the Court that in 1970 Mr Jacqmain was employed as a sales agent by the German company Hoffmann GmbH which subsequently adopted the name Elefanten Schuh GmbH; however, he actually worked in Belgium, in particular in the provinces of Antwerp, Brabant and Limburg, on instructions which he received from the Belgian subsidiary of that undertaking, Elefant NV. The main action arose as a result of difficulties which occurred in 1975 between Mr Jacqmain and the two companies concerning details of the transfer of the contract of employment from the German company to the Belgian company.

4. Mr Jacqmain brought an action in the Arbeidsrechtbank Antwerpen [Labour Tribunal, Antwerp] against the two companies. The defendant companies appeared before that court and by their first submissions they contested the substance of the applications lodged against them. In further submissions lodged nine months later the German company claimed that the Arbeidsrechtbank did not have jurisdiction on the ground that the contract of employment contained a clause stipulating that the court at Kleve in the Federal Republic of Germany was to have exclusive jurisdiction in the event of any dispute. The Arbeidsrechtbank dismissed that objection. It took the view that such a clause could not derogate from Article 627 of the Belgian Judicial Code which in disputes of this kind provides that the court of the place where the occupation is pursued is to have jurisdiction.

5. The Arbeidshof Antwerpen, to which an appeal from the judgment of the Arbeidsrechtbank was made, considered that pursuant to Article 17 of the Brussels Convention of 27 September 1968 the parties to the contract of employment could confer territorial jurisdiction on the court of Kleve by agreeing in writing to derogate from the rules on territorial jurisdiction contained in the Belgian Judicial Code. However, the Arbeidshof held that the German company could not rely on the jurisdiction clause on the ground that the contract of employment had to be written in Dutch by virtue of Article 10 of the Decree of 19 July 1973 governing the use of languages in relations between employers and employees, adopted by the Cultuurraad voor Nederlandse Cultuurgemeenschap [Culture Council for the Netherlands Cultural Community] (Moniteur Belge, p. 10089). The Arbeidshof took the view that Article 10, which provides that any act or document not written in Dutch is null and void, applies to documents drawn up before the decree entered into force. Consequently the contract of employment, drawn up in German, was null and void and the clause conferring jurisdiction contained therein was invalid.

6. The appeal in cassation lodged against the judgment of the Arbeidshof by the Belgian company was declared inadmissible by the Hof van Cassatie [Court of Cassation]. As the appeal in cassation lodged by the German company concerned the validity of the jurisdiction clause in particular the Hof van Cassatie decided in view of Article 17 of the Brussels Convention to put three questions to the Court of Justice.

Question 1

7. Question 1 is worded as follows: '1. (a) Is Article 18 of the Convention of 27 September 1968 on Jurisdiction and the Enforcement of Judgments in Civil and Commercial Matters applicable if parties have agreed to confer jurisdiction on a court within the meaning of Article 17? (b) Is the rule on jurisdiction contained in Article 18 applicable if the defendant has not only contested jurisdiction but has in addition made submissions on the action itself? (c) If it is, must jurisdiction then be contested *in limine litis?*'

8. Articles 17 and 18 form Section 6 of Title II of the Convention which deals with prorogation of jurisdiction; Article 17 concerns jurisdiction by consent and Article 18 jurisdiction implied from submission as a result of the defendant's appearance. The first part of the question seeks to determine the relationship between those two types of prorogation.

9. In the first sentence, Article 18 of the Convention lays down the rule that a court of a Contracting State before whom a defendant enters an appearance is to have jurisdiction and in the second sentence it provides that that rule is not to apply where appearance was entered solely in order to contest the jurisdiction, or where another court has exclusive jurisdiction by virtue of Article 16 of the Convention.

10. The case envisaged in Article 17 is not, therefore, one of the exceptions which Article 18 allows to the rule which it lays down. Moreover, neither the general scheme nor the objectives of the Convention provide grounds for the view that the parties to an agreement conferring jurisdiction within the meaning of Article 17 are prevented from voluntarily submitting their dispute to a court other than that stipulated in the agreement.

11. It follows that Article 18 of the Convention applies even where the parties have by agreement designated a court which is to have jurisdiction within the meaning of Article 17.

12. The second and third parts of the question envisage the case in which the defendant has appeared before a court within the meaning of Article 18 but contests the jurisdiction of that court.

13. The Hof van Cassatie first asks if Article 18 has application where

the defendant makes submissions as to the jurisdiction of the court as well as on the substance of the action.

14. Although differences between the different language versions of Article 18 of the Convention appear when it is sought to determine whether, in order to exclude the jurisdiction of the court seised, a defendant must confine himself to contesting that jurisdiction, or whether he may on the contrary still achieve the same purpose by contesting the jurisdiction of the court as well as the substance of the claim, the second interpretation is more in keeping with the objectives and spirit of the Convention. In fact, under the law of civil procedure of certain Contracting States a defendant who raises the issue of jurisdiction and no other might be barred from making his submissions as to the substance if the court rejects his plea that it has no jurisdiction. An interpretation of Article 18 which enabled such a result to be arrived at would be contrary to the right of the defendant to defend himself in the original proceedings, which is one of the aims of the Convention.

15. However, the challenge to jurisdiction may have the result attributed to it by Article 18 only if the plaintiff and the court seised of the matter are able to ascertain from the time of the defendant's first defence that it is intended to contest the jurisdiction of the court.

16. The Hof van Cassatie asks in this regard whether jurisdiction must be contested *in limine litis*. For the purposes of interpreting the Convention that concept is difficult to apply in view of the appreciable differences existing between the legislation of the Contracting States with regard to bringing actions before courts of law, the appearance of defendants and the way in which the parties to an action must formulate their submissions. However, it follows from the aim of Article 18 that if the challenge to jurisdiction is not preliminary to any defence as to the substance it may not in any event occur after the making of the submissions which under national procedural law are considered to be the first defence addressed to the court seised.

17. Therefore, the answer to the second and third parts of Question 1 should be that Article 18 of the Convention must be interpreted as meaning that the rule on jurisdiction which that provision lays down does not apply where the defendant not only contests the court's jurisdiction but also makes submissions on the substance of the action, provided that, if the challenge to jurisdiction is not preliminary to any defence as to the substance, it does not occur after the making of the submissions which under national procedural law are considered to be the first defence addressed to the court seised.

Question 2

18. Question 2 is as follows: '2. (a) In application of Article 22 of the Convention, can related actions which, had they been brought separately, would have had to be brought before courts of different Contracting States, be brought simultaneously before one of those courts, provided that the law of that court permits the consolidation of related actions and that court has jurisdiction over both actions? (b) Is that also the case if the parties to one of the disputes which have given rise to the actions have agreed, in accordance with Article 17 of the Convention, that a court of another Contracting State is to have jurisdiction to settle that dispute?'

19. Article 22 of the Convention is intended to establish how related actions which have been brought before courts of different Member States are to be dealt with. It does not confer jurisdiction; in particular, it does not accord jurisdiction to a court of a Contracting State to try an action which is related to another action of which that court is seised pursuant to the rules of the Convention.

20. The answer to Question 2 should, therefore, be that Article 22 of the Convention applies only where related actions are brought before courts of two or more Contracting States.

Question 3

21. The final question is worded as follows: '3. Does it conflict with Article 17 of the Convention to rule that an agreement conferring jurisdiction on a court is void if the document in which the agreement is contained is not drawn up in the language which is prescribed by the law of a Contracting State upon penalty of nullity and if the court of the State before which the agreement is relied upon is bound by that law to declare the document to be void of its own motion?'

22. From that wording it appears that the Hof van Cassatie is solely concerned with the validity of an agreement conferring jurisdiction which is rendered void by the national legislation of the court seised as having been written in a language other than that prescribed by that legislation.

23. Article 17 stipulates that the agreement conferring jurisdiction must take the form of an agreement in writing or an oral agreement evidenced in writing.

24. According to the Report on the Convention submitted to the Governments of the Contracting States at the same time as the draft Convention those formal requirements were inserted out of the concern not to impede commercial practice, yet at the same time to cancel out the effects of clauses in contracts which might go unread, such as clauses in printed forms for business correspondence or in invoices, if they were not agreed to by the party against whom they operate. For those reasons jurisdiction clauses should be taken into consideration only if they are the subject of a written agreement, and that implies the consent of all the parties. Furthermore, the draftsmen of Article 17 were of the opinion that, in order to ensure legal certainty, the formal requirements applicable to agreements conferring jurisdiction should be expressly prescribed.

25. Article 17 is thus intended to lay down itself the formal requirements which agreements conferring jurisdiction must meet; the purpose is to ensure legal certainty and that the parties have given their consent.

26. Consequently, Contracting States are not free to lay down formal requirements other than those contained in the Convention. That is confirmed by the fact that the second paragraph of Article 1 of the Protocol annexed to the Convention expressly prescribes special requirements of form with regard to persons domiciled in Luxembourg.

27. When those rules are applied to provisions concerning the language to be used in an agreement conferring jurisdiction they imply that the legislation of a Contracting State may not allow the validity of such an agreement to be called in question solely on the ground that the language used is not that prescribed by that legislation.

28. Moreover, any different interpretation would run counter to Article 17 of the Convention the very purpose of which is to enable a court of a Contracting State to be chosen by agreement where that court, if not so chosen, would not normally have jurisdiction. That choice must, therefore, be respected by the courts of all the Contracting States.

29. Consequently, the answer to Question 3 must be that Article 17 of the Convention must be interpreted as meaning that the legislation of a Contracting State may not allow the validity of an agreement conferring jurisdiction to be called in question solely on the ground that the language used is not that prescribed by that legislation.

On those grounds, the Court, in answer to the questions referred to it by the Hof van Cassatie by judgment of 9 June 1980, hereby rules:

1. Article 18 of the Convention of 27 September 1968 on Jurisdiction and the Enforcement of Judgments in Civil and Commercial Matters applies even where the parties have by agreement designated a court which is to have jurisdiction within the meaning of Article 17 of that Convention.

2. Article 18 of the Convention of 27 September 1968 must be interpreted as meaning that the rule on jurisdiction which that provision lays down does not apply where the defendant not only contests the court's jurisdiction but also makes submissions on the substance of the action, provided that, if the challenge to jurisdiction is not preliminary to any defence as to the substance, it does not occur after the making of the submissions which under national procedural law are considered to be the first defence addressed to the court seised.

3. Article 22 of the Convention of 27 September 1968 applies only where related actions are brought before courts of two or more Contracting States.

4. Article 17 of the Convention of 27 September 1968 must be interpreted as meaning that the legislation of a Contracting State may not allow the validity of an agreement conferring jurisdiction to be called in question solely on the ground that the language used is not that prescribed by that legislation.

OPINION OF ADVOCATE GENERAL SIR GORDON SLYNN

This case was referred to the Court by the Hof van Cassatie, Brussels by order dated 9 June 1980 in accordance with Article 3 of the Protocol of 3 June 1971 on the Interpretation of the Convention of 27 September 1968 on Jurisdiction and the Enforcement of Civil and Commercial Judgments ('the Convention'). It concerns three articles of the Convention: Articles 17 and 18, on prorogation of jurisdiction; and Article 22, on the consolidation of related actions.

The appellant in the proceedings before the court making the reference, Elefanten Schuh GmbH, is a company incorporated under German law. I refer to the appellant as 'the German Company'. It maintains its registered office in Kleve and is engaged in the shoe business. The respondent, Pierre Jacqmain, lives in Schoten in Belgium.

On 1 February 1970 the German Company engaged Mr Jacqmain as its commercial representative in Belgium (other than the provinces of Luxembourg, Namur and Hainaut). This Court has not seen the contract of employment but it is common ground that this was written in German and that it provided that any disputes arising thereunder would fall within the exclusive jurisdiction of the courts of Kleve in Germany.

From some time in 1974 Mr Jacqmain's basic salary was paid by Elefant NV, the appellant's Belgian associate which I refer to as 'the Belgian Company'. From the end of 1974 the Belgian Company paid his commission also. From 1 September 1975, he worked under the authority, direction and control of the Belgian Company. In December 1975 he was dismissed without notice.

Mr Jacqmain then instituted proceedings against the German and the Belgian Companies in the Arbeidsrechtbank at Antwerp. He put his claim under Belgian law. He sought damages for the termination of his contract under Article 20 of the Royal Decree of 20 July 1955, (M.B. 3-4 October 1955) and compensation for the extinction of his franchise pursuant to Article 15 of the Law of 30 July 1963, (M.B. 7 August 1963) together with cost of living increases, interest, pay for annual and public holidays and reimbursement of telephone charges.

The German Company contended that the Arbeidsrechtbank was without jurisdiction, in view of the choice of forum clause in the contract employment. The tribunal rejected this argument, basing its rejection on Articles 627 (9) and 630 of the Belgian Judicial Code. The former confers exclusive jurisdiction in labour disputes on the court or tribunal for the place in which the enterprise in question conducts its business or in which the relevant professional or commercial activity is conducted. The latter provides that any agreement contrary to Article 627 shall be null and void.

The Arbeidsrechtbank also rejected an argument, advanced by the Belgian Company, that Mr Jacqmain's contract was with the German Company alone. Citing many authorities, it took the view that under Belgian law any person under whose authority, direction or control an employee works, for reward, is treated as a party to his contract of employment; and concluded that in the circumstances of the case the German and the Belgian Companies shared liability jointly and severally. It awarded Mr Jacqmain damages amounting to BFR 3 064 160 plus interest, together with ancillary relief.

The two companies appealed to the Arbeidshof at Antwerp, where they relied again on the choice of forum clause in the contract of employment. That court accepted that Article 17 of the Convention authorizes the parties to a written contract to confer jurisdiction on a court of a Contracting State, even in the face of Articles 627 (9) and 630 of the Belgian Judicial Code. Nevertheless, it dismissed the companies' contention that the Belgian courts had no jurisdiction. It found that the written contract of employment between Mr Jacqmain and the appellant was void because it did not comply with Articles 5 and 10 of a Decree made by the Cultural Council of the Dutch-speaking Community governing the use of languages on 19 July 1973. Article 5 provides that employers of any persons working in the Dutch-speaking areas of Belgium shall use the Dutch language in all documents addressed to their staff or prescribed by law (including, it seems, contracts of employment). Article 10 provides that any document which fails to comply with the foregoing provisions shall be null and void. On the substance of the case, the court upheld the judgment of the Arbeidsrechtbank, with only a minor modification.

The two companies sought to appeal further to the Hof van Cassatie. That court ruled that the Belgian Company's appeal was inadmissible because it was out of time.

The Hof van Cassatie was of the opinion, in favour of the German Company, that a clause in a contract whereby the parties agree to submit disputes to a particular court could not be affected by rules adopted by a Member State concerning relations between employers and employees, since Article 17 of the Convention of 27 September 1968 applied in a uniform manner in all Contracting States.

It was, however, contended on behalf of Mr Jacqmain that the Arbeidsrechtbank at Antwerp had jurisdiction under Article 18 of the Convention because the appellant had entered an appearance before that tribunal for the purpose of making submissions both on jurisdiction and on the substance of the case.

Furthermore, Mr Jacqmain's representative questioned whether it was open to the German Company to invoke the choice of forum clause, since the proceedings were originally instituted against two companies, one of which (the Belgian Company) was not a party to the contract in which that clause was contained. It was suggested that, since the proceedings against the Belgian Company were admissible, Mr Jacqmain could rely, as against the German company, on Article 22 of the Convention. This envisages that whenever related actions are brought in courts of different Contracting States, any court other than the one first seised may decline jurisdiction if the law of its own State permits the consolidation of related actions and the court first seised has jurisdiction over both actions. Belgian law, specifically Articles 566 and 634 of the Judicial Code, permits the consolidation of related actions.

In the light of the issues raised the Hof van Cassatie referred to this Court six questions.

The *first* reads as follows: '1. (a) Is Article 18 of the Convention of 27 September 1968 on Jurisdiction and the Enforcement of Judgments in Civil and Commercial Matters applicable if the parties have agreed to confer jurisdiction on a court within the meaning of Article 17?'

Articles 17 and 18, so far as relevant to this case read as follows: '17. If the parties, one or more of whom is domiciled in a Contracting State, have, by agreement in writing or by an oral agreement evidenced in writing, agreed that a court or the courts of a Contracting State are to have jurisdiction to settle any disputes which have arisen or which may arise in connection with particular legal relationship, that court or those courts shall have exclusive jurisdiction.
Agreements conferring jurisdiction shall have no legal force if they are contrary to the provisions of Article 12 or 15, or if the courts whose jurisdiction they purport to exclude have exclusive jurisdiction by virtue of Article 16'.

'18. Apart from jurisdiction derived from other provisions of this Convention, a court of a Contracting State before whom a defendant enters an appearance shall have jurisdiction. This rule shall not apply where appearance was entered solely to contest the jurisdiction, or where another court has exclusive jurisdiction by virtue of Article 16'.

The Commission and the Government of the United Kingdom, contend in their observations to this Court, that this question must be answered in the affirmative. I am of the same opinion.

It seems to me that the opening words of Article 18 'apart from' in the English version, 'outre les cas' in the French version, clearly indicate that a basis of jurisdiction is being established by the Article which is additional to those derived from the provisions of the Convention. It is not limited to situations where jurisdictions not otherwise derived from the Convention. The German and Italian versions I believe to give the same indication.

The jurisdiction established by Article 18 is stated not to apply where another court has exclusive jurisdiction under Article 16. There is no such express reservation in respect of Article 17 and I can see no reason to imply one. One would not expect Articles 17 and 18 to be mutually exclusive and in the alternative, since they represent two ways in which a party may consent to jurisdiction, the one by contract, the other by the act of entering an appearance.

That this is the right approach to the interpretation of the Convention may, as is suggested in the observations submitted to the Court, receive support from the fact that, in a number of bilateral conventions between Member States which are specified in the observations, it is assumed or accepted that the entry of appearance by a defendant may confer jurisdiction even where the parties have agreed to submit their disputes to another forum. It is my understanding that this principle is also accepted in the national laws of many, if not all, of the Member States.

The *second* question posed by the Hof van Cassatie reads as follows: 'Is the rule on jurisdiction contained in Article 18 applicable if the defendant has not only contested jurisdiction but has in addition made submissions on the action itself?'

This question appears to arise from the fact, as I understand it to be, that in the Dutch, as in the German and the Italian, versions the second sentence of Article 18 contains words to the same effect as in the English version, namely that jurisdiction is not conferred if appearance is entered 'solely to contest the jurisdiction'. These words would suggest that the defendant must have entered appearance for no other purpose than to contest the jurisdiction. If there is an additional, albeit a subsidiary purpose, then the first sentence of Article 18 continues to apply. On the other hand the French text reads 'Cette règle n'est pas applicable si la comparution a pour objet de contester la compétence'. There is no equivalent of the word 'solely'. I understand that the Irish text is to the same effect.

It can, of course, be argued that properly construed these words in the French version produce the same result and that the intention is that the appearance must be entered only to contest the jurisdiction. I am not satisfied that this is necessarily so.

This Court has already observed that the Brussels Convention must be interpreted having regard both to its principles and objectives and to its relationship with the EEC Treaty (see e.g. Case 12/76 *Tessili* v *Dunlop* [1976] ECR 1473 at p. 1484). Where there is doubt about the specific words used, and where there is or may be a divergence between the different versions of the Convention it is clearly right to have regard to the objects and purposes of the Convention.

It would seem to be contrary to the spirit and intention of the Convention to place difficulties in the way of litigants. Substantial difficulties can arise in practice if a defendant is limited to entering an appearance on the question of jurisdiction alone. If he fails on that issue, he may deprive himself of the chance of contesting the claim against him on the merits or even on other procedural grounds. He cannot rely on those, either, if proceedings for enforcement of the judgment against him are begun in the State where he is or where he has assets, since Article 28 of the Convention provides, subject to exceptions, that the jurisdiction of the court of the State in which judgment is given may not be reviewed. Moreover, cases can arise in which the jurisdictional point is complex but the point on the merits is short. It would seem an unattractive result that a defendant who desires to contest the jurisdiction should be barred from raising a point on the merits which could speedily be dealt with if he failed on jurisdiction. This is particularly so in a case where a defendant desires to secure property seised or threatened with seizure, not least in the commercial field. It is no less unattractive a result that a court which concludes in the course of argument that it does not have jurisdiction should be required to take jurisdiction merely because a defendant has, in entering an appearance, raised a subsidiary point on the merits or some other procedural objection.

English law takes a stricter view on this question, as I understand it, than the law of certain other Contracting States where a defendant is not necessarily to be taken to have submitted to the jurisdiction merely because he advances arguments on the merits. There must be knowingly a conscious acceptance of jurisdiction. I refer to, without repeating, the extracts from commentaries included in the observations of the United Kingdom Government.

It is, perhaps, right to observe that the International Court of Justice took a similar view to that more generally adopted by Member States when it was called upon to decide, in accordance with general principles of law, whether the Iranian Government should be taken to have conferred jurisdiction on the Court by submitting to it for decision several questions which were not objections to its jurisdiction. The Court ruled that 'the principle of *forum prorogatum*, if it could be applied to the present case, would have to be based on some conduct or statement of the Government of Iran which involves an element of consent regarding the jurisdiction of the Court' (*Anglo-Iranian Oil Company Case*, 1952 I.C.J. Rep. 89 at 113-4).

In my opinion the answer to the second question is that a court of a Contracting State does not obtain jurisdiction, by virtue of Article 18 of the Convention, if the defendant enters an appearance for the purpose of contesting that jurisdiction, but avails himself of the opportunity of raising a subsidiary point on the merits of the case. So long as the initial purpose is to protest the jurisdiction, the defendant does not forfeit the right to object by raising arguments on the merits in the alternative.

The Hof van Cassatie asks the Court to answer its *third* question only if the second is answered in the affirmative: 'If it is, must jurisdiction be contested *in limine litis?*'

On the one hand, it is clear that the Convention does not regulate matters of procedure. In principle, therefore, the *lex fori* must determine the stage and manner in which any plea is to be raised. M. Jenard made this point explicitly in his Report (O.J. 1979, C. 59/1 at p. 38). Indeed, the Contracting States' laws on this point differ quite considerably. For instance, Article 854 of the Belgian Judicial Code, as I understand it, requires the defendant to take any objection to jurisdiction *in limine*; whereas the German Code of Civil Procedure enables him to take the objection at any stage before the first oral hearing. The Brussels Convention does not set out to harmonise such rules.

On the other hand, it must be acknowledged that the second sentence of Article 18, by its very wording, requires that the appearance be entered for the purpose of contesting the Court's jurisdiction. It cannot be maintained that the appearance was entered for that purpose when the jurisdiction was challenged after the appearance was made. Furthermore, a defendant who raises the plea at a late stage can scarcely contend that his arguments, directed to the merits of the case, were subsidiary or alternative to the issue of jurisdiction. It follows, if my opinion on the second question be accepted, that such a defendant would forfeit his right to plead to the jurisdiction. He would be met with the objection that his previous appearance amounted to a voluntary submission.

These considerations are not difficult to reconcile. The second sentence of Article 18 presupposes, in my view, that the defendant's object in the entry of an appearance was to contest the jurisdiction. Accordingly, the jurisdiction must be challenged no later than the date when the appearance is made. But it is for the *lex fori* to determine what constitutes an appearance.

The *fourth* and *fifth* questions posed by the Hof van Cassatie read as follows:

'(a) In application of Article 22 of the Convention can related actions which, had they been brought separately would have had to be brought before the courts of different Contracting States, be brought simultaneously before one of those courts, provided that the law of that court permits the consolidation of related actions and that court has jurisdiction over both actions?

(b) Is that also the case if the parties to one of the disputes which has given rise to the actions have agreed, in accordance with Article 17 of the Convention, that a court of another Contracting State is to have jurisdiction to settle that dispute?'

As the Government of the United Kingdom has observed, the wording of these questions gives rise to some difficulty. It is not merely that the first begins with the presumption that the actions, if brought separately, would have had to be brought in courts of different Contracting States, and ends with the presumption that a single court has jurisdiction over both actions. That obstacle could, perhaps, be overcome by reading the final proviso as a reference to national law which 'permits the consolidation of related actions and thereby invests the court with jurisdiction over both actions'. The central difficulty, to my mind, is the fact that both questions ask the Court whether Article 22 permits the assumption of jurisdiction in specified circumstances.

Article 22, however, is not concerned with the assumption of jurisdiction in related actions. For the rules on that subject one must refer to Article 6. Article 22 is concerned with the circumstances in which one court may stay proceedings or decline jurisdiction in favour of another, 'the court first seised'. It does not seem reasonable to infer from the wording of these questions that the Hof van Cassatie requires guidance on the circumstances in which it may stay proceedings or decline jurisdiction in favour of the Courts of Kleve, or any other 'court first seised'; for nothing in the file suggests that the courts of any Contracting State other than Belgium have been seised of the case: rather the contrary.

While this Court is, of course, free to read questions with such modifications of wording as may be necessary to enable it to perform its function, it seems to me that it would not be appropriate in the present case to consider the relationship between Articles 6 and 17 of the Convention, since Article 6 is not referred to in the questions. In these circumstances it seems to me that the right course is to say that the fourth and fifth questions call for no answer in this case.

By its final question the Hof van Cassatie asks: 'Does it conflict with Article 17 of the Convention to rule that an agreement conferring jurisdiction on a court is void if the document in which the agreement is contained is not drawn up in the language which is prescribed by the law of the Contracting State upon penalty of nullity and if the court of the State before which the agreement is relied upon is bound by that law to declare the document to be void of its own motion?'

The Court has already made clear that Article 17 imposes on the court before which the matter is brought the duty of examining, first, whether the clause conferring jurisdiction upon it was, in fact, the subject of consensus which must be clearly and precisely demonstrated. It has also indicated certain criteria which may establish, or which are necessary to establish, that there has been an agreement in writing or evidenced by writing. (See e.g. Case 24/76 *Estassis Salotti* v *RUWA* [1976] ECR 1831 and Case 25/76 *Galeries Segoura SPRL* v *Rahim Bonakdarian* [1976] ECR 1851). Insofar as conditions are prescribed in the Convention they must be interpreted independently of any particular national law. However, as was said by Mr Advocate General Capotorti in his opinion in Case 25/76 at p. 1868: 'All this is, of course, without prejudice to national requirements in other respects, whether of form or substance, which do not come within the ambit of the Convention rules subject to Community interpretation'. The question in the present case, as I see it, is which national law decides those other requirements as to whether there is a valid agreement.

One possibility is the national law of the forum in which proceedings are brought, being a forum other than that specified in writing upon which a defendant relies to challenge jurisdiction. As a general proposition it does not seem to me that that can be right. Such law may have no connection whatever with the agreement reached and the forum may have been chosen by a plaintiff simply because such national law would, if applied, render null the agreement relied upon. Another possibility is that the forum in which proceedings are brought should apply its own rules of private international law to choose the national law appropriate to determine the question. This clearly has more attraction since it seeks to choose a law which has a connection with the agreement alleged. It does, however, produce the result that different laws may be chosen by the courts of different Contracting States because of the different rules which they apply under their own conflict of laws rules. This is contrary to that maximum degree of legal certainty for those engaged in civil and commercial transactions across the borders of Contracting States upon which M. Jenard lays emphasis in his report on the Convention. It is also contrary to the principle stated by Mr Advocate General Capotorti in the opinion cited previously namely that 'it is clearly important that there should be uniform treatment in all Member States of private parties between whom there exist agreements assigning jurisdiction; this purpose would not be served if reference were made to this or that substantive law applicable to the form of instruments according to the private international law of each Member State' (page 1845).

The United Kingdom Government proposes a compromise solution - namely that if there is a separate agreement conferring jurisdiction, or an agreement conferring jurisdiction which is part of a wider contract, but which can be severed from it, then the court before which the question arises should decline jurisdiction so long as the formalities specified by Article 17 are satisfied. I find this difficult to accept partly because such an approach does not identify the national law which is to decide issues as to validity other than those subject to the formal rules set out in Article 17 itself. It also opens up questions which can be difficult, and as to which different courts might reach different opinions, as to whether the jurisdiction clause is 'clearly severable'. It leaves a residuary category where the jurisdiction clause is left to stand or fall with the validity of the contract as a whole, to be determined in accordance with the conflict of laws rules of the forum first seised of the question. This militates against that 'principle of uniformity which the Convention seeks to establish' to which Mr Advocate General Capotorti refers in another context in his opinion in the *Segoura* case at page 1868.

In my opinion, having regard to the objects and purposes of the Convention, Article 17 is to be read as implicitly laying down the rule that where a particular forum is referred to in writing, in what is alleged to be, or to be evidence of, a valid agreement, the law of that forum must decide whether the agreement is valid. Only in this way can any principle of uniformity be satisfied.

I do not consider that this view is vitiated by an argument that it is anticipating the Convention on the Law Applicable to Contractual Obligations opened for signature on 19 June 1980 (OJ 1980, L 266/1) which provides in Article 8(1) that 'the existence and the validity of a contract, or of any term of a contract, shall be determined by the law which would govern it under this Convention if the contract or term were valid', although that Convention is not dealing with the choice of jurisdiction clauses. Nor is the argument vitiated by the fact that it produces the same result as that set out in the draft of the Hague Convention on 'for contractuel': 'pour toutes les questions non reglées par les dispositions de la présente Convention l'accord d'élection de for est régi par la loi interne de l'État du tribunal élu' (Actes et documents de la conference de droit international privé de la Haye 10e Session 1964 IV, p. 18).

A further question arises as to which court decides the validity of the agreement under the national law of the named forum. One possibility is that the court in which the question is raised should immediately refer the matter to the named forum for decision under its own national law. There are advantages in this but I do not consider that it is right. It seems to me that the court seised of the challenge of jurisdiction must itself decide the validity of the agreement (other than in relation to the provisions as to form specified in Article 17 itself) under the national law of the named forum. If it decides that under such law the agreement is valid it will, subject to jurisdiction being established in some other way under the Convention, refer the dispute at that stage. If it decides that the agreement is invalid it will continue to adjudicate upon the dispute.

It is to be noted that Article 27 of the Convention permits the non-recognition of a judgment if such recognition is contrary to public policy in the State in which recognition is sought. There is no reference to 'ordre public' in that section of the Convention dealing with exclusive jurisdiction. It seems to me that the court seised of the question as to whether there is a valid agreement is not entitled to refuse to give effect to it if it decides that the agreement is valid under the domestic law of the forum named. Once the judgment has been given by the nominated forum "ordre public" may become relevant if the successful party seeks to enforce the judgment in another Contracting State, including the State in which the question was first raised; but it is not an issue to be raised at an earlier stage.

For these reasons I am of the opinion that the Hof van Cassatie's questions should be answered as follows:

1. (a) Article 18 of the Convention of 27 September 1968 on Jurisdiction and the Enforcement of Judgments in Civil and Commercial Matters applies although the parties have agreed to confer jurisdiction on a court within the meaning of Article 17.

(b) The rule on jurisdiction contained in Article 18 of the Convention applies whenever the defendant manifests by his appearance before the Court his submission to its jurisdiction. It is for the national court to determine as a question of fact whether the defendant has done so.

A defendant's act in advancing arguments on the substance of the action does not necessarily indicate that he has submitted to the jurisdiction, if these arguments are alternative to his primary submission that the court has no jurisdiction.

(c) To exclude the rule contained in the first sentence of Article 18 the Court must be satisfied that a defendant entered an appearance to contest the jurisdiction even if he adds submissions in the alternative. It is not sufficient that the defendant decides to protest the jurisdiction at a later stage. It is for national law to determine what constitutes an entry of appearance, what evidence establishes, and what procedure must be followed to establish, that the defendant did enter an appearance to contest the jurisdiction.

2. (a) ...(b) ...

3. A court of one Contracting State is not entitled to disregard an agreement, satisfying the conditions of Article 17 and valid under the law of the State chosen for the forum, conferring exclusive jurisdiction in relation to a dispute on the courts of another Contracting State on the ground that such an agreement is void by the law of the first such State.

Case 27/81 - 22 October 1981

Établissements Rohr Société Anonyme
v
Dina Ossberger

Article 18 - Agreement on jurisdiction - Appearance entered by the defendant in the court seised - Appearance entered not only to contest the jurisdiction but also to present a defence on the substance - Entering an appearance does not entail submission to the jurisdiction.

Summary

Article 18 of the Convention of 27 September 1968 must be interpreted as meaning that it allows the defendant not only to contest the jurisdiction but to submit at the same time in the alternative a defence on the substance of the action without, however, losing his right to raise an objection of lack of jurisdiction.

JUDGMENT OF THE COURT

Touffait, President of the Third Chamber, Lord Mackenzie Stuart and Everling, Judges

1. By a judgment of 26 November 1980, which was received at the Court on 16 February 1981, the Cour d'Appel [Court of Appeal], Versailles, referred to the Court for a preliminary ruling under the Protocol of 3 June 1971 on the Interpretation by the Court of Justice of the Convention of 27 September 1968 on Jurisdiction and the Enforcement of Judgments in Civil and Commercial Matters a question as to the interpretation of Article 18 of the Convention.

2. The question was asked within the framework of appeal proceedings instituted by Société anonyme Établissements Rohr (hereinafter referred to as 'Rohr'), having its registered office at Sarcelles, France, against a writ of execution issued by the President of the Tribunal de Grande Instance [Regional Court], Pontoise, on 5 June 1979. By that writ the court rendered enforceable, on the application of Ossberger Turbinenfabrik (hereinafter referred to as 'Ossberger'), having its place of business at Weissenburg, in the Federal Republic of Germany, a provisionally enforceable judgment of the Landgericht [Regional Court] Anshach of 15 December 1978, together with a taxing order in respect of the costs of that court of 5 February 1979.

3. The judgment in question was given by the Landgericht Ansbach following proceedings instituted by Ossberger against Rohr for payment of various accounts for goods supplied by Ossberger. Since Rohr merely argued before the Landgericht that the court had no jurisdiction *ratione loci* and did not submit any defence on the substance, and since the Landgericht considered that it had jurisdiction in accordance with Article 17 of the Convention by reason of a clause conferring jurisdiction contained in Ossberger's general conditions of sale, Rohr was ordered to settle the said accounts and pay the costs. Rohr submitted an appeal to the Oberlandesgericht Nürnberg [Higher Regional Court, Nuremberg], again relying upon the objection of lack of jurisdiction without submitting any defence on the substance; that appeal was dismissed by a judgment of 13 June 1979 since the Oberlandesgericht Nürnberg considered that the Landgericht had jurisdiction under the provisions of the Convention and that Rohr had still failed to submit a defence on the substance in the course of the appellate procedure. A further appeal on a point of law by Rohr to the Bundesgerichtshof [Federal Court of Justice] was dismissed as inadmissible by an order of 19 March 1980 because the grounds for the appeal were not stated within the prescribed time limits.

4. Rohr argued before the Cour d'Appel, Versailles, that the recognition and enforcement of the judgments of the Landgericht Ansbach were contrary to public policy within the meaning of Article 27(1) of the Convention: since Article 18 of the Convention made it impossible for Rohr to submit a defence on the substance before the German courts without losing the right to raise an objection of lack of jurisdiction, the fact that these courts did not restrict themselves to giving a ruling on jurisdiction but also give judgment on the substance of the case constituted a manifest infringement of the rights of the defence and thereby of public policy in France. Ossberger contended that Article 18

of the Convention, like the provisions of German law on civil procedure, did not prevent Rohr from submitting a defence on the substance but that Rohr voluntarily refrained from doing so.

5. The Cour d'Appel, Versailles, since it considered that this case raised a question concerning the interpretation of the Convention, referred to the Court a preliminary question which is essentially concerned to establish whether Article 18 of the Convention permits a defendant who contests the jurisdiction of the court before which an application has been brought to submit at the same time in the alternative a defence on the substance of the action without thereby losing his right to raise an objection of lack of jurisdiction.

6. The Italian Government and the Commission of the European Communities have argued that that question must be answered in the affirmative.

7. The Court of Justice has had occasion to give a preliminary ruling on a similar question in its judgment of 29 June 1981 (*Elefanten Schuh GmbH* v *Jacqmain*, Case 150/80, [1981] ECR 1671). In that judgment the Court declared: 'Although differences between the different language versions of Article 18 of the Convention appear when it is sought to determine whether, in order to exclude the jurisdiction of the court seised, a defendant must confine himself to contesting that jurisdiction, or whether he may on the contrary still achieve the same purpose by contesting the jurisdiction of the court as well as the substance of the claim, the second interpretation is more in keeping with the objectives and spirit of the Convention. In fact under the law of civil procedure of certain Contracting States a defendant who raises the issue of jurisdiction and no other might be barred from making his submissions as to the substance if the court rejects his plea that it has no jurisdiction. An interpretation of Article 18 which enabled such a result to be arrived at would be contrary to the right of the defendant to defend himself in the original proceedings, which is one of the aims of the Convention'.

8. This case has disclosed no factor of such a kind as to affect these findings. Accordingly the answer to the question submitted must be that Article 18 of the Convention of 27 September 1968 must be interpreted as meaning that it allows the defendant not only to contest the jurisdiction but to submit at the same time in the alternative a defence on the substance of the action without, however, losing his right to raise an objection of lack of jurisdiction.

On those grounds, the Court (Third Chamber), in answer to the question referred to it by the Cour d'Appel, Versailles, by judgment of 26 November 1980, hereby rules.

Article 18 of the Convention of 27 September 1968 must be interpreted as meaning that it allows the defendant not only to contest the jurisdiction but to submit at the same time in the alternative a defence on the substance of the action without, however, losing his right to raise an objection of lack of jurisdiction.

OPINION OF MR ADVOCATE GENERAL CAPOTORTI

1. This reference for a preliminary ruling raises a problem concerning the interpretation of Article 18 of the Convention on Jurisdiction and the Enforcement of Judgments in Civil and Commercial Matters, signed in Brussels on 27 September 1968. The same problem was recently encountered by the Court of Justice within the framework of another case of the same nature: the reference for a preliminary ruling in Case 150/80, *Elefanten Schuh*, in which judgment was given on 24 June 1981. I shall accordingly be able to deal with the matter very briefly.

First of all, I shall summarize the facts. The undertaking Ossberger Turbinenfabrik [hereinafter referred to as 'Ossberger'] which has its registered office in Weissenburg, Bavaria, instituted proceedings before the Landgericht [Regional Court] Ansbach against a French customer, Établissements Rohr SA [hereinafter referred to as 'Rohr'], Sarcelles, Val d'Oise, for an order that the latter should pay certain outstanding accounts. In order to establish that the Landgericht had jurisdiction the plaintiff invoked a clause conferring jurisdiction which was contained in its general conditions of sale. Rohr confined itself to contesting the jurisdiction *ratione loci* but did not submit any defence on the substance. By a judgment of 15 December 1978 the Landgericht Ansbach ruled that the clause conferring jurisdiction was valid (pursuant to Article 17 of the above-mentioned Brussels Convention); since the defendant had failed to submit a defence on the substance the court ordered it to pay the plaintiff the sum claimed together with the costs of the case.

Before the Oberlandesgericht Nürnberg [Higher Regional Court, Nuremberg], the court of second instance, Rohr repeated its objection of lack of jurisdiction and again did not submit any defence on the substance. Its appeal was dismissed by a judgment of 13 June 1979. A further appeal on a point of law by Rohr to the Bundesgerichtshof [Federal Court of Justice] was dismissed as inadmissible by an order of 19 March 1980 because the grounds for the appeal were not stated within the prescribed time-limits.

On the application of Ossberger the President of the Tribunal de Grande Instance [Regional Court], Pontoise, had meanwhile issued an order of 5 June

1979 declaring enforceable in France the judgment of the Landgericht Ansbach and the relative taxing order. In challenging the order of the President of the Tribunal de Grande Instance before the Cour d'Appel, Versailles, Rohr claimed that Article 18 of the Brussels Convention did not permit a defendant who wished to contest the jurisdiction of the court to submit a defence on the substance at the same time. The fact that the German court, in addition to dismissing the objection of lack of jurisdiction, also gave judgment on the substance of the case constitutes a manifest infringement of the rights of the defence and is accordingly contrary to public policy within the meaning of Article 27(1) of the Brussels Convention. On that argument the judgment of the Landgericht Ansbach should not be recognized in France.

By a judgment of 26 November 1980 the Court d'Appel, Versailles, decided to stay the proceedings, requested the Court of Justice to give a ruling pursuant to the Protocol of 3 June 1971 on the interpretation of the Brussels Convention and submitted the following preliminary question: 'Must it be held with regard to all the versions of the Convention of 27 September 1968 which are drawn up in the Dutch, French, German and Italian languages in accordance with Article 68 of the Convention either that Article 18 thereof prohibits the simultaneous submission in the alternative of a defence concerning the substance of the case where an objection contesting jurisdiction as allowed by that provision has been raised, in order that a final decision on jurisdiction must be reached before any argument on the substance of the action, or that the said Article 18 permits, although it does not say so expressly, the objection contesting jurisdiction for which it makes provision to be submitted at the same time as defence in the alternative regarding the substance of the action in order to permit the court before which the action is brought to give a decision in a single judgment, if that is appropriate, on both the objection and the substance of the action on the pattern of the express provisions of Article 76 of the Nouveau Code de Procédure Civile [New Code of Civil Procedure] together with the detailed procedures for the protection of rights of the defence?'

2. The provisions of Article 18 of the Brussels Convention are as follows:

'Apart from jurisdiction derived from other provisions of this Convention, a court of a Contracting State before whom a defendant enters an appearance shall have jurisdiction. This rule shall not apply where appearance was entered solely to contest the jurisdiction by virtue of Article 16'.

In setting out the reasons on which the judgment making the reference was based on the Cour d'Appel, Versailles, emphasized the difference existing between the French version of the above-mentioned provision and the Dutch, German and Italian versions. In fact the French version of the second sentence of Article 18 provides: 'Cette règle n'est pas applicable si la comparution a pour objet de contester la compètence ...', whilst according to the versions drawn up in the other three languages the provision contained in the first sentence does not apply 'where appearance was entered solely to contest the jurisdiction ...'.

That difference in the four language versions of Article 18 has already prompted the Belgian Hof van Cassatie, to request the Court, by an order of 9 June 1980, to reply to the following question: 'Is the rule on jurisdiction contained in Article 18 applicable if the defendant has not only contested jurisdiction but has in addition made submissions on the action itself?' As I recalled at the beginning that question was a subject of the reference for a preliminary ruling in Case 150/80, *Elefanten Schuh* and led to the judgment of 24 June 1981 in which it was held, *inter alia,* that the said article 'must be interpreted as meaning that the rule on jurisdiction which that provision lays down does not apply where the defendant not only contests the court's jurisdiction but also makes submissions on the substance of the action, provided that, if the challenge to jurisdiction is not preliminary to any defence as to the substance, it does not occur after the making of the submissions which under national procedural law are considered to be the first defence addressed to the court seised'.

In this connection the statement of the Court of Justice at paragraph 14 of the decision should be recalled: it was that the interpretation permitting a defendant to contest the jurisdiction of the court as well as the substance of the claim 'is more in keeping with the objectives and spirit of the Convention. In fact, under the law of civil procedure of certain Contracting States a defendant who raises the issue of jurisdiction and no other might be barred from making his submissions as to the substance if the court rejects his plea that it has no jurisdiction. An interpretation of Article 18 which enabled such a result to be arrived at would be contrary to the right of the defendant to defend himself in the original proceedings, which is one of the aims of the Convention'. The Court then added a single restrictive condition stating: 'However, the challenge to jurisdiction may have the result attributed to it by Article 18 only if the plaintiff and the court seised of the matter are able to ascertain from the time of the defendant's first defence that it is intended to contest the jurisdiction of the court'.

The views upheld in that judgment should, in my opinion, be fully confirmed. Article 18, as the Court is aware, is intended to govern 'jurisdiction implied from submission' (cf. the Report on the Convention, known as the Jenard Report, at page 38) and in that connection the entry of an appearance by the defendant is deemed to imply submission to the court seised of the proceedings which, it is supposed, the plaintiff selected without any regard for the cases provided for by the other provisions of the Convention. In order to prevent in particular cases entry of an appearance being considered as implying an intention to submit to the jurisdiction it is sufficient that a clear declaration that this is not so should be made: that is to say, an objection of lack of jurisdiction. Nevertheless, once the objection of lack of jurisdiction has been submitted there does not appear to be any reason why the defendant should be precluded from dealing in the alternative with the substance of the case lest the court should hold that it has jurisdiction. Clearly, the essential aim of entering an appearance remains that of raising an objection to the jurisdiction (the French version of Article 18 was thus well drafted, unlike the other versions); but what purpose is served by prohibiting the defendant from submitting arguments, as a precaution, to apply only if his objection is overruled?

3. In stating the reasons on which the judgment making the reference is based the French court properly points out that the interpretation of Article 18 is decisive in resolving the problem raised by Rohr in connection with the enforcement of the German judgment: namely whether or not recognition of that judgment is precluded by the fact that it is contrary to the public policy in the State in which recognition is sought (Article 27(1) of the Brussels Convention). We have seen that the objection concerning public policy is based, according to Rohr, on an interpretation of Article 18 whereby that provision precludes a defence concerning substance of the case (thereby violating, it is said, the principle that the rights of the defence must be respected); accordingly, the rejection as such of that interpretation means that there is no basis for holding the said Article 27(1) applicable to this case. In fact, it is Rohr which has misinterpreted Article 18 of the Convention and certainly not the German courts; it is clear that an error as to procedure committed by Rohr cannot and may not prevent recognition of the judgment against it.

I have, however, two considerations to add. First, the restriction concerning public policy may not be relied upon to obtain in the course of enforcement a sort of review of the jurisdiction of the courts of the State in which judgment was given: the last paragraph of Article 28 of the Convention expressly excludes such a review, subject to the provisions of the first paragraph, and states 'the test of public policy referred to in Article 27(1) may not be applied to the rules relating to jurisdiction'. For the purposes of the first paragraph of Article 28 the jurisdiction of the court, enforcement of whose judgment is sought, may be reviewed only where the provisions on jurisdiction contained in Sections 3, 4 and 5 of Title II (Articles 7 to 16) are infringed; the fact that Article 18 is not included amongst those provisions confirms that it is excluded from consideration in such a review. There does exist a case of infringement of the rights of the defence which may have the effect of precluding recognition of a foreign judgment but it concerns a well-defined situation: that is the case in which 'the defendant was not duly served with the document which instituted the proceedings or with an equivalent document in sufficient time to enable him to arrange for his defence' (Article 27(2)). It is clear that the foregoing does not apply to this case; all that may be inferred from it is that a particular aspect of the protection of the rights of the defence has been ensured by the authors of the Brussels Convention by means of a provision other than that concerning public policy.

Secondly - and this observation is even more relevant to the case under consideration - I do not see what basis there is for considering that Article 18 applies to the proceedings pending before the Cour d'Appel, Versailles. So far as the file indicates, Ossberger claimed that the German court had jurisdiction (and the claim was upheld by the Landgericht) pursuant to a clause expressly providing for submission to jurisdiction which had been agreed upon by the parties when delivery was made. Rohr could, of course, have contested the jurisdiction by challenging, on any ground whatever, the validity of the clause and by referring to Article 17 of the Brussels Convention; however, precisely because there was a clause in existence there was no reason to discuss the matter of implied submission to the jurisdiction which is the only matter covered by Article 18. In general, this makes clear that Article 18 does not concern all situations in which the defendant claims that he is entitled to raise an objection of lack of jurisdiction but only the case in which the defendant wishes to protect himself against the risk that his entry of an appearance may be interpreted as tacit submission to a jurisdiction which could not be founded on any other ground.

4. I accordingly suggest that the Court should rule, in reply to the reference for a preliminary ruling made to it by the Cour d'Appel, Versailles, by judgment of 26 November 1980, that Article 18 of the Brussels Convention on Jurisdiction and the Enforcement of Judgments in Civil and Commercial Matters permits a defendant who contests the jurisdiction of the court before which the plaintiff has brought proceedings to submit at the same time in the alternative a defence on the substance of the action.

Case 48/84 - 7 March 1985

Hannelore Spitzley
v
Sommer Exploitation SA

Articles 17 and 18 - Prorogation of jurisdiction - Entering an appearance without contesting the jurisdiction of the court seised of the proceedings - Claim for a set-off made by the defendant - Dispute on the substance of the case entered into by the applicant - Application of Article 18 - Clause conferring jurisdiction on another court - No effect.

Summary

The court of a Contracting State before which the applicant, without raising any objection as to the court's jurisdiction, enters an appearance in proceedings relating to a claim for a set-off which is not based on the same contract or subject-matter as the claims in his application and in respect of which there is a valid agreement conferring exclusive jurisdiction on the courts of another Contracting State within the meaning of Article 17 of the Convention of 27 September 1968 on Jurisdiction and the Enforcement of Judgments in Civil and Commercial Matters has jurisdiction by virtue of Article 18 of that Convention.

JUDGMENT OF THE COURT

Bosco, President of Chamber, Koopmans and Joliet, Judges

1. By an order of 3 February 1984, which was received at the Court on 24 February 1984, the Oberlandesgericht [Higher Regional Court] Koblenz referred to the Court for a preliminary ruling under the Protocol

of 3 June 1971 on the Interpretation by the Court of Justice of the Convention of 27 September 1968 on Jurisdiction and the Enforcement of Judgments in Civil and Commercial Matters several questions concerning the interpretation of Articles 17 and 18 of that Convention.

2. Those questions were raised in the context of an action between Sommer Exploitation SA (hereinafter referred to as 'Sommer'), a manufacturer of felt cloth, whose registered office is at Neuilly (France), and Hannelore Spitzley, the owner of an undertaking established in the Federal Republic of Germany, relating to payment for felt cloth purchased from Sommer by Mrs Spitzley.

3. In proceedings before the Landgericht [Regional Court] Koblenz Mrs Spitzley did not dispute that Sommer's application was well founded. However, she claimed a right to set off sums owed by Sommer to her husband, Wolfgang Spitzley.

4. She claimed that those sums were owed by Sommer to Mr Spitzley in respect of commission under a commercial agency contract concluded in 1976 and had subsequently been assigned to Mrs Spitzley.

5. In the proceedings before the Landgericht, Sommer contested the substance of the claim for a set-off made by Mrs Spitzley. The Landgericht, giving judgment on the merits of the case, allowed a set-off only in respect of a limited amount and ordered Mrs Spitzley to pay the remainder of the sum claimed by Sommer.

6. Both Mrs Spitzley and Sommer appealed to the Oberlandesgericht Koblenz which considered the question whether the German courts had jurisdiction to hear Mrs Spitzley's claim for a set-off. In that respect it noted that Clause VII of the commercial agency contract made between Mr Spitzley and Sommer conferred jurisdiction on the courts of the place where Sommer had its registered office, that is to say the French courts, in all disputes arising out of the contract.

7. In the order for reference the Oberlandesgericht states that while the presence and interpretation of that clause would seem to mean that the German courts do not have jurisdiction, the conduct of Sommer, which has not relied on that clause at all but has instead submitted arguments relating to the substance of the action, may have amounted to the conferring of jurisdiction on the German courts by virtue of the principle laid down in Article 18 of the Convention.

8. Consequently, the Oberlandesgericht considered it necessary to refer the following questions to the Court: (1) If a plaintiff, without raising any objection, enters an appearance in proceedings relating to a claim for a set-off which is not based on the same contract or subject matter as his application and in respect of which there is a valid agreement conferring exclusive jurisdiction within the meaning of Article 17 of the Convention, does such an appearance set aside any procedural prohibition against setting-off arising from that agreement conferring jurisdiction or its interpretation (judgment of the Court of Justice of 9 November 1978 in Case 23/78 *Meeth* v *Glacetal*)? (2) Or is the court prevented in such a case from giving judgment in respect of the claim for a set-off by the agreement conferring jurisdiction and the prohibition against setting-off contained therein notwithstanding the fact that the plaintiff has entered an appearance to the set-off without raising any objection?'

9. Pursuant to Article 20 of the Protocol on the Statute of the Court of Justice observations were lodged by the Government of the Federal Republic of Germany, the United Kingdom and the Commission of the European Communities which all took the view that the questions must be answered by affirming the first meaning proposed by the Oberlandesgericht.

10. By the questions it referred to the Court the Oberlandesgericht seeks to know, in substance, whether the prorogation of jurisdiction arising, according to the terms of Article 18 of the Convention, when a defendant enters an appearance before a court without contesting the jurisdiction of that court occurs in the following circumstances: when the lack of jurisdiction of the court seised of the proceedings does not relate to the application made by the plaintiff but to the claim for a set-off made by the defendant; when the lack of jurisdiction of the court seised of the proceedings arises from a clause conferring jurisdiction in accordance with the requirements laid down by Article 17 of the Convention.

11. Article 18 of the Convention states as follows: 'Apart from jurisdiction derived from other provisions of this Convention, a court of a Contracting State before whom a defendant enters an appearance shall have jurisdiction. This rule shall not apply where appearance was entered solely to contest the jurisdiction, or where another court has exclusive jurisdiction by virtue of Article 16'.

12. Article 17 provides as follows: 'If the parties, one or more of whom

is domiciled in a Contracting State, have, by agreement in writing or by an oral agreement evidenced in writing, agreed that a court or the courts of a Contracting State are to have jurisdiction to settle any disputes which have arisen or which may arise in connection with a particular legal relationship, that court or those courts shall have exclusive jurisdiction. Agreements conferring jurisdiction shall have no legal force if they are contrary to the provisions of Article 12 or 15, or if the courts whose jurisdiction they purport to exclude have exclusive jurisdiction by virtue of Article 16. If the agreement conferring jurisdiction was concluded for the benefit of only one of the parties, that party shall retain the right to bring proceedings in any other court which has jurisdiction by virtue of this Convention'.

13. Those two provisions form Section 6 - headed 'Prorogation of jurisdiction' - of Title II of the Convention. Whereas Article 17 is concerned with prorogation of jurisdiction by agreement, Article 18 deals with implied prorogation resulting from the defendant's entering an appearance without contesting the jurisdiction of the court seised of the proceedings.

14. The inclusion of those two provisions indicates that the Convention allows the parties, so far as is possible and subject to the limits laid down in the second paragraph of Article 17 and in the second sentence of Article 18, to choose the court to which they intend to submit the settlement of their disputes.

15. Article 18 in particular is based on the idea that, by entering an appearance before the court seised of the proceedings by the plaintiff, without contesting that court's jurisdiction, the defendant is by implication signifying his consent to the hearing of the case by a court other than that designated by the other provisions of the Convention.

16. The Oberlandesgericht asks first whether Article 18 is applicable to a case such as that before it, where it is the plaintiff who enters into a dispute on the substance of the case before the court seised of an action by the plaintiff himself in relation to a claim for a set-off made by the defendant and in respect of which the said court would otherwise have no jurisdiction.

17. The doubts expressed in that connection by the Oberlandesgericht arise from the wording of Article 18. That provision only refers expressly to the prorogation of jurisdiction as a consequence of the defendant's

entering an appearance before the court seised of the proceedings by the plaintiff.

18. Nevertheless, from an interpretation of Article 18 in the light of its purpose and context, as already defined, it may be concluded that a case such as that referred to by the Oberlandesgericht also falls within the scope of application of Article 18.

19. A plaintiff who, when faced with a claim for a set-off made by the defendant and in respect of which the court seised of the proceedings does not have jurisdiction, submits arguments relating to the substance of that claim without contesting the jurisdiction of the said court is in a similar position to that expressly referred to in Article 18 of a defendant who enters an appearance before the court seised of the proceedings by the plaintiff without contesting that court's jurisdiction.

20. Consequently, in a case such as that considered by the Oberlandesgericht, the plaintiff's conduct should be held to constitute the prorogation of jurisdiction, pursuant to Article 18 of the Convention, in favour of the court seised of the proceedings insofar as the other conditions for the application of that provision as defined in particular in the Court's judgment of 24 June 1981 (Case 150/80 *Elefanten Schuh* v *Jacqmain* [1981] ECR 1671) are fulfilled.

21. As the United Kingdom rightly points out that interpretation corresponds, moreover, to the need to avoid superfluous procedure which, as the Court recognised in its judgment of 9 November 1978 (Case 23/78 *Meeth* v *Glacetal* [1978] ECR 2133), forms the basis of the Convention as a whole of which Article 18 is part.

22. The aforementioned conclusion is not affected by the fact, emphasised in the order for reference, that the defendant's claim for a set-off is not based on the same contract or subject-matter as the main application. That fact relates to the admissibility of a claim for a set-off which depends on the law of the State in which the court seised of the proceedings is situated.

23. The second question considered by the Oberlandesgericht is whether Article 18 is applicable when the lack of jurisdiction of the court seised of the proceedings stems from the fact that there is, in relation to the subject-matter of the claim for a set-off, an agreement

conferring jurisdiction on the courts of a Contracting State other than that in which the court seised of the proceedings is situated.

24. It should be recalled that, according to the second sentence of Article 18, the rule in the first sentence does not apply where another court has exclusive jurisdiction by virtue of Article 16 of the Convention. The case envisaged in Article 17 is not therefore one of the exceptions which Article 18 allows to the rule which it lays down.

25. As the Court has already stated in the said judgment of 24 June 1981 neither the general scheme nor the objectives of the Convention provide grounds for the view that the parties to an agreement conferring jurisdiction within the meaning of Article 17 are prevented from voluntarily submitting their dispute to a court other than that stipulated in the agreement.

26. It follows that the fact that an agreement conferring jurisdiction within the meaning of Article 17 designates the court which is to have jurisdiction does not preclude the application, where appropriate, of Article 18 where another court is seised of the proceedings.

27. Consequently the reply to the questions referred to the Court by the Oberlandesgericht Koblenz must be that the court of a Contracting State before which the applicant, without raising any objection as to the court's jurisdiction, enters an appearance in proceedings relating to a claim for a set off which is not based on the same contact or subject-matter as the claims in his application and in respect of which there is a valid agreement conferring exclusive jurisdiction on the courts of another Contracting State within the meaning of Article 17 of the Convention, has jurisdiction by virtue of Article 18 of the Convention.

On those grounds, the Court (First Chamber), in answer to the questions referred to it by the Oberlandesgericht Koblenz, by order of 3 February 1984, hereby rules:

The court of a Contracting State before which the applicant, without raising any objection as to the court's jurisdiction, enters an appearance in proceedings relating to a claim for a set-off which is not based on the same contract or subject-matter as the claims in his application and in respect of which there is a valid agreement conferring exclusive jurisdiction on the courts of another Contracting State within the meaning of Article 17 of

the Convention of 27 September 1968 on Jurisdiction and the Enforcement of Judgments in Civil and Commercial Matters has jurisdiction by virtue of Article 18 of that Convention.

OPINION OF ADVOCATE GENERAL SIR GORDON SLYNN

This is a reference to the Court by the Oberlandesgericht Koblenz dated 3 February 1984 pursuant to Articles 2(2) and 3(2) of the Protocol of 3 June 1971 on the Interpretation of the Convention of 27 September 1968 on Jurisdiction and the Enforcement of Judgments in Civil and Commercial Matters ('the Convention'). It concerns Article 18 of the Convention, on the prorogation of jurisdiction by the act of entering an appearance, in relation not to the main action but to a set-off raised by the defendant as a defence to the plaintiff's claim.

The plaintiff in the proceedings before the national court is a company, Sommer Exploitation Société Anonyme, having its registered office in Neuilly-sur-Seine, France. Its business is the manufacture of felt cloth. The defendant is Mrs Hannelore Spitzley who owns the undertaking Filzvertrieb Hannelore Spitzley in Trimbs in the Federal Republic of Germany. That undertaking manufactures and sells felt products. Mrs Spitzley obtained supplies from Sommer Exploitation.

The defendant's husband, Wolfgang Spitzley, used to act as the plaintiff's commercial agent in Germany, first under a contract dated 21 October 1974, then under a contract dated 31 March 1976. Clause VII of the latter contract, which was drawn up in French, provided *inter alia* as follows: 'French law shall apply to this contract. The courts of the place where Sommer Exploitation SA has its registered office shall have exclusive jurisdiction in disputes arising out of this contract.' ('Le contrat est régi par le droit français. Il est fait attribution de jurisdiction pour tous litiges éventuels, émanant de ce contrat aux tribunaux compétents du Siege de la société Sommer Exploitation.')

At a meeting on 20 June 1978 between the plaintiff's export manager and Mr Spitzley, the contract was terminated orally. The plaintiff confirmed this termination by a letter dated 28 June 1978. By letter of 4 July 1978, Mr Spitzley accepted the notice of termination but said that he would come back to the matter of his outstanding commission. On 25 September 1978 the plaintiff, the defendant's husband and the defendant, represented by her husband, made a written agreement covering both the price of goods owed by the defendant to the plaintiff and amounts of commission owed by the plaintiff to the husband. By that agreement the defendant acknowledged that she owed DM 148 934.28 in respect of goods supplied, from which was to be deducted DM 63 760.89 in respect of commission due to her husband for the period from the third quarter of 1977 to the second quarter of 1978 inclusive, and the defendant undertook to pay the balance (DM 85 173.39) in five equal monthly instalments starting on 30 September 1978. As regards other amounts of commission due to the husband, the agreement provided that 'any further commission due to Mr Spitzley will be paid by cheque within 20 days of the end of the quarter after presentation of the usual commission claim'. This is a reference to commission arising outside the period covered by the agreement, a subject still in dispute between the parties.

The defendant paid DM 38 902.90 of the DM 85 173.39 in execution of the agreement, leaving DM 46 270.49 still outstanding thereunder. The plaintiff brought an action against the defendant for this amount before the Landgericht Koblenz. The defendant paid a further DM 3 145.35 in March 1980, and the plaintiff reduced its claim by that amount so that the plaintiff's claim was then for DM 43 125.14.

The defendant did not (and does not now) deny that she owed that amount to the plaintiff in respect of goods supplied, but she sought to set off against it the sum of DM 46 594.01 which she claimed was still outstanding in commission due to her husband under the commercial agency contract of 31 March 1976 and which, she maintained, had been assigned to her.

In the proceedings before the Landgericht the plaintiff did not rely on the jurisdiction clause in Clause VII of the 1976 commercial agency contract, but joined issue on the substance of the set-off. It contested the validity of the alleged assignment to the defendant of the husband's remaining claims to commission, and it challenged the claims themselves both as to their legal foundation and as to their amount.

In its judgment of 18 October 1982, the Landgericht Koblenz upheld the plaintiff's claim in full (i.e. DM 43 125.14). As regards the set-off, the court held that the defendant's husband had validly assigned his existing and future claims for commission to her by an oral declaration made in 1977, but it found on the evidence that only DM 6 258.59 were due to him by way of commission. Allowing the set-off to that extent, it gave judgment for the plaintiff in the amount of DM 36 866.55 with interest.

The defendant appealed against that decision to the Oberlandesgericht Koblenz, arguing that the plaintiff's claim should be dismissed in its entirety because commission was still due from the plaintiff to her husband, which she could set off against the plaintiff's claim. The plaintiff cross-appealed for DM 2 256.20 with interest.

The Oberlandesgericht Koblenz noted that by Clause VII of the commercial agency contract of 31 March 1976, the plaintiff and the defendant's husband had agreed that the courts of the place where the plaintiff had its registered office, namely Neuilly in France, were to have exclusive jurisdiction in relation to disputes arising in respect of that contract. It expressed the view that this was an agreement in writing whereby, under Article 17 of the Convention, the courts of Neuilly would have exclusive jurisdiction for 'claims' arising in respect of the commercial agency contract, the agreement actually using the word 'disputes' which is broader. It then considered the question whether the same rule applied to set-offs arising out of that contract. On the one hand, it interpreted the letter and spirit of the agreement conferring jurisdiction concluded in this case by the plaintiff and the defendant's husband to mean that no court other than the court of the place where the plaintiff has its registered office had jurisdiction to hear a claim for a set-off. On the other hand, it noted that the plaintiff had entered an appearance to the set-off to contest it on its substance and had not pleaded the existence of the agreement conferring exclusive jurisdiction. In these circumstances the Oberlandesgericht was concerned as to whether Article 18 of the Convention gave it jurisdiction on the basis that the plaintiff had submitted to its jurisdiction.

Article 18 provides: 'Apart from jurisdiction derived from other provisions of this convention, a court of a Contracting State before whom a defendant enters an appearance shall have jurisdiction. This rule shall not apply where appearance was entered solely to contest the jurisdiction, or where another court has exclusive jurisdiction by virtue of Article 16.' None of the provisions of Article 16 is in point here.

The difficulty felt by the Oberlandesgericht was that Article 18 does not apply in terms to a plaintiff but only a defendant, and it was not sure whether the plaintiff's conduct (in the light of Article 18) allowed it to override the jurisdiction clause in the interpretation which it had given it. To resolve these difficulties it asks the Court:

'(1) If a plaintiff, without raising any objection, enters an appearance in proceedings relating to a claim for a set-off which is not based on the same contract or subject matter as his application and in respect of which there is an agreement conferring exclusive jurisdiction within the meaning of Article 17 of the Convention, does such an appearance set aside any procedural prohibition against setting off arising from that agreement conferring jurisdiction or its interpretation (judgment of the Court of Justice of 9 November 1978 in Case 23/78 *Meeth* v *Glacetal*)?

(2) Or is the court prevented in such a case from giving judgment in respect of the claim for a set-off by the agreement conferring jurisdiction and the prohibition against setting-off contained therein notwithstanding the fact that the plaintiff has entered an appearance to the set-off claim without raising any objection?'

The second question posed (an alternative to the first) is based on the assumption that the jurisdiction clause in question contains a 'prohibition against setting-off'; but it should be pointed out that Clause VII does not expressly prohibit set-offs and this springs from the interpretation placed upon it by the Oberlandesgericht reading it in conjunction with Article 17 of the Convention.

Neither of the parties to the main action, nor the defendant's husband, have submitted written observations. The Commission, the Federal Republic of Germany and the United Kingdom have done so, and they have all come to the same conclusion, namely that the first limb of the question should be answered in the affirmative. In other words, they submit that where the plaintiff has appeared before a court to contest a set-off raised by the defendant without challenging the court's jurisdiction, then that court is competent by virtue of Article 18 to deal with the set-off, notwithstanding that the set-off is not based on the same contract or subject matter as the plaintiff's claim and is covered by a clause conferring exclusive jurisdiction under Article 17 of the Convention.

The Commission refers to the Court's judgment in Case 150/80 *Elefanten Schuh* v *Jacqmain* [1981] ECR 1671 (holding that Article 18 of the Convention applies even where the parties have by agreement designated a court which is to have jurisdiction within the meaning of Article 17) and argues that Article 18 should be read as applying to the case of a plaintiff who defends a claim for a set-off. It adduces four reasons for this. First, the conduct of the plaintiff in contesting the substance of the set-off without challenging the court's jurisdiction amounts to an implied prorogation of jurisdiction. Secondly, it is more convenient, particularly for the taking of evidence, if the set-off in the instant case is dealt with by the German court. Thirdly, applying Article 18 also to set-offs achieves one of the aims of that article, which is to extend the field of application of the Convention's rules on jurisdiction. Finally, such an extension would not substantially reduce the plaintiff's procedural safeguards.

The United Kingdom argues from the scheme of the Convention as a whole and from the purpose of Article 18. The scheme of the Convention (particularly Article 6(3) regarding counterclaims) is designed to avoid superfluous procedure, in particular by concentrating proceedings in a single court; and the purpose of Article 18 is, subject to the listed exceptions, to give maximum freedom of choice to the parties. On both points the United Kingdom relies on the judgment of the Court in Case 23/78 *Meeth* v *Glacetal* [1978] ECR 2133, in which the Court held that Article 17 did not prohibit a national court from entertaining a set-off in spite of reciprocal exclusive jurisdiction clauses entered into by the parties, and submits that Article 18 should apply as much to the party who is nominally the plaintiff but who is the defendant to a counterclaim as it does to the party who is the defendant to a principal claim. Hence, it submits that in the instant case the plaintiff's submission to the jurisdiction under Article 18 overrides any contrary provision of a jurisdiction agreement, thus giving the German court jurisdiction over the set-off.

The Federal Republic of Germany advances similar arguments. It submits that the parties' joining issue on the substance of a set-off without contesting jurisdiction constitutes a tacit conferment of jurisdiction, capable of modifying any earlier agreement to the contrary. This submission is based on two arguments: first, the freedom of the parties to choose the forum is paramount in the scheme of the Convention. The *Elefanten Schuh* judgment establishes that Article 17 does not prevent the parties from waiving a jurisdiction clause by submitting to the jurisdiction of another court. Secondly, the extension of Article 18 to set-offs and counterclaims is required for reasons of economy of procedure. The Federal Republic expressly submits (and the United Kingdom clearly implies) that this reasoning applies as much to counterclaims as to set-offs.

The first paragraph of Article 17 of the Convention provides: 'If the parties, one or more of whom is domiciled in a Contracting State, have, by agreement in writing or by an oral agreement evidenced in writing, agreed that a court or the courts of a Contracting State are to have jurisdiction to settle any disputes which have arisen or which may arise in Connection with a particular legal relationship, that court or those courts shall have exclusive jurisdiction'. Although it might be argued that Article 17 gives binding force to jurisdiction agreements concluded by the parties, so that, thereafter, the parties and any other courts seised are bound by their choice of forum, the Court has made it clear that this is not the case and that the parties remain free to change their choice of forum. At paragraph 10 of its decision in Case 150/80, *Elefanten Schuh* v *Jacqmain* at page 1684, the Court said: 'Neither the general scheme nor the objectives of the Convention provide grounds for the view that the parties to an agreement conferring jurisdiction within the meaning of Article 17 are prevented from voluntarily submitting their dispute to a court other than that stipulated in the agreement'. It is clear from this passage, as well as from paragraphs 5 and 8 of the decision in Case 23/78 *Meeth* v *Glacetal* at pages 2141 and 2142, emphasising the free will of the parties, that the parties can waive their jurisdiction agreement.

There is no doubt that if a plaintiff sues in a court other than one stipulated in an agreement as to jurisdiction, within the meaning of Article 17, the other party to the agreement may as defendant submit to the jurisdiction by entering an unconditional appearance. That court then has jurisdiction (*Elefanten Schuh* ruling, paragraph 1). Such a situation falls expressly within the wording of Article 18 since jurisdiction is conferred where 'a defendant enters an appearance'. There is no express provision that if, in an action not covered by an agreement as to jurisdiction, a defendant raises a counter-claim or set-off which is covered by an agreement as to jurisdiction, and the plaintiff resists the counterclaim or set-off without challenging the jurisdiction, the court has jurisdiction over the latter dispute.

In my opinion, however, the scheme and intendment of the Convention require that the same rules should apply to claims as to counterclaims and set-offs in this respect. Except where specific mandatory rules are laid down, the Convention recognises a margin of choice of jurisdiction in the parties to a dispute. Even if they agree a jurisdiction in advance they can subsequently, by respectively making and defending claims in some other court, confer jurisdiction on that court. That freedom of choice must apply equally whether the claim is raised in the initial proceedings or by way of counterclaim and set-off. Moreover, it is clear from Articles 6, 21, 22 and 23 of the Convention that multiplicity of proceedings is to be avoided and in its decision in *Meeth* v *Glacetal* (paragraph 8) the Court stressed the need to avoid superfluous procedures. If parties to disputes, both content to test them before some other court than that agreed in respect of one of the disputes, are obliged automatically to have the dispute covered by an agreement as to jurisdiction transferred to some other court, then clearly two sets of proceedings must follow. This is contrary to the objectives of the Convention.

This conclusion does not produce an unacceptable erosion of the effect of Article 17, since the plaintiff who is defendant to a counterclaim or set-off, like the defendant to a claim, can always challenge jurisdiction by relying on the agreement no later than the time of making submissions which under national procedural law are considered to be the first defence addressed to the court seised (*Elefanten Schuh* ruling, paragraph 2). This protection in particular is available where the dispute raised by the counterclaim or set-off relates to facts other that those in issue in the claim. There may, of course, in addition be national rules of procedure which limit the extent to which unrelated matters can be raised by way of set-off or counterclaim.

I can see no justification for distinguishing between the position of a plaintiff and a defendant in regard to submission to the jurisdiction, nor in distinguishing between a counterclaim and a set-off raised by a defendant. It should be added that in the instant case no problem arises from the fact that the parties to the action (Sommer Exploitation and Mrs Spitzley) are not the same as the parties to the agreement of 31 March 1976 (Sommer Exploitation and Mr Spitzley) since, as the Landgericht Koblenz found at first instance, Mr Spitzley had validly assigned his rights under that agreement to Mrs Spitzley.

Accordingly I am of the opinion that the questions put by the Oberlandesgericht Koblenz should be answered as follows: 'If a plaintiff enters an appearance before a court to contest a set-off or a counterclaim raised by the defendant without contesting the court's jurisdiction, that court has jurisdiction over the set-off or counterclaim by virtue of Article 18 of the Convention, notwithstanding that the set-off or counterclaim does not arise from the same contract or facts as the plaintiff's claim and is covered by a clause conferring exclusive jurisdiction on another court under Article 17 of the Convention'.

TITLE II *[Chapter II]*

JURISDICTION *[Jurisdiction]*

Examination as to jurisdiction and admissibility – Articles 19 - 20 *[Articles 25 - 26]*

See

TITLE II *[Chapter II]*

JURISDICTION *[Jurisdiction]*

Lis pendens - related actions – Articles 21 - 23 *[Articles 27 - 30]*

See also

Case 129/83 - 7 June 1984

Siegfried Zelger
v
Sebastiano Salinitri II

Article 21 - Lis pendens - Proceedings brought in the courts of different Contracting States - Court 'first seised' - Concept.

Summary

Article 21 of the Convention of 28 September 1968 must be interpreted as meaning that the court 'first seised' is the one before which the requirements for proceedings to become definitively pending are first fulfilled, such requirements to be determined in accordance with the national law of each of the courts concerned.

JUDGMENT OF THE COURT

Koopmans, President of Chamber, Bahlmann, Pescatore, O'Keeffe and Bosco, Judges

1. By an order of 22 June 1983, received at the Court on 8 July 1983, the Oberlandesgericht München referred to the Court for a preliminary ruling under the Protocol of 3 June 1971 on the Interpretation by the Court of Justice of the Convention of 27 September 1968 on Jurisdiction and Enforcement of Judgments in Civil and Commercial Matters (hereinafter referred to as 'the Convention') a question on the interpretation of Article 21 of that Convention.

2. The two parties in the main action are merchants, one of whom has his place of business in Munich in the Federal Republic of Germany and the other in Mascali in Sicily. The plaintiff in the main action brought proceedings against the defendant for repayment of an amount outstanding on a loan dating back to 1975 and 1976. The application which is the subject of the dispute was lodged at the Registry of the Landgericht München I on 5 August 1976 and served on the defendant in the main action on 13 January 1977. In addition, the plaintiff in the main action brought further proceedings with the same purpose and involving the same cause of action before the Tribunale Civile in Catania, Italy, by an application which was lodged with that court on 22 or 23 September 1976 and served on the defendant on 23 September 1976.

3. The Landgericht dismissed the proceedings on the ground that it lacked international jurisdiction. Before the Landgericht the proceedings were definitively instituted only on 13 January 1977, by service of the document initiating them (Paragraphs 261(1) and 253(1) of the Zivilprozeßordnung [Code of Civil Procedure]) whereas they had been definitively instituted before the court in Catania by service of an equivalent document on 23 September 1976. In the opinion of the Landgericht München the court in Catania had jurisdiction by virtue of Article 21 of the Convention.

4. The plaintiff appealed to the Oberlandesgericht contending that the decisive time was not the moment at which the document initiating the proceedings was served but the moment at which the court was seised of the proceedings.

5. The Oberlandesgericht München considered that the dispute raised questions concerning the interpretation of the aforesaid Convention. It therefore stayed the proceedings and by order of 22 June 1983 referred the following question to the Court for a preliminary ruling: 'For the purpose of resolving the question which court of a Contracting State was first seised of proceedings (Article 21 of the Convention) is it the moment at which the document initiating them was lodged with the court ('Anhängigkeit') that is decisive or the moment at which - by service of that document on the defendant - the proceedings have become fully instituted ('Rechtshangigkeit')?'

6. Article 21 of the Convention provides: 'Where proceedings involving the same cause of action and between the same parties are brought in the courts of different Contracting States, any court other than

the court first seised shall of its own motion decline jurisdiction in favour of that court. A court which would be required to decline jurisdiction may stay its proceedings if the jurisdiction of the other court is contested'.

7. The plaintiff in the main action considers that Article 21 of the Convention adopts as the moment at which the proceedings are brought the date on which the application is lodged at the court. The German text of the Convention uses the word 'anhängig' as being equivalent to the word 'formées' ['brought'] in the French version. An action is 'anhängig' in German law as soon as the document initiating the proceedings is lodged at the registry of the court. On the other hand, the word 'formées' in the French text of Article 22 of the Convention has been translated as 'erhoben' in the German text. The plaintiff in the main action concludes that the Convention intended to distinguish between the concept of the bringing of proceedings within the meaning of Article 21, in which case the mere lodging of the document initiating the proceedings is sufficient, and the concept of bringing an action within the meaning of Article 22, for which the action must be definitively pending according to the national law of the Member State concerned.

8. In the view of the plaintiff in the main action, service of the proceedings is, in German law, a matter for the court and not for the parties. The jurisdiction of the court seised thus cannot depend on delays in service effected by the court itself.

9. The defendant in the main action considers that the difference between the German words used in Articles 21 and 22 of the Convention as being equivalent to 'formées' in the French version cannot have any effect on the interpretation of the Convention. He contends that the concept of bringing proceedings within the meaning of Article 21 of the Convention must be interpreted as meaning the definitive initiation of the action and that that concept must be determined by reference to the *lex fori* of the court seised.

10. It should be pointed out that the rules of procedure of the various Contracting States are not identical as regards determining the date at which the courts are seised.

11. It appears from information on comparative law placed before the Court that in France, Italy, Luxembourg and the Netherlands the action is considered to be pending before the court from the moment at which the document initiating the proceedings is served upon the defendant. In

Belgium the court is seised when the action is registered on its general roll, such registration implying in principle prior service of the writ of summons on the defendant.

12. In the Federal Republic of Germany the action is brought, according to Paragraph 253(1) of the Zivilprozeßordnung, when the document initiating the proceedings has been served on the defendant. Service is effected of its own motion by the court to which the document has been submitted. The procedural stage between the lodging of the document at the registry of the court and service is called 'Anhängigkeit'. The lodging of the document initiating the proceedings plays a role as regards limitation periods and compliance with procedural time-limits but in no way determines the moment at which the action becomes pending. It is clear from the aforementioned Paragraph 253, read together with Paragraph 261(1) of the Zivilprozeßordnung, that an action becomes pending once the document initiating the proceedings has been served on the defendant.

13. It follows from the comparison of the legislation mentioned above that a common concept of *lis pendens* cannot be arrived at by a rapprochement of the various relevant national provisions. A *fortiori*, therefore, it is not possible to extend to all the contracting parties, as is proposed by the plaintiff in the main action, a concept which is peculiar to German law and which, because of its characteristics, cannot be transposed to the other legal systems concerned.

14. It may properly be inferred from Article 21, read as a whole, that a court's obligation to decline jurisdiction in favour of another court only comes into existence if it is established that proceedings have been definitively brought before a court in another State involving the same cause of action and between the same parties. Beyond that, Article 21 gives no indication of the nature of the procedural formalities which must be taken into account for the purposes of considering whether or not to recognise the existence of such an effect. In particular, it gives no indication as to the answer to the question whether a *lis pendens* comes into being upon the receipt by a court of an application or upon service or notification of that application on or to the party concerned.

15. Since the object of the Convention is not to unify those formalities, which are closely linked to the organisation of judicial procedure in the various States, the question as to the moment at which the conditions for definitive seisin for the purposes of Article 21 are met must be appraised

and resolved, in the case of each court, according to the rules of its own national law. That method allows each court to establish with a sufficient degree of certainty, by reference to its own national law, as regards itself, and by reference to the national law of any other court which has been seised, as regards that court, the order or priority in time of several actions brought within the conditions laid down by the Convention.

16. The answer to the question raised by the Oberlandesgericht München is therefore that Article 21 of the Convention must be interpreted as meaning that the court 'first seised' is the one before which the requirements for proceedings to become definitively pending are first fulfilled, such requirements to be determined in accordance with the national law of each of the courts concerned.

On those grounds, the Court (Fourth Chamber), in answer to the question referred to it by the Oberlandesgericht München, by order of 22 June 1983, hereby rules:

> **Article 21 of the Convention of 27 September 1968 on Jurisdiction and the Enforcement of Judgments in Civil and Commercial Matters must be interpreted as meaning that the court 'first seised' is the one before which the requirements for proceedings to become definitively pending are first fulfilled, such requirements to be determined in accordance with the national law of each of the courts concerned.**

OPINION OF MR ADVOCATE GENERAL MANCINI

1. The present reference for a preliminary ruling requires the Court to interpret Article 21 of the Brussels Convention on Jurisdiction and Enforcement of Judgments in Civil and Commercial Matters (27 September 1968). The Court must lay down the criteria according to which the court first seised is to be identified when, in the same case, the parties bring actions before two courts in different Member States. More specifically, the Court is called upon to define the concept of *lis pendens* recognized by the Convention and, therefore, to choose between two possible interpretations of Article 21. The first of those interpretations regards Article 21 as a uniform rule for the definition of *lis pendens* and the second views it as a rule of private international law, that is, a provision which refers to the legal systems applicable to one or the other court in order to ascertain, case by case, the concept of *lis pendens* to be applied in each action. Obviously, the second interpretation implies that there are as many concepts of *lis pendens* as there are legal system in the Contracting States.

Siegfried Zelger, merchant, owner of the undertaking of the same name, whose registered office is in Munich (Federal Republic of Germany), brought an action before the Landgericht [Regional Court], Munich, against Sebastiano Salinitri, also a merchant, who resides in Mascali, in Italy. He sought an order against Mr Salinitri for the repayment of the amount outstanding on a loan contracted in 1975 and 1976, and, as a justification for the international jurisdiction of the German court, he claimed that the contracting parties had verbally agreed that Munich should be the place of performance of the obligation to repay the loan. For his part, the defendant denies both the obligation and the existence of such an agreement. The Landgericht rejected the plaintiff's argument and declined jurisdiction. It stated that there was such an agreement but, since it was not in writing, as required by Article 17 of the Convention, it could not derogate from the general criteria relating to jurisdiction. Later, however, the Bundesgerichtshof [Federal Supreme Court] (to which the plaintiff had appealed after an unsuccessful appeal to the Oberlandesgericht [Higher Regional court], Munich) stayed the proceedings and asked this Court to decide whether, on the basis of Article 5(1) and Article 17 of the said Convention, an agreement on the place of performance of an obligation, concluded without observing the formalities specified in Article 17, was sufficient to found jurisdiction in that place.

By its judgment of 17 January 1980 ([1980] ECR 89), the Court replied that the problem was to determine if the clause by which the parties fixed the place of performance of a contractual obligation was valid according to the national law applicable to the contract. If it was, Article 5(1) gave the court for that place jurisdiction to take cognizance of disputes relating to that obligation irrespective of whether the formal conditions provided for under Article 17 had been observed. Since the clause at issue was valid under German law, that decision implied that the Munich court had jurisdiction in the principal action. Accordingly, the Bundesgerichtshof quashed the earlier decisions declining jurisdiction and remitted the case to the Landgericht for a fresh decision.

However, the story did not end there. Having heard new evidence and having requested an opinion from the Institute of Comparative Law of the University of Munich, the Landgericht once again declined jurisdiction, but this time on the ground that proceedings involving the same cause of action had been brought (and were still pending) before the Tribunale di Catania [District Court, Catania], the court which had jurisdiction for the place in which the defendant resided. In accordance with the criterion of priority, it was the court first seised which had jurisdiction, and there was no doubt that, at the time when proceedings were brought before the Landgericht, proceedings had already been initiated before the Italian court, the documents initiating the proceedings having been served on 13 January 1977 and 23 September 1976 respectively. The plaintiff did not accept that unfavourable decision and brought an appeal, contending that the decisive time for identifying the court having jurisdiction was not the moment at which the document initiating the proceedings was served but that at which the proceedings were brought before the court. The Oberlandesgericht therefore stayed the proceedings and referred the following question to the Court for a preliminary ruling: 'For the purposes of resolving the question which court of a Contracting State was first seised of proceedings (Article 21 of the Convention) is it the moment at which the document initiating them was lodged with the court ('Anhängigkeit') that is decisive or the moment at which - by service of that document on the defendant - the proceedings have become fully instituted ('*Rechtshängigkeit*')?'

2. Since it provided for a plurality of courts (general and special), the Brussels Convention allows several international jurisdictions to exist concurrently, and, as the Jenard Report (Official Journal, C 59, 5. 3. 1979, p. 41) observes, that made it necessary to regulate the question of *lis pendens*. That was done in Article 21 which provides that the courts of a Contracting State are of their own motion to decline jurisdiction in regard to proceedings brought before them when such proceedings are also pending before the courts of another State. The terms of that provision are clear: 'Where proceedings involving the same cause of action and between the same parties are brought in the courts of different States, any court other than the court first seised shall ... decline jurisdiction ...'.

The problem raised by the national court in this case concerns the expression 'court other than the court first seised'. The question which must be decided is whether the priority therein referred to is related to the lodging at the court registry of the document initiating the proceedings or to service of that document on the defendant. The doubt arises from the fact that the German version of Article 21 speaks of 'Anhängigkeit'. In the terminology of German legal writing on the law of procedure and of German case-law, that term designates pendency deriving from lodgment (and capable of producing certain effects, such as causing time to cease to run for the purposes of limitation periods as provided for in Paragraph 270(3) of the Zivilprozeßordnung [Code of Civil Procedure]) whereas pendency which derives from service and which removes jurisdiction from a court later seised is defined as Rechtshängigkeit. The national court suggests that it can be deduced from the foregoing that Article 21 was intended to make priority dependent on the simple lodging of the document initiating the proceedings.

That interpretation, which, obliviously, sees in the expression 'court other than the court first seised' a uniform concept of law, is confirmed, according to the national court, by the first paragraph of Article 22, which governs the staying of proceedings pending before any court other than the court first seised where the action in question is related to another action, brought before a court in a different State. In the German text of that provision, the past participle 'brought' is rendered as *erhoben* which, in the language of German procedure, designates the bringing of an action by means of service of the document initiating it (*Zustellung*). The Oberlandesgericht observes that the use of two different words allows the conclusion to be drawn that the authors of the Convention, modifying concepts peculiar to German law, intended to lay down two different types of pendency, one under Article 21, based on the lodging of the document initiating the proceedings, and the other under Article 22, based on service of that document on the party.

3. Let me say straight away that Article 21 cannot be interpreted as the national court proposes. I would exclude in particular the proposition that that provision lays down a concept of *lis pendens* which is valid for the legal systems of the six Contracting States and, even more, that the concept is based on a concept of the institution of proceedings coincident with the lodging of the originating document. Let us leave aside for the moment the obviously marginal argument derived from the German text of the Convention. A problem such as the one before the Court can only be resolved by (a) ascertaining what is meant by *lis pendens* in the context of Article 21, and (b) examining the six legal systems to see if they provide a uniform rule in this case and, therefore, if a uniform rule of law can be found in Article 21.

Let us begin therefore with (a). The concept of *lis [alibi] pendens* implies, on the one hand, that proceedings involving the same cause of action have been brought before different courts and, on the other, that there is a criterion for deciding which of the two courts is to be 'master' of the proceedings. However those criteria vary greatly. An English court, for example, can 'disregard the fact that proceedings may already be pending before foreign courts' and can even 'exceptionally ... refuse to hear or decide a case, if they believe it would be better for the case to be heard before a another State ... because this would increase the likelihood of an efficient and impartial hearing of the particular case' (see Schlosser Report, Official Journal, C 59, 5. 3. 1979. p. 97). As has been seen, however, the Brussels Convention employs the criterion of priority. It therefore resolves the conflict before the court to the disadvantage of the 'court other than the court first seised'. That, moreover, is the rule by which the national court must abide.

However, what does 'court other than the court first seised' mean? The question presupposes a definition of the moment at which proceedings are initiated and there are in theory two conceivable ways of carrying out that task. The first is to identify that moment without taking account of the many substantive and procedural effects which the various legal systems attach to it and the second is to determine it on the basis of the effects of a *lis pendens* and, therefore, deny jurisdiction in the proceedings to the court seised later.

In my opinion, the first method leads nowhere. Its purpose is to establish an autonomous and neutral concept of the institution of proceedings. It is futile, however, to seek support for that proportion in the Convention itself. The concept to which Article 21 refers when it speaks of 'court other than the court first seised' is, on the contrary, variable and divisible into its constituent parts according to the effects which are sought to be obtained from it, and the national legal systems offer us many examples of this. Let us take German law. When it is a question of time ceasing to run for the purposes of a period of limitation, reference is made purely to the lodging of the document initiating the proceedings. When it is a question of identifying the *lis pendens* that is, of saying which court is 'master' of the proceedings, it is service of that document which is decisive. For two different consequences, therefore, there are two different concepts of the institution proceedings.

I pointed out that, in the view of the Oberlandesgericht, a different conclusion can be drawn from the German text of Article 21. By defining *anhängig* (that is, pending from the moment of lodgment) as what Article 22 calls *erhoben* it would appear to be establishing an autonomous concept of the institution of proceedings. I do agree. I believe that the authors of the Convention did not employ the two terms to indicate different things. Nor did they use *anhängig* to lend credence to the idea that, for the purposes of *lis pendens*, proceedings must always and everywhere be considered initiated by the lodgment of the necessary document. Three factors militate in fact against the doubts of the national court. The first is that the distinction made in the German version is not to be found in the French, Italian or Dutch versions. The second is that a *lis pendens* does not arise in any of the other five countries prior to service of the document initiating proceedings upon the other party. The third is that, in German law itself, a *lis pendens* arises, as I have already said, from service of the document originating proceedings and that law relies upon the earlier moment of lodgment for various other purposes (such as, in certain cases, to stop time running for the purposes of limitation periods).

4. We have thus ascertained what Article 21 means by *lis pendens*. Turning now to the second aspect of the problem before the Court, it must be asked if the rule laid down in that article is a uniform rule of law, that is, common to all the Contracting States, or if it refers to the rules governing *lis pendens* under the legislation of each of those States. As we know, both possibilities are open (see in this context, as regards all the legal concepts to be found in the Convention, the judgment of 6 October 1976 in Case 12/76 *Tessili* v *Dunlop* 1976) ECR 1473, and in order to choose one or the other, there is no alternative but to examine successively each of the six legal systems. Can it be said that they contain a common concept of *lis pendens*? Better still, can it be said that they designate the same step in the procedure as the decisive moment for the purposes of identifying the court having jurisdiction when the proceedings have been brought at different times before different courts?

I stated at the end of part 3 of this Opinion that they have something in common: *none* of them places that moment in the procedural phase preceding service of the document initiating the proceedings on the defendant. According to Article 29 of the Belgian Judicial Code, the court first seised is identified by reference to the date of registration of the proceedings on the roll (an event, mind you, which follows and presupposes service of the document initiating the proceedings on the other party). Germany has already been spoken of several times (see Paragraph 253 (1) and Paragraph 261 (1), Zivilprozessordnung). In France, Article 100 of the New Code of Civil Procedure provides that 'si le même litige est pendant devant deux jurisdictions ... également compétences ..., la juridiction saisie en second lieu doit se dessaisir en faveur de l'autre'. Moreover, according to Article 54, 'la demande initiale' (which according to Article 53 'introduit l'instance') 'est formée par assignation ou par remise d'une requête conjointe au secrétariat de la jurisdiction'. However, it is not the mere unilateral lodging at the court registry of the document initiating the proceedings which gives rise to a *lis pendens*. For this to occur, according to the way in which Article 100 has been interpreted by the Cour de Cassation [Court of Cassation], it is essential that the document initiating the proceedings be notified to the other party (judgment of 24 April 1981, Bull. Civ., II, No 104). Italian law is clearer. According to the third paragraph of Article 39 of the Code of Civil Procedure, 'priority is determined by service of the document initiating proceedings', while registration of proceedings on the roll, which takes place after service and upon the initiative of the parties has no effect on that situation. The same is true in Luxembourg. A *lis pendens* arises upon service (Article 61 and 171 of the Code of Civil Procedure) and, as the Tribunal d'Arrondissement [District Court], Luxembourg and the Cour Supérieure de Justice [Supreme Court of Justice] have pointed out, it is in no way affected by registration of the proceedings on the roll (judgment of 21 November 1957, Pas. lux., Vol. 17 p. 207 and judgement of 9 November 1964, Pas. lux., Vol. 19, p. 426). The Netherlands rules are no different. According to the first paragraph of Article 158 of the Wetboek van Burgerlijke Rechtsvordering [Code of Civil Procedure], there is a *lis pendens* when the document initiating the proceedings is served on the defendant. Registration, which must take place at the latest on the day preceding the hearing for which the document initiating proceedings has been issued, is not relevant (first paragraph, Article 135).

5. There are similar tendencies, therefore, but not identical rules. That, principally because of the Belgian rules and of the ambiguity of the French provisions, seems to me to be the conclusion to which the comparative examination I have undertaken leads. If such is the case, it is not possible to elaborate a concept of *lis pendens* common to and valid for all the legal systems. Moreover, the Jenard Report takes the same view. It is stated in that report that the Committee of Experts which prepared the draft Convention decided that there was 'no need to specify in the text [of Article 21] the point in time from which the proceedings shold be considered to be pending' and decided, therefore, to leave 'this question to be settled by the internal law of each Contracting State'.

However, the result which we have arrived at does not provide the complete answer to which the national court is entitled. Having decided that the provision is a rule of private international law, it is now a question of ascertaining if *any* national rules on *lis pendens* are legitimate in the eyes of Community law and, therefore, capable of causing the renvoi provided for in Article 21 to become operative. I would doubt it. For example, I would not consider legitimate rules which limited the rights of the defence. In fact, the Convention attaches particular importance to those rights when it includes among the conditions which will prevent recognition of a foreign judgment the fact that the defendant was not 'duly served with the document which instituted the proceedings ... in sufficient time to enable him to arrange for his defence' (Article 27(2)).

It seems to me that to establish a link between a *lis pendens* and a procedural step preceding service of the document initiating the proceedings runs the risk of undermining the possibilities of defence open to the defendant from two points of view. In the first place, because he is unaware that proceedings have been initiated against him before another court, he cannot raise the plea of lis alibi pendens in time and, therefore, take prompt action to ensure that the case is heard by the court first seised; secondly, because the rights of the defence would also be undermined because the mere lodging by the plaintiff of the document initiating the proceedings would prevent the defendant, even before that document had been served on him, from taking proceedings before another court which also had jurisdiction. Thus, Article 21 only permits solutions which do not cause a *lis pendens* to arise before service. Obviously, that does not prevent the moment at which a *lis pendens* arises from being shifted to a later stage (such as, at the time of registration on the roll: Article 29 of the Belgian Civil Code).

Nor is that all. In my opinion, the only systems which are in conformity with the objectives of the Convention are those which make use of an automatic criterion to resolve the conflict between two courts before which proceedings involving the same cause of action have been brought. Leaving the choice to the discretion of those courts or to the parties would give rise to a situation of uncertainty and of competition between several authorities (what rule is to be applied, for example if two courts in two different States both accept or decline jurisdiction?) It is precisely that situation that the concept of *lis pendens* is intended to overcome and that the Convention intended to eliminate. I doubt, therefore, if the English, once they have ratified the Convention, can maintain in being the system to which I referred to in part 3 of this Opinion.

6. For all the foregoing reasons, I propose that the Court reply as follows to the question referred to it by the Oberlandesgericht, Munich, by order of 22 June 1983, in the proceedings brought by Siegfried Zelger against Sebastiano Salinitri: 'Article 21 of the Brussels Convention on Jurisdiction and the Enforcement of Judgment in Civil and Commercial Matters (27 September 1968), must be interpreted as meaning that the decisive time for determining the order of priority of two or more sets of proceedings involving the same cause of action and between the same parties brought in courts of different Contracting States, is the moment at which a *lis pendens* arises under the law of the court seised. That moment, however, must be identifiable by the application of objective criteria and must not precede service of the document initiating the proceedings on the defendant'.

Case 144/86 - 8 December 1987

Gubisch Maschinenfabrik KG
v
Giulio Palumbo

Article 21 - Lis pendens - Concept - Independent interpretation - Actions involving the same subject-matter and the same cause of action - Action for rescission or discharge of a contract and action to enforce the contract.

Summary

The terms used in Article 21 of the Convention of 27 September 1968 in order to determine whether a situation of *lis pendens* arises must be regarded as independent.

Lis pendens within the meaning of that article arises where a party brings an action before a court in a Contracting State for the rescission or discharge of an international sales contract whilst an action by the other party to enforce the same contract is pending before a court in another Contracting State.

JUDGMENT OF THE COURT

Due and Rodriguez Iglesias, Presidents of Chambers, Koopmans, Bahlmann and Kakouri, Judges

1. By an order of 9 January 1986, which was received at the Court Registry on 12 June 1986, the Corte Suprema di Cassazione (Supreme Court of Cassation), Rome, referred to the Court under the Protocol of 3 June 1971 on the interpretation by the Court of Justice of the Convention

of 27 September 1968 on Jurisdiction and Enforcement of Judgments in Civil and Commercial Matters (hereinafter referred to as 'the Convention') a question on the interpretation of Article 21 of the Convention.

2. That question arose in a dispute between Gubisch Maschinenfabrik KG (hereinafter referred to as 'Gubisch'), whose registered office is in Flensburg (Federal Republic of Germany), and Mr Palumbo, resident in Rome, relating to the validity of a contract of sale. Mr Palumbo brought proceedings against Gubisch before the tribunale di Roma (District Court, Rome) for a declaration that the contract was inoperative on the ground that his order had been revoked before it reached Gubisch for acceptance. In the alternative, the plaintiff claimed the contract should be set aside for lack of consent or, in the alternative, its discharge on the ground that Gubisch had not complied with the time-limit for delivery.

3. Gubisch objected that the tribunale di Roma lacked jurisdiction, in accordance with Article 21 of the Convention, on the ground that it had already brought an action before the Landgericht (Regional Court), Flensburg, to enforce performance by Mr Palumbo of his obligation under the contract, namely payment for the machine he had purchased.

4. The tribunale di Roma dismissed the objection of *lis pendens* based on Article 21 of the Convention; Gubisch appealed to the Corte suprema di cassazione, which stayed the proceedings and referred to the Court the following question for a preliminary ruling: 'Does a case where, in relation to the same contract, one party applies to a court in a Contracting State for a declaration that the contract is inoperative (or in any event for its discharge) whilst the other institutes proceedings before the courts of another Contracting State for its enforcement fall within the scope of the concept of *lis pendens* pursuant to Article 21 of the Brussels Convention of 27 September 1968?'

5. Reference is made to the Report for the Hearing for a fuller account of the facts of the case, the course of the procedure and the written observations submitted to the Court, which are mentioned hereinafter only insofar as is necessary for the reasoning of the Court.

6. In order to answer the question submitted, it is necessary to determine first of all whether the terms used in Article 21 of the Convention in order to describe the circumstances constituting *lis pendens* (an expression used solely in the heading of Section 8 of Title II)

are to be interpreted independently or are to be regarded as referring to the national law of one or other of the States concerned.

7. As the Court has already held in its judgment of 6 October 1976 in Case 12/76 Tessili v Dunlop [1976] ECR 1473, neither of those two options rules out the other since the appropriate choice can be made only in respect of each of the provisions of the Convention to ensure that it is fully effective having regard to the objectives of Article 220 of the EEC Treaty.

8. According to its preamble, which incorporates in part the terms of Article 220, the Convention seeks in particular to facilitate the recognition and enforcement of judgments of courts or tribunals and to strengthen in the Community the legal protection of persons therein established. Article 21, together with Article 22 on related actions, is contained in Section 8 of Title II of the Convention; that section is intended, in the interests of the proper administration of justice within the Community, to prevent parallel proceedings before the courts of different Contracting States and to avoid conflicts between decisions which might result therefrom. Those rules are therefore designed to preclude, insofar as is possible and from the outset, the possibility of a situation arising such as that referred to in Article 27(3), that is to say, the non-recognition of a judgment on account of its irreconcilability with a judgment given in a dispute between the same parties in the State in which recognition is sought.

9. Moreover, in its judgment of 30 November 1976 in Case 42/76 *De Wolf* v *Cox* [1976] ECR 1759, the Court acknowledged the importance of those objectives of the Convention even outside the narrow field of *lis pendens*, holding that it would be incompatible with the meaning of Article 26 *et seq.* on the recognition of judgments to accept the admissibility of an application concerning the same subject-matter and brought between the same parties as an application upon which judgment has already been delivered by a court in another Contracting State.

10. Furthermore, the concept of *lis pendens* is not the same in all the legal systems of the Contracting States and, as the Court has already held in its judgment of 7 June 1984 in Case 129/83 *Zelger* v *Salinitri* [1984] ECR 2397, a common concept of *lis pendens* cannot be arrived at by a combination of the various relevant provisions of national law.

11. Having regard to the aforesaid objectives of the Convention and to

the fact that Article 21, instead of referring to the term *lis pendens* as used in the different national legal systems of the Contracting States, lays down a number of substantive conditions as components of a definition, it must be concluded that the terms used in Article 21 in order to determine whether a situation of *lis pendens* arises must be regarded as independent.

12. That result does not conflict with the judgment of 7 June 1984, referred to earlier, in which the Court pointed out that the question as to the moment at which a court is to be considered seised of a case for the purposes of Article 21 of the Convention must be appraised and resolved, in the case of each court, according to the rules of its own national law. That reasoning was based on the absence of any indication in that Article of the nature of the relevant procedural formalities, since the Convention does not have the aim of unifying those formalities, which are closely connected with the procedural systems of the different Member States. Accordingly, it cannot prejudge the interpretation of the substantive scope of the conditions of *lis pendens* laid down in Article 21.

13. It is therefore in the light of the aforesaid objectives and with a view to ensuring consistency as between Articles 21 and 27(3) that the question whether a procedural situation of the kind at issue in this case is covered by Article 21 must be dealt with. The salient features of that situation are that one of the parties has brought an action before a court of first instance for the enforcement of an obligation stipulated in an international contract of sale; an action is subsequently brought against him by the other party in another Contracting State for the rescission or discharge of the same contract.

14. It must be observed first of all that according to its wording Article 21 applies where two actions are between the same parties and involve the same cause of action and the same subject-matter; it does not lay down any further conditions. Even though the German version of Article 21 does not expressly distinguish between the terms 'subject-matter' and 'cause of action', it must be construed in the same manner as the other language versions, all of which make that distinction.

15. In the procedural situation which has given rise to the question submitted for a preliminary ruling the same parties are engaged in two legal proceedings in different Contracting States which are based on the same 'cause of action', that is to say the same contractual relationship. The problem which arises, therefore, is whether those two actions have

the same 'subject-matter' when the first seeks to enforce the contract and the second seeks its rescission or discharge.

16. In particular, in a case such as this, involving the international sale of tangible moveable property, it is apparent that the action to enforce the contract is aimed at giving effect to it, and that the action for its rescission or discharge is aimed precisely at depriving it of any effect. The question whether the contract is binding therefore lies at the heart of the two actions. If it is the action for rescission or discharge of the contract that is brought subsequently, it may even be regarded as simply a defence against the first action, brought in the form of independent proceedings before a court in another Contracting State.

17. In those procedural circumstances it must be held that the two actions have the same subject-matter, for that concept cannot be restricted so as to mean two claims which are entirely identical.

18. If, in circumstances such as those of this case, the questions at issue concerning a single international sales contract were not decided solely by the court before which the action to enforce the contract is pending and which was seised first, there would be a danger for the party seeking enforcement that under Article 27(3) a judgment given in his favour might not be recognised, even though any defence put forward by the defendant alleging that the contract was not binding had not been accepted. There can be no doubt that a judgment given in a Contracting State requiring performance of the contract would not be recognised in the State in which recognition was sought if a court in that State had given a judgment rescinding or discharging the contract. Such a result, restricting the effects of each judgment to the territory of the State concerned, would run counter to the objectives of the Convention, which is intended to strengthen legal protection throughout the territory of the Community and to facilitate recognition in each Contracting State of judgments given in any other Contracting State.

19. The answer to the question submitted by the national court must therefore be that the concept of *lis pendens* pursuant to Article 21 of the Convention of 27 September 1968 covers a case where a party brings an action before a court in a Contracting State for the rescission or discharge of an international sales contract whilst an action by the other party to enforce the same contract is pending before a court in another Contracting State.

On those grounds, the Court (Sixth Chamber), in answer to the question referred to it by the Corte Suprema di Cassazione, by order of 9 January 1986, hereby rules:

The concept of *lis pendens* pursuant to Article 21 of the Convention of 27 September 1968 covers a case where a party brings an action before a court in a Contracting State for the rescission or discharge of an international sales contract whilst an action by the other party to enforce the same contract is pending before court in another Contracting State.

OPINION OF MR ADVOCATE GENERAL MANCINI

1. The Italian Court of Cassation seeks an interpretation of the concept of *lis pendens* pursuant to the first paragraph of Article 21 of the Brussels Convention of 27 September 1968 on Jurisdiction and Enforcement of Judgments in Civil and Commercial Matters (hereinafter referred to as 'the Convention').

By a summons served on 12 December 1974, Giulio Palumbo, an Italian citizen, brought proceedings against Gubisch Maschinenfabrik KG, whose registered office is in Flensburg (Federal Republic of Germany), before the Tribunale di Roma (District Court, Rome) for a declaration that the order he had placed with Gubisch for a machine tool was inoperative. Mr Palumbo argued that he had revoked the order even before it reached Gubisch for acceptance. In the event that the Tribunale should hold that a sales contract had been concluded, Mr Palumbo claimed in the alternative its rescission for lack of consent or in any event its discharge for failure to comply with the mandatory time-limit for delivery.

In entering an appearance Gubisch lodged a preliminary objection to the effect that the Italian court lacked jurisdiction on the ground that it had already instituted proceedings before the Landgericht Flensburg seeking payment from Mr Palumbo for the machine tool purchased by the latter on the basis of a valid contract. There was therefore a situation of *lis pendens* as between the two actions, which, pursuant to the first paragraph of Article 21 of the Convention, had to be resolved in favour of the German court, which was the court first seised.

The Tribunale di Roma dismissed the objection, stating that the two cases did not involve the same cause of action and it could not therefore decline jurisdiction in accordance with the aforesaid provision. Gubisch accordingly appealed to the Court of Cassation on the issue of jurisdiction. That court considered it necessary to submit the following question to the Court of Justice for a preliminary ruling: 'Does a case where, in relation to the same contract, one party applies to a court in a Contracting State for a declaration that the contract is inoperative (or in any event for its discharge) whilst the other institutes proceedings before the courts of another Contracting State for its enforcement fall within the scope of the concept of *lis pendens* pursuant to Article 21 of the Brussels Convention of 27 September 1968?'

In these proceedings, written observations were submitted by Gubisch, the Commission of the European Communities, the Government of the Federal Republic of Germany and the Government of the Italian Republic.

2. The view is generally held that the concept of *lis pendens* to which Article 21 refers must be interpreted independently, that is to say without reference to its definition under the lex fori. There is disagreement, however, as regards the conditions governing the operation of that provision. According to the Italian Government, that provision must be interpreted literally. In other words, for *lis pendens* to arise, the actions brought by the parties must involve 'the same subject-matter and the same cause of action'. Otherwise, the relationship, if any, between proceedings pending before the courts of different States is determined and regulated in the Convention by the rules on related actions. Consequently, and for the same reasons as those specified by the Tribunale di Roma, the question submitted for a preliminary ruling must be answered in the negative. However, the other interveners maintain that the objection of *lis pendens* is designed to prevent the same dispute from being brought before the courts of different States, with the result that judgments may be given which are irreconcilable and for that very reason incapable of being recognised (Article 27(3)). The provision under consideration therefore operates not only in the case of proceedings involving exactly the same subject-matter and cause of action but also in the case of actions which, whilst differing in scope, are based on the same legal circumstances.

In this case, for instance, it is common ground that in order to be able to consider the substance of the action for enforcement brought by Gubisch the German court will in the first place have to establish whether a valid contractual relationship exists between the parties, which is precisely the main issue to be resolved by the Italian court. Hence a literal interpretation of Article 21 leads to the same problem being raised in different courts, but that danger is avoided by a broad interpretation of Article 21 which requires the court other than the court first seised to decline jurisdiction. Moreover, only the latter interpretation is in conformity with the spirit of the Convention; that is to say, only that interpretation is capable of ensuring that proceedings are swift and straightforward, so as to improve the mobility of national judgments.

3. Both points of view are plausible and are skilfully argued. In my view, however, the first is more persuasive.

I would recall that, according to the first paragraph of Article 21, *lis pendens* arises 'where proceedings involving the same subject-matter and cause of action and between the same parties are brought in the courts of different Contracting States Under those conditions, 'any court other than the court first seised shall of its own motion decline jurisdiction' in favour of the court first seised. On the other hand, the third paragraph of Article 22 provides that actions are deemed to be related where they are so closely connected that it is expedient to hear and determine them together to avoid the risk of irreconcilable judgments resulting from separate proceedings'. In those circumstances, the court other than the court first seised 'may stay its proceedings'.

As I have said, on reading those two provisions it is clear in the first place that the authors of the Convention intended to regulate *lis pendens* and related actions in an independent manner, and took care to specify their constituent elements and their consequences. The two provisions are designed to prevent as far as possible any conflicts between judgments within the territory of the Community. Hence the need for a uniform definition of the situations to which they relate.

Turning to the substance of the rules, I would point out that the solutions they provide for diverge quite clearly from one another. Article 22 requires that the two actions should be 'so closely connected' as to make it expedient to join them. Moreover, the proceedings in question must 'be pending at the same level of adjudication, for otherwise the object of the proceedings would be different and one of the parties might be deprived of a step in the hierarchy of the courts' (Report by Mr P. Jenard on the Convention of 27 September 1968, Official Journal 1979, C 59, p. 41, under Article 22; my italics). In the case of *lis pendens*, it is not sufficient that the actions should be 'connected'; they must involve the same subject-matter, the same cause of action and the same parties. That explains the mandatory nature of the provision in question, which requires the court other than the court first seised to decline jurisdiction even in the absence of an application to that effect by one of the parties.

The first paragraph of Article 21 is therefore very strict. It is certainly stricter than the corresponding national rules or those in other conventions - and, I should add, quite innovative. In most of the Contracting States the objection of lis alibi pendens does not exist, and the conventions which do make provision for it impose the further requirement that the decision of the court first seised must be capable of being recognised in the State concerned. From the point of view of the consequences, moreover, the court first seised usually has the option of declining jurisdiction or is able to choose between declining jurisdiction and staying the proceedings (see, generally, Droz, Compétence judiciaire et effets des jugements dans le Marché commun, Paris, 1972, p. 179 *et seq.*; for international rules, see Article 20 of The Hague Convention of 1 February 1971 on the Recognition and Enforcement of Foreign Judgments in Civil and Commercial Matters).

In my view, those factors are decisive. It is clear that, with legislative traditions that are so unfavourable to the concept of *lis pendens*, the courts of the Contracting States would have complied with the obligation to decline jurisdiction only if that obligation had been conditional on straightforward and unequivocal criteria. Accordingly, the fact that the first paragraph of Article 21 makes the existence of proceedings involving the same subject-matter and cause of action and between the same parties' the basis for the objection does not reflect excessive formalism. On the contrary, the twofold or threefold use of the adjective 'same' ('samme', 'même', 'derselbe', 'idios', 'stesso' or 'medesimo', 'dezelfde') shows that that choice was dictated by a specific policy aim. If that is true, the broad interpretation according to which the provision should also be applicable in the case of actions which are different, although based on the same legal circumstances, ultimately confuses matters which the Convention was designed to keep apart, namely related actions and *lis pendens*.

Moreover, even from a practical point of view that interpretation does not provide all the advantages which are claimed for its exponents. With regard to obligations, for instance, it would be sufficient to challenge the validity of a contract in order to paralyse, by raising an objection of *lis pendens*, any subsequent action brought or the basis of that contract before the court of another State. That is certainly not the objective pursued by the first paragraph of Article 21 of the Convention.

4. With that in mind, I now turn to this case. It is clear from the order for reference that the action pending before the tribunale di Roma is for a declaration that a contract of sale is inoperative because the offer was revoked, whilst the action before the German court assumes the validity of the contract and seeks to obtain judgment for the amount of the price. As the Commission has pointed out, the two cases do not involve either the same subject-matter or the same cause of action. Both cases are indeed concerned with the question whether a contract exists and whether it is operative. In the case pending before the Landgericht Flensburg, however, that question is secondary or, to be more precise, preliminary to consideration of the substance of the action to enforce payment of the price. In such circumstances, it is impossible to endorse the argument of the German Government that, for the purposes of the first paragraph of Article 21, the action for a declaration that the contract is inoperative is substantially incorporated in the action to enforce the contract. From the procedural point of view, the relief sought by the plaintiff in the two cases differs widely in terms of its scope and its effects.

Instead, the two actions are 'so closely connected' - on a preliminary issue - 'that it is expedient to hear and determine them together' (third paragraph of Article 22). In other words, the actions are related, and since that does not permit the transfer of jurisdiction provided for by the first paragraph of Article 21 there are those - Germany and the Commission, to be precise - who see the risk of a conflict of decisions on the same question. That fear is exaggerated, to say the least. According to the second paragraph of Article 22, a court other than the court first seised 'may', on application by the parties, decline jurisdiction 'if the law of that court permits the consolidation of related actions and the court first seised has jurisdiction over both actions', and it may in any event stay the proceedings. Furthermore, those two possibilities do not imply that of disregarding an objection raised by one of the parties. On the contrary, the court other than the court first seised is required to rule on that objection. As I have said, in other words, the rules laid down in the case of related actions are also designed to prevent the delivery of conflicting judgments, and they do so by means which, whilst they may not be automatic like those provided for in the case of *lis pendens*, are not any the less effective.

5. In the light of all the foregoing considerations I suggest that the Court answer the question submitted by the Italian Court of Cassation by order of 28 May 1986 in proceedings brought by Gubisch Maschinenfabrik KG against

Giulio Palumbo as follows: 'The first paragraph of Article 21 of the Brussels Convention of 27 September 1968 on Jurisdiction and Enforcement of Judgments in Civil and Commercial Matters must be interpreted as meaning that *lis pendens* arises only where proceedings between the same parties involving the same subject-matter and the same cause of action are brought in the courts of different Contracting States. The term *lis pendens* does not cover a case where one party applies to a court in a Contracting State for a declaration that a contract is inoperative (or in any event for its discharge) whilst the other institutes proceedings before the court of another Contracting State for its enforcement.'

Case C-351/89 - 27 June 1991

Overseas Union Insurance Limited and Others
v
New Hampshire Insurance Company

Lis alibi pendens - Article 21 - Proceedings brought before courts in different Contracting States - Domicile of the parties to the two proceedings - Lack of effect on the application of the rules of the Convention - Options available to the court second seised where the jurisdiction of the court first seised is contested - Jurisdiction to be declined or proceedings to be stayed - Examination of the jurisdiction of the court first seised - Precluded.

Summary

Article 21 of the Convention of 27 September 1968 on Jurisdiction and the Enforcement of Judgments in Civil and Commercial Matters must be interpreted as meaning that the rules applicable to lis alibi pendens set out therein must be applied irrespective of the domicile of the parties to the two sets of proceedings.

Without prejudice to the case where the court second seised has exclusive jurisdiction under the Convention and in particular under Article 16 thereof, Article 21 of the Convention must be interpreted as meaning that, where the jurisdiction of the court first seised is contested, the court second seised may, if it does not decline jurisdiction, only stay the proceedings and may not itself examine the jurisdiction of the court first seised.

JUDGMENT OF THE COURT

Mancini, President of the Chamber, O'Higgins, Kakouris, Schockweiler and Kapteyn, Judges

1. By order dated 26 July 1989, which was received at the Court on 17 November 1989 the Court of Appeal, London, referred to the Court for a preliminary ruling pursuant to the Protocol of 3 June 1971 on the interpretation by the Court of Justice of the Convention of 27 September 1968 on Jurisdiction and the Enforcement of Judgments in Civil and Commercial Matters (hereinafter referred to as 'the Convention') a number of questions on the interpretation of Articles 7 to 12a and Article 21 of that Convention.

2. The questions arose in proceedings between Overseas Union Insurance Limited (hereinafter referred to as 'OUI'), Deutsche Ruck UK Reinsurance Limited ('Deutsche Ruck') and Pine Top Insurance Company Limited ('Pine Top'), on the one hand, and New Hampshire Insurance Company ('New Hampshire'), on the other, relating to the obligations which may arise on the part of OUI, Pine Top and Deutsche Ruck on account of insurance contracts which they concluded with New Hampshire.

3. It appears from the documents before the Court that New Hampshire, a company incorporated in the State of New Hampshire, USA, is registered in England as an overseas company pursuant to the provisions of the Companies Act 1985 and in France as a foreign company, since it has several offices in that country. In 1979 it issued a policy of insurance covering certain costs relating to the repair or replacement of electrical appliances sold with the benefit of a five-year warranty by Société Française des Nouvelles Galeries Réunies, a company incorporated in France with its registered office in Paris.

4. In 1980 New Hampshire reinsured a proportion of its risk under that policy inter alia with OUI, a company incorporated in Singapore and registered in England as an overseas company, and with Deutsche Ruck and Pine Top, companies incorporated in England with their registered offices in London.

5. After raising a number of queries with New Hampshire concerning the management of the insurance account OUI Deutsche Ruck and Pine Top first ceased all payment of claims and then purported to avoid their

respective insurance commitments on the grounds of non-disclosure, misrepresentation and breach of duty in both the placing and operation of the reinsurance policies.

6. On 4 June 1987 New Hampshire issued proceedings against Deutsche Ruck and Pine Top in the Tribunal de Commerce (Commercial Court) in Paris claiming monies due under the reinsurance policies. On February 1988 New Hampshire brought similar proceedings against OUI in the same court. Deutsche Ruck and Pine Top formally challenged the jurisdiction of the French court, whilst OUI made clear its intention to do likewise.

7. On 6 April 1988, OUI, Deutsche Ruck and Pine Top brought an action against New Hampshire in the Commercial Court of the Queen's Bench Division of the High Court of Justice in which they sought a declaration that they had lawfully avoided their obligations under the reinsurance policies. On 9 September 1988 the Commercial Court granted a stay of the proceedings pursuant to the second paragraph of Article 21 of the Convention until such time as the French court gave a decision on the question of its jurisdiction in the proceedings pending before it.

8. OUI, Deutsche Ruck and Pine Top appealed that order to the Court of Appeal. Taking the view that the dispute raised a question concerning the interpretation of the Convention, that court stayed the proceedings and submitted the following questions to the Court of Justice for a preliminary ruling:

'(1) Does Article 21 of the Convention apply: (a) irrespective of the domicile of the parties to the two sets of proceedings? or (b) only if the defendant in the proceedings before the court second seised is domiciled in a Contracting State, irrespective of the domicile of any other party? or (c) if at least one, and if so which, of the parties to the two sets of proceedings is domiciled in a Contracting State?

(2) Under Article 21, paragraph 2, of the Convention, where the jurisdiction of the court first seised is contested, is the court second seised obliged in all circumstances to stay its proceedings as an alternative to declining jurisdiction?

(3) (a) If the court second seised is not so obliged, is it (i) required or (ii) permitted for the purpose of deciding whether to stay its proceedings to examine whether the court first seised has jurisdiction? (b) If so, under what circumstances and to what extent may the second-seised court examine the jurisdiction of the first-seised court?

(4) If the answer to questions 3(a) and (b) indicate that the court second seised is required, or, if not required, is permitted, in circumstances which do, or may, include the present to examine whether the court first seised has jurisdiction, do the provisions of Title II Section 3 of the Convention apply as between an insurer (reassured) and a reinsurer under a contract of quota share reinsurance?'

9. In its order the Court of Appeal makes it clear that it is common ground between the parties that the French court was in each case the court first seised and that the proceedings before the courts of the two Contracting States involve in each case the same cause of action between the parties within the meaning of Article 21 of the Convention, as interpreted by the Court of Justice in the judgment of 8 December 1987 in Case 144/86 *Gubisch Maschinenfabrik* v *Palumbo* [1987] ECR 4861.

10. Reference is made to the Report for the Hearing for a fuller account of the legal and factual background to the main proceedings, the course of the procedure and the written observations submitted to the Court, which are mentioned or discussed hereinafter only in so far as is necessary for the reasoning of the Court.

The first question

11. In its first question the national court essentially seeks to establish whether Article 21 of the Convention applies irrespective of the domicile of the parties to the two sets of proceedings.

12. In order to answer that question it should be recalled that Article 21 of the Convention provides that: 'Where proceedings involving the use of action and between the same parties are brought in the courts of different contracting States any court other than the court first seised shall of its own motion decline jurisdiction in favour of that court.

A court which would be required to decline jurisdiction may stay its proceedings if the jurisdiction of the other court is contested.'

13. Thus, the wording of Article 21, unlike the wording of other provisions of the Convention, makes no reference to the domicile of the parties to the proceedings. Moreover, Article 21 does not draw any distinction between the various heads of jurisdiction provided for in the Convention. In particular, it does not provide for any derogation to cover a case where, in accordance with the provisions of Article 4 of the Convention, a court of a Contracting State exercises its jurisdiction by

virtue of the law of that State over a defendant who is not domiciled in a Contracting State.

14. Consequently, it appears from the wording of Article 21 that it must be applied both where the jurisdiction of the court is determined by the Convention itself and where it is derived from the legislation of a Contracting State in accordance with Article 4 of the Convention.

15. The interpretation suggested by the wording is borne out by an examination of the aims of the Convention. In the judgment of 11 January 1990 in Case C-220/88 *Dumez France and Tracoba* v *Hessische Landesbank and Others* [1990] ECR I-49, the Court held that essentially the aim of the Convention was to promote the recognition and enforcement of judgments in States other than those in which they were delivered and that it was therefore indispensable to limit the risk of irreconcilable decisions, which is a reason for withholding recognition or an order for enforcement by virtue of Article 27(3) of the Convention.

16. With regard in particular to Article 21, the Court observed in the judgment in *Gubisch*, cited above, that that provision, together with Article 22 on related actions, is contained in Section 8 of Title II of the Convention, which is intended, in the interests of the proper administration of justice within the Community, to prevent parallel proceedings before the courts of different Contracting States and to avoid conflicts between decisions which might result therefrom. Those rules are therefore designed to preclude, in so far as possible and from the outset, the possibility of a situation arising such as that referred to in Article 27(3), that is to say the non-recognition of a judgment on account of its irreconcilability with a judgment given in proceedings between the same parties in the State in which recognition is sought. It follows that, in order to achieve those aims, Article 21 must be interpreted broadly so as to cover, in principle, all situations of *lis pendens* before courts in Contracting States, irrespective of the parties' domicile.

17. In view of that conclusion, it is necessary to reject the argument of the appellants in the main proceedings to the effect that the very existence of Article 27(3) of the Convention shows that Articles 21 and 22 cannot prevent irreconcilable judgments from being given in certain cases in different Contracting States. The fact that the Convention makes provision for cases in which such situations might nevertheless arise cannot constitute an argument against an interpretation of Articles 21 and 22, which, according to the case-law of the Court (see the judgment in

Dumez France and Tracoba, cited above), have the specific aim of precluding or limiting the risk of irreconcilable judgments and non-recognition.

18. The answer to the first question submitted by the national court must therefore be that Article 21 of the Convention must be interpreted as applying irrespective of the domicile of the parties to the two sets of proceedings.

The second and third questions

19. By its second and third questions, the national court essentially seeks to establish whether Article 21 of the Convention must be interpreted as meaning that, if it does not decline jurisdiction, the court second seised may only stay its proceedings, or whether Article 21 permits or requires it to examine whether the court first seised has jurisdiction and, if so, to what extent.

20. In that connection, it must be observed in the first place that nothing in the documents before the Court suggests that the main proceedings fall within an exclusive head of jurisdiction laid down in the Convention, in particular in Article 16 thereof. The Court's ruling does not, therefore, have to cover cases in which the court second seised has such exclusive jurisdiction.

21. In the case of a dispute over which it is not claimed that the court second seised has exclusive jurisdiction, the only exception to the obligation imposed by Article 21 of the Convention on that court to decline jurisdiction is where it stays proceedings, an option which it may exercise only if the jurisdiction of the court first seised is contested.

22. It appears from the report of the committee of experts which drafted the Convention (Official Journal 1979 C 59, p. 1) that that rule was introduced so that the parties would not have to institute new proceedings if, for example, the court first seised of the matter were to decline jurisdiction. However, the objective of the provision, which is to avoid negative conflicts of jurisdiction, may be achieved without the court second seised examining the jurisdiction of another court.

23. Moreover, it should be noted that in no case is the court second seised in a better position than the court first seised to determine whether the latter has jurisdiction. Either the jurisdiction of the court first seised

is determined directly by the rules of the Convention, which are common to both courts and may he interpreted and applied with the same authority by each of them, or it is derived, by virtue of Article 4 of the Convention, from the law of the State of the court first seised, in which case that court is undeniably better placed to rule on the question of its own jurisdiction.

24. Moreover, the cases in which a court in a Contracting State may review the jurisdiction of a court in another Contracting State are set out exhaustively in Article 28 and the second paragraph of Article 34 of the Convention. Those cases are limited to the stage of recognition or enforcement and relate only to certain rules of special or exclusive jurisdiction having a mandatory or public-policy nature. It follows that, apart from those limited exceptions, the Convention does not authorize the jurisdiction of a court to be reviewed by a court in another Contracting State.

25. It therefore appears both from the wording of Article 21 and from the scheme of the Convention that the only other possibility available, as an alternative solution, to the court second seised, which should normally decline jurisdiction, is to stay the proceedings if the jurisdiction of the court first seised is contested. However, it cannot itself examine the jurisdiction of the court first seised.

26. The answer to the second and third questions submitted by the national court must therefore be that, without prejudice to the case where the court second seised has exclusive jurisdiction under the Convention and in particular under Article 16 thereof, Article 21 of the Convention must be interpreted as meaning that, where the jurisdiction of the court first seised is contested the court second seised may, if it does not decline jurisdiction, only stay the proceedings and may not itself examine the jurisdiction of the court first seised.

27. In view of the answers given to the first three questions, the fourth question is redundant.

On those grounds, the Court (Sixth Chamber), in reply to the questions submitted to it by the Court of Appeal, London, by order of 26 July 1989, hereby rules:

(1) Article 21 of the Convention of 27 September 1968 on Jurisdiction and the Enforcement of Judgments in Civil and Commercial Matters must be interpreted as applying

irrespective of the domicile of the parties to the two sets of proceedings;

(2) Without prejudice to the case where the court second seised has exclusive jurisdiction under the Convention and in particular under Article 16 thereof, Article 21 of the Convention must be interpreted as meaning that, where the jurisdiction of the court first seised is contested, the court second seised may, if it does not decline jurisdiction, only stay the proceedings and may not itself examine the jurisdiction of the court first seised.

OPINION OF MR ADVOCATE GENERAL VAN GERVEN

1. Under the Protocol of 3 June 1971 on the interpretation by the Court of Justice of the Convention of 27 September 1968 on jurisdiction and the enforcement of judgments in civil and commercial matters ('the Convention') the Court of Appeal in the United Kingdom has referred for a preliminary ruling a number of questions concerning the interpretation of some of the Convention's provisions, notably Article 21 which deals with the question of *lis pendens*.

2. The questions were raised in a dispute between three reinsurance companies (Overseas Union Insurance Limited, 'OUI'; Deutsche Ruck UK Reinsurance Limited, 'Deutsche Ruck'; Pine Top Insurance Company Limited, 'Pine Top') and the insurers New Hampshire Insurance Company ('New Hampshire') concerning the effects of a reinsurance policy.

OUI is a company incorporated in Singapore and registered in England as an overseas company. Deutsche Ruck and Pine Top are companies incorporated in England with their registered offices in London. New Hampshire is a company incorporated in the State of New Hampshire (U.S.A.) and has its head office in that State. New Hampshire carries on business not only in the United States but also in France and in England. It is registered in England as an overseas company. In France it is registered as a foreign company and it has several offices there. It conducts its business in France through the agency of American International Underwriters SARL, a company incorporated in France.

3. The facts of the case and the course of the procedure were described in the order making the reference as follows. In September 1979 New Hampshire issued a policy of insurance to Nouvelles Galeries Réunies, a company incorporated in France, to cover risks for that company incurred under the five year warranty it gives on sales of electrical appliances. In December 1980 New Hampshire reinsured a proportion of that risk with OUI, Deutsche Ruck and Pine Top. In July 1986 the reinsurers ceased paying claims after raising a large number of queries concerning the operation and management of the insurance account.

On 4 June 1987 New Hampshire issued proceedings against Deutsche Ruck and Pine Top in the Tribunal de Commerce in Paris seeking performance under the reinsurance policy. On 9 February 1988 it brought similar proceedings in that court against OUI. In the French proceedings Deutsche Ruck, Pine Top and OUI have contested the jurisdiction of the French court.

In a letter dated towards the end of March 1988 OUI, Deutsche Ruck and Pine Top claimed that they were no longer bound by the reinsurance agreement because of non-disclosure and/or misrepresentation or breach of duty in both the placing and operation of the agreement on the part of New Hampshire. On 6 April 1988 they brought an action in the Commercial Court of the Queen's Bench Division seeking a declaration from the English court that they are no longer bound by the reinsurance-policy. New Hampshire applied to the Court for a stay of the proceedings. That was granted by the Commercial Court, which decided pursuant to Article 21, second paragraph, of the Convention to stay the English proceedings pending the decision of the French court on the objection concerning its jurisdiction. OUI, Deutsche Ruck and Pine Top appealed against that order to the Court of Appeal. It is in the course of those proceedings that the Court of Appeal has referred to the Court of Justice for a preliminary ruling a number of questions concerning the interpretation of the Convention.

First question

4. The first question concerns the *applicability* of Article 21 of the Convention. The Court of Appeal seeks to know whether Article 21 applies regardless of the domicile of the parties.

Article 21 of the Convention provides as follows: 'Where proceedings involving the same cause of action and between the same parties are brought in the courts of different Contracting States, any court other than the court first used shall of its own motion decline jurisdiction in favour of that court. A court which would be required to decline jurisdiction may stay its proceedings if the jurisdiction of the other court is contested.'

5. This Court has already delivered two judgments concerning Article 21 of the Convention.

In *Gubisch* the Court explained what was to be understood by the words 'proceedings involving the same cause of action'. It was held that the concept of *lis pendens* for the purposes of that article covered the case in which one party had brought proceedings before an Italian court for a contract to be set aside, or in the alternative for the party's discharge therefrom, when an action for enforcement of the same contract was pending before a German court. Between the parties in the main dispute there is no dispute as regards that point. In the order making the reference the Court of Appeal states that it is common ground that the proceedings before the French and English courts involve the same cause of action within the meaning of Article 21 of the convention as explained by the Court of Justice in *Gubisch*.

In *Zelger* the Court explained the meaning of the words 'the court first seised'. The Court held that those words were to be interpreted as meaning: '[the court] before which the requirements for proceedings to become definitively pending are first fulfilled, such requirements to be determined in accordance with the national law of each of the courts concerned'.

In the order making the reference the Court of Appeal stated that it was common ground between the parties that the French court was the court first seised.

6. In the first question the Court of Appeal asks whether the applicability of Article 21 of the Convention depends on the domicile of the parties and if so, of which one of them. The question was raised as a result of one of the arguments put forward by OUI, Deutsche Ruck and Pine Top before the Court of Appeal: they maintain that Article 21 of the Convention does not apply in this case as New Hampshire is not domiciled in a Contracting State, and in particular is not domiciled in France.

Whether a company such as New Hampshire is in fact domiciled outside the Contracting States is a question which was not referred to this Court. Nevertheless, I will discuss that point briefly, since it was the origin, because of Article 4 of the Convention, to which I will refer later, of the dispute as regards the applicability of Article 21.

The first paragraph of Article 53 of the Convention provides as follows: 'For the purposes of this Convention, the seat of a company or other legal person or association of natural or legal persons shall be treated as its domicile. However, in order to determine that seat, the court shall apply its rules of private international law.'

The Court of Appeal states in the order making the reference that the national rules enabling the seat of a legal person to be determined for the purposes of Article 53 of the Convention are to be found in Section 42 of the Civil Justice and Judgments Act 1982. The section provides that a corporation has its seat in a Contracting State if and only if:

- it was incorporated or formed under the law of that State and has its registered office or some other official address there; or
- its central management and control is exercised in that State.

Consequently, the Court of Appeal is of the opinion that under the rules of private international law applicable by it New Hampshire does not have its seat in another Contracting State within the meaning of Article 53 of the Convention. However, the Court of Appeal adds that the question whether under French law New Hampshire is to be regarded as domiciled in France is a matter of dispute between the parties.

7. I now come back to the argument relied on by OUI, Deutsche Ruck and Pine Top as explained by them in their observations to this Court. They submit that Article 21 of the Convention applies solely if the defendant is domiciled in the territory of a Contracting State and not when, as the Court of Appeal assumed, he is not domiciled there. Whereas in the first case Article 2 and the provisions referred to in Article 3 of the Convention itself indicate which court has jurisdiction, jurisdiction in the second case is determined according to Article 4 of the Convention in each Contracting State by the law of that State. In that case English law provides that the principle of *forum conveniens* applies, according to which the English court itself may deal with the case if it is to be considered, in the circumstances of the case, as the most appropriate forum.

New Hampshire, the United Kingdom, the German Government and the

Commission take the view in their observations that Article 21 of the Convention does apply in the present procedural situation, that is to say, as the Court of Appeal does that New Hampshire is not domiciled in a Contracting State. I agree with them for the reasons I shall set out.

8. Article 21 of the Convention governs cases where proceedings involving the same cause of action and between the same parties are brought in the courts of different Contracting States. According to that article the court last seised (which I shall call the second court) must decline jurisdiction in favour of the court first seized (which I shall call the first court) unless it chooses to stay its proceedings where the jurisdiction of the first court is contested.

As regards the principle of *lis pendens* Article 21 of the Convention makes no distinction based on the provisions applied pursuant to the Convention to determine the jurisdiction of a court. More particularly it makes no special provision, as the representative of the reinsurers suggested at the hearing, for cases in which Article 4 of the Convention applies. Consequently, Article 21 must be read as meaning that its provisions applied both when the jurisdiction of the court is determined pursuant to Articles 2 and 3 of the Convention by the provisions of the Convention itself (that is to say when the defendant is domiciled in the territory of a Contracting State) and when jurisdiction is governed in accordance with Article 4 of the Convention by the legislation of the relevant Contracting State (that is to say, when the defendant is not domiciled in the territory of the Contracting State). Thus the *wording* of Article 21 of the Convention indicates that that article applies irrespective of the domicile of the parties.

9. That interpretation is in accordance with the *purpose* of the provision. In *Gubisch* the Court of Justice described that purpose as follows (paragraph 8 of the decision): 'Article 21, together with Article 22 on related actions, is contained in Section 8 of Title II of the Convention; that section is intended, in the interests of the proper administration of justice within the Community, to prevent parallel proceedings before the courts of different Contracting States and to avoid conflicts between decisions which might result therefrom. Those rules are therefore designed to preclude, in so far as is possible and from the outset, the possibility of a situation arising such as that referred to in Article 27(3), that is to say the non-recognition of a judgment on account of its irreconcilability with a judgment given in a dispute between the same parties in the State in which recognition is sought.'

That purpose is best served if Article 21 of the Convention is interpreted as broadly as possible in order to enable it to be applied in principle (granted that there may be an exception in the case of exclusive jurisdiction: see paragraph 13, below) in all cases of proceedings pending before the courts of different Contracting States which are capable of leading to irreconcilable decisions and thus, as I have said, regardless of whether those courts have jurisdiction pursuant to the provisions of Articles 2 and 3 or pursuant to those of Article 4 of the Convention.

Consequently, I see no reason connected with the purpose of Article 21 of the Convention, either, to exclude its application in cases where Article 4 applies.

I therefore conclude on the basis of both the wording and the purpose of Article 21 of the Convention that it applies regardless of the domicile of the parties.

Second and third question

10. The second and third questions concern the *interpretation* of the second paragraph of Article 21 of the Convention.

In the second question the Court of Appeal assumes that Article 21 of the Convention is applicable, that the jurisdiction of the first court is contested and that the second court, under the option given to it by the second paragraph of Article 21, has not declined jurisdiction in favour of the first court. The Court of Appeal wishes to know if in those circumstances the second court is obliged to stay its proceedings or whether it may consider the case directly itself.

The third question applies if the second is answered to the effect that the second court is not bound to stay the proceedings, but *may* deal with the case itself. In the third question the Court of Appeal wishes to know whether *in that case* the second court is required or permitted, in order to decide whether to stay its proceedings or decide the case itself, to examine whether the first court has jurisdiction, and, if so, in what circumstances and to what extent such an examination may or must be conducted.

11. Those questions arose as a result of an alternative argument relied on by OUI, Deutsche Ruck and Pine Top to the effect that the second paragraph of Article 21 of the Convention applies only where the first court has been *properly* seised, a fact which the second court must accordingly ascertain. If the English court did in fact examine the jurisdiction of the French court in their case, they maintain that it would be apparent that the French court is not entitled under the Convention to assume jurisdiction as regards Deutsche Ruck and Pine Top since they have their seat in England and ought therefore to have been sued there, and that as regards OUI, which is registered in England as an overseas company, the French court cannot derive jurisdiction from either the Convention or French law. New Hampshire contends, according to the order making reference, that the French courts do have jurisdiction on the ground that under French law it must be regarded as being domiciled in France for the purposes of the second paragraph of Article 4 of the Convention (or possibly the second paragraph of Article 8), and that such jurisdiction may in fact also be founded on Article 5(1) of the Convention.

12. The question whether the French courts have jurisdiction has not been put to this Court. The Court of Justice has been asked to give a preliminary ruling solely on the question whether the second court may or must examine the jurisdiction of the first.

The representative of OUI, Deutsche Ruck and Pine Top submitted at the hearing that the second court may in some cases proceed to hear itself a case pending before it without awaiting a declaration by the first court that it has no jurisdiction. That argument is based on the view held by some writers that Article 21 of the Convention does not apply where the second court has exclusive jurisdiction on one of the grounds set out in Article 16 of the Convention. That is said to indicate that the second court must in all cases consider whether the first court was *properly* seised.

13. Whether Article 16 of the Convention, like other articles (for instance Article 17) which confer exclusive jurisdiction, constitutes an exception to the rule laid down in Article 21 of the Convention is a question which I need not consider here. It has not been referred by the Court of Appeal. In any case, neither of the parties has suggested that this is a case of exclusive jurisdiction.

Whatever the answer to that question may be, it seems to me to be going too far to draw from the (possible) existence of an exception where there is exclusive jurisdiction the conclusion that the second court may or must in other cases, too, examine whether the first court has jurisdiction.

There is a radical difference between the two hypotheses. Where there is exclusive jurisdiction the second court examines solely the question of its own (exclusive) jurisdiction. That is not so in cases such as the present where there is no ground for exclusive jurisdiction. In such a case the second court, if one takes the view put forward by the reinsurers, would be led to examine the jurisdiction of the first court *in place of the latter* in order to assume jurisdiction itself if it takes the view that the first court has no jurisdiction. Given the difference between the two hypotheses, the *possible* existence of an exception to Article 21 of the Convention where there is exclusive jurisdiction is not relevant to the case in hand.

14. Now, as regards the questions actually referred, I agree with New Hampshire, the United Kingdom, the German Government and the Commission that the interpretation of the second paragraph of Article 21 of the Convention advocated by OUI, Deutsche Ruck and Pine Top (see paragraph 11, above) must be rejected. That is clear from the purpose of the provision, as just described.

The second paragraph of Article 21 of the Convention contains an exception to the general principle that jurisdiction must be declined in favour of the first court. The purpose of that exception was described in the Jenard Report as follows: 'This rule was introduced so that the parties would not have to institute new proceedings if, for example, the court first seised of the matter were to decline jurisdiction. The risk of unnecessary disclaimers of jurisdiction is thereby avoided.'

In view of that statement of its purpose I consider that if the second court does not wish to decline jurisdiction in favour of the first court when the jurisdiction of the first court is contested, it must confine itself to staying the proceedings before it without embarking on an examination of the matter itself. Staying the proceedings is entirely sufficient, indeed, to satisfy the aim of avoiding unnecessary disclaimers of jurisdiction as far as possible (that is to say, avoiding the possibility that whenever the first court declares that it has no jurisdiction, the second may no longer validly be seised). It is therefore unnecessary for the second court to proceed to make the examination and decide the case on that basis. Indeed, if it does so, conflicting decisions might arise, if the first court, too, declared that it had jurisdiction and ruled on the case, a result which the Convention seeks to avoid as far as possible (paragraph 9, above).

15. Consequently, the second court must in circumstances such as those of

the present case stay its proceedings, if it has not declined jurisdiction in favour of the first court. That also applies if the second court is of the opinion that the first court has no jurisdiction. In any case, whether the first court has jurisdiction or not is a matter not for the second court - leaving aside the case of exclusive jurisdiction - but for the first alone to decide. Any other conclusion would constitute an unjustified interference by the second court in the legal autonomy of the first.

That conclusion also accords best with the wording of the second paragraph of Article 21 of the Convention, which merely states that suspending the proceedings is an alternative to declining jurisdiction in favour of the first court, and does not provide for the possibility that the second court also chooses to proceed with the case.

Fourth question

16. The fourth question concerns the ambit of the provisions of Title II, Section 3, of the Convention with regard to reinsurance contracts. Since that question is asked only if the answer to the other questions indicates that the second court must or may examine the jurisdiction of the first court, I think that on the basis of the answers I have suggested up to now, this question needs no further consideration.

Conclusion

17. I suggest that the questions referred for a preliminary ruling should be answered as follows:

'(1) Article 21 of the Convention applies irrespective of the domicile of the parties who have brought proceedings involving the same course of action in the courts of different Contracting States.

(2) Where Article 21 of the Convention applies, and the jurisdiction of the court first seised is contested, the court second seised is obliged merely to stay its proceedings if it does not decline jurisdiction in favour of the court first seised pursuant to the second paragraph of that article.'

Case C-129/92 - 20 January 1994

Owens Bank Ltd
v
Fulvio Bracco and Bracco Industria Chimica SpA

Articles 21, 22, 23 - Proceedings for the recognition and enforcement in a Contracting State of judgments given in non-contracting States - Excluded - Need for a decision on a preliminary issue - Irrelevant.

Summary

The Convention of 27 September 1968 on Jurisdiction and the Enforcement of Judgments in Civil and Commercial Matters and, in particular, Articles 21, 22 and 23 thereof do not apply to proceedings, or to issues arising in proceedings, in Contracting States for the recognition and enforcement of judgments given in civil and commercial matters in non-contracting States.

First, it follows from Articles 26 and 31 of the Convention, which are to be read in conjunction with Article 25, that the procedures provided for in Title III of the Convention, which concerns recognition and enforcement, apply only to judgments given by the courts of Contracting States. Secondly, the rules on jurisdiction contained in Title II of the Convention do not establish the forum in which proceedings for the recognition and enforcement of judgments given in non-contracting States are to take place, having regard to the fact that Article 16(5), which provides that in proceedings concerned with the enforcement of judgments the courts of the Contracting State in which the judgment has been or is to be enforced are to have exclusive jurisdiction, is also to be read in conjunction with the definition of "judgment" contained in Article 25. No distinction can be drawn in that regard between an order for enforcement simpliciter and a judgment of a court of a Contracting State ruling on an issue arising in proceedings for the enforcement of a judgment given in a non-contracting State, since if the subject-matter of such a dispute is such that it falls outside the scope of the Convention, the existence of a preliminary issue on which the court has to give a ruling in order to decide the dispute cannot justify the application of the Convention, whatever the nature of that issue may be.

JUDGMENT OF THE COURT

Mancini, President of the Chamber, Díez de Velasco, Kakouris, Schockweiler and Kapteyn, Judges

1. By order of 1 April 1992, received at the Court on 22 April 1992, the House of Lords referred to the Court for a preliminary ruling pursuant to the Protocol of 3 June 1971 on the interpretation by the Court of Justice of the Convention of 27 September 1968 on Jurisdiction and the Enforcement of Judgments in Civil and Commercial Matters (Official Journal 1972 L 299, p.32) three questions on the interpretation of that Convention, as amended by the Convention of 9 October 1978 on the accession of the Kingdom of Denmark, Ireland and the United Kingdom of Great Britain and Northern Ireland (Official Journal 1978 L 304, p.l) and by the Convention of 25 October 1982 on the accession of the Hellenic Republic (Official Journal 1982 L 388, p.1) (hereinafter referred to as 'the Convention'), in particular Articles 21, 22 and 23, relating to lis pendens and related actions.

2. Those questions arose in proceedings between Owens Bank Ltd (hereinafter referred to as 'Owens Bank'), a company domiciled in the independent Caribbean State known as Saint Vincent and the Grenadines (hereinafter referred to as 'Saint Vincent') and Bracco Industria Chimica SpA, a company domiciled in Italy (hereinafter referred to as 'Bracco SpA'), and its chairman and managing director, Fulvio Bracco, domiciled in Italy.

3. Owens Bank claims to have lent SFR 9 000 000 in cash to Fulvio Bracco in 1979. According to a clause in the documentation relating to the loan, the High Court of Justice of Saint Vincent was to have jurisdiction to decide all disputes. On 29 January 1988 Owens Bank obtained from that court a judgment (hereinafter referred to as 'the Saint Vincent judgment') ordering Fulvio Bracco and Bracco SpA to repay the

loan. An appeal lodged by the last named parties was dismissed by the Court of Appeal of Saint Vincent on 12 December 1989.

4. In the course of those proceedings Fulvio Bracco and Bracco SpA denied that a loan was made. They alleged that the documents submitted by Owens Bank were forgeries and that certain witnesses had given false testimony.

5. On 11 July 1989 Owens Bank applied in Italy for an order for the enforcement of the Saint Vincent judgment. Before the Italian court Fulvio Bracco and Bracco SpA claimed, *inter alia*, that Owens Bank had obtained that decision by fraud.

6. On 7 March 1990 Owens Bank applied to an English court, pursuant to section 9 of the Administration of Justice Act 1920, for a declaration that the Saint Vincent judgment was enforceable in England. Fulvio Bracco and Bracco SpA maintained, as they had done in the Italian proceedings, that Owens Bank had obtained by fraud the judgment it was seeking to enforce. Relying on Articles 21 and 22 of the Brussels Convention, they also requested the English court to decline jurisdiction or to stay proceedings pending the conclusion of the Italian enforcement proceedings.

7. In support of their application the defendants relied on the fact that the question whether the plaintiff had obtained the Saint Vincent judgment by fraud had to be examined in both the English and the Italian enforcement proceedings.

8. The House of Lords, as court of last instance, considered that the case raised issues concerning the interpretation of the Convention and decided to stay the proceedings until the Court of Justice had given a preliminary ruling on the following questions:

'1. Does the 1968 Brussels Convention on Jurisdiction and the Enforcement of Judgments in Civil and Commercial Matters ("the 1968 Convention") have any application to proceedings, or issues arising in proceedings, in Contracting States concerning the recognition and enforcement of the judgments in civil and commercial matters of non-contracting States?

2. Do Articles 21, 22 or 23 of the 1968 Convention, or any of them, apply to proceedings, or issues arising in proceedings, which are brought in more than one Contracting State to enforce the judgment of a non-contracting State?

3. If the court in a Contracting State has the power to stay proceedings under the 1968 Convention on the grounds of lis pendens, what are the *communautaire* principles which should be applied by a national court in determining whether there should be a stay of the proceedings in the national court second seised?'

The first and second questions

9. Since the first and second questions are closely linked, they will be examined together.

10. Before answering them, the nature of the procedure before the national court needs to be described.

11. As the Advocate General explained in paragraphs 7 and 8 of his Opinion, there are a number of ways in which foreign judgments may be recognized and enforced under English law. The procedure followed in this case consisted in having the foreign judgment registered pursuant to section 9 of the Administration of Justice Act 1920 so that it could be enforced in the same way as a judgment given by an English court.

12. That section provides, *inter alia*, that a judgment shall not be registered if it was obtained by fraud or it was in respect of a cause of action which, for reasons of public policy, could not have been entertained by the registering court. Any such judgment, if registered, is open to challenge in legal proceedings. The court seised of the matter may then order the issue to be determined following a trial inter partes.

13. The first and second questions referred to the Court have therefore arisen in proceedings which are intended to pave the way in one of the States parties to the Convention (hereinafter referred to as 'Contracting States') to the execution of a judgment given in a civil and commercial matter in a State other than a Contracting State (hereinafter referred to as 'a non-contracting State').

14. In view of the purpose of such proceedings, the national court asks whether the Convention, in particular Articles 21, 22 or 23, applies to proceedings, or issues arising in proceedings, in Contracting States concerning the recognition and enforcement of judgments given in civil and commercial matters in non-contracting States.

15. Fulvio Bracco and Bracco SpA maintain that such proceedings

involve civil and commercial matters as defined in Article 1 of the Convention and that consequently they fall within the scope of the Convention.

16. That view cannot be accepted.

17. First, it follows from the wording of Articles 26 and 31 of the Convention, which must be read in conjunction with its Article 25, that the procedures envisaged by Title III of the Convention, concerning recognition and enforcement, apply only in the case of decisions given by the courts of a Contracting State.

18. Articles 26 and 31 refer only to 'a judgment given in a Contracting State' whilst Article 25 provides that, for the purposes of the Convention, 'judgment' means any judgment given by a court or tribunal of a Contracting State, whatever the judgment may be called.

19. Next, as regards the rules on jurisdiction contained in Title II of the Convention, the Convention is, according to its preamble, intended to implement provisions in Article 220 of the EEC Treaty by which the Member States of the Community undertook to simplify formalities governing the reciprocal recognition and enforcement of judgments of courts or tribunals.

20. Moreover, according to its preamble, one of the objectives of the Convention is to strengthen in the Community the legal protection of persons therein established.

21. The experts' report drawn up at the time when the Convention was drafted (Official Journal 1979 C 59, p.1, in particular at p.15), states in this regard that 'the purpose of the Convention is... by establishing common rules of jurisdiction, to achieve in the field which it was required to cover, a genuine legal systematization which will ensure the greatest possible degree of legal certainty. To this end, the rules of jurisdiction codified in Title II determine which State's courts are most appropriate to assume jurisdiction, taking into account all relevant matters...'.

22. To that end, Title II of the Convention establishes certain rules of jurisdiction which, after laying down the principle that persons domiciled in a Contracting State are to be sued in the courts of that State, go on to determine restrictively the cases in which that principle is not to apply.

23. So it is clear that Title II of the Convention lays down no rules determining the forum for proceedings for the recognition and enforcement of judgments given in non-contracting States.

24. Contrary to the arguments advanced by Fulvio Bracco and Bracco SpA, Article 16(5), which provides that in proceedings concerned with the enforcement of judgments the courts of the Contracting State in which the judgment has been or is to be enforced are to have exclusive jurisdiction, must indeed be read in conjunction with Article 25, which, it will be recalled, applies only to judgments given by a court or tribunal of a Contracting State.

25. The conclusion must therefore be that the Convention does not apply to proceedings for the enforcement of judgments given in civil and commercial matters in non-contracting States.

26. Fulvio Bracco and Bracco SpA argue that a distinction should be made between an order for enforcement *simpliciter* and a decision of a court of a Contracting State on an issue arising in proceedings to enforce a judgment given in a non-contracting State, such as the question whether the judgment in question was obtained by fraud. Decisions of the second type are, they argue, independent of the enforcement proceedings and should be recognized in the other Contracting States in accordance with Article 26 of the Convention.

27. According to the defendants, that interpretation follows from the principles and objectives of the EEC Treaty and of the Convention, as identified by the Court. It is therefore necessary, in the interests of the proper administration of justice, to prevent parallel proceedings before the courts of different Contracting States and the conflicting decisions which might result from them, and, similarly, to preclude as far as possible a situation where a Contracting State refuses to recognize a decision of another Contracting State on the ground that it is irreconcilable with a decision given between the same parties in the State in which recognition is sought. They refer in this regard to the judgments in Case 144/86 Gubisch Maschinenfabrik [1987] ECR 4861, Case C-220/88 *Dumez France and Tracoba* [1990] ECR I-49 and Case C-351/89 *Overseas Union Insurance and Others* [1991] ECR I-3317.

28. That interpretation cannot be accepted.

29. First, the essential purpose of a decision given by a court of a

Contracting State on an issue arising in proceedings for the enforcement of a judgment given in a non-contracting State, even where that issue is tried *inter partes*, is to determine whether, under the law of the State in which recognition is sought or, as the case may be, under the rules of any agreement applicable to that State's relations with non-contracting States, there exists any ground for refusing recognition and enforcement of the judgment in question. That decision is not severable from the question of recognition and enforcement.

30. Secondly, according to Articles 27 and 28 of the Convention, read in conjunction with Article 34, the question whether any such ground exists in the case of judgments given in another Contracting State falls to be determined in the proceedings in which recognition and enforcement of those judgments are sought.

31. There is no reason to consider that the position is any different where the same question arises in proceedings concerning the recognition and enforcement of judgments given in non-contracting States.

32. On the contrary, the principle of legal certainty, which is one of the objectives of the Convention (see the judgment in Case 38/81 *Effer* [1982] ECR 825, paragraph 6), militates against making the distinction advocated by Fulvio Bracco and Bracco SpA.

33. The rules of procedure governing the recognition and enforcement of judgments given in a non-contracting State differ according to the Contracting State in which recognition and enforcement are sought.

34. Lastly, it is clear from the judgment in Case C-190/89 *Rich* [1991] ECR I-3855, at paragraph 26, that if, by virtue of its subject-matter, a dispute falls outside the scope of the Convention, the existence of a preliminary issue which the court must resolve in order to determine the dispute cannot, whatever that issue may be, justify application of the Convention.

35. Fulvio Bracco and Bracco SpA also argue that, even assuming that the jurisdiction of the courts seised is not conferred by the Convention, the judgment in *Overseas Union Insurance*, cited above, shows that Articles 21, 22 and 23 of the Convention apply even where the courts seised derive their jurisdiction, not from the provisions of the Convention, but from the applicable national law.

36. In response to that argument, it is sufficient to state that the judgment

in *Overseas Union Insurance* relates to proceedings which, unlike those with which the present dispute is concerned, fell, by virtue of their subject-matter, within the scope of the Convention.

37. The answer to the first and second questions must therefore be that the Convention, in particular Articles 21, 22 and 23, does not apply to proceedings, or issues arising in proceedings, in Contracting States concerning the recognition and enforcement of judgments given in civil and commercial matters in non-contracting States.

The third question

38. In view of the answer given to the first and second questions, the third question does not call for a reply.

On those grounds, the Court (Sixth Chamber), in answer to the questions referred to it by the House of Lords, by order of 1 April 1992, hereby rules:

> **The Convention of 27 September 1968 on Jurisdiction and the Enforcement of Judgments in Civil and Commercial Matters, in particular Articles 21, 22 and 23, does not apply to proceedings, or issues arising in proceedings, in Contracting States concerning the recognition and enforcement of judgments given in civil and commercial matters in non-contracting States.**

OPINION OF MR ADVOCATE GENERAL LENZ

A - Introduction

1. The plaintiff in the proceedings before the national court, Owens Bank Limited (hereinafter referred to as 'the plaintiff'), is domiciled in St Vincent and the Grenadines, where it is registered as a company and as a bank.

Bracco Industria Chimica SpA is a pharmaceutical undertaking domiciled in Italy. The chairman and managing director of that undertaking is Dr Fulvio Bracco, who is domiciled in Italy. I will refer hereinafter to Dr Bracco and to the undertaking managed by him as 'the defendants'.

2. On 29 January 1988 the defendants were found liable by the High Court of Justice of St Vincent to repay a loan amounting to nine million Swiss francs which had allegedly been granted by the plaintiff to the defendants at the end of January 1979. In those proceedings the plaintiff relied in particular on certain documents showing the signature of Dr Bracco and on evidence given by one of its employees, who testified to the handing over of the money. The documents contained *inter alia* a clause providing that the High Court of St

Vincent should have jurisdiction to decide disputes arising from the grant of the loan.

The defendants asserted in the course of those proceedings that the documents submitted by the plaintiff were forgeries and that witnesses had given false evidence in the proceedings. However, the High Court of St Vincent held that the defendants had failed to raise that objection in good time, and found for the plaintiff. The defendants' appeal against that judgment was dismissed by the Court of Appeal of St Vincent on 12 December 1989.

3. On 11 July 1989 the plaintiff applied to a court in Milan for an order declaring the St Vincent judgment enforceable. The defendants pleaded before the Italian court *inter alia* that the plaintiff had obtained the judgment at issue by fraud. Those proceedings (hereinafter to as referred to as 'the Italian enforcement proceedings') had still not been concluded when the House of Lords ordered that the matter be referred for a preliminary ruling. According to information provided by the defendants, the Italian court, in a decision which is not yet final, has in the meantime rejected the plaintiff's application for a declaration as to the enforceability of the St Vincent judgment, but without thereby deciding the question whether the plaintiff obtained that judgment by fraud.

4. As long ago as November 1988 the defendants brought a civil action against the plaintiff in Italy (hereinafter referred to as 'the Italian civil proceedings'), in which they applied *inter alia* for a declaration that there was no debt owed by them to the plaintiff. At the time of the oral procedure before the Court of Justice, no final decision had yet been given in those proceedings either.

5. In addition to those proceedings and the enforcement proceedings in England, to which I propose imminently to turn my attention, the dispute between the defendants and the plaintiff has led to a series of further proceedings which do not need to be gone into further here. However, mention should be made of the (not yet final) judgment of a Milan court of 21 June 1991 in criminal proceedings against Mr Nano and Mr Layne. In a detailed and carefully reasoned decision, the Italian court concludes that the documents submitted by the plaintiff are forgeries.

6. On 7 March 1990 the plaintiff applied for an order for the enforcement in England, pursuant to Section 9 of the Administration of Justice Act 1920, of the St Vincent judgment. In those proceedings (hereinafter referred to as 'the English enforcement proceedings') too, the defendants asserted that the judgment to be enforced had been obtained by the plaintiff by fraud. At the same time, relying on Articles 21 and 22 of the Convention on Jurisdiction and the Enforcement of Judgments in Civil and Commercial Matters of 27 September 1968 (hereinafter referred to as 'the Brussels Convention'), they applied for a declaration by the English court declining jurisdiction or an order staying the English enforcement proceedings pending the conclusion of the Italian enforcement proceedings. The defendants based their application on the ground that the question whether the plaintiff had obtained the St Vincent judgment by fraud needed to be examined in both the English and the Italian enforcement proceedings.

7. Under English law there are a number of ways in which foreign

judgments (that is to say, judgments not given in England or Wales) may be recognized and enforced:

- Under section 9 of the Administration of Justice Act 1920, judgments of the courts of certain States (including St Vincent and the Grenadines) ordering the defendant to pay a sum of money may be recognized in England by means of entry in a register. The effect of such recognition is that the foreign judgment can in principle be enforced in the same way as a judgment given by an English court. Similar provisions are contained in the Foreign Judgments (Reciprocal Enforcement) Act 1933.
- Judgments of the courts of other Contracting States which are parties to the Brussels Convention and judgments of the courts of other parts of the United Kingdom may be recognized and enforced under the provisions of the Civil Jurisdiction and Judgments Act 1982.
- At common law, proceedings may be brought in certain cases on the basis of a foreign judgment. These are ordinary civil proceedings, the special characteristic of which is that the action is based not on the original claim (e.g. the claim for repayment of a loan) but on the foreign judgment ordering the defendant to make payment.

8. The registration and/or recognition of a foreign judgment pursuant to section 9 of the Administration of Justice Act 1920 is prohibited *inter alia* where the judgment in question has been obtained by fraud. The same applies where the recognition of a judgment would be contrary to English public policy. Where in such a case a judgment has nevertheless been initially recognized, such recognition can be challenged. The court seised of the matter may order any issue arising in such proceedings to be tried.

The court also enjoys a certain measure of discretion with regard to the way in which such interlocutory proceedings are organized. This is evident from the decision in the case of *Société Coopérative Sidmetal* v *Titan International Ltd.* That case concerned the registration in England of a Belgian judgment. The Belgian undertaking, which had been unsuccessful in the initial proceedings, had served in those proceedings a third party notice on an English company (its supplier). In the proceedings before the court in London the English company asserted that the Belgian court had not had jurisdiction in the matter. The English court ordered a trial of that question, in which the English company should stand as plaintiff.

9. On 7 March 1990 the High Court (Mr Justice Sheen) made two orders. The first order concerned a preventive measure (known as a *Mareva* injunction) which was granted on the plaintiff's undertaking to issue proceedings in the form approved by the High Court. Those proceedings, which sought the registration in England of the judgment given in St Vincent (and at the same time the continuation of the injunction), were issued in the High Court by the plaintiff on the same day.

The second order (hereinafter referred to as 'the registration order') ordered the St Vincent judgment to be registered immediately pursuant to the Administration of Justice Act 1920, but also gave liberty to the defendants to apply to set aside the registration if they had grounds for doing so. The High

Court further ordered execution on the judgment thus recognized should not issue until after the first hearing of the main proceedings or, if an application were made by the defendants to set aside the registration, until such application had been disposed of.

10. The defendants entered an appearance to those proceedings and made various applications, in which - as already mentioned - they relied in particular on the Brussels Convention. On 19 July 1990 the High Court (Sir Peter Pain) held that the Brussels Convention did not apply to the English enforcement proceedings. On 9 November 1990 the High Court further ordered that there be a trial of the issue between the parties on the question whether the registration order and all subsequent proceedings should be set aside on the ground that the St Vincent judgment fell within those cases in which, pursuant to section 9(2)(d) (fraud) or section 9(2)(f) (infringement of public policy) of the Administration of Justice Act 1920, a judgment may not be registered in England.

11. The plaintiff and the defendants appealed against those decisions (the defendants against the decision of 19 July and the plaintiff against the decision of 9 November 1990). The Court of Appeal dismissed the appeals on 27 March 1991. It held that the Brussels Convention had no application to proceedings for the recognition and enforcement of the judgments of non-contracting States and in particular to proceedings under the Administration of Justice Act 1920. Even if the Brussels Convention did apply, Articles 21 and 22 were not applicable to the present case.

The Court of Appeal further confirmed that there should be a trial of the question whether the St Vincent judgment had been obtained by the plaintiff by fraud.

12. The plaintiff and the defendants appealed to the House of Lords against those parts of the decision of the Court of Appeal which were not in their favour. The plaintiff's appeal was dismissed by the House of Lords on 1 April 1992. With regard to the defendants' appeal, the national court took the view that it was necessary to seek a ruling from the Court of Justice.

13. The House of Lords has consequently referred the following questions to the Court of Justice for a preliminary ruling:

(1) Does the 1968 Brussels Convention on Jurisdiction and the Enforcement of Judgments in Civil and Commercial Matters ('the 1968 Convention') have any application to proceedings, or issues arising in proceedings, in Contracting States concerning the recognition and enforcement of the judgments in civil and commercial matters of non-contracting States?

(2) Do Articles 21, 22 or 23 of the 1968 Convention, or any of them, apply to proceedings, or issues arising in proceedings, which are brought in more than one Contracting State to enforce the judgment of a non-contracting State?

(3) If the court in a Contracting State has the power to stay proceedings under the 1968 Convention on the grounds of *lis pendens*, what are the *communautaire* principles which should be applied by a national court in determining whether there should be a stay of the proceedings in the national court second seised?

B - Opinion

Preliminary observation

14. Before considering the questions referred by the House of Lords, I will attempt to define the problems needing to be dealt with in this case. This appears to me all the more necessary since at the hearing before this Court the defendants' representative alleged that the Commission and the United Kingdom were guilty of serious misunderstandings, and consequently denied that the arguments of those two parties were of relevance to these proceedings.

15. The defendants have rightly pointed out that this case concerns proceedings to establish the conditions in which a judgment given in a State which is not a party to the Brussels Convention (hereinafter referred to as a 'non-contracting State') may be enforced by execution. In other words, these are proceedings in which a judgment of a court of a non-contracting State is to be declared enforceable in one of the Contracting States which are parties to the Brussels Convention (hereinafter referred to as 'Contracting States'). The present case, however, does not concern execution consequent upon a declaration of enforceability, that is to say, the enforcement per se of the judgment.

16. The House of Lords seeks to know, first, whether the Brussels Convention has any application to proceedings for a declaration as to the enforceability in a State which is a party to the Brussels Convention of a judgment given in a non-contracting State (see the first question referred for a preliminary ruling). Following on from this is the further question whether - and if so, how - the provisions of the Brussels Convention concerning *lis pendens* and related actions (Articles 21 to 23) are to be applied where concurrent applications are made in more than one Contracting State for a declaration as to the enforceability of a judgment of a non-contracting State (see the second and third questions referred for a preliminary ruling).

17. However, the defendants have rightly asserted that the scope of the questions referred for a preliminary ruling is not limited to the foregoing. The House of Lords further seeks from the Court an answer to the question whether the provisions of the Brussels Convention (or some of them) can apply to 'issues' arising in proceedings for the recognition and enforcement of a judgment of a non-contracting State.

The significance of this in relation to the present case is as follows: the English courts have ordered that there should be a trial of the issue whether the plaintiff obtained the St Vincent judgment by fraud. That question is also occupying the Italian court, which has to decide whether to declare the judgment enforceable in Italy. Does this mean that one of those courts must decline jurisdiction in favour of the other court or stay the proceedings before it pursuant to the provisions of Articles 21 to 23 of the Brussels Convention until the other court has decided the question needing to be resolved? In the following paragraphs I propose to deal with both aspects of the questions referred for a preliminary ruling.

18. In their written observations, and particularly in the oral procedure before the Court, the defendants have asserted that the question of possible fraud was also raised in the Italian civil proceedings. It also appears to have been argued by the defendants in the proceedings before the High Court and the Court of Appeal.

The judgment of the House of Lords referring the questions for a preliminary ruling refers throughout to 'the English enforcement proceedings' and 'the Italian enforcement proceedings'. Since the Italian civil proceedings are mentioned only once in the judgment but are not otherwise referred to, it might be assumed that the House of Lords does not wish the Court to deal with that aspect in its answer to the questions referred for a preliminary ruling.

However, for the sake of completeness I propose briefly to consider that factor as well.

19. Finally, it should be borne in mind that the English enforcement proceedings are for a declaration as to the enforceability of a judgment pursuant to the provisions of the Administration of Justice Act 1920. However, the questions referred for a preliminary ruling by the House of Lords relate generally to proceedings concerning 'the recognition and enforcement of the judgments in civil and commercial matters of non-contracting States'. Consequently, I propose, in setting forth my arguments, to refer initially to the actual circumstances of this case but thereafter to suggest to the Court an answer to the preliminary questions which is applicable to all proceedings in which it is sought to enforce a judgment of a non-contracting State in Contracting States which are parties to the Brussels Convention.

Applicability of the Brussels Convention

Permissibility of double execution

20. The parties which have taken part in the proceedings before this Court are agreed that a decision by which a court in a Contracting State recognizes and declares enforceable a decision given in another State cannot itself be recognized and declared enforceable pursuant to Title III of the Brussels Convention in another Contracting State.

21. In so far as the original decision constitutes a decision of a court of a Contracting State which falls under the Brussels Convention, that position is clear from the Convention itself. Thus it is possible, for example, for a judgment of a Belgian court ordering the defendant to pay damages for breach of contract to be enforced in France pursuant to Article 31 of the Brussels Convention 'when... the order for its enforcement has been issued there'. The effects of that declaration of enforceability are restricted to the State in whose courts that declaration has been made. 'Where the judgment is also to be enforced in Spain, it must first be declared enforceable by the Spanish courts.

This is apparent both from the wording of Article 31 ('there') and from the nature of such proceedings. A declaration of enforceability enables the enforcement of a foreign judgment to take place in a given Contracting State.

Consequently, it must of necessity be reserved to the organs of the State in which the judgment is to be enforced. According to the second paragraph of Article 34 in conjunction with Article 27(1) of the Brussels Convention, an application for a declaration of enforceability may be refused *inter alia* where recognition of the judgment would be 'contrary to public policy in the State in which recognition is sought'. Of course, that concept does not have exactly the same meaning in each Contracting State. Consequently, in the example given above, the French courts' decision to declare the Belgian judgment enforceable in France cannot in any way bind the Spanish courts. If the judgment is also to be enforced in Spain, the judgment creditor must apply to the competent Spanish court for a declaration of enforceability. That court will then decide independently whether the judgment may be enforced in Spain.

22. The same applies in relation to the recognition and enforcement of judgments of the courts of non-contracting States. A decision by a Contracting State whereby a judgment of a non-contracting State is declared enforceable takes effect only in that Contracting State. 'Where the judgment of the non-contracting State is also to be enforced in another Contracting State, the judgment creditor must apply to the courts of that Contracting State for a declaration that the judgment of the non-contracting State is enforceable in that Contracting State. Both cases concern proceedings governed solely by the law of the Contracting State in question, including any conventions existing between that Contracting State and the non-contracting State. On the other hand, Title III of the Brussels Convention does not apply to those proceedings. This means, in particular, that the decision of Contracting State A by which the judgment of the non-contracting State is declared enforceable in that Contracting State cannot be enforced in Contracting State B pursuant to Article 31 et seq. of the Convention.

To permit such 'double execution' would as the United Kingdom has rightly pointed out - create the danger that a judgment creditor could circumvent the conditions laid down by a Contracting State for the recognition of judgments of the courts of the non-contracting State in question. If, for example, Contracting State A makes the recognition and enforcement of a judgment of the courts of a non-contracting State conditional on certain criteria, whereas judgments from that non-contracting State are declared enforceable unconditionally in Contracting State B, the judgment creditor could first obtain a declaration of enforceability in Contracting State B and then (pursuant to Article 31 of the Brussels Convention) enforce the judgment without difficulty in Contracting State A by virtue of the decision obtained in Contracting State B. I share the United Kingdom's view that it is not the aim of the Brussels Convention to enable judgment creditors to engage in such 'forum shopping'.

Support for the view that a decision given in a Contracting State by which a judgment given in another State is declared enforceable cannot itself be declared enforceable in another Contracting State is also to be found in the virtually unanimous opinions of legal writers.

23. In my view, this view also applies where the judgment of the non-contracting State is not declared enforceable as such in the Contracting State but is made the basis of civil proceedings. The decision regarding such an *actio*

judicati is also apt to facilitate the enforcement of the judgment of the non-contracting State in the Contracting State in question. If it were permissible for such a decision to be declared enforceable in another Contracting State on the basis of the provisions of Title III of the Brussels Convention, this would not only provide the judgment creditor with the opportunities, described above, of circumventing the rules applying to recognition but would also - as will be shown hereafter - throw into disarray the jurisdictional system laid down in the Convention.

Scope of the Brussels Convention

24. The defendants essentially put forward two arguments in support of their view that the provisions of the Brussels Convention apply to 'proceedings, or issues arising in proceedings, in Contracting States concerning the recognition and enforcement of the judgments in civil and commercial matters of non-contracting States'. They maintain, first, that this is apparent from the wording of Article 1 of the Convention. In their view, Article 16(5) also shows that proceedings concerning the enforcement of judgments fall within the scope of the Brussels Convention. Second, they submit that the principles and objectives of the Convention necessitate such an interpretation: the Convention is intended to facilitate the recognition and enforcement of decisions of the courts of Contracting States in civil and commercial matters and to strengthen the legal protection of persons established in the Community; in addition, it is intended to contribute to the proper administration of justice in the Community by preventing parallel proceedings before the courts of different Contracting States and precluding, in so far as possible and from the outset, the possibility of a situation arising where a Contracting State refuses to recognize a decision of another Contracting State on account of its irreconcilability with a decision given in a dispute between the same parties in the State in which recognition is sought.

The defendants draw attention in this connection to the adverse consequences which would, in their view, arise if the provisions of the Brussels Convention were not to apply. In their defence in both the English and the Italian enforcement proceedings, they raised the objection that the plaintiff obtained the St Vincent judgment by fraud. If the Brussels Convention, and in particular the provisions of Section 8 of Title II on lis pendens and related actions, were inapplicable, the defendants would be faced with having to prove in both sets of enforcement proceedings that their arguments represented the true facts. If the plaintiff were to apply for a declaration as to the enforceability of its judgment in yet another Contracting State, the defendants would have to prove yet again, in the enforcement proceedings before the courts of that State, that the plaintiff had obtained the St Vincent judgment by fraud. Thus the same question would have to be resolved by several different courts. The defendants would consequently incur considerable additional costs in the litigation.

The wording of Article 1

25. The first sentence of the first paragraph of Article 1 of the Brussels Convention provides that the Convention 'shall apply in civil and commercial matters whatever the nature of the court or tribunal'. Article 1 goes on to list various areas of law which do not fall within the scope of the Convention; these are of no relevance to the present case.

26. The defendants point out that the scope of the Brussels Convention was intended to be as wide as possible. The Jenard Report states in that connection: '... the solution adopted implies that all litigation and all judgments relating to contractual and non-contractual obligations which do not involve the status or legal capacity of natural persons, wills or succession, rights in property arising out of a matrimonial relationship, bankruptcy or social security must fall within the scope of the Convention, and that in this respect the Convention should be interpreted as widely as possible.'

27. The wording of the provision under consideration here and the statement quoted in the immediately preceding paragraph suggest that the proceedings in civil and commercial matters referred to therein must concern claims in civil or commercial law (for example a claim for repayment of a loan), but not proceedings for the recognition and enforcement of judgments. It is true, however, that the wording of Article 1 does indeed admit of the interpretation advanced by the defendants. In that regard, it should be noted in particular that Article 1 forms Title I of the Brussels Convention, which defines its scope. Since Title III of the Convention governs the recognition and enforcement of judgments, the view might be taken that analogous proceedings fall within the scope of the Convention.

The scheme and objectives of the Convention

28. In my view, however, it is apparent from the schematic context and objectives of the Brussels Convention that it is not applicable to proceedings of the kind with which we are here concerned. In that connection, I propose initially to deal below only with proceedings for the recognition and enforcement of judgments of non-contracting States.

29. I am of the view that the question how a judgment of a court of a non-contracting State can be declared enforceable and enforced in the Community is not dealt with, and should not be dealt with, by the Brussels Convention.

30. It should be pointed out, first of all, that according to Article 25 of the Convention, 'judgment' means, for the purposes of the Convention, any judgment given by a 'court or tribunal of a Contracting State'. As regards the relationship between such judgments and the judgments of non-contracting States, Article 27(5) contains an important indication. According to that provision, a judgment of a Contracting State may not be recognized in another Contracting State 'if the judgment is irreconcilable with an earlier judgment given in a non-contracting State involving the same cause of action and

between the same parties, provided that this latter judgment fulfils the conditions necessary for its recognition in the State addressed.'

That provision shows, first, that the Convention itself is based on the assumption that there are cases in which recognition of a judgment given on the basis of the Convention may be refused in another Contracting State on the ground that it is irreconcilable with a judgment given in a non-contracting State. Second, the reference in that provision to the conditions necessary for its recognition in the State addressed shows that the question of the recognition of judgments given in non-contracting States is intended to be reserved to the respective laws of the Contracting States. The Brussels Convention merely governs the consequences arising from the existence of a recognized or recognizable judgment of a non-contracting State and a judgment of a Contracting State which is irreconcilable with it - and that conflict is decided in favour of the earlier judgment given in the non-contracting State.

31. The Commission has in addition rightly pointed out that the Brussels Convention does not affect the right of Contracting States to conclude agreements with non-contracting States concerning the recognition and enforcement of judgments. Whether this results from Article 57, to which the Commission refers, or from other provisions and considerations is a question we need not go into here. At all events, it is clear in the final analysis that the recognition and enforcement of judgments of non-contracting States are matters reserved to the respective laws of the Contracting States (including any existing agreements with non-contracting States).

That interpretation also accords with the Convention's objective of simplifying the formalities governing reciprocal recognition and enforcement of judgments of courts or tribunals, as laid down in Article 220 of the EEC Treaty (which is the legal basis for the Brussels Convention) and in the preamble to the Convention. As I have already stated, decisions whereby a judgment is recognized and declared enforceable in one Contracting State may not be declared enforceable in another Contracting State.

Consequently, the application of the Convention to such proceedings would be of no relevance in that regard to the achievement of the aforesaid objective.

32. On the other hand, the reference by the Commission to the Court's judgment in the *Hagen* case seems to me to be less significant in the present context. In that judgment, the Court stated *inter alia*: 'It should be stressed that the object of the Convention is not to unify procedural rules but to determine which court has jurisdiction in disputes relating to civil and commercial matters in intra-Community relations (...).'

The Commission appears to be seeking to infer from that statement and from the wording of Article 220 of the EEC Treaty that the Convention is not applicable to proceedings having a connection with non-contracting States. I have reservations about subscribing to that view. However, it does not appear necessary to me to go further into that question here. First, it can hardly be denied that there exists in the present case the intra-Community link which is necessary according to the view mentioned, since the recognition and enforcement of the St Vincent judgment is a matter with which the courts of two

Contracting States are concerned. Second, the Court will probably have an opportunity of considering this question in the '*Harrods*' case now pending before it.

33. Furthermore, attention should be drawn to the connection between Title II ('Jurisdiction') and Title III ('Recognition and Enforcement') of the Brussels Convention. The simplified procedure laid down by the Convention for the enforcement of the judgments of one Contracting State in another Contracting State is 'the counterpart of Title II'. The establishment of rules concerning jurisdiction and of the procedural provisions consequent thereon (particularly Articles 21 to 23) serves to facilitate the recognition and enforcement of the decisions given in the respective proceedings. As I have already stated, however, a decision given in a Contracting State whereby a judgment of a non-contracting State is declared enforceable takes effect only in the territory of that Contracting State. Such an enforcement decision cannot itself be declared enforceable in another Contracting State. Consequently, no irreconcilability can ever arise between such decisions given in more than one Contracting State. If the judgment given in the non-contracting State is declared enforceable in Contracting State A but enforcement is refused in Contracting State B, the result is merely that the judgment creditor can enforce in Contracting State A but not in Contracting State B.

However, irreconcilability could of course arise between judgments given in different Contracting States with regard to the relationship between such an enforcement decision and a decision given on the basis of the Convention (in the Italian civil proceedings, for example) (see paragraph 60 below).

34. Above all, however, it appears to me significant that Title II of the Convention makes no reference to jurisdiction in proceedings of the type with which we are here concerned. If the Brussels Convention were applicable to proceedings for the recognition and enforcement of judgments given in non-contracting States, it would also, in accordance with its inherent logic, have laid down rules specifying which courts should have jurisdiction to decide such proceedings.

35. However, no such jurisdictional provisions exist. Article 2 of the Convention provides that persons domiciled in the territory of a Contracting State are in principle to be sued in the courts of that State. Clearly, that jurisdictional rule is not framed to cover proceedings for the recognition and enforcement of judgments given in non-contracting States. The adoption of a contrary view would mean that such a judgment could in principle be enforced only in the State in which the debtor is domiciled. However, not even the defendants are in any doubt that a judgment creditor is entitled to choose the State in which he wishes to enforce the judgment obtained by him, provided of course that the State in question recognizes that judgment. The United Kingdom rightly points out in that regard that there may certainly be cases in which a judgment is enforced in more than one State.

36. The only other jurisdictional provision of the Convention which could be taken into consideration here is Article 16(5). According to that provision, exclusive jurisdiction, regardless of domicile, is granted, 'in proceedings

concerned with the enforcement of judgments, [to] the courts of the Contracting State in which the judgment has been or is to be enforced.'

37. In the case of *AS-Autoteile Service* v *Malhé* the Court had an opportunity for the first time to state its view on the interpretation of that provision. The question at issue in that case was whether actions to oppose enforcement pursuant to Paragraph 767 of the German Code of Civil Procedure fall within Article 16(5). The Court answered that question in principle in the affirmative.

38. The decision in the case of *Reichert* and *Kockler*, concerning the French law concept of an *actio pauliana*, is much more illuminating. In its judgment the Court stated: 'In that regard, it is necessary to take into account the fact that the main reason for giving exclusive jurisdiction to the courts of the place of enforcement is that only the courts of the Member State in whose territory the enforcement is required may apply the rules concerning the action to be taken within that territory by the authorities responsible for carrying out such enforcement.

The Court went on to quote the Jenard Report, which states that the expression 'proceedings concerned with the enforcement of judgments' means those proceedings which can arise from 'recourse to force, constraint or distraint on movable or immovable property in order to ensure the effective implementation of judgments and authentic instruments'.

As Advocate General Gulmann stated in his Opinion, proceedings to which Article 16(5) of the Convention apply are thus proceedings relating directly to enforcement.

39. However, as the defendants' representative again emphasized in the oral procedure before the Court, proceedings for a declaration as to the enforceability of judgments concern not the enforcement itself but the stage in the proceedings which precedes such enforcement. Consequently, such proceedings do not fall within the ambit of Article 16(5). This also accords with the principle that, where any doubt exists, provisions such as Article 16(5) are - as an exception to the general rule laid down in Article 2 - to be narrowly interpreted.

40. Even if the foregoing is not accepted and it is sought instead to place a wide interpretation on the expression 'proceedings concerned with the enforcement of judgments', Article 16(5) could not be applied here. According to the definition contained in Article 25, the term 'judgment' means, for the purposes of the Convention, only a judgment given by a court or tribunal of a Contracting State, whereas the present case concerns the enforcement of a judgment of a non-contracting State.

41. The defendants are wholly conscious of the fact that the jurisdictional system laid down in Title II of the Convention is not appropriate to cases of the type with which we are here concerned. In order nevertheless to achieve the desired result, and in particular to establish the applicability of Articles 21 to 23 of the Convention, they suggest that the jurisdiction of the courts of the Contracting States in such cases is to be determined by analogy with Articles 57 and 4 of the Convention.

42. That construction cannot be accepted. In cases in which the Brussels Convention is applicable, the Convention itself lays down which court has jurisdiction. The Jenard Report states in this regard: 'Moreover, the purpose of the Convention is also, by establishing common rules of jurisdiction, to achieve, (...) in the field which it was required to cover, a genuine legal systematization which will ensure the greatest possible degree of legal certainty. To this end, the rules of jurisdiction codified in Title II determine which State's courts are most appropriate to assume jurisdiction, taking into account all relevant matters.'

As the Court has ruled, the Convention contains a number of jurisdictional rules aimed at achieving that objective, which list exhaustively those cases in which a person may be sued outside the State in which he is domiciled. According to those rules, the general principle is that a person is to be sued in the courts of the State in which he is domiciled (Article 2 of the Convention); derogation from that principle is permissible only in the cases expressly referred to in the Convention: 'Consequently, the jurisdictional rules derogating from that general principle may not give rise to an interpretation going beyond the hypotheses envisaged by the Convention.'

43. The solution suggested by the defendants is therefore irreconcilable with the objectives which the Brussels Convention aims to achieve, in particular the objective of legal certainty. Consequently it must follow that the Convention does not contain any appropriate jurisdictional provisions in respect of proceedings for the recognition and enforcement of the judgments of non-contracting States. This confirms that the Convention is not applicable to such proceedings.

44. The same applies in my view to cases in which the law of a Contracting State provides that a judgment of a non-contracting State can be enforced by means of an *actio judicati*. In respect of those cases also, the Convention manifestly does not contain any appropriate jurisdictional rules.

45. The question whether at least Articles 21, 22 or 23 of the Convention may nevertheless be applied to proceedings of this kind, and the arguments submitted in that regard, will be considered later.

46. The above considerations confirm my view that the jurisdictional rules contained in the Convention, and its Title II as a whole, are framed so as to cover only the 'original' proceedings in which no decision has yet been given, and not to proceedings for the enforcement of decisions which have already been given.

The only provision which could stand in the way of such an interpretation is Article 16(5), the contents of which are discussed above. As the United Kingdom has pointed out, that provision represents an extraneous element, which does not seem to fit in properly with the other provisions of Title II. Apart from the fact that that provision constitutes a basically self-evident rule, its subject-matter is such that its proper place is in Title III of the Convention. It only becomes applicable where a judgment which has already been given is to be enforced or has already been enforced. The only reason for the incorporation of that provision in Title II appears to have been a wish to itemize exhaustively in that Title all matters of jurisdiction. In my view, therefore, its existence does not alter the fact that, with the exception of Article 16(5), the matters of jurisdiction forming the substance of Title II of the Convention concern jurisdiction in the institution of original actions.

47. I now turn to the question whether the Brussels Convention is applicable to individual issues arising in proceedings for the recognition and enforcement of judgments given in non-contracting States. As mentioned above, in the proceedings in which the reference for a preliminary ruling was made the High Court ordered that two aspects of the enforcement proceedings should be tried, namely the question whether the plaintiff obtained the St Vincent judgment by fraud and the question whether it would be contrary to public policy to recognize that judgment in England.

48. On a purely formal view, it is indeed possible to conclude that those interlocutory proceedings concern proceedings in civil and commercial matters within the meaning of Article 1 of the Brussels Convention, and that the rules laid down in the Convention, including Articles 21 to 23, may be applicable to those proceedings.

That view was argued very eloquently by the defendants' representative in the oral procedure before the Court. However, it should not in my view be followed.

49. It should be borne in mind, first, that the application of the jurisdictional provisions of the Brussels Convention to individual issues or, more precisely, to proceedings concerning individual issues would have inappropriate results.

50. Were those proceedings to constitute proceedings in civil and commercial matters within the meaning of Article 1, the rules on jurisdiction contained in the Convention would also be applicable to those proceedings. As the defendants have quite rightly pointed out in their written observations, consideration would only have to be given to the jurisdiction, laid down in Article 2, of the courts of the State in which the defendant is domiciled. In the present case, this would mean that the Italian courts would have jurisdiction to decide the question whether the plaintiff obtained the St Vincent judgment by fraud. The English courts would then be entitled to decide that question only if they were competent to do so pursuant to a jurisdiction agreement. In normal circumstances, the result of this would be that in the event of the judgment debtor being a person domiciled in a Contracting State, the courts of a Contracting State in which it was sought to enforce a judgment of a non-contracting State would no longer be in a position to decide the question of enforceability on their own.

This cannot, however, be right. The facts of the original case need be altered only slightly for the absurdity of this solution to become apparent: were the defendants domiciled not in Italy but in France, for example, the French courts would have to decide the issue in question, although enforcement of the judgment of the non-contracting State is to take place in Italy and in England.

51. Above all, however, it should be noted that the defendants are rather arbitrarily breaking down the proceedings brought by the plaintiff for a declaration of enforceability into two or even more parts, and are suggesting that the trial ordered by the High Court constitutes completely separate proceedings. I am doubtful that such an approach is appropriate. The proceedings ordered by

the High Court are intended to settle points of doubt which have arisen in the course of the proceedings for a declaration of enforceability and fit into the context of those proceedings. In my view, therefore, it is much more natural to speak in that regard of interlocutory proceedings, as I have hitherto done. Consequently, the present case may be said to involve a single set of proceedings which admittedly comprises several stages but which can hardly be divided up into several separate sets of proceedings. At all events, I agree with the view, so expressively put by Sir Peter Pain, that the Convention is not applicable to such proceedings.

52. The question whether these proceedings constitute under English law an integral part of the enforcement proceedings, or whether they amount instead to separate proceedings, is of course a matter to be decided by the English courts alone. However, the question whether they constitute proceedings within the meaning of the Convention falls in my view to be decided solely on the basis of the Convention itself. It should be particularly borne in mind in that connection that otherwise the question whether the Convention is applicable would depend to a large extent on national law. Is the Convention applicable where, as in English law, a separate trial is held to decide an issue, but inapplicable where under the law of a Contracting State all questions arising have to be settled in one and the same set of proceedings? Were it accepted that even in the latter cases the Convention can be applied to individual issues, difficult problems of demarcation would result. The Commission and the United Kingdom have rightly pointed out the threat to legal certainty which those problems would present.

53. In my view, therefore, issues arising in proceedings for the recognition and enforcement of the judgments of non-contracting States are to be treated no differently from those proceedings themselves: the Brussels Convention is applicable in neither case. This is also the view of the United Kingdom and of the Commission.

The second question

54. In asking its second question, the House of Lords seeks to know whether Articles 21, 22 or 23 are applicable to proceedings of the kind with which we are here concerned. That question needs to be considered in the light of the decisions given in these proceedings in the courts below. Both the High Court and the Court of Appeal were of the view that Articles 21 to 23 of the Convention were inapplicable, even if the Convention itself were to apply.

The answer to the second question in itself results therefore, from the arguments relating to the first question. If the Convention itself is inapplicable, then the same should also apply to the provisions relating to lis pendens and related actions which fall to be considered here.

55. The defendants assert, however, that the Convention should be applicable even where its rules as to jurisdiction do not apply. In so saying, the defendants appear to be arguing that Articles 21 to 23 of the Convention can be applied even where the jurisdiction of the courts seised derives not from the

provisions of the Convention but from the national law of the State in question. They place particular reliance in that regard on the judgment of the Court in the case of *Overseas Union Insurance.*

56. That case concerned a dispute between a number of reinsurance undertakings domiciled in the Community and an insurance undertaking domiciled in the United States. The American undertaking brought an action against the reinsurers before the Paris Tribunal de Commerce for payment pursuant to the reinsurance contracts The reinsurers asserted that the French court did not have jurisdiction. They also applied to the High Court in London for a declaration that they were not liable to perform any of the obligations contained in the reinsurance contracts. The High Court stayed the proceedings pending before it pursuant to the second paragraph of Article 21 of the Convention until such time as the French court had decided whether it had jurisdiction.

The reinsurers appealed against that decision. The Court of Appeal thereupon sought from the Court a preliminary ruling *inter alia* on the question whether Article 21 applied irrespective of the domicile of the parties. The background to that question was the fact that the American undertaking was domiciled outside the Community and that the jurisdiction of the English courts therefore fell to be determined by English law in accordance with Article 4 of the Convention.

57. The Court pointed out that Article 21 contains no reference to the domicile of the parties to a dispute and concluded: 'Consequently, it appears from the wording of Article 21 that it must be applied both where the jurisdiction of the court is determined by the Convention itself and where it is derived from the legislation of a Contracting State in accordance with Article 4 of the Convention.'

58. In my view, however, that statement has no bearing on the present case. Contrary to the view advanced by the defendants, the decision in the *Overseas Union Insurance* case concerned a situation which is not comparable to that in this case. The Court was expressly concerned with proceedings in relation to which the jurisdiction of the courts in question derives - by virtue of Article 4 - *from the Convention itself.* That is not the position in the present case.

59. It is however true that the Court made a very general reference in that judgment to those provisions, and particularly Article 21, on which the defendants rely: '(That Section) is intended, in the interests of the proper administration of justice within the Community, to prevent parallel proceedings before the courts of different Contracting States and to avoid conflicts between decisions which might result therefrom. Those rules are therefore designed to preclude, in so far as possible and from the outset, the possibility of a situation arising such as that referred to in Article 27(3), that is to say the non-recognition of a judgment on account of its irreconcilability with a judgment given in proceedings between the same parties in the State in which recognition is sought. It follows that, in order to achieve those aims, Article 21 must be interpreted broadly so as to cover, in principle, all situations of lis pendens before the courts in Contracting States, irrespective of the parties' domicile.'

60. It therefore comes as no surprise to learn of the view expressed by legal writers that Article 21 of the Convention is generally applicable where the same dispute is pending before the courts of different Contracting States, irrespective of whether the courts seised derive their jurisdiction from the provisions of the Convention or from any other provisions. Articles 21 to 23 of the Brussels Convention could therefore be thought to apply to cases of the kind with which we are here concerned, either directly or analogously. Let us suppose that one of the Italian courts (either the court required to decide on the declaration of enforceability in Italy or the court before which the Italian civil proceedings are pending) comes to the conclusion that the plaintiff committed a fraud, and let us further assume that that decision can in principle be recognized in England. If the English courts have decided in the meantime that the St Vincent judgment can be enforced in England, one might expect that the Italian decision just referred to could no longer be recognized, since it would be irreconcilable with the English enforcement decision. A situation would then arise such as the Brussels Convention seeks to prevent. In order to avoid this risk, the (direct or analogous) application of Articles 21 to 23 is indeed conceivable.

61. There appears to me to be no doubt that Articles 21 to 23 constitute general rules which may in principle be applied even in cases where their application is not expressly laid down by the Convention. As evidence of this, it is necessary only to refer to the genesis of Article 25(2) of the 1978 Accession Convention. The aim of that provision was to ensure the uniform interpretation of Article 57. To that end, Article 25(2)(a) of the Accession Convention provides that a court which founds its jurisdiction on a special convention pursuant to Article 57 must in any event apply Article 20 of the Brussels Convention. It is to be inferred from the Schlosser Report that the question of the applicability of Article 21 was deliberately left open, in order to leave the solution 'to legal literature and case law'.

62. In my view, however, it is not necessary in the present case to consider further the construction advanced by the defendants. In order for Articles 21 to 23 to be applicable at all, it is in my view necessary for the proceedings in question to be covered by the Convention, at least as regards their subject-matter. As I have already stated, this is not the case where enforcement proceedings are concerned. The Convention is framed to cover ordinary 'original' actions. It does not cover proceedings for the recognition and enforcement of judgments given in non-contracting States. As regards individual issues requiring to be settled in such proceedings, these may be regarded as proceedings for the purposes of the Convention only where they are severed from their connection with the enforcement proceedings. For the reasons stated above, this does not appear to me to be appropriate.

63. Consequently, it is only *in the alternative* that I propose to consider below which of the provisions of Articles 21 to 23 might be relevant if it were assumed, contrary to the view put forward here, that those provisions were applicable to cases of this kind. It will also be shown in that connection that the argument advanced by the defendants in the oral procedure, to the effect that a

refusal to apply those provisions would result in a 'gaping hole' in the legal protection enjoyed by them, is not persuasive. Admittedly, the defendants are correct in saying that it would be inconvenient for them to have to prove in each Contracting State in which the plaintiff sought to enforce the St Vincent judgment that the plaintiff obtained that judgment by fraud. However, the United Kingdom has rightly pointed out that the resulting disadvantages can in many cases be offset by the application of national rules of procedure, without there being any need to apply the provisions of the Convention in respect of lis pendens and related actions. In my view, the present case illustrates this.

64. As regards the *enforcement proceedings* themselves, only Article 22 might then be relevant. The English enforcement proceedings are concerned solely with the question whether the St Vincent judgment can be enforced in *England.* Similarly, the Italian enforcement proceedings concern the question whether the judgment can be enforced in *Italy.* Consequently, even on a wide interpretation of Article 21, as endorsed by the Court, the subject-matter of the dispute is not the same, as it is required to be by that article. The same is true of the relationship between the English enforcement proceedings and the Italian civil proceedings. Here too, the subject-matter of the dispute might not be the same, within the meaning of Article 21.

65. Article 23 is inapplicable for the same reason. Admittedly, it is in the nature of things for the English courts to have exclusive jurisdiction to decide whether to allow enforcement to take place in England just as the Italian courts should have exclusive jurisdiction with regard to the question whether the judgment may be declared enforceable in Italy. To that extent it is understandable, given the circumstances, that the Commission should rely in its alternative submissions on Article 16(5). However, Article 23 appears to concern those cases (surely not very numerous) where the courts of different Contracting States have exclusive jurisdiction to decide the same dispute. Because the effects of an enforcement decision are restricted to the individual Contracting State, that is not the case here. It would clearly be inappropriate to apply Article 23: if the English courts subsequently seised in this case had to decline jurisdiction in favour of the Italian courts, the plaintiff would be unable, temporarily at any rate, to obtain a declaration in England that the judgment given in its favour was enforceable.

66. According to the first paragraph of Article 22, where related actions are brought before the courts of different Contracting States, any court other than the court first seised 'may, while the actions are pending at first instance, stay its proceedings'. For the purposes of that provision, actions are deemed to be related 'where they' are so closely connected that it is expedient to hear and determine them together to avoid the risk of irreconcilable judgments resulting from separate proceedings' (paragraph 3 of Article 22).

67. Consequently, Article 22 gives the court other than the court first seised the possibility of staying its proceedings, but does not oblige it to stay them. The result would be the same if the national rules of procedure were applied instead of Article 22 of the Convention.

Parker LJ, who delivered the unanimous judgment of the Court of Appeal in this case, pointed out that under English law a finding by the Italian courts that the plaintiff had committed a fraud could affect the English enforcement proceedings by creating an issue estoppel. It followed, in the Court of Appeal's view, that the English courts were empowered to stay the English proceedings on the question of fraud until that issue had been determined in Italy. Following careful reflection, the High Court had decided not to stay the English enforcement proceedings, since, first, there was in its opinion no certainty that the Italian courts would decide the question of fraud at all, and, second, it took the view that no such decision could be expected in the foreseeable future. Although the Court of Appeal was quite prepared to acknowledge the arguments in favour of having that issue decided by the Italian courts, and attached considerable weight to them, it upheld that decision.

The application of Article 22 of the Brussels Convention could very well have led to precisely the same result.

68. Within the context of these alternative observations, let us now turn to the question of which provisions could be applied to individual issues arising in proceedings for the recognition and enforcement of the judgments of non-contracting States. In principle, both Article 21 and Article 22 would fall to be considered here. I will be brief in this regard, since otherwise I would have to enter the realm of speculation. It is true that the defendants have repeatedly asserted that the question whether the plaintiff obtained the St Vincent judgment by fraud has arisen both in the Italian enforcement proceedings and in the Italian civil proceedings. However, as the High Court and the Court of Appeal have already stated, there is not even any certainty that the Italian courts will decide that question at all. Consequently it is not possible to determine whether Article 21 or Article 22 might be applicable in the present case. It can only be stated in general terms, therefore, that Article 21 would apply if the proceedings involved 'the same cause of action', whilst Article 22 would be applicable if the proceedings concerned only related actions.

69. If it is assumed that only Article 22 could be at all applicable in the present case (which seems likely to me), the result must be that the court second seised would have to decide in its discretion whether to stay its proceedings. It should be pointed out in that regard that the same result could very well be achieved on the basis of the respective national rules of procedure.

The position would of course be different if Article 21 of the Convention could be applied. It should be noted in that regard that, as is well known, the Court interprets that provision very widely. In particular, the judgment in the *Gubisch* case should be borne in mind here.

In that case the court second seised would have to decline jurisdiction of its own motion in favour of the court first seised.

70. In the present case, that would mean that in this respect - I am referring in this connection only to the issue of fraud - the English courts would have to decline jurisdiction in favour of the Italian courts since there is no dispute that the latter were seised first. There can hardly be any doubt that this would produce a sensible result. The issue would be decided by the Italian courts, which are probably in the best position to determine it: the native tongue of the most

important persons involved is Italian, as is that of most of the witnesses. The domicile or seat of the defendants and of most of the witnesses is in Italy. Almost all of the relevant documents are in Italian. Of those documents, the most important ones are in the custody of the Italian courts and apparently cannot be released until the conclusion of the criminal proceedings. In addition, the experts appointed by the Italian courts and by the parties are Italian and have produced their reports in their native language.

71. It is clear, though, that this result would be due only to the fact that the Italian courts were seised first. However, had the plaintiff applied to have its judgment declared enforceable in England or another Contracting State before those questions came before the Italian courts, then under Article 21 those courts would have had jurisdiction, and not the Italian courts, although the latter are much closer to the facts of the case which are to be determined. The application of the Brussels Convention would thus result in the issue in question being indeed decided by the courts of a single Contracting State, but they would not be the courts of the Contracting State which, in terms of proximity to the subject-matter, appears almost predestined to deal with the matter.

72. As one has already seen, Title II of the Brussels Convention lays down rules of jurisdiction to determine which courts should most appropriately decide the dispute, taking all relevant matters into account. For that reason, the conflict arising from the fact that pursuant to Title II two competent courts are seised of the same matter can be resolved quite simply by the Convention by conferring jurisdiction under Article 21 on the court first engaged. However, where, as in the present case, the jurisdiction of one (or both) of those courts derives not from the provisions of Articles 2 to 18 of the Convention but directly from national law, that relatedness will be lacking. In those circumstances, the application of Article 21 may produce appropriate results, but will not necessarily do so.

Here too therefore, we find confirmation that Articles 21 to 23 and the Convention as a whole are based on original jurisdiction and are not suited to proceedings for the recognition and enforcement of judgments given in non-contracting States or to issues arising in such proceedings.

73. Like the Commission, I am not convinced by the defendants' submission, upon which they place particular emphasis, that this could result in high costs for them because of the possible multiplicity of proceedings. The very reason for the fact that there could be many sets of proceedings lies in the fact that a judgment creditor can enforce, or can at least attempt to enforce, his judgment in more than one State.

The third question

74. The national court's third question seeks to ascertain the principles of Community law which are applicable where a court other than the court first seised is deciding whether to stay its proceedings. This is therefore a reference to the criteria to be observed in the context of Article 22 of the Convention. In the light of my proposed answer to the first preliminary question, I will deal only in the alternative with the problems addressed here.

75. The decision required in the context of Article 22 of the Convention is a discretionary decision. It goes without saying that the circumstances of each individual case are particularly important here. The national courts must bear in mind that the aim of this provision is 'to prevent parallel proceedings before the courts of different Contracting States and to avoid conflicts between decisions which might arise therefrom', as the Court stated in its judgment in *Overseas Union Insurance*. It would therefore be appropriate in case of doubt for a national court to decide to stay its proceedings under Article 22.

76. Furthermore, there are three factors which may be relevant to the exercise of the discretion vested in national courts by virtue of Article 22, but this does not mean that other considerations may not also be important: the extent of the relatedness and the risk of mutually irreconcilable decisions; the stage reached in each set of proceedings; and the proximity of the courts to the subject-matter of the case.

77. Clearly, the closer the connection between the proceedings in question, the more necessary it would appear for the court second seised to stay its proceedings. If other factors are of some relevance to the proceedings pending before the court first seised, it may be appropriate for the court second seised not to stay its proceedings. It would also appear sensible, for example, for a court to decline to stay its proceedings on the grounds that only an interim measure can be taken in those proceedings and that there is therefore no risk of irreconcilable decisions. The more the proceedings are related, however, and the greater the risk of the courts arriving at irreconcilable decisions, the more likely it will be that the court second seised should stay its proceedings in accordance with Article 22.

78. Contrary to the defendants' view, it is also legitimate for the court second seised to have regard, when reaching its decision regarding a possible stay, to the stage reached in the parallel proceedings. The proceedings before the court first seised should of course have reached a more advanced stage than the proceedings before the court subsequently seised of a related action. Where this is not the case, however, and where there is no prospect of a decision in the first set of proceedings there is nothing to prevent the court subsequently seised from taking account of this when arriving at its discretionary decision.

79. Finally, it goes without saying that in the exercise of such discretion regard may be had to the question of which court is in the best position to decide a given question.

C - Conclusion

80. I therefore propose that the Court should answer the questions submitted by the House of Lords for a preliminary ruling as follows: 'The Brussels Convention of 27 September 1968 on Jurisdiction and the Enforcement of Judgments in Civil and Commercial Matters is not applicable to proceedings concerning the recognition and enforcement of judgments in civil and commercial matters given in non-contracting States, nor to issues arising in such proceedings'.

Case C-406/92 - 6 December 1994

The owners of the cargo lately laden on board the Ship 'Tatry'
v
The owners of the Ship 'Maciej Rataj'

Articles 21 and 22 - Lis pendens - Related actions - Article 57 - Relationship with the International Convention relating to the arrest of seagoing ships.

Brussels Convention - Relationship to other conventions - Conventions on a specific matter - Convention including rules of jurisdiction - Exclusion of application of the Brussels Convention - Limits - Applicability of that convention to questions not governed by the specialized convention

Lis pendens - Actions brought between the same parties - Some but not all parties to the two sets of proceedings identical - Obligation of the second court seised to decline jurisdiction - Obligation limited solely to those parties who are also parties to the action previously commenced

Lis pendens - Actions involving the same cause of action and the same object - Concept - Action for a finding of liability with a claim for payment by the defendant of damages for the loss suffered, and action by that party for a declaration that he is not liable for the same loss - Inclusion - Distinction in national law between actions in personam and in rem - Irrelevance

Related actions - Concept - Independent interpretation - Risk of conflicting decisions - Actions brought against a shipowner by several groups of cargo owners seeking damages for loss which occurred during the shipment of the joint cargo and based on contracts which are separate but identical

Summary

1. On a proper construction, Article 57 of the Brussels Convention on Jurisdiction and Enforcement of Judgments in Civil and Commercial Matters, as amended by the Convention of 9 October 1978 on the Accession of the Kingdom of Denmark,Ireland and the United Kingdom of Great Britain and Northern Ireland, means that, where a Contracting State is also a contracting party to another convention on a specific matter containing rules on jurisdiction, that specialized convention precludes the application of the provisions of the Brussels Convention only in cases governed by the specialized convention and not in those to which it does not apply. Where a specialized convention contains certain rules of jurisdiction but no provision as to lis pendens or related actions, Articles 21 and 22 of the Brussels Convention accordingly apply.

2. On a proper construction of Article 21 of the Convention, where it requires, as a condition of the obligation of the second court seised to decline jurisdiction, that the parties to the two actions be identical, that cannot depend on the procedural position of each of them in the two actions. Where some but not all of parties to the second action are the same as the parties to the action commenced earlier in another Contracting State, that article requires the second court seised to decline jurisdiction only to the extent to which the parties to the proceedings before it are also parties to the action previously commenced; it does not prevent the proceedings from continuing between the other parties.

3. For the purpose of Article 21 of the Convention, the 'cause of action' comprises the facts and the rule of law relied on as the basis of the action and the 'object of the action' means the end the action has in view. An action seeking to have the defendant held liable for causing loss and ordered to pay damages has the same cause of action and the same object within the meaning of that article as earlier proceedings brought by that defendant seeking a declaration that he is not liable for that loss. A subsequent action does not cease to have the same cause of action and the same object and to be between the same parties s a previous action where the latter, brought by the owner of a ship before a court of a Contracting State, is an action *in personam* for a declaration that that owner is not liable for alleged damage to cargo transported by his ship, whereas the subsequent action has been brought by the owner of the cargo before a court of another Contracting State by way of an action *in rem* concerning an arrested ship, and has subsequently continued both *in*

rem and *in personam*, or solely *in personam*, according to the distinction drawn by the national law of that other Contracting State.

4. The concept of 'related actions' defined in the third paragraph of Article 22 of the Convention, which must be given an independent interpretation, must be interpreted broadly and, without its being necessary to consider the concept of irreconcilable judgments in Article 27(3) of the Convention, must cover all cases where there is a risk of conflicting decisions, even if the judgments can be separately enforced and their legal consequences are not mutually exclusive. It is accordingly sufficient, in order to establish the necessary relationship between, on the one hand, an action brought in a Contracting State by one group of cargo carried in bulk under separate but identical contracts, and, on the other, an action in damages brought in another Contracting State against the same shipowner by the owners of another part of the cargo shipped under the same conditions and under contracts which are separate from but identical to those between the first group and the shipowner, that separate trial and judgment would involve the risk of conflicting decisions, without necessarily involving the risk of giving rise to mutually exclusive legal consequences.

JUDGMENT OF THE COURT

Rodríguez Iglesias, President, Joliet, Schockweiler, Kapteyn, Presidents of Chambers, Mancini, Kakouris and Murray, Judges

1. By order of 5 June 1992, received at the Court on 4 December 1992, the Court of Appeal referred to the Court for a preliminary ruling under the Protocol of 3 June 1971 on the interpretation by the Court of Justice of the Convention of 27 September 1968 on jurisdiction and the enforcement of judgments in civil and commercial matters (hereinafter 'the Convention' or 'the Brussels Convention'), as amended by the Convention of 9 October 1978 on the accession of the Kingdom of Denmark, Ireland and the United Kingdom of Great Britain and Northern Ireland (OJ 1978 L 304, p. 1, and - amended text - p. 77) (hereinafter 'the Accession Convention'), several questions on the interpretation of Articles 21, 22 and 57 of the Convention.

2. Those questions were raised in two actions in which the facts and procedure before the national courts are summarized below.

3. In September 1988 a cargo of soya bean oil belonging to a number of owners (hereinafter 'the cargo owners') was carried in bulk aboard the vessel '*Tatry*', belonging to a Polish shipping company, Zegluga Polska Spolka Alceyjna - referred to in the order for reference as 'the shipowners'. The voyage was from Brazil to Rotterdam for part of the cargo and to Hamburg for the rest. The cargo owners complained to the shipowners that in the course of the voyage the cargo was contaminated with diesel or other hydrocarbons.

4. There are three groups of cargo owners:

- 'Group 1': owners of cargo carried to Rotterdam under separate bills of lading;
- 'Group 2': this is not a 'group', but simply the company Phillip Brothers Ltd (hereinafter 'Phibro'), whose registered office is in the United Kingdom, which owned another part of the cargo also carried to Rotterdam under separate bills of lading;
- 'Group 3': four owners of cargo carried to Hamburg under four separate bills of lading; the owners in the group were Phibro (in respect of parcels other than those covered by Group 2) and Bunge & Co. Ltd, whose registered office is likewise in the United Kingdom, Hobum Oele und Fette AG and Handelsgesellschaft Kurt Nitzer GmbH, both of whose registered offices are in Germany.

5. Various actions were commenced in courts in the Netherlands and the United Kingdom by the various cargo owners and the shipowners.

(a) Actions brought by the shipowners

6. On 18 November 1988, before any other proceedings had commenced, the shipowners brought an action before the Arrondissementsrechtbank (District Court), Rotterdam against Groups 1 and 3, with the exception of Phibro, seeking a declaration that they were not liable or not fully liable for the alleged contamination.

7. The cargo owners in Group 1 were sued in the Rotterdam District Court on the basis of Article 2 of the Convention, and those in Group 3 on the basis of Article 6(1).

8. In 1988, no action had been brought by the shipowners against Group 2 (Phibro). It was not until 18 September 1989 that the shipowners initiated separate proceedings in the Netherlands for a declaration that they were not liable for the contamination of the cargo delivered to Group

2 in Rotterdam. Those proceedings were brought against Phibro's agents in Rotterdam, who had presented the bills of lading on behalf of Phibro.

9. On 26 October 1990 the shipowners initiated proceedings in the Netherlands seeking to limit their liability in respect of the entire cargo. Those proceedings were brought under the International Convention of 10 October 1957 relating to the limitation of the liability of owners of sea-going ships [International Transport Treaties, suppl. 1-10 (January 1986), p. I-76].

(b) Actions brought by the cargo owners

10. The following actions were brought by the cargo owners in Groups 2 and 3 against the owners of the vessel *Tatry* seeking damages for their alleged loss.

11. After an unsuccessful attempt to arrest the *Tatry* in Hamburg, Group 3 brought an action *in rem* (hereinafter 'Folio 2006') before the High Court of Justice, Queens's Bench Division, Admiralty Court, against the *Tatry* and another ship, the *Maciej Rataj*, whose owners are the same as the owners of the *Tatry*. The writ was served on 15 September 1989 in Liverpool on the *Maciej Rataj*, which was arrested. Subsequently, the shipowners acknowledged service of the writ and, by providing a guarantee, secured the vessel's release from arrest. The action continued in accordance with English law. However, doubts exist under that law as to whether the proceedings continue in those circumstances only *in personam* or both *in rem* and *in personam*.

12. Group 2 (Phibro) also commenced an action *in rem* before the same court (hereinafter 'Folio 2007') against the ship Maciej Rataj. The writ was served on 15 September 1989 in Liverpool on the Maciej Rataj, which was likewise arrested. The course of events in Folio 2007 was the same as in Folio 2006.

13. For the arrest of the Maciej Rataj, the Admiralty Court based its jurisdiction on sections 20 to 24 of the Supreme Court Act 1981, which implement the International Convention for the unification of certain rules relating to the arrest of sea-going ships, signed at Brussels on 10 May 1952 [International Transport Treaties, suppl. 14 (March 1990), p. I-64, hereinafter 'the Arrest Convention'], to which the Netherlands is also a party.

14. Furthermore, as a precautionary measure in the event that the

English courts declined jurisdiction, Groups 2 and 3 (with the exception of Phibro) brought actions in the Netherlands on 29 September and 3 October 1989 respectively.

15. Group 1 brought no action before the English courts. However, on 29 September 1989 it brought an action for damages in the Netherlands against the shipowners.

16. As regards Folio 2006, the shipowners moved the Admiralty Court to decline jurisdiction in favour of the Netherlands court pursuant to Article 21 of the Brussels Convention relating to lis pendens or, in the alternative, pursuant to Article 22 on related actions. As regards Folio 2007, since they accepted that the Admiralty Court was the first seised, they did not rely on Article 21 of the Convention but none the less requested that the Admiralty Court decline jurisdiction on the basis of Article 22.

17. At first instance, the Admiralty Court decided that it was under no obligation to decline jurisdiction or stay proceedings in accordance with Article 21 of the Convention, since that provision was not applicable for the following reasons: (a) in Folio 2006, on the ground that that action and the proceedings previously brought in the Netherlands did not have the same cause of action, since the English proceedings sought compensation for the cargo owners while the Netherlands proceedings sought neither to protect nor to enforce a right but sought a declaration that the cargo owners were not entitled to claim damages from the owners of the *Tatry*; (b) in Folio 2007, on the ground that Group 2 was not a party to the proceedings commenced in the Netherlands.

18. The Admiralty Court accepted that Folio 2006 and Folio 2007 and the proceedings commenced in the Netherlands were related actions. It decided, however, that it was not appropriate to decline jurisdiction or stay proceedings in the two cases pending before it.

19. The shipowners appealed against that decision to the Court of Appeal.

20. The Court of Appeal, since it did not uphold the decision given at first instance and considered that the outcome of the proceedings depended on the interpretation of Articles 21, 22 and 57 of the Convention, decided to stay proceedings and refer the following questions to the Court for a preliminary ruling:

'1. For the purposes of the application of Article 21 of the Brussels Convention 1968 (as amended), where proceedings are brought in a Contracting State which involve the same cause of action as prior proceedings brought in another Contracting State, must the courts of the Contracting State second seised decline jurisdiction (a) only where there is a complete identity of parties between the two sets of proceedings; or (b) only where all the parties to the proceedings in the courts of the Contracting State second seised are also parties to the proceedings in the courts of the Contracting State first seised; or (c) whenever at least one of the plaintiffs and one of the defendants to the proceedings before the courts of the Contracting State second seised are also parties to the proceedings in the courts of the Contracting State first seised; or (d) whenever the parties in the two sets of proceedings are substantially the same?

2. In relation to the carriage of goods by sea in circumstances where goods are discharged in an allegedly damaged condition, does a claim brought by the cargo owners in a Contracting State in respect of such alleged damage in an action which was commenced *in rem* against either the carrying vessel or a sister ship thereof pursuant to the United Kingdom's admiralty jurisdiction involve the same parties and the same cause of action for the purposes of Article 21 of the Brussels Convention 1968 (as amended) as *in personam* proceedings previously brought in another Contracting State by the shipowner against the cargo owners in respect of such alleged damage if the shipowner acknowledges service and procures the release from arrest of the vessel upon provision of security and thereafter (a) the admiralty action continues both *in rem* and *in personam*; or (b) the admiralty action continues only *in personam*?

3. Where a Contracting State is party to the Brussels Arrest Convention 1952 and its merits jurisdiction has been invoked by the arrest of a vessel in accordance with the provisions of the Arrest Convention by cargo owners in respect of a claim for loss arising out of the discharge of cargo in an allegedly damaged condition, then in so far as proceedings have previously been brought by the shipowner against the cargo owners in respect of such alleged damage in another Contracting State, are the courts of the Contracting State in which merits jurisdiction has been founded by arrest entitled to retain such jurisdiction by virtue of Article 57 of the Brussels Convention 1968 (as amended by Article 25(2) of the Accession Convention) if (a) the two actions involve the same cause of action and same parties for the purposes of Article 21 of the Brussels Convention 1968 (as amended); or (b) the two actions are 'related actions' for the purposes of Article 22 of the Brussels Convention 1968 (as amended) and it would otherwise be appropriate for the court second seised to decline jurisdiction or to stay its proceedings thereunder?

4. For the purposes of Article 22 of the Brussels Convention 1968 (as amended): (a) Does the third paragraph of Article 22 provide an exclusive definition of 'related proceedings'? (b) In order for the courts of a Contracting State to decline jurisdiction or to stay their proceedings under Article 22, is it necessary for there to be a risk that if the two sets of proceedings are heard and determined separately, this might lead to legal consequences which are mutually exclusive? (c) If proceedings are brought in one Contracting State in respect of a claim by one group of cargo owners against a shipowner for damage to their portion of a bulk cargo carried under specified contracts of carriage and if separate proceedings are brought in another Contracting State against the same shipowner based on essentially similar issues of fact and law but by a different cargo owner for damage to its portion of the same bulk cargo carried under separate contracts of carriage on the same terms, do these proceedings, if heard and determined separately, involve the risk of giving rise to legal consequences which are mutually exclusive or are they otherwise related actions for the purposes of Article 22?

5. In relation to the carriage of goods by sea in circumstances where goods are discharged in an allegedly damaged condition, if (i) the shipowner commences proceedings in a Contracting State which involve a claim for a declaration of non-liability to cargo interests in respect of such alleged damage; and (ii) the cargo claimants subsequently commence the proceedings in another Contracting State in which they claim damages against the shipowner for negligence and/or breach of contract and/or duty in respect of such alleged damage to their cargo, do the latter proceedings involve the same cause of action as the former proceedings for the purposes of Article 21 of the 1968 Brussels Convention (as amended) so that the courts of the latter Contracting State must decline jurisdiction pursuant to Article 21?'

21. In the light of the interrelationship between the various questions referred, it is appropriate first to consider the third question, which concerns the scope of the Brussels Convention and of the special conventions. The first, fifth and second questions, all three of which seek an interpretation of Article 21 of the Convention, concerned with lis pendens, will be considered thereafter. Finally, the fourth question, which seeks an interpretation of Article 22 of the Convention, concerned with related actions, will be considered.

The third question

22. The national court's third question is essentially whether, on a proper

construction, Article 57 of the Convention, as amended by the Accession Convention, means that, where a Contracting State is also a contracting party to another convention on a specific matter containing rules on jurisdiction, that specialized convention always, subject to express exceptions, precludes the application of the Brussels Convention, or that the specialized convention precludes the application of the provisions of the Brussels Convention only in cases governed by it and not in those to which it does not apply.

23. Article 57 of the Convention, as amended by Article 25(1) of the Accession Convention, provides: 'This Convention shall not affect any conventions to which the Contracting States are or will be parties and which, in relation to particular matters, govern jurisdiction or the recognition or enforcement of judgments. This Convention shall not affect the application of provisions which, in relation to particular matters, govern jurisdiction or the recognition or enforcement of judgments and which are or will be contained in acts of the institutions of the European Communities or in national laws harmonized in implementation of such acts.'

24. Article 57 introduces an exception to the general rule that the Convention takes precedence over other conventions signed by the Contracting States on jurisdiction and the recognition and enforcement of judgments. The purpose of that exception is to ensure compliance with the rules on jurisdiction laid down by specialized conventions, since in enacting those rules account was taken of the specific features of the matters to which they relate.

25. That being its purpose, Article 57 must be understood as precluding the application of the provisions of the Brussels Convention solely in relation to questions governed by a specialized convention. A contrary interpretation would be incompatible with the objective of the Convention which, according to its preamble, is to strengthen in the Community the legal protection of persons therein established and to facilitate recognition of judgments in order to secure their enforcement. In those circumstances, when a specialized convention contains certain rules of jurisdiction but no provision as to lis pendens or related actions, Articles 21 and 22 of the Brussels Convention apply.

26. The cargo owners argue that the Arrest Convention contains provisions relating to lis pendens in Article 3(3), which provides: 'A ship shall not be arrested ... more than once in any one or more of the

jurisdictions of any of the Contracting States in respect of the same maritime claim by the same claimant'.

27. The cargo owners argument cannot be accepted. Where an arrest has already been made in the jurisdiction of a Contracting State, Article 3(3) of the Arrest Convention prohibits a second arrest by the same claimant in respect of the same claim in the jurisdiction, in particular, of another Contracting State. Such a prohibition has nothing to do with the concept of lis pendens within the meaning of Article 21 of the Brussels Convention. That provision is concerned with the situation where proceedings are brought before two courts both of which have jurisdiction and it governs only the question which of those two courts is to decline jurisdiction in the case.

28. The answer to the third question therefore is that, on a proper construction, Article 57 of the Convention, as amended by the Accession Convention, means that, where a Contracting State is also a contracting party to another convention on a specific matter containing rules on jurisdiction, that specialized convention precludes the application of the provisions of the Brussels Convention only in cases governed by the specialized convention and not in those to which it does not apply.

The first question

29. The national court's first question is essentially whether, on a proper construction, Article 21 of the Convention is applicable in the case of two sets of proceedings involving the same cause of action where some but not all of the parties are the same, at least one of the plaintiffs and one of the defendants to the proceedings first commenced also being among the plaintiffs and defendants in the second proceedings, or vice versa.

30. The question refers to the term 'the same parties' mentioned in Article 21, which requires as a condition for its application that the two sets of proceedings be between the same parties. As the Court held in Case 144/86 *Gubisch Maschinenfabrik* v *Palumbo* [1987] ECR 4861, the terms used in Article 21 in order to determine whether a situation of lis pendens arises must be regarded as independent (paragraph 11 of the judgment).

31. Moreover, as the Advocate General noted in his Opinion (paragraph 14), it follows by implication from that judgment that the question whether the parties are the same cannot depend on the procedural

position of each of them in the two actions, and that the plaintiff in the first action may be the defendant in the second.

32. The Court stressed in that judgment (paragraph 8) that Article 21, together with Article 22 on related actions, is contained in Section 8 of Title II of the Convention, a section intended, in the interests of the proper administration of justice within the Community, to prevent parallel proceedings before the courts of different Contracting States and to avoid conflicts between decisions which might result therefrom. Those rules are therefore designed to preclude, in so far as is possible and from the outset, the possibility of a situation arising such as that referred to in Article 27(3), that is to say the non-recognition of a judgment on account of its irreconcilability with a judgment given in a dispute between the same parties in the State in which recognition is sought.

33. In the light of the wording of Article 21 of the Convention and the objective set out above, that article must be understood as requiring, as a condition of the obligation of the second court seised to decline jurisdiction, that the parties to the two actions be identical.

34. Consequently, where some of the parties are the same as the parties to an action which has already been started, Article 21 requires the second court seised to decline jurisdiction only to the extent to which the parties to the proceedings pending before it are also parties to the action previously started before the court of another Contracting State; it does not prevent the proceedings from continuing between the other parties.

35. Admittedly, that interpretation of Article 21 involves fragmenting the proceedings. However, Article 22 mitigates that disadvantage. That article allows the second court seised to stay proceedings or to decline jurisdiction on the ground that the actions are related, if the conditions there set out are satisfied.

36. Accordingly, the answer to the first question is that, on a proper construction of Article 21 of the Convention, where two actions involve the same cause of action and some but not all of the parties to the second action are the same as the parties to the action commenced earlier in another Contracting State, the second court seised is required to decline jurisdiction only to the extent to which the parties to the proceedings before it are also parties to the action previously commenced; it does not prevent the proceedings from continuing between the other parties.

The fifth question

37. The national court's fifth question is essentially whether, on a proper construction of Article 21 of the Convention, an action seeking to have the defendant held liable for causing loss and ordered to pay damages has the same cause of action and the same object as earlier proceedings brought by that defendant seeking a declaration that he is not liable for that loss.

38. It should be noted at the outset that the English version of Article 21 does not expressly distinguish between the concepts of 'object' and 'cause' of action. That language version must however be construed in the same manner as the majority of the other language versions in which that distinction is made (see the judgment in *Gubisch Maschinenfabrik* v *Palumbo*, cited above, paragraph 14).

39. For the purposes of Article 21 of the Convention, the 'cause of action' comprises the facts and the rule of law relied on as the basis of the action.

40. Consequently, an action for a declaration of non-liability, such as that brought in the main proceedings in this case by the shipowners, and another action, such as that brought subsequently by the cargo owners on the basis of shipping contracts which are separate but in identical terms, concerning the same cargo transported in bulk and damaged in the same circumstances, have the same cause of action.

41. The 'object of the action' for the purposes of Article 21 means the end the action has in view.

42. The question accordingly arises whether two actions have the same object when the first seeks a declaration that the plaintiff is not liable for damage as claimed by the defendants, while the second, commenced subsequently by those defendants, seeks on the contrary to have the plaintiff in the first action held liable for causing loss and ordered to pay damages.

43. As to liability, the second action has the same object as the first, since the issue of liability is central to both actions. The fact that the plaintiff's pleadings are couched in negative terms in the first action whereas in the second action they are couched in positive terms by the defendant, who has become plaintiff, does not make the object of the dispute different.

44. As to damages, the pleas in the second action are the natural consequence of those relating to the finding of liability and thus do not alter the principal object of the action. Furthermore, the fact that a party seeks a declaration that he is not liable for loss implies that he disputes any obligation to pay damages.

45. In those circumstances, the answer to the fifth question is that, on a proper construction of Article 21 of the Convention, an action seeking to have the defendant held liable for causing loss and ordered to pay damages has the same cause of action and the same object as earlier proceedings brought by that defendant seeking a declaration that he is not liable for that loss.

The second question

46. The national court's second question is whether a subsequent action has the same cause of action and the same object and is between the same parties as a previous action where the first action, brought by the owner of a ship before a court of a Contracting State, is an action *in personam* for a declaration that that owner is not liable for alleged damage to cargo transported by his ship, whereas the subsequent action has been brought by the owner of the cargo before a court of another Contracting State by way of an action *in rem* concerning an arrested ship, and has subsequently continued both *in rem* and *in personam*, or solely *in personam*, according to the distinctions drawn by the national law of that other Contracting State.

47. In Article 21 of the Convention, the terms 'same cause of action' and 'between the same parties' have an independent meaning (see *Gubisch Maschinenfabrik* v *Palumbo*, cited above, paragraph 11). They must therefore be interpreted independently of the specific features of the law in force in each Contracting State. It follows that the distinction drawn by the law of a Contracting State between an action *in personam* and an action *in rem* is not material for the interpretation of Article 21.

48. Consequently, the answer to the second question is that a subsequent action does not cease to have the same cause of action and the same object and to be between the same parties as a previous action where the latter, brought by the owner of a ship before a court of a Contracting State, is an action *in personam* for a declaration that that owner is not liable for alleged damage to cargo transported by his ship, whereas the subsequent action has been brought by the owner of the cargo before a

court of another Contracting State by way of an action *in rem* concerning an arrested ship, and has subsequently continued both *in rem* and *in personam*, or solely *in personam*, according to the distinctions drawn by the national law of that other Contracting State.

The fourth question

49. The national court's fourth question is essentially whether, on a proper construction of Article 22 of the Convention, it is sufficient, in order to establish the necessary relationship between, on the one hand, an action brought in a Contracting State by one group of cargo owners against a shipowner seeking damages for harm caused to part of the cargo carried in bulk under separate but identical contracts, and, on the other, an action in damages brought in another Contracting State against the same shipowner by the owners of another part of the cargo shipped under the same conditions and under contracts which are separate from but identical to those between the first group and the shipowner, that separate trial and judgment would involve the risk of conflicting decisions, without necessarily involving the risk of giving rise to mutually exclusive legal consequences.

50. It is clear that that question arises only if the conditions for the application of Article 21 of the Convention are not satisfied.

51. The third paragraph of Article 22 provides that 'actions are deemed to be related where they are so closely connected that it is expedient to hear and determine them together to avoid the risk of irreconcilable judgments resulting from separate proceedings.'

52. The purpose of that provision is to avoid the risk of conflicting judgments and thus to facilitate the proper administration of justice in the Community (see the Report on the Convention on jurisdiction and the enforcement of judgments in civil and commercial matters, OJ 1979 C 59, p. 1, and in particular at p. 41). Furthermore, since the expression 'related actions' does not have the same meaning in all the Member States, the third paragraph of Article 22 sets out the elements of a definition (same report, p. 42). It follows that the concept of related actions there defined must be given an independent interpretation.

53. In order to achieve proper administration of justice, that interpretation must be broad and cover all cases where there is a risk of conflicting decisions, even if the judgments can be separately enforced and their legal consequences are not mutually exclusive.

54. The cargo owners and the Commission contend that the adjective 'irreconcilable', which is used both in the third paragraph of Article 22 and in Article 27(3) of the Convention, must be used in the same sense in both provisions, meaning that the decisions must have mutually exclusive legal consequences, as was held in Case 145/86 *Hoffmann* v *Krieg* [1987] ECR 645 (paragraph 22). They point out that the Court there held that a foreign judgment ordering a person to make maintenance payments to his spouse by virtue of his conjugal obligations to support her is irreconcilable, within the meaning of Article 27(3) of the Convention, with a national judgment pronouncing the divorce of the spouses (paragraph 25).

55. That argument cannot be accepted. The objectives of the two provisions are different. Article 27(3) of the Convention enables a court, by way of derogation from the principles and objectives of the Convention, to refuse to recognize a foreign judgment. Consequently the term 'irreconcilable ... judgment' there referred to must be interpreted by reference to that objective. The objective of the third paragraph of Article 22 of the Convention, however, is, as the Advocate General noted in his Opinion (paragraph 28), to improve coordination of the exercise of judicial functions within the Community and to avoid conflicting and contradictory decisions, even where the separate enforcement of each of them is not precluded.

56. That interpretation is supported by the fact that the German and Italian versions of the Convention use different terms in the third paragraph of Article 22 and in Article 27(3).

57. The conclusion is therefore inescapable that the term 'irreconcilable' used in the third paragraph of Article 22 of the Convention has a different meaning from the same term used by Article 27(3) of the Convention.

58. Consequently the answer to the fourth question is that, on a proper construction of Article 22 of the Convention, it is sufficient, in order to establish the necessary relationship between, on the one hand, an action brought in a Contracting State by one group of cargo owners against a shipowner seeking damages for harm caused to part of the cargo carried in bulk under separate but identical contracts, and, on the other, an action in damages brought in another Contracting State against the same shipowner by the owners of another part of the cargo shipped under the same conditions and under contracts which are separate from but identical to those between the first group and the shipowner, that separate

trial and judgment would involve the risk of conflicting decisions, without necessarily involving the risk of giving rise to mutually exclusive legal consequences.

On those grounds, the Court, in answer to the questions referred to it by the Court of Appeal by order of 5 June 1992, hereby rules:

1. On a proper construction, Article 57 of the Brussels Convention of 27 September 1968 on jurisdiction and the enforcement of judgments in civil and commercial matters, as amended by the Convention of 9 October 1978 on the accession of the Kingdom of Denmark, Ireland and the United Kingdom of Great Britain and Northern Ireland, means that, where a Contracting State is also a contracting party to another convention on a specific matter containing rules on jurisdiction, that specialized convention precludes the application of the provisions of the Brussels Convention only in cases governed by the specialized convention and not in those to which it does not apply.

2. On a proper construction of Article 21 of the Convention, where two actions involve the same cause of action and some but not all of the parties to the second action are the same as the parties to the action commenced earlier in another Contracting State, the second court seised is required to decline jurisdiction only to the extent to which the parties to the proceedings before it are also parties to the action previously commenced; it does not prevent the proceedings from continuing between the other parties.

3. On a proper construction of Article 21 of the Convention, an action seeking to have the defendant held liable for causing loss and ordered to pay damages has the same cause of action and the same object as earlier proceedings brought by that defendant seeking a declaration that he is not liable for that loss.

4. A subsequent action does not cease to have the same cause of action and the same object and to be between the same parties as a previous action where the latter, brought by the owner of a ship before a court of a Contracting State, is an action *in personam* for a declaration that that owner is not liable for alleged damage to cargo transported by his ship, whereas the

subsequent action has been brought by the owner of the cargo before a court of another Contracting State by way of an action *in rem* concerning an arrested ship, and has subsequently continued both *in rem* and *in personam*, or solely *in personam*, according to the distinctions drawn by the national law of that other Contracting State.

5. On a proper construction of Article 22 of the Convention, it is sufficient, in order to establish the necessary relationship between, on the one hand, an action brought in a Contracting State by one group of cargo owners against a shipowner seeking damages for harm caused to part of the cargo carried in bulk under separate but identical contracts, and, on the other, an action in damages brought in another Contracting State against the same shipowner by the owners of another part of the cargo shipped under the same conditions and under contracts which are separate from but identical to those between the first group and the shipowner, that separate trial and judgment would involve the risk of conflicting decisions, without necessarily involving the risk of giving rise to mutually exclusive legal consequences.

OPINION OF MR ADVOCATE GENERAL TESAURO

1. In the order for reference in the present case, the English Court of Appeal has submitted a number of questions on the interpretation of Articles 21, 22 and 57 of the Brussels Convention of 27 September 1968 on jurisdiction and the enforcement of judgments in civil and commercial matters, as amended by the 1978 Accession Convention ('the Brussels Convention').

2. To apprehend the precise scope of the questions, it is appropriate to summarize the - somewhat complex - facts of the main proceedings.

In September 1988 the Polish shipping company Zegluga Polska Spolka Alceyjna ('the shipowners') carried from Brazil to Rotterdam and Hamburg a cargo of soya bean oil in bulk aboard its vessel, the *Tatry*. The cargo belonged to various principals, and was carried under separate bills of lading in identical terms. On delivery of the cargo, both the part discharged in Rotterdam and the part discharged in Hamburg were found by its owners to have been contaminated by diesel oil and other hydrocarbons.

On 18 November 1988, the shipowners brought an action before the Arrondissmentsrechtbank (District Court), Rotterdam, for a declaration that they were not liable for the alleged contamination. The defendants in those proceedings are the Netherlands company Igeb International BV, which took delivery of the soya bean oil discharged in Rotterdam on behalf of several owners (hereinafter 'Group 1') and some of the owners of the oil discharged in Hamburg, namely the German companies Handelsgesellschaft Kurt Nitzer GmbH and Hobum Oele und Fette AG, and the English company Bunge & Co Ltd, as well as Daehn & Hamann GmbH, which took delivery of the cargo in question in Hamburg. The other owners of the cargo, the English company Phillip Brothers Ltd ('Phibro'), were not defendants in the proceedings (from here on I shall refer collectively to the owners of the cargo discharged in Hamburg as 'Group 3'). Nor was Phibro a defendant in the proceedings in respect of the parts of the cargo discharged in Rotterdam, of which it was also the owner and of which delivery was taken, on its behalf, by the Netherlands company ICM BV ('Group 2').

3. About ten months later, on 14 September 1989, Group 3 commenced an action *in rem* (hereinafter 'Action 2006') before the High Court of Justice, Queens's Bench Division, Admiralty Court, against the *Tatry* and the Maciej Rataj, the latter also belonging to the owners of the *Tatry*. The writ was served on 15 September 1989 and on the same date the arrest was authorized of the Maciej Rataj, which at that time was berthed in Liverpool. The shipowners subsequently secured its release by providing a guarantee; the proceedings then continued in the English court, in relation also to the merits of the dispute which gave rise to the application for arrest, namely compensation for the damage arising from the discharge of the soya bean oil in Hamburg in an allegedly contaminated state. The Admiralty Court based its merits jurisdiction on the legislation which gave effect in the United Kingdom to the International Convention relating to the arrest of seagoing ships signed in Brussels on 10 May 1952. Doubts exist under English law as to whether the proceedings continue in such cases both *in rem* and *in personam* or only *in personam*.

On the same day, 14 September 1989, Group 2 also commenced an action *in rem* before the same court (hereinafter 'Action 2007'); the course of events was the same as in Action 2006.

Finally, on 29 September 1989, Group 1, which had not instituted any proceedings before the English courts, brought proceedings in the Arrondissementsrechtbank, Rotterdam, for compensation for damage to the goods discharged in the Netherlands.

4. In Action 2006, the shipowners objected that the English court should have declined jurisdiction in favour of the Netherlands court, pursuant to Article 21 of the Brussels Convention, since proceedings involving the same cause of action were pending between the same parties in the Netherlands. In the alternative, if the lis pendens rule were not considered applicable, the Admiralty Court should, in the shipowners' view, have stayed the proceedings and, possibly, have declared, by virtue of Article 22 of the Convention, that it lacked jurisdiction in view of the connection which certainly existed between the action pending before the English courts and those pending before the Netherlands courts. Group 3 denied that there was a situation of lis pendens, considering that the two actions did not have the same parties or the same subject-matter; however, it conceded that the actions were related.

In Action 2007, on the other hand, recognizing that in fact the English court had been first seised, the shipowners asked it to stay the proceedings and, if appropriate, declare that it lacked jurisdiction under Article 22 of the Brussels Convention, concerning related actions - a view which was contested by Group 2.

5. The Admiralty Court rejected, at first instance, the shipowners' objection of lis pendens and, whilst admitting that the English and Netherlands actions were related, did not consider that it was obliged, under Article 22 of the Brussels Convention, to stay the proceedings. The shipowners appealed against that decision to the Court of Appeal.

In those proceedings, Group 3 claimed that Articles 21 and 22 of the Brussels Convention were not applicable to the case in any event, since the English court's jurisdiction was based on the Arrest Convention, the application of which, in so far as it related to 'particular matters', was assured by Article 57 of the Brussels Convention.

In those circumstances, the Court of Appeal, considering that the decision to be given in the proceedings depended on the interpretation of Articles 21, 22 and 57 of the Brussels Convention, stayed the proceedings and referred to the Court of Justice for a preliminary ruling several questions relating essentially to the following points:

(a) how, for the purposes of applying Article 21, the requirement of identity of parties in proceedings brought in different contracting States and having the same subject-matter and the same cause of action should be construed;

(b) whether, in relation to the carriage of goods by sea, a claim for compensation for damage allegedly caused to goods in transit brought by the cargo owners as an action *in rem* against the carrying vessel has the same parties and the same subject-matter and cause of action, for the purposes of Article 21, as an action *in personam* previously brought by the shipowner in relation to that damage; the national court asks, in particular, whether the answer to the question might differ according to whether the action *in rem* is proceeding, after acknowledgment of service by the shipowners, both *in rem* and *in personam* or only *in personam*;

(c) whether the derogation in favour of special conventions laid down in Article 57 means that, where the jurisdiction of a court is based on the provisions of such a convention, Articles 21 and 22 concerning lis pendens and related actions are inapplicable;

(d) what the term 'related actions' used in the third paragraph of Article 22 of the Brussels Convention actually means;

(e) whether, in relation to the carriage of goods by sea a case of lis pendens arises for the purposes of Article 21 where the shipowner brings proceedings in a Contracting State for a declaration that he is not liable to the owners of goods discharged in an allegedly damaged state and, subsequently, the owners of the goods commence another action in a different Contracting State in order to obtain compensation for the damage from the shipowner.

The relationship between the Brussels Convention and conventions on particular matters

6. I shall examine first the third issue raised by the national court - namely the relationship between the Brussels Convention and conventions on particular matters, as provided for by Article 57 of the former - since a negative answer to that question could in fact render the other questions wholly academic.

7. Article 57 lays down an important exception, concerning present and future conventions on particular matters, to the general rule that the Brussels Convention is intended to take precedence over other conventions concluded between the Contracting States concerning jurisdiction and the recognition and enforcement of judgments. The exception is justified by the need to uphold the specific choices made in this field and reflected in special conventions by virtue of the special features of the matters which they regulate. It follows that if such conventions lay down provisions concerning direct or exclusive jurisdiction, they must be complied with. Since, therefore, the Arrest Convention certainly falls within the category of special agreements, in any conflict between that convention and the Brussels Convention, in principle it is inevitable that the provisions of the Arrest Convention should prevail.

8. That said, there can in my view be no question of Article 57 being interpreted merely as a subordinating provision, that is to say one which purely and simply affirms the primacy of the provisions of a particular convention, whether already in existence or yet to be concluded - a provision by virtue of which, therefore, the existence of the connecting factors contemplated in the special convention means that the provisions of the Brussels Convention cannot be applied at all. I do not consider that to be the correct construction of the exception in favour of special conventions created by Article 57; on the contrary, a systematic reading of that provision shows that it is more in the nature of a coordinating provision, designed to allow the respective provisions to be applied in combination.

That follows in particular from the implementing provisions in Article 57(1), which were introduced into the Brussels Convention following the accession of the United Kingdom, Denmark and Ireland, and are now contained in paragraph 2. As is apparent from the text set out earlier, the first of those provisions stresses that precedence is to be given to the special convention, containing rules on direct jurisdiction, in any case where its rules conflict with those of the Brussels Convention; and where, by virtue of that convention, jurisdiction is given to a court other than that of the defendant's residence, which would normally have jurisdiction under the Brussels Convention, it requires that Article 20 thereof be applied in order to ensure observance of the rights of the defence. The other implementing provision provides for the applicability of the provisions of the convention regarding the recognition and enforcement of judgments delivered on the basis of the jurisdictional rules contained in a special convention; where, therefore, the special convention itself contains rules for the recognition and enforcement of judgments, the possibility exists of relying on the rules of that convention in the alternative.

9. The correctness of that interpretation of the relationship between the Brussels Convention and conventions on particular matters is also confirmed by the Schlosser Report, drawn up in connection with the accession of the United Kingdom, Denmark and Ireland, in which it is stated that: 'provisions in special conventions are special rules which every State may make prevail over the 1968 Convention by becoming a party to such a convention. *Insofar as a special convention does not contain rules covering a particular matter the 1968 Convention applies* (emphasis added). This is also the case where the special convention includes rules of jurisdiction which do not altogether fit the inter-connecting provisions of the various parts of the 1968 Convention ...' . It follows above all that '*the provisions on jurisdiction contained in special conventions are to be regarded as if they were provisions of the 1968 Convention itself,* even if only one Member State is a Contracting Party to such a special convention' (emphasis added).

It is true that at the time of the accession negotiations consideration was not given to all the questions stemming from the established principle that there should be a substantive connection between the provisions of the Brussels Convention and those of the conventions on particular matters - questions which are not therefore entirely answered by Article 57 but are left, as is apparent once again from the Schlosser Report, to legal literature and case-law. It nevertheless seems to me that there can be no doubt that the relationship between the various conventions is to be interpreted, by virtue of that article, as involving the reciprocal incorporation of their respective provisions. As a result, it is entirely legitimate to have recourse to the provisions of the general convention in order to supply any lacunae in those of the special convention.

10. That the foregoing observations are correct becomes entirely clear where, as in the present case, there are no provisions in the convention on a particular matter governing the situation where actions arising from the same facts are pending at the same time in two different States. The specific risk inherent in such cases of an overlap between proceedings concerning the same subject-matter and the possibility of conflicting decisions would in fact ultimately undermine the fundamental aim pursued by the Brussels Convention, namely that of 'strengthen[ing] in the Community the legal protection of persons therein established'. For those reasons, therefore, I am of the opinion - which coincides with that of many academic legal writers - that such cases call for the full application of Articles 21 and 22 of the Brussels Convention, the precise aim of which is to ensure that only one action is commenced in relation to the same subject-matter or to harmonize such decisions as may be arrived at by the courts in different Contracting States.

11. Furthermore, I cannot agree with the observations of the plaintiffs in Actions 2006 and 2007 to the effect that the Arrest Convention in fact contains provisions concerning lis pendens, in particular in Article 3(3); under that provision, arrest of the same vessel may not be ordered more than once in respect of the same maritime claim by the courts of one or more Contracting States. However, that provision is intended to prevent a plaintiff, who in principle is entirely at liberty to choose his forum, from bringing the same action before a

court other than the one first seised. It is, therefore, a device which, although certainly designed to preclude conflicting decisions, nevertheless relates to situations which differ from lis pendens. Once the plaintiff chooses a court by instituting proceedings for the arrest of a vessel, the court before which the same action is again brought later must do no more than simply dismiss it on the ground that the same proceedings have already been commenced elsewhere. Accordingly, it must not make any findings concerning fulfilment of the conditions for recognition of the judgment to be delivered by the court first seised; on the other hand, that is a matter which it must examine for the purpose of upholding the objection *lis alibi pendens.*

12. In order to determine the real content of Article 57, I think it is appropriate, finally, to refer to the relevant national case-law, which is extremely helpful in defining the scope of the provisions of an international agreement. And indeed, an examination of that case-law, in particular the English decisions on the relationship between the Brussels Convention and the Arrest Convention, confirms the wide acceptance of the view that they should be applied in an integrated manner or jointly in relation to the matter of lis pendens or the related nature of proceedings.

13. In conclusion, I consider that where a convention on a particular matter contains no provisions on lis pendens and related actions, Article 57 allows the application of Articles 21 and 22 of the Brussels Convention.

Lis pendens within the meaning of Article 21 of the Brussels Convention

14. Having regard to the conclusion arrived at regarding the relationship between the Brussels Convention and special conventions, it is necessary to answer the further questions submitted by the Court of Appeal. In its first, second and fifth questions, it asks essentially for a definition of the concept of lis pendens as used in the Brussels Convention, in other words, it seeks clarification as to when two actions have the same subject-matter and parties. Helpful guidance is available from the previous decisions of the Court on that point.

Of particular importance is, firstly, the judgment in *Gubisch Maschinenfabrik* v *Palumbo*, in which it was made clear that the terms used in Article 21 to describe the conditions characterizing lis pendens must be interpreted independently from those laid down in the various national procedural rules. In arriving at that conclusion, the Court laid particular emphasis on the aim in pursuit of which Article 21 was introduced, namely 'in the interests of the proper administration of justice within the Community, to prevent parallel proceedings before the courts of different Contracting States and to avoid conflicts between decisions which might result therefrom. Those rules are therefore designed to preclude, so far as is possible and from the outset, the possibility of a situation arising such as that referred to in Article 27(3), that is to say the non-recognition of a judgment on account of its irreconcilability with a judgment given in a dispute between the same parties in the State in which recognition is sought'. In that judgment, attention is also drawn to the fact that Article 21 does not refer to the term lis pendens as used in the different national legal systems but instead lays down a number of substantive conditions as components of a definition.

In the light of those considerations, the Court therefore concluded that lis pendens arose in a case such as the one before it, in which the annulment was sought of an international contract of sale in one Contracting State, whilst the action commenced previously in a court of another State sought enforcement of the same contract. That judgment shows, therefore, that it is necessary and sufficient, in order for Article 21 to be applicable, *for the parties to be the same, regardless of the procedural position of each of them in the two actions, and for the basic legal relationship from which the situations relied on by the parties derive to be the same*: the latter circumstance arises, in particular, where the issue raised in an action constitutes a logical precondition for the claim on which the other action is based, or where the origin of different actions is to be found in the same substantive situation.

15. The importance of the function of Article 21 in the context of the Brussels Convention, and the consequent need to take account of that function in expounding the concept of lis pendens used in it, was also highlighted by the Court of Justice in *Overseas Union Insurance.* In that decision, it is stated that, 'in order to achieve the aims attributed to it, Article 21 must be interpreted broadly so as to cover, in principle, all situations of lis pendens before courts in Contracting States': on that basis, the Court then answered the question put to it by saying that no account should be taken of the domicile of the parties to the two actions in applying the provision in question.

16. What consequences can therefore be drawn from that decision in relation to the problem now before us?

It should first be observed that in the main proceedings bills of lading in identical terms govern the contractual relationships between the various cargo owners and the shipowners and that the conditions of carriage, including the material circumstances thereof, the goods in question being soya bean oil in bulk, are the same in the various cases. It thus seems reasonable to conclude that the most important aspect of the legal situation to which the present preliminary question relates is the fact that the proceedings pending before the Arrondissementsrechtbank, Rotterdam, and the Admiralty Court, London, have the same 'cause of action', that is to say the same contractual relationship, and - at least partially, to the extent to be indicated shortly - the same 'subject-matter', in that in both cases the central issue is whether the shipowners are liable for the contamination of the soya bean oil through leakage of various hydrocarbons. In fact, both actions, the one in which it is sought to establish the liability of the shipowners and the one in which it is sought to establish non-liability, are nothing more than two sides of the same coin, as has been rightly pointed out by the Commission in the course of the present proceedings.

17. It is appropriate at this point to draw attention to a rather important difference between the facts of Gubisch Maschinenfabrik and those of the present case: whilst in the former case too, the relationship between the claims was attributable to their preliminary nature, the position in that case was the opposite of the one under review here, in that the proceedings brought before the

court first seised were wider in scope than those brought subsequently. Since the proceedings seeking enforcement of the international sale contract preceded those seeking the annulment or cancellation of the same contract, it was possible in the Court's view that the latter might 'even be regarded as simply a defence against the first action, brought in the form of independent proceedings before a court in another Contracting State'.

In the present case, on the other hand, the subject-matter of the action brought in the United Kingdom is not entirely covered by that of the previous action, in that it includes a claim for damages and determination of the amount thereof, which was not in issue (and in any case the position could not have been otherwise) in the proceedings initially commenced in the Netherlands court. In view of the fact, therefore, that Article 21 of the Brussels Convention does not lay down a procedure whereby proceedings are automatically consolidated, but merely requires a court subsequently seised to decline jurisdiction, application of the provision on lis pendens might give rise, in such cases, to a denial of justice. If it were not possible, under the rules applicable in the jurisdiction where the first action is pending, to extend its subject-matter by making further claims or raising new grounds of defence, there would be no opportunity to deal with all aspects of the dispute in all cases where an action of more limited scope was commenced first.

18. I therefore consider that, where the proceedings commenced before the court subsequently seised are wider in scope and where it is not possible to broaden the subject-matter of the first action (a circumstance which does not appear to have arisen in the present case, since all the cargo owners lodged a claim for damages, albeit merely by way of precaution, before the Netherlands court) that court should decline jurisdiction under Article 21 as regards the part of the subject-matter regarded as included within the action brought before the court first seised and may, on the other hand, stay the proceedings as regards the remainder of the subject-matter, relying also on Article 22 of the Convention.

19. However, for the purposes of resolving the present problem, namely identification of the circumstances in which it can be said that two actions have the same cause of action under the Brussels Convention, no importance should in my view be attached to the distinction drawn by English law between actions *in rem*, by means of which the plaintiff seeks to satisfy his claim by proceeding against specific assets, and actions *in personam* intended to produce binding effects as between individuals. The application of Article 21 cannot be made conditional upon the individual features of national procedural laws and differing forms of action: reference to the domestic laws of Contracting States, when rendered necessary by the incompleteness of the rules contained in the Brussels Convention, must be conducive to the applicability of the provisions of the convention and may not in any circumstances lead to results which conflict with its aims and rationale. The purpose of Article 21 is - as already indicated - to avoid the duplication of proceedings involving the same cause of action before courts in different Contracting States and the concomitant risk of judgments which are irreconcilable with each other and therefore, by virtue of Article 27(3), cannot be recognized. It seems to me in that connection, that the possibility of

conflicting judgments clearly exists in the present case, since the central issue in the proceedings pending in the United Kingdom and the Netherlands is the liability of the shipowners for contamination of the cargo. No importance must therefore be attached to the fact that the proceedings in question may possibly be of a different nature under the civil procedural law of one or other of the States concerned - what is important is whether or not the substantive issues which the Court is called upon to examine are the same.

A similar conclusion was recently arrived at by the Admiralty Court itself, in a judgment of April 1992 in proceedings which in certain respects are similar to those in the present case. Being called on to determine, specifically for the purpose of applying Articles 21 and 22 of the Brussels Convention, whether Netherlands proceedings brought by owners of goods for compensation for damage suffered by a ship's cargo involved the same subject-matter and cause of action as proceedings subsequently commenced by the same owners in the United Kingdom by arresting the vessel under the Arrest Convention, the English court concluded that the two actions involved the same subject-matter, notwithstanding the differences between actions *in rem* and actions *in personam*. It arrived at that conclusion by reference to the fact that the subject-matter of the action against the ship must necessarily be the same as that of the action against the owner and that, if service of the writ of arrest is not acknowledged by the owner, the plaintiff must, in order to obtain a decision against the vessel, prove the owner's liability.

20. A further precondition for the applicability of Article 21 is that the parties to the proceedings commenced before the courts in different Contracting States should be the same. As already stated, the Court has made clear that the parties remain the same even if, procedurally, their positions are reversed in the two cases, so that the plaintiff in the first is the defendant in the second, provided of course that the legal situation relied on in the two cases is the same. However, although - in the circumstances which gave rise to the present preliminary questions - the possibility must certainly be ruled out that a situation of lis pendens exists as between the action commenced by Phibro in the United Kingdom (Action 2007) and the earlier Netherlands action, since Phibro was not a party to the latter, what is the position regarding the other action pending before the English court (Action 2006) in which the plaintiffs, that is to say the Group 3 cargo owners, are only in part defendants in the proceedings commenced earlier in the Netherlands?

It seems to me, that in such circumstances, the risk of irreconcilable judgments, which would materialize if the English court ordered the shipowners to pay damages on the basis of their being held liable, whilst the Netherlands court concluded that the cargo owners were not entitled to proceed against the shipowners, is clearly envisageable as regards those who are parties to both sets of proceedings.

In view of the need to ensure that all parties are able to enforce their rights in legal proceedings and of the aim of Article 21 of the Brussels Convention, that provision should therefore be interpreted as meaning that, in such cases, the court second seised must decline jurisdiction to the extent to which the parties to the proceedings pending before it are also parties to the proceedings commenced earlier. The same court must continue the proceedings as between the other parties, nevertheless reserving the right to stay the proceedings as regards them if it is appropriate to do so by reason of the fact that the actions are related, in other words pursuant not to Article 21 of the Brussels Convention but to Article 22.

21. Finally, it is necessary to consider the last (the fifth) question submitted by the national court in relation to Article 21, which asks essentially whether the conclusions reached in interpreting the concept of lis pendens embodied in that provision may in some degree be modified where the plaintiff in the action brought before the court first seised seeks a declaration of non-liability. The cargo owners in particular contend, in that connection, that actions of that kind are in fact a cloak for forum shopping. In other words, the plaintiff has no claim whatsoever against the defendant and seeks only to preclude any possible action by the latter against him, thereby predetermining the competent court, in his own interests, and depriving a party with a genuine interest in bringing an action of the possibility of choosing the court of competent jurisdiction under the Brussels Convention or another special convention, the application of which is upheld by Article 57 of the Brussels Convention. Therefore, if Article 21 were interpreted as meaning that an action seeking a declaration of non-liability brought by the person allegedly responsible for damage is to be placed on the same footing as a claim for compensation made by the aggrieved party, the result would be, it is argued, that uncertainty would arise as regards determination of the court of competent jurisdiction, the right of a person with a real claim to choose the court in which to pursue it would be undermined and there would be an unjustified incentive to bring legal proceedings merely in order to secure a procedural advantage.

22. I do not agree with that argument or with the views put forward in support of it; in the light of the facts of the main proceedings, reference to it in this case seems to me to be entirely unjustified. It is true that the inclusion in the Brussels Convention and, it should not be forgotten, in the Arrest Convention, of alternative rules for determining jurisdiction and the consequent wide choice left open to the plaintiff in deciding which of the equally competent courts to approach for the examination of a particular dispute, may leave the way open for 'clever' manoeuvres. In particular, the possibility cannot be ruled out that efforts may be made to establish the jurisdiction of a particular court solely in order to take advantage of the substantive legislation which is applied by it and is regarded as more favourable by the plaintiff, or, again, in order to raise difficulties for the other party.

In that regard, it should be noted, however, that such efforts - constituting forum shopping - are easiest to deploy in systems in which priority is automatically given to the connecting factor of the *lex fori*, however disguised. Where, conversely, the rules of private international law or the case-law, or both, adopt connecting factors which better correspond to the nature and characteristics of the relationship, and to the expectations of the parties who originally created it and 'devised it', the possibilities of biased or even abusive use of procedural and private international law, as a whole, are also reduced. In any event, it will be incumbent upon the court seised to ensure that any abuse is thwarted.

In fact, I do not think that this problem can be resolved by interpreting Article 21 restrictively, in other words so as to exclude its application - as contended in the course of these proceedings - where a negative finding is sought by means of the proceedings commenced earlier in one of the Contracting States.

It would also be specious, as the Commission observes, to seek to draw a distinction according to whether an action seeking a declaration of non-liability is the first or the second to be brought; such a distinction, besides having no possible basis in the wording of Article 21, would not avoid the problem which that provision seeks to forestall, namely the possibility of conflicting judgments delivered by two courts called upon at the same time to examine the same matter.

23. It should also be borne in mind that the bringing of proceedings to obtain a negative finding, which is generally allowed under the various national procedural laws and is entirely legitimate in every respect, is an appropriate way of dealing with genuine needs on the part of the person who brings them. For example, he may have an interest, where the other party is temporizing, in securing a prompt judicial determination - if doubts exist or objections are raised - of the rights, obligations or responsibilities deriving from a given contractual relationship. That seems to be the case in the present proceedings, in view of the timing of the commencement of the actions.

24. Even in the light of those considerations, the cargo owner's reference to the risks allegedly inherent in the practice of forum shopping seems to me to be irrelevant, and indeed rather unusual. Quite apart from any other considerations, they may not be best placed to preach such a sermon. Whilst it is certainly possible that one of the reasons for the determination of the shipowners to have recourse to the Dutch courts was the intention to have applied to the case legislation which they regarded as more favourable to them, it is also a fact that their action in the Arrondissementsrechtbank, Rotterdam, was brought little more than one-and-a-half months after discharge of the cargo, whilst the action by the Group 2 and 3 owners was not commenced until ten months had elapsed and on the basis of a connecting factor which, I repeat, is wholly fortuitous. Furthermore, it has not been denied that the cargo owners were lawfully brought before the Netherlands court under the provisions of the Brussels Convention, specifically Articles 2 and 6(1). In that regard, it appears on the other hand to be entirely a matter of chance that the English court had jurisdiction, under Article 7(1) of the Arrest Convention, solely by virtue of the fact that a vessel belonging to the same owner happened to berth in an English port and the cargo owners were in a position to apply for its arrest. Having regard, therefore, to all the circumstances, it does not seem to me entirely out of place to ask who, in the present case, might be regarded as 'responsible' for recourse to forum shopping - if 'responsible' is the right word.

25. In view of those considerat-ions, I repeat that, in any event, Article 21 is not the place to look for a remedy for what might constitute a self-interested use of proceedings seeking a negative declaration. That seems to me to follow also from Gubisch Maschinenfabrik, mentioned several times earlier, from

which it is apparent that the concept of lis pendens used in the Brussels Convention extends to circumstances where a party has brought before a court of a Contracting State an action for the annulment or cancellation of a contract, whilst an action by the other party for the enforcement of that contract is pending before a court in another Contracting State. On that occasion, the Court disregarded the views of the Advocate General, who had expressly drawn attention to the possible risks deriving from that interpretation of Article 21, which might make it possible to use an action challenging the validity of a contract to paralyse, by raising an objection of lis pendens, any later action brought on the basis of that contract before a court in another Member State. Moreover, the most recent national case-law is adopting the same approach as that adopted in the above-mentioned judgment of the Court of Justice.

Related actions within the meaning of Article 22 of the Brussels Convention

26. With regard in particular, but not exclusively, to Action 2007, a final series of questions relates to the interpretation of Article 22 of the Brussels Convention. The national court asks the Court of Justice to clarify the concept of related actions in the third paragraph of Article 22, by virtue of which, it will be remembered, actions 'are deemed to be related where they are so closely connected that it is expedient to hear and determine them together to avoid the risk of irreconcilable judgments resulting from separate proceedings'.

27. It should be noted at the outset that that definition, like that of lis pendens, should be interpreted independently from those (which differ from each other) found in the various national procedural rules. In that regard, it is clear, in the first place, that two (or more) actions, in order to be related within the meaning of the third paragraph of Article 22, do not necessarily have to have the same parties and involve the same subject-matter and cause of action. Where those conditions are fulfilled, Article 21 will apply; on the other hand, in related actions, there is a difference as regards the subjective or objective elements (or possibly both).

Having regard to the subjective limits of judgments, which, of course, can produce effects only as regards the litigants, it is clear that no incompatibility, in the technical sense, can arise between the judgments delivered in related actions except where, although having a different cause of action or subject matter or both, they involve the same parties. In a case in which the Court examined Article 27(3) of the Brussels Convention, and which has been referred to by many of the parties involved in these proceedings, a foreign judgment ordering a husband to pay maintenance to his wife by virtue of his matrimonial obligations would be incompatible with a decision given in the State where enforcement of it was applied for, which dissolved the marriage of the same spouses. On that occasion, therefore, the Court observed that judgments of that kind '*have legal consequences which are mutually exclusive*. The foreign judgment, which necessarily presupposes the existence of the matrimonial relationship, would have to be enforced although that relationship has been dissolved by a judgment given in a dispute between the same parties in the State in which enforcement is sought' (emphasis added).

28. In view of the aim inherent in the concept of related actions in the Brussels Convention, I do not believe, however, that the expression 'irreconcilable judgments' contained in the third paragraph of Article 22 can be given the same restrictive meaning as the expression 'judgment ... irreconcilable with a judgment given in a dispute' at an earlier stage used in Article 27(3), as suggested by most of the parties to the present proceedings. The latter provision envisages the possibility, by way of derogation from the principles and objectives laid down in the Convention, of refusing, exceptionally, to recognize a foreign judgment, whilst the former is intended rather to improve coordination of the judicial function within the Community and to avoid conflicting and contradictory decisions, even where the separate enforcement of each of them is not precluded. An example, which I take from the Opinion of Advocate General Darmon in *Kalfelis*, seems to me to provide a clear illustration of the view just expressed: it is also a particularly appropriate illustration, because of its considerable factual similarity with the present case. If, after separate actions have been commenced against two persons allegedly responsible for an accident, two decisions are given, one of which upholds the action and the other dismisses it, on the ground that the damage suffered does not justify compensation, those decisions, although contradictory, may certainly be enforced at the same time, having been given in proceedings between different parties. Nevertheless, recognition of the fact that the two sets of proceedings were related and a possible stay of proceedings or, if the requisite conditions were fulfilled, a declaration by the court second seised that it lacked jurisdiction, under the first and second paragraphs of Article 22, would in any event have been conducive to the substantive uniformity of judicial decisions and would therefore have been in conformity with the objectives pursued by the Brussels Convention.

The rationale of the provision is therefore to encourage harmonious judicial decisions and thereby obviate the danger of judgments which conflict with each other, albeit only as regards their reasoning. The court second seised should therefore be able to have recourse to the machinery envisaged by that provision whenever it considers that the reasoning adopted by the court hearing the earlier proceedings may concern issues likely to be relevant to its own decision.

29. It seems to me that such a situation arises in the present case. Because the matters of fact and of law at issue in the proceedings pending in the Netherlands and in Action 2007 are the same, in that the transport operation to which the two actions relate is one and the same, the cargo was a bulk cargo and the bills of lading signed by the various cargo owners were in the same terms, it is clear that if the two actions were to proceed in parallel, the possibility could not be ruled out that 'conflicting' decisions might be arrived at, in the sense just described.

Conclusion

30. In the light of the foregoing considerations, I propose the following answers to the questions referred by the Court of Appeal on the interpretation of

the Brussels Convention of 27 September 1968 on jurisdiction and the enforcement of judgments in civil and commercial matters:

1. Article 57 of the Convention must be interpreted as meaning that, if - as in the present case - a convention on a particular matter contains no provisions concerning lis pendens and related actions, Articles 21 and 22 of the Convention are applicable.

2. Article 21 of the Convention must be interpreted as meaning that lis pendens arises whenever there is total or partial identity of subject-matter, cause of action and parties as between two (or more) actions. In particular:

- an action brought in one Contracting State, in order to obtain a declaration that the plaintiff is not liable for damage allegedly suffered by the defendants, has the same subject-matter and cause of action as an action subsequently commenced in another Contracting State by one of the defendants in the first action with a view to establishing that the plaintiff in the latter action is liable for the same damage;
- in that regard, the fact that the forms of the actions differ under the procedural laws of the two States concerned is unimportant;
- the obligation of the court second seised to decline jurisdiction under Article 21 applies only to that part of the proceedings which has the same subject-matter and parties as the proceedings commenced previously.

3. The third paragraph of Article 22 of the Convention is to be interpreted as meaning that two actions are to be regarded as related, in that they are so closely connected that it is expedient to hear and determine them together to avoid the risk of irreconcilable judgments, whenever they are concerned with essentially the same matters of fact and law, and there is therefore a risk that they might be decided in a conflicting manner, albeit only as regards their reasoning.

Case C-351/96 - 9 October 1997

Von Horn
v
Cinnamond

Accession of new Contracting States - Spain - Portugal - Transitional provisions - Lis pendens - Proceedings involving the same cause of action and between the same parties in two different Contracting States - First proceedings brought before and second proceedings after the entry into force of the Accession Convention between the two States - Application of Article 21 of the Convention on Jurisdiction and the Enforcement of Judgments by the court second seised - Conditions.

Summary

Article 29(1) of the Convention of 26 May 1989 on the Accession of the Kingdom of Spain and the Portuguese Republic to the Convention on Jurisdiction and the Enforcement of Judgments in Civil and Commercial Matters must be interpreted as meaning that where proceedings involving the same cause of action and between the same parties are pending in two different Contracting States, the first proceedings having been brought before the date of entry into force of the Brussels Convention between those States and the second proceedings after that date, the court second seised must apply Article 21 of the latter Convention if the court first seised has assumed jurisdiction on the basis of a rule which accords with the provisions of Title II of that Convention or with the provisions of a convention which was in force between the two States concerned when the proceedings were instituted; if the court first seised has jurisdiction, the court second seised must apply that article provisionally.

On the other hand, the latter court must not apply Article 21 of the Convention on Jurisdiction and the Enforcement of Judgements in Civil and Commercial matters if the court first seised has assumed jurisdiction on the basis of a rule which does not accord with the provisions of Title II of that Convention or with the provisions of a convention which was in force between those two States when the proceedings were instituted.

JUDGMENT OF THE COURT

Ragnemalm, President, Mancini, Rapporteur, Kapteyn, Murray and Hirsch, Judges

1. By order of 25 May 1995, received at the Court on 29 May 1995, the House of Lords referred to the Court for a preliminary ruling under the Protocol of 3 June 1971 on the interpretation by the Court of Justice of the Convention of 27 September 1968 on Jurisdiction and the Enforcement of Judgments in Civil and Commercial Matters (OJ 1978 L 304, p. 36, hereinafter 'the Brussels Convention') two questions on the interpretation of Article 21 of that Convention, as amended by the Convention of 9 October 1978 on the Accession of the Kingdom of Denmark, Ireland and the United Kingdom of Great Britain and Northern Ireland (OJ 1978 L 304, p. 1) and the Convention of 25 October 1982 on the Accession of the Hellenic Republic (OJ 1982 L 388, p. 1) and the Convention of 26 May 1989 on the Accession of the Kingdom of Spain and the Portuguese Republic (OJ 1989 L 285, p. 1, hereinafter 'the San Sebastian Convention'), and of Article 29 of the San Sebastian Convention.

2. Those questions were raised in proceedings between Freifrau von Horn, domiciled in Portugal, and Mr Cinnamond, domiciled in the United Kingdom, concerning the payment of a sum of money which she claims from him as constituting payment for the sale to a Gibraltar company of shares in a property company.

3. On 27 August 1991 Mr Cinnamond brought proceedings against Freifrau von Horn in the Tribunal de Círculo (Circuit Court), Portimão, Portugal, for a declaration that he did not owe the sum of £600 000 or the equivalent in escudos. In those proceedings Freifrau von Horn counterclaimed for a declaration that Mr Cinnamond owed her £600 000 and an order for payment.

4. On 9 November 1992 Freifrau von Horn issued a writ in the High Court of Justice, served on Mr Cinnamond on 18 November 1992, for

payment of £600 000 as the balance due for the shares or, in the alternative, for damages. On 27 November 1992 Mr Cinnamond issued a summons for a declaration that that court lacked jurisdiction. On 5 March 1993 the proceedings were stayed. On 21 April 1993 a judge of the High Court allowed Freifrau von Horn's appeal against the stay. Mr Cinnamond appealed against the judge's decision to the Court of Appeal, which dismissed his appeal by judgment of 25 February 1994. On 19 July 1994 the House of Lords granted Mr Cinnamond leave to appeal.

5. Since it considered that the dispute raised questions of the interpretation of the Brussels and San Sebastian Conventions, the House of Lords stayed proceedings and referred the following questions to the Court: 'In a case where:

(a) there are pending proceedings in two different Contracting States involving the same cause of action and between the same parties;

(b) the first such proceedings in time were initiated in Contracting State A before the Brussels Convention and/or any applicable accession convention came into force in that State;

(c) the second such proceedings are initiated in Contracting State B in accordance with Article 2 of the Brussels Convention after the Brussels Convention and/or any applicable accession convention has come into force in both State A and State B; and having regard to Article 29(1) of the San Sebastian Convention and the corresponding articles in any other applicable accession convention and Article 21 of the Brussels Convention (as amended):

(1) Does the Brussels Convention (as amended) and/or any applicable accession convention lay down any, and if so what, rules as to whether the proceedings in State B may or must be stayed, or jurisdiction declined, on the ground of pending proceedings in State A and in particular

(2) Is the Court second seised required or permitted, for the purpose of deciding whether or not to decline jurisdiction in respect of, or to stay, the proceedings before it, to conduct any and, if so, what examination of the basis upon which the court first seised assumed jurisdiction?'

6. In answering those questions, which should be taken together, it must be noted that under Article 21 of the Brussels Convention, as amended by Article 8 of the San Sebastian Convention,

'Where proceedings involving the same cause of action and between the same parties are brought in the courts of different Contracting States, any court other than the court first seised shall of its own motion stay its proceedings until such time as the jurisdiction of the court first seised is established.

Where the jurisdiction of the court first seised is established, any court other than the court first seised shall decline jurisdiction in favour of that court.'

7. Article 29 of the San Sebastian Convention reads as follows:

'1. The 1968 Convention and the 1971 Protocol, as amended by the 1978 Convention, the 1982 Convention and this Convention, shall apply only to legal proceedings instituted and to authentic instruments formally drawn up or registered after the entry into force of this Convention in the State of origin and, where recognition or enforcement of a judgment or authentic instrument is sought, in the State addressed.

2. However, judgments given after the date of entry into force of this Convention between the State of origin and the State addressed in proceedings instituted before that date shall be recognized and enforced in accordance with the provisions of Title III of the 1968 Convention, as amended by the 1978 Convention, the 1982 Convention and this Convention, if jurisdiction was founded upon rules which accorded with the provisions of Title II of the 1968 Convention, as amended, or with the provisions of a convention which was in force between the State of origin and the State addressed when the proceedings were instituted.'

8. In accordance with Article 32(2) thereof, the San Sebastian Convention entered into force between Portugal and the United Kingdom on the first day of the third month following the deposit of the last instrument of ratification, namely 1 July 1992.

9. The rule which governs the temporal application of Article 21 of the Brussels Convention is therefore that laid down in Article 29(1) of the San Sebastian Convention. However, that provision does not allow it to be determined with certainty whether the lis pendens provisions of Article 21 of the Brussels Convention apply where the first proceedings were brought in a Contracting State before the date of entry into force of the San Sebastian Convention and the second proceedings were brought in another Contracting State after that date, or whether both sets of proceedings must have been brought after the entry into force of the San Sebastian Convention.

10. First, while Article 21 is included in Title II of the Brussels Convention among the provisions which determine jurisdiction of the court seised, it requires that court to stay the proceedings before it and, as

the case may be, decline jurisdiction because of the existence of proceedings before a court of another Contracting State. In contrast to other procedural rules, it thus necessarily implies the taking into account of other proceedings, which may have been brought before or after the entry into force of the Convention.

11. While Article 29(1) of the San Sebastian Convention states that the Brussels Convention is to apply to legal proceedings instituted after its entry into force, it does not specify whether, in the case, referred to in Article 21 of the Brussels Convention, where several actions are pending before the courts of different Contracting States, it is necessary that all the proceedings should have been instituted after the date of entry into force or whether it is enough that the proceedings pending before the court last seised were so instituted.

12. Most of the language versions of Article 21 of the Brussels Convention admittedly refer to the institution of the proceedings and thus appear to suggest that Article 29(1) of the San Sebastian Convention is to be interpreted as providing that Article 21 is to apply only if all the proceedings were commenced after the entry into force of the Convention. However, the German ('werden ... anhängig gemacht') and Dutch ('aanhangig zijn') versions refer to the situation where the proceedings are pending, so that they permit the interpretation that by reason of Article 29(1) the rule in Article 21 applies where that situation is shown to exist before the court second seised after the entry into force of the San Sebastian Convention.

13. Second, the two interpretations mentioned in paragraph 9 above are both capable of leading to consequences which are unsatisfactory and contrary to the aims of the Brussels Convention as set out in its preamble, which are, in particular, to facilitate reciprocal recognition and enforcement of judgments of courts and tribunals and to strengthen the legal protection of persons established in the Community. With respect more particularly to Article 21, the Court has repeatedly observed that that provision, together with Article 22 on related actions, is contained in Section 8 of Title II of the Brussels Convention, a section which is intended, in the interests of the proper administration of justice within the Community, to prevent parallel proceedings before the courts of different Contracting States and to avoid conflicts between decisions which might arise therefrom. Those rules are therefore designed to preclude, in so far as possible and from the outset, a situation such as that referred to in Article 27(3), namely the non-recognition of a judgment on account of its

irreconcilability with a judgment given between the same parties in the State addressed (see Case 144/86 *Gubisch Maschinenfabrik* v *Palumbo* [1987] ECR 4861, paragraph 8, and Case C-351/89 *Overseas Union Insurance and Others* v *New Hampshire Insurance* [1991] ECR I-3317, paragraph 16).

14. The view that Article 21 applies where the second proceedings have been brought after the date of entry into force of the San Sebastian Convention, even if the first action was commenced before that date, could make it impossible for the parties to the proceedings to obtain a judgment enforceable in the Contracting State in which the second proceedings take place. The court second seised would have to stay the proceedings and, as the case may be, decline jurisdiction by reason of the existence of proceedings before a court of another Contracting State, even though recognition and enforcement of the judgment given in those proceedings might prove impossible in the State addressed. That would be the case in particular, under Article 29(2) of the San Sebastian Convention, if the jurisdiction of the court of the Contracting State of origin was founded on rules which did not accord with Title II of the Brussels Convention or with the provisions of a convention which was in force between the State of origin and the State addressed when the proceedings were instituted.

15. The contrary view, namely that Article 21 applies only if the two sets of proceedings were instituted after the entry into force of the San Sebastian Convention, on the other hand, would lead to their continuing, in the two Contracting States, and possibly resulting in two different judgments being delivered. If those decisions were irreconcilable, neither of them could be recognized in the other State, in accordance with Article 27(3) of the Brussels Convention.

16. In those circumstances, it may be seen that it is essential to interpret Article 29(1) of the San Sebastian Convention in the light of the structure and aims of that Convention and the Brussels Convention.

17. That provision should therefore be construed in such a way as to make it possible for the legal protection of persons established in the Community to be strengthened and recognition and enforcement of judicial decisions to be facilitated, in particular by reducing the danger of irreconcilable judgments being delivered, that being a ground for refusing recognition and enforcement under Article 27(3) and the second paragraph of Article 34 of the Brussels Convention (see Case C-220/88

Dumez France and Tracoba v *Hessische Landesbank and Others* [1990] ECR I-49, paragraph 18, and Overseas Union Insurance, paragraph 15).

18. In accordance with Article 29(2) of the San Sebastian Convention, judgments delivered in a Contracting State after the date of entry into force of that Convention in proceedings brought before that date must be recognized and enforced in accordance with Title III of the Brussels Convention if jurisdiction was founded on rules which accorded with the provisions of Title II of that Convention or with the provisions of a convention which was in force between the State of origin and the State addressed when the proceedings were instituted.

19. In such a case, therefore, the court second seised should, in accordance with Article 21, stay the proceedings of its own motion until the jurisdiction of the court first seised is established and, where the jurisdiction of the court first seised is established, decline jurisdiction in favour of that court. The production of parallel, potentially conflicting judgments which might prevent recognition and enforcement will thereby be avoided.

20. If, on the other hand, the jurisdiction of the court first seised is founded on rules which do not accord with the provisions of Title II of that Convention or with the provisions of a convention which was in force between the State of origin and the State addressed when the proceedings were instituted, its judgment could not be recognized in the Contracting State of the court second seised.

21. In such a case, the court second seised should disapply Article 21 and continue with the proceedings before it. In that way a judgment can be given in the Contracting State of the court second seised, in which the judgment of the court first seised cannot be recognized or enforced. Moreover, the judgment of the court second seised can be recognized and enforced in the Contracting State of the court first seised, provided always that it is not incompatible with a judgment given between the same parties in that State.

22. Further, if the court first seised has not yet ruled on whether it has jurisdiction, it is for the court second seised to apply Article 21 of the Brussels Convention provisionally and stay its proceedings. However, those proceedings may later be resumed if the court first seised declines jurisdiction or the rule on which it has founded its jurisdiction does not accord with the rules of Title II of the Brussels Convention or with a

convention which was in force between the State of origin and the State addressed when the proceedings were instituted.

23. That interpretation does admittedly mean that a court of a Contracting State will review the jurisdiction of a court of another Contracting State outside the cases expressly listed in Article 28 and the second paragraph of Article 34 of the Brussels Convention, even though, as the Court held in Overseas Union Insurance, paragraph 24, apart from those limited exceptions, the Convention does not authorize such a review. However, an exception to that principle appears justified in the situation referred to by the national court.

24. First, by virtue of the transitional provision contained in Article 29(2) of the San Sebastian Convention, application of the rules of that convention which concern the recognition and enforcement of judgments specifically depends on the basis of the jurisdiction of the court first seised.

25. Second, the court second seised must restrict itself to determining whether the jurisdiction of the court first seised accords with the rules of the Brussels Convention, or a convention concluded between the two States concerned, which are common to both courts and may be interpreted with equal authority by the courts of both Contracting States (see Overseas Union Insurance, cited above, paragraph 23). In the particular case where the jurisdiction of the court first seised derives, in accordance with Article 4 of the Brussels Convention, from the law of the State of that court, which would thus undeniably be better placed to rule on the question of its own jurisdiction, the court second seised should restrict itself to ascertaining whether the conditions for the application of that provision are satisfied, namely that the plaintiff is domiciled in a Contracting State and the defendant is not domiciled in such a State. In no case, therefore, may the court second seised assess the jurisdiction of the court first seised in the light of the law of the State of that court.

26. Lastly, it must be emphasized that the above rules apply only on a transitional basis to resolve the difficulties deriving from the entry into force of the Brussels Convention and only for so long as proceedings brought before that entry into force are still pending in a Contracting State. Consequently, the principle referred to in paragraph 23 above suffers no lasting injury.

27. The answer to the national court's questions must therefore be that

Article 29(1) of the San Sebastian Convention must be interpreted as meaning that where proceedings involving the same cause of action and between the same parties are pending in two different Contracting States, the first proceedings having been brought before the date of entry into force of the Brussels Convention between those States and the second proceedings after that date, the court second seised must apply Article 21 of the Brussels Convention if the court first seised has assumed jurisdiction on the basis of a rule which accords with the provisions of Title II of that Convention or with the provisions of a convention which was in force between the two States concerned when the proceedings were instituted, and must do so provisionally if the court first seised has not yet ruled on whether it has jurisdiction. On the other hand, the court second seised must not apply Article 21 of the Brussels Convention if the court first seised has assumed jurisdiction on the basis of a rule which does not accord with the provisions of Title II of that Convention or with the provisions of a convention which was in force between those two States when the proceedings were instituted.

On those grounds, the Court (Sixth Chamber), in answer to the questions referred to it by the House of Lords by order of 25 May 1995, hereby rules:

> **Article 29(1) of the Convention of 26 May 1989 on the Accession of the Kingdom of Spain and the Portuguese Republic to the Convention on Jurisdiction and the Enforcement of Judgments in Civil and Commercial Matters must be interpreted as meaning that where proceedings involving the same cause of action and between the same parties are pending in two different Contracting States, the first proceedings having been brought before the date of entry into force of the Brussels Convention between those States and the second proceedings after that date, the court second seised must apply Article 21 of the latter Convention if the court first seised has assumed jurisdiction on the basis of a rule which accords with the provisions of Title II of that Convention or with the provisions of a convention which was in force between the two States concerned when the proceedings were instituted, and must do so provisionally if the court first seised has not yet ruled on whether it has jurisdiction. On the other hand, the court second seised must not apply Article 21 of the Convention on Jurisdiction and the Enforcement of Judgments in Civil and Commercial Matters if the court first seised has assumed**

jurisdiction on the basis of a rule which does not accord with the provisions of Title II of that Convention or with the provisions of a convention which was in force between those two States when the proceedings were instituted.

OPINION OF MR ADVOCATE GENERAL JACOBS

1. The issue put to the Court by the House of Lords in this case concerns two sets of proceedings, involving the same cause of action and between the same parties, which are pending before courts in two States (Portugal and the United Kingdom) now party to the Brussels Convention of 1968 (hereafter 'the Brussels Convention' or 'the Convention'). The first set of proceedings was commenced in Portugal before the Convention entered into force between Portugal and the United Kingdom, whereas the second set of proceedings was commenced in the United Kingdom after the Convention had entered into force between the two States. The House of Lords wishes to know whether, in such circumstances, the court second seised (i.e. the United Kingdom court) may or must stay proceedings or decline jurisdiction and whether it is required or permitted, for the purpose of deciding whether to stay proceedings or to decline jurisdiction, to conduct an examination of the basis on which the court first seised (the Portuguese court) assumed jurisdiction.

Relevant provisions of the Brussels and San Sebastian Conventions

2. Title II of the Convention contains general and special rules governing the jurisdiction of courts of the Contracting States. Article 2 provides: 'Subject to the provisions of this Convention, persons domiciled in a Contracting State shall, whatever their nationality, be sued in the courts of that State.

Persons who are not nationals of the State in which they are domiciled shall be governed by the rules of jurisdiction applicable to nationals of that State.'

3. In Section 8 of Title II of the Convention, entitled 'Lis pendens - related actions', is to be found Article 21, which, as amended by Article 8 of the San Sebastian Convention of 26 May 1989, provides: 'Where proceedings involving the same cause of action and between the same parties are brought in the courts of different Contracting States, any court other than the court first seised shall of its own motion stay its proceedings until such time as the jurisdiction of the court first seised is established.

Where the jurisdiction of the court first seised is established, any court other than the court first seised shall decline jurisdiction in favour of that court.'

4. Title III of the Convention concerns recognition and enforcement of judgments given in other Contracting States. Article 26 lays down the general rule that a judgment given in a Contracting State is to be recognized in the other Contracting States without any special procedure being required. Article 27 specifies a number of cases in which a judgment is not to be recognized including, in paragraph 3, the case where: 'the judgment is irreconcilable with a

judgment given in a dispute between the same parties in the State in which recognition is sought'.

5. In Overseas Union Insurance the Court, referring to its judgment in Gubisch, held that Article 21 of the Convention was intended: 'to preclude, in so far as possible and from the outset, the possibility of a situation arising such as that referred to in Article 27(3), that is to say the non-recognition of a judgment on account of its irreconcilability with a judgment given in proceedings between the same parties in the State in which recognition is sought. It follows that, in order to achieve those aims, Article 21 must be interpreted broadly so as to cover, in principle, all situations of lis pendens before courts in Contracting States, irrespective of the parties' domicile.'

6. The Court held further that, without prejudice to the case where the court second seised had exclusive jurisdiction under the Convention, Article 21 of the Convention prevented the court second seised from examining the jurisdiction of the court first seised where the jurisdiction of the latter was contested; the only option for the court second seised, in the event of its not declining jurisdiction, was to stay proceedings.

7. Article 29 of the San Sebastian Convention provides:

'1. The 1968 Convention and the 1971 Protocol, as amended by the 1978 Convention, the 1982 Convention and this Convention, shall apply only to legal proceedings instituted and to authentic instruments formally drawn up or registered after the entry into force of this Convention in the State of origin and, where recognition or enforcement of a judgment or authentic instrument is sought, in the State addressed.

2. However, judgments given after the date of entry into force of this Convention between the State of origin and the State addressed in proceedings instituted before that date shall be recognized and enforced in accordance with the provisions of Title III of the 1968 Convention, as amended by the 1978 Convention, the 1982 Convention and this Convention, if jurisdiction was founded upon rules which accorded with the provisions of Title II of the 1968 Convention, as amended, or with the provisions of a convention which was in force between the State of origin and the State addressed when the proceedings were instituted.'

The facts and the national court's questions

8. Mrs von Horn is a German citizen domiciled in Portugal. Mr Cinnamond is a company director domiciled in England. Both sets of proceedings arise out of an agreement made on or about 19 December 1989 between Mrs von Horn and Mr Cinnamond whereby the latter agreed to pay Mrs von Horn an amount of £600 000, representing the balance of monies owed to Mrs von Horn in respect of the sale by her of shares in a Portuguese company to a Gibraltar company, and out of a further promise to pay that amount made on 23 April 1990. In the event Mr Cinnamond failed to pay Mrs von Horn the amount in question.

9. On 27 August 1991 Mr Cinnamond commenced proceedings against

Mrs von Horn before a Portuguese court, seeking a declaration that he was not liable to pay Mrs von Horn the £600 000 or the equivalent sum in Escudos. On 9 March 1992 Mrs von Horn served a defence and a counterclaim seeking a declaration that Mr Cinnamond was liable to pay her the amount in question and an order for payment.

10. Mrs von Horn subsequently commenced proceedings in England, issuing a writ on 9 November 1992 which was served on the defendant on 18 November 1992. Mr Cinnamond then issued a summons seeking a declaration that the English court had no jurisdiction; as the court second seised, it should stay proceedings and in due course decline jurisdiction pursuant to Article 21 of the Convention.

11. It is common ground that both sets of proceedings are between the same parties and concern the same cause of action within the meaning of Article 21. The problem in the case arises from the fact that Portugal's accession to the Convention, pursuant to the San Sebastian Convention, did not take effect until 1 July 1992, that is to say after the commencement of the Portuguese proceedings (but before the commencement of the English proceedings).

12. On 5 March 1993 the proceedings in the English High Court were stayed by order of a Master, but Mrs von Horn's appeal against that order was allowed by a Judge. Mr Cinnamond unsuccessfully appealed to the Court of Appeal and was subsequently granted leave to appeal to the House of Lords, which decided to seek a ruling from the Court on the following questions:

'In a case where:

(a) there are pending proceedings in two different Contracting States involving the same cause of action and between the same parties;

(b) the first such proceedings in time were initiated in Contracting State A before the Brussels Convention and/or any applicable Accession Convention came into force in that State;

(c) the second such proceedings are initiated in Contracting State B in accordance with Article 2 of the Brussels Convention after the Brussels Convention and/or any applicable Accession Convention has come into force in both State A and State B;

and having regard to Article 29(1) of the San Sebastian Convention and the corresponding articles in any other applicable Accession Convention and Article 21 of the Brussels Convention (as amended):

(1) Does the Brussels Convention (as amended) and/or any applicable Accession Convention lay down any, and if so what, rules as to whether the proceedings in State B may or must be stayed, or jurisdiction declined, on the ground of pending proceedings in State A

and in particular

(2) Is the Court second seised required or permitted, for the purpose of deciding whether or not to decline jurisdiction in respect of, or to stay, the proceedings before it, to conduct any and, if so, what examination of the basis upon which the Court first seised assumed jurisdiction?'

The arguments put forward before the Court

13. Mr Cinnamond's primary contention is that, notwithstanding Article 29(1) of the San Sebastian Convention, Article 21 of the Brussels Convention applies in the present case and that the English court is therefore required to decline jurisdiction. According to Mr Cinnamond, Article 29(1) of the San Sebastian Convention does not preclude that view because the Portuguese proceedings may still be considered to have been 'brought' for the purposes of Article 21 even though they are not proceedings to which the Convention 'shall apply' for the purposes of Article 29(1). Mr Cinnamond considers his view to be consistent with the scheme and purpose of the relevant provisions. Since by virtue of Article 29(2) any judgment in the Portuguese proceedings will be recognized and enforceable in the other Contracting States in accordance with Title III of the Convention, Article 21 must apply in order to avoid the risk of irreconcilable judgments in the Convention area.

14. In his written observations Mr Cinnamond also puts forward two subsidiary submissions. The first of those is that the lis pendens rule in Article 21 is a particular expression of a more general principle of law which must or, at the very least, may be applied by a court of a Contracting State in the event of parallel proceedings in another Contracting State. The rule in Article 21 must or may therefore be applied by analogy. It is open to the court second seised to investigate whether the proceedings in the court first seised were founded on a basis of jurisdiction which accords with the rules in Title II of the Convention.

15. Mr Cinnamond's second subsidiary submission is that, in the event of the lis pendens rule in the Convention not applying directly or by analogy, neither the Convention nor any Accession Convention precludes the court of a Contracting State from staying proceedings or declining jurisdiction in circumstances such as those of this case in accordance with its national procedural rules on the ground of forum non conveniens or lis alibi pendens.

16. Mrs von Horn, the United Kingdom and the Commission all take the view that Article 21 does not apply in the present case because the Portuguese proceedings are not proceedings brought in the courts of a Contracting State within the meaning of that provision. Article 21 allocates jurisdiction between two courts both of which are bound by the rules of the Convention. Where the court first seised assumed jurisdiction under rules applicable before the Convention took effect, it may have assumed jurisdiction considered by the Convention to be exorbitant; in such circumstances there would be no justification for requiring the court second seised, which, but for Article 21, would be entitled to assume jurisdiction in accordance with the rules of the Convention, to decline jurisdiction. The United Kingdom adds that a judgment of the court first seised might well be unenforceable before the courts of the Contracting States since Article 29(2) of the San Sebastian Convention would not require enforcement in such a case; the application of Article 21 in such circumstances could therefore lead to a denial of justice. In order to meet that point Mr Cinnamond conceded at the hearing that Article 21 did not apply to proceedings which were not capable of producing a judgment enforceable in the

other Contracting States because the court first seised did not assume jurisdiction on a basis which conformed to the rules of the Convention or with a convention in force at the material time between the State of origin and the State addressed as required by Article 29(2) of the San Sebastian Convention.

17. The Commission notes that, although the transitional provision in Article 29(2) of the Accession Convention allows the court of the State addressed to inquire into the basis on which the court of the State of origin assumed jurisdiction, no such provision is made in relation to lis pendens. The explanation, it suggests, is that it may not always be possible for the court second seised to verify whether the court first seised assumed jurisdiction on grounds compatible with the Convention; the operation of Article 29(2) is less problematic in that respect since the court before which enforcement is sought has available a judgment on the basis of which it can verify the grounds on which jurisdiction was assumed.

18. Although considering Article 21 of the Convention to be inapplicable, the United Kingdom suggested in its written observations that the obligation which Article 29(2) of the San Sebastian Convention imposed on Contracting States in certain circumstances to recognize and enforce a judgment given after the date of entry into force of the Convention in proceedings instituted before that date was relevant to the question whether, in the circumstances postulated by the referring court, the court second seised should exercise jurisdiction to decide the dispute.

19. Referring to that suggestion, the Court put a written question to Mrs von Horn, Mr Cinnamond, the United Kingdom and the Commission, asking whether, if Article 21 of the Convention did not apply, it might be inferred from Article 29(2) of the San Sebastian Convention that, so as to avoid frustrating the application of that provision by delivering a judgment which might be irreconcilable with that of the court first seised, the court second seised was obliged in circumstances such as the present to consider whether the court first seised had assumed jurisdiction on the basis of rules which accorded with the Brussels Convention and, where that appeared to be the case, to refrain from proceeding to judgment pending the judgment of the court first seised.

20. In its written reply to that question and also at the hearing, the United Kingdom stated that, having considered the matter further, it took the view that an implied obligation arose from Article 29(2) not to perform an act which would be likely to frustrate the operation of Article 29(2) and thereby prevent, in part, the achievement of the purposes of the San Sebastian Convention. That would be the case if, in the circumstances postulated by the referring court, the court second seised were to exercise jurisdiction. The judgment delivered by that court might be irreconcilable with the judgment of the court first seised, thus preventing recognition of the latter judgment in the State of the court second seised.

21. The Commission - although acknowledging at the hearing that the solution suggested by the United Kingdom in response to the Court's question would to a large extent resolve the conceptual and practical problems in the case - considers that the most appropriate solution is to treat Portugal as a non-

contracting State for the purposes of the present case. In its view the only possible construction of the Convention which will avoid undesirable results without undermining its effectiveness is to apply by 'effet réflexe' the derogations embodied in the Convention to non-contracting States. An example of the alleged 'effet réflexe' would be that the exclusive jurisdiction conferred on the courts of Contracting States in specified circumstances by Article 16 of the Convention could have an 'effet réflexe' as regards the courts of third countries: thus the courts of a Contracting State should decline jurisdiction over a defendant domiciled in that State where the proceedings relate to, for example, immovable property in a non-contracting State. Article 16 recognizes that, where the conditions laid down therein are fulfilled, the jurisdiction assigned by Article 2 is displaced. In the Commission's view the Convention allows such derogations in favour of a non-contracting State where the conditions are fulfilled in that State, thereby filling the void left by the fact that the Convention refers only to Contracting States. The consequence of the 'effet réflexe' in such a case, however, is to entitle rather than to oblige the courts of the Contracting State to decline jurisdiction if the conditions are met in the non-contracting State. The Commission considers that the question of lis pendens in a non-contracting State should be dealt with in the same manner. Where jurisdiction is based on an ordinary ground in a Contracting State, the courts of that State may decline jurisdiction, as if the lis pendens existed in a Contracting State, where the conditions provided for in Articles 21 to 23 are fulfilled in a non-contracting State.

22. At the hearing the United Kingdom considered that such a view, based on the 'effet réflexe' of the Convention, was open to objection on a number of grounds: first, the Convention was intended to regulate jurisdiction between Contracting States and not relations with non-contracting States; secondly, it would involve a radical re-drafting of the Convention and a massive extension of its provisions; thirdly, it would lead to legal uncertainty, thereby defeating one of the principal objectives of the Convention.

Appraisal of the issues

The effect of Article 21 of the Convention

23. I do not share Mr Cinnamond's view that Article 21 of the Convention is applicable in the present case. Article 21 states that, 'where proceedings ... are brought in the courts of different Contracting States, any court other than the court first seised shall ... stay its proceedings'. It is true that that wording does not wholly preclude Mr Cinnamond's construction. As Mr Cinnamond suggests, it would be possible to interpret Article 21 as requiring only that, at the moment at which the applicability of Article 21 arises (i.e. at the moment when the second set of proceedings is instituted), proceedings involving the same cause of action and between the same parties should be pending in another Contracting State, even if the Convention as a whole does not apply to those proceedings.

24. It seems to me however that a more natural construction of Article 21

is that the proceedings before the court first seised must be ones to which the Convention applies. Since by virtue of Article 29(1) of the San Sebastian Convention the Brussels Convention does not apply to the Portuguese proceedings in the present case, Article 21 is inapplicable. The terms of Article 21 ('Where proceedings ... are brought in the courts of different Contracting States') suggest that the proceedings must have been instituted before the court first seised after the entry into force of the Convention. That is consistent with the other language versions of the Convention. Only the Dutch and German versions use terms in Article 21 ('aanhangig zijn', 'anhängig gemacht') which might be considered to have a slightly different connotation. Contrary to Mr Cinnamond's suggestion, it does not assist to contrast the language of Article 21 of the Convention with that of Article 54, which contains a transitional provision similar to that in Article 29 of the San Sebastian Convention. Most language versions appear to use terms which are virtually synonymous in the two provisions.

25. That Article 21 is inapplicable in the present case also follows from the scheme of that provision.

26. In Overseas Union Insurance the Court held that, without prejudice to the case where the court second seised had exclusive jurisdiction under the Convention, Article 21 of the Convention prevented the court second seised from examining the jurisdiction of the court first seised where the latter court's jurisdiction was contested. The Court based that conclusion first on the wording of Article 21, which laid down a sole exception to the obligation to decline jurisdiction, to the effect that the court second seised should stay proceedings until the jurisdiction of the court first seised was established. It then added that the court second seised was never better placed than: 'the court first seised to determine whether the latter has jurisdiction. Either the jurisdiction of the court first seised is determined directly by the rules of the Convention, which are common to both courts and may be interpreted and applied with the same authority by each of them, or it is derived, by virtue of Article 4 of the Convention, from the law of the State of the court first seised, in which case that court is undeniably better placed to rule on the question of its own jurisdiction.

Moreover, the cases in which a court in a Contracting State may review the jurisdiction of a court in another Contracting State are set out exhaustively in Article 28 and the second paragraph of Article 34 of the Convention. Those cases are limited to the stage of recognition or enforcement and relate only to certain rules of special or exclusive jurisdiction having a mandatory or public-policy nature. It follows that, apart from those limited exceptions, the Convention does not authorize the jurisdiction of a court to be reviewed by a court in another Contracting State.'

27. Thus the premiss underlying Article 21 is that the court first seised has assumed jurisdiction under the rules of the Convention (or under national legislation in circumstances where that is expressly provided for by the Convention); if necessary its jurisdiction may be challenged in accordance with the procedures laid down by the law of the State of the court first seised. On that premiss it is unnecessary for the court second seised to examine the basis on

which jurisdiction was assumed by the court first seised. Accordingly, by contrast with Article 28 and the second paragraph of Article 34, Article 21 makes no provision for such an examination.

28. As Mrs von Horn, the United Kingdom and the Commission point out, the premiss underlying Article 21 does not apply where the Convention was not in force at the moment when the first proceedings were instituted. In such circumstances the court first seised would not be bound by the jurisdictional rules of the Convention and might assume jurisdiction on a basis which the Convention considers exorbitant. Moreover, as the United Kingdom points out, a judgment of the court first seised might be unenforceable before the courts of the Contracting States.

29. As already noted above, Mr Cinnamond, in response to that argument, conceded at the hearing that Article 21 applies only where the judgment of the court first seised would be capable of recognition and enforcement in the Contracting States. That concession does not however overcome the difficulty that Article 21, as interpreted by the Court in Overseas Union Insurance, does not allow the court second seised to examine the basis on which the court first seised assumed jurisdiction. Mr Cinnamond sought to meet that objection by arguing that, while the policy considerations underlying that rule were perfectly understandable in the context of the normal application of Article 21, the situation here was different inasmuch as the court first seised had not assumed jurisdiction on the basis of the Convention. By examining the basis on which the court first seised assumed jurisdiction the court second seised would not be questioning the jurisdiction of the court first seised in order to verify its correctness but would be merely ascertaining the basis on which jurisdiction was assumed in order to determine whether its judgment was capable of recognition and enforcement in the Contracting States.

30. That argument may deal with part of the Court's reasoning in Overseas Union Insurance, namely that both courts interpret and apply the Convention with equal authority and the court first seised is better placed to interpret its national law in cases where Article 4 applies. Even on that point, however, it might be replied that the Court was merely setting out the reasons for the omission from Article 21 of any provision for examination of jurisdiction; that those reasons do not apply merely serves to show that Article 21 was not intended to cover a case such as the present. In any event, the remainder of the Court's reasoning, based on the wording of Article 21 and the express provision for an examination of jurisdiction in Article 28 and the second paragraph of Article 34, applies with equal force. Mr Cinnamond's modified construction of Article 21 is difficult to reconcile with the wording of the provision.

31. I therefore consider that Article 21 does not apply.

The effect of Article 29(2) of the San Sebastian Convention

32. Contrary to the Commission's view, however, I do not think that it is possible to disregard for the purposes of this case the fact that Portugal acceded to the Convention before the English proceedings were instituted; indeed it is

that accession which has given rise to the essential problem in this case. Article 29(2) of the San Sebastian Convention requires the recognition and enforcement in the United Kingdom, in accordance with the provisions of Title III of the Convention, of judgments of Portuguese courts given after the date of entry into force of the Convention between Portugal and the United Kingdom in proceedings instituted before that date where the jurisdiction of the Portuguese court was founded upon rules which accorded with the provisions of Title II of the Convention, a requirement that is met in the present proceedings. Thus, although by virtue of Article 29(1) the Convention does not apply to the Portuguese proceedings in this case, it will apply to the judgment given in those proceedings.

33. It is true, as the Commission points out, that Article 29(2) is not itself a rule on lis alibi pendens. However, it seems to me that it inevitably has some bearing on the steps to be taken by the court second seised in circumstances such as the present. Article 27(3) of the Convention, contained in Title III to which Article 29(2) refers, provides that a judgment is not to be recognized where it is irreconcilable with a judgment given in a dispute between the same parties in the State in which recognition is sought. As the United Kingdom points out, if in circumstances such as the present the court second seised were to exercise jurisdiction without regard to the proceedings already pending before the court first seised, its judgment might prove to be irreconcilable with the judgment given subsequently by the court first seised, thereby preventing recognition of the latter judgment pursuant to Article 29(2). Such a result would be inappropriate where the court second seised was aware that there were proceedings pending before the court first seised which might give rise to a judgment that would otherwise require recognition and enforcement in the United Kingdom and in other Contracting States. I share the United Kingdom's view that in such circumstances Article 29(2) of the San Sebastian Convention imposes by implication on the court second seised an obligation not to perform an act which may frustrate the operation of the transitional provision in Article 29(2).

34. To give effect to that obligation it would seem appropriate (as suggested by the United Kingdom in its reply to the Court's written question) for the court second seised to proceed as follows:

(1) The court second seised should seek to ascertain the basis on which the court first seised assumed jurisdiction and, where it finds that the basis of jurisdiction accords with the rules of the Convention (or another convention between the States concerned applicable at the material time), it should decline jurisdiction.

(2) If the court second seised is as yet unable to ascertain the basis on which the court first seised assumed jurisdiction, it should stay proceedings pending the judgment of the court first seised, whereupon the disposal of the case will depend on the basis on which the court first seised exercised jurisdiction.

35. That solution overcomes the difficulty noted by the Commission that the court second seised may not be able to ascertain the basis on which the court first seised assumed jurisdiction in the absence of a judgment by the latter. Moreover, as the United Kingdom observed at the hearing, it has the merit of achieving a result which is consistent with the objectives of the Convention, while avoiding

the undesirable consequences which would flow from the direct application of Article 21 to cases where the Convention was not in force at the moment when the first proceedings were instituted. It also accords with legal principle. It does not entail a strained interpretation of the wording of the Convention or of the San Sebastian Convention. In addition it is consistent with the rules of public international law. Article 26 of the Vienna Convention of 22 May 1969 on the Law of Treaties embodies the universally recognized principle that treaties must be performed by the parties in good faith; and Article 18 of that Convention, which imposes an obligation of good faith on the signatories to a treaty even prior to its entry into force, prohibits States from performing 'acts which would defeat the object and purpose of a treaty'.

36. The above solution is also in conformity with that adopted by the general rules on lis alibi pendens of a number of Member States, according to which the court second seised must consider whether foreign pending proceedings are likely to give rise to a judgment capable of recognition in the State of that court.

37. Consequently, I do not think it necessary in this case to consider the question, raised by the Commission, of the possible effects of the Convention in relations with non-contracting States. That question in any event raises issues of broader significance which have not been fully debated in these proceedings.

Conclusion

38. Accordingly, I am of the opinion that the Court should give the following reply to the questions put by the House of Lords:

(1) In a case where there are proceedings pending in two States party to the Brussels Convention involving the same cause of action and between the same parties and the Brussels Convention entered into force in the first State by virtue of the San Sebastian Convention after proceedings were instituted in the first State but before proceedings were instituted in the second State, Article 29(2) of the San Sebastian Convention imposes by implication on the court second seised an obligation not to exercise jurisdiction in such a way as to frustrate the operation of that provision.

(2) In such circumstances:

(a) The court second seised should seek to ascertain the basis on which the court first seised assumed jurisdiction and, where it finds that the basis of jurisdiction accords with the rules of the Convention (or another convention between the States concerned applicable at the material time), it should decline jurisdiction.

(b) If the court second seised is as yet unable to ascertain the basis on which the court first seised assumed jurisdiction, it should stay proceedings pending the judgment of the court first seised, whereupon the disposal of the case will depend on the basis on which the court first seised exercised jurisdiction.

Case C-351/96 - 19 May 1998

Drouot Assurances
v
CMI and Others

Lis alibi pendens - Proceedings between the 'same parties' - Definition - Whether insurer and its insured are to be treated as the same party - Condition - Litigation concerning the obligation of the owner of the cargo of a vessel to contribute to the general average following the foundering of the vessel

Summary

An insurer and its insured must be considered to be one and the same party for the purposes of the application of Article 21 of the Convention on Jurisdiction and the Enforcement of Judgments in Civil and Commercial Matters, where there is such a degree of identity between their interests that a judgment delivered against one of them would have the force of *res judicata* as against the other. On the other hand, application of the said article cannot have the effect of precluding the insurer and its insured, where their interests diverge, from asserting their respective interests before the courts as against the other parties concerned.

Thus, Article 21 of the Convention is not applicable in the case of two actions for contribution to general average, one brought by the insurer of the hull of a vessel which has foundered against the owner and the insurer of the cargo which the vessel was carrying when it sank, the other brought by the latter two parties against the owner and the charterer of the vessel, unless it is established that, with regard to the subject-matter of the two disputes, the interests of the insurer of the hull of the vessel are identical to and indissociable from those of its insured, the owner and the charterer of that vessel.

JUDGMENT OF THE COURT

Gulmann, President, Wathelet, Moitinho de Almeida, Edward (Rapporteur) and Sevón, Judges.

1. By order of 8 October 1996, received at the Court on 25 October 1996, the Cour de Cassation (Court of Cassation), France, referred to the Court for a preliminary ruling under the Protocol of 3 June 1971 on the interpretation by the Court of Justice of the Convention of 27 September 1968 on Jurisdiction and the Enforcement of Judgments in Civil and Commercial Matters, a question on the interpretation of Article 21 of that Convention (OJ 1978 L 304, p. 36), as amended by the Convention of 9 October 1978 on the Accession of the Kingdom of Denmark, Ireland and the United Kingdom of Great Britain and Northern Ireland (OJ 1978 L 304, p. 1; amended version of the Convention, p. 77) and the Convention of 25 October 1982 on the Accession of the Hellenic Republic (OJ 1982 L 388, p. 1) (hereinafter 'the Convention').

2. That question was raised in proceedings brought by Drouot Assurances SA, a company incorporated under French law (hereinafter 'Drouot'), against Consolidated Metallurgical Industries (CMI Industrial Sites, hereinafter 'CMI') and Protea Assurance (hereinafter 'Protea'), companies incorporated under South African law, and Groupement d'Intérêt Économique (GIE) Réunion Européenne (hereinafter 'GIE Réunion'), on the subject of the cost of refloating a barge known as the 'Sequana' which foundered in the inland waters of the Netherlands on 4 August 1989.

3. Article 21 of the Convention provides: 'Where proceedings involving the same cause of action and between the same parties are brought in the courts of different Contracting States, any court other than the court first seised shall of its own motion decline jurisdiction in favour of that court.

A court which would be required to decline jurisdiction may stay its proceedings if the jurisdiction of the other court is contested.'

4. In 1989 CMI arranged with a Mr Velghe to transport on the Sequana a cargo of ferrochromium belonging to it from the Dutch port of

Rotterdam to the French port of Garlinghem-Aire-la-Lys on the Rhine. According to the referring court, at the time of these events, the Sequana belonged to a Mr Walbrecq and was chartered by Mr Velghe.

5. However, at the hearing the Court was informed that, according to CMI and Protea, following the death of Mr Walbrecq in 1981, Mr Velghe had become the owner of the Sequana and that, at the material time, the vessel was chartered by another company. Drouot stated that it had no information on those matters, but explained that, according to the custom followed on the Rhine, the master is the legal agent of the owner and he is responsible for checking that the vessel is fit to sail. Finally, according to CMI, Protea and Drouot, Mr Velghe was the master of the Sequana at the time of the events in issue.

6. On 4 August 1989 the Sequana foundered in the inland waters of the Netherlands. Drouot, the insurer of the hull of the vessel, had it refloated at its own expense, thereby enabling CMI's cargo to be salvaged.

7. On 11 and 13 December 1990, Drouot brought proceedings before the Tribunal de Commerce (Commercial Court), Paris, against CMI, Protea (the insurer of the cargo) and GIE Réunion (Protea's agent at the time of the expert's report on the salvaging costs), for payment of the sum of HFL 99 485.53, the figure set by the average adjuster as the amount of the contribution of CMI and Protea to the general average.

8. However, in the French court, CMI and Protea raised an objection of *lis alibi pendens* on the basis of an action they had brought on 31 August 1990 against Mr Walbrecq and Mr Velghe before the Arrondissementsrechtbank (District Court), Rotterdam, for a declaration, *inter alia*, that they were not obliged to contribute to the general average.

9. On 11 March 1992 the Tribunal de Commerce, Paris, rejected the plea of *lis alibi pendens* on the ground that, as Drouot was not a party to the Netherlands action and Mr Walbrecq and Mr Velghe were not parties to the French action, the parties to the two actions were not the same. Moreover, the Tribunal took the view that the subject-matter of the applications made in the two actions was not the same.

10. CMI, Protea and GIE Réunion then appealed to the Cour d'Appel (Court of Appeal), Paris. Before that court, CMI and Protea argued that the only reason Drouot was not a party to the Netherlands action was that procedural rules in the Netherlands did not permit insurers to be brought

into the action. They also argued that, since the subject-matter of the dispute before the Netherlands court encompassed that of the dispute before the French court, the subject-matter of the two disputes was the same.

11. In a judgment of 29 April 1994, the Cour d'Appel, Paris, first noted that it was common ground that Netherlands procedural rules restricted the opportunity for an insurer to be party to proceedings in which the insured is involved. It then considered that Drouot was in fact present in the Netherlands action 'through the intermediary of the insured'. Finally, it held that, in the light of the arguments put forward by CMI and Protea, the two disputes did have the same subject-matter. Accordingly the plea of *lis alibi pendens* was upheld.

12. Drouot then appealed to the Cour de Cassation against that judgment, contending that the parties to the two actions were not the same.

13. The Cour de Cassation, taking the view that the appeal before it raised a difficulty concerning the interpretation of Article 21 of the Convention, decided to stay proceedings and seek a ruling from the Court of Justice on the question 'Whether with regard in particular to the independent concept of "same parties" used in Article 21 of the Convention of 27 September 1968 on Jurisdiction and the Enforcement of Judgments in Civil and Commercial Matters, there is inter-State *lis alibi pendens* for the purposes of that provision where a court of one Contracting State is seised by the insurer of a vessel that has been shipwrecked with an action seeking from the owner and the insurer of the cargo on board partial reimbursement, by way of contribution to the general average, of the refloating costs, when a court of another Contracting State was seised previously by that owner and insurer with an action against the owner and the charterer of the vessel for a declaration that they were not obliged to contribute to the general average, and the court seised second declines jurisdiction, despite the parties in the two cases not being strictly identical, on the ground that the procedural law applicable before the court seised first "restricts the opportunity for an insurer to be party to proceedings in which the insured is involved" so that the insurer of the vessel is in fact also involved, through the intermediary of the insured, in the case brought first.'

14. By that question, the national court is asking essentially whether Article 21 of the Convention is applicable in the case of two actions for contribution to general average, one brought by the insurer of the hull of

a vessel which has foundered against the owner and the insurer of the cargo which the vessel was carrying when it sank, the other brought by the latter two parties against the owner and the charterer of the vessel.

15. As the parties to those two actions do not appear to be the same, it should be considered whether, in a case such as that in the main proceedings, the insurer of the hull of a vessel must be deemed to be the same person as its insured when applying the 'same parties' criterion contained in Article 21 of the Convention.

16. According to consistent case-law, the terms used in Article 21 of the Convention in order to determine whether a situation of lis pendens arises must be regarded as independent (Case C-406/92 *The 'Tatry'* [1994] ECR I-5439, paragraph 30).

17. In the '*Tatry*' judgment, cited above, at paragraph 32, the Court stressed that Article 21, together with Article 22 on related actions, is contained in Section 8 of Title II of the Convention, a section intended, in the interests of the proper administration of justice within the Community, to prevent parallel proceedings before the courts of different Contracting States and to avoid conflicts between decisions which might result therefrom. Those rules are therefore designed to preclude, in so far as is possible, the possibility of a situation arising such as that referred to in Article 27(3), that is to say the non-recognition of a judgment on account of its irreconcilability with a judgment given in a dispute between the same parties in the State in which recognition is sought.

18. In that same judgment, at paragraph 33, the Court held that, in the light of the wording of Article 21 of the Convention and the objective set out above, that article must be understood as requiring, as a condition of the obligation of the second court seised to decline jurisdiction, that the parties to the two actions be identical.

19. It is certainly true that, as regards the subject-matter of two disputes, there may be such a degree of identity between the interests of an insurer and those of its insured that a judgment delivered against one of them would have the force of *res judicata* as against the other. That would be the case, *inter alia*, where an insurer, by virtue of its right of subrogation, brings or defends an action in the name of its insured without the latter being in a position to influence the proceedings. In such a situation, insurer and insured must be considered to be one and the same party for the purposes of the application of Article 21 of the Convention.

20. On the other hand, application of Article 21 cannot have the effect of precluding the insurer and its insured, where their interests diverge, from asserting their respective interests before the courts as against the other parties concerned.

21. In the present case, CMI and Protea made clear at the hearing that, in the Netherlands action, they seek to have Mr Velghe declared exclusively liable for the foundering of the Sequana. As the insurer merely of the hull of the vessel, however, Drouot takes the view that it cannot be held liable for the fault of its insured and thus has no interest in the Netherlands action.

22. It appears, moreover, that, in the French action, Drouot has been acting not in its capacity as the representative of its insured but in its capacity as a direct participant in the refloating of the Sequana.

23. Thus, in this case, it does not appear that the interests of the insurer of the hull of the vessel can be considered to be identical to and indissociable from those of its insured, the owner and the charterer of that vessel. However, it is for the national court to ascertain whether this is in fact the case.

24. In those circumstances, the existence or otherwise of a national procedural rule such as that mentioned in the question referred for a preliminary ruling is of no relevance to the solution of the dispute.

25. The answer to the question raised must thus be that Article 21 of the Convention is not applicable in the case of two actions for contribution to general average, one brought by the insurer of the hull of a vessel which has foundered against the owner and the insurer of the cargo which the vessel was carrying when it sank, the other brought by the latter two parties against the owner and the charterer of the vessel, unless it is established that, with regard to the subject-matter of the two disputes, the interests of the insurer of the hull of the vessel are identical to and indissociable from those of its insured, the owner and the charterer of that vessel.

On those grounds, the Court (Fifth Chamber), in answer to the question referred to it by the Cour de Cassation, France, by order of 8 October 1996, hereby rules:

Article 21 of the Convention of 27 September 1968 on Jurisdiction and the Enforcement of Judgments in Civil and

Commercial Matters, as amended by the Convention of 9 October 1978 on the Accession of the Kingdom of Denmark, Ireland and the United Kingdom of Great Britain and Northern Ireland and by the Convention of 25 October 1982 on the Accession of the Hellenic Republic, is not applicable in the case of two actions for contribution to general average, one brought by the insurer of the hull of a vessel which has foundered against the owner and the insurer of the cargo which the vessel was carrying when it sank, the other brought by the latter two parties against the owner and the charterer of the vessel, unless it is established that, with regard to the subject-matter of the two disputes, the interests of the insurer of the hull of the vessel are identical to and indissociable from those of its insured, the owner and the charterer of that vessel.

OPINION OF ADVOCATE GENERAL FENNELLY

I - Introduction

1. The Court is asked, in this reference from the French Cour de Cassation, to interpret the notion of 'the same parties' in Article 21 of the Brussels Convention. The issue is whether, in the context of a claim in general average made by an insurer in a French court and an earlier claim for a negative declaration against the insured in a Dutch court that there is no such liability, there is a *lis alibi pendens* for the purposes of Article 21. Accordingly, the issue effectively is whether the insured should be treated as the 'same party' as its insurer.

II - The legal and factual background to the reference

A - The relevant provisions of the Convention

2. Title II of the Convention deals with 'jurisdiction'. Whereas the general rules are set out in section 1, various special rules qualifying those general rules are established by sections 2 to 9.

3. Section 8 is entitled '*Lis Pendens* - related actions' and consists of Articles 21 to 23. Prior to its amendment by the San Sebastian Convention, Article 21 of the Convention was worded as follows:

'Where proceedings involving the same cause of action and between the same parties are brought in the courts of different Contracting States, any court other than the court first seised shall of its own motion decline jurisdiction in favour of that court.

A court which would be required to decline jurisdiction *may* stay its proceedings if the jurisdiction of the other court is contested.'

4. In the case of 'related actions', the rule under Article 22 of the Convention is that the court other than that first seised may stay its proceedings. Related actions are defined as those which 'are so closely connected that it is expedient to hear and determine them together to avoid the risk of irreconcilable judgments resulting from separate proceedings'.

5. Title III of the Convention concerns 'recognition and enforcement'. In accordance with the general objective of the Convention, the general principle stated in Article 26 is that 'a judgment given in a Contracting State shall be recognised in the other Contracting States without any special procedure being required'. However, Article 27 prescribes a limited number of grounds upon which such recognition may be refused. For the purpose of the present case, only the third indent is potentially relevant: '3.[I]f the judgment is irreconcilable with a judgment given in a dispute between the same parties in the State in which recognition is sought.'

B - Factual background and procedure before the referring court

6. Consolidated Metal Industries (hereinafter 'CMI') charged Mr Velghe to transport on a barge, known as the Sequana, a cargo of ferrochromium from Rotterdam in the Netherlands to Garlinghem-Aire-la-Lys in France. The vessel, having begun to take in water, foundered in Netherlands inland waters early on 4 August 1989, but not before the captain was apparently able to steer it from the main channel. Drouot Assurances SA (hereinafter 'Drouot'), the insurer of the vessel (or hull), caused the ship to be refloated at its own expense, thus salvaging CMI's cargo. Drouot brought proceedings on 11 and 13 December 1990 before the Tribunal de Commerce (Commercial Court), Paris against CMI, Protea Assurance (hereinafter 'Protea', a South African company), the insurer of the cargo, as well as Protea's European representative, the Groupement d'intérêt économique (GIE) Réunion européenne (hereinafter 'GIE'), for payment of the sum of HFL 99 485.53, being the figure set by the average adjuster as the amount of the contribution of CMI and Protea to the general average. However, CMI and Protea pleaded, by way of a procedural objection to the French action, a *lis alibi pendens* arising out of an action which they had earlier brought against Mr Walbrecq and Mr Velghe before the Arrondissementsrechtbank (District Court), Rotterdam on 31 August 1990. According to the case-file and the observations submitted to the Court, CMI and Protea sought, in the Netherlands action, a declaration to the effect that they were not obliged to contribute to the general average. Such a negative declaration, which, apparently, could not have been sought if the action had been initiated in France, was sought in the alternative to a claim that Mr Velghe be held responsible for the occurrence of the accident on the ground that, as captain, he had permitted the barge to become unseaworthy by overloading it at Rotterdam.

7. The *lis alibi pendens* plea was rejected on 11 March 1992 by the Tribunal de Commerce on the basis that the parties to the two actions were not the same; viz. Drouot was not a party to the Netherlands action and Messrs Velghe and Walbrecq were not parties to the proceedings before it. Moreover, in

the view of the Tribunal de Commerce, the issues in the two actions were not the same. The defendants appealed to the Cour d'Appel (Court of Appeal), Paris.

8. According to the judgment of the Cour d'Appel, CMI and Protea contended before that court that the object of the two actions was the same and that Drouot was not a party to the Netherlands action only because Dutch procedural rules did not permit insurers to be named. In its judgment of 29 April 1994, the Cour d'Appel took the view that it was uncontested that Netherlands procedural rules precluded the possibility for an insurance company to be present in a case involving its insured. Having recited the broader scope of the Netherlands action (including, as it did, a claim regarding the owner's liability for the unseaworthy state of the vessel), it held that, in fact, it, none the less, encompassed the subject-matter of the French action. Furthermore, it held that Drouot could be regarded as a party to the Netherlands action 'through the intermediary of the insured'. Accordingly, the plea of *lis alibi pendens* was upheld.

9. On appeal to the Cour de Cassation (Court of Cassation), Drouot contended, primarily, that the Cour d'Appel should not have upheld the *lis alibi pendens* plea, since neither the nature of the proceedings nor the identity of the parties in the two actions was the same, and that the impugned judgment was incompatible with Article 21 of the Convention.

10. The Cour de Cassation, being of the view that the appeal before it turned on the interpretation of the concept of the 'same parties' used in Article 21 of the Convention, decided to refer the following question to the Court pursuant to Articles 1 to 3 of the Protocol of 3 June 1971 on the interpretation of the Convention: '... [W]hether, with regard in particular to the independent concept of "same parties" used in Article 21 of the Brussels Convention, there is inter-State *lis alibi pendens* for the purposes of that provision where a court of one Contracting State is seised by the insurer of a vessel that has been shipwrecked with an action seeking from the owner and the insurer of the cargo on board partial reimbursement, by way of contribution to the general average, of the refloating costs, when a court of another Contracting State was seised previously by that owner and insurer with an action against the owner and the charterer of the vessel for a declaration that they were not obliged to contribute to the general average, and the court seised second declines jurisdiction, despite the parties in the two cases not being strictly identical, on the ground that the procedural law applicable before the court seised first "restricts the opportunity for an insurer to be party to proceedings in which the insured is involved" so that the insurer of the vessel is in fact also involved, through the intermediary of the insured, in the case brought first.'

III - Observations

11. Written and oral observations have been submitted by Drouot, the French Republic and the Commission. On the other hand, GIE and the Federal Republic of Germany merely submitted written observations while CMI and Protea submitted joint oral observations. They may be summarised as follows.

12. At the hearing, counsel for Drouot pointed out that the general provisions of maritime law apply to fluvial transport on the Rhine and Moselle rivers, under which, he submitted, Drouot's contract of insurance, in the absence of an express stipulation to the contrary, must be regarded as merely covering the hull. Vessel insurance covers only liability for damage done by the vessel to other vessels or to port or riverside installations. Drouot also submitted that the maritime rules of general average (see further paragraphs 17 to 19 below) apply to navigation on the Rhine and Moselle rivers. Based on the case-law concerning Article 21 of the Convention Drouot submits that no *lis alibi pendens* may arise unless the same parties figure in both proceedings. The criteria set out in Article 21 must be construed autonomously from related concepts in the respective laws of the Contracting States. Both the judgment and the Advocate General's Opinion in *The Tatry* support the view that there is *lis alibi pendens* only when there is a strict identity of parties in the two procedures. At the hearing, Drouot submitted that, for parties to be identical, they must have a common interest to defend or, at least, a common argument to make, which, in its view, cannot be the case regarding its supposed representation by Mr Velghe in the Netherlands action. It claims that, as insurer of the hull, it was not responsible for the general presumed liability of the boat-owner. In its written observations, Drouot submits that the status of a person as a *party* before a court allegedly first seised must be determined by the law of the forum where the plea of *lis alibi pendens* is raised, i.e. by French law in the present case. Finally, Drouot submitted that, apart from the fact that it was neither voluntarily nor involuntarily a party to the Netherlands action, it had no interest in that action, since, as insurer of the *Sequana*, it was liable to reimburse Mr Velghe in respect of his contribution to the general average, notwithstanding the possible responsibility for the occurrence of the accident.

13. In their oral observations, CMI and Protea, first, contended that Drouot was not merely, as claimed, the insurer of the vessel but also of the personal liabilities of its captain and owner, namely Mr Velghe. Secondly, counsel for CMI and Protea pointed out that his clients had initially brought an action in France before the Tribunal de Commerce, Béthune (the place of Mr Velghe's residence) against both Mr Velghe and Drouot, in which, it was alleged, Drouot claimed that the action against it should have been brought in Rotterdam. Accordingly, CMI and Protea instituted the Netherlands action but did not cite Drouot because of the alleged Dutch procedural rules which prevent the insurer being a party to proceedings brought against its insured. As regards the interpretation of Article 21 of the Convention, CMI and Protea contended that the most important consideration was the avoidance of the adoption of incompatible decisions by courts in different Contracting States. They relied in particular on *Gubisch* as establishing the identity of two causes of action concerning, on the one hand, the annulment of a contract and, on the other, its enforcement.

14. France submits that the autonomy of the conditions required for the occurrence of a *lis alibi pendens* by Article 21 of the Convention would be undermined if the peculiarities of the procedural law of a Contracting State were

to determine whether the 'same parties' are present. It laid particular emphasis on the need to respect the rights of defence, or fair hearing, of the insured. An insurer is not represented in national proceedings by its insured. It does not have access to the court in legal proceedings involving its insured, so as to permit it to present its own arguments or defend its position, and the legal rights and interests of an insurer and its insured often do not coincide. Thus, even assuming identity between insurer and insured, the rights of defence of insurance companies could only properly be guaranteed if Article 21 of the Convention were interpreted as requiring, as a prerequisite to upholding a plea of *lis alibi pendens*, that the parties supposedly present in both actions actually be involved as principal parties.

15. Germany also stresses the importance of adopting an autonomous interpretation but argues for a broad concept of 'same parties' so as to avoid the occurrence of irreconcilable judgments within the meaning of the third indent of Article 27 of the Convention. Given the relationship between the concepts of *lis alibi pendens* and *res judicata*, Germany contends that parties to a second action, who are not formally identical to those involved in a first action, should not be regarded as being 'the same', unless they would be bound by the effects of the judgment given by the court first seised, so as to create a danger of irreconcilable judgments if the plea were not upheld. For this purpose, the second court seised should refer to either the substantive or procedural rules of the first court seised, as well as its own, in order to determine whether any binding third-party effects of the first court's judgment would be recognised. Finally, Germany emphasises the need to ensure that Article 21 be applied in a manner that respects the requirements of effective access to court. Thus, where a plea of *lis alibi pendens* is upheld but the first action is unsuccessful, it must remain possible for the party whose second action was affected by that plea subsequently to resume its action before the second court.

16. The Commission, though recognising that the question referred focuses only on the concept of the 'same parties', submits that the two actions may be regarded as having the same cause of action and object. On the identity of the parties, the Commission observes that the question referred raises the novel issue as to whether Article 21 of the Convention permits a court before which a plea of *lis alibi pendens* is raised to go beyond the formal identification of the parties in the proceedings before the court first seised. The concept of the 'same parties' should, in its view, be interpreted strictly. Besides the need to preserve the autonomy of that concept from the laws of the Contracting State concerning matters such as subrogation, there are various other reasons which militate against assimilating an insurer with its insured. The interests of an insured and an insurer are not necessarily identical; the efficient administration of justice may not be well served by making the insurer await the outcome of a first set of proceedings to which it is not a party whenever it wishes to claim, in a different action, that, for example, no subrogation actually arises. In the Commission's view the wording of Article 21, by referring to the *same* parties and not to other parties who may have rights or liabilities arising from the rights or liabilities of the actual parties, supports this approach. At the hearing, the

Commission's agent questioned the practicality of the approach suggested by Germany: if the second court seised were obliged systematically to assess the binding effects of a potential judgment to be given by the first court seised before upholding a plea, the practical application of the notion of *lis alibi pendens* in Article 21 would become unduly complicated.

IV - Analysis

A - Introduction

17. The disputed claim in the French action concerns a contribution to general average. Although, as France rightly points out, the Court has not been asked to assess the similarity of that cause of action with those involved in the Netherlands action, I think that it would still be helpful to take cognizance of the nature of a claim for general average contribution. A short review of the particularities of the legal doctrine of general average will, I think, assist the application in this particular case of the concept of identity of parties in Article 21 of the Convention.

B - The notion of general average

18. The notion of general average lies at the heart of both the proceedings instituted by Drouot in France and the alternative claim by Protea and CMI in the Netherlands. It is a notion of maritime law of great antiquity. Its origins can be traced to the Rhodian Sea Law, which also found later expression in Roman Law, whereby the owner of cargo subjected to jettison (*jactus factus levandae navis gratia*) to save a vessel could spread his loss, by claiming contribution, among the owner of the vessel and other cargo owners. It came, over time, to include claims based on other types of damage and expense incurred to avoid it. In modern times, it generally takes the form, in practice, of the incorporation into contracts of affreightment and policies of marine insurance of the conventional York-Antwerp Rules. These rules, regularly revised since the first International General Average Rules were adopted at York in 1864, appear to have been given effect in French law by a law of 1967. The nautical event giving rise to the claims at issue before the Dutch and French courts did not, however, take place at sea but on a part of the Rhine and Moselle waterway system. Counsel for Drouot explained at the hearing that, by virtue of a law of 1895, passed during the period of the attachment of Alsace to Germany, maritime law was applied to navigation on the Rhine and Moselle. The rules specifically applied in the charter-party in this case are those of Rhine, Antwerp and Rotterdam and, as appears from the case-file, general average is therein defined as the sacrifices and expenses reasonably made and incurred with the object of saving a boat and its cargo from common peril.

19. The gist, therefore, of the notion of general average is that participants in a common commercial adventure should contribute equitably to the damage or loss of one of the participants who has, for the benefit of all, suffered a

sacrifice or, by extension, reasonably incurred expense to prevent loss. Insurers of the hull and cargo are treated as participants and may claim or be liable for general average contribution. A claim for general average contribution is, therefore, not necessarily made by an insurer.

20. That conclusion seems to me to have a bearing on the question of the capacity of Mr Velghe (and Mr Walbrecq) before the Dutch court. It is true that an insurer, having fully discharged its liability to its insured, may in certain circumstances, by virtue of a right of subrogation, effectively step into the shoes of the insured so as to pursue claims (including a claim for general average contribution) against third parties. This right may, depending on the applicable law, be exercised either in the name of the insured or by the insurer in its own name, but only so as to invoke the rights of the insured and after payment. That clearly does not apply to the Netherlands action; nor does it apply to the French action where Drouot's claim is not based on subrogation to any rights of Mr Velghe but on its general average claim. The precise nature of the action before the Dutch court is known only indirectly; but it is generally agreed that it includes, as one element, a claim for a negative declaration that CMI and Protea be held not liable to contribute to general average. Thus, in the particular context of a general average claim, it is difficult to see how the prima facie lack of identity between Mr Velghe and Drouot should be merged into an identity of interest.

21. However, there are other problems of a practical nature to be addressed in considering whether a party should be treated as representing his insurers for the purposes of Article 21 of the Brussels Convention. The court in the Contracting State where the issue of *lis alibi pendens* in the sense of Article 21 of the Convention is raised, and which is informed of the existence of a prior action claimed to be between the same parties in another Contracting State, will need to conclude that an insured, a named party in the other contracting State, should be treated as being the same party as his insurer. To start with, that court will need to investigate the relationship between insurer and insured. It is notorious that disputes between insurer and insured take a great variety of forms. I will cite only a few. The very existence of the policy may be in dispute; if its existence is established or admitted its validity may be contested on grounds of fraud, misrepresentation or non disclosure; its application to the particular loss may be in doubt, as may be the quantum of the loss, the means of proving it or the time for payment. Even in the present case, there is a dispute between CMI and Protea, on the one hand, and Drouot, on the other (though not, so far as I am aware, between Drouot and Mr Velghe), regarding the scope of the cover under Drouot's policy of insurance. The second national court, in my hypothesis, might have to reach a conclusion on any of those potentially complex issues by reference to the law applicable in the other, or even a third, Contracting State.

22. The comparison of the capacity in which the claim for general average contribution is made by Drouot in the French court with that of Mr Velghe in the Dutch court is the key to the application of Article 21 of the Convention. The Drouot claim is made in its capacity as a party to the enterprise having made a sacrifice. It is not made as representative of Mr Velghe. Indeed, any claim made

by the owner of a vessel which had sunk against the owner of the damaged cargo would be met, to say the least, with surprise, unless it were itself based on general average, i.e. on sacrifice. However, in the present case, Mr Velghe would not appear to have participated in the salvage of the vessel and, thus, would scarcely have incurred any such sacrifice.

23. Consequently, viewing the matter exclusively within the context of the present claim for general average contribution, there is no such identity of interest between Drouot and Mr Velghe as would justify, even if that were permitted, overlooking their nominal and real differences of identity so as to treat them as the 'same party'.

C - The same parties

24. In upholding the plea of *lis alibi pendens* in the present case, the Cour d'Appel, in determining the identity of the parties to the Netherlands action, has relied upon a principle which, in its opinion, forms part of the procedural law of the Netherlands. It is right to point out that the provisions of the Convention were not cited to the Cour d'Appel. Nevertheless, the approach which it has adopted is not, in my opinion, compatible with the Court's decisions in *Gubisch* and *The Tatry*, where the Court declared unambiguously that the 'substantive conditions' prescribed by Article 21 of the Convention for a successful plea of *lis alibi pendens* 'must be regarded as independent'. These substantive conditions represent a considered choice and the implicit rejection of the possibility of referring to the term *lis alibi pendens* as used in the different national legal systems of the Contracting States. The application of the Convention concept of 'the same parties' cannot, in my view, depend on the existence and scope of the Netherlands-law principle relied upon by the Cour d'Appel, since that represents a consideration of the law of the first court seised.

25. Next, it is necessary to assess what guidance the Court's case-law furnishes in respect of the autonomous Convention concept of the 'same parties'. *Zelger* is not relevant because it only concerned the procedural formalities regulating the temporal point at which a court may be regarded as having been seised of an action. In *Gubisch*, the Court was concerned with a situation whose 'salient features' were that 'one of the parties [had] brought an action before a court of first instance for the enforcement of an obligation stipulated in an international contract of sale ... [while] an action was subsequently brought against him by the other party in another Contracting State for the rescission or discharge of the same contract'. The Court declared that the conditions laid down by Article 21 are exhaustive; namely, the two actions must be 'between the same parties and involve the same cause of action and the same subject-matter'. It proceeded, in circumstances where the present issue of identity of parties was not in doubt, to take the view that the concept of the same cause of action 'cannot be restricted so as to mean two claims which are entirely identical'. That the Court was clearly motivated by the need to avoid conflicting judgments emerges clearly from its statement that in circumstances such as those of the case before it:

'There can be no doubt that a judgment given in a Contracting State requiring performance of the contract would not be recognised in the State in which recognition is sought if a court in that State had given a judgment rescinding or discharging the contract. Such a result, restricting the effects of each judgment to the territory of the State concerned, would run counter to the objectives of the Convention, which is intended to strengthen legal protection throughout the territory of the Community and to facilitate recognition in each Contracting State of judgments given in any other Contracting State.'

26. CMI and Protea have argued from *Gubisch* for a broad and flexible interpretation of the concept of the 'same cause of action' and, by extension, of 'the same parties' as those terms are used in Article 21 of the Convention. It is true that, in *Gubisch*, the Court held that the concept of 'the same subject-matter', which, in effect, it interpreted into the English text by reference to the other language versions, could not 'be restricted so as to mean two claims which are entirely identical'. In practice, it applied that reasoning to the two actions one of which was brought to enforce and the other to rescind or discharge the same contract. In doing so, it attached great importance to the purpose expressed, *inter alia*, in Article 27(3) of the Convention of avoiding irreconcilable judgments between the same parties and how such judgments could arise if the competing claims had to be 'entirely identical' before a *lis alibi pendens* plea could be upheld. That reasoning is not, however, equally applicable to the concept of 'the same parties', since the judgment proceeds on the assumption that, whatever differences exist in the subject-matter, the parties are the same. Nothing in the judgment, in the text of Article 21 or in the purpose of the Convention requires that a flexible approach be adopted in that instance. The contrary is rather the case. Judgments are, in my view, truly irreconcilable only if they are contrary and given in actions between the same parties.

27. The judgment in *The Tatry* confirms this view and has the merit of having addressed the issue of identity of parties, albeit not in the radical form suggested in the instant case. The Court had to examine whether the Convention could be regarded as applicable in the case of two sets of proceedings involving the same cause of action but where some but not all of the parties were the same; i.e. where at least one of the plaintiffs and one of the defendants to the proceedings first commenced were among the plaintiffs and defendants in the second proceedings, or *vice versa*. The Court first agreed with the recommendation of its Advocate General to the effect that the identity of the parties 'cannot depend on the procedural position of each of them in the two actions, and that the plaintiff in the first action may be the defendant in the second'. Having regard to the wording and objective of Article 21, 'to prevent parallel proceedings...', the Court declared that Article 21 'must be understood as requiring, as a condition of the obligation of the second court seised to decline jurisdiction, that the parties to the two actions be identical'. It follows that this requirement must be strictly construed.

28. Thus, in *The Tatry*, the Court ruled that, 'where some of the parties are the same as the parties to an action which has already been started, Article 21 requires the second court seised to decline jurisdiction *only* to the extent to which

the parties to the proceedings pending before it are also parties to the action previously started before the court of another Contracting State'. I agree with the Commission's contention that the application of Article 21 of the Convention cannot depend on the court before which the plea of *lis alibi pendens* is raised carrying out an inquiry into the true capacity of parties before the court of a different Contracting State.

29. My view, therefore, is that the concept of 'same parties' is to be interpreted literally and strictly. The Court has used the word 'identical'. This means that not only must the parties to the two actions be the same in the literal sense of the same natural or legal person, but also that they must appear in the same right. In particular, a person suing in his own right and for his own benefit is obviously not to be equated with the same person suing or being sued in a purely representative capacity, for example, as the legal personal representative of a deceased person or a person under a disability, or in any of the wide range of cases where a person may, in law, be named to represent corporate bodies or their creditors in cases of insolvency.

30. This does not, to my mind, create too rigid a framework for the operation of Article 21 of the Convention. On the contrary, it is in conformity with the objective of 'simplification of formalities governing the reciprocal recognition and enforcement of judgments ...' found in Article 220 of the EC (formerly EEC) Treaty, which authorised the Member States, among other things, to enter into the Convention. Simple and transparent rules, capable of being applied on the basis of objective and readily accessible factors best serve this objective. Cases where a broader discretion is required to stay proceedings where related actions are brought in the courts of different Contracting States are catered for by Article 22 of the Convention. As Advocate General Tesauro explained in his Opinion in *The Tatry*, the idea of 'irreconcilable' judgments in the third paragraph of Article 22 does not bear 'the same restrictive meaning' as in Article 27(3). According to him, Article 22 'is intended rather to improve coordination of the judicial function within the Community and to avoid conflicting and contradictory decisions, even where the separate enforcement of each of them is not precluded'; that is to say, 'the rationale of the provision is therefore to encourage harmonious judicial decisions and thereby obviate the danger of judgments which conflict with each other, albeit only as regards their reasoning'. An unduly broad interpretation of the requirements of Article 21 would run the risk of confusing related actions with *lis alibi pendens*. No question has, however, been referred to the Court in this case with regard to the exercise of the discretionary power conferred by Article 22.

31. Moreover, I share the concerns expressed, particularly in the observations of France and the Commission, that a more flexible approach to the application of the condition that the parties must be the same in order for an obligation to decline jurisdiction to arise under Article 21 of the Convention could seriously imperil the right to a fair hearing and, in some cases, even the efficient administration of justice. In the instant case, it is apposite to recall that the principle of Netherlands procedural law which forms the basis for the supposed implicit presence of Drouot in the Netherlands action - at least if the

Court were to accept the uncontradicted description furnished by counsel for Drouot at the hearing - would appear to have 'slipped onto' the case-file before the Cour d'Appel. As Advocate General Tesauro pointed out in his Opinion in *The Tatry*, when 'reference to the domestic laws of Contracting States [is] rendered necessary by the incompleteness of the rules contained in the Brussels Convention, ... [it] must be conducive to the application of the provisions of the Convention and may not in any circumstances lead to results which conflict with its aims and rationale'. Accordingly, I do not think that the right of Drouot to a fair hearing would be served if Article 21 of the Convention were to be interpreted as imposing an obligation, in circumstances such as those of the present case, on the Cour d'Appel to decline jurisdiction in respect of its claim in the French action when its right to be heard in the Netherlands action would effectively depend on the attitude of Mr Velghe.

32. The conclusion which must, to my mind, be drawn in circumstances such as those of the present case is that no *lis alibi pendens* for the purposes of Article 21 of the Convention arises.

V - Conclusion

33. In the light of all the foregoing considerations, I recommend that the Court answer the question referred by the French Cour de Cassation as follows: No *lis alibi pendens* for the purposes of Article 21 of the Convention of 27 September 1968 on Jurisdiction and the Enforcement of Judgments in Civil and Commercial Matters, as amended by the Convention of 9 October 1978 on the Accession of the Kingdom of Denmark, Ireland and the United Kingdom of Great Britain and Northern Ireland, arises where a court of one Contracting State is seised by the insurer of a vessel that has been shipwrecked with an action seeking from the owner and the insurer of the cargo on board partial reimbursement, by way of contribution to the general average, of the refloating costs, when a court of another Contracting State was seised previously by that owner and insurer with an action against the owner of the vessel for a declaration that they were not obliged to contribute to the general average.

TITLE II *[Chapter II]*

JURISDICTION *[Jurisdiction]*

Provisional, including protective, measures – Article 24 *[Article 31]*

See also

Case C-391/95 - 17 November 1998

Van Uden Maritime BV
v
Kommanditgesellschaft

Arbitration clause - Interim payment - Meaning of 'provisional measures' - Jurisdiction in matters relating to a contract Scope - Jurisdiction to order provisional or protective measures - Included - Substance of the dispute subject to arbitration - Jurisdiction founded solely on Article 24 - Jurisdiction to order provisional or protective measures - Grant of measures - Conditions - Measure ordering an interim payment - 'Provisional measure' within the meaning of Article 24 - Conditions.

Summary

On a proper construction of Article 5, point 1, of the Convention of 27 September 1968 on Jurisdiction and the Enforcement of Judgements in Civil and Commercial Matters, as amended by the Convention of 9 October 1978 on the accession of the Kingdom of Denmark, Ireland and the United Kingdom of Great Britain and Northern Ireland, and by the Convention of 25 October 1982 on the accession of the Hellenic Republic, the court which has jurisdiction by virtue of that provision also has jurisdiction to order provisional or protective measures, without that jurisdiction being subject to any further conditions. However, whether the parties have validly excluded the jurisdiction of the courts in a dispute arising under a contract and have referred that dispute to arbitration, it is only under Article 24 of the Convention that a court may be empowered to order such measures, since it cannot do so as the court having jurisdiction on the substance of the dispute. In the connection, where the subject-matter of an application for provisional measures relates to a question falling within the scope *ratione materiae* of the Convention, that Convention is applicable and Article 24 thereof may confer jurisdiction on the court hearing that application even where proceedings have already been, or may be, commenced on the substance of the case and even where those proceedings are to be conducted before arbitrators.

The granting of provisional or protective measures on the basis of Article 24 of the Convention of 27 September 1968 is conditional on, *inter alia*, the existence of a real connecting link between the subject matter of the measures sought and the territorial jurisdiction of the Contracting State of the court before which those measures are sought. A measure ordering interim payment of a contractual consideration does not constitute a provisional measure within the meaning of that article unless, first, repayment to the defendant of the sum awarded is guaranteed if the plaintiff is unsuccessful as regards the substance of him claim and, second, the measure sought relates only to specific assets of the defendant located or to be located within the confines of the territorial jurisdiction of the court to which application is made.

JUDGMENT OF THE COURT

Presiding, Lecourt, President, Rodriguez Iglesias, Presidents of Chambers, Kapteyn, Puissochet, Hirsch and Jann, Rapporteur, Mancini, Moitinho de Almeida, Gulmann, Murray, Edward Ragnemalm, Judges, Sevon and Wathelet, Advocate General, Léger.

1. By judgment of 8 December 1995, received at the Court on 14 December 1995, the Hoge Raad der Nederlanden (Supreme Court of the Netherlands) referred to the Court for a preliminary ruling under the Protocol of 3 June 1971 on the interpretation by the Court of Justice of the Convention of 27 September 1968 on Jurisdiction and the Enforcement of Judgments in Civil and Commercial Matters eight questions on the interpretation of Article 1, second paragraph, point 4, Article 3, Article 5, point 1, and Article 24 of the Convention of 27 September 1968, cited above (OJ 1978 L 304, p. 36), as amended by the Convention of 9 October 1978 on the accession of the Kingdom of Denmark, Ireland and the United Kingdom of Great Britain and Northern Ireland (OJ 1978 L 304, p. 1, and - amended text - p. 77), and by the Convention of 25 October 1982 on the accession of the Hellenic Republic (OJ 1982 L 388, p. 1) (hereinafter 'the Convention').

2. Those questions were raised in the context of a dispute between Van Uden Maritime BV ('Van Uden'), established at Rotterdam, the Netherlands, and Kommanditgesellschaft in Firma Deco-Line and Another ('Deco-Line'), of Hamburg, Germany, concerning an application for interim relief (in kort geding proceedings) relating to the payment of debts arising under a contract containing an arbitration clause.

3. Under the first paragraph of Article 1, the Convention is to apply in civil and commercial matters. The second paragraph provides, however, under point 4, that it is not to apply to arbitration.

4. Under Article 2 of the Convention, the general rule of jurisdiction is that persons domiciled in a Contracting State are, whatever their nationality, to be sued in the courts of that State.

5. Persons domiciled in a Contracting State may be sued in the courts of another Contracting State only by virtue of the rules set out in the Convention. The second paragraph of Article 3 lists the rules of exorbitant jurisdiction which are not to be applicable against persons domiciled in another Contracting State, including Articles 126(3) and 127 of the Netherlands Code of Civil Procedure (Wetboek van Burgerlijke Rechtsvordering, hereinafter 'the Code of Civil Procedure').

6. Under Article 5, point 1, of the Convention, a person domiciled in a Contracting State may, in matters relating to a contract, be sued, in another Contracting State, in the courts for the place of performance of the obligation in question.

7. Article 24 of the Convention, which deals specifically with provisional and protective measures, provides: 'Application may be made to the courts of a Contracting State for such provisional, including protective, measures as may be available under the law of that State, even if, under this Convention, the courts of another Contracting State have jurisdiction as to the substance of the matter.'

8. In March 1993 Van Uden and Deco-Line concluded a 'slot/space charter agreement', under which Van Uden undertook to make available to Deco-Line cargo space on board vessels operated by Van Uden, either on its own account or in association with other shipping lines, on a liner service between northern or western parts of Europe and west Africa. In return, Deco-Line was to pay charter hire in accordance with the rates agreed between the parties.

9. Van Uden instituted arbitration proceedings in the Netherlands pursuant to the agreement, on the ground that Deco-Line had failed to pay certain invoices submitted to it by Van Uden.

10. Van Uden also applied to the President of the Rechtbank (District Court), Rotterdam, for interim relief on the grounds that Deco-Line was not displaying the necessary diligence in the appointment of arbitrators and that non-payment of its invoices was disturbing its cash flow. In its application, it sought an order against Deco-Line for payment of DM 837 919.13 to cover four debts due under the agreement.

11. In those proceedings, Deco-Line objected, first, that the Netherlands court had no jurisdiction to entertain the claims. Being established in Germany, it could be sued only before the German courts.

12. The President of the Rechtbank dismissed that objection on the ground that an order sought as interim relief must be regarded as a provisional measure within the meaning of Article 24 of the Convention.

13. Referring to Article 126(3) of the Code of Civil Procedure, he decided that, as court of the plaintiff's domicile, he had jurisdiction to entertain an application made by a plaintiff residing in the Netherlands against a defendant with no known domicile or recognised place of residence there. He further concluded that the case had the requisite minimum connection with Netherlands law, for two reasons: (i) Deco-Line was engaged in international trade and would thus become a creditor in the Netherlands, so that any judgment against it could be enforced there, and (ii) such a judgment could also be enforced in Germany.

14. Finally, the President of the Rechtbank took the view that his jurisdiction was in no way affected by the fact that the parties had agreed to have their dispute determined by arbitration in the Netherlands since, under Article 1022(2) of the Code of Civil Procedure, an arbitration clause cannot preclude a party's right to seek interim relief.

15. By provisionally enforceable judgment of 21 June 1994, the President of the Rechtbank, Rotterdam, therefore ordered Deco-Line to pay Van Uden the sum of DM 377 625.35, together with interest at the statutory rate.

16. On appeal by Deco-Line, the Gerechtshof te s'-Gravenhage (Regional Court of Appeal, The Hague) quashed that order. In its view,

the fact that the case had to have a sufficient connection with Netherlands law meant, in the context of the Convention, that it must be possible for the interim order applied for to be enforced in the Netherlands. The mere fact that Deco-Line could acquire assets there in the future was, it considered, insufficient for that purpose.

17. A further appeal against that decision was brought before the Hoge Raad der Nederlanden, which stayed proceedings and requested a preliminary ruling by the Court on the following questions:

(1) Where an obligation to pay a sum or sums due under a contract must be performed in a Contracting State - so that, under Article 5, point 1, of the Brussels Convention, the creditor is entitled to sue his defaulting debtor in the courts of that State with a view to obtaining performance, even though the debtor is domiciled in another Contracting State - do the courts of the first-mentioned State (for that same reason) have jurisdiction also to hear and determine a claim brought by the creditor against his debtor in interim [kort geding] proceedings for an order requiring the debtor, by provisionally enforceable judgment, to pay a sum which, in the view of the court hearing the interim application, is very probably due to the creditor, or do additional conditions apply in relation to the jurisdiction of the court hearing the interim application, for example the condition that the relief sought from that court must take effect (or be capable of taking effect) in the Contracting State concerned?

(2) Does it make any difference to the answer to Question 1 whether the contract between the parties contains an arbitration clause and, if so, what the place of arbitration is according to that clause?

(3) If the answer to Question 1 is that, in order for the court hearing the interim application to have jurisdiction, the relief sought from it must also take effect (or be capable of taking effect) in the Contracting State concerned, does that mean that the order applied for must be capable of enforcement in that State, and is it then necessary for this condition to be fulfilled when the interim application is made, or is it sufficient that it can be reasonably expected to be fulfilled in the future?

(4) Does the possibility, provided for in Article 289 *et seq.* of the Netherlands Code of Civil Procedure, of applying on grounds of pressing urgency to the President of the Arrondissementsrechtbank for a provisionally enforceable judgment constitute a 'provisional' or 'protective' measure within the meaning of Article 24 of the Brussels Convention?

(5) Does it make any difference to the answer to Question 4 whether substantive proceedings on the main issue are, or may become, pending and, if so, is it material that arbitration proceedings had started in the same case?

(6) Does it make any difference to the answer to Question 4 that the interim relief sought is an order requiring performance of an obligation of payment, as referred to in Question 1?

(7) If Question 4 must be answered in the affirmative, and 'the courts of another Contracting State have jurisdiction as to the substance of the matter', must Article 24, and in particular the reference therein to 'such provisional ... measures as may be available under the law of [a Contracting] State', be interpreted as meaning that the court hearing the application for interim measures has (for that same reason) jurisdiction if it has jurisdiction under provisions of its national law, even where those provisions are referred to in the second paragraph of Article 3 of the Brussels Convention, or is its jurisdiction in the latter case conditional on the fulfilment of additional conditions, for example that the interim relief sought from that court must take effect, or be capable of taking effect, in the Contracting State concerned?

(8) If the answer to Question 7 must be that, in order for the court hearing the application for interim relief to have jurisdiction, it is also required that the relief sought from it must take effect (or be capable of taking effect) in the Contracting State concerned, does that mean that the order applied for must be capable of enforcement in that State, and is it then necessary for this condition to be fulfilled when the application for interim relief is made, or is it sufficient that it can reasonably be expected to be fulfilled in the future?'

18. The questions raised relate to the jurisdiction, under the Convention, of a court hearing applications for interim relief. The national court wishes to know both whether such jurisdiction could be established on the basis of Article 5, point 1, of the Convention (Questions 1 to 3) and whether it could be established on the basis of Article 24 (Questions 4 to 8). In both cases, the national court's questions relate to:

- first, the relevance of the fact that the dispute in question is subject, under the terms of the contract, to arbitration,
- next, whether the jurisdiction of the court hearing the application for interim relief is subject to the condition that the measure sought must take effect or be capable of taking effect in the State of that court, in particular that it must be enforceable there, and whether it is necessary that such a condition should be met at the time when the application is made, and
- finally, the relevance of the fact that the case relates to a claim for interim payment of a contractual consideration.

19. The first point to be made, as regards the jurisdiction of a court

hearing an application for interim relief, is that it is accepted that a court having jurisdiction as to the substance of a case in accordance with Articles 2 and 5 to 18 of the Convention also has jurisdiction to order any provisional or protective measures which may prove necessary.

20. In addition, Article 24, in Section 9 of the Convention, adds a rule of jurisdiction falling outside the system set out in Articles 2 and 5 to 18, whereby a court may order provisional or protective measures even if it does not have jurisdiction as to the substance of the case. Under that provision, the measures available are those provided for by the law of the State of the court to which application is made.

21. Article 5, point 1, of the Convention provides that in matters relating to a contract a defendant may be sued, in a Contracting State other than that in which he is domiciled, in the courts for the place of performance of the obligation in question.

22. Thus, the court having jurisdiction as to the substance of a case under one of the heads of jurisdiction laid down in the Convention also has jurisdiction to order provisional or protective measures, without that jurisdiction being subject to any further conditions, such as that mentioned in the national court's third question.

23. However, in the present case, the contract signed between Van Uden and Deco-Line contains an arbitration clause.

24. Where the parties have validly excluded the jurisdiction of the courts in a dispute arising under a contract and have referred that dispute to arbitration, there are no courts of any State that have jurisdiction as to the substance of the case for the purposes of the Convention. Consequently, a party to such a contract is not in a position to make an application for provisional or protective measures to a court that would have jurisdiction under the Convention as to the substance of the case.

25. In such a case, it is only under Article 24 that a court may be empowered under the Convention to order provisional or protective measures.

26. In that connection, Deco-Line and the German and United Kingdom Governments agreed that, since the parties have agreed to submit their dispute to arbitration, interim proceedings also fall outside the scope of the Convention. The German Government argues in particular that

measures sought in interim proceedings, when they are intrinsically bound up with the subject-matter of an arbitration procedure, fall outside the scope of the Convention. In the United Kingdom Government's view, the measures sought in the present case may be regarded as ancillary to the arbitration procedure and are thus excluded from the scope of the Convention.

27. Van Uden and the Commission, however, contend that the existence of an arbitration clause does not have the effect of excluding an application for interim measures from the scope of the Convention. The Commission points out that the subject-matter of the dispute is decisive and that the issue underlying the interim proceedings concerns the performance of a contractual obligation - a matter which falls within the scope of the Convention.

28. It must first be borne in mind here that Article 24 of the Convention applies even if a court of another Contracting State has jurisdiction as to the substance of the case, provided that the subject-matter of the dispute falls within the scope ratione materiae of the Convention, which covers civil and commercial matters.

29. Thus the mere fact that proceedings have been, or may be, commenced on the substance of the case before a court of a Contracting State does not deprive a court of another Contracting State of its jurisdiction under Article 24 of the Convention.

30. However, Article 24 cannot be relied on to bring within the scope of the Convention provisional or protective measures relating to matters which are excluded from it (Case 143/78 *De Cavel* v *De Cavel* [1979] ECR 1055, paragraph 9).

31. Under Article 1, second paragraph, point 4, of the Convention, arbitration is excluded from its scope. By that provision, the Contracting Parties intended to exclude arbitration in its entirety, including proceedings brought before national courts (Case C-190/89 *Rich* v *Società Italiana Impianti* [1991] ECR I-3855, paragraph 18).

32. The experts' report drawn up on the accession of the Kingdom of Denmark, Ireland and the United Kingdom of Great Britain and Northern Ireland to the Convention (OJ 1979 C 59, p. 71, at pp. 92-93) specifies that the Convention does not apply to judgments determining whether an arbitration agreement is valid or not or, because it is invalid, ordering the

parties not to continue the arbitration proceedings, or to proceedings and decisions concerning applications for the revocation, amendment, recognition and enforcement of arbitration awards. Also excluded from the scope of the Convention are proceedings ancillary to arbitration proceedings, such as the appointment or dismissal of arbitrators, the fixing of the place of arbitration or the extension of the time-limit for making awards.

33. However, it must be noted in that regard that provisional measures are not in principle ancillary to arbitration proceedings but are ordered in parallel to such proceedings and are intended as measures of support. They concern not arbitration as such but the protection of a wide variety of rights. Their place in the scope of the Convention is thus determined not by their own nature but by the nature of the rights which they serve to protect (see Case C-261/90 *Reichert and Kockler* v *Dresdner Bank* [1992] ECR I-2149, paragraph 32).

34. It must therefore be concluded that where, as in the case in the main proceedings, the subject-matter of an application for provisional measures relates to a question falling within the scope ratione materiae of the Convention, the Convention is applicable and Article 24 thereof may confer jurisdiction on the court hearing that application even where proceedings have already been, or may be, commenced on the substance of the case and even where those proceedings are to be conducted before arbitrators.

35. Next, as regards the conditions set out in the Convention for the grant of an application under Article 24, Van Uden submits that no further condition need be fulfilled for the court hearing such an application to have jurisdiction provided that it has jurisdiction under provisions of its national law even where those provisions are among those listed in the second paragraph of Article 3 of the Convention. Deco-Line, however, maintains that the imposition of stricter conditions is clearly justified and that, in any event, the fact that Article 24 refers to national rules on jurisdiction implies that the court in question is free to hold that its jurisdiction is subject to such conditions.

36. In the German Government's view, Article 24 does not authorise a court acting on the basis of one of the rules of jurisdiction listed in the second paragraph of Article 3 of the Convention to order provisional measures unless the rule of jurisdiction in question is subject to the urgency of the decision or based upon that reasoning and unless the

provisional measure, at the time when it is ordered, has a sufficient connecting link with the State of that court. The latter condition is satisfied when the provisional measure can be enforced in that State.

37. In that regard, it must be remembered that the expression 'provisional, including protective, measures' within the meaning of Article 24 of the Convention is to be understood as referring to measures which, in matters within the scope of the Convention, are intended to preserve a factual or legal situation so as to safeguard rights the recognition of which is otherwise sought from the court having jurisdiction as to the substance of the case (*Reichert and Kockler*, cited above, paragraph 34).

38. The granting of this type of measure requires particular care on the part of the court in question and detailed knowledge of the actual circumstances in which the measures sought are to take effect. Depending on each case and commercial practices in particular, the court must be able to place a time-limit on its order or, as regards the nature of the assets or goods subject to the measures contemplated, require bank guarantees or nominate a sequestrator and generally make its authorisation subject to all conditions guaranteeing the provisional or protective character of the measure ordered (Case 125/79 *Denilauler* v *Couchet Frères* [1980] ECR 1553, paragraph 15).

39. In that regard, the Court held at paragraph 16 of Denilauler that the courts of the place - or, in any event, of the Contracting State - where the assets subject to the measures sought are located are those best able to assess the circumstances which may lead to the grant or refusal of the measures sought or to the laying down of procedures and conditions which the plaintiff must observe in order to guarantee the provisional and protective character of the measures authorised.

40. It follows that the granting of provisional or protective measures on the basis of Article 24 is conditional on, inter alia, the existence of a real connecting link between the subject-matter of the measures sought and the territorial jurisdiction of the Contracting State of the court before which those measures are sought.

41. It further follows that a court ordering measures on the basis of Article 24 must take into consideration the need to impose conditions or stipulations such as to guarantee their provisional or protective character.

42. With regard more particularly to the fact that the national court has in this instance based its jurisdiction on one of the national provisions listed in the second paragraph of Article 3 of the Convention, it must be borne in mind that, in accordance with the first paragraph of that article, persons domiciled in a Contracting State may be sued in the courts of another Contracting State only by virtue of the rules set out in Sections 2 to 6 of Title II, that is to say Articles 5 to 18, of the Convention. Consequently, the prohibition in Article 3 of reliance on rules of exorbitant jurisdiction does not apply to the special regime provided for by Article 24.

43. Finally, with regard to the question whether an interim order requiring payment of a contractual consideration may be classified as a provisional measure within the meaning of Article 24 of the Convention, Deco-Line and the Government of the United Kingdom argue that it cannot. The German Government considers that the main proceedings appear to fall outside the definition of provisional or protective measures.

44. Van Uden and the Commission do not share that view. In the Commission's view, provisional measures must be taken to mean those whose validity lapses when the main issue is determined or on the expiry of a specified period. They may comprise positive measures, that is to say an order to perform some act such as the handing-over of property or the payment of a sum of money.

45. Here, it must be noted that it is not possible to rule out in advance, in a general and abstract manner, that interim payment of a contractual consideration, even in an amount corresponding to that sought as principal relief, may be necessary in order to ensure the practical effect of the decision on the substance of the case and may, in certain cases, appear justified with regard to the interests involved (see, in the context of Community law, Case C-393/96 P(R) *Antonissen v Council and Commission* [1997] ECR I-441, paragraph 37).

46. However, an order for interim payment of a sum of money is, by its very nature, such that it may preempt the decision on the substance of the case. If, moreover, the plaintiff were entitled to secure interim payment of a contractual consideration before the courts of the place where he is himself domiciled, where those courts have no jurisdiction over the substance of the case under Articles 2 to 18 of the Convention, and thereafter to have the order in question recognised and enforced in the defendant's State, the rules of jurisdiction laid down by the Convention could be circumvented.

47. Consequently, interim payment of a contractual consideration does not constitute a provisional measure within the meaning of Article 24 unless, first, repayment to the defendant of the sum awarded is guaranteed if the plaintiff is unsuccessful as regards the substance of his claim and, second, the measure sought relates only to specific assets of the defendant located or to be located within the confines of the territorial jurisdiction of the court to which application is made.

48. In the light of the foregoing considerations, the answer to the first and second questions must be that:

- on a proper construction of Article 5, point 1, of the Convention, the court which has jurisdiction by virtue of that provision also has jurisdiction to order provisional or protective measures, without that jurisdiction being subject to any further conditions, and
- where the parties have validly excluded the jurisdiction of the courts in a dispute arising under a contract and have referred that dispute to arbitration, no provisional or protective measures may be ordered on the basis of Article 5, point 1, of the Convention.

The answer to the fifth question must be that

- where the subject-matter of an application for provisional measures relates to a question falling within the scope ratione materiae of the Convention, the Convention is applicable and Article 24 thereof may confer jurisdiction on the court hearing that application even where proceedings have already been, or may be, commenced on the substance of the case and even where those proceedings are to be conducted before arbitrators.

Finally, the answer to the fourth, sixth, seventh and eighth questions must be that

- on a proper construction, the granting of provisional or protective measures on the basis of Article 24 of the Convention is conditional on, inter alia, the existence of a real connecting link between the subject-matter of the measures sought and the territorial jurisdiction of the Contracting State of the court before which those measures are sought, and
- interim payment of a contractual consideration does not constitute a provisional measure within the meaning of Article 24 of the Convention unless, first, repayment to the defendant of the sum awarded is guaranteed if the plaintiff is unsuccessful as regards the substance of

his claim and, second, the measure sought relates only to specific assets of the defendant located or to be located within the confines of the territorial jurisdiction of the court to which application is made.

On those grounds, the Court, in answer to the questions referred to it by the Hoge Raad der Nederlanden by judgment of 8 December 1995, hereby rules:

1. On a proper construction of Article 5, point 1, of the Convention of 27 September 1968 on Jurisdiction and the Enforcement of Judgments in Civil and Commercial Matters, as amended by the Convention of 9 October 1978 on the accession of the Kingdom of Denmark, Ireland and the United Kingdom of Great Britain and Northern Ireland, and by the Convention of 25 October 1982 on the accession of the Hellenic Republic, the court which has jurisdiction by virtue of that provision also has jurisdiction to order provisional or protective measures, without that jurisdiction being subject to any further conditions.

2. Where the parties have validly excluded the jurisdiction of the courts in a dispute arising under a contract and have referred that dispute to arbitration, no provisional or protective measures may be ordered on the basis of Article 5, point 1, of the Convention of 27 September 1968.

3. Where the subject-matter of an application for provisional measures relates to a question falling within the scope ratione materiae of the Convention of 27 September 1968, that Convention is applicable and Article 24 thereof may confer jurisdiction on the court hearing that application even where proceedings have already been, or may be, commenced on the substance of the case and even where those proceedings are to be conducted before arbitrators.

4. On a proper construction, the granting of provisional or protective measures on the basis of Article 24 of the Convention of 27 September 1968 is conditional on, inter alia, the existence of a real connecting link between the subject-matter of the measures sought and the territorial jurisdiction of the Contracting State of the court before which those measures are sought.

5. Interim payment of a contractual consideration does not constitute a provisional measure within the meaning of Article 24 of the Convention of 27 September 1968 unless, first, repayment to the defendant of the sum awarded is guaranteed if the plaintiff is unsuccessful as regards the substance of his claim and, second, the measure sought relates only to specific assets of the defendant located or to be located within the confines of the territorial jurisdiction of the court to which application is made.

OPINION OF MR ADVOCATE GENERAL LÉGER

1. The reference for a preliminary ruling, made pursuant to Article 3 of the Protocol of 3 June 1971 by the Hoge Raad der Nederlanden (Supreme Court of the Netherlands), will undoubtedly give the Court occasion to consider a number of questions of principle concerning the Brussels Convention of 27 September 1968 on Jurisdiction and the Enforcement of Judgments in Civil and Commercial matters, as amended by the Convention of Accession of 1978 (hereinafter 'the Convention' or 'the Brussels Convention'). In particular, the Court is asked for a ruling on the interpretation of Articles 1, point 4, 5, point 1, and 24 of the Convention, the repercussions of which are likely to extend well beyond the context of this case.

2. The circumstances of this case are as follows.

I - Facts and procedure

3. In March 1993, the companies Van Uden Maritime (hereinafter 'Van Uden' or 'the applicant in the main proceedings'), established in Rotterdam, the Netherlands, and Kommanditgesellschaft in Firma Deco-Line, Peter Determann (hereinafter 'Deco-Line' or 'the defendant in the main proceedings'), established in Hamburg, Germany, concluded a 'slot/space charter agreement'. Under the agreement, Van Uden made available to Deco-Line cargo space on board vessels operated within the framework of a liner service, in return for payment of a charter hire (calculated according to rates agreed between the parties).

4. Deco-Line having failed to pay certain invoices, its contracting partner instituted arbitration proceedings against it in the Netherlands pursuance to the agreement.

5. It is pointed out by the court making the reference that Deco-Line does not possess any seizable assets in that country.

6. Taking the view that Deco-Line was procrastinating over the appointment of arbitrators and that the continuing non-payment of its outstanding invoices was seriously disturbing its cash flow, Van Uden made an interim application to the President of the Rechtbank (District Court), Rotterdam, seeking collection of four of the debts payable under the agreement. Its principal claim was for a sum of DM 830 919.13, together with interest

thereon at the statutory rate, and, in the alternative, an advance of DM 404 923.29 on the sum sought in the principal claim.

7. Deco-Line disputed the jurisdiction of the Netherlands court, claiming that the German courts, claiming that the German courts should hear the case under the general jurisdiction conferred, in principle, under the first paragraph of Article 2 of the Brussels Convention, on the courts of the State in which the defendant is domiciled. In the alternative, it disputed the urgency of the matter.

8. The President first of all rejected the objection that he did not have jurisdiction. He held that an application for interim relief, such as that made to him, must be regarded as seeking an order granting a 'provisional' measure within the meaning of Article 24 of the Convention, infering from that that his jurisdiction did not have to be based on the rules of principle contained in Articles 2 to 18 of the Convention, and that he fulfilled the criterion for the exercise of jurisdiction under his national law.

9. Article 126(3) of the Netherlands Code of Civil Procedure confers on the courts of the place where the plaintiff is domiciled jurisdiction to hear and determine proceedings brought against a defendant who has neither a fixed place of residence nor a recognised domicile in the Netherlands, provided that there are certain minimum connections with Netherlands law. The Netherlands court held that that criterion was fulfilled in this case for two reasons. Firstly, Deco-Line is engaged in international trade and thus acquires claims in the Netherlands, so that any judgment against it could be enforced in the Netherlands. Secondly, such a judgment could also be enforced in Germany.

10. The President further considered that the jurisdiction conferred on him under Netherlands law by Article 1022(2) of the Code of Civil Procedure was not affected by the fact that the parties had agreed to have recourse to arbitration in the Netherlands. Article 1022(2) of the Code of Civil Procedure is worded as follows: 'An arbitration agreement shall not preclude a party from applying to the ordinary courts for a protective measure or from making an application to the President of the court for interim relief pursuant to Article 289…'.

11. By a provisionally enforceable judgment of 21 June 1994, he therefore granted Van Uden's application to an amount of DM 377625,35m together with interest thereon at the statutory rate.

12. Hearing the case on appeal, the Gerechtshof (Regional Court of Appeal), The Hague, denied the Netherlands courts jurisdiction and set aside the contested judgment by judgment of 11 October 1994.

13. In that court's view, although Article 24 of the Convention allows the President to base his jurisdiction on Article 126(3) of the Code of Civil Procedure, the criteria for the application of which are, in principle, fulfilled in this case, that jurisdiction is nevertheless subject to the additional criterion that the matter must have sufficient connection with Netherlands law. However, in the context of the Brussels Convention, the Gerechtsof considered that this latter criterion is fulfilled only if the relief granted by the court hearing interlocutory applications is capable of taking effect within the territorial jurisdiction of that court, and if it is enforceable there. Under the scheme of the Brussels Convention, the latter condition must likewise be fulfilled in order for the

jurisdiction of the President also to be based, as in this case, on Article 5, point 1, of the Convention (in so far as Van Uden's claim is for the payment of a sum of money and the place where that contractual obligation is to be performed is in the Netherlands). However, in the Gerechtshof's view, the mere possibility that Deco-Line will acquire assets in Netherlands territory in the future is insufficient for that purpose.

14. Van Uden appealed in cassation. The Hoge Raad, considering it necessary to seek clarification concerning the interpretation of the Convention provisions relied on, stayed the proceedings and submitted the following questions to the Court for a preliminary ruling:

'(1) Where an obligation to pay a sum or sums due under a contract must be performed in a Contracting State–so that, under Article 5, point 1, of the Brussels Convention, the creditor is entitled to sue his defaulting debtor before the courts of that State with a view to obtaining performance, even though the debtor is domiciled in the territory of another Contracting State–do the courts of the first-mentioned State (for that same reason) have jurisdiction also to hear and determine a claim brought by a creditor against his debtor in interim (kort geding) proceedings for an order requiring the debtor, by provisionally enforceable judgment, to pay a sum which, in the view of the court hearing the interlocutory application, is very probably due to the creditor, or do additional conditions apply in relation to the jurisdiction of the court hearing the interim application, for example the condition that the relief sought from that court must take effect (or be capable of taking effect) in the Contracting State concerned?

(2) Does it make any difference to the answer to Question 1 whether the contract between the parties contains an arbitration clause and, if so, what the place of arbitration is according to that clause?

(3) If the answer to Question 1 is that, in order for the court hearing the interim application to have jurisdiction, the relief sought from it must also take effect (or be capable of taking effect) in the Contracting State concerned, does that mean that the order applied for must be capable of enforcement in that State, and is it then necessary for this condition to be fulfilled when the interim application is made, or is it sufficient that it can be reasonably expected to be fulfilled in the future?

(4) Does the possibility, provided for in Article 289 *et seq*. of the Netherlands Code of Civil Procedure, of applying on grounds of pressing urgency to the President of the Arrondissementsrechtbank for a provisionally enforceable judgment constitute a 'provisional' or 'protective' measure within the meaning of Article 24 of the Brussels Convention?

(5) Does it make any difference to the answer to Question 4 whether substantive proceedings on the main issue are, or may become, pending and, if so, is it material that arbitration proceedings had started in the same case?

(6) Does it make any difference to the answer to Question 4 that the interim relief sought is an order requiring performance of an obligation of payment, as referred to in Question 1?

(7) If Question 4 must be answered in the affirmative, and 'the courts of another Contracting State have jurisdiction as to the substance of the matter',

must Article 24, and in particular the reference therein to 'such provisional ... measures as may be available under the law of [a Contracting] State', be interpreted as meaning that the court hearing the application for interim measures has (for that same reason) jurisdiction if it has jurisdiction under the provisions of its national law, even where those provisions are referred to in the second paragraph of Article 3 of the Brussels Convention, or is its jurisdiction in the latter case conditional on the fulfilment of additional conditions, for example that the interim relief sought from that court must take effect, or be capable of taking effect, in the Contracting State concerned?

(8) If the answer to Question 7 must be that, in order for the court hearing the application for interim relief to have jurisdiction, it is also required that the relief sought from it must take effect (or be capable of taking effect) in the Contracting State concerned, does that mean that the order applied for must be capable of enforcement in that State, and is it then necessary for this condition to be fulfilled when the application for interim relief is made, or is it sufficient that it can reasonably be expected to be fulfilled in the future?'

II - Legal Framework

A - The relevant provisions of the Brussels Convention

15. The scope *ratione materiae* of the Convention (Title I), as defined in Article 1 thereof, includes civil and commercial matters. Under the second paragraph of that article, it does not apply to:

'1. the status or legal capacity of natural persons, rights in property arising out of a matrimonial relationship, wills and succession;

2. bankruptcy, proceedings relating to the winding-up of insolvent companies or other legal persons, judicial arrangements, compositions and analogous proceedings;

3. social security;

4. arbitration'.

16. Various grounds of jurisdiction (Title II) serve to determine the courts in which a person can validly be sued; the principle is that general jurisdiction lies with the forum of the place where the defendant is domiciled (Article 2). Under the second paragraph of Article 3, exorbitant jurisdiction and, in particular, 'in the Netherlands: Articles 126(3) and 127 of the code of civil procedure (Wetboek van Burgerlijke Rechtsvordering)', may not be invoked against him.

17. Under 'special jurisdiction' (Section 2 of Title II), other rules are laid down which the plaintiff may prefer to that in Article 2, on account of the close connecting link between particular court and a dispute. Thus, under Article 5, point 1: 'A person domiciled in a Contracting State may, in another Contracting State, be sued:

1. in matters relating to a contract, in the courts for the place of performance of the obligation in question ...'.

18. Finally, 'provisional, including protective, measures' are the subject of

Article 24 of the Convention, which is the sole provision of Section 9 of Title II. That article allows a court which does not have jurisdiction as to the substance of the matter to order such measures, within the scope *ratione materiae* of the Convention, if the plaintiff chooses to apply to that court rather than to the court of another Contracting State having jurisdiction as to the substance. The measures which may be ordered will be those available under the law of the State of the court to which the application is made.

B - National law

19. Interim civil proceedings, termed as *'kort geding'*, are dealt with by Article 289 *et seq*. of the Code of Civil Procedure.

20. The Commission gives the following details concerning them:'They consist of an application for interim relief made to the President of the Arrondissementsrechtbank. Such interim applications are in very widespread use in the Netherlands. The condition of urgency which governs them is applied flexibly. Although interim proceedings lead to the granting or refusal of the interim relief sought, a decision given in such proceedings is often regarding as final by the parties in that no substantive proceedings are initiated on the main issue. Although originally the interim relief sought could relate only to orders to act or refrain from acting, for some time now the Hoge Raad has also, within the certain limits, accepted pecuniary claims. It is thus possible to obtain, by interim proceedings, an advance on the payment of a debt, provided that the validity of that debt is indisputable or virtually indisputable.'

21. Although the Netherlands Government has not lodged any observations during these proceedings, reference may usually be made to the information which it supplied in the context of Case 25/81. *W.* v *H.* [1982] ECR 1189: '... the Netherlands Government states that interlocutory proceedings for interim relief are special arrangements for urgent cases which, if not protective in nature, are at all events provisional. The provisional nature of decisions on interlocutory applications referred to in Article 289 of the Netherlands Code of Civil Procedure finds expression in Article 292 of that Code which provides that: 'interlocutory judgments shall not affect the outcome of the main action'.'

III - The answers to the question

22. It is clear from reading the order for reference that the Netherlands court essentially envisages two possible ways in which the jurisdiction of the President hearing an application for interim relief could be established on the basis of the Convention: on the one hand (Questions 1 to 3), Article 5, point 1 (which provides for the possibility of a *forum speciale* for disputes in matters relating to a contract); on the other (Questions 4 to 8), Article 24 (which introduces a special jurisdictional rule for provisional or protective measures).

23. In both cases, the court raises the more specific question of whether the jurisdiction of a court to hear interim applications is subject to the condition that its decision will take effect within its territorial jurisdiction and, from that point

of view, whether that condition must be fulfilled when the application is made, or whether it is sufficient that it is merely likely to be fulfilled in the future.

24. With regard to both those possibilities, the court also asks, in particular, whether it is material that the case brought before it has been referred to arbitration (Questions 2 and 5).

25. I propose to deal with the questions referred from three angles in turn, corresponding to the three provisions of the Brussels Convention to which the national court relates its questions:

Article 1, point 4, 5, point 1, and 24.

A - Preliminary remarks on the applicability of the Brussels Convention despite the existence of an arbitration clause.

26. It should first be determined whether the existence of an arbitration clause has the effect of excluding proceedings such as those in this case from the scope of the Convention on the basis of Article 1, point 4, thereof.

27. The written observations submitted to the Court by the parties to the main proceedings, the German and United Kingdom Governments and the Commission consider this issue in their examination of Questions 2 and 5, even though those two questions do not relate directly to it. The arbitration clause and arbitration proceedings are mentioned by the national court more, it seems, in the context of determining any effect they may have on whether the decision given by the court hearing the application can take effect in the territory of its own State than in order to establish whether their existence is such as to preclude the application of the Convention.

28. It is, moreover, symptomatic that at no time during the national proceedings was it objected that the Netherlands courts hearing the case did not have jurisdiction on grounds of the existence of the arbitration clause. The objection of lack of jurisdiction raised by the dependant in the main proceedings before the court hearing the interim application was intended to secure recognition, *pursuant to the rules of the Convention*, of the principle that the German courts, within whose territorial jurisdiction the defendant is established, had general jurisdiction. The arbitration clause was not relied on, and it was merely as an incidental matter, it would appear, that the court hearing the appeal examined this question of its own motion in the light of the relevant provisions of its national law.

1. Article 17 of the Convention

29. That observation gives rise to a preliminary remark. The observations submitted with regard to the effect of the arbitration clause in this case have all hinged on an interpretation of Article 1, point 4, of the Convention. However, I think it best to reject immediately an argument which, although it has not been taken up during the proceedings, could nevertheless appear attractive.

30. It is tempting to regard the arbitration cause agreed upon between the parties as a voluntary prorogation of jurisdiction as referred to in Article 17 of the Convention, which provides as follows: 'If the parties, one or more of whom is

domiciled in a Contracting State, have agreed that a court or the courts of a Contracting State are to have jurisdiction to settle any disputes which have arisen or which may arise in connection with a particular legal relationship, that court or those courts shall have exclusive jurisdiction …'.

31. Without commenting on the issue of whether a clause conferring jurisdiction on an arbitration tribunal must be regarded as a clause conferring jurisdiction on 'a court or the courts of a Contracting State' within the meaning of that provision, and therefore whether Article 17 should apply in this case, it is sufficient to point out that, if that were the case, it would still not deprive the provisions of the Convention of their effect.

32. We would actually be faced with a choice between two possibilities.

33. On the one hand, the situation could be treated as that, envisaged by the academic writings, of a clause conferring jurisdiction on a court of a State not party to the Convention or a clause not fulfilling the conditions laid down in Article 17. It would then no longer be the Brussels Convention, but the law of each State, which would determine the scope of that clause, and it would be for the *lex fori* to state whether, if necessary, the clause is not to take effect. However, it was pursuant to the provisions of its national law (Article 1022(2) of the Code of Civil Procedure) that the court hearing the application rules out the operation of the clause at issue in the present case.

34. On the other hand, the designated arbitration tribunal could be simply treated in the same way as 'a court or the courts of a Contracting State' within the meaning of Article 17. However, the defendant's entry of a voluntary appearance in this case and the fact that no objection was raised in favour of the jurisdiction of the arbitration tribunal would then imply tacit prorogation of jurisdiction as provided for in Article 18 of the Convention, under which:'Apart from jurisdiction derived from other provisions of this Convention, a court of a Contracting State before whom a defendant enters an appearance shall have jurisdiction. This rule shall not apply where appearance was entered solely to contest the jurisdiction, or where another court has exclusive jurisdiction by virtue of Article 16.'

35. It is clear, in all events, that, even if Article 17 of the Convention had been relied on, the Convention would nevertheless have been applicable. It would, of course, still be necessary for the dispute to come substantively within the scope of the Convention. I therefore come back the problem raised by the arbitration clause in the light of Article 1, point 4, of the Convention.

2. Article 1, point 4, of the Convention

36. Although, as we have seen, this aspect of the proceedings has not been expressly considered by the court making the reference, it cannot be disregarded since, if it were to be held that the existence of the arbitration clause precluded the application of the Convention, there would be no point in answering the other questions.

37. Two arguments have been put forward in this regard, predicted on opposite interpretations of Article 1, point 4, of the Convention.

38. The first, put forward by Deco-Line, the United Kingdom Government and, less categorically, the German Government, leads to the conclusion that these proceedings cannot be governed by the provisions of the Convention since the parties have agreed, under the terms of the agreement, to submit their disputes to arbitration.

39. The second, put forward by Van Uden and the Commission, suggests that the scope of that exclusion should not be stretched too far.

40. Although this may be the first time that the Court has had occasion to rule on the effect of existence of an arbitration clause on the application of the provisions of the Brussels Convention to proceedings pending before a national court, the framers of the Convention were aware of these issues. The report by Professor P. Schlosser already identified the two ways in which the exclusion referred to in Article 1, point 4, could be understood: 'Two divergent basic positions which it was not possible to reconcile emerged from the discussion on the interpretation of the relevant provisions of Article 1, second paragraph, point (4). The point of view expressed principally on behalf of the United Kingdom was that this provision covers all disputes which the parties had effectively agreed should be settled by arbitration, including any secondary disputes connected with the agreed arbitration. The other point of view, defended by the original Member States of the EEC, only regards proceedings before national courts as part of 'arbitration' if they refer to arbitration proceedings, whether concluded, in progress or to be started.'

41. It is thus quite natural that those two 'divergent basic positions which it was not possible to reconcile' should have been stated and argued in detail before the Court.

42. The following considerations have been put forward in favour of the argument that the rules set out in the Convention are not applicable.

43. Deco-Line and the German Government, in particular, have highlighted the risk of a conflict of decisions which would be introduced if parallel jurisdiction of national courts hearing interim applications and arbitration tribunals adjudicating on the substance were allowed for the purpose of dealing with aspects of the same dispute. They have cited the danger that an arbitration clause could be easily circumvented by a party in favour of the ordinary courts.

44. Moreover, the German Government asserts that the interim relief sought is inseparably linked to the subject-matter of the arbitration proceedings in the sense that both concern the payment of a debt; since the arbitration proceedings are excluded from the scope of the Convention, the application for interim relief, which is ancillary to those proceedings, must be treated in the same way.

45. Finally, the United Kingdom Government has maintained that the application in this case to a court for provisional measures is part of court proceedings 'which are ancillary to arbitration proceedings' according to the definition given in the Schlosser report of proceedings excluded under Article 1, point 4, of the Convention.

46. Far from being convinced by that line of argument, I am of the opinion,

together with the Commission and the plaintiff in the main proceedings, that the exclusion of 'arbitration' from the scope of the Convention does not cover the circumstances of this case.

47. The first argument put forward by the German Government and Deco-Line, it should be noted, has already been set out in the *Rich* case cited above. I shall not re-examine it since the Court agreed with the view taken by Advocate General Darmon who proposed, in his Opinion in that case, that it should be rejected in these terms: '...irreconcilability between an arbitral award and a national judgment, although obviously not desirable, is susceptible of remedy. The ways of remedying the problem have been set out in a paper dealing with conflicts between judgments and arbitral awards [Schlosser, P. 'Conflicts entre judgment judiciaire et arbitrage', *Revue de l'arbitrage,* 1991, No 3, p. 371]. And its author considered in particular the situation where a judgment protected by the Brussels Convention and an arbitral award conflict and the solutions which would be applicable in such circumstances. In any event, it is clear from that paper that the applicable principles make it possible to say, according to the conflicting situations, whether the judgment or the award should prevail.'

48. I would add that, in the circumstances of this case, I see an advantage in allowing the application of the rules of the Convention, even though the risk of two courts both claiming jurisdiction cannot be discounted. If the Convention is not applied, it is difficult to see how a situation such as that which arose initially in this case, where arbitration could not be implemented due to the inertia of one of the parties, could be resolved. In line with the Court's judgment in *Rich*, cited above, any proceedings for the appointment of arbitrators would, in that case, certainly fall outside the scope of the Convention. The risk of both courts refusing jurisdiction could then not be discounted.

49. If we set out next to define the purpose of the exclusion referred to in Article 1, point 4, as it may be inferred from its logical basis in the mind of the drafters, that provision cannot be attributed the wide scope suggested by the German and United Kingdom Governments.

50. The reasons for the exclusion are very clear from the report by Mr P. Jenard: 'There are already many international agreements on arbitration. Arbitration is, of course, referred to in Article 220 of the Treaty of Rome. Moreover, the Council of Europe has prepared a European Convention providing a uniform law on arbitration, and this will probably be accompanied by a Protocol which will facilitate the recognition and enforcement of arbitral awards to an even greater extent than the New York Convention. This is why it seemed preferable to exclude arbitration.'

51. The objective was thus to prevent the Brussels Convention from duplicating pre-existing or future international provisions.

52. The purpose of the exclusion can therefore only be to ensure that the matter of arbitration, as regulated elsewhere, remains outside the scope of the Convention.

53. however, the abovementioned international agreements relate to very limited aspects of international disputes: those concerning arbitration as such. It is thus apparent from the study made of them by Advocate general Darmon in

his Opinion in the *Rich* case, cited above - to which I refer for fuller details - that they essentially concern 'the effectiveness of arbitration agreements and the enforcement of arbitration awards' or else 'the arbitration tribunal, the arbitration procedure, the making of awards, appeals against awards and recognition and enforcement thereof'. Those conventions are thus clearly not intended to deal with all matters which could constitute the *subject-matter* of a dispute submitted to arbitration. The extent of such matters is virtually limitless and, in any event, variable from one dispute to another.

54. Those are, moreover, the lines along which the Court has already defined the exclusion referred to, when it held that '... by excluding arbitration from the scope of the Convention on the ground that it was already covered by international conventions, the Contracting Parties intended to exclude *arbitration in its entirety ...*'.

55. That is why, as is clear from the experts' reports, the Convention cannot apply 'to the recognition and enforcement of arbital awards...; it does not apply for the purpose of determining the jurisdiction of courts and tribunals in respect of litigation relating to arbitration - for example, proceedings to set aside an arbitral award; and, finally, it does not apply to the recognition of judgments given in such proceedings'.

56. In actual fact, the matters covered by the exclusion are those which '...are ancillary to *arbitration proceedings*, for example the appointment or dismissal of arbitrators, the fixing of the place of arbitration, the extension of the time-limit for making awards or the obtaining of a preliminary ruling on questions of substance as provided for under English law known as 'statement of special case' (section 21 of the Arbitration Act 1950). In the same way a judgment determining whether an arbitration agreement is valid or not, or because it is invalid, ordering the parties not to continue the arbitration proceedings, is not covered by the 1968 Convention.' 'Nor does the 1968 Convention cover proceedings and decisions concerning applications *for the revocation, amendment, recognition and enforcement of arbitration awards*.'

57. However, it should be kept firmly in mind that 'matters falling outside the scope of the Convention do so only if they constitute the principal subject-matter of the proceedings'.

58. In particular, ''arbitration' refers only to arbitration *proceedings*. Proceedings before national courts would therefore be affected by Article 1, second paragraph point (4) of the 1968 Convention *only if they dealt with arbitration as a main issue* and did not have to consider the validity of an arbitration agreement merely as a matter incidental to an examination of the competence of the court of origin to assume jurisdiction'.

59. The Court has drawn attention to that consideration: 'In order to determine whether a dispute falls within the scope of the Convention, reference must be made *solely to the subject-matter of the dispute*. If, by virtue of its subject-matter, such as the appointment of an arbitrator, a dispute falls outside the scope of the Convention, the existence of a preliminary issue which the court must resolve in order to determine the dispute cannot, whatever the issue may be, justify application of the Convention.

60. Consequently, as the German Government and Deco-Line have rightly pointed out, we must concern ourselves in this case with the *subject-matter of the dispute* brought before the Netherlands courts, in order to determine whether it constitutes 'arbitration' as defined above and whether it must, therefore, be excluded from the application of the provisions of the Convention.

61. However, it is clear from the account of the facts and procedures that Van Uden made an interlocutory application to the Netherlands court for, principally, an order requiring its debtor to pay the amount of four unpaid invoices due under the terms of the agreement, and, in the alternative, a part only of the amount of those invoices.

62. Consequently, the subject-matter of its claim is in no way that of arbitration. It is, rather, a claim in a matter relating to a contract in the sense that 'the basis for [it] is the failure to comply with a contractual obligation'.

63. That consideration is not, in my view, affected in any way by the fact that the dispute brought before the Netherlands courts can be regarded, as the German Government and Deco-Line suggest, as ancillary to the principal arbitration proceedings.

64. The Court has held that '…the general scheme of the Convention does not necessarily link the treatment of an ancillary claim to that of a principal claim' in the sense that a claim to that of a principal claim' in the sense that a claim is not excluded from the scope of the Convention merely because the principal claim to which it is ancillary is excluded from it.

65. Once again, the decisive criterion is the subject-matter of the proceedings: 'Ancillary claims … come within the scope of the Convention according to the subject-matter with which they are concerned and not according to the subject-matter involved in the principal claim'.

66. I do not, therefore, find any argument capable of convincing the Court among those put forward in favour of holding the provisions of the Convention inapplicable.

67. I realise, of course, that it may be thought unsatisfactory that application might be made simultaneously to an arbitration tribunal and a national court in connection with the same dispute.

68. Nevertheless, I am of the view that, in such circumstances, reference should be made to the rules of national law 'since the Brussels Convention cannot be extended beyond what is covered by its subject-matter'.

69. Consequently, the objection that a court lacks jurisdiction over a dispute with which it is seised, the subject-matter of which concerns a matter covered by the Convention, and that a panel of arbitrators should have jurisdiction, falls outside the scope of the Court's supervision. The resolution of that issue is a matter solely for the national court, by application of the *lex fori*.

70. However, in this case it is sufficient to point out that the Netherlands court based its jurisdiction on Article 1022(2) of the Code of Civil Procedure, which expressly provides that an arbitration clause does not preclude the jurisdiction of a court to hear interim applications.

71. In any event, as the Schlosser report pointed out, such 'differing basis positions lead to a different result in practice only in one particular instance': 'If

a national court adjudicates on the subject-matter of a dispute, because it overlooked an arbitration agreement or considered it inapplicable, can recognition and enforcement of that judgment be refused in another State of the Community on the ground that the arbitration agreement was after all valid and that therefore, pursuant to Article 1, second paragraph, point (4), the judgment falls outside the scope of the 1968 Convention?' According to the expert, that difficulty alone is easily disposed of: 'the court in the State addressed can no longer re-open the issue of classification; if the court of the State of origin, in assuming jurisdiction, has taken a certain view as to the applicability of the 1968 Convention, this becomes binding on the court in the State addressed'.

72. I therefore conclude that the existence of arbitration proceedings does not preclude the application of the provisions of the Convention in this case.

73. Having dealt with that preliminary point, I now come to the questions referred by the national court.

B - The application of Article 5, point 1, of the Convention

74. By its first question, the Hoge Raad asks the Court whether Article 5, point 1, of the Convention confers jurisdiction on the court seised to hear and determine a claim brought in interim proceedings, as provided for by the Code of Civil Procedure, for an order requiring the debtor, as immediate provisional relief, to pay a sum due, or whether its jurisdiction to hear the interim application under that provision is subject to a condition that the debt be enforceable within its territorial jurisdiction.

75. The third question presupposes that the Court regards that condition as necessary for the application of Article 5, point 1, of the Convention: if so, must it be fulfilled when the application is made to the court, or is it sufficient that it will probably be fulfilled in the future?

76. It is, in fact, a question of determining whether interim proceedings such as those in this case fall within the scope of Article 5, point 1, of the Convention and, if so, under what conditions.

77. Although the wording of the first question shows that the Hoge Raad seems to consider it established that the Netherlands court has jurisdiction to hear and determine the substance of the dispute between the parties, it should nevertheless be briefly ascertained, before examining whether that jurisdiction extends to the interim proceedings, whether that is so.

78. I note at once, moreover, that, with the exception of Deco-Line, no one disputes that, short of excluding the application of the rules of the Convention by an interpretation, which I have not accepted, of Article 1, point, 4 of the Convention, the Netherlands court hearing interlocutory applications has jurisdiction under Article 5, point 1, to hear and determine Van Uden's claim.

79. As we know, that provision leaves it open to the plaintiff, if he prefers, to sue the defendant, not in the courts having general jurisdiction in principle of the place where the defendant is domiciled, but in the courts having the closest links created by a contract between the parties thereto, it should be possible for all the difficulties which may arise on the occasion of the performance of a

contractual obligation to be brought before the same court: that for the place of performance of the obligation'.

80. That additional, optional jurisdiction presupposes that a number of conditions are fulfilled, as they are in this case.

81. First, since Article 1, point 4, does not apply, there is no doubt that the dispute submitted for determination by the court constitutes a 'matter relating to a contract'. Although it is sometimes difficult to be certain that a dispute constitutes such a matter, which the Court regards as an independent concept, a claim for payment of the whole or part of a sum due under an agreement '... finds its very basis in that agreement and consequently constitutes a matter relating to a contract within the meaning of Article 5, point 1, of the Convention' since 'the basis for [it] is the failure to comply with a contractual obligation'.

82. Second, the 'place of performance of the obligation in question' can, in this case, be determined without difficulty. There is only one obligation in question in the present case: Deco-Line's financial obligation towards Van Uden, and '...the place of performance of the obligation to pay ... is to be determined pursuant to the substantive law governing the obligation in dispute under the conflict rules of the court seised'. However, the Netherlands appeal court found that 'payment of the charter hire owed by Deco-Line was to take place in the Netherlands'.

83. Consequently, the Netherlands court seised does have jurisdiction under Article 5, point 1, of the Convention. It is, in my opinion, of little relevance that Van Uden's application was made in interim proceedings.

84. In the first place, it must be remembered, Article 1 of the Convention provides that the Convention is to apply 'whatever the nature of the court or tribunal; seised.

85. Moreover, the nature of the relief sought is immaterial under the Convention. In its *De Cavel I* judgment cited above, the Court held that 'in relation to the matters covered by the Convention, no legal basis is to be found therein for drawing a distinction between provisional and definitive measures'.

86. In the same way, and irrespective of how the interim relief sought by Van Uden is to be classified for the purpose of the Convention, I see no reason to draw a distinction, in the context of the application of Article 5, point 1, according to the nature of the proceedings instituted. As Advocate General Warner pointed out in his Opinion in the *De Cavel I* case cited above, '[i]t would be odd if the applicability of the Convention depended on the particular forum or type of procedure chosen by the plaintiff, petitioner or other claimant'.

87. Article 24 of the Convention does not in any way affect that conclusion.

88. Even it if were to be considered that the interim relief sought by Van Uden is a 'provisional' or 'protective' measure within the meaning of Article 24, that provision is not intended to confer exclusive jurisdiction in the matter. It merely authorises a court which does not have jurisdiction as to the substance of the matter to take such measures, within the scope of the matters covered by the Convention, where the plaintiff chooses to apply to it rather than to the courts of another Contracting State which have jurisdiction as to the substance of the matter.

89. The fact remains that the plaintiff is perfectly entitled not to make use of that right and to abide by one of the other grounds of jurisdiction provided for by the Convention. Thus, the court which has jurisdiction as to the substance of the matter under Article 5, point 1, has, *a fortiori*, jurisdiction to hear and determine an application for a 'provisional' or 'protective' measure within the meaning of Article 24: '... Article 24 allows the plaintiff an *option*, but does not prevent him, if he so prefers, from applying for provisional or protective measures to the court having jurisdiction as to the substance of the matter; that jurisdiction as to the substance naturally always implying jurisdiction to order provisional or protective measures'.

90. The relief sought from the court applied to under Article 5, point 1, must, of course, fall within the scope of the Convention. Since, in my opinion, there were no grounds for applying Article 1, point 4, and since the subject-matter of the dispute brought before the Netherlands court was contractual, that was the case here.

91. The second part of the first question asks the Court to make it clear whether the jurisdiction exercised under Article 5, point 1, in interim proceedings for an order requiring the debtor to pay a sum of money is subject to the further condition that the decision given should be enforceable in the State of the court hearing the application.

92. This question raised by the Hoge Raad probably stems from the fact that the relevant provisions of its national law specify such a condition, whereas the defendant in the main proceedings does not possess any seizable assets in the Netherlands.

93. However, as the German Government points out, no such requirement is contained in Article 5, point 1.

94. Moreover, that provision makes no reference to national provisions. On the contrary, it designates directly the courts having jurisdiction. It would therefore be incompatible with that direct designation to make jurisdiction subject to requirements of national law.

95. Furthermore, as the Commission points out, it would be absurd to make jurisdiction under Article 5, point 1, dependent on the condition that the order granting interim relief should be capable of taking effect in the State of the court hearing the application, when the Brussels Convention was specifically drawn up in order to ensure the 'free movement of judgments' in the Common Market. In particular, Title III makes it possible to guarantee in the Contracting States the expeditious and summary recognition and enforcement of a decision given in another Contracting State.

96. I therefore conclude, with regard to the first question, without there thus being any need to answer the third question, that a court having jurisdiction under Article 5, point 1, of the Convention has that jurisdiction irrespective of the nature of the proceedings in which the application was made to it. It may therefore, by virtue of that jurisdiction, in interim proceedings order the payment of a sum of money as immediate provisional relief, without its jurisdiction being made subject to the condition that the order be enforceable in the State concerned.

97. Two conclusions must be drawn from that.

98. On the one hand, since the court hearing the interim application has jurisdiction, in its capacity as the court for the 'place of performance of the obligation in question', in matters relating to a contract, it is not required to refer to the grounds of jurisdiction provided for by its national law. In particular, it is not necessary to rely on Article 126(3) of the Code of Civil Procedure (which is included in the list of rules of exorbitant jurisdictions in the second paragraph of Article 3 of the Convention and may not, therefore, be relied on in order to sue a defendant in the Netherlands courts).

99. On the other hand, in so far as the Court holds, as I propose that it should, that the Netherlands court has jurisdiction under Article 5, point 1, to hear and determine the application for interim relief, it is not necessary to ascertain whether its jurisdiction can also be based on Article 24. There is, in principle, no need to answer Questions 4 to 8.

100. I therefore put forward only in the alternative the following arguments concerning that provision.

C - Article 24 of the Convention

101. During the national proceedings, the President of the Rechtbank, Rotterdam, held that he had jurisdiction to hear and determine the application made by Van Uden in *kort geding* proceedings, not under Article 5, point 1, of the Brussels Convention, even though, as we have just seen, that possibility was open to him, but under Article 24.

102. By its fourth to eighth questions, the court making the reference therefore seeks to ascertain whether Article 24 of the Convention covers an application such as that made in the main proceedings and, if so, under what conditions.

103. The Court is thus once again faced (fourth question) with the issue of whether immediate provisional relief, applied for on the grounds of pressing urgency and ordered in *kort geding* proceedings, may be regarded as a 'provisional' or 'protective' measure within the meaning of Article 24 of the Convention. That was also one of the questions referred to the Court by the Hoge Raad in the *W.* v *H.* case cited above. On that occasion, the Court was not required to rule on this issue.

104. The other questions submitted essentially ask the Courts to clarify the conditions of application of Article 24. They are of two types: two (Questions 4 and 6) are concerned with 'provisional' or 'protective' measures, the others (Questions 5, 7 and 8) with jurisdiction.

1. The concept of provisional or protective measures

105. Article 24 obviously applies only if the 'provisional' or 'protective' measures sought fall within the scope *ratione materiae* of the Convention: '[Article 24] cannot ... be relied on to bring within the scope of the Convention provisional or protective measures relating to matters which are excluded therefrom'. As we have seen, that is the case in this instance.

106. With regard to the measures envisaged by that provision, which, as the Court has held, may serve '... to safeguard a variety of rights', academic writers often draw attention to the difficulty of defining their content. Indeed, 'the absence of a uniform definition of the concept of provisional and protective measures established by the Brussels Convention is liable to result in appreciably different systems of legal protection in the member States'.

107. The Court has in any event opted for a 'Community' definition of the concept: 'The expression 'provisional, including protective, measures' within the meaning of Article 24 must ... be understood as referring to measures which, in matters within the scope of the Convention, are intended to preserve a factual or legal situation so as to safeguard rights the recognition of which is sought elsewhere from the court having jurisdiction as to the substance of the matter.'

108. Can measures ordered in proceedings on an application for interim relief under Netherlands law, as provided for by Article 289 *et seq.* of the Netherlands Code of Civil Procedure, be regarded as satisfying such a definition?

109. That question is justified, according to one writer, because '... the procedure of applying for interim relief (*kort geding*) has undergone very considerable changes in Netherlands practice. ... from an expeditious and *provisional* procedure, it has to a large extent become a procedure for urgent cases with definitive character ... Indeed, social or economic issues of major importance which demand an urgent solution, such as, for example, an injunction to end a strike, are often the subject-matter of an application for interim relief, the substance of which will not be further discussed by the ordinary courts. In fact, in the Netherlands, courts hearing applications for interim relief make very little use of the power available to them to enjoin the parties to bring an action on the substance of the matter within a certain time, which deprives the procedure of most of its provisional character'.

110. That is because, according to the classification proposed by another writer, the Netherlands *kort geding*, like the French *référé-provision,* for example, is one of those 'measures totally or partly anticipatory of the decision on the substance' which differ from the more conventional provisional measures which exist in other legal systems, such as 'protective measures in the narrow sense of the term [which] are designed to ensure performance or bring about an advance on performance', or 'temporary and protective measures for the provisional resolution of the factual situation in relation to a disputed legal relationship'.

111. According to certain writers, however, 'it may ... be considered that the letter of Article 24 imposes a rigorous distinction between provisional and substantive measures, so that any measure anticipating the decision on the substance would cease to be provisional within the meaning of the Brussels Convention'. That was also the opinion of the Commission in the *C.H.W.* v *G.J.H* case cited above.

112. However, I do not think that a measure such as that ordered in the interim proceedings in this case on the basis of Article 289 *et seq*. of the Code of Civil Procedure, requiring the debtor to pay a sum as immediate provisional

relief, can be regarded as 'intended to preserve a factual or legal situation so as to safeguard rights the recognition of which is sought elsewhere from the court having jurisdiction as to the substance of the matter'.

113. On the one hand, the pecuniary character of such a measure is not such as to preclude it from being characterised as 'provisional' or 'protective'.

114. That was, in any event, what the Court held in its judgment in Case 125/79 *Denilauler* [1980] ECR 1553. On that occasion, reference was made to the Court by a German appeal court asked to register for enforcement an order made by a French court, declared provisionally enforceable, authorising a creditor to freeze the account of a debtor at a bank in Germany. Although the Court did not expressly rule on the classification of such a measure in the light of Article 24, it refused to allow the enforcement order in that case only because the proceedings in the French court had not involved the hearing of both parties, and thus had not respected the rights of the defence. In so doing, it seems to me that the Court implicitly acknowledged that such measures, while capable of being classified as 'provisional' or 'protective' within the meaning of Article 24, could not be covered by the provisions of Title III unless they had been ordered pursuant to adversary proceedings.

115. Another example can be found in a recent order which, although not made in the context of the Brussels Convention but on appeal against an order of the President of the Court of First Instance made in interlocutory proceedings, seems to me to identify some principles which may guide the Court in giving the interpretation requested from it. While: '[t]he wording of the order under appeal ... appears to indicate that a measure granting (by way of advance) a part of the compensation claimed in the main proceedings and seeking to protect the applicant's interests until judgment is delivered in those proceedings is inconsistent with the conditions for or nature of an interim application, irrespective of the factual and legal circumstances of the individual case', it was held that: '[i]t is not possible ... to rule out in advance, in a general and abstract manner, that payment, by way of an advance, even of an amount corresponding to that sought in the main application, may be necessary in order to ensure the practical effect of the judgment in the main action and may, in certain cases, appear justified with regard to the interests involved'.

116. Moreover, the relief sought in the *kort geding* proceedings is certainly intended to achieve the 'recognition of rights sought elsewhere from the court having jurisdiction as to the substance of the matter', in the sense that it does not have definitive character.

117. Article 292 of the Code of Civil Procedure lays down that such relief must be without prejudice to the main action. It does not, therefore, constitute *res judicata*. Consequently, the proceedings provided for in Article 289 *et seq.* are intended by that legislation to be provisional in character.

118. The fact that the current trend of practice in the Netherlands courts frequently seems to mean that no proceedings on the substance of the matter are either pending when the application for interim relief is made or instituted subsequently does not in any way detract from the foregoing consideration.

119. Indeed, if, despite the merely provisional status which it is intended to

have, the measure acquires definitive character, that is only because of the attitude of the parties. As the Commission points out: 'If the defendant submits to the judgment, the fact that what is intended as a provisional measure acquires definitive character must be attributed to that submission. Similarly, where the defendant does not apply for the annulment of a measure ordered in interlocutory proceedings, although there are no proceedings pending on the substance of the matter, that decision is a matter for the defendant alone and does not alter the provisional character of the measure in any way.'

120. I therefore conclude, in answer to the fourth and sixth questions, that a provisionally enforceable measure requiring a debtor to pay a sum of money, ordered pursuant to Article 289 *et seq*. of the Code of Civil Procedure, is a 'provisional' or 'protective' measure within the meaning of Article 24 of the Brussels Convention.

2. Courts having jurisdiction

121. By allowing application to be made to the court of a Contracting State, 'even if, under this Convention, the courts of another Contracting State have jurisdiction as to the substance of the matter', Article 24 is intended to apply irrespective of which jurisdictional rule is laid down by the Convention for disposing of the substantive issues. Consequently, each court must determine its jurisdiction according to the *lex fori*.

122. Within the powers thus conferred on the national court by Article 24 of the Convention, the Court has held that the national court must '... make its authorisation subject to all conditions guaranteeing the provisional or protective character of the measure ordered'.

In particular, the Court emphasised that: '... the granting of this type of measure requires particular care of the part of the court and detailed knowledge of the actual circumstances in which the measure is to take effect. Depending on each case and commercial practices in particular, the court must be able to place a time-limit on its order or, as regards the nature of the assets or goods subject to the measure contemplated, require bank guarantees or nominate a sequestrator ...'.

123. Do more specific conditions apply to the exercise of jurisdiction?

(a) The requirement that proceedings should also be pending before another court having jurisdiction as to the substance of the matter

124. By its fifth question, the Hoge Raad seeks to ascertain whether the jurisdiction conferred pursuant to Article 24 necessarily presupposes that substantive proceedings on the main issue are, or may become, pending before another court.

125. In answer to this question, I concur with the opinion expressed by a number of writers: '... Article 24 applies regardless of whether substantive proceedings on the main issue are or are not pending before another court ... Of course, Article 24 does not require a substantive action on the main issue to have already been brought before one court in order for a provisional or protective measure to be sought from another court ...'

126. As the Commission points out, it is sufficient to refer to the wording of Article 24, which provides the applicant with an additional ground of jurisdiction, *'even if*, under this Convention, the Courts of another Contracting State have jurisdiction as to the substance of the matter'.

127. The jurisdiction conferred pursuant to Article 24 applies only to provisional or protective measures. The possibility of disposing of the substantive issues of the case therefore remains, as we have seen, unaffected by that provision. However, the court from which such provisional or protective measures are sought will not necessarily be the same as the court having jurisdiction pursuant to Sections 2 to 6 of Title II of the Convention to hear and determine the substantive issues of the case. That is why Article 24 makes it clear that the fact that another court has jurisdiction as to the substance of the matter does not in any way preclude the aforementioned court, which is '... best able to assess the circumstances which may lead to the grant or refusal of the measures sought or to the laying down of procedures and conditions which the plaintiff must observe in order to guarantee the provisional and protective character of the measures ordered ...', from ordering the measures at issue.

128. There is no point, in this context, in requiring that substantive proceedings on the main issue be already pending. It is sufficient in this regard that the possibility of disposing of the substantive issues exists. I have pointed out that Article 292 of the Code of Civil Procedure guarantees the principle that such proceedings may be brought.

129. In answer to the fifth question, I therefore conclude that the jurisdiction provided for under Article 24 of the Convention is not conditional upon the prior commencement of substantive proceedings on the main issue. It is sufficient in this regard that the possibility of bringing such proceedings exists.

(b) The possibility for the court to hold that it can hear the application under a rule of exorbitant jurisdiction.

130. If the court from which a provisional or protective measure is sought pursuant to Article 24 determines its jurisdiction according to the *lex fori,* it may be wondered whether all the international jurisdictional rules of the Contracting States can serve as the basis for the exercise of jurisdiction by their courts in matters relating to provisional or protective measures or whether, on the contrary, Article 24 leads to the exclusion of certain jurisdictions. Can a court having jurisdiction under Article 24, for example, be allowed to give judgment on the basis of a national legal rule of exorbitant jurisdiction of the kind referred to in Article 3 of the Convention? That is the substance of the first part of the seventh question.

131. The German Government points out that the answer to this question is particularly important because, 'under the third paragraph of Article 28 of the brussels Convention, the international jurisdiction of the court applied to may not be reviewed when recognising and ordering the enforcement of an interim measure, and because the rules relating to jurisdiction are not a matter of public policy within the meaning of Article 27, point 1, of the Brussels Convention'.

132. As we know, Article 3 establishes the principle that a defendant may be sued in the courts of a Contracting State other than that in which he is

domiciled 'only by virtue of the rules set out in Section 2 to 6 [of Title II of the Convention]'.

133. However, Article 24 is the sole provision in Section 9 of that title. Consequently, the provisions of Article 3 do not appear to be applicable to it.

134. To allow the exercise of an exorbitant jurisdiction in the context of the reference made by Article 24 to the *lex fori* does not appear to me to distort the meaning of the exclusion provided for in Article 3.

135. On the contrary, I see an advantage in it. In view of the urgency which generally underlies the making of such applications, the person seeking a measure intended to preserve a factual or legal situation must be able to apply to his nearest court.

136. The jurisdiction of the courts of the plaintiff's domicile is certainly accepted in such a case, contrary to the rule of principle established by Article 2. However, measures ordered under the jurisdiction conferred by Article 24 will necessarily have 'provisional' or 'protective' character. Once such measures have been ordered, it will then be for the party concerned - in some cases the defendant - to commence proceedings in the court having jurisdiction as to the substance of the matter, if that has not already been done.

(c) The requirements that the measure be capable of enforcement in the State of the court hearing the application

137. Certain writers sometimes add a further condition: that the court seised should not assume jurisdiction to adopt the measures referred to in Article 24, even though its law may give it such jurisdiction, where its decision could be complied with only by way of proceedings to obtain an enforcement order; on that view, the court would adopt such measures only if its decision could be complied with in the territory of its State.

138. The extremely general terms in which Article 25 is couched mean that decisions order provisional or protective measures fall within the scope of Title III of the Convention: 'Article 24 does not preclude provisional or protective measures ordered in the State of origin pursuant to adversary proceedings … from being the subject of recognition and an authorisation for enforcement on the conditions laid down in Articles 25 to 49 of the Convention.

139. A court of a Contracting State may thus have jurisdiction to order such a measure even if it can be enforced only in another Contracting State. Moreover, in the *De Cavel I* and *Denilauler* judgments cited above, the Court did not dispute that a French court can order protective measures relating to property situated in Germany (placing under seal and freezing of assets in the *De Cavel I* case; freezing of a bank account in the *Denilauler* case). And in both cases, although the French decisions did not come within the system of recognition and enforcement provided for by the Brussels Convention, that was for reasons connected with the matter at issue and the rights of the defence respectively.

140. Consequently, in answer to the second part of the seventh question, there can be no requirement making a court's jurisdiction under Article 24 dependent on fulfilment of the condition that the relief granted by the court must be capable of enforcement in the territory of its State.

141. The eighth question therefore becomes devoid of purpose.

IV - Conclusion

142. In the light of the foregoing I propose that the Court give the following replies to the Hoge Raad der Nederlanden:

(1) The jurisdiction in matters relating to a contract exercised by a court under Article 5, point 1, of the Convention on Jurisdiction and the Enforcement of Judgments in Civil and Commercial Matters, signed at Brussels on 27 September 1968, applies irrespective of the nature of the proceedings in which application is made to that court. In particular, a court of a Contracting State may have jurisdiction, under that provision, to hear and determine a claim brought in interim proceedings for an order requiring the debtor, as immediate provisional relief, to pay a sum to the creditor, without its jurisdiction being made dependent on the fulfilment of conditions other than those specified in Article 5, point 1, such as the condition that the decision given be capable of enforcement in the State of the court hearing the application.

(2) The fact that the parties have agreed on an arbitration clause is relevant, if at all, only under the *lex fori*, pursuant to which it is for the court hearing the application to make sure that it has jurisdiction.

143. In the alternative:

(3) In answer to the fourth and sixth questions: Article 24 of the Convention must be interpreted as meaning that the concept of 'provisional' or 'protective' measures to which it refers covers the possibility, as provided for in Article 289 *et seq.* of the Netherlands Code of Civil Procedure, of applying on grounds of pressing urgency to the President of the Arrondissementsrechtbank for an order requiring the debtor, as immediate provisional relief, to pay a sum of money in performance of a contractual obligation.

(4) In answer to the fifth question, it is immaterial, in the context of the application of Article 24 of the Convention, whether substantive proceedings on the main issue are, or may become, pending, provided that the possibility of bringing such proceedings before a court exists in national law.

(5) In answer to the seventh question: Likewise, it is immaterial whether the court bases its jurisdiction under Article 24 of the Convention on a provision of its national law referred to in the second paragraph of Article 3 of the Convention.

The court's jurisdiction under Article 24 of the Convention may not be made dependent on fulfilment of the condition that the measure which it adopts be capable of enforcement in the territory of its State.

TITLE III *[Chapter III]*

Recognition and Enforcement
[Recognition and Enforcement]

Definition of judgment – Article 25 *[Article 32]*

See also

Case C-414/92 - 2 June 1994

Solo Kleinmotoren GmbH
v
Emilio Boch

Recognition and enforcement - Article 25 - Definition of 'judgment' - Scope - Court settlement - Excluded - Recognition and enforcement - Article 27(3) - Grounds for refusal - Strict interpretation - Judgment irreconcilable with a judgment given in the State in which recognition is sought - Treatment of a Court settlement reached in the State in which recognition is sought as judgment given by a court of that State - Excluded.

Summary

1. The definition of a 'judgment' given in Article 25 of the Convention on Jurisdiction and the Enforcement of Judgments in Civil and Commercial Matters refers, for the purposes of the application of the various provisions of the Convention in which the term is used, solely to judicial decisions actually given by a court or tribunal of a Contracting State deciding on its own authority on the issues between the parties. That is not the case as far as a settlement is concerned, even if it was reached in a court of a Contracting State and brings legal proceedings to an end, because settlements in court are essentially contractual in that their terms depend first and foremost on the parties' intention.

2. Article 27 of the Convention must be interpreted strictly, inasmuch as it constitutes an obstacle to the achievement of one of its fundamental objectives, which is to facilitate, to the greatest extent possible, the free movement of judgments by providing for a simple and rapid enforcement procedure. Hence Article 27(3) of the Convention is to be interpreted as meaning that an enforceable settlement reached before a court of the State in which recognition is sought in order to settle legal proceedings

which are in progress does not constitute a 'judgment' within the meaning of that provision, 'given in a dispute between the same parties in the State in which recognition is sought' which, under the Convention may preclude recognition and enforcement of a judgment given in another Contracting State.

JUDGMENT OF THE COURT

Mancini, President of the Chamber, Kakouris, Schockweiler, Kapteyn and Murray, Judges

1. By order of 5 November 1992, received at the Court on 15 December 1992, the Bundesgerichtshof referred to the Court for a preliminary ruling pursuant to the Protocol of 3 June 1971 on the interpretation by the Court of Justice of the Convention of 27 September 1968 on Jurisdiction and the Enforcement of Judgments in Civil and Commercial Matters (OJ 1978 L 304, p. 36), as amended by the Convention of 9 October 1978 on the Accession of the Kingdom of Denmark, Ireland and the United Kingdom of Great Britain and Northern Ireland (OJ 1978 L 304, p. 1) (hereinafter the 'Convention'), two questions on the interpretation of Article 27(3) of the Convention.

2. The questions arose in proceedings between Solo Kleinmotoren GmbH ('Solo Kleinmotoren'), a company established in the Federal Republic of Germany, and Emilio Boch, the owner of an agricultural machinery retail sales company established in Italy, concerning an application for an order for enforcement in Germany of a final judgment delivered by a civil court in Italy.

3. The file shows that until 1966 Mr Boch sold in Italy, under the trade name 'Solo', agricultural machinery supplied to him by Solo Kleinmotoren. Subsequently, Solo Italiana SpA ('Solo Italiana') began to distribute in Italy the machinery manufactured by Solo Kleinmotoren, which consequently discontinued its supplies to Mr Boch's company. Mr Boch then brought two actions.

4. First, he sued Solo Kleinmotoren in the Tribunale Civile (District Court), Milan (Italy), for breach of the supply contract. In 1975 the Cotte d'Appello (Court of Appeal), Milan, ordered the defendant to pay an amount of over LIT 48 000 000, with interest. On Mr Boch's application, an order for enforcement was issued in Germany in accordance with the

provisions of the Convention. Following an appeal brought by Solo Kleinmotoren against that enforcement order, the parties concluded a settlement on 24 February 1978 in the Oberlandesgericht (Higher Regional Court) Stuttgart (Federal Republic of Germany). It was worded as follows: '1. On Monday 27 February 1978 (Solo Kleinmotoren) shall pay a sum of DM 160 000 (to Mr Boch) by handing over a banker's cheque to M. X. 2. (Solo Kleinmotoren) shall collect the goods described in the "packing list" at its own expense from the carrier Y by 31 March 1978 at the latest. Notification must be sent (to Mr Boch) one week before the goods are collected. (Mr Boch) guarantees that storage costs have been paid for the period until 31 March 1978 and that no other charge is payable on the goods. (Solo Kleinmotoren) waives the warranty on the goods recovered. 3. All the parties' claims against one another arising from their business relationship are hereby resolved. All claims between (Mr Boch) and Inter Solo at Zug are also resolved. (Mr Boch) undertakes not to assert the claims forming the subject-matter of the present legal dispute against Solo Italiana, Bologna. 4. (Solo Kleinmotoren) shall pay the legal costs, its own non-legal expenses and the costs of the legal agent (of Mr Boch) in the present proceedings; (Mr Boch) shall pay the other expenses himself.'

5. Mr Boch commenced a second action against Solo Kleinmotoren and Solo Italiana before the Tribunale Civile, Bologna (Italy), for infringement of the trade name 'Solo' and for unfair Competition. In 1979 the Corte d'Appello, Bologna, held that Solo Kleinmotoren and Solo Italiana were jointly liable for misuse of the trade name 'Solo' and acts of unfair competition prejudicial to Mr Boch and ordered the two defendant companies jointly to pay him damages, the quantum to be determined in separate proceedings. In the grounds of its judgment that court examined Solo Italiana's objection that the settlement reached in the German court had disposed of Mr Boch's claims, and held that the settlement could not be relied on in the proceedings before it because it had not been declared enforceable in Italy and because, according to its terms, the subject-matter of the dispute before the courts in Bologna was excluded from the settlement reached by the parties. That judgment of the Corte d'Appello, Bologna, subsequently became final.

6. In 1981 Mr Boch brought proceedings before the Tribunale Civile, Bologna for determination of the quantum of damages to be paid by Solo Kleinmotoren and Solo Italiana pursuant to the judgment of the Corte d'Appello, Bologna. On 18 February 1986 the Tribunale Civile ordered the two defendant companies to pay Mr Boch LIT 180 000 000 by way

of damages. The Corte d'Appello, Bologna, dismissed the appeal brought by Solo Kleinmotoren against that judgment. Both courts rejected Solo Kleinmotoren's argument that the settlement approved by the Stuttgart court resolved all the claims which the parties had against one another, and held that this question had been settled definitively by the judgment given in 1979 by the Corte d'Appello, Bologna.

7. Mr Boch then lodged an application in the Landgericht (Regional Court) Stuttgart to obtain enforcement in Germany of the judgment of the Tribunale Civile, Bologna, of 18 February 1986. The Landgericht granted the application. After the Oberlandesgericht Stuttgart had dismissed the appeal brought by Solo Kleinmotoren against the Landgericht's decision, Solo Kleinmotoren appealed on a point of law to the Bundesgerichtshof and asked it to annul the Oberlandesgericht's order and dismiss the application for an order for the enforcement of the Italian judgment.

8. Solo Kleinmotoren contended before the Bundesgerichtshof that Article 27(3) of the Convention precluded enforcement in Germany of the Italian judgment since it was incompatible with the settlement concluded by the parties on 24 February 1978 in the Oberlandesgericht Stuttgart. In support of that argument, Solo Kleinmotoren maintained that the settlement brought to an end all the parties' reciprocal rights and obligations arising from their previous business relationship, including Mr Boch's claims which had been upheld by the judgment delivered on 18 February 1986 by the Tribunale Civile, Bologna.

9. The Bundesgerichtshof, unsure whether a court settlement can be treated as a'judgment given in a dispute between the same parties in the State in which recognition is sought' for the purposes of Article 27(3) of the Convention and whether such a settlement therefore precludes, under the provisions of the Convention, recognition and enforcement of a judgment given in another Contracting State which is irreconcilable with that settlement, stayed the proceedings until the Court of Justice has given a preliminary ruling on the following questions: 'Can a judgment within the meaning of Article 27(3) of the Brussels Convention, with which the judgment whose recognition is sought is irreconcilable, also be an enforceable settlement which is reached by the same parties before a court of the State in which recognition is sought in order to settle legal proceedings which are in progress? If so, does that answer apply to all the terms of that settlement or only to those which are independently enforceable under Article 51 of the Brussels Convention and possibly only if the conditions for enforcement are met?'

The first question

10. In answering this question it must be borne in mind at the outset that in derogation from the principle laid down in the first paragraph of Article 26 of the Convention, according to which a judgment given in a Contracting State is to be recognized in the other Contracting States without any special procedure being required, Articles 27 and 28 of the Convention list exhaustively the grounds for refusing to recognize such a judgment.

11. Thus, according to Article 27 of the Convention, 'A judgment shall not be recognized: ... (3) if the judgment is irreconcilable with a judgment given in a dispute between the same parties in the State in which recognition is sought ...'.

12. The first paragraph of Article 31 of the Convention provides: 'A judgment given in a Contracting State and enforceable in that State shall be enforced in another Contracting State when, on the application of any interested party, the order for its enforcement has been issued there.'

13. The second paragraph of Article 34 of the Convention provides: 'The application may be refused only for one of the reasons specified in Articles 27 and 28.'

14. On the question whether a court settlement such as that at issue in the main proceedings constitutes a 'judgment' within the meaning of Article 27(3), it is to be noted that Article 25 of the Convention, which appears under Title III 'Recognition and Enforcement' - provides: 'For the purposes of this Convention, "judgment" means any judgment given by a court or tribunal of a Contracting State, whatever the judgment may be called, including a decree, order, decision or writ of execution, as well as the determination of costs or expenses by an officer of the court'.

15. The very wording, of Article 25 shows that the definition of 'judgment' given in that provision refers, for the purposes of the application of the various provisions of the Convention in which the term is used, solely to judicial decisions actually given by a court or tribunal of a Contracting State.

16. As is explained in the Report of the Committee of Experts on the Convention (OJ 1979 C 59, at the foot of p. 42), Article 25 expressly treats the determination of costs by an officer of the court as a judgment

since, under the German Code of Civil Procedure which makes provision for this, the registrar acts as an officer of the court which decided on the substance of the matter and, in the event of a challenge to the registrar's decision, the court decides the issue.

17. It follows from the foregoing that in order to be a 'judgment' for the purposes of the Convention the decision must emanate from a judicial body of a Contracting State deciding on its own authority on the issues between the parties.

18. That condition is not fulfilled in the case of a settlement, even if it was reached in a court of a Contracting State and brings legal proceedings to an end. Settlements in court are essentially contractual in that their terms depend first and foremost on the parties intention, as the Experts' Report explains (op. cit., p. 56).

19. Moreover, a different construction cannot be entertained where the application of Article 27(3) of the Convention is concerned.

20. As has already been stated in paragraph 15 of this judgment, the definition of 'judgment' given in Article 25 applies to all the provisions of the Convention in which that term is used. Moreover, Article 27 constitutes an obstacle to the achievement of one of the fundamental objectives of the Convention, which is to facilitate, to the greatest extent possible, the free movement of judgments by providing for a simple and rapid enforcement procedure. Article 27 must therefore be interpreted strictly, which precludes treating a court settlement as a judgment given by a court or tribunal.

21. The Report of the Committee of Experts states elsewhere (op. cit., p. 45), with regard to the ground for refusing recognition set out in Article 27(3) of the Convention, that 'the rule of law in a State would be disturbed if it were possible to take advantage of two conflicting judgments'. Such a risk of disturbance only assumes the gravity required to justify, under the Convention, refusal of recognition and enforcement of a judgment given in another Contracting State, whose irreconcilability with a judgment given between the same parties in the State where recognition is sought is pleaded, if the latter decision is a judgment of a court which itself determines a matter at issue between the parties.

22. Furthermore, the case of court settlements is governed expressly by Article 51 of the Convention, which falls under Title IV, headed

'Authentic Instruments and Court Settlements', and which lays down specific rules for their enforcement.

23. According to that provision: 'A settlement which has been approved by a court in the course of proceedings and is enforceable in the State in which it was concluded shall be enforceable in the State in which enforcement is sought under the same conditions as authentic instruments'.

24. In derogation from the system of rules governing enforcement of judgments, the first paragraph of Article 50 of the Convention provides that enforcement of an authentic instrument in a Contracting State other than the State in which it was formally drawn up or registered and is enforceable may be refused only if enforcement of the instrument is contrary to public policy in the State in which enforcement is sought.

25. In view of all the preceding considerations, the reply to the first question submitted by the Bundesgerichtshof must be that Article 27(3) of the Convention is to be interpreted as meaning that an enforceable settlement reached before a court of the State in which recognition is sought in order to settle legal proceedings which are in progress does not constitute a 'judgment', within the meaning of that provision, 'given in a dispute between the same parties in the State in which recognition is sought' which, under the Convention, may preclude recognition and enforcement of a judgment given in another Contracting State.

The second question

26. In view of the answer given to the first question, there is no need to answer the second question.

On those grounds, the Court (Sixth Chamber), in answer to the questions referred to it by the Bundesgerichtshof by order of 5 November 1992, hereby rules:

> **Article 27(3) of the Convention of 27 September 1968 on Jurisdiction and the Enforcement of Judgments in Civil and Commercial Matters is to be interpreted as meaning that an enforceable settlement reached before a court of the State in which recognition is sought in order to settle legal proceedings which are in progress does not constitute a 'judgment', within the meaning of that provision, 'given in a dispute between the**

same parties in the State in which recognition is sought' which, under the Convention, may preclude recognition and enforcement of a judgment given in another Contracting State.

OPINION OF MR ADVOCATE GENERAL GULMANN

1. The Bundesgerichtshof has submitted questions to the Court of Justice for a preliminary ruling on the interpretation of the Convention of 27 September 1968 on jurisdiction and the enforcement of judgments in civil and commercial matters ('the Brussels Convention'). The questions arose in a case before it between a German company, Solo Kleinmotoren, and an Italian businessman, Emilio Boch. The issue in dispute is whether a court settlement reached in Germany is a bar to Mr Boch's having a judgment delivered in Italy enforced in Germany.

2. The facts of the case are as follows: Mr Boch ran a business in Milan under the name 'SOLO', dealing in agricultural machinery which was supplied by Solo Kleinmotoren. In 1966 a company was formed in Bologna with the name SOLO Italiana SpA which subsequently took over the sales in Italy of the machinery manufactured by Solo Kleinmotoren; accordingly Solo Kleinmotoren discontinued its supplies to Mr Boch. Mr Boch thereupon brought two actions. One action, which was brought before the Tribunale Civile, Milan, concerned breach of the contract between the parties. The other action, brought before the Tribunale Civile, Bologna, against both Solo Kleinmotoren and SOLO Italiana, concerned misuse of the trade name and unfair competition.

3. The action in Milan ended in 1975, when the Corte d'Appello, Milan, ordered Solo Kleinmotoren to pay Emilio Boch approximately LIT 48 million, with interest. That judgment was, in accordance with the Brussels Convention, declared enforceable in Germany. Solo Kleinmotoren, however, appealed against the enforcement decision to the Oberlandesgericht Stuttgart. Before that court and at its suggestion, the parties reached a court settlement on 24 February 1975 which provided *inter alia* as follows: '1. The judgment debtor [Solo Kleinmotoren] shall pay the judgment creditor [Emilio Boch] ... DM 160 000; 2. The judgment debtor will collect ... goods ...; 3. All the parties' claims against one another arising from their business relationship are hereby resolved ... The judgment creditor undertakes not to assert the claims forming the subject-matter of the present legal dispute against SOLO Italiana, Bologna ....

4. The action brought in Bologna resulted in a judgment delivered in 1979 in which the Corte d'Appello, Bologna, held Solo Kleinmotoren and SOLO Italiana jointly liable for misuse of the trade name 'SOLO' and unfair competition. The Corte d'Appello stated that the decision on the quantum of damages should be dealt with in later proceedings. In its reasoning the Corte d'Appello considered a submission that Emilio Boch's claims should be regarded as having been satisfied in their entirety in Stuttgart on 24 February 1978. The court did not uphold that submission, stating *inter alia* that the court settlement had never been declared enforceable in Italy and, in any case, was

unrelated to the dispute being heard by the court. The judgment states *inter alia*: 'Moreover it is clear from the content of the minute of the settlement and the subject-matter of the dispute as expounded before the German courts and set out in the settlement deed that the matters at issue in the present dispute were excluded from the settlement of the relations which was there reached between Emilio Boch and the German company. The proceedings before the Oberlandesgericht Stuttgart were concerned with the enforcement of the judgment of the Court of Appeal, Milan, on the application brought by Emilio Boch ... for termination of the exclusive supply contract and for compensation for the damage resulting from the breach.'

5. In 1951 Emilio Boch brought proceedings before the Tribunale Civile, Bologna, to obtain payment of damages for infringement of his trade name and unfair competition. In 1986 the Tribunale Civile, Bologna, ordered Solo Kleinmotoren and SOLO Italiana to pay damages of approximately LIT 150 million. That judgment was upheld by the Corte d'Appello, Bologna. Before both courts, Solo Kleinmotoren contended that the court settlement reached before the Oberlandesgericht Stuttgart in 1978 put an end to the parties' differences. Each court rejected that submission, stating that the judgment delivered in 1979 by the Corte d'Appello, Bologna, had dealt with that question and it was therefore *res judicata*.

6. Emilio Boch then lodged an application in the Landgericht Stuttgart to obtain enforcement in Germany of the judgment ordering the payment of damages delivered in Bologna. The application was granted in an order of 4 December 1990. It was confirmed in an order of the Oberlandesgericht Stuttgart on 4 February 1992. It is against that order that Solo Kleinmotoren has appealed to the Bundesgerichtshof seeking to have it set aside and asking that Emilio Boch's application for an order for enforcement be dismissed.

7. Before the Bundesgerichtshof Solo Kleinmotoren contended that Point 3 of the court settlement reached in the Oberlandesgericht Stuttgart was aimed at precluding all claims that Emilio Boch might have against the company, including the claims on which he subsequently obtained judgment before the courts in Bologna; on that basis the company claimed that the court settlement was a bar to the recognition and enforcement of the judgment for damages delivered in Bologna. In that submission the company relied on Article 27(3) of the Brussels Convention, which provides: 'A judgment shall not be recognized: (3) if the judgment is irreconcilable with a judgment given in a dispute between the same parties in the State in which recognition is sought.'

The company takes the view that a court settlement is covered by Article 27(3).

8. The Bundesgerichtshof held that it had to decide whether a court settlement can be treated as a judgment barring recognition under Article 27(3) before it could decide whether there was a conflict between the content of the court settlement and the judgment in respect of which enforcement was sought. The Bundesgerichtshof therefore referred the following questions to the Court of Justice for a preliminary ruling: 'Can a judgment within the meaning of Article 27(3) of the Brussels Convention, with which the judgment whose recognition is

sought is irreconcilable, also be an enforceable settlement which is reached by the same parties before a court of the State in which recognition is sought in order to settle legal proceedings which are in progress? If so, does that answer apply to all the terms of that settlement or only to those which are independently enforceable pursuant to Article 51 of the Brussels Convention and possibly only if the conditions for enforcement are met?'

9. The parties to the main proceedings, the German Government, the Italian Government and the Commission have submitted observations to the Court.

10. Emilio Boch claimed that the Court of Justice should decline to answer the questions referred to it. He stated that the judgment of the Corte d'Appello, Bologna, was final on the question whether there was a conflict between the court settlement and the claim that he had raised before the court and that it had upheld. The correctness of such a judgment which has the force of *res judicata* cannot be disputed in connection with an application for an order for enforcement under the Brussels Convention, since the third paragraph of Article 34 of the Convention provides that under no circumstances may the foreign judgment be reviewed as to its substance.

11. Mr Boch's view is based on a particular interpretation of the Convention, namely that the third paragraph of Article 34 excludes application of Article 27(3) when, in the judgment in respect of which enforcement is sought, a position has been taken on whether it is irreconcilable with a 'judgment between the same parties' given in the State of enforcement.

12. The Bundesgerichtshof did not refer questions to the Court of Justice concerning the meaning of the third paragraph of Article 34. It chose to pose the questions quoted above concerning the interpretation of Article 27(3). The Bundesgerichtshof found it appropriate to seek a ruling on those questions because if they are answered in the negative application of Article 27(3) is in any case precluded.

13. In my opinion it would not be right, in the present case, for the Court of Justice to state its view on the correctness of the interpretation contended for by Mr Boch of the third paragraph of Article 34 of the Convention. No question has been raised in that regard and, as mentioned, a reply in the negative to the question referred to the Court will mean that a decision on the meaning of the third paragraph of Article 34 is rendered unnecessary.

14. The Bundesgerichtshof posed the question concerning the interpretation of Article 27(3) because Solo Kleinmotoren relied on that provision as a bar to enforcement of the judgment for damages delivered in Italy.

15. Under Article 31 of the Convention 'a judgment given in a Contracting State and enforceable in that State shall be enforced in another Contracting State when, on the application of any interested party, the order for its enforcement has been issued there' and under the second paragraph of Article 34 'the application may be refused only for one of the reasons specified in Articles 27 and 28'.

16. The provisions which are relevant to a decision in this case are to be found in Title III on recognition and enforcement. The first provision in Title III is Article 25, which lays down: 'For the purposes of this Convention, "judgment"

means any judgment given by a court or tribunal of a Contracting State, whatever the judgment may be called, including a decree, order, decision or writ of execution, as well as the determination of costs or expenses by an officer of the court'.

17. It is clear that definition does not cover a court settlement.

18. Special rules on the enforcement of court settlements are laid down in Title IV on authentic instruments and court settlements. Article 51 provides: 'A settlement which has been approved by a court in the course of proceedings and is enforceable in the State in which it was concluded shall be enforceable in the State in which enforcement is sought under the same conditions as authentic instruments.' Article 50, which concerns authentic instruments, provides that such a document 'which has been formally drawn up or registered as an authentic instrument shall, in another Contracting State, have an order for its enforcement issued there, on application made in accordance with the procedures provided for in Article 31 *et seq.*' and that 'the application may be refused only if enforcement of the instrument is contrary to public policy in the State in which enforcement is sought'.

19. Whilst there is no doubt but that, in respect of judgments whose recognition is sought, Article 27(3) operates on the basis of the definition given in Article 25, doubt has been raised in the present case whether the definition in Article 25 also applies to the 'judgment' which is relied upon as a bar to recognition of the foreign judgment.

20. The Bundesgerichtshof states in this connection that the definition in Article 25 applies directly only to the judgment to be recognized and that it is questionable whether the concept of a 'judgment' as a bar to recognition under Article 27(3) 'corresponds exactly to the term set out in Article 25 of the Brussels Convention in view of the difference between their objects'.

21. The Bundesgerichtshof's assumption is, in my view, not sustainable. The definition in Article 25 applies, on its terms, generally to the term 'judgment' when it is used in the convention - 'For the purposes of this Convention'. Neither in the *travaux préparatoires* nor elsewhere in the Convention is there any suggestion that the definition should not apply to judgments which bar recognition.

22. The very formulation of Article 27(3) militates against a judgment which is a bar to recognition including a court settlement. The English version of the provision thus also uses the term 'judgment' in respect of a bar to recognition. All the language versions speak of a 'judgment' 'given' in the State in which recognition is sought. Article 51 of the Convention speaks of a court settlement being 'approved' by the court in the course of proceedings.

23. To accept that a judgment barring recognition under Article 27(3) could be a court settlement would therefore necessitate a construction of the provision which is not warranted by the wording and context of the provision.

24. Such a broad interpretation is not appropriate given that Article 27(3) contains a derogation from the objective of the Convention, which is to promote the recognition and enforcement of judgments in the Contracting States, and on its wording Article 27(3) affords judgments given in 'the State of enforcement'

a particularly privileged position, since they can be a bar to recognition if they are given either before or after the judgment whose recognition and enforcement is sought.

25. In addition, as mentioned in the order for reference and in many of the observations, acceptance of a court settlement as a bar to recognition gives rise to particular problems, including the problems prompting the second of the questions referred to the Court.

26. Accordingly there would have to be particularly strong and cogent grounds for interpreting Article 27(3) to the effect that a court settlement can also constitute a bar to recognition.

27. According to the *travaux préparatoires*, the reason for the provision is that 'the rule of law in a State would be disturbed if it were possible to take advantage of two conflicting judgments'. It may be maintained that the rule of law in the State of enforcement will also be disturbed if there is a conflict between a foreign judgment and a domestic settlement, but it can equally truly be maintained that the disturbance is more pronounced and noticeable if the conflict is between two judgments.

28. In my view there is no reason to enter into a discussion of the arguments for a broad interpretation of Article 27(3) with reference to the lis pendens rules in Article 21 of the Convention which are based on the premise, *per se* correct, that the provisions should be given a consistent interpretation. There is nothing, in my opinion, in that line of reasoning which significantly advances the cause of a broad interpretation of Article 27(3).

29. Solo Kleinmotoren contended that only by acceptance of a court settlement as a bar to recognition can the necessary equal treatment of the various means by which proceedings may be concluded in the Contracting States be achieved.

In amplification the company stated that proceedings in all the Contracting States can be terminated by common agreement of the parties. According to Solo Kleinmotoren that happens, however, in many Contracting States not by way of a 'court settlement' but by a 'consent judgment'. That is the case in Belgium, Luxembourg, Ireland and the United Kingdom. In the result the same process occurs in practice, with the name given to it and its minor details merely varying from State to State. If, in such a situation more weight were attached to the name than the content, judgments from the Contracting States would indeed ostensibly be treated in the same way. In substance, however, it would be treating differently the States which call the termination of proceedings brought about *inter alia* by the parties' themselves a court settlement.

30. That argument does not, in my view, carry enough persuasive weight for the interpretation suggested by the company. According to the information available there is no support for the contention that the two alternative ways of concluding disputes differ from each other merely on minor details. On the evidence there are currently no Contracting States whose legal systems accord the status of *res judicata* to court settlements, whereas 'consent judgments' can acquire that status. The Convention does not lay down any requirement that a judgment should have become *res judicata* before it can be recognized, subject

to the first paragraph of Article 30, but it is nevertheless a significant difference between the two means of terminating proceedings generally that the one cannot acquire the status of *res judicata* whilst the other will generally become *res judicata* at some point.

Furthermore, there is the point that a settlement will typically not be afforded all the guarantees of a judgment and the authority of the law does not lie behind a court settlement as it does in the case of a court judgment.

31. It does not therefore appear to me possible to interpret Article 27(3) to the effect that that provision, despite its wording, includes a court settlement as a bar to recognition. If there should appear in practice to be a need for it to do so, the provision can be amended so as to achieve such a result.

32. As is also mentioned in the order for reference, it should not be overlooked in this connection that Article 27(1) contains a rule which can be applied in order to refuse to recognize and enforce foreign judgments, that is to say when recognition 'is contrary to public policy' in the State in which enforcement is sought, and if necessary that provision could be applied in a case where the circumstances are quite out of the ordinary.

33. As a consequence of the suggested interpretation of Article 27(3), there is no reason to reply to the second question referred to the Court.

Conclusion

34. On the basis of the foregoing, I would suggest that the Court answer the first question referred to it as follows: 'An enforceable settlement reached by the same parties before a court in the State in which recognition is sought to settle legal proceedings which are in progress does not constitute a judgment which, under Article 27(3) of the Brussels Convention, can preclude recognition of a foreign judgment'.

TITLE III *[Chapter III]*

Recognition and Enforcement
[Recognition and Enforcement]

Recognition – Articles 26 - 30 *[Articles 33 - 37]*

See also

Case 43/77 - 22 November 1977

Industrial Diamond Supplies v Luigi Riva

Recognition or grant of an order for enforcement in one Contracting State of a judgment given in another Contracting State - Stay of the proceedings for recognition or enforcement - Appeal lodged in the State in which the judgment was given against the foreign judgment - Concept of 'ordinary appeal' within the meaning of Articles 30 and 38 of the Convention - Differences in the legal concepts of the various Contracting States with regard to the distinction between 'ordinary' and 'extraordinary' appeals - Definition of the concept of 'ordinary appeal' solely within the framework of the Convention - Meaning.

Summary

1. Because of the differences in the legal concepts of the Member States which are parties to the Convention of 27 September 1968 with regard to the distinction between 'ordinary' and 'extraordinary' appeals, the meaning of the concept of 'ordinary appeal' cannot be determined by reference to a national legal system, whether that of the State in which the judgment was given or that of the State in which recognition or enforcement is sought. This concept may therefore be defined solely within the framework of the Convention itself.

2. In view of the structure of Articles 30 and 38 and of their function in the system of the Convention, any appeal which is such that it may result in the annulment or the amendment of the judgment which is the subject-matter of the procedure for recognition or enforcement under the Convention and the lodging of which is bound, in the State in which judgment was given, to a period which is laid down by the law and starts

to run by virtue of that same judgment constitutes an 'ordinary appeal' which has been lodged or may be lodged against a foreign judgment.

JUDGMENT OF THE COURT

Kutscher, President, Sorensen, Bosco, Presidents of Chambers, Donner, Mertens de Wilmars, Pescatore, Lord Mackenzie Stuart, O'Keeffe and Touffait, Judges

1. By judgment of 7 April 1977, which was received at the Court on 18 April 1977, the Rechtbank van Eerste Aanleg (Court of First Instance), Antwerp, referred to the Court of Justice under Articles 2(3) and 3(2) of the Protocol of 3 June 1971 two questions on the interpretation of the expression 'ordinary appeal' used in Articles 30 and 38 of the Convention of 27 September 1968 on Jurisdiction and the Enforcement of Judgments in Civil and Commercial Matters (hereinafter referred to as 'the Convention').

2. The file shows that Industrial Diamond Supplies, the plaintiff in the main action, having its registered office in Antwerp, was ordered by the Tribunale Civile e Penale (Civil and Criminal Court), Turin, to pay to Luigi Riva, the defendant in the main action, a commercial representative residing in Turin, the sum of Lit 53 052 980, as commission owed by the plaintiff to the defendant in the context of a contractual relationship between the parties, together with interest and legal costs.

3. The judgment, which was given on 23 September 1976 by the Turin Court on appeal from a decision of the Pretore of the same city, is at present enforceable.

4. On 25 November 1976 Mr Riva obtained from the Antwerp court a judgment authorizing the enforcement in Belgium of the judgment of the Turin court, in accordance with the provisions of Article 31 *et seq.* of the Convention.

5. On 15 December 1976, Industrial Diamond Supplies lodged an appeal against the order for enforcement before the Antwerp court under Articles 36 and 37 of the Convention.

6. On 27 December 1976 Industrial Diamond Supplies lodged an appeal in cassation before the Italian Corte Suprema di Cassazione

(supreme court of appeal) against the judgment given on appeal by the Turin court.

7. It is not in dispute that that appeal does not have the effect of suspending the enforceability of the judgment given by the Turin court.

8. It is also established that Industrial Diamond Supplies has not sought a stay of execution in Italy.

9. Industrial Diamond Supplies requested the Antwerp court principally to suspend the proceedings relating to the enforcement of the judgment given by the Turin court until final judgment has been delivered between the parties in Italy.

10. So as to be able to reach a decision on that request, the Antwerp court submitted to the Court of Justice the following two questions on the interpretation of Articles 30 and 38 of the Convention:

1. What appeals are regarded as 'ordinary' appeals in Articles 30 and 38 of the Convention of 27 September 1968 or, in other words, to what judgments are Articles 30 and 38 of the Convention applicable? or

2. Is the nature of the appeal lodged against the judgment in the State in which that judgment was given to be determined solely in accordance with the law of that State?

11. These questions ask in substance whether the expression 'ordinary appeal' used in Articles 30 and 38 of the Convention must be understood as a reference to national law or as an independent concept, the interpretation of which must be sought within the Convention itself.

12. In the second case, the questions submitted by the court ask what the meaning of that expression is within the context of the Convention.

13. During the procedure the view was expressed that Article 30 of the Convention, which relates to the recognition and not the enforcement of judgments, is not relevant to the proceedings and that the interpretation requested concerns only the meaning of the expression 'ordinary appeal' within the context of Article 38, which relates to enforcement.

14. There is no need to examine this question, especially since the connexity of the provisions of Title III of the Convention make it necessary to interpret the expression in question in the two above mentioned articles in the same way.

The nature of the expression 'ordinary appeal' as a reference to national law or as an independent concept

15. Under Article 30 of the Convention, 'A court of a Contracting State in which recognition is sought of a judgment given in another Contracting State may stay the proceedings if an ordinary appeal against the judgment has been lodged'.

16. Under the first paragraph of Article 38, 'The court with which the appeal under the first paragraph of Article 37 is lodged may, on the application of the appellant, stay the proceedings if an ordinary appeal has been lodged against the judgment in the State in which that judgment was given or if the time for such an appeal has not yet expired; in the latter case, the Court may specify the time within which such an appeal is to be lodged'.

17. According to Industrial Diamond Supplies, it is necessary to classify any appeal considered to be an ordinary appeal in the Contracting State in which the judgment the recognition or enforcement of which is sought was given as an 'ordinary appeal' within the meaning of the above mentioned provisions.

18. Under the law of the Italian Republic, the State in which the judgment in question was given, there is no doubt that an appeal in cassation (*ricorso per cassazione*) must, in fact, be considered as an ordinary appeal.

19. This view has been supported by the Government of the United Kingdom and by the Commission, which both agree that the nature of an appeal for the purposes of Articles 30 and 38 must be determined by reference to the national law of the Contracting State in which the original judgment was given.

20. Mr Riva, without contesting the fact that in Italy an appeal in cassation is considered to be an ordinary appeal, takes the view that in any case a judgment which is enforceable in Italy must also be considered as enforceable in Belgium so long as the enforceability of that judgment has not been suspended in the State in which the judgment was given.

21. Finally, it is necessary to note that the Government of the Federal Republic of Germany expressed the opinion that the expression 'ordinary appeal' used in Articles 30 and 38 must be interpreted within the context

of the Convention itself, regardless of the classification of appeals by the national law of the State in which the judgment was given.

22. It follows from a comparison of the legal concepts of the various Member States of the Community that although in some States the distinction between 'ordinary' and 'extraordinary' appeals is based on the law itself, in other legal systems the classification is made primarily or even purely in the works of learned authors while in a third group of States this distinction is completely unknown.

23. It is established, moreover, that in the legal systems in which the distinction between 'ordinary' and 'extraordinary' appeals is acknowledged by legislation or by learned authors, the classification of the various appeals for the purposes of that distinction gives rise to varying classifications.

24. It seems, therefore, that if the concept of 'ordinary appeal' were interpreted by reference to a national legal system, whether the legal system of the State in which the judgment was given or that of the State in which enforcement or recognition is sought, it would in certain cases be impossible to classify a specific appeal with the required degree of certainty for the purposes of Articles 30 and 38 of the Convention.

25. Moreover, reference to a particular national legal system might perhaps oblige the Court required to make a decision under Articles 30 and 38 of the Convention to classify appeals of the same type inconsistently according to whether they belonged to the legal system of one or other of the Contracting States.

26. The effect of the application of that criterion of interpretation would therefore be to create even greater legal uncertainty since Article 38 requires the Court before which an order for enforcement of the judgment is sought to take into consideration not only appeals which have been lodged at present but in addition appeals which may be lodged within specific periods.

27. It follows from these considerations that the interpretation of the concept of 'ordinary appeal' may only be usefully sought within the framework of the Convention itself.

28. It is, therefore, necessary to reply to the national court that the expression ordinary appeal' within the meaning of Articles 30 and 38 of

the Convention must be determined solely within the framework of the system of the Convention itself and not according to the law either of the State in which the judgment was given or of the State in which the recognition or enforcement of that judgment is sought.

The meaning of the expression 'ordinary appeal' within the framework of the Convention

29. The meaning of the expression 'ordinary appeal' may be deduced from the actual structure of Articles 30 and 38 and from their function in the system of the Convention.

30. Although, as a whole, the Convention is intended to ensure the rapid enforcement of judgments with a minimum of formalities when those judgments are enforceable in the State in which they were given, the specific purpose of Articles 30 and 38 is to prevent the compulsory recognition or enforcement of judgments in other Contracting States when the possibility that they might be annulled or amended in the State in which they were given still exists.

31. For this purpose Articles 30 and 38 reserve to the court before which a request for recognition or an appeal against a decision authorizing enforcement has been brought in particular the possibility of staying the proceedings where, in the State in which the judgment was given, the judgment is being contested or may be contested within specific periods.

32. According to the Convention, the Court before which recognition or enforcement is sought is not under a duty to stay the proceedings but merely has the power to do so.

33. This fact presupposes a sufficiently broad interpretation of the concept of 'ordinary appeal' to enable that court to stay the proceedings whenever reasonable doubt arises with regard to the fate of the decision in the State in which it was given.

34. It is possible by applying this criterion alone to decide the outcome of a request for recognition or enforcement based on a judgment which, in the State in which the judgment was given, is at present the subject of an appeal which may lead to the annulment or amendment of the judgment in question.

35. A court may be required to make a more difficult appraisal whenever

a request for a stay of the proceedings is lodged before it under Article 38 of the Convention when the periods for lodging appeals have not yet expired in the State in which the judgment was given.

36. In that case, it is also necessary to bear in mind, in addition to the criterion based on the possible effect of an appeal, all the relevant considerations arising from the nature and conditions for the application of the judicial remedies in question.

37. Considered from this point of view, the expression 'ordinary appeal' must be understood as meaning any appeal which forms part of the normal course of an action and which, as such, constitutes a procedural development which any party must reasonably expect.

38. It is necessary to consider that any appeal bound by the law to a specific period of time which starts to run by virtue of the actual decision whose enforcement is sought constitutes such a development.

39. Consequently, it is impossible to consider as 'ordinary appeals' within the meaning of Articles 30 and 38 of the Convention in particular appeals which are dependent either upon events which were unforeseeable at the date of the original judgment or upon the action taken by persons who are extraneous to the case, and who are not bound by the period for entering an appeal which starts to run from the date of the original judgment.

40. It is for a court before which a request is submitted under Article 36 at a date on which the period for entering an appeal in the State in which the judgment was given has not yet expired to exercise its discretion in this respect.

41. This freedom of discretion is implicit in the actual system of Article 38 which gives the court before which an order for enforcement is sought the power to specify with regard to a party which is opposed to enforcement, although it has not yet taken advantage of the possibility of lodging an appeal in the State in which the judgment was given, a time within which its appeal is to be lodged.

42. It is, therefore, necessary to reply that, within the meaning of Articles 30 and 38 of the Convention, any appeal which is such that it may result in the annulment or the amendment of the judgment which is the subject-matter of the procedure for recognition or enforcement

according to the Convention and the lodging of which is bound, in the State in which the judgment was given, to a period which is laid down by the law and starts to run by virtue of that same judgment constitutes an 'ordinary appeal' which has been lodged or may be lodged against a foreign judgment.

On those grounds, the court, in answer to the questions referred to it by the Rechtbank van Eerste Aanleg of the judicial district of Antwerp by judgment of 7 April 1977, hereby rules:

1. The expression 'ordinary appeal' within the meaning of Articles 30 and 38 of the Convention of 27 September 1968 on Jurisdiction and the Enforcement of Judgments in Civil and Commercial Matters must be defined solely within the framework of the system of the Convention itself and not according to the law either of the State in which the judgment was given or of the State in which recognition of enforcement of that judgment is sought.

2. Within the meaning of Articles 30 and 38 of the Convention, any appeal which is such that it may result in the annulment or the amendment of the judgment which is the subject-matter of the procedure for recognition or enforcement under the Convention and the lodging of which is bound, in the State in which the judgment was given, to a period which is laid down by the law and starts to run by virtue of that same judgment constitutes an 'ordinary appeal' which has been lodged or may be lodged against a foreign judgment.

OPINION OF MR ADVOCATE GENERAL REISCHL

The defendant in the proceedings which have given rise to the reference for a preliminary ruling which I must discuss today, an Italian commercial representative, obtained on 23 September 1976 from the Tribunale Civile e Penale (Civil and Criminal Court), Turin, a judgment ordering the plaintiff in the main action, a Belgian limited liability company, to pay a certain sum. On 27 December 1976 a *Kassationsbeschwerde* (appeal in cassation) was lodged against that judgment before the Corte Suprema di Cassazione (Supreme Court of Appeal) in Rome; under Italian law such an appeal does not suspend the execution of the contested judgment. Apparently no recourse was had to the possibility of applying to the Italian court which delivered the contested judgment for a stay of execution.

The defendant in the main action wishes to enforce in Belgium the judgment of the Tribunale Civile e Penale, Turin. For this purpose he obtained from the Rechtbank van Eerste Aanleg (Court of First Instance) in Antwerp an order for its enforcement in accordance with Article 31 of the Convention on Jurisdiction and the Enforcement of Judgments in Civil and Commercial Matters (hereinafter referred to as 'the Convention on Jurisdiction').

The plaintiff in the main action appealed against this decision, which was made on 25 November 1976, in accordance with Article 36 of the Convention on Jurisdiction. At the same time it requested a stay of the proceedings concerning the order for enforcement until a final judgment had been delivered in Italy or at least that the enforcement should be made conditional on the provision of security by the defendant. It based these requests on Article 38 of the Convention on Jurisdiction which provides that:

'The Court with which the appeal under the first paragraph of Article 37 is lodged may, on the application of the appellant, stay the proceedings if an ordinary appeal has been lodged against the judgment in the State in which that judgment was given or if the time for such an appeal has not yet expired; in the latter case, the Court may specify the time within which such an appeal is to be lodged. The Court may also make enforcement conditional on the provision of such security as it shall determine'.

The plaintiff takes the view that for the purpose of the appraisal of the question whether there has been an ordinary appeal the law of the State in which that judgment was given is important. In accordance with that law, in this case Italian law, an appeal in cassation is, however, considered as an ordinary appeal, in contrast to Belgian law, because it prevents the decision from having the force of *res judicata.*

The judgment creditor objects that the application of Article 38 of the Convention on Jurisdiction does not come into consideration because an appeal in cassation does not preclude enforcement under either Italian or Belgian law.

The decision on the application for a stay of the proceedings therefore depends on the question whether the appeal in cassation lodged in Italy is an ordinary appeal within the meaning of the Convention on Jurisdiction. Since the Convention is not in the view of the Belgian Court completely clear in this respect, it stayed the proceedings by judgment of 7 April 1977 and referred to the Court the following questions for a preliminary ruling under the Protocol of 3 June 1971 issued under the Convention on Jurisdiction:

1. What appeals are regarded as 'ordinary' appeals in Articles 30 and 38 of the Convention of 27 September 1968, or, in other words, to what judgments are Articles 30 and 38 of the Convention applicable? or

2. Is the nature of the appeal lodged against the judgment in the State in which that judgment was given to be determined solely in accordance with the law of that State?

I - I shall begin my opinion with two short observations.

1. The questions obviously go further than is necessary for the purposes

of the main action. They not only mention Article 38 of the Convention on Jurisdiction but also Article 30 thereof which relates to the recognition of a decision given in another Contracting State. In addition, the first part of the first question mentions appeals quite generally while only the second part of the question confines itself to judgments. Thus the problem arises whether I should simply adhere to the questions or whether I should restrict myself according to the known facts.

My opinion is that I should take the latter course and restrict my examination to appeals which can be lodged against judgments. The problem is already complex enough as it is. In addition, some of the problems relating to other judicial decisions are different so that, with regard to the present case, there is little to be gained from consideration of them. In this respect I shall merely recall the observation made by the Government of the Federal Republic of Germany that other judicial decisions are of lesser importance, normally serve other purposes and in addition often do not formally acquire the force of *res judicata.*

I should also confine myself in principle to the interpretation of Article 38, which relates to proceedings for enforcement. This does not, however, prevent Article 30 of the Convention on Jurisdiction, which relates to the recognition of foreign judgments and also uses the expression 'ordinary appeal', from being included in the examination too insofar as it is necessary to discuss an argument which the Commission has based upon it.

2. According to the wording of the questions chosen by the Court making the reference there are two possibilities of interpretation: the concept of 'ordinary appeal' may be an independent concept used in the Convention on Jurisdiction, or else the law of the State in which the judgment was given may be determinative in this respect. A third possibility was mentioned by the Government of the Federal Republic of Germany: the law of the State in which enforcement is sought might also be decisive with regard to the classification.

I consider, and I may say that from the beginning, that this third possibility should not be seriously taken into consideration. In fact, quite apart from other arguments which it will be necessary to examine later in connexion with the other possibilities an important objection to the feasibility of deciding according to the law of the State in which enforcement is sought immediately arises. Appeals obviously take different forms in the legal systems of the Member States. Thus, in many cases, in particular in the case of atypical appeals, consideration of the law of the State in which enforcement is sought would not enable an unequivocal statement to be made, but only the statement that a specific foreign appeal may more or less be equated with a specific national appeal. Such a classification would therefore not be clearcut. It would involve too much uncertainty and cannot therefore be seriously taken into consideration for the purposes of the interpretation of a convention in the application of which the principle of legal certainty ranks highly.

II - Turning next directly to the questions submitted by the court making the reference, there is on the one hand the view, and I shall confine myself to the arguments which were substantiated in detail in the proceedings for a preliminary ruling, that the important factor is the law of the State in which the judgment was given. This view is taken by the Government of the United Kingdom and, albeit with little force, by the Commission. On the other hand, the Government of the Federal Republic of Germany has declared itself in favour of the assumption that there is a common independent concept of 'ordinary appeal' in the Convention on Jurisdiction.

1. In the appraisal of this dispute I should like to discuss first an argument which tells strongly in favour of the first solution, classification according to the law of the State in which the judgment was given. It is based on the draft Convention by means of which the three new Member States are to accede to the Convention on Jurisdiction. In view of the fact that in the law of the United Kingdom and in Irish law there is a variety of appeals, that no distinction is made between them, even by learned authors, according to whether they are ordinary or extraordinary appeals, and that it is difficult to determine criteria for a distinction, that draft provides that a paragraph shall be added to Article 38, according to which if a decision has been given in Ireland or in the United Kingdom any appeal provided for in the original State must be considered as an ordinary appeal for the purpose of the application of the first paragraph of Article 38.

In addition, it was claimed that if the Convention is really based upon an independent concept of 'ordinary appeal' it must have been possible to apply the criteria applicable thereto also to the appeals known in the United Kingdom and in Ireland and to designate accordingly those which must be considered as ordinary or extraordinary. The fact that no attempt was made to do so tells against the assumption that there is an independent concept with specific criteria contained in the Convention. In addition it must seem strange that all appeals existing in the United Kingdom and in Ireland must be classified as ordinary. There are no doubt also those which correspond to extraordinary appeals in other Member States. Since nevertheless the abovementioned provision of the draft Convention has been decided upon, the assumption that the Convention on Jurisdiction contains an independent concept of ordinary appeal leads to the conclusion that exceptions have been permitted for two Member States. This must, however, appear incomprehensible.

I make no secret of the fact that this argument made a considerable impression on me. However, it does not seem to be completely conclusive. For example, it is simply impossible to overlook the fact that until now this is merely a draft; the proposed provision has not yet become binding. In addition, it is certainly conceivable that if the Court of Justice reaches the view that the Convention contains an independent concept of 'ordinary appeal' in respect of which specific criteria apply, an attempt will also be made to classify English and Irish law accordingly. I am therefore of the opinion that I can safely leave aside the argument based on the above mentioned draft convention.

2. An appraisal of the remaining considerations which have been put forward for and against a Community concept of 'ordinary appeal' reveals, and

I must say this immediately, more important reasons in favour of such a concept than reasons in favour of classification according to the law of the State in which the judgment was given.

(a) The Commission has itself referred to several advantages of a common concept:

(aa) An appeal in Cassation is regarded as an ordinary appeal in Italy and in the Netherlands but not in French, Belgian and Luxembourg law. If the law of the State in which the judgment was given were decisive for the purposes of Article 38 of the Convention on Jurisdiction the Convention would be applied in various different ways, whilst if it were accepted that there is an independent concept under Community law uniform legal effects would arise. This is an important aspect with regard to a multilateral Convention which, as the Government of the Federal Republic has correctly pointed out, represents a step towards the approximation of international procedural law. Since the Convention, as the Jenard Report shows, is intended to be as progressive as possible and therefore to be a contrast to the previous conventions on enforcement and since it aims, moreover, at uniform rules on jurisdiction and uniform proceedings for enforcement, this principle of uniform application must certainly take precedence over the fact that in many bilateral Conventions such as the Convention between Germany and Greece of 4 November 1961 (see Kerameus 'In Multitudo Legum lus Unum', in Honour of Wilhelm Wengler on the Occasion of his Sixty-Fifth Birthday, Volume 2, p. 383 *et seq.*) reference is made to the law of the State in which judgment was given in deciding what must be considered as an ordinary appeal.

(bb) It is, moreover, certain that *Revision* (second appeal or accelerated appeal on a point of law) and an appeal in cassation result if successful in the quashing of the contested judgment. It must therefore seem undesirable that there should be no stay of proceedings under Article 38 of the Convention on Jurisdiction if such an appeal is lodged. This would, however, be the result in some cases if the classification made by the State in which the judgment was given were considered as decisive.

(cc) The third consideration put forward by the Commission relates to the duty laid down in the Protocol to the Convention on Jurisdiction for the highest courts to refer questions of interpretation to the Court of Justice of the European Communities for a preliminary ruling. If the law of the State in which the judgment was given were decisive, with the result that it would be necessary, in accordance with that law, to regard a certain appeal as extraordinary, it would be possible to enforce the judgment and the duty to refer the matter to the Court of Justice for a preliminary ruling, which is an essential guarantee as far as the Convention is concerned, could not be put into practice.

(b) In addition to these considerations, there is an important argument which the Government of the Federal Republic has put forward. That Government refers to the fact that the Convention on Jurisdiction does not provide for any claim for damages in the event of the unjustified enforcement of a judgment. Article 38, therefore, performs the important function of protecting the judgment debtor from serious and possibly irreparable damage. This protection would, as the Commission has already stressed, be rather unequal if the necessary classification were to be made according to the law of the State in which the judgment was given. It might, however, also be inadequate, in as much as national rules on claims for damages in the law on the enforcement of judgments generally take into consideration only the field of interest of domestic cases. It is, therefore, impossible to refer to those rules in order to claim that there is no objection to the exclusion of a stay of execution under Article 38 because national claims for damages exist.

(c) Finally, it must be borne in mind in this connexion that a strong argument may be based upon the previous relevant case-law, that is, from the judgment in Case 29/76 (*LTU Lufttransportunternehment GmbH* v *Eurocontrol*, judgment of 14 October 1976, [1976] ECR 1541). As the Court will remember, that case concerned the meaning of the expression 'civil and commercial matters' contained in Article 1 of the Convention. The Court of Justice, contrary to my view that the important factor was the classification by the courts of the State in which the judgment was given - a view in support of which I still believe that good reasons may be put forward - found it necessary to assume that there was an independent concept contained in the Convention. The principal reason given for this was that it is necessary to ensure 'that the rights and obligations which derive from it for the Contracting States and the persons to whom it applies are equal and uniform'. This principle, which may likewise be deduced from the Jenard Report mentioned above, is certainly also important in respect of the law on the enforcement of judgments.

(d) Conversely, two other arguments which were used in support of the argument that the determinative factor is the law of the State in which the judgment was given can hardly be decisive.

(aa) The first referred to the important aspect of legal clarity and legal certainty in respect of the Convention, which must be applied promptly. Account would best be taken of this aspect if the law of the State in which the judgment was given were decisive with regard to the distinction between ordinary and extraordinary appeals. In all except the British and Irish legal systems this distinction has, in fact, been clearly made either in legislation, in academic studies or in special international conventions. Thus, no conceptual difficulties would arise for the court before which the enforcement of the judgment is sought if it simply adhered to that distinction.

In my opinion this is only apparently convincing. Thus, doubt may arise as to whether the very distinction between ordinary and extraordinary appeals under national law is actually so clear, straightforward and comprehensive as portrayed by the representative of the British Government. On the other hand reference may nevertheless be made to the so-called Schlosser Report which was drawn up with a view to the accession of the three new Member States to the Convention on Jurisdiction. Moreover, and this seems even more important, comparable certainty is possible even if an independent concept is accepted. It is only necessary to ensure that the criteria for that concept are laid down as clearly and simply as possible. If this happens, and an opportunity for this exists in the present proceedings, no inordinate difficulties can arise for the court before which the enforcement of the judgment is sought in determining whether an appeal must be considered as ordinary or extraordinary within the meaning of Community law.

(bb) The Commission deduced a second counter-argument from Article 30 of the Convention on Jurisdiction which, as I have already said, refers to the recognition of judgments and likewise uses the expression 'ordinary appeal'. The Commission, starting from the correct assumption that the expression used in Article 30 must have the same meaning as it has in Article 38, considers that there is a potential danger here if the argument in favour of an independent concept is accepted, in that accordingly in certain cases a stay of proceedings and thus prevention of recognition of a judgment might be precluded because of the classification of an appeal as an ordinary appeal, although in the State in which the judgment was given the judgment has not yet become effective because in that State the appeal is classified differently. This is incompatible with the objective of the Convention which is, so to speak, to make the effects of national judgments uniform within the Community which would exclude the possibility of the effects of the judgment being more extensive in the State in which recognition or enforcement of the judgment was sought than in the State in which the judgment was given.

This argument may, however, easily be countered. The supposed danger may be avoided immediately if the choice is made in favour of a broad interpretation of the concept of 'ordinary appeal' which covers everything which comes within this concept in the Member States. Such a solution seems perfectly possible and is, indeed, compulsory for other reasons too, which I shall have to examine later.

III - Consequently, since the examination has hitherto shown that there are important reasons for assuming the use of an independent concept of 'ordinary appeal' in the Convention on Jurisdiction, the task of establishing the criteria which are decisive with regard to the common concept still remains. This is certainly not easy since the Convention provides but few indications in this respect. If, however, these indications are evaluated and the objectives and structure of the Convention and the general principles which stem from the corpus of the national legal systems are taken into consideration, as stated in the above mentioned judgment in Case 29/76, sufficiently practicable statements may be made.

(a) It is necessary in this connexion to start by returning to a point which has already been mentioned, that is, the need to choose a wide interpretation of the concept in question.

It is true that it would be possible to state in opposition to this and in favour of a narrow interpretation that the objective of the Convention is to ensure the recognition and enforcement of foreign judgments on a broad scale, which seems to tell against making a stay of proceedings easier to obtain.

Other considerations however must take precedence.

I have already mentioned, and in this connexion reference should he made to the Jenard Report and to Droz (*Compétence Judiciaire et Effets des Jugements dans le Marché Commun*, (Jurisdiction and Effect of Judgments in the Common Market) p. 280), that the Convention concerns, so to speak, converting a national legal situation into a Community one; if a judgment is recognized it should have the effect in the State in which enforcement is sought which it also has in the State in which the judgment was given. A restrictive interpretation of the concept of 'ordinary appeal' would not meet that requirement; the danger would rather exist in this case that a judgment would be recognized abroad although a right has not arisen in the State in which the judgment was given because according to the view taken in that State an ordinary appeal has been lodged.

In addition, the fact that where ordinary appeals exist it is not compulsory to stay the proceedings but that this is at the discretion of the court before which enforcement is sought tells in favour of a broad interpretation. In this way it will be possible to avoid consequences which might arise in the case of a wide interpretation but which are considered undesirable. On the other hand, if a restrictive interpretation were adopted it is certain that in many cases the protective aim of the provision, and I recall once again that the Convention does not provide for any claims for damages in the event of unjustified enforcement of the judgment would not be fully attained.

Finally, it is also necessary in this connexion to come back once more to the draft which has been drawn up for the accession of the three new Member States to the Convention on Jurisdiction. As I have already mentioned, it was deemed appropriate to include therein a provision according to which in view of the difficulties of delimitation which exist in the United Kingdom and in Ireland all appeals in those States are considered to be ordinary appeals. This, as shown by the Schlosser Report, is considered justifiable because the discretion given to the courts under Article 38 may be so exercised that equilibrium may be achieved in the application of Articles 30 and 38 in all the Contracting States. However, if this is so it is necessary in the interests of this equilibrium also to interpret liberally provisions of the Convention which are already applicable.

(b) After this finding it is almost as easy to see in addition which criteria would be inappropriate in the present connexion. I must mention three criteria at this point which were also discussed extensively during the proceedings.

(aa) The question whether the enforcement of a judgment is suspended by an appeal should be disregarded. In any case, a judgment may only be enforced in another State if there is an enforceable right in the State in which the judgment was given. Article 38 is also based on this presupposition, which may be deduced from Article 31 of the Convention. Article 38 and the discretion which it confers on the court before which enforcement is sought would, therefore, be purposeless if only those appeals which suspend enforcement were to be considered as ordinary appeals.

It may also be said in this connexion that it is, likewise, impossible to make the question whether the lodging of an appeal might possibly lead to the suspension of the enforcement by the court the decisive factor. A decision of the court in the State in which the judgment was given on the suspension of execution is, in fact, provided for not only in the case of appeals which, like *Berufung*, must clearly be regarded as ordinary; it also occurs frequently in the case of extraordinary appeals, as the representative of the British Government stressed. Such a criterion would, therefore, certainly extend too far the bounds applicable to Article 38.

(bb) Further, it does not seem to me to be appropriate to make the question of *res judicata* the decisive factor, in other words whether the lodging of an appeal prevents the decision from having the force of *res judicata*. If the question of *res judicata* is made the decisive factor, one indefinite concept is replaced by another. In fact the concept of *res judicata* in the Member States does not actually seem to be uniform. In addition, in several Member States it is linked precisely to the concept of ordinary appeal; in those States a judgment is said to have the force of *res judicata* if no ordinary appeal is possible or if the periods for lodging an ordinary appeal have expired (for example in Belgian and in Netherlands law). The use of the criterion of *res judicata* would therefore be incompatible with the basic concern previously stated, that it is necessary for the definition of the concept of 'ordinary appeal' to be based, in the interests of legal certainty and legal uniformity, on criteria which are not only simple but also clear.

(cc) Finally, the question whether or not when certain appeals are lodged restrictions apply with regard to the reasons upon which the appeal is based, that is, the permissible 'moyens' (submissions), should also be disregarded. Otherwise, both an appeal in cassation in the Netherlands and in Italy and *Revision* in German law would have to be considered as extraordinary appeals. I have, however, already pointed out that in their case it is undesirable to exclude the possibility of staying the proceedings because they may lead to the annulment of a judgment.

(c) If we consider what criteria may positively come into consideration it appears quite quickly that there are really not many of them, in fact two or, at most, three. According to the meaning and purpose of the provision they should, however, also be sufficient and ensure a relatively easy application.

(aa) An important indication seems to me to be the fact that Article 38 itself speaks of the *time* for an appeal. It is necessary to conclude from this that periods of time must apply to the lodging of ordinary appeals and in principle, periods of time which begin to run with delivery or service of the judgment.

It is necessary, however, to go a step further and declare, as does the Government of the Federal Republic of Germany, that relatively short periods of time must be involved. It is impossible to object to this, as we attempted, that Article 38 thereby *loses its* raison d'être, for periods of about three months, which may come in question in this connexion, are nevertheless long enough to show the importance of the question whether there should be a suspension of enforcement or not. Conversely, it is possible to refer, with regard to the requirement of relatively short periods of time, to the fact that the Convention that, therefore, the suspension of enforcement must not be too protracted. Thus very short periods of time apply *Berufung* and *Widerspruch* in the case of default judgment which are generally considered as ordinary appeal. If I am correct, they are between two weeks and three months long, with the exception of Luxembourg law in which in the case of default judgments given against parties who are not legally represented the period for the lodging of a *Berufung*, three months, must apparently be added to a possible period for the lodging of a *Widerspruch*, up to six months.

It is likewise possible to determine what periods of time come into consideration in the case of an appeal in cassation, which is, the Court is aware, involved in the main action, with the aid of an examination of comparative law. In this connexion it appears that the periods of time which come into consideration here under the legal systems of the Member States are generally of between one month and three months from service or delivery of the judgment. Only in Italy, if I am correct, does the period of one year from 'pubblicazione della sentenza' (notification of the judgment) apply, and this, moreover, also in the case of a *Berufung*, if notice of the judgment is not served. This must, however, also be included in view of the above mentioned requirement that the concept of 'ordinary appeal' must be interpreted so that it covers everything which is classified as such under the national legal system.

Moreover, it becomes clear at the same time with these observations on the need to observe relatively short periods of time that appeals which amount to the re-opening of the proceedings cannot come into consideration. In fact, in such cases the relevant periods of time generally start to run from the moment at which the reason for the re-opening of the case becomes known and accordingly they do not preclude review of a judgment even after a considerable time. In addition, it is also important in this connexion that in the legal systems of the Member States such appeals are unanimously designated as extraordinary.

(bb) The question whether an appeal can have direct effects on the rights and duties of the parties which are concerned in the contested judgment should constitute a second important criterion. Accordingly, an ordinary appeal is involved only if the writ of execution may be amended when the appeal has been heard and it might thus happen that the judgment which has nevertheless been enforced was unjustified. In fact, only in such cases is there a need to protect the judgment debtor. *Cassation dans l'intérêt de la loi* (appeal in cassation in the interests of the law) under French law could, if the basic objective laid down in Article 38 were taken into consideration, therefore certainly not be held to be an ordinary appeal.

(cc) Finally, and this consideration may, however, be left open for the purposes of the dispute in the main action, it is still possible to consider attaching importance to the question whether an appeal brings the case before a court of the same level of jurisdiction and if it is, therefore, possible to speak of the continuation of the same proceedings but not of the start of fresh proceedings. This consideration, which was also put forward by the Government of the Federal Republic of Germany, obviously has in view appeals such as a complaint of unconstitutionality which may also be brought against judgments. It is, in fact, possible to consider attributing significance to it because in this connexion possibilities are involved which are only available in two Member States and which can certainly not be counted as ordinary appeals even in those States.

For similar reasons, and this must likewise merely be briefly touched upon, it would also be necessary to exclude appeals in which, as in the case of

Drittwiderspruchsklagen (objections raised by third parties) the interests of third parties are involved. Quite apart from the fact that in such cases too there are frequently no time-limits or very lengthy ones, a decisive factor with regard to this appraisal is that such appeals, where they exist, are likewise unanimously classified as extraordinary.

There can be very little more to say from the point of view of Community law with regard to the criteria for determining whether ordinary or extraordinary appeals are involved, within the meaning of the Convention.

IV - I therefore conclude that the following reply should be given to the questions referred for a preliminary ruling:

(a) The concept of 'ordinary appeal' within the meaning of Article 38 of the Convention on Jurisdiction is not determined according to the law of the State in which the judgment was given or according to the law of the State in which enforcement is sought but must be regarded as an independent concept of Community law.

(b) Ordinary appeals against judgment within the meaning of Article 38 of the Convention on Jurisdiction are those which must be lodged within relatively short periods of time after delivery or service of the judgment and which may lead to the annulment or amendment of the judgment with effect for parties to the proceedings for enforcement.

Case 125/79 - 21 May 1980

Bernard Denilauler
v
S.n.c. Couchet Frères

Provisions of Title II (Jurisdiction) and Title III (Recognition and Enforcement) of the Convention - Observance of rights of the defence - Consequences - Decisions with which the Convention is concerned - Decisions capable of being the subject of an inquiry in adversary proceedings in the State of origin - Recognition and enforcement of judgments - Decisions authorising provisional or protective measures - Exclusion from the procedure provided for by Title III - Conditions.

Summary

1. All the provisions of the Convention, both those contained in Title II on jurisdiction and those contained in Title III on recognition and enforcement, express the intention to ensure that, within the scope of the objectives of the Convention, proceedings leading to the delivery of judicial decisions take place in such a way that the rights of the defence are observed. It is because of the guarantees given to the defendant in the original proceedings that the Convention, in Title III, is very liberal in regard to recognition and enforcement. In the light of these considerations it is clear that the Convention is fundamentally concerned with judicial decisions which,before the recognition and enforcement of them are sought in a State other than the State of origin, have been, or have been capable of being, the subject in that State of origin and under various procedures, of an inquiry in adversary proceedings.

2. The conditions imposed by Title III of the Convention on the recognition and the enforcement of judicial decisions are not fulfilled in the case of provisional or protective measures which are ordered or

authorised by a court without the party against whom they are directed having been summoned to appear and which are intended to be enforced without prior service on that party. It follows that this type of judicial decision is not covered by the system of recognition and enforcement provided for by Title III of the Convention.

JUDGMENT OF THE COURT

Kutscher, President, O'Keeffe and Touffait, Presidents of Chambers, Mertens de Wilmars, Pescatore, Lord Mackenzie Stuart, Bosco, Koopmans and Due, Judges

1. By an order of 25 July 1979 received at the Court on 6 August 1979 the Oberlandesgericht [Higher Regional Court] Frankfurt am Main referred to the Court under the Protocol on the Interpretation by the Court of Justice of the Convention of 27 September 1968 on Jurisdiction and the Enforcement of Judgments in Civil and Commercial Matters (hereinafter referred to as 'the Convention') (Official Journal 1978, L 304, p. 36) four questions relating to the interpretation of Articles 24, 27(2), the second paragraph of Article 34, the first paragraph of Articles 36 and Articles 46(2) and 47(1) of the Convention.

2. In 1978 a dispute between a creditor, Couchet Frères, and its debtor, Denilauler, was brought before the Tribunal de Grande Instance [Regional Court], Montbrison (France). On 7 February 1979 the President of that court, exercising the powers conferred on him by Article 48 of the French Code of Civil Procedure at the request of the creditor and without the other party's having been summoned to appear, made an order which was declared provisionally enforceable, authorising the creditor to freeze the account of the debtor at a bank in Frankfurt am Main as security for a debt estimated at FF 130 000. Under French law such freezing of assets ['saisie conservatoire'] which the creditor was thus authorised to carry out may be affected without prior service of the order on the debtor whose assets are seized.

3. The questions before the Court have been referred to it pursuant to proceedings before German courts for the issue of an order for the enforcement of the French order and also for a 'Phandungsbeschluß' [attachment order] seizing the funds in the bank's possession. These proceedings were first before the President of the Landgericht [Regional Court] Wiesbaden who ordered enforcement on 23 March 1979 resulting

in seizure of the funds on 28 March, all without the debtor's having been a party to the proceedings. It seems that the order by the President of the Landgericht Wiesbaden was not served on the debtor until 3 May 1979; the debtor immediately appealed against it before the Oberlandesgericht Frankfurt am Main which referred to the Court the questions now under consideration.

4. These questions first seek to know whether decisions of the judicial authorities of a Contracting State ordering provisional and protective measures, where the party against whom they are directed has not been summoned to appear and does not become aware of them until after their enforcement, may be recognised and made enforceable in another Contracting State without prior service on the party against whom they are directed (Questions 1 and 2). They secondly seek clarification of the objections which the party against whom enforcement is sought may raise when lodging the appeal against the enforcement order as provided by Article 36 of the Convention (Questions 3 and 4).

Questions 1 and 2

5. Questions 1 and 2, which should be answered together, read as follows:

'1. Do Articles 27(2) and 46(2) also apply to proceedings in which provisional protective measures are taken without the opposite party's being heard?

2. Is Article 47(1) of the Convention to be interpreted as meaning that the party applying for enforcement must also produce the documents which establish that the judgment of which enforcement is sought has been served, even if that judgment concerns a provisional and purely protective measure?'

6. The Commission, the Italian government and the plaintiff in the main action express the opinion in their observations that such judgments must be recognised as enforceable in the Contracting State addressed without prior service on the party against which they are directed.

The specific object of this type of provisional or protective measure is thought to be to produce a surprise effect intended to safeguard the threatened rights of the party seeking them by preventing the party against whom they are directed from removing the assets in its possession, whether they be the subject-matter of the dispute or constitute the creditor's security. To stipulate that the recognition and the enforcement of such types of judgments must be subject to their prior service on the other party and from the stage of the proceedings in the

Contracting State of origin would, it is said, make them totally meaningless.

The United Kingdom government, on the other hand, is of the opinion that the recognition and the enforcement of these judgments must be subject to the conditions set out in Articles, 27, 46 and 47 as regards service on the other party. It acknowledges that this requirement removes the surprise effect peculiar to such decisions and destroys all their practical value so that it virtually amounts to a refusal to recognise and enforce the decisions in question. However, it feels that the effect of this is not so serious as what it regards the intolerable risks which would have to be run by undertakings having assets in different Contracting States as a result of a procedure which obliges the courts of the State addressed to authorise measures freezing assets located in that State without the owner of those assets having ever had the opportunity to put forward his version of the case either before the court of the State of origin or before the court of the State addressed when such assets may have been legitimately intended to meet other obligations. Only the court having jurisdiction in the State in which the assets are located is in a position to determine, in the full knowledge of the facts of the case, the necessity to authorise this type of provisional or protective measure. The United Kingdom government further contends that its point of view does not create a lacuna in the scheme of the Convention because Article 24 enables any party to apply to the courts of a Contracting State for such provisional or protective measures as may be available under the law of that State, even if the courts of another Contracting State have jurisdiction as to the substance of the matter.

7. Article 27 of the Convention sets out the conditions to be fulfilled for the recognition in a Contracting State of judgments given in another Contracting State. Under Article 27(2) a judgment shall not be recognised 'if the defendant was not duly served with the document which instituted the proceedings in sufficient time to enable him to arrange for his defence'. Article 46(2) stipulates that a party seeking recognition or applying for enforcement of a judgment given in default in another Contracting State must produce amongst other documents the document which establishes that the party in default was served with the document instituting the proceedings or notice thereof.

8. These provisions were clearly not designed in order to be applied to judgments which, under the national law of a Contracting State, are intended to be delivered in the absence of the party against whom they are directed and to be enforced without prior service on him. It is

apparent from a comparison of the different language versions of the words in question and in particular from the terms used to describe the party who does not appear that these provisions are intended to refer to proceedings in which in principle both parties participate but in which the court is nevertheless empowered to give judgment if the defendant, although duly summoned, does not appear.

9. The same applies to Article 47(1) of the Convention under which the party seeking enforcement must produce documents which establish that, according to the law of the State in which it has been given, the judgment is enforceable and has been served. This provision which relates to judgments in cases in which both parties participate as well as to judgments such as the type in dispute, which have a different character.

10. However, it cannot be inferred from the fact that Articles 27(2), 46(2) and 47(1) cannot apply to decisions of the type in question, save by distorting their substance and scope, that such decisions must nevertheless be recognised and enforced in the State addressed. It is necessary to consider whether judicial decisions of this type, having regard to the scheme and objects of the Convention, may be dealt with under the simplified procedure for recognition and enforcement provided by the Convention.

11. In favour of an affirmative answer, the Commission and the Italian government maintain that, according to Article 25, the Convention covers all decisions given by the courts of the Contracting States without distinguishing between those involving adversary proceedings and those given without the other party's being summoned to appear. As is apparent from Article 24 the field of application of the Convention embraces protective and provisional measures which, under the law of the different Contracting States and by reason of their very nature or their urgency are often adopted without the opposite party's having first been heard. The Contracting States cannot have intended to restrict the field of application of the Convention to such an extent without express mention being made to that effect. Finally, it may clearly be seen from Article 34 of the Convention, which states that in the proceedings for an enforcement order 'the party against whom enforcement is sought shall not at this stage of the proceedings be entitled to make any submissions on the application', that the Convention itself recognises that proceedings in which only one party is heard are, where circumstances justify them, in keeping with the basic principle of the rights of the defence.

12. These arguments cannot prevail over the scheme of the Convention and the principles underlying it.

13. All the provisions of the Convention, both those contained in Title II on jurisdiction and those contained in Title III on recognition and enforcement, express the intention to ensure that, within the scope of the objectives of the Convention, proceedings leading to the delivery of judicial decisions take place in such a way that the rights of the defence are observed. It is because of the guarantees given to the defendant in the original proceedings that the Convention, in Title III, is very liberal in regard to recognition and enforcement. In the light of these considerations it is clear that the Convention is fundamentally concerned with judicial decisions which, before the recognition and enforcement of them are sought in a State other than the State of origin, have been, or have been capable of being, the subject in that State of origin and under various procedures, of an inquiry in adversary proceedings. It cannot therefore be deduced from the general scheme of the Convention that a formal expression of intention was needed in order to exclude judgments of the type in question from recognition and enforcement.

14. Nor is the argument by analogy, based on Article 34 of the Convention, of such a nature as to turn the scale. Although enforcement proceedings may be unilateral - but only provisionally so - this fact has to be brought into accord with the liberal character of the Convention as regards the procedure for enforcement, which is justified by the guarantee that in the State of origin both parties have either stated their case or had the opportunity to do so. Whilst another reason for the unilateral character of the enforcement procedure under Article 34 is to produce the surprise effect which this procedure must have in order to prevent a defendant from having the opportunity to protect his assets against any enforcement measures, the surprise effect is attenuated since the unilateral proceedings are based on the assumption that both parties will have been heard in the State of origin.

15. An analysis of the function attributed under the general scheme of the Convention to Article 24, which is specifically devoted to provisional and protective measures, leads, moreover, to the conclusion that, where these types of measures are concerned, special rules were contemplated. Whilst it is true that procedures of the type in question authorising provisional and protective measures may be found in the legal system of all the Contracting States and may be regarded, where certain conditions are fulfilled, as not infringing the rights of the defence, it should however

be emphasised that the granting of this type of measure requires particular care on the part of the court and detailed knowledge of the actual circumstances in which the measure is to take effect. Depending on each case and commercial practices in particular the court must be able to place a time-limit on its order or, as regards the nature of the assets or goods subject to the measures contemplated, require bank guarantees or nominate a sequestrator and generally make its authorisation subject to all conditions guaranteeing the provisional or protective character of the measure ordered.

16. The courts of the place or, in any event, of the Contracting State, where the assets subject to the measures sought are located, are those best able to assess the circumstances which may lead to the grant or refusal of the measures sought or to the laying down of procedures and conditions which the plaintiff must observe in order to guarantee the provisional and protective character of the measures ordered. The Convention has taken account of these requirements by providing in Article 24 that application may be made to the courts of a Contracting State for such provisional, including protective, measures as may be available under the law of that State, even if, under the Convention, the courts of another Contracting State have jurisdiction as to the substance of the matter.

17. Article 24 does not preclude provisional or protective measures ordered in the State of origin pursuant to adversary proceedings - even though by default - from being the subject of recognition and an authorisation for enforcement on the conditions laid down in Articles 25 to 49 of the Convention. On the other hand, the conditions imposed by Title III of the Convention on the recognition and the enforcement of judicial decisions are not fulfilled in the case of provisional or protective measures which are ordered or authorised by a court without the party against whom they are directed having been summoned to appear and which are intended to be enforced without prior service on that party. It follows that this type of judicial decision is not covered by the simplified enforcement procedure provided for by Title III of the Convention. However, as the government of the United Kingdom has rightly observed, Article 24 provides a procedure for litigants which to a large extent removes the drawbacks of this situation.

18. The reply to Questions 1 and 2 should, therefore, be that judicial decisions authorising provisional or protective measures, which are delivered without the party against which they are directed having been summoned to appear and which are intended to be enforced without prior

service do not come within the system of recognition and enforcement provided for by Title III of the Convention.

Questions 3 and 4

19. In view of the answer to Questions 1 and 2 there is no longer any reason to examine Questions 3 and 4 which now have no purpose.

On those grounds, the court, in answer to the questions referred to it by the Oberlandesgericht Frankfurt am Main by order of 25 July 1979 received at the Court on 6 August 1979, hereby rules:

Judicial decisions authorising provisional or protective measures, which are delivered without the party against which they are directed having been summoned to appear and which are intended to be enforced without prior service do not come within the system of recognition and enforcement provided for by Title III of the Convention of 27 September 1968 on Jurisdiction and the Enforcement of Judgments in Civil and Commercial Matters.

OPINION OF MR ADVOCATE GENERAL MAYRAS

This reference for a preliminary ruling is made by the Oberlandesgericht [Higher Regional Court] Frankfurt am Main in the Federal Republic of Germany concerning a dispute between S.n.c. Couchet Frères, a French transport undertaking, and a German customer, Mr Denilauler. The questions put by the court making this reference concern the interpretation of the Brussels Convention of 27 September 1968 on Jurisdiction and the Enforcement of Judgments in Civil and Commercial Matters.

Since the report for the bearing by the Judge-Rapporteur has fully described the facts surrounding the dispute and the different procedural stages it has gone through, there is no need to waste the Court's time by recapitulating them here. So I take leave to come straight to the important problems raised by the Frankfurt Regional Court.

The first two questions submitted by that court concern the interpretation of Articles 27(2), 46(2) and 47(1) of the Convention.

Article 27(2) provides that 'a judgment shall not be recognized ... where it was given in default of appearance, if the defendant was not duly served with the document which instituted the proceedings in sufficient time to enable him to arrange for his defence'. This provision is made applicable to enforcement as a result of the second paragraph of Article 34 by which the application for such enforcement must be refused if it could not be recognised under Articles 27 and 28.

Article 46(2) pursues the matter as regards evidence by requiring that a party seeking recognition or applying for enforcement of a judgment shall produce, in the case of a judgment given in default, the original or a certified true copy of the document which establishes that the party in default was served with the document instituting the proceedings.

Article 47(1) deals with the actual judgment to be enforced. It makes it compulsory for the party applying for enforcement to produce 'documents which establish that, according to the law of the State in which it has been given, a judgment is enforceable and has been served'. The court making the reference asks whether these provisions apply where the judgment in the State of origin authorises a provisional or protective measure pursuant to proceedings which, in accordance with the law of that State, have been conducted *ex parte*. Is this the case here, especially when we are confronted with a decision such as an order of the President of a French court authorising a creditor to freeze the account of his debtor in Germany without the debtor's having been notified of the application and the decision which resulted therefrom, under Article 48 of the old Code de Procedure Civile [Code of Civil Procedure]?

I - In dealing with this question I shall concentrate first on the words actually used in the provisions requiring construction.

I think that it is necessary here to distinguish between Article 47(1) on the one hand and Articles 46(2) and 27(2) on the other.

Article 47(1) uses the word 'judgment' without any restriction. As may be seen from Article 25, this word was selected to cover all the possible forms of judicial decisions including those authorizing provisional or protective measures at the conclusion of *ex parte* proceedings.

Unless the word 'judgment' is used in Article 47 ,l) with a different meaning from that in Article 25, subparagraph (1) does apply to the judgments I have mentioned.

Whether Articles 27(2) and 46(2) apply to provisional or protective measures may on the other hand still be in some doubt in as much as the French text of the provisions contains the phrases 'défendeur défaillant' [defendant in default of appearance] and 'décision par défaut' [judgment given in default] respectively. As the court which made the reference points out, default proceedings are, in the technical meaning of the term, proceedings 'which are not, in their legal nature, *ex parte*, but which envisage the participation of the defendant'.

From an analysis of Article 46(2) the Commission comes to the same conclusion. It is true that default proceedings [procédure par défaut] are adversary proceedings for, in such a case, although he has not responded to them, the defendant has been notified of the action in which he is involved.

It is, however, far from certain that the terms used in Articles 27(2) and 46(2) of the Convention can apply only to default proceedings as understood *stricto sensu* in certain national legal systems.

I do not think it right to construe Article 27(2) as referring only to specific proceedings known to certain national legal systems. In my view such a construction would be too narrow and would fail to recognise the independent nature of the Convention, which is an instrument of international law, in relation to the multiplicity of proceedings under the national legal systems of the Contracting States.

This is confirmed by the English text of Article 27(2) which, by using the expression 'judgment ... given in default of appearance', is careful to avoid terminology calling to mind certain national proceedings and those alone. There can be no doubt that according to the ordinary meaning of the words any judgment given against a defendant without his having been heard is a judgment 'in default of his appearance'. The English term refers simply to the absence of the defendant from the course of the proceedings for whatever reason. It therefore covers not only the case of the defendant upon whom the document instituting the proceedings has been served and who does not respond to it, but also the case of the defendant upon whom, under the national rules of procedure, it has not been necessary to serve such a document.

Even though the English text of Article 47(2) uses the shorter expression 'given in default', we must not overlook the fact that this provision is secondary to Article 27(2) of which, as I have indicated, it is an extension from the point of view of evidence. Because of this link, 'given in default' can only mean 'given in default of appearance'.

As the court making the reference itself points out, the view that Articles 27(2) and 46(2) apply to any decision in proceedings of an *ex parte* nature is also supported by Bülow and Böckstiegel, the eminent specialists on the Convention (Der Internationale Rechtsverkehr in Zivil und Handelssachen, commentary on Article 27, III, 2, p. 606-208.209 - commentary on Article 46, II, 2, p. 606-276.277).

In short, from this textual analysis of the provisions in question I gain the impression that the argument that they apply to provisional or protective measures adopted at the conclusion of *ex parte* proceedings is more sound than the reverse argument. I must however admit that, except in the case of Article 47(1), I cannot find sufficient support for this to strengthen my belief.

II - I feel therefore that I can find a satisfactory solution to the important problem raised by the Oberlandesgericht Frankfurt only by examining it in the light of the object and purpose of the Convention.

The Convention is meant to strengthen legal protection and legal certainty in the Common Market and abolish obstacles which prevent it from working properly.

1. On the basis of that idea the plaintiff in the main action, Italy and the Commission are in favour of excluding the application of Article 27(2) to judgments ordering a provisional or protective measure at the conclusion of *ex parte* proceedings. They claim that judgments of this sort may be made at the national level in all Contracting States. It is also true, at the national level, for the United Kingdom, Ireland and Denmark in which the Convention is not yet in force. Since the object of the Convention is to make possible at Community level what is already possible at national level, they come to the conclusion that the recognition and enforcement of such measures must be possible at Community level.

For all its impeccable logic, it seems to me that this argument completely disregards the special character of *ex parte* provisional or protective measures.

That the authors of the Convention were aware of the specific features of these measures is clear from the special jurisdiction to deal with them provided in Article 24. According to that provision: 'Application may be made to the courts of a Contracting State for such provisional, including protective, measures as may be available under the law of that State, even if, under this Convention, the courts of another Contracting State have jurisdiction as to the substance of the matter'.

We should give particular attention to the all-embracing nature of this jurisdiction, indicated by the words 'even if'. Under the normal rules of the Convention conferring jurisdiction, a court has no jurisdiction to entertain disputes which, in substance, concern a court of another Contracting State. To my way of thinking the special jurisdiction in Article 24 would have been quite superfluous if the authors of the Convention had intended that judgments given in a State other than the State of the court having jurisdiction under Article 24 should automatically become enforceable within the territorial jurisdiction of the latter court.

I therefore draw some comfort in thinking that provisional and protective measures have a special nature from the text of The Hague Convention of 1 February 1971 drawn up under the auspices of The Hague Conference on Private International Law of which all the Community States are members. According to Article 2(2), that Convention does not apply to judgments ordering provisional or protective measures. The preparatory studies show that that provision was already included in the preliminary draft adopted by the commission charged with the drafting of the text and was not questioned thereafter. According to the rapporteur of the Convention that provision is in accord with the prevailing opinion to the effect that such measures must be considered as coming within the exclusive jurisdiction of the country in which they are to be applied.

However, it would not be right to conclude from the foregoing that I am adopting the opinion, expressed during the oral procedure by the United Kingdom representative, that under the Brussels Convention no provisional or protective measure, whether adopted in *ex parte* or in adversary proceedings, can have extra-territorial effect.

In my view it all depends on the nature of the judgment concerning the measure. If, on the one hand, the judgment by the court of origin is enforceable, it would be a clear breach of the universally recognised principle of the territoriality of the enforcement of judicial decisions.

In the Convention, such territoriality takes the form of the exclusive jurisdiction laid down in Article 16(5) under which: 'The following courts shall have exclusive jurisdiction, regardless of domicile: ... in proceedings concerned with the enforcement of judgments, the courts of the Contracting State in which the judgment has been or is to be enforced'.

If, on the other hand, the judgment is just a declaration by which a court authorizes the plaintiff to apply to a court in another Contracting State to have it enforced under the enforcement procedures provided for in that court's own law, then the jurisdiction of the court addressed seems to me to be respected.

In short, the special nature of provisional and protective measures calls for the adoption of an intermediate opinion. I think that if they have been adopted in the form I have just indicated and, in addition, at the conclusion of adversary proceedings, they may have extra-territorial effect by virtue of the rules of the Brussels Convention on enforcement. Conversely, this same special nature leads me to say that similar measures adopted at the conclusion of *ex parte* proceedings do not come under the rules of the Convention.

It is therefore this *ex parte* nature of the proceedings which, to my way of thinking, justifies this difference in treatment.

2. This is not, however, the opinion of those who contend that Article 27(2) does not apply to *ex parte* provisional and protective measures. In their view, requiring proof of service of the document instituting the proceedings to obtain an order for enforcement of those measures is tantamount to robbing them of all practical effect.

This is an argument which the Oberlandesgericht had in mind, too. It expresses its fear by stating that 'the surprise effect, obviously intended, of the protective measure decreed by the President of the Tribunal de Grande Instance, Montbrison, which in all probability would be decisive for the success of the enforcement of that measure, would be lost if, in that case too, the plaintiff's application instituting the proceedings and the judgment of the same date of the French court applied to were subject to the requirement of prior service in order to obtain an order for enforcement'.

It cannot be denied that speed and the surprise effect are essential for the success of measures of this type. However, I do not think that this is the only consideration to be taken into account; in international relations it is second in importance to the observance of the rights of the defence. Even in national legal systems judgments ordering *ex parte* provisional or protective measures have far-reaching effects. They are a seriously disturbing factor in the normal judicial order, of which the adage *audi alteram partem* is a cornerstone. In the field of commercial relationships the freezing of a bank account may result in serious consequences for the undertaking affected.

Moreover, third parties who are in a business relationship with the defendant are affected by the repercussions of such a measure. For example, a defendant's customers to whom a refused cheque or bill was payable may suffer serious injury owing to the impossibility of obtaining immediate payment. These risks seem to me to be particularly acute in certain international commercial sectors where very large sums or goods of great value may change hands several times within a short space of time.

Acting solely on the basis of the plaintiff's assertions, the court of origin will have no means of checking whether the goods whose seizure is sought still in fact belong to the defendant when they may have been sold just a moment before, or whether third parties have prior claim to them. If serious prejudice to the rights of third parties is to be prevented and if the risk of increasing the uncertainty of commercial transactions is not to be accepted, it is essential that measures such as 'saisie conservatoire' [attachment] in

French law should rapidly be brought to the notice of all concerned and that they should have the opportunity to take immediate counter-action.

A defendant wanting to obtain the release of his goods from the measures taken against them must be in a position to put forward his arguments in the shortest possible time. Can this be possible when a measure has been authorised by a court of one State and made enforceable by a court of another State? I do not think so.

What then can the debtor do? He may go to the court of origin. Let us imagine - the most favourable case - in order to highlight this, that he is domiciled in the State to which that court belongs. This will make his task easier from the linguistic and legal point of view. But one must not forget that since the measure was *ex parte*, the defendant will get to know of its enforcement through the foreign court which has ordered it, which may be the first cause of delay. Even if he obtains a rapid lifting of the measures against his goods, he will still have to contend with the transmission of that judgment to the country of enforcement, which may be a second cause of delay.

But the most frequent case will be the one where a defendant is not domiciled in the same State as the court of origin. For obvious practical reasons he will need a certain amount of time to make his application to it.

Can the defendant challenge the measure before the court of the place of enforcement? Article 29 of the Convention certainly does not allow him to rely on substantive arguments. No doubt he will be able to prove, as Jenard suggests in his commentary to Article 37 (Reports on the Convention (Official Journal of the European Communities C 59 of 5 March 1979, p. 51)), that he has paid his debt since the foreign judgment was delivered. But that possibility is indeed minimal and does not go very far towards ensuring appropriate protection in all cases.

If, for example, the debtor denies that he is the owner of the goods seized because he has just sold them, the exclusion of substantive review, which is justified in other circumstances, will prevent him from assessing that argument. Similarly, the third party acquiring the goods will have no right of access to the court.

It follows that a quick and effective appeal is not possible either in the court of origin or in the court addressed. To be effective, an appeal against enforcement of a preventive measure requires that the court which is to take cognizance of it shall have jurisdiction both in regard to the justification for this measure and the form it must take and it must also be able to give immediate effect to the decision at which it arrives, whatever it may be. I think that I have shown that these conditions are not met either in the court of origin or in the court of the place of enforcement.

3. This inability of a defendant to take quick and effective counter-action against a judgment from a foreign court at the conclusion of *ex parte* proceedings for a provisional or protective measure against him, is, I feel, an unjustified infringement of the rights of the defence.

However, the Brussels Convention is founded upon the strict observance of such rights. This is evidenced by Article 2 which is a straightforward application of the maxim *actor sequitur forum rei*. As Jenard explains, that the court of the defendant should in principle have jurisdiction 'is even more relevant in the international sphere than it is in national law. It is more difficult, generally speaking, to defend oneself in the courts of a foreign country than in those of another town in the country where one is domiciled' (Report on the Convention, Official Journal of the European Communities C 59 of 5 March 1979, p. 18).

Similarly, the second paragraph of Article 20 of the Convention which stipulates that 'the court shall stay the proceedings so long as it is not shown that the defendant has been able to receive the document instituting the proceedings in sufficient time to enable him to arrange for his defence, or that all necessary steps have been taken to this end', is also designed to safeguard the rights of the defendant, by recognizing the international importance of the service of judicial documents Jenard, Report on the Convention, p.39).

This strictness of the requirement that the rights of the defence must be observed is not without purpose. It is the counterpart to the extreme liberality of the Convention as regards the recognition and enforcement of judgments. It is possible to accept this liberality only if the court addressed can have full confidence in the judgment of the court of origin. The same thought is expressed by Jenard when he writes, at the start of his general considerations on recognition and enforcement (Report on the Convention, p. 42) that 'as a result of the safeguards granted to the defendant in the original proceedings, Title III of the Convention is very liberal on the question of recognition and enforcement'.

Consequently, the scheme of the Convention in my opinion rules out the possibility of the defendant's being taken by surprise by the enforcement of a judgment which has not been served on him and when he did not even know that the court had given it. The importance of observing the rights of the defence also makes me think that if the authors of the Convention had intended that a refusal of recognition and enforcement on the ground given in Article 27(2) should not apply in the case of decisions such as those in question in the main action, they would have said so expressly.

The possibility cannot even be excluded that courts in certain States which have a particularly strict concept of the rights of the defence would refuse to grant an enforcement order for judgments ordering a provisional or protective measure at the conclusion of *ex parte* proceedings on the ground that such judgments are contrary to national public policy.

III - Are we then to conclude that under the Brussels Convention it is not possible for a creditor to protect his interests by obtaining from a court an urgent measure taking his debtor by surprise?

1. Such a conclusion would overlook Article 24, referred to earlier, a corresponding provision to which is found in nearly all enforcement conventions (Jenard Report, at p 42). The terms of this provision do not in any way prevent provisional or protective measures which are sought from the courts of another Contracting State, even when a court of another Contracting State has jurisdiction as to the substance of the matter, from being granted at the conclusion of *ex parte* proceedings if the internal law of the court applied to makes provision for them.

The advantage of an application under Article 24 is that the court applied to not only has full power as far as the procedure is concerned; it also has cognizance of the facts of the case. Even if it makes only a cursory and provisional inquiry, it does in fact need to inquire into the circumstances of the case in order to decide upon the expediency of granting the measure which is sought. From the procedural point of view the choice of measure which it regards as the most appropriate from those available under national law of course is a matter for that court alone. The comprehensive view which it thus has of a case puts it alone in a position to adjudicate, in the full knowledge of the facts of the case, on any objections which the defendant may put forward against the measure which it has taken.

Clearly, a further necessary requirement enabling Article 24 to be actually used in a case such as the one in the main action is that all Contracting States should have a procedure of the 'saisie conservatoire' type under French law. The Commission has told us that is the case as regards the States between which the Convention is now in force.

The United Kingdom representative told us during the oral procedure about the 'Mareva injunction' named after a case decided by the Court of Appeal in 1975. By an injunction of that type a court restrains a defendant from taking the funds concerned out of its jurisdiction following proceedings which may be *ex parte*. The Agent of the British Government also informed us that under the legislation which his country is preparing with a view to its accession to the Convention the benefit of the 'Mareva injunction' will be extended to cases in which a court of another Contracting State has jurisdiction as to the substance of the matter.

In Denmark a measure similar to the French 'saisie conservatoire' may be obtained by virtue of the combined provisions of Articles 612 and 628 of the Law on the administration of justice ('Lov om rettens pleje').

According to my information it seems that the possibility also exists in Ireland of obtaining from the court the freezing of bank assets, to take the case here, without the defendant's being given prior notice.

There is therefore no practical obstacle preventing Article 24 from being invoked in bilateral relations between all States now members of the Community, once the Convention is also in force in the United Kingdom, Ireland and Denmark.

2. During the oral procedure the Commission pointed out a drawback to Article 24 which arises particularly when defendant has assets in several countries. A plaintiff wishing to seize them would therefore be obliged to seek urgent measures in each of these.

Practical difficulties would result out of all proportion to those arising from the solution advocated by the Commission. In the case of the latter solution the plaintiff's obligation is limited to seeking enforcement of the foreign judgment ordering a provisional or protective measure following *ex parte* proceedings under the summary procedure laid down by the Convention. On the other hand, under Article 24, every application for urgent measures would necessitate on the part of the court addressed the fuller inquiry of which I spoke.

It is true that this is a difficulty which the defendant must accept. But I regard it as a fair price to pay for obtaining from the court the extraordinary measures he is seeking and, conversely, an expression of the consideration which must be shown to the debtor. Moreover, it may be thought that in practice the creditors having to resort to these measures will in most cases have an organistion enabling them to overcome this drawback.

Above all I am not sure that plaintiffs will obtain an order for an enforcement as easily as the Commission thinks. Even with regard to relations between the six original members of the Community this case illustrates the hesitations of certain national courts. What will the position be in regard to the three States which have not yet ratified the Brussels Convention?

The novelty of the 'Mareva' injunction which, moreover, does not seem to have been accepted without some reticence, leads me to believe that the ordering of the enforcement of a judgment authorising a provisional or protective measure following *ex parte* proceedings will not be a straightforward matter for courts in Common Law countries, quite apart from the fact that, as their law now stands, the direct enforcement of foreign judgments is unknown.

In Denmark, even within the privileged context of the Nordic Council, a decision may not in principle be recognised and enforced by virtue of Law No 300 of 8 June 1977 unless it is definitive. It is true that the operation of that Law is extended, by way of exception, to a few judgments which are not definitive and are listed therein but judgments given pursuant to *ex parte* proceedings do not figure in the list.

In these circumstances I see some justification for fearing that, looking ahead to the welcome accession to the Convention of the United Kingdom, Ireland and Denmark, certain courts which are applied to may refuse to recognise or enforce judgments such as those which have given rise to this request for a preliminary ruling. Far from strengthening legal certainty and promoting the free movement of judgments within the Common Market, an effect contrary to that sought by the Brussels Convention would be the unfortunate outcome.

For these reasons I propose that the Court should rule that Articles 27(2), 46(2) and 47(1) apply to proceedings in which the adoption of provisional and protective measures is ordered without the other party's having been heard.

IV - In its third question the Oberlandesgericht Frankfurt asks the Court whether the first paragraph of Article 36 of the Convention enables a debtor, in his appeal against the order of the court authorising the enforcement of a provisional and protective measure, to plead objections to the claim itself irrespective of the time at which the grounds for the objections arose.

In particular can the debtor, in cases of this sort, set off a claim which he already possessed against the plaintiff before the provisional measure was adopted in the State of origin?

As the court making the reference itself points out, an objection based upon the set-off of two debts is an objection of substance or, to put it another way, a matter of substantive law. However, the whole essence of the Convention is not to allow the court addressed to have jurisdiction as to the substance of the case.

As the Jenard Report says (commentary on Article 37, at p. 51), this principle clearly applies to courts to which objections are made against judgments authorising enforcement.

Indeed one surely has to agree with Jenard that 'the appellant could, however, effectively adduce grounds which arose after the foreign judgment was given. For example, he may establish that he has since discharged the debt'. (Commentary on Article 37, at p. 51). But the scope of this exception cannot be extended. It cannot cover objections based on facts arising prior to the foreign judgment which is to be enforced.

If the Court which is asked to order enforcement were to take into account an objection as to the substance, there is no doubt that it would thereby encroach on the power of decision of the original court, which has jurisdiction to give a definite judgment on the claim in question. The courts with such jurisdiction are the courts having jurisdiction as to the substance which are therefore, by virtue of Article 29, the only courts of origin. As the Italian Government points out in its observations, it is inconceivable that the appeal provided for in Article 36 should have the effect of altering the normal criteria as regards jurisdiction between the courts of the various Contracting States.

Under the scheme of the Convention its object can be no more than ascertaining whether the conditions laid down by the Convention for issuing an order for enforcement are fulfilled and consequently ordering recourse to enforcement procedures.

To these cogent observations, whatever the nature of the judgment of the court of origin, it is necessary to add a comment specifically concerning judgments relating to measures of a provisional or protective nature. In any event new objections as to the substance could only be taken into consideration if the foreign proceedings were at an end.

However, where a provisional or protective measure has been ordered in a judicial decision, then, by definition, there has not yet been any definitive inquiry as to the claim concerned by this measure.

Moreover, taking the special case of the enforcement in Germany of a foreign judgment of this type, to admit an objection as to the substance would give the debtor more chance of resisting enforcement of the foreign judgment than of resisting enforcement of the same type of judgment given in Germany, as may be seen from Articles 916 and 917(1) of the Zivilprozeßordnung [Code of Civil Procedure]. Such a result is unacceptable.

For all these reasons the answer to the third question put by the court making the reference should, in my opinion, be in the negative.

V - In these circumstances, I regard its last question to be in the alternative, requiring an answer only should the previous question be answered in the affirmative. The question is based on the assumption that the court seised of the appeal against enforcement has jurisdiction to hear objections as to the substance and is concerned with whether the defendant can submit to the court objections which he has already raised in the proceedings instituted in the State of origin against the judgment ordering a provisional or protective measure against him.

It is clear that the rules on lis pendens stated in Article 21 of the Convention completely rule this out. According to that provision: 'Where proceedings involving the same cause of action and between the same parties are brought in the courts of differing Contracting States, any court other than the court first seised shall of its own motion decline jurisdiction in favour of that court'.

There is no reason for not applying that provision to the particular case described by the Oberlandesgericht in its question. The risk will thereby be avoided that the court seised of the appeal in the State of origin and the court in the country of enforcement will give conflicting rulings on the same question.

In conclusion, I propose that the questions referred to the Court by the Oberlandesgericht Frankfurt am Main be answered as follows:

1. Articles 27(2) and 46(2) apply to proceedings in which the adoption of provisional and protective measures is ordered without the other party's having been heard.

2. Article 47(1), in stipulating that the party seeking enforcement must produce the documents establishing that the judgment to be enforced has been served, also applies to judgments ordering a provisional or protective measure following *ex parte* proceedings.

3. A defendant in enforcement proceedings is not allowed to rely in those proceedings on a set-off arising before the judgment was given by the court of origin.

4. The same applies *a fortiori* if he has already raised that objection during an appeal against the judgment given in the State of origin.

Case 166/80 - 16 June 1981

Peter Klomps
v
Karl Michel

Recognition and enforcement of judgments - Grounds for refusal - Article 27, point 2 - Document which instituted the proceedings not served in due form and in sufficient time on defendant who fails to take appropriate action - Document which instituted the proceedings - Concept - Service in sufficient time - Appraisal of the court in which enforcement is sought - Period to be taken into consideration - Effect where there is an objection against the judgment in default which is declared inadmissible by a court of the State in which the judgment was given - Decision of a court of the State in which the judgment was given finding that service was duly effected - Duty of the court in which enforcement is sought to consider whether service was effected in sufficient time - Service in sufficient time - Appraisal of the court in which enforcement is sought - Beginning of time to be allowed the defendant.

Summary

1. The words 'the document which instituted the proceedings' contained in Article 27, point 2, of the Convention of 27 September 1968 on Jurisdiction and the Enforcement of Judgments in Civil and Commercial Matters cover any document, such as the order for payment [Zahlungsbefehl] in German law, service of which enables the plaintiff, under the law of the State of the court in which the judgment was given, to obtain in default of appropriate action taken by the defendant, a decision capable of being recognized and enforced under the provisions of the Convention. A decision such as the enforcement order

[Vollstreckungsbefehl] in German law, which is issued after service of the order for payment has been effected and which is enforceable under the Convention, is not covered by the words 'the document which instituted the proceedings'.

2. In order to determine whether the defendant has been enabled to arrange for his defence as required by Article 27, point 2, the court in which enforcement is sought must take account only of the time, such as that allowed under German law for submitting an objection [Widerspruch] to the order for payment, available to the defendant for the purposes of preventing the issue of a judgment in default which is enforceable under the Convention.

3. Article 27, point 2, of the Convention, which is addressed exclusively to the court before which proceedings are brought for recognition or enforcement in another Contracting State, remains applicable where the defendant has lodged an objection against the decision given in default and a court in the State in which the judgment was given has declared the objection inadmissible on the ground that the time for making such objection has expired.

4. Even if the court in which the judgment was given has held, in separate adversary proceedings, that service was duly effected, Article 27, point 2, of the Convention still requires the court in which enforcement is sought to examine whether service was effected in sufficient time to enable the defendant to arrange for his defence.

5. Article 27, point 2, of the Convention does not require proof that the document which instituted the proceedings was actually brought to the knowledge of the defendant. As a general rule the court in which enforcement is sought may accordingly confine its examination to ascertaining whether the period reckoned from the date on which service was duly effected allowed the defendant sufficient time to arrange for his defence. Nevertheless, the court must consider whether, in a particular case, there are exceptional circumstances which warrant the conclusion that, although service was duly effected, it was, however, inadequate for the purpose of causing time to begin to run.

JUDGMENT OF THE COURT

Mertens de Wilmars, President, Pescatore, Lord Mackenzie Stuart, O'Keeffe, Bosco, Touffait, Due, Everling, Chloros, Judges,

1. By judgment of 8 July 1980, which was received at the Court on 15 July 1980, the Hoge Raad der Nederlanden [Supreme Court of the Netherlands] referred to the Court for a preliminary ruling pursuant to the Protocol of 3 June 1971 on the interpretation by the Court of Justice of the Convention of 27 September 1968 on Jurisdiction and the Enforcement of Judgments in Civil and Commercial Matters, five questions, the first four of which concern the interpretation of Article 27, point 2, of that Convention whilst the fifth refers to Article 52.

2. These questions were submitted to the Court in the context of an appeal in Cassation against a judgment of the Arrondissementsrechtbank [District Court], Roermond, of 20 September 1979 overruling the objection submitted against an order of 27 June 1978 whereby the president of that court declared enforceable in the Netherlands, by virtue of the provisions of the Convention, an order for payment and the order for its enforcement issued by German courts in the context of summary proceedings for the recovery of debts or liquidated demands, known as 'Mahnverfahren'.

3. Personal service of the order for payment [Zahlungsbefehl] was not effected but in the absence of the defendant the order was lodged at the post office and written notification of the order was left at the address in the Federal Republic of Germany provided by the creditor, which, according to German law, constituted service at that address. Under the legislation in force at the time the defendant was allowed a period of not less than three days in order to submit an objection [Widerspruch] to the order for payment but that period was extended until such time as the Court issued an order for its enforcement [Vollstreckungsbefehl]. In the present case that period was six days. After service of the enforcement order, which was effected by the same method, the defendant had a second period of one week within which to lodge an objection [Einspruch] to the enforcement order. However, the defendant allowed four months to pass before submitting such an objection and claimed that at the time of the summary proceedings his habitual residence was in the Netherlands. The objection was dismissed as being out of time following adversary proceedings in which the German court considered the question of habitual residence in order to establish whether service was

duly effected and held that, according to German law, Mr Klomps was habitually resident at the address where service was effected.

4. It is clear from the file that under German law the objection to the order for payment might be made quite informally, without stating reasons, and even by a representative who was not required to prove that he was duly authorized for the purpose. Both the properly-introduced objection against an enforcement order and the objection to the order for payment had the effect of transforming the summary proceedings for obtaining that order into adversary proceedings but the enforcement order remained provisionally enforceable despite the objection and it was, thus, equivalent to a judgment in default.

5. In the course of the various proceedings before the Netherlands courts the defendant, who is the appellant in cassation, claimed that the recognition, and accordingly the enforcement, in the Netherlands, of the orders made against him by the German courts were contrary to Article 27, point 2, of the Convention which provides: 'A judgment shall not be recognized: ... 2. Where it was given in default of appearance, if the defendant was not duly served with the document which instituted the proceedings in sufficient time to enable him to arrange for his defence'.

6. In these circumstances the Hoge Raad decided to stay the proceedings and to request the Court of Justice to answer the following questions:

'(1) Must a 'Zahlungsbefehl' [order for payment], or a 'Vollstreckungsbefehl' [enforcement order], issued under German law as it was in 1976, be regarded as 'the document which instituted the proceedings' within the meaning of the opening words and point 2 of Article 27 of the EEC Convention on Jurisdiction and the Enforcement of Judgments in Civil and Commercial Matters?

(2) If it must be assumed that in a case such as the present one the 'Zahlungsbefehl' is the document which instituted the proceedings within the meaning of the opening words and point 2 of Article 27 is it necessary, with regard to the question whether that document was served on the defendant in sufficient time to enable him to arrange for his defence, to take account only of the period for submitting a 'Widerspruch' [objection] against the 'Zahlungsbefehl', or must account also be taken of the fact that after the expiry of that period the defendant still has a period for lodging an 'Einspruch' [objection] against the 'Vollstreckungsbefehl'?

(3) Are the opening words and point 2 of Article 27 applicable if the

defendant in the State of the court the recognition or enforcement of whose decision is sought (the court first seised) has objected to the decision given in default and the court first seised rules that the objection is inadmissible because it was not lodged within the period laid down for that purpose?

(4) If the court first seised has ruled that at the time of service of the document which instituted the proceedings the defendant had his habitual residence in the State of that court, with the result that in that respect service was duly effected, do the provisions of the opening words and point 2 of Article 27 require that a separate examination be carried out into the question whether the document was served in sufficient time to enable the defendant to arrange for his defence? If so, is that examination then confined to the question whether the document reached the defendant's habitual residence in good time or must, for example, the question also be examined whether service at that residence was sufficient to ensure that the document would reach the defendant personally in good time?

(5) In connection with the questions set out under (4), is the position altered, having regard to Article 52, by the question whether the court of the State in which recognition or enforcement is sought rules that under the law of that State at the time of service of the document which instituted the proceedings the defendant had his habitual residence in that State?'

7. Before a reply is given to those questions it must be recalled that Title II of the Brussels Convention contains provisions regulating directly and in detail the jurisdiction of the courts of the State in which judgment was given, and also provisions concerning the verification of that jurisdiction and of admissibility. These provisions, which are binding on the court in which judgment was given, are of such a nature as to protect the interests of defendants. This has made it possible, at the stage of recognition and enforcement which is governed by Title III of the Convention, to facilitate the free movement of judgments within the Community by simplifying the procedure for recognition and by reducing the number of grounds which may operate to prevent the recognition and enforcement of judgments. Amongst these grounds are that contained in Article 27, point 2, which, for the sole purpose of safeguarding the rights of the defendant, provides for refusal of recognition and, read together with Article 34, for refusal of enforcement, in exceptional cases where the guarantees contained in the law of the State in which the judgment was given and in the Convention itself are insufficient to ensure that the defendant has an opportunity of arranging for his defence before the court

in which judgment was given. It is in the light of these considerations that the provision relied upon by the appellant in cassation in the main proceedings must be interpreted.

The first two questions

8. By the first question the Hoge Raad asks whether, under a system like that which was in force in the Federal Republic of Germany in 1976 in accordance with which service on the defendant of an order for payment enables the plaintiff, where the defendant does not submit an objection to the order within the prescribed period, to obtain a decision which remains provisionally enforceable even after the submission of the objection against the enforcement order, but under which both that objection and the objection to the order for payment transform the procedure into adversary proceedings, the words 'the document which instituted the proceedings' refers to the order for payment [Zahlungsbefehl] or the enforcement order [Vollstreckungsbefehl].

9. As has been indicated above, Article 27, point 2, is intended to ensure that a judgment is not recognized or enforced under the Convention if the defendant has not had an opportunity of defending himself before the court first seised. It follows that a measure, such as the order for payment [Zahlungsbefehl] in German law, service of which on the defendant enables the plaintiff, where no objection to the order is made, to obtain a decision which is enforceable under the Convention, must be duly served on the defendant in sufficient time to enable him to arrange for his defence and accordingly that such a measure must be understood as being covered by the words 'the document which instituted the proceedings' in Article 27, point 2. On the other hand, a decision, such as the enforcement order [Vollstreckungsbefehl] in German law, which is issued following service of an order for payment and which is in itself enforceable under the Convention, is not covered by those words even although the lodging of an objection against the enforcement order, like the objection to the order for payment, transforms the procedure into adversary proceedings.

10. With regard to the second question the same considerations show that for the purpose of examining whether the defendant has been able to arrange for his defence within the meaning of Article 27, point 2, the court in which enforcement is sought must take account only of the time, such as that allowed under German law for submitting an objection to the order for payment, available to the defendant for the purposes of

preventing the issue of a judgment in default which is enforceable under the Convention.

11. The reply to those two questions must accordingly be that Article 27, point 2, must be interpreted as follows:

- The words 'the document which instituted the proceedings' cover any document, such as the order for payment [Zahlungsbefehl] in German law, service of which enables the plaintiff, under the law of the State of the court in which the judgment was given, to obtain, in default of appropriate action taken by the defendant, a decision capable of being recognized and enforced under the provisions of the Convention;
- A decision such as the enforcement order [Vollstreckungsbefehl] in German law, which is issued after service of the order for payment has been effected and which is enforceable under the Convention, is not covered by the words 'the document which instituted the proceedings';
- In order to determine whether the defendant has been enabled to arrange for his defence as required by Article 27, point 2, the court in which enforcement is sought must take account only of the time, such as that allowed under German law for submitting an objection [Widerspruch] to the order for payment, available to the defendant for the purposes of preventing the issue of a judgment in default which is enforceable under the Convention.

Third question

12. This question refers in substance to the jurisdiction of the courts of the State in which the judgment was given and the courts of another Contracting State before which proceedings have been brought for the recognition or enforcement of a judgment given in the former State. In this connection it should be emphasized that Article 27, point 2, is not addressed to the courts of the State in which the judgment was given, but only to the court before which proceedings have been brought for recognition or enforcement of the judgment in another Contracting State. In the case with which the question is concerned the defendant did not submit a defence as to the substance of the case before the court first seised. The dismissal of the objection to the enforcement order as inadmissible means that the decision given in default remains intact. For that reason the objective of Article 27, point 2, requires that in the case with which this question is concerned the court in the State in which enforcement is sought should carry out the examination prescribed by that provision.

13. The reply to the third question should therefore be that Article 27, point 2, remains applicable where the defendant has lodged an objection against the decision given in default and a court of the State in which the judgment was given has held the objection to be inadmissible on the ground that the time for lodging an objection has expired.

Fourth question

14. By this question the Hoge Raad asks first whether, where a court of the State in which the judgment was given has already found that service has been duly effected, the court seised in the other Contracting State is still required to consider whether service was effected in sufficient time to enable the defendant to arrange for his defence.

15. For the purposes of the reply to the first part of the question it should first of all be pointed out that Article 27, point 2, lays down two conditions, the first of which, that service should be duly effected, entails a decision based on the legislation of the State in which judgment was given and on the conventions binding on that State in regard to service whilst the second, concerning the time necessary to enable the defendant to arrange for his defence, implies appraisals of a factual nature. A decision concerning the first of those conditions made in the State in which the judgment was given accordingly does not release the court in the State in which enforcement is sought from its duty to examine the second condition, even if that decision was made in the context of separate adversary proceedings.

16. The reply to this part of the question must accordingly be that, even if the court in which the judgment was given has held, in separate adversary proceedings, that service was duly effected, Article 27, point 2, still requires the court in which enforcement is sought to examine whether service was effected in sufficient time to enable the defendant to arrange for his defence.

17. In the event of an affirmative reply to first part of the fourth question, the Hoge Raad asks further whether the examination in question must be limited to the finding that the document reached the habitual residence of the defendant in sufficient time or whether it is a further requirement, for example, that the service in question should provide a sufficient guarantee that the document would reach the defendant personally in good time.

18. The second condition contained in Article 27, point 2, is intended to ensure that the defendant has sufficient time to prepare his defence or to take the steps necessary to prevent judgment's being given in default. The question submitted to the Court is not concerned with how long this time is but rather with the point from which it begins to run. The Hoge Raad is, in fact, asking whether the court in which enforcement is sought must proceed on the assumption that a defendant is able to prepare his defence as soon as the document which instituted the proceedings reaches his habitual residence.

19. In this connection it must be stated first of all that Article 27, point 2, does not require proof that the document which instituted the proceedings was actually brought to the knowledge of the defendant. Having regard to the exceptional nature of the grounds for refusing enforcement and to the fact that the laws of the Contracting States on the service of court documents, like the international conventions on this subject, have as their objective the safeguarding of the interests of defendants, the court in which enforcement is sought is ordinarily justified in considering that, following due service, the defendant is able to take steps to defend his interests as soon as the document has been served on him at his habitual residence or elsewhere. As a general rule the court in which enforcement is sought may accordingly confine its examination to ascertaining whether the period reckoned from the date on which service was duly effected allowed the defendant sufficient time to arrange for his defence. Nevertheless, the court must consider whether, in a particular case, there are exceptional circumstances which warrant the conclusion that, although service was duly effected, it was, however, inadequate for the purposes of enabling the defendant to take steps to arrange for his defence and, accordingly, could not cause the time stipulated by Article 27, point 2, to begin to run.

20. In considering whether it is confronted with such a case the court in which enforcement is sought may take account of all the circumstances of the case in point, including the means employed for effecting service, the relations between the plaintiff and the defendant or the nature of the steps which had to be taken in order to prevent judgment from being given in default. If, for example, the dispute concerns commercial relations and if the document which instituted the proceedings was served at an address at which the defendant carries on his business activities the mere fact that the defendant was absent at the time of service should not normally prevent him from arranging his defence, above all if the action necessary to avoid a judgment in default may be taken informally and even by a representative.

21. The reply to that part of the fourth question should, therefore, be that the court in which enforcement is sought may as a general rule confine itself to examining whether the period reckoned from the date on which service was duly effected allowed the defendant sufficient time for his defence. However, the court is also required to consider whether, in a particular case, there are exceptional circumstances such as the fact that, although service was duly effected, it was, nevertheless, inadequate for the purpose of causing that time to begin to run.

Fifth question

22. This question concerns Article 52 of the Convention, the relevant provisions of which read as follows: 'In order to determine whether a party is domiciled in the Contracting State whose courts are seised of a matter, the court shall apply its internal law.
If a party is not domiciled in the State whose courts are seised of the matter, then, in order to determine whether the party is domiciled in another Contracting State, the court shall apply the law of that State'.

23. That article states which law is applicable where, according to the other provisions of the Convention, in particular those concerning jurisdiction, it is necessary to determine the habitual residence (or one of the habitual residences) of a party. In the context of Article 27, point 2, the habitual residence of the defendant may be a decisive factor for the purpose of considering whether service has been duly effected but that question must in any case be resolved by applying the internal law of the State in which the judgment was given and of the relevant conventions. The question whether service was effected in sufficient time involves, as has been indicated above, assessments of fact to which the concept of habitual residence is irrelevant.

24. The reply to the fifth question should therefore be that Article 52 of the Convention and the fact that the court of the State in which enforcement is sought concluded that under the law of that State the defendant was habitually resident within its territory at the date of service of the document which instituted the proceedings do not affect the replies given above.

On those grounds, the Court in answer to the questions referred to it by the Hoge Raad der Nederlanden by judgment of 8 July 1980, hereby rules:

Article 27, point 2, of the Brussels Convention of 27 September 1968 on Jurisdiction and the Enforcement of Judgments in Civil and Commercial Matters must be interpreted as follows:

1. The words 'the document which instituted the proceedings' cover any document, such as the order for payment [Zahlungsbefehl] in German law, service of which enables the plaintiff, under the law of the State of the court in which the judgment was given to obtain, in default of appropriate action taken by the defendant, a decision capable of being recognized and enforced under the provisions of the Convention.

2. A decision such as the enforcement order [Vollstreckungsbefehl] in German law, which is issued after service of the order for payment has been effected and which is enforceable under the Convention, is not covered by the words 'the document which instituted the proceedings'.

3. In order to determine whether the defendant has been enabled to arrange for his defence as required by Article 27, point 2, the court in which enforcement is sought must take account only of the time, such as that allowed under German law for submitting an objection [Widerspruch] to the order for payment, available to the defendant for the purposes of preventing the issue of a judgment in default which is enforceable under the Convention.

4. Article 27, point 2, remains applicable where the defendant has lodged an objection against the decision given in default and a court of the State in which the judgment was given has held the objection to be inadmissible on the ground that the time for lodging an objection has expired.

5. Even if a court of the State in which the judgment was given has held, in separate adversary proceedings, that service was duly effected Article 27, point 2, still requires the court in which enforcement is sought to examine whether service was effected in sufficient time to enable the defendant to arrange for his defence.

6. The court in which enforcement is sought may as a general rule confine itself to examining whether the period, reckoned from the date on which service was duly effected,

allowed the defendant sufficient time for his defence. It must, however, consider whether, in a particular case, there are exceptional circumstances such as the fact that, although service was duly effected, it was inadequate for the purposes of causing that time to begin to run.

7. Article 52 of the Convention and the fact that the court of the State in which enforcement is sought concluded that under the law of that State the defendant was habitually resident within its territory at the date of service of the document which instituted the proceedings do not affect the replies given above.

OPINION OF MR ADVOCATE GENERAL REISCHL

The case on which I shall give my views today concerns the interpretation of Article 27, point 2, of the Convention on Jurisdiction and the Enforcement of Judgments in Civil and Commercial Matters (hereinafter referred to as 'the Convention on Jurisdiction'), which is worded as follows: 'A judgment shall not be recognized: ... 2. where it was given in default of appearance, if the defendant was not duly served with the document which instituted the proceedings in sufficient time to enable him to arrange for his defence;...'.

The interpretation is requested in relation to the following facts. Mr Michel, the respondent in cassation in the main action, is an estate agent in Neuss. It appears that he has a claim, in respect of his agency fees, for a sum amounting to DM 63 270 against Mr Klomps, the appellant in cassation in the main action. In order to enforce his claim he had recourse to summary proceedings for the recovery of debts and liquidated demands known as 'Mahnverfahren' the details of which I shall discuss later. On the application of Mr Michel a court officer [Rechtspfleger] of the Amtsgericht [Local Court] Krefeld issued on 29 March 1976 a Zahlungsbefehl [order for payment], as it was then called, for DM 63 270 together with interest and costs. The method of service on the debtor, which took place on 3 April 1976, was by depositing the order at the Post Office at Willich and by leaving notification of this at the debtor's address, 34 Heiligenweg, Willich. This was considered to be substituted service for the purposes of Article 182 of the German Zivilprozebordnung [Code of Civil Procedure]. Since an objection to the order for [Widerspruch] payment was not made within the period of three days, the time-limit which was at that time prescribed by Articles 692 and 499 of the Code of Civil Procedure for debtors whose habitual residence was within the district of the court seised of the matter, an enforcement order [Vollstreckungsbefehl] was issued on 9 April 1976. It was served in the same way as the order for payment and the debtor was notified of it on 22 April 1976. In German law the enforcement order constitutes a provisionally enforceable title against which an objection [Einspruch] may be submitted within a period of one week, that is, in this case before 29 April 1976.

However, the objection to the enforcement order was not submitted until 1 September 1976. This gave rise to proceedings before the Amtsgericht Krefeld in the course of which investigations were carried out as to the habitual residence of the debtor since he claimed that he was not, in fact, residing at 34 Heiligenweg, Willich, but had his habitual residence in the Netherlands, as was established by an entry in the population register of Venlo of 31 December 1971 and another entry in the register of Meijel of 28 August 1976. However, the court found on the basis of the evidence of witnesses that the debtor's habitual residence for the purposes of Article 7 of the German Civil Code [Bürgerliches Gesetzbuch] and of Article 13 of the Code of Civil Procedure was in fact in Willich. The relevant factors on which the court based its finding were that the debtor's wife and children, who were not living apart from him, resided in Willich, the children attended school there, that the debtor ran a business in Willich, that his name was entered in the telephone directory for Willich and that he came regularly to Willich to collect post sent to him there. Accordingly, the court considered that the order for payment and enforcement order had been correctly served and, in its judgment of 19 April 1977, which became binding on 12 July 1977, dismissed the objection against the enforcement order as inadmissible on the ground that it was out of time. In the following year Mr Michel tried to have the order executed against Mr Klomps in the Netherlands. On the application of Mr Klomps the President of the Arrondissementsrechtbank [District Court] Roermond, issued, on the basis of Articles 31, 32 and 34 of the Convention on Jurisdiction, an order dated 27 June 1978, for the enforcement of the above-mentioned order for payment and execution of the enforcement order together with - in relation to the costs - the judgment of the Amtsgericht Krefeld of 19 April 1977. The debtor appealed in accordance with Article 36 of the Convention on Jurisdiction and the Arrondissementsrechtbank Roermond gave judgment on that appeal on 20 September 1979. In that judgment the court found that the order for payment and enforcement order were to be considered as 'judgments' within the meaning of Article 25 of the Convention on Jurisdiction, in particular since an enforcement order is stated by Article 700 of the Code of Civil procedure to be equivalent to a judgment in default declared to be enforceable. The procedure which preceded their issue was not irregular, service was not effected at a wrong address and there were no grounds for refusal of recognition under Article 27, point 2, of the Convention on Jurisdiction. Accordingly, the order for payment and the enforcement order could be recognized as being in accordance with Articles 25 and 26 of the Convention on Jurisdiction and an order for enforcement could be issued in accordance with Article 31 of that Convention. With regard to the judgment of the Amtsgericht Krefeld it was found that it might indeed be recognized that its enforcement was temporarily excluded since the costs were not specified, on which point the debtor's application, which as to the other heads was to be dismissed, must be allowed.

Thereafter, the case came before the Hoge Raad [the Supreme Court of the Netherlands] on an appeal in cassation. The appellant based his appeal on Article 27, point 2, of the Convention on Jurisdiction and claimed that the document which instituted the proceedings (the order for payment) was not served in due form, and not in sufficient time to enable him to arrange for his defence. At the time of service of the order for payment and of the enforcement order he was not residing in Willich but in Meijel in the Netherlands. He was entered on the population register in Meijel and was, in fact, staying there, as were his wife and children at the time. For that reason the order for payment and the enforcement order did not, in fact, reach him and, since he was unable to present his defence in regard to them in good time, they should not be recognized.

The Hoge Raad decided that the order for payment and the enforcement order must be considered as duly served within the meaning of Article 27, point 2, of the Convention on Jurisdiction. Doubt remained only on the point whether it might be considered that service was 'in sufficient time' for the purposes of the said provision since it had to be accepted that the order for payment and the enforcement order had not, in fact, reached the debtor because at the time of service he was in fact in the Netherlands, staying there with his wife and children.

Accordingly the Hoge Raad, by a decision of 8 July 1980, stayed the proceedings and referred the following questions to the Court for a preliminary ruling under Article 3 of the Protocol on the interpretation of the Convention on Jurisdiction and the Enforcement of Judgments in Civil and Commercial Matters:

'(1) Must a 'Zahlungsbefehl' [order for payment], or a 'Vollstreckungsbefehl' [enforcement order], issued under German law as it was in 1976, be regarded as 'the document which instituted the proceedings' within the meaning of the opening words and point 2 of Article 27 of the EEC Convention on Jurisdiction and the Enforcement of Judgments in Civil and Commercial Matters?

(2) If it must be assumed that in a case such as the present one the 'Zahlungsbefehl' is the document which instituted the proceedings within the meaning of the opening words and point 2 of Article 27 is it necessary, with regard to the question whether that document was served on the defendant in sufficient time to enable him to arrange for his defence, to take account only of the period for submitting a 'Widerspruch' [objection] against the 'Zahlungsbefehl', or must account also be taken of the fact that after the expiry of that period the defendant still has a period for lodging an 'Einspruch' [objection] against the 'Vollstreckungsbefehl'?

(3) Are the opening words and point 2 of Article 27 applicable if the defendant in the State of the court the recognition or enforcement of whose decision is sought (the court first seised) has objected to the decision given in default and the court first seised rules that the objection is inadmissible because it was not lodged within the period laid down for that purpose?

(4) If the court first seised has ruled that at the time of service of the document which instituted the proceedings the defendant had his habitual residence in the State of that court, with the result that in that respect service was duly effected, do the provisions of the opening words and point 2 of Article 27 require that a separate examination be carried out into the question whether the

document was served in sufficient time to enable the defendant to arrange for his defence? If so, is that examination then confined to the question whether the document reached the defendant's habitual residence in good time or must, for example, the question also be examined whether service at that residence was sufficient to ensure that the document would reach the defendant personally in good time?

(5) In connection with the questions set out under (4), is the position altered, having regard to Article 52, by the question whether the court of the State in which recognition or enforcement is sought rules that under the law of that State at the time of service of the document which instituted the proceedings the defendant had his habitual residence in that State?'

My opinion on these questions is as follows.

1. Let me begin with a few remarks on the course of the 'Mahnverfahren' which at the time was governed, by virtue of the Law of 12 September 1950, by Articles 688 to 703 of the Code of Civil Procedure. The procedure, which is appropriate only to certain claims, was initiated by an informal claim which was not communicated to the opposite party. It was processed by an officer of the Amtsgericht having jurisdiction in the matter [Rechtspfleger] who, after carrying out certain examinations, in particular as to jurisdiction and whether the claim was prima facie well-founded issued an order for payment, a demand enjoining the debtor to satisfy the claim. That order for payment was served by the court of its own motion, thus making it possible, in the absence of the debtor, for substituted service of the kind described above to be effected. An objection [Widerspruch] to the order for payment might be submitted within a period of (at that time) three days where the debtor had his habitual residence within the district of the court, a period of one week being allowed in other cases. In any case, by virtue of Article 694 of the Code of Civil Procedure an objection to the order for payment might be submitted as long as an enforcement order had not been issued. On the submission of an objection to the order for payment the action was transformed into normal adversary proceedings in which, in accordance with Article 596 of the Code of Civil Procedure, the order for payment was treated as equivalent to an originating application. If no such objection was made, then upon application by the creditor, which might be made even before the expiry of the period prescribed in the order for payment, there would be issued an enforcement order in the form of an endorsement on the order for payment, enabling enforcement to be carried out as if there had been a default judgment. An objection [Einspruch] might be lodged within a period, which at that time amounted to one week, against the enforcement order, service of which might be effected in the same manner as service of the order for payment. If no such objection was made no remedy lay against the enforcement order; if an objection was made the case was, likewise, transformed into a normal court action, which was deemed to have become a pending suit upon service of the order for payment. I have also to point out that this procedure was altered with effect from 1 July 1977 by the Law of 3 December 1976. The alteration consisted of an adaptation of the system to the requirements of data-processing and resulted, having regard in particular to the comprehensive nature

of a change of this kind, in an alteration of the relevant time-limits so that, thereafter, a period of 14 days was prescribed both for objections to orders for payment and objections to enforcement orders.

2. By its first question the Hoge Raad wishes to ascertain whether the order for payment or the enforcement order must be considered as the document which instituted the proceedings within the meaning of Article 27, point 2, of the Convention on Jurisdiction.

In answering that question it is unnecessary to consider further whether the words 'the document which instituted the proceedings' must be interpreted independently, in accordance with the system and objective of the Convention on Jurisdiction, as the respondent in the main action considers, or whether it is necessary to decide, in accordance with the law of the court first seised, what constitutes such a document, as the Commission considers, pointing out that the said words are already to be found in the second paragraph of Article 20(2) of the Convention on Jurisdiction which concerns the procedure to be observed by that court.

It is clear, in any event that, unlike the request for the issue of an order for payment, which request is not notified to the opposite party, the order for payment fulfils the requirements which, in accordance with the concepts forming the basis of the protective provisions in Article 27, are intended to provide such a party with an opportunity to put forward an effective defence to the document which instituted the proceedings. It contains particulars of the grounds of the claim, in regard to which a description of the relevant facts and their legal consequences is sufficient, it is served on the opposite party who then has a specified time-limit within which to contest it. If he does so the dispute is deemed, as I have already mentioned, to have become a pending suit as from the date of service of the order for payment. The order itself is considered as the originating application instituting the proceedings and forms the basis for the judgment of the court which is delivered at the conclusion of adversary proceedings.

Reference is also made in the first question to the enforcement order. In regard to this it may be stated in the first place that, although it is not issued by a judge it must be considered as fully equivalent to a judgment within the meaning of Article 25 of the Convention on Jurisdiction. This is emphasized in legal literature (Bülow-Böckstiegel 'Internationaler Rechtsverkehr in Zivilund Handelssachen', Note III (2) to Article 27 of the Convention on Jurisdiction), it is to be inferred from the Jenard Report (page 42 of Official Journal of the European Communities C 59 of 5.3.79) which also constitutes confirmation of the view that in any case the order for payment, which in fact forms the basis for the enforcement order, is to be considered as the document which instituted the proceedings within the meaning of Article 27 of the Convention on Jurisdiction. It is, then, difficult to argue that the enforcement order also constitutes the document which instituted the proceedings in accordance with Article 27, point 2, of the Convention on Jurisdiction. Even though, according to German procedural law, which must form the point of departure with regard to Article 27, it is clear that the lodging of an objection against the enforcement order leads to normal civil proceedings in which the decision as a whole (the order for payment and the enforcement order) is at issue, nevertheless, the essential point is that the claim is deemed, by virtue of Article 700 of the Code of Civil Procedure, to have become a pending suit as from the date of service of the order for payment. It follows from this that in such a case too the order for payment must be classified as the document which instituted the proceedings.

3. The Hoge Raad also wishes to know whether, if it is accepted that the order for payment constitutes the document which instituted the proceedings, as regards the question whether service was effected on the defendant in sufficient time to enable him to arrange for his defence, account is to be taken only of the period within which the objection to the order for payment may be made or also of the further period within which the objection to the enforcement order may be lodged.

In the view of the respondent in the main action the answer to that question is that account should also be taken of the period allowed for objecting to the enforcement order. In this connection it is pointed out that, after the objection has been lodged it is possible to put forward a full defence against the claim. In addition, it is noted that the execution of an enforcement order which is provisionally enforceable is usually carried out with some hesitation as there may be a claim for damages if an objection is successful and after the submission of an objection the debtor may have the execution stayed.

The Commission's view corresponds very closely to these conclusions. The Commission considers it important that an objection, made out of time, to an order for payment is treated as an objection to the enforcement order and that, as it were, through the latter objection the former can be restored. Following on from this, the Commission, too, refers to the possibility of putting forward a comprehensive defence after lodging an objection against the enforcement order, in which case detailed grounds of defence do not have to be lodged at the same time as the objection but, as a rule, only within a period which is subsequently fixed. However, if I have properly understood the Commission's arguments in the oral procedure, it apparently considers such a far-reaching proposition as applicable only where the circumstances of a particular case are as follows: when an enforcement order is not immediately executed and when it is clear, at the time of the proceedings for recognition, that no objection against the enforcement order has been lodged within the prescribed time-limit. The Government of the Federal Republic of Germany has, on the other hand, clearly opposed, at least in its written observations, taking into account the time for lodging an objection against the enforcement order. In this connection it is significant that the enforcement order provides the same authority for enforcement as a judgment in default. The protective purpose of Article 27 of the Convention on Jurisdiction requires, however, that it should be possible to put forward a defence before the authority for enforcement is issued, that is to say, that between service of the document which instituted the proceedings, in this case the order for payment, and the decision taken on the basis of it, there must be sufficient time to arrange for the defence.

In this matter I am in principle disposed to share the Federal Government's view, which, on the basis of the general scheme of the Convention on Jurisdiction and the objective of Article 27, clearly has very weighty arguments in its favour. In addition, it should not be forgotten that, according to Article 46 of the Convention on Jurisdiction, a party applying for enforcement is required to produce, in the case of a judgment in default, the original or certified copy of the document which establishes that the party in default was served with the document which instituted the proceedings. Accordingly, it ought to be clear that the last-mentioned document must be different from the one which constitutes the actual basis for enforcement. Since in the summary proceedings for recovery of a debt or liquidated demand the document which instituted the proceedings is the order for payment, what is important is what time remained after service of that order for preparing the defence. In that connection it is, of course, necessary to take into account a number of factors in ascertaining whether this period is reasonable. What is concerned is not a strict exclusionary time-limit. On the contrary, it was possible for an objection to the order for payment to be made until the enforcement order was issued, which, owing to the volume of work, was often not done until some considerable time had elapsed, in this case six days after the issue of the order for payment. It is also important that during that time the debtor is simply required to make it known that he does not admit the claim. That may be done without giving reasons and without observing any requirements as to form; for example, it may be done orally in the presence of the appropriate officer at the court registry or, as the representative of the Federal Government has informed the Court, by telephone or telegram and a representative is not in this connection required to establish his authority to act in the matter. In view of the fact that submission of the objection to the order for payment transforms the procedure into a legal action properly so-called there is sufficient time afterwards for detailed preparation of the defence which usually requires to be lodged before or at a hearing, the date of which is subsequently fixed.

Nevertheless, I should like to add that the views of the Commission are not to be dismissed out of hand. For the Commission what is important is that, in interpreting the Convention on Jurisdiction, the primary consideration should be its objective - the requirement of the free movement of judgments. On this basis, and also in view of the fact that Title II of the Convention on Jurisdiction already provides guarantees for the procedure to be followed before the court first seised and that in principle recognition is granted without any special procedure a restrictive application of the provisions of Articles 27 and 28 is appropriate. If this view is accepted it may, in fact, appear arguable that, in a case such as this, in which the enforcement order was served on 22 April 1976 and in which, during the procedure for recognition in 1978, it became clear that the time for lodging an objection to the enforcement order had expired without being used for that purpose, in answering the question whether the debtor had sufficient time to defend the claim made against him the time for lodging an objection to the enforcement order should also be taken into account. This would give twenty-five days in all for the defence.

4. Following on from these considerations it is further necessary to

consider what significance, for the purposes of the application of Article 27, point 2, of the Convention on Jurisdiction, should be ascribed to the fact that the respondent lodged an objection to the enforcement order in the State of the court first seised which was dismissed as inadmissible because it was out of time.

On this point the respondent in the main action expressed the view that the court in which recognition is sought is bound by the appraisal of the court first seised. Not only would it be contrary to the spirit and objective of the Convention on Jurisdiction if the court in which recognition is sought were to undertake a special examination based on Article 27, point 2, of the Convention. The principles of legal certainty and the uniformity of the enforcement also militate against such an examination. Nevertheless, the Federal Government and the Commission challenge that view. In my opinion their arguments are more persuasive.

Proceeding on the basis of the narrow interpretation of Article 27, point 2, which the Federal Government considers to be proper for the purposes of answering the question when it may rightly be said that the document which instituted the proceedings was served in sufficient time for the defendant to arrange for his defence, an important point is that the court first seised was required to decide on an objection lodged on 1 September 1976 against the enforcement order. Thus, what was concerned was not the submission of a defence before the issue of the authorization for enforcement but an attempt to put forward a defence subsequently. That attempt did not, in fact, result in an investigation of the claim in question but, because of the expiry of the period prescribed by national law, in a refusal to carry out that investigation and consequently in a refusal to examine any possible defects in the proceedings before the Court first seised. It must further be borne in mind that Article 27 of the Convention on Jurisdiction constitutes a protective provision within the framework of the procedure for recognition and enforcement which only comes into operation when an application is made under Article 31 of the Convention. The court in which the judgment was given, the court first seised, does not participate in that procedure. In principle it only applies its national law and does not carry out any verification such as that required by Article 27, point 2. It is, furthermore, clear, as reference to the Jenard Report confirms, that Article 27, point 2, constitutes an independent provision in relation to the national law of both the court first seised and the court in which recognition is sought. The court in which recognition is sought is thus required to ascertain independently whether both requirements mentioned in that provision have been fulfilled and, in connection with the question whether service was effected in good time, is perfectly entitled to criticize the time-limits prescribed by national law, because it is required to investigate what actually happened.

In my opinion it is clear that a reference to the principles of legal certainty and the uniformity of enforcement provides no answer to the foregoing considerations. If, in fact, these principles were required to form the decisive guidelines for the enforcement procedure under the Convention on Jurisdiction a provision like Article 27, point 2, of the Convention would not have been adopted. Instead, the observance of the rules to be applied by the court first seised would simply have been made the sole criterion and no additional protection for the debtor in the procedure for recognition and enforcement would have been provided.

5. The fourth question submitted to the Court by the Hoge Raad, which must now be considered, consists of two parts: it must first of all be considered whether, when the court first seised has reached the conclusion that when the document which instituted the proceedings was served the defendant had his habitual residence in the State of that court and that service was, thus, duly effected there, a further examination must be carried out by the court in which recognition is sought, namely as to whether service was effected 'in sufficient time' within the meaning of Article 27, point 2, of the Convention on Jurisdiction. If the answer to the first part of the fourth question is in the affirmative the Hoge Raad wishes to know, secondly, whether the examination may be confined to the question whether the document which instituted the proceedings reached the habitual residence of the defendant in good time or whether it must be ascertained in addition whether service of that nature provided a sufficient guarantee that the document would reach the defendant personally in good time.

(a) The first part of the fourth question appears to embody a problem relating to the matters covered by Article 27, point 2, of the Convention on Jurisdiction. It is natural, first of all, to consider whether that provision concerns only cases where it is necessary to effect service abroad, that is to say, that it does not apply to matters which appear to the court in which recognition is sought to constitute purely national cases since both the habitual residence of the parties and the place where the dispute occurs are on the national territory. In fact, it may indeed appear in the last-mentioned case that the application of Article 27, point 2, amounts to providing additional protection which may be considered unjustified. It might, in fact, be said that, when in such a situation enforcement under national law is perfectly possible because there is no reason to consider that the rights of the defence have been restricted, it is hard to see why a different criterion should apply with regard to the conservation of the rights of defence in the case of execution levied on assets situated abroad.

Nevertheless, the very general terms of Article 27 do not, in fact, appear to provide any grounds for a conclusion of that nature, especially when the are compared with Article 20 of the Convention on Jurisdiction which expressly concerns the case of a defendant who has his habitual residence in one Contracting State and who is sued in a court of another Contracting State. It also appears to be generally accepted in legal literature that the provision with which we are concerned applies even when the defendant is habitually resident in the State of the court first seised and all that is required for the transmission of the document which instituted the proceedings is service within the national territory (cf. Bülow-Böckstiegel, loc. cit. Note III to Article 27; Martha Weser, 'Convention Communautaire sur la Competénce Judiciaire et l'Exécution des Décisions', p. 332; Droz, 'Competénce Judiciaire et Effets des Jugements dans le Marché Commun', p. 315).

However, if this view is taken to be correct, that is to say, if it is accepted that Article 27, point 2, of the Convention on Jurisdiction applies in principle when enforcement is to be effected abroad the answer to the first part of the fourth question does not, for the rest, cause any difficulties. According to the Jenard Report it is clear that Article 27, point 2, must be considered as a provision providing special protection within the framework of the procedure for recognition, which requires the court in which recognition is sought to carry out an independent examination from two points of view which must be taken together. It follows from this not only that the second court is not bound by the findings of the court first seised as to whether the document which instituted the proceedings was duly served, a matter which is to be judged in accordance with the law of the court first seised and the international agreements which it must apply (cf. Bülow-Böckstiegel, loc. cit. Note III (4) (a) to Article 27). The court in which recognition is sought must in all cases also examine whether service was effected in sufficient time to enable the defendant to arrange for his defence. In this respect, as Bülow-Böckstiegel, loc. cit., for example, emphasizes, the court in which recognition is sought is not bound by the provisions which the court first seised had to apply and instead it must carry out the examination, of its own motion if necessary, independently and having regard to all the circumstances of the case (the kind of action, the parties to it, the need to obtain a legal adviser, whether translations are required, etc.).

(b) With regard to the second part of the fourth question I should like to emphasize in the first place that the view of those who in principle are in favour of a restrictive interpretation of Article 27, point 2, seems to me to be the correction. The decisive point in this connection is that as early as the procedure leading to judgment the Convention on Jurisdiction provides substantial guarantees which derive in particular from Article 20 and from The Hague Convention on Service of 1965. Accordingly, the Jenard Report states that Article 27 applies only in exceptional cases and this view is also taken by Martha Weser (loc. cit., p. 333) when she emphasizes that refusal of recognition under Article 27, point 2, will be unusual.

Further, it is an important factor in relation to this part of the question that, under the Convention on Jurisdiction or other relevant agreements, there is no principle that a procedural document must be communicated directly and personally to the person to whom it is addressed. Where such a requirement is contemplated it is expressly stated, as, for example, in Article 36 of the Convention on Jurisdiction which is concerned with service of the decision on the person against whom enforcement is sought either in person or at his residence. Accordingly, it may be accepted in principle that service at the habitual residence of the defendant is sufficient and that the question whether service has been effected in sufficient time does not depend on whether the document which instituted the proceedings was in fact brought to the knowledge of the defendant, but that it is enough that he should have the possibility of having knowledge of it. Linke ('Die Versäumnisentscheidungen im deutschen, österreichischen, belgischen und englischen Recht, ihre Anerkennung und Vollstreckbarerklärung', p. 157) and Bülow-Böckstiegel, (loc. cit., Note III (4)(b) to Article 27) stress this, emphasizing the similarity of the requirements of

Articles 20 and 27, and the same thing may also be inferred from the remarks made in the Jenard Report concerning Article 20 of the Convention on Jurisdiction. Anyone who became habitually resident in one or more places - possibly in different Member States - must accordingly be aware of the consequences of this. When service is effected in such circumstances it may in principle be expected that the addressee, particularly if he is a businessman, will take steps to ensure that he is informed of documents communicated in this way.

As was, however, emphasized in the proceedings, variations from this rule may be admitted only in rare cases. Only when, owing to special circumstances, such as sudden and necessary hospitalization, it cannot be expected that arrangements have been made for information to be obtained in good time of the service of documents, must it be held that service at the habitual residence is not sufficient for the purposes of Article 27 and its protective function and that arrangements must be made to effect personal service.

I consider that there is nothing more to be said in general on the problem to which the fourth question of the Hoge Raad gives rise. According to the information which we have obtained in the course of the proceedings it should accordingly be found, and this should be sufficient for the judgment in the main action, that the essential point is that service was effected at the German address of the appellant and that it is necessary to examine only whether as from the time of service there was sufficient time for a first, adequate defence to be prepared in accordance with the requirements of the 'Mahnverfahren'.

6. The last question is solely concerned to clarify the problem whether another answer to the fourth question would be obtained by taking into consideration Article 52 of the Convention on Jurisdiction. That article reads as follows: 'In order to determine whether a party is domiciled in the Contracting State whose courts are seised of the matter, the court shall apply its internal law.

If a party is not domiciled in the State whose courts are seised of the matter, then, in order to determine whether the party is domiciled in another Contracting State, the court shall apply the law of that State.

The domicile of a party shall, however, be determined in accordance with his national law if, by that law, his domicile depends on that of another person or on the seat of an authority'.

This question was put in case the court in the State in which enforcement is sought takes the view that at the time of service of the document which instituted the proceedings the defendant had his habitual residence, according to the law of that State, on its territory.

As the Federal Government and the Commission concurred in stating - the respondent in the main action did not give his views on the point - this question can immediately be answered in the negative.

The function of Article 52, in view of the fact that there is no uniform definition of the concept 'habitual residence' in the legal systems of the Contracting States, is to determine the proper law and thereby to make good a hiatus which would otherwise have existed in the application of the Convention on Jurisdiction. The article is, accordingly, relevant in all cases in which habitual residence is concerned under the Convention. This applies in particular in determining the jurisdiction of courts and also in the context of proceedings for enforcement (cf. Article 32 of the Convention on Jurisdiction). It also applies, for example, in the calculation of the time for appeals under Article 36 of the Convention. As has already been made clear, the determination of the habitual residence of the defendant has in principle no decisive influence on the question whether the document which instituted the proceedings was served in sufficient time in accordance with Article 27, point 2, of the Convention on Jurisdiction. If, as is generally emphasized, the actual circumstances in the individual case are important in this respect, there can clearly be no question of using as a basis a rule which relates to determining the law applicable to the question of habitual residence. It was accordingly properly pointed out in relation to the fifth question that the court in which enforcement is sought may not draw conclusions in regard to the question whether the document which instituted the proceedings was served in sufficient time on the basis of the provisions which it has to apply in relation to the question of habitual residence. In this matter that court should instead be bound by the findings in regard to habitual residence made by the court first seised, above all, because otherwise a situation might arise amounting almost to a review of the jurisdiction of the court first seised, which is precluded by Article 28 of the Convention on Jurisdiction.

7. I accordingly propose that the following answer should be given to the questions submitted by the Hoge Raad:

(a) An order for payment ['Zahlungsbefehl'; now 'Mahnbescheid'] issued in accordance with Article 688 *et seq.* of the German Code of Civil Procedure must also be regarded as 'a document which instituted the proceedings' within the meaning of Article 27, point 2, of the Convention on Jurisdiction.

(b) With regard to the question whether the document which instituted the proceedings was served on the defendant in sufficient time to enable him to arrange for his defence, in principle the only time to be taken into consideration is that within which the objection to the order for payment may be made. The fact that after the expiry of that time the defendant has a further period within which to lodge an objection to the enforcement order may also be taken into account if it is established at the time when the proceedings for recognition are instituted that the last-mentioned period has expired without an objection being lodged.

(c) Article 27, point 2, of the Convention on Jurisdiction is also applicable if the defendant in the State of the court the recognition or enforcement of whose decision is sought (the court first seised) has instituted proceedings for the judgment given in default of appearance to be set aside and the court first seised rules that the proceedings are inadmissible because they were not brought within the period prescribed for that purpose.

(d) A separate examination of the question whether the document which instituted the proceedings was served in sufficient time to enable the defendant to arrange for his defence is also required where the court first seised concluded that, at the time of service of that document, the defendant had his habitual residence in the State of the court first seised and that such service was duly effected. In this respect, since personal service on the defendant is not generally stipulated, examination of the question may usually be restricted to the point whether the document reached the habitual residence of the defendant in good time; a further examination is only appropriate where exceptional circumstances give reason to believe that the defendant was unable to make arrangements for the transmission to him of documents reaching his habitual residence during his absence.

(e) Article 52 of the Convention on Jurisdiction and the fact that the court of the State in which recognition is sought rules that under the law of that State at the time of service of the document which instituted the proceedings the defendant had his habitual residence in that State do not affect the answer to the preceding question.

Case 228/81 - 15 July 1982

Pendy Plastic Products BV
v
Pluspunkt Handelsgesellschaft mbH

Articles 27(2) and 20, third paragraph - Article 15, Hague Convention of 15 November 1965 - Recognition and enforcement of judgments - Grounds for refusal - Defendant in default of appearance not duly served with the document instituting the proceedings in sufficient time - Review by the court in which enforcement is sought - Scope - Judgment of the court of the original State establishing that service was effected properly and in sufficient time - No effect.

Summary

The court of the State in which enforcement is sought may, if it considers that the conditions laid down by Article 27(2) of the Convention of 27 September 1968 are fulfilled, refuse to grant recognition and enforcement of a judgment even though the court of the State in which the judgment was given regarded it as proven, in accordance with the third paragraph of Article 20 of that Convention in conjunction with Article 15 of the Hague Convention of 15 November 1965, that the defendant, who failed to enter an appearance, had an opportunity to receive service of the document instituting the proceedings in sufficient time to enable him to make arrangements for his defence.

JUDGMENT OF THE COURT

Due, President, Chloros and Grévisse, Judges

1. By order of 8 July 1981, which was received at the Court Registry

on 6 August 1981, the Bundesgerichtshof [Federal Court of Justice] referred to the Court for a preliminary ruling under the Protocol of 3 June 1971 on the interpretation by the Court of Justice of the Brussels Convention of 27 September 1968 on Jurisdiction and the Enforcement of Judgments in Civil and Commercial Matters a question on the interpretation of Article 27(2) of that Convention, having regard to the provisions of the third paragraph of Article 20 thereof in conjunction with those of Article 15 of the Hague Convention of 15 November 1965 on the Service Abroad of Judicial and Extra-judicial Documents in Civil or Commercial Matters (Tractatenblad 1966, No 91).

2. That question was raised in an appeal on a point of law lodged by Pendy Plastic Products (BV) (hereinafter referred to as 'Pendy'), whose registered office is in Helmond in the Netherlands, against a decision of the Oberlandesgericht [Higher Regional Court] Düsseldorf dismissing its application for the issue of an order for the enforcement of a judgment given in default by the Netherlands court in 's-Hertogenbosch on 14 September 1979 ordering Pluspunkt Handelsgesellschaft mbH (hereinafter referred to as 'Pluspunkt'), whose registered office is in Neuss in the Federal Republic of Germany, to pay Pendy the sum of HFL 29 979.25, plus interest calculated from 6 December 1978 and the costs of the proceedings until the date of that judgment, amounting to HFL 1 042.15.

3. It appears that the document instituting the proceedings which culminated in the judgment by default of the Netherlands court was transmitted on 26 March 1979 to the Netherlands Officier van Justitie for the purpose of service. That document, together with the summons to appear at the hearing on 27 April 1979, was to be served on the defendant at 36 Kaarster Strasse, Neuss. On 17 May 1979, the Amtsgericht [Local Court] Neuss issued a certificate, in accordance with Article 6(2) of the Hague Convention of 15 November 1965, ratified by the Kingdom of the Netherlands and by the Federal Republic of Germany, indicating that it had not been possible to serve the documents in question.

4. The defendant, Pluspunkt, failed to enter an appearance and the court in 's-Hertogenbosch enjoined the plaintiff, Pendy, by an interlocutory judgment dated 8 June 1979, to prove that the defendant had been able to receive the summons in sufficient time or that all necessary steps had been taken in that respect to enable it to make arrangements for its defence. At the hearing on 20 July 1979, the plaintiff lodged an extract from the commercial register and a communication from the Amtsgericht

Neuss to the effect that the files in its possession showed the defendant's address as 36 Kaarster Strabe.

5. On the basis of that information, the court in 's-Hertogenbosch considered that transmission of the document instituting the proceedings to the Officier van Justitie, as evidenced by the document issued on 26 March 1979, was sufficient and delivered a judgment in default on 14 September 1979, in respect of which Pendy applied to the German courts for the issue of an enforcement order.

6. In its order of 8 July 1981 the Bundesgerichtshof restated the findings of the Oberlandesgericht Düsseldorf. According to the latter court, the measures taken by the plaintiff to discover the defendant's business address and to give proof thereof to the Netherlands court were inappropriate, in view of the fact that the commercial register merely mentions the town where a company has its registered office, in this instance Neuss, a factor which had not changed in the case of the defendant. Therefore, the procedural principle of the right to a proper hearing was held to have been contravened with regard to the defendant. In the opinion of the Oberlandesgericht, the fact that the Netherlands court considered service to have been properly effected was not sufficient to justify the issue of an enforcement order under the Brussels Convention.

7. Those are the circumstances in which the Bundesgerichtshof decided to stay the proceedings and to request the Court of Justice to give a preliminary ruling on the following question: 'May recognition of a judgment be refused in accordance with Article 27(2) of the Brussels Convention where the defendant did not enter an appearance in the proceedings in the adjudicating State and he was not duly served with the document which instituted the proceedings in sufficient time to enable him to arrange for his defence, even where the court of the State in which the judgment was given established, in accordance with the third paragraph of Article 20 of the Convention in conjunction with Article 15 of the Hague Convention of 15 November 1965 on the Service Abroad of Judicial and Extra-judicial Documents in Civil or Commercial Matters, that the defendant had an opportunity to receive the writ in sufficient time to enable him to arrange for his defence?'

8. It must be observed *in limine* that, according to the grounds of the order making the reference, the dispute which the Bundesgerichtshof seeks to resolve by way of a reference for a preliminary ruling relates not

only to the recognition but also to the enforcement in the Federal Republic of Germany of a judgment given by a Netherlands court. In the present case, however, that necessary finding is of very limited scope. The recognition and enforcement of judicial decisions are both governed by Title III of the Brussels Convention. Article 34, which is concerned with enforcement, provides that an application for the issue of an enforcement order may be refused only for one of the reasons specified in Articles 27 and 28, which are concerned with the recognition of judicial decisions.

9. Thus, the question raised by the Bundesgerichtshof seeks in substance to ascertain whether, under the Brussels Convention, the court of the State in which enforcement is sought may rely on Article 27(2) of the Convention in order to justify a refusal to recognise or enforce a judgment given by the court of another State which has acceded to the Convention, or whether it is bound by the conclusions which the adjudicating court drew from the application of the third paragraph of Article 20 of the Brussels Convention and Article 15 of the Hague Convention of 15 November 1965.

10. Article 27(2) of the Brussels Convention provides that a judgment given by a court of another Contracting State 'shall not be recognised … where it was given in default of appearance, if the defendant was not duly served with the document which instituted the proceedings in sufficient time to enable him to arrange for his defence'. Furthermore, Article 46(2) of the same Convention requires a party seeking recognition or applying for enforcement, in one Member State, of a judgment given in default in another Member State to produce the original or a certified true copy of the document which establishes that the party in default was served with the document instituting the proceedings.

11. The second paragraph of Article 20 of the Brussels Convention provides that, where a defendant domiciled in one Contracting State is sued in a court of another Contracting State and does not enter an appearance, the court must stay the proceedings so long as it is not shown that the defendant has been able to receive the document instituting the proceedings in sufficient time to enable him to arrange for his defence, or that all necessary steps have been taken to that end. The third paragraph of Article 20 provides that the aforegoing provisions are to be replaced by those of Article 15 of the Hague Convention of 15 November 1965 if the document instituting the proceedings or notice thereof had to be transmitted abroad in accordance with that Convention.

12. As the Bundesgerichtshof has established, that was precisely the case in this instance, since both the Kingdom of the Netherlands and the Federal Republic of Germany are parties to the Hague Convention. Article 15 of that Convention specifies, in the same way as the second paragraph of Article 20 of the Brussels Convention but in accordance with rules which are far more detailed and more precise, the circumstances in which a document instituting proceedings may be regarded as having been served on a defendant who is domiciled abroad and has failed to enter an appearance.

13. Although they do not seek to harmonise the different systems of service abroad of legal documents which are in force in the Member States, the provisions of the Brussels Convention are designed to ensure that the defendant's rights are effectively protected. For that reason, jurisdiction to determine whether the document introducing the proceedings was properly served was conferred both on the court of the original State and on the court of the State in which enforcement is sought. Thus, in accordance with the objective of Article 27 of the Convention, the court of the State in which enforcement is sought must examine the question posed by paragraph (2) of that article, notwithstanding the decision given by the court of the original State on the basis of the second and third paragraphs of Article 20. That examination is subject only to the limitation set by the third paragraph of Article 34 of the Convention to the effect that the foreign judgment may under no circumstances be reviewed as to its substance.

14. Accordingly, the answer to the question submitted by the Bundesgerichtshof must be that the court of the State in which enforcement is sought may, if it considers that the conditions laid down by Article 27(2) of the Brussels Convention are fulfilled, refuse to grant recognition and enforcement of a judgment even though the court of the State in which the judgment was given regarded it as proven, in accordance with the third paragraph of Article 20 of that Convention in conjunction with Article 15 of the Hague Convention of 15 November 1965, that the defendant, who failed to enter an appearance, had an opportunity to receive service of the document instituting the proceedings in sufficient time to enable him to make arrangements for his defence.

On those grounds, the Court (Second Chamber), in answer to the question submitted to it by the Bundesgerichtshof by order of 8 July 1981, hereby rules:

The court of the State in which enforcement is sought may, if it considers that the conditions laid down by Article 27(2) of the Brussels Convention are fulfilled, refuse to grant recognition and enforcement of a judgment, even though the court of the State in which the judgment was given regarded it as proven, in accordance with the third paragraph of Article 20 of that Convention in conjunction with Article 15 of the Hague Convention of 15 November 1965, that the defendant, who failed to enter an appearance, had an opportunity to receive service of the document instituting the proceedings in sufficient time to enable him to make arrangements for his defence.

OPINION OF MR ADVOCATE GENERAL REISCHL

Pendy Plastic Products [hereinafter referred to as 'Pendy'], the appellant on a point of law in the main proceedings, which has its registered office in Helmond in the Netherlands, brought an action before the court in 's-Hertogenbosch in the spring of 1970 against Pluspunkt Handelsgesellschaft [hereinafter referred to as 'Pluspunkt'], which has its registered office in Neuss in the Federal Republic of Germany. Apparently, the action was initiated in the following manner: the writ and the summons to attend a hearing on 27 April 1979 were transmitted on 26 March 1979 to the Netherlands Officier van Justitie at the court in 's-Hertogenbosch, which is permissible under Netherlands law for the purpose of service abroad. Furthermore, aforementioned documents were to be served through official channels on the defendant at 36 Kaarster Strasse, Neuss, that is to say the address which the plaintiff, later the appellant on a point of law, knew at the time.

However, it proved impossible to effect service because in April 1979 the defendant had transferred its business premises to another address in Neuss, of which the plaintiff claims to have learnt from the Chamber of Commerce for the Central Lower Rhine towards the end of April 1979. The Amtsgericht [local court] Neuss, whose assistance had been requested, issued a certificate on 17 May 1979 - perhaps a little too hastily and without carrying out sufficient inquiries - indicating that it had not been possible to effect service in accordance with Article 6(2) of the Hague Convention of 15 November 1965 on the Service Abroad of Judicial and Extra-judicial Documents in Civil or Commercial Matters [hereinafter referred to as 'the Hague Convention']. On 8 June 1979 the court in 's-Hertogenbosch delivered an interlocutory judgment on account of the defendant's failure to enter an appearance. It enjoined the plaintiff to prove that the defendant had had an opportunity to receive the Summons in sufficient time or that all necessary steps had been taken to enable it to arrange for its defence. At the same time, it adjourned the proceedings until 20 July 1979.

The plaintiff complied with that order by submitting to the court the answers which it had received from the Residents Registration Office, Neuss, and the Commercial Register, Neuss, according to which the defendant's address was insofar as any details were given, '36 Kaarster Strasse, Neuss'. Accordingly, in the opinion of the court in 's-Hertogenbosch, the plaintiff had demonstrated to the court's satisfaction that it had taken all the necessary steps to locate the person on whom the documents were to be served. Their transmission to the Netherlands Officier van Justitie, as evidenced by the document issued on 26 March 1979, was thus regarded as sufficient. The Netherlands court then gave judgment in default on 14 September 1979 ordering the defendant to pay a certain sum, plus interest and the costs of the proceedings. That judgment was declared provisionally enforceable and served on the defendant by the Amtsgericht Neuss on 10 December 1979. That, it seems, is when the defendant heard for the first time that proceedings had been instituted against it. It apparently lodged an appeal against that judgment but we know nothing of the outcome.

In order to enforce that judgment the plaintiff subsequently applied to the Landgericht [Regional Court] Düsseldorf pursuant to Article 31 et seq. of the Convention on Jurisdiction and the Enforcement of Judgments in Civil and Commercial Matters [hereinafter referred to as 'the Brussels Convention'] for the issue of an enforcement order. The application was dismissed on 24 July 1980, essentially in reliance on the principle of the right to a proper hearing and on the ground that the defendant had had no knowledge of the proceedings instituted against it.

The appeal lodged against that decision was also dismissed. In its judgment of 6 January 1981 the Oberlandesgericht [Higher Regional Court] Düsseldorf held that, according to the second paragraph of Article 34 in conjunction with Article 27(2) of the Brussels Convention, it was for the court of the State in which enforcement was sought to establish whether service had been effected properly. In that regard it was clear that service had not been effected in accordance with the Hague Convention; it had merely been attempted, and since the Convention contained no other provisions which were relevant in those circumstances the proceedings had culminated in the issue of a certificate attesting that it had been impossible to effect service. Nor had the documents been served in compliance with the Netherlands provisions on service by public notice, since there had been no notification in a newspaper, as required by those provisions. Instead, the documents had merely been transmitted to the Officier van Justitie, which is sufficient under Netherlands law for the purpose of service abroad. In any event, Article 27(2) of the Brussels Convention provided that the principle of the right to a proper hearing must be observed. That principle had, however, been contravened because the defendant had not received any notice of the proceedings. In that respect, the steps taken by the plaintiff to discover the defendant's address were wholly inappropriate - as the plaintiff, which is a business undertaking, might have realized - since it should not have confined itself to approaching the Residents Registration Office, which does not record the addresses of commercial premises, and the Commercial Register, which does not list the addresses of undertakings, but should at least have applied to the Chamber of Commerce for information.

Pendy then appealed on a point of law to the Bundesgerichtshof [Federal Court of Justice]. It contended that, since service through official channels had proved impossible, as was apparent from the certificate issued by the Amtsgericht Neuss, the Netherlands court had been right to accept service by public notice. The only thing which mattered in those circumstances was that the Netherlands court had complied with Article 20 of the Brussels Convention in conjunction with Article 15 of the Hague Convention. Accordingly, it was no longer permissible for the court in which enforcement was sought to question whether the documents had been properly served under Netherlands law.

The Bundesgerichtshof, which proceeds on the assumption that the Hague Convention applies in the Federal Republic of Germany and in the Netherlands, is uncertain about the nature of the power of examination vested in the court in which enforcement is sought by Article 27(2) of the Brussels Convention. The Bundesgerichtshof's doubts stem from Article 20 of the Brussels Convention and Article 15 of the Hague Convention. It inclines to the view that the court in which enforcement is sought is entitled to examine the judgment if the court of the State in which it was given conducted an investigation under Article 20 of the Brussels Convention and Article 15 of the Hague Convention and disregarded essential matters. In the opinion of the Bundesgerichtshof, however, it may also be argued that where the court of the State in which the judgment was given endeavoured to ascertain in accordance with Article 20 of the Brussels Convention whether the defendant had an opportunity to arrange for his defence, the third paragraph of Article 34 of that Convention requires that its findings should be accepted without further inquiry by the court of the State in which enforcement is sought.

Accordingly, by decision of 8 July 1981 the Bundesgerichtshof stayed the proceedings and referred to the Court of Justice, under Article 3 of the Protocol on the interpretation by the Court of Justice of the Brussels Convention, the following question for a preliminary ruling: 'May recognition of a judgment be refused in accordance with Article 27(2) of the Brussels Convention where the defendant did not enter an appearance in the proceedings in the adjudicating State and he was not duly served with the document which instituted the proceedings in sufficient time to enable him to arrange for his defence, even where the court of the State in which the judgment was given established, in accordance with the third paragraph of Article 20 of the Convention in conjunction with Article 15 of the Hague Convention of 15 November 1965 on the Service Abroad of Judicial and Extra-judicial Documents in Civil or Commercial Matters, that the defendant had an opportunity to receive the writ in sufficient time to enable him to arrange for his defence?'

The Governments of the Federal Republic of Germany, the United Kingdom and the Italian Republic and the Commission of the European Communities have suggested that the question should be answered in the affirmative. In my opinion, there can be no other answer.

1. However, I should first like to remind the Court of the contents of the provisions which are relevant to these proceedings.

The second paragraph of Article 20 of the Brussels Convention provides that, where a defendant domiciled in one Contracting State is sued in a court of another Contracting State and does not enter an appearance: 'The Court shall stay the proceedings so long as it is not shown that the defendant has been able to receive the document instituting the proceedings in sufficient time to enable him to arrange for his defence, or that all necessary steps have been taken to this end'.

However, in the circumstances of this case, the aforesaid provision is, according to the third paragraph of Article 20, to be replaced by Article 15 of the Hague Convention, which provides that: 'Where a writ of Summons or an equivalent document had to be transmitted abroad for the purpose of service, under the provisions of the present Convention, and the defendant has not appeared, judgment shall not be given until it is established that -

(a) the document was served by a method prescribed by the internal law of the State addressed for the service of documents in domestic actions upon persons who are within its territory, or

(b) the document was actually delivered to the defendant or to his residence by another method provided for by this Convention, and that in either of these cases the service or the delivery was effected in sufficient time to enable the defendant to defend.

Each contracting State shall be free to declare that the judge, notwithstanding the provisions of the first paragraph of this article, may give judgment even if no certificate of service or delivery has been received, if all the following conditions are fulfilled:

(a) the document was transmitted by one of the methods provided for in this Convention,

(b) a period of time of not less than six months, considered adequate by the judge in the particular case, has elapsed since the date of the transmission of the document,

(c) no certificate of any kind has been received, even though every reasonable effort has been made to obtain it through the competent authorities of the State addressed.'

The Netherlands has made such a declaration. It was published in the Bundesgesetzblatt (1980, Part II, p. 912) and provides as follows: 'Notwithstanding the provisions of the first paragraph of Article 15 of the Convention, the Netherlands court may give judgment even if no certificate of service or delivery has been received, if all the following conditions are fulfilled:

(a) the document was transmitted by one of the methods provided for in the Convention,

(b) a period of time of not less than six months, laid down by the court in the particular case, has elapsed since the date of the transmission of the document,

(c) no certificate of service or delivery has been received, even though every reasonable effort has been made to obtain it through the competent authorities'.

It is also significant that, according to Article 34 of the Brussels Convention, an application to the court of the country in which enforcement is sought for the issue of an enforcement order may be refused only for one of the reasons specified in Articles 27 and 28. Article 27 provides, insofar as it is relevant, that:'A judgment shall not be recognized: 1. if such recognition is contrary to public policy in the State in which recognition is sought; 2. where it was given in default of appearance, if the defendant was not duly served with the document which instituted the proceedings in sufficient time to enable him to arrange for his defence'.

2. In order to solve the problem raised by the Bundesgerichtshof, reference may be made in particular to Case 166/80 [*Klomps* v *Michel*] which also involved Article 27(2). That occurred in connection with the enforcement in the Netherlands of a German order, equivalent to a judgment by default, which had been granted after the German court had established that the document instituting the proceedings had been duly served on the defendant at his address in Germany.

In this regard, it was stated in the preliminary ruling that the purpose of Article 27(2) of the Brussels Convention is to prevent the recognition and enforcement of judgments if the guarantees provided by the law of the State in which the judgment was given and by the Brussels Convention are not sufficient to ensure that the defendant had an opportunity to arrange for his defence. Under that provision the court of the State in which enforcement is sought must determine whether two requirements were satisfied: the first relates to the proper service of the document and the test is to be carried out by reference both to the law of the State in which the judgment was given and to the Convention, which is binding on that State: the second concerns the time required by the defendant to prepare his defence and necessitates findings of fact. A decision given in the original State in connection with the first of the aforementioned requirements does not release the court of the State in which enforcement is sought from the duty to ascertain whether the second requirement was complied with. The court in which enforcement is sought must establish in each case whether there are exceptional circumstances leading to the conclusion that service was sufficient to enable the defendant to arrange for his defence; for this purpose all the circumstances of the case, including the manner in which service was effected, must be taken into consideration.

Accordingly, it is clear that the fundamental purpose of Article 27(2) is to ensure that the defendant has an opportunity to prepare a proper defence or, in other words, that the principle of the right to a proper hearing is observed (see in that connection Geimer Anerkennung gerichtlicher Entscheidungen nach dem EWG-Übereinkommen vom 27. September 1968, Recht der Internationalen Wirtschaft 1976, p. 139 et seq.; Droz, Compétence judiciaire et effets des jugements dans le marché commun, 1972, No 500). Furthermore, in my opinion it is possible to deduce from that judgment a principle that the court in which enforcement is sought must act independently in assessing that matter and is not bound by the findings of the adjudicating court.

3. (a) It must, of course, be recognized that the provisions of Title II of the Brussels Convention, and indeed those of Article 15 of the Hague Convention, serve to protect the interests of the defendant.

However, it is clear from the rules as a whole, in the light of the declaration made by the Netherlands pursuant to Article 15, that no adequate guarantee is provided of the defendant's actually being notified of the document instituting the proceedings and having an opportunity to arrange for his defence accordingly. As the Jenard Report on the Brussels Convention (Official Journal C 59, 5. 3. 1979, p. 39) stated Netherlands law is characterised *inter alia* by the fact that the formalities connected with judicial documents intended for a person living abroad, are localised in the territory of the State of the forum, which means in effect that the documents are considered to have been duly served if they have been transmitted to the Procureur Generaal or Officier van Justitie at the competent Netherlands court or forwarded to the Ministry for Foreign Affairs. That was apparently the position even after the entry into force of the Hague Convention, as may be inferred from the German Government's memorandum thereon (Drucksache des Deutschen Bundestages, 8/217 II A 1 b), which was referred to by the Commission. That alone suffices to show that it is reasonable to assume that the examination by the court of the State in which the judgment was given of the question whether the defendant had an opportunity to arrange for his defence is not final and that a second, independent examination in the State in which enforcement is sought must be performed in order to determine whether the defendant genuinely had an opportunity to arrange for his defence before the judgment by default was given.

(b) I have already pointed out that Article 27(2) of the Brussels Convention reflects the basic concern to ensure observance of the principle of the right to a proper hearing. In order to clarify the meaning of that principle reference was made in the course of the proceedings to the Court's judgment in Case 125/79 [*Denilauler* v *Couchet Frères*], and to the fact that the principle is often regarded as a matter of public policy. In any event, that was emphasised in relation to English law and it also holds true for French law, according to the French Court of Cassation (judgment of 4 October 1967, cited by Droz, op. cit, p. 317). It may therefore be stated without further inquiry that provisions having such a content are not to be interpreted restrictively, that is to say they must not be construed as curtailing the powers of the courts which are responsible for their application.

(c) It was also argued - quite rightly - that according to an internationally recognized principle, the courts decision-making powers are unfettered and may not be assumed to be restricted as regards the determination and appraisal of the facts unless such a restriction has been expressly laid down.

Such a provision is indeed contained in the third paragraph of Article 34 of the Brussels Convention in relation to the review of the substance of a foreign judgment and in the second paragraph of Article 28, which provides as follows: 'In its examination of the grounds of jurisdiction referred to in the foregoing paragraph, the court or authority applied to shall be *bound by the findings of fact* on which the court of the State in which the judgment was given based its jurisdiction'.

Article 5 of the Convention of 30 August 1962 between Germany and the Netherlands contained a provision to the same effect.

However, as far as the inquiry to be conducted under Article 27(2) of the Brussels Convention is concerned, no restrictions whatsoever are imposed either by that or by any other provision of the Convention. In particular, it does not contain any proviso in relation to Article 20. Nor may it be said with certainty that the conclusion must perforce be drawn from the last mentioned article - as would be in view of the principle under discussion - that its purpose is to restrict the scope of the inquiry to be conducted by the court in which enforcement is sought.

4. Finally, it is also significant that Article 46 of the Brussels Convention requires, in the case of a judgment given in default, the party seeking recognition or applying for enforcement of the judgment to produce the document establishing that the party in default was served with the document instituting the proceedings. This, in particular the absence of any restriction, undoubtedly suggests that the court of the State in which enforcement is sought - must examine the manner in which service was effected and cannot therefore simply proceed on the assumption that the tests which were to be conducted by the court in which the judgment by default was given were sufficient.

Moreover, the opinion which I have expressed is also held by various academic lawyers.

I would refer to the above-mentioned article by Geimer, in which it is emphasised that the questions of public policy which must be considered include the question whether in the foreign proceedings any fundamental procedural requirements which may not be waived in the second State were infringed, and that in conducting such an inquiry the court of the second State is not bound by the findings of fact made by the first court.

Moreover, a number of interesting statements are contained in 'Internationaler Rechtsverkehr in Zivil- und Handelssachen, Erläuterungen zu dem Übereinkommen über die gerichtliche Zuständigkeit und die Vollstreckung gerichtlicher Entscheidungen in Zivil- und Handelssachen,' by Bülow-Böckstiegel. There it is pointed out (in Note III 4(a) to Article 27) that, precisely because certain forms of service, such as service by public notice, are fictitious, it is required - as a necessary corrective - that service should be effected in sufficient time and that the defendant should have an opportunity to arrange for his defence. It is also stated that, because of the disruptive impact of judgments by default, Article 27(2) contains an exception, concerning the proper service of documents, to the rule that the judgment may not be reviewed as to its substance. Moreover, even where the adjudicating court has already determined, pursuant to the second paragraph of Article 20 of the Brussels Convention or Article 15 of the Hague Convention, that service was effected in sufficient time, the court in which recognition is sought may, according to Bülow-Böckstiegel, re-examine the question and may arrive at quite different findings (Note III 4(b) to Article 27).

5. Accordingly, I propose that the court should answer the question submitted by the Bundesgerichtshof as follows: 'Article 27(2) of the Brussels Convention is to be interpreted as meaning that even where the court of the State in which the judgment was given established, pursuant to the third paragraph of

Article 20 of the Brussels Convention in conjunction with Article 15 of the Hague Convention, that the defendant had an opportunity to receive the writ in sufficient time to enable him to arrange for his defence, the court of the State in which enforcement is sought must, where the defendant failed to enter an appearance in the proceedings in the State in which the judgment was given, ascertain independently whether the defendant was duly served with the document instituting the proceedings in sufficient time to enable him to arrange for his defence; if it comes to the conclusion that that was not the case it must refuse to recognise the judgment'.

Case 49/84 - 11 June 1985

Leon Emile Gaston Carlos Debaecker and Berthe Plouvier
v
Cornelius Gerrit Bouwman

Article 27(2) - Recognition and enforcement of judgments - Grounds for refusal - The document which instituted the proceedings not served in sufficient time on a defendant in default of appearance - Service in sufficient time - Review by the court in which enforcement is sought - Scope - Exceptional circumstances - Taken into account - Conditions.

Summary

The requirement, laid down in Article 27(2) of the Convention on Jurisdiction and the Enforcement of Judgments in Civil and Commercial Matters, that service of the document which instituted the proceedings should have been effected in sufficient time is applicable where service was effected within a period prescribed by the court of the State in which the judgment was given or where the defendant resided, exclusively or otherwise, within the jurisdiction of that court or in the same country as that court.

In examining whether service was effected in sufficient time, the court in which enforcement is sought may take account of exceptional circumstances which arose after service was duly effected.

The fact that the plaintiff was apprised of the defendant's new address after service was effected, and the fact that the defendant was responsible for the failure of the duly serviced document to reach him are matters which the court in which enforcement is sought may take into account in assessing whether service was effected in sufficient time.

JUDGMENT OF THE COURT

Lord Mackenzie Stuart, President, Bosco, President of Chamber, Pescatore, Koopmans and Bahlmann, Judges

1. By a judgment dated 17 February 1984, which was received at the Court on 24 February 1984, the Hoge Raad der Nederlanden [Supreme Court of the Netherlands] requested a preliminary ruling, under the Protocol of 3 June 1971 on the Interpretation by the Court of Justice of the Convention of 27 September 1968 on Jurisdiction and the Enforcement of Judgments in Civil and Commercial Matters (hereinafter referred to as 'the Convention'), on several questions concerning the interpretation of Article 27(2) of the Convention.

2. Those questions were raised in the course of proceedings pending before that court between Mr and Mrs Debaecker on the one hand, and Mr Bouwman on the other hand.

3. Mr and Mrs Debaecker had let commercial premises in Antwerp to Mr Bouwman, a national of the Netherlands, for a period of nine years from 15 October 1980. On 21 September 1981 Mr Bouwman left the premises (in which he had established his residence), without giving prior notice and without leaving any forwarding address. On 24 September 1981 he was summoned to appear on 1 October 1981 before the Vrederechter [Cantonal Judge], Antwerp, by a writ which was served on him, pursuant to Article 37 of the Belgian Judicial Code, at the Politiecommissariat [police station], Antwerp, since he was still registered as a resident of Antwerp. In a letter dated 25 September 1981 and received by the plaintiffs' lawyer on 28 September 1981, Mr Bouwman terminated the tenancy, returned the keys of the premises and stated that his new address was a post office box number in Essen, Belgium. The plaintiffs' lawyer made no attempt to inform the defendant at that new address that he had been summoned to appear on 1 October before the Vrederechter in Antwerp, and on that date the defendant was ordered, by judgment in default of appearance, to pay to Mr and Mrs Debaecker damages of BFR 1 072 900.

4. On 30 November 1981 the President of the Arrondissementsrechtbank [District Court] in Breda (the Netherlands) made an order, on an application by Mr and Mrs Debaecker, for the enforcement of the judgment in default given by the Vrederechter in Antwerp. Mr Bouwman appealed against that order on 6 January 1982

and it was set aside by the Arrondissementsrechtbank on 12 October 1982.

5. Mr and Mrs Debaecker appealed to the Hoge Raad, which stayed the proceedings and referred to the Court the following questions for a preliminary ruling: '1. Is the requirement, laid down in Article 27(2) of the Convention on Jurisdiction and the Enforcement of Judgments in Civil and Commercial Matters, that service of the document which instituted the proceedings should have been effected in sufficient time inapplicable if service was effected within a period prescribed by the court of the State in which the judgment was given and/or the defendant resided, exclusively or otherwise, within the jurisdiction of that court or in the same country as that court?

If Question 1 is answered in the negative: 2(a) In relation to the question whether, in a particular case, there are exceptional circumstances which warrant the conclusion that, although due service was effected, as provided for in Article 27(2), it was nonetheless inadequate for the purpose of causing the time required in that provision to begin to run, is account to be taken only of circumstances which existed at the time of service and which the plaintiff could take into consideration at that time?

If Question 2(a) is answered in the negative: 2(b) Can the plaintiff be required as a result of circumstances which arose after service was effected, in particular notification to the plaintiff of the defendant's address, to take further steps to inform the defendant of the impending action, so that if such steps are not taken the time required by Article 27(2) does not begin to run?

If Question 2(b) is answered in the affirmative: 2(c) What criterion must be applied in that regard? In particular, does the fact that the defendant was responsible for the failure of the duly served document to reach him prevent the court, where, for example, the plaintiff was aware that the defendant had left the address stated to be his place of residence, from considering that further steps as referred to above were required?'

6. Written observations were submitted by the parties to the main proceedings the Governments of the Federal Republic of Germany, the United Kingdom and the Commission of the European Communities.

7. In Question 1 the Hoge Raad asks whether the requirement, laid down in Article 27(2) of the Convention, that service of the document which instituted the proceedings should have been effected in sufficient time is inapplicable if service was effected within a period prescribed by

the court of the State in which the judgment was given and/or the defendant resided in that State.

8. The plaintiffs in the main proceedings consider that the answer to the first question should be that Article 27(2) of the Convention is inapplicable where at the time of service of the document which instituted the proceedings, the defendant was resident within the jurisdiction of the adjudicating court or at least where (as in the present case) he had his sole residence there.

9. The defendant in the main proceedings disputes that interpretation, contending that there is nothing in the wording of Article 27(2) to suggest that the rules laid down by the Convention in order to guarantee the defendant's right to a fair hearing should be applied solely where the defendant is resident in a Contracting State other than that of the adjudicating court. If that were so, the court in which enforcement was sought would have no discretion to decide whether service was effected in sufficient time where both parties resided in the same Contracting State. The defendant's view is shared by the Commission, the Federal Republic of Germany and the United Kingdom, which stresses that in its judgment of 16 June 1981 in Case 166/80 (*Klomps* v *Michel* [1981] ECR 1593) the Court has already by implication acknowledged that Article 27(2) applies regardless of whether the parties reside in different States or in the same State.

10. First of all, it should be stated that there is nothing in the wording of Article 27(2) - which does not lay down any condition as regards the defendant's place of residence to suggest that the question asked by the Hoge Raad should be answered in the affirmative. Although the Convention is, as is clear from the preamble, intended to 'secure the simplification of formalities governing the reciprocal recognition and enforcement of judgments of courts or tribunals', that aim cannot, according to a series of decisions of the Court, be attained by undermining in any way the right to a fair hearing.

11. It follows from the wording of Article 27 that the courts of a Contracting State may refuse to recognise a judgment only on one of the grounds expressly mentioned in that provision. One of those grounds is that laid down in Paragraph (2), in order to ensure the adequate protection of the rights of a defendant against whom judgment is given in default of appearance abroad. Article 27(2) provides that a judgment shall not be recognised '... if the defendant was not duly served with the document

which instituted the proceedings in sufficient time to enable him to arrange for his defence'. That provision takes account of the fact that certain Contracting States make provision for the fictitious service of process where the defendant has no known place of residence. The effects that are deemed to follow from such fictitious service vary and the probability of the defendant's actually being informed of service, so as to give him sufficient time to prepare his defence, may vary considerably, depending on the type of fictitious service provided for in each legal system.

12. For that reason Article 27(2) must be interpreted as being intended to protect the right of a defendant to defend himself when recognition of judgment given in default in another Contracting State is sought, even if the rules on service laid down in that Contracting State were complied with.

13. The answer to the first question must therefore be that the requirement, laid down in Article 27(2) of the Convention, that service of the document which instituted the proceedings should have been effected in sufficient time is applicable even where service was effected within a period prescribed by the court of the State in which the judgment was given or where the defendant resided, exclusively or otherwise, within the jurisdiction of that court or in the same country as that court.

14. In Question 2(a) the Hoge Raad asks whether, in assessing whether there are exceptional circumstances which warrant the conclusion that, although due service was effected as provided for in Article 27(2), it was nonetheless inadequate for the purpose of causing the time required in that provision to begin to run, account is to be taken only of circumstances which existed at the time of service and which the plaintiff could take into consideration at that time.

15. The parties who have submitted observations to the Court refer on this point to the judgment in *Klomps* v *Michel* (cited above) in which the Court ruled that, although the court in which enforcement is sought may as a general rule confine itself to examining whether the period reckoned from the date on which service was duly effected allowed the defendant sufficient time for his defence, it is nonetheless also required to consider whether, in a particular case, there are exceptional circumstances which warrant the conclusion that, although service was duly effected, it was inadequate for the purposes of enabling the defendant to take steps to arrange for his defence and, accordingly, could not cause the time stipulated by Article 27(2) to begin to run.

16. The plaintiffs in the main proceedings interpret that ruling as meaning that no account may be taken of circumstances which did not become apparent until after service was effected, and that due service which at the date on which it was effected was considered adequate, in the light of the circumstances existing at that time, for the purpose of causing the time stipulated by Article 27(2) to begin to run, may not be invalidated as a result of circumstances which subsequently supervene. The serious consequences of deciding otherwise would be exacerbated by the fact that the defence provided for under Article 27(2) may be pleaded not only in proceedings for enforcement but also in proceedings in which the recognition of a judgment is sought.

17. The opinion of the plaintiffs in the main proceedings is in part shared by the Commission, on grounds relating to legal certainty, to the need for a restrictive interpretation of Article 27(2) - since it is an exception to the general rule prohibiting any fresh assessment of the facts at the enforcement stage - and to the fact that guarantees are already provided in the national rules on the service of process. The Commission concedes, however, that it may be possible to take into account certain wholly exceptional circumstances which occur after service and for which the defendant cannot be held responsible.

18. The defendant in the main proceedings, the Federal Republic of Germany and the United Kingdom all propose that the question should be answered in the negative, stressing in particular that Article 27(2) can only provide complete protection for a defendant if all the circumstances, including those occurring after service, are taken into account.

19. With regard to this question, it should be pointed out first that, if the circumstances to be taken into account were confined to those which were known at the time of service, there would be a danger of interpreting the requirement of service in sufficient time in such a restrictive and formalistic manner that it would, in fact, coincide with the requirement of due service, thus negating one of the safeguards laid down by the Convention for the protection of the defendant.

20. Accordingly, in order to ascertain whether the requirement of service in sufficient time was fulfilled - that requirement being laid down precisely in order to ensure that the defendant's rights are effectively protected - regard must be had to facts which, although occurring after service was effected, may nonetheless have had the effect that service did not, in fact, enable the defendant to arrange for his defence.

21. That view finds further support in *Klomps* v *Michel*, where the Court ruled that, in ascertaining whether service was effected in sufficient time, a court might take account 'of all the circumstances of the case in point, including the means employed for effecting service, the relations between the plaintiff and the defendant or the nature of the steps which had to be taken in order to prevent judgment from being given in default'. An appraisal of the steps which had to be taken in order to prevent judgment from being given in default is bound to concern factors arising after service was effected.

22. The answer to Question 2(a) must, therefore, be that the Court in which enforcement is sought may, in examining whether service was effected in sufficient time, take account of exceptional circumstances which arose after service was duly effected.

23. In Question 2(b) the Hoge Raad asks whether the plaintiff can be required, as a result of circumstances which arose after service was effected, to take further steps to inform the defendant of the impending action, so that if such steps are not taken the time required by Article 27(2) does not begin to run. Question 2(c) asks whether the fact that the defendant was responsible for the failure of the duly served document to reach him prevents the court where for example, the plaintiff was aware that the defendant had left the address stated to be his place of residence, from considering that further steps as referred to in Question 2(b) should have been taken.

24. With regard to Question 2(b), the plaintiffs in the main proceedings observe that no such obligation is provided for in the applicable national law or in the Convention itself and consider that a rule of that kind would impair legal certainty in the field of procedural law. In addition, they argue that there is no uniform practice in the legal systems of the Contracting States, some of which are more formalistic than others and thus less inclined to require any steps to be taken which are not prescribed by the law or the Convention, In any event, say the plaintiffs, although it may be expected that a lawyer might notify the opposite party or request an adjournment in a case such as this, a lawyer cannot be reproached for failing to do so.

25. The Commission also considers that such an obligation would seriously jeopardise legal certainty. In its view, no consequence under procedural law should flow from the fact that the plaintiff does not notify the defendant when he learns after service that the defendant may be contacted at another address.

26. The defendant in the main proceedings, the Federal Republic of Germany and the United Kingdom, on the other hand, propose an affirmative answer, stressing *inter alia* that the purpose of Article 27(2) is to guarantee not merely formal service but the right to be heard and thus the opportunity of presenting a defence, They therefore consider that every effort must be made to prevent judgment from being given against a defendant without his having had an opportunity of defending himself.

27. On that point it must be borne in mind that the question whether service was effected in sufficient time is a question of fact and therefore cannot be determined on the basis of the domestic law of the adjudicating court or on the basis of the domestic law of the court in which enforcement is sought. However, the Convention does not impose on the plaintiff any obligation to take steps such as those referred to in Question 2(b). The failure to take such steps is in reality merely a factor which must be taken into account in order to establish whether service was effected in sufficient time.

28. Seen in that light, the fact that the plaintiff, after service, learns of the defendant's new address does not compel him to take any further steps, but renders his subsequent behaviour important for the purpose of determining whether service was effected in sufficient time. By notifying the defendant at his new address, the plaintiff ensures that the court in which enforcement is sought cannot decide that the defendant's change of address is an exceptional circumstance which prevents the service effected at his former address from being regarded as having been effected in sufficient time.

29. As regards Question 2(c), the plaintiffs in the main proceedings consider that, even if the plaintiff is bound to take further steps to notify the defendant, failure to do so does not necessarily result in the refusal of recognition or enforcement of the judgment if it is the defendant's fault that the plaintiff was unaware at the time of service of the address at which the defendant could have been contacted. They argue that it is not enough for the defendant to give a post office box number. The Commission shares that view and considers that, if the defendant is responsible for the fact that he did not receive the document which was duly served, the plaintiff is under no obligation to take further steps, even if he subsequently discovers the defendant's new address.

30. The defendant in the main proceedings, the Federal Republic of Germany and the United Kingdom consider that the defendant's

behaviour is one of the circumstances which the court in which enforcement is sought may take into account in assessing whether service was effected in sufficient time, and its effect must be evaluated by that court in the light of the requirement that the defendant's rights should be effectively protected.

31. In view of the fact that Article 27(2), as has already been stated, seeks to enable a defendant to defend himself effectively, the defendant's behaviour may not be used as a basis for considering that service was effected in sufficient time even though the plaintiff subsequently became aware that the defendant could be reached at a new address. To admit such a proposition would be tantamount to acknowledging the existence of a presumption that service was effected in sufficient time. Although it may rightly be presumed that service was effected in sufficient time where the plaintiff did not know where to reach the defendant, such a presumption would clearly be contrary to the principle that the defendant's rights should be protected if, after service, the plaintiff learned where the defendant could be reached.

32. Thus the defendant's behaviour cannot automatically rule out the possibility of taking into account exceptional circumstances which warrant the conclusion that service was not effected in sufficient time, Instead, such behaviour may be assessed by the court in which enforcement is sought as one of the matters in the light of which it determines whether service was effected in sufficient time. It will, therefore, be for that court to assess, in a case such as the present, to what extent the defendant's behaviour is capable of outweighing the fact that the plaintiff was apprised after service of the defendant's new address.

33. In view of the foregoing considerations, the answer to Questions 2(b) and 2(c) must be that the fact that the plaintiff was apprised of the defendant's new address, after service was effected, and the fact that the defendant was responsible for the failure of the duly served document to reach him are matters which the court in which enforcement is sought may take into account in assessing whether service was effected in sufficient time.

On those grounds, the Court (Fourth Chamber), in answer to the questions submitted to it by the Hoge Raad der Nederlanden by judgment of 17 February 1984, hereby rules:

1. The requirement, laid down in Article 27(2) of the Convention on Jurisdiction and the Enforcement of Judgments in Civil and Commercial Matters, that service of the document which instituted the proceedings should have been effected in sufficient time is applicable where service was effected within a period prescribed by the court of the State in which the judgment was given or where the defendant resided, exclusively or otherwise, within the jurisdiction of that court or in the same country as that court.

2. In examining whether service was effected in sufficient time, the court in which enforcement is sought may take account of exceptional circumstances which arose after service was duly effected.

3. The fact that the plaintiff was apprised of the defendant's new address, after service was effected, and the fact that the defendant was responsible for the failure of the duly served document to reach him are matters which the court in which enforcement is sought may take into account in assessing whether service was effected in sufficient time.

OPINION OF THE ADVOCATE GENERAL VERLOREN VAN THEMAAT

1. Introduction

The Hoge Raad der Nederlanden [Supreme Court of the Netherlands] has referred to the Court a number of questions concerning Article 27(2) of the Convention of 27 September 1968 on Jurisdiction and the Enforcement of Judgments in Civil and Commercial Matters [hereinafter referred to as 'the Convention'].

Article 27 provides as follows: 'A judgment shall not be recognised: (1) if such recognition is contrary to public policy in the State in which recognition is sought; (2) where it was given in default of appearance, if the defendant was not duly served with the document which instituted the proceedings in sufficient time to enable him to arrange for his defence; ...'.

This case concerns in particular the rule laid down in that article that the defendant should receive service in sufficient time to ensure, as the Court stated in its judgment of 15 July 1982 in Case 228/81 *Pendy Plastic* v *Pluspunkt* [1982] ECR 2723, at p. 2736), 'that the defendant's rights are effectively protected' where recognition is sought in a State other than the State in which it was given. The Hoge Raad summarised the various questions in the following terms: 'May facts which occurred later - that is to say, after the service of the document which instituted the proceedings - compel the plaintiff to take further steps to inform the defendant of the impending action, so that if such steps are not taken the time required by Article 27(2) does not begin to run?'

The facts of the case

In setting out the facts of the case, I shall be guided largely by the lengthy remarks made by the Commission in its observations. I consider that a detailed description of the facts is warranted since it is necessary to appraise the facts in order to determine whether service was effected in sufficient time. Therefore, even a general answer to the questions submitted to the Court must, in order to be of use, take adequate account of those facts. Mr Bouwman, a Dutch national, signed a lease with Mr Debaecker and his wife Berta Plouvier, both of Belgian nationality, by which he agreed from 15 October 1980 to rent business premises situated at 18 Frankrijklei, Antwerp, where he intended to run an art gallery. On Monday, 21 September 1981, Mr Bouwman left without giving notice or leaving a forwarding address. On Thursday, 24 September 1981, the Debaeckers' lawyer, Mr Debaecker, who according to the Commission is their son, applied to the Vrederechter [Cantonal Judge], Antwerp, for leave to serve a writ on Mr Bouwman at reduced notice, alleging *inter alia* that Mr Bouwman had left, taking with him all his movable property, 'like a thief in the night'. The Vrederechter granted leave for Mr Bouwman to be summoned to appear at the sitting on Thursday, 1 October 1981, and a writ dated 24 September 1981 was served on the Politiecommissariaat, Antwerp, in accordance with Article 37 of the Gerechtelijk Wetboek [Belgian Judicial Code]. That course was followed because at the time of service the lawyer was not aware of Mr Bouwman's whereabouts. However, he assumed that Mr Bouwman still resided in Antwerp because he was registered there. The writ could not be served at his home address, 18 Frankrijklei, because neither he nor any member of his household was there.

On 25 September 1981 Mr Bouwman sent to the Debaeckers' lawyer a registered letter, in which he repudiated the lease, returned the keys and gave notice that he was to be reached 'through post office box number 24, 2190 Essen' (likewise in Belgium). That letter reached the Debaeckers' lawyer on 28 September 1981. He, however, took no action and therefore left Mr Bouwman unaware that a writ had been served on him at the Politiecommissariaat requiring him to appear before the Vrederechter on 1 October. On 1 October the Vrederechter gave judgment in default against Mr Bouwman, terminating the lease and awarding Mr and Mrs Debaecker compensation of BFR 1 072 900.

The Commission informed the Court that that judgment was itself served in the same way: as Mr Bouwman was not at his official place of residence in Frankrijklei, it was served at the Politiecommissariaat.

On 18 November the Registrar of the Vredegerecht, Antwerp, established that no appeal had been lodged against the judgment in default. On the same day Mr and Mrs Debaecker lodged an application with the President of the

Arrondissementsrechtbank [District Court] in Breda (the Netherlands) for an order freezing Mr Bouwman's bank account in Breda. It was presumably at about that time that Mr Bouwman discovered that proceedings had been brought against him.

On 30 November the President of the Arrondissementsrechtbank, Breda, authorised the enforcement of the judgment of the Vrederechter. Mr Bouwman appealed against that decision to the Arrondissementsrechtbank, Breda, on 6 January 1982. On 12 October 1982 that court held that the appeal was well founded and dismissed the application for the issue of an order for enforcement.

Mr Bouwman based his appeal *inter alia* on Articles 20 and 27 of the Convention. The Arrondissementsrechtbank found that the claim based on Article 20 could not succeed because that article covered the situation in which a defendant residing in one Contracting State was sued in a court of another Contracting State. In this case, however, Mr Bouwman was sued before a court in the same State and city as that in which he had his residence under Belgian law and the writ did not even have to leave the City of Antwerp in order to be validly served.

As regards Article 27(2), the Arrondissmentsrechtbank found that it was not disputed that the document which instituted the proceedings had been duly served in accordance with Belgian law. However, Mr Bouwman contended that, in order to satisfy the requirement that service should be effected in sufficient time, it would have been necessary not only to effect formal service in the prescribed manner but, in addition, to serve the writ requiring him to appear before the Vrederechter on 1 October 1981 through his post office box number, which was known to the Debaeckers' lawyer from 28 September 1981.

In that connection, in accordance with the judgment of the court in Case 166/80 (*Klomps* v *Michel* [1981] ECR 1593, at pp.1608 and 1609) the Arrondissementsrechtbank considered 'whether, in this particular case, there are exceptional circumstances which warrant the conclusion that, although service was duly effected, it was, however, inadequate for the purpose of causing the time needed for the defence to begin to run'.

On that question the Arrondissementsrechtbank considered: 'Although the applicant must himself be regarded as responsible for the fact that throughout the course of these proceedings he has retained as his official residence an address at premises of which he no longer even has the keys, and he will in principle have to bear the consequences, the question whether the summons to appear before the Vrederechter on 1 October 1981 gave the applicant sufficient time to arrange for his defence must be determined according to the particular circumstances obtaining at that time, The court considers that service exclusively on the Politiecommissariaat, when the applicant was not found at his official residence, which he was known to have left such service not being followed by notice of a different kind when before the sitting on 1 October 1981 the respondents became aware of how the applicant could be reached, was insufficient to cause the time for the defence to begin to run. It was in fact impossible for the applicant to enter any kind of defence. The judgment in default given by the Vrederechter, Antwerp, therefore cannot be recognised in the Netherlands'.

Mr and Mrs Debaecker appealed against that judgment to the Huge Raad, on two grounds which may be summarised as follows. In the first place they claimed that Article 27(2) was not applicable in this situation since service 'was effected in accordance with a period specified by the adjudicating court and the defendant's sole residence was within the jurisdiction of that court or in the same country as that court'. Secondly, they argued that facts which occurred later - that is to say, after service of the document which instituted the proceedings - did not compel the plaintiff to take further steps to inform the defendants of the impending action so that if steps were not taken the time required by article 27(2) did not begin to run.

The Hoge Raad submitted the following questions to the Court of Justice:
1. Is the requirement laid down in article 27(2) of the Convention on Jurisdiction and the Enforcement of Judgments in Civil and Commercial matters, that service of the document which instituted the proceedings should have been effected within a sufficient time inapplicable if service was effected within a period prescribed by the court of the State in which the judgment was given and/or the defendant resided, exclusively or otherwise, within the jurisdiction of that court or in the same country as that court?

If Question 1 is answered in the negative: 2(a) In relation to the question whether, in a particular case, there are exceptional circumstances which warrant the conclusion that, although due service was effected, as provided for in Article 27(2), it was nonetheless inadequate for the purpose of causing the time required in that provision to begin to run, is account to be taken only of circumstances which existed at the time of service and which the plaintiff could take into consideration at that time?

If Question 2(a) is answered in the negative: 2(b) Can the plaintiff be required as a result of circumstances which arose after service was effected, in particular notification to the plaintiff of the defendant's address, to take further steps to inform the defendant of the impending action, so that if such steps are not taken the time required by Article 27(2) does not begin to run.

If Question 2(b) is answered in the affirmative: 2(c) What criterion must be applied in that regard? In particular, does the fact that the defendant was responsible for the failure of the duly served document to reach him prevent the court, where, for example, the plaintiff was aware that the defendant had left the address stated to be his place of residence, from considering that further steps as referred to above were required?'

2. *Protection of the defendant*

Before discussing the questions referred to the Court, I consider it appropriate to make certain general remarks on the protection afforded to the defendant by Article 27(2). That Article forms part of Title III of the Convention, concerning 'Recognition and Enforcement' (Articles 25 to 49).

It should first be stated that the provision concerns a defendant against whom judgment has been given by default. The Convention makes special provision for judgments in default, owing to the drastic effects which they have.

The aim of the Convention, which is based on the assumption that the *audi alteram partem* principle will apply, is to achieve as far as possible the free movement of judgments. For that purpose, it is arranged in such a way as to provide, in Title II, for such safeguards in the original proceedings as to enable a judgment given in one State to be recognised in another State without any special procedure being required (Article 26), subject to an exhaustive list of exceptions set out in Articles 27 and 28.

One of the important safeguards in the original proceedings is contained in Article 20, which concerns a judgment in default where a defendant domiciled in one Contracting State is sued in a court of another Contracting State. The second paragraph of Article 20 provides that the court is to 'stay the proceedings so long as it did not shown that the defendant has been able to receive the document instituting the proceedings in sufficient time to enable him to arrange for his defence, or that all necessary steps have been taken to this end'. It is clear from the third paragraph that the second paragraph constitutes a transitional provision pending the application of the Hague Convention of 15 November 1965 on the Service Abroad of Judicial and Extrajudicial Documents in Civil or Commercial Matters. It seeks as far as possible to prevent judgment in default from being given against a defendant who is unaware of the proceedings, as is possible by virtue of the systems of fictitious service (such as the *'remise au parquet'*) which are accepted in most Contracting States other than Germany. As the Arrondissementsrechtbank rightly remarked, that article is not applicable in this case. Nonetheless, the fundamental principle of laws to which it gives effect, namely the right to a fair hearing, is in my opinion of indirect significance for the interpretation of Article 27(2), which is somewhat briefer on that point.

At the stage of the recognition of judgments, Article 27 provides for an exception, applicable to judgments in default, to the general scheme of the Convention, whereby judgments given in one Contracting State are recognised in the other Contracting States without any special procedure being required.

Where judgment is given abroad in default of appearance, the Convention affords the defendant double protection. In the first place, the document must have been duly served. In that connection reference must be made to the domestic law of the State in which the judgment was given and to the international conventions on the service of judicial documents. Secondly, even where service was duly effected, recognition may be refused if the court in which recognition is sought considers that the document was not served in sufficient time to enable the defendant to arrange for his defence. The question of 'sufficient time' is a question of fact to be determined by the court. The principle on which Articles 20 and 27 are based is described in legal writings in different ways, but the result is always the same. In France reference is made to 'the rights of the defence', whilst German writings speak of the principle that the court should hear both sides.

It is, in my view, important to realise that the principle of procedural laws in question is intended to afford protection in connection with an improper procedure, namely judgment in default given against a person who is unaware that proceedings are pending. In that regard I also refer to my previous remarks on the indirect significance which I consider that the second paragraph of Article 20 may have for the interpretation of Article 27(2).

From the judgment of the Court in *Klomps* v *Michel*, and in particular paragraphs 19 and 20, I infer that the mandatory examination of the question whether service was effected in sufficient time should also take into account the degree of care to be exercised by the parties. At least that is my understanding of the examples given by the Court of matters which may be taken into account, such as 'the means employed for effecting service, the relations between the plaintiff and the defendant or the nature of the steps which had to be taken in order to prevent judgment from being given in default'. Droz, in a commentary on a French judgment concerning Article 27(2), appears to share that view, stating *inter alia* that Article 27(2) '"moralise" les relations entre les parties en presence'.

The judgments of the Court on Article 27(2) (Case 166/80 *Klomps* v *Michel* and Case 228/81 *Pendy Plastic* v *Pluspunkt*) may be summarised as follows:

- Article 27(2) should be interpreted independently, as an autonomous provision of the Convention, notwithstanding the examination conducted by the adjudicating court under the second paragraph of Article 20;
- the aim of the requirement that service should have been effected in sufficient time is to ensure that the defendant's rights are effectively protected;
- in principle, that requirement is fulfilled where service was duly effected; however, the court should consider whether in a particular case, taking into account all the circumstances, there are exceptional reasons for considering that the requirement that service should be effected in sufficient time has not been fulfilled.

3. *The questions submitted by the Hoge Raad*

3.1. *The first question.* The first question asked by the Hoge Raad asks whether the requirement laid down in Article 27(2) that service should be effected in sufficient time is inapplicable if service was effected within a period prescribed by the court of the State in which the judgment was given and/or the defendant resided in the same country as that court. Mr and Mrs Debaecker's lawyer raised that ground of appeal because he considered that the Court of Justice had not yet given an express ruling on that point. Although the Hoge Raad had referred to that possibility in its fourth question referred to the Court in *Klomps* v *Michel*, the Court did not expressly rule on that part of the question.

In my view, however, the Court in that case implicitly decided that Article 27(2) is applicable in a case such as that described by the Hoge Raad. Thus, it may be noted that that case, as the United Kingdom has rightly recalled in its written observations in this case, was concerned with a judgment in default obtained in Germany following service in Germany on a defendant who, under German law, was resident in Germany. The judgment of the Court in no way implies that Article 27 is not applicable in that situation. On the contrary, it seems to me that the place of residence is of no relevance to the requirement that service should be effected in sufficient time.

In the judgment in *Klomps* v *Michel* the Court held that Article 27(2) laid down two conditions: (i) that service should be duly effected and (ii) that service should be effected in sufficient time to enable the defendant to arrange for his defence. The second condition requires the court to make appraisals of a factual nature which are independent of the examination as to whether there was due service (paragraph 15). In connection with the fifth question referred to the Court in that case. asking whether the question of service in sufficient time would be answered differently if the court in which enforcement was sought were to find that the defendant had his residence in that State, the Court stated that the residence was irrelevant since the question whether service was effected in sufficient time was a question of fact (paragraph 23).

That is consistent with the remarks made by Mr Advocate General Reischl in his opinion in that case, with which I entirely concur. He based his view on an interpretation of the wording of the provision in question. Article 27(2) is widely formulated and its application is not restricted by any reference to residence. It is therefore applicable to all interested parties irrespective of their residence. In that respect it differs from the second paragraph of Article 20 which applies only to a defendant resident in one Contracting State who is sued in a court of another Contracting State.

As Mr Advocate General Reischl stated in his opinion, having referred to the relevant legal writings, Article 27(2) applies whenever a writ served within national territory leads to a judgment in default which the plaintiff then seeks to enforce abroad.

As Weser has stated, the application of Article 27(2) is justified because national law alone will not necessarily provide the safeguards laid down in Article 20 of the Convention. Differences in the rules on service in the Contracting States, permitting fictitious service to a greater or a lesser extent, should be given particular consideration here. In that connection it may also be pointed out, as Droz observed in the commentary which I referred to earlier, that in purely national proceedings the disadvantages of the rules on fictitious service may be avoided by the possibility of contesting or appealing against a judgment, whereas the position is different in a case with an international dimension. Viewed in that light, Article 27(2) affords a welcome safeguard for the protection of the interests of the defendant where a judgment in default is to be recognised abroad.

Finally, the Court ruled in *Pendy Plastic* that the examination which Article 27(2) requires the enforcing court to undertake is independent of the decision taken on that point by the adjudicating court.

In conclusion, Article 27(2) must in my view be regarded as applicable in a case such as that referred to by the Hoge Raad in its first question.

3.2. *Question 2(a)* asks the Court whether, in determining whether there are exceptional circumstances which warrant the conclusion that, although due service was effected, it was nonetheless inadequate for the purpose of enabling the defendant to arrange for his defence and consequently causing the time required in Article 27(2) to begin to run, account is to be taken only of circumstances which existed at the time of service and which the plaintiff could take into consideration at that time.

As regards the answer to that question, the Court has been presented with the entire range of possibilities. Mr and Mrs Debaecker contend that the question should be answered in the affirmative, so that account should be taken only of circumstances which existed at the time of service. On the other hand, Mr Bouwman and the German and United Kingdom Governments consider that, in determining whether the requirement as to sufficient time has been fulfilled, account may also be taken of circumstances which arose after service was effected. The Commission adopts an intermediary position, stating that although in principle only circumstances which existed at the time of service may be taken into account, an exception may in its view be made for highly exceptional circumstances for which the defendant cannot be blamed.

Mr and Mrs Debaecker's contention that it is impossible at the time of service to take account of circumstances which only become apparent later is, in itself, correct so far as actual service is concerned. However, according to the judgment of the Court in *Klomps* v *Michel*, the court in which enforcement is sought must consider two separate questions, namely whether service was duly effected and whether it was effected in sufficient time. Mr and Mrs Debaecker do not consider the second question.

Mr Bouwman and the German a United Kingdom Governments base their observations, in my view rightly, on the judgment in *Klomps* v *Michel*. There the Court stated that, in view of the national laws and international provisions which also have as their objective the safeguarding of the interest of the defendant, the court in which enforcement is sought is ordinarily justified in considering that, if due service is established, the requirement that service should have been effected in sufficient time is fulfilled. Nonetheless, the court must consider whether, in a particular case, there are exceptional circumstances which warrant the conclusion that that requirement is not fulfilled (paragraph 19). In reaching its decision the court may take account of all the circumstances of the case, including the means employed for effecting service, the relations between the plaintiff and the defendant or the nature of the steps which had to be taken in order to prevent judgment from being given in default (paragraph 20).

It cannot, in my view, be inferred from that that the Court sought to restrict the examination undertaken by the national court to circumstances which were known at the time of service; otherwise there would be a risk of interpreting the requirement as to sufficient time in such a restrictive and formalistic manner that it would in practice coincide with the requirement that service should be duly effected.

I consider it important that the Court stated that the court in which enforcement is sought may take account of all the circumstances of the case. As the United Kingdom Government has rightly observed, one of the circumstances given by the Court as an example, namely the steps which the defendant would have needed to take in order to prevent judgment from being given in default, necessarily arises after service has been effected (paragraph 20). Further support is found in the Court's remark that an appraisal of the facts is required (paragraph 15). From that I infer that it may appear from the whole of the facts that, although service was duly effected, it was nonetheless inadequate for the purposes of enabling the defendant to prepare his defence or to take the necessary steps to prevent judgment from being given in default (summarising the criteria laid down in paragraphs 19 and 20). It is not acceptable, in the light of the purpose of the requirement that service should be effected in sufficient time, to confine the facts which the national court must appraise to those existing at the time of service. Since it is to appraise the effectiveness of service, the court should also examine the subsequent period.

By analogy with paragraph 20 of the Court's judgment in *Klomps* v *Michel*, the Court could mention in its judgment in this case, among other circumstances which the national court may take into account, the extent to which the defendant is himself to blame for his not being able to defend himself, the date of service and the particular way in which it was effected, the nature and timing of the steps which the defendant took, after leaving his official residence without stating his destination, in order to inform the other party to the contract (the plaintiff) of his new address, and the way in which the plaintiff reacted to those steps. Those factors elaborated by analogy with the examples given in paragraph 20 also take account of the circumstances which, as already stated, the Arrondissementsrechtbank, Breda, regarded as important in this case.

I wish now briefly to consider the Commission's proposed reply to this question. It regards the facts known at the time of service as decisive, on the basis of a number of arguments such as legal certainty, the need to interpret Article 27(2) restrictively and the safeguards afforded by the national rules in relation to the service of documents. The Commission considers, however, that there may be an exception to the general rule in the case of highly exceptional circumstances which cannot be considered to be the defendant's fault. In the list of examples recited in footnote 10, which was submitted by the Commission at the hearing, it adopted a much less restrictive view than that put forward in its written observations, where it mentioned only circumstances in the nature of *force majeure*, such as an accident caused by a third party or a general strike.

I would again emphasise that, according to the judgments of the Court, 'Article 27(2) should be interpreted as an independent provision. The safeguards afforded by national procedural law do not prevent the court in which enforcement is sought from reaching, on the basis of the facts, a different view on the requirement laid down in 'Article 27(2) that service should be effected in sufficient time. An identical view to that put forward by the Commission in its written observations was, in my view, rejected by the Court in paragraph 19 of the judgment in *Klomps* v *Michel*, Moreover, I infer from the judgments of the Court that Article 27(2) should not be interpreted as restrictively as the Commission maintains in this case. In that regard I refer to the judgment in Case 125/79 (*Denilauler* v *Couchet Frères* [1980] ECR 1553), in which the Court ruled that certain *ex parte* proceedings do not fall within Title III of the Convention, and to the judgments in *Klomps* v *Michel* and *Pendy Plastic* v *Pluspunkt*.

The nature of the exceptional circumstances which the Commission, in particular in its written observations, suggests may be taken into account after service is, in my view, too restricted. The court in which enforcement is sought may certainly take account of those matters, but more in the sense that, in weighing up the particular facts, it will give more weight to those matters than to others, in the light of the purpose of the requirement laid down in Article 27(2) that service should be effected in sufficient time. In conclusion, I consider that the answer to Question 2(a) should, be that the court in which enforcement is sought may, in examining whether the requirement as to sufficient time is fulfilled, take account of all the circumstances which are relevant to the exercise of the right to a fair hearing, even those which arose after service was effected.

3.3. *Question 2(b)* asks whether the plaintiff can be required as a result of circumstances which arose after service was effected, in particular notification to the plaintiff of the defendant's address, to take further steps to inform the defendant of the impending action, so that if such steps are not taken the time required by Article 27(2) does not begin to run.

Mr and Mrs Debaecker and the Commission consider that, since no such obligation is laid down in the Convention or expressly in the national law of the adjudicating court, an affirmative answer to that question would be inconsistent with the need for legal certainty. They take the view that such conduct can be demanded more as a rule of etiquette than as a rule of law. On the other hand, Mr Bouwman and the German and United Kingdom Governments infer from the purpose of the requirement of service in sufficient time that such an obligation does exist. I endorse that view. I have already observed, the requirement in question should be interpreted as an independent provision of the Convention and is thus not governed by the *lex fori* of the original State or of the State in which enforcement is sought, as Mr Advocate General Reischl stated in *Klomps* v *Michel* (at p.1619, right-hand column). It should be borne in mind that the provision in question requires an appraisal of the effectiveness of service, for the protection of the defendant in the case of a judgment in default in order to ensure that his rights are effectively protected and to prevent his being taken unawares by a judgment in default. The Court's statement in *Klomps* v *Michel* that service is not always adequate for the purposes of enabling the defendant to take steps to arrange for his defence implied that it may not be enough for the plaintiff duly to effect service. The very purpose of Article 27(2) is to lay down the principle that, in addition to formal service, the defendant's rights must be protected. Consequently the plaintiff must as far possible take account of the defendant's actual situation in order to give him an opportunity of defending himself according to the Court's judgment in *Klomps* v *Michel*, the document which instituted the proceedings need not actually be brought to the knowledge of the defendant. The position is somewhat different, however, where it is clear from the facts of the case that the plaintiff must have known that the defendant had no knowledge of the writ and was therefore unable to arrange for his defence. That applies particularly where the defendant, after service of a writ which he has not received, informs the plaintiff of a new address, albeit only a post box number, in a different area. Otherwise, it would be possible for a judgment in default to be sprung upon the defendant, even though the plaintiff knew where the defendant was to be reached. In that situation the fact that after service the plaintiff is apprised of a new address may, in my view, obliges him to take further steps to inform the defendant even at that stage of the forthcoming action, in order to give him an opportunity of arranging for his defence. As I have already observed, the national law of the adjudicating court is irrelevant here.

It is not, as the Commission has maintained, a mere question of etiquette. Admittedly, it is clear from the instructive information annexed to the Commission's written observations that in most Member States it is, in fact, considered proper for the defendant to be informed even at that stage of the imminent action. However, since the requirement laid down in Article 27(2) that service should be effected in sufficient time is not purely formal, but rather involves a question of fact - namely, whether service made it possible for the defendant to arrange for his defence - it may in principle be considered to entail a legal obligation to provide further information in such a case.

Whether failure to comply with that obligation necessarily means that the time stipulated by the requirement in question does not begin to run is a separate question and one which may in my view be difficult to answer in general terms, since that is merely one of the circumstances which may be taken into account. It seems to me that the correct reply is that it may prevent time from running but does not necessarily do so, since that will depend upon all the circumstances of the case which are relevant to the exercise of the right to a fair hearing.

3.4. In *Question 2(c)* the Hoge Raad asks the Court whether, if the defendant is responsible for the failure of the document to reach him, the plaintiff does not have to inform him if, after service is effected, he discovers where the defendant is to be reached.

This question concerns the conduct of the parties to the case. The starting point is that the principle that the defendant's rights should be protected must be given full effect. Breaches of that principle may be committed by either party. It is ultimately the court which must determine, on the basis of all the circumstances, the conduct which was chiefly responsible for the defendant's failure to enter an appearance and which therefore resulted in judgment being given in default.

I have already emphasised that the plaintiff should as far as possible take account of the defendant's actual situation. But the defendant may also be expected to co-operate as far as possible in order to prevent judgment from being given in default. As I observed in my introduction, the principle that the defendant's rights must be protected, in my view, presupposes that both parties should exercise care in the conduct of the case. It is for that reason that I have set out the facts in such detail.

That means that even if the defendant is himself to blame for the fact that the duly effected service was inadequate for the purpose of enabling him to arrange for his defence in time, the court may also, in examining whether service was effected in sufficient time, consider any breaches of procedural requirements on the part of the plaintiff. It is clear from the judgment of the Arrondissementsrechtbank that that court did in fact consider all the aspects of the case and weighed up the extent to which the parties were to blame. It regarded as decisive, however, the fact that in practice it was impossible for the defendant to enter any defence, whereas the plaintiffs became aware in advance of the hearing before the Vrederechter of how the defendant could be reached and informed of the imminent action. That seems to me to be entirely consistent with the principle under Article 27(2) that the defendant's rights should be protected.

4. Conclusion

In conclusion I propose that the questions submitted to the Court by the Hoge Raad should be answered as follows:

1. The court in which enforcement is sought must examine the question of compliance with the requirement, laid down in Article 27(2) of the Convention on Jurisdiction and the Enforcement of Judgments in Civil and Commercial Matters, that service of the document which instituted the proceedings should have been effected in sufficient time even if service was effected within a period prescribed by the court of the State in which the judgment was given and the defendant resided, exclusively or otherwise, within the jurisdiction of that court.

2(a) In examining whether the above-mentioned requirement is fulfilled, account may be taken of exceptional circumstances which arose after service was duly effected.

2(b) Circumstances which arose after service was effected, such as notification to the plaintiff of the defendant's address, may oblige the plaintiff to take further steps to inform the defendant of the impending action. In determining whether the plaintiff's breach of that obligation means that the time required by Article 27(2) does not begin to run, the court should take account of all the circumstances of the case which are relevant to the defendant's exercise of his right to defend himself.

2(c) Blameworthy conduct on the part of the defendant, as a result of which a duly served document failed to reach him, does not prevent the court, in taking account of all the circumstances of the case, from deciding that further steps were needed to inform the defendant of the impending action.

Case 145/86 - 4 February 1988

Horst Ludwig Martin Hoffmann
v
Adelheid Krieg

Article 26 - Recognition of judgments - Scope - Effects of a judgment in the State in which it was given - Same effects in the State in which enforcement is sought -Article 1, second paragraph and Article 31 - Enforcement - Judgment ordering maintenance payments - Obstacles to proceeding with enforcement - Circumstance falling outside the scope of the Convention - Divorce decreed in the State in which enforcement is sought - Recognition and enforcement - Article 27(3) - Grounds for refusing enforcement - Irreconcilable judgments - Foreign judgment making a matrimonial maintenance order - Decree of divorce granted in the State in which enforcement is sought - Article 36 - Enforcement - Failure to appeal against the judgment granting leave to enforce - Pleading, at the execution stage, of grounds for refusal - Not permitted - Obligations on the part of the court seised - Limits.

Summary

1. A foreign judgment which has been recognised by virtue of Article 26 of the Convention of 27 September 1968 on Jurisdiction and the Enforcement of Judgments in Civil and Commercial Matters must in principle have the same effects in the State in which enforcement is sought as it does in the State in which judgment was given.

2. A foreign judgment whose enforcement has been ordered in a Contracting State pursuant to Article 31 of the Convention and which remains enforceable in the State in which it was given must not continue to be enforced in the State where enforcement is sought when, under the law of the latter State, it ceases to be enforceable for reasons which lie outside the scope of the Convention.

The Convention does not preclude the court of the State in which enforcement is sought from drawing the necessary inferences from a national decree of divorce when considering the enforcement of the foreign order made in regard to maintenance obligations between spouses.

3. A foreign judgment ordering a person to make maintenance payments to his spouse by virtue of his conjugal obligations to support her is irreconcilable within the meaning of Article 27(3) of the Convention with a national judgment pronouncing the divorce of the spouses.

4. Article 36 of the Convention must be interpreted as meaning that a party who has not appealed against the enforcement order referred to in that provision is thereafter precluded, at the stage of the execution of the judgment, from relying on a valid ground which he could have pleaded in such an appeal, and that that rule must be applied of their own motion by the courts of the State in which enforcement is sought. However, that rule does not apply when it has the result of obliging the national court to make the effects of a national judgment which lies outside the scope of the Convention conditional on its recognition in the State in which the foreign judgment whose enforcement is at issue was given.

JUDGMENT OF THE COURT

Lord Mackenzie Stuart, President, Bosco and Rodríguez Iglesias, Presidents of Chambers, Koopmans, Bahlmann, Joliet and O'Higgins, Judges

1. By a judgment of 6 June 1986, which was received at the Court on 13 June 1986, the Hoge Raad der Nederlanden referred to the Court for a preliminary ruling under the Protocol of 3 June 1978 on the interpretation by the Court of Justice of the Convention of 27 September 1968 on Jurisdiction and the Enforcement of Judgments in Civil and Commercial Matters (hereinafter referred to as 'the Convention') five questions on the interpretation of a number of articles contained in that Convention.

2. The questions arose in the course of proceedings between H.L.M. Hoffmann (hereinafter referred to as 'the husband') and A. Krieg (hereinafter referred to as 'the wife'), concerning the enforcement in the Netherlands of a judgment of the Amtsgericht (Local Court), Heidelberg,

ordering the husband to make monthly maintenance payments to the wife.

3. It is apparent from the documents before the Court that the parties to the main proceedings are German nationals who were married in 1930 and that, in 1978, the husband left the matrimonial home in the Federal Republic of Germany and settled in the Netherlands. On application by the wife, the husband was ordered by a decision of the Amtsgericht, Heidelberg of 21 August 1979 to make maintenance payments to her as a separated spouse.

4. On the application of the husband, the Arrondissementsrechtbank (District Court), Maastricht, granted a decree of divorce by a judgment of 1 May 1980 given in default, applying German law in accordance with Netherlands rules on the conflict of laws. On 19 August the divorce was entered in the Civil Register at The Hague whereupon in the Netherlands the marriage was dissolved. The decree of divorce, which falls outside the scope of the Convention, had not been recognised in the Federal Republic of Germany at the time which the national court considers material for the purposes of the case.

5. On the application of the wife, the President of the Arrondissmentsrechtbank, Almelo, made an order on 29 July 1981 for the enforcement of the judgment of the Amtsgericht, Heidelberg, in accordance with Article 31 of the Convention. In April 1982 notice of that enforcement order was served on the husband who did not appeal against the order.

6. On 28 February 1983 the wife obtained an attachment of the husband's earnings paid by his employer. The husband brought interlocutory proceedings before the Arrondissementsrechtbank, Almelo, in order to have the attachment order discharged, or at least suspended. He was successful at first instance but on appeal the Gerechtshof (Regional Court of Appeal), Arnhem, dismissed his application. He appealed in cassation against that judgment to the Hoge Raad.

7. The Hoge Raad took the view that the resolution of the dispute depended on the interpretation of a number of articles in the Convention and referred the following questions to the Court for a preliminary ruling:

(1) Does the obligation imposed on the Contracting States to recognise a judgment given in another Contracting State (Article 26 of the Brussels Convention) mean that such a judgment must be given the

same effect in the other Contracting States as it has under the law of the State in which it was given and does this mean that it is therefore enforceable in the same cases as in that State?

(2) If Question 1 is answered in the affirmative: Must Articles 26 and 31 of the Brussels Convention, read together, be interpreted as meaning that the obligation to recognise a judgment given in a Contracting State requires that, because the judgment remains enforceable under the law of the State in which it was given, it is also enforceable in the same cases in the other Contracting State?

(3) If Question 2 is answered in the affirmative: In a case such as this, is it possible to plead that the German maintenance order is irreconcilable with the subsequent Netherlands decree of divorce or to plead public Policy (Article 27(1) and (3) of the Brussels Convention)?

(4) Does (the scheme of) the Brussels Convention require acceptance of the rule that, if the party against whom enforcement is sought of a judgment given in another Contracting State fails to plead, in the appeal against the order for enforcement of the judgment, matters of which he was aware before the end of the period referred to in the first paragraph of Article 36 of the Brussels Convention and which preclude (further) enforcement of that judgment, he may no longer plead those matters in subsequent execution proceedings in which he is appealing against (continued) enforcement?

(5) If Question 4 is answered in the affirmative: Does (the scheme of) the Brussels Convention require it to be assumed that the court of the State in which an enforcement order is issued must apply of its own motion the role referred to in the fourth question in subsequent execution proceedings, even if its own law makes no provision for the application of such a rule?

8. Reference is made to the Report for the Hearing for a fuller account of the facts, the course of the procedure and the written observations submitted to the Court, which are mentioned or discussed hereinafter only insofar as is necessary for the reasoning of the Court.

9. The national court's first question seeks, in essence, to establish whether a foreign judgment, which has been recognised pursuant to Article 26 of the Convention, must in principle have the same effects in the State in which enforcement is sought as it does in the State in which judgment was given.

10. In that regard it should be recalled that the Convention 'seeks to facilitate as far as possible the free movement of judgments, and should

be interpreted in this spirit'. Recognition must therefore 'have the result of conferring on judgments the authority and effectiveness accorded to them in the State in which they were given' (Jenard Report on the Convention on Jurisdiction and the Enforcement of Judgments in Civil and Commercial Matters, Official Journal 1979, C 59, pp. 42 and 43).

11. It follows that the answer to be given to the national court's first question is that a foreign judgment which has been recognised by virtue of Article 26 of the Convention must in principle have the same effects in the State in which enforcement is sought as it does in the State in which judgment was given.

12. In the circumstances of the main proceedings, as disclosed by the documents before the Court, the national court's second question seeks, in essence, to establish whether a foreign judgment whose enforcement has been ordered in a Contracting State pursuant to Article 31 of the Convention must continue to be enforced in all cases in which it would still be enforceable in the State in which it was given even when, under the law of the State in which enforcement is sought, the judgment ceases to be enforceable for reasons which lie outside the scope of the Convention.

13. In this instance, the judgment whose enforcement is at issue is one which orders a husband to make maintenance payments to his spouse by virtue of his obligations, arising out of the marriage, to support her. Such a judgment necessarily presupposes the existence of the matrimonial relationship.

14. Consideration should, therefore, be given to whether the dissolution of that matrimonial relationship by a decree of divorce granted by a court of the State in which the enforcement is sought can terminate the enforcement of the foreign judgment even when that judgment remains enforceable in the State in which it was given, the decree of divorce not having been recognised there.

15. In that connection it must be observed that indent (1) of the second paragraph of Article 1 of the Convention provides that the Convention does not apply *inter alia* to the status or legal capacity of natural persons. Moreover, it contains no rule requiring the court of the State in which enforcement is sought to make the effects of a national decree of divorce conditional on recognition of that decree in the State in which the foreign maintenance order is made.

16. That is confirmed by Article 27(4) of the Convention, which excludes in principle the recognition of any foreign judgment involving a conflict with a rule - concerning *inter alia* the status of natural persons - of the private international law of the State in which the recognition is sought. That provision demonstrates that, as far as the status of natural persons is concerned, it is not the aim of the Convention to derogate from the rules which apply under the domestic law of the court before which the action has been brought.

17. It follows that the Convention does not preclude the court of the State in which enforcement is sought from drawing the necessary inferences from a national decree of divorce when considering the enforcement of the foreign maintenance order.

18. Thus, the answer to be given to the national court is that a foreign judgment whose enforcement has been ordered in a Contracting State pursuant to Article 31 of the Convention and which remains enforceable in the State in which it was given must not continue to be enforced in the State where enforcement is sought when, under the law of the latter State, it ceases to be enforceable for reasons which lie outside the scope of the Convention.

19. The national court's third question seeks, in essence, to establish whether a foreign judgment ordering a person to make maintenance payments to his spouse by virtue of his conjugal obligations to support her is irreconcilable within the meaning of Article 27(3) of the Convention with a national judgment pronouncing the divorce of the spouses or, alternatively, whether such a foreign judgment is contrary to public policy in the State in which recognition is sought within the meaning of Article 27(1).

20. The provisions to be interpreted set out the grounds for not recognising foreign judgments. Under the second paragraph of Article 34, an enforcement order may be refused for those same reasons.

21. As far as the second part of the third question is concerned, it should be noted that, according to the scheme of the Convention, use of the public-policy clause, which 'ought to operate only in exceptional cases' (Jenard Report, cited above, at p. 44) is in any event precluded when, as here, the issue is whether a foreign judgment is compatible with a national judgment; the issue must be resolved on the basis of the specific provision under Article 27(3), which envisages cases in which the foreign

judgment is irreconcilable with a judgment given in a dispute between the same parties in the State in which enforcement is sought.

22. In order to ascertain whether the two judgments are irreconcilable within the meaning of Article 27(3), it should be examined whether they entail legal consequences that are mutually exclusive.

23. It is apparent from the documents before the Court that, in the present case, the order for enforcement of the foreign maintenance order was issued at a time when the national decree of divorce had already been granted and had acquired the force of *res judicata*, and that the main proceedings are concerned with the period following the divorce.

24. That being so, the judgments at issue have legal consequences which are mutually exclusive. The foreign judgment, which necessarily presupposes the existence of the matrimonial relationship, would have to be enforced although that relationship has been dissolved by a judgment given in a dispute between the same parties in the State in which enforcement is sought.

25. The answer to be given to the third question submitted by the national court is therefore that a foreign judgment ordering a person to make maintenance payments to his spouse by virtue of his conjugal obligations to support her is irreconcilable within the meaning of Article 27(3) of the Convention with a national judgment pronouncing the divorce of the spouses.

26. The national court's fourth and fifth questions ask whether Article 36 of the Convention must be interpreted as meaning that a party who has not appealed against the enforcement order in accordance with that provision is precluded, at the stage of the execution of the judgment, from relying on a valid argument which he could have raised in an appeal against the enforcement order, and whether that rule must be applied of their own motion by the courts of the State in which enforcement is sought.

27. In answering those questions it should first be pointed out that, in order to limit the requirements to which the enforcement of a judgment delivered in one Contracting State may be subjected in another Contracting State, the Convention lays down a very simple procedure for the issue of the enforcement order, which may be withheld only on the grounds exhaustively set out in Articles 27 and 28. However, the

Convention merely regulates the procedure for obtaining an order for the enforcement of foreign enforceable instruments and does not deal with execution itself, which continues to be governed by the domestic law of the court in which execution is sought (judgment of 2 July 1985 in Case 148/84 *Deutsche Genossenschaftsbank* v *Brasserie du Pêcheur* [1985] ECR 1981).

28. Consequently, a foreign judgment for which an enforcement order has been issued is executed in accordance with the procedural rules of the domestic law of the court in which execution is sought, including those on legal remedies.

29. However, the application, for the purposes of the execution of a judgment, of the procedural rules of the State in which enforcement is sought may not impair the effectiveness of the scheme of the Convention as regards enforcement orders.

30. It follows that the legal remedies available under national law must be precluded when an appeal against the execution of a foreign judgment for which an enforcement order has been issued is lodged by the same person who could have appealed against the enforcement order and is based on an argument which could save been raised in such an appeal. In those circumstances, to challenge the execution would be tantamount to again calling in question the enforcement order after the expiry of the strict time-limit laid down by the second paragraph of Article 36 of the Convention, and would thereby render that provision ineffective.

31. In view of the mandatory nature of the time-limit laid down by Article 36 of the Convention, the national court must ensure that it is observed. It should therefore of its own motion dismiss as inadmissible an appeal lodged pursuant to national law when that appeal has the effect of circumventing that time-limit.

32. Nevertheless, that rule, arising from the scheme of the Convention, cannot apply when - as in this case - it would have the result of obliging the national court to ignore the effects of a national decree of divorce, which lies outside the scope of the Convention, on the ground that the decree is not recognised in the State in which the foreign judgment whose enforcement is at issue was given.

33. As was established in the context of the reply to the second question, the Convention contains no rule compelling the courts of the State in

which enforcement is sought to make the effects of a national decree of divorce conditional on recognition of that decree in the State in which a foreign maintenance order - falling within the scope of the Convention - was made.

34. Accordingly, the answer to be given to the national court's fourth and fifth questions is that Article 36 of the Convention must be interpreted as meaning that a party who has not appealed against the enforcement order referred to in that provision is thereafter precluded, at the stage of the execution of the judgment, from relying on a valid ground which he could have pleaded in such an appeal against the enforcement order, and that that rule must be applied of their own motion by the courts of the State in which enforcement is sought. However, that rule does not apply when it has the result of obliging the national court to make the effects of a national judgment which lies outside the scope of the Convention conditional on its recognition in the State in which the foreign judgment whose enforcement is at issue was given.

On those grounds, the Court, in answer to the questions referred to it by the Hoge Raad by a judgment of 6 June 1986, hereby rules:

> **(1) A foreign judgment which has been recognised by virtue of Article 26 of the Convention must in principle have the same effects in the State in which enforcement is sought as it does in the State in which the judgment was given;**
>
> **(2) A foreign judgment whose enforcement has been ordered in a Contracting State pursuant to Article 31 of the Convention and which remains enforceable in the State in which it was given must not continue to be enforced in the State where enforcement is sought when, under the law of the latter State, it ceases to be enforceable for reasons which lie outside the scope of the Convention;**
>
> **(3) A foreign judgment ordering a person to make maintenance payments to his spouse by virtue of his conjugal obligations to support her is irreconcilable within the meaning of Article 27(3) of the Convention with a national judgment pronouncing the divorce of the spouses;**
>
> **(4) Article 36 of the Convention must be interpreted as meaning that a party who has not appealed against the**

enforcement order referred to in that provision is thereafter precluded, at the stage of the execution of the judgment, from relying on a valid ground which he could have pleaded in such an appeal against the enforcement order, and that that rule must be applied of their own motion by the courts of the State in which enforcement is sought. However, that rule does not apply when it has the result of obliging the national court to make the effects of a national judgment which lies outside the scope of the Convention conditional on its recognition in the State in which the foreign judgment whose enforcement is at issue was given.

OPINION OF MR ADVOCATE GENERAL DARMON

1. In the questions which it has referred to the Court for a preliminary ruling, the Hoge Raad of the Netherlands seeks an interpretation of a number of provisions of the Brussels Convention of 27 September 1968 on Jurisdiction and the Enforcement of Judgments in Civil and Commercial Matters. I shall begin by setting out the background to the main proceedings.

2. In 1978, after 28 years of marriage, a German national, Mr Hoffmann (hereinafter referred to as 'the husband'), went to live in the Netherlands. His wife, Mrs Krieg (hereinafter referred to as 'the wife'), also a German national, remained in the Federal Republic of Germany, where, by a judgment of the Amtsgericht (Local Court), Heidelberg of 21 August 1979, she obtained a maintenance order as a separated spouse.

3. An order for the enforcement of that judgment was granted pursuant to the Convention on 29 July 1981 by the President of the Arrondissementsrechtbank (District Court), Almelo (Netherlands), and was served on the husband on 29 April 1982. He did not appeal against that order.

4. On 1 May 1980, the Arrondissementsrechtbank, Maastricht, dissolved the marriage on application by the husband, the wife not having entered an appearance. The decree of divorce was entered in the Civil Register in The Hague on 19 August 1980. The divorce, which does not fall within the scope of application of the Convention, has not yet been recognised by the German authorities.

5. Relying on the decree of divorce, the husband instituted proceedings before the Amtsgericht, Heidelberg in order to terminate the maintenance order. His application was refused by a judgment of 25 January 1983 on the ground that the divorce had not been recognised in the Federal Republic of Germany but the amount of maintenance was reduced.

6. On 28 February 1983 the wife served an attachment of earnings order on the husband's employer in the Netherlands, pursuant to the German judgment, in respect of which an order for enforcement had been granted. The husband brought interlocutory proceedings and the attachment of earnings order was discharged by the President of the Arrondissements-rechtbank, Almelo, by an

order of 7 July 1982. On an appeal brought against that decision by the wife, the Gerechtshof (Regional Court of Appeal), Arnhem, quashed it by a judgment of 24 September 1984, which was the subject of an appeal in cassation.

7. It is in those proceedings that the Hoge Raad has submitted five questions to this Court. In examining them I shall be following a slightly different order from that chosen by the Netherlands court. It has asked the Court, first, two questions relating to the effects of a judgment which has been recognised, then a question on whether it is possible to plead grounds for refusing recognition or enforcement, and, lastly, two questions on the remedies available in proceedings subsequent to the order for enforcement. The procedural order, however, is the following:

(a) recognition, which takes place automatically under the terms of the Convention;

(b) the order for enforcement, granted according to the rules laid down in the Convention;

(c) execution proper, which is governed by the rules of national law as the Court confirmed in its judgment in *Deutsche Genossenschaftsbank*.

I shall therefore be examining, first, the circumstances in which it is possible to plead grounds for refusing recognition or an order for enforcement (I) before going on to try to ascertain the effect of a judgment which has been recognised (II). Lastly, I shall be considering Questions 4 and 5 which deal with the issues which may be raised in proceedings relating to execution (III).

I - Article 27 of the Convention (Question 3 submitted by the Hoge Raad)

8. I should, first of all, point out that the second paragraph of Article 34, which deals with the refusal of enforcement, refers expressly to the five grounds for non-recognition provided for in Article 27. The Hoge Raad is asking the Court to determine whether two of them, namely irreconcilability (subheading A below) and public policy (subheading B), are applicable in the main proceedings. For the time being, let me simply say that in this instance those grounds were raised at a procedural stage where an order for enforcement had already been granted and the appeal provided for by the Convention had not been exercised.

A - Irreconcilable judgments

9. Article 27(3) provides that a judgment is not to be recognised if it is irreconcilable with a judgment given in a dispute between the same parties in the State in which recognition is sought. That definition is clearly wider than the concept of res judicata. Should there be any possible doubt on that point it would be sufficient to compare paragraph (3) of Article 27 with paragraph (5), which requires recognition to be refused where the judgment is irreconcilable with a judgment given in a non-Contracting State involving the same cause of action and between the same parties, which are the traditional criteria for res judicata. What, then, are the characteristic elements of irreconcilability for the purposes of Article 27(3)?

10. Any approach based on the substantive content of judgments runs the risk of leading to an unduly restrictive result. For example, two judgments may be based on divergent reasoning without their effects being irreconcilable. For an example, I need only refer to the case where an appellate court upholds the judgment at first instance on different grounds, that is, on the basis of a different or even diametrically opposed legal reasoning.

11. In my view irreconcilability should therefore be sought at the level of the legal effects which recognition of the judgment would produce in the State of enforcement. More specifically, the question to be determined is whether the combined effects of the two judgments would lead to a contradiction incompatible with the logical consistency of the legal order of the State in which enforcement is sought.

12. A few examples, some fictitious and some taken from the judgments of national courts, will serve as illustrations of the solution which I am proposing. Thus a judgment ordering performance of a contract is clearly irreconcilable with a judgment declaring the contract invalid. Similarly, it would seem that a judgment granting a divorce and containing a maintenance order in favour of the ex-wife would be irreconcilable with a judgment refusing recognition of that judgment. The same is not the case, however, with a judgment ordering a purchaser to pay the purchase price and a judgment ordering the vendor to pay compensation for hidden defects, because the two judgments are not contradictory and the amounts may be set off.

13. I, therefore, think that it is for the court before which enforcement is sought to evaluate each individual case in the light of its own legal system.

14. In this instance the German maintenance order logically presupposed that the parties were married and that legal situation was terminated by the subsequent Netherlands judgment. The dissolution of the marriage takes effect only for the future and cannot call into question the automatic recognition enjoyed by the German order in the Netherlands as soon as it has become effective in the Federal Republic of Germany. The fact that that order was prior to the decree of divorce establishes that there was indeed a period during which the husband was liable to pay maintenance. In that regard the situation is no different from that under national law where a husband is ordered to pay maintenance and then obtains a divorce. The ex-husband clearly cannot rely on the decree of divorce as a ground for refusing the payment of maintenance for the period separating the two judgments.

15. I shall, therefore, take it to be an essential factor in favour of reconcilability that there was a period prior to the divorce when the maintenance could be enforced; as a result the ground set out in Article 27(3) can be held inapplicable and an order for enforcement granted. The abstract approach suggested by the Commission, which is to say that the decisions are reconcilable in themselves without considering what would be their combined effects within a given legal system, is not consistent in my view with Article 27(3). The irreconcilability of judgments for the purposes of that provision must be assessed in the specific context according to the criterion of legal consistency in the State in which enforcement is sought.

B - Public policy

16. Under the terms of Article 27(1), a judgment is not to be recognised if it is contrary to public policy. I do not think it necessary to suggest a reply on the application of that provision to this case; clearly it is for the national courts alone to define the scope of public policy.

17. Thus, I shall confine myself to making two general remarks with regard to Article 27(1):

(a) within the scheme of the Convention, that clause is intended to apply only in exceptional cases, which will be all the rarer in that from a statistical point of view judgments in property matters are unlikely to raise issues of public policy;

(b) it should be specified that the meaning of that provision is that the question is not whether a judgment is itself contrary to public policy but whether its recognition or an order for its enforcement would have that effect. That is an application of the doctrine known as the 'diluted effect of public policy', according to which a national court may order the enforcement of a judgment which it could not have delivered itself.

II - The effects of a judgment which has been recognised (Questions 1 and 2 submitted by the Hoge Raad)

18. Insofar as they ask for a ruling on the scope of a judgment which has been recognised, I shall be examining the first two questions jointly.

19. In the main proceedings there is a fundamental difference between the German and Netherlands legal systems as to the existence of the divorce and the correlative extinction of the duty to pay maintenance. It is therefore essential to ascertain whether the effects of a judgment which has been recognised are to be determined by the law of the State of origin or the law of the State in which enforcement is sought.

20. As G.A.L. Droz points out, the Convention is silent on that point. The Jenard Report explains: 'Recognition must have the result of conferring on judgments the authority and effectiveness accorded to them in the State in which they were given'; it further states: 'Article 31 does not purport to determine whether it is the judgment given in the State of origin, or the decision authorising the issue of the enforcement order, which is enforceable in the State in which enforcement is sought'. I agree with G.A.L. Droz that a dual limit should be imposed: the judgment cannot have greater effects in the State in which enforcement is sought than it would have in the State in which it was delivered, nor can it produce greater effects than similar local judgments would. That second limitation is founded on the need to harmonise interpretations and the desirability of preventing excessive recourse to the public policy exception.

21. I shall now try to ascertain the consequences of the approach which has been advocated in situations analogous to that in the main proceedings. First of all, it cannot be for the court before which enforcement is sought to determine the practical effects of a judgment which has been recognised; it must confine

itself to authorising or refusing its enforcement. The power to order partial enforcement is restricted to the two cases set out in Article 42 of the Convention: where enforcement is limited to certain heads of the application, which logically requires that they may be separated, or where the applicant requests partial enforcement. If, however, it is sought, as in this case, to determine the period during which the judgment which has been recognised is applicable, I think that it is then for the court dealing with execution to spell out the practical consequences of the authorisation of enforcement previously granted in the court where enforcement was sought. In my view that approach is dictated by the need to avoid extensive application of Article 42, which would present the obvious risk of a review of the substance, contrary to the express wording of Article 29.

22. On the other hand, it does not seem to me in any way contrary to the Convention for the court dealing with execution to seek to discover, applying its own national law - in accordance with the principles laid down by the Court in *Deutsche Genossenschaftsbank* - how the effects of the judgment which has been recognised can best be combined or reconciled with the effects of another measure of enforcement granted in the State in which execution is sought, as it would in the case of two national judgments. At all events, the Convention cannot lead to the result that a court in the State in which execution is sought is precluded from giving effect to a national judgment on the ground that it has not been recognised in the State in which the judgment to be executed was given.

23. According to the scheme of the Convention, recognition and the order for enforcement of a judgment have the effect of transposing the effects of that judgment into the legal system of other Contracting States. This does not of itself enable the legal system of the State of origin to take precedence over that of the State of execution by subjecting the execution of judgments given in the latter State within its own territory to the requirement of prior recognition in the legal system of the former. In the circumstances of this case such a requirement would effectively subordinate if not negate the Netherlands legal system. The Convention requires Contracting States to ensure the 'free movement' and execution of judgments in property matters but cannot on that account call into question the effect of national judicial decisions.

24. I am therefore unable to share the approach taken by the Commission, which would in practice make the legal effectiveness of a Netherlands decree of divorce in the Netherlands dependent on its recognition in the Federal Republic of Germany. It is not a question of recognising the divorce in that State but simply of drawing the necessary conclusions in the Netherlands where it was granted. Accordingly, the maintenance order must, like an analogous Netherlands judgment, be taken in conjunction in the State where execution is sought with the effects following from the divorce.

25. The solution which I am proposing would seem consistent with the logic of the Convention. The Convention provides that recognition or an order for enforcement is to be refused if the judgment given in another Contracting State is irreconcilable with a judgment given in the State where its enforcement is sought. Where that is not the case, the foreign judgment, being 'naturalised' by the order for enforcement - to use the terminology adopted by Premier

President Bellet - is incorporated into the national legal system in which it is to be executed, taking effect in conjunction with any national judgment. It would be no different in the case of two national enforceable instruments. If I may use a metaphor: where the Convention is intended to ensure the 'free movement of judgments', my analysis, *mutatis mutandis*, is the expression of the rule of 'national treatment'.

III - Objection to execution (Questions 4 and 5 submitted by the Hoge Raad)

26. The Hoge Raad has asked in essence the following question. Can the party against whom the order for enforcement was granted rely, in proceedings relating to execution, on grounds which would have been sufficient to prevent its being granted but which that party failed to put forward in proceedings relating to the order for enforcement within the period laid down by Article 36 of the Convention?

27. The appeal provided for by Article 36 must be brought, according to the circumstances, within one or two months from service of the order authorising enforcement. The appeal must be lodged with a court specified in Article 37 for each Contracting State. The judgment given on the appeal may be contested only by the procedure laid down for each State by the second paragraph of Article 37. Lastly, in any event it is only the grounds set out in Article 27 that may be adduced. Indeed the issue in this case is precisely whether it is possible to rely on one of those grounds outside the procedural system laid down by the Convention.

28. I should say at once that such a possibility, which would amount to allowing a defence to execution by means of an objection of non-recognition, would seem contrary to the scheme of the Convention as interpreted in the judgments of the Court. In its judgments in *Brennero* and *Deutsche Genossenschaftsbank*, the Court made it clear that the sights of appeal provided for by the Convention, which constitutes an autonomous and complete system, cannot be given effect outside the terms of its provisions or 'complemented' by the provisions of national law.

29. In its judgment in *Brennero*, the Court stated: 'The second paragraph of Article 37 provides that the judgment given on the appeal may be contested only by an appeal in cassation ... Under the general scheme of the Convention, and in the light of one of its principal objectives which is to simplify procedures in the State in which enforcement is sought, that provision cannot be extended so as to enable an appeal in cassation to be lodged against a judgment other than that given on the appeal.'

That passage makes it clear that since the Convention is intended to facilitate the procedure for recognition and enforcement, the rights of appeal for which it provides cannot be exercised outside the framework expressly laid down by Article 36 and those immediately following. It would be to disregard that rule to rely on grounds contained in the Convention in proceedings subsequent to the order for enforcement. Merely to hold a submission based on the grounds for non-recognition admissible in proceedings relating to execution would be to accept that it is possible to challenge the order for enforcement even though it had become definitive on the expiry of the period laid down by Article 36.

30. Furthermore, the Court expressed itself in particularly clear terms in its judgment in *Deutsche Genossenschaftsbank* when it said: 'The Convention merely regulates the procedure for obtaining an order for the enforcement of foreign enforceable instruments and does not deal with execution itself, which continues to be governed by the domestic law of the court in which execution is sought ...'.

31. In my view that principle is the logical corollary of the previous one in the sense that it creates a watertight partition between the Convention and national law. The former deals with recognition and orders for enforcement by laying down an exhaustive list of the rights of appeal which are available. Execution is governed solely by the latter. The logic of that framework precludes the possibility of lifting a particular ground of appeal out of the Convention and using it outside the scheme of its provisions. The system of the Convention necessarily means that any such 'transplant' would be rejected.

32. I should, however, define carefully the extent of that rule. The expiry of the period for appealing does indeed remove the right to rely on the grounds provided for by the Convention. Nevertheless, it does not negate the underlying factual situation, namely the situation which, from a legal point of view, corresponds to the provisions in question. After all, that is merely a logical consequence of the classical distinction between the legal rule and the operative event.

33. Thus, the irreconcilability of judgments can no longer be argued under Article 27(1) before the court dealing with execution. However, the situation which might have been characterised by that provision - in this instance the existence of a divorce - is not thereby affected. The decree of divorce is an established fact in the Netherlands legal system. For that reason there is nothing to prevent it from being relied upon in support of any objection which national law makes available against execution. Indeed, the Court stated as much in its judgment in *Deutsche Genossenschaftsbank* when, after pointing out that the Convention did not touch on execution proper, it went on: '...interested third parties may contest execution by means of the procedures available to them under the law of the State in which execution is levied'.

34. This does not necessarily make irrelevant the last question submitted by the Hoge Raad, which asks whether the court of the State in which execution is sought is required to apply of its own motion the rule that a submission pleading grounds contained in the Convention is inadmissible in proceedings against execution. The commentators point out that, until the final stage in the negotiations, the application of the Convention of a court's own motion was provided for in Article 1 and that its absence from the final text was the result of translation difficulties in one of the Contracting States. The Jenard Report, which refers to the binding nature of the Convention, states: '[The Convention] applies automatically ... It was decided by the committee of experts that the Convention should apply automatically'.

35. In its judgment in *De Wolf*, the Court did not fail to point out that the system instituted by the Convention precluded recourse to any other procedure and hence did not permit a request for a new judgment on the substance in the State in which execution was sought.

36. Reliance on one of the grounds contained in Article 27 outside the framework laid down by Articles 36 *et seq.* would seriously prejudice the autonomous and complete character of the provisions of the Convention. The inadmissibility which must operate as a bar to such a practice constitutes a sanction guaranteeing the balance of the mechanism instituted by the Convention. By the same token, its application by a national court of its own motion would appear to be the logical and necessary corollary of the rule requiring recourse to the Convention wherever it is sought to obtain recognition or an order for enforcement of a judgment. As is stated in the Jenard Report, 'The courts [of the Contracting States] must apply the rules of the Convention whether or not they are pleaded by the parties'.

37. Even though I have thought it necessary to examine all the questions submitted to the Court, I propose that in its reply to the Hoge Raad the Court address only the issues of law relevant to the determination of the main proceedings. In view of the fact that the proceedings before the Hoge Raad relate to execution, the questions of recognition and enforcement already being definitively settled, I propose that the Court rule as follows: 'The effects of a judgment recognised by virtue of the Convention of 27 September 1968 cannot go beyond those which a similar national judgment would have in the State in which execution is sought. Where necessary it is solely for the court dealing with execution to define those effects, if need be by combining the effects of the judgment which has been recognised with those of a national judgment. Grounds for non-recognition based on Article 27 of the Convention cannot be pleaded outside the framework defined by Articles 36 *et seq.* The inadmissibility of a submission based on such grounds, which must be declared by the court of the State in which execution is sought of its own motion even if its national law does not provide for such a possibility, does not preclude a party from relying on the facts or the situation which might have been covered by such grounds in exercising any other right of appeal against execution provided for by national law'.

Case C-305/88 - 3 July 1990

Isabelle Lancray SA
v
Peters und Sickert KG

Recognition and enforcement - Article 27(2) - Grounds for refusal - Document instituting the proceedings not served in due form and in sufficient time on a defendant who fails to appear - Concurrent nature of conditions of due form and sufficient time - Document served in sufficient time but not in due form - Refusal of recognition - Review of service by the courts of the State in which recognition is sought - Curing of defective service - To be determined in accordance with the law of the State in which judgment was given.

Summary

1. The conditions laid down in Article 27(2) of the Convention of 27 September 1968 on jurisdiction and the enforcement of judgments in civil and commercial matters, that a defendant who fails to appear must have been served with the document instituting the proceedings in due form and in sufficient time, must both be met in order for a foreign judgment given against that defendant to be recognized. That provision is therefore to be interpreted as meaning that a judgment given in default of appearance may not be recognized where the document instituting the proceedings was not served on the defendant in due form, even though it was served in sufficient time to enable him to arrange for his defence.

2. Article 27(2) of the Convention is to be interpreted as meaning that questions concerning the curing of defective service are governed by the law of the State in which judgment was given, including any relevant international agreements.

JUDGMENT OF THE COURT

Kakouris, President of the Chamber, Schockweiler, Mancini, O'Higgins and Díez de Velasco, Judges

1. By order dated 22 September 1988, which was received at the Court on 19 October 1988, the Bundesgerichtshof referred to the Court for a preliminary ruling pursuant to the Protocol of 3 June 1971 on the interpretation by the Court of Justice of the Convention of 27 September 1968 on jurisdiction and the enforcement of judgments in civil and commercial matters (hereinafter referred to as 'the Convention') two questions on the interpretation of Article 27(2) of the Convention.

2. Those questions arose in the context of proceedings pending before that court between Isabelle Lancray SA, a public limited liability company governed by French law whose registered office is at Neuilly-sur-Seine, France (hereinafter referred to as 'Lancray'), and Peters und Sicken KG, a limited partnership governed by German law whose registered office is at Essen, Federal Republic of Germany (hereinafter referred to as 'Peters').

3. It appears from the documents before the Court that the parties had business relations, based on a contract of 2 November 1983, in respect of which they had agreed to apply French law and to give jurisdiction to the Tribunal de commerce (Commercial Court), Nanterre. A number of problems led Lancray to bring legal proceedings against Peters, and on 18 July 1986 Lancray obtained an interim order from the Amtsgericht (Local Court) Essen prohibiting Peters from selling or delivering to third parties any products in its possession bearing Lancray's trade mark. On 30 July 1986, Lancray applied to the Tribunal de commerce, Nanterre, to have the Amtsgericht's order confirmed and for a number of additional measures. Also on 30 July 1986, the competent French authorities sent to the President of the Landgericht (Regional Court) Essen a summons to Peters, drawn up in French, to appear on 18 November 1986 before the French court, together with a request that the summons be served on Peters and that a certificate of service be returned to the French authorities.

4. By a certificate of service dated 19 August 1986 the competent German authority stated that the documents had been served by handing them to a secretary in Peters's offices. No German translation was appended to the documents. A further summons dated 19 September

1986, drawn up in French, to appear at a hearing before the Tribunal de commerce, Nanterre, on 16 December 1986 was sent to Peters by registered mail.

5. On 16 October 1986, on appeal by Peters, the Landgericht Essen quashed the interim order obtained by Lancray from the Amtsgericht on 18 July 1986. By a letter of 11 November 1986, Peters informed the Tribunal de commerce, Nanterre, of this fact and also stated that the summonses had not been duly served because they were not accompanied by a translation in German.

6. Peters did not appear at the hearing on 16 December 1986 and, by judgment of 15 January 1987, the Tribunal de commerce, Nanterre, upheld Lancray's application. That judgment was served on Peters by delivery to its managing partner on 9 March 1987. By order of 6 July 1987, the Landgericht Essen ruled that the judgment of the Tribunal de commerce, Nanterre, was to be recognized in the Federal Republic of Germany and authorized its enforcement in certain respects.

7. Peters then appealed against that judgment to the Oberlandesgericht (Higher Regional Court) on the ground that under Article 27(2) of the Convention Lancray's application should not have been allowed. The Oberlandesgericht allowed that appeal. Lancray then appealed to the Bundesgerichtshof against the latter judgment.

8. Article 27(2) of the Convention, in the version to which the Bundesgerichtshof refers, provides: 'A judgment shall not be recognized ... (2) where it was given in default of appearance, if the defendant was not duly served with the document which instituted the proceedings in sufficient time to enable him to arrange for his defence; ...'.

9. The Bundesgerichtshof agrees with the Oberlandesgericht that the summons was served on Peters in sufficient time to enable it to arrange for its defence. It further agrees with the Oberlandesgericht that the document instituting the proceedings was not served in due form. It considers that the summons was served not on the addressee who accepted it voluntarily but by delivery to a secretary in the addressee's offices, that is to say by substituted service. In accordance with the relevant international conventions, such service would have been acceptable only if the document served had been accompanied by a German translation, and that was not the case. The Bundesgerichtshof also notes that the Oberlandesgericht held that the national rules

concerning the curing of defective service were not applicable since the addressee did not have a command of the foreign language used.

10. The Bundesgerichtshof therefore decided to stay the proceedings and to seek a preliminary ruling from the Court on the following questions:

'(1) Is recognition of a judgment given in default of appearance to be refused in accordance with Article 27(2) of the pre-accession version of the Brussels Convention where the document instituting the proceedings was not served on the defendant in due form, even though it was served in sufficient time to enable him to arrange for his defence?

(2) In the event that a judgment given in default of appearance is not recognized because, although the defendant was served with the document instituting the proceedings in sufficient time to enable him to arrange for his defence, the service was not duly effected, does Article 27(2) of the pre-accession version of the Brussels Convention preclude recognition of the judgment even where the laws of the State in which recognition is sought permit the defective service to be cured?'

11. Reference is made to the Report for the Hearing for a fuller account of the facts of the case before the national court, the course of the procedure and the written observations submitted to the Court, which are mentioned or discussed hereinafter only insofar as is necessary for the reasoning of the Court.

The First question

12. The first question seeks to determine, in the light of the facts established by the national court, whether Article 27(2) of the Convention is to be interpreted as meaning that a judgment given in default of appearance may not be recognized where the document instituting the proceedings was not served on the defendant in due form, even though it was served in sufficient time to enable him to arrange for his defence.

13. In order to examine that question, it must first be determined whether the article in question lays down two mutually independent grounds for refusing to recognize a foreign judgment.

14. The Court observed in its judgment in Case 166/80 *Klomps* v *Michel* [1981] ECR 1593 that Article 27(2) lays down two conditions, the first of which, that service should be duly effected, entails a decision based on the legislation of the State in which judgment was given and on the conventions binding on that State in regard to service, whilst the second,

concerning the time necessary to enable the defendant to arrange for his defence, implies appraisals of a factual nature.

15. It must then be determined whether the conditions of due service and sufficient time laid down in the aforementioned provision must both be met concurrently for a foreign judgment to be recognized.

16. The wording of the different language versions of the provision in question suggests that question must be answered in the affirmative.

17. That interpretation is corroborated by the experts' report on the Brussels Convention (Official Journal 1979 C 59, p. 1) which observes, in relation to Article 27(2) of the Convention: 'Where judgment is given abroad in default of appearance, the Convention affords the defendant double protection.... Secondly, even where service has been duly effected, recognition can be refused if the court in which recognition is sought considers that the document was not served in sufficient time to enable the defendant to arrange for his defence'.

18. It must therefore be held that the requirements of due service and service in sufficient time constitute two separate and concurrent safeguards for a defendant who fails to appear. The absence of one of those safeguards is therefore a sufficient ground for refusal to recognize a foreign judgment.

19. The contrary view has been submitted that it is not necessary to insist on proper service if the defendant has, in any event, had sufficient time to arrange for his defence. According to that interpretation, due service is merely prima-facie evidence that service was effected in sufficient time, and failure to comply with the time requirement is the only true ground for refusing recognition.

20. That reasoning cannot be accepted. First, it is difficult to reconcile that interpretation with the wording of the relevant provision or with the Court's ruling cited above. Secondly, it would render completely inoperative the requirement of due service. If the sole issue were whether the document came to the defendant's attention in sufficient time, plaintiffs would be tempted to ignore the prescribed forms for due service, the requirements of which have in any event been considerably relaxed by international agreements. That would create considerable uncertainty as to whether documents had actually been served, thus thwarting the uniform application of the provisions of the Convention.

Finally, a defendant could not know with certainty whether proceedings which might lead to a finding against him had been properly instituted and whether it was therefore necessary to arrange for a defence, a situation which would also be inconsistent with the aims of the Convention.

21. It must be added that, as the Court held in its judgment in Case 49/84 *Debaecker* v *Bouwman* [1985] ECR 1779, although the Convention is, as is clear from the preamble, intended to secure the simplification of formalities governing the reciprocal recognition and enforcement of judgments of courts or tribunals, that aim cannot be attained by undermining in any way the right to a fair hearing.

22. It follows from all of the foregoing considerations that recognition of a foreign judgment should be refused if service has not been effected in due form, regardless of whether the defendant was actually aware of the document instituting the proceedings.

23. The answer to the first question must therefore be that Article 27(2) of the Convention of 27 September 1968 on jurisdiction and the enforcement of judgments in civil and commercial matters is to be interpreted as meaning that a judgment given in default of appearance may not be recognized where the document instituting the proceedings was not served on the defendant in due form, even though it was served in sufficient time to enable him to arrange for his defence.

The second question

24. The national court's second question seeks to determine whether Article 27(2) of the Convention is to be interpreted as authorizing the courts of the State in which enforcement is sought to cure defective service by applying their national law.

25. It must be pointed out first of all that Article 27(2) of the Convention does not itself contain any rule as to whether defective service may be cured.

26. The question must therefore be answered on the basis of the rules applicable to the service of foreign judgments.

27. The first paragraph of Article IV of the Protocol of 27 September 1968 (Official Journal 1978 L 304, p. 47), to which Article 65 of the

Convention refers, provides: 'Judicial and extra-judicial documents drawn up in one Contracting State which have to be served on persons in another Contracting State shall be transmitted in accordance with the procedures laid down in the conventions and agreements concluded between the Contracting States'.

28. In its judgment in Case 228/81 *Pendy Plastic Products* v *Pluspunkt* [1982] ECR 2723, the Court held that, although they do not seek to harmonize the different systems of service abroad of legal documents which are in force in the Member States, the provisions of the Brussels Convention are designed to ensure that the defendant's rights are effectively protected. For that reason, jurisdiction to determine whether the document instituting the proceedings was properly served was conferred both on the court of the State in which the judgment was given and on the court of the State in which enforcement is sought.

29. The Brussels Convention does not determine which law is to be applied to that question. Since the rules governing the service of the document instituting the proceedings form part of the procedure before the court of the State in which judgment was given, the question whether service was duly effected can only be answered by reference to the law to be applied by that court, including any relevant international conventions.

30. Consequently, questions concerning the curing of defective service are governed by that law.

31. The answer to the second question must therefore be that Article 27(2) of the Convention is to be interpreted as meaning that questions concerning the curing of defective service are governed by the law of the State in which judgment was given, including any relevant international agreements.

On those grounds, the Court (Sixth Chamber), in answer to the questions referred to it by the Bundesgerichtshof, by order of 22 September 1988, hereby rules:

(1) Article 27(2) of the Convention of 27 September 1968 on jurisdiction and the enforcement of judgments in civil and commercial matters is to be interpreted as meaning that a judgment given in default of appearance may not be recognized where the document instituting the proceedings was not served

on the defendant in due form, even though it was served in sufficient time to enable him to arrange for his defence.

(2) Article 27(2) of the Convention is to be interpreted as meaning that questions concerning the curing of defective service are governed by the law of the State in which judgment was given, including any relevant international agreements.

OPINION OF MR ADVOCATE GENERAL JACOBS

1. This case arises by way of a reference for a preliminary ruling from the Bundesgerichtshof (Federal Court of Justice) under the Protocol of 3 June 1971 on the interpretation by the Court of Justice of the Convention of 27 September 1968 on jurisdiction and the enforcement of judgments in civil and commercial matters ('the Brussels Convention'). The two questions referred ask for guidance on the meaning of Article 27 of the Brussels Convention in the version in force prior to the accession thereto of Denmark, Ireland and the United Kingdom. Article 27 is concerned with the circumstances in which the courts of one Contracting State are precluded from recognizing judgments given by the court of another Contracting State. The first question referred to the Court corresponds to that posed by the Bundesgerichtshof in Case 36/88, which was removed from the register after the main action was discontinued.

The facts

2. The facts of the case are as follows. On 2 November 1983, Isabelle Lancray SA ('Lancray'), a French company having its registered office at Neuilly-sur-Seine, entered into an agreement for the exclusive distribution of its products with Peters und Sickert KG ('Peters'), a limited partnership governed by German law and established at Essen. The contract was expressed to be subject to French law and conferred jurisdiction on the Tribunal de commerce (Commercial Court), Nanterre. Lancray subsequently terminated the contract, taking the view that Peters was no longer complying with it. In accordance with Article 24 of the Brussels Convention (which is the same in both the pre-accession and post-accession versions), Lancray then applied to the Amtsgericht (Local Court), Essen, for an interim injunction restraining Peters from disposing of any Lancray products in its possession. The injunction was granted on 18 July 1986. On 30 July 1986, Lancray commenced proceedings before the Tribunal de commerce, Nanterre, seeking confirmation of the injunction granted by the Amtsgericht and certain additional relief. On the same day, the competent French authorities sent to the President of the Landgericht (Regional Court), Essen, Lancray's application and a summons, drawn up in French, requiring Peters to appear before the French court on 18 November 1986. Those documents were accompanied by a form drawn up in French and English and partly completed in

French together with a request that they be served on Peters and that a record of service be returned to the French authorities.

3. On 19 August 1986, the application and the form drawn up in English and French were handed to a secretary at Peters' offices. Those documents were not accompanied by translations into German. Peters was subsequently sent by registered letter a further application drawn up in French and a summons dated 19 September 1986 to appear before the Tribunal de commerce in Nanterre on 16 December 1986.

4. On 16 October 1986, the Landgericht, Essen, lifted the injunction granted to Lancray by the Amtsgericht on 18 July. Peters informed the Tribunal de commerce of this development by letter dated 11 November 1986, in which it also pointed out that the previous documents had not been correctly served as they were not accompanied by translations into German. By a stroke of irony, the Tribunal de Commerce returned this letter with a recommendation that a document drawn up in French be submitted.

5. Peters failed to appear before the Tribunal de commerce which, on 15 January 1987, delivered a decision upholding Lancray's application. The judgment of the Tribunal de commerce was served on Peters' managing partner on 9 March 1987.

6. On 6 July 1987, the Landgericht, Essen, ordered that the judgment of the Tribunal de commerce dated 15 January 1987 be recognized in the Federal Republic of Germany and authorized its enforcement in certain respects. An appeal against that ruling brought by Peters before the Oberlandesgericht (Higher Regional Court) was successful. Lancray brought a further appeal against the decision of the Oberlandesgericht before the Bundesgerichtshof, which has referred two questions to this Court for a preliminary ruling.

7. In the main action, Peters claims that the judgment of the Tribunal de commerce should not be recognized in the Federal Republic by virtue of Article 27(2) of the Brussels Convention. This provides that a judgment given in default of appearance by the defendant by a court in one Contracting State shall not be recognized in other Contracting States 'if the defendant was not duly served with the document which instituted the proceedings [or with an equivalent document] in sufficient time to enable him to arrange for his defence'. The words in parentheses were added on the accession to the Convention of Denmark, Ireland and the United Kingdom to take account of peculiarities in the procedural law of the last two States and to indicate which documents must be served for the right to a hearing to be respected: see the Schlosser Report (Official Journal 1979 C 59, p. 71, at pp. 125, 126 and 128).

8. The Oberlandesgericht took the view that, although the application and summons to appear before the Tribunal de commerce on 18 November 1986 were delivered to Peters sufficiently early for it to prepare its defence, they had not been served in accordance with the relevant international conventions on the service abroad of legal documents as they were not accompanied by translations into German. Moreover, the Oberlandesgericht did not consider that it was at liberty to apply its national rules on curing defective service since Peters did not have a command of the language in which the documents in question had been drawn up.

The questions referred

9. On appeal, the Bundesgerichtshof referred the following questions to this Court for a preliminary ruling:

'(1) Is recognition of a judgment to be refused in accordance with Article 27(2) of the pre-accession version of the Brussels Convention where the defendant did not enter an appearance and, although he was served with the document which instituted the proceedings in sufficient time to enable him to conduct his defence, the service was not duly effected?

(2) In the event that a judgment where the defendant did not enter an appearance is not recognized because, although the defendant was served with the document which instituted the proceedings in sufficient time to enable him to conduct his defence, the service was not duly effected, does Article 27(2) of the pre-accession version of the Brussels Convention preclude recognition of the judgment even where the laws of the State in which recognition is sought permit the defect of service to be cured?'

10. Before examining the substance of the questions referred, it is necessary to consider which version of the Brussels Convention is applicable in the main action. The original version of that Convention was amended by the Convention of 9 October 1978 ('the Accession Convention'), by which Denmark, Ireland and the United Kingdom acceded to it. Articles 34 to 36 of the Accession Convention lay down a number of transitional provisions. The second paragraph of Article 34 provides: 'as between the six Contracting States to the 1968 Convention, judgments given after the entry into force of this Convention in proceedings instituted before that date shall be recognized and enforced in accordance with the provisions of Title III of the 1968 Convention as amended.'

11. The six original Contracting States to the Brussels Convention included France and the Federal Republic of Germany. As far as those States are concerned, the Accession Convention entered into force on 1 November 1986. Lancray instituted proceedings before the Tribunal de commerce in Nanterre on 30 July 1986 and judgment was given by that court on 15 January 1987. It would therefore appear, as the Commission points out, that it is the amended rules on recognition and enforcement rather than the pre-accession rules which apply in the present case.

12. The referring court has not asked for guidance on which version of the Brussels Convention is applicable. However, the substance of Article 27(2) was not changed in any relevant respect by the Accession Convention. I do not therefore consider it necessary for this Court to specify to which version of the Brussels Convention its ruling relates. In my view the questions referred fall to be answered in the same terms regardless of which version is applicable. In the remainder of this Opinion, I will indicate the changes made by the Accession Convention where necessary.

13. Article 27 of the Brussels Convention is contained in Title III, which is headed 'Recognition and Enforcement'. The general rule with regard to recognition is laid down in the first paragraph of Article 26. This provides that 'a judgment given in a Contracting State shall he recognized in the other

Contracting States without any special procedure being required'. Article 27 constitutes an exception to that general rule. Is sets out a number of situations in which a court in one Contracting State must (not merely may) refuse to recognize a judgment given by a court in another Contracting State. By virtue of Article 34 of the Brussels Convention, Article 27 also applies to applications before the courts of one Contracting State for the *enforcement* of a judgment given by a court in another Contracting State. Under Article 46(2) of the Brussels Convention, a party seeking recognition or applying for enforcement of a judgment given in default must produce 'the original or a certified true copy of the document which establishes that the party in default was served with the document instituting the proceedings [or with an equivalent document]' (the words in parentheses were added by the Accession Convention).

14. The purpose of the second paragraph of Article 37 of the Brussels Convention is to safeguard the rights of the defendant, as the Jenard Report (Official Journal 1979 C 59, p. 1, at p. 44) makes clear. The Court pointed out in Case 166/80 *Klomps* v *Michel* [1981] ECR 1593, paragraph 9, that it is 'intended to ensure that a judgment is not recognized or enforced under the Convention if the defendant has not had an opportunity of defending himself before the court first seised'. Although, as an exception to the general rule laid down in Article 26 of the Brussels Convention, Article 27 is not to be interpreted extensively, too restrictive an interpretation might undermine the defendant's right to a fair hearing. The Court emphasized in Case 49/84 *Debaecker* v *Bouwman* [1985] ECR 1779, paragraph 10, that this was not an acceptable way of achieving the objectives of the Brussels Convention.

15. The first question referred by the Bundesgerichtshof asks essentially whether the requirements laid down in Article 27(2) that service must have been effected properly and in good time are cumulative or whether the first requirement no longer applies where the second has been satisfied. On a literal interpretation, it is clear, at least from the English and French texts, that both requirements must be satisfied: the document which instituted the proceedings must have been served both properly and in good time if a judgment given in default of appearance is to be recognized in another Contracting State. That this was the interpretation intended by the authors of the Brussels Convention is apparent from the Jenard Report, which states (at p. 44) that: 'Where judgment is given abroad in default of appearance, the Convention affords the defendant double protection. First, the document must have been duly served ... Secondly, even where service has been duly effected, recognition can be refused if the court in which recognition is sought considers that the document was not served in sufficient time to enable the defendant to arrange for his defence.'

The Court itself recognized in *Klomps* v *Michel* paragraph 15, that Article 27(2) laid down two conditions, both of which had to be satisfied before a judgment given in default could be recognized.

16. Thus, in a case such as that pending before the referring court, recognition must in my view be refused where the document instituting the proceedings was not duly served, even though the defendant may in fact have received that document in sufficient time to enable it to arrange its defence.

Lancray urges a contrary interpretation on the basis that there is no need to insist on proper service where the defendant has in any event had sufficient time to prepare its defence. This view is difficult to reconcile with the wording of the French and English versions of Article 27(2) and is inconsistent with both the intentions of the authors of the Brussels Convention and the Court's case-law. It would also empty the requirement of due service of any substance. The German Government rightly observes that, if that view were adopted, plaintiffs would be tempted to depart from the usual channels for serving documents and assume responsibility for the service of documents themselves. This would create considerable uncertainty as to whether documents had in fact been served at all, thereby undermining the uniform application of the Convention's provisions. Moreover, as the Commission points out, defendants would be left in doubt as to whether proceedings which might result in a binding judgment had been commenced and whether it was therefore necessary to prepare a defence.

17. How, then, is a court before which recognition of a judgment given in another Contracting State is sought to determine whether the document instituting the proceedings was duly served? The first paragraph of Article IV of the Protocol annexed to the Brussels Convention provides that 'judicial and extra-judicial documents drawn up in one Contracting State which have to be served in another Contracting State shall be transmitted in accordance with the procedures laid down in the conventions and agreements concluded between the Contracting States'. The Jenard Report is more specific, stating in relation to Article 27(2) that 'reference must be made to the internal law of the State in which the judgment was given, and to the international conventions on the service abroad of judicial instruments' (p. 44). A similar statement is to be found in *Klomps* v *Michel* paragraph 15, where the Court said that this question was to be determined on the basis of the legislation of the State in which judgment was given and the international conventions binding on that State with regard to the service of judicial instruments abroad.

18. In cases where a defendant domiciled in one Contracting State is sued before a court of another Contracting State and does not enter an appearance, similar issues will have been considered by the court in which judgment was given under the second and third paragraphs of Article 20 of the Brussels Convention. In the present case, it appears to be the third paragraph of Article 20 which is relevant. That provision lays down that, where the document instituting proceedings or notice thereof had to be transmitted abroad in accordance with the Hague Convention of 15 November 1965 on the service abroad of judicial and extra-judicial documents in civil and commercial matters, Article 15 thereof is applicable. According to the referring court, this case is governed by the latter convention. Article 15 provides that where a writ of summons or an equivalent document had to be served abroad and the defendant has not entered an appearance, judgment shall not be given until it is established that the document was served on or delivered to the defendant in accordance with certain specified methods and that service or delivery was effected in sufficient time to enable the defendant to arrange for his defence. Contracting States have the right to declare that judgment may be given, even if no certificate of service or delivery has been

received, provided certain conditions are satisfied. The conditions relate to the manner in which the document was transmitted, the time which has elapsed since the date of transmission, and the efforts that have been made to obtain a certificate of service or delivery through the competent authorities of the State addressed.

19. The fact that, in circumstances such as those of the present case, the court which gave judgment will have considered the manner in which the document instituting proceedings was served on the defendant does not relieve the court in which recognition of that judgment is sought of its duty under Article 27(2) to examine this question itself. The Court made this clear in Case 228/81 *Pendy Plastic* v *Pluspunkt* [1982] ECR 2723, a case concerned with both recognition and enforcement. As the Court pointed out in its judgment (see paragraph 8) and as I indicated above, Article 27 applies to both. In the *Pendy Plastic* case, the Court stated: 'Although they do not seek to harmonize the different systems of service abroad of legal documents which are in force in the Member States, the provisions of the Brussels Convention are designed to ensure that the defendant's rights are effectively protected. For that reason, jurisdiction to determine whether the document introducing the proceedings was properly served was conferred both on the court of the original State and on the court of the State in which enforcement is sought. Thus, in accordance with the objective of Article 27 of the Convention, the court of the State in which enforcement is sought must examine the question posed by paragraph 2 of that article, notwithstanding the decision given by the court of the original State on the basis of the second and third paragraphs of Article 20' (paragraph 13).

20. In my view, the principles applied in those cases offer sufficient guidance to enable the second question posed by the referring court to be answered. That question asks essentially whether a court is required to refuse to recognize a judgment given in another Contracting State where the document instituting proceedings, although received by the defendant in good time, was not correctly served, notwithstanding the fact that the laws of the State in which recognition is sought permit the defect of service to be cured.

21. I consider that the answer to this question is a qualified 'yes'. The rules to be applied in determining whether the document instituting the proceedings was correctly served are, as already stated, those of the State in which judgment was given and the provisions of any international conventions on service applicable in that State. As the Commission suggests, it is only if those rules (which may incorporate by reference the rules applicable in the State in which recognition is sought) permit a defect of service to be cured that the document instituting the proceedings can be regarded as having been duly served for the purposes of Article 27(2). Otherwise, where recognition or enforcement is sought in several Contracting States, the outcome might depend on the domestic laws of each of the States concerned and the uniform application of Article 27(2) would be jeopardized.

22. The French Government has invited the Court to examine whether the document which instituted the proceedings at issue here was in fact served improperly. In my view, however, the questions referred fall to be answered on

the hypothesis that the document instituting proceedings was not duly served. It is not for this Court, in the context of a reference for a preliminary ruling, to examine whether this was so in the particular circumstances of the case pending before the Bundesgerichtshof. Whether that document was in fact properly served or not is a matter for the national courts.

23. The result is unfortunate for Lancray, who, apparently through no fault of its own, may find itself unable to secure the recognition of a judgment awarded against a defendant whose case, from the procedural point of view, seems somewhat lacking in merit. None the less, I believe the Court's case-law and the intentions of the authors of the Brussels Convention to be clear. The case emphasizes the need for those responsible for the service of judicial documents abroad to ensure strict compliance with the applicable rules.

Conclusion

24. I therefore consider that the questions referred by the Bundesgerichtshof should be answered as follows:

'(1) Article 27(2) of the Brussels Convention precludes a court in one Contracting State from recognizing a judgment given by a court in another Contracting State in default of appearance by the defendant where the document instituting the proceedings or an equivalent document was not duly served on the defendant, even where that document was received by the defendant in good time for it to arrange its defence.

(2) In deciding whether the document instituting the proceedings or an equivalent document was duly served on the defendant for the purposes of Article 27(2) of the Brussels Convention, a court of a Contracting State which is asked to recognize a judgment given by a court in another Contracting State must apply the provisions of the internal law of the second State and those of any international conventions on the service of documents abroad which are applicable in that State. A court in the first State may cure defects of service only if permitted by those provisions to do so.'

Case C-123/91 - 12 November 1992

Minalmet GmbH
v
Brandeis Ltd

Recognition and enforcement - Grounds of refusal - Defendant who failed to appear not served, or not duly served, with the document instituting the proceedings - Failure by defendant to have recourse to the remedies provided for in the State where judgment was delivered after becoming aware of the judgment delivered in default of appearance - Refusal of recognition.

Summary

Article 27(2) of the Brussels Convention of 27 September 1968 on jurisdiction and the enforcement of judgments in civil and commercial matters must be interpreted as precluding a judgment given in default of appearance in one Contracting State from being recognized in another Contracting State where the defendant was not duly served with the document which instituted the proceedings, even if he subsequently became aware of the judgment which was given and did not avail himself of the remedies provided for under the code of procedure of the State where the judgment was delivered.

JUDGMENT OF THE COURT

Kakouris, President of the Chamber, Diez de Velasco and Kapteyn, Judges

1. By order of 4 April 1991, received at the Court Registry on 26 April 1991, the Bundesgerichtshof referred to the Court of Justice for a

preliminary ruling under the Protocol of 3 June 1971 on the interpretation by the Court of Justice of the Brussels Convention of 27 September 1968 on jurisdiction and the enforcement of judgments in civil and commercial matters a question on the interpretation of Article 27(2) of that convention, as amended by the 1978 Convention of Accession (OJ 1978 L 304, p. 1, hereinafter 'the Brussels Convention').

2. That question was raised in proceedings between Minalmet GmbH, whose registered office is in Düsseldorf, Germany (hereinafter 'Minalmet'), and Brandeis Ltd, whose registered office is in London (hereinafter 'Brandeis').

3. It is apparent from the documents before the Court that Brandeis seeks the enforcement in Germany of a judgment delivered, in default of appearance, by the High Court of Justice, Queen's Bench Division, ordering Minalmet to pay it a certain sum.

4. The document instituting the proceedings which led to the judgment at issue was forwarded by the competent authorities in the United Kingdom to the competent judicial authority in Germany in order to be served in accordance with Article 5(a) of the Hague Convention of 15 November 1965 on the service and notification abroad of judicial and extrajudicial documents in civil and commercial matters.

5. The Amtsgericht (Local Court) Düsseldorf, the competent authority in Germany, then effected service by post. The postoffice employee, finding none at the Minalmet's premises, lodged the documents to be served at the appropriate post office and issued a certificate to the effect that he had left at the debtor's address a notice of such lodgment, in accordance with the procedure normally followed for the delivery of mail (substituted service under Paragraph 182 of the German Code of Civil Procedure). On the basis of that certificate, the Amtsgericht Düsseldorf issued a certificate recording due service and referring to the lodgment of the documents.

6. By order of 21 February, the Landgericht (Regional Court), Düsseldorf, ordered, at the request of Brandeis, that the judgment be certified as enforceable.

7. Minalmet brought an action for the annulment of that order before the Oberlandesgericht (Higher Regional Court), Düsseldorf, contending that the document instituting proceedings had not been served on it in

accordance with the formal requirements of German law and solemnly affirmed that it had no knowledge either of the notice of lodgment by the postoffice employee or of the said document. The Oberlandesgericht dismissed the application on 14 May 1990.

8. Minalmet then brought an appeal (Rechtsbeschwerde) against that decision before the Bundesgerichtshof. In its analysis of the case, that court found that the document instituting proceedings had not been validly served, the procedure being governed, by virtue of Article 5(a) of the Hague Convention, by the civil law of Germany, the State to which application had been made for service to be effected. It stated that substituted service could have been properly effected only at the private address of the statutory representative of the company, not at the debtor's premises.

9. In those circumstances, the Bundesgerichtshof decided to stay the proceedings pending a preliminary ruling by the Court on the following question: 'Is recognition of a judgment given in default of appearance to be refused under Article 27(2) of the Brussels Convention where it cannot be proved that the defendant was served with the document which instituted the proceedings or he was not duly served with that document, if he was nevertheless aware of the judgment delivered in the proceedings but availed himself of none of the legal remedies against the judgment provided for in the procedure of the State in which the judgment was delivered?'

10. Reference is made to the Report for the Hearing for a fuller account of the facts, the procedure and the written observations submitted to the Court, which are mentioned or discussed hereinafter only in so far as is necessary for the reasoning of the Court.

11. By its question, the national court wishes essentially to ascertain whether Article 27(2) of the Brussels Convention must be interpreted as precluding recognition in one contracting State of a judgment given in default of appearance in another contracting State where the document instituting the proceedings was not served in due form on the defaulting defendant, even if the latter subsequently had notice of the judgment in question but did not avail himself of the legal remedies against that judgment provided for under the procedure of the State where it was delivered.

12. It must be borne in mind first of all that Article 27 of the Brussels

Convention sets out the conditions for recognition in one contracting State of judgments given in another contracting State. According to Article 27(2), recognition must be refused 'if the defendant was not duly served with the document which instituted the proceedings or with an equivalent document in sufficient time to enable him to arrange for his defence'.

13. It must next be noted that, in its judgment in Case C-305/88 *Lancray* [1990] ECR I-2725, paragraph 18, the Court held that due service and service in sufficient time constituted two separate and concurrent safeguards for a defendant who fails to appear. The absence of one of those safeguards is therefore a sufficient ground for refusing to recognize a foreign judgment.

14. It follows that a decision given in default of appearance in a contracting State must not be recognized in another contracting State if the document instituting proceedings was not duly served on the defaulting defendant.

15. That interpretation is not invalidated by the fact that the defendant had notice of the judgment given in default and did not avail himself of the remedies provided for under the procedure of the State where it was delivered.

16. Any other conclusion would be difficult to reconcile with the wording and purpose of Article 27(2) of the Brussels Convention.

17. It follows from the wording of the aforesaid provision that service on the defendant of the document instituting proceedings in due form and in sufficient time is required by that provision for recognition of that decision in a contracting State.

18. Furthermore, as the Court held in its judgment in Case 166/80 *Klomps* [1981] ECR 1593, paragraph 9, Article 27(2) of the Brussels Convention is intended to uphold the rights of the defence and ensure that a judgment is not recognized or enforced under the Convention if the defendant has not had an opportunity of defending himself before the Court first seised.

19. It must be emphasized in that regard that, as is apparent from the provision at issue, the proper time for the defendant to have an opportunity to defend himself is the time at which proceedings are

commenced. The possibility of having recourse, at a later stage, to a legal remedy against a judgment given in default of appearance, which has already become enforceable, cannot constitute an equally effective alternative to defending the proceedings before judgment is delivered.

20. As correctly pointed out by the national court, once a judgment has been delivered and has become enforceable, the defendant can obtain suspension of its enforcement, if suspension is appropriate, only under more difficult circumstances and may also find himself confronted by procedural difficulties. The possibility for a defaulting defendant to defend himself is thus considerably diminished. Such a result would run counter to the purpose of the provision in question.

21. It follows from all the foregoing considerations that recognition in one contracting State of a judgment delivered in default of appearance in another contracting State must be refused where the document which instituted the proceedings was not duly served on the defendant, even if the defendant had notice of the judgment and did not have recourse to the available legal remedies.

22. It must therefore be stated in reply to the question submitted by the national court that Article 27 (2) of the Brussels Convention must be interpreted as precluding a judgment given in default of appearance in one Contracting State from being recognized in another Contracting State where the defendant was not duly served with the document which instituted the proceedings, even if he subsequently became aware of the judgment which was given and did not avail himself of the legal remedies available under the procedure of the State where the judgment was delivered.

On those grounds, the Court in answer to the question referred to it by the Bundesgerichtshof by order of 4 April 1991, hereby rules:

> **Article 27(2) of the Brussels Convention must be interpreted as precluding a judgment given in default of appearance in one Contracting State from being recognized in another Contracting State where the defendant was not duly served with the document which instituted the proceedings, even if he subsequently became aware of the judgment which was given and did not avail himself of the legal remedies provided for under the procedure of the State where the judgment was delivered.**

OPINION OF MR ADVOCATE GENERAL JACOBS

1. This case concerns the extent to which the Convention of 27 September 1968 on jurisdiction and the enforcement of judgments in civil and commercial matters, as amended by the Convention of Accession of 9 October 1978 of Denmark, Ireland and the United Kingdom (see OJ 1978 L 304), precludes a court in one Contracting State from recognizing a judgment given in default of appearance by a court in another Contracting State. I shall refer to the 1968 Convention, as amended, as 'the Brussels Convention'.

2. The case arises by way of a reference for a preliminary ruling made by the German Bundesgerichtshof (Federal Court of Justice) under the Protocol of 3 June 1971 on the interpretation by this Court of the Brussels Convention. The question referred is in the following terms: 'Is recognition of a judgment given in default of appearance to be refused under Article 27(2) of the Brussels Convention where it cannot be proved that the defendant was served with the document which instituted the proceedings or he was not duly served with that document, if he was nevertheless aware of the judgment delivered in the proceedings but availed himself of none of the legal remedies against the judgment provided for in the procedure of the State in which the judgment was delivered?'

The background

3. That question has arisen in the course of proceedings instituted by Brandeis Ltd, a company incorporated under English law the registered office of which is in London, against Minalmet GmbH, a company incorporated under German law and which has its place of business in Düsseldorf. Brandeis is seeking to enforce in Germany a judgment in default of appearance given by the Queen's Bench Division of the English High Court ordering Minalmet to pay Brandeis $36,533.50 plus interest and costs. Minalmet argues that the writ commencing the proceedings against it in the High Court was not duly served on it and that Article 27(2) of the Brussels Convention therefore prevents the High Court's judgment from being recognized in Germany.

4. Article 27 of the Brussels Convention is contained in Title III, which is headed 'Recognition and Enforcement'. The general rule with regard to recognition is laid down in the first paragraph of Article 26, which provides that 'A judgment given in a Contracting State shall be recognized in the other Contracting States without any special procedure being required.' Article 27 derogates from that general rule by setting out a number of situations in which a court of one Contracting State must refuse to recognize a judgment given by a court in another Contracting State. Thus, in accordance with Article 27(2), a judgment shall not be recognized: 'where it was given in default of appearance, if the defendant was not duly served with the document which instituted the proceedings or with an equivalent document in sufficient time to enable him to arrange for his defence.

By virtue of Article 34 of the Brussels Convention, Article 27 also applies to applications in one Contracting State for the enforcement of a judgment given in another Contracting State.

5. In the present proceedings, the referring court takes the view that the document which instituted the proceedings , that is the writ, was not properly served on Minalmet and that the defect in service cannot be cured. However, Brandeis argues that the judgment of the High Court should still be recognized on the basis that a defendant cannot rely on Article 27(2) if he was aware of the judgment against him and failed to avail himself of the remedies available in the State in which it was delivered. It appears that, in this case, the judgment of the High Court was served on Minalmet on 12 January 1990. Under the rules of procedure applicable in the English High Court (see the Rules of the Supreme Court, Order 13, rule 9), Minalmet could then have taken steps to have the judgment set aside or varied, but failed to do so.

The effect of Article 27(2)

6. As the referring court points out, the argument put forward by Brandeis enjoys the support of certain academic writers. The reasoning underlying it may be summarized as follows. The purpose of the Brussels Convention is to implement the provisions of Article 220 of the EEC Treaty, by virtue of which the Member States undertook to secure 'the simplification of formalities governing the reciprocal recognition and enforcement of judgments of counts or tribunals...'. The first paragraph of Article 26 of the Convention is intended to contribute to the realization of that objective. Article 27 constitutes an exception to the general rule set out in the first paragraph of Article 26 and as such must be strictly construed. The purpose of Article 27(2) is to safeguard the rights of the defendant. It should not be applied literally if that purpose can be achieved in other ways. Where provision is made for a judgment given in default of appearance to be set aside, it is not necessary to insist on strict compliance with the wording of Article 27(2) in order to protect the rights of the defendant.

7. Brandeis draws attention to the second subparagraph of Article 2(c) of the Convention between the Netherlands and Germany on the mutual recognition and enforcement of judgments and other enforceable instruments in civil and commercial matters, signed at The Hague on 30 August 1962, which expressly requires judgments given in default to be recognized in circumstances such as these.

8. It will be observed, however, that the text of Article 27(2) provides no support for the view that the requirements of that provision do not need to be satisfied where the defendant fails to avail himself of a remedy available in the State in which the default judgment was given. Moreover, the Jenard Report contains no suggestion that Article 27(2) was intended to be qualified in the manner advocated by Brandeis (see OJ 1979 C 59, p. 1 at pp. 44-45).

9. Where the defendant was not duly served with the document which instituted the proceedings, it is clear that service of the judgment itself cannot affect the position. As both the referring court and the United Kingdom Government rightly point out, the judgment cannot be considered the document

which instituted the proceedings or an equivalent document for the purposes of Article 27(2). This is evident from paragraph 9 of the judgment in Case 166/80 *Klomps* v *Michel* [1981] ECR 1593, where the Court explained that: '...Article 27, point 2, is intended to ensure that a judgment is not recognized or enforced under the Convention if the defendant has not had an opportunity of defending himself before the court first seised. It follows that a measure, such as the order for payment [Zahlungsbefehl] in German law, service of which on the defendant enables the plaintiff, where no objection to the order is made, to obtain a decision which is enforceable under the Convention, must be duly served on the defendant in sufficient time to enable him to arrange for his defence and accordingly that such a measure must be understood as being covered by the words "the document which instituted the proceedings" in Article 27, point 2. On the other hand a decision, such as the enforcement order [Vollstreckungsbefehl] in German law, which is issued following service of an order for payment and which is itself enforceable under the Convention, is not covered by those words even although [sic] the lodging of an objection against the enforcement order, like the objection to the order for payment, transforms, the procedure into adversary proceedings'.

10. A variant of the view put forward by Brandeis in these proceedings was advanced in Case C-305/88 *Lancray* v *Peters und Sickert* [1990] ECR I-2725, where the plaintiff contended that the defendant's rights were adequately protected where he received the document which instituted the proceedings in sufficient time to enable him to arrange for his defence, and that it was not necessary in such circumstances to require it to be established in addition that that document was duly served. That argument was rejected by the Court, which made it clear that both the conditions laid down in Article 27(2) had to be satisfied before a judgment given in default could be recognized. The Court pointed out, at paragraph 20 of the judgment, that the opposite view: 'would render completely inoperative the requirement of due service. If the sole issue were whether the document came to the defendant's attention in sufficient time, plaintiffs would be tempted to ignore the prescribed forms for due service, the requirements of which have in any event been considerably relaxed by international agreements. That would create considerable uncertainty as to whether documents had actually been served, thus thwarting the uniform application of the provisions of the Convention. Finally, a defendant could not know with certainty whether proceedings which might lead to a finding against him had been properly instituted and whether it was therefore necessary to arrange for a defence, a situation which would also be inconsistent with the aims of the Convention.'

11. While it is true that it is one of the purposes of the Brussels Convention to facilitate the recognition of judgments, the Court has made it clear that this cannot be achieved at the expense of the defendant's right to a fair hearing: see Case 49/84 *Debaecker* v *Bouwman* [1985] ECR 1779; *Lancray*, already cited. To interpret Article 27(2) in accordance with the view put forward by Brandeis would be liable to have this result, for, as the referring court points out, the possibility of challenging a judgment given in default which has already become

enforceable cannot be considered a satisfactory alternative to entering a defence before the judgment is delivered, since the remedies available afterwards may be more limited or more difficult to exercise. Article 27(2) seems implicitly to recognize this point by seeking to protect the defendant's right to be heard before judgment is given against him.

12. I therefore consider that, in the light of the wording of Article 27(2), the intentions of the authors of that provision and the case-law of the Court, the question referred can only be answered in the affirmative. In other words, a judgment given in default may not be recognized if the document which instituted the proceedings was not duly served on the defendant. It is irrelevant that the defendant was aware of the judgment and has failed to avail himself of the remedies available in the State in which the judgment was delivered.

13. The Convention between the Netherlands and Germany of 30 August 1962 does not affect the conclusion I have reached on the proper interpretation of Article 27(2). As the Commission points out, that Convention has now been superseded by the Brussels Convention pursuant to Article 55 of the latter. If it had any relevance at all in the present context, it might in any event be taken to support the view that, had the authors of the Brussels Convention intended to qualify Article 27(2) in the manner advocated by Brandeis, they would have done so expressly.

Conclusion

14. I am therefore of the opinion that the question referred to the Court in this case should be answered as follows: 'Under Article 27(2) of the Brussels Convention, a judgment given in default of appearance in one Contracting State must not be recognized in another Contracting State if the defendant was not duly served with the document which instituted the proceedings, even if he was aware of the judgment concerned but failed to avail himself of any remedies available under the law of the first State which might have led to that judgment being set aside or varied'.

Case C-474/93 - 13 July 1995

Hengst Import BV
v
Anna Maria Campese

Article 27(2) - Concept of document instituting the proceedings or equivalent document.

Summary

The term 'document instituting the proceedings or equivalent document' within the meaning of Article 27(2) of the Convention of 27 September 1968 on Jurisdiction and the Enforcement of Judgments in Civil and Commercial Matters, as amended by the Convention of 9 October 1978 on the accession of the Kingdom of Denmark, Ireland and the United Kingdom of Great Britain and Northern Ireland, means the document or documents which must be duly and timeously served on the defendant in order to enable him to assert his rights before an enforceable judgment is given in the State of origin. The decreto ingiuntivo within the meaning of Book IV of the Italian Code of Civil Procedure (Articles 633 to 656), together with the application instituting the proceedings, must therefore be regarded as 'the document which instituted the proceedings or ... an equivalent document' within the meaning of that provision, since their joint service starts time running for the defendant to oppose the order and since the plaintiff cannot obtain an enforceable order before the expiry of that time-limit.

JUDGMENT OF THE COURT

Gulmann, President of the Chamber, Moitinho de Almeida and Edward, Judges

1. By order of 15 December 1993, received at the Court on 20 December 1993, the Arrondissementsrechtbank Zwolle (Zwolle District Court) referred to the Court for a preliminary ruling under the Protocol of 3 June 1971 on the interpretation by the Court of Justice of the Convention of 27 September 1968 on Jurisdiction and the Enforcement of Judgments in Civil and Commercial Matters a preliminary question on the interpretation of Article 27(2) of that Convention (OJ 1978 L 304, p.36) as amended by the Convention of 9 October 1978 on the accession of the Kingdom of Denmark, Ireland and the United Kingdom of Great Britain and Northern Ireland (OJ 1978 L 304, p.1 and - amended text - p. 77; hereinafter 'the Convention').

2. That question was raised in proceedings between Mrs Campese, domiciled in Italy, and Hengst Import BV ('Hengst'), whose registered office is in the Netherlands, concerning partly unpaid bills relating to shoe deliveries in 1987 and 1988.

3. Using the *procedimento d'ingiunzione*, a summary procedure for recovery of debts, Mrs Campese applied to the President of the Tribunale di Trani (Trani District Court, Italy) on 28 March 1989 for a *decreto ingiuntivo* (order for payment) requiring Hengst to pay her the sum of LIT 11 214 875 with statutory interest and costs.

4. The *procedimento d'ingiunzione* is a summary procedure which allows a creditor by ex parte application to obtain an enforceable court order against the debtor.

5. The creditor applies to the court, with all supporting written evidence, for an order against the debtor for payment of the sum claimed or delivery of the goods within a period of - generally - 20 days (Article 641 of the Italian Code of Civil Procedure, hereinafter 'CCP'). The second paragraph of Article 643 provides that copies of the order and the application are to be served on the defendant. The third paragraph of Article 643 provides that that joint service marks the start of the proceedings. After service, the defendant may oppose the order until the end of the period set under Article 641 of the CCP for voluntary compliance.

6. In principle, the order is not enforceable without more: authorisation of the court, given on the application of the plaintiff after expiry of the period for opposing the order, is necessary to make it enforceable. On application by the creditor, however, the order may be made enforceable on an interim basis where the debt is based on a bill of exchange, a banker's draft, a cheque, a certificate of stock-market liquidation (in cases where a stockbroker has become insolvent) or an instrument made before a notary or other authorised public officer (Article 642(1) of the CCP). The court may also make the order enforceable on an interim basis if delay would give rise to a risk of serious harm (Article 642(2) of the CCP).

7. If the debtor opposes the order within the prescribed period, the ordinary *inter partes* civil procedure is followed (Article 645 of the CCP). Otherwise, the court declares the order enforceable on application by the creditor. It must, however, first order fresh service where it is probable that the debtor was not aware of the order (Article 647 of the CCP).

8. In this case, the President of the Tribunale di Trani made an order for payment on 1 April 1989. On 23 May 1989, that order, together with the application, was served on Hengst in the Netherlands by the Office of the Public Prosecutor at the Arrondissementsrechtbank Zwolle in accordance with the Hague Convention of 15 November 1965 on the service abroad of judicial and extrajudicial documents in civil or commercial matters.

9. On 31 July 1989, noting that the *decreto ingiuntivo* had been duly served on the defendant and that the period of 20 days had expired without Hengst's opposing it, the President of the Tribunale di Trani declared the order enforceable. That decision was recorded on 27 June 1989 in the form of a declaration by the clerk of the Tribunale di Trani, inscribed on the *decreto ingiuntivo*.

10. By order of 20 November 1990, the President of the Arrondissementsrechtbank Zwolle authorised enforcement of the *decreto ingiuntivo* in accordance with Article 31 of the Brussels Convention, which provides: 'A judgment given in a Contracting State and enforceable in that State shall be enforced in another Contracting State when, on the application of any interested party, the order for its enforcement has been issued there'. On 6 December 1990, Mrs Campese served that order on Hengst.

11. Hengst opposed the order before the Arrondissementsrechtbank Zwolle on the basis of Article 27(2) of the Convention which provides that a judgment is not to be recognised where it was given in default of appearance, if the defendant was not duly served with the document which instituted the proceedings or with an equivalent document in sufficient time to enable him to arrange for his defence. According to Hengst, service of the copy of the order together with that of the application cannot be considered to be a document which instituted the proceedings or an equivalent document within the meaning of that provision. The order for payment made by the Tribunale di Trani cannot therefore be recognised and enforced on the basis of the Convention.

12. Unsure of the interpretation to be given to the Convention, the Arrondissementsrechtbank referred the following question to the Court for a preliminary ruling: 'Must a *decreto ingiuntivo* within the meaning of Book IV of the Italian Code of Civil Procedure (Articles 633 to 656), together with the application instituting the proceedings or on its own, be regarded as "the document which instituted the proceedings or ...an equivalent document" within the meaning of Article 27(2) or Article 46(2) or the second paragraph of Article 20 of the Convention on Jurisdiction and the Enforcement of Judgments in Civil and Commercial Matters?'

13. It must be noted first that only Article 27(2) of the Convention is to be interpreted, since Articles 20 and 46(2) of the Convention, also referred to in the question, are irrelevant to the main proceedings. Article 20 is addressed to the courts of the State in which the judgment was given and not to those of the State in which enforcement is sought. With regard to Article 46, the main proceedings do not appear to be concerned with the question whether, as required by that provision in the case of judgments in default, Mrs Campese, in the course of the procedure for recognition and enforcement, produced a document proving that the document which instituted the proceedings had been duly served in the original action.

14. It should also be noted that the order at issue is undoubtedly a judgment capable of recognition and enforcement under Title III of the Convention since there could have been an *inter partes* hearing in the State where it was made before recognition and enforcement were sought in the Netherlands (see Case 125/79 *Denilauler* v *Couchet Frères* [1980] ECR 1553, paragraph 13).

15. By virtue of Article 645 of the CCP, Hengst could have opposed the order before the Tribunale di Trani within 20 days of service of the d*ecreto ingiuntivo,* which would have converted the matter into ordinary contentious proceedings.

16. In order to construe the term 'document which instituted the proceedings or ... equivalent document' used in Article 27(2) of the Convention, it must first be noted that the provisions of the Convention as a whole, both in Title II on jurisdiction and in Title III on recognition and enforcement, manifest an intention to ensure that, within the scope of the objectives of the Convention, proceedings culminating in judicial decisions are conducted in such a way that the rights of the defence are observed (*Denilauler*, paragraph 13).

17. That requirement is particularly crucial where the defendant fails to respond. Article 27(2) is specifically intended to ensure that a judgment given in default can be recognised or enforced under the Convention only if the defendant had the opportunity to put his defence before the court which gave the judgment (Case 166/80 *Klomps* v *Michel* [1981] ECR 1593, paragraph 9, and Case C-123/91 *Minalmet* v *Brandeis* [1992] ECR I-5661, paragraph 18). To that end, the provision requires that the document which instituted the proceedings or an equivalent document be duly and timeously served on the defendant.

18. It is clear from Minalmet, paragraphs 19 and 20, that in order to enable the defendant to arrange for his defence, service of the document which instituted the proceedings or an equivalent document within the meaning of Article 27(2) of the Convention must be effected before an enforceable judgment is given in the State of origin.

19. It follows that the term 'document which instituted the proceedings or ...an equivalent document' within the meaning of Article 27(2) of the Convention means the document or documents which must be duly and timeously served on the defendant in order to enable him to assert his rights before an enforceable judgment is given in the State of origin.

20. Since their joint service starts time running for the defendant to oppose the order and since the plaintiff cannot obtain an enforceable order before the expiry of the time-limit, the decreto ingiuntivo and the plaintiff's application constitute a document which instituted the proceedings or an equivalent document within the meaning of Article 27(2) of the Convention.

21. It must be stressed that in this case the document which instituted the proceedings is constituted by the combination of the order to pay and the application. The decreto ingiuntivo is just a form which to be comprehensible must be read with the application. Conversely, service of the application alone would not enable the defendant to decide whether to defend the action since, without the decreto ingiuntivo, he would not know whether the court had granted or refused the application. Moreover, the requirement for joint service of the decreto ingiuntivo and the application is confirmed by Article 643 of the CCP, according to which it marks the start of the proceedings.

22. In its written observations to the Court, the Commission puts forward an argument against the recognition and enforcement of the judgment of the Tribunale di Trani which was not raised before the national courts. According to the final paragraph of Article 633 of the CCP, 'the order may not be made if service on the defendant pursuant to Article 643 must be effected outside Italy or the territories under Italian sovereignty'. Noting that in this case service was effected in the Netherlands, the Commission submits that the order cannot be a document which instituted the proceedings within the meaning of Article 27(2) of the Convention. Hence, the Netherlands court could refuse to recognise the order of the Tribunale di Trani on the ground of lack of proper service of the document which instituted the proceedings.

23. That argument cannot be upheld.

24. Firstly, the sole aim of Article 27(2) is to ensure that a document which instituted the proceedings or an equivalent document was duly served on the defendant in sufficient time to enable him to arrange for his defence. It does not entitle the court of the State in which recognition is sought to refuse recognition and enforcement of a judgment because of a possible breach of provisions of the law of the State in which it was given other than those governing proper service.

25. Secondly, disregard by the court in which the judgment was given of the final paragraph of Article 633 of the CCP is neither one of the grounds for refusing recognition laid down elsewhere in Article 27 nor one of the situations exhaustively listed in Article 28 of the Convention, in which the court of the State in which recognition is sought is authorised to review the jurisdiction of the court of the State in which the judgment was given.

26. The reply to the national court should accordingly be that the decreto ingiuntivo within the meaning of Book IV of the Italian Code of Civil Procedure (Articles 633 to 656), together with the application instituting the proceedings, must be regarded as 'the document which instituted proceedings or ... an equivalent document' within the meaning of Article 27(2) of the Convention.

On those grounds, the Court (Third Chamber), in answer to the question referred to it by the Arrondissementsrechtbank te Zwolle by judgment of 15 December 1993, hereby rules:

The decreto ingiuntivo within the meaning of Book IV of the Italian Code of Civil Procedure (Articles 633 to 656), together with the application instituting the proceedings, must be regarded as 'the document which instituted proceedings or ... an equivalent document' within the meaning of Article 27(2) of the Convention of 27 September 1968 on Jurisdiction and the Enforcement of Judgments in Civil and Commercial Matters, as amended by the Convention of 9 October 1978 on the accession of the Kingdom of Denmark, Ireland and the United Kingdom of Great Britain and Northern Ireland.

OPINION OF MR ADVOCATE GENERAL JACOBS

1. This case concerns the interpretation of Article 27(2) of the Convention on Jurisdiction and the Enforcement of Judgments in Civil and Commercial Matters of 27 September 1968 (hereinafter 'the Brussels Convention' or simply 'the Convention') as amended by the Convention of 9 October 1978 on the accession of Denmark, Ireland and the United Kingdom. The point raised is whether a decreto ingiuntivo - a summary order provided for in Italian law - may be enforced in another Contracting State under the Brussels Convention.

2. The question referred by the Arrondissementsrechtbank Zwolle is worded as follows: 'Must a decreto ingiuntivo within the meaning of Book IV of the Italian Code of Civil Procedure (Articles 633 to 656), together with the application instituting the proceedings or on its own, be regarded as 'the document which instituted the proceedings or ...an equivalent document' within the meaning of Article 27(2) or Article 46(2) or the second paragraph of Article 20 of the Brussels Convention?'

The facts

3. Mrs Campese, domiciled in Italy, sold consignments of shoes to Firma

Hengst BV ('Hengst'), a company established in the Netherlands. Mrs Campese alleged that Hengst had not paid the full purchase price. On 28 March 1989 she applied, under Article 638 of the Italian Code of Civil Procedure ('CCP'), to the Tribunale di Trani, in Italy, for a decreto ingiuntivo requiring Hengst to pay her the sum of LIT 11 214 875 with interest and costs. On 1 April 1989 the President of the Tribunale di Trani made such an order under Article 641 of the CCP. On 23 May 1989 the order, together with the application which instituted the proceedings before the court in Trani, was served on Hengst pursuant to Article 643 of the CCP in the manner prescribed by Article 15 of the Hague Convention of 15 November 1965 on the service abroad of judicial and extrajudicial documents in civil and commercial matters. In accordance with Article 641 of the CCP, Hengst then had 20 days either to pay the amount specified in the order or to oppose the order before the court in Trani. It did neither. On 31 July 1989 the President of the court in Trani declared the order to be executory in accordance with Article 647 of the CCP and that declaration was inscribed on the order by the clerk of the court on 27 September 1989. Mrs Campese applied to the President of the Arrondissementsrechtbank Zwolle to have the order enforced against Hengst in the Netherlands under Article 32 of the Brussels Convention. Enforcement was authorised on 20 November 1990. Hengst appealed against the decision authorising enforcement to the Arrondissementsrechtbank Zwolle, which referred the question reproduced above.

The decreto ingiuntivo

4. The procedure by which the decreto ingiuntivo is obtained is a rapid, simple, ex parte procedure by which a creditor may obtain an enforceable court order against a debtor. The creditor applies, with all supporting written evidence, for an order for payment of the sum of money owed or for delivery of specified goods (Article 633 of the CCP). Where all the conditions of Article 633 are fulfilled, the court makes an order that the sum claimed shall be paid or the goods delivered within 20 days (Article 641). That period can be reduced to five days if the applicant shows just cause or it can be increased to 30 days.

According to Article 643 of the CCP a copy of the order together with a copy of the application is served on the defendant who then has until the end of the period set in accordance with Article 641 to oppose the order. Article 643, paragraph 3, states that the joint service of the order and the application mark the start of the proceedings: it is only upon that joint service that the defendant is made aware that proceedings have been commenced against him. In normal circumstances, the order itself is not executory until after the expiry of the period set and until the court has declared it to be executory, but the applicant may request that it be made executory on an interim basis if the action is based on a cheque or a negotiable instrument or in other specified cases (Article 642). If the defendant does not oppose the order within the time specified or if the court finds that the opposition is unfounded, the applicant can apply to the court, either orally or in writing, for a declaration that the order is executory. The court must require that the order be served again if it knows or has reason to believe that the defendant did not know of it (Article 647, paragraph 1, in fine). According to Article 650, the defendant may oppose the order after the expiry of the period laid down in the order if he can demonstrate that he did not know of it because of an irregularity in the service or for reasons amounting to force majeure. If the defendant opposes the order, the procedure becomes a normal adversary procedure before the court seised (Article 645, paragraph 2). Finally, it may be noted that Article 633, paragraph 3, specifies that the order cannot be made if it has to be served outside Italy or the Italian sovereign territories.

The relevant provision of the Brussels Convention

5. The referring court is concerned essentially with the interpretation of Article 27(2) of the Brussels Convention, which provides that: 'A judgment shall not be recognised: [...] 2. Where it was given in default of appearance, if the defendant was not duly served with the document which instituted the proceedings or with an equivalent document in sufficient time to enable him to arrange for his defence'.

The purpose of the question referred is to ascertain whether the referring court must refuse to recognise the decreto ingiuntivo granted to Mrs Campese in accordance with Article 27(2). To that end, the referring court needs to know whether the decreto ingiuntivo, either alone or together with the application commencing the proceedings, constitutes the 'document which instituted the proceedings' within the meaning of Article 27(2).

6. The question referred also mentions Article 20, second paragraph, and 46(2) of the Convention, in which the same expression occurs. However, those articles are not directly relevant. Article 20 is addressed to the court in which the original proceedings are commenced in the State of adjudication, while Article 46(2) is concerned with the obligation of the party requesting recognition or enforcement of a judgment in default to produce documentary evidence establishing service of the document instituting the proceedings. The proceedings before the referring court do not appear to be concerned with the issue whether Mrs Campese produced such evidence. I shall therefore concentrate on the interpretation of Article 27(2).

Legal analysis

7. I am of the opinion that service of the 'document which instituted the proceedings' referred to in Article 27(2) means service of both the decreto ingiuntivo and the application as required by Article 643 of the CCP. The fundamental concern of Article 27(2) of the Convention is to ensure that the rights of the defence are adequately protected. The Court stated in *Denilauler* v *Couchet Frères* that: 'All the provisions of the Convention, both those contained in Title II on jurisdiction and those contained in Title III on recognition and enforcement, express the intention to ensure that, within the scope of the objectives of the Convention, proceedings leading to the delivery of judicial decisions take place in such a way that the rights of the defence are observed. It

is because of the guarantees given to the defendant in the original proceedings that the Convention, in Title III, is very liberal in regard to recognition and enforcement'.

Thus, the important element is whether the defendant has had an opportunity to put in a defence or not. Indeed, the Court continued: 'In the light of these considerations it is clear that the Convention is fundamentally concerned with judicial decisions which, before the recognition and enforcement of them are sought in a State other than the State of origin, have been, or have been capable of being, the subject in that State of origin and under various procedures, of an inquiry in adversary proceedings'. (emphasis added).

8. It is clear from an examination of the provisions of the Italian Code of Civil Procedure that the decreto ingiuntivo was indeed capable of being 'the subject of an inquiry in adversary proceedings'. Hengst could have opposed the order before the Tribunale de Trani under Article 645 of the CCP. Had Hengst done so, the procedure would, according to the second paragraph of Article 645, have become a normal adversary one.

9. In addition to allowing the defendant to oppose the decreto ingiuntivo within a period of (normally) 20 days, Italian law contains further procedural safeguards in order to ensure that the rights of the defence are respected. As stated above, Article 650 of the CCP provides that the defendant can oppose the order out of time in certain circumstances. Article 647 of the CCP obliges the court to order fresh service of the decreto ingiuntivo and the application if it knows or has reason to believe that the defendant did not know of it.

10. In *Klomps* v *Michel* the Court had to determine whether a similar kind of order for payment (*Zahlungsbefehl*) which existed in German law was 'the document which instituted proceedings' within the meaning of Article 27(2) of the Convention. It is clear from the description given in the Opinion of Advocate General Reischl that the procedure in issue in that case was similar to the procedure described above in the Italian Code of Civil Procedure. Under the German procedure, a creditor could make an *ex parte* application to a court officer, who, after making a prima facie examination of the claim, issued an order for payment. The order was then served on the debtor, who then had three days in which to oppose the order. That period was subsequently changed to 14 days. On the lodging of an objection to the order the action was transformed into normal adversary proceedings. However, if no objection was made, the creditor could apply for an enforcement order. An objection could be made to that enforcement order also.

11. In Klomps v Michel the Court had no difficulty in interpreting 'the document which instituted the proceedings' in Article 27(2) as covering the order for payment (*Zahlungsbefehl*) in German law. The Court stated that: 'It follows that a measure, such as the order for payment [*Zahlungsbefehl*] in German law, service of which on the defendant enables the plaintiff, where no objection to the order is made, to obtain a decision which is enforceable under the Convention, must be duly served on the defendant in sufficient time to enable him to arrange for his defence, and accordingly that such a measure must be understood as being covered by the words "the document which instituted the proceedings" in Article 27(2)'.

12. One point raised in the order for reference which remains to be dealt with is whether the *decreto ingiuntivo* alone or together with the application constitutes 'the document which instituted the proceedings'. Given that Article 643 of the CCP requires service on the defendant of both the *decreto ingiuntivo* and the application, I am of the opinion that it is the conjunction of those documents which constitutes 'the document which instituted the proceedings' within the meaning of Article 27(2). Indeed, as stated in the third paragraph of Article 643 of the CCP, the service of both of those documents marks the start of the time in which to oppose the order. The Italian Government has pointed out in its observations that the court making the order must check whether service was carried out properly before declaring the *decreto ingiuntivo* executory. If one of the two documents is missing, the court would have to order fresh service pursuant to Article 647 of the CCP.

13. Before concluding, I address one matter which the Commission has raised, although I do not consider that it affects the answer which should be given to the question referred. The Commission has raised the issue whether the *decreto ingiuntivo* given in this case comes within the meaning of the term used in Article 27(2) because it was served on a defendant domiciled outside Italy. Article 633 of the CCP states that the Italian court cannot make the order if it has to be served outside Italy. The Commission concludes than only a *decreto ingiuntivo* served on a defendant domiciled in Italy constitutes, together with the application, 'the document which instituted the proceedings' within the meaning of Article 27(2).

14. I disagree. In Article 27(2), the important element is whether the defendant was duly served with the relevant document or its equivalent in sufficient time to enable him to arrange for his defence. That provision seeks to ensure that default judgments given in circumstances in which the defendant had no opportunity of defending himself do not come within the simplified rules on recognition and enforcement laid down in Title III of the Convention. Whether the Italian court was right or wrong in making the order in the present case is a different issue.

15. The answer proposed by the Commission would have the effect of allowing the Dutch court to refuse to enforce (or recognise) the Italian order because of a possible mistake contrary to Italian law. That would lead the Dutch court to examine whether the Italian court had been correct as a matter of Italian law in making the order. Article 29 of the Convention precludes the court of the State in which enforcement is sought from undertaking such an examination.

16. It is true that in *Pendy Plastic* v *Pluspunkt* the Court ruled that jurisdiction to determine whether the document instituting proceedings was properly served was conferred both on the court of the original State and on the court of the State in which enforcement was sought. However, the examination that may be carried out by the latter court is limited, in my opinion, to the question whether service was duly effected in such a way that the defendant was put in a position to be able to organise his defence. That interpretation accords with the fundamental purpose of Article 27(2), namely to ensure that the rights of the defence are protected.

Conclusion

17. Accordingly, I am of the opinion that the question referred by the Arrondissementsrechtbank Zwolle should be answered as follows:
'Article 27(2) of the Brussels Convention of 27 September 1968 on Jurisdiction and the Enforcement of Judgments in Civil and Commercial Matters as amended by the Convention of 9 October 1978 on the accession of Denmark, Ireland and the United Kingdom must be interpreted as meaning that the words 'the document which instituted the proceedings or... and equivalent document' cover any document, such as the order known as the *decreto ingiuntivo* under Italian law together with the application initiating the procedure for obtaining it, service of which enables the plaintiff, under the law of the State of the court in which judgment was given, to obtain, in default of appropriate action taken by the defendant, a decision capable of being recognised and enforced under the provisions of the Convention'.

Case C-78/95 - 10 October 1996

Bernardus Hendrikman and Maria Feyen
v
Magenta Druck & Verlag GmbH

Recognition and enforcement - Grounds for refusal - Defendant who is not properly served with or notified of the document instituting proceedings in sufficient time and who fails to appear - Definition of "in default of appearance" - Defendant unaware of proceedings initiated against him and represented by a lawyer without his authority - Included - Remedy available in the State in which judgment was given, allowing it to be contested on the ground of lack of representation - Not material

Summary

Where proceedings are initiated against a person without his knowledge and a lawyer appears before the court first seised on his behalf but without his authority, such a person is quite powerless to defend himself and must be regarded as a defendant in default of appearance, within the meaning of Article 27(2) of the Convention of 27 September 1968 on jurisdiction and the enforcement of judgments in civil and commercial matters, even if the proceedings before the court first seised became, in point of form, proceedings inter partes. That conclusion is not affected by the fact that the defendant may apply to have the judgment in question annulled on the ground of lack of representation, since the proper time for a defendant to have an opportunity to defend himself is the time at which proceedings are commenced.

Article 27(2) of the Convention therefore applies to judgments given against a defendant who was not duly served with, or notified of, the document instituting proceedings in sufficient time and who was not validly represented during those proceedings, albeit the judgments given were not given in default of appearance because someone purporting to represent the defendant appeared before the court first seised.

JUDGMENT OF THE COURT

Moitinho de Almeida, President of the Chamber, Gulmann, Edward, Jann (Rapporteur), and Wathelet, Judges

1. By judgment of 10 March 1995, which was received at the Court on 16 March 1995, the Hoge Raad der Nederlanden (Supreme Court of the Netherlands) referred to the Court for a preliminary ruling pursuant to the Protocol of 3 June 1971 on the interpretation by the Court of Justice of the Convention of 27 September 1968 on jurisdiction and the enforcement of judgments in civil and commercial matters three questions on the interpretation of Article 27(1) and (2) and Article 29 of that Convention (OJ 1972 L 299, p. 32), cIS amended by the Convention of 9 October 1978 relating to the accession of the Kingdom of Denmark, Ireland and the United Kingdom of Great Britain and Northern Ireland (OJ 1978 L 304, p. 1 and, for the amended text, p. 77; hereinafter 'the Convention).

2. Those questions arose in proceedings between Bernardus Hendrikman and Maria Feyen (hereinafter 'Mr and Mrs Hendrikman'), residing at The Hague, and Magenta Druck & Verlag GmbH (hereinafter 'Magenta'), a German company whose seat is in Krefeld, Germany. Those proceedings concern the enforcement in the Netherlands of a judgment delivered on 2 April 1991 by the Landgericht (Regional Court), Krefeld, and of an order on taxation of costs made on 12 July 1991 by the Amtsgericht (Local Court) Nettetal (Germany) against Mr and Mrs Hendrikman. That judgment and that order were both served on Mr and Mrs Hendrikman on 17 September 1991.

3. By order of 14 January 1992, the acting President of the Arrondissementsrechtbank (District Court), The Hague, gave leave for the enforcement of the German judgment and order in the Netherlands. In their appeal against that order for leave, Mr and Mrs Hendrikman relied on Article 27(1) and (2) of the Convention contending that they had never received the documents instituting the proceedings and had not been validly represented before the German courts.

4. Article 27 of the Convention provides that: 'A judgment shall not be recognized:

1. if such recognition is contrary to public policy in the State in which recognition is sought;

2. where it was given in default of appearance, if the defendant was not duly served with the document which instituted the proceedings or with an equivalent document in sufficient time to enable him to arrange for his defence;

3. if the judgment is irreconcilable with a judgment given in a dispute between the same parties in the State in which recognition is sought; ...'

5. According to Mr and Mrs Hendrikman, the proceedings leading to the German judgment and order had been instituted by Magenta in Germany without their knowledge. They concerned an unpaid invoice for stationery which had been ordered on behalf of Mr and Mrs Hendrikman by two persons who had DC) authority to do so. The same two persons also instructed lawyers in the name of Mr and Mrs Hendrikman, but again without their authority, to represent the couple in the proceedings.

6. By judgment of 2 February 1994, the Arrondissementsrechtbank, The Hague, dismissed the appeal as unfounded. It held that Article 29 of the Convention, which provides that 'under no circumstances may a foreign judgment be reviewed as to its substance', precluded it from judging whether the German courts were entitled to assume that the conduct of the proceedings by the lawyers in question amounted to valid representation.

7. The Arrondissementsrechtbank also took the view that Article 27(1) could only apply where, under the law of the country in which the judgment was given, no remedy was available to a party who was unaware of the proceedings initiated against him and who was not validly represented, or where that party could not in practice exercise that remedy. In the present case, Paragraphs 579(4) and 586 of the Zivilprozessordnung (German Code of Civil Procedure) would have allowed Mr and Mrs Hendrikman to apply for annulment of the German judgment and order on the ground of lack of representation within one month of service. However, they did not avail themselves of that remedy.

8. Lastly, according to the Arrondissementsrechtbank, Mr and Mrs Hendrikman could not rely on Article 27(2) of the Convention because

their case did not concern a judgment delivered against a defendant in default of appearance.

9. Mr and Mrs Hendrikman appealed in cassation to the Hoge Raad der Nederlanden against the Arrondissementsrechtbank's decision.

10. The Hoge Raad decided to stay proceedings and request a preliminary ruling from this Court on the following questions:

'(1) Must Article 29 of the Brussels Convention be interpreted as meaning that the court of the State in which recognition is sought must refrain from making any inquiry into the question whether the defendant to the proceedings conducted in the State in which judgment was given was validly represented, even if the court of the State in which judgment was given made no ruling in that regard'?

(2) (a) Must Article 27(1) of the Brussels Convention be interpreted as precluding recognition of a judgment given in another Contracting State where the defendant in the relevant proceedings was not validly represented and had no knowledge of the proceedings, even if he later had cognizance of the judgment which was given and availed himself in that regard of none of the legal remedies afforded by the procedural law of the State in which judgment was given'?

(2) (b) Is it relevant in that connection that the time within which the legal remedy must be exercised is one month from the day on which the defendant has cognizance of the judgment which has been given?

(3) Must Article 27(2) of the Brussels Convention be interpreted as meaning that that provision is also applicable in a case in which, although the defendant was not declared to be in deflault of appearance, the document instituting the proceedings or an equivalent document was not duly served on, or notified to, him in sufficient time and the defendant was not validly represented in the proceedings?'

11. Since the court making the reference has not described the facts found in any great detail, the answers given by this Court will be apposite only in so far as the description of the circumstances on which the appellants in the main case rely corresponds to the facts.

12. The third question should be addressed first.

The third question

13. By this question, the national court is essentially asking whether Article 27(2) of the Convention applies to judgments delivered against a

defendant who was not duly served with, or notified of, the document instituting proceedings in sufficient time and who was not validly represented during those proceedings, albeit the judgments given were not given in default of appearance, because someone purporting to represent the defendant appeared before the court first seised.

14. Under Article 27(2), a court from which recognition is sought may decline to recognize a judgment only if certain conditions are satisfied: the document instituting proceedings was not duly served on, or notified to, the defendant in sufficient time and he failed to appear in the proceedings conducted before the court first seised. The national court inquires only about the second condition.

15. According to settled case-law, the purpose of Article 27(2) of the Convention is to ensure that a judgment is not recognized or enforced under the Convention if the defendant has not had an opportunity of defending himself before the court first seised (see Case 166/80 *Klomps* v *Michel* [1981] ECR 1593, paragraph 9, and Case C-172/91 *Sonntag* v *Waidmann* [1993] ECR 1-1963, paragraph 38).

16. The German Government submits that the rights of the defence are observed even if a lawyer who is not authorized to act appears for the defendants because the court must rely on what is stated by that lawyer until such time as he is shown to have no authority.

17. That argument cannot be accepted.

18. Where proceedings are initiated against a person without his knowledge and a lawyer appears before the court first seised on his behalf but without his authority, such a person is quite powerless to defend himself. That person must therefore be regarded as a defendant in default of appearance, within the meaning of Article 27(2), even if the proceedings before the court first seised became, in point of form, proceedings *inter partes*. It is for the court from whom recognition is sought to ascertain whether those exceptional circumstances exist.

19. That conclusion is not affected by the fact that, under Paragraphs 579(4) and 586 of the German Code of Civil Procedure, Mr and Mrs Hendrikman were entitled to apply, within one month of service of the judgment and order, for their annulment on the ground of lack of representation.

20. The proper time for a defendant to have an opportunity to defend himself is the time at which proceedings are commenced. The possibility of having recourse, at a later stage, to a legal remedy against a judgment given in default of appearance, which has already become enforceable, cannot constitute an equally effective alternative to defending proceedings before judgment is given (see Case C-123/91 *Minalmet* v *Brandeis* [1992] ECR 1-5661, paragraph 19).

21. The answer to the third question must therefore be that Article 27(2) of the Convention applies to judgments given against a defendant who was not duly served with, or notified of, the document instituting proceedings in sufficient time and who was not validly represented during those proceedings, albeit the judgments given were not given in default of appearance because someone purporting to represent the defendant appeared before the court first seised.

The first and second questions

22. In view of the reply given to the third question, there is no need to answer the first question.

23. As regards the second question, it should be noted that the public-policy clause in Article 27(1) of the Convention 'ought to operate only in exceptional cases' (see the Report on the Convention on jurisdiction and the enforcement of judgments in civil and commercial matters, OJ 1979 C 59, p. 1, at p. 44). Recourse to it is in any event precluded when the issue must be resolved on the basis of a specific provision such as Article 27(2) (see, in connection with Article 27(3), Case 145/86 *Hoffmann* v *Krieg* [1988] ECR 645, paragraph 21).

24. In view of the foregoing considerations, there is no need to reply to the second question.

On those grounds, the court, in answer to the questions referred to it by the Hoge Raad der Nederlanden, by judgment of 10 March 1995, hereby rules:

> **Article 27(2) of the Convention of 27 September 1968 on jurisdiction and the enforcement of judgments in civil and commercial matters, as amended by the Convention of 9 October 1978 relating to the accession of the Kingdom of Denmark, Ireland and the United Kingdom of Great Britain**

and Northern Ireland, applies to judgments given against a defendant who was not duly served with, or notified of; the document instituting proceedings in sufficient time and who was not validly represented during those proceedings, albeit the judgments given were not given in default of appearance because someone purporting to represent the defendant appeared before the court first seised.

OPINION OF MR ADVOCATE GENERAL JACOBS

1. The issue raised by the Netherlands Hoge Raad (Supreme Court) in this case is essentially whether a judgment given by a German court in ostensibly *inter partes* proceedings must be enforced under the Brussels Convention on Jurisdiction and the Enforcement of Judgments in Civil and Commercial Matters by a Netherlands court in circumstances where the defendants were not aware of the proceedings in Germany and were represented before the German court without their authority.

Relevant provisions of the Brussels Convention

2. The provisions at issue are contained in Title III of the Brussels Convention, which is headed 'Reecognition and Enforcement'.

3. The general rule with regard to recognition is laid down in the first paragraph of Article 26, which provides: 'A judgment given in a Contracting State shall be recognised in the other Contracting States without any special procedure being required.'

4. Article 27 derogates from that general rule by setting out a number of situations in which a court of one Contracting State must refuse to recognise a judgment given by a court in another Contracting State, of which the first two are:

'(1) if such recognition is contrary to public policy in the State in which recognition is sought;

(2) where it was given in default of appearance, if the defendant was not duly served with the document which instituted the proceedings or with an equivalent document in sufficient time to enable him to arrange for his defence'.

5. Article 28 provides further exceptions to the general requirement of recognition, relating to insurance and consumer contracts, to cases in respect of which the Convention provides for exclusive jurisdiction, and to certain judgments which a Contracting State may agree with a third State not to recognise.

6. Article 29 states: 'Under no circumstances may a foreign judgment be reviewed as to its substance'.

7. Article 34, which concerns applications in one Contracting State for the enforcement of a judgment given in another Contracting State, states in its

second paragraph that an application for enforcement 'may be refused only for one of the reasons specified in Articles 27 and 28' and continues in its third paragraph: 'Under no circumstances may the foreign judgment be reviewed as to its substance'.

8. The grounds on which a court must refuse to recognise a judgment are accordingly identical to those on which it may refuse to order enforcement. The national court's questions are framed in terms of recognition; the parties in their observations and the Court in its judgments in various cases cited in this Opinion sometimes use one term, sometimes the other and sometimes both.

Background and questions referred

9. Very few facts figure in the order for reference. Most of the following account is, in the absence of any other information, drawn from the observations of the appellants in the main proceedings and hence cannot be regarded as corroborated.

10. At the time of the events giving rise to the judgment sought to be enforced, Mr and Mrs Hendrikman, the appellants in the main proceedings, both resident in the Netherlands, were sole shareholders in the Netherlands company Hendrikman BV (subsequently dissolved). The company was in the business of cosmetics wholesaling. In 1989, negotiations took place with Mr Conrad and Mr Ernst of the Düsseldorf firm Partnership Management with a view to Conrad and Ernst handling the company's marketing in Germany. Conrad and Ernst ordered stationery, business cards and a stamp, all printed with 'Dekor Display' and 'Markenvertried Hendrikman & Hendrickman, Ben & Ria Hendrikman (...) Düsseldorf (...)', from Magenta Druck & Verlag GmbH, a company incorporated in Germany. The invoice for that order, received by Conrad and Ernst in April 1989, was never paid. Magenta subsequently brought an action against Mr and Mrs Hendrikman before the Amtsgericht (local court), Düsseldorf, in June 1989. It appears that service of the writ, citing the defendants as 'Herr und Frau Ben & Ria Hendrikman, handelnd unter der Firma Dekor Display, Markenvertrieb Hendrikman & Hendrikman (...) Per adresse Werner Conrad (...) Düsseldorf', was effected at Conrad's address and that in October 1989 Conrad or Ernst, using the stationery, instructed local lawyers to arrange for a defence.

11. According to Mr and Mrs Hendrikman, they had no knowledge of either the writ or the response to it.

12. The action was dismissed for reasons which are apparently not known to Mr and Mrs Hendrikman, but that judgment was reversed on appeal by the Landgericht (Regional Court), Krefeld, in April 1991; the Amtsgericht, Nettetal (to which the proceedings had been referred by the Amtsgericht, Düsseldorf), made an order for costs against Mr and Mrs Hendrikman in July 1991.

13. The Landgericht's judgment and the order for costs were served on Mr and Mrs Hendrikman in the Netherlands in September 1991 with a notification that failure to pay would lead to an application for enforcement. In January 1992 the President of the Arrondissementsrechtbank (District Court), The Hague, gave leave to Magenta to enforce the judgment and order against Mr and Mrs

Hendrikman in the Netherlands. The judgment and order together with the President's order granting leave were served on them on 11 February 1992 with an order to comply and notification of execution in the event of non-compliance. On 10 March 1992 they lodged an appeal against the President's order to the Arrondissementsrechtbank, The Hague, invoking Article 27(1) and (2) of the Brussels Convention.

14. According to the order for reference, Mr and Mrs Hendrikman contended on appeal that (i) they were represented in the German proceedings without their authority; (ii) they had never received the documents instituting the proceedings; (iii) Conrad and Ernst acted without their authority in their name to instruct local lawyers to represent them; (iv) consequently Conrad and Ernst were, substantively, parties to the proceedings and not Mr and Mrs Hendrikman; (v) the German courts wrongly assumed that Mr and Mrs Hendrikman were validly represented before them; (vi) as a result, decisions were delivered against them against which they could not defend themselves; (vii) to recognise and, in this case, enforce the decisions would be contrary to public policy since it would be an unacceptable breach of the fundamental principle of the autonomy of the human person and the fundamental principle *audi alteram partem*.

15. The appeal was dismissed in February 1994. According to the order for reference, the Arrondissementsrechtbank held that (i) Article 29 of the Brussels Convention precluded it from judging whether the German courts were entitled to assume that the representation in question was valid; (ii) Article 27(1) of the Brussels Convention should be given a narrow interpretation, although public policy might be at issue if the law of the country in which judgment was given against a defendant who was not aware of proceedings instituted against him and not validly represented conferred no remedy, or if a remedy was not available in the circumstances; (iii) however, even if Mr and Mrs Hendrikman were not aware of the proceedings and not validly represented, they could not invoke Article 27(1) since they could have sought annulment of the judgment and order on the ground of lack of representation within one month of the initial service in September 1991 pursuant to Article 586 of the German code of civil procedure; and (iv) Article 27(2) of the Brussels Convention did not apply since there was no question of a defendant's having been declared in default of appearance.

16. On an appeal in cassation, the Hoge Raad referred the following questions to the Court of Justice:

'(1) Must Article 29 of the Brussels Convention be interpreted as meaning that the court of the State in which recognition is sought must refrain from making any inquiry into the question whether the defendant to the proceedings conducted in the State in which judgment was given was validly represented, even if the court of the State in which judgment was given made no ruling in that regard'

(2)(a) Must Article 27(1) of the Brussels Convention be interpreted as precluding recognition of a judgment given in another Contracting State where the defendant in the relevant proceedings was not validly represented and had no knowledge of the proceedings, even if he later had cognisance of the judgment which was given and availed himself in that regard of none of the legal remedies afforded by the procedural law of the State in which judgment was given?

(2)(b) Is it relevant in that connection that the time within which the legal remedy must be applied is one month from the day on which the defendant has cognisance of the judgment which has been given?

(3) Must Article 27(2) of the Brussels Convention be interpreted as meaning that that provision is also applicable in a case in which, although the defendant was not declared to be in default of appearance, the document instituting the proceedings or an equivalent document was not duly served on or notified to him in sufficient time and the defendant was not validly represented in the proceedings?'

17. As the Commission points out, it does not appear from the order for reference whether in fact Mr and Mrs Hendrikman knew of the proceedings in Germany or were validly represented: thus if the Court were to conclude that lack of knowledge or valid representation could in principle preclude automatic recognition and enforcement in the Netherlands of the German judgment, the Netherlands courts would have first to ascertain whether those circumstance had been proved before refusing to authorise enforcement.

18. Nor is it apparent why the German courts had jurisdiction in proceedings brought against persons domiciled in the Netherlands. I assume, although it is nowhere stated, that those courts exercised special jurisdiction in accordance with Article 5(1) of the Convention, on the basis that they were the courts for the place of performance of the contractual obligation in dispute.

19. I propose to address the various issues in a different order from that adopted in the questions referred. I will first consider the national court's final question, concerning Article 27(2) of the Convention (judgments delivered in default of appearance), since I think that my proposed answer to that question resolves its other questions.

The scope of Article 27(2): judgments delivered in default of appearance

20. The national court's final question essentially asks whether a judgment delivered in proceedings where, although the defendant was not declared to be in default of appearance, he was not validly represented and had no knowledge of the proceedings is a judgment 'given in default of appearance' for the purpose of Article 27(2).

21. If that question is answered in the affirmative, the national court will be required to examine whether the two conditions set out in that provision were met before it enforces the judgment. Those conditions are separate and cumulative: the first requirement, of due service, is to be determined by reference to the procedural law of the State in which the judgment was delivered together with any relevant international conventions; the second requirement, of service in sufficient time to enable a defence to be arranged, is a question of fact to be assessed by the court before which enforcement is sought taking into consideration the circumstances of the case before it.

22. The wording of the question suggests that the national court is

assuming that neither condition was met. It therefore needs to know whether the defendants were in default of appearance, in which case Article 27(2) applies and it may not recognise the judgment. Although the German Government has suggested in these proceedings that there was due service under German law, it would still be possible for the referring court to find that the second condition was not met. The issue in this case is therefore whether the judgment was given in default of appearance within the meaning of Article 27(2).

23. The only case in which the Court has specifically considered the question of what constitutes 'appearance' for the purposes of Article 27(1) is *Sonntag*. That case concerned criminal proceedings brought in Italy against Mr Sonntag, a German schoolteacher, for causing the death by negligence of a pupil who had suffered a fatal accident on a school trip to Italy. The deceased pupil's parents and brother joined the criminal proceedings as civil parties seeking an order against Mr Sonntag for compensation for the loss caused by the accident. The civil parties' declaration of intention to make a civil claim against him was served on Mr Sonntag. He was legally represented at the trial before the criminal court at which he was found guilty on the criminal count and ordered to pay compensation to the civil parties. The relevant German court granted the civil parties' application to enforce the civil law part of the judgment. Mr Sonntag appealed to the Oberlandesgericht, which dismissed the appeal; he appealed against that dismissal to the Bundesgerichtshof, which referred a number of questions to the Court including the following: 'Has a defendant appeared for the purposes of Article 27(2) of the Convention where the case concerns a civil claim for damages in connection with charges brought before a criminal court ... and the person against whom enforcement is sought, through defence counsel of his choice, answered the criminal charges but did not express a view on the civil claim, on which oral argument was also submitted in the presence of his counsel'?

24. Advocate General Damon favoured a restrictive interpretation of the exception, stating: 'In order to be applicable, Article 27(2) necessarily implies, in my view, that the defendant is in default of appearance, *and must have been found to be so by the court of the State where the proceedings were first brought* ... ' (Emphasis added). That statement should, however, be seen in its context: it was not disputed in *Sonntag* that the defendant had been aware of the proceedings as a whole and had been represented at the hearing by counsel of his choice.

25. The Court did not follow the Advocate General's approach. The Court stressed that Article 27(2) was intended to ensure that a judgment was not recognised or enforced under the Convention if the defendant had not had an opportunity of defending himself before the court first seised. Non-recognition under Article 27(2) is accordingly possible only where the defendant was in default of appearance at the original proceedings: 'Consequently, that provision may not be relied upon where the defendant appeared, at least if he was notified of the elements of the claim and had the opportunity to arrange for his defence .... A defendant is deemed to have appeared for the purposes of Article 27(2) of the Convention where, in connection with a claim for damages made in the

context of criminal proceedings pending before the criminal court, the defendant, through defence counsel of his own choice, answered the criminal charges at the trial but did not express a view on the civil claim, on which oral argument was also submitted in the presence of his counsel.'

26. Although the factual context of *Sonntag* was entirely different, it is instructive to note the Court's readiness to develop an autonomous interpretation of the concept of a judgment 'given in default of appearance' without reference to the relevant national law of the court which delivered the judgment in question. That echoes the view of Advocate General VerLoren van Themaat, who stated in *Debaecker* v *Bouwman* after reviewing the earlier cases that 'Article 27(2) should be interpreted independently, as an autonomous provision of the Convention'.

27. I consider that the Court's dicta in *Sonntag* as to scope of Article 27(2), and in particular as to the meaning of 'appeared' for that purpose, support the view that that provision applies where the defendant was not in fact notified of the elements of the claim and did not answer the claim through counsel of his own choice, even though the court which delivered the judgment did not formally declare it to be given in default of appearance.

28. Such a construction is to my mind consistent with the Court's readiness in earlier cases to give a broad interpretation to Article 27(2). Although as I stated in my Opinion in *Lancray*, 'as an exception to the general rule laid down in Article 26 of the Brussels Convention, Article 27 is not to be interpreted extensively', that proposition is, as I made clear, subject to the important caveat that 'too restrictive an interpretation might undermine the defendant's right to a fair hearing [which is] not an acceptable way of achieving the objectives of the Brussels Convention'.

29. The clearest authority for a broad interpretation may be found in the Court's statements in *Klomps* v *Michel* and *Minalmet* that Article 27(2) is intended to ensure that a judgment is not recognised or enforced under the Convention if the defendant has not had an opportunity of defending himself before the court first seised.

30. Similarly in *Pendy Plastic* v *Pluspunkt* Advocate General Reischl stated that Article 27(2): 'reflects the basic concern to ensure observance of the principle of the right to a proper hearing ... the principle is often regarded as a matter of public policy ... provisions having such a content are not to be interpreted restrictively'.

31. The case-law concerning the proper balance to be struck between the Convention's aim of ensuring the free movement of judgments and the need to ensure observance of the principle of *audi alteram partem* contains numerous further statements by the Court stressing the fundamental nature of the guarantee in Article 27(2) that the rights of the defence have been observed, supporting an interpretation of the provision which extends it beyond proceedings in default *stricto sensu* where that is necessary for the protection of the rights of the defence.

32. Such an interpretation accords with that advocated by the Commission and the Greek Government as well as by the appellants in the main proceedings.

33. The contrary view would have the perverse consequence that defendants to proceedings which, albeit nominally *inter partes*, were in fact conducted without their knowledge and without their being validly represented would not benefit from the additional safeguards provided by Article 27(2), whereas a defendant to a judgment given in default of appearance who had in fact received the document instituting the proceedings although it was not served according to the relevant procedural requirements, as in *Lancray*, would so benefit. As the Commission's representative pointed out at the hearing, if the rights of the defence are regarded as prejudiced in the latter situation, then *a fortiori* they should be so regarded in the former.

34. The contrary view would, moreover, entail the risk that a judgment delivered after proceedings which did not comply with the safeguards required by Article 6 of the European Convention on Human Rights, which guarantees the right to a fair hearing, would require recognition and enforcement throughout the Community.

35. Furthermore, it would mean that a judgment delivered by a court in proceedings brought without their knowledge against defendants domiciled in another Contracting State in circumstances where there was no jurisdiction under the Convention might be treated as enforceable, which would be contrary to the fundamental principles underlying the Convention.

36. Although the construction which I advocate runs counter to the view of Advocate General Darmon in *Sonntag*, mentioned above, the Advocate General was - understandably in the circumstances of the case before him, where neither improper presentation nor the defendant's lack of awareness of the proceedings was at issue - clearly influenced by the fact that the essence of an *inter partes* hearing before the court is that 'the defendant, or his counsel, had the opportunity before that court to raise the possible unlawfulness of the document instituting the proceedings and to submit defence arguments going to admissibility and the merits'. That is precisely the opportunity which the appellants in the main proceedings in this case deny having had.

37. It may be noted that Advocate General Mayras came to a similar view to that which I propose in *Denilauler* v *Couchet Frères*, a case concerning the application of the Convention to an interim order obtained *ex parte*. The Advocate General, considering whether Article 27(2) applied to proceedings in which such an order was obtained, stated: 'It is, however, far from certain that the terms used in [Article 27(2)] can apply only to default proceedings as understood *stricto sensu* in certain national legal systems.

I do not think it right to construe Article 27(2) as referring only to specific proceedings known to certain national legal systems. In my view such a construction would be too narrow and would fail to recognise the independent nature of the Convention, which is an instrument of international law, in relation to the multiplicity of proceedings under the national legal systems of the Contracting States.

This is confirmed by the English text of Article 27(2) which, by using the expression 'judgment ... given in default of appearance', is careful to avoid terminology calling to mind certain national proceedings and those alone. There can be no doubt that according to the ordinary meaning of the words any judgment given against a defendant without his having been heard is a judgment 'in default of his appearance'. The English term refers simply to the absence of the defendant from the course of the proceedings for whatever reason.'

38. The Court did not adopt Advocate General Mayras' analysis of Article 27(2), ruling instead that *ex parte* orders were outside the scheme of the Convention as a whole.

39. The court before which enforcement is sought will, of course, require evidence of wholly exceptional circumstances to establish that an ostensibly *inter partes* judgment in fact falls within the scope of Article 27(2). However, where that provision applies that court is already required to satisfy itself not only that service was duly effected but also whether, in a particular case, there are exceptional circumstances which warrant the conclusion that service was nonetheless inadequate for the purposes of enabling the defendant to arrange for his defence. In considering whether it is confronted with such a case the court may take account of all the circumstances, including the means employed for effecting service and the relations between the plaintiff and the defendant. It does not seem to be unduly burdensome, or to make too great an inroad into the system set in place by the Convention, to require the court to undertake a comparable preliminary appraisal in situations such as that at issue in this case in order to ascertain whether the provision applies.

40. Finally, it should be mentioned that it is clearly irrelevant for the purposes of Article 27(2) that the appellants in the main proceedings became aware of the judgment once it had been served on them and failed to avail themselves of the possibility under German law of applying to have the judgment set aside on grounds of lack of representation. As the Court stated in *Minalmet*: 'the proper time for the defendant to have an opportunity to defend himself is the time at which proceedings are commenced. The possibility of having recourse, at a later stage, to a legal remedy against a judgment given in default of appearance, which has already become enforceable, cannot constitute an equally effective alternative to defending the proceedings before judgment is delivered'.

41. I accordingly conclude that a judgment delivered in ostensibly *inter partes* proceedings of which the defendant was unaware and in which he was not validly represented is a judgment given in default of appearance within the meaning of Article 27(2).

The limits of Article 29: prohibition of a review of the substance of a judgment

42. The national court's first question asks essentially whether Article 29 prohibits the court before which recognition is sought from making any inquiry into whether the defendant was validly represented.

43. Once it is accepted that a judgment delivered in proceedings in which the defendant was not validly represented may constitute a judgment in default of appearance for the purposes of Article 27(2), it is clear that Article 29 cannot

have the effect posited in the national court's first question since if it had that effect Article 27(2) would be wholly undermined: the national court would be precluded by one provision from making inquiries relevant to determining whether another provision applied in a particular case.

44. Thus, to my mind, to the extent that the invalidity of representation is being pleaded by the defendant with a view to establishing that the judgment sought to be enforced is a judgment in default and hence that the safeguards in Article 27(2) apply, the court before which enforcement is sought is clearly competent to investigate the issue (although as stated above it will require evidence of wholly exceptional circumstances to justify a finding that a judgment expressed to have been delivered in *inter partes* proceedings falls within Article 27(2)).

45. Nonetheless, I consider that it is worth briefly reviewing the scope of Article 29, if only to avoid unwarranted generalisation of the conclusion that in this case the court before which enforcement is sought may review a procedural aspect of the judgment sought to be enforced.

46. In my view, it would be stretching normal usage to construe the concept of the substance of a judgment as encompassing such unequivocally procedural elements as service and representation. The question accordingly arises whether, merely because procedural irregularities do not go to the substance of a judgment and hence do not fall within the prohibition in Article 29, the court before which enforcement is sought is at liberty to investigate any alleged procedural irregularity.

47. I consider that the answer to that general question is clearly in the negative, notwithstanding the answer to be given to the question put in the specific circumstances of this case.

48. In my view, the grounds for refusing enforcement are set out exhaustively in Articles 27 and 28 and hence procedural irregularities cannot be investigated except to the extent that they fall within one of the grounds set out in those articles, notwithstanding the fact that such irregularities do not go to the substance of the judgment and hence are not covered by Article 29.

49. The cumulative effect of the relevant provisions strongly supports the view that the types of irregularity which must lead the court before which recognition or enforcement is sought to refuse the application are set out exhaustively in Articles 27 and 28.

50. Title III of the Convention is headed 'Recognition and Enforcement'. Section 1, 'Recognition', consists of Articles 26 to 30. Article 26 sets out the basic rule that a judgment given in a Contracting State is to be recognised without any special procedure being required. Article 27 states that a judgment 'shall not be recognised' in a number of specified circumstances; Article 28 states: 'Moreover, a judgment shall not be recognised' on further specified grounds. Article 29 states unequivocally that under no circumstances may a foreign judgment be reviewed as to its substance. (Article 30 provides for a stay of recognition proceedings in the event of an appeal against the judgment at issue).

51. In that context, Article 29 serves as a full stop: it reminds the court

before which recognition is sought of the cornerstone of the whole edifice of the free movement of judgments, the bedrock principle that *prima facie* it must recognise the judgment. In the words of Advocate General Mayras in *Denilauler* v *Couchet Frères:* 'the whole essence of the Convention is not to allow the court addressed to have jurisdiction as to the substance of the case'.

52. The pattern, moreover, is reflected in Section 2 of Title III, headed 'Enforcement': Article 31 provides that a judgment is to be enforced when on the application of any interested party it has been declared enforceable; Articles 32 and 33 prescribe the procedure for obtaining such a declaration; Article 34 provides that the application 'may be refused *only* for one of the reasons specified in Articles 27 and 28' (emphasis added) and immediately thereafter, in its third paragraph, reiterates that under no circumstances may the foreign judgment be reviewed as to its substance. (The remainder of Section 2 is taken up with further procedural matters, principally to do with appeals against enforcement).

53. The wording of the relevant provisions of Section 2, which is clearly designed substantially to mirror the scheme of Section 1, is to my mind unequivocal and hence supports a parallel construction of Section 1, the drafting of which is unfortunately less unambiguous.

54. Thus the scheme and objectives of the Convention support the view that the grounds for refusing recognition and enforcement are set out exhaustively in Articles 27 and 28 and that procedural irregularities may constitute such a ground only if they fall within those articles.

The scope of Article 27(1): public policy

55. In its second question, the Hoge Raad asks whether Article 27(1) precludes recognition of a judgment where the defendant was not validly represented and had no knowledge of the proceedings, even if he later had cognisance of the judgment and availed himself of none of the legal remedies afforded by the procedural law of the State in which the judgment was given.

56. This question does not arise if my view that Article 27(2) applies is correct since the public policy exception does not apply to situations covered elsewhere in Article 27: see *Hoffmann* v *Krieg*. One question in that case was whether recognition of a German maintenance order should be refused pursuant to Article 27(1) or 27(3) (which prohibits recognition of a judgment which is irreconcilable with a prior judgment in a dispute between the same parties in the State applied to). The Court stated unequivocally that: 'according to the scheme of the Convention, use of the public-policy clause ... is in any event precluded when, as here, the issue is whether a foreign judgment is compatible with a national judgment; the issue must be resolved on the basis of the specific provision under Article 27(3)'.

57. I can see no reason not to apply the Court's ruling that use of the public policy exception is precluded when the issue is specifically covered by Article 27(3) to cases where the issue has been held to fall within Article 27(2).

58. That approach, moreover, finds support in Advocate General

Capotorti's comment in *Rohr* v *Ossberger* to the effect that, where the circumstances fall within the scope of Article 27(2), 'a particular aspect of the protection of the rights of the defence has been ensured by the authors of the Brussels Convention by means of a provision other than that concerning public policy'.

59. Although it may appear to conflict with the words of Advocate General Reischl in *Pendy Plastics* v *Pluspunkt* quoted in paragraph 30 above, to the effect that the principle of the right to a proper hearing is often regarded as a matter of public policy and as such is not to be interpreted restrictively, it is apparent from Advocate General Reischl's Opinion that he is referring to the submission of the United Kingdom that 'Article 27(2) is intended to ensure observance of a principle of natural justice whereby recognition of a judgment must be withheld if the defendant did not have an opportunity to acquaint himself with the content of the instrument served'. He is accordingly using the concept of public policy in the specific sense of the principle *audi alteram partem.*

60. To my mind, therefore, that statement merely confirms that, as argued above, the principle of the right to a proper hearing embodied in Article 27(2) is so fundamental that the provision should be interpreted as encompassing the circumstances alleged in these proceedings. That makes it unnecessary to bring the matter within the scope of the public policy exception.

Conclusion

61. I consider therefore that, in the light of the proposed answer to the third question, there is no need to answer the first and second questions.

62. In view of the terms of the national court's questions, and hence of my proposed answer, it should be emphasised once more that the alleged circumstances which have prompted that court to seek a preliminary ruling from this Court cannot at this stage be regarded as more than hypothetical. Accordingly, it is for the appropriate national court, before deciding the case before it in the light of this Court's answer to the questions referred, to satisfy itself of the facts.

63. I am of the opinion that the Court should rule as follows on the questions put by the Hoge Raad:

Article 27(2) of the Brussels Convention applies in a case which, although the defendant was not declared to be in default of appearance, the document instituting the proceedings or an equivalent document was not duly served on or notified to him in sufficient time and the defendant was not validly represented in the proceedings.

Case C-7/98 - 28 March 2000

Dieter Krombach
v
André Bamberski

Recognition and enforcement of judgments – Article 27(1) - Notion of public policy.

Summary

1. The court of the State in which enforcement is sought cannot, with respect to a defendant domiciled in that State, take account, for the purposes of the public-policy clause in Article 27, point 1, of the Convention, of the fact, without more, that the court of the State of origin based its jurisdiction on the nationality of the victim of an offence.

2. The court of the State in which enforcement is sought can, with respect to a defendant domiciled in that State and prosecuted for an intentional offence, take account, in relation to the public-policy clause in Article 27, point 1, of the Convention, of the fact that the court of the State of origin refused to allow that person to have his defence presented unless he appeared in person.

JUDGMENT OF THE COURT

Iglesias, President, Moitinho de Almeida, Edward, Sevón, Schintgen, Presidents, Kapteyn, Gulmann, Puissochet, Hirsch, Jann (Rapporteur) and Ragnemalm, Judges

1. By order of 4 December 1997, received at the Court on 14 January

1998, the Bundesgerichtshof (Federal Court of Justice), Germany, referred to the Court for a preliminary ruling pursuant to the Protocol of 3 June 1971 on the interpretation by the Court of Justice of the Convention of 27 September 1968 on Jurisdiction and the Enforcement of Judgments in Civil and Commercial Matters three questions concerning the interpretation of Article 27, point 1, of the abovementioned Convention of 27 September 1968 (OJ 1978 L 304, p. 36), as amended by the Convention of 9 October 1978 on the Accession of the Kingdom of Denmark, Ireland and the United Kingdom of Great Britain and Northern Ireland (OJ 1978 L 304, p. 1 and - amended version - p. 77) and by the Convention of 25 October 1982 on the Accession of the Hellenic Republic (OJ 1982 L 388, p. 1) (hereinafter 'the Convention').

2. Those questions have arisen in proceedings between Mr Bamberski, who is domiciled in France, and Mr Krombach, who is domiciled in Germany, relating to the enforcement, in the latter Contracting State, of a judgment delivered on 13 March 1995 by the Cour d'Assises de Paris (Paris Assizes) which ordered Mr Krombach to pay to Mr Bamberski, the plaintiff in a civil claim, compensation in the amount of FRF 350 000.

The Convention

3. The first paragraph of Article 1 provides that the Convention 'shall apply in civil and commercial matters whatever the nature of the court or tribunal'.

4. With regard to jurisdiction, the rule of principle, set out in the first paragraph of Article 2 of the Convention, states that persons domiciled in a Contracting State shall, whatever their nationality, be sued in the courts of that State. The second paragraph of Article 3 prohibits a plaintiff from relying on certain rules of exorbitant jurisdiction, in particular, so far as France is concerned, those based on nationality which derive from Articles 14 and 15 of the Code Civil (Civil Code).

5. The Convention also sets out special rules of jurisdiction. Thus, Article 5 of the Convention provides:

'A person domiciled in a Contracting State may, in another Contracting State, be sued: ... 4. as regards a civil claim for damages or restitution which is based on an act giving rise to criminal proceedings, in the court seised of those proceedings, to the extent that that court has jurisdiction under its own law to entertain civil proceedings'.

6. In matters relating to the recognition and enforcement of judgments, the rule of principle, set out in the first paragraph of Article 31 of the Convention, provides that a judgment given in a Contracting State and enforceable in that State is to be enforced in another Contracting State when, on the application of any interested party, it has been declared enforceable there.

7. Under the second paragraph of Article 34, '[t]he application may be refused only for one of the reasons specified in Articles 27 and 28'.

8. Article 27, point 1, of the Convention states: 'A judgment shall not be recognised: 1. if such recognition is contrary to public policy in the State in which recognition is sought'.

9. Article 28, third paragraph, of the Convention states: 'Subject to the provisions of the first paragraph, the jurisdiction of the court of the State of origin may not be reviewed; the test of public policy referred to in point 1 of Article 27 may not be applied to the rules relating to jurisdiction'.

10. Article 29 and the third paragraph of Article 34 of the Convention provide: 'Under no circumstances may a foreign judgment be reviewed as to its substance.'

11. Article II of the Protocol annexed to the Convention (hereinafter 'the Protocol'), which, according to Article 65 of the Convention, forms an integral part thereof, provides: 'Without prejudice to any more favourable provisions of national laws, persons domiciled in a Contracting State who are being prosecuted in the criminal courts of another Contracting State of which they are not nationals for an offence which was not intentionally committed may be defended by persons qualified to do so, even if they do not appear in person.

However, the court seised of the matter may order appearance in person; in the case of failure to appear, a judgment given in the civil action without the person concerned having had the opportunity to arrange for his defence need not be recognised or enforced in the other Contracting States.'

The dispute in the main proceedings

12. Mr Krombach was the subject of a preliminary investigation in Germany following the death in Germany of a 14-year-old girl of French

nationality. That preliminary investigation was subsequently discontinued.

13. In response to a complaint by Mr Bamberski, the father of the young girl, a preliminary investigation was opened in France, the French courts declaring that they had jurisdiction by virtue of the fact that the victim was a French national. At the conclusion of that investigation, Mr Krombach was, by judgment of the Chambre d'Accusation (Chamber of Indictments) of the Cour d'Appel de Paris (Paris Court of Appeal), committed for trial before the Cour d'Assises de Paris.

14. That judgment and notice of the introduction of a civil claim by the victim's father were served on Mr Krombach. Although Mr Krombach was ordered to appear in person, he did not attend the hearing. The Cour d'Assises de Paris thereupon applied the contempt procedure governed by Article 627 et seq. of the French Code of Criminal Procedure. Pursuant to Article 630 of that Code, under which no defence counsel may appear on behalf of the person in contempt, the Cour d'Assises reached its decision without hearing the defence counsel instructed by Mr Krombach.

15. By judgment of 9 March 1995 the Cour d'Assises imposed on Mr Krombach a custodial sentence of 15 years after finding him guilty of violence resulting in involuntary manslaughter. By judgment of 13 March 1995, the Cour d'Assises, ruling on the civil claim, ordered Mr Krombach, again as being in contempt, to pay compensation to Mr Bamberski in the amount of FRF 350 000.

16. On application by Mr Bamberski, the President of a civil chamber of the Landgericht (Regional Court) Kempten (Germany), which had jurisdiction *ratione loci*, declared the judgment of 13 March 1995 to be enforceable in Germany. Following dismissal by the Oberlandesgericht (Higher Regional Court) of the appeal which he had lodged against that decision, Mr Krombach brought an appeal on a point of law ('Rechtsbeschwerde') before the Bundesgerichtshof in which he submitted that he had been unable effectively to defend himself against the judgment given against him by the French court.

17. Those are the circumstances in which the Bundesgerichtshof decided to stay proceedings and to refer the following questions to the Court for a preliminary ruling:

'1. May the provisions on jurisdiction form part of public policy within the meaning of Article 27, point 1, of the Brussels Convention where the State of origin has based its jurisdiction as against a person domiciled in another Contracting State (first paragraph of Article 2 of the Brussels Convention) solely on the nationality of the injured party (as in the second paragraph of Article 3 of the Brussels Convention in relation to France)?

If Question 1 is answered in the negative:

2. May the court of the State in which enforcement is sought (first paragraph of Article 31 of the Brussels Convention) take into account under public policy within the meaning of Article 27, point 1, of the Brussels Convention that the criminal court of the State of origin did not allow the debtor to be defended by a lawyer in a civil-law procedure for damages instituted within the criminal proceedings (Article II of the Protocol of 27 September 1968 on the interpretation of the Brussels Convention) because he, a resident of another Contracting State, was charged with an *intentional* offence and did not appear in person?

If Question 2 is also answered in the negative:

3. May the court of the State in which enforcement is sought take into account under public policy within the meaning of Article 27, point 1, of the Brussels Convention that the court of the State of origin based its jurisdiction solely on the nationality of the injured party (see Question 1 above) and *additionally* prevented the defendant from being legally represented (see Question 2 above)?'

Preliminary observations

18. By its questions, the national court is essentially asking the Court how the term 'public policy in the State in which recognition is sought' in point 1 of Article 27 of the Convention should be interpreted.

19. The Convention is intended to facilitate, to the greatest possible extent, the free movement of judgments by providing for a simple and rapid enforcement procedure (see, *inter alia*, Case C-414/92 *Solo Kleinmotoren* v *Boch* [1994] ECR I-2237, paragraph 20, and Case C-267/97 *Coursier* v *Fortis Bank* [1999] ECR I-2543, paragraph 25).

20. It follows from the Court's case-law that this procedure constitutes an autonomous and complete system independent of the legal systems of the Contracting States and that the principle of legal certainty in the Community legal system and the objectives of the Convention in accordance with Article 220 of the EC Treaty (now Article 293 EC), on which it is founded, require a uniform application in all Contracting

States of the Convention rules and the relevant case-law of the Court (see, in particular, Case C-432/93 *SISRO* v *Ampersand* [1995] ECR I-2269, paragraph 39).

21. So far as Article 27 of the Convention is concerned, the Court has held that this provision must be interpreted strictly inasmuch as it constitutes an obstacle to the attainment of one of the fundamental objectives of the Convention (*Solo Kleinmotoren*, cited above, paragraph 20). With regard, more specifically, to recourse to the public-policy clause in Article 27, point 1, of the Convention, the Court has made it clear that such recourse is to be had only in exceptional cases (Case 145/86 *Hoffmann* v *Krieg* [1988] ECR 645, paragraph 21, and Case C-78/95 *Hendrikman and Feyen* v *Magenta Druck & Verlag* [1996] ECR I-4943, paragraph 23).

22. It follows that, while the Contracting States in principle remain free, by virtue of the proviso in Article 27, point 1, of the Convention, to determine, according to their own conceptions, what public policy requires, the limits of that concept are a matter for interpretation of the Convention.

23. Consequently, while it is not for the Court to define the content of the public policy of a Contracting State, it is none the less required to review the limits within which the courts of a Contracting State may have recourse to that concept for the purpose of refusing recognition to a judgment emanating from a court in another Contracting State.

24. It should be noted in this regard that, since the Convention was concluded on the basis of Article 220 of the Treaty and within the framework which it defines, its provisions are linked to the Treaty (Case C-398/92 *Mund & Fester* v *Hatrex Internationaal Transport* [1994] ECR I-467, paragraph 12).

25. The Court has consistently held that fundamental rights form an integral part of the general principles of law whose observance the Court ensures (see, in particular, Opinion 2/94 [1996] ECR I-1759, paragraph 33). For that purpose, the Court draws inspiration from the constitutional traditions common to the Member States and from the guidelines supplied by international treaties for the protection of human rights on which the Member States have collaborated or of which they are signatories. In that regard, the European Convention for the Protection of Human Rights and Fundamental Freedoms (hereinafter 'the ECHR') has

particular significance (see, *inter alia*, Case 222/84 *Johnston* v *Chief Constable of the Royal Ulster Constabulary* [1986] ECR 1651, paragraph 18).

26. The Court has thus expressly recognised the general principle of Community law that everyone is entitled to fair legal process, which is inspired by those fundamental rights (Case C-185/95 P *Baustahlgewebe* v *Commission* [1998] ECR I-8417, paragraphs 20 and 21, and judgment of 11 January 2000 in Joined Cases C-174/98 P and C-189/98 P *Netherlands and Van der Wal* v *Commission* [2000] ECR I-0000, paragraph 17).

27. Article F(2) of the Treaty on European Union (now, after amendment, Article 6(2) EU) embodies that case-law. It provides: 'The Union shall respect fundamental rights, as guaranteed by the European Convention for the Protection of Human Rights and Fundamental Freedoms signed in Rome on 4 November 1950 and as they result from the constitutional traditions common to the Member States, as general principles of Community law'.

28. It is in the light of those considerations that the questions submitted for a preliminary ruling fall to be answered.

The first question

29. By this question, the national court is essentially asking whether, regard being had to the public-policy clause contained in Article 27, point 1, of the Convention, the court of the State in which enforcement is sought can, with respect to a defendant domiciled in that State, take into account the fact that the court of the State of origin based its jurisdiction on the nationality of the victim of an offence.

30. It should be noted at the outset that it follows from the specific terms of the first paragraph of Article 1 of the Convention that the Convention applies to decisions given in civil matters by a criminal court (Case C-172/91 *Sonntag* v *Waidmann and Others* [1993] ECR I-1963, paragraph 16).

31. Under the system of the Convention, with the exception of certain cases exhaustively listed in the first paragraph of Article 28, none of which corresponds to the facts of the case in the main proceedings, the court before which enforcement is sought cannot review the jurisdiction

of the court of the State of origin. This fundamental principle, which is set out in the first phrase of the third paragraph of Article 28 of the Convention, is reinforced by the specific statement, in the second phrase of the same paragraph, that 'the test of public policy referred to in point 1 of Article 27 may not be applied to the rules relating to jurisdiction'.

32. It follows that the public policy of the State in which enforcement is sought cannot be raised as a bar to recognition or enforcement of a judgment given in another Contracting State solely on the ground that the court of origin failed to comply with the rules of the Convention which relate to jurisdiction.

33. Having regard to the generality of the wording of the third paragraph of Article 28 of the Convention, that statement of the law must be regarded as being, in principle, applicable even where the court of the State of origin wrongly founded its jurisdiction, in regard to a defendant domiciled in the territory of the State in which enforcement is sought, on a rule which has recourse to a criterion of nationality.

34. The answer to the first question must therefore be that the court of the State in which enforcement is sought cannot, with respect to a defendant domiciled in that State, take account, for the purposes of the public-policy clause in Article 27, point 1, of the Convention, of the fact, without more, that the court of the State of origin based its jurisdiction on the nationality of the victim of an offence.

The second question

35. By this question, the national court is essentially asking whether, in relation to the public-policy clause in Article 27, point 1, of the Convention, the court of the State in which enforcement is sought can, with respect to a defendant domiciled in its territory and charged with an *intentional* offence, take into account the fact that the court of the State of origin refused to allow that defendant to have his defence presented unless he appeared in person.

36. By disallowing any review of a foreign judgment as to its substance, Article 29 and the third paragraph of Article 34 of the Convention prohibit the court of the State in which enforcement is sought from refusing to recognise or enforce that judgment solely on the ground that there is a discrepancy between the legal rule applied by the court of the State of origin and that which would have been applied by the court of

the State in which enforcement is sought had it been seised of the dispute. Similarly, the court of the State in which enforcement is sought cannot review the accuracy of the findings of law or fact made by the court of the State of origin.

37. Recourse to the public-policy clause in Article 27, point 1, of the Convention can be envisaged only where recognition or enforcement of the judgment delivered in another Contracting State would be at variance to an unacceptable degree with the legal order of the State in which enforcement is sought inasmuch as it infringes a fundamental principle. In order for the prohibition of any review of the foreign judgment as to its substance to be observed, the infringement would have to constitute a manifest breach of a rule of law regarded as essential in the legal order of the State in which enforcement is sought or of a right recognised as being fundamental within that legal order.

38. With regard to the right to be defended, to which the question submitted to the Court refers, this occupies a prominent position in the organisation and conduct of a fair trial and is one of the fundamental rights deriving from the constitutional traditions common to the Member States.

39. More specifically still, the European Court of Human Rights has on several occasions ruled in cases relating to criminal proceedings that, although not absolute, the right of every person charged with an offence to be effectively defended by a lawyer, if need be one appointed by the court, is one of the fundamental elements in a fair trial and an accused person does not forfeit entitlement to such a right simply because he is not present at the hearing (see the following judgments of the European Court of Human Rights: judgment of 23 November 1993 in *Poitrimol* v *France*, Series A No 277-A; judgment of 22 September 1994 in *Pelladoah* v *Netherlands*, Series A No 297-B; judgment of 21 January 1999 in *Van Geyseghem* v *Belgium*, not yet reported).

40. It follows from that case-law that a national court of a Member State is entitled to hold that a refusal to hear the defence of an accused person who is not present at the hearing constitutes a manifest breach of a fundamental right.

41. The national court is, however, unsure as to whether the court of the State in which enforcement is sought can take account, in relation to Article 27, point 1, of the Convention, of a breach of this nature having

regard to the wording of Article II of the Protocol. That provision, which involves extending the scope of the Convention to the criminal field because of the consequences which a judgment of a criminal court may entail in civil and commercial matters (Case 157/80 *Rinkau* [1981] ECR 1391, paragraph 6), recognises the right to be defended without appearing in person before the criminal courts of a Contracting State for persons who are not nationals of that State and who are domiciled in another Contracting State only in so far as they are being prosecuted for an offence committed unintentionally. This restriction has been construed as meaning that the Convention clearly seeks to deny the right to be defended without appearing in person to persons who are being prosecuted for offences which are sufficiently serious to justify this (*Rinkau*, cited above, paragraph 12).

42. However, it follows from a line of case-law developed by the Court on the basis of the principles referred to in paragraphs 25 and 26 of the present judgment that observance of the right to a fair hearing is, in all proceedings initiated against a person which are liable to culminate in a measure adversely affecting that person, a fundamental principle of Community law which must be guaranteed even in the absence of any rules governing the proceedings in question (see, *inter alia*, Case C-135/92 *Fiskano* v *Commission* [1994] ECR I-2885, paragraph 39, and Case C-32/95 P *Commission* v *Lisrestal and Others* [1996] ECR I-5373, paragraph 21).

43. The Court has also held that, even though the Convention is intended to secure the simplification of formalities governing the reciprocal recognition and enforcement of judgments of courts or tribunals, it is not permissible to achieve that aim by undermining the right to a fair hearing (Case 49/84 *Debaecker and Plouvier* v *Bouwman* [1985] ECR 1779, paragraph 10).

44. It follows from the foregoing developments in the case-law that recourse to the public-policy clause must be regarded as being possible in exceptional cases where the guarantees laid down in the legislation of the State of origin and in the Convention itself have been insufficient to protect the defendant from a manifest breach of his right to defend himself before the court of origin, as recognised by the ECHR. Consequently, Article II of the Protocol cannot be construed as precluding the court of the State in which enforcement is sought from being entitled to take account, in relation to public policy, as referred to in Article 27, point 1, of the Convention, of the fact that, in an action for

damages based on an offence, the court of the State of origin refused to hear the defence of the accused person, who was being prosecuted for an *intentional* offence, solely on the ground that that person was not present at the hearing.

45. The answer to the second question must therefore be that the court of the State in which enforcement is sought can, with respect to a defendant domiciled in that State and prosecuted for an *intentional* offence, take account, in relation to the public-policy clause in Article 27, point 1, of the Convention, of the fact that the court of the State of origin refused to allow that person to have his defence presented unless he appeared in person.

The third question

46. In light of the reply to the second question, it is unnecessary to answer the third question.

On those grounds, the Court, in answer to the questions referred to it by the Bundesgerichtshof by order of 4 December 1997, hereby rules:

> **Article 27, point 1, of the Convention of 27 September 1968 on Jurisdiction and the Enforcement of Judgments in Civil and Commercial Matters, as amended by the Convention of 9 October 1978 on the Accession of the Kingdom of Denmark, Ireland and the United Kingdom of Great Britain and Northern Ireland and by the Convention of 25 October 1982 on the Accession of the Hellenic Republic, must be interpreted as follows:**
>
> **(1) The court of the State in which enforcement is sought cannot, with respect to a defendant domiciled in that State, take account, for the purposes of the public-policy clause in Article 27, point 1, of that Convention, of the fact, without more, that the court of the State of origin based its jurisdiction on the nationality of the victim of an offence.**
>
> **(2) The court of the State in which enforcement is sought can, with respect to a defendant domiciled in that State and prosecuted for an intentional offence, take account, in relation to the public-policy clause in Article 27, point 1, of that Convention, of the fact that the court of the State of origin**

refused to allow that person to have his defence presented unless he appeared in person.*

* Opinion of AG not yet available in English.

TITLE III *[Chapter III]*

Recognition and Enforcement
[Recognition and Enforcement]

Enforcement – Articles 31 - 45
[Articles 38 - 52]

See also

Case 42/76 - 30 November 1976

Jozef de Wolf
v
Harry Cox B.V.

Judgment obtained in a Member State - Enforcement in another Contracting State possible by virtue of Article 31 of the Convention - Application concerning the same subject-matter and between the same parties brought before a court of that State - Prohibition - Costs of procedure.

Summary

The provisions of the Convention on Jurisdiction and the Enforcement of Judgments in Civil and Commercial Matters of 27 September 1968 prevent a party who has obtained a judgment in his favour in a Contracting State, being a judgment for which an order for enforcement under Article 31 of the Convention may issue in another Contracting State, from making an application to a Court in that other State for a judgment against the other party in the same terms as the judgment delivered in the first State. The fact that there may be occasions on which, according to the national law applicable, the procedure set out in Articles 31 *et seq.* of the Convention may be found to be more expensive than bringing fresh proceedings on the substance of the case does not invalidate these considerations.

JUDGMENT OF THE COURT

Kutscher, President, Donner and Pescatore, Presidents of Chambers, Mertens de Wilmars, Sorensen, Lord Mackenzie Stuart and O'Keeffe, Judges

1. By judgment of 7 May 1976, received at the Court Registry, on the following 14 May, the Hoge Raad of the Netherlands has referred to the Court a question on the interpretation, in particular, of Article 31 of the Convention on Jurisdiction and the Enforcement of Judgments in Civil and Commercial matters of 27 September 1968, hereinafter referred to as 'the Convention'.

2. It appears from the file that the plaintiff in the main action, resident in Belgium, having obtained a judgment from the juge de paix of Turnhout (Belgium) ordering the defendant in the main action, having its head office in the Netherlands, to pay an invoice, lodged an application before the Kantonrechter (juge de paix) of Boxmeer (The Netherlands) against the same defendant and in respect of the same matter.

3. The Kantonrechter, having heard the defendant, held that the application was admissible and gave judgment on the substance of the case in the same terms as the Belgian court.

4. In so doing, the Dutch court took the view, *inter alia*, on the one hand, that it was required to recognise the Belgian judgment under Article 26 of the Convention but that, on the other, under the legislation of the Netherlands, the procedure chosen by the applicant was less expensive for the parties than the procedure under Articles 31 *et seq.* of the Convention would have been. Under the latter procedure an application for an order for the enforcement of the judgment delivered by the Belgian court would have been brought before the President of the Arrondissementrechtbank which had jurisdiction.

5. The Attorney-General of the Hoge Raad brought an appeal against the judgment of the Kantonrechter before the Hoge Raad on the ground that the Kantonrechter ought to have declared the application inadmissible, because the procedure under Article 31 of the Convention is the only means available to the applicant for the purpose of enforcing the judgment of the Belgian court.

6. The Hoge Raad is asking the Court, in substance, to rule whether the Convention prevents a plaintiff who has obtained a judgment in his favour in a Contracting State, being a judgment for which an order for enforcement under Article 31 of the Convention may issue in another Contracting State, from making an application to a court in that other State for a judgment against the other party in the same terms as the judgment delivered in the first State.

7. The first paragraph of Article 26 of the Convention provides: 'A judgment given in a Contracting State shall be recognized in the other Contracting States without any special procedure being required'.

8. Although Articles 27 and 25 lay down certain exceptions to this duty of recognition, Article 29 nevertheless provides that 'under no circumstances may a foreign judgment be reviewed as to its substance'.

9. When an application for a review as to substance is declared admissible, the court before which the application is heard is required to decide whether it is well founded, a situation which could lead that court to conflict with a previous foreign judgment and, therefore, to fail in its duty to recognise the latter.

10/11. To accept the admissibility of an application concerning the same subject-matter and brought between the same parties as an application upon which judgment has already been delivered by a court in another Contracting State would therefore be incompatible with the meaning of the provisions quoted. It also results from Article 21 of the Convention, which covers cases in which proceedings 'involving the same cause of action and between the same parties are brought in the courts of different Contracting States' and requires that a court other than the first seised shall decline jurisdiction in favour of that court, that proceedings such as those brought before the Kantonrechter of Boxmeer are incompatible with the objectives of the Convention.

12. That provision is evidence of the concern to prevent the courts of two Contracting States from giving judgment in the same case.

13. Finally, to accept the duplication of main actions such as has occurred in the present case might result in a creditor's possessing two orders for enforcement on the basis of the same debt.

14. The fact that there may be occasions on which, according to the national law applicable, the procedure set out in Articles 31 *et seq.* of the Convention may be found to be more expensive than bringing fresh proceedings on the substance of the case does not invalidate these considerations.

15. In this respect, it must be observed that the Convention, which, in the words of the preamble thereto, is intended 'to secure the simplification of formalities governing the reciprocal recognition and enforcement of

judgments of courts or tribunals,' ought to induce the Contracting States to ensure that the costs of the procedure described in the Convention are fixed so as to accord with that concern for simplification.

16. The question raised by the Hoge Raad of the Netherlands should therefore be answered in the affirmative.

On those grounds, the court in answer to the question referred to it by Hoge Raad of the Netherlands by judgment of 7 May 1976, hereby rules:

> **The provisions of the Convention on Jurisdiction and the Enforcement of Judgments in Civil and Commercial Matters of 27 September 1968 prevents a party who has obtained a judgment in his favour in a Contracting State, being a judgment for which an order for enforcement under Article 31 of the Convention may issue in another Contracting State, from making an application to a court in that other State for a judgment against the other party in the same terms as the judgment delivered in the first State.**

OPINION OF MR ADVOCATE GENERAL MAYRAS

The dispute between Jozef de Wolf, a Customs agent at Turnhout (Belgium) and the Harry Cox undertaking, whose registered office is at Boxmeer (the Netherlands) was a very small one. It concerned the recovery of a bill for Fl 8.30, which, the agent claimed, was owed to him by the Netherlands undertaking. But that does not matter. This tiny case is at the origin of a reference for a preliminary ruling made by the Hoge Raad of the Netherlands on the interpretation of the provisions of the Convention of Brussels of 27 September 1968 on the recognition and enforcement of judgments; in examining them you will decide an important point of Community law.

Mr de Wolf began by suing his debtor before the juge de paix of the First Canton of Turnhout, the court of his own domicile. That court, considering itself to have jurisdiction, gave judgment by default ordering the defendant to pay the said bill, damages assessed by way of penalty at FB 500 together with the costs of service of formal notice to pay, fixed at 15 guilders, and to pay legal interest and costs, assessed at a total of FB 913.

It may be supposed that notice of this judgment was served on the defendant, but the latter did not react. A comparison of its date, the date on which notice thereof was served on the defendant and the time-limit for bringing an appeal should enable it to be stated that it had the force of *res judicata* and had become enforceable in Belgium.

However, whether it was possible to enforce it is another matter. It is necessary to beware of confusing the effects of a judgment and the practical measures or the means to be used in order for its enforcement to become a reality. The latter depend, as regards both form and substance, on the legislation of the country where enforcement must take place, on the place where the goods on which execution is to be levied are situated, and, most of all, on the very existence of goods against which execution may be levied. It is probable that the Netherlands undertaking offered no opportunity for enforcement in Belgium. This is why the plaintiff had to apply to the courts of the Netherlands.

Instead, however, of contenting himself with applying for the enforcement of that judgment in that country pursuant to the procedure laid down by Article 31 *et seq.* of the Convention, Mr de Wolf preferred to take up the case *ab ovo* and to sue his opponent before the Kantonrechter of Boxmeer, the court of the domicile of the latter (first paragraph of Article 2 of the Convention). He relied on the Belgian judgment delivered in his favour, and claimed that the said court should deliver judgment as to substance, that is, once more order the Harry Cox undertaking to pay the principal sums due and interest. For this purpose he relied on Article 431 of the Netherlands Code of Civil Procedure, which permits such an action when it is not possible to enforce the judgment of the foreign court.

This time, the defendant appeared. But the Netherlands court doubted whether the plaintiff had an interest in obtaining a decision as to substance from itself, since he was entitled, in its opinion, to rely on articles 11 and 12 of the Convention between Belgium and the Netherlands on Enforcement of 28 March 1925, which make it possible to obtain the enforcement in the Netherlands of judgments delivered in Belgium. It decided, by interlocutory judgment of 7 February 1975, to hear the plaintiff again on the reasons which induced him to obtain a judgment from the Netherlands court, for him a foreign court, in addition to the judgment of the Belgian court.

In its final judgment of 8 July 1975, the court at Boxmeer began by rectifying an obvious mistake which it had made in its judgment of 7 January: it was not the Convention between Belgium and the Netherlands on which the applicant could rely, but the Community Convention of 27 September 1968, which, by virtue of Article 55 thereof, supersedes the bilateral Convention, and the Netherlands Law on Enforcement of 4 May 1972, which entered into force on 1 February 1973.

Next, the Court found that 'there is nothing to say that the Belgian decision must not be recognised in the Netherlands without any special procedure being required within the meaning of the first paragraph of Article 26 of the Convention'. However, since the provisions of the Convention and of the Netherlands law of 4 May 1972 were applicable, if Mr de Wolf requested, in accordance with the procedure laid down by those provisions, that an order for the enforcement of the Belgian judgment be issued and that it be enforced, the cost thereof, as the plaintiff explained, would be a least 340 guilders, to be borne by the *defendant*.

This is why, the court continued, the plaintiff was right not to apply for the issue of an order for the enforcement of the Belgian judgment. He was entitled to request the Netherlands court to *deliver judgment afresh as to substance* by virtue of Article 431(2) of the Netherlands Code of Civil Procedure, because enforcement by this means would be less costly *for the defendant*. Therefore it was in the interests of *both parties* to obtain a judgment of the Netherlands court in addition to the judgment of the Belgian court.

Next, the Netherlands court went on formally to 'recognize' the judgment of the Belgian court. The court stressed that since the defendant had not alleged that the recognition of that judgment would be contrary to public order in the Netherlands (Article 27 of the Convention), given that the rules relating to the jurisdiction of the court of the State in which the judgment was given did not concern public policy (last paragraph of Article 28), and since the defendant had not produced evidence that it had duly paid its debt, the plaintiff had a legitimate interest in having the existence of his claim recognized. The Court found that the Belgian judgment had to be 'recognized', and from this it immediately deduced that the claim was well founded. It ordered the defendant to pay the plaintiff the amount settled by the Belgian court. However, as the plaintiff had, during the proceedings, reduced his debt, made up of the principal and interest, to the sum of Fl 1500, the Court limited the sum that the defendant was to pay to that amount, ordered that its judgment was to be enforceable provisionally even in the event of appeal, and, finally, ordered the defendant to bear the costs. The costs incurred by the plaintiff were assessed at Fl 105.30, of which Fl 30 represented the fees of his representative *ad litem*.

Previously, basing himself on another judgment of the same court at Turnhout delivered on that same 28 May 1974, Mr de Wolf had attempted to use the same procedure by applying to the Kantonrechter of Tilburg for the recovery of a debt of the same sort from another Netherlands undertaking. But that court found that *in fact* the plaintiff was asking for the enforcement in the Netherlands of a judgment delivered in Belgium while ostensibly claiming recognition of that judgment. The said court took the view that for such purpose the plaintiff could *only* lodge an application for enforcement in accordance with Title III of the Convention. It held that the common law provisions in Article 431(2) of the Netherlands Code of Civil Procedure, which enable Netherlands courts to deliver judgment afresh on the substance of a dispute upon which judgment has already been given by a foreign court, could not apply, because the Netherlands courts had jurisdiction by virtue of the Convention to issue an order for the enforcement of a judgment delivered by a court of a Contracting State. Accordingly, the court at Tilburg had declared that the plaintiff's claim was not admissible.

Alerted by the court officer who had represented Mr de Wolf's interests before the court at Tilburg, the Procureur General of the Hoge Raad of the Netherlands, acting as *amicus curiae*, brought an appeal before the Hoge Raad against the judgment, which had become definitive, of the court at Boxmeer, which was manifestly in conflict with the judgment delivered by the court at Tilburg.

Thus, the highest court of the Netherlands requests you to rule whether Article 31 of the Brussels Convention, by itself or in conjunction with other provisions of that Convention, prevents a plaintiff who has obtained a judgment in his favour in a Contracting State, being a judgment for which an order for enforcement within the meaning of Article 31 may issue in another Contracting

State, from making an application to a court in that other State, in accordance with Article 26 of the Convention, for a fresh judgment as to substance against the other party on the same terms as the judgment delivered in the first State, assuming, of course, that under the provisions of the Convention that court has jurisdiction to hear the application.

Put like that, the problem seems to me to concern Article 26 of the Convention much more than Article 31. I shall therefore interpret that provision.

The so called 'second limb' of the Convention to which we must direct our attention, concerns the *enforcement* of judgments in civil and commercial matters. However, as Mr. Droz has written: 'the provisions of the Convention as to *recognition* are fundamental. For it is those provisions which make it possible to achieve the "circulation of judgments" within the Community which is one of the foremost objectives of the Convention. Although the rules of procedure with regard to enforcement laid down in the Convention spring from the same intention, they are entirely subordinate to the rules of substance laid down with regard to recognition. Recognition can occur without enforcement, whereas enforcement can never be obtained without recognition.' 'The Convention', and I am still quoting Mr Droz, 'establishes the distinction between recognition and enforcement. Recognition gives the foreign judgment the force of *res judicata*. Enforcement consists in giving the foreign judgment enforceability in addition'.

The authors of the Convention directed their minds first to simplifying, accelerating and standardising the ways and means necessary for obtaining recognition. They have attempted to make the conditions governing recognition of judgments independent of the concept of territoriality and to make the recognition involved uniform throughout the Community by laying down the procedure to be followed to obtain recognition.

According to both the report of Mr Jenard and the opinions of the commentators who have had access to the preparatory drafts, up to the last stage prior to the signing of the Convention, Article 1 thereof was worded as follows: 'This Convention shall apply *directly* in civil and commercial matters whatever the nature of the court or tribunal.'

The word 'directly' was omitted at the last minute at the request of the German delegation because of problems of translation. Anyhow, in the present case I do not think that it is the 'direct' applicability of the Convention that matters, but rather whether Article 26 must be said to be *exclusive*.

However, that may be, the system laid down by the Convention as regards recognition appears to me to be as follows: the first paragraph of Article 26 provides that a judgment given in a Contracting State *shall be* recognised in the other Contracting States 'without any special procedure being required'. Thus the intention of the authors of the Convention was to state most categorically that judgments given in the six States automatically have the force of *res judicata* throughout the territory of the Community, with effect from the date on which judgment was given in the first State.

However, this principle of automatic recognition is immediately moderated and amended by the remainder of Article 26. In fact recognition only takes effect automatically in so far as it is not contested.

The remainder of that article therefore deals with the recognition of judgments the authority of which may be contested.

First of all I shall leave aside the case where recognition is only raised as an *incidental question* before the court of a Contracting State or, as the German text says, the case where the decision of that court *depends* ('abhängt') on recognition: in such a case the third paragraph of Article 26 provides that the court shall have jurisdiction over that question.

Where recognition of a judgment is sought *as the principal issue* and the authority of that judgment is contested, the second paragraph of Article 26 implies that the party in whose favour judgment has been given in the first State is left with a choice. He *may* either apply for the *enforcement* of the decision pursuant to Sections 2 and 3 of Title III, or apply for a decision that the judgment be recognised, but again in accordance with the procedures provided for in Sections 2 and 3 of Title III. In any event, the authority of the foreign judgment prevents a *fresh* application concerning the *same* subject-matter being brought by the *same* parties before the courts of another Contracting State.

For a party to have an interest in applying for recognition as the principal issue it is necessary to assume that the judgment concerned is not capable of enforcement properly so called, that is to say, that it is not possible to enforce it on the territory of the Contracting State in which it was given. Such appears to me to be indeed the case with regard to the judgment given by the Belgian court.

This is the situation which the second paragraph of Article 26 expressly covers. The authors of the Convention did not wish to leave this case outside the Treaty. Indeed, their silence on this point would undoubtedly have obliged the six States, or their national courts, as before, either to maintain or to introduce national procedures which would necessarily have differed from one State to another.

If the Convention had not settled this case and if no 'action for recognition as the principal issue' existed under the law of a Contracting State, the courts of that State would have had to 'widen' the rules of that Convention to include a judgment given in another Contracting State to enable it to take effect in their State. In certain States, it seems that it is possible to bring what is called a 'direct action on the foreign judgment'. A foreign judgment is invoked in support of an application concerning the same subject-matter as that upon which judgment has been given abroad. The plaintiff instead of applying for the enforcement or recognition of the foreign judgment, prefers to submit a fresh application relying of the foreign judgment.

In order to avoid these doubts the second paragraph of Article 26 of the Convention provides that any interested party who raises the recognition of a judgment as the principal issue *may*, in accordance with the procedures provided for in Section 2 and 3 of Title III, apply for a decision that the judgment be recognised, unless he prefers to use the procedure for enforcement of a foreign judgment.

The word 'may' used in the second paragraph of Article 26 must not be misconstrued. Admittedly, any interested party is free to use or not to use that procedure. But if his intention is simply to have a foreign judgment recognised, and not merely to plead its conclusive force, which after all may be taken into consideration regardless of any 'recognition', and if that judgment is contested as the principal issue ('as such' says the German version of the second paragraph of Article 26), he *may* only obtain recognition thereof by using the procedure laid down by the Convention.

Seen thus, the use of the word 'may' does not, therefore, leave the option of a third method. Again, no conclusions should be drawn from the use of this term ('kunnen') in the Dutch version of Article 31, whereas in the other versions, enforcement is presented as automatic, provided of course that the conditions laid down by the Convention are complied with. Similarly, in the German version of the last paragraph of Article 26, the word 'kann', that is to say 'may', is used as meaning that if the outcome of proceedings in a court of a Contracting State depends of the determination of an incidental question of recognition that court is empowered to deal with that question. The other versions, however, make such jurisdiction mandatory. Nobody would therefore consider arguing that the court concerned has discretion as to whether to accept jurisdiction or not.

As for the reasons why Mr de Wolf acted as he did, he stated that the said procedure was less expensive than the procedure under Sections 2 and 3 of the Title III. Since this ground was considered decisive by the court at Boxmeer and as it is causing the Hoge Raad doubts, I should explain my views on it.

Firstly, for whom was the procedure less expensive?

It should be noted that while the procedure before the Kantonrechter cost the plaintiff Fl 105.30, that sum was finally borne by the *defendant*, who was the unsuccessful party.

Similarly, while the costs of an application for the issue of an order for enforcement (or obtaining recognition) pursuant to the procedure under Sections 2 and 3 of Title III and those of enforcement come to at least Fl 340, this sum would have finally be borne by the *defendant*.

It is touching to see the plaintiff becoming the champion of the defendant's interests, unless he considers that in following the procedure under the Convention, he caused his opponent needless and unreasonable costs which he might well have been ordered to bear. If the plaintiff was really so concerned to save his opponent costs there was a very simple course open to him, which was to bring an action against it before the court of the place of the defendant's domicile in the Netherlands from the first. It was open to him to do so even if there had been an agreement between the parties that the Belgian courts should have jurisdiction. The defendant, for its part, had a very simple means for avoiding needless costs, which was to pay its bill, at the latest when the Belgian judgment had been given.

The authors of the Convention, for their part, have done their utmost to reduce the costs involved in the procedure for enforcement to a minimum compatible with the speed, certainty and effectiveness of that procedure. Article III of the Protocol annexed to the Convention provides: 'In proceedings for the issue of an order for enforcement, no charge, duty or fee calculated by reference to the value of the matter in issue may be levied in the State in which enforcement is sought'.

Nevertheless, by virtue of Article 7(3) of the Netherlands Law on Enforcement, Articles 56 to 58 of the Code of Civil Procedure are applicable to the Community procedure for enforcement of a foreign judgment. Those provisions govern, in a general way, the scale of costs relating to the enforcement of foreign judgments.

Furthermore, under Article 2 of the Law on Enforcement it remains compulsory to be represented by an advocate before the Arrondissementsrechbank. Since it seems to have been shown that the effect of these provisions is to render the procedure for enforcement relatively expensive, at least as regards the recovery of small debts, it would be desirable to make amendments to them in the future in order to make the said procedure more accessible.

It seems to me, in fact, that the Contracting States are under a duty to take all measures necessary to facilitate the practical implementation of the Convention.

But even supposing that the use of the *ad hoc* procedure laid down by the Convention is more expensive *for the plaintiff*, that consideration cannot be an impediment.

The conclusion of the Convention between the Contracting States connotes a *priori*, at least so it may be supposed, the organisation of a system which is on the whole *better* than the previous bilateral or multilateral systems. Admittedly, the Convention fits into the national systems of procedure with which it must coordinate. Although, as a whole, the provisions of the Convention bring about a system more favourable than the system under the common law of the Netherlands, it is possible, as I freely admit, that on certain particular points the latter contained more liberal provisions.

As the Commission points out, the provisions of a Convention on enforcement are, however, indivisible. In order to prevent recognition from coming into conflict with decisions varying with the state of national law, the Convention has established a system of automatic recognition. The only documents which need be produced are those mentioned in Article 46, that is to say, an authentic copy of the judgment relied upon and a document which proves that the party in default was duly served with the document instituting the proceedings. It is not even necessary to prove that the judgment is enforceable. However, the *quid pro quo* for these facilities and for the obvious advantage of the fact that there is no right of review (Article 29), or review of the rules of conflict of laws and jurisdiction (Article 28), is that the procedure under Sections 2 and 3 of Title III must be strictly complied with and that this procedure is exclusive.

The balance achieved by the Convention would be upset if a party could, at his own convenience, use both the system laid down by the Convention and the common law on enforcement of foreign judgments in the State concerned.

To accept that it is possible to use, as the plaintiff has done, this form of 'simplified recognition' under the private international law of the Netherlands would imply that it would also be necessary to apply the ordinary rules of such law as regards the grounds for refusing recognition and not the simplified rules of the Convention. As Mr. Droz says, 'it seems that concern for good administration of the justice requires that the rules of common law must not be intermingled in any way with those of the Convention' such that the latter would be 'applied *à la carte*'. Thus, nobody is entitled to invoke the principles of common law on the subject as a means of escaping the system laid down by the Convention, with which all the Contracting States must comply. The effect of the Convention cannot vary according to the Member States, for otherwise its effectiveness and the uniformity of its application, which are essential, would be seriously jeopardized.

In one of the States where the bringing of a 'direct action on a foreign judgment' appears to be accepted, the legislature has expressly excluded the possibility of bringing such an action in respect of mutual relationships with counties to which that State is bound by a convention on execution. I have in mind the Foreign Judgments Act, 1933, which is still applicable as regards the relationship arising under the Convention on Enforcement made in 1967 between the United Kingdom and the Netherlands.

It appears from Article 6 of that law that judgments ordering payment which are capable of recognition cannot be made enforceable in the United Kingdom except by way of the procedure of registration, which, in that State, is applied instead of issuing an order for enforcement and which constitutes, in the present state of the law in force in the United Kingdom, the counterpart of the Community procedure on enforcement.

Therefore, under the guise of a fresh main action Mr de Wolf obtained by means of nothing other than an abuse of procedure a judgment in which the principal issue was the recognition of a judgment given in his favour by a Belgian court.

If the court at Boxmeer meant to consider the application before it as an application for a fresh judgment, it should have kept outside the scope of application of the Convention and have admitted the Belgian judgment only as a piece of evidence in coming to its own decision.

But in reality the said court expressly applied Article 26, considering first, that it was bound to recognise the foreign judgment as the principal issue. In accepting that the said judgment had the force of *res judicata*, it placed itself within the field of Title III of the Convention. In so doing, it ought simply to have acted in accordance with Article 31 and to have issued an order for enforcement, assuming that it had the power to do so, which in fact it did not.

That court adopted the judgment of the Belgian court unaltered. Not only was the influence of the latter judgment overwhelming in deciding the case, but it constituted the only argument for the plaintiff. Admittedly, it amended the operative words of the foreign judgment by limiting the sum awarded and by converting it into national currency, but it is not really a fresh judgment upon an application genuinely distinguishable from the first.

Moreover, the said court *also partially* applied the Convention. In accordance with Article 27 of the Convention, it examined whether the recognition sought was contrary to public policy in the Netherlands. It noted that the defendant had not even argued that there was any such incompatibility and it found that in the case in question no such incompatibility existed. Yet although a foreign judgment may not under any circumstances be reviewed as to its substance (Article 29), the Netherlands court heard the observations of the defendant, which is prohibited by the first paragraph of Article 34. Although in this case that review led to the upholding of the foreign judgment, that new examination as to substance might have led to a conflicting or partially conflicting result apart, of course, from the possibility that the debt might have been paid meanwhile which would have been brought about a result incompatible with the first judgment.

Naturally enough, I am only giving my opinion on the judgment against which an appeal has been brought, and it will be for the Hoge Raad to decide the matter.

For my part, I am of the opinion that this Court should rule that: where the recognition of a judgment is raised as the principal issue within the meaning of Article 26 of the Convention of 27 September 1968, that judgment may only be recognised by following the procedure laid down in Sections 2 and 3 of Title III of the same Convention.

Case 178/83 - 12 July 1984

Firma P.
v
Firma K.

Article 40, second paragraph - Enforcement - Appeal against dismissal of an application for enforcement - Obligation to hear the party against whom enforcement is sought - Scope.

Summary

The Court hearing an appeal by the party seeking enforcement is required to hear the party against whom enforcement is sought, pursuant to the first sentence of the second paragraph of Article 40 of the Convention of 27 September 1968 on Jurisdiction and the Enforcement of Judgments in Civil and Commercial Matters, even though (a) the application for an enforcement order was dismissed simply because documents were not produced at the appropriate time and (b) the enforcement order is applied for in a State which is not the State of residence of the party against whom enforcement is sought.

JUDGMENT OF THE COURT

Bahlmann, President of Chamber, Pescatore and Due, Judges

1. By an order of 12 August 1983, which was received at the Court Registry on 18 August 1983, the Oberlandesgericht [Higher Regional Court] Frankfurt am Main referred to the Court of Justice for a preliminary ruling under Articles 2(2) and 3(2) of the Protocol of 3 June 1971 on the interpretation by the Court of Justice of the Convention of 27

September 1968 on Jurisdiction and the Enforcement of Judgments in Civil and Commercial Matters (hereinafter referred to as 'the Convention') a question on the interpretation of the first sentence of the second paragraph of Article 40 of the Convention.

2. That question was raised in the course of litigation between Firma P. (hereinafter referred to as 'the plaintiff') and Firma K. (hereinafter referred to as 'the defendant'); it concerns the necessity or otherwise of summoning the defendant to appear before the Oberlandesgericht in proceedings for the enforcement of a default judgment given on 20 January 1982 by the Arrondissementsrechtbank, Rotterdam.

3. By that judgment the defendant was ordered to pay to the plaintiff the sum of 678 095 Saudi riyals or the equivalent of that sum in US dollars, together with interest as required by law. On the ground that the defendant had a bank account in Frankfurt am Main, the plaintiff applied to the Landgericht [Regional Court] Frankfurt am Main for an order for the enforcement of the judgment.

4. By an order made on 10 January 1983 without the defendant's having been summoned to appear, the President of the Third Civil Division of that court dismissed the application on the ground that the plaintiff had failed to produce the documents required by Article 46(2), namely: 'The original or a certified true copy of the document which establishes that the party in default was served with the document instituting the proceedings', and by Article 47(1) of the Convention, namely: 'Documents which establish that, according to the law of State in which it has been given, the judgment is enforceable and has been served'.

5. The plaintiff appealed against that order to the Oberlandesgericht; in support of its appeal it produced supplementary documents which, in its view, showed that the statement of claim and the default judgment had been properly served.

6. Considering that the result of the proceedings before it depended on the interpretation of Article 40 of the Convention, the Oberlandesgericht stayed the proceedings and referred the following question to the Court of Justice: 'Is the appellate court required to hear the party against whom enforcement is sought under the first sentence of the second paragraph of Article 40 of the Convention on Jurisdiction and the Enforcement of Judgments in Civil and Commercial Matters if (a) the application for an

enforcement order was dismissed simply because documents were not produced at the appropriate time and (b) the enforcement order is applied for in a State which is not the State of residence of the party against whom enforcement is sought, so that the latter person will normally be able to establish against which asset (in the present case: a claim against a bank) enforcement is to take place in that State and thus be in a position to dispose of that asset before execution is levied?'

7. Article 40 of the Convention provides that: 'The party against whom enforcement is sought shall be summoned to appear before the appellate court. If he fails to appear, the provisions of the second and third paragraphs of Article 20 shall apply even where he is not domiciled in any of the Contracting States'.

8. It should be noted that the wording of that article does not provide for any exception.

9. The Oberlandesgericht, nonetheless, asks whether such an exception should be acknowledged to exist by reason of the fact that, on the one hand, the Landgericht dismissed the application for an enforcement order for the sole reason that the documents were not produced by the plaintiff at the proper time and, on the other hand, the system postulated by Article 40 is unsuited to this case since enforcement is to take place in a State which is not the State of domicile of the party against whom it is sought.

10. In the context of this case, the position taken by the Oberlandesgericht may be explained by the fact that, in order to fully safeguard the surprise effect of the enforcement proceedings at that level, the Landgericht could have gone further in its examination of the case and sought to obtain the information which was lacking in order to arrive at a decision on the substance of the case.

11. It is, nonetheless, true that the Convention formally requires that both parties should be given a hearing at the appellate level, without regard to the scope of the decision in the lower court. That provision is in accordance with the spirit of the Convention, which seeks to reconcile the necessary surprise effect in proceedings of this nature with respect for the defendant's right to a fair hearing (see the judgment of the Court of 21. 5. 1980, Case 125/79, *Denilauler* v *Couchet Frères*, [1980] ECR 1553). That is why the defendant is not entitled to be heard in the lower court, whereas on appeal he must be given a hearing. There can be no exception to that rule in a situation where, for reasons which may be ascribed to the

plaintiff, the lower court has dismissed an application for enforcement on purely formal grounds. There is no ground for approaching this matter differently according to whether the defendant's habitual residence or registered office is in the State where enforcement is sought or in another State.

12. As a result, the reply to the question referred by the national court should be that the court hearing an appeal by a party seeking enforcement is required to hear the party against whom enforcement is sought, pursuant to the first sentence of the second paragraph of Article 40 of the Convention, even though the application for an enforcement order was dismissed simply because documents were not produced at the appropriate time and the enforcement order is applied for in a State which is not the State of residence of the party against whom enforcement is sought.

On those grounds, the Court (Second Chamber), in answer to the question referred to it by the Oberlandesgericht Frankfurt am Main by order of 12 August 1983, hereby rules:

> **The court hearing an appeal by the party seeking enforcement is required to hear the party against whom enforcement is sought, pursuant to the first sentence of the second paragraph of Article 40 of the Convention on Jurisdiction and the Enforcement of Judgments in Civil and Commercial Matters, even though the application for an enforcement order was dismissed simply because documents were not produced at the appropriate time and the enforcement order is applied for in a State which is not the State of residence of the party against whom enforcement is sought.**

OPINION OF MR ADVOCATE GENERAL DARMON

1. The preliminary question which has been referred to you concerns the interpretation of the first sentence of the second paragraph of Article 40 of the Brussels Convention of 27 September 1988, hereinafter referred to as 'the Convention'. Let us recall the facts and the course of the procedure.

On 20 January 1982 the Netherlands firm P. obtained a default judgment from the Arrondissementsrechtbank, Rotterdam, ordering the firm K., whose registered office is in Jeddah, Saudi Arabia, to pay it the sum of 678 095 Saudi riyals or the equivalent of that sum in dollars, together with interest as required by law.

The judgment is provisionally enforceable, subject, in the event of an appeal, to the provision by the firm P. of adequate financial or other security.

With a view to the enforcement of the judgment in the Federal Republic of Germany, where the firm K. has a bank account, the firm P. applied to the Landgericht Frankfurt am Main for an order for enforcement (Articles 31 and 32 of the Convention).

By an order of 10 January 1983 made without the firm K. having been summoned to appear, the President of the Third Civil Division of the German court refused to grant an order for enforcement on the ground that the documents required by Articles 46(2)
and 47(1) of the Convention had not been produced.

The documents in question are. 'The original or a certified true copy of the document which establishes that the party in default was served with the document instituting the proceedings' and 'Documents which establish that, according to the law of the State in which it has been given, the judgment is enforceable and has been served.'

The judgment notes, moreover, that, although the President of the court gave the firm P. time to produce the documents referred to, at the hearing that firm only produced the documents which the court did not consider of sufficient probative value. The firm P., therefore, brought an appeal ('Beschwerde') before the Oberlandesgericht Frankfurt am Main, pursuant to the first paragraph of Article 40 of the Convention.

The second paragraph of Article 40 provides that: 'The party against whom enforcement is sought shall be summoned to appear before the appellate court...'. The Oberlandesgericht asks whether that provision must be applied 'even' in the circumstances of this case. It inclines to the view that the provision need not be applied on two grounds, corresponding to the two elements of the preliminary question referred to you:

(i) The application for an enforcement order was dismissed simply because the documents were not produced by the firm P. at the proper time.

(ii) The system provided for by the second paragraph of Article 40 is unsuited to a case where enforcement is to take place in a State other than that in which the party against whom enforcement is sought is domiciled, since in such a case that party can, in general, identify the asset threatened by enforcement and thus dispose of it before it is seized.

2. A decision must first be made on the admissibility of the case.

Article 20 of the Protocol on the Statute of the Court of Justice provides that: 'In the cases governed by Article 177 of this Treaty, the decision of the court or tribunal of a Member State which suspends its proceedings and refers a case to the Court shall be ... notified by the Registrar of the Court to the parties ...'.

In this case the firm K., the defendant in the main proceedings, has not been notified of the decision. It was considered that the firm K. should not be considered a party within the meaning of Article 20 so long as the national court excluded it from the proceedings pending before that court.

That opinion corresponds to that of the Commission. It must be endorsed, since the question referred to you is whether or not the defendant in the main proceedings must be summoned to appear before the Oberlandesgericht, that is to say, whether or not it is a party to the action. The notification to the firm K. of the request for a preliminary ruling would thus prejudge your decision, or at least make that of the Oberlandesgericht entirely otiose.

Finally, it should be noted in this regard that the Oberlandesgericht is dealing with the 'Beschwerde' brought by the firm P. against the order of the Landgericht of 10 January 1913 dismissing its application. The Oberlandesgericht is therefore sitting in an appellate capacity and has referred the matter to you pursuant to Article 2(2) (not Article 2(3)) and Article 3(2) of the Protocol of 3 June 1971 on the Interpretation of the Convention by the Court of Justice.

3. Let us return to the question referred by the Oberlandesgericht. The Court is asked whether, taking into account certain circumstances, the rule set out in the first sentence of the second paragraph of Article 40 of the Convention may admit of an exception. In this respect the wording of Article 40 leaves no room for any restriction. It provides that if the application for enforcement is refused the applicant may bring an appeal, and specifies, as I have already pointed out, that: 'The party against whom enforcement is sought shall be summoned to appear before the appellate court'.

So much for the letter. Moreover, it faithfully reflects the spirit of the Convention, according to Mr P. Jenard's explanatory report, which was submitted to the governments at the same time as the draft Convention and is the authorised commentary.

Mr Jenard first describes the enforcement procedure in general terms. The application, accompanied by the required documents, must be submitted to the competent court, which: 'must give its decision without delay, and is not able to summon the other party. At this stage no contentious proceedings are allowed'.

The decision given by that court may be challenged in an appeal by the party against whom enforcement has been ordered, or in an appeal by the party whose application for enforcement has been refused.

Such appeals are brought before the competent court in proceedings in which both parties are given a hearing. The judgment given on the appeal can be contested only by an appeal in cassation or, in the Federal Republic of Germany, by *Rechtsbeschwerde*.

Simply stated, then the enforcement procedure is *ex parte* in the first instance but if an appeal is brought against the decision given at the first instance both parties must be given a hearing.

In his commentary on Articles 34, 37, 40 and 41 of the Convention, Mr Jenard justifies the system chosen, which in his view reconciles the element of surprise which is necessary in an enforcement procedure with respect for the defendant's right to a fair hearing. He goes on to state that, although at first instance 'the Convention does not allow the court to which application is made to ask the respondent to make submissions, even in exceptional cases', once the application has been refused and an appeal is lodged both parties must be given a hearing in order 'to avoid numerous appeals' and 'to protect the rights of the defendant'.

The spirit of the Convention is thus in accord with its letter, which is not surprising since the principle of *audi alteram partem* is a fundamental rule of civil procedure; a restrictive interpretation should be given not to the application of that principle but rather to the exceptions which are expressly made to it.

My views on the matter are thus similar to those expressed by the Commission and by the German Government, and I therefore propose that the question referred to the Court by the Oberlandesgericht Frankfurt am Main should be answered as follows:

The court hearing an appeal brought under Article 40 of the Brussels Convention of 27 September 1968 must, pursuant to the provisions of the first sentence of the second paragraph of that article, hear the party against whom enforcement is sought, even though the application for an enforcement order was dismissed simply because documents were not produced at the appropriate time, and the enforcement order is applied for in a State which is not the State of residence of the party against whom enforcement is sought.

Case 258/83 - 27 November 1984

Calzaturificio Brennero sas
v
Wendel GmbH Schuhproduktion International

Article 38, second paragraph - Enforcement - Appeal against a decision authorising enforcement - Possibility for the court with which an appeal has been lodged of making enforcement conditional on the provision of security - Conditions - Article 37, second paragraph - Enforcement - Remedies - Appeal in cassation and Rechtsbeschwerde - Judgments contestable by an appeal in cassation.

Summary

1. The second paragraph of Article 38 of the Convention of 27 September 1968 on Jurisdiction and the Enforcement of Judgments in Civil and Commercial Matters must be interpreted as meaning that a court with which an appeal has been lodged against a decision authorising enforcement, given pursuant to the Convention, may make enforcement conditional on the provision of security only when it gives judgment on the appeal.

2. The second paragraph of Article 37 of the Convention of 27 September 1968 must be interpreted as meaning that an appeal in cassation and, in the Federal Republic of Germany, a Rechtsbeschwerde may be lodged only against the judgment given on the appeal lodged pursuant to Article 36.

JUDGMENT OF THE COURT

Bosco, President of Chamber, Pescatore, O'Keeffe, Koopmans and Bahlmann, Judges

1. By order of 12 October 1983, which was received at the Court Registry on 18 November 1983, the Bundesgerichtshof [Federal Court of Justice] referred to the Court of Justice for a preliminary ruling under the Protocol of 3 June 1971 on the interpretation by the Court of Justice of the Convention of 27 September 1968 on Jurisdiction and the Enforcement of Judgments in Civil and Commercial Matters (hereinafter referred to as 'the Convention') two questions concerning the interpretation of Articles 37 and 38 of the Convention.

2. Those questions arose in a dispute between two shoe manufacturers, Brennero and Wendel, which have their registered offices in Italy and the Federal Republic of Germany respectively. Brennero obtained judgment against Wendel in an Italian court and is now seeking to have that judgment enforced in the territory of the Federal Republic of Germany, in accordance with the provisions of the Convention.

3. The President of the Fourth Civil Chamber of the Landgericht [Regional Court], Detmold, issued an order for the enforcement of the judgment in question and, at the same time, authorised the adoption of protective measures covering the assets of the German undertaking. Wendel appealed against that decision under the first paragraph of Article 36 of the Convention whereupon the Oberlandesgericht [Higher Regional Court], Hamm, before giving judgment on the appeal, made enforcement of the Italian judgment conditional on Brennero providing security even if enforcement was restricted to the adoption of protective measures.

4. Brennero lodged a Rechtsbeschwerde (appeal on a point of law) against the Oberlandesgericht's order under the second paragraph of Article 37 of the Convention. It contended that a court with which an appeal has been lodged against a decision authorising enforcement cannot require security to be provided without at the same time giving judgment on the appeal.

5. The Bundesgerichtshof, before which the Rechtsbeschwerde was brought, held that the Oberlandesgericht had not given judgment on the appeal against the decision authorising enforcement but had instead, in accordance with Wendel's suggestion, given a preliminary decision

concerning the provision of security. Since, in those circumstances, the decision given by the Oberlandesgericht was an interim order, it was uncertain whether it could be contested by a Rechtsbeschwerde. Under the German law of civil procedure, an appeal of that kind is inadmissible if its purpose is to challenge an interim order issued by an Oberlandesgericht. It can, therefore, be reviewed by the Bundesgerichtshof only if the Convention provides for such an appeal.

6. Taking the view that in that regard an interpretation of Articles 37 and 38 of the Convention was necessary to enable it to give judgment, the Bundesgerichtshof referred the following questions to the Court for a preliminary ruling:

'1. May the Oberlandesgericht in the Federal Republic of Germany with which an appeal against a decision authorising enforcement has been lodged by a debtor under Articles 36 and 37 of the Convention issue an order under the second paragraph of Article 38 of the Convention making enforcement conditional on the provision of security only as part of its final judgment on the appeal or may it also issue the order as an interim measure during the appeal proceedings?

2. May a Rechtsbeschwerde (appeal on a point of law) be lodged with the Bundesgerichtshof either directly under the second paragraph of Article 37 of the Convention, or by analogy therewith, against an order concerning the provision of security issued by the Oberlandesgericht on the basis of the second paragraph of Article 38 of the Convention as an interim measure during the appeal proceedings?'

First question (Article 38)

7. Brennero, the Italian Government and the Commission of the European Communities consider that under Article 38 of the Convention a court with which an appeal has been lodged against a decision authorising enforcement could not make an interim order requiring security to be provided without giving judgment on the appeal. The power to make an order of that kind excluded by the wording of Article 38 which states that the court with which the appeal was lodged could make 'enforcement' conditional on the provision of security, such enforcement being possible only after the dismissal of the appeal. Moreover, in their view, the exercise by the court with which the appeal had been lodged of the power to make an interim order requiring security to be provided is contrary to one of the objectives of the Convention which is intended precisely to render the procedure for the enforcement of a judgment given in another Contracting State as straightforward and as rapid as possible.

8. The German Government considers that the power of the court with which the appeal had been lodged to make an order for the provision of security during the appeal proceedings was such as to prevent the debtor from being exposed to risks inherent in the uncertainty surrounding the outcome of the proceedings in the State in which the original judgment was given, since Article 38 applied only where the judgment to be enforced did not yet have the force of res judicata in the State in which it was given.

9. At the hearing, Wendel expressed its agreement with that view particularly on the ground that although Article 38 applies to cases where the judgment to be enforced could still be contested by an appeal in the State in which that judgment was given, Article 39, which authorises the adoption of interim protective measures, applies only in cases where that judgment had become final under the law of the State in which it was given. In cases such as the present, therefore, only Article 38 is relevant whilst Article 39 is inapplicable.

10. It is appropriate to recall in the first place that the purpose of the Convention is to limit the number of requirements to which the enforcement of a judgment may be subjected in another Contracting State. The Convention accordingly provides for a very simple enforcement procedure whilst giving the party against whom enforcement is sought an opportunity to lodge an appeal. Unlike the initial proceedings concerning the decision authorising enforcement, the proceedings on the appeal are adversary proceedings.

11. Article 39 of the Convention governs the rights of the party who obtained the decision authorising enforcement which is contested by the appeal. Until judgment is given on that appeal, that party may, according to that provision, take only 'protective measures ... against the property of the party against whom enforcement is sought'. It follows that no enforcement measures may be taken until the court with which the appeal has been lodged gives judgment thereon.

12. That is the context in which the second paragraph of Article 38 of the Convention, under which the court with which the appeal has been lodged may 'make enforcement conditional on the provision of such security as it shall determine', must be set. The whole significance of that provision lies in the fact that, as soon as the court gives judgment on the appeal, the restrictions provided for by Article 39 cease to be applicable. Enforcement measures may therefore be taken while that judgment can

still be contested by an appeal in cassation or by a Rechtsbeschwerde, in accordance with the second paragraph of Article 37, and while even the original judgment given in the first State can still be contested by an appeal, which is a possibility expressly provided for by Article 38. That is the time when the protection of the debtor's interests may require enforcement to be made conditional on the provision of security.

13. It follows that the second paragraph of Article 38 of the Convention must be interpreted as meaning that a court with which an appeal has been lodged against a decision authorising enforcement, given pursuant to the Convention, may make enforcement conditional on the provision of security only when it gives judgment on the appeal.

Second question (Article 37)

14. Brennero observes that the uniform interpretation of the Convention would be jeopardised if an interim or interlocutory order issued by the court with which the appeal has been lodged could not be contested by an appeal in cassation or by a Rechtsbeschwerde. However, according to the Commission and the German Government, the second paragraph of Article 37 of the Convention states categorically that a Rechtsbeschwerde can be lodged only against the final judgment given on the appeal.

15. The second paragraph of Article 37 provides that the judgment given on the appeal may be contested only by an appeal in cassation and, in the Federal Republic of Germany, by a Rechtsbeschwerde. Under the general scheme of the Convention, and in the light of one of its principal objectives which is to simplify procedures in the State in which enforcement is sought, that provision cannot be extended so as to enable an appeal in cassation to be lodged against a judgment other than that given on the appeal, for instance against a preliminary or interlocutory order requiring preliminary inquiries to be made.

16. Therefore, the answer to the second question must be that the second paragraph of Article 37 of the Convention must be interpreted as meaning that an appeal in cassation and, in the Federal Republic of Germany, a Rechtsbeschwerde may be lodged only against the judgment given on the appeal.

17. If, in the present case, the answer to the second question should lead the Bundesgerichtshof to declare the Rechtsbeschwerde lodged against the Oberlandesgericht's order inadmissible, while the order should be

regarded as unlawful in the light of the answer to the first question, it is for the Oberlandesgericht, when the case again comes before it, to revoke the interim order insofar as it required security to be provided without giving judgment on the appeal.

On those grounds, the Court (Fourth Chamber), in reply to the questions submitted to it by the Bundesgerichtshof by order of 12 October 1983 hereby rules:

1. The second paragraph of Article 38 of the Convention of 27 September 1968 on Jurisdiction and the Enforcement of Judgments in Civil and Commercial Matters must be interpreted as meaning that a court with which an appeal has been lodged against a decision authorising enforcement, given pursuant to the Convention, may make enforcement conditional on the provision of security only when it gives judgment on the appeal;

2. The second paragraph of Article 37 of the Convention of 27 September 1968 must be interpreted as meaning that an appeal in cassation and, in the Federal Republic of Germany, a Rechtsbeschwerde may be lodged only against the judgment given on the appeal.

OPINION OF ADVOCATE GENERAL SIR GORDON SLYNN

In the course of proceedings brought before the District Court at Verona, in Italy, by an Italian company ('Brennero') against a German company ('Wendel'), the former sought and obtained what has been described as a 'protective seizure order'.

The Court has been told that, under Italian law, such an order may be made either before proceedings have commenced or pending judgment when it is considered necessary in order to ensure enforcement of the judgment. It must be executed within 30 days and takes the form of a seizure of the debtor's goods. The creditor cannot actually enforce the seizure by selling the goods and keeping the proceeds. The goods are under the control of the court making the protective seizure order. If the creditor's action is upheld, he can enforce the order immediately by seizing the goods. If his action is dismissed, the order ceases to have effect automatically.

The order made in this case covered the movable and immovable property and assets in Wendel's possession up to an amount of LIT 700 000 000 plus interest. It is not disputed that it was made inter partes and that, for this reason, it is in principle, enforceable under the Convention of 27 September 1968 on

Jurisdiction and the Enforcement of Judgments in Civil and Commercial Matters (hereafter 'the Convention'): see Case 125/79 Denilauler v Couchet Frères 1980 ECR 1553 at para. 17. According to counsel for Brennero, Wendel had no property or assets in Italy and it was necessary to enforce the order in Germany. To this end the Italian court declared for the purposes of Article 47 of the Convention that the order was enforceable in Italy. Pursuant to Article 32 of the Convention, Brennero applied to the President of the Fourth Civil Chamber of the Landgericht at Detmold in Germany, Wendel's domicile, for an order for the enforcement of the protective seizure order. The order for enforcement was made on 7 July 1983 and notified to Brennero under Article 35 of the Convention.

Article 36 provides that, if enforcement is authorised, as it was here, 'the party against whom enforcement is sought may appeal against the decision' (i.e. the decision authorising enforcement) 'within one month of service thereof'. By Article 39: 'During the time specified for an appeal pursuant to Article 36 and until any such appeal has been determined, no measures of enforcement may be taken other than protective measures taken against the property of the party against whom enforcement is sought. The decision authorising enforcement shall carry with it the power to proceed to any such protective measures'.

For this reason, the present order authorising enforcement contained the proviso that enforcement should not go beyond 'protective measures' until Brennero produced a certificate showing that enforcement could proceed without limit. Due to the protective nature of the order made by the Italian court, it does not seem that Brennero could produce such a certificate until final judgment in its action against Wendel.

On 12 July 1983, Wendel lodged an appeal under Article 36 with the Oberlandesgericht against the order authorising enforcement. At the same time, Wendel sought an interim order that enforcement of the Italian court order should be made conditional on the lodgment by Brennero of a security which, so the Court has been informed, was to be equal in amount to the sum covered by the Italian court's order.

Wendel based its application on Article 38 of the Convention, which provides that the court with which an appeal against an order authorising enforcement has been lodged 'may, on the application of the appellant, stay the proceedings if an ordinary appeal has been lodged against the judgment in the State (in) which that judgment was given or if the time for such an appeal has not yet expired; in the latter case, the court may specify the time within which such an appeal is to be lodged. The court may also make enforcement conditional on the provision of such security as it shall determine'. So far as can be seen, Wendel did not appeal against the order of the Italian court - indeed, the Court has been informed that no appeal against it is possible under Italian law. That order may be revoked by the trial judge and is, it seems, superseded by the final judgment delivered in the action. Wendel did not apply for a stay under Article 38 and if no appeal is possible under Italian law there is no room for the application of the first paragraph of Article 38 which depends on there being an appeal, or at any rate the possibility of an appeal.

By decision dated 15 July 1983, the Oberlandesgericht made enforcement of the Italian court's order conditional on provision of the security requested by Wendel, in the event DM 1 200 000. The order for reference made by the Bundesgerichtshof, to which Brennero appealed on a point of law, states that this was an interim order. The Oberlandesgericht had not given judgment on Wendel's appeal by the time that the order for reference was made. Brennero decided that it could not give the security required because of the time it would take to transfer funds from Italy. It therefore appealed to the Bundesgerichtshof against the decision of the Oberlandesgericht by way of a Rechtsbeschwerde. In the order for reference it is stated that Brennero would not, under German law, have a right of appeal against the decision of the Oberlandesgericht. Article 37 of the Convention, however, states that a judgment given on the appeal against the decision authorising enforcement may be contested in the Federal Republic of Germany by and only by a Rechtsbeschwerde.

Two questions are referred, though they are inter-related. The first is as follows: 'May the Oberlandesgericht in the Federal Republic of Germany with which an appeal against a decision authorising enforcement has been lodged by a debtor under Articles 36 and 37 of the Convention issue an order under the second paragraph of Article 38 of the Convention making enforcement conditional on the provision of security only as part of its final judgment on the appeal or may it also issue the order as an interim measure during the appeal proceedings?'

The provisions of Article 31 et seq. of the Convention envisage that a foreign judgment may only be reviewed as to its substance in the State in which it was given, not that in which it is to be enforced. The role of the courts in the enforcing State is correspondingly limited. Articles 38 and 39 affect the immediate enforceability of the judgment in two specific cases. In the first place, when the judgment sought to be enforced is not final in the sense that it is still subject to an ordinary appeal, the court in the enforcing State may stay the proceedings under Article 38; there is a discretion. In the second case, when an appeal is made against the authorisation of enforcement (or the time for making such an appeal is still running) the court of the enforcing State can only issue protective measures; it has neither the discretion nor the power to do more. I do not accept the view put forward by counsel for Wendel that Article 38 applies to judgments which do not have the force of res judicate, Article 39 to judgments which do have such force, and that Article 38 takes precedence over Article 39. In my view Article 39 applies whether or not the judgment sought to be enforced is final.

By 'protective measures' Article 39 of the Convention envisages those forms of relief available under the law of the enforcing State to prevent the judgment debtor from removing the assets on which execution is to be levied (see the Jenard Report at page 52). By 'measures of enforcement' which may not be taken, Article 39 means, in consequence, all other measures of enforcement, which usually take the form of the sequestration of the judgment debtor's property.

The present case does not concern a judgment which is enforced by sequestration. The furthest it goes is to place the judgment debtor's property under the control of the court making the order. It does not entitle the judgment creditor to seize the property. It follows that such a judgment could not be validly enforced in another Contracting State by an order for enforcement enabling the judgment creditor to seize the property. It could only be enforced by the appropriate protective measure available under the law of the enforcing State to assist what is itself a protective measure adopted in the original judgment. The object of Article 39 is 'to ensure at the enforcement stage a balance between the rights and interests of the parties concerned, in order to avoid either of them suffering any loss as a result of the operation of the rules of procedure' (the Jenard Report at page 52). That balance may be safeguarded, not threatened, by the adoption of protective measures. Article 39, thus, does not exclude protective measures which have the same effect as an order for protective measures in the judgment sought to be enforced merely because they do give effect to that order. These are not the sort of measures which are prohibited by Article 39.

Whereas Article 39 is dealing with the period before the time for lodging an appeal in the enforcing State has expired, or the appeal has been determined, Article 38 is dealing with the period before the time for lodging an appeal in the State where the judgment has been given has expired, or by implication the appeal has been determined. In the latter case proceedings in the enforcing State may be stayed, as I see it, before the hearing of the appeal or on the hearing of the appeal in that State. Whether and when proceedings should be stayed under Article 38, may depend on whether protective measures are required under Article 39; it does not seem to me, however, that a stay under Article 38 deprives the court of the power to grant protective measures under Article 39.

The second paragraph of Article 38, after giving power to grant a stay, provides that the court may 'also' make enforcement conditional on the provision of security. It is curious that this paragraph should follow on the provision for grant of a stay in this way, since it seems to me plain that it is not intended that a court should, when it grants a stay, at the same time make enforcement (which ex hypothesi it is not at that stage ordering) in the future dependent on the provision of security. On the other hand, it seems to me equally plain that the provision of security is not to be treated as part of or as the corollary of protective measures being granted under Article 39. Protective measures merely freeze the assets in the enforcing State; they do not amount to enforcement. There is no provision that security may be made a condition of protective measures. 'Enforcement' is the carrying out of the original judgment. It is only when the court hearing the appeal decides that enforcement may proceed that it has power to require security. That decision is only taken on the final hearing of the appeal; only on the final determination of the appeal can security be ordered. It is a protection to the debtor alternative to granting a stay, so that if an appeal is allowed in the State where the judgment is given, the debtor may have a remedy if his goods have been taken and used or dispersed.

The power to order security exists, as does the power to grant a stay, only where an appeal has been lodged or the time for appealing is still running in the State where the judgment was granted.

In the case of judgments which enforcement conditional on the provision constitute protective measures, the question has been raised as to whether enforcement may ever be made conditional on provision of security even as part of the final decision on the appeal. It is argued that it may not. Although this question is not expressly included in the order for reference, it is relevant to the present case and it seems desirable to deal with the argument. It does not seem to me that as a matter of interpretation a judgment ordering protective measures is excluded from the scope of what the courts of the enforcing State can do on the final hearing of the appeal. It is not excluded expressly and I do not think that it should be regarded as excluded by necessary implication. On the contrary, it is clear that an order freezing assets on the application of a creditor may cause loss to the debtor, even if the goods cannot be used or dissipated. If the court making the original order has considered and rejected an application for security, then the policy of the Convention would seem to indicate that, in the normal way, the enforcing court should not review that decision in the absence of a change in circumstances. It has, however, power to do so. Where there has been a change in circumstances the enforcing court may order security where an appeal has been lodged even if the security has been refused. These considerations, however, apply as well to cases where the order is not for protective measures as to where it is. Accordingly, subject to the court of the enforcing State taking into account, when it exercises its discretion, the fact that the court giving the judgment has refused security, I would reject the suggestion that security cannot be ordered if the judgment is only for protective measures.

The second question referred is as follows: 'May a Rechtsbeschwerde be lodged with the Bundesgerichtshof either directly under the second paragraph of Article 37 of the Convention or by analogy therewith, against an order concerning the provision of security issued by the Oberlandesgericht on the basis of the second paragraph of Article 38 of the Convention as an interim measure during the appeal proceedings?'

Article 37 provides for a further appeal against 'the judgment given on the appeal' against the decision authorising enforcement. There is no express reference to interim decisions delivered by the Court under Article 37 pending 'the judgment given on the appeal' from this, Wendel, the German Government and the Commission have inferred that 'the judgment given on the appeal' means the final judgment determining the appeal and that there is no possibility of appealing against an interim decision.

If, as in my view was the case, the draughtsmen of the Convention precluded the making of an interim decision allowing enforcement subject to provision of security pending the outcome of the appeal by providing that Article 39 should govern the position, the words in Article 37, 'judgment given on the appeal', must be construed starting from the premise that the only decision 'given on the appeal', is the final decision determining the appeal, not an interim decision of this nature. Article 37 does not, therefore, apply where such an interim decision is made. This means that the position is covered by the normal remedies available under the domestic law of the enforcing State in cases where a court purports to make an interim order although it has no jurisdiction to do so, whether by way of appeal if an appeal exists, or on application to the court which made the original order if there is no right of appeal.

The fact that there is no provision in the Convention for such an appeal in my view supports the conclusion reached in answer to the first question that there is no jurisdiction under the Convention to make such an interim order.

For these reasons it is my opinion that the questions referred should be answered on the following lines:

1. The Oberlandesgericht in the Federal Republic of Germany with which an appeal against a decision authorising enforcement has been lodged by a debtor under Articles 36 and 37 of the Convention cannot issue an order under the second paragraph of Article 38 of the Convention making enforcement conditional on the provision of security as an interim measure during the appeal proceedings;

2. The second paragraph of Article 37 of the Convention does not apply to interim orders of this kind purporting to be made during appeal proceedings on the basis of the second paragraph of Article 38; in such a situation the parties are entitled to rely on those remedies normally available, in the national jurisdiction, where an interim order is made in the absence of jurisdiction to do so.

Case 148/84 - 2 July 1985

Deutsche Genossenschaftsbank
v
SA Brasserie du Pêcheur

Article 36 - Enforcement - Procedures for challenging an enforcement order - Autonomous and complete system established by the Convention - Procedures available to interested third parties under domestic law - Exclusion.

Summary

The Convention of 27 September 1968 on Jurisdiction and the Enforcement of Judgments in Civil and Commercial Matters established an enforcement procedure which constitutes an autonomous and complete system, including the matter of appeals. It follows that Article 36 of the Convention excludes procedures whereby interested third parties may challenge an enforcement order under domestic law.

JUDGMENT OF THE COURT

Due, President of Chamber, Kakouris, Everling, Galmot and Joliet, Judges

1. By a judgment of 16 May 1984, which was received at the Court on 14 June 1984, the Cour d'appel [Court of Appeal], Colmar, referred to the Court for a preliminary ruling, under the Protocol of 3 June 1971 on the Interpretation by the Court of Justice of the Convention of 27 September 1968 on Jurisdiction and the Enforcement of Judgments in Civil and Commercial Matters (hereinafter referred to as 'the Convention'), a question concerning the interpretation of Article 36 of that Convention.

2. That question was raised in the context of proceedings between Deutsche Genossenschaftsbank, whose registered office is at Frankfurt am Main (Federal Republic of Germany), and Brasserie du Pêcheur, whose registered office is at Schiltigheim (France). Those proceedings relate to the question whether Brasserie du Pêcheur, in its capacity as an interested third party, is entitled to apply for the setting aside of an order for the enforcement of an instrument attested by a German notary. The enforcement order was obtained in France by Deutsche Genossenschaftsbank against its debtor, Deutsche Getreideverwertung und Rheinisehe Kraftfutterwerke (hereinafter referred to as 'DGV'), whose registered office is at Frankfurt am Main.

3. It appears from the documents forwarded by the Cour d'appel that, by an authentic instrument drawn up by a German notary on 5 April 1972, DGV created an Eigentümergrundschuld (a land charge registered in the name of the property owner) in the sum of DM 2 000 000 plus interest at the rate of 10% from the date the instrument was drawn up. DGV consented thereby to immediate enforcement against the land charged by future assignees of the land charge. It also consented to immediate enforcement, if necessary, by such assignees against all its property. By a declaration dated 11 January 1976, attested by a German notary, DGV assigned the land charge and the additional guarantee therein contained to Deutsche Gewerbe- und Landkreditbank AG, whose registered office is at Frankfurt am Main, and whose direct successor in title is Deutsche Genossenschaftsbank.

4. On 8 February 1982 Deutsche Genossenschaftsbank gave instructions for a copy of the instrument of 5 April 1972 to be delivered to it for the purpose of enforcement in the Federal Republic of Germany. Since it also wished to enforce it against DGV's assets in France, it applied to the president of the Tribunal de grande instance [Regional Court], Strasbourg, for an order for the enforcement of the translation into French of the instrument of 5 April 1972. By an order dated 24 March 1982 the president of the Tribunal de grande instance granted the application and in doing so relied, in particular, on Article 50 of the Convention.

5. Brasserie du Pêcheur, another of DGV's creditors, then also applied to the president of the Tribunal de grande instance in an attempt to have that order set aside. The procedural basis for its application was Article 496 of the new French Code of Civil Procedure, which permits any person affected by a judicial decision given ex parte to make an application to the court which made the decision.

6. As regards the substance of its application, Brasserie du Pêcheur contended, with reference to Articles 31 and 50 of the Convention, that the enforcement order had wrongly been granted in respect of a translation of the authentic instrument in question rather than the instrument itself. The president of the Tribunal de grande instance upheld that argument and, by an order dated 13 October 1983, set aside his previous order.

7. Deutsche Genossenschaftsbank appealed against that decision to the Cour d'appel, Colmar, arguing that Article 36 of the Convention provided for no appeal against an enforcement order except on the part of the party against whom enforcement was sought.

8. The Cour d'appel stayed the proceedings and requested the Court of Justice to give a preliminary ruling 'on the interpretation of Article 36 of the Convention and in particular on the question whether Article 36, which, in cases where enforcement is authorised, provides for an appeal only by the party against whom enforcement is sought, thereby excludes any redress for interested third parties, even where the domestic law of one of the Contracting States allows such parties to challenge an order for enforcement'.

9. Since it appears from the documents before the Court that the authentic instrument in respect of which an enforcement order was initially granted under Article 50 of the Convention was drawn up before the Convention came into force, it is necessary to state first that the Court's reply to the question referred to it by the Cour d'appel is without prejudice to the question whether the Convention is, in fact, applicable to that authentic instrument in view of the terms of Article 54 of the Convention.

10. As regards the question of interpretation referred to the Court, the parties to the main proceedings, the Commission and two Member States adopted the following positions.

11. Deutsche Genossenschaftsbank states that the Convention is complete in itself and may not be supplemented by provisions of national law. In its opinion, Article 36 only makes provision for an appeal by the defendant against whom an order for enforcement is granted. It is true that that provision derogates from domestic provisions which also allow interested third parties to contest such an order. However, the Convention governs the order for enforcement, not execution itself. The interests of

third parties may be safeguarded in an appropriate case at the latter stage of the procedure.

12. Brasserie du Pêcheur contends that Article 36 of the Convention provides for an ordinary appeal by the party against whom an order for enforcement is granted. It does not exclude the possibility that an enforcement order may be challenged under domestic law by means of exceptional procedures, such as an objection raised by a third party.

13. The Commission considers that the Convention constitutes a complete system which seeks to place a foreign instrument on an equal footing with a domestic instrument in order that it may be executed in the same manner as a domestic instrument. The issue of an enforcement order is governed directly and exclusively by the provisions of the Convention, whilst execution, in the narrow sense, is governed by the domestic law of the court where execution is sought. The effect of Article 36 of the Convention is that domestic law may not be relied upon to supplement the right of appeal provided for by that provision. Any action by a third party would only prolong the enforcement procedure, which would be contrary to the spirit of the Convention.

14. The German Government takes the view that the exclusive nature of the appeals provided for by the Convention may be inferred from the objective of Article 31 *et seq.*, which is to ensure in a speedy, simple and uniform manner that foreign enforceable instruments are equated with domestic enforceable instruments. There is no means of challenging an enforcement order apart from the right of appeal provided for by Article 36 of the Convention. Nevertheless, the German Government emphasises that all remedies provided for by domestic law remain available in relation to the measures to be taken by the competent authority to execute an enforcement order, since such measures are governed exclusively by the law of the State where execution is levied.

15. The Italian Government states that the wording of Article 36 of the Convention does not exclude procedures whereby enforcement orders may be challenged under domestic law by persons other than the party against whom enforcement is ordered. In its opinion, the Convention could not logically provide guarantees solely in favour of the party against whom enforcement is sought without taking account of the protection of the rights of third parties who might be affected.

16. It is appropriate to recall first that in its judgment of 27 November 1984 (Case 258/83, *Calzaturificio Brennero sas* v *Wendel GmbH Schuhproduktion International*, [1984] ECR 3971) the Court stated that the Convention 'provides for a very simple enforcement procedure whilst giving the party against whom enforcement is sought an opportunity to lodge an appeal'. It also stated that the principal objective of the Convention 'is to simplify procedures in the State in which enforcement is sought'.

17. In order to attain that objective the Convention established an enforcement procedure which constitutes an autonomous and complete system, including the matter of appeals. It follows that Article 36 of the Convention excludes procedures whereby interested third parties may challenge an enforcement order under domestic law.

18. The Convention merely regulates the procedure for obtaining an order for the enforcement of foreign enforceable instruments and does not deal with execution itself, which continues to be governed by the domestic law of the court in which execution is sought, so that interested third parties may contest execution by means of the procedures available to them under the law of the State in which execution is levied.

19. For those reasons, the reply to the preliminary question raised by the Cour d'appel, Colmar, must be that Article 36 of the Convention of 27 September 1968 on Jurisdiction and the Enforcement of Judgments in Civil and Commercial Matters excludes any procedure whereby interested parties may challenge an enforcement order, even where such a procedure is available to third parties under the domestic law of the State in which the enforcement order is granted.

On those grounds, the Court (Fifth Chamber), in answer to the question referred to it by the Cour d'appel, Colmar, by a judgment of 16 May 1984, hereby rules:

Article 36 of the Convention of 27 September 1986 on Jurisdiction and the Enforcement of Judgments in Civil and Commercial Matters excludes any procedure whereby interested third parties may challenge an enforcement order, even where such a procedure is available to third parties under the domestic law of the State in which the enforcement order is granted.

OPINION OF MR ADVOCATE GENERAL LENZ

A. The proceedings which have resulted in the present reference to the Court for a preliminary ruling relate to the enforceability in France of an instrument drawn up by a German *notary*.

Insofar as they are relevant to these proceedings, the contents of the instrument, which was drawn up by a notary in Neuss on 5 April 1972, may be summarised as follows:

1. Grant of a charge on land in the sum of DM 2 000 000 plus interest at the rate of 100%;

2. Consent by Deutsche Getreideverwertung und Rheinische Kraftfutterwerke GmbH (hereinafter referred to as 'DGV') and future owners of the land charged to immediate enforcement in respect of claims arising under the charge;

3. Assumption of personal liability by DGV as against future assignees of the land charge;

4. Consent by DGV to immediate enforcement of that instrument against the whole of its assets.

The land charge, which was created originally as an *Eigentümergrundschuld* (a land charge registered in the name of the property owner), was assigned to the Deutsche Gewerbe- und Landkreditbank AG in January 1976 in a declaration attested by a notary. The assignee's *successor* in title, Deutsche Genossenschaftsbank, is now seeking enforcement of that instrument. To that end, on 8 February 1982, it instructed the successor of the notary in Neuss to provide it with a copy of the instrument which could be used in enforcement proceedings. It then applied to the president of the Tribunal de grande instance (Regional Court), Strasbourg, for an order for enforcement in France.

By an order dated 24 March 1982 the president of the Tribunal de grande instance, Strasbourg, *issued an order for enforcement* of the *French translation* of the notarial instrument. An application was made to the same court for the setting aside of that order by Brasserie du Pêcheur SA, another of DGV's creditors. By an interlocutory order dated 13 October 1983 the president set aside his order of 24 March 1982 and ordered Deutsche Genossenschaftsbank to pay the costs. Deutsche Genossenschaftsbank appealed against that order to the Cour d'appel, Colmar, on the ground that Brasserie du Pêcheur had no right to contest the previous order. It took the view that apart from the right of appeal provided for in Article 36 of the Convention of 27 September 1968 on Jurisdiction and the Enforcement of Judgments in Civil and Commercial Matters no other, exceptional form of appeal was permissible. Only DGV could have appealed to the Cour d'appel, Colmar, which had jurisdiction under Article 37 of the Convention. Brasserie du Pêcheur, on the other hand, took the view that, in addition to the right of appeal available under Article 36 of the Convention, further exceptional procedures available under French law were permissible.

Considering that the outcome of the appeal depended on the interpretation of Article 36 of the Convention, the Cour d'appel referred the following question to the Court of Justice for a preliminary ruling:

'Does Article 36 of the Brussels Convention of 27 September 1968, which, in cases where enforcement is authorised, provides for an appeal only by the party against whom enforcement is sought, thereby exclude any redress for interested third parties, even where the domestic law of one of the Contracting States allows such parties to challenge an order for enforcement?'

B. My views on that question are as follows.

The Court of Justice could give a theoretical reply to the question whether or not Article 36 of the Convention excludes additional forms of appeal available under domestic law. That is what is proposed by the parties to the main proceedings, by the German and Italian Governments and by the Commission of the European Communities, although with different results.

However, the Court of Justice could also restrict itself to providing the Cour d'appel with the criteria for interpreting Community law to enable it to make a decision in the legal dispute before it. In my opinion, that is what the Court should do.

In order to reply to the question in the manner that I propose, no more is required than a reference to the first paragraph of Article 54 of the Convention. That provision states as follows:

'The provisions of this Convention shall apply only to legal proceedings instituted and to documents formally drawn up or registered as authentic instruments after its entry into force.'

The instrument which is to be enforced clearly states that it was drawn up on 5 April 1972. However, the Brussels Convention, following ratification by the six original members of the Communities, only came into force on 1 February 1973 in accordance with Article 62 thereof (see the first footnote to the Convention, Journal Official 1972, L 299, p.32, and Décret No 73/63 of 13 January 1973 concerning publication of the Convention, Journal Official de la République Francaise of 17 January 1973, p. 677, footnote 1).

Since counsel for Deutsche Genossenschaftsbank, surprised by the questions put to him by the Court concerning the applicability of the Brussels Convention, sought to argue that, in reality, the assignment of 1976 and not the instrument of 1972 should be enforced since DGV's liability had not yet arisen in 1972, I consider it necessary to clarify the German legal position briefly. The purpose of that clarification is not to judge the validity of the instrument drawn up in 1972 but to decide the date from which such an instrument, considered in the abstract, can be effective.

The main provision of the instrument of 5 April 1972 was, without doubt, the creation of a charge on land. However, it also contained other matters which are of importance in this case since it is not possible to enforce the charge itself in this case because the land charged is situated in Neuss and not in French territory. Instead the claim that is to be enforced is based on the assumption of personal liability by DGV and the corresponding consent to immediate enforcement.

In German law such an acknowledgement of liability, linked to consent to immediate enforcement, can be made even in respect of claims that have not yet arisen. If the person who grants a charge on land in an enforceable instrument at the same time accepts personal liability for the payment of the sum charged and if he consents to immediate enforcement, that is to be regarded as an admissible abstract recognition of liability, within the meaning of Paragraph 780 of the Bürgerliches Gesetzbuch [German Civil Code], which is intended to facilitate enforcement of the creditor's claim.

Accordingly, in a case where a charge on land is granted and personal liability is assumed in respect of the claim secured by the charge and where consent is given to immediate enforcement, German law does *not* lay down that the claim to be secured must already exist. To that extent the legal position with regard to a charge on land differs from that relating to a mortgage, which is dependent upon a pre-existing claim.

Since, as has been stated, the instrument to be enforced was drawn up on 5 April 1972, whereas the Brussels Convention only came into force on 1 February 1973, the Convention is not applicable to this case under Article 54 thereof. At the hearing, however, the Commission's representative raised the question whether, in the case of authentic instruments, it was such a serious matter, as it was in relation to court judgments, if it were presumed that the Brussels Convention applied in this case. I consider that that question must be answered in the affirmative because I consider such a result, following from a literal interpretation of the Convention, to be appropriate. Consent to immediate enforcement which is intended to apply initially to the territory of a specific Member State has a different scope if the instrument is subsequently capable of enforcement in the other Member States by means of the simplified procedure provided for by the Brussels Convention. I therefore take the view that the Brussels Convention can only be applied to authentic instruments which are drawn up after its entry into force.

C. In view of the foregoing I propose that the Court of Justice should reply to the question referred to it by the Cour d'appel, Colmar as follows: 'According to Article 54 of the Brussels Convention of 27 September 1968 on Jurisdiction and the Enforcement of Judgments in Civil and Commercial Matters, the Convention is only applicable to authentic instruments which were drawn up after its entry into force, that is to say after 1 February 1973'.

D. Should the Court nonetheless consider giving a reply to the substance of the question referred to it by the Cour d'appel, Colmar, - the question is worded generally and does not consider whether or not the Brussels Convention is applicable - I beg leave to add some observations on the forms of appeal available when an order for enforcement is issued.

The parties to the proceedings expressed differing views on the question whether the right of appeal available under Article 36 of the Brussels Convention excludes other forms of appeal available to interested third parties under national law. Deutsche Genossenschaftsbank, the Government of the Federal Republic of Germany and the Commission took the view that Article 31 *et seq.* of the Convention provide an exhaustive set of rules concerning possible forms of appeal and that provisions of national law are only available where express reference is made to them, such as in the first paragraph of Article 33 and in Article 35. Brasserie du Pêcheur and the Government of the Italian Republic, however, take the view that procedures available under national law are permissible in addition to the appeal provided for in Article 36 of the Convention; they state that it cannot be supposed that the Convention was intended to provide an appeal solely for the party against whom enforcement is sought and thereby exclude any means of redress for third parties whose rights might be affected.

Since neither the wording of the Convention nor the travaux préparatoires indicate clearly how that question is to be answered, it is necessary for me to have recourse to the spirit and purpose of the Convention. In its judgment of 27 November 1984, the Court of Justice recalled that: '... the purpose of the Convention is to limit the number of requirements to which ... enforcement may be subjected in another Contracting State. The Convention accordingly provides for a very simple enforcement procedure whilst giving the party against whom enforcement is sought an opportunity to lodge an appeal'.

The Court went on to state as follows: 'The second paragraph of Article 37 provides that the judgment given on the appeal may be contested only by an appeal in cassation and, in the Federal Republic of Germany, by a *Rechtsbeschwerde*. Under the general scheme of the Convention, and in the light of one of its principal objectives which is to simplify procedures in the State in which enforcement is sought, that provision cannot be extended so as to enable an appeal in cassation to be lodged against a judgment other than that given on the appeal, for instance against a preliminary or interlocutory order requiring preliminary inquiries to be made'.

The Court's argument, which leads to the exclusion of all appeals not provided for in the Convention, is applicable *a fortiori* to this case. The aim of simplifying procedures in the State in which enforcement is sought and in particular the aim of harmonising the laws of the Contracting States in that area would fail to be attained if procedures available under national law were admissible in addition to the appeals provided for in the Convention. Foreign enforceable instruments are to be equated with national enforceable instruments in a speedy, simple and uniform manner. It would be inconsistent with that objective if, in addition to the right of appeal under Article 36 of the Convention, further national appeals against an order for enforcement which differed in each Member State were admissible. If that were the case a party seeking enforcement in another Contracting State of an instrument drawn up in his favour in his own State would be faced in proceedings for enforcement by a multitude of national procedural obstacles in the form of additional forms of appeal. Accordingly, foreign enforceable instruments would not equated in an uncomplicated manner with national enforceable instruments.

In Article 220 of the EEC Treaty the Member States undertook to simplify the formalities governing the reciprocal recognition and enforcement of judgments of courts or tribunals. The extension in intra-Community trade has necessarily led to an increase in the number of legal relationships involving parties in different countries and therefore inevitably in the number of situations where a conflict of laws may arise. For that reason the simplified recognition and enforcement of judgments of courts or tribunals - and authentic instruments - is in fact a necessary legal concomitant of the creation of a common market corresponding as closely as possible to an internal market. Of course, the exclusion of procedures available under national law does not extend beyond the field of application of the uniform rules provided for in the Convention. Those rules simply relate to the issue of an order for enforcement of the foreign instrument and not the levying of execution itself. At that stage the law of the State in which the enforcement is effected is applicable.

If the Court should decide to answer the substance of the question referred to it by the Cour d'appel, Colmar, I propose that the reply be given in the following manner: 'The only permissible procedure for challenging an order for enforcement in one Contracting State of an instrument drawn up in another Contracting State is the right of appeal provided for in Article 36 of the Convention. That principle also applies where the national rules of procedure in one Contracting State provide that interested third parties may contest an order for enforcement'.

Case 119/84 - 3 October 1985

P. Capelloni and F. Aquilini
v
J. C. J. Pelkmans

Enforcement - Article 39 - Protective measures against the property of the person against whom enforcement is sought - Application of such measures - Relevant legislation - Specific authorisation not required - Article 36 - Period within which the protective measures may be applied - Confirmatory judgment required by national law - Not obligatory.

Summary

1. Article 39 of the Convention of 27 September 1968 merely lays down the principle that the party who has applied for enforcement may, during the period indicated in that article, proceed to apply measures to protect the property of the party against whom enforcement is sought. By contrast, the Convention leaves the matter of resolving any question not covered by specific provisions of the Treaty to the procedural law of the court hearing the proceedings. It must, nevertheless, be made clear that the application of the requirements of the national procedural law of the court hearing the proceedings must not in any circumstances lead to frustration of the principles laid down in that regard, whether expressly or by implication, by the Convention itself and by Article 39 thereof in particular. Accordingly, the question whether any given provision of the national procedural law of the court hearing the proceedings is applicable to protective measures taken pursuant to Article 39 depends upon the scope of each provision of national law and upon the extent to which it is compatible with the principles laid down by Article 39.

2. By virtue of Article 39 of the Convention a party who has applied for

and obtained authorisation for enforcement may proceed directly with protective measures against the property of the party against whom enforcement is sought and is under no obligation to obtain specific authorization. Such measures may be taken up to the expiry of the period for lodging an appeal prescribed in Article 36 and, if such an appeal is lodged, until a decision is given thereon.

A party who has proceeded with the protective measures referred to in Article 39 of the Convention is under no obligation to obtain in respect of such measures any confirmatory judgment required by the national law of the court in question. However, Article 39 does not prevent the party against whom those measures have been applied from taking legal proceedings in order to secure, by recourse to the appropriate procedures laid down in the national law of the court dealing with the matter, adequate protection the rights which he alleges to have been infringed by the measures in question.

JUDGMENT OF THE COURT

Bosco, President of Chamber, Pescatore, Koopmans, Bahlmann and O'Higgins, Judges

1. By an order of 9 November 1983, which was received at the Court on 8 May 1984, the Corte suprema di cassazione referred to the Court under the Protocol of 3 June 1971 on the interpretation by the Court of Justice of the Convention of 27 September 1968 on Jurisdiction and the Enforcement of Judgments in Civil and Commercial Matters (hereinafter referred to as 'the Convention') three questions on the interpretation of Article 39 of the Convention.

2. The questions were raised in proceedings instituted by Messrs Capelloni and Aquilini against Mr Pelkmans. It is apparent from the documents before the Court that Mr Pelkmans secured from the Corte d'Appello [Court of Appeal], Brescia, a decision dated 19 December 1980 whereby, pursuant to Article 31 et seq. of the Convention, the enforcement was authorised in Italy of a judgment delivered on 8 May 1979 by a court in Breda (Netherlands) ordering Messrs Capelloni and Aquilini to pay Mr Pelkmans the sum of HFL 127 400, together with interest and costs.

3. Messrs Capelloni and Aquilini appealed against that decision to the

same Corte d'Appello pursuant to Article 36 of the Convention. On 13 March 1981, before any decision had been given on that appeal, Mr Pelkmans arranged for protective sequestration of immovable property belonging to Messrs Capelloni and Aquilini under Article 39 of the Convention.

4. Mr Pelkmans then requested the Corte d'Appello, Brescia, to confirm the sequestration in accordance with Article 680 of the Italian Code of Civil Procedure. Messrs Capelloni and Aquilini objected to any such confirmation, claiming that certain provisions of that Code regarding protective sequestration had not been complied with, and the Corte d'Appello expressed the view, in its judgment of 14 July 1981, that the provisions of the Italian Code of Civil Procedure cited above were not applicable to a sequestration carried out under Article 39 of the Convention. For the same reason, the Corte d'Appello also held that Mr Pelkmans' application for confirmation was unacceptable on the ground that Article 680 of the Italian Code of Civil Procedure, which provides for such confirmation, did not cover sequestrations of the type in question.

5. The case was brought before the Corte suprema di cassazione, which stayed the proceedings and submitted the following questions to the Court:

'(1) Are the protective measures against the property of the debtor which may be proceeded with in the event of his appealing against an order for the enforcement of decisions given in another Member State of the European Community subject to the procedural rules of municipal law, as regards the procedures for their implementation and the conditions for their validity and effectiveness, or did the States which acceded to the Brussels Convention intend to adopt a single legal instrument, identical in all the Contracting States, whose purpose is to ensure that the debtor cannot dispose of his property in the meantime, that purpose being satisfied once execution is levied after dismissal of an appeal under Article 37 of the Brussels Convention, without the need, in particular, for a court ruling to confirm the protective measure?

(2) Notwithstanding that an order has already been made in a Contracting State declaring enforceable a judgment given in another Contracting State, is authorisation required from the same court to enable protective measures to be taken against the property of the party against whom enforcement is sought, or may the applicant proceed directly with the protective measures without the need for specific authorisation?

(3) Are cases governed by Article 39 of the Brussels Convention also subject to the procedural rules of the State in which protective measures are adopted, which rules prescribe a non-extendable period, running from the

date on which the party applying for those measures is in a position to proceed with them, within which protective measures against property must be commenced or completed, or may that party proceed with such measures, without limitation as to time, until such time as the competent judicial authority has adjudicated on the appeal referred to in Article 37 of the Convention?'

6. The United Kingdom and the Commission of the European Communities have submitted observations on those questions pursuant to Article 20 of the Protocol on the Statute of the Court.

7. By order of the Court of 12 December 1984, the case was assigned to the Fourth Chamber.

8. Article 39 of the Convention provides as follows: 'During the time specified for an appeal pursuant to Article 36 and until any such appeal has been determined, no measures of enforcement may be taken other than protective measures taken against the property of the party against whom enforcement is sought.

The decision authorising enforcement shall carry with it the power to proceed to any such protective measures'

9. In the first part of its first question, the national court seeks, in substance, to establish whether, and if so to what extent, it is necessary, in order to determine what rules govern the protective measures referred to in Article 39, to refer to the provisions of the various national laws applicable to similar measures.

10. In the other questions submitted to the Court, the national court is concerned more particularly with the applicability to the protective measures referred to in Article 39 of the provisions of the Italian Code of Civil Procedure which apply the following principles to protective sequestration:

(i) Any sequestration of that kind must be authorised by a decision of the competent court and, therefore, the debtor may not proceed with it directly;

(ii) Protective sequestration must be carried out within a non-extendable period which commences on the date on which the party applying for the measure is in a position to proceed with it;

(iii) Any such sequestration must, after being carried out, be the subject of proceedings for confirmation thereof.

Applicability to the protective measures referred to in Article 39 of the national provisions applicable to similar measures

11. With respect to the question whether in general the court to which application is made may refer to its own internal procedural law in order to determine the rules applicable to the protective measures referred to in Article 39, the Commission states that the requirements laid down in that article are not complete. More specifically, according to the Commission, neither Article 39 nor any other provision of the Convention gives a list of the measures in question, the type and value of the goods in respect of which they may be adopted, the conditions to be satisfied for such measures to be valid or the detailed provisions for implementing them and ensuring that they are proper. As regards those matters and any other matter not dealt with in a uniform manner by the Convention itself, the Commission considers that the national court has no alternative but to apply the relevant provisions of its national code of procedure, to which the Convention refers by implication.

12. The United Kingdom shares the Commission's view and considers that the question of how a national court must exercise the power to grant protective measures provided for in Article 39 is a matter falling wholly within the domain of its national procedural law. The United Kingdom considers that all the questions raised by the national court should be resolved by application of Italian procedural law, since the Convention does not lay down specific rules.

13. Before a reply is given to the question submitted on that point by the national court, it is necessary to examine the context of Article 39 and the aim which it pursues.

14. Article 39 appears in Section 2 of Title III of the Convention, which is concerned with the enforcement in one Contracting State of decisions given in another Contracting State.

15. As the Court has already indicated in its judgment of 27 November 1984 (Case 258/83 *Brennero* [1984] ECR 3971), the Convention is intended to limit the requirements to which the enforcement of a judicial decision may be made subject in another Contracting State and for that purpose lays down a very summary procedure for obtaining authorisation for enforcement, whilst at the same time giving the party against whom enforcement is sought an opportunity to appeal against that decision.

16. However, the Convention confines itself to governing the procedure for obtaining authorisation for enforcement, and does not contain any provisions concerning enforcement properly so called, which, as stated in the judgment of 2 July 1985 (Case 148/84 *Deutsche Genossenschafsbank* [1985] ECR 1987), is subject to the national law of the court hearing the proceedings.

17. In that context, Article 39 governs, during the period laid down in Article 36 within which an appeal may be lodged and until that appeal has been determined, the rights of the party who has applied for and obtained authorisation for enforcement.

18. As is apparent from the first paragraph of Article 39, the party in question may not, during that time, take any measures of enforcement properly so called but must confine itself to taking, if it considers that there is a need for them, protective measures against the property of the party against whom enforcement is sought. The authorisation to take such protective measures flows, as indicated in the second paragraph, from the decision authorising enforcement.

19. The obvious purpose of that provision is to offer the party who has obtained authorisation for enforcement, but who cannot yet proceed with measures of enforcement, a means of preventing the party against whom enforcement is sought from disposing of his property in the meantime so as to render future enforcement fruitless or indeed impossible.

20. However, as in the case of enforcement properly so called, the Convention confines itself, with respect to the protective measures referred to in Article 39, to laying down the principle that the party who has applied for enforcement may, during the period indicated in that article, proceed with such measures. By contrast, the Convention leaves the matter of resolving any question not covered by specific provisions of the Treaty to the procedural law of the court hearing the proceedings.

21. It must, nevertheless, be made clear that the application of the requirements of the national procedural law of the court hearing the proceedings must not in any circumstances lead to frustration of the principles laid down in that regard, whether expressly or by implication, by the Convention itself and by Article 39 thereof in particular. Accordingly, the question whether any given provision of

the national procedural law of the court hearing the proceedings is applicable to protective measures taken pursuant to Article 39 depends upon the scope of each provision of national law and upon the extent to which it is compatible with the principles laid down by Article 39.

22. Consequently, it is impossible to reply in general terms to the questions submitted by the national court: it is necessary to consider in each individual case whether the national provisions mentioned by the Italian court in its other questions are compatible with Article 39.

The need to obtain a specific decision authorising the protective measures

23. In its second question the national court asks whether there applies to protective measures taken pursuant to Article 39 the principle embodied in its own national law whereby a person seeking to proceed with protective sequestration must first be authorised to do so by a specific decision of the court of competent jurisdiction.

24. As the Commission has correctly stated, the effect of Article 39 is that a party who has obtained authorisation for enforcement is under no obligation to obtain specific and separate judicial authorisation in order to proceed with protective measures during the period mentioned in that article, even though such authorisation may normally be required by the national procedural law of the court in question.

25. That conclusion follows from the very wording of the second paragraph of Article 39 which states that the decision authorising enforcement 'shall carry with it' the power to proceed with protective measures. That expression indicates that the right to proceed with such measures derives from the decision allowing enforcement and therefore that a second decision, which could not in any event undermine that right, would not be justified.

26. It must, therefore, be stated in reply to the second question submitted by the national court that by virtue of Article 39 of the Convention a party who has applied for and obtained authorisation for enforcement may, by virtue of that article and during the period mentioned therein, proceed directly with protective measures against the property of the party against whom enforcement is sought and is under no obligation to obtain specific authorisation.

The period during which measures of enforcement may be taken

27. In its third question, the national court asks whether the protective measures referred to in Article 39 are subject to the rule embodied in its national law whereby a protective measure must be taken within a non-extendable period running from the date on which the party applying for those measures is in a position to proceed with them.

28. It must be stated, in conformity with the view put forward by the Commission, that the reply to that question is to be inferred from the very wording of the first paragraph of Article 39. Since the Convention provides that 'during the time specified for an appeal pursuant to Article 36 and until any such appeal has been determined, no measures of enforcement may be taken other than protective measures', the right to proceed with the measures in question cannot be restricted in time by the application of national measures prescribing a shorter period.

29. Consequently, such provisions are not applicable to the cases governed by Article 39.

30. It must, therefore, be stated in reply to the third question submitted by the national court that a party who has obtained authorisation for enforcement may proceed with the protective measures referred to in Article 39 until the expiry of the period for lodging an appeal prescribed in Article 36 and, if such an appeal is lodged, until a decision is given thereon.

The need for a judgment confirming the protective measures

31. In the second part of its first question the national court asks whether a party who has proceeded with protective measures under Article 39 must obtain in respect of such measures any confirmatory judgment required by its national procedural law.

32. The Commission considers that neither the wording nor the purpose of the article in question prevents the requirement of such a confirmatory judgment from extending to protective measures adopted under Article 39. According to the Commission, provided that such measures are allowed automatically and without prior examination by the judicial authority, a procedure for examination of the measures *ex post facto*, such as the confirmatory procedure required by Italian law, constitutes the only way of averting the risk that irrelevant or vexatious protective measures might be adopted.

33. It must be noted in that connection that the confirmatory procedures laid down by the law in several Contracting States are intended to ensure ex post facto that the decision authorising the protective measures is subject to examination in order to establish whether it was well founded, in view of the fact that the procedure preceding the adoption of such decisions is normally summary in character.

34. An examination of that kind is unjustified and even superfluous in the case of protective measures adopted under Article 39. Those measures are granted not on the basis of a summary procedure for authorisation but rather on the basis of the legal effect with which a decision adopted in another Contracting State is endowed by the Convention.

35. It is to be noted in that connection that the only means of challenging the decision authorising enforcement afforded by the Commission is the appeal referred to in Article 36. Consequently, any other remedy provided for by the national law of the court in question, even if limited to the part of the decision which implicitly authorises the protective measures, is excluded.

36. As regards the argument put forward by the Commission to the effect that the procedure of subsequent examination enables any irregularities or abuses committed in the application of the protective measures in question to be rectified, it must be observed that Article 39 does not prevent the party against whom those measures have been applied from taking legal proceedings in order to secure, by recourse to the appropriate procedures laid down in the national law of the court dealing with the matter, adequate protection of the rights which he alleges to have been infringed by the measures in question.

37. It must, therefore, be stated in reply to the second part of the first question submitted by the national court that a party who has proceeded with the protective measures referred to in Article 39 of the Convention is under no obligation to obtain in respect of such measures any confirmatory judgment required by the national law of the court in question.

On those grounds, the Court (Fourth Chamber), in reply to the questions submitted to it by the Corte suprema di cassazione by order of 9 November 1983, hereby rules:

(1) By virtue of Article 39 of the Convention, a party who has applied for and obtained authorisation for enforcement may, within the period mentioned in that article, proceed directly with protective measures against the property of the party against whom enforcement is sought and is under no obligation to obtain specific authorisation.

(2) A party who has obtained authorisation for enforcement may proceed with the protective measures referred to in Article 39 until the expiry of the period prescribed in Article 36 for lodging an appeal and, if such an appeal is lodged, until a decision is given thereon.

(3) A party who has proceeded with the protective measures referred to in Article 39 of the Convention is under no obligation to obtain, in respect of those measures, any confirmatory judgment required by the national law of the court in question.

OPINION OF ADVOCATE GENERAL SIR GORDON SLYNN

In these proceedings the Italian Supreme Court of Cassation has referred three questions relating to the interpretation of Article 39 of the Convention on Jurisdiction and the Enforcement of Judgments in Civil and Commercial Matters.

The background to the reference can be shortly stated.

In 1979 Mr Pelkmans obtained a judgment from a court at Breda in the Netherlands for HFL 127 400 plus interest and costs against Messrs Capelloni and Aquilini. Mr Pelkmans then obtained from the Court of Appeal in Brescia an order rendering that judgment enforceable in Italy. The judgment debtors appealed against that order in accordance with Article 36 of the Convention.

Mr Pelkmans' next step was to obtain, pursuant to Article 39, an order for protective measures authorising him to sequester the immovable property of Messrs Capelloni and Aquilini. Sequestration of the property followed. He then sought confirmation of these measures under the procedure prescribed by Italian law and dismissal of the appeal by the two defendants. The defendants opposed the application for confirmation of the sequestration and asked that the order of sequestration be lifted. The Court of Appeal declared Mr Pelkmans' application to be inadmissible but rejected the applications by Messrs Capelloni and Aquilini, without apparently dealing with the appeal against the order authorising enforcement. The defendants brought an appeal in cassation against that judgment and Mr Pelkmans cross-appealed.

The questions referred by the Supreme Court of Cassation are these:

'(1) Are the protective measures against the property of the debtor which may be proceeded with in the event of his appealing against an order for the enforcement of decisions given in another Member State of the European Community subject to the procedural rules of municipal law, as regards the procedures for their implementation and the conditions for their validity and effectiveness, or did the States which acceded to the Brussels Convention intend to adopt a single legal instrument, identical in all the Contracting States, whose purpose is to ensure that the debtor cannot dispose of his property in the meantime, that purpose being satisfied once execution is levied after dismissal of an appeal under Article 37 of the Brussels Convention, without the need, in particular, for proceedings to confirm the protective measure?

(2) Notwithstanding that an order has already been made in a Contracting State declaring enforceable a judgment given in another Contracting State, is authorisation required from the same court to enable protective measures to be taken against the property of the party against whom enforcement is sought, or may the applicant proceed directly with protective measures without the need for specific authorisation?

(3) Are cases governed by Article 39 of the Brussels Convention also subject to the procedural rules of the State in which protective measures are adopted, which rules prescribe a non-extendible period, running from the date on which, the party applying for those measures is in a position to proceed with them within which protective measures against property must be commenced or completed, or may that party proceed with such measures without limitation as to time, until such time as the competent judicial authority has adjudicated on the appeal referred to in Article 37 of the Convention?'

Article 39 reads as follows: 'During the time specified for an appeal pursuant to Article 36 and until any such appeal has been determined, no measures of enforcement may be taken other than protective measures taken against property of the party against whom enforcement is sought. The decision authorising enforcement shall carry with it the power to proceed to any such protective measures.'

Article 36 provides for an appeal against an order authorising enforcement and lays down the periods within such an appeal may be instituted.

The first question begins by asking quite generally whether Article 39 creates a single Community procedure for protective measures or whether the protective measures envisaged by that provision are to be taken according to the national rules of civil procedure.

The United Kingdom maintains that the procedure concerned is governed entirely by municipal law. It appears to take the view that this principle is unqualified. The Commission also considers that in principle national law applies. In support of this contention it cites the following as examples of matters on which the Convention gives no guidance and which must, therefore, be governed by municipal law: the kind of protective measures to be taken, the assets which may be seized and their value, the question whether the judgment creditor may carry out the measures himself or whether he is required to act through the medium of an officer of the court or other agent, and so on. Nevertheless, it claims that there are exceptions to this rule: in addition to the exceptions which the Commission has set out in its answers to its second and third questions, it suggests that there may be other respects in which the wording of the Convention requires one and the same procedure to be followed in all the Contracting States. The view that in principle the procedure in question is a matter of national law is also expressed in the Jenard Report (Official Journal 1979, C 59/1, p. 52).

As a general rule this seems to me to be right since clearly there are many matters relating to protective measures which are not dealt with by the Convention and which, in my view, can thus only be dealt with by the rules of national law. On the other hand, there are equally clearly exceptions to this general rule. Thus, for example, the judgment creditor on an application for protective measures cannot be required to prove or even make out a *prima facie* case on the merits, even if he might otherwise have to do so under national law apart from the Convention. Such a requirement would run counter to the whole purpose of the Convention which, subject to certain specified exceptions, seeks to ensure that judgments falling within its terms may be recognised and enforced in the territory of other Contracting States with the minimum of formality and delay. Nor can the Court on such an application go into the factors relevant to the decision as to whether an order for enforcement should be made. They fall within the province of the court hearing the appeal under Article 36. There may be other exceptions which have not been adverted to in this case.

Subject to these matters, the procedure on an application for protective measures and the factors to be taken into account (e.g. the relevance of urgency and the risk of the judgment debtor's assets being removed from the jurisdiction) are for the national court to decide under national law and practice.

More specifically, the first question also asks whether national provisions requiring protective measures to be confirmed *ex post facto* by a second judicial decision can apply to measures taken under Article 39. This question is asked because under the Italian Code of Civil Procedure protective measures are taken in a number of stages. Initially a provisional court order is made after a summary consideration of the facts and arguments. That order, which may or may not be made *ex parte*, authorises the judgment creditor to take the measures concerned within thirty days. A second hearing then takes place *inter partes*. In certain cases the judgment debtor is summoned to this hearing by the judgment creditor, whereas in other cases the court carries out this function. In either case the court must decide at the second hearing whether to confirm or set aside its initial order. It will adopt the latter course if it finds that the requirement of urgency is lacking.

Such a procedure of confirmatory orders is not peculiar to Italy. A similar procedure is apparently required to be followed in every case in Denmark. Netherlands, French and Luxembourg law also provide for such a procedure in many cases.

Both the Commission and the United Kingdom agree that such a procedure is not precluded by the Convention. Accordingly, in their view the normal provisions of national law apply to this matter.

I agree that the wording of the Convention does not oust the rules of municipal law on this matter either expressly or by necessary implication. I therefore accept the view put forward by the Commission and the United Kingdom. However, for the reasons that I have already given, during the confirmatory procedure the court may not require the judgment creditor to make out a *prima facie* case on the substance; nor may it have regard to matters which might preclude a judgment of another Contracting State being enforced under the Convention.

On the second question the Commission and the United Kingdom are not agreed.

The Commission takes the second paragraph of Article 39 to mean that the decision authorising enforcement is the order authorising protective measures. On this view that decision automatically confers on the judgment creditor the power to proceed to protective measures. No further judicial order or decision is said to be necessary. The Commission claims to find support for this construction in the Jenard Report (p. 52) and the Schlosser Report (Official Journal 1979, C 59/71 pp. 134-135).

In line with its submissions on the first question, the United Kingdom claims, on the other hand, that this matter is governed entirely by domestic procedural law. It construes the provision concerned to mean that after the decision authorising enforcement the appropriate court may authorise protective measures according to the national rules of procedure. Thus a separate judicial order relating specifically to protective measures will be necessary, in, those States where the rules of civil procedure require it. The United Kingdom, nevertheless, accepts that, if there are Contracting States in which a decision for the enforcement of a judgment automatically authorises the judgment creditor to take protective measures, then no separate judicial order authorising protective measures will be necessary in those States.

That both of these positions are arguable is reflected in the implementing measures adopted by the Contracting States. The majority appear to have adopted the approach advocated by the United Kingdom. That interpretation has also been upheld by a number of Italian courts. On the other hand, under the German legislation implementing the Convention the decision authorising enforcement automatically contains within it the authorisation to the judgment creditor to take protective measures. Some Italian courts have also adopted the same view as the Commission.

In my opinion, however, the correct reading of the Article is that during the period provided for appealing against an order made under Article 31, no measures of enforcement may be taken other than such protective measures (against the property of the party against whom enforcement is sought) as are available under national law. A plaintiff who has obtained an order for enforcement may, under the Convention, proceed to those measures by whatever route national law provides. If national rules enable him, e.g., to seize property without further order, he may do so. If national rules require a further order of the court, such an order must be obtained either from the court authorising enforcement or from some other competent court. In some Member States such protective measures may be made in precise terms, in respect of specific property and subject to well-established conditions; they may vary according to the circumstances. Some property may not be available for seizure as a matter of national law. I cannot see that the Convention has abolished the power of the national courts to go into these questions by enabling protective measures to be automatically taken merely because an enforcement order has been made. Thus in the present case it seems to me that the Italian confirmatory procedure is not rendered inapplicable in a case to which the Convention applies by a provision as general and imprecise as that contained in the second paragraph of Article 39. I therefore take the view that whether a further application is needed for protective measures is a matter of national law.

The background to the third question is that under Article 675 of the Italian Code of Civil Procedure an order authorising protective measures lapses after 30 days if it is not executed within that period. Messrs Capelloni and Aquilini have argued that the protective measures taken by Mr Pelkmans were unlawful in that they did not comply with this provision.

Once again the United Kingdom maintains that the answer is to be found exclusively in national law. The Commission, on the other hand, maintains that the right of the judgment debtor to carry out the protective measures subsists throughout the period specified in the opening words of Article 39.

I do not accept the Commission's view. The primary purpose of the opening words of Article 39 is to define the period during which no measures of enforcement may be taken. Article 39 then goes on to provide that during that period protective measures may be taken. It does not follow, however, that the judgment creditor must be entitled to take such measures throughout the period concerned.

The Commission also argues that to apply the 30-day rule to protective measures taken under Article 39 would lead to unfair consequences. The reason is said to be that the judgment debtor might appeal against the enforcement order more than 30 days after the protective measures have been authorised. Thus, the Commission argues, the judgment creditor may not know whether he needs to take protective measures until it is too late. This may be so. The remedy is for the plaintiff who has obtained an order for protective measures to carry them out within the period prescribed by national law, in the instant case 30 days.

Accordingly, I take the view that the matter referred to in the third question is governed exclusively by national law.

In the light of these considerations I am of the opinion that the questions referred by the Supreme Court of Cassation should be answered as follows:

(1) The protective measures provided for by Article 39 of the Convention on Jurisdiction and the Enforcement of Judgments in Civil and Commercial Matters are governed by the procedural rules of national law except to the extent that the Convention expressly or by necessary implication requires otherwise. Thus, at no stage of the procedure relating to protective measures may the judgment creditor be required to make out a *prima facie* case on the substance; nor may the court have regard to matters which might preclude a judgment of another Contracting State being enforced under the Convention. Subject to that overriding principle, a rule of national law whereby protective measures are subject to confirmation by the courts may be applied to measures taken pursuant to Article 39.

(2) Whether or not, after obtaining a decision authorising enforcement, a judgment creditor requires specific authorisation to take protective measures is a matter of national law.

(3) Article 39 does not preclude a provision of national law prescribing a non-extendible period during which protective measures may be carried out from applying to cases governed by that Article.

Case 198/85 - 10 July 1986

Fernand Carron
v
Federal Republic of Germany

Enforcement - Article 33 - Procedure - Furnishing of an address for service of process - Rules - Applicable law - Law of the State in which enforcement it sought - Principles which apply when that law is silent as to the time at which an address for service is to be given - Failure to comply with the rules on the furnishing of an address for service - Consequences.

Summary

The second paragraph of Article 33 of the Convention of 27 September 1968 on Jurisdiction and the Enforcement of Judgments in Civil and Commercial Matters must be interpreted as meaning that the obligation to give an address for service of process laid down in that provision must be fulfilled in conformity with the rules laid down by the law of the State in which enforcement is sought, and if that law is silent as to the time at which that formality must be observed, no later than the date on which the decision authorising enforcement is served.

The consequences of a failure to comply with the rules on the furnishing of an address for service are, by virtue of Article 33 of the Convention, governed by the law of the State in which enforcement is sought, provided that the aims of the Convention are respected.

JUDGMENT OF THE COURT

Everling, President of the Chamber, Joliet, Galmot, Schockweiler and

Moitinho de Almeida, Judges

1. By an order of 14 June 1985, which was received at the Court on 26 June 1985, the Hof van Cassatie [Court of Cassation] of Belgium referred to the Court for a preliminary ruling under the Protocol of 3 June 1971 on the interpretation by the Court of Justice of the Convention of 27 September 1968 on Jurisdiction and the Enforcement of Judgments in Civil and Commercial Matters (hereinafter referred to as 'the Convention') three questions concerning the interpretation of the second paragraph of Article 33 of the Convention.

2. The questions arose in the course of an appeal in cassation brought by Mr Carron against a judgment of 14 June 1984 in which the Rechtbank van Eerste Aanleg [Court of First Instance], Antwerp, dismissed his application to set aside the order made by the same court on 27 July 1982.

3. That order, issued on the application of the Federal Republic of Germany, authorised the enforcement in Belgium of a judgment of 9 March 1982 in which the Landgericht [Regional Court] Duisburg ordered Mr Carron to pay the Federal Republic of Germany damages in the sum of DM 5 240 000.

4. In support of his application to set aside the enforcement order Mr Carron argued that the proceedings were void on the ground that in the application initiating the proceedings the Federal Republic of Germany had failed to give an address for service. In its judgment of 14 June 1984 the Rechtbank van Eerste Aanleg held, dismissing Mr Carron's application, that the requirements of the second paragraph of Article 33 of the Convention had indeed been fulfilled, by the inclusion of an address for service in the document giving notice of the enforcement order.

5. The Hof van Cassatie decided to refer the following questions to the Court for a preliminary ruling:

'1. Is the question of the time at which and the manner in which an address for service of process is to be given, for the purposes of the second paragraph of Article 33 of the Convention on Jurisdiction and the Enforcement of Judgments in Civil and Commercial Matters to be determined by the law of the State in which enforcement is sought?

2. If Question 1 is answered in the affirmative, are the rules concerning the imposition of a penalty also governed by the State in which enforcement is sought?

3. If Question 1 is answered in the negative, at what time and in what manner is an address for service of process to be given and what penalty, if any, is to be imposed for failure to comply?'

The first question

6. Mr Carron and the Commission emphasise that the Convention seeks to put into effect a standard enforcement procedure in all the Member States; hence the court in the State in which enforcement is sought may not apply national rules of procedure except where the Convention expressly calls on it to do so. Since Article 33 contains no such provision as regards the time at which an address for service should be given, the first question must be answered in the light of the aims of that article. It seeks to enable the defendant to appeal against the enforcement order at the earliest opportunity, and accordingly requires that an address for service of process be given, at the latest, before the order granting enforcement is issued.

7. The German Government and the United Kingdom, on the other hand, take the view that according to the very words of Article 33 of the Convention the rules governing the furnishing of an address for service are to be laid down by the law of the State in which enforcement is sought. In view of the vagueness of the article as to the time at which the address for service should be given, the German Government and the United Kingdom believe that regard should be had to the fact that the furnishing of such an address is of no importance to the party against whom enforcement is sought until the commencement of the period allowed for lodging an appeal against the enforcement order under Article 36 of the Convention - that is to say, until the order is due to be served on him.

8. It must be pointed out that in Articles 31 to 49 the Convention establishes an enforcement procedure common to all Member States. At the initial ex parte stage, that procedure enables the applicant seeking enforcement of a judgment in another Member State to obtain satisfaction swiftly. At the second stage, involving proceedings *inter partes*, it guarantees the rights of the party against whom enforcement is sought by setting up an appeal procedure. Under that system the duty on the applicant's part to give an address for service or to appoint a representative *ad litem* must enable the party against whom enforcement has been ordered to lodge an appeal under the Convention without having to embark on formalities outside the confines of his home jurisdiction.

Although the Convention sets those aims, to which effect must be given in all Member States, it must be observed that it does not lay down detailed roles for implementing the procedure but refers expressly, on several points, to the law of the State in which enforcement is sought.

9. Thus, the first and second paragraphs of Article 33 of the Convention read as follows; 'The procedure for making the application shall be governed by the law of the State in which enforcement is sought. The applicant must give an address for service of process within the area of jurisdiction of the court applied to. However, if the law of the State in which enforcement is sought does not provide for the furnishing of such an address, the applicant shall appoint a representative *ad litem.'*

10. It is clear from those provisions that the law of the State in which enforcement is sought governs the entire procedure for making the application and that the furnishing by the applicant of an address for service of process is part of that procedure. Where the law of the State in which enforcement is sought does not indicate the exact time at which an address for service is to be given, it must be held, in accordance with the aims of the Convention, that it must be given sufficiently early to ensure that the proceedings are not improperly delayed and that the rights of the party against whom enforcement is sought are safeguarded. At the latest it must be given when the decision authorising enforcement is served.

11. The answer to be given to the first question submitted by the national court must therefore be that the second paragraph of Article 33 of the Convention of 27 September 1968 on Jurisdiction and the Enforcement of Judgments in Civil and Commercial Matters must be interpreted as meaning that the obligation to give an address for service of process laid down in that provision must be fulfilled in conformity with the rules laid down by the law of the State in which enforcement is sought, and if that law is silent as to the time at which that formality must be observed, no later than the date on which the decision authorising enforcement is served.

The Second question

12. Mr Carron takes the view that since it is Community law which requires that an address for service should be given before a decision authorising enforcement has been issued, it is likewise Community law which determines the sanction attaching to any failure to do so. In view of the imperative wording of the second paragraph of Article 33, and the

requirement under Article 35 of the Convention that the court to which application is made must 'without delay' notify its decision to the applicant, the sanction can only be that the application is held to be void.

13. The Court must agree with the German Government and the United Kingdom that inasmuch as the Convention provides no sanction for failure to comply with Article 33 that sanction must, like the other procedural rules referred to in that article, be determined by the law of the State in which enforcement is sought.

14. The law of the State in which enforcement is sought must, however, conform to the aims of the Convention; thus the sanction provided for may neither cast doubt on the validity of the enforcement order nor in any way prejudice the rights of the party against whom enforcement is sought.

15. The answer to the second question submitted by the national court must therefore be that the consequences of a failure to comply with the rules on the furnishing of an address for service are, by virtue of Article 33 of the Convention, governed by the law of the State in which enforcement is sought, provided that the aims of the Convention are respected.

Third question

16. In view of the answers to the first two questions raised by the national court, it is unnecessary to answer the third question.

On those grounds, the Court (Fifth Chamber), in answer to the questions submitted to it by the Hof van Cassatie by order of 14 June 1985, hereby rules as follows:

> **(1) The second paragraph of Article 33 of the Convention of 27 September 1968 on Jurisdiction and the Enforcement of Judgments in Civil and Commercial Matters must be interpreted as meaning that the obligation to give an address for service of process laid down in that provision must be fulfilled in conformity with the rules laid down by the law of the State in which enforcement is sought, and if that law is silent as to the time at which that formality must be observed, no later than the date on which the decision authorising enforcement is served.**

(2) The consequences of a failure to comply with the rules on the furnishing of an address for service are, by virtue of Article 33 of the Convention, governed by the law of the State in which enforcement is sought, provided that the aims of the Convention are respected.

OPINION OF MR ADVOCATE GENERAL MANCINI

1. Article 31 of the Convention of 27 September 1968 on Jurisdiction and Enforcement of Judgments in Civil and Commercial Matters provides that: 'A judgment given in a Contracting State and enforceable in that State shall be enforced in another...State when, on the application of any interested party, the order for its enforcement has been issued there.' The first paragraph of Article 33 provides: 'The procedure for making the application shall be governed by the law of the State in which enforcement is sought', and the second paragraph continues: 'The applicant must give an address for service of process within the area of jurisdiction of the court applied to. However, if the law of the State in which enforcement is sought does not provide for the furnishing of such an address,.....[he] shall appoint a representative *ad litem.*'

The Belgian Hof van Cassatie [Court of Cassation], seized of a dispute concerning the application of the latter paragraph, has raised the following issues in a reference for a preliminary ruling:

(a) Is it for the law of the State in which enforcement is sought to determine how and when the address for service of process required by the second paragraph of Article 33 is to be given and to penalise any failure to comply with the obligation in question?

(b) If not, how and when is an address for service of process to be given and what penalty, if any, is to be imposed for non-compliance?

The facts of the dispute in the main proceedings go back to 27 July 1982. On that date the Rechtbank van Eerste Aanleg [Court of First Instance], Antwerp, issued an order for the enforcement of a judgment of the Landgericht [Regional Court], Duisburg, in which Fernand Carron, a Belgian national, was ordered to pay damages of DM 5 240 000 to the Federal Republic of Germany. Mr Carron's application to set aside the enforcement order was dismissed, and he thereupon lodged an appeal in cassation, claiming that the proceedings were void. In his opinion, the first and second paragraphs of Article 33 require the address for service of process to be given when the application for enforcement is made, and in any event before the decision authorising enforcement is issued. The German authorities, however, fulfilled that obligation within the jurisdiction of the Rechtbank only on the document notifying the order to the appellant.

That is the background to the questions set out above.

2. Written observations were submitted by the appellant in the main proceedings, the Commission of the European Communities, the Federal Republic of Germany and the United Kingdom. Two arguments are adduced.

According to the Commission and Mr Carron, the duty to give an address for service and the enforcement proceedings of which that duty is a part are governed by Community law. A national court cannot therefore apply its own procedural rules without jeopardising the uniformity of those proceedings. Furthermore, the requirements of simplicity and speed which underlie the provisions of the Convention mean that the address for service of process should normally be given when the application for enforcement is made; an applicant who fails to do so, thus, frustrates the whole procedure, to his own detriment.

Germany and the United Kingdom take the opposite point of view. In their opinion there can be no doubt that the obligation to give an address for service is of general application. The time at which and the manner in which an address for service must be given and the penalty for non-compliance, however, are merely rules for fulfilling that obligation and are thus governed by the law of the State in which enforcement is sought. That is made clear by the second paragraph of Article 33, according to which '...if the law of the State in which enforcement is sought does not provide for the furnishing of an address for service' (and hence makes no provision for the relevant rules regarding formalities and timing), then the obligation is satisfied by the applicant's appointment of a representative *ad litem*.

However, the general scheme of the Convention does not require an address for service to be given at the same time as the application is made. Indeed, before the decision authorising enforcement is served the party against whom enforcement is sought may not 'make any submissions' and therefore has no interest in knowing the applicant's address for service.

3. The argument of the appellant and the Commission cannot be accepted. It should be pointed out that, in view of the considerable safeguards enjoyed by the defendant in the substantive proceedings, the authors of the Convention thought it equitable to confer on a party wishing to enforce a judgment in his favour the benefit of a speedy procedure in which the debtor would be precluded from raising fresh objections and the court's role would be limited to considering issues of public policy. To that end, no reference was allowed to the procedure of the State in which enforcement was sought (which does not always confer on the creditor the advantages mentioned above), and it was decided to adopt a common system. The system chosen from amongst the various possibilities under consideration was the one based on an application by the successful party, precisely because it enables the court to give a ruling on the basis of the documents supplied by him, without hearing the other party.

In short, it may be said that the essential elements of the procedure under the Convention are the following:

(a) an application for enforcement made by the person concerned to the court within whose jurisdiction the persons against whom enforcement is sought is domiciled (see Articles 31 and 32);

(b) the obligation, on the part of that person, to give an address for service of process within the jurisdiction of the court applied to (second paragraph of Article 33) and

(c) the decision on the application, which 'the appropriate officer of the court shall without delay bring ... to the notice of the applicant [alone] ...'(Article 38).

With regard to the rules on the time-limits and formal requirements governing those steps, on the other hand, the legislature preferred not to lay down an *ad hoc* set of rules but to leave such matters to the law of the State in which enforcement is sought. That is expressly laid down in respect of the application for enforcement (first paragraph of Article 33) and the notification of the decision authorising enforcement (Article 35) - that is, the steps which initiate and close the proceedings. It is obvious, however, that the same criterion holds good for the furnishing of an address for service. That is made clear, moreover, by (a) the plain words of the article (rightly relied on by the governments participating in the proceedings before this court), (b) the remarks made in the Jenard Report (Official Journal 1979, C 59 at pp. 49 and 50, second and sixth paragraphs under the heading 'Article 33') and (c) a simple argument *a contrario*: where the legal system of the State in which enforcement is sought makes no provision for an address for service, the act which takes its place, namely the appointment of a representative *ad litem*, can only be carried not in accordance with the rules governing procedural steps *intuitu personae*.

As regards the question of penalties, it seems advisable to draw a distinction according to whether the applicant fails to comply with the obligations laid down by Articles 32 and 33 or with the rules established by the *lex fori* to ensure that they are observed in good time. In the first case the court hearing the application for enforcement will dismiss it for breach of those two articles (see Jenard Report, under the heading 'Article 34'), and in the second it will take the measures required by its own rules of procedure. From the point of view of the Convention, that entails better supervision by the national court, which will be quite familiar with its own procedural rules. At the same time the applicant has every interest in complying with them in order not to jeopardise the result which he hopes to achieve.

In those circumstances the reply to the first question cannot be other than affirmative. The second question thereby becomes otiose.

4. In view of the foregoing considerations I propose that the Court should give the following answer to the questions referred to it by the Hof van Cassatie in its order of 14 June 1982 in the proceedings between Mr Carron and the Federal Republic of Germany: 'The second paragraph of Article 33 of the Convention of 27 September 1968 on Jurisdiction and Enforcement of Judgments in Civil and Commercial Matters should be interpreted as meaning that the obligation to give an address for service of process must be fulfilled in conformity with the rules laid down by the law of the State in which enforcement is sought. That law also determines the procedural consequences of any failure to observe those rules.'

Case C-183/90 - 4 October 1991

Berend Jan van Dalfsen and Others
v
Bernard van Loon and Theodora Berendsen

Enforcement - Article 37, second paragraph and Article 38 - Legal remedies - Appeal in cassation - Judgments which may be contested by an appeal in cassation - Decision by the court with which the appeal against the enforcement order is lodged as to a stay of proceedings or the provision of security - Excluded - Enforcement - Article 31, Article 34, third paragraph and Article 38, first paragraph - Appeal against the enforcement order - Power of the court with which the appeal is lodged to stay the proceedings - Exercise - Taking into consideration only submissions not already put forward by or known to the applicant at the time of the proceedings before the court of the State in which the judgment was given.

Summary

1. The second paragraph of Article 37 of the Convention of 27 September 1968 on Jurisdiction and the Enforcement of Judgment in Civil and Commercial Matters is to be interpreted as meaning that a decision taken under Article 38 of the Convention by which the court with which an appeal has been lodged against an order for the enforcement of a judgment given in another Contracting State has refused to stay the proceedings and has ordered the party to whom the enforcement order was granted to provide security does not constitute a 'judgment given on the appeal' within the meaning of the second paragraph of Article 37 of the Convention and may not, therefore, be contested by an appeal in cassation or similar form of appeal. The position is the same where the decision taken under Article 38 of the Convention and the 'judgment given on the appeal' within the meaning

of the second paragraph of Article 37 of the Convention are given in a single judgment.

2. The first paragraph of Article 38 of the Convention is to be strictly interpreted so as not to prejudice the effectiveness either of Article 31, which lays down the principle that a judgment given in a Contracting State and enforceable in that State may be enforced in another Contracting State even if it has not yet become *res judicata*, or of the third paragraph of Article 34, which prohibits the courts of the State in which enforcement is sought from reviewing the substance of the judgment given in the first State.

Hence the first paragraph of Article 38 of the Convention is to be interpreted as meaning that a court with which an appeal is lodged against an order for the enforcement of a judgment given in another Contracting State may take into consideration, in a decision concerning an application for the proceedings to be stayed under that paragraph, only such submissions as the appellant was unable to put before the court of the State in which the judgment was given.

JUDGMENT OF THE COURT

Mancini, President of the Chamber, O'Higgins, Kakouris, Schockweiler and Kapteyn, Judges

1. By order dated 1 June 1990, which was received at the Court on 11 June 1990, the Hoge Raad der Nederlanden referred to the Court for a preliminary ruling pursuant to the Protocol of 3 June 1971 on the interpretation by the Court of Justice of the Convention of 27 September 1968 on Jurisdiction and the Enforcement of Judgments in Civil and Commercial Matters (Official Journal 1978 L 304, p. 36) (hereinafter referred to as 'the Convention') three questions on the interpretation of the second paragraph of Article 37 and the first paragraph of Article 38 of the Convention.

2. Those questions arose in the context of proceedings pending before that court between B. J. Van Dalfsen, J. Timmerman, H. Van Dalfsen, J. Harmke and G. Van Dalfsen (hereinafter referred to as 'Van Dalfsen'), residing in the Netherlands, on the one hand, and B. Van Loon and T. Berendsen (hereinafter referred to as 'Van Loon'), residing in Belgium, on the other.

3. It appears from the documents before the Court that, by judgment of 21 October 1986, the Vrederechter van bet Kanton Herentals (Belgium) dismissed the principal claim, for the annulment of a tenancy agreement between the parties to the main action, brought by Van Dalfsen against Van Loon, and accepted in principle the substance of Van Dalfsen's alternative claim that Van Loon should be ordered to repay the cost of Van Dalfsen's capital expenditure on the premises rented, and ordered an expert's report to determine the exact amount thereof. Giving judgment on Van Loon's counterclaim, the Vrederechter ordered Van Dalfsen to pay to Van Loon the sum of BFR 2 700 000 arrears of rent plus interest. The court declared the judgment to be 'provisionally enforceable notwithstanding any appeal and without security'.

4. On 17 December 1986, Van Dalfsen appealed to the Rechtbank van Eerste Aanleg te Turnhout (Belgium) against the part of the judgment relating to the counterclaim.

5. Van Loon, for their part, applied to the presiding judge of the Arrondissementsrechtbank te Zwolle (Netherlands) pursuant to Article 31 of the Convention for an order for the enforcement in the Netherlands of the Belgian Vrederechter's judgment. By decision of 23 January 1987 the presiding judge of the Arrondissementsrechtbank made the order requested.

6. On 2 April 1987 Van Dalfsen, pursuant to Article 36 of the Convention, appealed to the Arrondissementsrechtbank te Zwolle against that decision, applying merely for a stay of the proceedings on that appeal in pursuance of the first paragraph of Article 38 of the Convention, on the ground that they had appealed against the judgment given by the Vrederechter te Herentals and provided a bank guarantee as security for the amount which they had been ordered by that judgment to pay to Van Loon; they also emphasized that their alternative claim for payment had been accepted in principle and assessed in a provisional expert report at BFR 477 954.

7. By judgment of 13 April 1988, the Arrondissementsrechtbank te Zwolle dismissed the application to stay the proceedings on the ground that Van Dalfsen had not cited, in support of their application, any arguments other than those which the foreign court had been able to consider in its decision. By the same judgment the Arrondissementsrechtbank declared the appeal unfounded and hence ordered enforcement in the Netherlands of the judgment given by the

Belgian Vrederechter, whilst deciding, of its own motion, to make enforcement conditional, under the third paragraph of Article 38 of the Convention, upon the provision by Van Loon of a bank guarantee in the sum of BFR 478 000 until the final judgment on Van Dalfsen's alternative claim.

8. Van Dalfsen appealed in cassation against that judgment to the Hoge Raad der Nederlanden under the second paragraph of Article 37 of the Convention. Their sole submission was to the effect that the Arrondissementsrechtbank based its decision on an incorrect interpretation of the scope of the powers conferred by Article 38 of the Convention on the 'court with which the appeal... is lodged'. According to Van Dalfsen, a court giving judgment under that article must take account of all the circumstances which the foreign court has already been able to take into account in its decision and must in particular assess the chances of success of the ordinary appeal which has been or is to be lodged in another Contracting State.

9. The Hoge Raad der Nederlanden first considered whether the judgment appealed against must be regarded as a 'judgment given on the appeal' within the meaning of the second paragraph of Article 37 of the Convention. If not, Van Dalfsen's appeal in cassation would be inadmissible. On the other hand, if that question is answered in the affirmative, it would be necessary to consider the substance of the appeal in cassation and the question of the scope of the powers conferred by Article 38 of the Convention on the 'court with which the appeal is lodged' would then arise.

10. The Hoge Raad, taking the view that the action therefore raised questions concerning the interpretation of the Convention, decided, by order of 1 June 1990, in pursuance of the Protocol of 3 June 1971 on the interpretation by the Court of Justice of the Convention, to stay the proceedings until the Court had given a preliminary ruling on the following questions:

'1. Can decisions of "the court with which the appeal under the first paragraph of Article 37 is lodged" as to whether or not use should be made, or whether use should be made in a particular way, of the powers conferred on it by Article 38 of the Brussels Convention be regarded as "the judgment given on the appeal" against which an appeal in cassation may be lodged in the Netherlands under the second paragraph of Article 37 of the Brussels Convention?

2. Does it make any difference to the answer given to Question (1)

whether or not the decisions based on Article 38 of the Brussels Convention which are referred to in that question are set out in the (final) judgment ruling on the appeal?

3. May "the court with which the appeal under the first paragraph of Article 37 is lodged" make use of the powers conferred on it by the first paragraph of Article 38 of the Brussels Convention: (a) where the party lodging the appeal states no grounds for its application for the proceedings to be stayed or for enforcement to be made conditional on the provision of security other than grounds that the foreign court could have taken into account in its decision; (b) only where the application in question is based partly or exclusively on submissions not put forward in the proceedings before the foreign court; or (c) only where the application is based partly or exclusively on submissions which could not have been put forward in the proceedings before the foreign court because the party lodging the appeal was at that time unaware of the facts on which those submissions are based?'

11. Reference is made to the Report for the Hearing for a fuller account of the facts of the case before the national court, the course of the procedure and the written observations submitted to the Court, which are hereinafter mentioned or discussed only in so far as is necessary for the reasoning of the Court.

12. It should first be recalled that the second paragraph of Article 37 and the first paragraph of Article 38 of the Convention are part of Section 2 of Title III of the Convention, on enforcement of judgments which are enforceable in the Contracting State in which they have been given.

13. Under Article 31 of the Convention, such decisions are to be enforced in another Contracting State when, on the application of any interested party, the order for its enforcement has been issued there, by the competent court referred to in Article 32 of the Convention and in accordance with the rules laid down in Articles 33 to 35 and 42 to 45 thereof. It should be observed in particular that under Article 34 of the Convention the party against whom enforcement is sought is not, at this stage of the proceedings, entitled to make any submissions, that the application for enforcement may be refused only for one of the reasons specified in Articles 27 and 28 of the Convention and that the foreign judgment may in no circumstances be reviewed as to its substance.

14. If enforcement is authorized, the party against whom enforcement is sought may, under Article 36 of the Convention, appeal against the

decision to one of the courts referred to in the first paragraph of Article 37 thereof. Article 39 of the Convention provides that, during the time specified for an appeal and until any such appeal has been determined, no measures of enforcement may be taken other than protective measures taken against the property of the party against whom enforcement is sought.

15. If an ordinary appeal has been lodged in the State in which the foreign judgment was given against its enforcement, or if the time for such an appeal has not yet expired, Article 38 of the Convention provides that the court of the State in which enforcement is sought may, on the application of the party who has lodged the appeal under Article 36, stay the proceedings thereon. In pursuance of the third paragraph of Article 38 of the Convention, that court may however also make enforcement subject to the provision of security by the party seeking the enforcement order.

16. Under the second paragraph of Article 37 of the Convention, the judgment given on the appeal may be contested only by an appeal in cassation or a similar form of appeal.

The first and second questions

17. The court of reference, in its first two questions, which it is appropriate to consider together, substantially seeks to determine whether the second paragraph of Article 37 of the Convention is to be interpreted as meaning that a decision taken under Article 38 of the Convention, by which the court with which the appeal is lodged against an order for the enforcement of a judgment given in another Contracting State has refused to stay the proceedings and has ordered the party to whom the enforcement order was granted to provide security, constitutes 'judgment given on the appeal' under the second paragraph of Article 37 of the Convention and may accordingly be contested by an appeal in cassation or a familiar form of appeal. The court also asks whether the answer to that question according to whether or not the decision based on Article 38 of the Convention and the 'judgment given on the appeal' within the meaning of the second paragraph of Article 37 of the Convention are set out in the same judgment.

18. It should first be observed that the Convention gives no definition of what is to be understood by 'judgment given on the appeal' within the meaning of the second paragraph of Article 37.

19. Secondly it should be noted that the Court has stated in the judgment in Case 258/83 (*Brennero* v *Wendel* [1984] ECR 3971, paragraph 15), that the concept of 'judgment given on the appeal' appearing in the second paragraph of Article 37 of the Convention must be restrictively interpreted and has ruled that under the general scheme of the Convention, and in the light of one of its principal objectives which is to simplify procedures in the State in which enforcement is sought, that provision cannot be extended so as to enable an appeal in cassation to be lodged against a judgment other than that given on the appeal, for instance against a preliminary or interlocutory order requiring preliminary inquiries to be made.

20. The committee of experts set up on the occasion of the drafting of the Convention (Official Journal 1979 C 59, p.1) also emphasized the need for a strict interpretation of the second paragraph of Article 37 of the Convention. According to that report, 'an excessive number of avenues of appeal might be used by the losing party purely as delaying tactics, and this would constitute an obstacle to the free movement of judgments which is the object of the Convention'.

21. It follows from the foregoing that, since the object of the Convention is to facilitate the free movement of judgments by establishing a simple and rapid procedure in the Contracting State in which application is made for the enforcement of a foreign judgment, the expression 'judgment given on the appeal' in the second paragraph of Article 37 of the Convention must be interpreted as denoting only judgments deciding on the substance of the appeal lodged against an order for the enforcement of a judgment given in another Contracting State to the exclusion of judgments given under Article 38 of the Convention.

22. It should be added that even where the decision refusing to stay the proceedings or requiring the provision of security is contained in the same judgment as the decision on the substance of the appeal against the enforcement order, the procedure under Article 36 and that under Article 38 nevertheless have a different object.

23. In fact the appeal procedure envisaged by Article 36 relates to the legal question of whether, regard being had to the reasons exhaustively specified in Articles 27 and 28 of the Convention, the enforcement order has been lawfully issued, whereas the decision relating to a stay of proceedings or the provision of security under Article 38 constitutes a subsidiary measure designed to settle the subsequent course of the

procedure, which implies a balancing of the respective interests of the creditor and the debtor.

24. In those circumstances, a judgment given under Article 38 of the Convention cannot be assimilated to a judgment allowing or dismissing the appeal lodged against the order for enforcement despite the fact that in form it constitutes part of the same judgment.

25. It follows that, even when a decision based on Article 38 of the Convention appears in the same judgment as the decision on the substance of the appeal lodged against the enforcement order such a decision is not to be regarded as a 'judgment given on the appeal' within the meaning of the second paragraph of Article 37 of the Convention and cannot therefore be the subject of an appeal in cassation.

26. The answer to the first and second questions of the court of reference should therefore be that the second paragraph of Article 37 of the Convention is to be interpreted as meaning that a decision taken under Article 38 of the Convention by which the court with which an appeal has been lodged against an order for the enforcement of a judgment given in another Contracting State has refused to stay the proceedings and has ordered the party to whom the enforcement order was granted to provide security does not constitute a 'judgment given on the appeal' within the meaning of the second paragraph of Article 37 of the Convention and may not, therefore, be contested by an appeal in cassation or similar form of appeal. The position is the same where the decision taken under Article 38 of the Convention and the 'judgment given on the appeal' within the meaning of the second paragraph of Article 37 of the Convention are in fact given in a single judgment.

The third question

27. In its third question, the court of reference seeks substantially to determine whether the first paragraph of Article 38 of the Convention is to be interpreted as meaning that the court with which the appeal is lodged against an order for the enforcement of a judgment given in another Contracting State may take into consideration, in its decision concerning an application for the proceedings to be stayed under that paragraph, only such submissions as the appellant was unable to make before the court of the State in which the judgment was given, or whether that court may also take into consideration in such a decision submissions which were already before the foreign court, as well as arguments of

which the court was unaware at the time of its judgment because the party lodging the appeal had failed to put them before it.

28. It must first be pointed out that the first paragraph of Article 31 of the Convention lays down the principle that a judgment given in a Contracting State and enforceable in that State may be enforced in another Contracting State even if it has not yet become *res judicata.*

29. An exception is made to that principle by the power to stay the proceedings, conferred by the first paragraph of Article 38 of the Convention on the court with which the appeal was lodged against an order for the enforcement of a judgment given in another Contracting State. As may be seen from the report of the committee of experts prepared on the occasion of the drafting of the Convention, the object of that exception is to protect the party against whom enforcement is sought against any damage which might result from the enforcement of a judgment which has not yet become res judicata and might be amended, and it therefore serves as a counterbalance to the unilateral nature of the procedure for enforcement laid down by Article 31 *et seq.* of the Convention.

30. It follows that the first paragraph of Article 38 of the Convention, since it constitutes a derogation, must be strictly interpreted so as not to prejudice the effectiveness of Article 31 of the Convention and detract from its object, namely to permit the free movement of judgments by allowing judgments given in a Contracting State and enforceable in that State to be enforced in another Contracting State.

31. It should next be recalled that the basic principle of the third paragraph of Article 34 of the Convention is that a foreign judgment may in no circumstances be reviewed as to its substance by the courts of the State in which enforcement is sought.

32. If the court with which the appeal is lodged were able to take into consideration, in giving its decision on an application for a stay of proceedings under the first paragraph of Article 38 of the Convention, submissions already put before the foreign court, there would be a real risk of its proceeding, directly or indirectly, to review the foreign judgment as to its substance, which is expressly prohibited by the Convention. The position would be the same if that court were empowered to assess the chances of success of an ordinary appeal lodged or to be lodged in the State in which the judgment was given.

33. In those circumstances, the first paragraph of Article 38 of the Convention cannot be interpreted as meaning that the court with which the appeal is lodged may take into consideration, in a decision concerning an application for a stay of proceedings, submissions already put before the foreign court.

34. As regards the question whether the court with which the appeal is lodged may take into consideration, in a decision concerning an application for a stay of proceedings under the first paragraph of Article 38 of the Convention, arguments unknown to the foreign court at the time of its judgment because the appellant had failed to put them before it, it should be remembered that in its judgment in Case 145/86 (*Hoffmann* v *Krieg* [1988] ECR 645) the Court ruled, in connection with Article 36 of the Convention, that a party who had not appealed was precluded, at a later stage in the proceedings, from relying on a ground which he could have pleaded in such an appeal.

35. It must be stated that this principle applies equally as regards the first paragraph of Article 38 of the Convention. The scheme of the Convention and in particular the principle of the free movement of judgments, which is one of the Convention's essential objects, prevents a party from invoking before the court called upon to decide, under the first paragraph of Article 38, upon an application for a stay of the proceedings in the appeal lodged against the enforcement order, grounds which he could have pleaded before the foreign court.

36. Accordingly, the first paragraph of Article 38 of the Convention cannot be interpreted, either, as meaning that the court with which the appeal is lodged can take into consideration, in a decision regarding a stay of proceedings under that paragraph, submissions which were not known to the foreign court at the time of its judgment because the appellant had failed to put them before it.

37. It follows from all the foregoing considerations that the answer to the third question from the court of reference must be that the first paragraph of Article 38 of the Convention is to be interpreted as meaning that a court with which an appeal is lodged against an order for the enforcement of a judgment given in another Contracting State may take into consideration, in a decision concerning an application for the proceedings to be stayed under that paragraph, only such submissions as the appellant was unable to put before the court of the State in which the judgment was given.

On those grounds, the Court (Sixth Chamber), in answer to the questions referred to it by the Hoge Raad der Nederlanden, by order of 1 June 1990, hereby rules:

1. The second paragraph of Article 37 of the Convention on Jurisdiction and the Enforcement of Judgments in Civil and Commercial Matters is to be interpreted as meaning that a decision taken under Article 38 of the Convention by which the court with which an appeal has been lodged against an order for the enforcement of a judgment given in another Contracting State has refused to stay the proceedings and has ordered the party to whom the enforcement order was granted to provide security does not constitute a 'judgment given on the appeal' within the meaning of the second paragraph of Article 37 of the Convention and may not, therefore, be contested by an appeal in cassation or similar form of appeal. The position is the same where the decision taken under Article 38 of the Convention and the 'judgment given on the appeal' within the meaning of the second paragraph of Article 37 of the Convention are given in a single judgment.

2. The first paragraph of Article 38 of the Convention is to be interpreted as meaning that a court with which an appeal is lodged against an order for the enforcement of a judgment given in another Contracting State may take into consideration, in a decision concerning an application for the proceedings to be stayed under that paragraph, only such submissions as the appellant was unable to make before the court of the State in which the judgment was given.

OPINION OF MR ADVOCATE GENERAL VAN GERVEN

1. This case concerns a reference from the Hoge Raad der Nederlanden (hereinafter referred to as 'the court of reference') for a preliminary ruling under Article 177 of the EEC Treaty on the interpretation of Article 37(2) and the first paragraph of Article 38 of the Convention of 27 September 1968 on Jurisdiction and the Enforcement of Judgments in Civil and Commercial Matters (hereinafter referred to as 'the Brussels Convention'). The questions put to the Court arose in the context of an appeal in cassation brought before the court of reference by B. J. Van Dalfsen, J. Timmermann, H. Van Dalfsen, J. Harmke and G. Van Dalfsen (hereinafter referred to as Van Dalfsen') against a judgment of the Arrondissements-rechtbank te Zwolle (Netherlands). They concern the

procedure laid down under the articles of the Brussels Convention already referred to with regard to an appeal against the order for the enforcement of judgments given in another Contracting State.

2. By the first two questions, which are of a general nature, the Hoge Raad actually wishes to know, so as to decide on the admissibility of the appeal in cassation, whether an appeal in cassation within the meaning of the second paragraph of Article 37 of the Brussels Convention may be lodged against the refusal of the Arrondissementsrechtbank to stay the proceedings on the appeal against the order for enforcement. In its third question the Hoge Raad asks, so as to decide on Van Dalfsen's ground of appeal in cassation, if it is admissible, what arguments the Arrondissements-rechtbank could have taken into account in the context of a decision under the *first paragraph* of Article 38 of the Brussels Convention on whether or not to stay the proceedings on the appeal.

Legal background

3. Article 37(2) and Article 38 of the Brussels Convention, which are under discussion in these proceedings, are part of Section 2 of Title III of the Brussels Convention (Articles 31 to 45) concerning the enforcement of judgments which are enforceable in the State in which they are given. Under Article 31 of the Brussels Convention, such judgments may be enforced in another Contracting State when, on the application of any interested party, the order for enforcement has been issued there by the court having jurisdiction in pursuance of Article 32 of the Convention and in accordance with the rules laid down in Articles 33 to 35 and 42 to 45 thereof. It is particularly important to note that at this stage of the proceedings before the aforementioned court the party against whom enforcement is sought is not entitled to make any submissions on the application, that an application for enforcement may be refused only for one of the reasons specified in Articles 27 and 28 of the Convention and that the foreign judgment may under no circumstances be reviewed as to its substance (Article 34).

4. If the order for enforcement is refused, the applicant may, under Article 40 of the Brussels Convention, appeal to the court mentioned in that article, whose judgment may, in turn, be contested in cassation or by a similar form of appeal.

If, however, enforcement is authorized, the party against whom enforcement is sought may, in accordance with Article 36 of the Brussels Convention, appeal against the judgment within one month of the service thereof to the court mentioned in Article 37(l). Since under Article 34 the application for enforcement could have been refused only for one of the reasons specified in Articles 27 and 28, the appeal against the enforcement order must also be based on one of those reasons. According to Article 39, during the time specified for an appeal and until any such appeal has been determined, no measures of enforcement may be taken other than protective measures taken against the property of the party against whom enforcement is sought; the decision authorizing enforcement carries with it the power to proceed to any such protective measures.

If in the meantime an ordinary appeal has been lodged in the State of origin against the judgment whose enforcement is sought or if the time for such an appeal has not yet expired, the court with which the appeal is lodged may, under the first paragraph of Article 38 of the Brussels Convention, on the application of the appellant, stay the proceedings. However, under the last paragraph of that article, the court may also make enforcement conditional on the provision of such security as it may determine on behalf of the party against whom enforcement is sought.

Under the second paragraph of Article 37 of the Brussels Convention, the 'judgment given on the appeal' may be contested only by an appeal in cassation or by a similar form of appeal.

Facts and procedure

5. By judgment of 21 October 1986 given by the Vredegerecht van het Kanton Herentals (Belgium), Van Dalfsen were ordered to pay B. Van Loon and T. Berendsen (hereinafter referred to as Van Loon') arrears of rent amounting 'to BFR 2 700 000 plus interest. In the same judgment the Vredegerecht recognized in principle Van Dalfsen's right to repayment of the cost of capital expenditure they had incurred in respect of the premises' rented and ordered that an expert's report be drawn up to determine the amount of these costs. The court declared the judgment 'provisionally enforceable notwithstanding any appeal and without security'.

6. On 17 December 1986 Van Dalfsen appealed against this judgment to the Rechtbank van Eerste Aanleg te Turnhout (Belgium). Van Loon, for their part, applied to the presiding judge of the said Arrondissementsrechtbank, previously referred to, in accordance with Article 31 of the Brussels Convention, for an order for enforcement in the Netherlands of the judgment which in Belgium had been declared provisionally enforceable. By judgment of 23 January 1987 the presiding judge of the Arrondissementsrechtbank authorized enforcement. Pursuant to Article 36 of the Convention, Van Dalfsen appealed to the Arrondissementsrechtbank against the order for enforcement. They also requested the court to stay the proceedings on the appeal in view of the fact that an appeal had meanwhile been lodged in Belgium against the Vredegerecht's judgment and the fact that the claim for compensation for capital expenditure, which the Vredegerecht had accepted in principle, had in the meantime, been assessed in a provisional expert report at BFR 477954.

7. By judgment of 13 April 1988, that is, 'the judgment given on the appeal', within the meaning of the second paragraph of Article 37, the Arrondissementsrechtbank found that Van Dalfsen's appeal was clearly not based on a challenge to the legality of the order for enforcement which had been issued, but solely on the application to stay the proceedings on the appeal. It therefore declared the appeal unfounded, dismissed the application for a stay of proceedings, but attached to the order for enforcement, of its own motion, the condition that Van Loon should provide a bank guarantee in the sum of BFR 478 000 until such time as the court from whose decision the appeal was made had given judgment on Van Dalfsen's alternative claim.

8. Van Dalfsen appealed in cassation to the court of reference. In that appeal they state that the Arrondissementsrechtbank proceeded on the basis of an erroneous interpretation of the scope of its powers pursuant to Article 38 of the Brussels Convention as the court with which the appeal is lodged. Van Dalfsen's view is that it was open to the Arrondissementsrechtbank, in its decisions on the stay of proceedings on the appeal and making enforcement conditional on the provision of security, to take account of circumstances which the foreign court could already have taken into account in its judgment and to base such decisions, inter alia, on its estimate of the chance of success of the ordinary appeal lodged, or which might still be lodged, in the State in which the judgment was given.

9. The court of reference raises the following questions:

'(1) Can decisions of "the court with which the appeal under the first paragraph of Article 37 is lodged" as to whether or not use should be made, or whether use should be made in a particular way, of the powers conferred on it by Article 38 of the Brussels Convention be regarded as "the judgment given on the appeal" against which an appeal in cassation may be lodged in the Netherlands under the second paragraph of Article 37 of the Brussels Convention?

(2) Does it make any difference to the answer given to Question (1) whether or not the decisions based on Article 38 of the Brussels Convention which are referred to in that question are set out in the (final) judgment ruling on the appeal?

(3) May "the court with which the appeal under the first paragraph of Article 37 is lodged" make use of the powers conferred on it by the first paragraph of Article 38 of the Brussels Convention: (a) where the party lodging the appeal states no grounds for its application for the proceedings to be stayed or for enforcement to be made conditional on the provision of security other than grounds that the foreign court could have taken into account in its decision; (b) only where the application in question is based partly or exclusively on submissions not put forward in the proceedings before the foreign court; (c) only where the application is based partly or exclusively on submissions which could not have been put forward in the proceedings before the foreign court because the party lodging the appeal was at that time unaware of the facts on which those submissions are based?'

The second paragraph of Article 37 of the Brussels Convention

10. To enable it to decide as to the admissibility of the appeal in cassation, the court of reference wishes to know whether under Article 37(2) of the Brussels Convention an appeal in cassation may be lodged against a judgment given under Article 38 by the court with which the appeal is lodged, in which the latter refused to stay the proceedings and required the provision of security.

Article 37(2) provides for the possibility of lodging an appeal in cassation (or a similar form of appeal) against 'the judgment given on the appeal'. In its judgment in Case 258/83 *Brennero* v *Wendel* the Court stated that these words must be strictly interpreted and ruled that a preliminary or interlocutory decision requiring the creditor (wrongly in the Court's opinion) to provide security did not constitute 'a judgment given on the appeal' and could not therefore be challenged by an appeal in cassation (in that case by a 'Rechtsbeschwerde'). In that connection the Court stated: 'Under the general scheme of the Convention, and in the light of one of its principal objectives which is to simplify procedures in the State in which enforcement is sought, that provision cannot be extended so as to enable an appeal in cassation to be lodged against a judgment other than that given on the appeal, for instance against a preliminary or interlocutory order requiring preliminary inquiries to be made' (paragraph 15).

11. In my view, it follows from that judgment that a decision by the court with which the appeal is lodged to stay the proceedings likewise cannot be regarded as a 'judgment given on the appeal' in view of the fact that such a decision to stay the proceedings can naturally only be taken by an interlocutory judgment. However, the position is different in the case of a judgment refusing to stay the proceedings or requiring the provision of security, since such decisions pre-suppose a judgment on the appeal and are thus (as in this case) normally laid down in the final judgment declaring the appeal unfounded and ordering enforcement.

The question therefore is whether, in the light of *Brennero* v *Wendel* the conclusion must be drawn that these judgments, which are not interlocutory decisions but are a formal part of the final decision, may be regarded as judgments 'given on the appeal'. In other words, does it follow from *Brennero* v *Wendel* that an appeal in cassation may be brought against any final decision of the court with which the appeal is lodged (formal criterion) or can an appeal in cassation be brought against the final decision only in so far as it concerns the actual judgment on the appeal, that is, in so far as it concerns the justification for, in this case, the dismissal of the appeal, which pre-supposes a judgment on one of the reasons specified in Articles 27 and 28 (material criterion)?

12. The strict interpretation of the expression 'judgment given on the appeal' which the Court advocates is justified in *Brennero* v *Wendel* by a reference to one of the principal objectives of the Brussels Convention, namely to simplify enforcement procedures in the State in which enforcement is sought. This consideration is also an argument, as rightly observed by the Netherlands and German Governments, for using the expression 'judgment given on the appeal' to denote only judgments which concern the appeal itself and not the judgments referred to in Article 38 of the Convention.

In the Jenard Report, too, the need for a strict interpretation of the second paragraph of Article 37 is emphasized and it is pointed out that: 'An excessive number of avenues of appeal might be used by the losing party purely as delaying tactics, and this would constitute an obstacle to the free movement of judgments which is the object of the Convention.'

13. In its observations to the Court, the Commission puts forward another point of view. It thinks that a decision by the court with which the appeal is lodged to stay the proceedings is clearly not a judgment given on the appeal. On the other hand, a decision refusing to stay the proceedings and a decision to make enforcement conditional on the provision of security are indeed judgments given on the appeal because they imply the possibility of proceeding to enforcement.

I do not agree with that. In my view, the Commission's idea fails to recognize that, although the last-mentioned decisions are normally taken at the same time as the judgment on the substance of the appeal and are accordingly combined in a single judgment, they nevertheless have a different aim. The procedure on appeal envisaged in Article 36 of the Brussels Convention concerns the substance of the appeal and has a clearly legal aim: the question is whether the order for enforcement must be annulled because it ought not to have been made in view of the reasons exhaustively set out in Articles 27 and 28, to which Article 34 refers. The possibility envisaged in Article 38 of staying the proceedings or requiring the provision of security is intended, on the other hand, to preserve a balance between the interests of creditor and debtor: by staying the proceedings the court with which the appeal is lodged prevents the creditor from taking other than protective measures. Making enforcement conditional on the provision of security means that the interests of the debtor in the event of enforcement are protected in view of the possibility of a modification of the foreign court's judgment on appeal. In other words, decisions taken in this respect by the court with which the appeal is lodged lay down the details of the enforcement. Consequently, if it refuses a postponement or requires provision of security it is taking a decision regarding the details of enforcement. Of course, such a judgment implies that a decision is taken at the same time as to the substance of the appeal, but should be distinguished from it.

14. In view of the need to keep the procedure in the State in which enforcement is sought as simple as possible and of the different object of the procedures referred to in Articles 36 and 38, I therefore think I can say, in answer to the first preliminary question, that the expression 'judgment given on the appeal' refers to judgments directly concerning the substance of the appeal. These seem to me, moreover, to be the only judgments which lend themselves wholly to an appeal in cassation since they concern questions of law in the strict sense, whilst judgments in the context of the procedures referred to in Article 38 are intended basically to balance interests.

I therefore give preference to a criterion based on content rather than exclusively on the formal nature of the decision. The answer to the second preliminary question should therefore be that, even when a decision based on Article 38 is contained in the same (final) decision as the actual judgment on the appeal, an appeal in cassation against such a (final) decision will lie only in so far as it concerns the substance of the appeal.

An additional advantage of this solution is that in the appeal procedure it treats the parties to the dispute equally. If the possibility of an appeal in cassation were to be rejected when a decision taken under Article 38 was given in an interlocutory judgment (which is bound to be the case with a decision to stay the proceedings) but to be accepted when such a decision is included in a final decision (which is normally the case with a decision refusing to stay the proceedings and ordering enforcement, where appropriate with the provision of security) then the appellant is in a position to lodge an appeal in cassation against the said final decision, but the respondent is not entitled to appeal in cassation against the aforementioned interlocutory judgment.

First paragraph of Article 38 of the Brussels Convention

15. The Arrondissementsrechtbank refused the application to stay the proceedings on the appeal on the ground that Van Dalfsen, in support of their application, put forward no arguments other than those which the foreign court could already have taken into account in its judgment and that to consider such arguments would mean that the appeal court would essentially be reviewing the substance of the foreign judgment. The Arrondissementsrechtbank made the order for enforcement conditional on the provision of security, taking into consideration a new fact which had arisen since the foreign judgment, namely the production in the meantime of the legal expert's report in which Van Dalfsen's counterclaim was evaluated.

As I have already said, Van Dalfsen raise the point with the court of reference that in this way the Arrondissementsrechtbank proceeded on the basis of an erroneous interpretation of the scope of the powers conferred on it by Article 38 of the Brussels Convention. According to Van Dalfsen, it is open to the court with which the appeal is lodged to take into account in its decisions under Article 38 circumstances which the foreign court could already have taken into account in its judgment and the court with which the appeal is lodged must in particular base those decisions on its estimate of the chances of success of the ordinary appeal which has been or may still be lodged against the judgment.

16. In the third preliminary question the court of reference asks the Court to give its views on this point, whilst restricting the question to a decision taken in connection with an application to stay the proceedings, as referred to in the first paragraph of Article 38.

In their observations to the Court the Netherlands and German Governments associate themselves on this point with Van Dalfsen's interpretation, whilst the Commission takes the opposite point of view. I agree with the Commission, for the following reasons.

17. The possibility, envisaged in the first paragraph of Article 38, of staying proceedings on the appeal, with the consequence that, under Article 39, only protective measures may still be taken by the creditor just like the possibility, envisaged in the last paragraph of Article 38, of making the order for enforcement conditional on the provision of security) has as its object to: 'protect the judgment debtor against any loss which could result from the enforcement of a judgment which has not yet become *res judicata* and may be amended'.

In its judgment in Case 43/77 *Industrial Diamond Supplies* v *Luigi Riva* the Court stated, in clarification of Article 38 of the Brussels Convention, that the State in which enforcement is sought 'is not under a duty to stay the proceedings but merely has the power to do so' (paragraph 32) and that the court may 'stay the proceedings whenever reasonable doubt arises with regard to the fate of an appeal which may lead to the annulment or amendment of the judgment in question' (paragraph 33).

In assessing the damage which a party may suffer as a result of the enforcement of the judgment, the court with which the appeal is lodged must naturally take into account the chance which, in the abstract, always exists, that the judgment under appeal may be wholly or partially revised on further appeal. It must draw up a balance between this chance and the extent and possibly irreversible nature of the damage which enforcement may inflict on the debtor. So, in drawing up this balance, may the competent court also take account of facts and arguments which the foreign court has or might have already considered in its judgment so that it can assess specifically the chance of revision on appeal, or can it take into account only arguments and facts which were not and could not be known to the foreign court?

18. For an answer to this question it must be stressed in the first place that the first paragraph of Article 31 is based on the principle that judgments which are enforceable in the State in which the judgment was given, even though they have not the force of *res judicata*, are also enforceable in the State in which enforcement is sought. This means, as the Commission stated at the hearing, that the rules applicable between Contracting States must be as similar as possible to the rules applying within their national territory with regard to a judicial decision which has been declared enforceable.

A stay of proceedings on the appeal and the resulting prohibition of measures other than protective measures (like a requirement to provide security, though to a lesser extent) represent in some degree a derogation from this principle. It follows that the powers conferred for this purpose must be applied sparingly or with reservations. This is itself an indication that only facts and arguments which the foreign court did not and could not know may be taken into account.

19. That this is indeed so follows above all, however, (as was also observed by the Arrondissementsrechtbank), from the rule laid down in the third paragraph of Article 34 according to which the foreign judgment may 'under no circumstances ... be reviewed as to its substance' by the courts of the State in which enforcement is sought. If the court with which the appeal is lodged, in its decision regarding a stay of proceedings (or a requirement to provide security), could take into account arguments and facts already known to the foreign court, there would be a real risk of its proceeding to review the substance of the foreign judgment and in particular of the declaration of the provisional enforceability of that judgment, a declaration made *inter alia* on the strength of the conviction arrived at by the foreign court regarding the substance of the case.

I think that to avoid that risk the court with which the appeal is lodged, weighing up the chances of success of the appeal brought against the foreign judgment on the one hand against the damage to the debtor in, the event of complete enforcement (perhaps not protected by security) on the other, can only be guided by considerations which the foreign court could not take into account.

These are, in the first place, the lodging of an appeal, the manifest inadmissibility of the appeal lodged abroad (but not the fact that it is manifestly unfounded) or the length of time which the procedure in such an appeal might be expected to take and, in the second place, the nature, the extent and the reversibility or otherwise of the damage suffered by the other party in the event of complete enforcement or, on the other hand, the insufficiency of the protective measures for the party applying for enforcement if the proceedings are stayed. The provisional estimate accepted by the Arrondissementsrechtbank of the compensation due to Van Dalfsen in respect of capital expenditure (see paragraph 7) may in my view be regarded as belonging to the category of considerations which the court with which the appeal is lodged may take into account, in view of the fact that this is a factor affecting the extent of the damage with which the court from whose judgment the appeal is lodged was not acquainted and which is of such a kind as to influence the balance to be drawn up of the interests involved in the enforcement of the judgment.

20. A special problem arises with regard to the facts and arguments of which the foreign court was unaware at the time of its judgment but which were known to the appellant, who did not, however, bring them before the foreign court. My view is that the court with which the appeal is lodged cannot take these facts and arguments into account either. As the Commission observes, rightly I think, only in this way is it possible to avoid the enforcement of a judgment given abroad and declared enforceable there from being obstructed by an omission by the appellant and the effectiveness of Article 31 of the Brussels Convention being thus diminished.

The Court has not yet ruled on this problem, but reference may be made, in support of the opinion expressed here, to the judgment in Case 145/86 *Hoffmann* v *Krieg* in which the Court ruled: 'Article 36 of the Convention must be interpreted as meaning that a party who has not appealed against the enforcement order referred to in that provision is thereafter precluded, at the stage of the execution of the judgment, from relying on a valid ground which he could have pleaded in such an appeal against the enforcement order, [...].'

From this it appears that the omission by a party to lodge an appeal, whatever the cause may be, deprives that party of the opportunity to avail himself subsequently of a further ground which would have supported that appeal. By analogy it should in my view be stated in this case that a party who has neglected to put facts and arguments before the foreign court can no longer put them before the court deciding as to a stay of proceedings on the appeal (or as to the provision of security).

21. Having regard to the foregoing considerations, I propose that the questions submitted should he answered as follows:

'1. A Judgment given under Article 38 of the Brussels Convention by the court with which the appeal is lodged cannot be regarded as a "judgment given on the appeal" within the meaning of the second paragraph of Article 37 of that Convention and accordingly cannot be the subject of an appeal in cassation.

2. When a judgment given under Article 38 of the Brussels Convention and a 'judgment given on the appeal" are contained in a single judgment, an appeal in cassation against that judgment will lie only in so far as the second judgment is concerned.

3. The first paragraph of Article 38 of the Brussels Convention must be interpreted as meaning that the court with which the appeal is lodged, in its judgment regarding a stay of the proceedings, may take account only of considerations other than those taken into account by the foreign court or those which it could have taken into account if the appellant had not failed to put them forward.'

Case C-423/93 - 11 August 1995

Société d'Informatique Service Réalisation Organisation (SISRO)
v
Ampersand Software BV

Articles 36, 37 and 38 - Enforcement - Judgment given on an appeal against authorization of enforcement - Appeal on a point of law - Stay of proceedings.

Summary

Article 37(2) and the first paragraph of Article 38 of the Convention of 27 September 1968 on Jurisdiction and the Enforcement of Judgments in Civil and Commercial Matters, as amended by the Convention of 9 October 1978 on the Accession of the Kingdom of Denmark, Ireland and the United Kingdom of Great Britain and Northern Ireland, are to be interpreted as meaning that a decision by which a court of a Contracting State, seised of an appeal against authorisation to enforce an enforceable judgment of a court in another Contracting State, refuses a stay or lifts a stay previously ordered does not constitute a 'judgment given on the appeal' within the meaning of the said Article 37(2) and therefore cannot be contested by an appeal in cassation or similar form of appeal limited to the examination of points of law only. Moreover, the court seised of such an appeal on a point of law under Article 37(2) of the Convention does not have jurisdiction to impose or reimpose such a stay.

JUDGMENT OF THE COURT

Shockweiler, President of the Chamber, Mancini, Kakouris, Murray and Hirsch, Judges

1. By order of 14 July 1993, received at the Court Registry on 3 November 1993, the Court of Appeal referred to the Court for a preliminary ruling under the Protocol of 3 June 1971 on the interpretation by the Court of Justice of the Convention of 27 September 1968 on Jurisdiction and the Enforcement of Judgments in Civil and Commercial Matters (OJ 1978 L 304, p. 36), as amended by the Convention of 9 October 1978 on the Accession of the Kingdom of Denmark, Ireland and the United Kingdom of Great Britain and Northern Ireland (OJ 1978 L 304, p. 1 and - as amended - p. 77) (hereinafter 'the Convention'), three questions on the interpretation of Article 37(2) and the first paragraph of Article 38 of the Convention.

2. Those questions arose in proceedings between Société d'Informatique Service Réalisation Organisation ('SISRO'), governed by French law and established in France, and Ampersand Software BV ('Ampersand'), a company incorporated under Netherlands law and established in the Netherlands.

3. It appears from the case-file that on 8 April 1987 SISRO obtained from the Tribunal de Grande Instance, Paris, a provisionally enforceable judgment against Ampersand for damages for infringement of its copyright in a computer program.

4. Ampersand appealed against that judgment to the Cour d'Appel, Paris, on the ground that the French courts did not have jurisdiction to hear the case and that the judgment of 8 April 1987 had been given on the basis of an expert's report which was fraudulent. The appeal is still pending, the Cour d'Appel having stayed the proceedings pending the outcome of the criminal proceedings for forgery brought following complaints lodged by several defendants in the first instance proceedings, other than Ampersand, against the expert appointed by the Tribunal de Grande Instance.

5. Ampersand twice applied to the Paris Cour d'Appel for a stay of enforcement of the judgment of 8 April 1987. The applications were dismissed, the first on procedural grounds and the second on the merits.

6. On 15 December 1987 SISRO obtained in England, where Ampersand has assets, an order for registration of the judgment in order to enforce it in England, in accordance with Article 31 of the Convention.

7. On 8 April 1988 Ampersand appealed to the High Court of Justice

against that order, arguing that it was contrary to public policy for a foreign judgment obtained by fraud to be enforced in England. Although the period of two months laid down in the second paragraph of Article 36 of the Convention for lodging such an appeal had expired, the High Court declared it admissible under national procedural rules.

8. By order of 9 October 1989, the High Court, pursuant to the first paragraph of Article 38 of the Convention, stayed Ampersand's appeal against the English order for registration pending the determination of the appeal brought in France.

9. SISRO then appealed to the Court of Appeal against that order. In view of the second decision of the Paris Cour d'Appel refusing a stay of enforcement of the French judgment of 8 April 1987, the Court of Appeal authorized SISRO to request the High Court to lift the stay it had ordered on 9 October 1989.

10. On 23 January 1992 the High Court lifted the stay on the ground that the application for a stay of enforcement of the judgment of 8 April 1987 had been dismissed on the merits in France. It also dismissed Ampersand's appeal against the order for registration of that judgment in England, on the ground that Ampersand had remedies available in France to establish that it had been obtained by fraud and that its enforcement in England was therefore not contrary to public policy.

11. Ampersand thereupon appealed to the Court of Appeal against those two decisions.

12. The Court of Appeal held that the High Court's decision to dismiss the appeal against the order for registration of the French judgment in England could not be criticized, since no ground under Articles 27 and 28 of the Convention for refusing registration under Article 34 could be relied on.

13. Insofar as concerned the lifting of the stay of proceedings, on the other hand, the Court of Appeal examined the question of its jurisdiction and considered whether, and to what extent, the court of the State in which enforcement is sought must, when assessing whether a stay of proceedings is appropriate, take into account the outcome in the State of origin of an application for a stay of enforcement of the judgment in question and the reasons for the decision thereon.

14. The Court of Appeal was unsure how the Convention should be interpreted in that respect and referred the following three questions to the Court for a preliminary ruling:

'1. Is an appellant in the United Kingdom who has lodged an appeal under Article 36 of the 1968 Convention on Jurisdiction and the Enforcement of Judgments in Civil and Commercial Matters entitled to seek the relief provided by Article 38, if he is unable to advance successfully one of the reasons specified in Articles 27 and 28 for refusal of an application for registration for enforcement of a judgment given in another Contracting State, and, if so, what are the "proceedings" in respect of which a stay may be ordered?

2. Is the fact that there has been a refusal of a stay on the enforcement of a judgment in the State where the judgment was given (i) relevant to and/or (ii) decisive of the way in which the power to stay registration proceedings provided for by Article 38 of the Convention should be exercised?

3. If one of the courts referred to in the first paragraph of Article 37 of the Convention (a) refuses to grant a stay, or (b) removes a stay imposed under Article 36 of the Convention, does the court to which an *appeal on a point of law* is made under the second paragraph of Article 37 have the power to impose or reimpose such a stay?'

15. It must be observed to begin with that since the appeal against the registration order was lodged after the period of two months laid down in the second paragraph of Article 36 of the Convention had expired (see paragraph 7 above), the Court is answering the questions referred to it without prejudice to the issue whether the court with which the appeal was lodged could nevertheless declare it admissible pursuant to national procedural rules.

16. It should also be noted that Articles 36, 37 and 38 of the Convention, referred to in the national court's questions, form part of Section 2 of Title III of the Convention, which deals with the enforcement of judgments which are enforceable in the Contracting State in which they have been given.

17. Under Article 31 of the Convention, such judgments are to be enforced in another Contracting State after having been declared enforceable there or, in the United Kingdom, registered for enforcement, on application by any interested party, by the court with jurisdiction specified in Article 32 of the Convention and in accordance with the rules in Article 33 et seq. of the Convention. In England and Wales, the

application is made to the High Court, except in the case of a maintenance judgment.

18. Article 34 of the Convention provides that the party against whom enforcement is sought cannot submit observations at this stage. Moreover, the application for enforcement can be refused only for one of the reasons set out in Articles 27 and 28 of the Convention; under no circumstances may the foreign judgment be reviewed as to its substance.

19. If enforcement has been authorized, the party against whom enforcement is sought may, under Article 36 of the Convention, appeal against that decision within one month of service thereof. The period is two months if the party is domiciled in a Contracting State other than that in which the decision authorizing enforcement was given. No extension of time may be granted on account of distance.

20. Under Article 37(1) of the Convention, in England and Wales, the appeal is to be lodged, in accordance with the rules governing procedure in contentious matters, with the High Court, except in the case of a maintenance judgment. Article 39 provides that during the time allowed for an appeal and until any appeal is determined, the only measures which may be taken are protective measures against the property of the person against whom enforcement is sought.

21. Under Article 37(2) of the Convention, the judgment given on the appeal may be contested only by an appeal in cassation or similar form of appeal. In the case of the United Kingdom, Article 37(2) specifies that the judgment can be contested only 'by a single further appeal on a point of law'. Pursuant to the Civil Jurisdiction and Judgments Act 1982, whose object is to bring the Convention into force in the United Kingdom, the court with jurisdiction for England is the Court of Appeal.

22. Under Article 38 of the Convention, 'The court with which the appeal under Article 37(1) is lodged may, on the application of the appellant, stay the proceedings if an ordinary appeal has been lodged against the judgment in the State of origin or if the time for such an appeal has not yet expired; in the latter case, the court may specify the time within which such an appeal is to be lodged. ... The court may also make enforcement conditional on the provision of such security as it shall determine.'

23. As regards the particular circumstances in which the present

reference was made, it should be noted that an 'appeal on a point of law' has been lodged with the Court of Appeal, in accordance with Article 37(2) of the Convention, against the High Court's decision on the appeal brought under Article 36 of the Convention against the registration for enforcement in England of an enforceable judgment given in another Contracting State.

24. In that appeal the Court of Appeal is asked by the party against whom enforcement is sought in England to rule both on the lawfulness of the High Court's dismissal of the appeal against the order for registration and on whether the High Court was right to lift the stay of proceedings previously ordered.

25. The Court of Appeal's uncertainty as to the interpretation of the Convention extends, however, only to the stay of proceedings referred to in the first paragraph of Article 38. It thus asks the Court of Justice whether the court with which an appeal in cassation or similar appeal on a point of law is lodged under Article 37(2) has power to impose or reimpose a stay under the first paragraph of Article 38 (Question 3). If so, it requests the Court to specify the extent and conditions of exercise of the power to grant or refuse such a stay (Questions 1 and 2).

26. In those circumstances, Question 3 should be examined first.

Question 3

27. By this question the national court seeks essentially to know whether Article 37(2) and the first paragraph of Article 38 of the Convention are to be interpreted as meaning, firstly, that a decision by which a court of a Contracting State, seised of an appeal against authorization to enforce an enforceable judgment given in another Contracting State, refuses a stay or lifts a stay previously ordered can be contested by an appeal in cassation or similar form of appeal limited to the examination of points of law only and, secondly, that the court seised of such an appeal on a point of law under Article 37(2) of the Convention has jurisdiction to impose or reimpose such a stay of proceedings.

28. In answering that question, it must first be noted that the experts' reports written when the Convention was drawn up and when it was amended emphasized the need for Article 37(2) of the Convention to be interpreted strictly: 'An excessive number of avenues of appeal might be used by the losing party purely as delaying tactics, and this would

constitute an obstacle to the free movement of judgments which is the object of the Convention' (Jenard Report, OJ 1979 C59, p. 52). The Convention 'limit[s] the number of appeals, in the interests of rapid enforcement, to a single appeal which may involve a full review of the facts and a second one limited to points of law' (Schlosser Report, OJ 1979 C59, p. 133). 'Only the court seised of the appeal [the first appeal under Articles 36 and 37(1) of the Convention] has the power to stay the proceedings' (Jenard Report, p. 52).

29. Moreover, the Court has on several occasions favoured a restrictive interpretation of the phrase 'judgment given on the appeal' in Article 37(2) of the Convention.

30. In Case 258/83 *Brennero* v *Wendel* [1984] ECR 3971, paragraph 15, it held that under the general scheme of the Convention and in the light of one of its principal objectives, namely to simplify procedures in the State in which enforcement is sought, that provision cannot be extended so as to enable an appeal in cassation to be lodged against a judgment other than that given on the appeal, such as a preliminary or interlocutory order requiring preliminary inquiries to be made.

31. Similarly, in Case C-183/90 *van Dalfsen* v *van Loon* [1991] ECR I-4743, paragraph 21, the Court held that since the object of the Convention is to facilitate the free movement of judgments by establishing a simple and rapid procedure in the Contracting State in which the enforcement of a foreign judgment is sought, the expression 'judgment given on the appeal' in Article 37(2) of the Convention is to be understood as denoting only judgments deciding on the substance of the appeal lodged against an order for the enforcement of a judgment given in another Contracting State, to the exclusion of judgments given under Article 38.

32. The Court accordingly held in that judgment that a decision taken under Article 38 of the Convention by which the court seised of an appeal against an order for the enforcement of a judgment given in another Contracting State has refused to stay the proceedings does not constitute a 'judgment given on the appeal' within the meaning of Article 37(2) of the Convention, and may not, therefore, be contested by an appeal in cassation or similar form of appeal.

33. That interpretation applies to any decision on a stay of proceedings taken by the court with which an appeal has been lodged against the

authorization of enforcement or registration for enforcement of a judgment given in another Contracting State, including a decision to lift a stay previously ordered.

34. Both the wording of the Convention and its general scheme show that it distinguishes between the 'court with which the appeal ... is lodged' within the meaning of the first paragraph of Article 38 and the court in which 'the judgment given on the appeal' is contested within the meaning of Article 37(2), the former term relating to Articles 36 and 37(1) to the exclusion of Article 37(2).

35. Furthermore, since the effect of procedural issues is to delay the enforcement in one Contracting State of a judgment given in another Contracting State, they represent a derogation from the Convention's object of establishing a simple and rapid machinery for the enforcement of judgments which are enforceable in the State of origin, and hence the rules relating to them must be interpreted strictly.

36. For the same reasons, the court referred to in Article 37(2) of the Convention does not have jurisdiction to decide on a stay of proceedings under Article 38.

37. The United Kingdom observes, however, that that court must have jurisdiction to decide on the stay provided for in the Convention, if it possesses that power under its own procedural rules. It bases this argument on the specific features of its own legal system. In most of the original Contracting States, if a court hearing an appeal in cassation quashes the decision of an inferior court, it simply remits the case to another court for a decision on the substance; the latter court may then stay the proceedings under Article 38 of the Convention. In the United Kingdom, on the other hand, the superior court cannot remit the case, but always decides on the substance. It must therefore, in the United Kingdom's view itself be able to decide on the stay.

38. That argument cannot be accepted.

39. As the Advocate General has explained in point 37 of his Opinion, it follows from the case-law (see Joined Cases 9/77 and 10/77 *Bavaria Fluggesellschaft and Germanair* v *Eurocontrol* [1977] ECR 1517, paragraph 4, and Case 148/84 *Deutsche Genossenschaftsbank* v *Brasserie du Pêcheur* [1985] ECR 1981, paragraph 17), firstly, that the Convention established an enforcement procedure which constitutes an

autonomous and complete system independent of the legal systems of the Contracting States and, secondly, that the principle of legal certainty in the Community legal system and the objectives of the Convention in accordance with Article 220 of the EEC Treaty, which is at its origin, require a uniform application in all Contracting States of the Convention rules and the relevant case-law of the Court.

40. Moreover, the adjustments required for the accession of the United Kingdom to the Convention because of the particular features of that State's legal system were effected by the Convention of 9 October 1978.

41. In those circumstances, a court in the United Kingdom with which an appeal on a point of law has been lodged, within the meaning of Article 37(2) of the Convention, cannot have more extensive powers under Article 38 of the Convention than any other court of a Contracting State which, as a court of cassation, restricts its review to points of law without reappraising the facts of the case. Uniform application of the Convention in all the Contracting States precludes parties against whom enforcement is sought in some States from enjoying greater procedural possibilities than in other Contracting States for delaying the enforcement of an enforceable judgment given in the Contracting State of origin.

42. In view of all the foregoing, the reply to Question 3 should be that Article 37(2) and the first paragraph of Article 38 of the Convention must be interpreted as meaning that a decision by which a court of a Contracting State, seised of an appeal against authorization to enforce an enforceable judgment of a court in another Contracting State, refuses a stay or lifts a stay previously ordered cannot be contested by an appeal in cassation or similar form of appeal limited to points of law only. Moreover, the court seised of such an appeal on a point of law under Article 37(2) of the Convention does not have jurisdiction to impose or reimpose such a stay.

Questions 1 and 2

43. In view of the answer to Question 3, there is no need to rule on Questions 1 and 2 submitted by the national court.

On those grounds, the Court (Sixth Chamber), in answer to the questions referred to it by the Court of Appeal by order of 14 July 1993, hereby rules:

Article 37(2) and the first paragraph of Article 38 of the Convention of 27 September 1968 on Jurisdiction and the Enforcement of Judgments in Civil and Commercial Matters, as amended by the Convention of 9 October 1978 on the Accession of the Kingdom of Denmark, Ireland and the United Kingdom of Great Britain and Northern Ireland, are to be interpreted as meaning that a decision by which a court of a Contracting State, seised of an appeal against authorization to enforce an enforceable judgment of a court in another Contracting State, refuses a stay or lifts a stay previously ordered cannot be contested by an appeal in cassation or similar form of appeal limited to the examination of points of law only. Moreover, the court seised of such an appeal on a point of law under Article 37(2) of the Convention does not have jurisdiction to impose or reimpose such a stay.

OPINION OF MR ADVOCATE GENERAL LÉGER

1. The Court of Appeal asks the Court of Justice, pursuant to Article 3 of the Protocol of 3 June 1971, for a preliminary ruling on the interpretation of Articles 36, 37 and 38 of the Brussels Convention of 27 September 1968 on Jurisdiction and the Enforcement of Judgments in Civil and Commercial Matters as amended by the Accession Convention of 9 October 1978 (hereinafter 'the Convention'), in the context of an 'appeal on a point of law' (or an 'appeal in cassation', to use the terms of the Convention) brought by a party against whom the enforcement in England of a French judgment has been authorized.

2. When the authors of the Convention, in accordance with the objective set out in Article 220 of the EEC Treaty, established a simplified machinery for the recognition and enforcement of judgments, their first priority was to speed up procedures. The procedural complexity which has come about in the present case might cast doubt on whether such an objective has been achieved, were it not due in part to the poor application of the Convention rules by the courts concerned. I shall examine the course of the proceedings after noting the provisions of the Convention which are relevant in this case.

The enforcement procedure established by the Convention

3. The Convention sets up a unified system for determining jurisdiction (Title II), together with a simplified machinery for the recognition and enforcement of the judgments of the courts of the Contracting States (Title III) within the field covered by the Convention (Title I). Title III ('Recognition and Enforcement') seeks to ensure 'the free movement of judgments' by facilitating the recognition (Section 1) and enforcement (Section 2) of foreign judgments.

Section 2 (Articles 31 to 45) thus provides for a summary enforcement procedure with the following characteristics.

4. The first stage of the procedure is ex parte. It starts with the lodging of an application by any interested party for the enforceable judgment given in the State of origin to be declared enforceable - or, in the United Kingdom, to be 'registered for enforcement' - in the State in which recognition is sought (Article 31). The application is submitted to the court specified in Article 32, which gives its decision without being able to review the foreign judgment as to its substance (Article 34). The court can give only two kinds of decision: either to authorize enforcement or to refuse it. It can refuse enforcement only for one of the reasons set out in Articles 27 and 28 or for failure to take into account the requirements of Articles 31 (enforceability of the judgment in the State of origin), 32 and 33 (designated courts and formal rules) of the Convention. If the application is thus refused, the applicant can appeal (Article 40 et seq.).

5. If enforcement is authorized, the party against whom it is sought can oppose it by bringing an appeal (Article 36) within the prescribed time-limit. At this stage the procedure becomes inter partes. The appeal is heard by the court designated in Article 37(1). Enforcement is not possible during the time allowed for an appeal and until any appeal is determined; the only measures which may be taken by the applicant are protective measures against the property of the person against whom enforcement is sought (Article 39).

The court with which the appeal is lodged may decide:

- to refuse enforcement, on the same grounds as in the initial ex parte stage of the procedure (based on Articles 27 and 28 or Article 31); or
- to authorize enforcement, thus upholding the decision given on the application.

Two other possibilities are available to that court, under Article 38:

- to stay the proceedings (first paragraph of Article 38), subject to two cumulative conditions: the stay must have been applied for by the appellant, and an 'ordinary' appeal must have been brought against the foreign judgment in the State of origin or such an appeal must still be capable of being brought;
- to make enforcement conditional on the provision of security (third paragraph of Article 38).

6. The Convention provides, finally, for a possible third stage of the procedure (Article 37(2)). Depending on the national legal system, this is an 'appeal in cassation' (for example, in France) or an 'appeal on a point of law' (for example, in the United Kingdom). Such an appeal is, however, available only against 'the judgment given on the appeal'. While the judgment of the court hearing the appeal referred to in Article 37(1) authorizing or refusing enforcement undoubtedly constitutes such a 'judgment given on the appeal', is that also true of decisions under Article 38 relating to a stay of proceedings or the provision of security? That precisely is one of the questions raised by the national court, in proceedings whose background is as follows.

Facts and procedure of the present case

7. On 8 April 1987 SISRO, a French company established in France, obtained from the Tribunal de Grande Instance, Paris, a provisionally *enforceable judgment* against Ampersand, a Netherlands company established in the Netherlands, for damages for infringement of its copyright on certain computer programs. Ampersand then appealed against that judgment to the Cour d'Appel, Paris; the appeal is still pending, the Cour d'Appel having stayed the proceedings pending the outcome of the parallel criminal proceedings.

8. On *application* by SISRO, and in accordance with the Convention rules, the High Court of Justice on 15 December 1987 authorized 'registration' of the French judgment for enforcement in England, where Ampersand has assets.

9. Ampersand then brought an appeal against the decision on the application, relying on Article 27(1) of the Convention. That appeal, lodged on 8 April 1988, was in principle inadmissible in view of the rules on time-limits in Article 36. It was nevertheless declared admissible by the High Court of Justice.

On application by Ampersand, *the court with which the appeal was lodged stayed the proceedings* on 9 October 1989, pending the determination of the appeals brought in France, thus using its power under the first paragraph of Article 38 of the Convention.

In France, the Cour d'Appel on 11 May and 21 December 1989 dismissed successively two applications by Ampersand for a stay of enforcement of the judgment of the Tribunal de Grande Instance. The French judgment thus remains enforceable and therefore still complies with the requirements of Article 31 of the Convention.

10. On 9 May 1990 SISRO appealed to the Court of Appeal against the order of 9 October 1989 granting the stay of proceedings. In view of the latest decision of the French appellate court refusing a stay of enforcement of the 1987 judgment, the Court of Appeal authorized SISRO to apply to the High Court to lift the stay of proceedings it had ordered on 18 December 1990.

11. The High Court, to which the matter had been remitted by the Court of Appeal, gave judgment on 23 January 1992 on two points:

- it *lifted the stay of proceedings* previously ordered, considering that for reasons of 'comity' it should follow the French court's decision refusing a stay of enforcement of the 1987 judgment 'on the merits';
- it *dismissed* the appeal by Ampersand against the order of registration (that being a 'judgment given on the appeal' within the meaning of the Convention).

12. Ampersand then brought two appeals to the Court of Appeal, one against the lifting of the stay, the other against the dismissal of its appeal against the 'registration' order (note that that court, with which an '*appeal on a point of law*' has been lodged, has jurisdiction under Article 37(2) of the Convention to decide on the 'judgment given on the appeal').

13. The Court of Appeal stayed both appeals, and now refers the following three questions to the Court for a preliminary ruling:

'1. Is an appellant in the United Kingdom who has lodged an appeal under Article 36 of the 1968 Convention on Jurisdiction and the Enforcement of Judgments in Civil and Commercial Matters entitled to seek the relief provided by Article 38, if he is unable to advance successfully one of the reasons specified in Articles 27 and 28 for refusal of an application for registration for enforcement of a judgment given in another Contracting State, and, if so, what are the 'proceedings' in respect of which a stay may be ordered?

2. Is the fact that there has been a refusal of a stay on the enforcement of a judgment in the State where the judgment was given (i) relevant to and/or (ii) decisive of the way in which the power to stay registration proceedings provided for by Article 38 of the Convention should be exercised?

3. If one of the courts referred to in the first paragraph of Article 37 of the Convention (a) refuses to grant a stay, or (b) removes a stay imposed under Article 36 of the Convention, does the court to which an appeal on a point of law is made under the second paragraph of Article 37 have the power to impose or reimpose such a stay?'

Preliminary observations

14. In its written observations the Commission expressed doubts as to whether the Court of Justice has jurisdiction in this case. Although its representative withdrew those reservations at the hearing, I consider it useful to remove any ambiguity which might remain on this point.

15. The Commission was uncertain, firstly, as to the application of the Convention ratione temporis.

16. Since the United Kingdom was not one of the original parties to the Brussels Convention, only the version as amended by the 1978 Accession Convention could be applicable as between the two countries at the material time in the present case. That Convention entered into force on 1 November 1986 in France, the State of origin, and 1 January 1987 in the United Kingdom, the State in which enforcement is sought. The transitional provisions in Article 34(3) of the Accession Convention provide that the Convention is to apply to judgments given after the date of entry into force of the Convention in proceedings instituted before that date (as in the present case), if the jurisdiction of the court of the State of origin was founded upon rules which accorded with the provisions of Title II as amended or with provisions of a convention which was in force between the State of origin and the State addressed when the proceedings were instituted.

17. The question is thus whether the French court founded its jurisdiction on rules which accorded with the provisions of Title II as amended or provisions of a convention binding the two States.

18. That point was considered by the Paris Cour d'Appel in its judgment of 11 May 1989, which held that the French courts had jurisdiction on the basis both of the Berne Convention and of the Brussels Convention. It is therefore not for the Court of Justice, any more than it is for the courts of the State in which enforcement is sought, to review whether the Convention rules were applied

correctly by the courts of the State of origin, otherwise the Court would depart from the very basis of the Convention: confidence in the court of the State of origin, which is to permit recognition and easy enforcement of judgments. Moreover, the Court has already endorsed that view, when stating that 'the Court's reply to the question referred to it by the Cour d'Appel is without prejudice to the question whether the Convention is in fact applicable [in this case] in view of the terms of Article 54 of the Convention' in the *Brasserie du Pêcheur* judgment.

19. Finally, the Commission's observation that if the High Court had not disregarded the time-limits prescribed in Article 36 of the Convention, the case would not have reached the Court of Appeal and the problems raised by the questions referred would not have arisen, is indeed correct, but is not capable of calling into question the principle of the Court's jurisdiction in the present case.

20. Accordingly, I have no doubts as to the applicability of the Convention in this case or as to the jurisdiction of the Court. I shall therefore turn to consideration of the questions raised.

The answers to the questions

21. Since the questions are all essentially concerned with the interpretation of Article 38 of the Convention, in so far as it relates to a stay of proceedings, it should first be examined whether the national court, before which an 'appeal on a point of law' has been brought in accordance with Article 37(2), has jurisdiction to rule on such a stay. I shall therefore answer the third question first.

The third question

22. Article 37(2) of the Convention reads as follows: 'The judgment given on the appeal may be contested only: - in Belgium, France, Italy, Luxembourg and in the Netherlands, by an appeal in cassation, ... - in the United Kingdom, by a single further appeal on a point of law'.

23. In the light of that provision, the question before the Court is thus whether the decision to lift a stay of proceedings previously ordered, taken on the basis of Article 38 of the Convention by the court with which the appeal has been lodged, constitutes a 'judgment given on the appeal', which alone can be contested by an appeal in cassation or similar form of appeal. A negative answer appears to me to follow both from the reports on the Convention and from the Court's case-law.

24. According to the Jenard Report, the aim of the authors of the Convention was to avoid an 'excessive number of avenues of appeal... [which would] constitute an obstacle to the free movement of judgments which is the object of the Convention'. That is why it is provided that 'only the court seised of the appeal has the power to stay the proceedings ...'. It thus appears, a contrario, that neither the court to which the application is made nor the court before which an appeal in cassation or a similar appeal is brought may order a stay. The Schlosser Report is clearer still. It gives a very precise definition of the

nature of the appeal which can be brought before the court specified in Article 37(2): 'The purpose of [the rule in Article 37] is to limit the number of appeals, in the interests of rapid enforcement, to a single appeal which may involve a full review of the facts and a *second one limited to points of law*'. It also states that only 'the judgment of the court which [has] *ruled out an appeal* made by either the debtor or the creditor' can be the subject of a second appeal.

25. It thus appears that the authors of the reports favoured a strict interpretation of Articles 37(2) and 38 of the Convention. That is, moreover, how the Court interpreted those provisions in two judgments dealing with questions with a marked similarity to those in the present case.

26. In the *Brennero* case the Bundesgerichtshof, with which an appeal had been lodged in accordance with Article 37(2), was uncertain whether it had jurisdiction to hear a Rechtsbeschwerde against a decision under the last paragraph of Article 38 ordering security to be provided. The Court interpreted Article 37(2) in view of 'the general scheme of the Convention, and in the light of one of its principal objectives which is to simplify procedures in the State in which enforcement is sought' as meaning that: 'that provision cannot be extended so as to enable an appeal in cassation to be lodged against a judgment other than that given on the appeal, for instance against a preliminary or interlocutory order requiring preliminary inquiries to be made'.

27. While Advocate General Sir Gordon Slynn had already said in his Opinion that such a 'judgment given on the appeal' must be understood as 'the final decision determining the appeal', the Court still had to define that expression precisely, in order to determine whether it could cover decisions taken under Article 38. The Court addressed the point in the *Van Dalfsen* judgment, also taking the opportunity to confirm the solution reached in Brennero. The *Van Dalfsen* case exhibited such similarities to the present case that it is worth recalling.

28. A Belgian judgment had been declared enforceable in the Netherlands. Mr Van Dalfsen had thereupon appealed against that decision, pursuant to Article 36, and applied for a stay of proceedings on that appeal pending the outcome of the appeal lodged in Belgium. The Netherlands court declared the appeal unfounded, dismissed the application for a stay and ordered security to be provided. Mr Van Dalfsen brought an appeal in cassation. The court which made the reference, being the court with which the appeal was lodged under Article 37(2), then asked the Court whether it could, under Article 38, rule on such a decision *inter alia* refusing a stay.

29. The Court, once again basing itself on the Convention's essential objective of rapidity, adopted a strict interpretation of the phrase 'judgment given on the appeal' and ruled out any possibility of appealing under Article 37(2) of the Convention against decisions taken under Article 38: '... since the object of the Convention is to facilitate the free movement of judgments by establishing a simple and rapid procedure in the Contracting State in which application is made for the enforcement of a foreign judgment, the expression "judgment given on the appeal" in the second paragraph of Article 37 of the Convention must be interpreted as *denoting only judgments deciding on the*

substance of the appeal lodged against an order for the enforcement of a judgment given in another Contracting State, *to the exclusion of judgments given under Article 38 of the Convention'.*

30. The answer to the question submitted by the Court of Appeal in the present case must therefore be the same as that given to the Netherlands court in Van Dalfsen. Its wording is sufficiently general for it to be taken as a decision of principle: '... *a decision taken under Article 38 of the Convention* by which the court with which an appeal has been lodged against an order for the enforcement of a judgment given in another Contracting State has refused to stay the proceedings does not constitute a "judgment given on the appeal" within the meaning of the second paragraph of Article 37 of the Convention and may not, therefore, *be contested by an appeal in cassation or similar form of appeal*'.

31. That interpretation must be approved, especially as in the present case the party resisting enforcement of the judgment has - as can be seen from the length and complexity of the procedure - continually brought application on application, in order, one may fear, to postpone any final decision whether in the State of origin or in the State in which enforcement is sought. If that party were able once more to bring before the Court of Appeal an appeal analogous to an appeal in cassation against a decision to lift a stay of proceedings, that would entirely disregard the warning set out in the following terms in the Jenard Report: 'An excessive number of avenues of appeal might be used by the losing party purely as delaying tactics, and this would constitute an obstacle to the free movement of judgments which is the object of the Convention.'

32. For that reason I cannot accept the United Kingdom's argument based on the particular nature of its national law.

33. As justification of an affirmative answer to the third question, the United Kingdom submits that the appeal in cassation provided for in Article 37(2) for five of the original six Contracting States is a different concept from the 'single further appeal on a point of law' in the case of the United Kingdom. If a court hearing an appeal in cassation quashes the judgment of an inferior court, it always has the possibility of remitting the case to another court of the same rank with jurisdiction under Article 37(1) for it to rule on the substance. The latter court could thus again make a ruling under Article 38. That is not possible in the United Kingdom, however, where the superior court (in this case the Court of Appeal) cannot remit the case, but always rules on the substance, and must thus have an opportunity to rule on the stay.

34. Admittedly, as Professor Schlosser points out, 'the 1968 Convention implicitly proceeded from a legal background common to the original Member States of the EC' and 'by contrast the legal systems of the new Member States unmistakably contain certain special structural features'. But the 1978 Accession Convention precisely endeavoured to implement the necessary 'adjustments' for the accession of the United Kingdom. Thus it was necessary, for example, to reconsider the distinction drawn in Articles 30 and 38 between ordinary and extraordinary appeals, and the *exequatur* system, preference being given instead in that State to the system of 'registration'. Similarly, it

was stated that the Convention may require normal rules of domestic law not to be applied, as for instance the 'doctrine of the *forum conveniens*'.

35. More specifically, as the author of the Report himself admits, 'the adjustment of the second paragraph of Article 37... gave rise to difficulties'. The distinction between points of law and matters of fact familiar to continental legal systems is less clear-cut in the United Kingdom. It was therefore agreed that 'the United Kingdom will have to adapt [its] appeal system to the requirements of the 1968 Convention', in view of the fact that 'the concept of "appeal on a point of law" is the nearest equivalent as far as United Kingdom law is concerned to the "Rechtsbeschwerde" of German law and the appeal in cassation in the legal systems of the other original Member States of the Community, the common feature of which is a restriction of the grounds of appeal to an incorrect application of the law (as opposed to an incorrect assessment of the facts)'.

36. Consequently, while the concepts of 'appeal in cassation' and 'appeal on a point of law' are indeed not absolutely identical, it is for the court with which an appeal under Article 37(2) of the Convention is lodged to decide as any other national court would when hearing an appeal in cassation. More precisely, although in the legal system of England and Wales the Court of Appeal normally has to rule on the substance in its capacity as an appellate court, the function of court of cassation assigned it by the Brussels Convention is quite different, and it cannot on that basis have to rule on grounds of appeal not based directly on an incorrect application of the law, such as a stay of proceedings.

37. That is the only solution which ensures that the primacy of the Convention over domestic law is respected, a primacy the Court has justified as follows: 'The principle of legal certainty in the Community legal system and the objectives of the Brussels Convention in accordance with Article 220 of the EEC Treaty, which is at its origin, require in all Member States a uniform application of the legal concepts and legal classifications developed by the Court in the context of the Brussels Convention.'

The Court has explained that in particular Section 2 of Title III *as a whole* constitutes an autonomous system independent of the various systems of domestic law: '... the Convention established an enforcement procedure which constitutes an autonomous and complete system, including the matter of appeals'.

For that reason the United Kingdom's argument based on the specific nature of its domestic law cannot succeed.

38. I should like to make one final remark on the United Kingdom's argument. As in the case of recognition (Articles 26 to 30) and in accordance with the judgment in *Hoffmann*, the foreign judgment must have the effect and the authority it would have had in the State of origin, but cannot have more effect than local judgments of the same type. In the present case the French judgment is enforceable in the State of origin but, without there being a judgment on appeal, it is not *res judicata*. In practice, that means that the creditor SISRO can take enforcement measures in France, but *at its own risk*. If it takes such measures in France and the judgment is subsequently overturned, it will have to restore the original position. That must be the same in England. The fact that the Court of Appeal cannot decide on the lifting of a stay of proceedings therefore

does not involve the parties in any more risks in England than in France, even if the French judgment were subsequently to be quashed. On the basis of the 'registration' of the French judgment in England, SISRO can take enforcement measures, but *at its own risk*, just as in France.

39. I therefore conclude that the Court of Appeal, exercising jurisdiction under Article 37(2) of the Convention, can rule only on challenges relating to incorrect application of the law, and not on appeals against decisions refusing to stay the proceedings or lifting a stay previously ordered.

40. I now turn to the other two questions.

The first and second questions

41. Since I consider that the court designated in Article 37(2) of the Convention does not have jurisdiction to rule on a decision relating to a stay of proceedings, examination of the other two questions, which aim essentially to define the scope of the power to stay the proceedings, is purely hypothetical. I therefore make observations on this point only in the alternative, on the understanding that the following remarks are in any event applicable only to the court with jurisdiction under Article 37(1) before which the appeal is brought.

42. The first and second paragraphs of Article 38 of the Convention read as follows:

'The court with which the appeal under Article 37(1) is lodged may, on the application of the appellant, stay the proceedings if an ordinary appeal has been lodged against the judgment in the State of origin or if the time for such an appeal has not yet expired; in the latter case, the court may specify the time within which such an appeal is to be lodged.
Where the judgment was given in Ireland or the United Kingdom, any form of appeal available in the State of origin shall be treated as an ordinary appeal for the purposes of the first paragraph.'

The first question

43. By its first question the national court asks whether an appellant can seek a stay of proceedings on the appeal (Article 38) even though he is unable to rely on any of the grounds for refusal of recognition and enforcement of the foreign judgment (Articles 27 and 28).

44. I consider that the answer must be in the affirmative.

45. I have noted that the party against whom enforcement of a judgment is sought must put forward one of the grounds for refusal listed exhaustively in Articles 27 and 28, *for the court hearing the appeal to be able to rule on the substance, under Article 36*, that is, refuse enforcement of the foreign judgment in the State in which enforcement is sought. Is it then possible to draw a parallel with that situation and, as the applicant suggests, consider that the party against whom enforcement is sought must similarly put forward one of the grounds for refusal listed exhaustively in Articles 27 and 28, *for the court hearing the appeal to be able to grant a stay of proceedings, under Article 38?*

46. I think not, for at least three reasons.

47. To begin with, it would be vain to seek any textual argument to support SISRO's view. On the contrary, a reading of the Convention confirms my conclusion. Thus the text of Article 38 contains no reference to Articles 27 and 28, unlike the second paragraph of Article 34 (whose link with Article 36 I have pointed out), which provides: 'The application may be refused only for one of the reasons specified in Articles 27 and 28'. I consider that that should not be seen as an oversight on the part of the authors of the Convention, since elsewhere - as I have stated - they took care to make the power to stay the proceedings, provided for in Article 38, subject to two very precise conditions. It thus seems to me that if the authors of the Convention had wished to make the power to stay the proceedings subject to a third condition, such as the existence of a ground for refusing recognition and enforcement, they would have mentioned that in the text of Article 38. That view is confirmed by consulting the reports on the Convention and the Court's case-law, neither of which supports a presumption of such a requirement.

48. Quite apart from that textual analysis, I think that in any case Article 38 and Article 36 should be clearly differentiated. Those two articles give the court hearing the appeal two independent powers, which can be exercised at different times, and involve the consideration of completely distinct facts and questions.

The court designated in Article 37(1) has jurisdiction under Article 36 to hear an appeal against the decision given on the application authorizing enforcement. It *must* allow the appeal if one of the grounds for refusal listed in Articles 27 and 28 is present, otherwise it *must* dismiss it.

Under Article 38 that court *may* stay the appeal proceedings, but is not obliged to do so, as the Court has held: '... the court before which ... enforcement is sought is not under a duty to stay the proceedings but merely has the power to do so'. That provision, unlike the preceding one, is not in any way concerned with reaching a decision on the substance. Its purpose is different, as the Court stated: '... the specific purpose of [Article] 38 is to prevent the compulsory recognition or enforcement of judgments in other Contracting States when the possibility that they might be annulled or amended in the State in which they were given still exists'.

49. In the *Van Dalfsen* case the Court had occasion to draw a clear distinction between the two possibilities. Following the Opinion of the Advocate General, it emphasized that '... the procedure under Article 36 and that under Article 38 ... have a different object'.

The Court then stated: 'In fact the appeal procedure envisaged by Article 36 relates to the *legal question* of whether, regard being had to the reasons exhaustively specified in Articles 27 and 28 of the Convention, the enforcement order has been lawfully issued, whereas the decision relating to a stay of proceedings or the provision of security under Article 38 constitutes a *subsidiary measure* designed to settle the subsequent course of the procedure ...'.

50. Finally, I would rely on the *practical effect* of Article 38. If SISRO's view were followed and it was accepted that to obtain a stay of the appeal

proceedings one must be able to put forward one of the grounds set out in Articles 27 and 28, what purpose would Article 38 then still have? Let us suppose that a party against whom enforcement of a judgment is sought is able successfully to advance one of those grounds of refusal. He will undoubtedly rely on it for an appeal under Article 36. In that case, as I have stated, the court hearing that appeal will be obliged to refuse enforcement of the judgment in the State in which enforcement is sought. But if a decision has been given on the substance of the appeal, the question of a stay of those appeal proceedings *ipso facto* no longer arises, and there is no longer any need for Article 38.

51. For those reasons, I conclude that Article 38 of the Convention may be relied upon regardless of the absence of grounds for refusing recognition and enforcement of the foreign judgment as provided for in Articles 27 and 28 of the Convention.

The second question

52. By its second question the national court asks whether the refusal by the courts of the State of origin to order a stay of enforcement of the judgment is binding on the court of the State in which enforcement is sought when hearing an application for a stay under Article 38 of the Convention.

53. I note again that the power to stay proceedings under Article 38 is merely a *power* within the discretion of the court of the State in which enforcement is sought, so that the 'freedom of discretion [of the court hearing the application for enforcement] is implicit in the actual system of Article 38 ...'. The decision of the court of the State of origin not to order a stay of enforcement of the judgment cannot therefore by any means be *decisive* as regards the exercise of the power to stay proceedings in the State in which enforcement is sought, if that discretion is not to be called into question.

54. Is that decision of the court of the State of origin relevant?

55. The object of Article 38 is to enable the court with which the appeal is lodged to 'stay the proceedings whenever reasonable doubt arises with regard to the fate of the decision in the State in which it was given'. The exercise of that power must therefore enable the court to 'protect the judgment debtor against any loss which could result from the enforcement of a judgment which has not yet become *res judicata* and may be amended'. In exercising that power to order a stay, the court will thus in practice have occasion to take into account the chances of success of the appeal lodged in the State of origin. To do that, it seems to me that the refusal by the court of the State of origin to order a stay of enforcement of the judgment even though an appeal is still pending may constitute a factor of relevance for the court of the State in which enforcement is sought when making its assessment of the appeal's chances of success.

56. I therefore consider that a refusal to order a stay of enforcement in the State of origin is never decisive for the purposes of the power of the court of the State in which enforcement is sought to stay proceedings, but may be relevant.

57. For the above reasons, I suggest that the Court answer as follows: 'The court with which an appeal, limited to the examination of points of law

only, is lodged, pursuant to Article 37(2) of the Brussels Convention of 27 September 1968 on Jurisdiction and the Enforcement of Judgments in Civil and Commercial Matters, does not have jurisdiction to impose or reimpose a stay of proceedings which has been refused or lifted by one of the courts referred to in Article 37(1).

In the alternative,

- A person who has brought an appeal in a Contracting State under Article 36 of the Convention may apply for a stay of proceedings under Article 38, even though he is unable to rely on one of the grounds for refusing recognition and enforcement provided for in Articles 27 and 28.
- The refusal to stay the enforcement of a judgment in the State of origin, while never decisive, may be relevant for the exercise of the power to stay proceedings, provided for in Article 38 of the Convention, of the court with which the appeal is lodged in the State in which enforcement is sought.'

Case C-275/94 - 14 March 1996

Roger Van der Linden
v
Berufsgenossenschaft der Feinmechanik und Elektrotechnik

Recognition and enforcement procedure - Application for an enforcement order - Documents to be produced - Service of the judgment for which an enforcement order is sought - Production after the application has been lodged - Whether permissible - Conditions.

Summary

Article 47(1) of the Convention of 27 September 1968 on Jurisdiction and the Enforcement of Judgments in Civil and Commercial Matters, as amended by the Convention of 9 October 1978 on the Accession of the Kingdom of Denmark, Ireland and the United Kingdom of Great Britain and Northern Ireland, is to be interpreted as meaning that, where the domestic procedural rules of the State in which application is made so permit, proof of service of the judgment delivered in the State or origin may be produced after the application has been made, in particular during the course of appeal proceedings subsequently brought by the party against whom enforcement is sought, provided that that party is given a reasonable period of time in which to satisfy the judgment voluntarily and that the party seeking enforcement bears all costs unnecessarily incurred.

JUDGMENT OF THE COURT

Edward, President of the Chamber, Puissochet, Moitinho de Almeida, Gulmann and Jann, Judges

1. By order of 30 September 1994, received at the Court on 11 October 1994, the Hof van Cassatie van BelWe (Belgian Court of Cassation) referred to the Court for a preliminary ruling, under the Protocol of 3 June 1971 on the interpretation by the Court of Justice of the Convention of 27 September 1968 on Jurisdiction and the Enforcement of Judgments in Civil and Commercial Matters, two questions on the interpretation of Article 47(1) of that convention (OJ 1978 L 304, p. 17), as amended by the Convention of 9 October 1978 on the accession of the Kingdom of Denmark, Ireland and the United Kingdom of Great Britain and Northern Ireland (OJ 1978 L 304, p. 1 and - in its amended form - p. 77, hereinafter 'the Convention').

2. Those questions were raised in proceedings between Mr Van der Linden, a Belgian national, at the material time engaged in the resale of motor vehicles at Blankenberge (Belgium), and the Berufsgenossenschaft der Feinmechanik und Elektrotechnik, a German insurance company (hereinafter 'the insurer'). Those proceedings concern the enforcement in Belgium of two judgments given in default on 25 May and 1 September 1976 by the Landgericht (Regional Court) Bonn, ordering Mr Van der Linden to pay the insurer, first, the sum of DM 45 428.25 together with interest at the rate of 4% from 12 March 1976 and, second, the sum of DM 2 190.75 together with interest at the rate of 4% from 20 August 1976.

3. The first of those sums represents the medical expenses incurred as a result of injuries caused to Mr Rudolf Lempges, a policy-holder with the insurer, in a collision which occurred in Germany on 5 February 1973 between his vehicle and that of Mr Van der Linden, which was being driven by a third person. The second sum represents the legal costs incurred in those proceedings.

4. On 2 February 1982, upon application by the insurer, those judgments were rendered enforceable in Belgium by decision of the Rechtbank van Eerste Aanleg (Court of First Instance), Bruges (hereinafter 'the Rechtbank').

5. Mr Van der Linden lodged an appeal against that decision. He complained, in particular, that the Rechtbank had allowed the application for enforcement despite the fact that, contrary to the requirements of Article 47(1) of the Convention, no document had been produced to show that the default judgments had been served and were enforceable.

6. By judgment of 30 June 1993 the Rechtbank declared Mr Van der Linden's appeal admissible but unfounded. It found that, although Mr Van der Linden had probably been entitled to plead that no proof of service of the default judgments of 25 May and 1 September 1976 had been produced when the *ex parte* application was made, the insurer had proceeded on 6 January 1987 (that is to say, during the course of the appeal proceedings) to reserve the judgments in accordance with the rules of Belgian domestic law. According to the Rechtbank, Article 47(1) of the Convention had thus been complied with, so that the judgment challenged should be upheld, even though it had been given on the basis of incomplete documentation.

7. Mr Van der Linden appealed against that decision to the Hof van Cassatie van Belgie. He contended that, as a matter of law, the Rechtbank could not decide that the insurer could still regularize the procedure by effecting service during the course of the appeal proceedings, since it follows from Articles 46(1) and 47(I) of the Convention that a copy of the judgment and the record of service must be lodged at the same time as the application for enforcement of the judgment, and that service of the judgment must be effected before the application for enforcement is lodged.

8. The Hof van Cassatie van Belgïe decided to stay proceedings and to refer the following questions to the Court for a preliminary ruling:

'1. Must Article 47(1) of the Convention of 27 September 1968 between the Member States of the European Economic Community on Jurisdiction and the Enforcement of Judgments in Civil and Commercial Matters be interpreted as meaning that the court before which enforcement is sought may order the enforcement of a judgment given in another State only if, either together with the application or before a decision is given on the application, the document referred to in Article 47(1) and in particular proof of service are also produced?

2. If the answer to Question 1 is in the negative must that Article be interpreted as meaning that, notwithstanding provisions of national law, the requirement to produce the document is not satisfied where the decision is served only after the application was made and the document evidencing service was drawn up and produced only after a decision was given by the court before which enforcement is sought on the application and the party against whom enforcement is sought has lodged an appeal?'

9. By those questions, the national court is essentially asking whether Article 47(1) of the Convention is to be interpreted as meaning that proof

of service of the judgment of which enforcement is sought can be produced after the application has been lodged, in particular during the course of appeal proceedings subsequently brought by the party against whom that application is made.

10. The third paragraph of Article 33 of the Convention reads: 'The documents referred to in Articles 46 and 47 shall be attached to the application', whereas Article 47(1) provides: 'A party applying for enforcement shall also produce: (1) documents which establish that, according to the law of the State of origin, the judgment is enforceable and has been served ...'.

11. Article 48 of the Convention further provides: 'If the documents specified in point 2 of Articles 46 and 47 are not produced, the court may specify a time for their production, accept equivalent documents or, if it considers that ii has sufficient information before it, dispense with their production.

12. Mr Van der Linden and the Austrian Government maintain that those provisions clearly show that proof of service of the judgment must be produced, at the latest, when the application is lodged. According to Mr Van der Linden, such an interpretation is confirmed by Article 48, since that article makes no provision for the setting of a time-limit, the acceptance of equivalent documents or the exemption of the applicant from his obligation to produce the documents specified in Article 47(1), whereas it expressly provides for that possibility in the case of the documents referred to in Articles 46(2) and 47(2).

13. That view cannot be accepted.

14. Although, according to the third paragraph of Article 33, the documents referred to in Articles 46 and 47 must be attached to the application, that does not mean that the domestic procedural rules, to which the first paragraph of Article 33 refers as regards determination of the time when the application is to be made and of the form which it is to take, may not provide for the procedure to be regularized by production of proof of service after the application has been lodged, provided that the objective pursued by the Convention in the third paragraph of Article 33 and Article 47(1) is respected.

15. In that regard, the experts' report on the Convention (OJ 1979 C 59, p. 1, at p. 55) states that the purpose of serving the judgment on the

defendant is to inform him of the judgment given against him and to give him the opportunity to satisfy it voluntarily before enforcement can be applied for.

16. Domestic rules of procedure allowing the court to which application is made' to take into consideration, in *ex parte* proceedings, proof that the judgment has been served are not incompatible with such an objective, provided that the party against whom enforcement is sought, who is not represented at this stage of proceedings, is given a reasonable period of time in which to satisfy the judgment voluntarily and that the party seeking enforcement bears all costs unnecessarily incurred.

17. Contrary to the arguments advanced by Mr Van der Linden, that interpretation of the Convention is not invalidated by Article 48 of the Convention. Whilst it is true that that article, which allows the court to specify a time for the production of certain documents, does not relate to proof of service as provided for in Article 47(1), it also provides that the court may accept equivalent documents. However, that last possibility is excluded as regards proof of service of the judgment of which enforcement is sought. As the Advocate General observes in point 18 of his Opinion, Article 48 is merely a special provision whose scope is limited to the sphere which it governs, and which cannot therefore attach any other limitations to the general principle that domestic procedural rules which respect the essential requirements of the Convention will normally be applicable.

18. It should be added that this reasoning also applies in relation to the possibility of regularizing the application by producing proof of service in the course of appeal proceedings subsequently brought by the party against whom execution was sought. At that stage, the enforcement procedure is *inter partes*, thereby affording an additional safeguard for the party against whom enforcement is sought.

19. In those circumstances, the reply to the national court must be that Article 47(1) of the Convention is to be interpreted as meaning that, where the domestic procedural rules so permit, proof of service of the judgment may be produced after the application has been made, in particular during the course of appeal proceedings subsequently brought by the party against whom enforcement is sought, provided that that party is given a reasonable period of time in which to satisfy the judgment voluntarily and that the party seeking enforcement bears all costs unnecessarily incurred.

On those grounds, the Court, in answer to the questions referred to it by the Hof van Cassatie van Belgïe by order of September 1994, hereby rules:

Article 47(1) of the Convention of 27 September 1968 on Jurisdiction and the Enforcement of Judgments in Civil and Commercial Matters, as amended by the Convention of 9 October 1978 on the Accession of the Kingdom of Denmark, Ireland and the United Kingdom of Great Britain and Northern Ireland, is to be interpreted as meaning that, where the domestic procedural rules so permit, proof of service of the judgment may be produced after the application has been made, in particular during the course of appeal proceedings subsequently brought by the party against whom enforcement is sought, provided that that party is given a reasonable period of time in which to satisfy the judgment voluntarily and that the party seeking enforcement bears all costs unnecessarily incurred.

OPINION OF ADVOCATE GENERAL FENNELLY

Introduction

1. This case involves the interpretation of the Brussels Convention on Jurisdiction and Enforcement of Judgments in Civil and Commercial Matters of 27 September 1968 (hereinafter 'the Convention'). Where a judgment has not been served on its addressee, and an applicant nonetheless wins an *ex parte* order for its enforcement in another Contracting State, can the applicant be permitted to effect and to prove service during appeal proceedings instigated by the addressee on that basis?

Factual and legal context

2. An insurance providet, the Berufsgenossensehaft der Feinmechanik und Elektrotechnik, the respondent in the main proceedings (hereinafter 'the respondent'), paid the medical expenses of a person injured in 1973 in a road accident in Germany by a car owned by Roger Van Der linden, the appellant in the main proceedings (hereinafter 'the appellant'), who lives in Belgium. It obtained a judgment in a German court in 1976 to recoup these costs from the appellant, and later that year a further judgment requiring him to pay its legal costs. Both these judgments were obtained by default.

3. The respondent applied *ex parte* to the Rechtbank van Eerste Aanleg, the court specified in Article 32 of the Convention, at Bruges, for enforcement of the first German judgment in July 1980 and was permitted in October 1980 to

amend its application in a number of respects, including its extension to the second German judgment on costs. The respondent was granted an enforcement order in respect of both judgments in February 1982. The appellant appealed against this decision in May 1982, pursuant to Article 37 of the Convention, to the Rechtbank van Eerste Aanleg at Bruges, relying on the fact that no proof was supplied with the application for enforcement that he had been served with the German judgments. It appears that the court, on examining the appeal, specified a time-limit for the produc tion of proof of service of the judgment. The appeal was rejected in June 1993, on the ground that the respondent had served the German judgments on the appellant in accordance with Belgian law in January 1987, and that the incompleteness of the original application could no longer prevent the confirmation of the enforcement order. The appellant appealed against this decision in February 1994 to the Hof van Cassatie, pursuant to Article 37, second indent, of the Convention. He submitted that the enforcement order could not, at the stage of an appeal pursuant to Article 37 of the Convention, be cured of defects arising from the respondent's failure to produce essential proofs with its original application. An extraordinary length of time has passed since this case was commenced, but this has not given rise to any direct question from the national court.

4. Title III, Section 2 of the Convention governs enforcement in one Contracting State of judgments given in another Article 32 of the Convention sets out the courts in each of the Contracting States to which an application for enforcement must be made. Article 34 provides that an initial decision be taken on enforcement, at which stage the party against whom enforcement is sought shall not be entitled to make any submissions on the application. Article 37 sets out the avenues of appeal in the various Contracting States against a decision authorizing enforcement. As has been indicated, the appeal to set aside the *ex parte* order is not taken to a higher court in all Contracting States.

5. Article 33 of the Convention states, in its first and third paragraphs: 'The procedure for making the application [for enforcement] shall be governed by the law of the State in which enforcement is sought .... .

The documents referred to in Articles 46 and 47 shall be attached to the application'.

6. Articles 46 and 47 of the Convention list certain documents which must be produced by a party applying for enforcement of a judgment. Article 46 states: 'A party seeking recognition or applying for enforcement of a judgment shall produce:

1. a copy of the judgment which satisfies the conditions necessary to establish its authenticity;

2. in the case of a judgment given in default, the original or a certified true copy of the document which establishes that the party in default was served with the document instituting the proceedings or with an equivalent document.'

Article 47 of the Convention states: 'A party applying for enforcement shall also produce:

1. documents which establish that, according to the law of the State in which it has been given, the judgment is enforceable and has been served;

2. where appropriate, a document showing that the applicant is in receipt of legal aid in the State in which judgment was given.'

7. The first paragraph of Article 48 of the Convention provides for a degree of discretion in the application of certain aspects of these requirements. It states: 'If the documents specified in Articles 46(2) and 47(2) are not produced, the court may specify a time for their production, accept equivalent documents or, if it considers that it has sufficient information before it, dispense with their production.'

The present case does not come within that dispensing power. It concerns a failure to produce the proof of service of the judgment required by Article 47(1) of the Convention.

8. The Hof van Cassatie is of the view that a ruling on the interpretation of the Convention is necessary for it to give judgment in the appeal before it, and has referred the following questions to the Court, pursuant to Articles 1 to 3 of the Protocol of 3 June 1971 on the interpretation of the Convention (hereinafter 'the Protocol'):

'1. Must Article 47(1) of the Convention of 27 September 1968 between the Member States of the European Economic Community on Jurisdiction and the Enforcement of Judgments in Civil and Commercial Matters, be interpreted as meaning that the court before which enforcement is sought may order the enforcement of a judgment given in another State only if, either together with the application or before a decision is given on the application, the document referred to in Article 47(1) and in particular proof of service are also produced?

2. If the answer to Question 1 is in the negative ~ must that article be interpreted as meaning that, notwithstanding provisions of national law, the requirement to produce the document is not satisfied where the decision is served only after the application was made and the document evidencing service was drawn up and produced only after a decision was given by the court before which enforcement is sought on the application and the party against whom enforcement is sought has lodged an appeal?'

Written observations

9. Written observations were submitted by the parties to the proceedings in the Hof van Cassatie, by the German and Austrian Governments and by the Commission. Pursuant to Article 5 of the Protocol, and to Article 44a of its Rules of Procedure, the Court decided, with the consent of the parties, to dispense with an oral hearing.

10. The appellant argues for an affirmative response to the first question (requiring that proof of service should be produced with an application for enforcement), and an affirmative response to the second. Because the judgment must be enforceable in the State of origin before it can be given effect in any other State, and the appellant submits that the proof of enforceability must appear in the same document as the proof of service, he argues that this document cannot be introduced for the first time on appeal. While the Convention is designed to minimize formalities, the power to dispense with

certain documentary proofs found in Article 48 is implicitly excluded in respect of documents not mentioned. The appellant relies upon the Jenard Report on the Convention to suggest that a national court may refuse to entertain an application which is not accompanied by the document in question. The Report gives as the reason for the requirement of service the Interest in promoting voluntary' compliance.' The appellant alleges that he was denied this opportunity by the tardy service of the judgment, after he had appealed against the enforcement order against him, but does not indicate that he was in any way prejudiced as a result.

11. The respondent relies on the objective of the Convention to reduce formalism and to facilitate 'free movement of judgments, and argues that an application for enforcement is not inadmissible merely because of the omission of accompanying documents. It cites the Jenard Report's statement that 'enforcement should not be refused, but the court may Stay the proceedings and allow the applicant time to produce the documents'. Article 48 of the Convention provides only a further degree of flexibility, by allowing the national court to accept equivalent documents to those specified in Articles 46(2) and 47(2), or to dispense with them altogether. Service of a judgment should allow the addressee time voluntarily to comply, so that enforcement proceedings will not be necessary. There has been plenty of time for this, even though service was effected only during the appeal proceedings. The appellant's argument amounts simply to obstruction.

12. The German Government argues that a positive response should be given to the first question (requiring proof of service to he introduced at the latest by the moment of decision at first instance), and a negative response to the second. Although an enforcement order should not be granted at the *ex parte* stage without securing proof of service of the judgment at issue, the objectives of the Convention permit correction even after this stage, if national law so provides. The Convention should not be so construed as to make enforcement more difficult; Article 48 should not be read as excluding flexibility on points other than those it governs. If the documents specified in Article 47(l) of the Convention cannot be produced even after the applicant is invited to do so, the application should then be rejected. At the appeal stage, the applicant should not be prejudiced by the failure of the court at the *ex parte* stage to invite such production. Rejection of the possibility of production at the appeal stage would be excessively formalist, as the applicant could simply introduce a new application.

13. The Austrian Government also argues for an affirmative response to the first question (requiring production of proof of service with the original application), but says that the second question does not require a response. It submits that a literal interpretation of Article 47(i) of the Convention requires that proof of service accompany the application when it is deposited. Nothing suggests that this requirement should be distinguished from that of proof of enforceability, which must be produced at the outset.

14. The Commission argues for an affirmative response to the first question (requiring proof of service at the latest by the moment of decision at

first instance), but says that there should be a negative response to the second. It invokes the twin objectives of the Convention, as identified by the Court: a flexible and rapid enforcement procedure facilitating free movement of judgments, and the importance of the rights of the defence. The interests of the defence are substantially protected during the initial period, before judgment is reached, in order that the obstacles to the later enforcement phase can be reduced. Furthermore, the Convention does not establish a complete enforcement system; its minimum requirements are supplemented, for example, by national procedural rules. Article 48 of the Convention should not be deemed, merely by implication, to restrict the application of permissive national rules to evidentiary requirements outside the scope of that article, so long as the objectives of the Convention are respected. In the instant case, both flexibility and the interests of the defence are secured if the addressee of a judgment has an opportunity voluntarily to comply with it. Where the judge at the *ex parte* stage gives a period for production of documents omitted from the original application for enforcement, these objectives are fully secured so long as a reasonable period is also specified for voluntary compliance after service. As a new application for enforcement can be introduced in the event of rejection, it is better to allow the application to be amended than to eause the entire procedure to be restarted.

Analysis

15. I am in broad agreement with the arguments and suggested answers put forward by the respondent, the German Government and the Commission in respect of the Hof van Cassatie's two questions. In my opinion, proof of service should be introduced at the latest by the seised of the *ex parte* enforcement proceedings. None the less, national rules may, in certain circumstances, permit rectification of an omission in this regard after that point. I will address initially the position as regards the *ex parte* Stage of the enforcement procedure, which is the subject-matter (of the Hof van Cassatie's first question. I will then discuss the appropriate response to its second question, on the possibility of adding to the application at the appeal or *inter partes* stage.

(i) *The* ex parte *stage*

16. It is clear, I think, that proof of service of the judgment in question should ordinarily accompany the application for its enforcement. As well as being consistent with the wording of the third indent of Article 33 of the Convention, this is obviously in the interest of the party seeking enforcement, as it will minimize delay in securing the order sought. It will also ensure that the addressee of the judgment will have had an opportunity to satisfy the judgment voluntarily; if he does not do so, he must anticipate an application for enforcement. However, a failure, for whatever reason, to comply at this stage with the requirement of service, need not be fatal for the application.

17. Article 33 of the Convention requires that the documents referred to in

Articles 46 and 47 be attached to the application. This is a practical direction and will assist the court in its task of checking the proofs required for an order for enforcement. However, the first paragraph of Article 33 of the Convention states that the application procedure is governed by the law of the State in which enforcement is sought. If the law of that State permits attachment of documents to the application during the proceedings, in circumstances which do not undermine other requirements of the Convention, this cannot be said to be excluded by the text of Article 33. Indeed, I would go further and state that the obligation in Article 33 to attach documents to the originating application is, to call in aid a common-law concept, merely directory and not mandatory, and does not affect the validity of the application.

18. The real issue is whether and when the proof in question must be produced. The latest point during the *ex parte* procedure at which the various documents specified in Articles 46 and 47 of the Convention must be produced may vary with the content and function of those documents. This point is governed in part, of course, by Article 48, which gives the court three options in the event of failure to produce any of the documents referred to in Articles 46(2) and 47(2) of the Convention: it can set a deadline for their production, it can accept equivalent documents, or, where it feels it has sufficient information, it can dispense with them entirely. However, this provision does not, in my view, define exhaustively the procedural discretion of the national court, in particular in respect of documents not governed by it, such as that proving service of the judgment. It is evident that the Convention does not establish a complete system of enforcement. This is clear from the provision for what might nowadays be called procedural subsidarity in Article 33. Article 48 should be seen as qualifying that principle of subsidiarity, by setting a minimum degree of flexibility, at the discretion of the court, which must be permitted by the applicable national procedural rules. As a special provision, Article 48 cannot be read as limiting in any other way the general principle that national procedural rules, whether flexible or rigid, which respect the essential requirements of the Convention, apply to the enforcement process.

19. I am not convinced by the arguments either that proof of enforceability and of service should appear in the same document, or that the requirements as to the point of production of the one should determine those of the other. With regard to the first point, the text of the Convention indicates the possibility of multiple documents in all but one language version. Even if the text were in the singular, requiring both proofs to be contained in a single document would be excessively formalist, and without function under the scheme of the Convention. In respect of the second point, the function of a document in the enforcement proceedings determines the latest point at which it must be produced. While I do not need to express an opinion on the possibility of rectifying an omission of the proof that a judgment is enforceable at the time of application, or of continuing with enforcement proceedings, after any appropriate period of delay for service and compliance, in respect of a judgment which became enforceable only after their commencement, I think it is clear that proof of enforceability is a condition precedent to enforcement which is different in nature and function to proof of

Service. Enforceability in the Contracting State of origin is, as can be seen from Article 31 of the Convention, a *sine qua non* of any judgment whose enforcement, as distinct from recognition, is sought. Proof of prior service of the judgment has the more limited function of ensuring that the judgment debtor has had an opportunity of voluntary compliance.

20. Different Statements from a passage in the Jenard Report were relied upon to different effect in the written observations. It is worthwhile quoting the passage in full:

'In the view of the Committee, if the applicant does not produce the required documents, enforcement should not be refused, but the court may stay the proceedings and allow the applicant time to produce the documents. If the documents produced are not sufficient and the court cannot obtain sufficient information, it may refuse to entertain the application.'

21. This passage from the Report indicates that the Convention is, at the very least, permissive of flexibility on aspects of the application other than those which benefit from Article 48. As I have already stated, the court does not prejudice the various interests served by the Convention merely by permitting an applicant to rectify his application during the *ex parte* proceedings. However, the court should respect the interest of the addressee of the judgment (and the general interest) in avoiding enforcement proceedings through voluntary compliance. The Jenard Report indicates that this interest underlies the requirement of proof of service in Article 47(i) of the Convention.

22. The above-quoted passage from the Jenard Report also indicates that there are limits to the flexibility of the court in accommodating the applicant. If, after a period of grace has been given to effect service, the relevant proof cannot be attached to the application, the application should not be entertained. As the addressee of the judgment is not represented, it is for the court to ensure that he is not subjected to an enforcement order in respect of a judgment which he might happily have satisfied without further compulsion. The applicant should bear the consequences, financial or otherwise, of refusal.

23. The position I have taken thus far is reinforced by consideration of the general objectives of the Convention, and by the case-law of the Court on analogous questions. The Court has stated that 'the object of the Convention is to facilitate free movement of judgments by establishing a simple and rapid procedure in the Contracting State in which application is made for enforcement'. This objective is particularly served through the suppression of excessive formalism. 17 The Court has also highlighted the protection of the rights of the defence, while emphasizing that, within the scheme of the Convention, this protection is at its greatest during the court proceedings leading to the original judgment. Where there exists a judgment, against which no substantive or procedural objection can be raised, it is clearly in keeping with the objective of simple and rapid enforcement that the court hearing the application for enforcement should permit errors or omissions in the application to be remedied. No prejudice is done thereby to the rights of the defence. The national court can ensure, in accordance with national law, that the applicant is responsible for any unnecessary costs, and that (in a case such as the present,

involving an apparent failure to serve the judgment in question) the addressee of the judgment is given an appropriate period of time to comply voluntarily with the judgment once he is notified of it.

24. In *Carron* v *Germany*, the Court gave a preliminary ruling on two points which are relevant in the present context. The applicant in that case had failed to comply with the requirement in the second paragraph of Article 33 of the Convention, that an applicant for an enforcement order must give an address for service of process within the area of jurisdiction of the court applied to. The Court stated that it is clear from Article 33 'that the law of the State in which enforcement is sought governs the entire procedure for making the application'.

25. The Court went on to hold in Carrori that 'the obligation to give an address for service of process laid down in [Article 33 of the Convention] must be fulfilled in conformity with the rules laid down by the law of the State in which enforcement is sought, and if that law is silent as to the time at which that formality must be observed, no later than the date on which the decision authorizing enforcement is served'. As I have already observed, the point in the *ex parte* proceedings at which procedural requirements must be fulfilled varies with the function of the requirement in question. An address for service of appeal proceedings is clearly not needed until the addressee of an enforcement order is made aware of it; the Convention requires proof of service of a judgment, and of the opportunity of voluntary compliance, before such an order is made. Subject to that different requirement, the point in *Carron* applies equally to the present case, that national procedural rules apply to all aspects of the enforcement application.

26. To conclude this section, I would answer the first question referred by the Hof van Cassatie as follows:

Article 47(1) of the Convention must be interpreted as meaning that the court before which enforcement is sought may order the enforcement of a judgment given in another Contracting State only if proof of service of the judgment is also produced. Where national procedural rules permit, such proof may be accepted at any point before a decision is given on the application, provided that the addressee has had an adequate opportunity after service voluntarily to comply with the judgment, and that the applicant bears responsibility for any unnecessary proceedings.

(ii) *The* inter partes *stage*

27. The second question referred to the Court by the Hof van Cassatie relates more specifically to the facts of the instant case, where the procedural requirements I set out in answer to the first question were not fully observed in the context of the *ex parte* application. Can such a defect be cured? It can, in my view, provided, as before, that national procedural rules permit this, and the terms and objectives of the Convention are complied with. The general interest in the free movement of judgments which are, in themselves, in conformity with the requirements of the Convention, must counter any tendency to read the Convention as requiring an over-formalist distinction between the *ex parte* and

inter partes stages in this regard. As long as the position of the addressee of the judgment is not prejudiced by a late attempt to rectify the application during the appeal proceedings, no provision of the Convention prevents the operation of national rules permitting such rectification.

28. Two decisions of the Court are helpful in answering this point. In *Carron*, the Court held that 'the consequences of a failure to comply with the rules on the furnishing of an address for service are, by virtue of Article 33 of the Convention, governed by the law of the State in which enforcement is sought, provided that the aims of the Convention are respected'.

29. In *Lancray*, the Court considered the requirement in Article 27(2) of the Convention that a judgment not be recognized, where it was given in default of appearance, if the defendant was not duly served with the document which instituted the proceedings in sufficient time to enable him to arrange for his defence. The Court held that Article 27(2) 'is to be interpreted as meaning that questions concerning the curing of defective service are governed by the law of the State in which judgment was given'. Therefore, the possibility of rectifying an omission (in that case, to serve a translation of the document instituting the proceedings) is acknowledged even in respect of the first, prejudgment stage, during which, as we have seen, the protection of the rights of the defence is given greater priority.

30. National procedural rules permitting the applicant to remedy his application during an appeal pursuant to Article 37 should also, by analogy, be consistent with the Convention, provided that the position of the defence is not thereby prejudiced. I do not accept that permitting the rectification of the application at this stage would encourage negligence on the part of the applicant, or a lack of vigilance on the part of the court on behalf of the absent addressee of the judgment during the *ex parte* proceedings. As to the former argument, the applicant will almost certainly be burdened by greater costs by his negligence. With regard to the second, the possibility of rectification at the appeal stage of applications or pleadings, under the national procedural laws of a Contracting State, is evidence, if it were needed, that such a lack of vigilance is not to be feared. Interpretative questions may not be referred to the Court at the *ex parte* stage. The first point at which this can be done is the appeal stage, which suggests that a court in a Contracting State, hearing an appeal pursuant to Article 37, may seek guidance as to the conduct of the proceedings before it. Of course, the same does not apply to an appeal such as that to the Hof van Cassatie in the present case, which is limited by Article 41 to points of law.

31. I would therefore answer the second question referred by the Hof van Cassatie as follows: Article 47(1) of the Convention must be interpreted as meaning that the court before which an appeal is taken against an order for the enforcement of a judgment given in another Contracting State, on the grounds that the order was made without proof of service of the judgment, may confirm that order only if proof of service is produced, and national procedural rules permit such production at the appeal stage, and provided that the addressee has had an adequate opportunity after service voluntarily to comply with the judgment, that the applicant bears responsibility for any unnecessary

proceedings, and that the addressee is not otherwise prejudiced by the rectification of the application at that stage.

Conclusion

32. I would therefore answer the questions referred by the Hof van Cassatie as follows:

(1) Article 47(1) of the Convention must be interpreted as meaning that the court before which enforcement is sought may order the enforcement of a judgment given in another Contracting State only if proof of service of the judgment is also produced. Where national procedural rules permit, such proof may be accepted at any point before a decision is given on the application, provided that the addressee has had an adequate opportunity after service voluntarily to comply with the judgment, and that the applicant bears responsibility for any unnecessary proceedings.

(2) Article 47(1) of the Convention must be interpreted as meaning that the court before which an appeal is taken against an order for the enforcement of a judgment given in another Contracting State, on the grounds that the order was made without proof of service of the judgment, may confirm that order only if proof of service is produced, and national procedural rules permit such production at the appeal stage, and provided that the addressee has had an adequate opportunity after service voluntarily to comply with the judgment, that the applicant bears responsibility for any unnecessary proceedings, and that the addressee is not otherwise prejudiced by the rectification of the application at that stage.

Case C-267/97 - 29 April 1999

Éric Coursier
v
Fortis Bank and Martine Coursier, née Bellami

Enforcement - Judgments 'enforceable' in the State of origin - Meaning - Enforceability in formal terms - proceedings for enforcement in the State in which enforcement is sought - Effect of a subsequent decision falling outside the scope of the Convention and granting immunity from enforcement in the State of origin - Appraisal by the court of the State in which enforcement is sought.

Summary

The term 'enforceable' in the first paragraph of Article 31 of the Convention of 27 September 1968 on Jurisdiction and the Enforcement of Judgments in Civil and Commercial Matters is to be interpreted as referring solely to the enforceability, in formal terms, of foreign decisions and not to the circumstances in which such decisions may be executed in the State of origin. It is for the court of the State in which enforcement is sought, in appeal proceedings against the order for enforcement of such a decision brought under Article 36 of the Convention, to determine, in accordance with its domestic law, including the rules of private international law, the legal effects in its territory of another decision given in the State of origin in relation to a court-supervised liquidation, a matter not falling within the scope of the Convention.

JUDGMENT OF THE COURT

Puissochet, President, Jann, Moitinho de almeida, Gulmann and Edward, (Rapporteu), Judges

1. By judgment of 26 June 1997, received at the Court Registry on 22 July 1997, the Cour Supérieure de Justice (High Court of Justice), Luxembourg, referred to the Court for a preliminary ruling under the Protocol of 3 June 1971 on the interpretation by the Court of Justice of the Convention of 27 September 1968 on Jurisdiction and the Enforcement of Judgments in Civil and Commercial Matters a question on the interpretation of the first paragraph of Article 31 of the abovementioned Convention of 27 September 1968 (OJ 1975 L 204, p. 28), as amended by the Convention of 9 October 1978 on the Accession of the Kingdom of Denmark, Ireland and the United Kingdom of Great Britain and Northern Ireland (OJ 1978 L 304, p. 1), by the Convention of 25 October 1982 on the Accession of the Hellenic Republic (OJ 1982 L 388, p. 1) and by the Convention of 26 May 1989 on the Accession of the Kingdom of Spain and the Portuguese Republic (OJ 1989 L 285, p. 1, hereinafter 'the Brussels Convention').

2. That question was raised in proceedings brought by Éric Coursier, who lives in France, against Fortis Bank SA ('Fortis'), established in Luxembourg, and Mrs Coursier, née Bellami, who lives in France, concerning the enforcement in Luxembourg of a judgment delivered on 6 January 1993 by the Cour d'Appel (Court of Appeal), Nancy (France) ('the contested judgment'), ordering Mr and Mrs Coursier to repay to Fortis a loan granted by it to them.

3. On 13 August 1990 Fortis granted a loan of LUF 480 000 to Mrs and Mrs Coursier. Following their failure to meet their obligations, on 22 March 1991 Fortis called the loan in and commenced proceedings against them before the courts of the State in which they were domiciled pursuant to Articles 13 and 14 of the Brussels Convention, which concern jurisdiction in respect of contracts concluded by consumers. The contested judgment granted Fortis an order requiring Mr and Mrs Coursier to repay the sum of LUF 563 282 together with interest at the contractual rate and costs. That judgment was served on the debtors on 24 February 1993.

4. By judgment of 1 July 1993, the Tribunal de Commerce (Commercial Court), Briey (France), converted the court-supervised receivership of Mr Coursier's business - a bar in Rehon (France) - into a court supervised liquidation, in the context of which Fortis gave notice of a claim.

5. By judgment of 16 June 1994, the Tribunal de Commerce closed the

court-supervised liquidation on the ground that there were insufficient assets and stated that 'the right of creditors to bring individual proceedings shall be reinstated only under the conditions specified in Article 169 of the Law of 25 January 1985'.

6. The first paragraph of Article 169 of Law No 85-98 of 25 January 1985 on liquidation of assets and court-supervised liquidation of undertakings, which forms part of Section II, headed 'Discontinuation of court-supervised liquidation proceedings', is worded as follows, in the version in force from 1 October 1994, which does not, for the purposes of this case, change the meaning of the earlier version: 'A judgment closing liquidation proceedings as a result of insufficient assets does not reinstate the right of creditors to bring proceedings individually against the debtor unless their claim derives from:

1. a finding against the debtor in criminal proceedings relating either to circumstances not connected with the profession or occupation of the debtor or to tax evasion, such right in the latter case being available only to the public revenue authorities;
2. rights vested in the creditor personally.

However, a surety or co-obligor who has made payment for the debtor may take proceedings against the latter.'

7. Mr Coursier having thereafter obtained employment in Luxembourg, as a frontier worker, Fortis instituted proceedings before the Justice de Paix, Luxembourg, for attachment of Mr Coursier's salary. In those proceedings, the President of the Tribunal d'Arrondissment, Luxembourg, granted an order on 2 July 1996 for enforcement of the contested judgment under the Brussels Convention.

8. By applications of 9 and 14 August 1996, Mr Coursier appealed, in accordance with Article 36 of the Brussels Convention, against that order to the Cour Supérieure de Justice, contending that since, by virtue of the first paragraph of Article 169 of Law No 85-98, the contested judgment was no longer enforceable in France, no order for its enforcement could be granted in Luxembourg under Article 31 of the Brussels Convention.

9. The Brussels Convention, pursuant to the first paragraph of Article 1 thereof, is to apply in civil and commercial matters whatever the nature of the court or tribunal. However, according to subparagraph 2 of the second paragraph of that article, bankruptcy, proceedings relating to the winding up of insolvent companies or other legal persons, judicial arrangements, compositions and analogous proceedings are excluded from its scope.

10. The first paragraph of Article 31, which is in Section 2, entitled 'Enforcement', of Title III of the Brussels Convention, provides: 'A judgment given in a Contracting State and enforceable in that State shall be enforced in another Contracting State when, on the application of any interested party, it has been declared enforceable there.'

11. Considering that the dispute raised a problem concerning the interpretation of the Brussels Convention, the Cour Supérieure de Justice stayed proceedings pending a preliminary ruling from the Court of Justice on the following question: 'Does a judgment delivered in the State of origin in the context of a court-supervised liquidation - a matter which is excluded from the scope of the Brussels Convention - and which is not open to recognition under the national law of the State in which enforcement is sought, but which, in the State in which it was given, confers on one of the parties immunity from execution of the judgment whose enforcement is sought, affect the quality of enforceability which, according to the first paragraph of Article 31 of the Convention, a judgment must possess in order to be recognised and enforced?'

The scope of the question

12. In replying to the question submitted, it is appropriate to focus first on the aspects of the case relating to the scope and legal effects of the contested judgment and those of the insolvency judgment.

13. It is clear from the terms of the contested judgment that it bears an order for enforcement. That judgment was served on Mr and Mrs Coursier on 24 February 1993 and, in the absence of any appeal against it, has become final.

14. It is common ground that a decision of that kind falls within the scope of the Brussels Convention and, as such, can qualify for recognition and enforcement under the rules contained in Title III thereof.

15. It is clear from the documents before the Court that Mr and Mrs Coursier do not contend that the obligation to pay the debt, which has been judicially recognised, has been extinguished through payment of the debt or some other cause, such as expiry of a limitation period.

16. The insolvency judgment, for its part, concerns a matter (insolvency) which is expressly excluded from the scope of the Brussels Convention by subparagraph 2 of the second paragraph of Article 1 thereof.

17. The documents on the file of the Tribunal de Commerce de Briey show that the latter declared the court-supervised liquidation closed, under Article 167 of Law No 85-98, because the lack of assets made further proceedings impossible.

18. Under the first paragraph of Article 169 of Law No 85-98, the judgment closing the court-supervised liquidation for lack of assets has the effect of preventing creditors individually from bringing actions against the debtor. According to the information before the Court, that provision does not extinguish the debtor's obligation to pay, so that a natural obligation continues to attach to him, and if, on his own initiative, he discharges his debt, such payment cannot be deemed to be one that was not due and so subject to repayment.

The question on which a ruling is sought

19. According to Fortis, Article 169 of Law No 85-98 confers a degree of immunity from enforcement on Mr Coursier alone - and only in France - which does not divest the contested judgment of its intrinsic enforceability under the first paragraph of Article 31 of the Brussels Convention.

20. Mr Coursier considers that the contested judgment has, by virtue of Article 169 of Law No 85-98, ceased to be enforceable against him. It is clear, in his view, particularly from the wording of the first paragraph of Article 31 of the Brussels Convention that the personal immunity from enforcement that he enjoys in France also operates in his favour in the other Contracting States.

21. According to the Commission, the contested judgment does not fulfil the condition laid down in the first paragraph of Article 31 of the Brussels Convention whereby a decision must be duly enforceable in the State of origin. The contested judgment cannot be accorded greater authority and effectiveness than it already has in the State of origin. Even if the insolvency judgment is excluded from the scope of the Brussels Convention by virtue of subparagraph 2 of the second paragraph of Article 1 thereof, its effect is inseparable from enforcement of the contested judgment.

22. In view of the terms of the question submitted, it is important to note that a judgment such as the contested judgment is, in principle, one to which the rules on recognition of decisions contained in Section I of Title III (Articles 26 to 30) of the Brussels Convention apply.

23. The rules on enforcement of decisions are contained in Section 2 of Title III (Articles 31 to 45) of the Brussels Convention. It is clear from the first paragraph of Article 31, which forms part of those rules, that the enforceability of a decision in the State of origin is a precondition for its enforcement in the State in which enforcement is sought.

24. However, the question whether a decision is, in formal terms, enforceable in character must be distinguished from the question whether that decision can any longer be enforced by reason of payment of the debt or some other cause.

25. The Brussels Convention is intended to facilitate the free movement of judgments by establishing a simple and rapid procedure in the Contracting State where enforcement of a foreign decision is applied for. That enforcement procedure constitutes an autonomous and complete system (see to that effect Case 148/84 *Deutsche Genossenschaftsbank* v *Brasserie du Pêcheur* [1985] ECR 1981, paragraph 17, and Case C-172/91 *Sonntag* v *Waidmann* [1993] ECR I-1963, paragraphs 32 and 33).

26. Thus, under Article 34 of the Brussels Convention, the procedure for obtaining authorisation for enforcement is carried out with the utmost speed, without the party against whom enforcement is sought being able, at that stage of the procedure, to make submissions.

27. Under Article 36 of the Brussels Convention, the party against whom enforcement is sought may make submissions only at a later stage in the procedure, namely in an appeal against the decision authorising enforcement before one of the courts mentioned in Article 37(1) of the Convention.

28. Thus, the Court has held that the Brussels Convention merely regulates the procedure for obtaining an order for the enforcement of foreign enforceable instruments and does not deal with execution itself, which continues to be governed by the domestic law of the court in which execution is sought (see *Deutsche Genossenschaftsbank*, cited above, paragraph 18, and Case 145/86 *Hoffmann* v *Krieg* [1988] ECR 645, paragraph 27).

29. In those circumstances, it follows from the general scheme of the Brussels Convention that the term 'enforceable' in Article 31 thereof refers solely to the enforceability, in formal terms, of foreign decisions

and not to the circumstances in which such decisions may be executed in the State of origin.

30. That interpretation is supported by the Report on the Convention of 26 May 1989 (OJ 1990 C 189, p. 35). According to paragraph 29 of that report, although the expression 'when it has been declared enforceable' in Article 31 of the Brussels Convention replaced the expression 'when the order for its enforcement has been issued' which appeared in its original version in order to bring the convention into line with the Lugano Convention of 16 September 1988 on Jurisdiction and the Enforcement of Judgments in Civil and Commercial Matters (OJ 1988 L 319, p. 9), those two expressions may be considered virtually equivalent.

31. It follows that a decision such as the contested judgment, which bears a formal order for enforcement, must, in principle, be covered by the rules on enforcement in Title III of the Brussels Convention.

32. As regards a judgment such as the insolvency judgment which concerns a matter expressly excluded from the purview of the Brussels Convention, it is for the court of the State in which enforcement is sought, in appeal proceedings brought under Article 36 of the Brussels Convention, to determine, in accordance with its domestic law including the rules of private international law, the legal effects of that judgment within its territory.

33. The answer to the question submitted must therefore be that the term 'enforceable' in the first paragraph of Article 31 of the Brussels Convention is to be interpreted as referring solely to the enforceability, in formal terms, of foreign decisions and not to the circumstances in which such decisions may be executed in the State of origin. It is for the court of the State in which enforcement is sought, in appeal proceedings brought under Article 36 of the Brussels Convention, to determine, in accordance with its domestic law including the rules of private international law, the legal effects of a decision given in the State of origin in relation to a court-supervised liquidation.

On those grounds, the Court in answer to the questions referred to it by the Cour Supérieure de Justice by judgment of 26 June 1997, hereby rules:

The term 'enforceable' in the first paragraph of Article 31 of the Convention of 27 September 1968 on Jurisdiction and the Enforcement of Judgments in Civil and Commercial Matters, as amended by the Convention of 9 October 1978 on the Accession of the Kingdom of Denmark, Ireland and the United Kingdom of Great Britain and Northern Ireland, by the Convention of 25 October 1982 on the Accession of the Hellenic Republic and by the Convention of 26 May 1989 on the Accession of the Kingdom of Spain and the Portuguese Republic, is to be interpreted as referring solely to the enforceability, in formal terms, of foreign decisions and not to the circumstances in which such decisions may be executed in the State of origin. It is for the court of the State in which enforcement is sought, in appeal proceedings brought under Article 36 of the Brussels Convention, to determine, in accordance with its domestic law including the rules of private international law, the legal effects of a decision given in the State of origin in relation to a court-supervised liquidation.

OPINION OF MR ADVOCATE GENERAL LA PERGOLA

Facts of the case and legal background

1. The question submitted to the Court for a preliminary ruling in these proceedings relates to the concept of 'enforceable judgment' for the purposes of the first paragraph of Article 31 of the Convention on Jurisdiction and the Enforcement of Judgments in Civil and Commercial Matters, signed at Brussels on 27th September 1968 (hereinafter 'the Convention'). 'The first paragraph of Article 31 of the Convention states that '[a] judgment given in a Contracting State and enforceable in that State shall be enforced in another Contracting State when, on the application of any interested party, it has been declared enforceable there'.

In accordance with Articles 1 and 2(2) of the Protocol on the interpretation of the Convention, the Cour Superieure de Justice (High Court of Justice) of the Grand Duchy of Luxembourg has referred the following question to the Court of Justice:

'Does a judgment delivered in the State of origin in the context of a court-supervised liquidation - a matter which is excluded from the scope of the [Convention] - and which is not open to recognition under the national law of the State in which enforcement is sought, but which, in the State in which it was given, confers on one of the parties immunity from execution of the judgment whose enforcement is sought, affect the quality of enforceability which, according to the first paragraph of Article 31 of the Convention, a judgment must possess in order to be recognised and enforced?'

2. The facts at the origin of the dispute in the main proceedings can be summarised as follows. By judgment of 6 January 1993 of the Cour d'Appel (Court of Appeal), Nancy, the spouses Eric Coursier and Martine Bellami, both of French nationality and resident in France, were ordered to pay to the Luxembourg company Fortis Bank (hereinafter 'Fortis') the equivalent in French Francs of LUF 563 282 together with statutory interest and the costs of the proceedings. The claim of Fortis recognised by the French court stemmed from the failure of the Coursier-Bellami couple to meet their obligation to repay the sum of LUF 480 000, which they had been lent in August 1990. It does not appear from the case-file that the debtors appealed against the judgment, which was served on them on 24 February 1993.

By judgment of 1 July 1993, the Tribunal de Commerce (Commercial Court), Briey, brought simplified proceedings for court-supervised receivership (*redressement judiciaire*) against Mr Coursier, who ran a bar in Rehon (France). On the same date the receivership was converted into a court-supervised liquidation (*liquidation judiciaire*), in view of the cessation of business activities by the debtor, his inability to offer creditors a serious recovery plan and the impossibility of other recovery options. Under this procedure, Fortis registered its claim as an unsecured creditor.

3. The court-supervised liquidation was finally terminated for lack of sufficient assets by judgment of the Tribunal de Commerce of 16 June 1994. The judgment stated 'that the right of creditors to bring individual proceedings shall be reinstated only under the conditions specified in Article 169 of the Law of 25 January 1985'. Under the first paragraph of Article 169: 'a judgment terminating, for lack of sufficient assets, a liquidation under supervision of the court shall not reinstate the right of creditors to bring individual actions against the debtor, except in so far as the debt arises:

1. from a criminal conviction in respect of facts unrelated to the occupational activity of the debtor or in respect of tax fraud, in which case only the public treasury may benefit;

2. from rights attaching to the person of the debtor. The debtor may, however, be sued by a surety or joint debtor who has paid in his stead.'

4. Subsequently, as Mr Coursier had found paid employment in Luxembourg while continuing to reside in France, Fortis applied to the Tribunal de Paix (Magistrate's Court) in Luxembourg for a writ attaching the wages which its debtor earned there. In order to obtain an enforceable instrument for the purposes of securing the attachment, Fortis requested and obtained an order for the enforcement of the judgment, which order was made in accordance with Articles 31 and 32 of the Convention by the presiding judge of the Tribunal d'arrondissement (District Court) Luxembourg on 2 July 1996 (hereinafter 'the enforcement order').

5. *Mr Coursier* appealed to the national court in accordance with Articles 36 to 39 of the Convention (see point 14 below), claiming that the order enforcing the judgment was void. In his opinion, the judgment is not enforceable as Fortis' claim does not come within the exceptions specifically laid down in Article 169 of Law No 85-98 and the bank's right to bring individual

proceedings for enforcement had therefore not been reinstated either in France or in another Contracting State. Article 31 of the Convention makes enforcement (hereinafter referred to by that term in order to distinguish it from compulsory execution in the proper sense of the word) subject to the condition that the decision to be enforced is of an enforceable nature. The appellant maintains that that requirement is not satisfied in the present case because the court-supervised liquidation procedure under French law grants the insolvent debtor 'immunity from enforcement', which in his view makes the judgment delivered by the court in that country unenforceable in Luxembourg. Under the procedure in question, no international validity can be conferred on a decision which under the internal law of the State of origin has ceased to be valid vis-a-vis the debtor on account of the immunity from enforcement which the law grants to the latter. Those arguments are endorsed by the *Commission*, as is clear from the observations it has submitted to the Court of Justice.

6. By contrast, *Fortis* maintains that the immunity from enforcement deriving from Article 169 of Law No 85-98 applies only to the person of Mr Coursier (and therefore does not extend to Mrs Bellami) and has territorial effects which are confined to France. The fact that the right to bring individual enforcement proceedings against a debtor previously subject to court-supervised liquidation is not reinstated does not, however, detract in any way from the enforceable nature of judgments *predating* the opening of the bankruptcy proceedings. The applicant in the main proceedings is therefore wrong to rely on Article 31 of the Convention. In the view of Fortis, the article in question does not permit enforcement to be refused in the light of the effects of other decisions that may have been adopted against the respondent in the State of origin if they relate to issues falling outside the scope of the Convention. This, the bank maintains, is precisely the case of the French order terminating the court-supervised liquidation for lack of sufficient assets. Furthermore, Article 34 of the Convention provides that the application for enforcement may be refused 'only for one of the reasons specified in Articles 27 and 28', none of which applies in the present case, even according to Mr Coursier. If the Court were to hold that the alleged defence of unenforceability of the judgment in France were well founded and if the enforcement order were quashed, Fortis would have no possibility of taking action for the compulsory execution of its rights as creditor, either in Luxembourg, the State in which Mr Coursier earns income from employment that is (at least partly) attachable, or in France, where Fortis had duly obtained judgment against the debtor as required by the provisions of the Convention regarding territorial jurisdiction. Fortis adds that in France bankruptcy proceedings are governed by the principle of territoriality; hence, even if the liquidation were to be reopened - which is theoretically possible - it could not lead to assets or income held by the debtor in other Contracting States being added to the assets in bankruptcy.

Legal analysis

7. In my view, the question submitted by the national court calls for a preliminary inquiry. Above all, it is necessary to examine the procedure for reviewing the enforcement in one Contracting State of enforceable judgments delivered in another Contracting State. It is also necessary to ascertain what effects can be accorded in the legal system of one Contracting State to foreign decisions of the same type as the judgment delivered on 16 June 1994 by the Tribunal de Commerce, Briey. That judgment in turn refers to Article 169 of Law No 85-98 (see point 3 above); the *rationale* and scope of that provision therefore also warrant a brief analysis for the purposes of these proceedings.

The extinction of individual actions for enforcement by creditors, provided for by Article 169 of Law No 85-98

8. I shall commence with the latter point. Article 169 - which lays down that the termination of court-supervised liquidation for lack of sufficient assets does not reinstate the right of either unsecured or preferential creditors to bring individual actions against the debtor in respect of claims predating the commencement of the recovery procedure except in the cases specifically laid down by law - is understood in academic writing as providing for the definitive *extinction* of the creditors' rights, and not simply for their suspension. However, such extinction applies not to creditors' substantive rights but to their ability to take legal action against the debtor to obtain satisfaction of those rights. This distinction is important, because the counterpart to the extinction of the action is that it creates a natural obligation on the part of the debtor: consequently, spontaneous repayment to a creditor cannot be regarded as an undue payment liable to recovery. The provision in question does not appear to have an equivalent in any other Member State; particular relevance for the purposes of this Opinion attaches to the fact that Luxembourg bankruptcy law (see Article 536 of the Commercial Code) applies the opposite principle, which permits creditors to resume individual actions for enforcement if the proceedings are terminated, and on which the French system was based before the adoption of Law No 85-98. By distinguishing between the debtor and the undertaking, the *rationale* behind Article 169 appears to be to bring the treatment of sole traders, who otherwise would be liable up to the value of their entire assets for debts contracted in the conduct of business, into line with that of shareholders in joint stock companies, who are not personally liable for the company's debts, which are extinguished when the company is dissolved. However, legal writers have raised the question whether or not the provision at issue serves its intended purpose: it is one thing to rehabilitate the undertaking of a debtor in difficulties and another to allow him to free himself immediately of all his residual debts and to start again from scratch, resulting in a kind of 'advance rehabilitation' of his future enterprise which excludes the risk of another insolvency. It has been observed, more specifically, that the major sacrifice in terms of creditor rights and the serious harm to freedom of contract caused by Article 169 cannot be

justified on grounds of the survival of the undertaking, which by definition has ceased to exist at the liquidation stage. Conversely, if the debtor submits a plan for the continued operation of the undertaking, he is actually prevented from relying upon Article 169. This leads some authors to argue that the article in question which, 'in disregard of a judgment that has acquired the force of *res judicata*, divests of his rights a creditor who had fulfilled all the obligations imposed upon him', is unconstitutional.

The procedures laid down by the Convention for the recognition and enforcement of enforceable foreign judgments

9. Article 169 of Law No 85-98 is relied upon by Mr Coursier in the main proceedings to block the attempt by the creditor bank to obtain the compulsory execution (in Luxembourg) of its claim which is legally recognised (in France), after having obtained recognition of the foreign judgment as equivalent to the domestic enforcement instrument, in accordance with the domestic rules for compliance with the Convention (see point 5 above).

10. As we know, the object of facilitating the recognition and enforcement of judgments between Member States (endorsed by Article 220 of the EC Treaty) is of such importance that it prompted this Court to affirm that the Convention should be interpreted in the spirit of promoting the free movement of judgments within the single market. It was precisely in order to pursue that objective more effectively that the authors of the Convention did not confine themselves to establishing simplified procedures for the recognition and enforcement of foreign judgments but also laid down rules of *direct* jurisdiction (see Articles 2 to 24), that is to say rules that are also applicable in the State of origin (and not only by the court of the State in which recognition or enforcement is sought when the jurisdiction of the foreign court is reviewed for those purposes).

11. The recognition and enforcement procedures are purely declaratory and rest on the fundamental principle of reciprocal confidence among the Contracting States. The powers of the court of the State in which recognition is sought are confined to a much simpler and speedier review of the 'international legality' of the foreign judgment than that laid down by the rules of ordinary law. In the light of the guarantees accorded to the respondent in the original proceedings by the uniform rules on direct jurisdiction referred to above and the safeguards provided for the rights of the defence, again within the framework of the objectives pursued by the Convention, the foreign judgment is presumed to be in order, to K.D. Kerameus, 'By having almost all jurisdictional issues determined in the court of origin, the Convention has been able to relieve the recognition and enforcement proceedings from that most serious obstacle confronting all other bilateral or multilateral treaties. Thus upgrading the relevance of rules on jurisdiction ends up in significantly improving recognition and enforcement itself' (see Basic rules relating to recognition and enforcement of foreign judgments under the Brussels Convention, in Studia Juridica, 1995, *even if it has not acquired the force of res judicata* in the State of origin. Judgments enforceable by law against which there is a right of appeal or which

the court has declared to be provisionally enforceable may be treated in this way; so too may provisional and protective measures, as Article 24 of the Convention shows. As has been observed, this system 'leads to a considerable simplification for the creditor, enabling him to avoid those delaying tactics that often lie at the root of appeals [made in the State of origin] in purely financial disputes and which are lodged for the sole purpose of delaying enforcement of the claim. The Convention has, as a rule, given priority to the position of the creditor over that of the debtor', although naturally without denying protection to the latter (see points 14 and 17 below).

12. The concepts of 'recognition' (see Articles 26 to 30) and 'enforcement' (see Articles 31 to 45) are not expressly defined in the Convention. In this regard, I would point out that the former automatically confers substantive validity on the foreign judgment in the State in which recognition is sought as well. This State therefore agrees to incorporate automatically the legal situation enshrined in the measure in question (a declaratory judgment, for example) into its own legal system without the need for judicial review. The intervention of the court is prescribed only if recognition is sought: (i) as the principal issue, where there is dispute between the parties as to the legality of the decision in question (in which case the party applying for recognition may request application of the enforcement procedure; see point 16 below); or (ii) as an ancillary matter (for example, to support an objection of *res judicata* or the offsetting of a claim), in which case jurisdiction rests with the court hearing the main application.

13. The enforcement procedure which relates solely to measures requiring material execution - that is to say, typically judgments establishing and documenting a claim as being certain, liquidated and enforceable, including, for example, judgments ordering th eunsuccessful party to pay the costs of the proceedings–is designed to render the foreign judgment enforceable by means of a domestic order. In this way, the beneficiary of the judgment is enabled to satisfy in the State addressed – by using legal instruments appropriate to its system, if necessary by having recourse to public authority – the substantive right found to exist and to be compulsorily enforceable in the State of origin.

14. Among the conditions for the legality of the foreign judgment, particular importance attaches here to its enforceability. 'If a judgment from which an appeal still lies or against which an appeal has been lodged in the State in which it was given [see point 11 above] cannot be provisionally enforced in that State, it cannot be enforced in the State in which enforcement is sought. It is *an essential requirement of the instrument whose enforcement is sought* that it should be enforceable in the State in which it originates.... there is no reason for granting to a foreign judgment rights which it does not have in the country in which it was given'. For the same reason, if at the time of the application the foreign judgment has *ceased* to be enforceable in the legal system of origin - for example, because it has been quashed or as a result of prescription _ the view must be taken that the substantive condition laid down by Article 31 for the granting of enforcement is not fulfilled.

15. The enforcement procedure is a summary one: the competent court (indicated for each Contracting State in Article 32 of the Convention) decides

upon application by the interested party, without delay and without hearing the other party. The rights of the defence of the party against whom enforcement is sought are safeguarded, however, as there is provision for a hearing to be held at a later date if the respondent lodges an appeal within one or two months of service of the measure granting enforcement (depending on the addressee's State of domicile). Such an appeal may be based, *inter alia*, on the fact that the decision is not yet enforceable or is the subject of an appeal in the State of origin or does not fall within the scope of the Convention. The debtor can also effectively raise objections on the ground of lack of interest on the part of the creditor in bringing proceedings because of events arising after the judgment was given (for example, evidence that the debt to which the foreign judgment relates has been discharged). However, the *substance* of the judgment to be enforced or the procedure on the basis of which the judgment was reached may be reviewed only to the extent provided for in Articles 27 and 28 (see point 16 below).

16. Although the method of lodging the application for enforcement or recognition (such as the information it must contain or the number of copies to be submitted) is determined by the procedural law of the State addressed, the Convention requires the production of certain documents, in particular an authenticated copy of the foreign judgment 'which satisfies the conditions necessary to establish its authenticity' and, in the case of a judgment given in default, the document which establishes that the party in default was served with the document instituting the proceedings (see Article 46).

Under Article 47(1) of the Convention, a provision which applies only to applications for enforcement, the applicant must also produce documents which establish that (i) the judgment is enforceable according to the law of the State of origin and (ii) has been served on the other party in order to give him the opportunity to comply voluntarily. It need hardly be pointed out that the provision in question, by requiring proof of the enforceability of the foreign judgment - which may be deduced from the enforcement order or other references in the same measure, or else from separate documents, and in particular from a comparison of the date of the judgment, the date of service and the time allowed for lodging an appeal - is clearly linked to the first paragraph of Article 31 of the Convention (see point 14 above).

17. If the foreign judgment of which the applicant seeks recognition is only provisionally enforceable and an appeal is lodged, the court of the State in which recognition is sought may stay the proceedings (see Article 30 of the Convention), where appropriate after having first ascertained that the grounds for refusal set out in Articles 27 and 28 (see point 16 above) do not apply. Similarly, under Article 38 of the Convention, if the enforceable foreign judgment is the subject of an appeal *in the State of origin* (or if the time for lodging such an appeal has not yet expired), the court of the State in which an objection has been lodged may (a) stay the proceedings, upon application by the appellant, or (b) confirm the enforcement order, even of its own motion, but make it conditional on the provision of such security as it shall determine.

18. Recognition and enforcement of the foreign judgment may be refused (or, if granted, revoked by the ruling on the appeal) only for one of the reasons

specified in Articles 27 and 28 of the Convention, that is to say if (i) recognition (or enforcement) is contrary to public policy in the State in which recognition is sought; (ii) the rights of the defence of a respondent who has not entered an appearance are infringed (failure to serve the document which instituted the proceedings in sufficient time); (iii) the judgment is irreconcilable with a ruling given in a dispute between the same parties in the State in which recognition is sought; (iv) the court of the State of origin has decided a preliminary question concerning certain matters lying outside the scope of the Convention in a way that conflicts with a rule of private international law of the State in which recognition is sought; (v) the judgment is irreconcilable with an earlier judgment given in a non-contracting State involving the same cause of action and between the same parties, provided that this latter judgment fulfils the conditions necessary for its recognition in the State addressed (Article 27); (vi) the judgment conflicts with special or binding provisions regarding jurisdiction (for example, in matters relating to insurance and consumer contracts) or rules of exclusive jurisdiction contained in the Convention; and (vii) recognition or enforcement is prohibited under a previous convention concluded by the State addressed with a third State in which the respondent was domiciled or normally resident when the judgment was delivered, if the jurisdiction of the court of the State of origin was based solely on one of the 'anomalous' rules of jurisdiction listed in the second paragraph of Article 3 of the Convention (Article 28).

19. In particular, under no circumstances may a foreign judgment be reviewed as to its substance (see Articles 29 and 34 of the Convention): even if the court of the State addressed considers that a point of fact or of law has been wrongly decided by the court of origin, or if the defendant in the foreign proceedings does not enter an appearance, that court cannot refuse recognition or enforcement, substituting its own discretion for that of the foreign court. This prohibition, which is an expression of the respect and confidence which the legal system of the State addressed vests in the juridical sovereignty of the State of origin and which is accompanied by an almost total prohibition on reviewing the jurisdiction of the original court, constitutes, in my view, the central principle of the entire Convention.

20. Finally, as to the precise scope of the effects of the 'naturalised' foreign judgment, the Court has stated, on the basis of the Jenard Report, that in principle a foreign judgment should not be accorded greater authority and effectiveness than it would have in the State of origin (the so-called extension of effects theory). Some academic writers, however, add a caveat, which received authoritative approval from Advocate General Darmon in the case of *Hoffmann* v *Krieg* to which I have referred: a foreign judgment cannot have greater effects *in the State in which enforcement is sought* than those of similar *national* judgments (the so-called equivalence of effects theory).

Judgments in bankruptcy cases are outside the scope of the Convention

21. In the light of the characteristics of the system of reciprocal recognition of judgments established by the Convention, which I have described

above (see points 10 to 20), it is easier, in my view, to understand the reasons that led Mr Coursier to adopt the position described earlier (see point 5) in challenging the enforcement order in the main proceedings. As stated in the order for reference, the judgment falls within the scope of the Convention and as such is capable of enforcement -at least in theory, without reference to the solution to be adopted in the individual case. By contrast, the judgment terminating the appellant's court-supervised liquidation for lack of sufficient assets, which was delivered on 16 June 1994 by the Tribunal de Commerce, Briey, cannot enjoy automatic recognition under Luxembourg law by virtue of Article 26, as it turns on a matter that lies outside the scope of the Convention ('bankruptcy, proceedings relating to the winding-up of insolvent companies or other legal persons, judicial arrangements, compositions and analogous proceedings': see indent (2) of the second paragraph of Article 1).

As we know, the exclusion of insolvency proceedings from the scope of the Convention was due historically to what at the time appeared to be the insurmountable difficulty of arriving at a solution acceptable to all Member States on a matter as complex as bankruptcy. In the light of this difficulty, and in order not to delay unduly the conclusion of the Convention, the committee of national experts appointed by the Council considered it advisable to 'excise' the matter in question from the draft convention. Separate negotiations were begun in parallel with a view to concluding a separate convention relating solely to bankruptcy, the scope of which would have had to 'dovetail almost completely' with that of the Convention. Moreover, as the Court of Justice has long since made clear, this exclusion relates to all proceedings based, under the various laws of the Contracting States, on cessation of payments, insolvency or lack of creditworthiness of the debtor, which involve the intervention of the courts culminating in compulsory collective liquidation of assets or simply in judicial supervision. Moreover, 'it is necessary, if decisions relating to bankruptcy and winding-up are to be excluded from the scope of the Convention, that they must derive *directly* from the bankruptcy or winding-up and be closely connected with the proceedings for the liquidation of assets or supervision by the court.'

It therefore seems indisputable to me that the judgment terminating Mr Coursier's court-supervised liquidation - which derives directly from the judgment opening the insolvency proceedings and constitutes the culmination of those proceedings - cannot be relied upon by the debtor to block Fortis' claim for satisfaction of its rights as creditor. In other words, the Convention works solely to the disadvantage of the applicant in these proceedings, exposing him to the risk of attachment of his income despite his immunity from enforcement under the French legal system, in which both of the judgments relevant to the main proceedings originated. As the Jenard Report so states, 'pending the conclusion of the separate Convention covering bankruptcy, proceedings arising directly from bankruptcy will be governed by the legal rules currently in force, or by the conventions which already exist between certain Contracting States'.

22. France and Luxembourg are not bound by any bilateral or multilateral convention on jurisdiction and the recognition and enforcement of judgments in bankruptcy cases. Moreover, the Bankruptcy Convention 51 has not yet entered

into force. Article 25 of that Convention (entitled 'Recognition and enforceability of other judgments') states in the first paragraph of indent 1: 'Judgments handed down by a court whose judgment concerning the opening of proceedings is recognised [in accordance with the Convention's rules on jurisdiction] and which concern the course and *closure* of insolvency proceedings ... shall also be recognised with no further formalities. Such judgments shall be enforced in accordance with Articles 31 to 51 of the Convention ..., with the exception of Article 34(2)' (emphasis added).

23. As to the possibility of the judgment of 16 June 1994 of the Tribunal de Commerce, Bricy, being recognised in Luxembourg at least *under the ordinary law*, this is obviously a matter which the Court may analyse purely as an ancillary issue. In order to examine this possibility, it would be necessary to interpret not the rules of the Convention but national law: it therefore falls not only outside the scope of the question referred by the national court but also outside the jurisdiction of the Court of Justice.

I shall therefore confine myself to recalling that, in the order for reference, the Cour Superieure de Justice observed that in practice - in the light of the 'universalist' approach of Luxembourg private international law regarding bankruptcy proceedings - the possibility cannot be excluded that, under certain conditions, decisions of foreign courts regarding an insolvent debtor's capacity or assets may be recognised as having the same effects in Luxembourg as they produce in the State of origin, irrespective of whether a formal order enforcing the foreign decision has been granted. According to the national court, however, that principle is not applicable to judgments delivered in a country whose legal system is based on the opposite principle of the 'territoriality and multiple nature' of bankruptcy proceedings, as is the case of French law. A French judgment delivered in insolvency proceedings and relied upon in Luxembourg can therefore have only strictly territorial effects; in the case in point, that principle means that the judgment cannot prevent the insolvent person's property situated in the Grand Duchy from being subject to individual enforcement proceedings.

Answer to the question referred in the present case

24. I believe I have now brought into focus the precise contours of the problem, for the solution of which the national court has sought a ruling on interpretation. In my view, the question raised by the Cour Superieure de Justice must be answered in the negative, for the following reasons.

25. The case under review does not exhibit any special feature that distinguishes it substantially from others in which the problem arises of ensuring the cross-border movement of judgments involving property: given the inadequacy of the debtor's property in the State of origin - ascertained by the court in the decision to terminate the court-supervised liquidation *for lack of sufficient assets* - the interested party has evaded the order to meet his obligations issued in that jurisdiction and has therefore been summoned to comply in the territory of the State in which enforcement is sought, where by

contrast he has assets that can be seized. This duty to comply exists and, in my opinion, can be relied upon. Indeed, the judicial position (including immunity from enforcement) relating to the subsequent collective enforcement to which the debtor was subject by virtue of his individual undertaking in the legal system of origin, *the effects of which were confined to the national territory*, does not suggest otherwise. On the other hand, by taking up paid employment in another Contracting State, Mr Coursier incurred the objective risk of losing the protection afforded to him in France by the 'shield' of personal immunity. It was doubtful, to say the least, whether his legal immunity from enforcement proceedings, stemming in the jurisdiction of origin from the judgment of the Tribunal de Commerce, Briey, could automatically be extended from France to the host State.

26. More precisely, the claim adduced by the debtor in the main proceedings does not appear to me to derive support from either the text or the spirit of the Convention. Under the simplified system of enforcement established by the Convention, the requirement that the judgment must be enforceable according to the law of the State of origin - as provided for in the first paragraph of Article 31 and the first indent of Article 47, upon which Mr Coursier relies in today's proceedings is justified exclusively by the fact that the Convention does not make enforcement dependent on the foreign judgment having acquired the force of *res judicata*. I have already explained how the system established by the Convention operates (see point 11 above). It is true that even a judgment that is fully enforceable (whether automatically or by virtue of a clause affixed by the court), which has been equated to a national judgment for the purposes of compulsory execution in another Contracting State, may cease to be valid in the jurisdiction of origin as a result of a subsequent judgment partially reversing or quashing it. Under the system established by the Convention, a case of this kind is catered for by stipulating that the host State must automatically recognise the new foreign judgment, which can then produce its extinctive effects there. However, if the new foreign decision with extinctive effects cannot be recognised (for example, because the application initiating the proceedings was not properly and promptly served on the respondent who failed to enter an appearance), Article 31 of the Convention will again come into play, in the sense that it will invalidate the enforcement order or the registration of the judgment subsequently quashed or amended.

27. That said, it must be pointed out at once that this case undoubtedly differs from the one I have just described, and from more than one angle: the judgment, which established that Fortis had a liquidated claim that had fallen due (in that it was not subject to time-limits or conditions), became final well before the action and order for enforcement; nor does the obligation arising out of the legally recognised debt appear to have been extinguished as a result of payment or any another reason. the bank's interest in bringing an action must therefore be assumed to be unchanged (see point 15 above). The Luxembourg court hearing the application for enforcement was accordingly justified, when examining the legality of the judgment, in holding that it exhibited the same 'quality as the instrument' for the purposes of enforcement that French law

prescribes for all judgments of that type. Therefore, under the legal system of the Grand Duchy, the judgment was not accorded any 'rights' (for my part, I would prefer to speak of 'effects') 'which it does not have in the State of origin'.

Although it is true that in France Fortis would be prevented from obtaining compulsory execution of the claim in question, this stems from a distinct measure (the judgment of the Tribunal de Commerce, Briey) which relates (like the substantive provision on which it rests) to a matter outside the scope of the Convention - to be precise, bankruptcy and similar proceedings - and cannot therefore benefit from freedom of movement for the purposes of recognition, in this case in Luxembourg (see points 21 and 22 above). This exclusion stems from the clear and unambiguous decision of the Contracting States, and in my view there is no doubt that the rules defining the substantive scope of the Convention take precedence over those which, *equally within the scope so defined,* concern the enforceable nature of foreign judgments, the execution of which has been sought. Furthermore, Luxembourg legislation does not grant extraterritorial validity to the aforementioned judgment of the French court (see point 23 above). That ruling is therefore of no relevance to the national court. If it were otherwise, and if the arguments of the applicant in the present case were accepted, the result would be illogical, as Fortis has correctly pointed out: the French judgment terminating the court-supervised liquidation, while falling outside the substantive scope of the Convention, would automatically be accorded recognition under Luxembourg law, while at the same time enforcement of the judgment to which, by contrast, the Convention is clearly applicable, would be prevented.

28. Permit me to clarify one further point. In contrast to the fear expressed by the Commission, the solution proposed in this Opinion, which permits the creditor's claim to be enforced in the State addressed, dow not impair the right to equal treatment of creditors who have previously participated in bankruptcy proceedings that have run their course in the State of origin. Other creditors who have obtained an enforcement instrument from a court (including a court settlement) or an authentic instrument (see Article 50 and 51 of the Convention) - even if they have been divested of the right to bring individual actions for enforcement in the State of origin as a result of a decision of the type reached by the Tribunal de Commerce, Briey - will be able, subject to their instrument being declared enforceable, to intervene in the enforcement proceedings initiated by the speediest creditor in the State in which enforcement is sought, and thus to participate collectively and on an equal footing in the subsequent distribution of the assets (without prejudice to the effects of substantive rules regarding preferential claims or granting preferential treatment to the first creditor to seek attachment).

Conclusions

For the reasons set out above, I propose that the Court reply as follows to the question submitted for a preliminary ruling by the Cour Supérieure de Justice:

A judgment ordering the payment of a sum of money does not lose the quality of enforceability, which Article 31 of the Convention on Jurisdiction and the Enforcement of Judgments in Civil and Commercial Matters requires a judgment to possess in order to be enforced in another Contracting State, if the party against whom enforcement is sought is permanently protected in the State of origin from individual proceedings for enforcement as a result of another judgment delivered in that State in the context of insolvency proceedings which is not open to recognition in the State in which enforcement is sought either under the Convention or under that State's national law.

Case C-260/97 - 17 June 1999

Unibank A/S
v
Flemming G. Christensen

Enforcement of a document which has been formally drawn up and registered as an authentic instrument and is enforceable in a Contracting State - Definition of 'authentic instruments' - Document drawn up without any involvement of a competent authority - Excluded.

Summary

An acknowledgment of indebtedness enforceable under the law of the State of origin whose authenticity has not been established by a public authority or other authority empowered for that purpose by that State does not constitute an authentic instrument within the meaning of Article 50 of the Convention of 27 September 1968 on Jurisdiction and the Enforcement of Judgments in Civil and Commercial Matters.

The authentic nature of such instruments must be established beyond dispute so that the court in the State in which enforcement is sought is in a position to rely on their authenticity, since the instruments covered by Article 50 are enforced under exactly the same conditions as judgments.

JUDGMENT OF THE COURT

Puisochet, President, Moitinho de Almeida, Edward (Rapporteaur), Sevón and Wathelet, Judges

1. By order of 26 June 1997, received at the Court on 18 July 1997, the

Bundesgerichtshof (Federal Court of Justice) referred to the Court for a preliminary ruling under the Protocol of 3 June 1971 on the interpretation by the Court of Justice of the Convention of 27 September 1968 on jurisdiction and the enforcement of judgments in civil and commercial matters, two questions on the interpretation of Articles 32, 36 and 50 of that Convention (OJ 1972 L 299, p. 32), as amended by the Convention of 9 October 1978 on the accession of the Kingdom of Denmark, Ireland and the United Kingdom of Great Britain and Northern Ireland (OJ 1978 L 304, p. 1 and - amended text - p. 77) and by the Convention of 25 October 1982 on the accession of the Hellenic Republic (OJ 1982 L 388, p. 1) (hereinafter 'the Brussels Convention').

2. Those questions have been raised in proceedings between Unibank A/S ('Unibank') and Mr Christensen concerning the former's application for three acknowledgements of indebtedness to be declared enforceable.

Legal background

3. Article 32(2) of the Brussels Convention provides: 'The jurisdiction of local courts shall be determined by reference to the place of domicile of the party against whom enforcement is sought. If he is not domiciled in the State in which enforcement is sought, it shall be determined by reference to the place of enforcement.'

4. Article 36 of the Brussels Convention states: 'If enforcement is authorised, the party against whom enforcement is sought may appeal against the decision within one month of service thereof.

If that party is domiciled in a Contracting State other than that in which the decision authorising enforcement was given, the time for appealing shall be two months and shall run from the date of service, either on him in person or at his residence. No extension of time may be granted on account of distance.'

5. Article 50 of the Brussels Convention provided: 'A document which has been formally drawn up or registered as an authentic instrument and is enforceable in one Contracting State shall, in another Contracting State, have an order for its enforcement issued there, on application made in accordance with the procedures provided for in Article 31 *et seq*. The application may be refused only if enforcement of the instrument is contrary to public policy in the State addressed.

The instrument produced must satisfy the conditions necessary to establish its authenticity in the State of origin.

The provisions of Section 3 of Title III shall apply as appropriate.'

6. The first sentence of the first paragraph of Article 50 of the Brussels Convention was amended by Article 14 of the Convention of 26 May 1989 on the accession of the Kingdom of Spain and the Portuguese Republic (OJ 1989 L 285, p. 1, hereinafter 'the Third Accession Convention'), as follows: 'A document which has been formally drawn up or registered as an authentic instrument and is enforceable in one Contracting State shall, in another Contracting State, be declared enforceable there, on application made in accordance with the procedures provided for in Article 31 *et seq*.'

7. Following that amendment, the wording of Article 50 of the Brussels Convention coincides exactly with that of Article 50 of the Convention of 16 September 1988 on jurisdiction and the enforcement of judgments in civil and commercial matters (OJ 1988 L 319, p. 9, hereinafter 'the Lugano Convention').

8. Under Article 478(1)(5) of the Retsplejelov (Danish Code of Civil Procedure), execution may be levied on the basis of written acknowledgements of indebtedness provided that they contain an express provision to that effect.

The dispute in the main proceedings and the questions referred to the Court

9. Between 1990 and 1992 Mr Christensen signed in favour of Unibank, a bank established under Danish law in Arhus (Denmark) three acknowledgments of indebtedness (*Gældsbrev*) for DKK 270 000, DKK 422 000 and DKK 138 000, together with interest thereon. The three documents are typewritten and also bear the signature of a third person, apparently an employee of Unibank, who witnessed the debtor's signature. The documents expressly state that they may be used, pursuant to Article 478 of the Retsplejelov, as a basis for execution to be levied.

10. When the acknowledgments of indebtedness were drawn up, the debtor resided in Denmark. He then moved to Weiterstadt, Germany, where the acknowledgments of indebtedness were presented to him for payment. At the request of Unibank, the Landgericht Darmstadt, in whose jurisdiction Weiterstadt is located, authorised enforcement of those documents. Mr Christensen appealed against that decision to the Oberlandesgericht (Higher Regional Court) Frankfurt am Main. In the

course of the proceedings, Mr Christensen had indicated that he had left Germany, but had not disclosed his new address. The appeal court thereupon held that Unibank no longer had an interest in pursuing proceedings since it could no longer levy execution in respect of the acknowledgments of indebtedness in Germany and, accordingly, upheld the appeal.

11. Unibank appealed to the Bundesgerichtshof, which stayed proceedings pending a preliminary ruling from the Court of Justice on the following questions:

'1. Is an acknowledgment of indebtedness signed by a debtor without the involvement of a public official - such as the *Gældsbrev* under Danish law (Paragraph 478(1)(5) of the Danish Code of Civil Procedure) - an authentic instrument within the meaning of Article 50 of the Brussels Convention, if that acknowledgment of indebtedness expressly specifies that it can serve as the basis for enforcement and if it can constitute the basis for enforcement under the law of the State in which it was drawn up, albeit subject to the condition that the court with jurisdiction to enforce it may refuse the creditor's application for enforcement if, as a result of objections to the basis for enforcement, there are doubts as to whether enforcement proceedings should be continued?

If the answer to Question 1 is in the affirmative:

2. Can an application for recognition of a decision or authentic instrument submitted to a court having local jurisdiction within the meaning of Article 32(2) of the Brussels Convention be rendered inadmissible or unfounded by reason of the fact that, while appeal proceedings (Article 36 of the Brussels Convention) are pending, the debtor has left the State in which the proceedings were instituted and his new place of residence is unknown?'

The first question

12. By its first question, the national court seeks essentially to ascertain whether an enforceable acknowledgment of indebtedness which has been drawn up without the involvement of a public authority constitutes an authentic instrument within the meaning of Article 50 of the Brussels Convention.

13. Unibank submits that the answer to that question should be in the affirmative. Conversely, Mr Christensen, the German and United Kingdom Governments and the Commission contend that the adjective

'authentic' means that the procedures for enforcement provided for by the Brussels Convention apply not to every instrument but only to those whose authenticity has been established by a competent public authority.

14. It must be borne in mind at the outset that Article 50 of the Brussels Convention treats a 'document which has been formally drawn up or registered as an authentic instrument and is enforceable in one Contracting State' in the same way, with regard to its enforceability in the other Contracting States, as judgments within the meaning of Article 25 of that Convention, in that it declares that the provisions on enforcement contained in Article 31 *et seq.* thereof also to be applicable to such documents. The purpose of those provisions is to achieve one of the fundamental objectives of the Brussels Convention, which is to facilitate, to the greatest possible extent, the free movement of judgments by providing for a simple and rapid enforcement procedure (see Case 148/84 *Deutsche Genossenschaftsbank* [1985] ECR 1981, paragraph 16, and Case C-414/92 *Solo Kleinmotoren* [1994] ECR I-2237, paragraph 20).

15. Since the instruments covered by Article 50 of the Brussels Convention are enforced under exactly the same conditions as judgments, the authentic nature of such instruments must be established beyond dispute so that the court in the State in which enforcement is sought is in a position to rely on their authenticity. Since instruments drawn up between private parties are not inherently authentic, the involvement of a public authority or any other authority empowered for that purpose by the State of origin is needed in order to endow them with the character of authentic instruments.

16. That interpretation of Article 50 of the Brussels Convention is supported by the Jenard-Möller Report on the Lugano Convention (OJ 1990 C 189, p. 57, hereinafter 'the Jenard-Möller Report').

17. Paragraph 72 of the Jenard-Möller Report states that the representatives of the Member States of the European Free Trade Area (EFTA) requested that the conditions which had to be fulfilled by authentic instruments in order to be regarded as authentic within the meaning of Article 50 of the Lugano Convention should be specified. In that connection the report mentions three conditions, namely: 'the authenticity of the instrument should have been established by a public authority; this authenticity should relate to the content of the instrument and not only, for example, the signature; the instrument has to be enforceable in itself in the State in which it originates'.

18. According to the same report, the involvement of a public authority is therefore essential for an instrument to be capable of being classified as an authentic instrument within the meaning of Article 50 of the Lugano Convention.

19. It is true that Article 50 of the Brussels Convention and Article 50 of the Lugano Convention were not identically worded at the material time in the present case and that the Jenard Report on the Brussels Convention (OJ 1979 C 59, p. 1) does not indicate the criteria to be fulfilled by authentic instruments but merely reproduces the conditions laid down by Article 50 of the latter Convention.

20. However, the only difference in the wording of the two Conventions on that point was that the Brussels Convention used the expression 'have an order for its enforcement issued' whereas the Lugano Convention used the expression 'declared enforceable'. Moreover, it is clear from paragraph 29 of the De Almeida Cruz, Desantes Real and Jenard Report on the Third Accession Convention (OJ 1990 C 189, p. 35) that the latter Convention, by adopting for Article 50 of the Brussels Convention the same wording as that of Article 50 of the Lugano Convention, sought to bring the wording of the two Conventions into line with each other on that point, the two expressions cited above being considered virtually equivalent.

21. It follows from all the foregoing that the answer to the first question must be that an acknowledgment of indebtedness enforceable under the law of the State of origin whose authenticity has not been established by a public authority or other authority empowered for that purpose by that State does not constitute an authentic instrument within the meaning of Article 50 of the Brussels Convention.

The second question

22. In view of the answer given to the first question, it is unnecessary to answer the second.

On those grounds, the Court (Fifth Chamber) in answer to the questions referred to it by the Bundesgerichtshof by order of 26 June 1997, hereby rules:

> **An acknowledgment of indebtedness enforceable under the law of the State of origin whose authenticity has not been established**

by a public authority or other authority empowered for that purpose by that State does not constitute an authentic instrument within the meaning of Article 50 of the Convention of 27 September 1968 on jurisdiction and the enforcement of judgments in civil and commercial matters, as amended by the Convention of 9 October 1978 on the accession of the Kingdom of Denmark, Ireland and the United Kingdom of Great Britain and Northern Ireland and by the Convention of 25 October 1982 on the accession of the Hellenic Republic.*

* Opinion of AG not yet available in English.

Miscellaneous

Joined Cases 9 and 10/77 - 14 July 1977

Bavaria Fluggesellschaft Schwabe & Co. KG and Germanair Bedarfsluftfahrt GmbH & Co. KG
v
Eurocontrol

Concepts and legal classifications laid down by the Court - Uniform application in the Member States - Judgments excluded from the scope of the latter - Articles 55 and 56(1) - Bilateral agreements - Application - Exclusive jurisdiction of national court - Protocol of interpretation of the Convention.

Summary

1. The principle of legal certainty in the Community legal system and the objectives of the Brussels Convention in accordance with Article 220 of the EEC Treaty, which is at its origin, require in all Member States a uniform application of the legal concepts and legal classifications developed by the Court in the context of the Brussels Convention.

2. A national court must not apply the Brussels Convention so as to recognize or enforce judgments which are excluded from its scope as determined by the Court of Justice. On the other hand, it is not prevented from applying to the same judgments one of the special agreements referred to in Article 55 of the Brussels Convention, which may contain rules for the recognition and enforcement of such judgments. As the first paragraph of Article 56 of the Brussels Convention recognizes, these agreements continue to have effect in relation to judgments to which the Brussels Convention does not apply. Since Article 1 of the Protocol of 3 June 1971 gives the Court jurisdiction to interpret only the Brussels Convention and the Protocol, it is solely for the national courts to judge the scope of the above-mentioned agreements in relation to judgments to which the Brussels Convention does not apply. This may lead to the same

expression in the Brussels Convention and in a bilateral agreement being interpreted differently.

JUDGMENT OF THE COURT

Kutscher, President, Donner, Pescatore, Presidents of Chambers, Mertens de Wilmars, Sorensen, Lord Mackenzie Stuart, O'Keeffe, Bosco, Touffait, Judges

1. By orders dated 22 December 1976, received at the Court on 25 January 1977, the Bundesgerichtshof referred to the Court pursuant to Article 3 of the Protocol of 3 June 1971 on the interpretation by the Court of Justice of the Convention of 27 September 1968 on Jurisdiction and the Enforcement of Judgments in Civil and Commercial Matters (hereinafter referred to as 'the Brussels Convention') the question whether under Article 56 of the Brussels Convention the treaty and conventions referred to in Article 55 continue to have effect in relation to judgments which do not fall under the second paragraph of Article 1 of the Brussels Convention but are excluded from its scope.

2. The question has arisen in two actions concerned with the enforcement in the Federal Republic of Germany of two judgments by the Tribunal de Commerce, Brussels; the judgments concern claims by Eurocontrol against Bavaria and Germanair for charges due for the use of the equipment and services of Eurocontrol. In its judgment of 14 October 1976 in Case 29/76, *Lufttransportunternehmen GmbH & Co. KG* v *Eurocontrol* [1976] ECR 1541, the Court on a reference by the Oberlandesgericht Düsseldorf in an action pending before that court in relation to charges of a similar nature to those in the present case ruled as follows:

1. 'In the interpretation of the concept "civil and commercial matters" for the purposes of the application of the Convention of 27 September 1968 on Jurisdiction and the Enforcement of Judgments in Civil and Commercial Matters, in particular Title III thereof, reference must not be made to the law of one of the States concerned but, first, to the objectives and scheme of the Convention and, secondly, to the general principles which stem from the corpus of the national legal systems;

2. A judgment given in an action between a *public authority* and a person governed by private law, in which the *public authority* has acted in the exercise of its powers, is excluded from the area of application of the Convention.'

The Bundesgerichtshof referred its question to the Court with particular regard to that judgment and to the Convention between the Federal Republic of Germany and the Kingdom of Belgium on the Mutual Recognition and Enforcement of Judgments, Arbitration Awards and Authentic Instruments in Civil and Commercial Matters, signed at Bonn on 30 June 1958. A ruling is sought whether and how far the legal concepts laid down by the Court in relation to the Brussels Convention are binding on national courts in respect of the application of a bilateral agreement such as the one mentioned above in matters excluded from the scope of the Brussels Convention. It appears from the orders for reference that in German law the question whether a case concerns a civil or commercial matter has for purposes of the recognition and enforcement of a foreign judgment traditionally been decided according to the law of the State in which the judgment was given.

3. Article 55 of the Brussels Convention provides ... this Convention shall, for the States which are parties to it, supersede the following conventions concluded between two or more of them ...'. The fifth convention to be listed is the said German-Belgian Convention of 30 June 1958. The first paragraph of Article 56 of the Brussels Convention, however, makes clear that these conventions 'shall continue to have effect in relation to matters to which this Convention does not apply'. The first paragraph of Article 1 of the Brussels Convention provides that it shall apply 'in civil and commercial matters'; on the other hand the German-Belgian Convention of 30 June 1958, as shown by the first paragraph of Article 1 thereof, covers the recognition of 'judgments given in civil and commercial matters' according to the criteria laid down by that convention itself.

4. The Court in the above-mentioned judgment of 14 October 1976 has determined the scope of the Brussels Convention in relation to a judgment of the present kind by interpreting 'civil and commercial matters' as an independent concept and not as a reference to the internal law of one or other of the States concerned. This interpretation is based on the desire to ensure in relation to Community law that the Contracting States and parties concerned have equal and uniform rights and duties under the Brussels Convention. The principle of legal certainty in the Community legal system and the objectives of the Brussels Convention in accordance with Article 220 of the EEC Treaty, which is at its origin, require in all Member States a uniform application of the legal concepts and legal classifications developed by the Court in the context of the Brussels Convention.

5. For this reason a national court must not apply the Brussels Convention so as to recognize or enforce judgments which are excluded from its scope as determined by the Court of Justice. On the other hand it is not prevented from applying to the same judgments one of the special agreements referred to in Article 55 of the Brussels Convention, which may contain rules for the recognition and enforcement of such judgments. As the first paragraph of Article 56 of the Brussels Convention recognizes, these agreements continue to have effect in relation to judgments to which the Brussels Convention does not apply. Since Article 1 of the Protocol of 3 June 1971 gives the Court jurisdiction to interpret only the Brussels Convention and the Protocol, it is solely for the national courts to judge the scope of the above-mentioned agreements in relation to judgments to which the Brussels Convention does not apply. The jurisdiction thus left to the national courts is the more readily justifiable insofar as the supplementary application of these bilateral agreements contributes to the objective pursued by the Brussels Convention of facilitating the recognition and enforcement of judgments between Member States.

6. The answer must therefore be that the first paragraph of Article 56 of the Brussels Convention does not prevent a bilateral agreement such as the German-Belgian Convention, which is the fifth to be listed in Article 53, from continuing to have effect in relation to judgments which do not fall under the second paragraph of Article 1 of the Brussels Convention, but to which, nevertheless, that Convention does not apply.

7. Although this result may lead to the same expression in the Brussels Convention and in a bilateral agreement being interpreted differently, this is due to the different systems in which the concept 'civil and commercial matters' is used. In relation to a bilateral agreement the acceptance of a classification, made by the court first giving judgment, by the courts of another State could lead to an appropriate result having regard to the fact that the courts of the various States are independent one of another. On the other hand, if this occurred in a system such as the Brussels Convention, the interpretation of which is entrusted to a court common to all parties, it would lead to undesirable divergencies.

On those grounds, the court in answer to the question referred to it by the Bundesgerichtshof by orders dated 22 December 1976, hereby rules:

The first paragraph of Article 56 of the Convention on Jurisdiction and the Enforcement of Judgments in Civil and

Commercial Matters does not prevent a bilateral agreement such as the German-Belgian Convention, which is the fifth to be listed in Article 55, from continuing to have effect in relation to judgments which do not fall under the second paragraph of Article 1 of the Convention first above-mentioned, but to which nevertheless that Convention does not apply.

OPINION OF MR ADVOCATE GENERAL MAYRAS

On 14 October 1976 in Case 29/76 referred to the Court for a preliminary ruling by the Oberlandesgericht Düsseldorf in an action between Eurocontrol and Lufttransport-unternehmen GmbH & Co. KG in relation to the recovery of route charges claimed by Eurocontrol the Court considered ([1976] ECR at p. 1551) that the words 'in civil and commercial matters' used in Article 1 of the Convention of 27 September 1968 on Jurisdiction and the Enforcement of Judgments in Civil and Commercial Matters did not depend on the classification given by the court which delivered the judgment to be enforced but must be regarded as an independent concept.

On this basis the Court decided that 'although certain judgments given in actions between a public authority and a person governed by private law may fall within the area of application of the Convention, this is not so where the public authority acts in the exercise of its powers'. 'Such is the case', the Court added, 'in a dispute which, *like that between the parties to the main action*, concerns the recovery of charges payable by a person governed by public law to a national body governed by public law for the use of equipment and services provided by such body, in particular where such use is obligatory and exclusive' (*ibid.* at p. 1551). 'This applies in particular', the judgment continues, 'where the rate of charges, the methods of calculation and the procedures for collection are fixed unilaterally in relation to the users, *as is the position in the present case* where the body in question unilaterally fixed the place of performance of the obligation at its registered office and selected the national Courts with jurisdiction to adjudicate, upon the performance of the obligation'.

The Court's judgment, which appears to me to be an illustration of the theory of *administrative* contracts containing clauses derogating from the general law thus necessarily rejected the view of the Tribunal de Commerce, Brussels, before which the case had been brought by Eurocontrol and which, to confirm its jurisdiction, had decided on 7 March 1974 that the charges claimed were not akin to taxes and were of a *commercial* nature.

At the same time however the Court clearly rejected the view of the German Bundesgerichtshof (Federal Court of Justice) in a judgment given on 26 November 1975 between the same parties, Eurocontrol and LTU, which was limited to referring the case back to the Oberlandesgericht Düsseldorf and in consequence of which the Oberlandesgericht referred to the Court of Justice on 16 February 1976 the question on which the Court ruled in its judgment of 14 October 1976.

The Bundesgerichtshof took the view that its decision did not involve an interpretation of the Convention of 1968 and it did not therefore regard itself as bound to bring the matter before this Court in accordance with Article 3(1) of the Protocol on the Interpretation by the Court of Justice of the Convention of 27 September 1968, which, however, had entered into force on 1 September 1975.

The Bundesgerichtshof rules that as regards the question whether a foreign judgment had been given in a 'civil and commercial matter' the classification given by the court which had given the judgment to be enforced was decisive for the purposes of the enforcement procedure. This judgment of the Bundesgerichtshof was upheld by the Bundesverfassungsgericht (Federal Constitutional Court) in an order of 23 June 1976.

Apparently the Bundesgerichtshof has changed its opinion since it now considers that the judgment which it is now required to give in two parallel cases which are in every respect identical save for the names of the airlines and the amount of the charges claimed from them by Eurocontrol, does, in fact, require an interpretation of the Convention of 1968. It therefore asks the Court whether under Article 56 of the Convention the treaty and conventions referred to in Article 55 continue to have effect in relation to judgments which do not fall under the second paragraph of Article 1 of the Convention but are excluded from the scope of the Convention as a result of the first paragraph of Article 1 thereof as interpreted by the Court's judgment of 14 October 1976.

As a result of this question the 'dialogue' which began between the Bundesgerichtshof in Karlsruhe and the Oberlandesgericht Düsseldorf, which rightly made use of the unlimited right which the Court of Justice recognizes, as being vested in national courts, to bring the matter before this Court (Case 166/73, *Rheinmühlen* [1974] ECR 33 and Case 146/73, *Rheinmühlen* [1974] ECR 139), is now directly between the Bundesgerichtshof and this Court. This indicates the importance of the judgment which the Court is called upon to give and which must provide the basis of the decision in the three cases between Eurocontrol and three German companies: apart from the two cases which have given rise to the present reference by the Bundesgericht, the judgment of this Court is awaited with interest by the Oberlandesgericht Düsseldorf which has indicated that it has still not given judgment 'on the basis of the Court's judgment of 14 October 1976 and that it was waiting to do so until a ruling had been given in the parallel proceedings with which we are concerned today.

Let me add that the judgment in the present case will necessarily have an effect upon the result of certain cases brought before the administrative courts of the Federal Republic of Germany: there is the action brought by LTU before the Oberverwaltungsgericht (Higher Administrative Court) Nordrheinwestfalen, claiming that the charges made by Eurocontrol are not due, and the appeal brought by LTU before the Bundesverwaltungsgericht (Federal Administrative Court) against the decision of the aforementioned Oberverwaltungsgericht declaring the action for annulment brought by LTU inadmissible insofar as the accounts of charges made by Eurocontrol were not actionable administrative measures within the meaning of German law.

1. In the case of a preliminary ruling the Court always refuses on

principle to consider the relevance of the question submitted by the national Court or whether it is necessary to enable it to give judgment in the case with which it is concerned. However, the Court does endeavour to set out in the answer the factors which seem likely to be 'helpful' in deciding the case. In this spirit let me observe that it is not a question in the abstract whether all the agreements referred to in Article 55 of the Convention of 1968 continue to have effect in respect of judgments to be given in relation to all matters which are expressly excluded by the second paragraph of Article 1 (status of persons, bankruptcy, social security and arbitration).

Although the Bundesgerichtshof does not mention in its order requesting a preliminary ruling the Convention between the Federal Republic of Germany and the Kingdom of Belgium on the Mutual Recognition and *Enforcement of Judgments*, Arbitration Awards and Authentic Instruments in *Civil and Commercial Matters*, signed at Bonn on 30 June 1958, it is obvious that when it speaks of 'the treaty and conventions referred to in Article 55' it is thinking in the first place of that bilateral German-Belgian agreement and since the judgment in question cannot be governed by the Convention of 1968 according to your judgment in the LTU case, It is necessary for it to know whether certain judgments (with the exception naturally of those referred to in the second paragraph of Article 1) while not being of a civil or commercial nature within the meaning of the Convention of 1968, could be so within the meaning of the bilateral convention of 1958. The only matter therefore which it is necessary for the Bundesgerichtshof to know is whether the Convention of 1968 has replaced for Belgium and the Federal Republic of Germany the bilateral convention signed between the two countries in 1958 in the very special case of judgments relating to the recovery of charges by Eurocontrol or whether there remain in some way 'residual' civil and commercial matters which might come under the bilateral convention.

2. This question must therefore obviously be related to the answer given by the Court in Case 29/76. I think that the Court will wish first of all to confirm this case-law. Several commentators have criticized this judgment, given contrary to the opinion of Mr Advocate General Reischl, but for the present I shall assume that it is to stand. Moreover having regard to the 'guidelines' indicated by your judgment, the working party entrusted with making the necessary adjustments for the accession of the new Member States to the Convention of 1968 has laid down that at present revenue, customs and *administrative* matters are not civil and commercial matters within the meaning of the Convention.

3. The Bundesgerichtshof assumes that there are judgments which, while not falling within the classes expressly excluded by the second paragraph of Article I of the Convention and not relating to civil and commercial matters within the meaning of this expression in the Court's case-law, might continue to be civil and commercial matters within the meaning of the bilateral convention; the question put to the Court necessarily calls, it seems to me, for a definition of the respective fields of application of the Convention of 1968 and of the bilateral convention of 1958 having regard to the charges claimed by Eurocontrol.

Article 55 of the Brussels Convention states 'this Convention shall, for the States which are parties to it, *supersede* the following conventions concluded between two or more of them', namely in particular the German-Belgian Convention of 1958. However, this supersession is subject to the provisions of the second paragraph of Article 54 and of Article 56'.

Article 56 States that 'the treaty and the conventions referred to in Article 55 shall continue to have effect *in relation to matters* to which this Convention does not apply'.

Judgments given *before* the entry into force of the Convention, that is to say before 1 February 1973, even if given in matters to which the Convention applies, are not affected by the provisions of the Convention of 1968 (second paragraph of Article 56).

Judgments given *after* the date of entry into force of the Convention of 1968 in proceedings instituted *before* that date 'shall be recognized and enforced in accordance with the provisions of Title III [of the Convention of 1968] if jurisdiction was founded upon rules which accorded with those provided for either in Title II of this Convention or in a convention concluded between the State in which the judgment was given and the State in which recognition or enforcement is sought and which was in force when the proceedings were instituted' (second paragraph of Article 54). It is also necessary, of course, that the proceedings should relate to 'civil and commercial matters' within the meaning of the Convention of 1968 but this is so obvious that the article does not even say so expressly.

In other words, to know whether the European Convention has 'superseded' the bilateral Convention or whether on the other hand the latter 'continues to have effect' it is necessary to ascertain whether the matters to which the two Conventions respectively apply are the same, that is, whether the 'civil and commercial matters' referred to in Article 1 of the Convention of 1968 are the same as the 'civil and commercial matters' referred to in Article 3 of the bilateral convention.

4. In general the provisions of the bilateral agreements cannot be interpreted by the Court of Justice save under Article 182 of the Treaty and the jurisdiction of the Court is limited to the Community provisions (Article 164). This rule which the Court has developed in relation to regulations concerning social security for migrant workers applies likewise, it seems to me, to the interpretation of the Convention of 1968. The Court had a similar problem in the sphere of social security where the Community regulations also have a provision to the effect that 'Save as otherwise expressly stated herein, the provisions of this regulation shall ... replace the provisions of: (a) the social security conventions concluded between two or more Member States .. .' (Article 5 of Regulation No 3) and 'The provisions of this regulation notwithstanding, the following shall continue to apply: ... (e) such other provisions of social security conventions as are listed in Annex D to this regulation' (Article 6 of Regulation No 3).

It is clear from these provisions, as the Court decided in its judgment of 7 June 1973 in Case 82/72, *Walder* ([1973] ECR at p. 604), that the principle that the provisions of social security conventions concluded between Member States are *replaced* by Regulation No 3 is *mandatory* in nature and does not allow of exceptions save for the cases expressly laid down by the regulation. Not even the fact that social security conventions concluded between Member States are *more advantageous* to persons covered by Regulation No 3 than the regulation itself is sufficient to justify an exception to this principle unless such conventions are expressly preserved by the regulation. This fact to which the Court refused to attach crucial significance in relation to social security should not be decisive in the sphere covered by the Convention either if, as I said in my opinion in Case 42/76, *De Wolf* ([1976] ECR at p. 1774), the conclusion of the Convention between the Contracting States connotes *a priori*, at least so it may be supposed, the organization of a system which is on the whole better than the previous bilateral or multilateral systems.

A confirmation of this supposition is furnished by the fact that, unless I am mistaken, Eurocontrol has always relied solely on the provisions of the Convention of 1968 and not on those of the bilateral convention to obtain enforcement of the decisions given in its favour in Belgium. In brief, Eurocontrol, which had begun legal proceedings before the entry into force of the Convention of 1968 to recover its charges, once armed with the judgment of the Tribunal de Commerce of Brussels given after the said entry into force, has attempted at first to enforce it in the Federal Republic of Germany by alleging that the judgment was given in accordance with the jurisdiction provided for by the bilateral convention and relying on the second paragraph of Article 54 of the Convention of 1968; now it prefers to fall back on the Convention of 1958 since the Court has decided that the recovery of such debts is not a 'civil and commercial matter' within the meaning of the Brussels Convention.

As I said in my opinion in the *De Wolf* case it does not appear to me possible to apply the Convention of 1968 'à la carte'; the balance achieved by the Convention would be upset if a party could, at his own convenience, use either the Community system laid down by the Convention or the traditional treaty rights under bilateral conventions.

5. It nevertheless appears to me necessary to carry the analysis a little further and to refer, at least indirectly, to the provisions of the bilateral convention of 1958 to give a helpful answer to the national court.

It is, moreover, necessary to interpret the bilateral conventions, at least in certain respects, for the purpose of the interpretation and application of the Convention of 1968. The first paragraph of Article 54, as I have said, provides that the provisions shall apply only to legal proceedings instituted *after* the entry into force of the Convention. Nevertheless, the second paragraph thereof provides, in relation to enforcement, that the fact that enforcement proceedings have been instituted *before* the entry into force of the Convention is of no consequence provided that the court of the State in which judgment was given delivered judgment *after* such date 'if jurisdiction was founded upon rules which *accorded with those provided* for either in Title II of this Convention or *in a convention* concluded between the State in which the judgment was given and the State in which recognition or enforcement is sought and which was in force when the proceedings were instituted'.

In Case 29/76 the Commission and Mr Advocate General Reischl following it relied on the existence of the German-Belgian Convention of 30 June 1958 to claim jurisdiction ratione loci for the Tribunal de Commerce of Brussels (court of the State in which the judgment was given) in accordance with the Convention of 1958, which obviously implies an interpretation of that Convention. The Court itself, by implication, acted in the same manner, for it would not have answered the question referred to it if it had not taken the view that the rules on jurisdiction under the Convention of 1958 were applicable ratione temporis in the case in question.

Following this precedent I think that with regard to the recovery of the charges of Eurocontrol the Convention of 1968, as interpreted by you, has replaced, in relations between the Federal Republic of Germany and Belgium, the bilateral convention signed in 1958 between those two countries.

This is so not only because the Brussels Convention has been signed between these two countries, the signatories to the Convention of 1958, not only because the words used in this respect by the two instruments are identical, but above all because the second paragraph of Article 54 postulates *the equal standing of the rules of jurisdiction* provided for by the bilateral convention with those provided for by Title II of the Brussels Convention, since this is the justification for enforcement in conformity with the provisions of the Brussels Convention of judgments given as a result of proceedings begun even before the Convention entered into force.

6. Whether it be by means of the Brussels Convention or by means of the bilateral Convention, the enforcement of the judgment given in the original country would meet with the same kind of obstacles.

An enforcement by means of the Brussels Convention comes up against the Court's judgment of 14 October 1976. The proceedings initiated in the first country concerned the recovery of charges payable by a person governed by private law to a national or international body governed by public law for the use of equipment and services provided by such body, their use being obligatory and exclusive (cf. paragraph 4 of the part of the Court's judgment headed 'Law'). *In that case* the rate of charges, the methods of calculation and the procedures for collection were fixed *unilaterally* in relation to the users, the public body having *unilaterally* fixed the place of performance of the obligation at its registered office and selected the national courts with jurisdiction to adjudicate upon the performance of the obligation. In brief the proceedings were between a *public authority* and a person governed by private law in which the *public authority* was acting in the exercise of its *powers* (paragraph 5).

Since it relates to an application for enforcement of an enforceable judgment given in a civil and commercial matter within the meaning of the Brussels Convention, the procedure is very simple: the party against whom the enforcement is sought cannot at this stage of the proceedings make any submissions on the application; under no circumstances may the judgment be reviewed as to its substance (Article 34). It is true the application may be refused but only for one of the reasons specified in Articles 27 and 28, that is to say in particular if the enforcement is contrary to *public policy* in the State in which recognition is sought (Article 27(1)). But the last paragraph of Article 28 provides that '*the jurisdiction* of the court of the State in which the judgment was given *may not be reviewed*; the test of public policy referred to in Article 27(1) *may not be applied* to the rules relating to jurisdiction' (that is to say those referred to in Title II).

The reason underlying the Court's judgment of 14 October 1976 therefore appears to me to be the following: to include a claim for recovery such as that which was the subject of the action before the national court in civil and commercial matters would have had the result that the court of the State in which recognition was sought and which had asked for a preliminary ruling would have been bound by the classification given of its jurisdiction by the court of the State in which judgment was given and this jurisdiction, not being a matter of *public policy* (third paragraph of Article 28) could not have been reviewed by the court of the State in which enforcement was sought. The Court of Justice itself considered that the main action raised, in fact, a question of *public policy* and for this reason felt it necessary to reject the classification of the action as a 'civil or commercial matter' within the meaning of the Brussels Convention.

Recourse to the bilateral convention appears at first sight simpler, but this is not so. It is true that, as distinct from the Brussels Convention, the bilateral convention covers the enforcement of arbitration awards but subject to their being in accord with public policy (Article 13). In the same way the definition of what must be understood by 'judgment' (Article 1(3), Article 2(2)) or by 'matter' (Articles 3 and 4) within the meaning of the bilateral convention appears wider than the expressions in Articles 25 and 1 of the Brussels Convention.

But this liberality is tempered by a serious restriction. According to Article 10, the judgment of which enforcement is requested may not be reviewed in any way save as specified in Article 2. Under that article, even if there can be no review of the substance of the judgment (last sentence of Article 10(1)), the court before which enforcement is sought - contrary to the position in relation to recognition (Article 5(1)) - is not bound by the findings of fact on which the court in which judgment was given based its jurisdiction and recognition may be refused if, but only if, it is contrary to the public policy of the State where it is sought (first subparagraph of Article 2(1)) and if the courts of the State where the judgment was given are not recognized as having jurisdiction under the convention (third subparagraph of Article 2(1)): in this respect reference should be made in particular to the provisions of the second subparagraph of Article 3(1) and to Article 3(2). With regard to enforcement the court applied to may, and indeed must, review the jurisdiction of the court where judgment was given and, as distinct from the Brussels Convention, the *rules for jurisdiction* are put on the same level as public policy and the court must review them of its own motion.

Consequently, the practical result appears to me to be the same whether the application for enforcement is based on the Brussels Convention or on the bilateral convention: through the expedient of the objection based on public policy and the review, of the court's own motion, of the jurisdiction of the court before which judgment was given, the court in which the enforcement is sought under the bilateral convention must review the classification of the subject-matter of the action brought before the original court and, having regard to what was laid down in the judgment of the Court of Justice of 14 October 1976, I cannot see how the German courts could still include in the field of application of the bilateral convention actions for the recovery of the charges of Eurocontrol without involving German public policy or refusing to review the jurisdiction of the courts where judgment was given, which comes to the same thing. It seems to me that this is what the Bundesverfassungsgericht decided in an order of 2 December 1974.

Of course, as it is customary to state, it is for the national court to decide this issue.

My opinion is that the Court should rule that Article 56 of the Brussels Convention of 1968 must be interpreted as meaning that the bilateral convention listed fifthly in Article 55 of the Brussels Convention continues to have effect in relation to the enforcement of judgments including such as are given after the entry into force of the Convention as a result of actions begun before such date, provided that that application does not prejudice the classification of 'civil and commercial matter' within the meaning of the first paragraph of Article 1 of the Convention.

Case 784/79 - 6 May 1980

Porta-Leasing GmbH
v
Prestige International S.A.

Protocol, Article I, second paragraph - Prorogation of jurisdiction - Agreements conferring jurisdiction - Validity with respect to a person domiciled in Luxembourg - Special requirements as to form - Express and specific agreement - Concept.

Summary

The second paragraph of Article I of the Protocol annexed to the Convention of 27 September 1968 on Jurisdiction and the Enforcement of Judgments in Civil specifically agreed to by a person and Commercial Matters must be interpreted as meaning that a clause conferring jurisdiction within the meaning of that provision may not be considered to have been expressly and specifically agreed to by a person domiciled in Luxembourg unless that clause, besides being in writing as required by Article 17 of the Convention, is mentioned in a provision specially and exclusively meant for this purpose and which has been specifically signed by the party domiciled in Luxembourg; in this respect the signing of the contract as a whole does not in itself suffice. It is not however necessary for that clause to be mentioned in a document separate from the one which constitutes the written instrument of the contract.

JUDGMENT OF THE COURT

Kutscher, President, Mertens de Wilmars and Lord Mackenzie Stuart, Judges

1. By an order of 12 October 1979 which was received at the Court on 23 October 1979 the Oberlandesgericht [Higher Regional Court] Koblenz asked the Court under Article 1 of the Protocol on the interpretation by the Court of Justice of the Convention of 27 September 1968 on Jurisdiction and the Enforcement of Judgments in Civil and Commercial Matters (Official Journal 1975, L 204, p. 28) for a preliminary ruling on the interpretation of the second paragraph of Article I of the Protocol annexed to the above-mentioned Convention of 27 September 1968.

2. This question arises out of a dispute between a leasing undertaking, the plaintiff in the main action, whose registered office is at Trier, Federal Republic of Germany, and one of its customers, the defendant in the main action, whose registered office is in the Grand Duchy of Luxembourg. The contracts made between the parties were drawn up in advance as standard printed contracts and contain a clause conferring jurisdiction on the courts of the place where the plaintiff in the main action has its seat. When sued by the plaintiff in the Landgericht [Regional Court] Trier the Luxembourg firm disputed the jurisdiction on grounds of locality of the German court by relying on the second paragraph of Article I of the Protocol annexed to the Convention of 27 September 1968.

3. The second paragraph of Article I provides that: 'An agreement conferring jurisdiction within the meaning of Article 17 (of the Convention) shall be valid with respect to a person domiciled in Luxembourg only if that person has expressly and specifically so agreed'.

4. In order to enable it to resolve the problem of jurisdiction which thus arose the Oberlandesgericht Koblenz, having been asked to rule on appeal, put the following question: 'Does an agreement conferring jurisdiction which is contained in a standard form contract concluded with and signed by a person resident in Luxembourg but to which his attention has not specifically been brought satisfy the requirements as to validity contained in the second paragraph of Article 1 of the Protocol annexed to the Convention of 27 September 1968 on Jurisdiction and the Enforcement of Judgments in Civil and Commercial Matters?'

5. In order to reply to this question the provision which it is sought to interpret should be put in perspective in regard to Article 17 of the Convention. According to Article 17 a prorogation of jurisdiction (Vereinbarung über die Zuständigkeit) agreed to between the parties must be by agreement in writing or by an oral agreement evidenced in writing. It follows from the judgments given by the Court of Justice on 14

December 1976 (Case 24/76 *Estasis Salotti* and Case 25/76 *Segoura* ECR 1831 and 1851) that the purpose of the requirement of a writing under Article 17 serves to ensure that the consensus between the parties, who, by a prorogation of competence, depart from the general rules for determining jurisdiction laid down in Articles 2, 5 and 6 of the Convention, is clearly and precisely demonstrated and has actually been reached. The second paragraph of Article 1 of the Protocol which it is sought to interpret goes further. By expressly providing that an agreement conferring jurisdiction shall be valid with respect to a person domiciled in Luxembourg only if that person has 'expressly and specifically so agreed' that provision imposes more special and more strict conditions which are superimposed on those in Article 17 of the Convention.

6. This interpretation accords with the purpose of the second paragraph of Article I of the Protocol annexed to the Convention of 27 September 1968. Indeed, in view of the fact that many contracts concluded by persons resident in the Grand Duchy of Luxembourg are international contracts, the authors of the Convention of 27 September 1968 thought that it was absolutely necessary to make clauses conferring jurisdiction which were likely to be used against persons domiciled in Luxembourg subject to more stringent conditions than those contained in Article 17 of the Convention. This aim can only be completely achieved if the clause in question has been accepted both expressly and specifically by the person domiciled in Luxembourg.

7. In regard to persons domiciled in Luxembourg there are therefore two requirements in addition to the conditions contained in Article 17 of the Convention; these must be cumulatively fulfilled, that is to say, first, express agreement and, secondly, specific agreement. A comparison between the words used in Article 17 and those used in Article I of the Protocol indicates that the first of these conditions is not satisfied unless the agreement conferring jurisdiction is contained in a provision which is specially and exclusively devoted to it.

8. In order to meet the requirement of specific agreement it is further necessary for the Luxembourg party specifically to sign the clause conferring jurisdiction as an indication of his agreement; his mere signing of the contract is not sufficient to secure the safeguards which the second paragraph of Article I of the Protocol has in view. It is not, however, necessary for that clause to be mentioned in a document separate from the one which constitutes the written instrument of the contract.

9. On the basis of the foregoing considerations it is appropriate to answer that the second paragraph of Article I of the Protocol annexed to the Convention of 27 September 1968 must be interpreted as meaning that a clause conferring jurisdiction within the meaning of that provision may not be considered to have been expressly and specifically agreed to by a person domiciled in Luxembourg unless that clause, besides being in writing as required by Article 17 of the Convention, is mentioned in a provision specially and exclusively meant for this purpose and specifically signed by the party domiciled in Luxembourg; in this respect the signing of the contract as a whole does not in itself suffice. It is not, however, necessary for that clause to be mentioned in a document separate from the one which constitutes the written instrument of the contract.

On those grounds, the court (Third Chamber), in answer to the question referred to it by the Oberlandesgericht Koblenz (Second Civil Chamber) by order of 12 October 1979, received at the Court on 23 October 1979, hereby rules:

The second paragraph of Article I of the Protocol annexed to the Convention of 27 September 1968 on Jurisdiction and the Enforcement of Judgments in Civil and Commercial Matters must be interpreted as meaning that a clause conferring jurisdiction within the meaning of that provision may not be considered to have been expressly and specifically agreed to by a person domiciled in Luxembourg unless that clause, besides being in writing as required by Article 17 of the Convention, is mentioned in a provision specially and exclusively meant for this purpose and specifically signed by the party domiciled in Luxembourg; in this respect the signing of the contract as a whole does not in itself suffice. It is not however necessary for that clause to be mentioned in a document separate from the one which constitutes the written instrument of the contract.

OPINION OF MR ADVOCATE GENERAL REISCHL

The present proceedings concern the interpretation of the second paragraph of Article 1 of the Protocol annexed to the Convention on Jurisdiction and Enforcement of Judgments in Civil and Commercial Matters (hereinafter referred to as 'the Brussels Convention'), according to which: 'An agreement concerning jurisdiction, within the meaning of Article 17 [of the Brussels Convention] shall be valid with respect to a person domiciled in Luxembourg only if that person has *expressly and specifically* so agreed'.

In 1977 the parties to the main action concluded a series of leasing contracts for motor vehicles on the basis of which the German company Porta-Leasing GmbH, the plaintiff in the main action, submitted claims, according to its own statements, for performance of the contracts and damages against the Luxembourg company Prestige International S.A., the defendant in the main action.

The relevant printed contract forms include the following agreement conferring jurisdiction: '? 12 General ... (5) The place of performance and of jurisdiction for all the obligations arising under this contract shall be the place where the lessor has its seat'.

In the proceedings instituted before the Landgericht Trier the defendant claimed that the Court had no jurisdiction as the clause concerning jurisdiction was not *expressly and specifically* agreed upon by it in accordance with the second paragraph of Article 1 of the Protocol annexed to the Brussels Convention.

The Landgericht Trier dismissed the case for want of jurisdiction and stated in the reasons for its decision that an agreement concerning jurisdiction is binding on a person domiciled in Luxembourg only if it is contained in a separate document apart from the other terms in the agreement.

The Second Civil Senate of the Oberlandesgericht, Koblenz, before which the case went on appeal, made an order on 28 September 1979 staying the proceedings and referring the following question to the Court of Justice for a preliminary ruling in accordance with Articles 1 and 2(2) of the Protocol of 3 June 1971 on the interpretation by the Court of Justice of the Convention of 27 September 1968 on Jurisdiction and the Enforcement of Judgments in Civil and Commercial Matters: 'Does an agreement conferring jurisdiction which is contained in a standard form contract concluded with and signed by a person resident in Luxembourg but to which his attention has not specifically been brought satisfy the requirements as to validity contained in the second paragraph of Article 1 of the Protocol annexed to the Convention of 27 September 1968 on Jurisdiction and the Enforcement of Judgments in Civil and Commercial Matters?'

Contrary to the plaintiff's view, that question should be answered in the negative for the following reasons and giving them I shall in essence be following what has been said by the Commission.

In general, an agreement conferring jurisdiction is only effective according to the provisions in Article 17 of the Brussels Convention if there is an agreement in writing or an oral agreement evidenced in writing. In the case of a party domiciled in Luxembourg the effectiveness of an agreement concerning jurisdiction is subject to the additional requirement of form, according to the second paragraph of Article 1 of the Protocol annexed to the Brussels Convention, that it has been *expressly and specifically* so agreed by that party. As is clear from the Jenard Report (Official Journal 1979 C 59, p. 63), that requirement of form is a protective measure in favour of persons resident in Luxembourg who, on account of the large number of international contracts concluded by them, run the risk of actions being brought against them in foreign courts far more often than parties in the other Contracting States. As the Commission rightly points out, the object of protecting them has already been partly achieved insofar as the validity of an agreement conferring jurisdiction is subject to its being expressly agreed to by the party domiciled in Luxembourg. On the other hand, one cannot ignore the fact that many international contracts, as in the present case, contain in a standard form, along with numerous other clauses in the contract, express clauses conferring jurisdiction, with the result that even though the latter are specifically indicated, insufficient attention is paid to them. That is why the Contracting States made the effectiveness of an agreement conferring jurisdiction for a person domiciled in Luxembourg dependent, under the second paragraph of Article 1 of the Protocol annexed to the Brussels Convention, on its being expressly *and* specifically agreed. The word 'and' linking the two requirements is sufficient to show that specific agreement constitutes a further requirement for effectiveness in addition to the conditions mentioned regarding an agreement conferring jurisdiction.

The Commission is therefore of the opinion that the requirement 'specifically so agreed' is only satisfied if the agreement conferring jurisdiction forms the subject-matter of a written, separate declaration of acceptance by the Luxembourg party, and that that declaration must not contain any contractual provisions apart from the agreement conferring jurisdiction.

I would not go that far, however. It must be conceded on behalf of the plaintiff that the wording of the provision in question does not stipulate the requirement of a separate document. In my opinion the protection envisaged in favour of the Luxembourg party is satisfied if he expressly acknowledges the agreement conferring jurisdiction in a separate written declaration. The acknowledgment may be made in a separate document, but it can also be made by the party declaring acceptance of the agreement conferring jurisdiction, in addition to the other stipulations in the agreement, by means of a separate signature on the same document.

Therefore I suggest that the question which has been referred to the Court for a preliminary ruling should be answered as follows:

An agreement conferring jurisdiction included without specific indication in a standard form contract concluded with and signed by a person resident in Luxembourg does not satisfy the requirements as to validity contained in the second paragraph of Article 1 of the Protocol annexed to the Convention of 27 September 1968 on Jurisdiction and the Enforcement of Judgments in Civil and Commercial Matters. In order to satisfy the requirements as to validity in that provision there must be a separate written declaration whereby the party resident in Luxembourg expressly accepts the agreement conferring jurisdiction.

Case 157/80 - 26 May 1981

Criminal proceedings against Siegfried Ewald Rinkau

Article II of the Protocol annexed to the Convention - Special provisions as regards criminal proceedings - Right to be defended without appearing in person in criminal proceedings relating to an offence which was not intentionally committed - Concept of an 'offence which was not intentionally committed' - Independent concept - Definition - Scope - Criminal proceedings relating to an offence which was not intentionally committed raising the issue of the accused's civil liability.

Summary

1. The concept of an offence which was not intentionally committed appearing in Article II of the Protocol annexed to the Convention of 27 September 1968 on Jurisdiction and the Enforcement of Judgments in Civil and Commercial Matters must be regarded as an independent concept which must be explained by reference, first, to the objectives and scheme of the Convention and, secondly, to the general principles which the national legal systems have in common. It covers any offence the legal definition of which does not require, either expressly or as appears from the nature of the offence defined, the existence of intent on the part of the accused to commit the punishable act or omission.

2. The right to be defended without appearing in person, granted by Article II of the aforementioned Protocol, applies in all criminal proceedings concerning offences which were not intentionally committed, in which the accused's liability at civil law, arising from the elements of the offence for which he is being prosecuted, is in question or on which such liability might subsequently be based.

JUDGMENT OF THE COURT

Mertens de Wilmars, President, Pescatore, Lord Mackenzie Stuart, Koopmans, O'Keeffe, Bosco, Touffait, Everling and Chloros, Judges

1. By a judgment dated 17 June 1980 which was received at the Court on 3 July 1980 the Hoge Raad [Supreme Court] of the Netherlands referred to the Court for a preliminary ruling under the Protocol of 3 June 1971 on the Interpretation by the Court of Justice of the Convention of 27 September 1968 on Jurisdiction and the Enforcement of Judgments in Civil and Commercial Matters (hereinafter referred to as 'the Convention') two questions as to the interpretation of Article II of the Protocol annexed to the Convention (hereinafter referred to as 'the Protocol').

2. After being summoned to appear before the Politierechter [Magistrate] of the Arrondissementsrechtbank [District Court], Zutphen (Netherlands), for driving in the Netherlands a vehicle equipped with a radio-electrical transmitting device without holding the requisite licence, Siegfried Rinkau, resident in the Federal Republic of Germany, did not appear at the hearing. His Counsel asked for leave to defend him. Notwithstanding the opinion of the Public Prosecutor the Magistrate took the view that the accused should be allowed to avail himself of the right granted by the first paragraph of Article II of the Protocol and gave his Counsel leave to defend him. Mr Rinkau was sentenced in his absence to a fine or failing payment thereof to one day's imprisonment and the radio-electrical device was ordered to be confiscated.

3. Following an appeal by the Public Prosecutor, the Gerechtshof [Regional Court of Appeal], Arnhem, held in its interlocutory judgment of 28 August 1979 that Article II of the Protocol had application in all criminal proceedings concerning offences which were not intentionally committed but that the offence with which the accused was charged was not such an offence. The Gerechtshof accordingly decided not to grant the accused's Counsel leave to defend him in his absence and, as regards the substance of the case, by a judgment of 11 September 1979 upheld the judgment given at first instance.

4. Mr Rinkau appealed in cassation against those two judgments. He claimed that Article II of the Protocol had been infringed. The Hoge Raad decided before making any further ruling to refer the following questions to the Court for an interpretation:

'1. Must the expression 'an offence which was not intentionally committed' appearing in the first paragraph of Article II of the said Protocol be understood as including any offence for which the legal definition does not require specific intent in regard to any element of the offence, or should the expression be understood in a narrower sense as relating only to offences in the definition of which there is reference to some element of guilt (*culpa*) on the part of the offender?

2. If the conditions set out in Article II of the said Protocol are fulfilled, does the right granted to 'the accused' by that article apply without restriction, or does the accused person have that right only where he has to defend himself against a civil claim made in the relevant criminal proceedings, or at any rate where the interests of the accused under civil law are affected by the outcome of the criminal proceedings?'

General considerations

5. According to Article 65 of the Convention the Protocol forms an integral part thereof. The scope of the Convention, which is defined in Article 1, is confined to civil and commercial matters. The question to be asked at the outset, therefore, is why a rule of criminal procedure like Article II of the Protocol came to be inserted in a Convention on civil and commercial matters. That article reads: 'Without prejudice to any more favourable provisions of national laws, persons domiciled in a Contracting State who are being prosecuted in the criminal courts of another Contracting State of which they are not nationals for an offence which was not intentionally committed may be defended by persons qualified to do so, even if they do not appear in person.

However, the court seised of the matter may order appearance in person; in the case of failure to appear, a judgment given in the civil action without the person concerned having had the opportunity to arrange for his defence need not be recognised or enforced in the other Contracting States.'

6. In the report submitted to the national governments at the same time as the draft Convention (Official Journal 1979, C 59, p. 1) that extension to the criminal field is justified by reference to the consequences which a judgment of a criminal court may entail in civil and commercial matters if those consequences themselves come within the ambit of the Convention.

7. The first paragraph of Article II of the Protocol appears to have been the transposition into the Convention of Article II of the Protocol annexed

to the Treaty between Belgium, the Netherlands and Luxembourg on Jurisdiction, Bankruptcy and the Validity and Enforcement of Judgments, Arbitration Awards and Authentic Instruments. That provision, in fact, provides: 'Without prejudice to any more favourable provisions of national laws the nationals of any one of the three countries who are resident in their country may appear before the courts of the other two countries by special attorney if they are being prosecuted there for an offence other than one which was intentionally committed'.
The commission responsible for drawing up the draft Benelux Treaty explained in its report that it believed that it was 'essential' that the accused 'should be able to conduct his defence during the criminal stage of the proceedings' without having to appear in person.

8. That same reason is also cited in the report on the Brussels Convention in connection with Article II of the Protocol annexed to the Convention. However, that right is conferred by the Convention only on accused persons being prosecuted for an 'offence which was not intentionally committed' That concept is not further defined or clarified in the Convention. However, the report does say that it 'includes road accidents' which thus appear to be a particularly important area of application of Article II of the Protocol.

9. It is necessary to stress once more that, as Article II expressly provides, the right granted to the accused person to be defended without appearing in person does not prejudice the court's power to order appearance in person. If, notwithstanding such an order, the accused person does not appear, the court may deliver judgment without granting the accused's Counsel leave to defend him. The result of the absence of a defence, according to the second paragraph of Article II of the Protocol, is that a judgment given in the civil action need not be recognised or enforced in the other contracting States.

10. The questions framed by the Hoge Raad of the Netherlands must be answered in the light of those various considerations.

The concept of an 'offence which was not intentionally committed'

11. Although the concept of an 'offence which was not intentionally committed' is not defined in the Convention, in order to ensure as far as possible that the rights and obligations of the Contracting States and of the persons concerned arising from the Convention are equal and uniform, it must nevertheless be regarded as an independent concept

which must be explained by reference, first, to the objectives and scheme of the Convention and, secondly, to the general principles which the national legal systems have in common. That is all the more necessary where, as in this case, terminological differences exist between the various language versions of the Convention.

12. The aim of the Convention to cover offences connected with road accidents through its use of the concept of an offence which was not intentionally committed has already been mentioned in connection with the objectives of the Convention. Another more general guide is the fact that by restricting the right to be defended without appearing in person, which is made available to persons who have committed certain offences, the Convention clearly seeks to deny that right to persons being prosecuted for offences which are sufficiently serious to justify its denial.

13. It is therefore necessary to ascertain whether there is a criterion for classification which is common to the national legal systems of all the Contracting States, by which offences may de distinguished according to their seriousness and on the basis of which most, if not all, of the offences connected with road accidents may be classified amongst the less serious offences.

14. The national laws of most of the Contracting States distinguish in one way or another between offences committed intentionally and those not so committed. Even though that distinction may lead to the classification of offences into categories of which the content may vary appreciably from one legal system to another, it still serves the aforementioned purpose.

15. Whereas offences which were intentionally committed, if they are to be punishable, require an intent to commit them on the part of the person concerned, offences which were not intentionally committed may result from carelessness, negligence or even the mere objective breach of a legal provision. They are therefore, first, generally less serious in nature and, secondly, cover most offences connected with road accidents which are to be ascribed to carelessness, negligence or the mere actual breach of a legal provision.

16. Consequently, the answer to the first question of the Hoge Raad must be that the expression 'an offence which was not intentionally committed' within the meaning of Article II of the Protocol annexed to the Convention of 27 September 1968 on Jurisdiction and the

Enforcement of Judgments in Civil and Commercial Matters should be understood as meaning any offence the legal definition of which does not require, either expressly or as appears from the nature of the offence defined, the existence of intent on the part of the accused to commit the punishable act or omission.

The second question

17. The Hoge Raad asks in the second place whether the right granted to the accused by Article II of the Protocol has application in all criminal proceedings which affect the accused's interests at civil law or only in those in which a criminal court has to decide a civil claim at the same time.

18. The Netherlands Government points out in its observations that the scope of the Convention is restricted to civil and commercial matters. It considers that that restriction should be borne in mind when Article II of the Protocol is construed, as appears from the second paragraph of that article. The Netherlands Government accordingly concludes that the right granted to the accused by the first paragraph has application only if the criminal court has to decide a civil claim at the same time.

19. The Commission does not deny that the aim of Article II of the Protocol is to lay down a rule of criminal procedure insofar as criminal proceedings may have an effect on the accused's interests at civil law. However, having regard to the fact that a rule of criminal procedure which is for the benefit of the accused should receive a wide interpretation and in view of the difficulty which frequently exists, in the Commission's view, in deciding whether or not criminal proceedings are likely to affect the accused's interests at civil law, the Commission considers that the right granted to the accused by Article II of the Protocol must apply in all criminal proceedings.

20. Although it is not expressly provided by the first paragraph of Article II of the Protocol that the right therein granted to the accused applies only during criminal proceedings in which his liability at civil law (arising from the elements of the offence for which he is being prosecuted) is in question or on which such liability might subsequently be based, it should nevertheless not be forgotten that that was the actual intention behind the insertion in the Protocol of the provision in question. That intention precludes the right to be defended without appearing in person from having application in criminal proceedings in which the accused is not open to a civil claim in the circumstances described above.

21. The answer to the second question of the Hoge Raad should, therefore, be that the accused's right to be defended without appearing in person, granted by Article II of the Protocol annexed to the Convention of 27 September 1968 on Jurisdiction and the Enforcement of Judgments in Civil and Commercial Matters, applies in all criminal proceedings concerning offences which were not intentionally committed, in which the accused's liability at civil law, arising from the elements of the offence for which he is being prosecuted, is in question or on which such liability might subsequently be based.

On those grounds, the Court, in answer to the questions referred to it by the Hoge Raad by judgment of 17 June 1980, hereby rules:

1. The expression 'an offence which was not intentionally committed' within the meaning of Article II of the Protocol annexed to the Convention of 27 September 1968 on Jurisdiction and the Enforcement of Judgments in Civil and Commercial Matters should be understood as meaning any offence the legal definition of which does not require, either expressly or as appears from the nature of the offence defined, the existence of intent on the part of the accused to commit the punishable act or omission.

2. The accused's right to be defended without appearing in person granted by Article II of the Protocol annexed to the Convention of 27 September 1968 on Jurisdiction and the Enforcement of Judgments in Civil and Commercial Matters, applies in all criminal proceedings concerning offences which were not intentionally committed, in which the accused's liability at civil law, arising from the elements of the offence for which he is being prosecuted, is in question or on which such liability might subsequently be based.

OPINION OF MR ADVOCATE GENERAL REISCHL

This reference concerns a German national, a resident of the Federal Republic of Germany, who was summoned before the Politierechter [Magistrate], Zutphen (Netherlands), for driving on 10 March 1977 in the District of Aalten a vehicle equipped with a radio-electrical transmitting device without possessing the licence which is required for that purpose in the Netherlands.

Whilst a licence for the possession and use of such a device is required in the Federal Republic of Germany, it appears that the accused did have one. No action was taken against him when he crossed the border between the Federal Republic and the Netherlands. What is more, the device was switched off at the time in question, the car aerial was retracted and the microphone lay on the back seat.

The accused was not ordered to appear in person and he did not appear at the hearing. However, Counsel from Maastricht (Netherlands) appeared and sought leave to defend him. Contrary to the submissions of the Officer van Justitie [Public Prosecutor], the Politierechter gave Counsel leave to defend the accused pursuant to Article II of the Protocol annexed to the Convention of 27 September 1968 on Jurisdiction and the Enforcement of Judgments in Civil and Commercial Matters since the accused was resident in a State signatory to that Convention and was being prosecuted in another State signatory to that Convention; nevertheless the accused was still sentenced in his absence.

The Magistrate rejected the defence argument that Mr Rinkau was not guilty owing to his pardonable misapprehension as to the existence of a prohibition. The Magistrate further took the view that the offence was an 'offence which was not intentionally committed' and sentenced Mr Rinkau to a fine of 50 guilders or, failing payment thereof, to one day's imprisonment and ordered the confiscation of the equipment seized, the value of which far exceeded the amount of the fine.

The Public Prosecutor's Office appealed against that judgment to the Gerechtshof [Regional Court of Appeal], Arnhem.

That court did not follow a proposal of the Public Prosecutor's Office to refer a question to the Court of Justice as to what was to be understood by an 'offence which was not intentionally committed' for the purposes of Article II of the Protocol. In an interim judgment it held that the act with which the accused was charged did not constitute an 'offence which was not intentionally committed' for the purposes of that article and that the Magistrate was wrong to grant Counsel leave to defend the accused in his absence.

In its final judgment the court upheld the Magistrate's decision on the substance of the case.

Mr Rinkau then lodged an appeal in cassation. Contrary to the opinion of the Procureur-Generaal [Public Prosecutor], the Hoge Raad referred the following questions to the Court in accordance with Article 3(1) of the Protocol of 3 June 1971 on the Interpretation by the Court of Justice of the Convention of 27 September 1968:

'1. Must the expression 'an offence which was not intentionally committed' appearing in the first paragraph of Article II of the said Protocol be understood as including any offence for which the legal definition does not require specific intent in regard to any element of the offence, or should the expression be understood in a narrower sense as relating only to offences in the definition of which there is reference to some element of guilt (culpa) on the part of the offender?

2. If the conditions set out in Article II of the said Protocol are fulfilled,

does the right granted to 'the accused' by that article apply without restriction, or does the accused person have that right only where he has to defend himself against a civil claim made in the relevant criminal proceedings, or at any rate where the interests of the accused under civil law are affected by the outcome of the criminal proceedings?'

My opinion on those questions is as follows, and I deal with the second question first, which I consider to be expedient.

I - Article II of the Protocol annexed to the Convention, which, according to Article 65, forms an integral part of the Convention, reads as follows: 'Without prejudice to any more favourable provisions of national laws, persons domiciled in a Contracting State who are being prosecuted in the criminal courts of another Contracting State of which they are not nationals for an offence which was not intentionally committed may be defended by persons qualified to do so, even if they do not appear in person.

However, the court seised of the matter may order appearance in person; in the case of failure to appear, a judgment given in the civil action without the person concerned having had the opportunity to arrange for his defence need not be recognised or enforced in the other Contracting States.'

For the purpose of construing this provision reference to the preparatory documents is of considerable help.

1. The provisions of the Protocol are based largely on considerations which were taken into account by the Benelux countries; that is particularly so in the case of Article II.

Article 13 of the Treaty signed in Brussels on 24 November 1961 between Belgium, the Netherlands and Luxembourg on Jurisdiction, Bankruptcy and the Validity and Enforcement of Judgments, Arbitration Awards and Authentic Instruments provides: '(1) Judgment given in civil or commercial matters in any one of the three countries shall be recognised in the other two even if delivered by a criminal Court, provided that they fulfil the following conditions: ... (4) The parties were duly represented or their default after a summons had been duly served was established and, if they had a known address, the summons to appear reached them in good time. ...'.

Article 14(1) provides: 'Judgments given in civil or commercial matters in any one of the three countries even if delivered by a criminal court and including those ordering penalty payments may be enforced in the other two countries when they have been declared enforceable in those countries. ...'.

Article 2 of the Protocol annexed to that Treaty reads as follows: 'Without prejudice to any more favourable provisions of national laws the nationals of any one of the three countries who are resident in their country may appear before the courts of the other two countries by special attorney if they are being prosecuted there for an offence other than one which was intentionally committed (in Dutch: 'een niet opzettelijk gepleegd strafbaar feit')'.

According to the preamble to the Netherlands Law of 1961 ratifying that Treaty, application for the enforcement of judgments in civil and commercial matters may be made under Articles 11 and 12 of the Agreement of 28 March 1925 made between the Netherlands and Belgium on the enforcement of judgments: the question arose whether that provision also covered an order to pay damages made by a criminal court upon application by the person injured.

In a judgment of 16 March 1931 (Nederlandse Jurisprudentie 1931, p. 689) the Hoge Raad of the Netherlands held that a judgment given by a criminal court requiring payment of damages could not be regarded as a judgment in a civil or commercial matter for the purposes of the Agreement. The preamble further explained that in order to avoid the Agreement's being interpreted differently in the Contracting States the new Treaty expressly provided that judgments given by a criminal court in civil and commercial matters came under the Treaty as well.

The preamble continues: 'The Netherlands Bar Council, whose views were heard by the Netherlands Delegation to the Benelux Study Commission, favoured the adoption of the view of the Hoge Raad, one of its reasons being that the rule proposed would have resulted in compelling a Netherlands national suspected of committing an offence on the territory of another Contracting State to appear in person before the Belgian or Luxembourg court which would be irreconcilable with the general principle that Netherlands nationals are not extradited and are free to decide whether to appear before a foreign criminal court. That objection was met by Article 2 of the Protocol which gives a national of any of the three States who is being prosecuted for an offence which was not committed intentionally the right to be defended before the courts of the other two States by duly qualified persons'.

2. The report by P. Jenard on the Convention of 27 September 1968 (Official Journal C 59 of 5 March 1979, p. 1) confirms that the experts who drew up the draft Convention had the same considerations in mind: 'The Convention covers civil proceedings brought before criminal courts, both as regards decisions relating to jurisdiction, and also as regards the recognition and enforcement of judgments given by criminal courts in such proceedings. It thereby takes into account certain laws in force in the majority of the Contracting States, tends to rule out any differences of interpretation such as have arisen in applying the Convention between Belgium and the Netherlands and, finally, meets current requirements arising from the increased number of road accidents.

The formula adopted by the Committee reflects the current trend in favour of inserting in conventions clauses specifying that they apply to judgments given in civil or commercial matters by criminal courts. This can in particular be seen in the Benelux Treaty of 24 November 1961 and in the work of the Hague Conference on private international law. ...

As regards both jurisdiction and recognition and enforcement, the Convention affects only civil proceedings of which those courts are seised, and judgments given in such proceedings.

However, in order to counter the objection that a party against whom civil proceedings have been brought might be obstructed in conducting his defence if criminal sanctions could be imposed on him in the same proceedings, the Committee decided on a solution identical to that adopted in the Benelux Treaty. Article II of the Protocol provides that such persons may be defended or represented in criminal courts. Thus they will not be obliged to appear in person to defend their civil interests'.

The report contains these further comments on Article II of the Protocol: 'Article II of the Protocol also has its origin in the Benelux Treaty. The latter applies *inter alia* to judgments given in civil matters by criminal courts, and this puts an end to a controversy between Belgium and the Netherlands on the interpretation of the 1925 Convention between Belgium and the Netherlands. As the report annexed to the Treaty explains, the reluctance of the Netherlands authorities to enforce judgments given by foreign criminal courts in civil claims is due to the fact that a Netherlander charged with a punishable offence committed in a foreign country may be obliged to appear in person before the foreign criminal court in order to defend himself even in relation to the civil claim, although the Netherlands does not extradite its nationals. This objection is less pertinent than would appear at first sight under certain systems of law, and in particular in France, Belgium and Luxembourg, the judgment in a criminal case has the force of *res judicata* in any subsequent civil action.

In view of this, the *subsequent* civil action brought against a Netherlander convicted of a criminal offence will inevitably go against him. It is therefore essential that he should be able to conduct his defence during the criminal stage of the proceedings.

For this reason the Convention, like the Benelux Treaty, provides (see the Protocol) that a person domiciled in a Contracting State may arrange for his defence in the criminal courts of any other Contracting State.

Under Article II of the Protocol, that person will enjoy this right even if he does not appear in person and even if the code of criminal procedure of the State in question does not allow him to be represented. However, if the court seised of the matter should specifically order appearance in person, the judgment given without the person concerned having had the opportunity to arrange for his defence, because he did not appear in person, need not be recognised or enforced in the other Contracting States.

This right is, however, accorded by Article II of the Protocol only to persons who are prosecuted for an offence which was not intentionally committed; this includes road accidents'.

3. It may be readily seen from that commentary that Article II of the Protocol requires application not only in criminal proceedings as part of which civil claims are also to be tried but also in criminal proceedings in which the judgment of the criminal court may have the force of *res judicata* in a subsequent civil action under the relevant national law. On the other hand the provision may not be extended so far as to apply to *all* criminal proceedings. The first paragraph of Article II of the Protocol may not in fact be removed from its context; it may not be treated as a general rule of *criminal* procedure applicable in the Contracting States. The scope of its application is restricted to that of the Convention which, according to Article 1 thereof, 'shall apply in civil and commercial matters' and to those matters *only*. It is only from that point of view that criminal proceedings could have concerned the draughtsmen of the Convention.

The first paragraph of Article II of the Protocol must, therefore, be read together with the second paragraph. It then becomes apparent that the right granted in the first paragraph is available only if 'a civil action' must or might have to be tried. Such a civil claim will be for compensation for the damage caused by a criminal act to the person injured or his successors in law.

The person injured may bring that claim for damages:

- *Either* before the criminal court having jurisdiction to decide upon the charge - in which case one speaks of 'Adhasionsverfahren' [action for damages which may be joined with criminal proceedings] in the Federal Republic of Germany and of 'constitution de partie civile' in France, Belgium and Luxembourg; as a prerequisite for such proceedings, damage to property, personal injury or non-material damage must have been caused to the victim as a direct result of the criminal act; it is not sufficient for the damage or injury to have occurred simply on the occasion of the criminal act;
- Or *later* before a civil court - here again a distinction must be drawn between the actual claim for damages and other civil claims which may have been occasioned by the criminal act and which may be based on breaches of contract for example.

The meaning and object of the provision is, however, to safeguard the opportunity of being heard, which the Convention on Jurisdiction and the Enforcement of Judgments in Civil and Commercial Matters guarantees in all civil actions, even where a decision is being taken in criminal proceedings on 'civil and commercial matters'.

In the cases in which a civil action is not brought before a civil court until later it must indeed be assumed as a matter of principle that the general provisions of the Convention on the protection of the accused operate in the last-mentioned case. But the problem of legal protection then arises if the civil court is bound by the earlier judgment of the criminal court since those general provisions are then redundant. It is only in such cases that the provision in question allows an accused person to be defended by persons suitably qualified if the conditions set out therein are fulfilled.

The Commission makes the point here that it may be assumed that all the States which signed the Convention recognise the unwritten rule that rules concerning the defence of the accused must be construed broadly and in his favour. To support that argument it adduces in evidence the report in connection with the 1961 Treaty drawn up by the joint Belgian, Netherlands and Luxembourg Study Commission on the Harmonisation of Laws.

Commenting on Article 13 of the Treaty that report states at p. 63 that under Belgian and Luxembourg law 'the judgment in a criminal case has the force of *res judicata* in any *subsequent* civil action ... In view of this, the *subsequent* civil action brought against a Netherlander convicted of a criminal offence will inevitably go against him. It is therefore essential that he should be able to conduct his defence during the criminal stage of the proceedings'. Those observations were adopted word for word in the Jenard report. The report on the Benelux Treaty contains this additional comment on Article II of the Protocol: 'Since this provision is meant to protect the rights of the defence it is to be construed in favour of the accused'. Those comments must, however, be viewed in their context; they are qualified by the phrase 'in relation to any subsequent civil action'. So their scope may not be considered to be absolute: They apply only where a civil claim for damages is tried together with criminal proceedings or in a subsequent civil action for compensation for the damage caused to a third party by the accused himself.

Therefore, Article II may have application only where a third person who is injured as a result of an offence which was not intentionally committed brings or may bring claims in conjunction with the criminal proceedings as long as the criminal court has not arrived at a final verdict with regard to the charge, or where the accused's liability at civil law is at any rate already in question at that stage.

4. Returning to the case in point, I am unable to see, subject to the findings of the trial judge, how a third party could have been injured as a direct result of an offence of the type in question or how that party could at a later date bring an action in which the issue of the accused's criminal liability could play a decisive part in determining any consequences in civil law.

It cannot be argued that the accused might later be sued by the owner of the seized equipment with which the vehicle was equipped if the accused had borrowed or rented that vehicle. That is not a 'civil action' within the meaning of Article II of the Protocol. The assumption underlying Article II is that the legal interests of a third party have been infringed by the *unintentional offence* and that that infringement may also lead to civil claims being brought on the part of the third party or his successors in title. However, the legal interest infringed by the offence with which the main proceedings were concerned does not consist in the property rights of a third party. The protection of radio communications, which is in the public interest, or the monopoly in postal services might possibly have been jeopardised, but that is all.

Moreover, no private individual appeared as plaintiff in any concurrent civil action in the main proceedings; except for the sentence itself, no judgment has been or is to be delivered in the Netherlands which could be recognised or enforced in another Member State.

II - As a result of this conclusion in regard to Question 2 I believe that consideration of Question 1 is unnecessary. In the event of the Court's taking a different view I should like to make the following brief remarks on Question 1.

In view of the considerable differences existing between the relevant legal provisions of the Member States I do not feel that it is practicable to give an exhaustive definition of what is meant by an 'offence which was not intentionally committed' in the first paragraph of Article II of the Protocol.

The Jenard report does not address itself to this question. The expression 'fahrlässig begangene Straftat' [offence which was not intentionally committed] which is the same in both the 1961 and 1968 Protocols (subject to the Dutch variation of 'niet opzettelijk' for 'onopsettelijk') varies in the French wording of the two provisions - from 'infraction autre qu'une infraction intentionnelle' in the 1961 version to 'infraction involontaire' in the 1968 version. In my opinion the concept 'infraction autre qu'une infraction intentionnelle' is to be preferred from the legal point of view.

The draughtsmen of the 1968 provision, like the draughtsmen of the 1961 provision, intended the provision to cover *less serious* 'offences'. The question whether such acts, which, in order to reduce the number of criminal offences, particularly traffic offences, are no longer treated as 'offences' but as contraventions, in other words as infringements of administrative rules, still fall under that provision does not need to be resolved for the purposes of this case. In any case the draughtsmen of the 1968 Convention appear to have assumed that, irrespective of the differences existing between the legal systems of the Member States, *deliberate* acts should not fall under Article II of the Protocol.

The term 'an offence which was not intentionally committed' appearing in the first paragraph of Article II of the Protocol should therefore be construed as covering any act which is punishable even if it is *not deliberately* committed. It, thus, covers not only offences which were not committed 'intentionally' but also those which do not require criminal guilt to exist or to be proved in order to be punishable.

III - In my opinion, therefore, the Court should rule that the right accorded under the first paragraph of Article II of the Protocol annexed to the Convention of 1968 on Jurisdiction and the Enforcement of Judgments in Civil and Commercial Matters is available only if a person suffering injury as a result of an offence which was not deliberately committed has brought a claim for damages in criminal proceedings or it is to be expected that the accused's liability at civil law might later be invoked by that injured person or his successors in title.

Case C-398/92 - 10 February 1994

Mund & Fester
v
Hatrex Internationaal Transport

Article 220 of the EEC Treaty - Brussels Convention on Jurisdiction and Enforcement of Judgments - Connection of the EEC Treaty with both the Convention and the national provisions referred to by the Convention - Community law - Principles - Equal treatment - Discrimination on grounds of nationality - National provision authorizing seizure based on the presumption of foreseeable difficulties in the event of a judgment being enforced abroad - Presumption not justified where enforcement takes place in a Member State party to the Brussels Convention - Unlawful.

Summary

1. By providing that the Member States shall, so far as is necessary, enter into negotiations with each other with a view to ensuring for the benefit of their nationals the simplification of formalities governing the reciprocal recognition and enforcement of judgments of courts and tribunals, the purpose of the fourth indent of Article 220 of the Treaty is to facilitate the working of the common market through the adoption of rules of jurisdiction for disputes relating thereto and the elimination, as far as is possible, of difficulties concerning the recognition and enforcement of judgments in the territory of the Contracting States. It follows that the provisions of the Brussels Convention of 27 September 1968 on Jurisdiction and the Enforcement of Judgments in Civil and Commercial Matters, concluded on the basis of that article and within the framework defined by it, and also the national provisions to which the Convention refers, are linked to the EEC Treaty.

2. Article 7 of the Treaty, read in conjunction with Article 220 thereof and the Brussels Convention, precludes a national provision of civil procedure which, in the case of a judgment to be enforced within national territory, authorizes seizure only on the ground that it is probable that enforcement will otherwise be made impossible or substantially more difficult but, in the case of a judgment to be enforced in another Member State, authorizes seizure simply on the ground that enforcement is to take place abroad.

The distinction made by such a provision is not justified by objective circumstances, since all the Member States are Contracting Parties to the Brussels Convention and the conditions for enforcing judgments and the risks attached to the difficulties raised by enforcement are the same.

JUDGMENT OF THE COURT

Mancini, President of the Chamber, Kakouris, Schockweiler, Kapteyn, Murray, Judges

1. By order of 16 November 1992, which was received at the Court on 23 December 1992, the Hanseatisches Oberlandesgericht (Higher Regional Court), Hamburg, referred to the Court for a preliminary ruling under Article 177 of the EEC Treaty a question on the interpretation of Article 7 of the EEC Treaty, read in conjunction with Article 220 of the Treaty and the Convention of 27 September 1968 on Jurisdiction and the Enforcement of Judgments in Civil and Commercial Matters (OJ 1972 L 299, p. 32), as subsequently amended (hereinafter referred to as the 'Brussels Convention').

2. That question was raised in the course of proceedings brought by Mund & Fester, a German company, against Hatrex Internationaal Transport (hereinafter referred to as 'Hatrex'), an international carrier having its registered office in the Netherlands, for a seizure order against assets of Hatrex in Germany.

3. Hatrex transported hazelnuts from Carsamba (Turkey) to Hamburg which were damaged in transit by moisture arising from failure to make the lorry transporting them watertight.

4. Mund & Fester, which acquired rights by subrogation as the result of the transfer of the debt, claimed damages and, to ensure that the debt was recovered, lodged an application on 23 June 1992 at the Landgericht

(Regional Court), Hamburg, pursuant to Paragraph 917 of the Zivilprozebordnung (German Code of Civil Procedure, hereinafter referred to as 'ZPO'), for a seizure order against the lorry belonging to Hatrex which was used to carry the hazelnuts and which was still in Germany.

5. Paragraph 917 of the ZPO provides as follows: '(1) An order for the seizure of assets shall be made when it is to be feared that enforcement of the judgment would otherwise be made impossible or substantially more difficult. (2) The fact that judgment is to be enforced abroad shall be considered sufficient grounds for a seizure order.'

6. By order of the same day the Landgericht Hamburg refused to authorize seizure. It considered that the grounds laid down in Paragraph 917(2) of the ZPO did not exist because the judgment in question was to be enforced in a Contracting State party to the Brussels Convention.

7. Mund & Fester appealed against the order of the Landgericht Hamburg to the Hanseatisches Oberlandesgericht Hamburg, claiming inter alia that the interpretation of Paragraph 917(2) of the ZPO was not affected by the Brussels Convention.

8. Considering that judgment on the application for a seizure order depended on whether the grounds for seizure laid down in Paragraph 917(2) of the ZPO existed where a judgment was to be enforced in the Netherlands, the Hanseatisches Oberlandesgericht Hamburg decided to stay the proceedings and to refer the following question to the Court of Justice for a preliminary ruling: 'Does the need to enforce a seizure order abroad (Paragraph 917 (2) of the Zivilprozebordnung) also constitute grounds for seizure where such enforcement would take place in a State which has adhered to the EEC Convention on Jurisdiction and the Enforcement of Judgments in Civil and Commercial Matters of 27 September 1968 (the Brussels Convention)?'

9. By its question, the national court is essentially asking whether Article 7 of the EEC Treaty, read in conjunction with Article 220 of the Treaty and the Brussels Convention, precludes a national provision of civil procedure which, in the case of a judgment to be enforced within the national territory, authorizes seizure only on the ground that it is probable that enforcement will otherwise be made impossible or substantially more difficult, but, in the case of a judgment to be enforced in another Member State, authorizes seizure simply on the ground that enforcement is to take place abroad.

10. In order to answer that question, it must first be considered whether that provision falls within the ambit of the EEC Treaty.

11. The fourth indent of Article 220 of the EEC Treaty provides that the Member States shall, so far as is necessary, enter into negotiations with each other with a view to securing for the benefit of their nationals the simplification of formalities governing the reciprocal recognition and enforcement of judgments of courts or tribunals, although it is not intended to lay down a legal rule directly applicable as such but merely to mark out the framework of negotiations between the Member States (see judgment in Case 137/84 *Mutsch* [1985] ECR 2681, at paragraph 11). Its purpose is this: to facilitate the working of the common market through the adoption of rules of jurisdiction for disputes relating thereto and through the elimination, as far as is possible, of difficulties concerning the recognition and enforcement of judgments in the territory of the Contracting States.

12. It is on the basis of that article and within the framework defined by it that the Member States concluded the Brussels Convention. Consequently, the provisions of that Convention relating to jurisdiction and to the simplification of formalities concerning the recognition and enforcement of judgments and also the national provisions to which the Convention refers are linked to the EEC Treaty.

13. In this case, it must be considered whether the national provision at issue in the main proceedings introduces discrimination on grounds of nationality prohibited by Article 7 of the Treaty.

14. The Court has consistently held that that provision prohibits any discrimination on grounds of nationality within the field of application of the Treaty. The article forbids not only overt forms of discrimination based on nationality, but also all covert forms of discrimination which, by the application of other criteria of differentiation, lead in fact to the same result (see judgment in Case 22/80 *Boussac* [1980] ECR 3427 at paragraph 9).

15. The national provision at issue in the main proceedings entails a covert form of discrimination.

16. While examination of Paragraph 917(2) of the ZPO reveals no overt discrimination based on nationality, since it applies in all cases where a judgment is to be enforced abroad, even if the assets forming the subject

of the seizure belong to a German national, it is nevertheless the case that, as the Commission correctly points out, the latter situation is rare, the great majority of enforcements abroad being against persons who are not of German nationality or against legal persons not established in the Federal Republic of Germany. It follows that the national provision in question leads in fact to the same result as discrimination based on nationality.

17. However, that finding is not sufficient to conclude that a provision such as that at issue in the main proceedings is incompatible with Article 7 of the Treaty. For that it would also be necessary that the provision in question should not be justified by objective circumstances.

18. In that connection, it must be borne in mind that a seizure order guarantees the creditor the opportunity of enforcing a subsequent judgment against the debtor effectively and within the prescribed time. According to Paragraph 917(1) of the ZPO, seizure is to be authorized where it is reasonable to fear, in the light of the circumstances of the case, that enforcement of the subsequent judgment would otherwise be made impossible or substantially more difficult. By virtue of Paragraph 917(2), such difficulties are presumed from the mere fact that enforcement is to take place in a State other than the Federal Republic of Germany.

19. While such a presumption is justified where the subsequent judgment is to be enforced in the territory of a non-member country, it is not justified where enforcement is to take place in the territory of the Member States of the Community. All those States are Contracting Parties to the Brussels Convention whose territories may be regarded as forming a single entity, as indicated in the Report on the Brussels Convention (Official Journal 1979 C 59, p. 1, particularly at p. 13).

20. Consequently, although the conditions for enforcing judgments and the risks attached to the difficulties raised by enforcement are the same in all the Member States, Paragraph 917(2) of the ZPO in essence considers those risks and difficulties to be sure and certain solely because enforcement will take place in the territory of a Member State other than Germany.

21. It follows that the national provision is not justified by objective circumstances.

22. In the light of the foregoing, the answer to the question submitted

must be that Article 7 of the EEC Treaty, read in conjunction with Article 220 of the Treaty and the Brussels Convention, precludes a national provision of civil procedure which, in the case of a judgment to be enforced within the national territory, authorizes seizure only on the ground that it is probable that enforcement will otherwise be made impossible or substantially more difficult, but, in the case of a judgment to be enforced in another Member State, authorizes seizure simply on the ground that enforcement is to take place abroad.

On those grounds, the Court (Sixth Chamber), in answer to the question referred to it by the Hanseatisches Oberlandesgericht Hamburg by order of 16 November 1992, hereby rules:

> **Article 7 of the EEC Treaty, read in conjunction with Article 220 of the Treaty and the Brussels Convention of 27 September 1968 on Jurisdiction and the Enforcement of Judgments in Civil and Commercial Matters, precludes a national provision of civil procedure which, in the case of a judgment to be enforced within national territory, authorizes seizure only on the ground that it is probable that enforcement will otherwise be made impossible or substantially more difficult, but, in the case of a judgment to be enforced in another Member State, authorizes seizure simply on the ground that enforcement is to take place abroad.**

OPINION OF MR ADVOCATE GENERAL TESAURO

1. By order of 16 November 1992, the Hanseatisches Oberlandesgericht (Higher Regional Court), Hamburg, asked the Council whether a provision such as Paragraph 917(2) of the *Zivilprozebordnung* (German Code of Civil Procedure, hereinafter referred to as 'the ZPO'), pursuant to which the fact that the judgment to be delivered in due course will have to be enforced abroad is a sufficient ground for authorizing a seizure order, even if enforcement is to take place in a country which is a party to the Brussels Convention on Jurisdiction and the Enforcement of Judgments in Civil and Commercial Matters of 27 September 1968, is contrary to the prohibition of discrimination laid down by Article 7 of the EEC Treaty (which has become Article 6 under the new numbering resulting from the Maastricht Treaty, which entered into force on 1 November 1993).

2. The facts of the present case may be summarized as follows. Hatrex Internationaal Transport ('Hatrex'), an international carrier whose registered office is in the Netherlands, had carried goods on behalf of a German principal. Since the goods were damaged whilst in transit, the German company Mund &

Fester, which was subrogated to the principal's rights by virtue of an assignment of a debt, claimed damages. In order to ensure recovery of the debt in question, Mund & Fester applied to the Landgericht (Regional Court), Hamburg, pursuant to Paragraph 917 of the ZPO, for a seizure order against the lorry - which was still in Germany - used by Hatrex for the transport operation. According to the first paragraph of the German provision in question, a seizure order may be made where there is reason to believe that, without such a measure, the enforcement of the judgment would be made impossible or considerably more difficult; according to the second sub-paragraph, the fact that the judgment will have to be enforced abroad is in itself a sufficient reason for granting such a measure.

3. Mund & Fester appealed to the Hanseatisches Oberlandesgericht against the dismissal of its application, one of the reasons given for which was that Paragraph 917(2) was no longer applicable to the enforcement of decisions in States which are parties to the Brussels Convention. The Hanseatisches Oberlandesgericht considered itself under an obligation to stay the proceedings and to refer to the Court of Justice a question on the interpretation of the first paragraph of Article 7 of the EEC Treaty.

4. The order for reference must be construed as meaning that the national court wishes to know whether the provisions of the Brussels Convention, alone or in conjunction with Article 7 or other provisions of the EEC Treaty, prevent the application of a national provision which automatically allows a seizure order to be made, at the request of the interested party, on the sole ground that the judgment will have to be enforced abroad, where the country in question is a Member State, whilst if the judgment is to be enforced within national territory the measure in question can be granted only if there is a risk that enforcement will be made impossible or considerably more difficult.

5. Paragraph 917 (2) of the ZPO is not in fact incompatible with any specific provision of the Brussels Convention. Moreover, it would be difficult to envisage any such incompatibility since the provision at issue does not come within the objective scope of the Convention, whose purpose is not to unify procedural rules but to determine which court has jurisdiction in disputes relating to civil and commercial matters in intra-Community relations and to facilitate the enforcement of judgments. In the present case, on the contrary, the court was called on to adopt protective measures, an area not covered by the Convention - Article 24 of it refers, in that connection, to the national legislation of the countries concerned, and likewise as regards the determination of jurisdiction.

6. It may be true that the Court has held that limits apply to the application of national procedural rules since the latter must not impair the effectiveness of the Convention, in particular the rules on jurisdiction laid down in it; however, it can hardly be contended that Paragraph 917(2) of the ZPO entails that result.

In the first place, it cannot be asserted that that provision is contrary to the Convention's objective, which is 'to facilitate recognition and to introduce an expeditious procedure for securing the enforcement of judgments ...', since enforcement would in any event be guaranteed by the seizure order and it would therefore be inappropriate to use the machinery provided for by the Convention.

Indeed, the latter, as rightly pointed out by the Commission in its observations, is not intended to raise to the maximum the number of occasions on which judgments are enforced in Member States other than those in which they were delivered but merely to facilitate their free movement to the greatest possible extent.

Secondly, it likewise cannot be affirmed that Paragraph 917(2) of the ZPO has an impact on the rules on jurisdiction laid down by the Convention: as far as provisional and protective measures are concerned, the Convention confines itself to allowing application to be made for such measures to the judicial authorities of a Contracting State, even if a court of another Contracting State has jurisdiction as to the substance of the matter (Article 24).

7. It thus being clear that the provision in question is not incompatible with the Convention, it is necessary to consider whether the general principle of non-discrimination embodied in Article 7 of the Treaty prevents its application.

Article 7 provides that 'Within the scope of application of this Treaty, and without prejudice to any special provisions contained therein, any discrimination on grounds of nationality shall be prohibited'. It will therefore be necessary to decide first whether the provision at issue concerns a matter governed by Community law and secondly whether there is inherent in it any discrimination based on nationality.

8. As regards the first point, it must be noted that Article 220 of the Treaty, in so far as it is relevant to the present case, includes among the types of further action conducive to the attainment and development of a common market, as provided for in Article 2 of the Treaty, the simplification of formalities governing the reciprocal recognition and enforcement of judgments. The fact that that article entrusts to the Member States, and not to the Community institutions, the task of attaining the objectives which it sets is due to the fact that jurisdiction in civil and commercial matters remains, in any event, a matter within the sovereignty of the Member States; however, that does not preclude the conclusion that the rules with which it is concerned fall within the scope of application of the Treaty, for the purposes of Article 2. The free movement of judgments is of fundamental importance to the avoidance of the difficulties which can arise for the functioning of the common market when it proves impossible to secure the acceptance of, and easily enforce, even by judicial means, the individual rights that derive from the multiplicity of legal relationships which come into being in that market.

9. In reply to the objection that Article 220 merely sets out a programme or, to use the Court's words, 'is not intended to lay down a legal rule directly applicable as such, but merely defines a number of matters on which the Member States are to enter into negotiations with each other "so far as necessary"', it can be stated without difficulty that, in the sphere relevant to this case, those matters are set out by the 1968 Brussels Convention. It is therefore by virtue of the Convention that the provisions concerning jurisdiction and the simplication of formalities for the recognition and enforcement of judgments now fall within the scope of the Treaty. That said, it is clear that - on the basis of the traditional rules governing the hierarchy of sources of law - neither the provisions of the

Convention nor the national provisions to which they refer, in particular as regards seizure orders, can conflict with the rules of the Treaty.

10. I shall therefore move on to consider the second point, namely whether Paragraph 917(2) of the ZPO involves any discrimination on grounds of nationality which cannot be justified by objective reasons of the kind laid down in the case-law of the Court.

11. No manifest discrimination is apparent in the provision at issue. Since a seizure order is automatically granted in all cases in which the judgment to be delivered in due course has to be enforced abroad, such an order may also be made against a German national who has no assets in Germany of sufficient value for the judgment given against him to be enforced.

In that connection it must nevertheless be pointed out that the Court has consistently held that 'the rules regarding equality of treatment forbid not only overt discrimination by reason of nationality but also all covert forms of discrimination which, by the application of other criteria of differentiation, lead to the same result'; and in my view, it is difficult to deny that Paragraph 917(2) of the ZPO can be invoked only rarely - and in wholly exceptional cases - against a German undertaking or national and that that provision therefore leads to the same result as discrimination on grounds of nationality.

12. That finding is not, however, sufficient in itself to demonstrate the existence in this case of discrimination prohibited by Article 7 of the Treaty.

It is necessary to consider whether the provision at issue may be justified by objective reasons and therefore whether the differing rules laid down for seizure orders, depending on whether a judgment is to be enforced inside the country in question or abroad, reflects a genuine difference between the factual circumstances of the two cases.

In that regard I think it is appropriate to bear in mind the function of a measure such as a seizure order. A seizure assures the person in whose favour the measure was granted of the possibility of securing the enforcement, in due time, of a judgment to be delivered subsequently, where there are solid grounds for believing that the debtor may attempt to dispose of the assets which might be seized. Whilst, therefore, it is appropriate to adopt a provisional measure of that kind - as is in fact stated in Paragraph 917(1) of the ZPO - where it is reasonable to fear, having regard to the circumstances of the case, that without such a measure enforcement of the judgment delivered in due course would be rendered impossible or considerably more difficult, that greater difficulty cannot be presumed if enforcement is to take place in a Member State of the Community.

Indeed, whilst such a presumption might have been justified before the entry into force of the Brussels Convention, and may without doubt continue to be justified in cases where enforcement is to take place in a non-member country, in view of the delays and problems associated with the need to secure the recognition of a judgment and an order for enforcement in a foreign country, those reasons can no longer be relied on with regard to countries that are signatories to the Convention. The reduction in the number of obstacles to the recognition and enforcement of decisions given in another Contracting State and also the simplification of the procedures for obtaining an order for enforcement ensure, within the scope of the Convention, enforcement of judgments which is not in practice less rapid or less certain than when the judgment is enforced within the country in which it is delivered but within the territorial jurisdiction of another court. Since, therefore, there is no objective reason justifying the differing rules for which Paragraph 917 of the ZPO provides - at least as it is interpreted in practice - regarding the conditions required for the issue of a seizure order in cases where a judgment is to be enforced in another Member State of the Community, that difference in fact creates discrimination contrary to the first paragraph of Article 7 of the Treaty.

13. In view of the foregoing considerations, I therefore suggest that the Court reply as follows to the question submitted by the Hanseatisches Oberlandesgericht: 'By virtue of Articles 7 and 220 of the EEC Treaty, read in conjunction with the Brussels Convention of 27 September 1968 on Jurisdiction and the Enforcement of Judgments in Civil and Commercial Matters, a national provision which authorizes the seizure of an asset if the judgment to be delivered in due course is to be enforced abroad may not be interpreted to the effect that the fact of enforcement abroad in itself provides sufficient grounds for the court to grant that provisional measure even where the judgment is to be enforced against a national of a Member State and falls within the scope of application of that Convention'.

Case C-346/93 - 28 March 1995

Kleinwort Benson Ltd
v
City of Glasgow District Council

National legislation modelled on the Convention - Interpretation - Questions submitted for a preliminary ruling - Competence of the Court - Interpretation of Article 5(1) and (3) - Action for restitution of a sum of money paid under a contract declared null and void ab initio - Lack of jurisdiction of the Court.

Summary

The function of the Court, as envisaged by the Protocol of 3 June 1971 on the interpretation by the Court of Justice of the Convention of 27 September 1968 on jurisdiction and the enforcement of judgments in civil and commercial matters, is that of a court whose judgments are binding on the national court. That function would be altered if the replies given by the Court to the courts of the Contracting States were permitted to be purely advisory and without binding effect.

However, that would be the case if the Court were to declare that it had jurisdiction to provide interpretation of the Convention requested of it by a national court before which proceedings are pending and to which not the Convention but national legislation is applicable, where that legislation takes the Convention as a model, by reproducing certain of its provisions but without incorporating them as such into the domestic legal order, and expressly providing for the possibility of adopting modifications in order to produce divergence in relation to Convention provisions as interpreted by the Courts, and where that legislation merely requires national courts in applying the convention provision to have regard to the Court's interpretation of the corresponding provisions of the Convention without giving binding effect to that interpretation.

For that reason the Court does not have jurisdiction to give a preliminary ruling on a question arising in such a context.

JUDGMENT OF THE COURT

Rodríguez Iglesias, President, Schockweiler, Kapteyn and Gulmann, Presidents of Chambers, Mancini, Kakouris, Moitinho de Almeida, Murray, Edward, Puissochet and Hirsch, Judges

1. By decision of 18 May 1993 received at the Court on 6 July 1993, the Court of Appeal referred to the Court for a preliminary ruling under the Protocol of 3 June 1971 on the interpretation by the Court of Justice of the Convention of 27 September 1968 on jurisdiction and the enforcement of judgments in civil and commercial matters a question on the interpretation of Article 5(1) and (3) of the above-mentioned Convention of 27 September 1968 (OJ 1972 L 299, p. 32), as amended by the Convention of 9 October 1978 on the Accession of the Kingdom of Denmark, Ireland and the United Kingdom of Great Britain and Northern Ireland (OJ 1978 L 304, p. 1 and - text of the Convention as amended - p. 77, hereinafter 'the Convention').

2. That question was raised in the course of proceedings between Kleinwort Benson Ltd (hereinafter 'Kleinwort Benson'), a bank established in England, and the City of Glasgow District Council (hereinafter 'the District Council') concerning the determination of the court with jurisdiction to hear an action for restitution of sums of money paid in performance of contracts declared void.

3. It is apparent from the documents before the Court that as from 7 September 1982 Kleinwort Benson and the District Council entered into seven interest-rate swap contracts under which Kleinwort Benson, between 9 March 1983 and 10 September 1987, made payments to the District Council totalling £807,230.31.

4. On 24 January 1991 the House of Lords held in a test case that it was *ultra vires* local authorities such as the District Council to enter into contracts of that kind and that the contracts entered into were consequently void *ab initio* owing to the lack of capacity of one of the parties.

5. On 6 September 1991 Kleinwort Benson brought an action against the District Council founded on unjust enrichment before the Commercial Court of the Queen's Bench Division of the Court of Justice for restitution of sums of money paid in performance of contracts entered into between the parties.

6. The District Council challenged the jurisdiction of the English courts to determine Kleinwort Benson's claim arguing that the action for restitution had to be brought before the courts of the place of the defendant's domicile in Scotland.

7. On the other hand, Kleinwort Benson argued before the High Court that the District Council was being sued either 'in matters relating to a contract' or 'in matters relating to tort, delict or quasi-delict', and that the English courts therefore had jurisdiction under either Article 5(1) or Article 5(3) of Schedule 4 to the Civil Jurisdiction and Judgments Act 1982 ('the 1982 Act').

8. The principal purpose of the 1982 Act is to render the Convention applicable in the United Kingdom, but it also provides for the allocation of civil jurisdiction as between the separate jurisdictions within the United Kingdom (England and Wales, Scotland, Northern Ireland).

9. To that end Schedule 4 to the 1982 Act contains certain provisions modelled on the Convention. Thus, Article 2 enshrines the principle that the courts of the defendant's domicile are to have jurisdiction. Article 5(1) and (3) respectively confer special jurisdiction in matters relating to a contract on the courts for the place of performance of the obligation in question and, in matters relating to tort, delict or quasi-delict, on the courts for the place where the harmful event occurred or in the case of a threatened wrong is likely to occur.

10. Section 16(3)(a) provides that, in determining any question as to the meaning or effect of any provision contained in Schedule 4, 'regard shall be had to any relevant principles laid down by the European Court in connection with Title II of the 1968 Convention and to any relevant decision of that court as to the meaning or effect of any provision of that Title.'

11. Section 47(1) and (3) makes provision for amendments in particular of Schedule 4 'in view of any principle laid down by the European Court in connection with Title II of the 1968 Convention or of any decision of

that court as to the meaning or effect of any provision of that Title', including 'modifications designed to produce divergence between any provision of Schedule 4 ... and a corresponding provision of Title II of the 1968 Convention.'

12. On 27 February 1992 the High Court ruled that it did not have jurisdiction to determine the action. On 26 March 1992 Kleinwort Benson appealed against that decision to the Court of Appeal.

13. Considering that the resolution of the dispute required a decision on the scope of Article 5(1) and (3) of Schedule 4 to the 1982 Act and on the interrelationship between those two provisions, whose wording was substantially the same as that of Article 5(1) and (3) of the Convention, and on whose interpretation the Court of Justice had not yet ruled, the Court of Appeal on 18 May 1993 decided to stay the proceedings and refer the following question to the Court for a preliminary ruling under Article 3 of the Protocol of 3 June 1971: 'Where proceedings are brought against a defendant for restitution in respect of a sum of money paid to that defendant by the plaintiff under a contract which is a nullity because one of the parties did not have capacity to enter into it, (a) is the defendant being sued "in matters relating to a contract" within the meaning of Article 5(1) of the Convention on Jurisdiction and the Enforcement of Judgments in Civil and Commercial Matters signed in Brussels on 27 September 1968 (as amended)? or (b) is the defendant being sued "in matters relating to tort, delict or quasi-delict" within the meaning of Article 5(3) of the Convention?'

Jurisdiction of the Court

14. It is common ground that the purpose of the interpretation which the Court is asked to give of the Convention provisions at issue is to enable the national court to decide on the application not of the Convention but of the national law of the contracting state to which that court belongs.

15. Under those circumstances the question arises as to the jurisdiction of the Court to give a preliminary ruling on the question submitted by the Court of Appeal.

16. Far from containing a direct and unconditional *renvoi* to provisions of Community law so as to incorporate them into the domestic legal order, the 1982 Act takes the Convention as a model only, and does not wholly reproduce the terms thereof'.

17. Though certain provisions of the 1982 Act are taken almost word for word from the Convention, others depart from the wording of the corresponding Convention provision. That is true in particular of Article 5(3).

18. Moreover, express provision is made in the 1982 Act for the authorities of the contracting state in question to adopt modifications 'designed to produce divergence' between any provision of Schedule 4 and a corresponding provision of the Convention, as interpreted by the Court.

19. Accordingly, the provisions of the Convention which the Court is asked to interpret cannot be regarded as having been rendered applicable as such, in cases outwith the scope of the Convention, by the law of the contracting state concerned.

20. The 1982 Act does not require the courts of the contracting state to decide disputes before them by applying absolutely and unconditionally the interpretation of the Convention provided to them by the Court.

21. Indeed, in terms of the 1982 Act, when national courts apply provisions modelled on those of the Convention, they are required only to have regard to the Court's case-law concerning the interpretation of the corresponding provisions of the Convention. In contrast, when the Convention applies to the dispute, Article 3(1) of the 1982 Act provides that 'any question as to the meaning or effect of any provision of the Convention shall, if not referred to the European Court in accordance with the 1971 Protocol, be determined in accordance with the principles laid down by and any relevant decision of the European Court.'

22. In a case such as that in the main proceedings, where the Convention is not applicable, the court of the Contracting State in question is therefore free to decide whether the interpretation given by the Court is equally valid for the purposes of the application of the national law based on the Convention.

23. Accordingly, if the Court were to declare that it had jurisdiction to give a ruling in regard to this question, its interpretation of the provisions of the Convention would not be binding on the national court which would be bound by the interpretation of the Court only if the Convention were applicable to the dispute.

24. It cannot be accepted that the replies given by the Court to the courts of the Contracting States are to be purely advisory and without binding effect. That would be to alter the function of the Court, as envisaged in the Protocol of 3 June 1971, cited above, namely that of a court whose judgments are binding (see Opinion 1/91 [1991] ECR I-6079, paragraph 61).

25. In the light of all the foregoing considerations the Court does not have jurisdiction to give a preliminary ruling on the question submitted by the Court of Appeal.

On those grounds, the Court, in answer to the question submitted to it by the Court of Appeal, by decision of 18 May 1993, hereby rules:

The Court does not have jurisdiction to give a preliminary ruling on the question submitted by the Court of Appeal.

OPINION OF MR ADVOCATE GENERAL TESAURO

1. The questions referred to the Court by the Court of Appeal concern the interpretation of Article 5(1) and (3) of the Convention of 27 September 1968 on Jurisdiction and the Enforcement of Judgments in Civil and Commercial Matters ('the Convention'), as amended by the Convention of 9 October 1978 on the Accession of the Kingdom of Denmark, Ireland and the United Kingdom of Great Britain and Northern Ireland.

More specifically, the national court is asking whether, in proceedings for restitution in respect of money paid to the defendant by the plaintiff under a contract which is a nullity because one of the parties did not have capacity to enter into it, the defendant must be sued in the courts for the place of performance of the obligation in question, the case concerning a matter relating to a contract within the meaning of Article 5(1) of the Convention, or before the courts for the place where the harmful event occurred, since the dispute is a matter relating to tort, delict or quasi-delict, within the meaning of Article 5(3) of the Convention.

2. It should be pointed out straight away that, although the national court is seeking a ruling on the interpretation of the aforementioned provisions of the Convention, in the main proceedings the question to be determined is whether the London courts or the Glasgow courts have jurisdiction. Thus the case involves a conflict of territorial jurisdiction between the courts of a contracting State, namely the United Kingdom.

In order to assess the reasons which prompted the national court to make this reference it will be helpful to give a brief account of the relevant national legislation and of the facts underlying the main proceedings.

National legislation

3. Section 2 of the Civil Jurisdiction and Judgments Act 1982 provides that the Convention is to have the force of law in the United Kingdom (Section 2(1)) and that any question as to the meaning or effect of any provision of the Convention, if not referred to the European Court, is to be determined in accordance with the principles laid down by and any relevant decision of the European Court (Section 3(1)), together with the assistance, if necessary, of the Reports of Messrs Jenard and Schlosser (Section 3(3)).

The Convention, contained in Schedule 1 to that legislation, manifestly applies only to the Member States. In order to resolve problems stemming from the fact that in the United Kingdom there are separate jurisdictions in civil matters (England and Wales, Scotland and Northern Ireland), the Civil Jurisdiction and Judgments Act 1982 lays down a scheme for resolving possible territorial conflicts of jurisdiction within the United Kingdom.

4. That scheme is contained in Section 16 of the legislation. As far as is relevant for these purposes, it provides:

'(1) The provisions set out in Schedule 4 (which contains a modified version of Title II of the 1968 Convention) shall have effect for determining, for each part of the United Kingdom, whether the courts of law of that part, or any particular court of law in that part, have or has jurisdiction in proceedings where:

(a) the subject-matter of the proceedings is within the scope of the 1968 Convention as determined by Article 1 (whether or not the Convention has effect in relation to the proceedings); and

(b) the defendant or defender is domiciled in the United Kingdom or the proceedings are of a kind mentioned in Article 16 (exclusive jurisdiction regardless of domicile).

(2) ...

(3) In determining any question as to the meaning or effect of any provision contained in Schedule 4:

(a) regard shall be had to any relevant principles laid down by the European Court in connection with Title II of the 1968 Convention and to any relevant decision of that Court as to the meaning or effect of any provision of that Title; and

(b) without prejudice to the generality of paragraph (a), the reports mentioned in Section 3(3) may be considered and shall, so far as relevant, be given such weight as is appropriate in the circumstances.'

Article 2 of the aforementioned Schedule 4 provides: 'subject to the provisions of this Title, persons domiciled in a part of the United Kingdom shall be sued in the courts of that part.'

Article 5 of Schedule 4 provides: 'a person domiciled in a part of the United Kingdom may, in another part of the United Kingdom, be sued:

(1) in matters relating to a contract, in the courts for the place of performance of the obligation in question;

(2) ...

(3) in matters relating to tort, delict or quasi-delict, in the courts for the

place where the harmful event occurred or in the case of a threatened wrong is likely to occur.'

5. Article 2 and Article 5(1) and (3) of Schedule 4 thus reproduce more or less verbatim the corresponding articles of the Convention, in the version contained in the 1978 Convention on Accession. Even if it is not apparent from the documents in the case, it should be stated that whilst the modifications to Article 5(1) made by the Convention on Accession of 1989 entered into force in the United Kingdom on 1 December 1991, Schedule 4 was amended insofar as is relevant with effect from 1 April 1993. That fact deserves to be underlined inasmuch as it shows that the provisions in question contained in Schedule 4 reproduce the corresponding provisions of the Convention but in a rigid, non-dynamic way in the sense that although the text of that schedule was that in force at a given time it may well not correspond to the current text of the Convention.

It should also be remembered that the 1982 legislation provides for the possibility of modifications to Schedule 4 'in view of any principle laid down by the European Court in connection with Title II of the 1968 Convention or of any decision of that Court as to the meaning or effect of any provision of that title' (Section 47(1)(b)). It is further stated that the modifications which may be made in that manner also include 'modifications designed to produce divergence between any provision of Schedule 4 (...) and a corresponding provision of Title II of the 1968 Convention', such as any interpretation given by the Court of Justice (Section 47(3)).

Facts

6. I now turn to the facts underlying these proceedings. As from September 1982 Kleinwort Benson Ltd (hereinafter 'Kleinwort Benson'), an English merchant bank, and the City of Glasgow District Council (hereinafter the 'District Council') entered into seven interest-rate swap contracts. In performance of these contracts, Kleinwort Benson between 9 March 1983 and 10 September 1987 made payments to the District Council totalling £807,230.31.

On 24 January 1991 the House of Lords held that interest-rate swap contracts entered into by local authorities such as the District Council were unlawful since they were *ultra vires* the local authorities. As a result of this judgment there is a dispute between the local authorities in question and the banks which are seeking to withhold sums not already paid or to recover payments made in performance of all the contracts held to be *ultra vires*. The District Council became involved in one such dispute.

7. It was against the District Council that on 6 September 1991 Kleinwort Benson brought an action before the High Court of Justice, Queen's Bench Division, Commercial Court, for restitution based on the principle of unjust enrichment. The District Council contested the jurisdiction of the London courts and contended that in accordance with Article 2 of the aforementioned Schedule 4, the courts of the place in which the defender was domiciled had jurisdiction, and that the action should be brought before the Glasgow courts. That line of

argument was upheld at first instance but Kleinwort Benson appealed against that decision to the Court of Appeal.

It was specifically in order to establish which court within the United Kingdom has jurisdiction to determine the dispute that the Court of Appeal made the reference to this Court. It asks whether an action for restitution, regard being had to the fact that it concerns contracts which are null and void *ab initio*, can be regarded as an action in a matter relating to a contract within the meaning of Article 5(1) of the Convention, or whether it comes within the terms of Article 5(3) which governs matters relating to non-contractual wrongs.

8. It is common ground between the parties that the contracts in question entered into in London are governed by English law and that England is 'the place of performance of the obligation in question' (Article 5(1) of Schedule 4) or the 'place where the harmful event occurred or in the case of a threatened wrong is likely to occur' (Article 5(3) of Schedule 4). It is therefore obvious that in either case, whether it is a matter relating to a contract or one relating to tort or quasi-delict, the English courts have jurisdiction to determine the dispute. It follows that the claim by the District Council that it should be sued in the courts of its domicile, that is to say in the Scottish courts, can be upheld only if it is concluded that an action for restitution based on the principle of unjust enrichment, such as that at issue in the main proceedings, is not covered by either Article 5(1) or (3) of the Convention.

Competence of the Court of Justice

9. As a preliminary observation I would point out that the Brussels Convention does not apply to the jurisdictional conflict underlying the main proceedings, as moreover is recognized by the parties and by the national court. Furthermore, the Convention itself states in its preamble that it refers to the determination of the *international* jurisdiction of the courts of the contracting States ('to determine the international jurisdiction of their courts') and not to internal conflicts as to territorial jurisdiction.

Therefore, however closely one examines the particular features of the United Kingdom's procedural system (in particular the division into three jurisdictions, save for the jurisdiction of the House of Lords in civil matters), no other conclusion as to the applicability of the Convention as such to the case before the national court may reasonably be contemplated. In any event it is not possible for the United Kingdom, even for the purposes of the Brussels Convention, to be deemed to be anything but a single contracting State, and for disputes as to territorial jurisdiction to come therefore within the scope of the Convention.

10. In the case before the Court, therefore, the dispute is governed by a national provision of law and not by a provision of the Brussels Convention. It follows therefore, as a preliminary matter, that it must be established whether the Court has jurisdiction to provide an interpretation of a Convention provision where the national provision, which is the one applicable, reproduces almost verbatim the corresponding Convention provisions, and where the national court

on the basis of the same legislation is obliged to take account of the Court's case-law in the matter (Article 16(3)(a)) but is not obliged to apply it.

That is a new problem only with regard to the interpretation of the Convention. On several occasions, in fact, the Court has been requested under Article 177 of the Treaty to interpret Community law in regard to factual situations which are not governed by Community law but by national law, where the latter contains a *renvoi* to provisions of Community law in order to determine the provisions applicable to a purely internal situation. On those previous occasions the Court declared that it had jurisdiction to give a ruling.

11. The parties to the main proceedings, together with the German and Spanish Governments, pleading in favour of the Court's jurisdiction, referred precisely to those judgments in which, although it was accepted that only domestic situations were involved, that is situations not governed by Community law but by national law, the Court declared itself competent to interpret the Community law. The French Government and the United Kingdom, together with the Commission, underlining the differences between the case before the Court in contrast to those decided on previous occasions, alleged that the Court did not have jurisdiction.

It is therefore appropriate, I think, to give a brief account of that case-law.

12. The line of decisions began with the *Thomasdünger* judgment of 26 September 1985. The Court first reaffirmed the principle that it is for the national court 'to determine in relation to the facts of each case whether the preliminary ruling is necessary in order to decide the dispute pending before it'. It therefore provided the national court with an interpretation of certain chapters of the common customs tariff, although it was common ground that this was being done in a context to which Community law did not apply, and that the customs chapters whose interpretation was sought had been used by the competent national authority for reference purposes in order to regulate various factual situations, that is the importation of goods not from non-member States but between Member States.

The Court's reasoning was more detailed and elaborate in the subsequent *Dzodzi* and *Gmurzynska-Bscher* judgments in which it declared itself competent to rule on the interpretation of Community provisions to which the national legislation of a Member State referred in order to determine the rules applicable to situations purely internal to that State. More specifically, in the *Dzodzi* judgment the Court provided the national court with the interpretation of certain provisions of Directive 64/221/EEC, notwithstanding the fact that Article 2 of that directive expressly excludes from its scope a situation such as that of the applicant in the main proceedings. Then, in *Gmurzynska-Bscher*, it ruled on the interpretation of certain chapters of the common customs tariff in relation to a dispute not directly concerning the common customs tariff but in the purely domestic context of the national law of a Member State which expressly referred to the Community customs nomenclature in order to establish the amount of turnover tax.

13. In both cases, the Court pointed out that Article 177 constitutes an instrument for cooperation between the Community judicature and national

courts and that it is always for the latter to assess the relevance and pertinence of the questions which they submit. It went on to justify its own jurisdiction on the basis essentially of two arguments. On the one hand, it stressed the fact that 'it is manifestly in the interest of the Community legal order that, in order to forestall future differences of interpretation, every Community provision should be given a uniform interpretation irrespective of the circumstances in which it is to be applied'. On the other hand, it pointed out that Article 177 of the Treaty does not exclude from its scope situations such as that under discussion, and more specifically that 'it does not appear either from the wording of Article 177 or from the aim of the procedure introduced by that article that the authors of the Treaty intended to exclude from the jurisdiction of the Court requests for a preliminary ruling on a Community provision in the specific case where the national law of a Member State refers to the content of that provision in order to determine rules applicable to a situation purely internal to that State'.

The same reasoning, moreover, has prompted the Court to declare itself competent to give a preliminary ruling on a provision of Community law to which reference was made not by a provision of national law but by a contractual provision. That was in order to determine the limit to the financial liability of one of the parties to the contract.

14. An account should also be specifically given of the *Fournier* judgment in which the Court ruled on the interpretation of the concept of the 'territory in which the vehicle is normally based' contained in a Community directive, though it was common ground that it was not the directive which was being applied in that case but an agreement between national insurers' bureaux, which reproduces verbatim certain provisions of the directive including those concerning the concept in question. However, the national court requested the Court to interpret that concept in order to establish which of the insurers' bureaux involved was obliged to pay compensation, a question entirely outside the scope of the directive.

Without examining its competence to give a ruling in a case of that kind and although it pointed out that 'the terms used in the agreement must not necessarily be interpreted as having the same meaning as those used in the directive', the Court nevertheless provided the national court with the interpretation requested. Owing to the fact that the scope of the directive and that of the agreement are not identical the Court was however careful to point out that it was in the final analysis 'for the national court which alone is competent to interpret the agreement between national bureaux to give to the terms of that agreement the meaning which it considers most appropriate, without being bound by the meaning to be conferred on the same term appearing in the directive' (paragraph 23).

15. In brief, in the cases examined it was sufficient for the questions raised by the national court to concern in some way the interpretation of Community law for the Court to declare itself competent to give a ruling. This it has done in full awareness of the fact that its interpretation may be only of contingent *future* usefulness to the Community legal order and may possibly even lack usefulness for the national court itself.

16. The case before the Court is not specifically envisaged in the case-law referred to. In the first place, this is a reference not under Article 177 of the EEC Treaty but under the 1971 Protocol on the Interpretation of the Brussels Convention. Secondly, the majority of cases recalled above concerned a *renvoi* by national law to Community law, whereas in the case before the Court we are confronted with an almost verbatim reproduction of the Convention provisions.

It must be determined whether these two factors are such as to place the issues in a different light and thus, as maintained by the United Kingdom, the French Government, and by the Commission, to militate in favour of a different solution.

17. Having regard to the criteria and the reasoning underlying the case-law recalled above, I consider that the reply must be in the negative. Above all, the difference between the two preliminary-ruling procedures under the 1971 Protocol and Article 177 of the EEC Treaty respectively appears to be formal rather than substantive, not to say artificial. It is difficult to see why there should be a different solution according to whether the subject-matter is outside the scope of the Convention, as in the case before the Court, or outside the scope of Community law, as in *Dzodzi*. In both cases, in fact, the logical requirements and the legal basis for the request for a preliminary ruling are the same: to provide the national court with the interpretation it seeks in order to ensure the uniform interpretation and application of Community law, or of the Convention, as the case may be, where that is necessary in order to enable a judgment applying the provision (of Community law *strictu senso* or of the Convention) to be given.

I do not think any particular importance needs to be attached to the fact that the case before us does not involve a simple *renvoi* to Community law, but a reproduction of certain Convention provisions. What is important, in fact, is not the content of the provision or its literal wording, but whether it is a provision either of Community law or another provision (be it internal, contractual or contained in a Convention). Moreover, as was seen in regard to the *Fournier* case already referred to, the Court did not identify any difference between the situation where there is a *renvoi* to the content of a Community provision and the situation where a Community provision is reproduced verbatim.

18. Having said that, I would say straightaway that I do not intend to propose that the Court should extend the *Dzodzi* solution to the case before us, but rather that it should adopt precisely the opposite solution. The arguments which follow, although centred on the facts of the case before the Court, substantively also apply to the preliminary-ruling procedure under Article 177.

I thus turn to the reasons, each one decisive in itself, which lead me to consider that the Court should not reply to the question submitted by the national court.

19. In the first place the Convention is not intended to be applied to conflicts as to territorial jurisdiction between the courts of the same contracting State; it was so stipulated. The Convention, as has already been emphasized, is applicable only to international conflicts of jurisdiction, an expression designating in the specialized literature, as has been noted, conflicts of jurisdiction between the courts of different countries.

In the present case the relevant provision of the Convention does not apply as such but is the model on which the national provision applicable to this case was formulated. In any event there are two provisions - the national one and the provision of the Convention on which it was based - and these are absolutely distinct. They are not only distinct as to their origin and the context in which they apply, but also the factual situations which they govern are different. Yet, the Court's competence to rule on the interpretation of the Convention under the 1971 Protocol can only be based on the scope of the Convention. It should generally be clear that when the Convention does not apply, the Court does not have jurisdiction.

20. Not only does the Court not have jurisdiction but it would make no sense if it did. In fact the machinery for 'centralized' interpretation by the Community judicature is conditioned, as is well known, by the need for uniform rules on conflict and the mutual recognition of judgments in all the Community Member States which are parties to the Convention. In its turn uniformity is the corollary of the requirement that judgments should move freely within the common market in line with its characteristic fundamental freedoms. In both cases the sole objective pursued is that of integration.

What is important is that a conflict between the courts of Heidelberg and the courts of Naples should be settled in the same manner as a conflict between the courts of Trier and the courts of Venice, inasmuch as within the Community it is useful and necessary that analogous conflicts should be resolved in an analogous manner. However, where that requirement does not have to be satisfied there is no longer any need for, or even utility in, a uniform and centralized interpretation. In resolving a conflict of territorial jurisdiction between the courts of Heidelberg and the courts of Trier there is no requirement to find the same solution as that which resolves the conflict between the courts of Naples and those of Venice. It follows that in such a case since the Brussels Convention does not apply there is no longer any room for the interpretative competence of the Community judicature. That would still hold true, even were the German or Italian conflict rule formulated in the same terms as the relevant provision of the Convention since there is no requirement that a provision based on a model must necessarily be interpreted in the same manner as its model. The 'scheme' of the Convention taken as a whole is indifferent to purely internal situations such as a conflict of territorial jurisdiction between the courts of the same country.

21. I am not thereby denying that in order to resolve the different situation of conflicts of territorial jurisdiction, the best solution may not be inspired by that adopted at international or Community level for conflicts of international jurisdiction. Indeed that may frequently occur in countries with a judicial system structured differently in the various geographical regions or administrative areas. But none of that requires the provision based on a model to receive the same interpretation as the model provision has in its own system. On the contrary, when a legislature takes as its model a provision already existing in another legal order it certainly cannot expect its 'own' provision at all costs to receive in its 'own' country the same interpretation as is given in the State of origin of the

model provision (consider for example the Napoleonic Code), to the point where the courts of the State of origin are requested to ensure its interpretation.

Finally, it seems to me perfectly normal that in the legal systems of different countries there should be different rules as to conflicts of territorial jurisdiction. Just as it is normal that, where different countries have adopted the same legislative solution by means of a provision of the same tenor, each of those countries may arrive at a different interpretation of the same provision.

22. The Court's case-law corroborates these arguments. On several occasions the Court has reaffirmed that provisions of the EC Treaty must and thus may be interpreted differently in the case of provisions of agreements having the same content, even to the letter, entered into with non-member States.

Moreover, it is significant that that approach was reaffirmed specifically in regard to facts analogous to those before the Court. In the *Fournier* judgment, cited above, it will be recalled that in providing the interpretation of a provision of a directive reproduced in a private agreement between the insurers' bureaux of the Member States, the Court in fact was careful to state that 'the terms used by the agreement must not necessarily be interpreted as having the same meaning as those used by the directive'.

23. The second reason why I am inclined to conclude that the Court does not have jurisdiction is that the request for interpretation of Article 5 of the Convention not only does not satisfy the conditions mentioned in Article 3 of the 1971 Protocol, inasmuch as it is not necessary for the judgment to be given in the main proceedings, but also would not be binding.

That is already clear from a reading of the relevant national provision itself which as summarized expressly provides for the possibility of adopting modifications intended to produce divergence between any provision of Schedule 4 and the corresponding provisions of the Convention, as affected by any interpretation provided by the Court of Justice. Furthermore, there is no obligation on the national court to resolve the dispute with the interpretation provided to it by the Community judicature. Moreover, even if a national provision could make provision for binding effect it would be as if it did not exist, inasmuch as it would not be a requirement which the national legislature could or would be obliged to sanction. In fact, the binding effect can stem only from a provision of the Protocol or of the Convention which, in terms of this case, is non-existent.

24. It is, then, worthy of note that on one occasion the Court of Justice affirmed that its interpretation was not binding when the provision forming the subject-matter of its interpretation was not as such applicable to the dispute before the national court. In the *Fournier* case, mentioned above, the Court in fact provided the national court with the interpretation sought by it and which the parties had submitted to arbitration pursuant to their agreement; at the same time, the Court acknowledged that such interpretation could be non-binding on the national court, since the same terms in the directive and in the agreement were capable of not having the same meaning and that, finally, it was 'for the national court which alone is competent to interpret the agreement between national bureaux to give to the terms of that agreement the meaning which it considers

most appropriate, *without being bound by the meaning to be given to the same expression appearing in the directive*'. To that extent, the Court thus recognized that its ruling under Article 177 could be non-binding.

The fact that the Court in that case gave the interpretation requested, though recognizing that it was not binding on the national court, cannot but raise serious doubts. In fact indeed, it is contrary to the very logic of the preliminary-ruling machinery to acknowledge that the interpretation of the Convention or of Community law requested and given is not binding on the national court. That is all the more so since less than a year earlier in a statement concerning questions of principle the Court rightly pointed out in that regard that 'it is unacceptable that the answers which the Court of Justice gives to the courts and tribunals in the EFTA States are to be purely advisory and without any binding effects. Such a situation would change the nature of the function of the Court of Justice as it is conceived by the EEC Treaty, namely that of a Court whose judgments are binding'.

25. Moreover, to accept that the Court may provide an interpretation of a provision for future reference ('to forestall future differences of interpretation'), though not necessary for the solution of the dispute before the national court and not binding on it, seems to me to be in open contradiction with the Court's well-settled case-law on hypothetical or analogous questions. The cooperation between the national court and the Community judicature and the preliminary-ruling machinery may not be availed of for purposes other than that of giving judgment in a specific case. Technical assistance, or in other words a legal advisory role, are manifestly outside the system adopted by the 1971 Protocol, just as they are outside the machinery of Article 177 of the Treaty.

In the latter connection I regard as unfounded the statement by the Court that it does not appear either from the wording of Article 177 or from the aims pursued thereby that the authors of the Treaty intended to exclude from the jurisdiction of the Court the interpretation of a Community provision when it is not applicable to the case in question, that is to say when the question clearly falls outside the scope of Community law. The situations not expressly excluded are in fact numerous: they cannot on that ground be deemed to be included; and that is all the more so in the Community system which, I hardly need recall, is based on the principle of the assignment of powers.

26. Finally, when the various provisions inspired by Community law or by the Convention itself are borne in mind - and these are no longer exceptional - there is no denying the risks that would be created by a ruling differing from that which is here canvassed. Specifically in relation to the subject-matter before the Court, suffice it to cite the Lugano Convention entered into between the Member States of EFTA and the Member States of the Community: the majority of the articles of that Convention are in fact reproduced verbatim from the provisions of the Brussels Convention. It should not therefore be thought that the Community judicature has automatically acquired jurisdiction to interpret the provisions of the Convention when a court of a Member State submits questions in the matter, and the conflict of jurisdiction is between the Community judicature and the court of an EFTA country. For an example taken from

Community law *strictu senso*, Article 85 of the Treaty may be cited. It was taken as the model, for example, for the Italian legislation on competition, is reproduced, *mutatis mutandis*, as Article 2, and contains an express reference to the principles of the Community case-law. I do not believe that the Italian court could ask the Community judicature for an interpretation of Article 85 of the Treaty in order to apply the corresponding national provision; and I am even more certain that in any event it would not receive the reply from the Court that it was seeking.

27. The considerations hitherto developed lead me therefore to propose that the Court should not provide the national court with the answers it seeks. Since the Convention is not applicable, neither is the Protocol, with the result that there is no legal basis for the Court's jurisdiction.

It is clear, moreover, that the view I have formed covers not only a reference under the 1971 Protocol but also the case of a reference under Article 177 of the Treaty. In even clearer terms, I suggest that the Court should - substantively, and however detailed its reply reconsider its *Dzodzi* judgment which I am unable to endorse, above all because in terms of general legal theory it flies in the face of the logic of the preliminary-ruling procedure, actually resulting - let us admit it - in a misuse of procedure; but also, to put it in more restrained but equally obvious terms, it is in contradiction with the Court's most recent case-law on the preliminary-ruling procedure.

28. In conclusion, for all the reasons I have stated, I am of the opinion that the Court should declare that it does not have jurisdiction to rule on the questions referred to it for a preliminary ruling by the Court of Appeal. Moreover, I consider, having regard to the foregoing, that it would be otiose to embark on an examination of the substance of the case.

29. In the light of the foregoing considerations, I therefore propose that the Court should give the following answer to the questions submitted by the national court: 'The provisions of the Convention of 27 September 1968 on Jurisdiction and the Enforcement of Judgments in Civil and Commercial Matters are not applicable in order to resolve conflicts of territorial jurisdiction between the courts of a single Member State. It follows that the Protocol of 3 June 1971 on the interpretation of that Convention is not applicable and that the questions raised under Article 3 of that Protocol are outside the Court's jurisdiction.'

APPENDIX I

1968 Brussels Convention on jurisdiction and the enforcement of judgments in civil and commercial matters

1968 Brussels Convention on jurisdiction and the enforcement of judgments in civil and commercial matters*

Preamble

The High Contracting Parties to the Treaty Establishing the European Economic Community,

Desiring to implement the provisions of Article 220 of that Treaty by virtue of which they undertook to secure the simplification of formalities governing the reciprocal recognition and enforcement of judgments of courts or tribunals;

Anxious to strengthen in the Community the legal protection of persons therein established;

Considering that it is necessary for this purpose to determine the international jurisdiction of their courts, to facilitate recognition and to introduce an expeditious procedure for securing the enforcement of judgments, authentic instruments and court settlements;

Have decided to conclude this Convention and to this end have designated as their Plenipotentiaries:

[Plenipotentiaries designated by the Member States] *who*, meeting within the Council, having exchanged their full powers, found in good and due form, *have agreed as follows*:

* This is the consolidated version of the text of the Brussels Convention on jurisdiction and the enforcement of judgments in civil and commercial matters.The text printed in this volume was drawn up by the General Secretariat of the Council (*OJ C 027, 26/01/1998, p. 1 - 27*), in whose archives the originals of the instruments concerned are deposited. It should be noted, however, that this text has no binding force.

TITLE I

SCOPE

Article 1

This Convention shall apply in civil and commercial matters whatever the nature of the court or tribunal. It shall not extend, in particular, to revenue, customs or administrative matters.

The Convention shall not apply to:

1. the status or legal capacity of natural persons, rights in property arising out of a matrimonial relationship, wills and succession;
2. bankruptcy, proceedings relating to the winding-up of insolvent companies or other legal persons, judicial arrangements, compositions and analogous proceedings;
3. social security;
4. arbitration.

TITLE II

JURISDICTION

Section 1

General provisions

Article 2

Subject to the provisions of this Convention, persons domiciled in a Contracting State shall, whatever their nationality, be sued in the courts of that State.

Persons who are not nationals of the State in which they are domiciled shall be governed by the rules of jurisdiction applicable to nationals of that State.

Article 3

Persons domiciled in a Contracting State may be sued in the courts of another Contracting State only by virtue of the rules set out in Sections 2 to 6 of this Title.

In particular the following provisions shall not be applicable as against them:

- in Belgium: Article 15 of the civil code (Code civil - Burgerlijk Wetboek) and Article 638 of the judicial code (Code judiciaire - Gerechtelijk Wetboek),

- in Denmark: Article 246 (2) and (3) of the law on civil procedure (Lov om rettens pleje),
- in the Federal Republic of Germany: Article 23 of the code of civil procedure (Zivilprozeßordnung),
- in Greece, Article 40 of the code of civil procedure (Κώδικας Πολιτικής Δικονομίας),
- in France: Articles 14 and 15 of the civil code (Code civil),
- in Ireland: the rules which enable jurisdiction to be founded on the document instituting the proceedings having been served on the defendant during his temporary presence in Ireland,
- in Italy: Articles 2 and 4, Nos 1 and 2 of the code of civil procedure (Codice di procedura civile),
- in Luxembourg: Articles 14 and 15 of the civil code (Code civil),
- in Austria: Article 99 of the Law on Court Jurisdiction (Jurisdiktionsnorm),
- in the Netherlands: Articles 126 (3) and 127 of the code of civil procedure (Wetboek van Burgerlijke Rechtsvordering),
- in Portugal: Article 65 and 65A of the code of civil procedure (Código de Processo Civil) and Article 11 of the code of labour procedure (Código de Processo de Trabalho),
- in Finland: the second, third and fourth sentences of the first paragraph of Section 1 of Chapter 10 of the Code of Judicial Procedure (oikeudenkäy miskaari/rättegångsbalken),
- in Sweden: the first sentence of the first paragraph of Section 3 of Chapter 10 of the Code of Judicial Procedure (rättegångsbalken),
- in the United Kingdom: the rules which enable jurisdiction to be founded on:
  (a) the document instituting the proceedings having been served on the defendant during his temporary presence in the United Kingdom; or
  (b) the presence within the United Kingdom of property belonging to the defendant; or
  (c) the seizure by the plaintiff of property situated in the United Kingdom.

Article 4

If the defendant is not domiciled in a Contracting State, the jurisdiction of the courts of each Contracting State shall, subject to the provisions of Article 16, be determined by the law of that State.

As against such a defendant, any person domiciled in a Contracting State may, whatever his nationality, avail himself in that State of the rules of jurisdiction there in force, and in particular those specified in the second paragraph of Article 3, in the same way as the nationals of that State.

Section 2

Special jurisdiction

Article 5

A person domiciled in a Contracting State may, in another Contracting State, be sued:

1. in matters relating to a contract, in the courts for the place of performance of the obligation in question; in matters relating to individual contracts of employment, this place is that where the employee habitually carries out his work, or if the employee does not habitually carry out his work in any one country, the employer may also be sued in the courts for the place where the business which engaged the employee was or is now situated;
2. in matters relating to maintenance, in the courts for the place where the maintenance creditor is domiciled or habitually resident or, if the matter is ancillary to proceedings concerning the status of a person, in the court which, according to its own law, has jurisdiction to entertain those proceedings, unless that jurisdiction is based solely on the nationality of one of the parties;
3. in matters relating to tort, delict or quasi-delict, in the courts for the place where the harmful event occurred;
4. as regards a civil claim for damages or restitution which is based on an act giving rise to criminal proceedings, in the court seised of those proceedings, to the extent that that court has jurisdiction under its own law to entertain civil proceedings;
5. as regards a dispute arising out of the operations of a branch, agency or other establishment, in the courts for the place in which the branch, agency or other establishment is situated;
6. as settlor, trustee or beneficiary of a trust created by the operation of a statute, or by a written instrument, or created orally and evidenced in writing, in the courts of the Contracting State in which the trust is domiciled;
7. as regards a dispute concerning the payment of remuneration claimed in respect of the salvage of a cargo or freight, in the court under the authority of which the cargo or freight in question:
   (a) has been arrested to secure such payment, or
   (b) could have been so arrested, but bail or other security has been given;

provided that this provision shall apply only if it is claimed that the defendant has an interest in the cargo or freight or had such an interest at the time of salvage.

Article 6

A person domiciled in a Contracting State may also be sued:

1. where he is one of a number of defendants, in the courts for the place where any one of them is domiciled;
2. as a third party in an action on a warranty or guarantee or in any other third party proceedings, in the court seised of the original proceedings, unless these

were instituted solely with the object of removing him from the jurisdiction of the court which would be competent in his case;
3. on a counter-claim arising from the same contract or facts on which the original claim was based, in the court in which the original claim is pending;
4. in matters relating to a contract, if the action may be combined with an action against the same defendant in matters relating to rights in rem in immovable property, in the court of the Contracting State in which the property is situated.

Article 6a

Where by virtue of this Convention a court of a Contracting State has jurisdiction in actions relating to liability from the use or operation of a ship, that court, or any other court substituted for this purpose by the internal law of that State, shall also have jurisdiction over claims for limitation of such liability.

Section 3

Jurisdiction in matters relating to insurance

Article 7

In matters relating to insurance, jurisdiction shall be determined by this Section, without prejudice to the provisions of Articles 4 and 5 point 5.

Article 8

An insurer domiciled in a Contracting State may be sued:
1. in the courts of the State where he is domiciled, or
2. in another Contracting State, in the courts for the place where the policy-holder is domiciled, or
3. if he is a co-insurer, in the courts of a Contracting State in which proceedings are brought against the leading insurer.
An insurer who is not domiciled in a Contracting State but has a branch, agency or other establishment in one of the Contracting States shall, in disputes arising out of the operations of the branch, agency or establishment, be deemed to be domiciled in that State.

Article 9

In respect of liability insurance or insurance of immovable property, the insurer may in addition be sued in the courts for the place where the harmful event occurred. The same applies if movable and immovable property are covered by the same insurance policy and both are adversely affected by the same contingency.

Article 10

In respect of liability insurance, the insurer may also, if the law of the court permits it, be joined in proceedings which the injured party had brought against the insured.

The provisions of Articles 7, 8 and 9 shall apply to actions brought by the injured party directly against the insurer, where such direct actions are permitted. If the law governing such direct actions provides that the policy-holder or the insured may be joined as a party to the action, the same court shall have jurisdiction over them.

Article 11

Without prejudice to the provisions of the third paragraph of Article 10, an insurer may bring proceedings only in the courts of the Contracting State in which the defendant is domiciled, irrespective of whether he is the policy-holder, the insured or a beneficiary.

The provisions of this Section shall not affect the right to bring a counterclaim in the court in which, in accordance with this Section, the original claim is pending.

Article 12

The provisions of this Section may be departed from only by an agreement on jurisdiction:

1. which is entered into after the dispute has arisen, or
2. which allows the policy-holder, the insured or a beneficiary to bring proceedings in courts other than those indicated in this Section, or
3. which is concluded between a policy-holder and an insurer, both of whom are domiciled in the same Contracting State, and which has the effect of conferring jurisdiction on the courts of that State even if the harmful event were to occur abroad, provided that such an agreement is not contrary to the law of that State, or
4. which is concluded with a policy-holder who is not domiciled in a Contracting State, except in so far as the insurance is compulsory or relates to immovable property in a Contracting State, or
5. which relates to a contract of insurance in so far as it covers one or more of the risks set out in Article 12a.

Article 12a

The following are the risks referred to in point 5 of Article 12:

1. any loss of or damage to:
   (a) sea-going ships, installations situated offshore or on the high seas, or aircraft, arising from perils which relate to their use for commercial purposes;

(b) goods in transit other than passengers' baggage where the transit consists of or includes carriage by such ships or aircraft;

2. any liability, other than for bodily injury to passengers or loss of or damage to their baggage:

(a) arising out of the use or operation of ships, installations or aircraft as referred to in point 1 (a) above in so far as the law of the Contracting State in which such aircraft are registered does not prohibit agreements on jurisdiction regarding insurance of such risks;

(b) for loss or damage caused by goods in transit as described in point 1 (b) above;

3. any financial loss connected with the use or operation of ships, installations or aircraft as referred to in point 1 (a) above, in particular loss of freight or charter-hire;

4. any risk or interest connected with any of those referred to in points 1 to 3 above.

Section 4

Jurisdiction over consumer contracts

Article 13

In proceedings concerning a contract concluded by a person for a purpose which can be regarded as being outside his trade or profession, hereinafter called 'the consumer', jurisdiction shall be determined by this Section, without prejudice to the provisions of point 5 of Articles 4 and 5, if it is:

1. a contract for the sale of goods on instalment credit terms; or

2. a contract for a loan repayable by instalments, or for any other form of credit, made to finance the sale of goods; or

3. any other contract for the supply of goods or a contract for the supply of services, and

(a) in the State of the consumer's domicile the conclusion of the contract was preceded by a specific invitation addressed to him or by advertising; and

(b) the consumer took in that State the steps necessary for the conclusion of the contract.

Where a consumer enters into a contract with a party who is not domiciled in a Contracting State but has a branch, agency or other establishment in one of the Contracting States, that party shall, in disputes arising out of the operations of the branch, agency or establishment, be deemed to be domiciled in that State.

This Section shall not apply to contracts of transport.

Article 14

A consumer may bring proceedings against the other party to a contract either in the courts of the Contracting State in which that party is domiciled or in the courts of the Contracting State in which he is himself domiciled.

Proceedings may be brought against a consumer by the other party to the contract only in the courts of the Contracting State in which the consumer is domiciled.

These provisions shall not affect the right to bring a counter-claim in the court in which, in accordance with this Section, the original claim is pending.

Article 15

The provisions of this Section may be departed from only by an agreement:
1. which is entered into after the dispute has arisen; or
2. which allows the consumer to bring proceedings in courts other than those indicated in this Section; or
3. which is entered into by the consumer and the other party to the contract, both of whom are at the time of conclusion of the contract domiciled or habitually resident in the same Contracting State, and which confers jurisdiction on the courts of that State, provided that such an agreement is not contrary to the law of that State.

Section 5

Exclusive jurisdiction

Article 16

The following courts shall have exclusive jurisdiction, regardless of domicile:
1. (a) in proceedings which have as their object rights in rem in immovable property or tenancies of immovable property, the courts of the Contracting State in which the property is situated;
   (b) however, in proceedings which have as their object tenancies of immovable property concluded for temporary private use for a maximum period of six consecutive months, the courts of the Contracting State in which the defendant is domiciled shall also have jurisdiction, provided that the landlord and the tenant are natural persons and are domiciled in the same Contracting State;
2. in proceedings which have as their object the validity of the constitution, the nullity or the dissolution of companies or other legal persons or associations of natural or legal persons, or the decisions of their organs, the courts of the Contracting State in which the company, legal person or association has its seat;
3. in proceedings which have as their object the validity of entries in public registers, the courts of the Contracting State in which the register is kept;
4. in proceedings concerned with the registration or validity of patents, trade marks, designs, or other similar rights required to be deposited or registered, the courts of the Contracting State in which the deposit or registration has been applied for, has taken place or is under the terms of an international convention deemed to have taken place;

5. in proceedings concerned with the enforcement of judgments, the courts of the Contracting State in which the judgment has been or is to be enforced.

Section 6

Prorogation of jurisdiction

Article 17

If the parties, one or more of whom is domiciled in a Contracting State, have agreed that a court or the courts of a Contracting State are to have jurisdiction to settle any disputes which have arisen or which may arise in connection with a particular legal relationship, that court or those courts shall have exclusive jurisdiction. Such an agreement conferring jurisdiction shall be either:

(a) in writing or evidenced in writing; or

(b) in a form which accords with practices which the parties have established between themselves; or

(c) in international trade or commerce, in a form which accords with a usage of which the parties are or ought to have been aware and which in such trade or commerce is widely known to, and regularly observed by, parties to contracts of the type involved in the particular trade or commerce concerned.

Where such an agreement is concluded by parties, none of whom is domiciled in a Contracting State, the courts of other Contracting States shall have no jurisdiction over their disputes unless the court or courts chosen have declined jurisdiction.

The court or courts of a Contracting State on which a trust instrument has conferred jurisdiction shall have exclusive jurisdiction in any proceedings brought against a settler, trustee or beneficiary, if relations between these persons or their rights or obligations under the trust are involved.

Agreements or provisions of a trust instrument conferring jurisdiction shall have no legal force if they are contrary to the provisions of Articles 12 or 15, or if the courts whose jurisdiction they purport to exclude have exclusive jurisdiction by virtue of Article 16.

If an agreement conferring jurisdiction was concluded for the benefit of only one of the parties, that party shall retain the right to bring proceedings in any other court which has jurisdiction by virtue of this Convention.

In matters relating to individual contracts of employment an agreement conferring jurisdiction shall have legal force only if it is entered into after the dispute has arisen or if the employee invokes it to seise courts other than those for the defendant's domicile or those specified in Article 5 (1).

Article 18

Apart from jurisdiction derived from other provisions of this Convention, a court of a Contracting State before whom a defendant enters an appearance shall have jurisdiction. This rule shall not apply where appearance was entered solely to contest the jurisdiction, or where another court has exclusive jurisdiction by virtue of Article 16.

Section 7

Examination as to jurisdiction and admissibility

Article 19

Where a court of a Contracting State is seised of a claim which is principally concerned with a matter over which the courts of another Contracting State have exclusive jurisdiction by virtue of Article 16, it shall declare of its own motion that it has no jurisdiction.

Article 20

Where a defendant domiciled in one Contracting State is sued in a court of another Contracting State and does not enter an appearance, the court shall declare of its own motion that it has no jurisdiction unless its jurisdiction is derived from the provisions of the Convention.

The court shall stay the proceedings so long as it is not shown that the defendant has been able to receive the document instituting the proceedings or an equivalent document in sufficient time to enable him to arrange for his defence, or that all necessary steps have been taken to this end.

The provisions of the foregoing paragraph shall be replaced by those of Article 15 of the Hague Convention of 15 November 1965 on the service abroad of judicial and extrajudicial documents in civil or commercial matters, if the document instituting the proceedings or notice thereof had to be transmitted abroad in accordance with that Convention.

Section 8

Lis pendens - related actions

Article 21

Where proceedings involving the same cause of action and between the same parties are brought in the courts of different Contracting States, any court other than the court first seised shall of its own motion stay its proceedings until such time as the jurisdiction of the court first seised is established.

Where the jurisdiction of the court first seised is established, any court other than the court first seised shall decline jurisdiction in favour of that court.

Article 22

Where related actions are brought in the courts of different Contracting States, any court other than the court first seised may, while the actions are pending at first instance, stay its proceedings.

A court other than the court first seised may also, on the application of one of the parties, decline jurisdiction if the law of that court permits the consolidation of related actions and the court first seised has jurisdiction over both actions.

For the purposes of this Article, actions are deemed to be related where they are so closely connected that it is expedient to hear and determine them together to avoid the risk of irreconcilable judgments resulting from separate proceedings.

Article 23

Where actions come within the exclusive jurisdiction of several courts, any court other than the court first seised shall decline jurisdiction in favour of that court.

Section 9

Provisional, including protective, measures

Article 24

Application may be made to the courts of a Contracting State for such provisional, including protective, measures as may be available under the law of that State, even if, under this Convention, the courts of another Contracting State have jurisdiction as to the substance of the matter.

TITLE III

RECOGNITION AND ENFORCEMENT

Article 25

For the purposes of this Convention, 'judgment' means any judgment given by a court or tribunal of a Contracting State, whatever the judgment may be called, including a decree, order, decision or writ of execution, as well as the determination of costs or expenses by an officer of the court.

Section 1

Recognition

Article 26

A judgment given in a Contracting State shall be recognized in the other Contracting States without any special procedure being required.

Any interested party who raises the recognition of a judgment as the principal issue in a dispute may, in accordance with the procedures provided for in Sections 2 and 3 of this Title, apply for a decision that the judgment be recognized.

If the outcome of proceedings in a court of a Contracting State depends on the determination of an incidental question of recognition that court shall have jurisdiction over that question.

Article 27

A judgment shall not be recognized:

1. if such recognition is contrary to public policy in the State in which recognition is sought;
2. where it was given in default of appearance, if the defendant was not duly served with the document which instituted the proceedings or with an equivalent document in sufficient time to enable him to arrange for his defence;
3. if the judgment is irreconcilable with a judgment given in a dispute between the same parties in the State in which recognition is sought;
4. if the court of the State of origin, in order to arrive at its judgment, has decided a preliminary question concerning the status or legal capacity of natural persons, rights in property arising out of a matrimonial relationship, wills or succession in a way that conflicts with a rule of the private international law of the State in which the recognition is sought, unless the same result would have been reached by the application of the rules of private international law of that State;
5. if the judgment is irreconcilable with an earlier judgment given in a non-contracting State involving the same cause of action and between the same parties, provided that this latter judgment fulfils the conditions necessary for its recognition in the State addressed.

Article 28

Moreover, a judgment shall not be recognized if it conflicts with the provisions of Sections 3, 4 or 5 of Title II, or in a case provided for in Article 59.

In its examination of the grounds of jurisdiction referred to in the foregoing paragraph, the court or authority applied to shall be bound by the findings of fact on which the court of the State of origin based its jurisdiction.

Subject to the provisions of the first paragraph, the jurisdiction of the court of the State of origin may not be reviewed; the test of public policy referred to in point 1 of Article 27 may not be applied to the rules relating to jurisdiction.

Article 29

Under no circumstances may a foreign judgment be reviewed as to its substance.

Article 30

A court of a Contracting State in which recognition is sought of a judgment given in another Contracting State may stay the proceedings if an ordinary appeal against the judgment has been lodged.

A court of a Contracting State in which recognition is sought of a judgment given in Ireland or the United Kingdom may stay the proceedings if enforcement is suspended in the State of origin, by reason of an appeal.

Section 2

Enforcement

Article 31

A judgment given in a Contracting State and enforceable in that State shall be enforced in another Contracting State when, on the application of any interested party, it has been declared enforceable there.

However, in the United Kingdom, such a judgment shall be enforced in England and Wales, in Scotland, or in Northern Ireland when, on the application of any interested party, it has been registered for enforcement in that part of the United Kingdom.

Article 32

1. The application shall be submitted:
- in Belgium, to the 'tribunal de première instance' or 'rechtbank van eerste aanleg',
- in Denmark, to the 'byret',
- in the Federal Republic of Germany, to the presiding judge of a chamber of the 'Landgericht',
- in Greece, to the 'Μονομελές Πρωτοδικείο',
- in Spain, to the 'Juzgado de Primera Instancia',
- in France, to the presiding judge of the 'tribunal de grande instance',
- in Ireland, to the High Court,
- in Italy, to the 'Corte d'appello',
- in Luxembourg, to the presiding judge of the 'tribunal d'arrondissement',
- in Austria, to the 'Bezirksgericht',
- in the Netherlands, to the presiding judge of the 'arrondissementsrechtbank',
- in Portugal, to the 'Tribunal de Comarca',
- in Finland, to the 'käräjäoikeus/tingsrätt',
- in Sweden, to the 'Svea hovrätt',
- in the United Kingdom:
  (a) in England and Wales, to the High Court of Justice, or in the case of maintenance judgment to the Magistrates' Court on transmission by the Secretary of State;

(b) in Scotland, to the Court of Session, or in the case of a maintenance judgment to the Sheriff Court on transmission by the Secretary of State;

(c) in Northern Ireland, to the High Court of Justice, or in the case of a maintenance judgment to the Magistrates' Court on transmission by the Secretary of State.

2. The jurisdiction of local courts shall be determined by reference to the place of domicile of the party against whom enforcement is sought. If he is not domiciled in the State in which enforcement is sought, it shall be determined by reference to the place of enforcement.

Article 33

The procedure for making the application shall be governed by the law of the State in which enforcement is sought.

The applicant must give an address for service of process within the area of jurisdiction of the court applied to. However, if the law of the State in which enforcement is sought does not provide for the furnishing of such an address, the applicant shall appoint a representative ad litem.

The documents referred to in Articles 46 and 47 shall be attached to the application.

Article 34

The court applied to shall give its decision without delay; the party against whom enforcement is sought shall not at this stage of the proceedings be entitled to make any submissions on the application.

The application may be refused only for one of the reasons specified in Articles 27 and 28.

Under no circumstances may the foreign judgment be reviewed as to its substance.

Article 35

The appropriate officer of the court shall without delay bring the decision given on the application to the notice of the applicant in accordance with the procedure laid down by the law of the State in which enforcement is sought.

Article 36

If enforcement is authorized, the party against whom enforcement is sought may appeal against the decision within one month of service thereof.

If that party is domiciled in a Contracting State other than that in which the decision authorizing enforcement was given, the time for appealing shall be two months and shall run from the date of service, either on him in person or at his residence. No extension of time may be granted on account of distance.

Article 37

1. An appeal against the decision authorizing enforcement shall be lodged in accordance with the rules governing procedure in contentious matters:

- in Belgium, with the 'tribunal de première instance' or 'rechtbank van eerste aanleg',
- in Denmark, with the 'landsret',
- in the Federal Republic of Germany, with the 'Oberlandesgericht',
- in Greece, with the 'Εφετείο',
- in Spain, with the 'Audiencia Provincial',
- in France, with the 'cour d'appel',
- in Ireland, with the High Court,
- in Italy, with the 'corte d'appello',
- in Luxembourg, with the 'Cour supérieure de justice' sitting as a court of civil appeal,
- in Austria with the 'Bezirksgericht',
- in the Netherlands, with the 'arrondissementsrechtbank',
- in Portugal, with the 'Tribunal de Relação',
- in Finland, with the 'hovioikeus/hovrätt',
- in Sweden, with the 'Svea hovrätt',
- in the United Kingdom:
  (a) in England and Wales, with the High Court of Justice, or in the case of a maintenance judgment with the Magistrates' Court;
  (b) in Scotland, with the Court of Session, or in the case of a maintenance judgment with the Sheriff Court;
  (c) in Northern Ireland, with the High Court of Justice, or in the case of a maintenance judgment with the Magistrates' Court.

2. The judgment given on the appeal may be contested only:

- in Belgium, Greece, Spain, France, Italy, Luxembourg and in the Netherlands, by an appeal in cassation,
- in Denmark, by an appeal to the 'højesteret', with the leave of the Minister of Justice,
- in the Federal Republic of Germany, by a 'Rechtsbeschwerde',
- in Austria, in the case of an appeal, by a 'Revisionsrekurs' and, in the case of opposition proceedings, by a 'Berufung' with the possibility of a revision,
- in Ireland, by an appeal on a point of law to the Supreme Court,
- in Portugal, by an appeal on a point of law,
- in Finland, by an appeal to 'korkein oikeus/högsta domstolen',
- in Sweden by an appeal to 'Högsta domstolen',
- in the United Kingdom, by a single further appeal on a point of law.

Article 38

The court with which the appeal under Article 37 (1) is lodged may, on the application of the appellant, stay the proceedings if an ordinary appeal has been lodged against the judgment in the State of origin or if the time for such an appeal has not yet expired; in the latter case, the court may specify the time within which such an appeal is to be lodged.

Where the judgment was given in Ireland or the United Kingdom, any form of appeal available in the State of origin shall be treated as an ordinary appeal for the purposes of the first paragraph.

The court may also make enforcement conditional on the provision of such security as it shall determine.

Article 39

During the time specified for an appeal pursuant to Article 36 and until any such appeal has been determined, no measures of enforcement may be taken other than protective measures taken against the property of the party against whom enforcement is sought.

The decision authorizing enforcement shall carry with it the power to proceed to any such protective measures.

Article 40

If the application for enforcement is refused, the applicant may appeal:

- in Belgium, to the 'cour d'appel' or 'hof van beroep',
- in Denmark, to the 'landsret',
- in the Federal Republic of Germany, to the 'Oberlandesgericht',
- in Greece, to the '΄Εφετείο',
- in Spain, to the 'Audiencia Provincial',
- in France, to the 'cour d'appel',
- in Ireland, to the High Court,
- in Italy, to the 'corte d'appello',
- in Luxembourg, to the 'Cour supérieure de justice' sitting as a court of civil appeal,
- in Austria, to the 'Bezirksgericht',
- in the Netherlands, to the 'gerechtshof',
- in Portugal, to the 'Tribunal de Relação',
- in Finland, to 'hovioikeus/hovrätten',
- in Sweden, to the 'Svea hovrätt',
- in the United Kingdom:
  (a) in England and Wales, to the High Court of Justice, or in the case of a maintenance judgment to the Magistrates' Court;
  (b) in Scotland, to the Court of Session, or in the case of a maintenance judgment to the Sheriff Court;
  (c) in Northern Ireland, to the High Court of Justice, or in the case of a maintenance judgment to the Magistrates' Court.

2. The party against whom enforcement is sought shall be summoned to appear before the appellate court. If he fails to appear, the provisions of the second and third paragraphs of Article 20 shall apply even where he is not domiciled in any of the Contracting States.

Article 41

A judgment given on an appeal provided for in Article 40 may be contested only:
- in Belgium, Greece, Spain, France, Italy, Luxembourg and in the Netherlands, by an appeal in cassation,
- in Denmark, by an appeal to the 'højesteret', with the leave of the Minister of Justice,
- in the Federal Republic of Germany, by a 'Rechtsbeschwerde',
- in Ireland, by an appeal on a point of law to the Supreme Court,
- in Austria, by a 'Revisionsrekurs',
- in Portugal, by an appeal on a point of law,
- in Finland, by an appeal to 'korkein oikeus/högsta domstolen',
- in Sweden, by an appeal to 'Högsta domstolen',
- in the United Kingdom, by a single further appeal on a point of law.

Article 42

Where a foreign judgment has been given in respect of several matters and enforcement cannot be authorized for all of them, the court shall authorize enforcement for one or more of them.

An applicant may request partial enforcement of a judgment.

Article 43

A foreign judgment which orders a periodic payment by way of a penalty shall be enforceable in the State in which enforcement is sought only if the amount of the payment has been finally determined by the courts of the State of origin.

Article 44

An applicant who, in the State of origin has benefited from complete or partial legal aid or exemption from costs or expenses, shall be entitled, in the procedures provided for in Articles 32 to 35, to benefit from the most favourable legal aid or the most extensive exemption from costs or expenses provided for by the law of the State addressed.

However, an applicant who requests the enforcement of a decision given by an administrative authority in Denmark in respect of a maintenance order may, in the State addressed, claim the benefits referred to in the first paragraph if he presents a statement from the Danish Ministry of Justice to the effect that he fulfils the economic requirements to qualify for the grant of complete or partial legal aid or exemption from costs or expenses.

Article 45

No security, bond or deposit, however described, shall be required of a party who in one Contracting State applies for enforcement of a judgment given in another Contracting State on the ground that he is a foreign national or that he is not domiciled or resident in the State in which enforcement is sought.

Section 3

Common provisions

Article 46

A party seeking recognition or applying for enforcement of a judgment shall produce:
1. a copy of the judgment which satisfies the conditions necessary to establish its authenticity;
2. in the case of a judgment given in default, the original or a certified true copy of the document which establishes that the party in default was served with the document instituting the proceedings or with an equivalent document.

Article 47

A party applying for enforcement shall also produce:
1. documents which establish that, according to the law of the State of origin the judgment is enforceable and has been served;
2. where appropriate, a document showing that the applicant is in receipt of legal aid in the State of origin.

Article 48

If the documents specified in point 2 of Articles 46 and 47 are not produced, the court may specify a time for their production, accept equivalent documents or, if it considers that it has sufficient information before it, dispense with their production.

If the court so requires, a translation of the documents shall be produced; the translation shall be certified by a person qualified to do so in one of the Contracting States.

Article 49

No legalization or other similar formality shall be required in respect of the documents referred to in Articles 46 or 47 or the second paragraph of Article 48, or in respect of a document appointing a representative ad litem.

TITLE IV

AUTHENTIC INSTRUMENTS AND COURT SETTLEMENTS

Article 50

A document which has been formally drawn up or registered as an authentic instrument and is enforceable in one Contracting State shall, in another Contracting State, be declared enforceable there, on application made in accordance with the procedures provided for in Article 31 *et seq.* The application may be refused only if enforcement of the instrument is contrary to public policy in the State addressed.

The instrument produced must satisfy the conditions necessary to establish its authenticity in the State of origin.

The provisions of Section 3 of Title III shall apply as appropriate.

Article 51

A settlement which has been approved by a court in the course of proceedings and is enforceable in the State in which it was concluded shall be enforceable in the State addressed under the same conditions as authentic instruments.

TITLE V

GENERAL PROVISIONS

Article 52

In order to determine whether a party is domiciled in the Contracting State whose courts are seised of a matter, the Court shall apply its internal law.

If a party is not domiciled in the State whose courts are seised of the matter, then, in order to determine whether the party is domiciled in another Contracting State, the court shall apply the law of that State.

Article 53

For the purposes of this Convention, the seat of a company or other legal person or association of natural or legal persons shall be treated as its domicile. However, in order to determine that seat, the court shall apply its rules of private international law.

In order to determine whether a trust is domiciled in the Contracting State whose courts are seised of the matter, the court shall apply its rules of private international law.

TITLE VI

TRANSITIONAL PROVISIONS

Article 54

The provisions of the Convention shall apply only to legal proceedings instituted and to documents formally drawn up or registered as authentic instruments after its entry into force in the State of origin and, where recognition or enforcement of a judgment or authentic instruments is sought, in the State addressed.

However, judgments given after the date of entry into force of this Convention between the State of origin and the State addressed in proceedings instituted before that date shall be recognized and enforced in accordance with the provisions of Title III if jurisdiction was founded upon rules which accorded with those provided for either in Title II of this Convention or in a convention concluded between the State of origin and the State addressed which was in force when the proceedings were instituted.

If the parties to a dispute concerning a contract had agreed in writing before 1 June 1988 for Ireland or before 1 January 1987 for the United Kingdom that the contract was to be governed by the law of Ireland or of a part of the United Kingdom, the courts of Ireland or of that part of the United Kingdom shall retain the right to exercise jurisdiction in the dispute.

Article 54a

For a period of three years from 1 November 1986 for Denmark and from 1 June 1988 for Ireland, jurisdiction in maritime matters shall be determined in these States not only in accordance with the provisions of Title II, but also in accordance with the provisions of paragraphs 1 to 6 following. However, upon the entry into force of the International Convention relating to the arrest of sea-going ships, signed at Brussels on 10 May 1952, for one of these States, those provisions shall cease to have effect for that State.

1. A person who is domiciled in a Contracting State may be sued in the courts of one of the States mentioned above in respect of a maritime claim if the ship to which the claim relates or any other ship owned by him has been arrested by judicial process within the territory of the latter State to secure the claim, or could have been so arrested there but bail or other security has been given, and either:
   - (a) the claimant is domiciled in the latter State; or
   - (b) the claim arose in the latter State; or
   - (c) the claim concerns the voyage during which the arrest was made or could have been made; or
   - (d) the claim arises out of a collision or out of damage caused by a ship to another ship or to goods or persons on board either ship, either by the execution or non-execution of a manoeuvre or by the non-observance of regulations; or

(e) the claim is for salvage; or
(f) the claim is in respect of a mortgage or hypothecation of the ship arrested.

2. A claimant may arrest either the particular ship to which the maritime claim relates, or any other ship which is owned by the person who was, at the time when the maritime claim arose, the owner of the particular ship. However, only the particular ship to which the maritime claim relates may be arrested in respect of the maritime claims set out in 5 (o), (p) or (q) of this Article.

3. Ships shall be deemed to be in the same ownership when all the shares therein are owned by the same person or persons.

4. When in the case of a charter by demise of a ship the charterer alone is liable in respect of a maritime claim relating to that ship, the claimant may arrest that ship or any other ship owned by the charterer, but no other ship owned by the owner may be arrested in respect of such claim. The same shall apply to any case in which a person other than the owner of a ship is liable in respect of a maritime claim relating to that ship.

5. The expression 'maritime claim' means a claim arising out of one or more of the following:

(a) damage caused by any ship either in collision or otherwise;
(b) loss of life or personal injury caused by any ship or occurring in connection with the operation on any ship;
(c) salvage;
(d) agreement relating to the use or hire of any ship whether by charterparty or otherwise;
(e) agreement relating to the carriage of goods in any ship whether by charterparty or otherwise;
(f) loss of or damage to goods including baggage carried in any ship;
(g) general average;
(h) bottomry;
(i) towage;
(j) pilotage;
(k) goods or materials wherever supplied to a ship for her operation or maintenance;
(l) construction, repair or equipment of any ship or dock charges and dues;
(m) wages of masters, officers or crew;
(n) mater's disbursements, including disbursements made by shippers, charterers or agents on behalf of a ship or her owner;
(o) dispute as to the title to or ownership of any ship;
(p) disputes between co-owners of any ship as to the ownership, possession, employment or earnings of that ship;
(q) the mortgage or hypothecation of any ship.

6. In Denmark, the expression 'arrest' shall be deemed as regards the maritime claims referred to in 5 (o) and (p) of this Article, to include a 'forbud', where that is the only procedure allowed in respect of such a claim under Articles 646 to 653 of the law on civil procedure (lov om rettens pleje).

TITLE VII

RELATIONSHIP TO OTHER CONVENTIONS

Article 55

Subject to the provisions of the second subparagraph of Article 54, and of Article 56, this Convention shall, for the States which are parties to it, supersede the following conventions concluded between two or more of them:

- the Convention between Belgium and France on jurisdiction and the validity and enforcement of judgments, arbitration awards and authentic instruments, signed at Paris on 8 July 1899,
- the Convention between Belgium and the Netherlands on jurisdiction, bankruptcy, and the validity and enforcement of judgments, arbitration awards and authentic instruments, signed at Brussels on 28 March 1925,
- the Convention between France and Italy on the enforcement of judgments in civil and commercial matters, signed at Rome on 3 June 1930,
- the Convention between the United Kingdom and the French Republic providing for the reciprocal enforcement of judgments in civil and commercial matters, with Protocol, signed at Paris on 18 January 1934,
- the Convention between the United Kingdom and the Kingdom of Belgium providing for the reciprocal enforcement of judgments in civil and commercial matters, with Protocol, signed at Brussels on 2 May 1934,
- the Convention between Germany and Italy on the recognition and enforcement of judgments in civil and commercial matters, signed at Rome on 9 March 1936,
- the Convention between the Kingdom of Belgium and Austria on the reciprocal recognition and enforcement of judgments and authentic instruments relating to maintenance obligations, signed at Vienna on 25 October 1957,
- the Convention between the Federal Republic of Germany and the Kingdom of Belgium on the mutual recognition and enforcement of judgments, arbitration awards and authentic instruments in civil and commercial matters, signed at Bonn on 30 June 1958,
- the Convention between the Kingdom of the Netherlands and the Italian Republic on the recognition and enforcement of judgments in civil and commercial matters, signed at Rome on 17 April 1959,
- the Convention between the Federal Republic of Germany and Austria on the reciprocal recognition and enforcement of judgments, settlements and authentic instruments in civil and commercial matters, signed at Vienna on 6 June 1959,
- the Convention between the Kingdom of Belgium and Austria on the reciprocal recognition and enforcement of judgments, arbitral awards and authentic instruments in civil and commercial matters, signed at Vienna on 16 June 1959,
- the Convention between the United Kingdom and the Federal Republic of

Germany for the reciprocal recognition and enforcement of judgments in civil and commercial matters, signed at Bonn on 14 July 1960,

- the Convention between the United Kingdom and Austria providing for the reciprocal recognition and enforcement of judgments in civil and commercial matters, signed at Vienna on 14 July 1961, with amending Protocol signed at London on 6 March 1970,
- the Convention between the Kingdom of Greece and the Federal Republic of Germany for the reciprocal recognition and enforcement of judgments, settlements and authentic instruments in civil and commercial matters, signed in Athens on 4 November 1961,
- the Convention between the Kingdom of Belgium and the Italian Republic on the recognition and enforcement of judgments and other enforceable instruments in civil and commercial matters, signed at Rome on 6 April 1962,
- the Convention between the Kingdom of the Netherlands and the Federal Republic of Germany on the mutual recognition and enforcement of judgments and other enforceable instruments in civil and commercial matters, signed at The Hague on 30 August 1962,
- the Convention between the Kingdom of the Netherlands and Austria on the reciprocal recognition and enforcement of judgments and authentic instruments in civil and commercial matters, signed at The Hague on 6 February 1963,
- the Convention between France and Austria on the recognition and enforcement of judgments and authentic instruments in civil and commercial matters, signed at Vienna on 15 July 1966,
- the Convention between the United Kingdom and the Republic of Italy for the reciprocal recognition and enforcement of judgments in civil and commercial matters, signed at Rome on 7 February 1964, with amending Protocol signed at Rome on 14 July 1970,
- the Convention between the United Kingdom and the Kingdom of the Netherlands providing for the reciprocal recognition and enforcement of judgments in civil matters, signed at The Hague on 17 November 1967,
- the Convention between Spain and France on the recognition and enforcement of judgment arbitration awards in civil and commercial matters, signed at Paris on 28 May 1969,
- the Convention between Luxembourg and Austria on the recognition and enforcement of judgments aud authentic instruments in civil and commercial matters, signed at Luxembourg on 29 July 1971,
- the Convention between Italy and Austria on the recognition and enforcement of judgments in civil and commercial matters, of judicial settlements and of authentic instruments, signed at Rome on 16 November 1971,
- the Convention between Spain and Italy regarding legal aid and the recognition and enforcement of judgments in civil and commercial matters, signed at Madrid on 22 May 1973,
- the Convention between Finland, Iceland, Norway, Sweden and Denmark

on the recognition and enforcement of judgments in civil matters, signed at Copenhagen on 11 October 1977,

- the Convention between Austria and Sweden on the recognition and enforcement of judgments in civil matters, signed at Stockholm on 16 September 1982,
- the Convention between Spain and the Federal Republic of Germany on the recognition and enforcement of judgments, settlements and enforceable authentic instruments in civil and commercial matters, signed at Bonn on 14 November 1983,
- the Convention between Austria and Spain on the recognition and enforcement of judgments, settlements and enforceable authentic instruments in civil and commercial matters, signed at Vienna on 17 February 1984 ,
- the Convention between Finland and Austria on the recognition and enforcement of judgments in civil matters, signed at Vienna on 17 November 1986, and, in so far as it is in force:
- the Treaty between Belgium, the Netherlands and Luxembourg in jurisdiction, bankruptcy, and the validity and enforcement of judgments, arbitration awards and authentic instruments, signed at Brussels on 24 November 1961.

Article 56

The Treaty and the conventions referred to in Article 55 shall continue to have effect in relation to matters to which this Convention does not apply.

They shall continue to have effect in respect of judgments given and documents formally drawn up or registered as authentic instruments before the entry into force of this Convention.

Article 57

1. This Convention shall not affect any conventions to which the Contracting States are or will be parties and which in relation to particular matters, govern jurisdiction or the recognition or enforcement of judgments.

2. With a view to its uniform interpretation, paragraph 1 shall be applied in the following manner:

   (a) this Convention shall not prevent a court of a Contracting State which is a party to a convention on a particular matter from assuming jurisdiction in accordance with that Convention, even where the defendant is domiciled in another Contracting State which is not a party to that Convention. The court hearing the action shall, in any event, apply Article 20 of this Convention;

   (b) judgments given in a Contracting State by a court in the exercise of jurisdiction provided for in a convention on a particular matter shall be recognized and enforced in the other Contracting State in accordance with this Convention.

Where a convention on a particular matter to which both the State of origin and the State addressed are parties lays down conditions for the recognition or enforcement of judgments, those conditions shall apply. In any event, the provisions of this Convention which concern the procedure for recognition and enforcement of judgments may be applied.

3. This Convention shall not affect the application of provisions which, in relation to particular matters, govern jurisdiction or the recognition or enforcement of judgments and which are or will be contained in acts of the institutions of the European Communities or in national laws harmonized in implementation of such acts.

Article 58

Until such time as the Convention on jurisdiction and the enforcement of judgments in civil and commercial matters, signed at Lugano on 16 September 1988, takes effect with regard to France and the Swiss Confederation, this Convention shall not affect the rights granted to Swiss nationals by the Convention between France and the Swiss Confederation on jurisdiction and enforcement of judgments in civil matters, signed at Paris on 15 June 1869.

Article 59

This Convention shall not prevent a Contracting State from assuming, in a convention on the recognition and enforcement of judgments, an obligation towards a third State not to recognize judgments given in other Contracting States against defendants domiciled or habitually resident in the third State where, in cases provided for in Article 4, the judgment could only be founded on a ground of jurisdiction specified in the second paragraph of Article 3.

However, a Contracting State may not assume an obligation towards a third State not to recognize a judgment given in another Contracting State by a court basing its jurisdiction on the presence within that State of property belonging to the defendant, or the seizure by the plaintiff of property situated there:

1. if the action is brought to assert or declare proprietary or possessory rights in that property, seeks to obtain authority to dispose of it, or arises from another issue relating to such property; or

2. if the property constitutes the security for a debt which is the subject-matter of the action.

TITLE VIII

FINAL PROVISIONS

Article 60

...

Article 61

This Convention shall be ratified by the signatory States. The instruments of ratification shall be deposited with the Secretary-General of the Council of the European Communities.

Article 62

This Convention shall enter into force on the first day of the third month following the deposit of the instrument of ratification by the last signatory State to take this step.

Article 63

The Contracting States recognize that any State which becomes a member of the European Economic Community shall be required to accept this Convention as a basis for the negotiations between the Contracting States and that State necessary to ensure the implementation of the last paragraph of Article 220 of the Treaty establishing the European Economic Community.

The necessary adjustments may be the subject of a special convention between the Contracting States of the one part and the new Member States of the other part.

Article 64

The Secretary-General of the Council of the European Communities shall notify the signatory States of:

(a) the deposit of each instrument of ratification;
(b) the date of entry into force of this Convention;
(c) . . . ;
(d) any declaration received pursuant to Article IV of the Protocol;
(e) any communication made pursuant to Article VI of the Protocol.

Article 65

The Protocol annexed to this Convention by common accord of the Contracting States shall form an integral part thereof.

Article 66

This Convention is concluded for an unlimited period.

Article 67

Any Contracting State may request the revision of this Convention. In this event, a revision conference shall be convened by the President of the Council of the European Communities.

Article 68

This Convention, drawn up in a single original in the Dutch, French, German and Italian languages, all four texts being equally authentic, shall be deposited in the archives of the Secretariat of the Council of the European Communities. The Secretary-General shall transmit a certified copy to the Government of each signatory State.

PROTOCOL

The High contracting Parties have agreed upon the following provisions, which shall be annexed to the Convention:

Article I

Any person domiciled in Luxembourg who is sued in a court of another Contracting State pursuant to Article 5 (1) may refuse to submit to the jurisdiction of that court. If the defendant does not enter an appearance the court shall declare of its own motion that it has no jurisdiction.

An agreement conferring jurisdiction, within the meaning of Article 17, shall be valid with respect to a person domiciled in Luxembourg only if that person has expressly and specifically so agreed.

Article II

Without prejudice to any more favourable provisions of national laws, persons domiciled in a Contracting State who are being prosecuted in the criminal courts of another Contracting State of which they are not nationals for an offence which was not intentionally committed may be defended by persons qualified to do so, even if they do not appear in person.

However, the court seised of the matter may order appearance in person; in the case of failure to appear, a judgment given in the civil action without the person concerned having had the opportunity to arrange for his defence need not be recognized or enforced in the other Contracting States.

Article III

In proceedings for the issue of an order for enforcement, no charge, duty or fee calculated by reference to the value of the matter in issue may be levied in the State in which enforcement is sought.

Article IV

Judicial and extrajudicial documents drawn up in one Contracting State which have to be served on persons in another Contracting State shall be transmitted in accordance with the procedures laid down in the conventions and agreements concluded between the Contracting States.

Unless the State in which service is to take place objects by declaration to the Secretary-General of the Council of the European Communities, such documents may also be sent by the appropriate public officers of the State in which the document has been drawn up directly to the appropriate public officers of the State in which the addressee is to be found. In this case the officer of the State of origin shall send a copy of the document to the officer of the State applied to who is competent to forward it to the addressee. The document shall be forwarded in the manner specified by the law of the State applied to. The forwarding shall be recorded by a certificate sent directly to the officer of the State of origin.

Article V

The jurisdiction specified in Articles 6 (2) and 10 in actions on a warranty or guarantee or in any other third-party proceedings may not be resorted to in the Federal Republic of Germany or in Austria. Any person domiciled in another Contracting State may be sued in the courts:

- of the Federal Republic of Germany, pursuant to Articles 68, 72, 73 and 74 of the code of civil procedure (Zivilprozessordnung) concerning third-party notices,
- of Austria, pursuant to Article 21 of the code of civil procedure (Zivilprozessordnung) concerning third-party notices.

Judgments given in the other Contracting States by virtue of Article 6 (2) or 10 shall be recognized and enforced in the Federal Republic of Germany and in Austria in accordance with Title III. Any effects which judgments given in those States may have on third parties by application of the provisions in the preceeding paragraph shall also be recognized in the other Contracting States.

Article Va

In matters relating to maintenance, the expression 'court' includes the Danish administrative authorities.

In Sweden, in summary proceedings concerning orders to pay (betalningsföreläggande) and assistance (bandräckning), the expression 'court' includes the 'Swedish enforcement service' (kronofogdemyndighet).

Article Vb

In proceedings involving a dispute between the master and a member of the crew of a sea-going ship registered in Denmark, in Greece, in Ireland or in Portugal, concerning remuneration or other conditions of service, a court in a Contracting State shall establish whether the diplomatic or consular officer responsible for the ship has been notified of the dispute. It shall stay the proceedings so long as he has not been notified. It shall of its own motion decline jurisdiction if the officer, having been duly notified, has exercised the powers accorded to him in the matter by a consular convention, or in the absence of such a convention has, within the time allowed, raised any objection to the exercise of such jurisdiction.

Article Vc

Article 52 and 53 of this Convention shall, when applied by Article 69 (5) of the Convention for the European patent for the common market, signed at Luxembourg on 15 December 1975, to the provisions relating to 'residence' in the English text of that Convention, operate as if 'residence' in that text were the same as 'domicile' in Articles 52 and 53.

Article Vd

Without prejudice to the jurisdiction of the European Patent Office under the Convention on the grant of European patents, signed at Munich on 5 October 1973, the courts of each Contracting State shall have exclusive jurisdiction, regardless of domicile, in proceedings concerned with the registration or validity of any European patent granted for that State which is not a Community patent by virtue of the provisions of Article 86 of the Convention for the European patent for the common market, signed at Luxembourg on 15 December 1975.

Article Ve

Arrangements relating to maintenance obligations concluded with administrative authorities or authenticated by them shall also be regarded as authentic instruments within the meaning of the first paragraph of Article 50 of the Convention.

Article VI

The Contracting States shall communicate to the Secretary-General of the Council of the European Communities the text of any provisions of their laws which amend either those articles of their laws mentioned in the Convention or the lists of courts specified in Section 2 of Title III of the Convention.

APPENDIX II

Council Regulation (EC) No 44/2001 of 22 December 2000 on jurisdiction and the recognition and enforcement of judgments in civil and commercial matters

Council Regulation (EC) No 44/2001 of 22 December 2000 on jurisdiction and the recognition and enforcement of judgments in civil and commercial matters*

THE COUNCIL OF THE EUROPEAN UNION,

Having regard to the Treaty establishing the European Community, and in particular Article 61(c) and Article 67(1) thereof,

Having regard to the proposal from the Commission,

Having regard to the opinion of the European Parliament,

Having regard to the opinion of the Economic and Social Committee,

Whereas:

(1) The Community has set itself the objective of maintaining and developing an area of freedom, security and justice, in which the free movement of persons is ensured. In order to establish progressively such an area, the Community should adopt, amongst other things, the measures relating to judicial cooperation in civil matters which are necessary for the sound operation of the internal market.

(2) Certain differences between national rules governing jurisdiction and recognition of judgments hamper the sound operation of the internal market. Provisions to unify the rules of conflict of jurisdiction in civil and commercial matters and to simplify the formalities with a view to rapid and simple recognition and enforcement of judgments from Member States bound by this Regulation are essential.

(3) This area is within the field of judicial cooperation in civil matters within the meaning of Article 65 of the Treaty.

(4) In accordance with the principles of subsidiarity and proportionality as set out in Article 5 of the Treaty, the objectives of this Regulation cannot be sufficiently achieved by the Member States and can therefore be better achieved

---

* *OJ L 012, 16/01/2001, p. 1 - 23.*

by the Community. This Regulation confines itself to the minimum required in order to achieve those objectives and does not go beyond what is necessary for that purpose.

(5) On 27 September 1968 the Member States, acting under Article 293, fourth indent, of the Treaty, concluded the Brussels Convention on Jurisdiction and the Enforcement of Judgments in Civil and Commercial Matters, as amended by Conventions on the Accession of the New Member States to that Convention (hereinafter referred to as the "Brussels Convention"). On 16 September 1988 Member States and EFTA States concluded the Lugano Convention on Jurisdiction and the Enforcement of Judgments in Civil and Commercial Matters, which is a parallel Convention to the 1968 Brussels Convention. Work has been undertaken for the revision of those Conventions, and the Council has approved the content of the revised texts. Continuity in the results achieved in that revision should be ensured.

(6) In order to attain the objective of free movement of judgments in civil and commercial matters, it is necessary and appropriate that the rules governing jurisdiction and the recognition and enforcement of judgments be governed by a Community legal instrument which is binding and directly applicable.

(7) The scope of this Regulation must cover all the main civil and commercial matters apart from certain well-defined matters.

(8) There must be a link between proceedings to which this Regulation applies and the territory of the Member States bound by this Regulation. Accordingly common rules on jurisdiction should, in principle, apply when the defendant is domiciled in one of those Member States.

(9) A defendant not domiciled in a Member State is in general subject to national rules of jurisdiction applicable in the territory of the Member State of the court seised, and a defendant domiciled in a Member State not bound by this Regulation must remain subject to the Brussels Convention.

(10) For the purposes of the free movement of judgments, judgments given in a Member State bound by this Regulation should be recognised and enforced in another Member State bound by this Regulation, even if the judgment debtor is domiciled in a third State.

(11) The rules of jurisdiction must be highly predictable and founded on the principle that jurisdiction is generally based on the defendant's domicile and jurisdiction must always be available on this ground save in a few well-defined situations in which the subject-matter of the litigation or the autonomy of the parties warrants a different linking factor. The domicile of a legal person must be defined autonomously so as to make the common rules more transparent and avoid conflicts of jurisdiction.

(12) In addition to the defendant's domicile, there should be alternative grounds of jurisdiction based on a close link between the court and the action or in order to facilitate the sound administration of justice.

(13) In relation to insurance, consumer contracts and employment, the weaker party should be protected by rules of jurisdiction more favourable to his interests than the general rules provide for.

(14) The autonomy of the parties to a contract, other than an insurance,

consumer or employment contract, where only limited autonomy to determine the courts having jurisdiction is allowed, must be respected subject to the exclusive grounds of jurisdiction laid down in this Regulation.

(15) In the interests of the harmonious administration of justice it is necessary to minimise the possibility of concurrent proceedings and to ensure that irreconcilable judgments will not be given in two Member States. There must be a clear and effective mechanism for resolving cases of *lis pendens* and related actions and for obviating problems flowing from national differences as to the determination of the time when a case is regarded as pending. For the purposes of this Regulation that time should be defined autonomously.

(16) Mutual trust in the administration of justice in the Community justifies judgments given in a Member State being recognised automatically without the need for any procedure except in cases of dispute.

(17) By virtue of the same principle of mutual trust, the procedure for making enforceable in one Member State a judgment given in another must be efficient and rapid. To that end, the declaration that a judgment is enforceable should be issued virtually automatically after purely formal checks of the documents supplied, without there being any possibility for the court to raise of its own motion any of the grounds for non-enforcement provided for by this Regulation.

(18) However, respect for the rights of the defence means that the defendant should be able to appeal in an adversarial procedure, against the declaration of enforceability, if he considers one of the grounds for non-enforcement to be present. Redress procedures should also be available to the claimant where his application for a declaration of enforceability has been rejected.

(19) Continuity between the Brussels Convention and this Regulation should be ensured, and transitional provisions should be laid down to that end. The same need for continuity applies as regards the interpretation of the Brussels Convention by the Court of Justice of the European Communities and the 1971 Protocol should remain applicable also to cases already pending when this Regulation enters into force.

(20) The United Kingdom and Ireland, in accordance with Article 3 of the Protocol on the position of the United Kingdom and Ireland annexed to the Treaty on European Union and to the Treaty establishing the European Community, have given notice of their wish to take part in the adoption and application of this Regulation.

(21) Denmark, in accordance with Articles 1 and 2 of the Protocol on the position of Denmark annexed to the Treaty on European Union and to the Treaty establishing the European Community, is not participating in the adoption of this Regulation, and is therefore not bound by it nor subject to its application.

(22) Since the Brussels Convention remains in force in relations between Denmark and the Member States that are bound by this Regulation, both the Convention and the 1971 Protocol continue to apply between Denmark and the Member States bound by this Regulation.

(23) The Brussels Convention also continues to apply to the territories of the Member States which fall within the territorial scope of that Convention and which are excluded from this Regulation pursuant to Article 299 of the Treaty.

(24) Likewise for the sake of consistency, this Regulation should not affect rules governing jurisdiction and the recognition of judgments contained in specific Community instruments.

(25) Respect for international commitments entered into by the Member States means that this Regulation should not affect conventions relating to specific matters to which the Member States are parties.

(26) The necessary flexibility should be provided for in the basic rules of this Regulation in order to take account of the specific procedural rules of certain Member States. Certain provisions of the Protocol annexed to the Brussels Convention should accordingly be incorporated in this Regulation.

(27) In order to allow a harmonious transition in certain areas which were the subject of special provisions in the Protocol annexed to the Brussels Convention, this Regulation lays down, for a transitional period, provisions taking into consideration the specific situation in certain Member States.

(28) No later than five years after entry into force of this Regulation the Commission will present a report on its application and, if need be, submit proposals for adaptations.

(29) The Commission will have to adjust Annexes I to IV on the rules of national jurisdiction, the courts or competent authorities and redress procedures available on the basis of the amendments forwarded by the Member State concerned; amendments made to Annexes V and VI should be adopted in accordance with Council Decision 1999/468/EC of 28 June 1999 laying down the procedures for the exercise of implementing powers conferred on the Commission,

HAS ADOPTED THIS REGULATION:

CHAPTER I

Scope

Article 1

1. This Regulation shall apply in civil and commercial matters whatever the nature of the court or tribunal. It shall not extend, in particular, to revenue, customs or administrative matters.
2. The Regulation shall not apply to:
   (a) the status or legal capacity of natural persons, rights in property arising out of a matrimonial relationship, wills and succession;
   (b) bankruptcy, proceedings relating to the winding-up of insolvent companies or other legal persons, judicial arrangements, compositions and analogous proceedings;
   (c) social security;
   (d) arbitration.
3. In this Regulation, the term “Member State” shall mean Member States with the exception of Denmark.

CHAPTER II

Jurisdiction

Section 1

General provisions

Article 2

1. Subject to this Regulation, persons domiciled in a Member State shall, whatever their nationality, be sued in the courts of that Member State.
2. Persons who are not nationals of the Member State in which they are domiciled shall be governed by the rules of jurisdiction applicable to nationals of that State.

Article 3

1. Persons domiciled in a Member State may be sued in the courts of another Member State only by virtue of the rules set out in Sections 2 to 7 of this Chapter.
2. In particular the rules of national jurisdiction set out in Annex I shall not be applicable as against them.

Article 4

1. If the defendant is not domiciled in a Member State, the jurisdiction of the courts of each Member State shall, subject to Articles 22 and 23, be determined by the law of that Member State.
2. As against such a defendant, any person domiciled in a Member State may, whatever his nationality, avail himself in that State of the rules of jurisdiction there in force, and in particular those specified in Annex I, in the same way as the nationals of that State.

Section 2

Special jurisdiction

Article 5

A person domiciled in a Member State may, in another Member State, be sued:

1. (a) in matters relating to a contract, in the courts for the place of performance of the obligation in question;
   (b) for the purpose of this provision and unless otherwise agreed, the place of performance of the obligation in question shall be:
   - in the case of the sale of goods, the place in a Member State where,

under the contract, the goods were delivered or should have been delivered,

- in the case of the provision of services, the place in a Member State where, under the contract, the services were provided or should have been provided,

(c) if subparagraph (b) does not apply then subparagraph (a) applies;

2. in matters relating to maintenance, in the courts for the place where the maintenance creditor is domiciled or habitually resident or, if the matter is ancillary to proceedings concerning the status of a person, in the court which, according to its own law, has jurisdiction to entertain those proceedings, unless that jurisdiction is based solely on the nationality of one of the parties;

3. in matters relating to tort, delict or quasi-delict, in the courts for the place where the harmful event occurred or may occur;

4. as regards a civil claim for damages or restitution which is based on an act giving rise to criminal proceedings, in the court seised of those proceedings, to the extent that that court has jurisdiction under its own law to entertain civil proceedings;

5. as regards a dispute arising out of the operations of a branch, agency or other establishment, in the courts for the place in which the branch, agency or other establishment is situated;

6. as settlor, trustee or beneficiary of a trust created by the operation of a statute, or by a written instrument, or created orally and evidenced in writing, in the courts of the Member State in which the trust is domiciled;

7. as regards a dispute concerning the payment of remuneration claimed in respect of the salvage of a cargo or freight, in the court under the authority of which the cargo or freight in question:

(a) has been arrested to secure such payment, or

(b) could have been so arrested, but bail or other security has been given; provided that this provision shall apply only if it is claimed that the defendant has an interest in the cargo or freight or had such an interest at the time of salvage.

Article 6

A person domiciled in a Member State may also be sued:

1. where he is one of a number of defendants, in the courts for the place where any one of them is domiciled, provided the claims are so closely connected that it is expedient to hear and determine them together to avoid the risk of irreconcilable judgments resulting from separate proceedings;

2. as a third party in an action on a warranty or guarantee or in any other third party proceedings, in the court seised of the original proceedings, unless these were instituted solely with the object of removing him from the jurisdiction of the court which would be competent in his case;

3. on a counter-claim arising from the same contract or facts on which the original claim was based, in the court in which the original claim is pending;

4. in matters relating to a contract, if the action may be combined with an

action against the same defendant in matters relating to rights in rem in immovable property, in the court of the Member State in which the property is situated.

Article 7

Where by virtue of this Regulation a court of a Member State has jurisdiction in actions relating to liability from the use or operation of a ship, that court, or any other court substituted for this purpose by the internal law of that Member State, shall also have jurisdiction over claims for limitation of such liability.

Section 3

Jurisdiction in matters relating to insurance

Article 8

In matters relating to insurance, jurisdiction shall be determined by this Section, without prejudice to Article 4 and point 5 of Article 5.

Article 9

1. An insurer domiciled in a Member State may be sued: (a) in the courts of the Member State where he is domiciled, or (b) in another Member State, in the case of actions brought by the policyholder, the insured or a beneficiary, in the courts for the place where the plaintiff is domiciled, (c) if he is a co-insurer, in the courts of a Member State in which proceedings are brought against the leading insurer.
2. An insurer who is not domiciled in a Member State but has a branch, agency or other establishment in one of the Member States shall, in disputes arising out of the operations of the branch, agency or establishment, be deemed to be domiciled in that Member State.

Article 10

In respect of liability insurance or insurance of immovable property, the insurer may in addition be sued in the courts for the place where the harmful event occurred. The same applies if movable and immovable property are covered by the same insurance policy and both are adversely affected by the same contingency.

Article 11

1. In respect of liability insurance, the insurer may also, if the law of the court permits it, be joined in proceedings which the injured party has brought against the insured.

2. Articles 8, 9 and 10 shall apply to actions brought by the injured party directly against the insurer, where such direct actions are permitted.
3. If the law governing such direct actions provides that the policyholder or the insured may be joined as a party to the action, the same court shall have jurisdiction over them.

Article 12

1. Without prejudice to Article 11(3), an insurer may bring proceedings only in the courts of the Member State in which the defendant is domiciled, irrespective of whether he is the policyholder, the insured or a beneficiary.
2. The provisions of this Section shall not affect the right to bring a counter-claim in the court in which, in accordance with this Section, the original claim is pending.

Article 13

The provisions of this Section may be departed from only by an agreement:
1. which is entered into after the dispute has arisen, or
2. which allows the policyholder, the insured or a beneficiary to bring proceedings in courts other than those indicated in this Section, or
3. which is concluded between a policyholder and an insurer, both of whom are at the time of conclusion of the contract domiciled or habitually resident in the same Member State, and which has the effect of conferring jurisdiction on the courts of that State even if the harmful event were to occur abroad, provided that such an agreement is not contrary to the law of that State, or
4. which is concluded with a policyholder who is not domiciled in a Member State, except in so far as the insurance is compulsory or relates to immovable property in a Member State, or
5. which relates to a contract of insurance in so far as it covers one or more of the risks set out in Article 14.

Article 14

The following are the risks referred to in Article 13(5):
1. any loss of or damage to:
    (a) seagoing ships, installations situated offshore or on the high seas, or aircraft, arising from perils which relate to their use for commercial purposes;
    (b) goods in transit other than passengers' baggage where the transit consists of or includes carriage by such ships or aircraft;
2. any liability, other than for bodily injury to passengers or loss of or damage to their baggage:
    (a) arising out of the use or operation of ships, installations or aircraft as referred to in point 1(a) in so far as, in respect of the latter, the law of the Member State in which such aircraft are registered does not

prohibit agreements on jurisdiction regarding insurance of such risks;
(b) for loss or damage caused by goods in transit as described in point 1(b);

3. any financial loss connected with the use or operation of ships, installations or aircraft as referred to in point 1(a), in particular loss of freight or charter-hire;
4. any risk or interest connected with any of those referred to in points 1 to 3;
5. notwithstanding points 1 to 4, all "large risks" as defined in Council Directive 73/239/EEC, as amended by Council Directives 88/357/EEC and 90/618/EEC, as they may be amended.

Section 4

Jurisdiction over consumer contracts

Article 15

1. In matters relating to a contract concluded by a person, the consumer, for a purpose which can be regarded as being outside his trade or profession, jurisdiction shall be determined by this Section, without prejudice to Article 4 and point 5 of Article 5, if:
   (a) it is a contract for the sale of goods on instalment credit terms; or
   (b) it is a contract for a loan repayable by instalments, or for any other form of credit, made to finance the sale of goods; or
   (c) in all other cases, the contract has been concluded with a person who pursues commercial or professional activities in the Member State of the consumer's domicile or, by any means, directs such activities to that Member State or to several States including that Member State, and the contract falls within the scope of such activities.
2. Where a consumer enters into a contract with a party who is not domiciled in the Member State but has a branch, agency or other establishment in one of the Member States, that party shall, in disputes arising out of the operations of the branch, agency or establishment, be deemed to be domiciled in that State.
3. This Section shall not apply to a contract of transport other than a contract which, for an inclusive price, provides for a combination of travel and accommodation.

Article 16

1. A consumer may bring proceedings against the other party to a contract either in the courts of the Member State in which that party is domiciled or in the courts for the place where the consumer is domiciled.
2. Proceedings may be brought against a consumer by the other party to the contract only in the courts of the Member State in which the consumer is domiciled.
3. This Article shall not affect the right to bring a counter-claim in the court in which, in accordance with this Section, the original claim is pending.

Article 17

The provisions of this Section may be departed from only by an agreement:

1. which is entered into after the dispute has arisen; or
2. which allows the consumer to bring proceedings in courts other than those indicated in this Section; or
3. which is entered into by the consumer and the other party to the contract, both of whom are at the time of conclusion of the contract domiciled or habitually resident in the same Member State, and which confers jurisdiction on the courts of that Member State, provided that such an agreement is not contrary to the law of that Member State.

Section 5

Jurisdiction over individual contracts of employment

Article 18

1. In matters relating to individual contracts of employment, jurisdiction shall be determined by this Section, without prejudice to Article 4 and point 5 of Article 5.
2. Where an employee enters into an individual contract of employment with an employer who is not domiciled in a Member State but has a branch, agency or other establishment in one of the Member States, the employer shall, in disputes arising out of the operations of the branch, agency or establishment, be deemed to be domiciled in that Member State.

Article 19

An employer domiciled in a Member State may be sued:
1. in the courts of the Member State where he is domiciled; or
2. in another Member State:
   (a) in the courts for the place where the employee habitually carries out his work or in the courts for the last place where he did so, or
   (b) if the employee does not or did not habitually carry out his work in any one country, in the courts for the place where the business which engaged the employee is or was situated.

Article 20

1. An employer may bring proceedings only in the courts of the Member State in which the employee is domiciled.
2. The provisions of this Section shall not affect the right to bring a counter-claim in the court in which, in accordance with this Section, the original claim is pending.

Article 21

The provisions of this Section may be departed from only by an agreement on jurisdiction:
1. which is entered into after the dispute has arisen; or
2. which allows the employee to bring proceedings in courts other than those indicated in this Section.

Section 6

Exclusive jurisdiction

Article 22

The following courts shall have exclusive jurisdiction, regardless of domicile:
1. in proceedings which have as their object rights in rem in immovable property or tenancies of immovable property, the courts of the Member State in which the property is situated.

However, in proceedings which have as their object tenancies of immovable property concluded for temporary private use for a maximum period of six consecutive months, the courts of the Member State in which the defendant is domiciled shall also have jurisdiction, provided that the tenant is a natural person and that the landlord and the tenant are domiciled in the same Member State;
2. in proceedings which have as their object the validity of the constitution, the nullity or the dissolution of companies or other legal persons or associations of natural or legal persons, or of the validity of the decisions of their organs, the courts of the Member State in which the company, legal person or association has its seat. In order to determine that seat, the court shall apply its rules of private international law;
3. in proceedings which have as their object the validity of entries in public registers, the courts of the Member State in which the register is kept;
4. in proceedings concerned with the registration or validity of patents, trade marks, designs, or other similar rights required to be deposited or registered, the courts of the Member State in which the deposit or registration has been applied for, has taken place or is under the terms of a Community instrument or an international convention deemed to have taken place. Without prejudice to the jurisdiction of the European Patent Office under the Convention on the Grant of European Patents, signed at Munich on 5 October 1973, the courts of each Member State shall have exclusive jurisdiction, regardless of domicile, in proceedings concerned with the registration or validity of any European patent granted for that State;
5. in proceedings concerned with the enforcement of judgments, the courts of the Member State in which the judgment has been or is to be enforced.

Section 7

Prorogation of jurisdiction

Article 23

1. If the parties, one or more of whom is domiciled in a Member State, have agreed that a court or the courts of a Member State are to have jurisdiction to settle any disputes which have arisen or which may arise in connection with a particular legal relationship, that court or those courts shall have jurisdiction. Such jurisdiction shall be exclusive unless the parties have agreed otherwise. Such an agreement conferring jurisdiction shall be either:
   (a) in writing or evidenced in writing; or
   (b) in a form which accords with practices which the parties have established between themselves; or
   (c) in international trade or commerce, in a form which accords with a usage of which the parties are or ought to have been aware and which in such trade or commerce is widely known to, and regularly observed by, parties to contracts of the type involved in the particular trade or commerce concerned.
2. Any communication by electronic means which provides a durable record of the agreement shall be equivalent to "writing".
3. Where such an agreement is concluded by parties, none of whom is domiciled in a Member State, the courts of other Member States shall have no jurisdiction over their disputes unless the court or courts chosen have declined jurisdiction.
4. The court or courts of a Member State on which a trust instrument has conferred jurisdiction shall have exclusive jurisdiction in any proceedings brought against a settlor, trustee or beneficiary, if relations between these persons or their rights or obligations under the trust are involved.
5. Agreements or provisions of a trust instrument conferring jurisdiction shall have no legal force if they are contrary to Articles 13, 17 or 21, or if the courts whose jurisdiction they purport to exclude have exclusive jurisdiction by virtue of Article 22.

Article 24

Apart from jurisdiction derived from other provisions of this Regulation, a court of a Member State before which a defendant enters an appearance shall have jurisdiction. This rule shall not apply where appearance was entered to contest the jurisdiction, or where another court has exclusive jurisdiction by virtue of Article 22.

Section 8

Examination as to jurisdiction and admissibility

Article 25

Where a court of a Member State is seised of a claim which is principally concerned with a matter over which the courts of another Member State have exclusive jurisdiction by virtue of Article 22, it shall declare of its own motion that it has no jurisdiction.

Article 26

1. Where a defendant domiciled in one Member State is sued in a court of another Member State and does not enter an appearance, the court shall declare of its own motion that it has no jurisdiction unless its jurisdiction is derived from the provisions of this Regulation.
2. The court shall stay the proceedings so long as it is not shown that the defendant has been able to receive the document instituting the proceedings or an equivalent document in sufficient time to enable him to arrange for his defence, or that all necessary steps have been taken to this end.
3. Article 19 of Council Regulation (EC) No 1348/2000 of 29 May 2000 on the service in the Member States of judicial and extrajudicial documents in civil or commercial matters shall apply instead of the provisions of paragraph 2 if the document instituting the proceedings or an equivalent document had to be transmitted from one Member State to another pursuant to this Regulation.
4. Where the provisions of Regulation (EC) No 1348/2000 are not applicable, Article 15 of the Hague Convention of 15 November 1965 on the Service Abroad of Judicial and Extrajudicial Documents in Civil or Commercial Matters shall apply if the document instituting the proceedings or an equivalent document had to be transmitted pursuant to that Convention.

Section 9

Lis pendens - related actions

Article 27

1. Where proceedings involving the same cause of action and between the same parties are brought in the courts of different Member States, any court other than the court first seised shall of its own motion stay its proceedings until such time as the jurisdiction of the court first seised is established.
2. Where the jurisdiction of the court first seised is established, any court other than the court first seised shall decline jurisdiction in favour of that court.

Article 28

1. Where related actions are pending in the courts of different Member States, any court other than the court first seised may stay its proceedings.
2. Where these actions are pending at first instance, any court other than the court first seised may also, on the application of one of the parties, decline jurisdiction if the court first seised has jurisdiction over the actions in question and its law permits the consolidation thereof.
3. For the purposes of this Article, actions are deemed to be related where they are so closely connected that it is expedient to hear and determine them together to avoid the risk of irreconcilable judgments resulting from separate proceedings.

Article 29

Where actions come within the exclusive jurisdiction of several courts, any court other than the court first seised shall decline jurisdiction in favour of that court.

Article 30

For the purposes of this Section, a court shall be deemed to be seised:

1. at the time when the document instituting the proceedings or an equivalent document is lodged with the court, provided that the plaintiff has not subsequently failed to take the steps he was required to take to have service effected on the defendant, or
2. if the document has to be served before being lodged with the court, at the time when it is received by the authority responsible for service, provided that the plaintiff has not subsequently failed to take the steps he was required to take to have the document lodged with the court.

Section 10

Provisional, including protective, measures

Article 31

Application may be made to the courts of a Member State for such provisional, including protective, measures as may be available under the law of that State, even if, under this Regulation, the courts of another Member State have jurisdiction as to the substance of the matter.

CHAPTER III

Recognition and Enforcement

Article 32

For the purposes of this Regulation, "judgment" means any judgment given by a court or tribunal of a Member State, whatever the judgment may be called, including a decree, order, decision or writ of execution, as well as the determination of costs or expenses by an officer of the court.

Section 1

Recognition

Article 33

1. A judgment given in a Member State shall be recognised in the other Member States without any special procedure being required.
2. Any interested party who raises the recognition of a judgment as the principal issue in a dispute may, in accordance with the procedures provided for in Sections 2 and 3 of this Chapter, apply for a decision that the judgment be recognised.
3. If the outcome of proceedings in a court of a Member State depends on the determination of an incidental question of recognition that court shall have jurisdiction over that question.

Article 34

A judgment shall not be recognised:

1. if such recognition is manifestly contrary to public policy in the Member State in which recognition is sought;
2. where it was given in default of appearance, if the defendant was not served with the document which instituted the proceedings or with an equivalent document in sufficient time and in such a way as to enable him to arrange for his defence, unless the defendant failed to commence proceedings to challenge the judgment when it was possible for him to do so;
3. if it is irreconcilable with a judgment given in a dispute between the same parties in the Member State in which recognition is sought;
4. if it is irreconcilable with an earlier judgment given in another Member State or in a third State involving the same cause of action and between the same parties, provided that the earlier judgment fulfils the conditions necessary for its recognition in the Member State addressed.

Article 35

1. Moreover, a judgment shall not be recognised if it conflicts with Sections 3, 4 or 6 of Chapter II, or in a case provided for in Article 72.
2. In its examination of the grounds of jurisdiction referred to in the foregoing paragraph, the court or authority applied to shall be bound by the findings of fact on which the court of the Member State of origin based its jurisdiction.
3. Subject to the paragraph 1, the jurisdiction of the court of the Member State of origin may not be reviewed. The test of public policy referred to in point 1 of Article 34 may not be applied to the rules relating to jurisdiction.

Article 36

Under no circumstances may a foreign judgment be reviewed as to its substance.

Article 37

1. A court of a Member State in which recognition is sought of a judgment given in another Member State may stay the proceedings if an ordinary appeal against the judgment has been lodged.
2. A court of a Member State in which recognition is sought of a judgment given in Ireland or the United Kingdom may stay the proceedings if enforcement is suspended in the State of origin, by reason of an appeal.

Section 2

Enforcement

Article 38

1. A judgment given in a Member State and enforceable in that State shall be enforced in another Member State when, on the application of any interested party, it has been declared enforceable there.
2. However, in the United Kingdom, such a judgment shall be enforced in England and Wales, in Scotland, or in Northern Ireland when, on the application of any interested party, it has been registered for enforcement in that part of the United Kingdom.

Article 39

1. The application shall be submitted to the court or competent authority indicated in the list in Annex II.
2. The local jurisdiction shall be determined by reference to the place of domicile of the party against whom enforcement is sought, or to the place of enforcement.

Article 40

1. The procedure for making the application shall be governed by the law of the Member State in which enforcement is sought.
2. The applicant must give an address for service of process within the area of jurisdiction of the court applied to. However, if the law of the Member State in which enforcement is sought does not provide for the furnishing of such an address, the applicant shall appoint a representative ad litem.
3. The documents referred to in Article 53 shall be attached to the application.

Article 41

The judgment shall be declared enforceable immediately on completion of the formalities in Article 53 without any review under Articles 34 and 35. The party against whom enforcement is sought shall not at this stage of the proceedings be entitled to make any submissions on the application.

Article 42

1. The decision on the application for a declaration of enforceability shall forthwith be brought to the notice of the applicant in accordance with the procedure laid down by the law of the Member State in which enforcement is sought.
2. The declaration of enforceability shall be served on the party against whom enforcement is sought, accompanied by the judgment, if not already served on that party.

Article 43

1. The decision on the application for a declaration of enforceability may be appealed against by either party.
2. The appeal is to be lodged with the court indicated in the list in Annex III.
3. The appeal shall be dealt with in accordance with the rules governing procedure in contradictory matters.
4. If the party against whom enforcement is sought fails to appear before the appellate court in proceedings concerning an appeal brought by the applicant, Article 26(2) to (4) shall apply even where the party against whom enforcement is sought is not domiciled in any of the Member States.
5. An appeal against the declaration of enforceability is to be lodged within one month of service thereof. If the party against whom enforcement is sought is domiciled in a Member State other than that in which the declaration of enforceability was given, the time for appealing shall be two months and shall run from the date of service, either on him in person or at his residence. No extension of time may be granted on account of distance.

Article 44

The judgment given on the appeal may be contested only by the appeal referred to in Annex IV.

Article 45

1. The court with which an appeal is lodged under Article 43 or Article 44 shall refuse or revoke a declaration of enforceability only on one of the grounds specified in Articles 34 and 35. It shall give its decision without delay.
2. Under no circumstances may the foreign judgment be reviewed as to its substance.

Article 46

1. The court with which an appeal is lodged under Article 43 or Article 44 may, on the application of the party against whom enforcement is sought, stay the proceedings if an ordinary appeal has been lodged against the judgment in the Member State of origin or if the time for such an appeal has not yet expired; in the latter case, the court may specify the time within which such an appeal is to be lodged.
2. Where the judgment was given in Ireland or the United Kingdom, any form of appeal available in the Member State of origin shall be treated as an ordinary appeal for the purposes of paragraph 1.
3. The court may also make enforcement conditional on the provision of such security as it shall determine.

Article 47

1. When a judgment must be recognised in accordance with this Regulation, nothing shall prevent the applicant from availing himself of provisional, including protective, measures in accordance with the law of the Member State requested without a declaration of enforceability under Article 41 being required.
2. The declaration of enforceability shall carry with it the power to proceed to any protective measures.
3. During the time specified for an appeal pursuant to Article 43(5) against the declaration of enforceability and until any such appeal has been determined, no measures of enforcement may be taken other than protective measures against the property of the party against whom enforcement is sought.

Article 48

1. Where a foreign judgment has been given in respect of several matters and the declaration of enforceability cannot be given for all of them, the court or competent authority shall give it for one or more of them.

2. An applicant may request a declaration of enforceability limited to parts of a judgment.

Article 49

A foreign judgment which orders a periodic payment by way of a penalty shall be enforceable in the Member State in which enforcement is sought only if the amount of the payment has been finally determined by the courts of the Member State of origin.

Article 50

An applicant who, in the Member State of origin has benefited from complete or partial legal aid or exemption from costs or expenses, shall be entitled, in the procedure provided for in this Section, to benefit from the most favourable legal aid or the most extensive exemption from costs or expenses provided for by the law of the Member State addressed.

Article 51

No security, bond or deposit, however described, shall be required of a party who in one Member State applies for enforcement of a judgment given in another Member State on the ground that he is a foreign national or that he is not domiciled or resident in the State in which enforcement is sought.

Article 52

In proceedings for the issue of a declaration of enforceability, no charge, duty or fee calculated by reference to the value of the matter at issue may be levied in the Member State in which enforcement is sought.

Section 3

Common provisions

Article 53

1. A party seeking recognition or applying for a declaration of enforceability shall produce a copy of the judgment which satisfies the conditions necessary to establish its authenticity.
2. A party applying for a declaration of enforceability shall also produce the certificate referred to in Article 54, without prejudice to Article 55.

Article 54

The court or competent authority of a Member State where a judgment was given shall issue, at the request of any interested party, a certificate using the standard form in Annex V to this Regulation.

Article 55

1. If the certificate referred to in Article 54 is not produced, the court or competent authority may specify a time for its production or accept an equivalent document or, if it considers that it has sufficient information before it, dispense with its production.
2. If the court or competent authority so requires, a translation of the documents shall be produced. The translation shall be certified by a person qualified to do so in one of the Member States.

Article 56

No legalisation or other similar formality shall be required in respect of the documents referred to in Article 53 or Article 55(2), or in respect of a document appointing a representative ad litem.

CHAPTER IV

Authentic Instruments and Court Settlements

Article 57

1. A document which has been formally drawn up or registered as an authentic instrument and is enforceable in one Member State shall, in another Member State, be declared enforceable there, on application made in accordance with the procedures provided for in Articles 38, *et seq*. The court with which an appeal is lodged under Article 43 or Article 44 shall refuse or revoke a declaration of enforceability only if enforcement of the instrument is manifestly contrary to public policy in the Member State addressed.
2. Arrangements relating to maintenance obligations concluded with administrative authorities or authenticated by them shall also be regarded as authentic instruments within the meaning of paragraph 1.
3. The instrument produced must satisfy the conditions necessary to establish its authenticity in the Member State of origin.
4. Section 3 of Chapter III shall apply as appropriate. The competent authority of a Member State where an authentic instrument was drawn up or registered shall issue, at the request of any interested party, a certificate using the standard form in Annex VI to this Regulation.

Article 58

A settlement which has been approved by a court in the course of proceedings and is enforceable in the Member State in which it was concluded shall be enforceable in the State addressed under the same conditions as authentic instruments. The court or competent authority of a Member State where a court settlement was approved shall issue, at the request of any interested party, a certificate using the standard form in Annex V to this Regulation.

CHAPTER V

General Provisions

Article 59

1. In order to determine whether a party is domiciled in the Member State whose courts are seised of a matter, the court shall apply its internal law.
2. If a party is not domiciled in the Member State whose courts are seised of the matter, then, in order to determine whether the party is domiciled in another Member State, the court shall apply the law of that Member State.

Article 60

1. For the purposes of this Regulation, a company or other legal person or association of natural or legal persons is domiciled at the place where it has its:
   (a) statutory seat, or
   (b) central administration, or
   (c) principal place of business.
2. For the purposes of the United Kingdom and Ireland "statutory seat" means the registered office or, where there is no such office anywhere, the place of incorporation or, where there is no such place anywhere, the place under the law of which the formation took place.
3. In order to determine whether a trust is domiciled in the Member State whose courts are seised of the matter, the court shall apply its rules of private international law.

Article 61

Without prejudice to any more favourable provisions of national laws, persons domiciled in a Member State who are being prosecuted in the criminal courts of another Member State of which they are not nationals for an offence which was not intentionally committed may be defended by persons qualified to do so, even if they do not appear in person. However, the court seised of the matter may order appearance in person; in the case of failure to appear, a judgment given in the civil action without the person concerned having had the opportunity to arrange for his defence need not be recognised or enforced in the other Member States.

Article 62

In Sweden, in summary proceedings concerning orders to pay (betalningsföreläggande) and assistance (handräckning), the expression "court" includes the "Swedish enforcement service" (kronofogdemyndighet).

Article 63

1. A person domiciled in the territory of the Grand Duchy of Luxembourg and sued in the court of another Member State pursuant to Article 5(1) may refuse to submit to the jurisdiction of that court if the final place of delivery of the goods or provision of the services is in Luxembourg.
2. Where, under paragraph 1, the final place of delivery of the goods or provision of the services is in Luxembourg, any agreement conferring jurisdiction must, in order to be valid, be accepted in writing or evidenced in writing within the meaning of Article 23(1)(a).
3. The provisions of this Article shall not apply to contracts for the provision of financial services.
4. The provisions of this Article shall apply for a period of six years from entry into force of this Regulation.

Article 64

1. In proceedings involving a dispute between the master and a member of the crew of a seagoing ship registered in Greece or in Portugal, concerning remuneration or other conditions of service, a court in a Member State shall establish whether the diplomatic or consular officer responsible for the ship has been notified of the dispute. It may act as soon as that officer has been notified.
2. The provisions of this Article shall apply for a period of six years from entry into force of this Regulation.

Article 65

1. The jurisdiction specified in Article 6(2), and Article 11 in actions on a warranty of guarantee or in any other third party proceedings may not be resorted to in Germany and Austria. Any person domiciled in another Member State may be sued in the courts:
   (a) of Germany, pursuant to Articles 68 and 72 to 74 of the Code of Civil Procedure (Zivilprozessordnung) concerning third-party notices,
   (b) of Austria, pursuant to Article 21 of the Code of Civil Procedure (Zivilprozessordnung) concerning third-party notices.
2. Judgments given in other Member States by virtue of Article 6(2), or Article 11 shall be recognised and enforced in Germany and Austria in accordance with Chapter III. Any effects which judgments given in these States may have on third parties by application of the provisions in paragraph 1 shall also be recognised in the other Member States.

CHAPTER VI

Transitional Provisions

Article 66

1. This Regulation shall apply only to legal proceedings instituted and to documents formally drawn up or registered as authentic instruments after the entry into force thereof.
2. However, if the proceedings in the Member State of origin were instituted before the entry into force of this Regulation, judgments given after that date shall be recognised and enforced in accordance with Chapter III,
   (a) if the proceedings in the Member State of origin were instituted after the entry into force of the Brussels or the Lugano Convention both in the Member State or origin and in the Member State addressed;
   (b) in all other cases, if jurisdiction was founded upon rules which accorded with those provided for either in Chapter II or in a convention concluded between the Member State of origin and the Member State addressed which was in force when the proceedings were instituted.

CHAPTER VII

Relations with other Instruments

Article 67

This Regulation shall not prejudice the application of provisions governing jurisdiction and the recognition and enforcement of judgments in specific matters which are contained in Community instruments or in national legislation harmonised pursuant to such instruments.

Article 68

1. This Regulation shall, as between the Member States, supersede the Brussels Convention, except as regards the territories of the Member States which fall within the territorial scope of that Convention and which are excluded from this Regulation pursuant to Article 299 of the Treaty.
2. In so far as this Regulation replaces the provisions of the Brussels Convention between Member States, any reference to the Convention shall be understood as a reference to this Regulation.

Article 69

Subject to Article 66(2) and Article 70, this Regulation shall, as between Member States, supersede the following conventions and treaty concluded between two or more of them:

- the Convention between Belgium and France on Jurisdiction and the Validity and Enforcement of Judgments, Arbitration Awards and Authentic Instruments, signed at Paris on 8 July 1899,
- the Convention between Belgium and the Netherlands on Jurisdiction, Bankruptcy, and the Validity and Enforcement of Judgments, Arbitration Awards and Authentic Instruments, signed at Brussels on 28 March 1925,
- the Convention between France and Italy on the Enforcement of Judgments in Civil and Commercial Matters, signed at Rome on 3 June 1930,
- the Convention between Germany and Italy on the Recognition and Enforcement of Judgments in Civil and Commercial Matters, signed at Rome on 9 March 1936,
- the Convention between Belgium and Austria on the Reciprocal Recognition and Enforcement of Judgments and Authentic Instruments relating to Maintenance Obligations, signed at Vienna on 25 October 1957,
- the Convention between Germany and Belgium on the Mutual Recognition and Enforcement of Judgments, Arbitration Awards and Authentic Instruments in Civil and Commercial Matters, signed at Bonn on 30 June 1958,
- the Convention between the Netherlands and Italy on the Recognition and Enforcement of Judgments in Civil and Commercial Matters, signed at Rome on 17 April 1959,
- the Convention between Germany and Austria on the Reciprocal Recognition and Enforcement of Judgments, Settlements and Authentic Instruments in Civil and Commercial Matters, signed at Vienna on 6 June 1959,
- the Convention between Belgium and Austria on the Reciprocal Recognition and Enforcement of Judgments, Arbitral Awards and Authentic Instruments in Civil and Commercial Matters, signed at Vienna on 16 June 1959,
- the Convention between Greece and Germany for the Reciprocal Recognition and Enforcement of Judgments, Settlements and Authentic Instruments in Civil and Commercial Matters, signed in Athens on 4 November 1961,
- the Convention between Belgium and Italy on the Recognition and Enforcement of Judgments and other Enforceable Instruments in Civil and Commercial Matters, signed at Rome on 6 April 1962,
- the Convention between the Netherlands and Germany on the Mutual Recognition and Enforcement of Judgments and Other Enforceable Instruments in Civil and Commercial Matters, signed at The Hague on 30 August 1962,
- the Convention between the Netherlands and Austria on the Reciprocal Recognition and Enforcement of Judgments and Authentic Instruments in Civil and Commercial Matters, signed at The Hague on 6 February 1963,
- the Convention between France and Austria on the Recognition and Enforcement of Judgments and Authentic Instruments in Civil and Commercial Matters, signed at Vienna on 15 July 1966,
- the Convention between Spain and France on the Recognition and

Enforcement of Judgment Arbitration Awards in Civil and Commercial Matters, signed at Paris on 28 May 1969,

- the Convention between Luxembourg and Austria on the Recognition and Enforcement of Judgments and Authentic Instruments in Civil and Commercial Matters, signed at Luxembourg on 29 July 1971,
- the Convention between Italy and Austria on the Recognition and Enforcement of Judgments in Civil and Commercial Matters, of Judicial Settlements and of Authentic Instruments, signed at Rome on 16 November 1971,
- the Convention between Spain and Italy regarding Legal Aid and the Recognition and Enforcement of Judgments in Civil and Commercial Matters, signed at Madrid on 22 May 1973,
- the Convention between Finland, Iceland, Norway, Sweden and Denmark on the Recognition and Enforcement of Judgments in Civil Matters, signed at Copenhagen on 11 October 1977,
- the Convention between Austria and Sweden on the Recognition and Enforcement of Judgments in Civil Matters, signed at Stockholm on 16 September 1982,
- the Convention between Spain and the Federal Republic of Germany on the Recognition and Enforcement of Judgments, Settlements and Enforceable Authentic Instruments in Civil and Commercial Matters, signed at Bonn on 14 November 1983,
- the Convention between Austria and Spain on the Recognition and Enforcement of Judgments, Settlements and Enforceable Authentic Instruments in Civil and Commercial Matters, signed at Vienna on 17 February 1984,
- the Convention between Finland and Austria on the Recognition and Enforcement of Judgments in Civil Matters, signed at Vienna on 17 November 1986, and
- the Treaty between Belgium, the Netherlands and Luxembourg in Jurisdiction, Bankruptcy, and the Validity and Enforcement of Judgments, Arbitration Awards and Authentic Instruments, signed at Brussels on 24 November 1961, in so far as it is in force.

Article 70

1. The Treaty and the Conventions referred to in Article 69 shall continue to have effect in relation to matters to which this Regulation does not apply.
2. They shall continue to have effect in respect of judgments given and documents formally drawn up or registered as authentic instruments before the entry into force of this Regulation.

Article 71

1. This Regulation shall not affect any conventions to which the Member States are parties and which in relation to particular matters, govern jurisdiction or the recognition or enforcement of judgments.

2. With a view to its uniform interpretation, paragraph 1 shall be applied in the following manner:

(a) this Regulation shall not prevent a court of a Member State, which is a party to a convention on a particular matter, from assuming jurisdiction in accordance with that convention, even where the defendant is domiciled in another Member State which is not a party to that convention. The court hearing the action shall, in any event, apply Article 26 of this Regulation;

(b) judgments given in a Member State by a court in the exercise of jurisdiction provided for in a convention on a particular matter shall be recognised and enforced in the other Member States in accordance with this Regulation.

Where a convention on a particular matter to which both the Member State of origin and the Member State addressed are parties lays down conditions for the recognition or enforcement of judgments, those conditions shall apply. In any event, the provisions of this Regulation which concern the procedure for recognition and enforcement of judgments may be applied.

Article 72

This Regulation shall not affect agreements by which Member States undertook, prior to the entry into force of this Regulation pursuant to Article 59 of the Brussels Convention, not to recognise judgments given, in particular in other Contracting States to that Convention, against defendants domiciled or habitually resident in a third country where, in cases provided for in Article 4 of that Convention, the judgment could only be founded on a ground of jurisdiction specified in the second paragraph of Article 3 of that Convention.

CHAPTER VIII

Final Provisions

Article 73

No later than five years after the entry into force of this Regulation, the Commission shall present to the European Parliament, the Council and the Economic and Social Committee a report on the application of this Regulation. The report shall be accompanied, if need be, by proposals for adaptations to this Regulation.

Article 74

1. The Member States shall notify the Commission of the texts amending the lists set out in Annexes I to IV. The Commission shall adapt the Annexes concerned accordingly.

2. The updating or technical adjustment of the forms, specimens of which appear in Annexes V and VI, shall be adopted in accordance with the advisory procedure referred to in Article 75(2).

Article 75

1. The Commission shall be assisted by a committee.
2. Where reference is made to this paragraph, Articles 3 and 7 of Decision 1999/468/EC shall apply.
3. The Committee shall adopt its rules of procedure.

Article 76

This Regulation shall enter into force on 1 March 2002.

This Regulation is binding in its entirety and directly applicable in the Member States in accordance with the Treaty establishing the European Community.

Done at Brussels, 22 December 2000.

For the Council

The President

C. PIERRET

Annex I

Rules of jurisdiction referred to in Article 3(2) and Article 4(2). The rules of jurisdiction referred to in Article 3(2) and Article 4(2) are the following:

- in Belgium: Article 15 of the Civil Code (Code civil/Burgerlijk Wetboek) and Article 638 of the Judicial Code (Code judiciaire/Gerechtelijk Wetboek);
- in Germany: Article 23 of the Code of Civil Procedure (Zivilprozessordnung),
- in Greece, Article 40 of the Code of Civil Procedure (Κώδικας Πολιτικής Δικονομίας);
- in France: Articles 14 and 15 of the Civil Code (Code civil),
- in Ireland: the rules which enable jurisdiction to be founded on the document instituting the proceedings having been served on the defendant during his temporary presence in Ireland,
- in Italy: Articles 3 and 4 of Act 218 of 31 May 1995,
- in Luxembourg: Articles 14 and 15 of the Civil Code (Code civil),
- in the Netherlands: Articles 126(3) and 127 of the Code of Civil Procedure (Wetboek van Burgerlijke Rechtsvordering),
- in Austria: Article 99 of the Court Jurisdiction Act (Jurisdiktionsnorm),
- in Portugal: Articles 65 and 65A of the Code of Civil Procedure (Código de Processo Civil) and Article 11 of the Code of Labour Procedure (Código de Processo de Trabalho),
- in Finland: the second, third and fourth sentences of the first paragraph of Section 1 of Chapter 10 of the Code of Judicial Procedure (oikeudenkäymiskaari/rättegångsbalken),
- in Sweden: the first sentence of the first paragraph of Section 3 of Chapter 10 of the Code of Judicial Procedure (rättegångsbalken),
- in the United Kingdom: rules which enable jurisdiction to be founded on:
  (a) the document instituting the proceedings having been served on the defendant during his temporary presence in the United Kingdom; or
  (b) the presence within the United Kingdom of property belonging to the defendant; or
  (c) the seizure by the plaintiff of property situated in the United Kingdom.

Annex II

The courts or competent authorities to which the application referred to in Article 39 may be submitted are the following:

- in Belgium, the "tribunal de première instance" or "rechtbank van eerste aanleg" or "erstinstanzliches Gericht",
- in Germany, the presiding judge of a chamber of the "Landgericht",
- in Greece, the 'Μονομελές Πρωτοδικείο',
- in Spain, the "Juzgado de Primera Instancia",
- in France, the presiding judge of the "tribunal de grande instance",
- in Ireland, the High Court,
- in Italy, the "Corte d'appello",
- in Luxembourg, the presiding judge of the "tribunal d'arrondissement",
- in the Netherlands, the presiding judge of the "arrondissementsrechtbank";
- in Austria, the "Bezirksgericht",
- in Portugal, the "Tribunal de Comarca",
- in Finland, the "käräjäoikeus/tingsrätt",
- in Sweden, the "Svea hovrätt",
- in the United Kingdom:

(a) in England and Wales, the High Court of Justice, or in the case of a maintenance judgment, the Magistrate's Court on transmission by the Secretary of State;
(b) in Scotland, the Court of Session, or in the case of a maintenance judgment, the Sheriff Court on transmission by the Secretary of State;
(c) in Northern Ireland, the High Court of Justice, or in the case of a maintenance judgment, the Magistrate's Court on transmission by the Secretary of State;
(d) in Gibraltar, the Supreme Court of Gibraltar, or in the case of a maintenance judgment, the Magistrates' Court on transmission by the Attorney General of Gibraltar.

Annex III

The courts with which appeals referred to in Article 43(2) may be lodged are the following:

- in Belgium,
  - (a) as regards appeal by the defendant: the "tribunal de première instance" or "rechtbank van eerste aanleg" or "erstinstanzliches Gericht",
  - (b) as regards appeal by the applicant: the "Cour d'appel" or "hof van beroep",
- in the Federal Republic of Germany, the "Oberlandesgericht",
- in Greece, the 'Εφετείο',
- in Spain, the "Audiencia Provincial",
- in France, the "cour d'appel",
- in Ireland, the High Court,
- in Italy, the "corte d'appello",
- in Luxembourg, the "Cour supérieure de Justice" sitting as a court of civil appeal,
- in the Netherlands:
  - (a) for the defendant: the "arrondissementsrechtbank",
  - (b) for the applicant: the "gerechtshof",
- in Austria, the "Bezirksgericht",
- in Portugal, the "Tribunal de Relação",
- in Finland, the "hovioikeus/hovrätt",
- in Sweden, the "Svea hovrätt",
- in the United Kingdom:
  - (a) in England and Wales, the High Court of Justice, or in the case of a maintenance judgment, the Magistrate's Court;
  - (b) in Scotland, the Court of Session, or in the case of a maintenance judgment, the Sheriff Court;
  - (c) in Northern Ireland, the High Court of Justice, or in the case of a maintenance judgment, the Magistrate's Court;
  - (d) in Gibraltar, the Supreme Court of Gibraltar, or in the case of a maintenance judgment, the Magistrates' Court.

Annex IV

The appeals which may be lodged pursuant to Article 44 are the following:

- in Belgium, Greece, Spain, France, Italy, Luxembourg and the Netherlands, an appeal in cassation,
- in Germany, a “Rechtsbeschwerde”,
- in Ireland, an appeal on a point of law to the Supreme Court,
- in Austria, a “Revisionsrekurs”,
- in Portugal, an appeal on a point of law,
- in Finland, an appeal to the “korkein oikeus/högsta domstolen”,
- in Sweden, an appeal to the “Högsta domstolen”,
- in the United Kingdom, a single further appeal on a point of law.

Annex V

Certificate referred to in Articles 54 and 58 of the Regulation on judgments and court settlements (English, inglès, anglais, inglese, …)

1. Member State of origin
2. Court or competent authority issuing the certificate
    - 2.1. Name
    - 2.2. Address
    - 2.3. Tel./fax/e-mail
3. Court which delivered the judgment/approved the court settlement (*)
    - 3.1. Type of court
    - 3.2. Place of court
4. Judgment/court settlement (*)
    - 4.1. Date
    - 4.2. Reference number
    - 4.3. The parties to the judgment/court settlement (*)
        - 4.3.1. Name(s) of plaintiff(s)
        - 4.3.2. Name(s) of defendant(s)
        - 4.3.3. Name(s) of other party(ies), if any
        - 4.4. Date of service of the document instituting the proceedings where judgment was given in default of appearance
        - 4.5. Text of the judgment/court settlement (*) as annexed to this certificate
5. Names of parties to whom legal aid has been granted

The judgment/court settlement (*) is enforceable in the Member State of origin (Articles 38 and 58 of the Regulation) against:

Name:

Done at . . . . , date . . . .

Signature and/or stamp . . . .

Annex VI

Certificate referred to in Article 57(4) of the Regulation on authentic instruments (English, inglés, anglais, inglese ....)

1. Member State of origin
2. Competent authority issuing the certificate
    2.1. Name
    2.2. Address
    2.3. Tel./fax/e-mail
3. Authority which has given authenticity to the instrument
    3.1. Authority involved in the drawing up of the authentic instrument (if applicable)
        3.1.1. Name and designation of authority
        3.1.2. Place of authority
    3.2. Authority which has registered the authentic instrument (if applicable)
        3.2.1. Type of authority
        3.2.2. Place of authority
4. Authentic instrument
    4.1. Description of the instrument
    4.2. Date
        4.2.1. on which the instrument was drawn up
        4.2.2. if different: on which the instrument was registered

4.3. Reference number

4.4. Parties to the instrument
    4.4.1. Name of the creditor
    4.4.2. Name of the debtor

5. Text of the enforceable obligation as annexed to this certificate

The authentic instrument is enforceable against the debtor in the Member State of origin (Article 57(1) of the Regulation)

Done at . . . . , date . . . .

Signature and/or stamp . . . .

INDEX